Christian Writers' Market Guide 2008

The Essential
Reference Tool
for the
Christian Writer

Includes CD-ROM with Contacts for 1,200+ Markets

Sally E. Stuart

WATERBROOK
PRESS

Christian Writers' Market Guide 2008
PUBLISHED BY WATERBROOK PRESS
12265 Oracle Boulevard, Suite 200
Colorado Springs, Colorado 80921
A division of Random House Inc.

ISSN 1080-3955

ISBN 978-1-4000-7461-7

Published in association with the literary agency of Janet Kobobel Grant, Books & Such, 4788 Carissa Avenue, Santa Rosa, CA 95405.

Printed in the United States of America
2008—First edition

10 9 8 7 6 5 4 3 2 1

CONTENTS

INTRODUCTION

What did we ever do without publisher Websites? I asked myself that question more than once while preparing this update. This year I noticed that many publisher Websites have improved in their value to the freelance writer. I would encourage you to spend some time reviewing the sites of the publishers you want to write for. More and more of them include their guidelines, and the general information about each company is very helpful. Many of the publishers who provide guidelines on their Website no longer provide them by e-mail or mail, in fact. It is becoming even more critical that you read and follow those guidelines exactly in order to be seriously considered by an editor.

Another thing I've noticed this year is that even more publishers have eliminated an e-mail address and ask instead that authors use an online submission form for that initial submission. Other publishers have eliminated a mailing address since the majority of their correspondence is now handled by e-mail.

Another change is that more publishers prefer accepted manuscripts to be sent by e-mail rather than on CD. In the periodical section you'll note even more online publications as print publications struggle to survive. In this edition I also indicate which publishers have a blog—often written by the editors—that gives you more insight into their current needs and what's happening in the industry. By next year I anticipate that we'll see a great many more of those.

This year I asked conference leaders to indicate which conferences offer full or partial scholarships, so you'll want to check out those if finances are preventing you from attending a conference.

This edition has 406 book publishers (43 new) and 677 periodicals (53 new). It seems each year there are more nonpaying markets, but even those can be important in establishing your reputation in a specific genre and developing your writing career.

As usual, a few new topics appear in the book and periodical lists. More listings indicate what formats the book publishers produce, and more of them indicate that they are open to photographs or art work.

You will also find over 280 new entries to the Resources for Writers section. (My special thanks to Pat Mohney, a former assistant, for again doing a great job updating the listings in that section, plus adding all those new ones.) I encourage you to spend some time in that section identifying those listings that will help you do your job better and more easily. This year we added a section for women writers. Notice that the section on publicists is still growing (see Promotion: Publicists).

The section on Contests for Writers includes updates on previous contests plus information on a number of new ones. At the end of that section you will find a list of major contests—such as Nobel, Pulitzer, and Caldecott—with their Websites.

This year I want to remind you again not to rely entirely on the topical listings for potential markets. Many good markets never fill out their list of topics, so you are likely to miss many good opportunities if you rely only on that list. As time permits, start checking out those markets that indicate they are not listed in the topical listings. You may find some real gems that perfectly fit your skills.

Last year e-book publishers rose from twenty-six to thirty-eight, but this year the number dropped to thirty-seven. Print-on-demand publishers gained, going from forty-three last year to fifty-three this year.

Since a number of periodical publishers are now making assignments only, it is even more important that you establish a reputation in your areas of interest and expertise. Once you have acquired a number of credits in a given field, write to some of those assignment-only editors, giving your credits, and ask for an assignment. In general, you will be better off striving to get some of those assignments rather than hoping to fill one of the few slots left for unsolicited material.

Although agents seem to come and go, we manage to keep the list at about 120—with 15 new this year. It is crucial that you carefully check out agents before signing a contract or committing to work with them. See the introduction to the agent section for some tips on how to do that. (Do not assume that because they are listed I can personally vouch for them. I am not able to check out each one as thoroughly as you need to.) The prevailing consensus is that agents should not charge fees other than actual office expenses—such as long-distance phone calls and photocopying. Because contacting agents has become more important in a writer's quest for publication, I indicate which conferences have agents, as well as editors, on staff.

If you are new to the guide—or have limited yourself to finding specific markets for your work—you'll want to discover the supplementary lists available throughout the book. Read through the glossary and spend a few minutes learning terms you are not familiar with. Review the lists of writers' groups and conferences and mark those you might be interested in pursuing. The denominational listing and corporate-family listing will help you start connecting periodicals and book publishers with their different denominations or publishing groups. With so many publishers being bought out or merging, this will help keep you up to date with the new members of these growing families.

Also be sure to carefully study the "How to Use This Book" section. It will save you a lot of time and frustration in trying to understand the meaning of all the notations in the primary listings, and it's full of helpful hints. Remember to send for a catalog and guidelines for any of the publishers or periodicals you are not familiar with. Then study those carefully before submitting anything to that publisher. Also remember that publishers who make their guidelines available on their Website often include a great deal more information than you get in the usual guidelines sheet.

Editors tell me repeatedly that they are looking for writers who understand them, their periodical or publishing house, and, most of all, their unique approach to the marketplace. One of the biggest complaints I've gotten from publishers over the years is that the material they receive is often not appropriate for their needs. Those complaints are coming less often these days, so I hope that is an indication that writers are doing a better job of market research. With a little time and effort, you can meet an editor's expectations, distinguish yourself as a professional, and sell what you write.

As always, I wish you well as you embark on this exciting road to publication, whether for the first time or as a longtime veteran. And as I remind you every year, each of you has been given a specific mission in the field of writing. You and I often feel inadequate to the task, but I learned a long time ago that the writing assignments God has given me cannot be written quite as well by anyone else.

Sally E. Stuart
1647 S.W. Pheasant Dr.
Aloha, OR 97006
(503)642-9844 (Please call after 9 a.m. Pacific time.)
Fax (503)848-3658
E-mail: stuartcwmg@aol.com
Website: www.stuartmarket.com

For information on how to receive the market guide automatically every year and freeze the price at $34.99, plus postage, for future editions, or for information on getting the guide at a discounted group rate or getting books on consignment for your next seminar or conference, contact me at the address, e-mail, or numbers above.

HOW TO USE THIS BOOK

The purpose of this market guide is to make your marketing job easier and more targeted. It will only serve you well, however, if you use it as a springboard for becoming an expert on those publishers best suited to your writing topics and style. Keeping the following explanations and guidelines in mind will help you become an expert on marketing yourself:

1. Spend time getting acquainted with the setup of this resource book. You cannot make the best use of it until you know exactly what it has to offer. Study the contents pages, where you will find listings of all the periodical and book topics.

2. When looking at the topical section, be sure to check topics *related* to your primary subject. Some cross-referencing may be helpful. For example, if you have a novel that deals with doctor-assisted suicide, you might look at the list for adult novels and the list for controversial issues and see which publishers are on both lists. Those would be good potential markets. In the topical sections you will find a letter R following publishers who accept reprints (pieces that have been printed in other publications but for which you retain the rights). You will find a dollar sign ($) in front of the paying markets. That will help you pick those out quickly when getting paid is your primary goal for a particular piece.

3. In each **book publisher listing** you will find the following information (as available) in this format:

a) Name of publisher

b) Address, phone and fax numbers, e-mail address, Website

c) Denomination or affiliation

d) Name of editor—This may include the senior editor's name, followed by the name of another editor to whom submissions should be sent. In a few cases, several editors are named with the type of books each is responsible for. Address to appropriate editor.

e) A statement of purpose

f) A list of imprint names

g) Number of inspirational/religious titles published per year, followed by formats of books published (hardcover, trade paperbacks, mass-market paperbacks, coffee-table books). Note that coffee-table books have a listing in the Book Topical Listings.

h) Number of submissions received annually

i) Percentage of books from first-time authors

j) Most listings indicate whether they accept, prefer, require, or don't accept manuscripts through agents.

k) The percentage of books from freelance authors they subsidy publish (if any). This does not refer to percentage paid by author. If percentage of subsidy is over 50%, the publisher will be listed in a separate section under Subsidy Publishers.

l) Whether they reprint out-of-print books from other publishers

m) Preferred manuscript length in words or pages; *pages* refers to double-spaced manuscript pages.

n) Average amount of royalty, if provided. If royalty is a percentage of wholesale or net, it is based on price paid by bookstores or distributors. If it is on retail price, it is based on cover price of the book.

o) Average amount paid for advances. Whether a publisher pays an advance or not is noted in the listing; if they did not answer the question, there is no mention of it.

p) Whether they pay flat fees (in these cases the author receives no royalties)

q) Average first printing (number of books usually printed for a first-time author)

r) Average length of time between acceptance of a manuscript and publication of the work

s) Whether they consider simultaneous submissions. This means you can send a query or complete manuscript simultaneously to more than one publisher, as long as you advise everyone involved that you are doing so.

t) Length of time it should take them to respond to a query/proposal or to a complete manuscript (when two lengths of time are given, the first refers to a query and the latter to a complete manuscript). Give them a one-month grace period beyond that and then send a polite follow-up letter if you haven't heard from them.

u) Whether a publisher "accepts," "prefers," or "requires" the submission of an accepted manuscript on disk. (Do not send your unsolicited manuscripts/submissions on disk). Most publishers now do accept or require that books be sent on a computer disk (usually along with a hard copy) or by e-mail, but since each publisher's needs are different, that information will be supplied to you by the individual publisher when the time comes. This section also indicates if they accept submissions by e-mail and whether they want it sent as an attachment or copied into the message.

v) If they have a preference, it will indicate what Bible version they prefer.

w) It will also indicate if they do print-on-demand publishing.

x) Availability and cost for writer's guidelines and book catalogs. If the listing says "guidelines," it means guidelines are available for a #10 (business size) SASE with a first-class stamp. The cost of the catalog (if any), the size of envelope, and amount of postage are given, if specified (affix stamps to envelope; don't send loose). Tip: If postage required is more than $2.13, I suggest you put $2.13 in postage on the envelope and clearly mark it "Media Mail." (That is enough for up to 1 pound.) If the listing says "free catalog," it means you need only request it; they do not ask for payment or SASE. Note: If sending for both guidelines and catalog, it is not necessary to send two envelopes; guidelines will be sent with catalog. If guidelines are available by e-mail or Website, that will be indicated.

y) Nonfiction and Fiction Sections—Preference for query letter, book proposal, or complete manuscript, and if they accept phone, fax, or e-queries (if it does not say they accept them, assume they do not; this reference applies to fiction as well as nonfiction). If they want a query letter, send just a letter describing your project. If they want a query letter/proposal, you can add a chapter-by-chapter synopsis and sample chapters. If not specified, send from one to three chapters. This data is often followed by a quote from them about their needs or what they don't want to see.

z) Special Needs—If a publisher has specific needs, especially those that are not included in the subject listings, they are indicated here.

aa) Ethnic Books—Usually specifies which ethnic groups they target

bb) Also Does—Indicates which publishers also publish booklets, pamphlets, tracts, or e-books

cc) Photos/Artwork—Indicates if they accept freelance photos for book covers. If interested, contact them for details or photography guidelines. This year I have also added information on whether a publisher will accept queries about artwork from freelancers.

dd) Tips—Specific tips provided by the editor/publisher

Note: At the end of some listings you will find an indication that the publisher receives mailings of book proposals from The Writer's Edge (see Editorial Services/Illinois for an explanation of that service) and/or ChristianManuscriptSubmissions.com (see Website or index).

4. In each periodical listing you will find the following information (as available) in this format:
   a) Name of periodical
   b) Address, phone, fax, e-mail address, Website
   c) Denomination or affiliation
   d) Name of editor and editor to submit to (if different)
   e) Theme of publication

f) Format of publication, frequency of publication, number of pages and size of circulation—Tells whether magazine, newsletter, journal, tabloid, newspaper, or take-home paper. Frequency of publication indicates quantity of material needed. Number of pages usually indicates how much material they can use. Circulation indicates the amount of exposure your material will receive and often indicates how well they might pay or the probability that they will stay in business.

g) Subscription rate—Amount given is for a one-year subscription in the country of origin. I suggest you subscribe to at least one of your primary markets every year to become better acquainted with its specific focus.

h) Date established—Included only if 2004 or later

i) Openness to freelance; percentage freelance written. This year, this information has been expanded to indicate the percentage of unsolicited freelance and the percentage of assigned articles. Since not all publishers have responded to this question, some will still give the two percentages combined or indicate only the unsolicited number. If they buy only a small percentage, it often means they are open but receive little material that is appropriate. When you have a choice, choose those with the higher percentage of freelance-written, but only if you have done your homework and know they are an appropriate market for your material.

j) Preference for query or complete manuscript also tells if they want a cover letter with complete manuscripts and whether they will accept phone, fax, or e-mail queries. (If it does not mention cover letters or phone, fax, or e-mail queries, assume they do not accept them.)

k) Payment schedule, payment on acceptance (they pay when the piece is accepted) or publication (they pay when it is published), and rights purchased. (See glossary for definitions of different rights.)

l) If a publication does not pay, or pays in copies or subscription, that is indicated in bold capital letters.

m) If a publication is not copyrighted, you should ask for your copyright notice to appear on your published piece so your rights will be protected.

n) Preferred word lengths and average number of manuscripts purchased per year (in parentheses)

o) Response time—The time they usually take to respond to your query or manuscript submission (add at least two weeks for delays for mailing)

p) Seasonal material (also refers to holiday)—Holiday or seasonal material should reach them at least the specified length of time in advance.

q) Acceptance of simultaneous submissions and reprints—If they accept simultaneous submissions, it means they will look at submissions (usually timely topic or holiday material) sent simultaneously to several publishers. Best to send to nonoverlapping markets (such as denominational), and be sure to indicate that it is a simultaneous submission. Reprints are pieces you have sold previously, but to which you hold the rights (which means you sold only first or one-time rights to the original publisher and the rights reverted to you as soon as they were published).

r) If they accept, prefer, or require submissions on disk or by e-mail. Many now prefer an e-mail submission, rather than on disk. Most will want a query or hard copy first. If it does not say they prefer or require disks, you should wait and see if they ask for them. If they accept an e-mail submission, it will indicate whether they want it as an attached file or copied into the message. If it says they accept e-mail submissions, but doesn't indicate a preference, it usually means they will take it either way.

s) Average amount of kill fee, if they pay one (see glossary for definition)

t) Whether or not they use sidebars (see glossary for definition), and whether they use them regularly or sometimes

u) Their preferred Bible version is indicated. The most popular version is the NIV (New International Version). If no version is indicated, they usually have no preference. See glossary for Bible Versions list.

v) Whether they accept submissions from children or teens. Young writers will find a list of the publishers open to submissions from them in the topical listings under "Young Writer Markets."

w) Availability and cost for writer's guidelines, theme list, and sample copies—If the listing says "Guidelines," it means they are available for a #10 SASE (business size) with a first-class stamp. Many more now have guidelines available by e-mail or Website, and the listing will indicate that. The cost for a sample copy, the size of envelope, and number of stamps required are given, if specified (affix stamps to envelope; don't send loose). Tip: If postage required is more than $2.13, I suggest you put $2.13 in postage on the envelope and clearly mark it "Media Mail." (That is enough for up to one pound.) If the listing says "free sample copy," it means you need only to request them; they do not ask for payment or SASE. Note: If sending for both guidelines and sample copy, it is not necessary to send two envelopes; guidelines will be sent with sample copy. If a listing doesn't mention guidelines or sample copy, they probably don't have them.

x) "Not in topical listings" means the publisher has not supplied a list of topics they are interested in. Send for their guidelines or study sample copies to determine topics used.

y) Poetry—Name of poetry editor (if different). Average number of poems bought each year. Types of poetry; number of lines. Payment rate. Maximum number of poems you may submit at one time.

z) Fillers—Name of fillers editor (if different). Types of fillers accepted; word length. Payment rate.

aa) Columns/Departments—Name of column editor. Names of columns in the periodical (information in parentheses gives focus of column); word length requirements. Payment rate. Be sure to see sample before sending ms or query. Most columns require a query.

bb) Special Issues or Needs—Indicates topics of special issues they have planned for the year or unique topics not included in regular subject listings

cc) Ethnic—Any involvement they have in the ethnic market

dd) Contest—Information on contests they sponsor or how to obtain that information. See Contest section at back of book for full list of contests.

ee) Tips—Tips from the editor on how to break into this market or how to be successful as an author

ff) At the end of some listings you will find a notation as to where that particular periodical placed in the Top 50+ Christian Periodical list in 2007, and/or their place in previous years. This list is compiled annually to indicate the most writer-friendly publications. To receive a complete listing, plus a prepared analysis sheet and writer's guidelines for the top 50 of those markets, send $25 (includes postage) to: Sally Stuart, 1647 S.W. Pheasant Dr., Aloha, OR 97006, or order from www.stuartmarket.com.

gg) Some listings also include EPA winners. These awards are made annually by the Evangelical Press Association (a trade organization for Christian periodicals). This section also indicates the top ten best-selling magazines in Christian retail stores.

5. It is important that you adhere closely to the guidelines set out in these listings. If a publisher asks for a query only, do not send a complete manuscript. Following these guidelines will mark you as a professional.

6. If your manuscript is completed, select the proper topical listing and target audience, and make up a list of possible publishers. Check first to see which ones will accept a complete manuscript (if you want to send it to those that require a query, you will have to write a query letter or book proposal to send first). Please do not assume that your manuscript will be appropriate

for all those on the list. Read the primary listing for each, and if you are not familiar with a publisher, read their writer's guidelines and study one or more sample copies or book catalog. (The primary listings tell how to get these.) Be sure the slant of your manuscript fits the slant of the publisher.

7. If you have an idea for an article, short story, or book but you have not written it yet, a reading of the appropriate topical listing will help you decide on a possible slant or approach. Select some publishers to whom you might send a query about your idea. If your idea is for an article, do not overlook the possibility of writing on the same topic for a number of different periodicals listed under that topic, either with the same target audience or another from the list. For example, you could write on money management for a general adult magazine, a teen magazine, a women's publication, or a magazine for pastors. Each would require a different slant, but you would get a lot more mileage from that idea.

8. If you do not have an idea, simply start reading through the topical listings or the primary listings. They are sure to trigger any number of book or magazine article ideas you could go to work on.

9. If you run into words or terms you are not familiar with, check the glossary at the back of the book for definitions.

10. If you need someone to look at your material to evaluate it or to give it a thorough editing, look up the section on Editorial Services and find someone to send it to for such help. That often will make the difference between success or failure in publishing.

11. If you are a published author with other books to your credit, you may be interested in finding an agent. Some agents will consider unpublished authors (their listing will indicate that), but many require an author to have a completed manuscript before being considered (see agent list). Christian agents are at a premium, so it can be hard to find an agent unless you have had some success in book writing. The agent list also includes secular agents who handle religious/inspirational material.

12. Check the Group list to find a group to join in your area. Go to the Conference list to find a conference you might attend this year. Attending a conference every year or two is almost essential to your success as a writer, especially when you get into book writing.

13. Send an SASE with every query or manuscript. If you do not want your manuscript returned, indicate that in your cover letter and send a #10 SASE for their acceptance or rejection

14. Do not rely solely on the information provided in this guide! It is just that—a guide—and is not intended to be complete by itself. It is important to your success as a freelance writer that you learn how to use writer's guidelines and study book catalogs or sample copies before submitting to any publisher.

ADDITIONAL RESOURCES TO HELP WITH YOUR WRITING AND MARKETING

Note: Here are additional resources to help with your writing needs. They are divided into interest areas to help you make the best selections. See instructions for ordering at the end of the list. (All prices include postage unless otherwise noted.)

GENERAL HELPS

1. *Sally Stuart's Guide to Getting Published*—The author of the *Christian Writers' Market Guide* has compiled all the information you need to understand and function in the world of Christian publishing. Takes you through all the steps needed to be successful as a freelance writer. Serves as both a text and a reference book. One of the most important and useful resources you'll ever find for your writing library. Special price: $10 (retails at $17.95). Special group offer on this book for writer's groups or classes—five or more copies to one address $6 each, plus postage.

2. *The Making of a Christian Bestseller*—$16
3. *Write What You Love and Make a Living at It*—$16
4. *The Little Style Guide to Great Christian Writing and Publishing*—An up-to-date style guide that deals with style concerns unique to Christian writing and editing. $16
5. *Just Write! An Essential Guide for Launching Your Writing Career*—Information on how to do research, common grammatical pitfalls, writing for children, interviewing, and short stories—plus much more. $15
6. *The Complete Guide to Christian Writing and Speaking*—A how-to handbook for beginning and advanced writers and speakers written by the nineteen members of the editorial staff of *The Christian Communicator.* $18
7. *The Complete Guide to Writing for Publication*—Written by top experts in the field. Contains chapters on fiction, marketing tips, and writing for children, plus everything you wanted to know about writing for publication. $18
8. *Small, Easy Ways to Break into Print*—Becoming a columnist, writing and selling microfiction, holiday articles, using an almanac, and publication release forms. $5
9. *The Real American Dream: Creating Independence and Running a One-Person Business*—Let this workbook coach you, step by step, through creating a one-person business to take control of your life as a professional writer. $15
10. *Writers on Writing*—Top Christian writers share their secrets for getting published. Chapters by Jerry B. Jenkins, Liz Curtis Higgs, James Scott Bell, Karen Ball, Sally Stuart, Dennis Hensley and others. $18
11. *The Write Start: Practical Advice for Successful Writing*—A well-rounded handbook for all Christian writers. $20

FICTION RESOURCES

12. *How to Write and Sell a Christian Novel*—$15
13. *The Professional Way to Write Dialogue*—$5
14. *The Professional Way to Create Characters*—$5
15. *How to Create Fictional Characters*—$5
16. *Developing Plots for Novels and Short Stories*—$5

LEGAL CONCERNS

17. Permissions Booklet—Sixteen pages of information compiled directly from publishers on how and when to ask permission to quote from other people's material or from Bible paraphrases. Information not available elsewhere in printed form. $6
18. *Totally Honest Tax Tips for Writers*—Answers all those tax questions specifically applicable to the Christian writer. $10
19. *Author Law: A to Z*—A desktop guide to writers' rights and responsibilities. Helpful advice organized alphabetically and extensively cross-referenced. Discussions of legal issues related to the business of writing and publishing are supplemented with useful tips, author experiences, practical advice, examples, case notes, and more. $25

MARKETING RESOURCES

20. 2008 Top 50+ Christian Periodical Publishers Packet—Includes a list of the Top 50+ "writer-friendly" periodicals, pre-prepared analysis sheets, and publisher's guidelines for each of the top fifty, plus a master form for analyzing your own favorite markets. Saves more than $40 in postage and 25-30 hours of work. New packet every year. $25
21. *A Market Plan for More Sales*—A step-by-step plan to help you be successful in marketing. Includes five reproducible forms. $5

22. *Keeping Track of Your Periodical Manuscripts*—These pages can be duplicated to keep track of every step involved in sending out your periodical manuscripts to publishers. $5

23. *Keeping Track of Your Book Manuscripts*—A booklet summarizing the steps in tracking a book manuscript from idea to publication. $5

24. *How to Submit a Book Proposal to a Publisher*—Contains all you need to know to present a professional-looking book proposal to a publishing house. $5

25. *Book Proposals That Sell*—An inside look at the process from a successful writer and acquisitions editor. $17

26. *A Sample Book Proposal*—Includes a sample of the chapter-by-chapter synopsis. $5

27. *How to Submit an Article or Story to a Publisher*—Shows how to write a query, prepare a professional-looking manuscript, and more. $5

28. *Marketing Manuscripts*—Locating the markets, analyzing magazines, page setup, book proposals, query letters, and literary agents. $5

NONFICTION RESOURCES

29. *Train-of-Thought Writing Method*—Practical, user-friendly help for beginning article writers. $18

30. *Perfecting the Art of Christian Writing*—$17

31. *Effective Magazine Writing*—$14

32. *How to Write That Sure-Sell Magazine Article*—Contains a three-step writing plan for articles, a list of article types, twelve evaluation questions, a sample manuscript page, and more. $5

33. *How to Write Personal Experience Articles*—Includes how to write a query letter/ sample, components of the personal experience article, interviewing tips, and more. $5

34. *How to Write and Sell Interviews and Personality Profiles*—Effective listening skills, open-ended questions, sample interview, photo release form, and basics of interviewing. $5

35. *Writing with Scripture*—Shows you step-by-step how to apply practical writing techniques to any writings that include scripture. Includes writing tips on how to cite your resources and format correctly. $22

SELF PROMOTION

36. *Guide to Marketing Christian Books.* $21

37. *You Can Market Your Book: All the Tools You Need to Sell Your Published Book*—$18

SPECIALTY AREAS

38. *Poetry: Taking Its Course*—A successful poetry writing course, now available in book form. $23

39. *You Can Do It: A Guide to Christian Self-Publishing*—Takes you step-by-step through the process of self-publishing, including the preparation, cost, and promotion of the book. $13

40. *Preparing for a Writing Conference*—A spiral-bound pamphlet that helps you prepare effectively for your first—or next—writer's conference. $7

41. *How to Write a Picture Book*—An inside look at how to write, format, and lay out a children's picture book, with tips for those all-important finishing touches. $5

42. *Writing and Selling Devotionals*—Includes the basic format and patterns for daily devotionals, marketing tips, collecting ideas, and polishing. $5

43. *Agents: What You Need to Know*—Includes why an agent would want you for a client, whether or not you need an agent, and signing with an agent. $5

44. *Writing and Selling Comedy and Humor*—Includes forms of comedy, markets for humor, how to be funny, and how to stimulate humorous thinking. $5

45. *Ghostwriting, Co-Authoring and Collaborations*—Ghostwriting basics, expense sheets, payment guidelines, multiauthor contracts, breaking in, working with book editors, and using a pen name. $5

46. *2008 Internet Directory of Christian Publishers*—A handy listing of nearly 900 Christian publishers who have Websites or e-mail addresses. This resource comes spiral bound for easier reference. $10

47. *Writing Junior Books the Professional Way*—Writing for ages 8-12. $5

48. *Writing for Young Adults the Professional Way*—$5

49. *The Complete Guide to Writers Groups That Work*—$17

SPIRITUAL/PERSONAL HELPS

50. *For the Write Reason*—Drawing on the wisdom of experienced writers, agents, and editors, this in-depth Bible study offers writers a valuable source of encouragement and wisdom. $21

51. *Write His Answer: A Bible Study for Christian Writers*—A Bible-study guide that deals specifically with the struggles of the Christian writer. $15

52. *Writers in the Spirit*—An encouraging and practical help in finding daily inspiration and creativity as a writer. $15

53. *Writing to Give God the Glory*—A potpourri of devotions, encouragement, and tips for the Christian who writes. Timely advice with a dose of laughter to keep you progressing along the journey to publication. $20

54. *Managing Stress as a Freelance Writer*—Stress response, self-assessment exercise, coping, handling anger and stress from editors. $5

55. *Time Management for Writers*—How to make time for writing, including a time-management contract and life map. $5

Note: Any of the above $5 booklets may be purchased at 2 for $9, 4 for $17, 6 for $25, 8 for $33, 10 for $40, or 12 for $47.

To order any of the above resources, send a list of what you want with your check or money order to: Sally E. Stuart, 1647 S.W. Pheasant Dr., Aloha OR 97006, (503)642-9844. Fax (503)848-3658; stuartcwmg@aol.com. Or order by credit card through PayPal on www.stuartmarket.com. All the above prices include postage.

RESOURCES FOR WRITERS

Below you will find a variety of resources that will help you carry out your work as a freelance writer. Also check out the separate listings for groups, conferences, editorial services, and contests. Spend time exploring these resources, as they represent a wealth of knowledge and contacts that will help you be more successful in the publishing business.

(*) New category this year

(+) New listing this year

CONNECTING WITH OTHER WRITERS

+AMERICAN WRITERS AND ARTISTS INC. Copywriting courses and travel writing. Website: www.awaionline.com.

AUTHOR'S DEN. Website: www.authorsden.com. Where authors and readers come together. Discover and meet thousands of authors and readers from around the world.

BACKSPACE. Offers critique forums, tips, and writing resources, plus agents, authors, and editors as guest speakers in discussion forums. Forums have a $30 annual membership fee and offer a free five-day trial. Website: www.bksp.org.

CHRISTIAN MARKET LISTSERV. Designed for networking and discussing issues around publication/marketing to the Christian marketplace. To join, send a message to christian publishers-subscribe@yahoogroups.com or visit Christian Small Publishers group at Yahoo Groups.

+CHRISTIAN STORY TELLER. Nonprofit site that highlights up-and-coming Christian authors and books. Website: http://christianstoryteller.com.

CHRISTIAN WRITERS' GROUP INTERNATIONAL (CWGI). Website: http://christianwriters group.org. An international organization of born-again Christians who write. Purpose: To assist Christians as they fulfill their call to write by offering resources, information, education, support, networking, and interaction with Christian writers, editors, and publishers. Includes critique and prayer sub groups for members only. Periodically offers CWGI members scholarships to writers' conferences. Editors and publishers are welcome. To join, send a blank e-mail to: CWG-subscribe@yahoogroups.com or sign up at http://groups .yahoo.com/group/CWGI. Executive Director: Brandy Brow. Membership (700+) open.

DISCUSSION FORUMS. Freelance Writing. Website for Today's Working Writers: www.free lancewriting.com. Numerous forums to meet and network with other writers.

+EIGHTEENQUESTIONS.COM. This site asks authors to answer 18 questions. When finished, it posts them for all to read. Website: http://eighteenquestions.com.

+FAITHWRITERS. Website: www.faithwriters.com.

FCW's FREE LIST SERVE (Fellowship of Christian Writers). To join, go to the Website: http://groups.yahoo.com/group/fcw or send an e-mail to FCW-subscribe@yahoo.com. Must apply online at Yahoo groups and fill out questionnaire. 750+ members. Has Monday goal setting and Friday praise, weekly writer's devotional, weekly topics, daily interaction, markets, encouragement, writing exercises, tips, prayer, contests, and more. Online-moderated critique groups for fiction, nonfiction, and poetry for list members 3 mos. after you join the main list. Website: www.fellowshipofchristianwriters.org. List owner/moderator Lavon Hightower Lewis.

FORWARD MOTION. Free site that offers 40 forums covering different genres, workshops, critique circles, and more. Website: www.fmwriters.com.

INTERNATIONAL@WRITERS CLUB. Website: http://members.tripod.com/~awriters/iwc.htm. Provides writers worldwide with services/opportunities, including networking, job opportunities, and invaluable writing resources.

KINGDOM WRITERS. Leaders: Marilyn Phemister and Sue Hoover. E-mail critique group and fellowship for Christian writers. Submit work for critique and critique the works of others in return. To subscribe, send a blank e-mail message to KingdomWriters-subscribe@egroups.com. Website: www.angelfire.com/ks/kingwrit/index.html. Membership open.

+MSN WRITERS' GROUP. A site for all writers. Website: http://groups.msn.com/universal writersgroup.

THE MUSE IT UP CLUB. For anyone who enjoys writing anything from flash fiction to novels. Main goal is to match up critique partners with authors who are willing to revise a fellow writer's work. Website: http://museitupclub.tripod.com.

+RELAY WRITING. Join other writers and complete 800 to 1,600 words of an online story.

SMALL PUBLISHERS, ARTISTS, AND WRITERS NETWORK (SPAWN). Forum, market updates, member discounts, free member Web page. Website: www.spawn.org.

+LAURAINE SNELLING. This popular Christian fiction author has resources for writers. Website: www.laurainesnelling.com.

+SPOILEDINK.COM. Workshop your short stories and poems prior to submitting. Website: www.spoiledink.com.

+WORDTRIP.COM. Discuss your writing or what's hot in bookstores in one of the many forums this site offers. Website: http://wordtrip.com.

+WRITERS HELPING WRITERS. A group for working writers, The philosophy of this site is that when someone helps you, you help the next person in the chain. Website: http://groups.yahoo.com/group/league_xrevisionists.

+THE WRITERS LIFE. You can enjoy the solitary writer's life and access the site's articles and interviews or get involved through the forums.

WRITERS SUITE. An online publishing community of writers, readers, and educators featuring 50,000 registered members, 400 blogs, tens of thousands of articles, and 150 courses. Website: www.suite101.com.

THE WRITERS VIEW. Website: http://groups.yahoo.com/group/TheWritersView. Over 600 members. A network of authors, editors, agents, freelance writers, journalists, publicists, and publishers. Offers focused panel discussions with 19 CBA professionals on advanced writing topics and issues. Now has added The Writers View 2 for beginning and intermediate writers.

+THE WRITING BRIDGE. Requires membership. Offers a forum, writing prompts, and critique sections. Website: http://thewritingbridge.org.

WRITING.COM. Website: www.writing.com. The online community for readers and writers of all ages and interests. Over 481,000 active members.

+WRITING EXERCISE BOARD. iVillage group where you can work on your writing skills. Website: www.ivillage.com/community/0,,8h6xjsqb,00.html or search "Writing" on www.ivillage.com.

WRITING GROUPS. Website: www.6ftferrets.com. Tips for starting and maintaining a group.

+WWFORUMS. A forum for fiction and greeting-card writers, as well as journalists. Website: http://wwforums.com/eve/ubb.x.

YAHOO WRITING GROUPS. (1) Christian Writers Club. Website: http://clubs.yahoo.com/clubs/christianwritersclub. A place to learn and share about Christian writing and publishing. Over 500 members. (2) http://groups.yahoo.com/group/mikeswritingworkshop. Over 7,000 members. (3) http://groups.yahoo.com/group/writercircle. Has a "discipline=success=progress" philosophy.

DENOMINATIONS

AMERICAN ANGLICAN COUNCIL. Read what is happening in the 77 million member Anglican Communion. Website: www.americananglican.org.

CHRISTIANITY, CULTS & RELIGIONS. Rose Publishing, 4733 Torrance Blvd., #259, Torrance CA 90503. (310)353-2100. Toll-free (800)532-4278. Fax (310)353-2116. E-mail: info@rose-publishing.com. Website: www.rose-publishing.com. Wall chart or pamphlet compares 18 world religions/cults at a glance.

COMPARISON CHART OF CHRISTIAN BELIEFS. Website: www.saintaquinas.com/christian_comparison.html.

THE UNAUTHORIZED GUIDE TO CHOOSING A CHURCH, by Carmen Renee Berry, (Brazos Press, 2003), ISBN 13: 978-1587430367. Conversational guide that discusses the nuances between denominations. Purchase from www.alibris.com or www.amazon.com.

WORLD RELIGIONS. Virtual Religion Index. Website: http://virtualreligion.net/vri. Analyzes and highlights content of religion-related Websites. Click on "Confessional Agencies."

ELEMENTS OF STYLE

THE ASSOCIATED PRESS STYLEBOOK AND BRIEFING ON MEDIA LAW. Edited by Norm Goldstein, (Perseus Books Group, 2007), ISBN 13: 978-0465004898, $17.95.

THE CHICAGO MANUAL OF STYLE. Website: www.chicagomanualofstyle.org/home/html. The definitive guide (15th edition) online.

A CHRISTIAN WRITER'S MANUAL OF STYLE, by Hudson & Townsend, (Zondervan, 2004), ISBN 13: 978-0310487715. Focuses on unique spellings, capitalization, etc., of religious terms.

CITATION SITE. Citation Styles Online. Website: www.bedfordstmartins.com/online/citex.html. Lists all the correct versions of citation style and related links.

CLEAR ENGLISH. Website: www.clearenglish.net/grammar.htm. Online references/resources to help with grammar/usage.

COLUMBIA GUIDE TO ONLINE STYLE, by Janice R. Walker and Todd Taylor, (Columbia University Press, New York, 1998), ISBN 13: 978-0231132107, $45 hardback, $19.50 paperback. Available at local bookstores. Website: www.columbia.edu/cu/cup/cgos2006/basic.html.

ELEMENTS OF STYLE. William Strunk Jr.'s classic online. Websites: (1) www.diku.dk/hjemmesider/studerende/myth/EOS; (2) www.crockford.com/wrrrld/style.html; (3) www.bartleby.com/141.

+THE GREGG REFERENCE MANUAL, by William A. Sabin (McGraw-Hill), ISBN 13: 978-0072936537.

THE LITTLE STYLE GUIDE TO GREAT CHRISTIAN WRITING AND PUBLISHING, by Leonard & Carolyn Goss. A style guide written especially for those writers writing in the Christian publishing industry, including helps for dealing with Christian/religious terms and references. Available at www.stuartmarket.com.

ONLINE ENGLISH COURSES. Purdue University's Online Writing Lab (OWL). Website: http://owl.english.purdue.edu/sitemap.html.

STYLE AND PROOFREADING HELPS. Websites: (1) www.proofread.com; (2) www.theslot.com; (3) www.webgrammar.com; (4) www.editavenue.com/writingtip.asp?cid=1600. (5) For more scholarly works, www.mla.org; (6) http://uwadmnweb.uwyo.edu/Pubrel/publications/StyleManual.htm.

WHAT'S THE RULE? Quick, easy, and practical reference guide to business English. Free trial version. Website: www.whatstherule.com.

FIND: BOOKS

ABEBOOKS.COM. Website: www.abebooks.com. Find which stores carry the book you want. Then work directly with the appropriate store to order the book.

ABSTRACTS. Get 3,000 word abstract book summaries. Website: www.getabstract.com.

ALIBRIS BOOKS. Website: www.alibris.com. Over 60 million new, used, out-of-print, and hard-to-find books.

ALLBOOKS4LESS.COM. Website: www.AllBooks4Less.com. Provides inexpensively priced books.

BIBLIOFIND. Website: www.bibliofind.com. Partnering with Amazon.com. Searches over 10 million used/rare/out-of-print books offered for sale by thousands of booksellers worldwide.

+BISAC SUBJECT HEADINGS. Publishers apply labels to a finished book so booksellers know where to shelve them. Find out technical aspects of this process at Website: www.bisg.org/publications/bisac_subj_faq.html.

BOOK FINDERS. (1) Find over 100 million new/used/rare/out-of-print books. Website: www.bookfinder.com. (2) Find books by category or author. Website: http://amaztype.tha.jp.

BOOKSINPRINT.COM. The world's most inclusive/accurate/up-to-date database of book, audiobook, and video titles. (1) For subscription information, visit Website: www.bowker.com. Links to U.S. ISBN agency. (2) www.booksinprint.com or call toll-free (888)269-5372.

BOOKSTORE LOCATOR. To find a Christian bookstore anywhere, go to: http://cba.know-where.com/cba.

BOOK WIRE. Website: www.bookwire.com. Comprehensive online portal into the book industry.

CHRISTIAN AUTHORS NETWORK (CAN) BOOK CLUB. Online book club. "Test drive" a book before buying. Website: www.christianauthorsnetwork.com. For your free subscription, go to https://app.quicksizzle.com/survey.aspx?sfid=9604.

CHRISTIAN BOOK DISTRIBUTORS (CBD). Website: www.christianbook.com. Check out what's selling in the marketplace. Books found by publisher, author, or subject.

DISCOUNT BOOKS. (1) Offers new/used book price comparison from 110 online bookstores worldwide at: www.alldiscountbooks.net. (2) Compare book prices at over 100 bookstores at: www.cheapbooks.com.

FETCHBOOK. Website: www.fetchbook.info. A quick way to compare prices of new/used books.

FIND YOUR BOOK. If you have a published book, go to this site to see if your book cover is anywhere on the Internet. Type in your ISBN number without the hyphens. Website: http://images.google.com.

FREE ONLINE BOOKS. (1) Site offers thousands of free online books for students, teachers, and the classic enthusiast. Website: www.readprint.com. (2) Site offers more than 20,000 free e-books at: http://gutenberg.org.

FROOGLE BOOK SEARCH. Go to www.froogle.com and type in the title of a book. Lists stores carrying the book and compares prices.

HALF.COM. Inexpensive source for both Christian and general books. Also a place to sell books you no longer need. Not an auction. Sellers list their books and their asking price, and you pick the ones you want. Refer to Help Desk for details. Website: www.Half.com.

KREGEL BOOKS. Website: http://kregel.gospelcom.net. Offers new/used/hard-to-find Christian books/publications/resources.

POWELL'S BOOKS. Website: www.powells.com. New & used titles.

READERS READ. Website: www.readersread.com. Contains hundreds of categorized links to the best book-related sites on the Web.

TEXTBOOKS AND MEDICAL BOOKS. For discounted new and used textbooks/medical/professional books, go to: www.discounttextbooks.net. Offers book price comparison from 110 online bookstores worldwide.

FIND: INFORMATION

ABOUT.COM. When you don't know anything about a topic, search: www.about.com for hundreds of information links.

AREA CODES. For a numerical listing of telephone area codes, go to: http://bennetyee.org/ucsd-pages/area.html.

ASK-AN-EXPERT SITES. (1) Website: www.K12Science.org/askanexpert.html. (2) www.askanexpert.com; (3) www.askjeeves.com. (4) The Yearbook of Experts, Authorities, and Spokespersons: www.yearbook.com.

BIOGRAPHICAL INFORMATION. (1) Website: www.biography.com. Short biographies on 25,000+ personalities. (2) This biographical dictionary covers more than 28,000 notable men and women who have shaped our world from ancient times to the present day: http://s9.com/biography.

+BRITANNICA. Website: www.britannica.com. The Encyclopedia Britannica's Website. Includes the Britannica blog, all of the articles in the Encyclopedia Britannica, a newsletter, and more.

COUNTRIES. These sites give information on various countries of the world: (1) CIA's World Factbook: www.cia.gov/cia/publications/factbook; (2) Library of Congress's Portals to the World: www.loc.gov/rr/international/portals.html; (3) Country Reports: www.countryreports.org; (4) www.economist.com/countries.

EXPERTS. (1) Website: www.experts.com. A diverse source of experts, academic and otherwise. (2) Directory that lists expertise of more than 1,000 University of Southern California scientists/scholars/administrators/physicians as a service to editors/reporters/producers can be found at www.usc.edu/uscnews/newsroom/. (3) Also, check out: www.profnet.com. Site contains 14,000 expert profiles.

FACT PORTAL. Colin Powell's favorite site links to sources of information on a multitude of topics. Website: www.refdesk.com.

FEDERAL CITIZEN INFORMATION CENTER SITES. (1) www.info.gov. Brochures on just about any subject. News, links, topics, resources, fun stuff, and more; (2) www.pueblo.gsa.gov. Information about anything and everything one could need. Free and low-cost booklets.

HOLIDAYS/FESTIVALS. (1) To find information on holidays/festivals worldwide, visit: www.holidays.net, or (2)www.wilstar.com/holidays.

HOW STUFF WORKS. (1) Website: www.howstuffworks.com. Explains how things work from vacuum cleaners to earthquakes, using text/pictures/animation. (2) See also: www.ehow.com.

INFORMATION PLEASE. Website: www.InfoPlease.com. This 50-year-old print resource now available on the Internet.

LOOKUPS. Amazing site with 30 databases for the demographic seeker: www.melissadata.com/Lookups.

MAG PORTAL. Website: www.MagPortal.com. Lets you search for articles online simultaneously, without having to visit each magazine's Website individually.

PHONE BOOK SEARCH USA. Websites: (1) www.switchboard.com; (2) www.infobel.com/teldir.

PUBLIC RECORDS. (1) To find public records online, go to: www.oatis.com. (2) To find financial information/background checks/birthdays/occupations of people, go to: www.pretrieve.com.

REFERENCE SITES. List of free reference sites useful to writers and anyone looking for free information: www.writers-free-reference.com.

+STINK LIT. Find books that reveal in graphic detail the underbelly of a particular locale, time period, or culture, such as poverty/dyspepsia/general squalor. (1) *A Journal of the Plague Year* by Daniel Defoe; (2) *The Jungle* by Upton Sinclair; (3) *Down and Out in Paris and London* by George Orwell.

WRITERS' KNOWLEDGE SWAP. Website: http://groups.yahoo.com/group/writerswap. An information-exchange mailing list for writers doing research.

FIND: QUOTES

ALL ABOUT QUOTES. Website: www.allaboutquotes.com/Daily.asp. If you use quotations in your writing and speaking, subscribe to this free daily e-mail quote service.

BARTLETT'S FAMILIAR QUOTATIONS. Website: www.bartleby.com/100. Enter the word or words and it gives you the quotations.

JOURNALISM QUOTES. Website: www.schindler.org/quote.shtml.

+MOVIE QUOTES. Locate a quote from just about any movie ever made at: www.imdb.com.

THE QUOTABLE WRITER, by William A. Gordon (McGraw Hill), ISBN 13: 978-0071355766. Quotes by writers on writing. Available at local bookstore. To read excerpts from this book, go to: http://members.aol.com/williamagordon/writers_quotations.html.

WEBSITES FOR QUOTATIONS. (1) www.itools.com. Go to "Research Tools" section, enter word in "Quotations" box. Search by topic, author, etc., including Bible quotations; (2) www.quotationspage.com; (3) www.quoteland.com; (4) www.aphids.com/quotes/index.shtml; (5) www.brainyquote.com; (6) www.startingpage.com/html/quotations.html; (7) www.cybernation.com/victory/quotations/directory.html; (8) http://members.aol.com/Jainster/Quotes/quotes.html; (9) www.motivationalquotes.com; (10) www.thinkexist.com/English; (11) www.madwed.com. Click on the "Quotations" section. The quotations are numbered. Authors are in alphabetical order under each topic. (12) www.quotegarden.com.

WORD CRAFTERS. Bob Kelly, 10225 E. Stoney Vista Dr., Sun Lakes AZ 85248. (480)895-7617. Fax (480)895-7618. E-mail: quotes@robsoncom.net. Website: www.wordcrafters.info. Free quotation search service and newsletter.

FIND: STATISTICS

BARNA RESEARCH GROUP. Website: www.barna.org/FlexPage.aspx?Page=Home. Click on "Ministry Resources" for information about the intersection of faith and culture in the U.S. Subjects include: church health, discipleship, stewardship, youth, evangelism, leaders, and trends.

BOOK INDUSTRY STATISTICS. (1) To find statistics about the book industry (i.e. how many books sold last year), check out Website: www.publishers.org/industry/index.cfm. (2) Also visit Dan Poynter's Website: http://parapub.com/. Click on "Resources" to find statistics.

BUREAU OF JUSTICE STATISTICS. Website: www.ojp.usdoj.gov/bjs.

+DEMOGRAPHICS. (1) Find population data on age, gender, households, families, housing units, plus social, economic, and more at www.demographics.com; or (2) www.aecf.org/kidscount/census/.

FEDERAL STATISTICS. Statistics from over 100 U.S. federal agencies: www.fedstats.gov.

INTERNET STATISTICS. Website: www.clickz.com/showPage.html?page=stats. "The world's leading resource for Internet trends and statistics."

THE PEW FORUM ON RELIGION & PUBLIC LIFE. Research and discussion of issues about the intersection of religion and public affairs: www.pewforum.org.

STATISTICS SOURCE. Website: www.nilesonline.com/data. How to find data on the Internet and access stats of all kinds.

TRACK BOOK SALES BY PHONE. The Ingram Book Group distributes more than a million titles to more than 30,000 stores. You can track the sales of a title by calling (800)937-8000. Press 4 and enter extension 36803. You will be asked for the book's ISBN or UPC number. When prompted, enter it and you'll be given recent and year-to-date sales.

UNIVERSITY OF MICHIGAN'S DOCUMENTS CENTER STATISTICAL RESOURCES ON THE WEB. Website: www.lib.umich.edu/govdocs/stats.html.

FREELANCE JOBS

ABOUT.COM. Offers market information/job search: http://freelancewrite.about.com.

THE CHRISTIAN PEN: PROOFREADERS AND EDITORS NETWORK. Kathy Ide, 203 Panorama Ct., Brea CA 92821. (714)529-1212. Fax (714)529-5267. Website: www.TheChristianPEN.com. Contact: Kathy@kathyide.com. Provides proofreaders and editors with a venue for "cooperative competition" through mutual support and exchange of information, leads, and resources. Has a free online group where members can exchange ideas, tips, news, findings, questions/answers, resources, and suggestions, as well as pass on job leads. Also offers online courses of interest to editorial freelancers. For $30/yr., contributing members can post their bios/résumés on the Christian PEN Website, receive a quarterly e-newsletter, get discounts on online courses, receive active job leads, and more. Open to anyone who is a full-time or part-time proofreader or editor (at any level), is seriously planning to become an editorial freelancer, or is simply investigating the possibility. If you're a writer looking for an editor or proofreader, check the "Members" page or contact Kathy Ide by e-mail for a referral.

+CRAIGSLIST.COM. Browse employment listings under "Writing/editing" or "Part-time." Website: www.craigslist.com.

CREATIVE FREELANCERS. Connecting freelancers and clients for over twenty years: www.freelancers.com.

ECPA CAREER CENTER. The Evangelical Christian Publishers Assoc. (ECPA) offers a free online resource to connect publishers and other industry employers with the largest, most qualified audience of publishing industry professionals. Employment opportunities include editorial, marketing, executive, operations, production, rights, sales, and administrative positions. Receive automatic notification of new jobs matching your criteria. Post your résumé, confidentially if preferred, so employers can actively search for you. Website: www.ecpa.org/careers.

FREELANCE COPYEDITING/PROOFREADING. This site provides insight into the ins and outs of the copyediting profession: http://freecontent.janktheproofer.com/BeaProofreader.htm.

FREELANCE SUCCESS. Website: www.freelancesuccess.com.

FREELANCE WRITING. (1) Website for "Today's Working Writers." Job Bank at: www.freelancewriting.com/careercenter.php. (2) Freelance Writers Resource: www.thegoldenpencil.com.

FREELANCE WRITING ORGANIZATION INT'L. Free site hosts thousands of writing resources, including funds for writers and job listings: www.fwointl.com.

HOW TO LAND HIGH-PAYING ASSIGNMENTS. E-book encourages writers to "seek the assignment, NOT the sale." Shows aspiring writers how to get an editor's attention without spending hours, days, and weeks on a manuscript: www.dougschmidt.com.

JOB SITES. Websites: (1) www.writerfind.com/freelance_jobs; (2) www.writejobs.com/jobs; (3) www.writersdigest.com; (4) www.epassoc.org/jobs; (5) www.prostogo.com; (6) http://allfreelance.com; (7) www.freelanceworkexchange.com; (8) www.nytimes.com/pages/jobs/

index.html; (9) www.mediabistro.com; (10) www.writersweekly.com/markets_and_jobs.php; (11) www.justmarkets.com. (12) Search terms like "Writer," "Journalist," "Editor," or "Public Relations." Website: www.monster.com. See also: (13) www.hotjobs.com; (14) http://writersrow.com/deborahng/freelancewritingjobs.html.

JOURNALISM JOBS & SIMILAR SITES. Websites: (1) www.journalismjobs.com; (2) www.newsjobs.net; (3) www.sunoasis.com/intern.html; (4) www.writejobs.com; (5) www.newslink.org/joblink.html; (6) www.iwantmedia.com/jobs/index.html. (7) Jobs and communities for journalists of color: www.journalismnext.com.

+ONLINE STORE FOR FREELANCE WORK. Write about any topic, name your price, and place it on this site. Folks in need of Web content can browse the work and buy what they want at this online store for freelance work. Cost is 35 percent commission but no up-front costs, and you can work at your own pace. Website: http://constant-content.com.

PR LEADS. Website: www.prLeads.com. Learn about articles before they are written. Dan Janal will supply you with target leads on the subjects you select. Then you contact the editor or freelancer to help him or her with the article. E-mail: Dan@prLeads.com.

+SALARIES IN THE PUBLISHING INDUSTRY. (1) http://tinyurl.com/tzzcj; (2) http://tinyurl.com/yyn53v; (3) http://news.shelf-awareness.com.

SNAPDRAGON GROUP EDITORIAL SERVICES, PO Box 3024, Tulsa OK 74101-3024. (918)245-0559. E-mail info@snapdragongroup.com. This group aims to provide the best professional freelancers for publishers' outsourced projects. For details: www.snapdragongroup.com.

WASHINGTON D.C. AREA OPPORTUNITY. Check out the DC WritersCorps: http://dcwriterscorps.org. They send writers to teach middle/junior high/high school students throughout the DC area.

WORLDWIDE FREELANCE. Website: www.worldwidefreelance.com. Extensive lists of travel writing markets/Christian markets/technology markets/and more. Subscribe to free newsletter online.

THE WRITER GAZETTE. Market listings and information on freelance jobs: www.writergazette.com.

WRITERS AND EDITORS FOR HIRE. Elizabeth Lyon of M. Evans & Company has compiled a national directory of editors and writers for hire. ISBN 13: 978-1590770696, $18.95. To order, call (800)462-6420. Website: www.rlpgtrade.com/mevans.

WRITING EMPLOYMENT. (1) www.poewar.com/jobs/. (2) This site has searchable classifieds so you can find a writing-related job in your area: http://editorandpublisherjobs.com.

FULL-TIME FREELANCING

ABOUT FREELANCING. Website: www.freelancewrite.about.com. Provides the essentials for freelance writers.

THE E-MYTH REVISITED, by Michael E. Gerber (Collins), ISBN 13: 978-0887307287. This book looks at and dispels myths involved with starting and maintaining your own business. Available at Amazon.com.

FREELANCE BIDDING SERVICES. Websites: (1) www.elance.com. Writers, editors, and other professionals in a broad range of fields bid for projects posted by companies looking for freelance workers. (2) An online marketplace for freelance talent: www.guru.com.

+FULL-TIME CAREER. This site shows realistic ways to build a writing career: www.tarakharper.com/k_living.htm.

FUNDS FOR WRITERS. Helping writers earn a living doing what they love: www.fundsforwriters.com.

HEALTH INSURANCE CONCERNS. These sites are not insurance sites; but rather biblically based Medi-Share alternatives: www.christianet.com/blessed; or www.biblicalhealthcare.com.

HEALTH SAVINGS ACCOUNTS. Golden Rule Insurance, 712 Eleventh St., Lawrenceville IL 62439-2395. Website: www.goldenrule.com. Provides a health insurance alternative to the self-employed.

WRITING FOR DOLLARS NEWSLETTER. Information for the business side of freelance writing: www.writingfordollars.com.

GRANTS

+AMERICAN GRANTS AND LOANS BOOK. Information on grants and loans offered by the U.S. federal government. Available on CD ($69.95) or printed ($149.95). To order call (819)322-7533.

CANADIAN SUBSIDY DIRECTORY. A guide containing more than 3,000 direct and indirect financial subsidies/grants/loans offered by government departments, agencies, foundations, associations, and organizations. Cost is $49.95. Order from Canadian Business Publications at: www.mgpublishing.net, or Fureteur Bookstore at (450)465-5597 or fax (450)465-8144.

EDUCATIONAL INSTITUTIONS GRANTS. (1) Michigan State University Libraries: www.lib.msu.edu/harris23/grants/3writing.htm; (2) University of Wisconsin at Madison: http://grants.library.wisc.edu; (3) University of Wisconsin funds fellows to assist resident professors: www.wisc.edu/writing/wf/main.html; (4) Duke University: http://scriptorium.lib.duke.edu/grants.html. (5) Artist in the Schools program sponsors visiting artists in schools: www.nwrdc.org/artsgrants.htm. (6) Kentucky Arts Council funds two-year residencies for writers to work, teach and share their creativity with students: http://artscouncil.ky.gov.

FELLOWSHIPS. Fine Arts Work Center in Provincetown, MA: www.fawc.org

THE FOUNDATION CENTER. (1) www.fdncenter.org. (2) Also check out The Chronicle of Philanthropy newspaper: www.philanthropy.com.

FULBRIGHT SCHOLARSHIPS. Website: www.state.gov/history.

GRANT WRITING. Website: www.writethisinstant.com. Click on "Writing." Then click on "Grants" in the right side bar. Lots of sites on grants and grant writing.

INTERNATIONAL WRITERS. (1) Arts Councils of Scotland: www.sac.org.uk; (2) Canada: www.canadacouncil.ca/grants; (3) Australia: www.ozco.gov.au; (4) England: www.artscouncil.org.uk.

JOURNALISM GRANTS & FELLOWSHIPS. Website: www.newswise.com/grants.htm.

NATIONAL ASSEMBLY OF STATE ARTS AGENCIES. For another funding source, check out: www.nasaa-arts.org.

NATIONAL ENDOWMENT FOR THE ARTS. (1) Find stipends for travel and learning as a writer: www.nea.gov. (2) To fund conference expenses, find your state's art commission at: www.nea.gov.

NATIONAL PARKS RESIDENCY. Become an artist-in-residence at one of 29 national parks: www.nps.gov. Enter "Residency" in search box.

NEWSWRITING GRANTS. (1) For journalists with a medical focus, contact The Kaiser Media Fellowships: www.kff.org/mediafellowships. For other newswriting grants, check out these Websites: (2) McCormick Tribune Foundation, www.rrmtf.org/journalism/index.htm; (3) Fund for Investigative Journalism, http://fij.org; (4) National Arts Journalism Program, www.najp.org.

OVERSEAS GRANTS. Gladys Krieble Delmas Foundation supports individuals who want to live in Venice and study its culture: www.delmas.org/guidelines/.

PEN AMERICAN CENTER, 588 Broadway, Ste. 303, New York NY 10012. (212)334-1660. Fax (212)334-2181. E-mail: pen@pen.org. Website: www.pen.org. For information on finding grants for writers, subscribe to online version of *Pen Grants and Awards Available to American Writers.* $12/yr. subscription.

RESIDENCIES. (See more residencies under "Services for Writers.") (1) Virginia Center for the Creative Arts in the Blue Ridge Mountains: www.vcca.com; (2) Shaw Guides link at Writer's Digest's site: www.writersdigest.com/conferences.

SPECIAL INTEREST GRANTS. (1) The International Association of Culinary Professionals for food writers: www.iacpfoundation.org. (2) National Endowment for the Humanities: www.neh.gov/grants/grants.html; (3) Bush Artist Fellowship: www.bushfoundation.org; (4) Montana Committee for the Humanities: www2.umt.edu/lastbest/default.htm. (5) Verizon Foundation offers grants for disaster relief, education, employment training, and literacy. Writing potential exists in all these areas. Website: http://foundation.verizon.com. (6) Arizona Humanities Council offers grants to nonprofit groups that preserve the humanities. The council's grants directly compensate individuals for work in these fields. Website: www.azhumanities.org. (7) To fund book festivals, go to Tennessee Arts Commission: www.arts.state.tn.us.

GROUPS/ORGANIZATIONS OF INTEREST

AMERICAN ACADEMY OF RELIGION. Find an expert on virtually any aspect of religion: www.aarweb.org.

AMERICAN BOOKSELLERS ASSN. Website: www.bookweb.org. A not-for-profit trade organization devoted to meeting the needs of its core members of independently owned bookstores with retail store-front locations through advocacy, education, research, and information dissemination.

AMERICAN CHRISTIAN WRITERS. Reg Forder, dir., PO Box 110390, Nashville TN 37222. Toll-free (800)21-WRITE. E-mail: ACWriters@aol.com. Website: www.ACWriters.com. Ministry with a goal to provide full service to Christian writers and speakers. Publishes two writers' periodicals (*Christian Communicator* and *Advanced Christian Writers*), operates two correspondence schools, hosts an annual conference in 24 cities across America, offers a critique service and book publishing division, and has a mail-order learning center that offers a huge selection of books, cassette tapes, and CDs for writers. Writers' chapters throughout the U.S.

AMERICAN SELF-PUBLISHING ASSN., PO Box 232233, Sacramento CA 95823. (916)422-8435. Toll-free (800)929-7889. Website: http://members.aol.com/ASPublish/members.html. Offers free email consulting, a newsletter, exhibition and book festival services, and more. Dues are $45/yr. E-mail: ASPublish@aol.com.

AMERICAN SOCIETY OF JOURNALISTS AND AUTHORS, 1501 Broadway, Ste. 302, New York NY 10036. (212)997-0947. Fax (212)937-2315. Will answer your questions or review your contract: www.asja.org. Dues: $195/yr.

AMERICAN SOCIETY OF MAGAZINE EDITORS (ASME), 810 Seventh Ave., Fl. 24, New York NY 10019. (212) 872-3700. E-mail: mpa@magazine.org. Website: www.magazine.org/Editorial.

THE AMY FOUNDATION. Sponsors the Amy Writing Awards, which is a call to present spiritual truth reinforced with biblical references in general, nonreligious publications. First prize is $10,000 with a total of $34,000 given annually. The Amy Writing Awards are designed to recognize creative, skillful writing that presents in a sensitive, thought-provoking manner a biblical position on issues affecting the world today. To be eligible, submitted articles must be published in a general, nonreligious publication and must be reinforced with at least one passage of Scripture. To request guidelines and a copy of last year's winning entries, go to the order information page or write: The Amy Foundation, PO Box 16091, Lansing MI 48901-6091. (517)323-6233. E-mail: amyfoundtn@aol.com. Website: www.amyfound.org.

ASSOCIATED CHURCH PRESS, PO Box 621001, Oviedo FL 32762-1001. (407)341-6615. Fax (407)386-3236. Joe Thoma, exec. dir. E-mail: contactACP@aol.com. Website: www.theacp.org. Individual membership in ACP is open to freelance writers/journalists/Web designers/marketers, as well as former ACP editors. Dues: $40/yr.

ASSOCIATED PRESS. Website: www.ap.org.

ASSN. OF AMERICAN PUBLISHERS. The principal trade association of the book publishing industry: www.publishers.org.

THE ASSN. OF AUTHOR'S REPRESENTATIVES. Assists agents in representing their client's interests: www.aar-online.org.

ASSN. OF HEALTH CARE JOURNALISTS (AHCJ). Website: www.ahcj.umn.edu/jour_basics.htm.

ASSN. OF WRITERS & WRITING PROGRAMS (AWP), George Mason University, MSN 1E3, Fairfax VA 22030. (703)993-4301. E-mail: services@awpwriter.org. Website: www.awpwriter.org. Nonprofit organization of teachers, writers, writing programs, and lovers of literature.

AUTHOR'S GUILD, 31 E. 32nd St., 7th Fl., New York NY 10016. (212)563-5904. Fax (212)564-5363. E-mail: staff@authorsguild.org. Website: www.authorsguild.org. The nation's leading advocate for writers' interests. Provides contract reviews, legal assistance, and access to group health insurance.

BOOK GROUPS. Find a book group in your area and tips for starting and leading book clubs. (1) www.generousbooks.com; (2) Barnes & Noble Online: www.bn.com. Click on "Book Clubs."

R. R. BOWKER, 630 Central Ave., New Providence NJ 07974. Toll-free (888)269-5372. E-mail: isbn-san@bowker.com. Website: www.bowker.com. This company issues International Standard Book Numbers (ISBN), Standard Account Numbers (SAN), and Advanced Book Information forms. Forms can be printed off their Website.

CANADIAN AUTHORS ASSN., Box 419, Campbellford ON K0L 1L0, Canada. Toll-free (866)216-6222. (705)653-0323. Fax (705)653-0593. E-mail: admin@canauthors.org. Website: www.canauthors.org. Addresses the needs of writers at all stages of development through meetings, workshops, and an annual conference. Publishes *The Canadian Writer's Guide.*

CANADIAN CHURCH PRESS, 8 Macdonald Ave., Hamilton ON L8P 4N5, Canada. Contact: Sue Newbery. (905)521-2240. E-mail: cdnchurchpress@hotmail.com. Website: www.Canadianchurchpress.com.

CANSCAIP (Canadian Society of Children's Authors, Illustrators, and Performers): www.canscaip.org.

CATHOLIC PRESS ASSN., 3555 Veterans Memorial Hwy., Unit O, Ronkonkoma NY 11779. (631)471-4730. Fax (631)471-4804. Helen Osman, pres.

CBA INTERNATIONAL. (1) Bill Anderson, pres., PO Box 62000, Colorado Springs CO 80962-2000. Toll-free (800)252-1950. E-mail: info@cbaonline.org. The international trade association of Christian retailers and product suppliers. Visit their newly redesigned, completely overhauled Website: www.cbaonline.org. (2) For their International Christian Retail Show schedule of events, go to: www.christianretailshow.com.

CHRISTIANBOOK.COM. Website: www.Christianbook.com. The largest e-commerce business site for Christian books and merchandise. Customer service: Toll-free (800)247-4784.

CHRISTIAN SMALL PUBLISHERS ASSOCIATION (CSPA), PO Box 481022, Charlotte NC 28269. (704)277-7194. Fax (704)717-2928. E-mail: cspa@christianpublishers.net. Website: www.christianpublishers.net.

CHRISTIANWRITERS.COM. Website: http://christianwriters.com. A free online writers' resource community. Their mission is to provide a supportive, family atmosphere where writers may easily access the tools and resources to create, market, and publish their work.

CHRISTIAN WRITERS FELLOWSHIP INTL. Sandy Brooks, 1624 Jefferson Davis Rd., Clinton SC 29325-6401. (864)697-6035. E-mail: cwfi@cwfi-online.org. To contact Sandy Brooks personally, e-mail: sandybrooks@cwfi-online.org. Website: www.cwfi-online.org. Offers market consultations, critique service, writers' instructional materials, and conference workshop tapes. Connects writers living in the same area and helps to start writers' groups. *Cross & Quill* is the organizational newsletter.

COUNCIL FOR INTERNATIONAL EXCHANGE OF SCHOLARS. The Fulbright Scholar Program for faculty and professionals is offering more than 70 awards in communications and journalism for lecturing and/or doing research abroad during the academic year: www.iie.org/cies.

COUNCIL OF LITERARY MAGAZINES AND PUBLISHERS (CLMP). *Literary Press and Magazine Directory,* $15. Order online: www.clmp.org.

THE DRAMATISTS GUILD OF AMERICA, 1501 Broadway, Ste. 701, New York NY 10036. (212)398-9366. Fax (212)944-0420. E-mail: from Website: www.dramaguild.com. Professional association of playwrights, composers, and lyricists with over 6,000 members.

EDITORIAL FREELANCERS ASSN. A national, nonprofit, professional organization of self-employed workers in the publishing and communications industry: www.the-efa.org.

EVANGELICAL CHRISTIAN PUBLISHERS ASSN. (ECPA). Mark Kuyper, pres./CEO, 9633 S. 48th St., Ste. 140, Phoenix AZ 85044. (480)966-3998. Fax (480)966-1944. E-mail: info@ecpa.org. Website: www.ecpa.org. Proclaiming the gospel through books, Bibles, gifts, curriculum, video, and audio products. Also offers a submission service on the Internet where Christian publishers who are members of this association can review your book proposal. Cost is $98 for six months. Visit their Website and click on "Christian Manuscript Submissions" for more information.

EVANGELICAL PRESS ASSN. Doug Trouten, exec. dir., PO Box 28129, Crystal MN 55428. (763)535-4793. Fax (763)535-4794. E-mail: director@epassoc.org. Website: www.epassoc.org. The professional association for the evangelical periodical publishing industry. EPA offers memberships to writers and tools to help freelancers connect with editors.

FREEDOM FORUM ONLINE. News about free press: www.freedomforum.org.

INTERNATIONAL ASSN. OF CRIME WRITERS (North American Branch). Mary A. Frisque, exec. dir., PO Box 8674, New York NY 10116. Email: info@crimewritersna.org. Promotes communication among crime writers worldwide: www.crimewritersna.org.

INTERNATIONAL CHRISTIAN WRITERS. Stanley C. Baldwin, dir., 12900 S.E. Nixon, Milwaukie OR 97222 (include SASE for reply). E-mail: SCBaldwin@icwriters.com. A point of contact for writers around the world. Contact Prayer Fellowship Coordinator: Joyce Tomanek through Website: www.icwriters.com.

INTERNATIONAL JOURNALISTS' NETWORK. Online source for media assistance, news, and journalism training opportunities: www.ijnet.org.

JERRY B. JENKINS CHRISTIAN WRITERS GUILD. Les Stobbe, ed-in-chief, 5525 N. Union Blvd., Ste. 200, Colorado Springs CO 80918. Toll-free (866)495-5177. E-mail: ContactUs@ChristianWritersGuild.com. Website: www.ChristianWritersGuild.com. This International organization owned by Jerry B. Jenkins, author of more than 150 books including the best-selling Left Behind series, has more than 2,000 members worldwide. The Guild offers annual memberships, mentor-guided correspondence and e-mail courses for adults (two-year Apprentice and advanced one-year Journeyman) and youth (Pages: ages 9-12 and Squires: 13 and up), writing contests (winners receive a book contract with a major CBA publisher), Writing for the Soul conferences, critique service, writers' resource books, monthly newsletter, and more. For a free Starter Kit, e-mail from Website.

MYSTERY WRITERS OF AMERICA, 17 E. 47th St., Fl. 6, New York NY 10017. (212)888-8171. Website: www.mysterywriters.org.

NATIONAL ASSN. OF SCIENCE WRITERS, PO Box 890, Hedgesville WV 25427. (304)754-5077. E-mail: diane@nasw.org. Website: www.nasw.org.

NATIONAL BOOK FOUNDATION. To find out about National Book Awards: www.nationalbook.org.

NATIONAL RELIGIOUS BROADCASTERS, 9510 Technology Dr., Manassas VA 20110. (703)330-7000. Fax (703)330-7100. E-mail: info@nrb.org. Website: www.nrb.org.

NATIONAL SPEAKERS ASSN., 1500 S. Priest Dr., Tempe AZ 85281. (480)968-2552. Fax (480)968-0911. Email: information@nsaspeaker.org. Website: www.nsaspeaker.org. Conventions and training for professional speakers. Puts out *Professional Speaker Magazine.*

NATIONAL WRITERS ASSN. (NWA), 10940 S. Parker Rd., #508, Parker CO 80134. (303)841-0246. E-mail: anitaedits@aol.com. Website: www.nationalwriters.com.

NATIONAL WRITERS UNION, 113 University Pl., 6th Fl., New York NY 10003. (212)254-0279. Fax (212)254-0673. E-mail: nwu@nwu.org. Website: www.nwu.org. The National Writers Union is the only U.S. trade union for freelance writers. Offers contract advice, grievance resolution, health and dental plans, member education, Job Hotline, and networking. Employers list contract and freelance jobs for free and deal directly with writers. See Website for list of local groups.

NEWSPAPER ASSN. OF AMERICA. Focuses on strategic issues such as marketing, public policy, diversity, industry development, electronic publishing, and newspaper operations: www.naa.org.

OUTDOOR WRITERS ASSN. OF AMERICA. Kevin Rhoades, exec. dir., 121 Hickory St., Ste. 1, Missoula MT 59801. Toll-free (800)692-2477. (406)728-7434. E-mail: krhoades@owaa.org. Website: www.owaa.org.

+PEACE RIVER CENTER FOR WRITERS. Carol Mahler, exec. dir., Punta Gorda History Park, 01 Shreve St., Punta Gorda, FL 33950. (941)575-1976. Fax (413)653-6681. E-mail: peaceriverwriters@comcast.net. Offers an array of educational and informational programs, services, and events. Monthly newsletter. Website: www.peaceriverwriters.org.

PEN AMERICAN CENTER, 588 Broadway, Ste. 303, New York NY 10012. (212)334-1660. Fax (212)334-2181. E-mail: pen@pen.org. Website: www.pen.org. Membership open to playwrights/editors/essayists/novelists. For information on finding grants for writers, subscribe to online version of *Pen Grants and Awards Available to American Writers.* $12 for one year.

PEN CENTER USA, c/o Antioch University, 400 Corporate Pointe, Culver City CA 90230. (310)862-1555. Fax (310)862-1556. E-mail: pen@penusa.org. Members work to defend the rights of writers nationally and internationally and to foster a literary community among the diverse writers living in the western United States: http://penusa.org/go.

+PROFESSIONAL WRITERS ASSOCIATION OF CANADA. www.pwac.ca.

PUBLISHERS WEEKLY. The international news magazine and trade journal for the general book publishing and bookselling industry: www.publishersweekly.com.

RELIGION NEWS SERVICE, 1101 Connecticut Ave. N.W., Ste. 350, Washington DC 20036. (202)463-8777. Toll-free (800)767-6781. Fax (202)463-0033. E-mail: info@religionnews.com. Website: www.religionnews.com. A general news service devoted to unbiased coverage of religion and ethics.

RELIGION NEWSWRITERS ASSN. Helping journalists cover religion with balance, accuracy, and insight: www.rna.org.

RELIGION NEWSWRITERS FOUNDATION (RNF). Website: www.rna.org.

ROMANCE WRITERS OF AMERICA. (832)717-5200. Fax (832)717-5201. E-mail: info@rwanational.org. Website: www.rwanational.org.

SCIENCE FICTION AND FANTASY WRITERS OF AMERICA, PO Box 877, Chestertown MD 21620. (207)861-8078. E-mail: execdir@sfwa.org. Website: www.sfwa.org.

SMALL PUBLISHERS ASSN. OF NORTH AMERICA (SPAN), 1618 W. Colorado Ave., Colorado Springs CO 80904. (719)475-1726. Fax (719)471-2182. E-mail: Span@SPANnet.org. Website: www.SPANnet.org. A nonprofit professional trade association for independent presses, self-publishers, and authors.

SOCIETY OF AMERICAN TRAVEL WRITERS. Provides support and development for its 1,200 members. Application fee $250. Annual membership $130. Website: www.satw.org.

SOCIETY OF CHILDREN'S BOOK WRITERS & ILLUSTRATORS. Lin Oliver, exec. dir., 8271 Beverly Blvd., Los Angeles CA 90048. (323)782-1010. E-mail: scbwi@scbwi.org. Website: www.scbwi.org.

SOCIETY OF PROFESSIONAL JOURNALISTS. Offers its members career training and support. E-mail from Website: www.spj.org.

WESTERN WRITERS OF AMERICA. Paul Andrew Hutton, exec. dir., e-mail: wwa@unm.edu. 500 members who write everything from mainstream fiction to local history. Annual conference last week in June in a western city attended by members, editors, and agents. Website: www.westernwriters.org.

WRITERS GUILD OF AMERICA EAST, 555 W. 57th St., Ste. 1230, New York NY 10019. (212)767-7800. Fax (212)582-1909. Website: www.wgaeast.org.

WRITERS GUILD OF AMERICA WEST, 7000 W. 3rd St., Los Angeles CA 90048. (323)951-4000. Toll-free (800)548-4532. Fax (323)782-4800. Website: www.wga.org.

WRITERS INFORMATION NETWORK, PO Box 11337, Bainbridge Island WA 98110. (206)842-9103. Fax (206)842-0536. Contact: Elaine Wright Colvin. E-mail: writersinfo network@juno.com. Website: www.Christianwritersinfo.net. A professional association for Christian writers. Newsletter, seminars, editorial services. Annual membership $49.95, includes the bimonthly magazine *WIN-Informer.*

WRITERS' UNION OF CANADA, 90 Richmond St. E., Ste. 200, Toronto ON M5C 1P1, Canada. (416)703-8982. Fax (416)504-9090. E-mail: info@writersunion.ca. Website: www.writers union.ca.

HELP FOR NEW WRITERS

+ABSOLUTEWRITE.COM. Great site for beginning writers by Writer's Digest contributing editor Jenna Glatzer: www.absolutewrite.com.

ADVICE FOR NEW WRITERS. (1) *No Fear Strategies for Publishing Your First Articles and Book.* David Sanford's 45-minute audio seminar. For a copy of the seminar, send a check for $15 to: Sanford Communications Inc., 16778 S.E. Cohiba Ct., Damascus OR 97015-6827. (2) Stephen L. Blain offers original book reviews, inspiring writing prompts, book giveaway contests, and advice for new writers. Also subscribe to *Writing Sparks* newsletter. Website: www.oncewritten.com.

BUSINESS HELP. (1) *Shelf-Awareness* is a free newsletter to help the writer learn more about business aspects of writing. (2) A community for small-business owners where you can get answers to key business questions: www.work.com.

+BOOKS AND AUTHORS. Website: www.booksandauthors.net.

CHRISTIAN WRITERS SEMINAR. Offers tapes of its conference and workshops on a wide variety of writing instruction targeted toward beginning-to-intermediate writers. Print order from Website and mail to Christian Writers Seminar, 19300 Redwood Rd., Castro Valley CA 94546-3465 or e-mail Jon Drury at jdrury@redwoodchapel.org. Website: www.christianwriter.org.

FIRSTWRITER.COM. Find information about contests, classes, agents, markets, tips, and more: www.firstwriter.com.

+FROM THE EDITOR'S DESK. This article will be especially helpful for beginning writers. Site also offers video clips and other articles on writing: www.aspire2.com/writing.htm.

+GET ORGANIZED. How to be an organized writer: www.organizedwriter.com/index.htm.

MANUSCRIPT GUIDELINES. (1) Site features a chart containing a variety of manuscript types and lists average word count and average number of pages for each type: www.pwcwriters.org/penpoints4.htm; (2) www.shunn.net/writing/coach/format.html.

+NOVICE WRITERS. For beginning writers, this is a place to test the waters: http://novicewriters.net.

OVERCOMING WRITERS BLOCK. (1) Lisa Cohen's helpful site for the writer: http://sff.net/people/LisaRC. (2) This site features a ton of generators for ideas, characters, and names: www.seventhsanctum.com/index-writ.php. (3) For more inspiration, go to: www.profitable-pen.com.

+RELEVANTPROSE. A site for aspiring writers: www.relevantprose.com.

+WHAT TO EXPECT WHEN YOU GET PUBLISHED. Website: www.jennybent.com/expect/what_to_expect_when_you_get_published.pdf.

WRITERS SUITE. An online publishing community of writers, readers, and educators featuring 40,000 discussion threads, 400 blogs, 75,000 articles, and 120 courses: www.suite101.com.

+WRITER TO WRITER. Covers marketing, promotion, writing techniques, finding ideas, submissions, getting a Website, publicity, and more. This online magazine is written and produced by award-winning, multipublished Australian writer, Cheryl Wright: www.writer2writer.com.

+WRITING BASICS. E-books that integrate faith and writing: www.write4christ.com.

WRITING CORNER. Links to author Web pages, markets, newsletters, writing schools, recommended books, and grammar tips: www.writingcorner.com.

WRITING WORLD. Good site for new writers. A step-by-step guide to launching a writing career and other important tips: www.writing-world.com.

ILLUSTRATION SOURCES

+ASSOCIATED PRESS PHOTO ARCHIVE. Website: www.apimages.com/eng/index.html?photoarchive.

BOOK COVERS AND MORE. For made-to-order, original illustration, layout, and design of book covers, contact Mike Bennett Graphics at (860)627-9772. Visit Mike's Website to see many examples of his cover designs and additional graphic arts including logo designs, Website designs, and more: www.mikebennettgraphics.com.

BUREAU OF LAND MANAGEMENT PHOTOS. For historical pictures of the Western United States from the 1890s to 1970, go to: www.photos.blm.gov/hist_index.html. This site is currently offline. Check back from time to time. It is worth the wait. E-mail: woinfo@blm.gov.

CARTOONS. (1) Contact: Ron Wheeler. E-mail: ron@cartoonworks.com. Website: www.cartoonworks.com. Provides cartoon illustrations for articles. (2) See latest portfolio additions: www.ronwheeler.com. (3) For Christian cartoons, visit Dan Rosandich's site: www.danscartoons.com. He offers existing images to license for usage in newsletters, presentations, magazines, Websites, books, calendars, etc.

CELEBRITY PHOTOS. If you need pictures of famous folks, try these two Websites: (1) www.mptv.net or (2) www.celebritypictures.co.uk.

CORBIS. Stock photography and digital pictures: www.corbis.com.

GOVERNMENT PHOTOS. (1) In the U.S., weather-related photographs are available at the National Oceanic and Atmospheric Administration: www.photolib.noaa.gov. (2) The United States Library of Congress site includes historical photographs and American celebrities: www.loc.gov.

GRAPHIC ARTIST. Contact Barbara McDonald at logolady1@aol.com. For an example of her work, go to Amazon.com and search for a book entitled *Gourmet Meetings on a Microwave Schedule.* She did the cover for the book.

+GRAPHIC DESIGNER. Carrie Fossati specializes in women's ministry designs. Offers bookmarks, postcards, brochures, conference marketing materials, CD jackets, DVD covers, and more. E-mail: cfdesigns@cox.net.

INTERNET PHOTO SOURCES. (1) AP Wide World Photos offers an online collection of 700,000 photos of people and events around the world. Price varies. Website: www.apwideworld.com. (2) Fotosearch combines several major online stock photo supplies into one site: www.fotosearch.com. (3) Getty Image. Around the world current photos: www.gettyimages.com. (4) MGN Online has fewer images but lower prices than Getty: www.mgnonline.com. (5) Newscom brings together images from many news agencies: www.newscom.com. (6) Photos to Go has a library of a half-million digital images available for licensing. This company also offers collections of royalty-free images on CD. Images now provided by Indexopen.com and IndexStock. Website: www.photostogo.com. Other stock photo sites include: (7) www.blackstar.com; (8) www.comstock.com; (9) www.images.com; (10) www.indexstock.com ; (11) www.mira.com; (12) www.photodisc.com; (13) www.picturequest.com; (14) www.stockphoto.com; (15) www.istockphoto.com; (16) http://images.google.com.

LIDIA SIMEONOVA. Available for designing book covers for writers and publishers. E-mail: from Website: absolutearts.com/portfolios/s/simlinstudio.

MAZZOCCHI GROUP GRAPHIC DESIGN, PO Box 68, Three Rivers MI 49093. (269)273-7070. Specializes in custom, full-color designs for the book cover of your self-published book. Designed by a Christian artist with over 20 years' experience.

MINISTRY PHOTOS. Worldwide Challenge Photo Gallery offers real life "ministry in action" photos: www.wwcmagazine.org/photos.

THE NATIONAL CARTOON MUSEUM (formerly International Museum of Cartoon Art). Website: www.cartoon.org /home.htm. E-mail: inquiry@cartoon.org.

PHOTOGRAPHERS. (1) If you are looking for a photographer rather than a photograph, go to: www.christiansinphotojournalism.org. (2) Also visit: www.photographers.com. (3) For a high quality photo resource, check out: www.whitmers.com or e-mail jim@whitmers.com.

PHOTOSOURCEBANK. PhotoSource Intl., Rohn Engh, dir. (715)248-3800. E-mail: info@photosource.com. Good source of stock photos. Offers an opportunity for you to post a description of the photos you have for sale on this Website: www.photosource.com.

RELIGIOUS STOCK PHOTOGRAPHY. Ponkawonka Inc. specializes in Christianity and other world religions. Contributions from professional photographers. Includes 500,000 images: www.ponkawonka.com.

RON ANDERSON PHOTO. Outdoor photography for book covers, book content, inspirational calendars, or daily journals: www.ronandersonphoto.com. E-mail: randerson7@charter.net.

SKJOLD PHOTOGRAPHS. Steve and Mary Skjold. Toll-free (800)484-9655, Security Code 9750. E-mail: skjfoto@skjoldphotographs.com. Website: www.skjoldphotographs.com. Interactive site with large, clear pictures available for downloading and placement. Features over 5000 stock photos of children, teens, classrooms, homeless, religious, and holidays.

SPORTS PHOTOS. Sports photos are available at Websites: (1) www.empics.com; (2) www.allsportusa.com.

TIPS ON FINDING & USING PHOTOS. For useful information, visit Sree's Tips on finding and using photos: www.sree.net/tips/graphics.html.

LANGUAGE/VOCABULARY

ACRONYM AND ABBREVIATION LIST. Allows you to search for over 530,000 acronyms, abbreviations, and definitions about all subjects, including information technology, business, telecommunications, military, government, and much more: www.AcronymFinder.com.

ANAGRAMS. An anagram is a word or phrase formed by rearranging the letters of another word or phrase: www.wordsmith.org/anagram.

APHORISMS. Website: www.aphorismsgalore.com.

AUSTRALIAN SLANG DICTIONARY. Website: www.koalanet.com.au/australian-slang.html.

+BAD METAPHORS. Do you know a bad metaphor when you see one? Check out this site for poorly written metaphors in student essays: www.mistupid.com/people/page027.htm.

+CLICHÉ CLEANER. www.cliches.biz/clichecleaner/index.html.

CLICHÉ FINDER. (1) Over 3,000 clichés listed: www.westegg.com/cliche. (2) Also see: www.plainenglish.co.uk for the Plain English Campaign against clichés; (3) www.copydesk.org/words; (4) www.jprof.com/writing/cliches.html.

COMMON ERRORS IN ENGLISH. (1) www.wsu.edu/~brians/errors/errors.html; (2) www.askoxford.com/betterwriting/classicerrors.

CONJUGATE VERBS. Check out this site for languages, modern and ancient: www.verbix.com/webverbix.

DE-MYSTIFYING BUZZWORDS. Website: www.buzzwhack.com. Sign up for the buzzword of the day.

THE DIALECTIZER. Converts English to Redneck, Jive, Cockney, Elmer Fudd, Swedish Chef, or Pig Latin: www.rinkworks.com/dialect.

DICTIONARY.COM. Type in the word you are looking for, and if there is no match, it makes suggestions that are hyperlinked so you can check the meaning to make sure it is the word you are actually seeking: www.dictionary.com.

DO YOU SPEAK AMERICAN? PBS program on American English: www.pbs.org/speak.

ENGLISH LESSONS. Free online English lessons: www.englishpage.com.

ENGLISH WORDS AND PHRASES. What words mean, where they came from, how they have evolved, and the ways people misuse them: www.worldwidewords.org.

ETYMOLOGY DICTIONARY. What did a word mean 600 or 2,000 years ago? Check out: www.etymonline.com.

FUN WITH WORDS. (1) www.fun-with-words.com. "The Wordplay Website." (2) Bob Kelly's newsletters contain word puzzles and memorable quotes: www.wordcrafters.

THE GLOSSARIST. A searchable directory of glossaries and topical dictionaries: www.glossarist.com.

GOOGLE TOOLS. (1) Language Tools allows you to search by specific languages or countries and translates texts: www.google.com/language_tools?hl=en. (2) Another Google feature when you need a quick word definition: Type "define:word" (no spaces), and Google will define the word.

GRAMMAR WEBSITES. (1) www.grammarcheck.com. Free weekly e-mail newsletter that helps improve your grammar, punctuation, and writing skills. See also: (2) www.edufind.com/english/grammar; (3) www.grammarlady.com; (4) www.writingenglish.com; (5) http://finance.groups.yahoo.com/group/writing-tips; (6) www.webgrammar.com.

IDIOMS. Learn the origin of phrases that have found their way into our everyday language: www.idiomsite.com.

LANGUAGE CONSTRUCTION KIT. Create your own language: www.zompist.com/kit.html.

LEXICAL SITE. Website: www.lexfn.com. Goes beyond giving synonyms; it also links words so that synonyms, antonyms, or words related by any of 16 different criteria may be found.

LINGUISTICS. Website: www.sfwa.org/members/elgin/Linguistics/RWL05.html. *A Lesson, Real World Linguistics 101,* by Suzette Haden Elgin.

MISSPELLED WORDS. For a list of 100 most commonly misspelled words, visit: http://your dictionary.com/library/misspelled.html.

OXYMORON: CONTRADICTORY WORDS. Website: www.oxymoronlist.com. Here's a self-proclaimed "Largest List of Oxymorons Ever Collected Online!"

THE PHRASE FINDER. Index of over 2,000 English sayings, phrases, and idioms: www.phrases .org.uk/index.html.

PRONUNCIATION GUIDE. The Voice of America Pronunciation Guide: http://ibb7.ibb.gov/ pronunciations.

QUIZZES. To improve your craft, check out these Websites: (1) www.edufind.com; (2) http:// grammar.ccc.commnet.edu/grammar; (3) www.copydesk.org/quizzes/quiz26.htm; (4) www .copydesk.org/quizzes/quiz48.htm; (5) www.dailygrammar.com/archive.shtml; (6) http:// grammar.ccc.commnet.edu/grammar/quiz_list.htm; (7) www.spelling-tests.com; (8) www .sentex.net/~mmcadams/spelling.html.

SLANG. (1) Website: www.slangsite.com. Here's a site where you can find the latest hip lingo. (2) Hip-Hop Lyrics Archive: www.ohhla.com; (3) For UK slang: www.peevish.co.uk/ slang/index.htm; (4) Rap Dictionary: www.rapdict.org; (5) Urban Dictionary: www.urban dictionary.com. Books on slang: (6) *Random House Historical Dictionary of American Slang,* ISBN 13: 978-0394544274; (7) *The Thesaurus of Slang,* by Esther Lewin and Albert E. Lewin (Checkmark Books), ISBN 13: 978-0816036615.

SYNONYMS AND ANTONYMS. (1) Website: http://wordweb.info. Downloadable program from almost any Windows-based program; (2) www.rhymezone.com.

TEEN LINGO. Website: www.thesourcefym.com/teenlingo.

TEXT ANALYSER. This site will analyze your text for word count, readability, sentence count, average sentence length, and most frequently used words: http://textalyser.net.

TRANSLATIONS. Websites: (1) http://babelfish.altavista.com/translate.dyn. Babelfish Translations. Type anything in English and it will translate it into either Spanish, French, Portuguese, Italian, German or the other way around; (2)http://translate.google.com/translate_t. Instantly translates from English to German, Spanish, French, Italian, and Portuguese, and from each of these into the others. Will even translate Website addresses; (3) http://translation2 .paralink.com. English, French, German, Russian, and Spanish; (4) Logos translates 188 languages at: www.logos.it.

THE VERB E-ZINE. Offers an active guide to better writing: www.readingwriters.com. Subscribe from Website.

THE VOCABULA REVIEW. An online journal about the state of the English language, with tips on grammar, articles, and more: www.vocabula.com.

WEBSTER'S ONLINE DICTIONARY. Search over 3 million words and expressions and find background origins, definitions, crosswords, rhyming words, quotations, and more: www.websters-online-dictionary.org.

A WORD A DAY. (1) Website: www.wordsmith.org/awad/index.html. Sign up to get a new word and its definition sent each day. (2) The Merriam-Webster Website also offers a word-a-day: www.m-w.com. (3) To subscribe to Hebrew word-a-day: http://HebrewResources.com. (4) Another site: www.vocabvitamins.com. It features a word-a-day with definitions, word origins, and an example of the word in text. Check out the "Reference" page for more links to interesting sites. Also see: (5) http://dictionary.reference.com.

+WORD AND PHRASE ORIGINS. Website: www.wordwizard.com.

WORD COUNTER. (1) Website: www.wordcounter.com. Ranks the most frequently used words in any body of text. (2) Another interesting site ranks words in order from the most to least frequently used: www.wordcount.org/main.php.

WORD POLICE. Website: www.theatlantic.com/unbound/wordpolice/six.

WORDS. (1) Source of popular new words or new uses: www.wordspy.com. Other word sites: (2) www.verbatimmag.com; (3) www.wordplays.com/p/index; (4) http://susettewilliams.com.

+WORD USAGE. Check this site out for word usage clarification: www.sparknotes.com/writing/style/.

WORTHLESS WORD OF THE DAY. Website: http://home.comcast.net/~wwftd/.

LEGAL CONCERNS

ASJA CONTRACTS WATCH. Offers free e-newsletter from the American Society of Journalists and Authors that keeps writers up to date on latest contract developments: www.asja.org.

AUTHORSLAWYER.COM. Find resources on copyright, literary scams, and more: www.authorslawyer.com.

BETTER BUSINESS BUREAU. If you are the victim of fraud or have questions/concerns about an agent or publisher, contact the Better Business Bureau in their town, as well as their local attorney general or their state attorney general's office of consumer protection. You can also contact the Better Business Bureau online to see if a certain company has any complaints on file. Website: www.bbb.org.

BOOKS FOR LEGAL CONCERNS. Books available through local retailer. (1) *The Copyright Permission and Libel Handbook: A Step-by-Step Guide for Writers, Editors, and Publishers* by Lloyd J. Jassin and Steve C. Schecter; (2) *The Practical Guide to Libel Law* by Neil J. Rosini; (3) *The Writer's Legal Companion* by Brad Bunnin and Peter Beren. Covers contracts, agents, copyright, taxes, libel, permissions, and more. (4) *How to Form a Limited Liability Company* by Mark Warda (Sphinx Publishing), ISBN 13: 978-1572482227; (5) *Incorporate Your Business: A Legal Guide to Forming a Corporation in Your State* by Anthony Mancuso (NOLO), ISBN 13: 978-1413306361.

CODE OF FAIR PRACTICE. Ethical standards and contract guidelines for editorial freelancers and clients: www.the-efa.org/res/code_TOC.html.

COPYRIGHT AND COPY WRONGS. Website: www.education-world.com/a_curr/curr280a.shtml. Multipart article for teachers and writers.

COPYRIGHT AND PUBLISHING LAW ATTORNEY. Law Office of Sallie G. Randolph, 520 Franklin St., Buffalo NY 14202. (716)885-1847. E-mail: sallie@authorlaw.com. Website: www.authorlaw.com. Available to consult with writers or their attorneys about publishing law issues. Available for speaking and teaching. Coauthor of *Author Law A to Z* (available at www.stuartmarket.com).

COPYRIGHT INFORMATION. Websites: (1) www.templetons.com/brad/copymyths.htm. Brad Templeton's article gives important information on copyrights. (2) www.writing-world.com/rights/topten.shtml. Answers the top ten questions about copyright permissions. (3) www.writersweekly.com/stamford.html; (4) www.copyrightauthority.com/poor-mans-copyright/; (5) www.bitlaw.com/copyright/duration.html; (6) Copyright Navigator: http://navigator.carolon.net. (7) "Taking the Mystery Out of Copyright" is designed for kids but can help everyone understand it more easily: www.copyright.gov.

COPYRIGHT LAW—LIBRARY OF CONGRESS COPYRIGHT OFFICE, 101 Independence Ave. S.E., Washington DC 20559-6000. (202)707-3000. (1) Website: www.copyright.gov. Available in Spanish: www.copyright.gov/espanol. You may call or write for forms or get them from the Website. To view the most current copyright rates, go to: www.copyright.gov/docs/fees.html. Also check out these copyright information sites: (2) www.benedict.com; (3) www.whatiscopyright.org. (4) To check on status of your copyrights, go to: www.copyright.gov/records/cohm.html.

COPYRIGHT PIRACY. Website: www.sharpwriter.com/content/piracy.htm. Offers one writer's experience with pirates.

+DISAPPEARING COPYRIGHT REGISTRATION. Check the U.S. Copyright Office site (www.copyright.gov) to make sure your copyright is listed. If not, go to www.asja.org/cw/cw.php and send an e-mail to the ASJA Contracts Committee.

ELECTRONIC RIGHTS. Concerned about electronic rights? Check out ASJA discussion at: www.asja.org/pubtips/ewrongs.php.

+ETHICS SITES. (1) American Society of Business Publication Editors. Sheds light on preferred practices for writers, too: www.asbpe.org/about/code.htm; (2) Association of Authors' Representatives: www.aar-online.org. (3) For travel writers, go to: www.satw.org/satw/index.asp?SId=81; (4) Society of Professional Journalists: www.spj.org/ethicscode.asp.

FAIR BUSINESS PRACTICES BRANCH, COMPETITION BUREAU, INDUSTRY CANADA. (1) Website: http://competition.ic.gc.ca. Contact about illegal or unethical behavior by an agent or publisher in Canada. (2) You also might notify or contact The Canadian Author's Assn., Box 419, Campbellford ON K0L 1L0, Canada. (705)653-0323. Toll-free (866) 216-6222. Fax (705)653-0593. E-mail: admin@canauthors.org. Website: www.canauthors.org.

THE FEDERAL TRADE COMMISSION, BUREAU OF CONSUMER PROTECTION. (1) Consumer Response Center (CRC). Toll-free (877)382-4357. (202)326-2222. Website: www.ftc.gov. Contact about illegal or unethical behavior by an agent or publisher in the U.S. Click "File a Complaint" in the menu bar to access FTC's Public Complaint Form. (2) Federal, state, and local government site: www.govengine.com.

FREEDOM OF INFORMATION ACT BY THE SOCIETY OF PROFESSIONAL JOURNALISTS. Website: http://spj.org/foi.asp?.

+HOW MUCH CAN YOU QUOTE? Find helpful information at: http://en.wikipedia.org/wiki/Fair_use.

+HUMAN RESOURCES. (1) Check FAQ on a variety of legal topics, including "Hiring Your First Employee." Website: www.nolo.com. (2) For modules on operations and personnel, check out: www.cbaonline.org.

+HYMNAL COPYRIGHTS. To determine if a hymn is in public domain: www.cyberhymnal.org.

INTELLECTUAL PROPERTY LAW. Look up copyrights or connect to legal reference sites: www.intelproplaw.com.

INTERNATIONAL TRADEMARK ASSN. Website: www.inta.org. Offers free information about trademarks. (212)642-1700. Fax (212) 768-7796. E-mail: info@inta.org.

ISBN CHANGES. Beginning January 1, 2007, ISBN agencies all over the world assigned new ISBN numbers that are 13 digits long, replacing the 10 digit numbers currently provided. The bar codes will not change. For more information: www.isbn-13.info.

JOURNALISM CONTRACTS. Website: www.nwu.org. Click on "Journalists" in the left margin.

LEGAL SITE FOR WRITERS. Daniel N. Steven, publishing attorney and consultant. Website: www.publishlawyer.com. The legal resource for publishing professionals.

NOLO: Law for All. Includes comprehensive legal explanations about trademarks and copyrights: www.nolo.com/encyclopedia/tc_ency.html.

PATENT CAFÉ. Website: www.patentcafe.com. "Intellectual Property Management."

PERMISSIONS CONTACTS. Websites: (1) www.publist.com. Lists over 150,000 publications with basic information, including who to contact for permissions. (2) www.ucpress.edu/press/Rights&Permissions.html.

PLAGIARISM. (1) For articles dealing with plagiarism: www.writersweekly.com/search.html and enter the search word "Plagiarism." (2) Another Website: www.web-miner.com/plagiarism.

PROTECTING YOUR SCRIPT/COPYRIGHT. Registration facts and fiction: www.writersstore.com/article.php?articles_id=532&discount=ezine@source=ezine.

PUBLIC DOMAIN CHART. (1) This chart will help you determine if a work has gone into public domain or not: www.bromsun.com/practices/copyright-portfolio-development/flowchart.htm. Also see: (2) www.unc.edu/~unclng/public-d.htm; (3) www.copyright.cornell.edu/training/Hirtle_Public_Domain.htm.

THE PUBLISHING LAW CENTER. Lloyd L. Rich, Property Rights Attorney, 1163 Vine St., Denver CO 80206. (303)388-0291. Fax (303)388-0477. E-mail: rich@publishingattorney.com. Offers a free newsletter and articles that concern publishing law (copyright, trademarks, contracts, Internet law) and other issues regarding the protection of intellectual property: www.publaw.com.

+SCAMS AND PREDITORS. Website: www.anotherrealm.com/preditors/pubwarn.htm.

SMALL BUSINESSES. (1) Launched by the Small Business Administration to provide indexes in one central location and links to credible sources of information such as licenses, permits, e-commerce, and exporting. The site also includes information specific to each state and territory: www.businesslaw.gov. (2) For forms, go to: http://sba.gov/starting_business/legal/forms.html. (3) To select the legal structure for your business, visit: http://sba.gov/library/pubs/mp-25.doc.

TRADE BOOK PUBLISHING AGREEMENT CHECKLIST. A good overview of items commonly found in a book publishing agreement: www.copylaw.com/forms/pubchk.html.

U.S. PATENT AND TRADEMARK OFFICE. Trademark process information in easy terms: www.uspto.gov.

VOLUNTEER LAWYERS FOR THE ARTS, 1 East 53rd St., 6th Fl., New York NY 10022. (212)319-2787, ext. 1. Fax (212)752-6575. Website: www.vlany.org.

WARNINGS. (1) A site to check out when you are having trouble getting payment or wondering about the legitimacy of a publisher: www.writersweekly.com/search.html. Enter the search words "Whispers and Warnings." (2) Also see: www.nwu.org. Click on "Writer Alerts" on sidebar.

MARKET SOURCES

ANTHOLOGIES ONLINE. Website: www.anthologiesonline.com. A listing of anthologies looking for contributors. Writers should subscribe and send in brief bio and best writing sample (up to 1,200 words total) to apply to become a feature writer.

AREOPAGUS GUIDE TO UK CHRISTIAN PUBLICATIONS. Published quarterly. U.S. price $17. Order from: www.areopagus.org.uk/index1.html.

ASK THE EXPERTS. (1) Hosted on Maureen McMahon's site, click on "Ask the Experts" link. Ask a book marketing question and a response will be e-mailed back to you within 4 working days. Experts include authors, editors, book reviewers, book coaches, ghostwriters, publicists, and publishers: www.maureenmcmahon.com. (2) Marketing message boards where you can ask questions: www.jorlanpublishing.com/phpBB2/.

BOOK MARKETING/PROMOTION CHECKLIST. *22 Ways to Promote and Sell Books,* by John B. McHugh. Free. Website: www.johnbmchugh.com. Click on "Free McHugh Publications."

BOOK MARKETING UPDATE. Bimonthly publication by subscription. For sample issue, go to: www.bookmarketingupdate.com.

BOOK PROMOTION NEWSLETTER. A biweekly e-zine for authors of all genres. Authors, publicists, publishers, editors, literary agents, book reviewers, and book coaches are welcome to contribute articles, promotional coups, announcements, and feedback. $7.50 annual fee. Website: www.bookpromotionnewsletter.com.

BOOK PROPOSALS. (1) To purchase a copy of *Book Proposals that Sell: 21 Secrets to Speed Your Success* by W. Terry Whalin, go to: www.stuartmarket.com. (2) To download e-book

Writing a Winning Book Proposal from Thomas Nelson Publishers, go to: www.thomas nelson.com/consumer/downloads/writingabookproposal.pdf.

+BOOK PUBLISHING REPORT. Source of news, objective analysis, and insight into the book publishing industry, including revenue and product strategies of competitors, how technology is changing content development and delivery, and exclusive industry rankings. Purchase at www.simbanet.com/trade/info.asp. $715/50 issues (electronic or print).

BOOKSCHRISTIAN.COM. To promote your book, go to: www.bookschristian.com. E-mail: customerservice@bookschristian.com.

+BOOKS ON MARKETING. (1) *Marketing to Moms* by Maria T. Bailey (Prima Lifestyles), ISBN 13: 978-0761563662; (2) *How to Write a Successful Book Proposal in 8 Days or Less* by Patricia L. Fry (Matilija Press), ISBN 13: 978-0961264291; (3) *The Frugal Book Promoter* by Carolyn Howard-Johnson (Star Publishing), ISBN 13: 978-1932993103; (4) *How to Write a Book Proposal* (Third Edition) by Michael Larsen (Writer's Digest Books), ISBN 13: 978-1582972510; (5) *Write the Perfect Book Proposal: 10 That Sold and Why* by Jeff Herman and Deborah Levine Herman (Wiley), ISBN 13: 978-0471353126; (6) *How to Publish Your Articles* by Shirley Kawa-Jump (Square One Publishers), ISBN 13: 978-0757000164; (7) *The Insider's Guide to Getting an Agent* by Lori Perkins (Writer's Digest Books), ISBN 13: 978-1582973685; (8) *Techniques of the Selling Writer* by Dwight V. Swain, (University of Oklahoma Press), ISBN 13: 978-0806111919; (9) *1001 Ways to Market Your Books* by John Kremer (Open Horizons), ISBN 13: 978-0912411491; (10) *Becoming the Brand of Choice* by Jason Hartman (Lifestyles Press), ISBN 13: 978-1583200049; (11) *Tested Advertising Methods* by John Caples and Fred E. Hahn (Prentice Hall), ISBN 13: 978-0130957016.

+BRADY MAGAZINE. Offers everything from free online content critiques to marketing and publicity advice: www.bradymagazine.com.

CANADIAN MARKETS. (1) PWAC members have exclusive access to *Canadian Writers' Market,* a searchable directory. Website: www.pwac.ca/resources/publications.htm. Also order *PWAC Guide to Roughing It in the Market: A Survival Toolkit for the Savvy Writer.* (2) Directory of members at www.writers.ca is a free searchable database.

+CHRISTIAN AUTHORS NETWORK BLOG. A blog for authors marketing their books: http://canblog.typepad.com.

CHRISTIAN MANUSCRIPT SUBMISSIONS.COM (formerly First Edition). Website: www.ChristianManuscriptSubmissions.com. This is an online submission service provided by ECPA publishing houses. Fee is $98 for 6 months in database.

CHRISTIAN WRITERS' MARKET GUIDE WEBSITE. Sally Stuart's Website with information on the latest guide, links to the Websites or e-mail of all the Christian publishers or publications that have them, a listing of conferences for the year, and a bookstore with more than 60 books and pamphlets specifically for writers: www.stuartmarket.com.

DIRECTORY OF PUBLISHERS AND VENDORS. Search for publishers' Websites using this handy subject directory: http://acqweb.org.

GUIDELINES DATABASE. Writer's Digest has the Web's largest database of guidelines provided by book and magazine editors. Searchable by keyword, specific words, or phrases: www.writersdigest.com/guidelines.asp.

IDEAMARKETERS.COM. Contact: Marnie L. Pehrson, dir., 514 Old Hickory Ln., Ringgold GA 30736. (706)866-2295. E-mail: webmaster@ideamarketers.com. Website: www.ideamarketers.com. A media-matching service that unites writers and publishers. Writers post their articles for free, and they are stored in a searchable database. Publishers, Web masters, and e-zine editors can then search for content. There is a link at the top of each article to ask author's permission to use the article.

LINKS TO FOREIGN MAGAZINES & NEWSPAPERS. Websites: (1) http://dir.yahoo.com/News_and_Media/By_Region/countries; (2) www.vicnet.net.au/~ozlit (Australian); (3) www.newsdirectory.com.

LITERARY JOURNALS. Links to literary journals, journal response times, statistics, ranking, and more: www.jefferybahr.com/Publications/default.htm.

LITERARY MARKETPLACE. Website: www.literarymarketplace.com. General market guide put out by Information Today Inc., 143 Old Marlton Pike, Medford NJ 08055. Toll-free (800)300-9868. E-mail: custserv@infotoday.com. Cost $399 annually or $19.95 for weekly subscription.

+MARKETING PLANS FOR BOOK PROPOSALS. Contact Jan Coates through her Website: www.jancoates.com/ccms. Jan partners with Helen Cook, former VP of B&B Media, focusing on Christian publishers and authors.

+MARKETING SITE. Terry Whalin's blog often tackles marketing issues: http://terrywhalin.blogspot.com.

NICHE PUBLISHING. Find the best ways to publish to niche markets. Go to Gordon Burgett's site and click on his book titled *Niche Marketing for Writers and Speakers*: www.gordonburgett.com.

PAYING MARKETS. (1) For hard-to-find markets that aren't published all over the net. Also includes "how-to" advice and tips: www.justmarkets.com. (2) Paying markets newsletter archive: www.writer-on-line.com/markets.

PUBLISHER'S CATALOGS. Website: www.lights.com/publisher. Includes over 7,700 publishers. Search by publisher's name or city; takes you to the publisher's Website.

PUBLISHERS MARKETING ASSOCIATION ONLINE. Lists basic contact information on hundreds of publishers: http://pma-online.org.

PUBLISHERS OF CHRISTIAN MATERIALS. Lists Websites of Christian publishers: www.idisciple.net/christianpublishers.shtml.

ROSEDOG.COM. Website: www.rosedog.com. Connects writers, agents, and publishers. Service is $24.95/yr. for writers; free to agents and publishers.

WEB-ZINE ARTICLE DISTRIBUTION SITES. (1) www.ideamarketers.com; (2) Free content for your e-zine or Website: www.EzineArticles.com.

WOODEN HORSE PUBLISHERS. Market database for nonfiction writers, plus a glossary for writers: www.woodenhorsepub.com.

WORLDWIDE FREELANCE. Dozens of market links: www.worldwidefreelance.com/markets.htm.

+THE WRITER. This magazine site features 2,500+ markets: www.writermag.com.

WRITER'S DIGEST WEBSITE. (1) Website: www.writersdigest.com. Lots of writer's helps, including copies of writer's guidelines you can print right off the site. Website for guidelines: (2) www.writersdigest.com/guidelines.asp.

WRITER'S EDGE. Submissions service: www.WritersEdgeService.com. Their listing goes to 75 participating publishers. Evaluation $95.

WRITER'S GUIDELINES DATABASE. Lists over 600 writer's guidelines to paying markets: www.freelancewriting.com/guidelines/pages/index.html.

WRITERS MARKET. Website: www.writersmarket.com. A searchable database of over 6,000 writing markets; updated daily. Also includes Submission Tracker, *Expert Advice* articles, Agent Q&A, rate chart, industry news, and more.

WRITER'S RELIEF INC., 409 S. River St., Hackensack NJ 07601. Toll-free (866)405-3003. Fax (201)641-1253. E-mail: Ronnie@wrelief.com. Website: www.wrelief.com. An author's submission service, handling your manuscript submissions for an hourly rate of $50-70 plus postage and copying (after initial free reading), or a flat fee after completing review. Prepares manuscripts, proofreads, writes query and cover letters, tracks submissions, keeps records, etc.

MONEY-SAVING TIPS FOR WRITERS

COMPUTERS AND SUPPLIES. (1) www.overstock.com; (2) www.walmart.com; (3) www.newegg.com; (4) www.saveontoner.com.

CRAIGSLIST. Price compare just about everything; check out their "free" category: www.craigslist.com.

FREECYCLER. Pass on things you no longer need and find things you do need, absolutely free: www.freecycle.org.

FROOGLE. (1) Price compare just about everything: www.froogle.com; (2) www.mysimon.com.

+HEALTH INSURANCE. Investigate group-health-insurance rates. Fee to join, and insurance details are not explained up-front, so be wary: www.pma-online.org/benefits/insurance.cfm.

MAILING LISTS. GoDaddy's Express E-mail. For example, 250 for $3.59 per month yearly rate or 2500 for $11.69 per month yearly rate. Website: www.godaddy.com.

OFFICE SUPPLIES. (1) Staples offers bonus coupons and a discount on your next ink cartridge when you bring in your empty ink cartridge: www.staples.com; (2) Office Depot offers free delivery for online orders of $50 or more: www.officedepot.com; (3) OfficeMax will give you a discount on your next ink cartridge when you bring in your empty ink cartridge: www.officemax.com. (4) In Canada go to www.redflagdeals.com to find the latest coupons and sales.

OVERSTOCK.COM. Discount prices for home office furniture: www.overstock.com.

PHONE CARDS FROM COSTCO. Verizon rechargeable phone cards cost .029 per minute or $19.99 for 700 minutes: www.costco.com.

PROMOTIONAL SUPPLIES. (1) A great place to order bookmarks: www.printingforless.com; or try (2) http://platinumprinters.com; (3) www.iconix.biz; (4) www.qualityprintingcheap.com. (5) For other printing needs: http://gotprint.net; (6) www.onlineprinthouse.com/index.html.

SHIPPING. If you cannot get your conference planner to handle shipping back your books after the event, set up your own shipping accounts through (1) www.ups.com or (2) www.fedex.com. Find the nearest UPS or FedEx store near your conference center or hotel and ship returns from there. Be aware that Mail Boxes Etc. or other subcontractor stores may have a 30% to 40% markup.

THRIFT STORE. Salvation Army: www.satruck.com/FindStore.aspx.

USED BOOKS. (1) www.addall.com; (2) www.paperbackswap.com; (3) www.frugalreader.com; (4) www.titletrader.com.

WEB HOSTING AND DOMAINS. GoDaddy's basic rate is $36/yr. Buy domains for as little at $1.99 each. Some of GoDaddy's Websites may be objectionable, but if your focus is savings, give them a try: www.godaddy.com.

PROMOTION

ADDRESS LABELS. Add your photo or book cover to address labels: www.colorfulimages.com.

AMAZON RATINGS. To see how your book is doing on Amazon.com and to understand sales rankings, visit these sites: (1) www.greententacles.com/articles/2/18; (2) www.murdermustadvertise.com/FAQ/amazon.html; (3) www.fonerbooks.com/surfing.htm.

ARTICLES AND BOOKS OF INTEREST. (1) *The Art of Creating an Unfair Advantage: 200+ Ideas to Market Yourself and Your Books* edited by Ted Decorte. To read article, go to www.geocities.com/MadisonAvenue/Boardroom/4278/aaideas.html. (2) *35 Ways to Make Your Next Book Signing an Event* by Larry James. Website: www.writerswrite.com/journal/jan00/james.htm. (3) See other book-signing articles at: www.writing-world

.com/promotion/james.shtml. (4) *You CAN Market Your Book!* by Carmen Leal (ACW Press 2003): www.stuartmarket.com; (5) *Sell Yourself Without Selling Your Soul* by Susan Harrow (HarperCollins, 2002): www.prsecrets.com.

AUTHORLINK. Where editors, agents, writers, and readers get connected. The newly enhanced site includes Writer's Registry open to all published authors: www.authorlink.com. Includes a place to advertise/sell self-published books.

AUTHORS@YOUR LIBRARY. Free, online database connecting librarians with authors and book publicists looking to promote their books: www.ala.org/ala/ppo/progresources/authors/authorsyour.htm.

+BAMW. Taken from e-book *A Business Approach to Marketing Your Work,* this electronic newsletter mixes product, place, promotion, and price to help writers develop unique marketing plans. E-mail: akinemily@gmail.com.

BANNERS/POSTERS. (1) www.poster.com; (2) www.brittenmedia.com.

BOOK MARKETING. Dozens of resources for marketing/selling your book. Search John Kremer's Book Publishing Resource File Cabinet: www.bookmarket.com. E-mail: info@bookmarket.com.

BOOK PROMOTION NEWSLETTERS. (1) A biweekly interactive e-zine for authors of all genres. $7.50/yr. Offers tips, encouragement, and networking opportunities: www.bookpromotionnewsletter.com. (2) Another site: www.earthlycharms.com/ecpromo.htm. (3) For a list of articles on online and offline promotion by Judy Cullins, go to www.bookcoaching.com. E-mail: from Website.

BOOKWIRE. Website: www.bookwire.com. Lets general public and industry professionals know about authors touring in their area. Click on "Calendar of Events."

BROCHURES/BUSINESS CARDS. Website: www.vistaprint.com.

CD OR DVD DUPLICATION. (1) Visit Website: www.tapeanddisc.com/site.html. (2) Also contact Toby Russell, Velocity AVS, in San Diego. E-mail: toby@velocityavs.com.

CHRISTIAN AUTHORS NETWORK. Cooperative of CBA authors dedicated to promoting Christian fiction/nonfiction will promote affiliate authors through retailer events/promotions/media campaigns/distribution of a monthly e-zine, speaker's bureau. For more information, send e-mail from Website: www.christianauthorsnetwork.com.

CHRISTIAN AUTHORS PROMOTIONAL ALLIANCE (CAPA). Helps small press authors connect with retail outlets; also has interactive CD catalog: www.capalliance.org. Membership $30/yr.

CHRISTIAN E-AUTHORS. Website: http://christianeauthor.com. Purpose of site is to promote the electronic works of inspirational authors from around the world. Site offers a variety of e-books in different genres. Author links take you directly to member Websites for more information on each author. A links page offers a glimpse into the world of e-books and e-publishing. A banner and link exchanges are also available.

DEARREADER.COM. Suzanne Beeches has encouraged over 300,000 people to read. Subscribers receive 5-minute read from a chapter of a featured book. For information on getting your book listed, e-mail Suzanne Beeches at Suzanne@dearreader.com. Website: http://dearreader.com.

DESIGN SERVICES. DzinDNA.com, Mark Combs, art dir., 7802 S. Hwy 97, Sapulpa OK 74066. (918)510-8972. This is a full service design/illustration shop, specializing in logo design, illustration, print design, and production of collateral material: www.dzindna.com. Email: creative@dzindna.com.

FREE PUBLICITY. Free expert radio advertising advice for people wanting to be interviewed on radio shows to talk about their businesses: www.freepresspublicity.com.

FRUGAL MARKETING. Website: www.frugalmarketing.com. Shel Horowitz offers tips, information, and his book, *Grassroots Marketing: Getting Noticed in a Noisy World.*

GUERRILLA MARKETING FOR WRITERS, by Jay Conrad Levinson, Rick Frishman, and Michael Larsen. Ideas on how to promote your book on the Internet, including using your own Website to increase sales. Available at local bookstores, Writer's Digest Book Club, or find information at: www.writersdigest.com/store/booksearch.asp.

GUIDE TO FREELANCERS. Website: www.epassoc.org. Click on "Freelance Guide" or call (763)535-4793. A joint project of the Evangelical Press Association, Associated Church Press, and Fellowship of Christian Newspapers. Annual guide is distributed free to hundreds of Christian periodical editors; designed to help them find freelance writers, photographers, and artists. Indexed by specialty and location. Listings available to professional freelancers for a small fee.

INTERVIEWS. (1) For food writers: www.willwrite4food.com. For author interviews: (2) www.writersweekly.com; (3) www.robinfriedman.com; (4) www.olswanger.com. Both of these author sites have wonderful interviews with editors and agents.

MAILING LISTS. ParaLists, Dan Poynter, PO Box 8206-240, Santa Barbara CA 93118-8206. (805)968-7277. Toll-free (800)727-2782. Fax (805)968-1379. ParaLists offers many categories of book promotion and how to obtain mailing lists: www.parapub.com. E-mail: info@ParaPublishing.com

MARKETING HELP. (1) Website: http://cba.know-where.com/cba. Search for Christian bookstores in your area, or any area you might want to target. (2) Tips on marketing yourself without money: www.stretcher.com/stories/01/010409j.cfm.

MARKETING TIP OF THE WEEK NEWSLETTER. Plus other helps for promoting your book: http://bookmarket.com.

MEDIA LISTS. Call toll-free (888)330-4919. E-mail: listsyoucanafford@excite.com.

MINI-CD BUSINESS CARDS. Website: www.cardiscs.com.

ONLINE PRESS RELEASE DISTRIBUTION SERVICE. Also offers press release tips and templates: www.prweb.com.

PREMIER MARKETING PUBLIC RELATIONS, W6439 Lakeview Ct., Menasha WI 54952-9706. (920)991-2614. Fax (920)991-2614. E-mail: PremierMktgPR@aol.com. For customized marketing tools advertising your book, such as business cards, luggage tags, bookmarks, postcards and more, contact Judy Waggoner.

PREMIUM POSTCARDS. The U.S. Post Office will print and mail customized postcards: www.usps.com/netpost/sendpremiumpostcards_business.htm.

PRESS KITS. Advice on what a press kit should contain and how to make yours stand out: www.murdermustadvertise.com/FAQ/PressKit.html.

PRESS RELEASES. Websites: (1) www.prsa.org. Offers information about chapters and other resources. (2) A weekly magazine, offering news of interest to PR writers: www.prweek.com; (3) Free news release samples: www.imediafax.com; (4) www.stetson.edu/~rhansen/prhowto.html; (5) www.press-release-writing.com/10_essential_tips.htm; (6) www.thewritemarket.com/articles/shtm. Insert "Press Releases" in search box. (7) Book: *Handbook of Strategic Public Relations and Integrated Communications* edited by Clarke L. Caywood (McGraw-Hill). ISBN 13: 978-0786311316.

PRINTING. Websites: (1) www.megacolor.com; (2) www.qualityprintingcheap.com.

PROMOTIONAL PRODUCTS. (1) A source for creative paper products/special printing for promotion pieces: www.flourishgreetings.com. (2) For bookmarks: www.qualityprintingcheap.com. (3) To create a book cover or to put your picture on a stamp: http://photo.stamps.com. (4) For CD cases, call for a free sample pack at (800)426-8664. (5) Find gifts for writers: www.coolstuff4writers.com. (6) Find hilarious sayings about the writing life on T-shirts, mugs, notebooks, and more: www.writesideout.com.

+PROMOTIONAL SITE. Website: www.promotesomething.com.

PUBLICITY HOUND. Joan Stewart, 3434 County KK, Port Washington WI 53074. (262)284-7451. Fax (262)284-1737. E-mail: jstewart@publicityhound.com. Excellent site for publicity solutions/tips/tricks/tools for free publicity: www.publicityhound.com.

RADIO STATIONS. Find radio stations doing interviews; sorted by city, state or station: www.radio-locator.com.

RADIO-TV INTERVIEW REPORT (RTIR). E-mail: from Website: www.rtir.com. Authors pay to have their profile included in this publication that goes to over 4,000 radio and TV producers who are looking for talk-show guests.

+RELIGIOUS PRESS RELEASES. Gary McCullough, dir. (202)546-0054. Releases sent to Christian radio, TV, and print outlets as well as radio talk-show hosts: www.christiannewswire.com.

STICKERS. Websites: (1) www.maysmall.com/order.htm (10 for $3.00); (2) www.spannet.org/stickers.htm (200 for $10); (3) www.abflink.com/abflink/product_page.asp; (4) www.bookweb.org/graphics/pdfs/ABABS.pdf (500 for $5).

TALK RADIO STATIONS. Websites: (1) http://newslink.org/rneradi.html; (2) www.radio-locator.com.

PROMOTION: BOOK REVIEWERS

+AUTHOR MANIA. This site is seeking book reviews. To submit a review, go to: www.authormania.com/bookreviews.html.

BOOK CONNECTOR. Match your book's characteristics with reviewers, review sites, book clubs, and reading venues using this free database: www.bookconnector.com.

BOOK CROSSING. Book Crossing encourages people to leave books in public places for anyone to pick up and read for free. Register your book online, then "release" it. When someone picks up your book and reads it, he/she is then encouraged to go to the site and leave feedback about it. Over a million books are registered: www.bookcrossing.com.

BOOK PROMOTION MAILING LISTS. Lists magazines, newsletters, and newspapers with book review columns. Use these lists to send review copies of books and news releases. List questions? Call 800-PARAPUB. Website: http://parapub.com/maillist.cfm.

+BOOK REVIEWERS WANTED. The European Christian Writers' Resources: www.christianwriter.co.uk. Features author Ms. Abidemi Sanusi, ed.

BOOK TALK RADIO. Looking for authors to interview. Send your book synopsis, author bio, and contact information to: RadioTalkers@aol.com.

+BOOKWIRE. Publishes *BookWire Christian Publishing News & Reviews* with a distribution to more than 12,000 book professionals: www.bookwire.com.

CHRISTIAN BOOK PREVIEWS.COM. Features book excerpts, reviews, author bios, and interviews. Also offers a price comparison tool for buyers who want to find the best prices online before purchasing: www.christianbookpreviews.com.

CHRISTIAN NEWS NORTHWEST. This publication reviews local Christian authors' books, meaning Washington, Oregon, and possibly Idaho. Contact Gail Welborn. E-mail: Gail.d.welborn@verizon.net. Website: www.cnnw.com.

EXTREME CHRISTIANITY. Brian Groce, pub. Reviews original articles, poetry, musical material, and Christian artwork to consider for future publication. See submission guidelines on site: www.extremechristianity.com.

FAITHFULREADER.COM. Edited for Christian readers, site includes book reviews, author interviews, book excerpts, and study guides: www.faithfulreader.com.

GLORY GIRLS, 33290 W. 14 Mile Rd., #482, West Bloomfield MI 48322. Reading groups for African American Christian women who love God and like to read: www.glorygirlsread.net. If you would like your book considered, send 3 copies/press kit/contact information to the address above.

+HISTORICAL FICTION REVIEW. Showcasing Christian historical fiction: http://home.midsouth.rr.com/ochsner/index.html.

+HOW TO MAKE THE MOST OF YOUR INTERVIEWS. Article by J. M. Cornwell: http://members.aol.com/Raven763/article42interview.html.

+I NEED A BOOK. Website: www.ineedabook.net/Gerlach/RP.html.

THE MIDWEST BOOK REVIEW, 278 Orchard Dr., Oregon WI 53575. (608)835-7937. E-mail: mbr@execpc.com. Website: www.midwestbookreview.com. James Cox, ed-in-chief. Send copy of your book to be reviewed for library resource newsletters, etc.

TCM REVIEWS. If you wish to have your book or e-book featured on this Website, take advantage of promotional packages, or wish to donate a book for a contest, see the information on the "For Authors" page: http://tcm-ca.com/authors.html. E-mail: info@tcm-ca.com.

WEBSITES FOR BOOK REVIEWS. (1) www.barnesandnoble.com; (2) www.christianbook.com; (3) www.amazon.com; (4) www.churchfolk.com (click on "Mall" for Churchfolk books). Other Websites: (5) www.christianitytoday.com/books (includes a free newsletter). (6) www.cbaonline.org. Click on "CBA Retailers+Resources" (7) www.romantictimes.com; (8) www.libraryjournal.com. (9) The Author's Choice Book Review site for book/movie reviews for the conservative Christian. Maintained by Carolyn R. Scheidies. Refer to Book Review Guidelines. E-mail: crscheidies@mail2faith.com. Website: http://IDealinHope.com/bookreviews.

PROMOTION: PUBLICISTS

AIRLEAF PUBLISHING & BOOKSELLING. Represents your self-published or print-on-demand book in bookstores: www.airleaf.com. Toll-free (800)342-6068. E-mail: information@airleaf.com, to request author's information packet.

+F. L. ANDERSON. Christian PR that targets African American consumers: www.flanderson.com/advertise.htm.

B & B MEDIA GROUP. Contact: Tina Jacobson. Toll-free (800)927-0517. E-mail: tbbmedia@tbbmedia.com. Full service publicity and public relations media communications firm that works with publishers/speakers/writers/organizations: www.tbbmedia.com.

+KATHLEEN CAMPBELL, PUBLICIST, 1255 Lake Plaza Dr., Ste. 244, Colorado Springs CO 80906. Toll-free (877)540-6022. E-mail: kcampbell@thecompletesolution.com.

CELEBRATION RADIO (KAMB 101.5), 90 E. 16th St., Merced CA 95340. (209)723-1015. E-mail: from Website: www.celebrationradio.com.

CHRISTIAN WRITER, AUTHOR AND SPEAKER NETWORK (CAN). Fee of $79 includes your personal page creation and listing. Reaches 125,000 readers/event and conference planners/librarians/radio/TV/print media worldwide: www.goodgirlbookclubonline.com/can/index.html.

CLASS PROMOTIONAL SERVICES INC., 2201 San Pedro Drive N.E., Albuquerque NM 87110. (505)899-4283. Fax (505)899-9282. Toll-free (800)433-6633. Contact: Marita Littauer. E-mail: marita@classervices.com. Christian leaders, authors, and speaker services. Website: www.classervices.com. Click on "Promotional Services." Specializing in radio and TV interview coverage for Christian authors, speakers, and ministries. Contact: Kim Garrison. E-mail: interviews@classervices.com.

+HELEN COOK, PUBLICIST. (979)922-1512. Toll-free (800)792-1512. E-mail: helen.cook@primestarpublicity.com. Former VP of B&B Media, she provides customized media mailing and follow-up: www.primestarpublicity.com.

CREATIVE RESOURCES. Contact: Susan Otis, PO Box 1665, Sandpoint ID 83864. (208)263-8055. Toll-free (800)858-9388. E-mail: CMResource@aol.com. A Christian consulting and publicity firm that schedules 2,000 broadcast interviews annually and arranges numerous reviews, articles, and interviews in major publications. Provides services for communications and media relations to parachurch groups, publishers, broadcast ministries, and others: www.cmresourceinc.com.

+THE BLYTHE DANIEL AGENCY, 4044 Cherry Plum Dr., Colorado Springs CO 80920. (719)213-3427. E-mail: blythe@theblythedanielagency.com. Website: www.theblythedanielagency.com.

DECHANT HUGHES ASSOCIATES INC. Public Relations/Media Tours. Contact: Kelly Hughes, pres., 1440 N. Kingsbury, Chicago IL 60622. (312)280-8126. Fax (312)280-8362. E-mail: dha@dechanthughes.com. Website: www.dechanthughes.com.

EVENT MANAGEMENT SERVICES, 1127 Grove St., Clearwater FL 33755. (727)443-7115, ext. 201. Contact Marsha or Steve Friedman. Reviews your book, writes 400-600 word review, mass newspaper distribution, and clipping service. Will also help you promote your book through radio talk shows. E-mail: mfriedman@event-management.com. Website: www.event-management.com.

GLASS ROAD PUBLIC RELATIONS. Rebeca Seitz, pres., 7926 State Rte. 166 E., Fulton KY 42041. (615)986-9516. Fax (615)986-9517. E-mail: rebeca@glassroadpr.com. Website: www.GlassRoadPR.com.

GOOD GIRL BOOK CLUB ONLINE. Reading group reaching over 125,000 worldwide. Receive exposure in your target market. Rates $299 per month/per title. E-mail: advertising@goodgirlbookclubonline.com. Website: www.goodgirlbookclubonline.com/promo/index.html.

GUEST FINDER.COM. NewsBuzz Inc., PO Box 40304, Raleigh NC 27629. A place to get noticed for possible interviews, plus tips on being a better guest: www.guestfinder.com. E-mail: lorilynbailey@gmail.com. For free newsletter, e-mail: newsletter@guestfinder.com.

THE IDEA NETWORK. Contacts: Erin Saxton & Jennifer Urezzio. Visit Website: www.theideanetwork.net. E-mail: info@theideanetwork.net.

+JANE JARRELL, PUBLICIST. E-mail: Jane.Jarrell@Prodigy.net.

ANNIE JENNINGS, PUBLICIST. Offers TV, radio, and print publicity opportunities, and extensive book promotion. (908)281-6201. Fax (908)431-9296. E-mail: annie@anniejenningspr.com. Website: www.anniejenningspr.com.

M&M PUBLIC RELATIONS. Contact: Jana Muntsinger. (281)251-0480. Fax (281)251-6775. E-mail: jana@mmpublicrelations.com. Or Pam McClure (615)595-8321. Fax (615)595-8322. E-mail: pamela@mmpublicrelations.com. Website: www.mmpublicrelations.com.

MCALLISTER COMMUNICATIONS. Margaret McAllister. E-mail: info@mcallcom.com. Website: www.mcallcom.com.

MICHELE BUC. Specializes in the Christian market and worked with the publisher of *Chicken Soup for the Christian Woman's Soul.* (615)297-2379. E-mail: michele@michelerbuc.com. Website: www.michelebuc.com.

MINISTRY MARKETING SOLUTIONS. Pamela Perry, Publicist. (248)426-2300. Fax (248)471-2422. E-mail: info@ministrymarketingsolutions.com. Website: www.ministrymarketingsolutions.com. A consulting firm that provides a blend of services in marketing and public relations, targeting the African American Christian Market (AACM).

+MOSAIC PR. LaVenia LaVelle has 12 years' experience in public relations and provides public relations, special events, media training, and multicultural communications: www.mosaicpublicrelations.com. E-mail: lavenia@mosaicpublicrelations.com.

PHENIX & PHENIX, 2100 Kramer Ln., Ste. 300, Austin TX 78758. (512)478-2028. Fax (512)478-2117. E-mail: info@bookpros.com. Website: www.bookpros.com.

PR-LINK PUBLIC RELATIONS, 8190 Beechmont Ave., #361, Cincinnati OH 45255. (513)233-9090. E-mail: pgiechrist@pr-link.com. Website: www.pr-link.com.

PROMOTE YOURSELF PUBLIC RELATIONS. Raleigh Pinskey, PO Box 701, Carefree AZ 85377. (480)488-4840. E-mail: raleigh@promoteyourself.com. Website: www.promoteyourself.com.

PR/PR PUBLIC RELATIONS. Publicist Pam Lontos worked with the publisher of *Chicken Soup for the Caregiver's Soul.* (407)299-6128. E-mail: pam@prpr.net. Website: www.prpr.net.

PS MEDIA RELATIONS. Contact: Paige Harvey at paige@psmediarelations.com or Shannon Davis at Shannon@psmediarelations.com. Fax (615)523-1368. Website: www.psmedia relations.com.

PUBLICITY HOUSE. Tim Shook, 2770 Haystack Dr., Colorado Springs CO 80922. (719)579-6472. E-mail: publicityhouse1@hotmail.com or Shook_t@yahoo.com. Website: www.publicity house.com.

+PUBLIST. Lists over 150,000 publications with basic contact information: www.publist.com.

PURE PUBLICITY. Ben Lauro, Tracy Cole, and Melinda Adair. Website: www.purepublicity.com.

BEVERLY RYKERD PUBLIC RELATIONS. Beverly Rykerd, PO Box 88180, Colorado Springs CO 80908. (800)481-0405. E-mail: brykerd@ix.netcom.com.

+TC PUBLIC RELATIONS. Tom Ciesielka, pres., 333 N. Michigan Ave., Ste. 2116, Chicago IL 60601. (312)422-1333. Fax (312)422-1533. E-mail: TC@tcpr.net, or ian@tcpr.net. Website: www.tcpr.net.

VERITAS COMMUNICATIONS. Don Otis, PO Box 2075, Canon City CO 81215. (208)255-8290 or (719)275-7775. E-mail: Info@veritasincorporated.com. Website: www.veritasincorporated .com. Provides communications services that help provide corporate, nonprofit, or author exposure in the marketplace: www.veritasincorporated.com/index.htm.

+WDC MEDIA: PR with a Higher Purpose. Carole Marie. (303)248-9650. E-mail: carole@ wdcmedia.com. Website: www.wdcmedia.com.

+WILDFIRE MARKETING. Ron Eager, 3625 Chartwell Dr., Suwanee GA 30024. Toll-free (800)267-2045. E-mail: ron@StartaWildFire.com. Website: www.StartaWildFire.com.

WYNN-WYNN MEDIA. Jeane Wynn, 2105 Walnut Hill Ln., Claremore OK 74019. (918)283-1834. Fax (918)512-4409. E-mail: info@WynnWynnMedia.com. Website: www.wynnwynn media.com.

REFERENCE TOOLS

ALMANACS. Topics include history, government, biography, sports, arts, entertainment, business, finance, health, science, and weather. There is even a "Fact Monster" for kids: www .infoplease.com/almanacs.html.

AMERICAN DIALECT SOCIETY. Offers e-mail discussion list, Words of the Year, and reference links: www.americandialect.org.

BARTLEBY'S REFERENCE LIBRARIES. (1) www.bartleby.com; (2) American Heritage Dictionary: www.bartleby.com/61. (3) The Columbia Encyclopedia: www.bartleby.com/65. (4) Strunk's Elements of Style: www.bartleby.com/141. (5) The Encyclopedia of World History: www.bartleby.com/67. (6) Roget's II: The New Thesaurus: www.bartleby.com/62. (7) Quotations: www.bartleby.com/quotations. (8) Gray's Anatomy: www.bartleby.com/107.

BIOGRAPHICAL DICTIONARY. Dictionary covers more than 33,000 notable men and women who have shaped our world from ancient times to the present day. Searchable by birth years, death years, professions, literary and artistic works, achievements, and other keywords: www.s9.com.

COMPUTER-USER HIGH-TECH DICTIONARY. Includes emoticons, file types, chat stuff, domains, HTML tags, and much more: www.computeruser.com/resources/dictionary.

+CURRENCY CONVERTER. A visit to the Universal Currency Converter will answer your currency questions: http://askbobrankin.com/currency_converter.html.

DEPT. OF DEFENSE DICTIONARY OF MILITARY TERMS. Website: www.dtic.mil/doctrine/ jel/doddict.

DICTIONARY.COM. Type in the word you are looking for, and if there is no match, it makes hyperlinked suggestions so you can check the meaning to make sure it is the word you are actually seeking: www.dictionary.com.

DICTIONARY DATABASE. A dictionary for everything: www.onelook.com/browse.shtml#all_gen.

ENCYCLOPEDIA BRITANNICA. Website: www.britannica.com.

LAW DICTIONARY. Website: www.duhaime.org/diction.htm. Also offers references to many other law topics. Use search feature to find the "Law Fun" page for jokes and great dumb stuff.

MERRIAM-WEBSTER ONLINE DICTIONARY/THESAURUS. Website: http://m-w.com.

ONELOOK DICTIONARIES. Definitions from over 900 dictionaries: www.onelook.com.

OXFORD ENGLISH DICTIONARY. Website: www.oed.com.

REFERENCE BOOKS ONLINE. (1) Website: www.xrefer.com. (2) Before you purchase your next research book, check out Direct Textbook: www.directtextbook.com.

+REFERENCE SOFTWARE. This site reviews writing-reference software and books: www.thescriptorium.net.

RHYMING DICTIONARY. Website: www.rhymezone.com.

ROGET'S DESCRIPTIVE WORD FINDER: *A Dictionary/Thesaurus of Adjectives and Adverbs* by Barbara Ann Kipfer (Writer's Digest Books, 2003), ISBN 13: 978-1582971704.

ROGET'S ONLINE THESAURUS. Website: www.thesaurus.com.

SUPER SEARCHER, AUTHOR, SCRIBE: *Successful Writers Share Their Internet Research Secrets* by Loraine Page. A book that features in-depth interviews with 14 writers who regularly use the Internet as a research tool. Website links to hundreds of Internet resources including search engines/mailing lists/online databases/software. Available at your local bookstore. ISBN 13: 978-0910965583. Website: www.supersearchers.com.

VISUAL THESAURUS. A visual representation of the English language with a Guided Tour: www.visualthesaurus.com.

A WEB OF ONLINE DICTIONARIES. Linked to more than 2500 dictionaries in over 300 different languages: www.yourdictionary.com.

WEBOPEDIA. Online dictionary/search engine for computer and Internet technology definitions: www.webopedia.com.

WORD WEB. A free trial version and download of a dictionary: www.wordweb.info.

WORLD BOOK ONLINE. Website: www.worldbook.com.

WORLD FACTBOOK. Published by the U.S. Central Intelligence Agency, it offers data on every country in the world, including maps/background/geography/people/government/economy/military: www.odci.gov/cia/publications/factbook.

WRITER'S FREE REFERENCE. Maps/encyclopedias/copyright information/zip codes/telephone directories/currency conversions/and more: www.writers-free-reference.com.

RESEARCH: BIBLE

ARCHAEOLOGY. Links related to archaeology and Bible scholarship: www.bib-arch.org.

BIBLE ANSWER MACHINE. Website: http://BibleAnswerMachine.ww7.com.

BIBLE GATEWAY. Searches different Bible versions in 30 translations and languages: http://bible.gospelcom.net.

BIBLEPROBE. A nondenominational reference site for Christians and Jews: www.bibleprobe.com.

BIBLE PROPHECY. Over 175 Bible prophecy sites on the Web: www.armageddonbooks.com.

THE BIBLE STUDIES FOUNDATION. Home of the Net Bible: www.bible.org.

BIBLE STUDY TOOLS. (1) www.biblestudytools.net; (2) www.e-sword.net. Free Bible Study software.

BIBLE TIMES & CUSTOMS. Includes topics such as Customs and Manners, Bible Measurements, Eating and Dressing, Transportation and Communication, Farming, Animals, Occupations, and Holidays: www.middletownbiblechurch.org/biblecus/biblec.htm.

CHRISTIAN INFORMATION MINISTRIES/RESEARCH SERVICE, 2050 N. Collins Blvd., Ste. 100, Richardson TX 75080. (972)690-1975. E-mail: info@christianinformation.org. Provides research links, including topics related to the Bible, theology, and Christian living: www.christianinformation.org/links.asp.

CHURCHLINK. Christian Resource Networking. Pages include Bible studies, Mini-Book Library, and a review of the latest Christian training manuals: www.churchlink.com.au.

CONCORDANCE. *Where to Find It in the Bible: The Ultimate A-Z Resource* by Ken Anderson (Thomas Nelson Publishers), ISBN 13: 978-0785251941. A topical concordance listing contemporary topics and issues. Available at local bookstores.

CROSS DAILY. Website: www.crossdaily.com. Click on "Bible Search."

+GUIDELINES FOR BIBLE QUOTES. Find guidelines for quoting the Amplified, NASB, and other Lockman translations: http://lockman.org/tlf/copyright.php.

+HEBREW BIBLE ONLINE. Features words in English and Hebrew with capability of listening in Hebrew. Great for hearing how Bible names and places are pronounced: www.mechon-mamre.org/index.htm.

ONEPLACE.COM. Provides Bible study tools, such as words in Greek and Hebrew, and Strong's Concordance: www.oneplace.com.

ONLINE BIBLE. Website: www.onlinebible.net.

+STRONG'S CONCORDANCE AND LEXICON. Find Hebrew and Greek name and place spellings and more: www.eliyah.com/lexicon.html.

STUDY LIGHT. Study resources, daily devotions, and more: www.studylight.org.

UNBOUND BIBLE. A collection of searchable Bibles, consisting of ten English versions, Greek and Hebrew versions, four ancient versions, and 42 other languages: http://unbound.biola.edu.

VINE'S EXPOSITORY DICTIONARY OF NEW TESTAMENT WORDS. Website: www.menfak.no/bibel/vines.html.

VIRTUAL CHRISTIANITY. A comprehensive list of online Bibles in English and other languages: www.internetdynamics.com/pub/vc/bibles.html.

RESEARCH: LIBRARIES

BARTLEBY. Website: www.bartleby.com.

THE BIBLIOGRAPHIC LIBRARY. Indexes hundreds of collections from libraries and museums with raw material of social history, including diaries, manuscripts, pictures, sheet music, campaign buttons, oral histories, films, recordings, etc.: www.hti.umich.edu/cgi/b/bib/bib-idx?c-dlfcoll.

CENTER FOR RESEARCH LIBRARIES. Website: www.crl.edu. Consortium of North American universities, colleges, and independent research libraries. The consortium acquires and preserves traditional and digital resources for research and teaching and makes them available to member institutions through interlibrary loan and electronic delivery.

E-LIBRARY. Search magazines, books, newspapers, maps, TV and radio transcripts. Over 35 million documents from more than 3,000 sources, going back 20 years: www.highbeam.com.

INTERNET PUBLIC LIBRARY (IPL). Online library of and for the Internet community: http://ipl.sils.umich.edu.

THE LIBRARY OF CONGRESS. Website: www.loc.gov.

LIBRARYSPOT. A free gateway to more than 5,000 libraries worldwide, the world's largest newspaper archive, reference desk, and more: www.libraryspot.com.

READING ROOMS. (1) IPL Reading Room: http://ipl.sils.umich.edu/div/reading; (2) Catalog of electronic texts: www.infomotions.com/alex; (3) English Server Drama Collection: http://drama.eserver.org; (4) Internet Classics Archive: http://classics.mit.edu.

REFDESK. Well-organized and useful information: www.refdesk.com.

RESEARCH LIBRARY. A subscription based service: www.researchlibrary.net.

RESEARCH: NEWS

ABYZ NEWS LINKS. Portal to online news sources from around the world: www.abyznews links.com.

AMERICAN SOCIETY OF NEWSPAPER EDITORS (ASNE). For careers in newspapers: http://asne.org/index.cfm?id=2.

ARCHIVED NEWSPAPERS. (1) To find something in an archived newspaper, check out "Newspaper Links": www.newspaperlinks.com. News Archives on the Web: (2) www.ibiblio .org/slanews/internet/archivesindex.html; (3) http://newslibrary.com; (4) www.library spot.com.

ASSIST NEWS SERVICE. Provides a wide variety of national and international stories that go to 2,400 media and Christian leaders around the world. For free subscription, e-mail from Website: www.assistnews.net.

BBC NEWSLINE. Desktop news center delivering updates automatically throughout the day: www.bbc.co.uk/newsline.

CHRISTIAN EXAMINER. So. California Christian newspaper: www.christianexaminer.com. (619)668-5100. E-mail info@christianexaminer.com.

CHRISTIAN SCIENCE MONITOR NEWS SITE. Website: www.csmonitor.com.

DAILY ROTATION. Collects and displays links to the latest tech news stories: www.daily rotation.com.

DEMOSSNEWSPOND.COM. Offers primary news about some of the major faith-based organizations, leaders, and enterprises in the world: www.DeMossNewsPond.com.

EDITOR & PUBLISHER. America's oldest journal covering the newspaper industry: www.editor andpublisher.com.

EP NEWS SERVICE. Features 6,000 words of national and world news each week emailed to subscribers; news can be printed in your publication or posted on your Website. To subscribe, call (704)295-7906. Website: www.epnews.com/epnews/services.html.

FIND ARTICLES. 10,000,000 articles not found on any other search engine: www.find articles.com.

JOURNALISM NET (UK). Portal of online tools and worldwide news: www.journalismnet.com/uk/index.htm.

+NEWS LINKS. Links to U.S. newspapers, radio/TV, blogs, and magazines by city or state: http://newslink.org.

NEWSPAPER DIRECTORY. Website: www.newsd.com.

NEWSPAPERS.COM. Exceptional tool for referencing the world's newspapers: www.news papers.com.

THE NEWSROOM HOMEPAGE. Connect to virtually any newspaper in the world: http://assignment editor.com.

NEWS STORY SOURCES. (1) www.ap.org; (2) http://dailynews.yahoo.com; (3) www.slate .com/code/todayspapers/todayspapers.asp; (4) www.newshub.com; (5) http://totalnews .com; (6) www.newsindex.com; (7) www.all-links.com/newscentral; (8) http://news.google .com; (9) www.newseum.org/todaysfrontpages; (10) http://newslink.org.

JLAR CHRISTIAN NEWS SITES. According to Alexa, a Web information company, here are the most visited Christian sites in "News & Media" categories: (1) www.christianpost.com; (2) www.christiantoday.com; (3) www.christianitytoday.com; (4) www.agapepress.org; (5) www.firstthings.com; (6) www.religionnewsblog.com; (7) www.worthynews.com; (8) www.assistnews.net; (9) www.sojo.net; (10) www.earnedmedia.org.

REGIONAL REPORTERS ASSOCIATION (RRA). To-do list for new reporters in Washington, D.C.: www.rra.org/dc_guide.html.

RELIGIONLINK.ORG. Linking journalists to ideas and sources for reporting today's news: http://religionlink.org.

TV STATIONS AND PUBLICATIONS. Website: www.greattv.com/hotlinks.htm.

USA WEEKEND. Website: www.usaweekend.com. Click on "Newspaper Sites." Links to over 600 newspapers listed by state.

VANDERBILT TELEVISION NEWS ARCHIVE. Website: http://tvnews.vanderbilt.edu.

THE WHY FILES. This site uses news and current events as springboards to explore science, health, environment, and technology: http://whyfiles.org.

RESOURCES: CHILDREN'S WRITING

AWARDS. The Paul A. Witty Short Story Award is given to the author of an original short story published for the first time in a periodical for children. Prize: $1,000. The short story should serve as a literary standard that encourages young readers to read periodicals. Website: www.reading.org/association/awards/childrens_witty.html.

BECOME A CHILDREN'S BOOK AUTHOR. Visit http://FabJob.com to order *Become a Children's Book Author* by Jeannie Harmon (previous editor at Cook Communications, Kid's Book Division, for 15 years) and Sheila Seifert. Book topics include how to come up with a book idea that will attract an editor's attention; step-by-step advice on how to write picture books, nonfiction books and juvenile fiction; what you need to know about format, plotting, illustrations, research, characterization, and more: www.fabjob.com/childauthor.asp?affiliate=262.

BLUE PHANTOM CRITIQUE GROUP FOR CHILDREN'S WRITERS. Offers Children's Literature forum, online support teams, and calendar of events: www.bluephantomwriters.com.

BOOKS OF INTEREST. (1) *Children's Writer Guide to 2007,* ISBN 13: 978-1889715346; (2) *Book Market for Children's Writers 2007,* ISBN 13: 978-1889715322; (3) *Magazine Market for Children's Writers 2007,* ISBN 13: 978-1889715339. Order at www.writersbookstore.com. Also check out: (4) *Books to Grow With: A Guide to Using the Best Children's Fiction for Everyday Issues and Tough Challenges,* ISBN 13: 978-0974802572. The book includes more than 500 recommended books, tips on how to use fiction to help children, helpful indexes by author and title, and multicultural books. Published children's writers can contact Lutra Press and request that they include their book in Lutra's online newsletter which lists updates and new books not included in *Books to Grow With.* Also, subscribe to *Children's Newsletter.* Website: www.lutrapress.com.

+CHILDREN'S BOOK CATEGORIES. (1) Descriptions of children's book categories by Laura Backes. Website: www.talewins.com/kidcats.htm. (2) Definitions for the different children's genres: www.write4kids.com/colum44.html.

THE CHILDREN'S BOOK COUNCIL. (1) 12 W. 37th St., 2nd Fl., New York NY 10018-7480. (212)966-1990. Fax (212)966-2073. E-mail: from Website: www.cbcbooks.org. Go to "Getting Your Book Published/FAQs" page for marketing information and beginner instruction for writers and illustrators of children's books, plus lots of good links. (2) Children's Book Council of Australia, presenters of the Children's Book of the Year Awards: www.cbc.org.au/publish.htm.

CHILDREN'S BOOK PUBLISHERS. (1) Website: www.scils.rutgers.edu/%7Ekvander/Children Lit/publish.html. Lists links to various children's book publishers. (2) Also visit the Colossal Directory of Children's Publishers: www.signaleader.com.

THE CHILDREN'S LITERATURE WEB GUIDE. Internet resources related to books for children and young adults: www.acs.ucalgary.ca/~dkbrown.

+CHILDREN'S PUBLISHING MARKET FORECAST. Order current edition: www.simbanet .com/trade/info.asp. Toll-free (888)297-4622.

CHILDREN'S WRITER NEWSLETTER. A monthly newsletter featuring reports on the marketplace for children's writing: www.childrenswriter.com.

+CHILDREN'S WRITING. The Blue Oasis Online Support Teams have everything for children's writers. If you're feeling worse than Alexander on his terrible, no-good day, read the "Good News" section about fellow writers for a pick-me-up: www.boost4writers.com.

CHILDREN'S WRITING SUPERSITE. Children's Book Insider LLC, 901 Columbia Rd., Fort Collins CO 80525. (970)495-0056. Toll-free (800)807-1916 (orders only). E-mail: mail@ write4kids.com. To subscribe to the free e-zine *Children's Book Insider,* and for more free offers, go to the Website: www.write4kids.com.

CONTESTS. Check the "Contests" section in this guide for "Writing for Children/Young Adult Contests."

+DIRECTORY OF CHILDREN'S AUTHORS AND ILLUSTRATORS. Authors and illustrators available for school visits, book signings, and other public appearances: www.smart writers.com.

GLORY PRESS/PROF. DICK BOHRER. Forty years as a national magazine, book and newspaper editor, teacher for grades 3-18, and managing editor of *Moody Monthly* magazine; author of 16 books. Contact: Glory Press, 2174 S.W. Mossy Brae Road, West Linn OR 97068. (503)638-7711. E-mail: dickbohrer@comcast.net. Website: www.professordick.com. The site offers 24 lessons on how to write stories for children. Lessons are free. His site also features his eight juvenile mysteries.

INSTITUTE OF CHILDREN'S LITERATURE, 93 Long Ridge Rd., West Redding CT 06896. (203)792-8600. Toll-free (800)243-9645. Fax (203)792-8406. E-mail: information services@InstituteChildrensLit.com. Website: www.InstituteChildrensLit.com.

KIDBIBS.COM. Bringing kids and books together, this site features award winning books and reading lists. It also has dozens of sites reporting on statistics and topics related to education: http://kidbibs.com.

KID MAGAZINE WRITERS. Great site for children's magazine writers; features market guides, interviews with editors, articles, and more: www.kidmagwriters.com.

NATIONAL SCHOLASTIC PRESS ASSOC. Contests: www.studentpress.org/nspa/contests.html.

PICTURE-BOOK.COM. "The online resource for children's illustrators, publishers, and book lovers." Dozens of links for writers: www.picture-book.com.

+RESOURCES FOR CHILDREN'S WRITERS. Features news, resources, links, articles, and book reviews for children's writers and illustrators: www.yellapalooza.com.

+SCHOOLBOOKINGS.COM, PO Box 6988, Chandler, AZ 85246-6698. Toll-free (866)471-0777. E-mail: info@schoolbookings.com. This organization offers tools to connect to student audiences. Fee is $99/yr. or $198 for 2 yrs.; first month free.

THE SOCIETY OF CHILDREN'S BOOK WRITERS AND ILLUSTRATORS, 8271 Beverly Blvd., Los Angeles CA 90048. (323)782-1010. Fax (323)782-1892. E-mail: membership@ scbwi.org. Site includes a newsletter, critique groups, workshops, market resources, and other general information: www.scbwi.org.

TRENDS IN CHILDREN'S PUBLISHING. Website: www.underdown.org/trends.htm.

VERLA KAY'S WEBSITE FOR CHILDREN'S WRITERS. Website: www.verlakay.com.

+WRITE BOOKS A CHILD WILL LOVE. Website: www.right-writing.com/child.html.

WRITING FOR CHILDREN WORKSHOP. Writer quotes, tips, FAQs, resources, book recommendations, and a directory of children's authors and illustrators: www.bethany roberts.com.

RESOURCES: ETHNIC WRITERS

AFRICAN-AMERICAN GUIDE TO WRITING AND PUBLISHING NONFICTION, by Jewell Parker Rhodes (Broadway Books), ISBN 13: 978-0767905787.

ASIAN AMERICAN JOURNALISTS ASSN. (AAJA), 1182 Market St., Ste. 320, San Francisco CA 94102. (415)346-2051. Fax (415)346-6343. E-mail: National@aaja.org. A nonprofit organization whose mission is to encourage Asian Pacific Americans to enter ranks of journalism, to work for fair and accurate coverage of Asian Pacific Americans, and to increase the number of Asian Pacific American journalists and news managers in the industry; 2,300 members: www.aaja.org.

BLACK WRITERS (formerly Black Writers United). Exists to promote fellowship and the sharing of resources and information among writers: www.blackwriters.org/forum.

COPYRIGHT INFORMATION IN SPANISH. Website: www.copyright.gov/espanol.

ETHNIC MARKETS. National Black Theatre Institute of Action Arts (formerly National Black Theatre Inc.), 2031-33 National Black Theatre Way at Fifth Ave., Harlem NY 10035. (212) 722-2031. Contact NBT's Theatre Arts Program for more information. E-mail: nbitca@ aol.com. Website: www.nationalblacktheatre.org.

+HISPANIC MARKETS. (1) Former editor for Simon & Schuster helps Latinos get into print with her newsletter that highlights markets open to Hispanic writers: http://groups .yahoo.com/group/marcelalandres; (2) *Emerging Trends in Publishing: The Hispanic Market,* ISBN 0-88709-322-1. Order from www.simbanet.com/trade/info.asp or call 1-888-Bowker2.

+JEWISH WRITERS. This site will help connect you with Jewish writers: http://geocities.com/ jewishwriting/Start.html.

MAYNARD INSTITUTE, Robert C. Maynard Institute for Journalism Education, 1211 Preservation Pkwy., Oakland CA 94612. (510)891-9202. Fax (510)891-9565. E-mail: mije@ maynardije.org. Advanced training and services nationally to help news organizations better reflect their diverse communities: www.maynardije.org.

MULTICULTURAL MARKETING RESOURCES. Lists annual seminars and conferences of interest to marketing professionals targeting all ethnic backgrounds: www.multicultural.com.

NATIONAL ASSN. OF BLACK JOURNALISTS (NABJ), 8701-A Adelphi Rd., Adelphi MD 20783. Toll-free (866)479-NABJ. Fax (301)445-7101. E-mail: nabj@nabj.org. Serves African American journalists, providing professional development and training. 3,300 members: www .nabj.org.

NATIONAL ASSN. OF HISPANIC JOURNALISTS (NAHJ), 1000 National Press Building, 529 14th St. N.W., Washington DC 20045-2100. Toll-free (888)346-6245. (202)662-7145. Fax (202)662-7144. E-mail: nahj@nahj.org. Website: www.nahj.org. Dedicated to the recognition and professional advancement of Hispanics in the news industry; approx. 2,300 members.

NATIVE AMERICAN JOURNALISTS ASSN. (NAJA), 555 N. Dakota St., Vermillion SD 57069. (605)677-5282. Fax (866)694-4264. E-mail: info@naja.com. Serves and empowers Native journalists through programs and actions designed to enrich journalism and to promote Native cultures; includes news articles, media resources, and links: www.naja.com.

ORGANIZATION OF BLACK SCREENWRITERS. E-mail from Website: www.obswriter.com. Represents African American writers in the entertainment industry.

+RAWSISTAZ. A literary group that focuses on reading, writing, and discussing books primarily by African American authors: www.rawsistaz.com.

UNITY: JOURNALISTS OF COLOR, 7950 Jones Branch Dr., McLean VA 22107. (703)854-3585. Fax (703)854-3586. E-mail: info@unityjournalists.org. Four national minority journalism associations (AAJA, NABJ, NAHJ, NAJA) seeking to promote diversity within the nation's media: www.unityjournalists.org.

RESOURCES: FICTION WRITING

ADVANCED FICTION WRITING. (1) According to successful fiction author Randy Ingermanson, you need only three things to get your novel published: content, craft, and connections. For his free e-zine, go to www.advancedfictionwriting.com or (2) www.rsingermanson.com/html/on_writing.html.

AMERICAN CHRISTIAN FICTION WRITERS (ACFW). ACFW is geared toward meeting the needs of new and seasoned authors alike, as well as offering a venue for readers of Christian fiction to learn more about their favorite authors and discover the vast array of choices available from the Christian fiction market in general. E-mail: president@acfw.com. Features online workshops/e-zine/book club/sponsors an annual conference/writing contest: www.acfw.com.

AMERICAN CRIME WRITERS LEAGUE. To be eligible for membership, a writer must have published at least one full-length book or three short stories, the most recent published within two years of applying. E-mail: membership@acwl.org.

AMERICAN WRITERS & ARTISTS INSTITUTE. Learn the insider secrets and techniques of being a published romance writer. Toll-free (866)879-2924 or visit Website: www.theromancewriterslife.com.

AT-HOME WRITING WORKSHOPS. Marlene Bagnull, LittD, dir., Write His Answer Ministries, 316 Blanchard Rd., Drexel Hill PA 19026. (610)626-6833. E-mail: mbagnull@aol.com. Website: www.writehisanswer.com. Fiction and nonfiction, 10 units, each unit $272. Units may also be purchased individually from $30-$34.

+AUTHOR MANIA. Listed as one of Writer's Digest Top 101 Sites. Offers ideas on how to create your story or novel, build believable characters, and more: www.authormania.com.

BOOKS OF INTEREST. (1) *Self-Editing for Fiction Writers: How to Edit Yourself into Print* by Renni Browne and Dave King (Collins), ISBN 13: 978-0060545697; (2) *The First Five Pages: A Writer's Guide to Staying Out of the Rejection Pile* by Noah Lukeman (Fireside 2000), ISBN 13: 978-0684857435, $13; (3) *Behind the Stories* by Diane Eble (Bethany House 2002), ISBN 13: 978-0764224638. (4) *Sometimes the Magic Works: Lessons from a Writing Life* by Terry Brooks, (Del Rey 2004), ISBN 13: 978-0345465511; (5) *The Breakout Novel* and *The Breakout Novel Workbook* by Donald Maass (WDB), ISBN 13: 978-1582971827 and ISBN 13: 978-1582972633; (6) *Save the Cat!* By Blake Snyder (Michael Wiese Productions), ISBN 13: 978-1932907001. (7) *Creating Unforgettable Characters* by Linda Seger (Owl Books), ISBN 13: 978-0805011715; (8) *Techniques of the Selling Writer* by Dwight Swain (University of Oklahoma Press), ISBN 13: 978-0806111917.

CHARACTER BIOGRAPHY. Use these Websites to help develop a character biography or personality profile for your fiction characters: (1) www.queendom.com/tests/personality/index.html; (2) www.2h.com/personality-tests.shtml.

CHARACTER DEVELOPMENT. (1) Do you need an occupation for your character or does your character need to do something in an emergency? Here is a site that will tell you all about anything and everything your character might need to know: www.ehow.com. (2) Hundreds of job descriptions at Dictionary of Occupational Titles: www.wave.net/upg/immigration/dot_index.html. (3) For background: www.greatmuseums.org/museumworld.html. (4) www.wordsmithshoppe.com/char_wrksheet.htm.

CHARACTER NAME SOURCES. (1) Link to the U.S. Census Bureau to find lists of male and female first and last names: www.craigcentral.com/names.asp. Other Websites: (2) www.babynames.com; (3) www.census.gov/genealogy/names; (4) www.ssa.gov.; (5) http://parenting.ivillage.com/namefinder; (6) www.babycenter.com/babyname/index.html; (7) www.babynamenetwork.com; (8) www.behindthename.com; (9) www.thinkbabynames.com; (10) www.geocities.com/edgarbook/names/welcome.html. (11) Medieval names: www.s-gabriel.org/names/english.shtml; (12) www.parenthood.com; (13) Fantasy names: www.rinkworks.com/namegen; (14) http://babynamewizard.com; (15) http://members.cox.net/sandiept/name-generator.html.

CHARACTER NAME SOURCES OF DIFFERENT NATIONALITIES. (1) African names: www.namesite.com/namesite/mainpage.html; (2) Afrocentric names: www.swagga.com/name.htm; (3) Arabic names, masculine: www.ummah.net/family/masc.html; (4) Arabic names, feminine: www.ummah.net/family/fem.html; (5) Chinese names: www.mandarintools.com/chinesename.html.

CHARACTER TRAITS. Useful poster of an alphabetical listing of character traits from Able to Zealous; $10: www.anecdote.com.au//shop.php?prodid=2.

CHRISTIAN CHICK LIT. USA Today ran an article on one of the newest genres in Christian publishing: "Chick Lit." Explains the terms and mentions some specific Christian books that fall into this genre. Read at: www.usatoday.com/life/books/news/2003-10-29-church-lit_x.htm.

+COMIC SITES. (1) www.scottmccloud.com; (2) www.onlinecomics.net; (3) www.comicsontheweb.ocm; (4) www.ozcomics.com; (5) www.serializer.net; (6) www.topwebcomics.com.

CONTESTS. Check the "Contest" section in this guide for "Fiction Contests."

CRIME MYSTERY WRITING/FORENSIC SITES. Websites: (1) www.visualexpert.com; (2) www.tritechusa.com; (3) www.crime-scene-investigator.net; (4) www.pimall.com/nais/home.html. (5) http://dir.yahoo.com/Society_and_Culture/Crime. Yahoo's Crime Directory. (6) www.officer.com. Offers links to agencies, criminal justice, investigations, special ops, most-wanted worldwide, and other law enforcement sites. (7) http://foia.fbi.gov. This Freedom of Information Act site offers an electronic reading room with categories such as espionage, famous persons, gangster era, historical interests, unusual phenomena, and violent crimes. (8) Also visit S. G. R. MacMillan, Barrister, for links to resources about organized crime, fraud, and financial scandals: www.sgrm.com; (9) Forensics & Faith, www.forensicsandfaith.blogspot.com; (10) Int'l Assoc. of Crime Writers: www.crimewritersna.org.

ECLECTIC FICTION. (1) Website: www.eclectics.com. (2) Offers a form to use in laying out the characteristics of characters in your stories: www.eclectics.com/articles/character.html.

EDITORIAL SERVICES FOR FICTION WRITERS. (1) Dave King's site features articles and a free "Ask the Editor" section: www.davekingedits.com; (2) also of interest is this book *Self-Editing for Fiction Writers,* Renni Brown (Collins 2004), ISBN 13: 978-0060545697.

+ENVIRONMENTAL FICTION. Is your character involved in the environment, like preserving our natural resources, pollution, or global warming? Check out the U.S. Environmental Protection Agency: www.epa.gov/epahome/commsearch.htm.

ESPIONAGE LINGO. Website: www.spymuseum.org/educate/loe.asp.

FAITH, HOPE & LOVE (1) The inspirational chapter of Romance Writers of America. Dues for the chapter are $24/yr., but you must also be a member of RWA to join (dues $75/yr.). Chapter offers online list of services for members, bimonthly newsletter, annual contest, and latest romance market information. Connects critique partners by mail or e-mail. To join, fill out PDF file application and mail to RWA National Office, 16000 Stuebner Airline Rd., Ste. 140, Spring TX 77379. (832)717-5200. Fax (832)717-5201. Website: www.rwanational.org. (2) Or go to FHL Website: www.faithhopelove-rwa.org. E-mail: info@rwanational.com. Over 180 members in FHL, over 9,000 in RWA.

FEDERAL CITIZEN INFORMATION CENTER. Website: www.pueblo.gsa.gov. Need information about your character's livelihood? The Center offers free and low-cost booklets on a myriad of topics.

FEELINGS & EMOTIONS. Looking for exactly the right word to show feelings and emotions? Go to: http://eqi.org/elit.htm.

+FICTION AND POETRY MARKET. This database contains more than 1,525 current markets for short fiction, poetry, and novels with ability to search by pay scale and submission length: http://duotrope.com.

FICTION AND SCI-FI/FANTASY E-GROUPS. (1) Website: http://groups.yahoo.com. Type into box "Christian_fic2" (for genre fiction), or "ChristSF" (for science fiction and Christianity). (2) A Christian fantasy site: www.christianfantasy.com. (3) A Christian sci-fi site: www .christian-fandom.org. Also check out: (4) www.critters.org; (5) The Charis Connection blog: http://charisconnection.blogspot.com. (6) Interactive fiction writing site where people write with others: www.morethannovellas.com.

+FICTION BLOGSPOT. Subscribe to Novel Journey, an online community helping writers grow: www.noveljourney.blogspot.com.

FICTION FACTOR. (1) Website: www.fictionfactor.com. Free monthly newsletter, plus tips and articles on writing better fiction, promoting and marketing your work, and more. (2) Christian Fiction Factor. Offers resources, links, and a bookstore for dedicated Christian writers: http://christian.fictionfactor.com.

FICTION FIX NEWSLETTER. *The Nuts and Bolts of Crafting Fiction:* www.coffeehousefor writers.com/news.html.

FICTION HOW-TO ESSAYS. Website: www.storyispromise.com.

FICTION LINKS. (1) Website: http://story.exis.net/masterlink. Writers Supercenter joins with StoryCraft software to offer 1,001 links to articles on writing. (2) See what other readers think of already published books, movies, and games or post a story of your own and see how you rate: www.sffworld.com.

FICTION WRITER'S CONNECTION. Provides help with novel writing and information on finding agents/editors and getting published. Website includes a newsletter, critiquing, editor/agent information, free tip sheets and consultations, and scam warnings: www.fictionwriters .com. Toll-free (800)248-2758. E-mail: Bcamenson@aol.com.

FICTION WRITING CLASSES. Website: www.writewords.org.uk/courses.asp.

FREE CHRISTIAN FICTION. Fiction writer Elizabeth Delayne's site offers free fiction as well as links to other Christian fiction sites: www.edelayne.com.

THE HISTORICAL NOVEL SOCIETY. Founded in 1997, this group aims to promote all aspects of historical fiction; offers an annual conference, discussion list, book reviews, and more. E-mail from Website: www.historicalnovelsociety.org.

HISTORY DATABASE. (1) What happened in 1014 AD? Here's an interactive timeline database extending from 1000 AD to the present: www.sbrowning.com/whowhatwhen/index.php; (2) Medieval Calendar Calculator: www.wallandbinkley.com/mcc/mcc_main.html.

+IMPROVE YOUR FICTION. See ten surefire suggestions to improve your fiction: www3.baylor .edu/~Greg_Garrett/writing/hints.html.

LEGAL INFORMATION INSTITUTE. (1) Website: www4.law.cornell.edu/uscode. Is your character in trouble with the law? Click on "Crimes & Criminal Procedures." Learn about court processes and other legalities. (2) For other useful legal links: www.findlaw.com.

LEGENDS & RUMORS. Visit www.snopes.com for 25 hottest urban legends, and more.

THE MARKET LIST. Offers markets, articles, links, touching on anything you might need to know about fiction writing: www.marketlist.com.

MYSTERYNET NETWORK, 3616 Far West Blvd., #117-298, Austin TX 78731. (512)342-8377. E-mail: notify@MysteryNet.com. Website: www.mysterynet.com.

MYSTERY WRITERS OF AMERICA, 17 E. 47th St., 6th Fl., New York NY 10017. (212)888-8171. Fax (212)888-8107. E-mail: mwa@mysterywriters.org. Website: www.mysterywriters.org.

MYSTERY WRITERS SITES OF INTEREST. Websites: (1) www.cluelass.com; (2) www.crime.org; (3) http://crime.about.com; (4) www.MurderMustAdvertise.com; (5) www.deadlypleasures.com.

NATIONAL NOVEL WRITING MONTH. Each year in November, participants begin writing a 50,000 word novel. Check site for specific dates of this yearly competition: www.nanowrimo.org.

NICHOLAS SPARKS' ADVICE. Advice for writers from Nicholas Sparks (*A Walk to Remember, The Notebook*): www.nicholassparks.com/WritersCorner/index.html.

ONLINE NEWSLETTER. Website: www.fictionaddiction.net.

+PECULIAR PEOPLE: INTERNATIONAL FICTION COLLABORATIONS. Sponsors books written by a number of different authors—each writing one chapter. Contact: Amy Michelle Wiley, founder & dir., PO Box 822281, Vancouver WA 98682. (360)909-2595. E-mail: contact@peculiarpeoplebooks.com. Website: www.peculiarpeoplebooks.com. Visit Website for details.

+PHOTOS FOR CHARACTERS. Website: www.photos.com/en/index.

+PLOTS. Creating a plot is a piece of cake with this Interactive Instant Plot Creator: www.writingfix.com.

PUBLIC RECORDS. (1) People Finder. Site offers help with public records. Careful, not all searches are free: www.peoplefinders.com; (2) U.S. Locate. More access to public records and special search techniques: www.uslocate.com.

ROBIN'S NEST. Offers links, articles, online courses, and workshops for all genres of fiction writers: www.robinsnest.com.

ROMANCE WRITERS. (1) Harlequin actually helps writers of romance learn to write better: www.eHarlequin.com/cms/learntowrite/ltwToc.jhtml; (2) This site boasts of more than 1,400 members: www.charlottedillon.com/writingromance.html; (3) Award-winning Website: www.romancedivas.com; (4) Be a founding member of this new sister site to Cata Romance.com: www.catauniversity.com; (5) http://groups.msn.com/romancewritingtips.

ROMANCE WRITERS OF AMERICA, (832)717-5200. Fax (832)717-5201. E-mail: info@rwanational.org. Website: www.rwanational.org.

SCIENCE FICTION AND FANTASY WRITERS OF AMERICA. Jane Jewell, exec. dir., PO Box 877, Chestertown MD 21620. (207)861-8078. E-mail: from Website: www.sfwa.org.

SCIENCE FICTION LANGUAGE. Website: www.langmaker.com.

SCIENCE FICTION SITE. Ralan Conley's SpecFic & Humor Webstravaganza: www.ralan.com. Science fiction romance.

SHAKESPEARE'S COMPLETE WORKS. Find a sonnet or a play for inspiration: http://mit.edu/works.html.

SHORT MYSTERY FICTION SOCIETY. Website: www.thewindjammer.com/smfs.

SISTERS IN CRIME, PO Box 442124, Lawrence KS 66044-8933. (785)842-1325. E-mail: sistersincrime@juno.com. Website: www.sistersincrime.org.

+SNOWFLAKE METHOD. Try out Randy Ingermanson's "Snowflake Method" for writing a novel: www.rsingermanson.com/html/the_snowflake.html. Highly recommended.

SPECULATIVE (Sci-fi & Fantasy) **FICTION LINK.** Spicy Green Iguana Inc. Website: www.spicygreeniguana.com.

STORYBOARDING. Fiction writers may be interested in story development software. To order, go to: www.writerssupercenter.com.

STORYCRAFT STORY DEVELOPMENT SOFTWARE. Guides writers through the entire process of writing novels, screenplays, teleplays, plays, and short stories: www.writerspage.com.

STORYTELLING TECHNIQUES. To get a better grasp of storytelling techniques, visit these Websites: (1) For a cross-cultural history of fairy tales: www.surlalunefairytales.com; (2) www.storyteller.net; (3) www.storynet.org. Books include: (4) *Telling Your Own Stories* by Donald Davis, ISBN 13: 978-0874832358; (5) *Telling Time: Angels, Ancestors and Stories* by Nancy Willard, ISBN 13: 978-0156931304; (6) *Steering the Craft* by Ursula K. Le Guin, ISBN 13: 978-0933377462; (7) *Zen in the Art of Writing* by Ray Bradbury, ISBN 13: 978-0553296341; (8) *Take Joy* by Jane Yolen, ISBN 13: 978-1582973852; (9) *On Writing* by Eudora Welty, ISBN 13: 978-0679642701.

SUBSTANCE SIDE EFFECTS. Writing a mystery and your character has a side effect or deadly reaction to a substance? On this Website you can read about side effects, interactions, and warnings about certain herbs and supplements: www.personalhealthzone.com/herbsafety.html.

SYNOPSES. Conquering the Dreaded Synopsis, online workshop by Lisa Gardner: www.rosecity romancewriters.com.

TIME TICKER. Keep track of characters in other time zones: www.timeticker.com.

TOP 100 FICTIONAL CHARACTERS. (1) Features the most influential characters in world literature and legend: www.fictional100.com. (2) Also: www.npr.org/programs/totn/features/2002/mar/020319.characters.html, for *Book* magazine's list of the top 100 fictional characters since 1900.

TRADEMARK SEARCHES. (1) If you are concerned that you may have chosen a name for a fictitious business or brand in your story that exists in real life, go to: www.uspto.gov/main/trademarks.htm and click "Search." (2) In Canada, go to: http://strategis.ic.gc.ca/sc_mrksv/cipo/tm/tm_main-e.html.

U.S. CITIZENSHIP. Does your character long to become a naturalized U.S. citizen? Check out this site so you will know some of the questions that might be asked on the U.S. Citizenship Test: www.usacitizen.com/?a=18kw=us+citizenship+test.

VICTORIAN SETTING. Websites: (1) www.victorianweb.org. (2) www.victorianlondon.org.

WESTERN WRITERS OF AMERICA. Website: www.westernwriters.org. For membership information, contact Rod Miller, 1665 E. Julho St., Sandy UT 84093. E-mail: rod@holmesco.com. Current membership over 500 published writers.

WRITER'S BLOCKS 3.0. Organize story elements for your fiction: www.writersblocks.com.

WRITER'S DIGEST, 4700 E. Galbraith Rd., Cincinnati OH 45236. Toll-free (800)759-0963. Fax (513)531-0798. E-mail: wdwowadmin@fwpubs.com. Website: www.writersonlineworkshops .com. Fiction Writing workshop, Marketing Your Writing, and others. This is a general course, but you may request a Christian instructor. Note that Writer's Digest School is shifting its focus to Web-based workshops.

XIANWORLDVIEW.COM. From a Christian world-view, this site provides book reviews, articles, interviews, forums, and other science fiction and fantasy resources: www.xianworldview.com.

RESOURCES: POETRY WRITING

ACADEMY OF AMERICAN POETS, 584 Broadway, Ste. 604, New York NY 10012-5243. (212) 274-0343. Fax (212)274-9427. E-mail: academy@poets.org. Website: www.poets.org.

ALBANY POETRY WORKSHOP. Website: www.sonic.net/poetry/albany.

+CATHOLIC POETS AND WRITERS. Site offers writing tips as well as information about writing for Catholic readers and/or about Catholicism: www.catholicpoetsandwriters.com.

CONTESTS. Check the Contest section in this guide for "Poetry Contests." (2) Also www.winning writers.com/tompoetry.htm.

CREATIVE-POEMS.COM. Website: www.creative-poems.com. "Join the world's friendliest free poetry site."

CROSSHOME.COM. A site where Christian poetry is featured: www.crosshome.com/poetry .shtml. E-mail: webmaster@crosshome.com.

DIRECTORY OF POETRY PUBLISHERS, Len Fulton, ed., ISBN 13: 978-0913218419.

FELLOWSHIP OF CHRISTIAN POETS, John and Marilyn Marinelli, cofounders, PO Box 831413, Ocala FL 34483. Offers books, a newsletter, and contests. Members are guaranteed publication of 52 poems per year, one per week, in the Library of Poetic Expression. Poems are copyright protected and may be used without charge for noncommercial use. One time membership fee $25. Website: www.christianpoets.com.

HAIKU. Websites devoted to haiku: (1) www.gardendigest.com/poetry/index.htm; (2) www.everypoet.com/absurdities/index.htm. The following organizations also provide additional resources for haiku writers: (3) British Haiku Society, 38 Wayside Ave., Hornchurch, Essex RM 12 4LL, England. Website: www.haikusoc.ndo.co.uk; (4) Haiku Oz, e-mail: secretary@haikuoz.org. Website: www.haikuoz.org; (5) Haiku Society of America, Lane Parker, 578 3rd Ave., San Francisco CA 94118-3903. E-mail: lstparker@cs.com. Website: www.hsa-haiku.org. (6) Also check out *The Haiku Box* by Lonnie Hull DuPont (Journey Editions 2001), ISBN 13: 978-1582900308.

HOW TO MAKE A LIVING AS A POET by Gary Mex Glazner (Soft Skull Press 2005), ISBN 13: 978-1932360691.

+NATIONAL FEDERATION OF STATE POETRY SOCIETIES. Dedicated to furthering poetry on the national level and uniting poets: http://nfsps.com.

ONLINE COMMUNITIES FOR POETS. (1) Utmost Christian Writers exists solely to encourage Christian poets; features contests: www.utmostchristianwriters.com. (2) The Belvedere Room is a place where you can enjoy and discuss poetry with other poets: www.belvederepoets.com. (3) Today's Woman, a community where over 1,200 writers/poets/columnists meet and exchange ideas, rate, review, and help each other succeed in the writing industry: www.todays-woman.net. (4) Another online community: www.allpoetry.com.

ONLINE POETRY CLASSROOM. Online classes geared toward high school poetry teachers, but helpful for all poets: www.onlinepoetryclassroom.org.

POETRY AND WRITERS PORTAL. Offers an international contest, forums, an e-zine, self-publishing options, and more: www.voicesnet.com.

POETRY ARCHIVES. An educational resource to aid students, educators, and writers seeking a poem. A searchable database by first line, author, and poem title: www.emule.com/poetry.

POETRY CONTEST SCAMS AND RIP-OFFS. (1) This site warns about poetry scams and is provided as a public service. Poets seeking recognition for their work might consider submitting to literary magazines rather then poetry contests: www.windpub.com/literary.scams/ripoffs.htm. See also (2) www.winningwriters.com/warningsigns.htm; (3) www.sfwa.org/beware/contests.html; (4) www.todays-woman.net/poetry-scams-blacklist.html; (5) www.absolutewrite.com/specialty_writing/poetry_scams.htm; (6) http://poetrynot com.tripod.com/index.htm#scam.

THE POETRY LIST. A free up-to-date listing of domestic, foreign, and online literary journals that regularly publish poetry: www.thepoetrylist.com.

+THE POETRY MARKET. Free, not-for-profit, monthly e-zine features poetry markets, contests, poetry reviews, and news: http://thepoetrymarket.com.

POETRY SOCIETY OF AMERICA, 15 Gramercy Park, New York NY 10003. (212)254-9628. Website: www.poetrysociety.org. Annual membership $45.

POETRY: TAKING ITS COURSE. Written by poetry editor and instructor Mary Harwell Sayler, this book covers techniques of free verse, syllabic, and traditional metered poetry. Order from: www.stuartmarket.com.

POETS & WRITERS. (1) Information, support, guidance, grants and awards, literary links, news from the writing world, and resources: www.pw.org. (2) www.utmostchristianwriters.com/utmost.htm.

RHYMING DICTIONARY. Website: www.rhymer.com.

THE SCROLL. E-mail: thescroll@christian-poetry.com. Online Christian magazine designed to share Christian poetry, creative writing, and articles: www.Christian-poetry.com/thescroll.html.

UNIVERSITY OF NEW YORK AT BUFFALO POETRY LINKS. Website: http://wings.buffalo.edu/epc/connects/poetrywebs.html.

WRITING POETRY, by Shelly Tucker (GoodYear Books), ISBN 13: 978-1596470934. A very "reader-friendly" book with clear examples of imagery, figures of speech, and guidelines for free and rhymed verse. Find a copy at www.amazon.com.

RESOURCES: SCREENWRITING/SCRIPTWRITING

ACADEMY OF MOTION PICTURE ARTS AND SCIENCES, 8949 Wilshire Blvd., Beverly Hills CA 90211-1972. (310)247-3000. Script library, Academy Players Directory, and listings for industry events: www.oscars.org.

ACADEMY WRITERS CLINIC, 2118 Wilshire Blvd., Ste. 160A, Santa Monica CA 90403. E-mail: info@academywriters.com. For screenwriters who wish to improve their art, sell their material, and be discovered: www.academywriters.com.

ACT ONE: WRITING FOR HOLLYWOOD, 2690 Beachwood Dr., Lower Fl., Hollywood CA 90068. (323)464-0815. E-mail: info@ActOneprogram.com. Offering two programs: Writing for Hollywood for aspiring film and TV writers; Executive Program for aspiring entertainment executives. See Website for dates and for information about weekend seminars: www.ActOneprogram.com.

ADVICE FOR SCREENWRITERS. (1) Website: www.jamesrussellpublishing.biz/screenwriting.html. (2) James Stevens-Arce, a successful screenwriter, novelist, and songwriter. Site features links to subjects such as agents, contests, articles, markets, general manuscript preparation, and more: www.stevens-arce.com.

AMERICAN SCREENWRITERS ASSOCIATION, 269 S. Beverly Dr., Ste. 2600, Beverly Hills CA 90212-3807. Toll-free phone/fax (866)265-9091. E-mail: asa@goasa.com. Nonprofit group that is committed to the international support and advancement of all screenwriters; no unsolicited scripts: www.asascreenwriters.com.

ART WITHIN. Bryan Coley, artistic dir., 1080 Holcomb Bridge Rd., Bldg. 200, Ste. 140, Roswell GA 30076, (770)558-8185. Fax (770)558-8198. E-mail: artwithin@artwithin.org. A professional theater company whose emphasis is new works that uniquely blend hope and truth from a Christian perspective and that are relevant to a contemporary audience: www.artwithin.org.

BOOKS OF INTEREST. (1) *The Writers Journey: Mythic Structure for Writers* by Christopher Vogler (Michael Weise Productions), ISBN 13: 978-0941188708; (2) *Screen Play: The Foundations of Screenwriting* by Syd Field (Dell Books), ISBN 13: 978-0385339032; (3) *The Writer's Guide to Writing Your Screenplay,* ISBN 13: 978-0871161918 and *The Writer's Guide to Selling Your Screenplay,* ISBN 13: 978-0871161925, by Cynthia Whitcomb (Kalmbach Publishing); (4) *How to Build a Great Screenplay: A Master Class in Storytelling for Film* by David Howard (St. Martin's Press), ISBN 13: 978-0312352622; (5) *Screenwriting Is Storytelling: Creating an A-List Screenplay That Sells!* by Kate Wright (Perigee Trade), ISBN 13: 978-0399530241; (6) *Pitching Hollywood: How to Sell Your TV and Movie Ideas* by Jonathan Koch and Robert Kosberg (Quill Driver Books), ISBN 13: 978-1884956317; (7) *Writing the Killer Treatment: Selling Your Story Without a Script* by Michael Halperin (Michael Wiese Productions), ISBN 13: 978-0941188401; (8) *Behind the Screen: Hollywood Insiders on Faith, Film, and Culture* by Spencer Lewerenz and Barbara Nicolosi, (Baker Books), ISBN 13: 978-0801065477; (9) *Advanced Screenwriting: Raising Your Script to the Academy Award Level* (Silman-James Press), ISBN 13: 978-1879505735; (10) *Making a Good Writer Great: A Creativity Workbook for Screenwriters* (Silman-James Press), ISBN 13: 978-1879505490; (11) *How to Be Your Own Script Doctor* by Jennifer Kenning (Continuum), ISBN 13: 978-0826417473; (12) *I Liked It, Didn't*

Love It: Screenplay Development from the Inside Out by Rona Edwards and Monika Skerbelis (Lone Eagle), ISBN 13: 978-1580650627; (13) *The Savvy Screenwriter: How to Sell Your Screenplay (and Yourself) Without Selling Out!* by Susan Kouguell (St. Martin's Griffin), ISBN 13: 978-0312355753; (14) *Author! Screenwriter! How to Succeed as a Writer in New York and Hollywood* by Peter Miller (Adams Media), ISBN 13: 978-1593375539.

BOOKS TO FILM. Some of the best movies have been based on books: www.readersread .com/bookstofilm.

CHRISTIAN DRAMA NORTHWEST. An e-mail group for those interested in drama: http:// groups.yahoo.com/groups/CDNW.

CHRISTIANS IN HOLLYWOOD. (1) Hollywood agent reveals secrets of "show biz." Contact: Victorya Rogers Communications, PO Box 92522, Southlake TX 76092. (214)257-8716. E-mail: victorya@victorya.com. Website: www.victorya.com. (2) A site for Christians interested in breaking into Hollywood: www.thrillinglife.com. Click on "Seminars."

CHRISTIANS IN THEATER ARTS, PO Box 26471, Greenville SC 29616. (864)679-1898. E-mail: information@cita.org. Website: www.cita.org. Holds an annual conference.

COLLABORATOR. Software and services for screenwriters and novelists: www.collaborator.com.

THE COMPLETE BOOK OF SCRIPTWRITING by J. Michael Straczynski (Writer's Digest Books), ISBN 13: 978-1582971582. Order from www.writersdigest.com or through local bookstore.

CREATIVE SCREENWRITING, 6404 Hollywood Blvd., Ste. 415, Los Angeles CA 90028. Toll-free (800)727-6978. (323)957-1405. Fax (323)957-1406. E-mail: info@creativescreen writing.com. A magazine for professional screenwriters: www.creativescreenwriting.com.

DONE DEAL. A wealth of resources for screenwriters: www.scriptsales.com.

DRAMASHARE CHRISTIAN DRAMA THEATRE RESOURCES, 82 St. Lawrence Crescent, Saskatoon SK S7K 1G5, Canada. Toll-free (877)363-7262. Fax (306)653-0653. E-mail: from Website. Supports those involved in Christian drama ministry worldwide with how-to manuals, scripts, seminars, and newsletters: www.dramashare.org.

THE DRAMATISTS GUILD OF AMERICA, 1501 Broadway, Ste. 701, New York NY 10036. (212)398-9366. Fax (212)944-0420. E-mail: from Website: www.dramaguild.com. Professional association of playwrights, composers, and lyricists with over 6,000 members.

DRAMA WORKSHOP. Nuts & Bolts of Dramatic Writing. Includes dramatic structures, script formats, screenwriting, reading list, and exercises: http://Chdramaworkshop.homestead.com/ Home.html.

ESSAYS. An index of essays on the craft of dramatic writing: www.storyispromise.com.

ETHNIC MARKET. National Black Theatre Inc., 2031-33 National Black Theatre Way at Fifth Ave., Harlem NY 10035. Open to historical and inspirational dramas, musicals, and children's plays. Scripts must reflect the African and African American lifestyle. E-mail: from Website: www.nationalblacktheatre.org.

FADE IN ONLINE. Annual screenplay and fiction competition: www.fadeinonline.com.

+FREE SCRIPTS. (1) www.scriptcrawler.net; (2) www.simplyscripts.com; (3) www.script-o-rama .com.

GARDNER'S GUIDES. Order from Garth Gardner Company: www.ggcinc.com/publrt.htm.# screenwriting. (1) Gardner's Guide to Animation Scriptwriting: The Writer's Road Map; (2) *Gardner's Guide to Television Scriptwriting;* (3) *Gardner's Guide to Screenwriting.*

GETTING YOUR ACTS TOGETHER by Frank V. Priore. A complete step-by-step guide on how to write and sell a full-length play for the school market. ISBN 13: 978-0963749840. Available at local bookstores.

GRIZZLY ADAMS PRODUCTIONS, PO Box 298, Baker City OR 97814. (208)683-0593. Fax (208)683-3009. E-mail: julie@grizzlyadams.tv. Website: www.grizzlyadams.tv. Producers of network television *Encounters with the Unexplained* (PAX-TV Network), home videos, and family-friendly and faith-based feature films. Producer for a variety of networks. Occasionally on the lookout for beginning screenwriters.

+HOLLYWOODCONNECT. Serving Christians in the arts, media, and entertainment industry: www.hollywoodconnect.com.

HOLLYWOOD CREATIVE DIRECTORY. (1) 5055 Wilshire Blvd., Hollywood CA 90036-4396. (323)525-2348 (research). Toll-free (800)815-0503. Fax (323)525-2393. Website: www.hcdonline.com. Updated 3 times a year. Lists production companies and staff (the ones who option or buy screenplays for production). Commonly referred to as "The Phone Book to Hollywood." (2) They also publish the *Hollywood Representation Directory.* Lists talent agents, management companies, and attorneys; (3) view other books on this site, including *The Blu-Book Production Directory.*

HOLLYWOOD JESUS. Movie reviews and pop culture from a spiritual point of view: www.hollywoodjesus.com.

HOLLYWOOD LIT SALES. A place to submit screenplays and to learn how to write them: www.hollywoodlitsales.com.

HOLLYWOOD SCRIPTWRITING. Teaches how to go from idea, to screenplay, to sale; includes free newsletter and links: www.HowToWriteScripts.com.

ILLINOIS/CHICAGO SCREENWRITING COMPETITION. Website: www.illinoisbiz.biz/film/index.html. This is a biennial event sponsored by the Chicago and Illinois Film Offices to support and promote local screenwriters. It is offered exclusively to Illinois resident writers who have completed a feature-length script. Winners receive a cash prize and their scripts are sent to a select group of production companies and Hollywood producers and studios. (312)814-3600. Application, rules, and regulations download available on site.

INKTIP.COM. Website: www.InkTip.com. "The fastest and easiest way to give your screenplays more exposure."

INTER-MISSION. A community of Christians involved in the entertainment industry: www.inter-mission.net.

INTERNATIONAL SCREENPLAY COMPETITION. Sponsored by the American Screenwriters Association and Writer's Digest: http://writersdigest.com/contests/internat_screenplay.asp.

+MOVIE SITES. (1) Website: www.moviebytes.com. Screenwriting contests and markets online. Lists rules and advance information on contests held monthly, yearly, internationally, and those which charge no fees to enter. (2) Movie Parables: www.christiancritic.com; (3) www.movieguide.org; (4) www.hollymcclure.com.

ONLINE SCREENWRITING AND WRITING COURSES. (1) Go to Website to see currently featured courses: www.absoluteclasses.com/courses.htm. (2) UCLA offers a one-year graduate-level certificate screenwriting program online: www.filmprograms.ucla.edu; (3) www.screenplay.com.

ORGANIZATION OF BLACK SCREENWRITERS, 1999 W. Adams Blvd., Los Angeles CA 90018. (323)735-2050. Fax (323)735-2051. E-mail: from Website. Helps African American writers get their work presented to Hollywood: www.obswriter.com.

THE PLAYWRIGHTS GUILD OF CANADA. (416)703-0201. Fax (416)703-0059. E-mail: info@playwrightsguild.ca. A national association of professional playwrights: www.playwrightsguild.com/pgc.

PLAYWRITING. (1) Website: www.vcu.edu/artweb/playwriting. "An Opinionated Web Companion on the Art & Craft of Playwriting." Offers playwriting seminars. (2) For playwriting opportunities: www.playwritingopportunities.com.

PROVIDENCE SCRIPT 2 SUCCESS, 555 W. Beech St., Ste. 225, San Diego CA 92101-2957. (619)238-8234. E-mail: Success@Script2Success.com. A consulting service to transform creative story ideas into viable business opportunities: www.Script2Success.com.

+QUESTIONS ABOUT SCRIPTWRITING. Professional screenwriters provide answers and articles: www.wordplayer.com.

SCREENPLAY COMPETITION. Print screenwriting application from the Web: http://americanaccolades.com/contest_rules.htm. E-mail info@americanaccolades, for current application.

SCREENPLAY FESTIVAL. Website: www.screenplayfestival.com.

SCREENPLAY MASTERY. Michael Hauge offers coaching and consultation services dedicated to the art, craft, and business of screenwriting: www.screenplaymastery.com. (818)995-4209. E-mail: contact@screenplaymastery.com.

+SCREENWRITER SITES. (1) www.online-communicator.com/toppage.html; (2) www.screentalk.org; (3) www.tvwriter.com; (4) http://visualwriter.com.

SCREENWRITER'S UTOPIA. Features dozens of resources and classes: www.screenwritersutopia.com.

THE SCRIPTJOURNAL. This free online publication gives an inside look at the film-making community. Their newsletter features screenplay tips, guest articles, pro screenwriting profiles, and more: www.scriptjournal.com/newsletter.htm.

SCR(i)PT MAGAZINE. The magazine for the craft and business of screenwriting: www.scriptmag.com.

SCRIPTSHARK, 520 Broadway St., Ste. 230, Santa Monica CA 90401. (310)260-5645. E-mail: scriptshark@blssi.com. Helps screenwriters connect to studios, agents, managers, and production companies: www.scriptshark.com.

SCRIPT VIKING. Provides evaluations and agent services for script writers: www.scriptviking.com.

SCRIPTWRITERS SITES. (1) www.screenwriters.com; (2) www.screenwriter.com; (3) www.hollywoodawards.com; (4) http://scriptwritersnetwork.com. (5) A site for writers of comics, radio, television, or movies: www.scrypticstudios.com.

SCRIPTWRITING CONFERENCES. (1) Website: www.writersdigest.com/conferences. Type in "Scriptwriting" in the Search box. (2) www.screenplay.com; (3) Nashville Screenwriters Conference: www.nashscreen.com/nsc.

SCRIPTWRITING RECOMMENDED BOOKS. Also see "Books of Interest" in this section. (1) *Making a Good Script Great* by Linda Seger (Samuel French), ISBN 13: 978-0573699214; (2) *Writing Screenplays That Sell* by Michael Hauge (Collins), ISBN 13: 978-0062725004; (3) *Story: Structure, Substance, Style and the Principles of Screenwriting* by Robert McKee (Regan), ISBN 13: 978-0060391683; (4) *The Writer's Journey* by Chris Vogler (Michael Wiese Productions), ISBN 13: 978-0941188708; (5) *Writing Treatments That Sell* by Kenneth Atchity (Owl Books), ISBN 13: 978-0805072785; (6) *The Complete Guide to Standard Script Formats* by Hilis R. Cole (CMC), ISBN 13: 978-0941710237; (7) *The Screenwriter's Bible: A Complete Guide to Writing, Formatting and Selling Your Script* by David Trottier (Silman-James Press), ISBN 13: 978-1879505841; (8) *Screenwriting on the Internet: Researching, Writing and Selling Your Script on the Web* by Christopher Wehner (Michael Wiese Productions), ISBN 13: 978-0941188364; (9) *Crafty TV Writing: Thinking Inside the Box* by Alex Epstein (Owl Books), ISBN 13: 978-0805080285.

SELLING TO HOLLYWOOD. American Screenwriters Assn. International Screenwriters Conference: www.sellingtohollywood.com.

+SELLING YOUR SCREENPLAY. Learn how to get your screenplay into the hands of producers and directors who can turn it into a movie. Instant online access to the e-book *Selling Your Screenplay:* www.sellingyourscreenplay.com?aff=aw2.

SOFTWARE FOR SCREEN/SCRIPT WRITERS. (1) ScreenStyle: www.screenstyle.com; (2) ScriptWizard: www.warrenassoc.com; (3) HollyWord: www.hollyword.com; (4) FinalDraft: www.finaldraft.com; (5) Movie Magic Screenwriter: www.screenplay.com; (6) Scriptware: www.scriptware.com; (7) Page 2 Stage: www.page2stage.com. (8) More software: www.writersstore.com/products.php?cPath=22; (9) http://indelibleink.com. (10) Sophocles Screenwriting Software: www.sophocles.net; (11) Idea Tracker: www.intellectusenterprises.com; (12) enLighter Professional: www.enliter.com; (13) Quick Query Tracker: www.quickquery tracker.com; (14) Thinkmap Visual Thesaurus: www.visualthesaurus.com; (15) Writer's Café: www.writerscafe.co.uk. (16) Hollywood Screenwriter software: www.write-bros.com; (17) Scriptwriter's Suite: www.finaldraft.com.

STORIE ARTS INC., 407 S. Vail Ave., Arlington Heights IL 60005. (630)561-6502. E-mail: GSI LAGI@storie.com. A Christian film/video company looking for original scripts to be produced as film shorts, half-hour shows for broadcast/video, or feature-length films: www .storie.com.

STUDIO NOTES. E-mail: info@writerssupercenter.com. A place where aspiring writers can receive professional feedback and evaluation: www.studionotes.com.

+THEATRE RESOURCES. Check out: www.dramasource.com and click on "Author Area" for submission information.

WRITE BROTHERS INC., 138 N. Brand Blvd., Ste. 201, Glendale CA 91203. (818)843-6557. Fax (818)843-8364. This company hosts two Websites: www.screenplay.com; (2) www.write-bros.com. Excellent software for writing screenplays and stories.

WRITERS BOOT CAMP. An immersion program to help writers turn an idea into a fully developed first draft in one month's time: www.writersbootcamp.com. Toll-free: (800)800-1733.

THE WRITERS STORE. Essentials for writers and filmmakers: www.writersstore.com.

ZOETROPE. Website: www.zoetrope.com. The Virtual Studio is a complete motion picture production studio on the Web. Membership free.

RESOURCES: SONGWRITING

Note: Also see "Music Markets" in Periodical section.

ADORATION PUBLISHING, CO. Website: www.adorationpublishing.com. E-mail: larry@ adorationpublishing.com. Publishes choral and instrumental music for Christian worship. Click on "Submit Your Music."

THE ART OF WRITING GREAT LYRICS by Pamela Phillips Oland (Allworth Press), ISBN 1581150938. Order this book and many others at: www.allworth.com.

CHORDANT MUSIC GROUP. EMI Music/Chordant Music Group Distribution: www .chordant.com. Click on "Products," then "Labels" for Chordant labels.

+CHRISTIAN COPYRIGHT LICENSING INTERNATIONAL (CCLI). For copyright issues around using song lyrics and phone numbers of all music publishing companies: www .ccli.com. E-mail: support@ccli.com.

CHRISTIAN MUSIC DIRECTORIES/CHRISTIAN MUSIC FINDER. Resource Publications Inc., 160 E. Virginia St., #290, San Jose CA 95112-5876. Toll-free (888)273-7782. Fax (408)287-8748. E-mail: info@rpinet.com. Website: www.rpinet.com/products/cmf.html. A comprehensive information source for Christian music.

CHRISTIAN MUSIC ONLINE. Website: www.cmo.com.

CHRISTIAN SONGWRITING ORGANIZATION. A group for songwriters to share ideas/ experiences and to critique each other's work: www.christiansongwriting.org.

CONTEST FOR SONGWRITERS. Contact The American Dream Group: http://achieve-the-dream .net. Click on "Contests."

THE DRAMATISTS GUILD OF AMERICA, 1501 Broadway, Ste. 701, New York NY 10036. (212)398-9366. Fax (212)944-0420. E-mail: from Website. Professional association of playwrights, composers, and lyricists: www.dramaguild.com.

FINDING A COLLABORATOR. Helpful article: www.writersdigest.com/articles/excerpts/99 songmarket_find_collaborator.asp.

GETTING STARTED IN CHRISTIAN MUSIC, Reed Arvin, ed. (Harvest House Publishers), ISBN 13: 978-0736902670. Find a balance between music, ministry, and fame; how to record with a major label or on your own; learn basic poetic techniques for lyric writers.

GOSPEL MUSIC ASSN., 1205 Division St., Nashville TN 37203. (615)242-0303. Fax (615)254-9755. Website: www.gospelmusic.org. Annual GMA conference, advocacy, and resources.

+GRANDVIEW RECORDS. Christian record label. Contains links to the best Christian Websites and resources on the Web: www.grandviewrecords.com/arts/literature.htm.

HOLLYWOOD CREATIVE DIRECTORY BOOKS. *Hollywood Music Industry Directory.* Website: www.hcdonline.com.

+HYMNAL COPYRIGHTS. To determine if a hymn is in public domain, go to: www.cyber hymnal.org.

INDIEHEAVEN. Information and resources for independent Christian artists, radio stations, venues. Do a site search for "50 Point Tune-up" song evaluation: www.indieheaven.com.

LYRICS FINDER. Can't remember lyrics to a song? Does your character need a song to sing? Go to: www.findmeatune.com, for searchable source.

+MUSIC RESOURCES. (1) Summary of news and events affecting the Christian Retail Channel, including music news: www.cbaonline.org; (2) www.ccmmagazine.com; (3) www.christian musicplanet.com; (4) www.christianradioweekly.com; (5) www.gospelcity.com; (6) www .singingnews.com.

THE NASHVILLE SONGWRITERS ASSOCIATION INTL., 1710 Roy Acuff Pl., Nashville TN 37203. Toll-free (800)321-6008. (615)256-3354. Fax (615)256-0034. E-mail: from Website. Offers workshops in 100 cities throughout the world: www.nashvillesongwriters.com.

PERFORMING RIGHTS SOCIETIES. These three groups collect royalties due their members from radio, TV, and concert performances:(1) ASCAP (American Society of Composers, Authors and Publishers), 1 Lincoln Plaza, New York NY 10023. (212)621-6000. E-mail: info@ascap.com. Website: www.ascap.com; (2) BMI (Broadcast Music Inc.), 320 W. 57th St., New York NY 10019-3790. (212)586-2000. Website: http://bmi.com; (3) SESAC (not an acronym), 55 Music Square E., Nashville TN 37203. (615)320-0055. Fax (615)329-9627. Website: www.sesac.com.

PROVIDENT MUSIC GROUP, 741 Cool Springs Blvd. E., Franklin TN 37067. Site provides links to retailers, Provident labels, artists, concerts, jobs, FAQs, features, and more: www.provident music.com.

PUBLICIST SITE. Devon O'Day, radio publicist, and Kim McLean, Dove Award–winning singer/songwriter, team up to provide creative, affordable, and effective artist-songwriter-author services. Hippie Chick Twang: www.hippiechicktwang.com.

THE RECORDING ACADEMY, 3402 Pico Blvd., Santa Monica CA 90405. (310)392-3777. Fax (310)399-3090. E-mail: from Website. Presents the Grammy Awards. Also engages in professional development activities; offers associate memberships: www.grammy.com/academy.

RESOURCES. Website: www.musesmuse.com. Order Songwriter's Toolkit.

RHYMING DICTIONARY. Website: www.rhymer.com.

SONGWRITERS GUILD OF AMERICA, 209—10th Ave. S., Ste. 534, Nashville TN 37203. (615)742-9945. Fax (615)742-9948. E-mail: nash@songwritersguild.com. Protects the rights of songwriters: www.songwritersguild.org.

THE SONGWRITER'S MARKET GUIDE. Website: www.writersdigest.com.

SONGWRITING COMPETITION. International Songwriting Competition, 1307 Eastland Ave., Nashville TN 37206. (615)251-4441. Fax (615)251-4442. E-mail: info@songwriting competition.com. Website: www.songwritingcompetition.com.

SONGWRITING LINKS. Website: www.lyricist.com.

YOU CAN WRITE SONG LYRICS, by Terry Cox (Writer's Digest Books), ISBN 13: 978-0898799897. Order from local bookstores.

*RESOURCES: WOMEN WRITERS

BABY BOOMER'S ONLINE COMMUNITY. See how wise, warm, and witty baby-boomer women are connecting, encouraging, and supporting one another: www.boomerwomenspeak.com.

DOMESTIC ABUSE. An outreach recovery program for domestic and intimate partner abuse: www.womeninspiration.org.

INTERNATIONAL WOMEN'S WRITING GUILD. Hannelore Hahn, exec. dir., PO Box 810, Gracie Station, New York NY 10028-0082. (212)737-7536. Fax (212)737-9469. E-mail: dirhahn@aol.com. Website: www.iwwg.com. A network for the personal and professional empowerment of women through writing; annual membership $45.

MOM WRITERS. (1) Support, encouragement, and tips for mothers who write. Discussion group at http://groups.yahoo.com/group/momwriters. (2) Includes a weekly talk-radio show. Website: www.momwriterslitmag.com; (3) www.thedabblingmum.com/writing/index.htm; (4) www.writefromhome.com.

NATIONAL ASSN. OF WOMEN WRITERS, 24165 IH-10 W., Ste. 217-637, San Antonio TX 78257. Toll-free (866)821-5829. Email: naww@onebox.com. Offers an e-book library, online critique and discussion groups, and industry-related legal advice. Subscribe to a weekly e-zine from Website: www.naww.org.

ONLINE GROUP FOR WOMEN WRITERS. Website: http://groups.yahoo.com/group/WritingWomenWisdom.

RESIDENCY. Soapstone offers a quiet space for women writers away from jobs, children, and other responsibilities. Thirty writers each year are given residencies that are offered at no charge. For further information and applications, go to: www.soapstone.org.

SHELOVESGOD.COM. Contact: Marnie L. Pehrson, dir., 514 Old Hickory Ln., Ringgold GA 30736. (706)866-2295. E-mail: webmaster@SheLovesGod.com. A community for Christian women. Read and/or submit faith-promoting articles, stories, testimonies, and poems. Writers post their submissions for free, and they are stored in a searchable database: www.SheLovesGod.com.

SISTERS IN CRIME. Rochelle Krich, pres., PO Box 442124, Lawrence KS 66044. (785)842-1325. E-mail: sinc@sistersincrime.org. Fights discrimination against women in the mystery field. Educates publishers and the public about inequalities in the treatment of female authors: www.sistersincrime.org.

TODAY'S WOMAN WRITING COMMUNITY. Supportive, online writing community with articles, short stories, poems, interactive forums, blogs, and more: www.todays-woman.net.

WOMEN'S MINISTRY. Ideas, resources, and information exchange among Christian women and worldwide ministry organizations: www.womensministry.net.

WOMEN'S WRITING RESOURCES. Website: www.womensministry.net.

RESOURCES: YOUNG WRITERS

AWARDS & CONTESTS. (1) Chattanooga Writers Guild sponsors an annual contest with adult and student (grades 6-12) divisions. Children's categories include poetry, fiction, and personal essay. Contact Ray Zimmerman, pres., PO Box 3087, Chattanooga TN 37404, to get information on current contest. E-mail: cwg@chattanoogawritersguild.org. Website: www.chattanoogawritersguild.org. (2) The Kenyon Review sponsors the Patricia Grodd Poetry Prize for Young Writers. The award recognizes outstanding young poets and is open to high school sophomores and juniors throughout the world. The winner receives a full scholarship to the Kenyon Review Young Writers Workshop. In addition, the winning poem will be published in *The Kenyon Review*. E-mail: kenyonreview@kenyon.edu. Check Website for submission guidelines and application: www.kenyonreview.org/programs/ywpp.php.

BOOK PUBLISHER. SynergEbooks publishes all genres of e-books written for children: www.synergebooks.com.

CONFERENCES. Check "Christian Writers' Conferences and Workshops" section in this guide for those that provide a separate track or sessions for young writers.

FUNDS FOR YOUNG WRITERS. Website: www.fundsforwriters.com/writingkid.htm.

GENERAL PERIODICAL MARKETS. (1) *Stone Soup* publishes stories, poems, and art by kids 13 and under: www.stonesoup.com/writing-by-children; (2) *Insight* magazine publishes stories and profiles for teens ages 13 to 19: www.insightmagazine.org; (3) *Creative Kids:* www.prufrock.com. Click "Journals & Magazines." (4) *Potluck Children's Literary Magazine:* http://members.aol.com/_ht_a/potluckmagazine; (5) *Merlyn's Pen:* www.merlynspen.com; (6) *Skipping Stones:* www.efn.org/~skipping/submissions.htm; (7) *Teen Ink* magazine: http://teenink.com; (8) *The Writers' Slate:* www.writingconference.com; (9) *I Love Cats:* www.iluvcats.com. (10) www.jhu.edu/~gifted/ts/writing_resources.htm.

IPL KIDSPACE. Features Culture Quest, Story Hour, Science Fair project ideas, a learning HTML guide, and subject collections with links ranging from art to sports. All selected to be age-appropriate for preteens: http://ipl.sils.umich.edu/div/kidspace.

JUST4TEENS. Site where teens can post stories and poems: www.lovepoetscafe.net/teens.

LISSA EXPLAINS IT ALL. An excellent site for learning HTML (the language in which Web pages are written), especially for kids, but equally helpful for any HTML novice: www.lissaexplains.com.

MYSTERY WRITING. Mystery writing lesson plans for kids: http://kids.mysterynet.com.

PERIODICAL MARKETS. Check "Periodical Topics" in this guide for "Young Writer Markets."

SCI-FI & FANTASY WRITING FOR TEENS. A great list of resources including contests, workshops, and markets: http://snipurl.com/9wda.

STORYBOOK WEAVER DELUXE. A CD for children ages 8-12 that encourages writing. Students author/illustrate stories with easy-to-use word processor and graphic features: www.riverdeep.net. Do site search for "Storybook Weaver."

UPPER ROOM MINISTRIES. Online community where young adults can explore their relationship with God and with others through young adult forums, networks, and blogs: www.MethodX.org.

THE WRITE STUFF. A club for young adult writers ages 13 to 23: www.geocities.com/writestuffclub.

WRITING WITH WRITERS. Students complete online activities to develop their writing skills: http://teacher.scholastic.com/activities. Do search for "Writing with Writers."

YAHOOLIGANS. Search engine for kids geared toward elementary age children or adults seeking information in a simple format: www.yahooligans.com.

YOUNG AUTHOR EDITION OF WRITING SMARTER NOT HARDER. (1) By Colleen Reece. A how-to book for elementary-school-age children. Great for children's writing classes or homeschoolers. To order a copy, send $7.95, plus $1.50 shipping to: Kaleidoscope Press, 2507—94th Ave. E., Edgewood WA 98371, or call (253)848-1116. (2) *Writing Smarter Not Harder* (for jr. high through adults) is available for $13.95 plus $1.50 shipping. You may also order from: www.pennylent.vpweb.com.

YOUNG WRITERS CLUBS. (1) Real Kids, Real Adventures, PO Box 461572, Garland TX 75046-1572. Website: www.realkids.com. From author Deborah Morris: tips on how to get started writing, a writing contest, and a critique group for kids. (2) The Young Writers Club: www.cs.bilkent.edu.tr/~david/derya/ywc.html.

+YOUNG WRITER SITE. Thirteen- to 20-year-olds can drop in to talk about their writing; no ID required: www.absynthemuse.com.

YOUNG WRITERS SERIES. *Young Writers Contest Manual, Young Writers Market Manual* and *Young Writers Manuscript Manual* by Penny Lent. For kindergarten to college-age students interested in selling nonfiction, poetry, photos, and art. To order, send $7.95, plus $1.50 shipping, for each book to: Kaleidoscope Press, 2507—94th Ave. E., Edgewood WA 98371, or call (253)848-1116. Or order from: www.pennylent.vpweb.com.

+YOUNG WRITERS SOCIETY. Online community where young writers can share work, chat, and create a blog: http://youngwriterssociety.com.

SEARCH ENGINES & BROWSERS

ALTAVISTA. Website: www.altavista.com.

+ALTERNATIVE BROWSER. The U.S. Computer Emergency Readiness Team, a branch of the U.S. Department of Homeland Security, has recommended that you "use a different Web browser" other than Internet Explorer, especially if you still have Windows 98, Windows 98 SE, or Windows ME. Instead, install Mozilla Firefox, available for free at: www.mozilla.com/firefox. You can't uninstall Internet Explorer—just stop using it.

A9. Website: http://a9.com. Amazon.com's search engine. In addition to Web search results, you can search books carried by Amazon.com.

+BOOKMARKING SERVICES. (1) Free service where you can store a complete copy of any Web page to create your personal online full-text-searchable library: www.furl.net. Similar sites: (2) www.blinklist.com; (3) http://snipurl.com/vcm9; (4) http://del.icio.us.

CHRISTIAN SEARCH ENGINES. Websites: (1) www.christianlink.com; (2) www.crosssearch.com; (3) www.crosswalk.com; (4) www.everythingchristian.org; (5) www.ibelieve.com; (6) www.injesus.com; (7) www.praize.com; (8) www.religiousresources.org; (9) www.chritech.com; (10) www.worthylinks.com; (11) www.his-net.com.

CLUSTY.COM. Similar to Google but offers alternate categories: www.clusty.com.

CNET. A conglomeration of dozens of tech sites and tools: http://cnet.com.

COPERNIC. A metasearch engine: www.copernic.com.

DIRECT SEARCH. A growing compilation of links to the find resources not easily searchable from general search tools: www.freepint.com/gary/direct.htm.

DITTO. A visual search engine: www.ditto.com.

DOGPILE. Uses over a dozen search engines to find your search topic: www.dogpile.com.

EXPERT CLICK. Search for experts by topic, geography, or organization: www.expertclick.com.

FREEALITY INTERNET SEARCH ENGINES. Website: www.freeality.com.

GOOGLE. Sorts hits based on how "popular" they are: www.google.com.

GOOGLE BOOKS. Search for full text books and discover new ones: http://books.google.com/print/faq.html.

GOOGLE TIPS. Check out an article entitled *Better Googling: Things You Didn't Know Google Does* at: www.sreetips.com/google.html.

GOOGLE WEBQUOTES. Enter quote in search box. Annotates the results of your Google search with comments from other Websites: www.google.com.

HOTBOT. Website: www.hotbot.com.

HOTWIRED. Website: hotwired.com/webmonkey.

INFO. Displays results from leading search engines: www.info.com.

LOOKSMART. Find resources for improving your writing and getting published: www.looksmart.com.

LYCOS. Website: www.lycos.com.

MSN SEARCH. Website: www.search.msn.com.

QUICKBROWSE. Service that combines your favorite sites into a single page for faster viewing: www.quickbrowse.com.

SEARCH ENGINE OPTIMIZATION. Website: http://thedabblingmum.com/business/seo/index.htm.

SEARCH ENGINE WATCH. Good site to learn information about search engines: www.searchenginewatch.com. Click on "Web Searching Tips" to learn how to search the Web.

711.NET. A Christian-oriented search engine that includes categories such as apologetics, Bible, faith, church, and theology: www.711.net.

TURBO10 METASEARCH ENGINE. Topics are generated for each search and are listed in a pull-down menu at the top of the search results to help refine it to the most specific search: http://turbo10.com.

VIVISIMO. New clustering search engine: http://vivisimo.com.

YAHOO! Website: www.yahoo.com; http://search.yahoo.com.

SELF-PUBLISHING

AIRLEAF PUBLISHING & BOOKSELLING. This firm represents your self-published or print-on-demand book in bookstores. Website: www.airleaf.com. Toll-free (800)342-6068. E-mail: information@airleaf.com, to request author's information packet.

AMERICAN SELF-PUBLISHING ASSN., PO Box 232233, Sacramento CA 95823. (916)422-8435. Toll-free (800)929-7889. Website: http://members.aol.com/ASPublish/members.html. Offers free e-mail consulting, a monthly newsletter, and reduced rates on many services, such as Websites and charge card capability. Dues are $45/yr. E-mail: ASPublish@aol.com.

IUNIVERSE.COM/SELF-PUBLISHING GUIDE. (1) Website: www.iuniverse.com. (2) Article: *Get Your Book Reviewed* (click on "Tips for Authors"). Website: www.iunivers.com/author toolkit.

MAGAZINE ARTICLE. Website: www.pcmag.com/article2/0,4149,1043161,00.asp. Article from *PC Magazine* about print-on-demand (POD). *PC Magazine* has rated six POD firms and lists the results.

PRINT-ON-DEMAND. (1) Website: www.booksandtales.com/pod. *An Incomplete Guide to Print on Demand Publishers* by Clea Saal compares different POD publishers and their services. (2) A series of interviews with the presidents of IUniverse and AuthorHouse and former VP from Xlibris. Offers inside information on how POD books actually sell: http://wbjbradio.com/series/pod.php; (3) Instant Publishing. You can print as few as 25 books: www.instantpublishing.com.

SELF-PUBLISHING SITES. (1) Website: www.parapublishing.com. (2) Check out Dan Poynter's book *The Self-Publishing Manual* (Para Publishing), ISBN 13: 978-1568601342. Also check out (3) www.instantpublisher.com; (4) www.selfpublishers.com; (5) www.selfpublishing.com; (6) www.go-publish-yourself.com; (6) www.wellfedsp.com. (7) http://lulu.com.

SERVICES FOR WRITERS

Note: Check out these services before hiring any of them. Their listing here in no way indicates an endorsement.

ABC'S OF POD. Order *The ABC's of POD: A Beginner's Guide to Fee-Based Print-on-Demand Publishing* from author Dehanna Bailee's Website: www.dehanna.com. The site also features a POD database.

+ADVICE FOR WRITERS. A site to categorize published writers and to help writers answer where they are in their writing careers: www.ingermanson.com/writing/freshman.php.

AGENT ADDRESSES. See: http://tinyurl.com/6vcq5 for a free list of agent e-mail addresses.

+AGENT BLOGS. Voted among the 101 Best Websites for Writers by Writer's Digest: (1) Literary agent Jennifer Jackson gives writing advice and her thoughts on the publishing industry:

http://arcaedia.livejournal.com. (2) Q&A sessions where you can ask questions of authors and agents: http://knightagency.blogspot.com; (3) http://pubrants.blogspot.com. (4) Tips for looking for an agent: http://raleva31.livejournal.com.

AGENT QUERY. (1) The Internet's largest and most current database of literary agents: www.agentquery.com. (2) See also Nebraska Center for Writers: http://mockingbird .creighton.edu/NCW/litag.htm.

AGENT RESEARCH & EVALUATION INC. (1) Website: www.agentresearch.com. 425 N. 20th St., Philadelphia PA 19130. (215)563-1867. E-mail: info@agentresearch.com. Tracks public record of literary agents for the sale of dramatic and other subsidiary rights involving books and manuscripts. Publishes a free e-mail newsletter. (2) See also http://agent research.com/agent_ver.html. Let this site do the work for you by researching public records for negative reports on an agency's business practices.

+BOOKS OF INTEREST. (1)*Partnerships, 2nd Edition: Small Business Start-Up Kit* by Daniel Sitarz (Nova Publishing Co.), ISBN 13: 978-1892949073; (2)*How to Form a Limited Liability Company* by Mark Warda (Sphinx Publishing), ISBN 13: 978-1572482227; (3)*Incorporate Your Business: A Legal Guide to Forming a Corporation in Your State* by Anthony Mancuso (NOLO), ISBN 13: 978-1413306361; (4)*Getting Everything You Can Out of All You've Got* by Jay Abraham (St. Martin's Griffin), ISBN 13: 978-0312284541.

BUSINESS CARDS. They offer 250 free business cards: www.VistaPrint.com.

+CHRISTIAN EDITOR NETWORK. 203 Panorama Ct., Brea CA 92821. (714)529-1212. Fax 714-529-5267. Website: www.christianeditor.com. Contact Kathy Ide, Kathy@kathyide.com. An editorial matchmaking service to connect authors, publishers, and agents with qualified, professional, editorial freelancers. Service is free to authors, publishers, and agents. Editors who pass the screening qualifications pay a one-time setup fee and a 15% referral fee for the first year working with a referred client.

CHRISTIAN MANUSCRIPT SUBMISSIONS.COM (formerly First Edition Manuscript Service). Now your book can be submitted to over 80 Christian publishers in one simple step by logging on to: www.ecpa.org. This is an online manuscript service of the Evangelical Christian Publishers Assn. Fee is $98 for six months.

CLASS PERSONAL MENTOR. Toll-free (800)433-6633. Fax (505)899-9282. Florence Littauer, who founded CLASS (Christian Leaders and Speakers Seminars), is offering to be a personal mentor to a limited number of CLASS graduates. This will be done in small classes in various locations. For more information, e-mail: info@classervices.com. Website: www .classervices.com.

COMPUTER HELP. (1) To clean up your computer so Windows will start quicker, run more reliably, and go faster: www.askbobrankin.com/make_windows_xp_run_faster.html. (2) Smart Computing. Free trial issue of Plain English, answers to your computer questions: www.smartcomputing.com. (3) Free Computer Performance Scan will help identify any problem areas: http://pcpitstop.com/tinylink.asp?id=244291.

+CORNERSTONE FULFILLMENT SERVICE LLC, PO Box 44, 35 Beaver St., Bondville VT 05340. (802)297-3771. Fax (802)297-3326. E-mail: cornerstoneorders@adelphia.net. Provides Website order processing and order fulfillment; mail, phone, and fax order processing; warehousing and shipping, and more: www.cornerstonefulfillmenservice.com.

CORRESPONDENCE COURSE FOR MANUSCRIPT EDITING. The University of Wisconsin offers a correspondence course in manuscript editing for those wanting to do editing on a professional level or for writers wanting to improve their personal editing skills. Contact: University of Wisconsin Learning Innovations, 505 S. Rosa Rd., Madison WI 53719-1257. Toll-free (877)895-3276. (608)262-2011. Fax (608)262-4096. E-mail: info@learn .uwsa.edu. Ask about Manuscript Editing C350-A52 or go to "Fundamentals of Manuscript Editing" under Independent Learning section: http://learn.wisconsin.edu/il.

+CSN CHRISTIAN BOOK PUBLISHERS. Toll-free (866)484-6184. Helps writers at any point in the book writing process from "vision to completion." Services include ghost writing, list management, distribution, preselling, order processing, and warehousing: www.csn books.com.

+DIGITAL BULLETIN BOARD. This screen saver features to-do lists, alarms, clocks, and countdown calendars. Free download at: www.mycorkboard.com.

EDITORIAL SERVICES. Lynda Lotman offers various services to writers and editors. Find the specific service you need in one of these Websites she coordinates: (1) www.English Edit.com; (2) www.ManuscriptEditing.com. Other editorial sites: (3) www.StatisticsTutors .com; (4) www.WritingNetwork.com; (5) www.Book-Editing.com.

E-MAIL LIST. Free mailing list company: www.topica.com.

+E-MAIL SERVICE. Free service allows you to create and maintain e-mail lists and avoid SPAM: www.christianemailservice.com.

FAX SERVICES WHEN YOU DON'T HAVE A FAX. You can now receive faxes through an existing e-mail address. Check out these sites: (1) www.efax.com and (2) www.faxaway.com. Both offer free trials.

FREE E-MAIL SERVICES. (1) Website: www.juno.com. Provides a free service to those who want the ability to correspond with others by e-mail, but don't need additional access to the Internet. Sign up online or call toll-free (800)390-5866 to order a Juno CD for $9.95. (2) For another option to set up a free e-mail address: www.mail.com. (3) Guide to free e-mail providers: www.fepg.net.

HOW MUCH TO CHARGE. Check this site out for low-medium-high rates for copywriting, ghostwriting, magazine editing, etc.: www.writersmarket.com/content/howmuch1.asp

+LITERARY AGENCIES. Database of more than 650 literary agencies: http://firstwriter.com.

LOGOS RESEARCH SYSTEMS, 1313 Commercial St., Bellingham WA 98225-4307. (360)527-1700. Toll-free (800)875-6467. Fax (360)527-1707. E-mail: customerservice@logos.com. Publishes comprehensive Logos Bible Software Series3: www.logos.com.

MANAGEMENT CONSULTANTS FOR WRITERS. Kamen & Co. Group Services. Print and digital media appraisers and brokers. Kevin B. Kamen, pres. & CEO, 3009 Grand Blvd., Baldwin NY 11510-4719. (516)379-2797. E-mail: info@kamengroup.com. Website:www.kamen group.com.

MANUSCRIPT BOXES. To obtain rugged boxes for mailing manuscripts, contact: Papyrus Place, 2210 Goldsmith Ln., Louisville KY 40218. (502)451-9748. Fax (502)451-5487. E-mail: info@papyrusplace.com. Website: www.papyrusplace.com.

MANUSCRIPT TRACKING PROGRAMS. (1) Website: www.sandbaggers.8m.com/samm.htm. Free download. (2) M3Pro—Manuscript & Marketing Manager. To order, call (918)451-4017 or e-mail jrw1@valornet.com.

MARKETING LISTS. Toll-free (888)330-4919. E-mail: sendlistinfo@netscape.net. If they don't have the list you need, they will compile a custom list according to your specifications. Lists include libraries, bookstores, media, and more.

THE NATIONAL DIRECTORY OF EDITORS AND WRITERS FOR HIRE. Elizabeth Lyon of M. Evans & Company has compiled a national directory of editors and writers for hire. ISBN 13: 978-1590770696, $18.95. To order, call (800)462-6420. Website: www.rlpgtrade .com/mevans.

PERSONAL WRITING COACH. Expert help for those seeking a life coach to guide them in their writing career. E-mail: info@maryanndiorio.com. Website: www.maryanndiorio.com.

POSTAGE CHARTS. Writer's Postage Chart: www.mirror.org/terry.hickman/index.htm. Click on "Postage Chart."

POSTAGE RATES WORLDWIDE. (1) Website: www.geocities.com/wallstreet/exchange/ 1161/index.htm. International postage rates. Writers living in foreign countries seeking U.S.

postage can order online at: www.usps.gov. (2) Canadian postal rates: www.canadapost .ca/personal/rates/default-e.asp.

+PROJECT & TIME MANAGEMENT. (1) Functionfox offers free newsletter and an online project management system that helps small businesses track expenses and workflow: www.functionfox.com. (2) Hemphill Productivity Institute offers free resources including the *Paper Tiger* e-newsletter containing tips on organizing time, space, and information: http://productiveenvironment.com. (3) For time management help: http://getmoredone .com. (4) For recommendations on how to boost retention, performance, and productivity: www.gevityinstitute.com.

RESEARCH HELP. Mignon Morse, librarian of 20 years, is interested in doing research for authors. 7919 Visa Creek Ln., Sachse TX 75048. E-mail: mmorse62@verizon.net.

RESIDENCIES. (See more residencies under "Grants.") (1) Soapstone offers a quiet space for women writers away from jobs, children, and other responsibilities. Thirty writers each year are given residencies which are offered at no charge. For further information and applications; www.soapstone.org. (2) Located in New Orleans, A Studio in the Woods provides residencies of two-to-four weeks to literary, visual, and performing artists, during which time the artist lives on site, is provided with a private studio, meals, and uninterrupted work time. Small fee to cover food costs. Shorter residencies of one day to a week are possible and happen throughout the year on an informal basis. Also offers Restoration Residencies to support work of artists studying the hurricane aftermath in the woods. Visit Website: www.astudiointhewoods.org.

P. L. SCHLACHTER CONSULTING INC., PO Box 22443, Denver CO 80222. (303)809-7231. E-mail: software@livebytheword.com. Offers personal Website management and database design at affordable prices. Developed database for the *Christian Writers' Market Guide*. Website: www.softwaredesignshop.com.

SCORE (Service Corps of Retired Executives). Offers free advice to small businesses by e-mail: www.score.org.

STAMPS.COM. Free software for printing postage on your computer: www.stamps.com.

SUBMISSION SERVICE. A site to connect writers with publishers, editors, and agents: www .publishersandagents.net.

TELEPHONE HANDSET RECORDING CONTROL. To record phone calls for interviewing purposes. Available at Radio Shack: www.radioshack.com. Enter Product #43-1237.

TO PRESS AND BEYOND. As "book shepherds," this publisher takes your book project through the writing, editing, design, layout, distribution, sales, and promotion stages: www.topress andbeyond.com.

TRANSLATORS. (1) Julia Borovik. E-mail: boroviki@mail.ru. Charges $4/page or $3.50/page for more than 100 pages. She provides services over the Internet as she is a Ukrainian resident. (2) Lean Terentyeva. E-mail: terentyeva@ukr.net. A professional Christian translator with 8 years of experience. Russian/English. (3) Francisco Chavarria. E-mail: inspanish@ juno.com. Translator and registered court interpreter. Spanish/English. (4) Sergey Rozhkove from Penza, Russia. Christian interpreter and translator for missionaries. Wants to translate Christian literature (books, articles, and sermons), especially from English into Russian. Letters of recommendations on request. E-mail: Rozhkov_sergey@mail.ru.

ULINE. Sells a variety of mailing supplies: www.uline.com.

VIRTUAL ASSISTANT. Gayle DeSalles, WordCount, PO Box 765, Hayden ID 83835. (208)664-0683. E-mail: wordcount.biz@gmail.com. Website: www.wordcount.biz.

WRITER-REMINDERS. E-zine to organize your writing with free daily, weekly, and monthly checklists, tips, and resources: http://groups.yahoo.com/group/writer-reminders. To subscribe: writer-reminders-subscribe@yahoogroups.com.

WRITERS' EDGE. Website: www.WritersEdgeService.com. Submission and critique service. Their list includes 80 participating publishers. Charge is $95.

WRITER'S HAVEN. Contact: Beverly Caruso. (951)245-4082. E-mail: Rancho@across2u.com. Website: www.across2u.com/haven.html. A haven near Lake Elsinore where Christian writers who need time and solitude to write will not be interrupted. Room and board included. E-mail for available dates and for information about upcoming writer's seminars.

WRITERS RESOURCE EXCHANGE. Buy, sell, or trade your books and other writing resources, but it is not to promote your own book. To subscribe, send a blank e-mail to: writers_resource-subscribe@yahoogroups.com.

SPEAKING

AMERICAN SPEAKERS BUREAU, 10151 University Blvd., #197, Orlando FL 32817. (407)826-4248. Fax (407)629-7752. E-mail: info@speakersbureau.com. Website: www.speakersbureau.com.

PAMELA CHRISTIAN. Professional speaker, author, and media personality. 18032-C Lemon Dr., PMB 206, Yorba Linda CA 92886. (714)624-0914. E-mail: plchristian@integrity.com. Website: www.pamelachristianministries.com. Speaker's bureau.

+CHRISTIAN SPEAKERS SERVICES. Free speaker's bureau: www.christianspeakerservices.com.

CLASS PERSONAL MENTOR. Toll-free (800)433-6633. Fax (505)899-9282. Florence Littauer, who founded CLASS (Christian Leaders and Speakers Seminars), is offering to be a personal mentor to a limited number of CLASS graduates. This will be done in small classes in various locations. For more information, e-mail info@classervices.com. Website: www.classervices.com.

CLASS SERVICES INC. (Christian Leaders, Authors & Speakers Services), 2201 San Pedro Drive NE, Albuquerque NM 87110. (505)899-4283. Fax (505)899-9282. E-mail: info@classervices.com. Specializing in radio and TV interview campaigns for Christian authors, speakers, and ministries. Provides resources, training, and promotion for Christian authors and speakers: www.classervices.com.

DAYBOOK NEWS. Information and updates on press releases, conferences, speaking engagements, conventions, and book release dates: www.expertclick.com/daybook.

+INVISIBLE CLOCK. The size of a pager, this clock has a vibrate setting where you can set twelve different alarms so you can have it go off at different times during your presentation: www.invisibleclock.com. Toll-free (888)602-2588. $39.95.

+MEDIA TRAINING. (1) www.mediatrainingworldwide.com; (2) www.robertagale.com; (3) www.starstyleproductions.com.

NATIONAL SPEAKERS ASSN., 1500 S. Priest Dr., Tempe AZ 85281. (480)968-2552. E-mail: from Website. Website: www.nsaspeaker.org. Convention and training for professional speakers. Puts out *Professional Speaker Magazine.*

ONE-SHEET PRINTING. Website: www.cfre.com. Click on "Personal Brochures."

ONLINE SPEAKERS BUREAU. Website: www.espeakersbureau.com. Allows speakers to register their background information online so meeting planners have greater access to available talent and can contact speakers directly. For more information, contact pjdoland@espeakersbureau.com.

SERMON AND SPEECH ILLUSTRATIONS. Over 40,000 illustrations in their database: www.bible.org/illus.php.

SPEAKER SPOTLIGHT, 7247 W. Colt, #300, Boise ID 83709. (208)362-6611. Website: www.speakerspotlight.com. Add your link to their directory.

SPEAKING.COM. Website: www.speaking.com. Speaker's platform. (415)861-1700. E-mail: speaker@speaking.com.

SPEECH & TRANSCRIPT CENTER. (1) For current and historical transcripts: www.freepint.com/gary/speech.htm. (2) www.historychannel.com. Click on "Speeches."

SPEECH COACHING. (1) http://fripp.com/forspeaker.html; (2) www.professionalspeaker.com/catalog.htm.

TOASTMASTERS. Worldwide speaking organization offering tips for professionals and nonprofessionals alike: www.toastmasters.org.

VOICE COACHING. Contact: Roy Hanschke. (303)507-9326. E-mail: voiceperson@msn.com. Website: www.voicepersonality.com. Ron Hanschke does voice coaching via audiotape. He listens to your tape, critiques it, and records instructions to you, which are cut into your tape where the correction is needed. Also offers workshops for groups and organizations.

WRITERSPEAKER.COM. Website: www.writerspeaker.com. Contact: Carmen Leal.

TAX HELP FOR WRITERS

AOL TAX CENTER. For expert advice, tax forms, and more: http://money.aol.com/tax/basics.

+BOOKS OF INTEREST. *Partnerships, 2nd Edition: Small Business Start-Up Kit* by Daniel Sitarz (Nova Publishing co.), ISBN 13: 978-1892949073.

CPA DIRECTORY. Website: www.cpadirectory.com.

SMALL BUSINESS ADMINISTRATION. Loads of help for self-employed writers: www.sba.gov.

+TAX FORMS & INFORMATION. (1) www.irs.gov; (2) www.irs.gov/pub/irs-pdf/p541.pdf.

TAX PLANNING. (1) CNN Money.com, http://money.CNN.com; (2) MSN Money, www.moneycentral.msn.com/tax/workshop/welcome.asp. Search these sites for tax help: (3) National Retail Federation: www.nrf.com; (4) Business Owner's Toolkit: www.toolkit.cch.com; (5) Fortune: www.fortune.com; (6) Forbes: www.forbes.com; (7) AllBusiness: www.allbusiness.com; (8) U.S. Assoc. for Small Business and Entrepreneurship: www.usasbe.org; (9) Bizjournals: www.bizjournals.com; (10) BusinessWeek Online: www.businessweek.com; (11) Dun & Bradstreet: www.dnb.com/us; (12) U.S. Chamber of Commerce Small Business Center: www.uschamber.com/sb/default.

TOTALLY HONEST TAX TIPS FOR WRITERS, by Sandy Cathcart (former licensed tax preparer). Determining when to claim your writing as a business, record keeping, deductions, travel, home office, a business plan, purchasing office equipment, phone calls, and much more. Recently updated. To order, go to www.stuartmarket.com.

WRITER'S POCKET TAX GUIDE. An annual tax guide book: www.foolscap-quill.com.

WEB PAGE DEVELOPMENT/RESOURCES

ADDING LINKS. (1) To add Google search to your site, go to: www.google.com/services/websearch.html. (2) To add Gospelcom to your site, go to: www.biblegateway.com/usage.

CHRISTIAN WEB DESIGN AND HOSTING. WebTech Design Group. Full service Christian company offering site design, hosting, domain registration, and more: www.webtechdg.com.

CREATE-IT 101: Basic HTML. Great tutorial on making Web pages: www.geocities.com/Karenw/index.html.

CROSSWAY CHRISTIAN ISP. A family-friendly and Christian filtered Internet service: http://crosswayisp.net.

DOMAIN NAMES. To see if the domain name you want to use is already in use, go to (1) www.networksolutions.com/whois/index.jsp. (2) To learn about domain names, read the articles at http://thedabblingmum.com/business/domainnames/index.htm. To register your domain name, go to (3) www.networksolutions.com; (4) www.rcomexpress.com; or (5) www.namezero.com. For domain name system management and a list of accredited registrars, go to: (6) www.icann.org/registrars/accredited-list.html. Other sites for domain names include: (7) http://domains.aplus.net; (8) www.godaddy.com; (9) www.homewithgod.com; (10) www.westhost.com.

FREE COUNTERS. Websites: (1) www.sitemeter.com. Other fee-based counters: (2) www.mycomputer.com and (3) www.thecounter.com.

FREE ELECTRONIC GREETING CARDS. Create your own e-card: http://associates.123greetings.com.

FREE HOSTING. (1) www.freehostingdirectory.com; (2) www.free-webhosts.com; (3) www.flashwebhost.com/favorite/free_hosting.php; (4) www.AmericanAuthor.com. (5) Easy to maintain. Website: www.freewebs.com.

FREE ONLINE CUSTOMER SERVICE. Website: http://humanclick.com.

FREE POLLS. Website: www.freepolls.com.

+FREE TARGETED TRAFFIC TO YOUR SITE. Website: www.Free-Targeted-Traffic.com.

FREE WEB-BASED E-MAIL SERVICE. Website: www.zzn.com.

+FREE WEBSITE. Book Treasure House Inc. Have your own Web address and multipage book Website with its own e-commerce. Unconditional guarantee, no costs, fees, or book-sales fees; not a trial or limited offer: http://booktreasurehouse.com.

FREE WEB TOOLS. (1) Some tools include guest books, message forums, counters, polls, site searches, audio clips, and more: www.bravenet.com. (2) www.wordpress.org.

HELPFUL WEBSITE. www.BigNoseBird.com.

HOMESTEAD WEB SERVER. Website: www.homestead.com.

HOW TO PROMOTE YOUR WEBSITE. Website: www.wilsonweb.com.

LISSA EXPLAINS IT ALL. An excellent site for learning HTML (the language in which Web pages are written), especially for kids, but equally helpful for any HTML novice: www.lissaexplains.com.

MAINTAINING YOUR WEBSITE. Website: www.workz.com.

MEDIA BUILDER. Offers free fonts and Web graphics to use on your Web page: www.mediabuilder.com.

OURCHURCH.COM. Free Christian Web server; easy to use: www.OurChurch.com.

SCRIPT ARCHIVE. Website: www.scriptarchive.com. Interactive Website gadgets. Site includes working CGI scripts that you can install on your server. Some programming skills required, as well as permission from your ISP or Web-hosting service to install and run your own CGI programs.

SEARCH ENGINE OPTIMIZATION & SUBMISSION. Website: www.webtechdg.com. Click on "Free Resources." Before you submit your site to search engines, let them evaluate your site for search-engine readiness. After they let you know what is needed to make your site rank higher in major search engines, you can submit your site to over 200 search engines from their site for free.

SITE BUILDING. For Site Build It software: www.sitesell.com.

WEB HOSTS. Websites: (1) www.wyenet.com; (2) www.arkwebs.com; (3) www.halfpricehosting.com; (4) www.catalog.com; (5) www.freepagehosting.com; (6) www.westhost.com; (7) www.christianwebhost.com/index.html; (8) www.truepath.com; (9) http://smallbusiness.yahoo.com/webhosting. (10) http://100best-web-hosting.com. (10)www.icdsoft.com.

WEB PAGE DESIGN. Websites: (1) www.webaim.org/standards/508/checklist; (2) www.fresnostate.edu/webaccess/users/default.html; (3) www.webposition.com; (4) www.webstyleguide.com/index.html?/contents.html. (5) Web page design for writers. Website: www.sky-bolt.com/writers/resources.htm. (6) To learn more about web design, read the articles at: http://thedabblingmum.com/business/webdesign/index.htm; (7) www.realEZsites.com; (8) www.pulsepointdesign.com.

WEBSITE OPTIMIZATION. Website Optimization (WSO) is a series of techniques that minimize Web page file sizes and maximize page display speeds: http://websiteoptimization.com/speed/toc.

WEBSITE WORKSTATION. All kinds of advice on Website design, etc.: www.davesite.com/webstation.

+WEB STORAGE. (1) Brady Storage is an online system where you can upload your writing to a server: www.bradymagazine.com/services/storage/index.html; (2) www.stream load.com.

+WEB TOOLS. (1) Create audio messages on your Website with Audio Generator: http:// members.audiogenerator.com/specialinfo.asp?x=92278. (2) Web Hosting Glossary: www .halfpricehosting.com/web-hosting-glossary.aspx.

WEB-ZINE ARTICLE DISTRIBUTION SITES. (1) www.ideamarketers.com/publishers.cfm; (2) www.EzineArticles.com. Free articles to put on your Web page.

WRITERSPEAKER WEB DESIGN AND DEVELOPMENT. Gary Scott, 1254 Ulupii St., Kailua HI 96734. E-mail: Gary@writerspeaker.com. A Christian company whose focus is helping writers and speakers set up effective Websites: www.writerspeaker.com.

WEBSITES: BLOGGING

Blog is a word made from *Web* plus *log*. A Web log, or blog, is a chronicle of the writings and thoughts of one individual. For a writer, it is a place to muse, usually about a particular theme, which is the best way to gather devoted readers and to develop a niche.

+AMAZONCONNECT. A new program that allows readers to receive messages directly from their favorite authors. Participating authors can post messages on their book detail pages and to the home page of readers who have bought their books on Amazon.com: www.Amazon .com/connect.

+BLOG CONTENT. Update your blog more often with free "sticky" content (writing prompts) offered by this site: http://oncewritten.com.

BLOG FOR FUN AND PROFIT. (1) This site contains a wealth of information about blogging sites, newest developments, and how to use blogs for profit: http://blogforfunandprofit .blogware.com. (2) www.writersweekly.com/success_stories/003897_02142007.html; (3) www.thedabblingmum.com/writing/successtories/blogtopublication.htm.

BLOGGING ABOUT BLOGS. (1) Ken Leebow reports on incredible blogs: http:// www.revolution 30.com.com. (2) http://tourbus.com/blognews.html.

BLOG SITES FOR WRITERS. (1) Writers Suite. An online publishing community of writers, readers, and educators. Site boasts of 4 million visitors a month, 2,000 live and archived topics, tens of thousands of articles, and 150 free courses: www.suite101.com; (2) www .relevantblog.blogspot.com.

BOOK BLOG. Book club with online discussions: www.bookblog.net.

+CHRISTIAN FICTION BLOG ALLIANCE. An organization of 150+ member blogs who do weekly blog tours for the latest in mainstream published Christian fiction. Usually books the tours as soon as there is a publication date, preferably 8-10 months ahead of time. Contact by e-mail: BonnieCalhoun@christianfictionblogalliance.com, or visit Website: www.christian fictionblogalliance.com.

CREATE YOUR OWN BLOG. This site shows you how to create your own blog in three easy steps: www.blogger.com/start.

GOOGLE BLOG SEARCH. Website: http://blogsearch.google.com.

+TRACKING BLOGS. (1)This site tracks more than 55.8 million blogs: http://technorati.com. (2)Searches LiveJournal blogs for information on your book: www.LjSeek.com.

WEB BLOGGING SERVER. Website: www.typepad.com.

+WINDOWS LIVE WRITER. Free, downloadable program to add rich content to your blog posts. Capability to see exactly what your blog will look like before you publish it to the Web. Also helps manage multiple blogs: http://ideas.live.com. Click on "Live Writer Beta" for a full description.

WEBSITES OF INTEREST TO WRITERS: GENERAL

AMERICAN CHRISTIAN WRITERS. Offers conferences, critique service, courses, and more: www.ACWriters.com.

ANGEL IN YOUR INKWELL. Site features workshops, coaching, other services, and fun stuff for writers by Carol Newman: www.angelinyourinkwell.com.

AUTHOR WEBSITES. If you are planning an author Website, you may want to check out these sites for ideas: (1) www.traciepeterson.com; (2) http://BrandilynCollins.com; (3) www.charlottedillon.com (for romance writers); (4) http://victoriagaines.com; (5) http://windowstomysoul.blogspot.com. (6) Christina Katz delivers a monthly newsletter, including interviews: www.writersontherise.com.

BEST OF THE BEST. Find the "best of" books, movies, and music: http://listsofbests.com.

BESTSELLERS LIST. USA Today offers a searchable-only database of its weekly top 150 best-seller lists since October 1993: http://asp.usatoday.com/life/books/booksdatabase/default.aspx.

BOOKPROPOSALS.WS. On this site, learn more about the secrets of getting published from author/editor W. Terry Whalin. The site includes information about what editors, literary agents, and best-selling authors are saying about it: www.bookproposals.ws.

+BOOKS OF INTEREST. (1) *Bird by Bird* by Anne Lamott (Anchor), ISBN 13: 978-0385480016; (2) *Writing Articles about the World Around You* by Marcia Yudkin, ISBN 13: 978-0898798142; (3) *How to Write What You Love* by Dennis Hensley (Shaw), ISBN 13: 978-0877881742; (4) *Effective Magazine Writing* by Roger C. Palms (Shaw), ISBN 13: 978-0877882114. (5) *On Writing Well: The Classic Guide to Writing Nonfiction* by William Zinsser (Collins), ISBN 13: 978-0060891541. Also available in audio cassette. (6) For books by writers for writers, visit: www.gryphonbooksforwriters.com/GMC.htm.

BURRYMAN WRITERS CENTER. Lists freelance jobs, resources for fiction and nonfiction writers, working professionals and beginners: www.burryman.com.

+CANADIAN SITES. (1) Comprehensive site that focuses on contests: www.placesforwriters.com; (2) Canadian Book Trade news: www.quillandquire.com; (3) Professional Writers Association of Canada: www.pwac.ca.

+CHRISTIAN COMPUTING MAGAZINE. Christian Computing Magazine's mission is to apply "Tomorrow's Technology to Today's Ministry": http://ccmag.gospelcom.net.

CHRISTIAN E-AUTHORS. Offers support to Christian authors with a specific call to write for the Internet: www.christianeauthor.com.

CHRISTIAN MINISTRY LINKS. Website: www.CrossSearch.com.

CHRISTIAN RETAILING. Website: www.christianretailing.com. Monitors the heartbeat of the Christian retail industry. Offers digital newsletter.

CHRISTIANWRITERS.COM. A free online writers' resource community. Their mission is to provide a supportive, family atmosphere where writers may easily access the tools and resources to create, market, and publish their work: http://christianwriters.com.

COFFEEHOUSE FOR WRITERS. For writers of all genres. Online writing workshops, critique groups, discussion lists, reader's corner: www.coffeehouseforwriters.com.

COPY EDITOR HELP, by Bill Walsh, business-desk copy chief at the Washington Post. Covers everything that any copyeditor could want to know. Offers advice in areas that AP Stylebook overlooks: www.theslot.com.

COURSE MATERIALS. MIT's OpenCourseWare site; writing course materials from MIT classes at no charge: http://ocw.mit.edu.

CREATIVITY SITES. (1) Eric Maisel's *Creativity Newsletter:* www.ericmaisel.com; (2) www.creativity-portal.com.

+CRITIQUE CIRCLE. (1) Voted among the 101 Best Websites for Writers by Writer's Digest, this site is open to all genres: http://critiquecircle.com. (2) www.urbis.com.

+DANCING WORD WRITERS NETWORK: WRITERS INK. Provides articles, interviews, columns, live chats, and writing workshops to encourage and equip Christian writers: www.dancingword.net.

ECONOMY INFORMATION. Website: www.dismal.com.

+EDIT RED. Voted among the 101 Best Websites for Writers by Writer's Digest, this site offers writing tips and a free personal Web page, promotion and marketing tools: http://editred.com.

THE EUROPEAN CHRISTIAN WRITERS' RESOURCES. Website: www.christianwriter.co.uk. Features author Ms. Abidemi Sanusi, ed. Book reviewers wanted.

E-ZINES. (1) www.zinebook.com. (2) Features free e-zine builder tool and a tutorial: www.e-zinez.com; (3) www.apollos-lyre.com.

FAITHFUL READER. Helps a writer keep track of current market trends by providing book reviews, author interviews, excerpts, study guides, and more: www.faithfulreader.com.

FAITH WRITERS. Offers free services and information for writers, readers, and publishers: www.faithwriters.com.

FAMILY LINKS. Find dozens of links to topics related to families: www.thewritingfamily.com/index.shtml.

FEDWORLD INFORMATION NETWORK. Website: www.fedworld.gov.

FIRST LINES. There are lots of sites that feature first lines of books and poems. Check these sites: (1) http://people.cornell.edu/pages/jad22; (2) http://bridge.lexingtonma.org/library/lines.html; (3) www.bookreporter.com/community/trivia/1996-triv.asp.

FOG INDEX FOR READABILITY. Website: www.tech-head.com/fog.htm.

FREELANCE WRITING ORGANIZATION. This site offers thousands of writing resources and writing links, including all genres, funds for writers, job listings, submission calls, and a research library. Also publishes an e-zine: www.fwointl.com.

THE GENDER GENIE. Find out if your writing voice is male or female for developing your fiction characters: www.bookblog.net/gender/genie.html.

GUIDELINES FOR WRITERS. (1) Search 1,400 magazine and book publishers' guidelines: www.powerpenmarketsearch.com. (2) Includes Christian markets from biweekly e-zine: www.powerpenmarketsearch.com/Articles/magazinemarkets.htm.

GUIDE TO LITERARY AGENTS. Website: http://literaryagents.org.

THE HOLLYWOOD PRAYER NETWORK. Website: www.hollywoodprayernetwork.org.

+HUMOR WRITING. Erma Bombeck Writers' Workshop for humor writing, human-interest writing, and more: www.humorwriters.org.

IBELIEVE.COM. Forums covering the gamut of fun, theology, faith, and life: www.ibelieve.com.

+I DEAL IN HOPE. Information and links for authors and speakers: http://idealinhope.com/author/forwriters.html.

INDEPENDENT CHRISTIAN MEDIA NETWORK. For writers, photographers, recording artists, painters, and any independent Christian artist to showcase his/her talents to the world: www.christianindy.com. Click on the recently launched "Christian Writer's Ebook Net."

INTERNET FOR CHRISTIANS. Website: www.gospelcom.net. Includes hyperlinks to all listed sites. Browse by "Ministry" or "Interest."

INTERNET-RESOURCES.COM. Website: www.internet-resources.com/writers.

JOURNALISM GUIDES & TIPS. (1) Check out Pulitzer-winner Bill Dedman's suggestions at: www.powerreporting.com. Thousands of free research tools for journalists. (2) Sponsored by the American Press Institute, JournalistToolBox offers API news, seminars, writing tips, and more: www.americanpressinstitute.org/pages/toolbox. (3) The Journalist Guide provides links to 16 categories of information and resources: http://reporter.umd.edu. (4) For an investigative guide to Internet research, go to: www.journalism.org. (5) IRE Tip Sheets offer 20,000 investigative stories at: www.ire.org/resourcecenter. (6) Skim this site for hundreds of publications to help you find what's important for your articles: www.journalist express.com.

+LIBRARY OF WRITING LINKS. Hundreds of links for writing helps and research. Web URL is case sensitive: www.terryburns.net/LIBRARY.htm.

MAGAZINES FOR WRITERS. (1) The Writer: www.writermag.com; (2) Writer's Digest: www.writersdigest.com. (3) Writer's Chronicle. Each issue of this magazine is full of information, in-depth advice, and inspiration for writers of fiction, poetry, and nonfiction. Call (703)993-4301 to subscribe. One yr., $59.

MAGAZINE SUBSCRIPTIONS. A great source for really cheap magazines, including 16 religious magazines: www.magazinevalues.com.

MR. MAGAZINE. Provides the latest information on consumer magazines, including the 30 Most Notable Launches of the previous year: www.mrmagazine.com.

MY HIDDEN TALENT. A place to read other writers' work and get your work reviewed: www.myhiddentalent.com.

NOVEL ADVICE. Offers contests and resources for writers: www.noveladvice.com.

101 BEST WEBSITES FOR WRITERS. For the Writer's Digest annual list of best Websites for writers, go to: www.writersdigest.com/101sites/2006_index.asp. Check back for a listing of current year sites. Search by one of these categories or by the A-Z list: articles, tips and discussion boards, creativity, general resources, genres, jobs, just for fun, media resources, niches, online writing and critique groups, online writing groups offering classes, organizations, and publishing resources.

101 WRITING ANSWERS. Website: www.101writinganswers.com. A directory of writing and related sources. Lists associations, forums, groups, writing by genre, markets, showcasing, and much more. Has a link to publishing and media resources.

ON THIS DAY IN HISTORY. (1) Details about any period in history: www.dmarie.com/timecap. (2) For a search engine to look up any date, any month, any year in history or a birth date: www.scopesys.com/today.

OPENING HOOKS. Lesson plan for learning how to write opening hooks: www.readwrite think.org/lessons/lesson_view.asp?id=969.

OVERCOMING WRITER'S BLOCK. (1) This site features a ton of generators for ideas, characters, and names: www.seventhsanctum.com/index-writ.php. (2) www.profitable-pen.com; (3) www.writersdock.co.uk.

PAGE ONE LITERARY NEWSLETTER. Website: www.pageonelit.com.

PAGE WISE. Website: www.essortment.com/in/hobbies.writing.

PARENTING PUBLICATIONS OF AMERICA. PPA-Writers, 4929 Wilshire Blvd., Ste. 428, Los Angeles CA 90010. E-mail: tracey@parentingpublications.org. Though membership is for member publications only, there are opportunities for writers, including a mailing list of PPA membership for $50. Writer's fee is $35 and provides writers an opportunity to submit information about themselves and their work to the Annual Convention's Resource Table: www.parentingpublications.org.

PUBLIC OPINION POLLS. Website: www.pollingreport.com.

+PUBLISHING INDUSTRY. (1) For current news and information about the publishing industry: www.writenews.com. (2) Book Publishing Report delivers weekly insight and analysis into the world of book publishing. Request free trial issue. Website: www.simbanet .com/publications/news_bpr.htm. (3) Visit this site for news and information on all things independent—bookstores, publishers, and more: www.newpages.com; (4) www.askabout writing.net; (5) http://publisherslunch.com.

RADIO STATIONS. Website: www.radio-locator.com. The MIT List of Radio Stations on the Internet or "radio-locator." Over 10,000 radio stations from all around the world.

REJECTIONS. (1) A place to post your rejections and vent your frustrations: www.rejection collection.com.

RESEARCH & RESOURCES FOR WRITERS. Website: www.fontayne.com/ink.

RIGHT WRITING. W. Terry Whalin, best-selling author and longtime editor, wants to help anyone with his/her written communication from novels to thank-you letters. Offers the e-zine Right Writing News: www.right-writing.com.

SCAMS. This site offers warnings about several scams: www.anotherrealm.com.

SHARP WRITER. Website: www.johncullen.com/sharpwriter.

SPARE TIME NOVELIST. Website: http://sparetimenovelist.netfirms.com/stntitanic.html.

SPECIAL INVESTIGATIONS AGENCY. www.us-sia.org.

SPIRIT-LED WRITER. Named as one of 101 Best Websites for Writers in 2003 and 2004: www.spiritledwriter.com.

TIME WARNER CHRISTIAN BOOKS NEWSLETTER. Free monthly newsletter: www.twbook mark.com. Click on "Excerpts" to read an excerpt from the books listed for free.

TIME ZONE SITES. (1) www.timezoneconverter.com; (2) www.disastercenter.com/time.htm.

TOASTED CHEESE. Excellent site providing forums, chats, news, musings, book reviews, and the Toasted Cheese Literary Journal: www.toasted-cheese.com.

TOURBUS. (1) Website: www.TOURBUS.com. An informative e-newsletter about what's happening on the Internet, including information on current Internet viruses and hoaxes. (2) Also check out "The Best of Everything": www.tourbus.com/best.html.

USA COMMUNITIES. To get information on any community in the USA, go to the Power of Place. Search out demographics, crime, economy, special events, and more: www.epodunk.com.

WILLWRITE4FOOD.COM. Geared toward creating community between writers: www.willwrite 4food.com.

WORDWISE. Free e-zine. Provides monthly writing and marketing tips. E-mail: kathywidenhouse@ att.net. Website: www.kathywidenhouse.com.

WRITE FROM HOME. Here you will find a collection of articles to help you juggle your home life with your writing career: www.writefromhome.com.

THE WRITER GAZETTE. Offers free articles for writers, market listings, contests, e-books, and a free newsletter: www.writergazette.com.

WRITERS' BREAK. Articles, online courses, interviews, and links: www.writersbreak.com.

+WRITERS.NET. Use this site to have other writers, agents, and editors answer your writing questions or to search for an agent or editor: www.writers.net.

WRITERS SUITE. An online publishing community of writers, readers, and educators featuring 50,000 registered members, 400 blogs, tens of thousands of articles, and 150 courses: www.suite101.com.

WRITE TO INSPIRE.COM. A site for inspirational and Christian writers: www.writetoinspire.com.

WRITING CORNER. Links to author Web pages, markets, newsletters, writing workshops, recommended books, and grammar tips: www.writingcorner.com.

WRITING FOR DOLLARS. www.writingfordollars.com.

WRITING-PORTAL.COM DIRECTORY. Lists links for fiction, freelancing, screenwriting, nonfiction, and hundreds of other sites for writers: www.writing-portal.com.

WRITING RESOURCES. For lists of publishers, writing links, resources, and research sites. (1) www.seliterary.homestead.com/links.html; (2) www.write-resource.com; (3) www.writers home.com/index.htm; (4) http://thinkers.net; (5) www.forwriters.com; (6) http://write success.com.

YOU CAN WRITE. Good site for nonfiction writers but with a boatload of good information for others too: www.youcanwrite.com.

+ZONDERVAN FREE PUBLICATIONS. Free e-newsletters. Topics include Zondervan News Bulletin, AuthorTracker, Bible devotionals, academic updates, Zonderkidz news, and more: www.zondervan.com/cultures/en-us/home.htm, and click on "Newsletters."

WEBSITES OF INTEREST TO WRITERS: SPECIALTY TOPICS

ADHD. (1) U.S. Library of Medicine Medline Plus. Do a search for "ADHD": www.nlm.nih.gov/medlineplus/. (2) National Institute of Mental Health. Click on "ADHD" for a wealth of articles, books, and several videos: www.ldonline.org/ld_indepth. (3) Children and Adults with ADHD. This advocacy organization offers online articles, a bookstore, fact sheets, and referrals to local support groups: www.chadd.org; (4) ADD Toronto: www.add-toronto.org. (5) U.S. Department of Education. In the Quick Search box type "Attention Deficit" to find dozens of ADHD-related articles: www.ed.gov; (6) Learning Disabilities Resource Community: http://ldrc.ca.

ADOPTION RESOURCES. (1) Adoption Yellowpages.com: http://yellow-pages.adoption.com; (2) All God's Children Intl.: www.allgodschildren.org; (3) America World Adoption Assoc.: www.awaa.org; (4) Bethany Christian Services: www.bethany.org; (5) Christian World Adoption: www.cwa.org; (6) North American Council on Adoptable Children: www.nacac.org; (7) http://members.shaohannahshope.org. (8) Free adoption posters, videos, radio spots: www.davethomasfoundation.com. (9) Holt International who pioneered Korean adoptions in the U.S. over 50 years ago (now reaching into many countries, not just Korea). Submit adoption stories to their bimonthly magazine: www.holtintl.org.

AMERICAN SIGN LANGUAGE. Website: http://commtechlab.msu.edu/sites/aslweb/browser.htm.

ASSN. OF PERSONAL HISTORIANS. Website: www.personalhistorians.org. Memoir writing.

AUSTRALIA. For information about writers in the "land down under," visit the Australian Society of Authors: www.asauthors.org.

BIBLICAL VERSUS EASTERN RELIGIOUS VIEWS. Free chart comparing biblical and eastern religious views and a book review of *The Dark Side of Karate* by Linda Nathan: www.logosword.com/karate.htm.

BRITISH ROYALTY. Website: www.royal.gov.uk.

CARTOONING. Website for the National Cartoon Museum. Includes information on how to become a cartoonist: www.cartoon.org. Click on "Advice."

CHRISTIAN HISTORY. (1) www.christianhistory.net; (2) www.gospelcom.net. Click on "Browse by Interest," then "Church History."

CLOTHING OF PAST ERAS. Covers everything from ancient Greece to the Middle Ages to the 1950s: www.costumepage.org/tcpinfo2.html.

COMIC BOOKS. Offers information for aspiring comic book writers with interviews, reviews, message board, and classifieds: www.jazmaonline.com.

COMIX35 CHRISTIAN COMICS TRAINING. Nathan Butler, PO Box 27470, Albuquerque NM 87125-7470. (505)232-3500. Fax (775)307-8202. E-mail: comix35@comix35.org. Website: www.comix35.org. Sponsors The Christian Comics Competition, a biannual event.

CREATIVE CHRISTIAN MINISTRIES, PO Box 12624, Roanoke VA 24027. E-mail: ccmbbr@juno.com. Website: www.CreativeChristianMinistries.com. Features resources for church leaders, including *Ideas Unlimited: The Ultimate Encyclopedia for Children's Ministry.*

DEMOLITION SCENES. If you have a demolition in your novel and you need to describe what happens when the detonation is triggered, you can study pictures of all kinds of implosions on this site to see how they fall: www.implosionworld.com/gallery.htm.

E-BOOK PUBLISHING. *How to Get Your E-Book Published: An Insider's Guide to the World of Electronic Publishing* by Richard Curtis and William Thomas Quick, ISBN 13: 978-1582970974.

EDUCATORS. (1) www.teacherfocus.com. Unique lesson plans submitted by teachers. (2) MERLOT, the Multimedia Educational Resource for Learning and Online Teaching, is a free, peer-reviewed collection of over 16,000 different online learning tools and simulations developed mostly by college professors around the world: www.merlot.org.

GLASS BLOWING. Check here for answers to your questions about mouth-blown glass and lots of other kinds of glass (i.e. restoration, flashed, crackled, cathedral), and glass around the world: www.lamberts.de/elambhom.htm.

HISTORY ONLINE. (1) Site lists all kinds of information by type, geographical area, or time period: www.history.ac.uk/hr/resources/historical/index.html. (2) www.historynet.com; (3) www.historychannel.com. Historical research by topic, time, event, etc. (4) Life in the Middle Ages: www.mnsu.edu/emuseum/history/middleages/contents.html.

HOMESCHOOLING. (1) www.homeschoolheadquarters.com; (2) www.hsrc.com; (3) www.crosswalk.com/homeschool; (4) Christian Homeschool Fellowship: www.chfweb.net; (5) www.lifeway.com. Click "Family/Homeschool"; (6) Nat'l African American Homeschoolers Alliance: www.naaha.com; (7) Nat'l Home Education Research Institute: www.nheri.org.

INDEPENDENT CHRISTIAN MEDIA NETWORK. A Website for writers, photographers, recording artists, painters, and any independent Christian artists: www.christianindy.com.

INTERNET IMAGES. Make sure your book's cover is on the Internet. Go to: http://images.google.com. Type in your book's ISBN number without hyphens.

MAPS. (1) For Ancient World maps, check out this site of cartography and geographic study: www.unc.edu/awmc/. (2) For Civil War maps, go to: www.msnbc.msn.com/id/6807551. (3) For "online maps to everywhere," go to: www.multimap.com. (4) For topographical state maps, click on "Topo Maps." Get names of mountain ranges, canyons, rivers, forests, etc.: www.wildernet.com/index.cfm.

MEDICAL & FORENSICS LAB. Archives of crime scenes where you can ask questions about related topics: www.dplylemd.com.

MEDICAL SITES. (1) For information to construct your character's medical condition: www.webmd.com. Click on "Diseases & Conditions." (2) www.mayoclinic.com.

MEDLINE PLUS. From a medical encyclopedia to all kinds of drug information: www.nlm.nih.gov/medlineplus/.

MEMOIRS. A resource for memoirs: www.turningmemories.com.

MINISTRY RESOURCES. If writing for pastors, Christian education leaders, or music directors, you may find some helpful resources at (1) www.woodlakebooks.com (2) www.logosproductions.com.

MOVIES. (1) Internet Movie Database: www.imdb.com. Free, searchable database of over 260,000 film and television productions made since 1910. Search by movie or TV title, cast, or character name. (2) www.metacritic.com. Movie Reviews.

MUSIC LOVERS. If you are a music lover or have a character who is a music lover, check out this site from the Rock and Roll Hall of Fame and Museum: www.rockhall.com.

ONE MINUTE MOTIVATOR. Offers free, daily e-mails tips that cover goals, setbacks, time management, stress reduction, motivation, and more: www.brightmoment.com.

PARENT SOUP. Website: http://parenting.ivillage.com. For writers of parenting articles.

PEN NAME. Here's a fun site to find your own pen name by supplying personal info: www.testcafe.com/pen/.

PROPHETIC NEWS SITES. (1) www.prophezine.com; (2) Discussion group: http://groups.yahoo.com/group/zincisrael. News about Israel from a Zionist perspective.

REGENCY ERA. Research materials: www.regencylibrary.com.

RESEARCH SITES. (1) Encyclopedia Mythica has 7,000 articles on mythology, folklore, and religion: www.pantheon.org (2) From ancient times the sun has been a major factor in civilizations. This site explores the worship, treatment, and traditions of the sun: www.traditionsofthesun.org.

REVIEW COPY HELPER. A site for book reviewers to get publisher contact information: www.lindaformichelli.com/reviewcopy.

TRAVELWRITERS.COM. E-source for travel writers. Contact info on over 500 travel publications plus 200 newspaper travel sections: www.travelwriters.com.

TRAVEL WRITING TIPS. (1) www.travelwritingtips.com. (2) For useful tips and sites for the travel writer: www.sree.net/tips/travel.html.

U.S. MILITARY INFORMATION. Websites: (1) www.usmilitary.com; (2) www.defenselink.mil; (3) www.dtic.mil/doctrine/jel/doddict. Army Websites: (4) www.army.mil; (5) www.goarmy.com; (6) www.armyreserve.army.mil; (7) www.qmfound.com/army_heraldry.htm. Navy Websites: (8) www.navy.mil; (9) www.navy.com; (10) www.navyseals.com. Air force Websites: (11) www.af.mil; (12) www.airforce.com. Marine Websites: (13) www.usmc.mil; (14) www.marines.com; (15) www.marinecorps.com; (16) www.usmc.mil/marinelink/ind.nsf/ranks. Coast Guard Websites: (17) www.uscg.mil; (18) www.gocoastguard.com; (19) www.cgaux.org. Special Ops Website: (20) www.specialoperations.com.

VICTORIAN ERA. (1) www.victorianlondon.org; (2) www.victorianweb.org; (3) http://dept.kent.edu/museum/costume.

+WHITE PAPERS. Learn how to write white papers (proposed government policies) with this free guide: http://whitepapersource.com.

WORD COUNT. *What Is a Word?* Article by Chuck Rothman: www.sfwa.org/writing/wordcount.htm.

WORLD WAR II INFO. Websites: www.ibiblio.org/pha; www.worldwar2history.info.

WRITERS' SOFTWARE

DRAMATICA PRO. Website: http://storymind.com.

+ENDNOTE. Interfaces with your Word document. Type your citation into a new EndNote directory, and it inserts the citation correctly in your document. Cost: $300. Website: www.endnote.com.

GOOGLE SEARCH. This Web address is case sensitive: http://directory.google.com/Top/Arts/Writers_Resources/Software.

MANUSCRIPT TRACKING. Website: www.sandbaggers.8m.com/samm.htm.

NEWNOVELIST. Software tools draw out your ideas, giving body to your characters, strength to your story lines. It also keeps notes alongside each element of your work: www.newnovelist.com/?source=aw10.

OUTLOOK EXPRESS ADD-INS. Website: www.SperrySoftware.com.

QUICKPLOT. Software programs to help organize your thoughts in the planning stages: www.typingchimp.com/index.html.

+QUICKSTORY. Website: www.quickstory.com.

SCREEN/SCRIPT WRITING SOFTWARE. See Resources section: "Screenwriting/Scriptwriting."

SOFTWARE WEBSITES: (1) Character Pro: www.characterpro.com; (2) Dramatic Pro and Movie Magic Screenwriter, Writer's DreamKit: www.write-bros.com; (3) Final Draft: www.finaldraft.com; (4) LifeJournal: www.lifejournal.com; (5) Personal Knowbase: www.bitsmithsoft.com; (6) Power Structure, Power Tracker, and Power Writer: www.write-brain.com; (7) TextAloud MP3: www.textaloud.com; (8) Truby's Blockbuster: www.truby.com; (9) Writer's Blocks: www.writersblocks.com; (10) WriteItNow: www.ravensheadservices.com.

STORYBASE. Website: www.storybase.net.

STORYCRAFT STORY DEVELOPMENT SOFTWARE. Guides writers through the entire process of writing novels, screenplays, teleplays, plays, and short stories. Visit the "Photo Gallery" and "Products and Services": www.storycraft.org.

STORYVIEW 2.0. A writing tool that lets you create the elements of your story and arrange them on a timeline. You add the building blocks of your story in any order and immediately see any gaps: www.storyview.com.

STORYWEAVER. Website: http://storymind.com.

WORD MENU. Website: www.wordmenu.com. Word Menu by Write Brothers Inc. organizes words by the way we actually use them (by subject matter). Cost: $34.95.

+WRITE AGAIN. Website: www.write-again.com.

+WRITEBOARD. Website: www.writeboard.com.

WRITE-BRAIN. Software to help you plot and write your stories: www.write-brain.com.

WRITE PRO. Website: www.writepro.com. Also, FictionMaster by Sol Stein and WritePro.

WRITER'S BLOCKS 3.0. Organize story elements for your fiction: www.writersblocks.com.

WRITER'S SUPERCENTER. Offers a wide variety of software to help writers of all genres and forms: www.writerssupercenter.com.

WRITING MANAGEMENT SOFTWARE. Website: www.write-again.com. Download on trial basis. Costs $49.95.

WRITING INSTRUCTION: CDs/CASSETTE TAPES

THE CHRISTIAN COMMUNICATOR MANUSCRIPT CRITIQUE SERVICE CASSETTE HANDS-ON COURSE. For information contact: Susan Titus Osborn, 3133 Puente St., Fullerton CA 92835-1952. (714)990-1532. Toll-free (877)428-7992. E-mail: Susanosb@aol.com. Website: www.christiancommunicator.com. Offers basic writing course available by cassette. Includes 6 lessons on cassettes, handouts, and critiqued assignments. Cost $200. By the lesson, $40.

CHRISTIAN WRITERS LEARNING CENTER. Website: www.ACWriters.com. Over 2,000 cassette tapes. Request free catalog from American Christian Writers, PO Box 110390, Nashville TN 37222. (800)21-WRITE. E-mail: ACWriters@aol.com.

CHRISTIAN WRITERS SEMINAR. Offers tapes of its conference and workshops on a wide variety of writing instruction. Targeted toward beginning-to-intermediate writers. Print order from Website and mail to Christian Writers Seminar, 19300 Redwood Rd., Castro Valley CA 94546-3465 or e-mail Jon Drury at jdrury@redwoodchapel.org. Website: www.christianwriter.org.

NO FEAR STRATEGIES FOR PUBLISHING YOUR FIRST ARTICLES AND BOOK. David Sanford's 45-minute audio seminar. For a copy of the seminar, send a check for $15 to: Sanford Communications Inc., 16778 S.E. Cohiba Ct., Damascus OR 97015-6827.

RADIO PUBLICITY TRAINING COURSE. Become the expert that radio hosts and producers need: www.sabahradioshows.com.

WRITE HIS ANSWER MINISTRIES. Marlene Bagnull, LittD, dir., 316 Blanchard Rd., Drexel Hill PA 19026. E-mail: mbagnull@aol.com. Website: www.writehisanswer.com. Tapes and books on 20+ topics, including: You Can Take the Pain out of Marketing, Writing Devotional/Inspirational Books, The Power of Story. Tapes of Marlene's 8.5-hour Write His Answer Seminar are $27.95 and include handouts.

WRITE-TO-PUBLISH CONFERENCE. Lin Johnson, dir., 9118 W. Elmwood Dr., Ste. 1G, Niles IL 60714-5820. E-mail: lin@writetopublish.com. Website: www.writetopublish.com. Bring speakers from the Write-to-Publish Conference into your home and car via these cassettes. Tapes from past conferences on all aspects of writing and publishing, as well as editors' panels telling what they are looking for now. $5 each or $4 each for 21 or more. Lists are available on the Website or send SASE to above address.

WRITING INSTRUCTION: CORRESPONDENCE COURSES

AMERICAN SCHOOL OF CHRISTIAN WRITING. Website: www.ACWriters.com. This division of American Christian Writers offers a 3-year, 36-lesson correspondence course that covers the entire field of Christian writing. Students may purchase full course or selected portions. Several payment plans available. For school brochure, call (800)21-WRITE or e-mail: ACWriters@aol.com.

ASSOCIATED WRITING PROGRAMS. George Mason University, MS 1E3, Fairfax VA 22030. (703)993-4301. Fax (703)993-4302. E-mail: awp@awpwriter.org. Website: www.awp writer.org.

AT-HOME WRITING WORKSHOPS. Marlene Bagnull, LittD, dir., Write His Answer Ministries, 316 Blanchard Rd., Drexel Hill PA 19026. E-mail: mbagnull@aol.com. Website: www.write hisanswer.com. Offers 3 courses of study with 5-10 study units in each: (1) Putting Your Best Foot Forward (lays foundation for your writing ministry), 5 units, $145; (2) Nonfiction (articles, tracts, curriculum, devotionals, how-tos, etc., plus planning a nonfiction book and book proposal), 10 units, $272; (3) Fiction, 10 units, $255. Units may also be purchased individually for $30-$34.

CHRISTIAN WRITERS INSTITUTE CORRESPONDENCE COURSES. Website: www.AC Writers.com. This 60-year-old institution, founded by veteran publisher Robert Walker, is a division of American Christian Writers. Offers six 1-year courses with an assigned instructor/mentor. Writing assignments are given with a goal of having a publishable manuscript by the end of each course. Two payment plans available. Contact: Christian Writers Institute, PO Box 110390, Nashville TN 37222. (800)21-WRITE. E-mail: ACWriters@aol.com.

CORRESPONDENCE COURSE FOR MANUSCRIPT EDITING. The University of Wisconsin offers a correspondence course in manuscript editing for those wanting to do editing on a professional level or for writers wanting to improve their personal editing skills. Contact: University of Wisconsin Learning Innovations, 505 S. Rosa Rd., Madison WI 53719-1257. Toll-free (877)895-3276. (608)262-2011. Fax (608)262-4096. E-mail: info@learn .uwsa.edu. Ask about Manuscript Editing C350-A52 or go to Fundamentals of Manuscript Editing under Independent Learning section. Website: http://learn.wisconsin.edu/il.

GLORY PRESS/PROF. DICK BOHRER. Forty years as a national magazine, book and newspaper editor, teacher for grades 3-18, and managing editor of *Moody Monthly* magazine; author of 16 books. Contact: Glory Press, 2174 S.W. Mossy Brae Road, West Linn OR 97068. (503)638-7711. E-mail: dickbohrer@comcast.net. Website: www.professordick.com. Offers 24 lessons on how to write stories for children, 24 on how to write feature articles, and 24 on how to writer your opinions (letters to editors, reviews, columns, etc.). Lessons are free. His site also features his eight juvenile mysteries as well as free downloads of Bible studies and commentaries by Dr. John G. Mitchell and a selection by Dr. Willard M. Aldrich.

THE INSTITUTE OF CHILDREN'S LITERATURE, 93 Long Ridge Rd., West Redding CT 06896. Toll-free (800)243-9645. (203)792-8600. Fax (203)792-8406. E-mail: information services@InstituteChildrensLit.com. Website: www.InstituteChildrensLit.com. Offers a writing program and a writing aptitude test; also a chat room and other resources for writers.

JERRY B. JENKINS CHRISTIAN WRITERS GUILD. Les Stobbe, ed-in-chief, 5525 N. Union Blvd., Ste. 200, Colorado Springs CO 80918. Toll-free (866)495-5177. E-mail: Contact Us@ChristianWritersGuild.com. Website: www.ChristianWritersGuild.com. This International organization owned by Jerry B. Jenkins, author of the best-selling Left Behind series, has more than 2,000 members worldwide. The Guild offers annual memberships, mentor-guided correspondence and e-mail courses for adults (two-year Apprentice and advanced one-year Journeyman) and youth (Pages: ages 9-12 and Squires: 13 and up), writing contests (winners receive a book contract with a major CBA publisher), Writing for the Soul conferences, critique service, writers' resource books, monthly newsletter, and more. For a Free Starter Kit, e-mail from Website.

LONG RIDGE WRITERS GROUP, 91 Long Ridge Rd., West Redding CT 06896. Toll-free (800)624-1476. Fax (203)792-8406. E-mail: informationservice@longridgewriters group.com. Website: www.longridgewritersgroup.com. General correspondence course, but you may request a Christian instructor. Offers a free writing test.

THE WRITING ACADEMY SEMINAR. Inez Schneider, New Member Coordinator, 4010 Singleton Rd., Rockford IL 61114. (815)877-9675. E-mail: pattyk@wams.org. Website: www .wams.org. Sponsors year-round Christian correspondence writing program and annual seminar in various locations.

WRITING INSTRUCTION: E-MAIL/INTERNET COURSES

ABOUT.COM. Offers free writing e-courses, and more: http://freelancewrite.about.com.

ABSOLUTE WRITE UNIVERSITY. Online courses in journalism, travel writing, writing children's picture books, creativity, screenwriting, and more: www.absoluteclasses.com.

+ANTIOCH UNIVERSITY. Offers MFA in Creative Writing. Combines intensive ten-day residencies with online instruction: www.antiochla.edu. Toll-free (800)726-8462.

+CERTIFICATE IN CREATIVE WRITING. Certificate of Advanced Studies in Creative Writing is a 24-credit-hour program. A bachelor's degree is required for admission. Credits earned may be applied toward a master's degree in Liberal Studies at the University of Denver's University College: www.universitycollege.du.edu. Toll-free (800)347-2042.

THE CHRISTIAN COMMUNICATOR MANUSCRIPT CRITIQUE SERVICE E-MAIL HANDS-ON COURSE. For information contact: Susan Titus Osborn, 3133 Puente St., Fullerton CA 92835-1952. Toll-free (877)428-7992. (714)990-1532. E-mail: Susanosb@aol.com. Website: www.christiancommunicator.com. Offers basic writing course available by e-mail. Includes 6 lessons online, handouts, and critiqued assignments. Cost for entire course, $180. By the lesson, $40.

COFFEEHOUSE FOR WRITERS. Website: http://members.tripod.com/coffeehouse4writers. Offers a variety of four-week writing workshops for $80.

E-MAIL NEWSLETTERS FOR WRITERS. (1) www.publishersweekly.com; (2) www.parapub.com.

GOTHAM WORKSHOPS. Most comprehensive creative writing classes online and in New York City: www.writinglcasses.com.

LIFE WRITE. Website: http://LifeWrite.com. Veteran writer Steven Barnes: The Lifewriting Year-Long writing course, $199.

ONLINE WORKSHOPS BY MARY EMMA ALLEN, 55 Binks Hill Rd., Plymouth NH 03264. Fax (603)536-4851. E-mail: me.allen@juno.com. Website: http://homepage.fcgnetworks .net/jetent/mea. Topics include: Column Writing 101, Introduction to Self-Publishing, Writing for Children, Writing Your Family History, Writing for Regional Markets, Writing for the Weekly Newspaper, Travel Writing, Marketing Your Manuscripts, Poetry Writing, Writing & Publishing on the Internet, Writing Life Essays, and Scrapbooking Your Family History. Mary Emma offers these workshops at conferences, in schools and libraries, as well as online. She also develops writing workshops for children.

ONLINE WRITING COURSES. (1) Website: www.ed2go.com/courses.html. For a list of online writing classes, put "Writing" in the search box. (2) Long Story Short School of Writing now offers online classes: www.LssWritingSchool.com; (3) The Nature of Writing: www.the natureofwriting.com; (4) E-script: www.singlelane.com/escript.

PARADIGM ONLINE WRITING ASSISTANT. An interactive, menu-driven, online writer's guide. Useful for all writers, from inexperienced to advanced: www.powa.org.

PERELANDRA COLLEGE. Offers online degrees in Creative Writing (short in-residence may be required) to fill the need for skilled, imaginative, thoughtful Christian writers to offer alternatives to the primarily formulaic offerings of Christian publishers and books of general presses: www.perelandra.info.

TRINITY COLLEGE WRITING CENTER ONLINE. Some good tips and lots of help: www.trincoll.edu/depts/writcent.

VIRTUAL UNIVERSITY. Website: http://vu.org/calendar.html. Offers online courses for writers.

WRITER'S DIGEST SCHOOL, 4700 E. Galbraith Rd., Cincinnati OH 45236. Toll-free (800)759-0963. Fax (513)531-0798. Refer to Writer's Digest Web-based workshops: www.writersdigest.com/wds.

WRITERS' ONLINE WORKSHOPS, 4700 E. Galbraith Rd., Cincinnati OH 45236. Toll-free (800)759-0963. (513)531-0798. Website: www.WritersOnlineWorkshops.com. Beginning to advanced workshops in fiction, nonfiction, proposal writing, and more. This is a general Internet-based course, but you may request a Christian instructor. Sponsored by Writer's Digest. Courses to improve your writing and advance your career. First Steps: The Basic Elements, Fundamentals Workshops: Skills & Techniques; Focus Workshops: Specific Projects; Marketing Your Writing; Advanced Writers' Workshops. Some workshops offer an extended option to give you more time to complete the course.

WRITERS WEEKLY UNIVERSITY. Website: http://writersweekly.com/wwu/courses. Offers online courses for writers. Topics include: plot, characters, life stories, marketing, newsletter writing, and novels.

WRITING BASICS. E-books that integrate faith and writing: www.write4christ.com.

THE WRITING SCHOOL HOME PAGE. Website: www.mythbreakers.com/writingschool.

WRITING INSTRUCTION: MISCELLANEOUS HELPS

ARTICLE IDEA GAME. Offers a classroom method for generating ideas for magazine articles: www.longleaf.net/ggrow/articlegame.html.

A TO Z WRITING. Writing tips for every writing need: www.atozwriting.com.

+AUTHORSBYDESIGN.COM. Stop by this site if you support its "Believe and Achieve" motto or simply need some motivation: www.authorsbydesign.com.

+AUTOCRIT. Voted among the 101 Best Websites for Writers by Writer's Digest, this site automatically identifies weak words and structures: http://autocrit.com.

BOOK PROPOSALS. (1) Nonfiction: http://co.essortment.com/bookproposal_rjwi.htm; (2) www.studiob.com/authors/winning_proposals.cfm.

BOOKS ON WRITING. (1) *Art and Soul* by Pam Grout (Andrews McNeel Pub. 2000), ISBN 13: 978-0740704826; (2) *On Writing: A Memoir of the Craft* by Stephen King (Scribner), ISBN 13: 978-0641597435; (3) *Forest for the Trees: An Editor's Advice to Writers* by Betsy Lerner (Riverhead Trade), ISBN 13: 978-1573228575; (4) *Feature & Magazine Writing: Action, Angle and Anecdotes* by David E Sumner and Holly G. Miller (Blackwell Publishing), ISBN 13: 978-0813805191.

+COPYWRITING TUTORIALS. www.adcopywriting.com/Tutorials_List.htm.

+CRITIQUE AND DISCUSSION FORUMS. Website: www.writersbbs.com.

THE EASY WAY TO WRITE. Excellent resources for writers of any genre and level of writing skill. Offers free writing lessons and a newsletter: www.easywaytowrite.com?hop=bizwings.

THE ECLECTIC WRITER. How-to articles for writers: www.eclectics.com/writing/writing.html.

+FANSTORY.COM. Share your writing and receive detailed feedback for everything you post. Includes fantasy, science fiction, poetry, humor, mystery, nonfiction, and children's stories. Also offers contests. Website: www.fanstory.com. No submission fees. $6.95 per month is the only charge.

FIFTEEN WRITING EXERCISES. Scroll down the page to "Exercises": www.poewar.com.

FONT IDENTIFYER. Need to find the name of a typeface? See "What the Font" tab: www.myfonts.com.

GETTING ORGANIZED. (1) www.onlineorganizing.com; (2) www.succeedinginbusiness.com/catalog. Offers many e-books, including *Winning the Fight between You and Your Desk* by Jeffrey Mayer.

+HOW MUCH TIME? To estimate your time to complete writing projects, such as brochures or feature articles: www.writersmarket.com/information.asp?Pricing. Must be a subscriber of www.writersmarket.com to access.

MANUSCRIPT FORMAT. For a sample and instructions on format for an article or a book, go to: (1) www.shunn.net/format.html; (2) www.sfwa.org/writing/format_betancourt.htm. (3) Chart containing manuscript types, average word count, and average number of pages for each type: www.pwcwriters.org/penpoints4.htm.

ME WRITE A SYNOPSIS? This site might help to handle that dreaded sales tool: www.vivianbeck.com/writingtips.htm.

NEWSTHINKING. Thoughts on writing by Bob Baker, LA Times ed.: www.newsthinking.com.

PROFESSIONAL WRITING DEGREE. Website: http://fw.taylor.edu/academics/departments/engwrit/programs/pwr_ba.shtml. Taylor University Fort Wayne has initiated the country's first Professional Writing major at an accredited Christian university. The four-year Bachelor of Arts program includes freelance writing, fiction, business and technical writing, journalism, fiction, public relations, editing, television, poetry writing, and literature. Write to Office of Admissions, TUFW, 1025 W. Rudisill Blvd., Fort Wayne IN 46807. Toll-free (800)233-3922. (260)744-8600. E-mail: online form.

PROVIDENCE JOURNAL TIPS. Writing tips from the *Providence Journal* include weekly lessons on the craft of newspaper writing: www.projo.com/words.

Q&A COLUMN. The University of Chicago Press (publisher of the *Chicago Manual of Style*, 15th edition) has a Q&A column written by their Manuscript Editing Department on their Website: www.chicagomanualofstyle.org/home.html.

QUERY LETTERS. (1) www.writing-world.com/basics/query.shtml. How to Write a Successful Query Letter. (2) www.writing-world.com/basics/email.shtml. Preparing E-mail Queries. (3) www.eclectics.com/articles/query.html; (4) www.jkelman.com/misc/queryletter.html; (5) www.charlottedillon.com/query.html; (6) www.relevantprose.com/Adobe/unlockingmysteriesofthequeryletter.pdf.

RENSSELEAR WRITING CENTER ONLINE HANDOUTS. Website: www.rpi.edu/web/writingcenter/handouts.html. Includes 18 handouts on Basic Punctuation and Mechanics under "Revising Prose" heading.

SALLY STUART'S GUIDE TO GETTING PUBLISHED. This book tells you everything you need to know about how to write for publication and how to get published. Special $10 postpaid from Christian Writers Marketplace, 1647 S.W. Pheasant Dr., Aloha OR 97006. Website: www.stuartmarket.com. Groups or teachers wanting to use it as a textbook can order 5 or more copies for $6 each, plus postage for the box (to one address). E-mail: stuartcwmg@aol.com.

SUBMISSIONS. Website: www.yudkin.com/publish.htm.

TEACHING RESOURCES. (1) *You Can Improve Your Students' Writing Skills Immediately* by David Melton, ISBN 13: 978-0933849679; (2) *Writing Toward Home* by Georgia Heard,

ISBN 13: 978-0435081249; (3) *Where I'm From* by George Ella Lyon, ISBN 13: 978-1888842128.

+TRACK CHANGES. Use Microsoft Word's "Track Changes" feature under the "Tools" menu. If you turn it on, it highlights in red everything that you have changed and shows the original version in bubbles on the margin.

TYPEFACE FOR MANUSCRIPTS. Website: www.right-writing.com/insight-typeface.html.

WRITERS CONFERENCE GUIDELINES. Website: www.WritersConferenceGuidelines.com. A Website dedicated to helping writers master the conference submissions process. Learn what goes into writing your submission package, and how to do it right. Information on cover letters, queries, book proposals, article and manuscript formats, genre tips, meeting with faculty, making the most of your conference, and much more. Contributions from editors, publishers, agents, and experienced writers.

WRITERS RESOURCE CENTER. (1) Find "Fifteen Craft Exercises for Writers": www.poewar.com. (2) See also University of Richmond's writer's helps: http://writing2.richmond.edu/writing/wweb.html.

WRITER'S ULTIMATE RESOURCE GUIDE. This site contains 1,600 conferences, writing books that belong on your shelf, specific contact information and Website links, and much more: www.writersdigest.com.

WRITERS WEEKLY. Website: www.writersweekly.com/index-starterkit.htm. Free Internet newsletter for writers. Subscribe and receive the free e-book *How to Be a Freelance Writer* (with 103 paying markets).

WRITING ARTICLES. Website: www.writing.org.

+WRITING CHALLENGES. These sites were voted among the 101 Best Websites for Writers by Writer's Digest: (1) http://book-in-a-week.com. (2) Write 270 pages of your novel in 90 days: http://community.livejournal.com/novel_in_90/profile. (3) Hundreds of writing prompts: http://dragonwritingprompts.blogsome.com; (4) http://creativewritingprompts.com. (5) Write 50,000 words in 30 days: www.nanowrimo.org. (6) Write using only six words: http://smithmag.net/sixwords.

+WRITING FOR MAGAZINES. Articles on how to make money writing for magazines by Mridu Khullar: www.mridukhullar.com/forwriters.

WRITING UPDATE FROM WRITER'S DIGEST. Periodic, free e-mail newsletter from the editors at *Writer's Digest;* includes up-to-date writing-related news/tips. Subscribe at: www.writersdigest.com.

WRITING WORLD. Good site for writers, including a step-by-step guide to launching a writing career and other important tips: www.writing-world.com.

YOU CAN BE A COLUMNIST by Charlotte Digregorio (Baker & Taylor), ISBN 13: 978-0962331817. Available at www.alibris.com.

TOPICAL LISTINGS OF BOOK PUBLISHERS

One of the most difficult aspects of marketing is trying to determine which publishers might be interested in the book you want to write. This topical listing was designed to help you do just that. First, look up your topic of interest in the following lists. If you don't find the specific topic, check the list of topics in the table of contents, find any related topics, and pursue those. Once you have discovered which publishers are interested in a particular topic, secure writer's guidelines and book catalogs from those publishers. Just because a particular publisher is listed under your topic, don't assume that it would automatically be interested in your book. It is your job to determine whether your approach to the subject will fit within the unique scope of that publisher's catalog. It is also helpful to visit a Christian bookstore to see some of the books produced by each publisher you are interested in pursuing. Note that the primary listings for each publisher indicate what the publisher prefers to see in the initial contact—a query, book proposal, or complete manuscript.

An R indicates which publishers reprint out-of-print books from other publishers.

An asterisk (*) following a topic indicates it is a new topic this year.

An (s) before a listing indicates it is a publisher listed in the Subsidy Publishers' section and does at least 50% subsidy publishing or print-on-demand. Please note that some of these publishers do some royalty publishing as well (check their listings), so if you aren't interested in a subsidy deal, you can contact them indicating you are interested only in a royalty contract.

APOLOGETICS

Aadeon Publishing—R
Abingdon Press
Ambassador-Emerald—R
(s)-American Binding—R
AMG Publishers—R
Baal Hamon—R
Baylor Univ. Press
Bethany House
(s)-Black Forest/Tennessee—R
Blue Dolphin
BMH Books
(s)-Booklocker.com—R
(s)-Brown Books—R
Chalice Press
Christian Family—R
Christian Heritage—R
College Press—R
Continuum Intl.—R
(s)-Creation House—R
CSS Publishing—R
Discovery House—R
Earthen Vessel—R
(s)-Elderberry Press
Emmaus Road—R
(s)-Essence—R
Fair Havens—R
(s)-Fairway Press—R
Forward Movement
Good News Pub.
Green Key Books
GRQ—R
Guardian Angel
Harvest House
Hensley Publishing
Hidden Brook Press—R
(s)-Holy Fire Publishing—R
Hope Publishing—R
Howard Books
(s)-IMD Press—R
InterVarsity Press—R
Kregel—R
Lighthouse Publishing—R
Lighthouse Trails—R
Lutheran Univ. Press
Magnus Press—R
Master Books
Messianic Jewish—R
Monarch Books
NavPress Th1nk—R
New Leaf
New Seeds—R
(s)-One World—R
Our Sunday Visitor—R
P & R Publishing—R
Parson Place—R
Parsons Publishing—R
Pauline Books—R
(s)-Pleasant Word—R
Randall House
(s)-Reformation Publishers—R
Reformation Trust
Regal
Rose Publishing
Salt Works
(s)-Scribe Book—R
St. Anthony Mess. Press—R
(s)-Star Bible Public.
(s)-Tate Publishing—R
(s)-Trafford Publishing—R
Victor Books
Whitaker House
(s)-WinePress—R
(s)-Word Alive
World Publishing

ARCHAEOLOGY

(s)-American Binding—R
Baker Academic
Baker Books
Baker Trittin
Baker's Plays—R
(s)-Black Forest/Tennessee—R
Blue Dolphin
BMH Books
(s)-Booklocker.com—R
Boyds Mills Press—R
(s)-Brentwood—R
(s)-Brown Books—R
Christian Writer's Ebook—R
Conciliar Press—R
(s)-Creation House—R
Doubleday—R
Dover Publications—R
Eerdmans Pub., Wm. B.—R
(s)-Elderberry Press
(s)-Essence—R
Facts on File
Fair Havens—R
(s)-Fairway Press—R
FaithWalk
Fordham Univ. Press—R

Gollehon Press
Green Key Books
HarperOne
Hidden Brook Press—R
Hill Street Press—R
(s)-Holy Fire Publishing—R
InterVarsity Press—R
Johns Hopkins—R
Knight George Pub.
Kregel—R
Lighthouse Publishing—R
Master Books
Messianic Jewish—R
Monarch Books
Mt. Olive College Press
New Leaf
New Seeds—R
(s)-One World—R
Pacific Press
Parsons Publishing—R
(s)-Pleasant Word—R
(s)-Reformation Publishers—R
Rose Publishing
T & T Clark—R
(s)-Tate Publishing—R
Third World Press—R
(s)-Trafford Publishing—R
Univ. Press of America—R
(s)-WinePress—R
(s)-Word Alive
World Publishing

ART—FREELANCE

Aadeon Publishing—R
Anglicans United—R
Baal Hamon—R
BelleBooks—R
BJU/Journey Forth—R
(s)-Booklocker.com—R
(s)-Brown Books—R
Carson-Dellosa
Chelsea House—R
Christian Ed. Pub.
Dove Inspirational
Earthen Vessel—R
Eerdmans/Yg Readers
Fair Havens—R
FamilyLife (books)—R
Fifth Estate—R
Focus on the Family
Guardian Angel
(s)-Holy Fire Publishing—R
(s)-IMD Press—R
Jebaire Publishing
Judson Press
Knight George Pub.
Lift Every Voice—R
Lighthouse Publishing—R
Lighthouse Trails—R
Liturgy Training—R
Marshall Trumann
Messianic Jewish—R
Mission City Press
Monarch Books
Mt. Olive College Press
Parson Place—R
Parsons Publishing—R
(s)-Path Publishing in Christ—R
(s)-Path Publishing—R
Pauline Books—R
Pelican Publishing—R
Players Press—R
(s)-Providence Pub.—R
Quintessential Books—R
Randall House
Ravenhawk Books—R
(s)-Reformation Publishers—R
Rose Publishing
Salt Works
(s)-Scribe Book—R
Sheed & Ward—R
White Stone Books—R
Wilshire Book—R
WindRiver—R

AUTOBIOGRAPHY

Ambassador-Emerald—R
(s)-American Binding—R
Baal Hamon—R
Baker Books
Believe Books
(s)-Black Forest/Tennessee—R
(s)-Book Publishers—R
(s)-Booklocker.com—R
Boyds Mills Press—R
(s)-Brentwood—R
(s)-Brown Books—R
Carey Library, Wm.—R
Christian Heritage—R
Christian Writer's Ebook—R
Continuum Intl.—R
(s)-Creation House—R
(s)-Dean Press, Robbie—R
Doubleday—R
(s)-Elderberry Press
(s)-Essence—R
Evergreen Press
(s)-Fairway Press—R
Friends United Press
Genesis Press—R
Georgetown Univ. Press
Greenwood/Praeger
Guernica Editions—R
HarperOne
Hidden Brook Press—R
Hill Street Press—R
(s)-Holy Fire Publishing—R
(s)-IMD Press—R
Kirk House
Life Changing Media
(s)-Lifevest Publishing
Lighthouse Publishing—R
Lighthouse Trails—R
(s)-Lightning Star Press—R
Living Books for All
Marshall Trumann
(s)-McDougal Publishing—R
Monarch Books
New Seeds—R
(s)-One World—R
Pacific Press
Parson Place—R
Parsons Publishing—R
(s)-Path Publishing in Christ—R
(s)-Pleasant Word—R
(s)-Providence Pub.—R
(s)-Reformation Publishers—R
Regal
Regnery
(s)-Selah Publishing—R
(s)-So. Baptist Press—R
Still Waters Revival—R
(s)-Tate Publishing—R
(s)-TEACH Services—R
(s)-Trafford Publishing—R
Univ. Press of America—R
(s)-VMI Publishers
WaterBrook Press—R
WindRiver—R
(s)-WinePress—R
(s)-Word Alive
(s)-Zoe Life Publishing

BIBLE/BIBLICAL STUDIES

Aadeon Publishing—R
Abingdon Press
ACTA Publications
Alba House—R
Ambassador Books
Ambassador-Emerald—R
(s)-American Binding—R
AMG Publishers—R
Anglicans United—R
B & H Publishing
Baal Hamon—R
Baker Academic
Baker Books
Baker Trittin
Baylor Univ. Press
Bethany House
BMH Books
(s)-Booklocker.com—R
(s)-Brentwood—R
Bridge Resources
(s)-Brown Books—R
Canticle Books—R
Carey Library, Wm.—R
Catholic Answers—R
Chalice Press
Christian Ed. Pub.
Christian Family—R
Christian Focus—R
Christian Liberty Press
Christian Writer's Ebook—R
College Press—R

Conciliar Press—R
Congregational Life
Contemporary Drama
Continuum Intl.—R
(s)-Creation House—R
(s)-CrossHouse—R
CSS Publishing—R
(s)-DCTS Publishing
(s)-Dean Press, Robbie—R
Discovery House—R
Doubleday—R
Editorial Portavoz
Educational Ministries
Eerdmans Pub., Wm. B.—R
(s)-Elderberry Press
Emmaus Road—R
(s)-Essence—R
Evergreen Press
(s)-Fairway Press—R
Faith Alive
FaithWalk
Fifth Estate—R
First Fruits of Zion
Fortress Press
Foursquare Media
Geneva Press
Good Book—R
Gospel Publishing
Greenwood/Praeger
Group Publishing
GRQ—R
Grupo Nelson
(s)-Hannibal Books—R
Harcourt Religion
Harrison House
Hensley Publishing
Hidden Brook Press—R
(s)-Holy Fire Publishing—R
(s)-IMD Press—R
Inkling Books—R
InterVarsity Press—R
Jubilant Press—R
Judson Press
(s)-Kindred Books—R
Knight George Pub.
Kregel—R
Libros Liguori
Lighthouse Publishing—R
Magnus Press—R
Marshall Trumann
(s)-McDougal Publishing—R
MegaGrace Books
Mercer Univ. Press—R
Messianic Jewish—R
Monarch Books
Morehouse—R
NavPress
NavPress Th1nk—R
New Hope—R
New Leaf
New York Univ. Press
(s)-One World—R
Our Sunday Visitor—R
P & R Publishing—R
Pacific Press
Paradise Research—R
Parson Place—R
Parsons Publishing—R
Pathway Press
Pauline Books—R
Paulist Press
Pilgrim Press—R
(s)-Pleasant Word—R
Presbyterian Pub.
(s)-Providence Pub.—R
Randall House Digital
(s)-Reformation Publishers—R
Regal
Rose Publishing
Salt Works
(s)-Scribe Book—R
Sheed & Ward—R
Smyth & Helwys
(s)-So. Baptist Press—R
St. Anthony Mess. Press—R
(s)-Star Bible Public.
T & T Clark—R
(s)-Tate Publishing—R
(s)-Trafford Publishing—R
UMI Publishing—R
Univ. Press of America—R
Victor Books
(s)-VMI Publishers
Walk Worthy—R
WaterBrook Press—R
Wesleyan Publishing
Westminster John Knox
Whitaker House
WindRiver—R
(s)-WinePress—R
Woodland Gospel
(s)-Word Alive
World Publishing
Youth Specialties
(s)-Zoe Life Publishing
Zondervan

BIBLE COMMENTARY

Abingdon Press
ACTA Publications
Alba House—R
Ambassador Books
Ambassador-Emerald—R
(s)-American Binding—R
AMG Publishers—R
Anglicans United—R
Baal Hamon—R
Baker Books
Bethany House
(s)-Black Forest/Tennessee—R
BMH Books
(s)-Booklocker.com—R
Bridge-Logos—R
(s)-Brown Books—R
Carey Library, Wm.—R
Catholic Answers—R
Chalice Press
Chapter Two—R
Christian Family—R
Christian Focus—R
Christian Writer's Ebook—R
College Press—R
Conciliar Press—R
Continuum Intl.—R
Cook, David C.
(s)-Creation House—R
CSS Publishing—R
Discovery House—R
Doubleday—R
Editorial Portavoz
Eerdmans Pub., Wm. B.—R
(s)-Elderberry Press
(s)-Essence—R
(s)-Fairway Press—R
Fifth Estate—R
Greenwood/Praeger
GRQ—R
Grupo Nelson
Harrison House
Hidden Brook Press—R
(s)-Holy Fire Publishing—R
(s)-IMD Press—R
Inkling Books—R
InterVarsity Press—R
Intl. Awakening—R
Kregel—R
Libros Liguori
Lighthouse Publishing—R
Lutheran Univ. Press
Messianic Jewish—R
Monarch Books
New Canaan—R
New Leaf
New Seeds—R
(s)-One World—R
Our Sunday Visitor—R
P & R Publishing—R
Parsons Publishing—R
Pauline Books—R
Paulist Press
(s)-Pleasant Word—R
(s)-Providence Pub.—R
(s)-Reformation Publishers—R
Reformation Trust
Rose Publishing
Sheed & Ward—R
St. Anthony Mess. Press—R
(s)-Star Bible Public.
(s)-Synergy Publishers—R
(s)-Tate Publishing—R
(s)-Trafford Publishing—R
Tyndale House—R
UMI Publishing—R
Westminster John Knox
WindRiver—R
(s)-WinePress—R

(s)-Word Alive
World Publishing
(s)-Zoe Life Publishing
Zondervan

BIOGRAPHY

Ambassador-Emerald—R
(s)-American Binding—R
American Book
Baal Hamon—R
Baker Books
Baker Trittin
Baker's Plays—R
Ballantine
Believe Books
BJU/Journey Forth—R
(s)-Black Forest/Tennessee—R
(s)-Book Publishers—R
(s)-Booklocker.com—R
Boyds Mills Press—R
Branden Publishing—R
(s)-Brentwood—R
(s)-Brown Books—R
Carey Library, Wm.—R
Catholic Answers—R
Chalice Press
Chapter Two—R
CharismaKids
Christian Family—R
Christian Focus—R
Christian Heritage—R
Christian Liberty Press
Christian Writer's Ebook—R
College Press—R
Conciliar Press—R
Continuum Intl.—R
(s)-Creation House—R
Cumberland House
(s)-Dean Press, Robbie—R
Discovery House—R
Doubleday—R
Earthen Vessel—R
Eerdmans Pub., Wm. B.—R
(s)-Elderberry Press
(s)-Essence—R
Facts on File
(s)-Fairway Press—R
FaithWalk
Fordham Univ. Press—R
Genesis Press—R
Georgetown Univ. Press
Good Book—R
Greenwood/Praeger
GuidepostsBooks
(s)-Hannibal Books—R
HarperOne
Hidden Brook Press—R
Hill Street Press—R
(s)-Holy Fire Publishing—R
Hope Publishing—R
Inkling Books—R
(s)-J and J Publishing
Kaleidoscope Press—R
Kirk House
(s)-Lifevest Publishing
Lighthouse Publishing—R
Lighthouse Trails—R
Living Books for All
Magnus Press—R
Marshall Trumann
(s)-McDougal Publishing—R
Mercer Univ. Press—R
Mission City Press
Monarch Books
Mt. Olive College Press
New Hope—R
New Seeds—R
(s)-One World—R
One World/Ballantine
P & R Publishing—R
Pacific Press
Paradise Research—R
Parson Place—R
Parsons Publishing—R
Pauline Books—R
(s)-Pleasant Word—R
(s)-Providence Pub.—R
Quintessential Books—R
(s)-Reformation Publishers—R
Reformation Trust
Regal
Regnery
Rose Publishing
Scepter Publishers—R
(s)-Scribe Book—R
(s)-Selah Publishing—R
Sheed & Ward—R
(s)-So. Baptist Press—R
Still Waters Revival—R
Strang Book Group—R
(s)-Tate Publishing—R
(s)-TEACH Services—R
(s)-Trafford Publishing—R
Univ. of AR Press—R
Univ. Press of America—R
(s)-VMI Publishers
W Publishing
WaterBrook Press—R
Whitaker House
WindRiver—R
(s)-WinePress—R
Woodland Gospel
(s)-Word Alive
Yale Univ. Press—R
(s)-Zoe Life Publishing

BOOKLETS

(s)-American Binding—R
Baal Hamon—R
Catholic Answers—R
Chapter Two—R
Christian Writer's Ebook—R
Concordia
(s)-Creation House—R
(s)-Dean Press, Robbie—R
(s)-Essence—R
Evergreen Press
Fair Havens—R
FamilyLife (books)—R
Forward Movement
(s)-FruitBearer Pub.
Good Book—R
Gospel Publishing
(s)-Holy Fire Publishing—R
(s)-Insight Publishing—R
InterVarsity Press—R
Intl. Awakening—R
(s)-J and J Publishing
Judson Press
Libros Liguori
Life Cycle Books—R
(s)-Lightning Star Press—R
Liguori—R
Living Books for All
Marshall Trumann
MegaGrace Books
(s)-One World—R
Our Sunday Visitor—R
P & R Publishing—R
Pacific Press
Paulist Press
(s)-Providence Pub.—R
Randall House
(s)-Reformation Publishers—R
Rose Publishing
Salt Works
(s)-Tate Publishing—R
Trinity Foundation—R
(s)-WinePress—R
(s)-Word Alive
(s)-Xulon Press—R

CANADIAN/FOREIGN

Ambassador-Emerald—R
Canadian Inst. for Law—R
Chapter Two—R
Christian Focus—R
(s)-Essence—R
Guernica Editions—R
Hidden Brook Press—R
(s)-Kindred Books—R
Lighthouse Publishing—R
Living Books for All
Lutterworth Press—R
Mission World Library—R
Monarch Books
Northstone
(s)-One World—R
Ponder Publishing
Skysong Press
Still Waters Revival—R
(s)-Trafford Publishing—R
Wood Lake Books—R

(s)-Word Alive

CELEBRITY PROFILES

(s)-American Binding—R
Baker Books
(s)-Booklocker.com—R
Branden Publishing—R
(s)-Brown Books—R
Christian Writer's Ebook—R
(s)-Creation House—R
(s)-Elderberry Press
(s)-Essence—R
(s)-Fairway Press—R
FaithWalk
Greenwood/Praeger
Hay House
Hidden Brook Press—R
Hill Street Press—R
(s)-Holy Fire Publishing—R
Life Changing Media
Lighthouse Publishing—R
Monarch Books
(s)-One World—R
(s)-Pleasant Word—R
Ravenhawk Books—R
(s)-Reformation Publishers—R
Salt Works
(s)-Selah Publishing—R
(s)-Tate Publishing—R
TowleHouse—R
(s)-Trafford Publishing—R
(s)-VMI Publishers
Whitaker House
(s)-WinePress—R
Woodland Gospel
(s)-Word Alive

CHARISMATIC

(s)-American Binding—R
Anglicans United—R
Baal Hamon—R
Bethany House
(s)-Black Forest/Tennessee—R
Blue Dolphin
(s)-Booklocker.com—R
Bridge-Logos—R
(s)-Brown Books—R
(s)-Creation House—R
CSS Publishing—R
(s)-Elderberry Press
(s)-Essence—R
(s)-Fairway Press—R
FaithWords
Gospel Publishing
Hidden Brook Press—R
(s)-Holy Fire Publishing—R
(s)-IMD Press—R
Life Changing Media
Lighthouse Publishing—R
Magnus Press—R
Marshall Trumann
Monarch Books
Nelson Ignite
(s)-One World—R
Paradise Research—R
Parsons Publishing—R
Pauline Books—R
(s)-Pleasant Word—R
(s)-Providence Pub.—R
(s)-Reformation Publishers—R
Regal
Rose Publishing
Salvation Publisher—R
Strang Book Group—R
(s)-Synergy Publishers—R
(s)-Tate Publishing—R
(s)-Trafford Publishing—R
Whitaker House
(s)-WinePress—R
(s)-Word Alive
World Publishing
(s)-Zoe Life Publishing

CHILDREN'S BOARD BOOKS

Big Idea
Candy Cane Press
Eerdmans/Yg Readers
(s)-Elderberry Press
Ideals Publications
Kregel Kidzone
Lift Every Voice—R
(s)-One World—R
Pauline Books—R
(s)-Tate Publishing—R
(s)-Trafford Publishing—R
(s)-WinePress—R
(s)-Word Alive

CHILDREN'S EASY READERS

Ambassador Books
Atheneum/Yg Readers
Baker Books
Big Idea
(s)-Booklocker.com—R
Boyds Mills Press—R
Branden Publishing—R
(s)-Brown Books—R
CharismaKids
Conciliar Press—R
Cook, David C.
(s)-Creation House—R
(s)-Dean Press, Robbie—R
E-Digital Books
(s)-Elderberry Press
(s)-Essence—R
Evergreen Press
(s)-Fairway Press—R
FaithKidz
Guardian Angel
Harvest Day
Hidden Brook Press—R
(s)-Holy Fire Publishing—R
Howard Books
Ideals Publications
(s)-IMD Press—R
Inkling Books—R
Journey Stone—R
Knight George Pub.
Legacy Press—R
Lift Every Voice—R
Lighthouse Publishing—R
(s)-Lightning Star Press—R
Master Books
McRuffy Press
(s)-One World—R
Our Sunday Visitor—R
Pacific Press
Pauline Books—R
(s)-Providence Pub.—R
(s)-Reformation Publishers—R
Reformation Trust
Salt Works
Salty's Books
Standard Publishing
Strang Book Group—R
(s)-Tate Publishing—R
(s)-Trafford Publishing—R
Tyndale House—R
(s)-VMI Publishers
(s)-Word Alive
(s)-Zoe Life Publishing

CHILDREN'S PICTURE BOOKS

ACTA Publications
Ambassador Books
Atheneum/Yg Readers
Augsburg—R
Baker Books
Big Idea
(s)-Black Forest/Tennessee—R
(s)-Book Publishers—R
Boyds Mills Press—R
(s)-Brown Books—R
Candy Cane Press
CharismaKids
Christian Focus—R
Conciliar Press—R
Cook, David C.
E-Digital Books
Editorial Portavoz
Eerdmans/Yg Readers
(s)-Elderberry Press
(s)-Essence—R
Evergreen Press
Extreme Diva
Faith Communications
FaithKidz
Grupo Nelson
Guardian Angel
Harvest Day

Howard Books
Ideals Publications
Illumination Arts
(s)-IMD Press—R
Journey Stone—R
Judson Press
Kaleidoscope Press—R
Knight George Pub.
Kregel—R
Kregel Kidzone
(s)-Lifevest Publishing
Lighthouse Publishing—R
(s)-Lightning Star Press—R
Living Books for All
Master Books
Monarch Books
(s)-One World—R
(s)-Path Publishing—R
Pauline Books—R
Pelican Publishing—R
(s)-Pleasant Word—R
(s)-Providence Pub.—R
Random Hs./Golden Bks
Salt Works
Salty's Books
(s)-Selah Publishing—R
(s)-Tate Publishing—R
Third World Press—R
(s)-Trafford Publishing—R
Tyndale House—R
WaterBrook Press—R
White Stone Books—R
WindRiver—R
(s)-WinePress—R
(s)-Zoe Life Publishing

CHRIST

(s)-American Binding—R
Atheneum/Yg Readers
Baal Hamon—R
Baker Trittin
Baker's Plays—R
Barbour
Bethany House
(s)-Black Forest/Tennessee—R
Blue Dolphin
BMH Books
(s)-Booklocker.com—R
Bridge-Logos—R
(s)-Brown Books—R
Canticle Books—R
Catholic Answers—R
CharismaKids
Christian Family—R
Christian Focus—R
Christian Heritage—R
Christian Writer's Ebook—R
Continuum Intl.—R
Cook, David C.
(s)-Creation House—R
CSS Publishing—R
Discovery House—R
Doubleday—R
(s)-Elderberry Press
(s)-Essence—R
(s)-Fairway Press—R
FaithWords
Fifth Estate—R
Gollehon Press
Good News Pub.
Guardian Angel
GuidepostsBooks
Hidden Brook Press—R
(s)-Holy Fire Publishing—R
Howard Books
(s)-IMD Press—R
InterVarsity Press—R
Jebaire Publishing
Judson Press
Kregel—R
Lift Every Voice—R
Lighthouse Publishing—R
Lutheran Univ. Press
Magnus Press—R
Marshall Trumann
Monarch Books
NavPress Th1nk—R
New Seeds—R
(s)-One World—R
Our Sunday Visitor—R
P & R Publishing—R
Paradise Research—R
Parson Place—R
Parsons Publishing—R
(s)-Path Publishing in Christ—R
Pauline Books—R
Pilgrim Press—R
(s)-Pleasant Word—R
Presbyterian Pub.
(s)-Providence Pub.—R
Quintessential Books—R
(s)-Reformation Publishers—R
Reformation Trust
Regal
Rose Publishing
Salt Works
St. Anthony Mess. Press—R
(s)-Star Bible Public.
(s)-Synergy Publishers—R
(s)-Tate Publishing—R
Torch Legacy
(s)-Trafford Publishing—R
(s)-VMI Publishers
WindRiver—R
(s)-WinePress—R
(s)-Word Alive
World Publishing
(s)-Zoe Life Publishing

CHRISTIAN BUSINESS

ACTA Publications
Ambassador-Emerald—R
(s)-American Binding—R
American Book
Anglicans United—R
Baal Hamon—R
(s)-Black Forest/Tennessee—R
BMH Books
(s)-Booklocker.com—R
Bridge-Logos—R
(s)-Brown Books—R
Chalice Press
Christian Family—R
Christian Writer's Ebook—R
Cook, David C.
(s)-Creation House—R
CSS Publishing—R
Dabbling Mum Press
Doubleday—R
(s)-Elderberry Press
(s)-Essence—R
Evergreen Press
Fair Havens—R
(s)-Fairway Press—R
Forward Movement
Green Key Books
GRQ—R
Grupo Nelson
(s)-Hannibal Books—R
Hidden Brook Press—R
(s)-Holy Fire Publishing—R
Hourglass Books—R
Howard Books
(s)-IMD Press—R
InterVarsity Press—R
Jubilant Press—R
Judson Press
Kirk House
Lift Every Voice—R
Lighthouse Publishing—R
Living Books for All
Lutheran Univ. Press
Marshall Trumann
Millennium III—R
Mission World Library—R
Monarch Books
Nelson, Thomas
New Leaf
(s)-One World—R
Parson Place—R
Parsons Publishing—R
Pilgrim Press—R
(s)-Pleasant Word—R
Power Publishing
PREP Publishing—R
(s)-Providence Pub.—R
Quintessential Books—R
(s)-Reformation Publishers—R
Regal
Rose Publishing
Salvation Publisher—R
(s)-Scribe Book—R
St. Anthony Mess. Press—R
(s)-Star Bible Public.
Starik Publishing
Strang Book Group—R

(s)-Synergy Publishers—R
(s)-Tate Publishing—R
(s)-Trafford Publishing—R
Trinity Foundation—R
(s)-VMI Publishers
WaterBrook Press—R
Westminster John Knox
Whitaker House
WindRiver—R
(s)-WinePress—R
(s)-Word Alive
World Publishing
(s)-Zoe Life Publishing

CHRISTIAN EDUCATION

Ambassador-Emerald—R
(s)-American Binding—R
B & H Publishing
Baal Hamon—R
Baker Academic
Baker Books
Baker Trittin
Big Idea
(s)-Booklocker.com—R
(s)-Brentwood—R
Bridge Resources
(s)-Brown Books—R
Carson-Dellosa
Chalice Press
Christian Ed. Pub.
Christian Family—R
Christian Heritage—R
Christian Liberty Press
Christian Writer's Ebook—R
Church Growth Inst.
College Press—R
Congregational Life
Contemporary Drama
Cook, David C.
(s)-Creation House—R
CSS Publishing—R
(s)-DCTS Publishing
(s)-Dean Press, Robbie—R
Doubleday—R
Educational Ministries
(s)-Elderberry Press
(s)-Essence—R
ETC Publications
(s)-Fairway Press—R
Faith Alive
Fifth Estate—R
Group Publishing
Harcourt Religion
Harvest Day
Hensley Publishing
Hidden Brook Press—R
Hill Street Press—R
(s)-Holy Fire Publishing—R
(s)-IMD Press—R
Judson Press
Kirk House
Knight George Pub.
Lighthouse Publishing—R
Liturgical Press
Lutheran Univ. Press
Master Books
Millennium III—R
Mission World Library—R
Monarch Books
Morehouse—R
New Canaan—R
New Hope—R
New Leaf
Northwestern
(s)-One World—R
Our Sunday Visitor—R
Our Sunday Visitor (bks.)—R
Pacific Press
Parson Place—R
Parsons Publishing—R
Pathway Press
Pauline Books—R
Pflaum Publishing
Pilgrim Press—R
(s)-Pleasant Word—R
(s)-Providence Pub.—R
Quintessential Books—R
Rainbow Publishers—R
Randall House
Reference Service
(s)-Reformation Publishers—R
Religious Education
Rose Publishing
Salvation Publisher—R
Smyth & Helwys
(s)-So. Baptist Press—R
Standard Publishing
(s)-Star Bible Public.
Starik Publishing
Still Waters Revival—R
(s)-Tate Publishing—R
Torch Legacy
(s)-Trafford Publishing—R
Trinity Foundation—R
UMI Publishing—R
Univ. Press of America—R
(s)-WinePress—R
Wood Lake Books—R
(s)-Word Alive
(s)-Zoe Life Publishing

CHRISTIAN HOMESCHOOLING

(s)-American Binding—R
B & H Publishing
Baker Books
Big Idea
(s)-Booklocker.com—R
(s)-Brentwood—R
(s)-Brown Books—R
Carson-Dellosa
Chalice Press
Christian Family—R
Christian Focus—R
Christian Writer's Ebook—R
(s)-Creation House—R
CSS Publishing—R
(s)-Dean Press, Robbie—R
(s)-Elderberry Press
Emmaus Road—R
(s)-Essence—R
ETC Publications
(s)-Fairway Press—R
(s)-Hannibal Books—R
Harcourt Religion
Hidden Brook Press—R
Hill Street Press—R
(s)-Holy Fire Publishing—R
(s)-IMD Press—R
Inkling Books—R
Jubilant Press—R
Judson Press
Kaleidoscope Press—R
Lift Every Voice—R
Lighthouse Publishing—R
Marshall Trumann
Master Books
Mission City Press
Mission World Library—R
Monarch Books
New Leaf
(s)-One World—R
P & R Publishing—R
Pacific Press
Parsons Publishing—R
(s)-Path Publishing in Christ—R
Pauline Books—R
(s)-Pleasant Word—R
(s)-Providence Pub.—R
(s)-Reformation Publishers—R
Rose Publishing
Standard Publishing
(s)-Star Bible Public.
Starik Publishing
Still Waters Revival—R
(s)-Tate Publishing—R
(s)-Trafford Publishing—R
Virginia Pines Press
(s)-WinePress—R
(s)-Word Alive
(s)-Zoe Life Publishing

CHRISTIAN LIVING

Aadeon Publishing—R
Abingdon Press
ACTA Publications
Ambassador Books
Ambassador-Emerald—R
(s)-American Binding—R
B & H Publishing
Baal Hamon—R
Baker Books
Baker Trittin
Barbour
Beacon Hill Press—R
Bethany House

(s)-Black Forest/Tennessee—R
(s)-Booklocker.com—R
(s)-Brentwood—R
Bridge-Logos—R
(s)-Brown Books—R
Canticle Books—R
Chalice Press
Christian Family—R
Christian Focus—R
Christian Writer's Ebook—R
Cladach Publishing
Cook, David C.
(s)-Creation House—R
CSS Publishing—R
(s)-DCTS Publishing
Dimensions for Living
Discovery House—R
Doubleday—R
Editorial Portavoz
Eerdmans Pub., Wm. B.—R
(s)-Elderberry Press
Elijah Press
(s)-Essence—R
Evergreen Press
Fair Havens—R
(s)-Fairway Press—R
FaithWalk
FaithWords
Forward Movement
Friends United Press
(s)-FruitBearer Pub.
Good News Pub.
Green Key Books
Greenwood/Praeger
GRQ—R
GuidepostsBooks
HarperOne
Harrison House
Harvest House
Haworth Pastoral—R
HeartSpring Pub.—R
Hendrickson—R
Hidden Brook Press—R
Hill Street Press—R
(s)-Holy Fire Publishing—R
Hope Publishing—R
Howard Books
(s)-IMD Press—R
(s)-Impact Christian—R
InterVarsity Press—R
(s)-J and J Publishing
Jebaire Publishing
Jireh Publishing
Jossey-Bass
Judson Press
(s)-Kindred Books—R
Kregel—R
Life Changing Media
Life Cycle Books—R
Lift Every Voice—R
Lighthouse Publishing—R
Liturgical Press
Living Books for All
Magnus Press—R
Marshall Trumann
(s)-McDougal Publishing—R
MegaGrace Books
Mission World Library—R
Monarch Books
Moody Publishers
Morehouse—R
Multnomah
NavPress
NavPress Th1nk—R
Nelson Ignite
Nelson, Thomas
New Hope—R
(s)-One World—R
Our Sunday Visitor—R
P & R Publishing—R
Parson Place—R
Parsons Publishing—R
(s)-Path Publishing in Christ—R
Pathway Press
Pauline Books—R
Pilgrim Press—R
(s)-Pleasant Word—R
Presbyterian Pub.
(s)-Providence Pub.—R
Quintessential Books—R
Ragged Edge—R
Randall House
(s)-Reformation Publishers—R
Reformation Trust
Regal
Revell
RiverOak
Rose Publishing
Salvation Publisher—R
(s)-Scribe Book—R
(s)-Selah Publishing—R
Smyth & Helwys
St. Anthony Mess. Press—R
Standard Publishing
(s)-Star Bible Public.
Starik Publishing
Still Waters Revival—R
Strang Book Group—R
(s)-Synergy Publishers—R
(s)-Tate Publishing—R
Tau-Publishing—R
(s)-TEACH Services—R
Torch Legacy
(s)-Trafford Publishing—R
Tyndale House—R
UMI Publishing—R
Univ. Press of America—R
(s)-VMI Publishers
W Publishing
WaterBrook Press—R
Wesleyan Publishing
Westminster John Knox
White Stone Books—R
(s)-WinePress—R
(s)-Winer Foundation—R
Woodland Gospel
(s)-Word Alive
World Publishing
(s)-Zoe Life Publishing

CHRISTIAN SCHOOL BOOKS

(s)-American Binding—R
B & H Publishing
Baker Books
Baker Trittin
Big Idea
(s)-Booklocker.com—R
(s)-Brown Books—R
Carson-Dellosa
Christian Liberty Press
Christian Writer's Ebook—R
CSS Publishing—R
(s)-Dean Press, Robbie—R
(s)-Elderberry Press
(s)-Essence—R
ETC Publications
(s)-Fairway Press—R
Hidden Brook Press—R
(s)-Holy Fire Publishing—R
(s)-IMD Press—R
Inkling Books—R
Kaleidoscope Press—R
Knight George Pub.
Lighthouse Publishing—R
Master Books
Mission World Library—R
Monarch Books
New Canaan—R
New Leaf
(s)-One World—R
Our Sunday Visitor—R
Pacific Press
Parsons Publishing—R
(s)-Pleasant Word—R
(s)-Providence Pub.—R
(s)-Reformation Publishers—R
Rose Publishing
(s)-So. Baptist Press—R
(s)-Star Bible Public.
(s)-Tate Publishing—R
(s)-Trafford Publishing—R
Trinity Foundation—R
(s)-WinePress—R
Wood Lake Books—R
(s)-Word Alive
(s)-Zoe Life Publishing

CHURCH HISTORY

Abingdon Press
ACTA Publications
Ambassador-Emerald—R
(s)-American Binding—R

Anglicans United—R
B & H Publishing
Baal Hamon—R
Baker Books
Baker Trittin
Baker's Plays—R
Baylor Univ. Press
(s)-Black Forest/Tennessee—R
(s)-Booklocker.com—R
(s)-Brown Books—R
Canticle Books—R
Carey Library, Wm.—R
Catholic Answers—R
Chalice Press
Chapter Two—R
Christian Family—R
Christian Focus—R
Christian Heritage—R
Christian Writer's Ebook—R
College Press—R
Continuum Intl.—R
(s)-Creation House—R
(s)-CrossHouse—R
Crossroad Publishing—R
CSS Publishing—R
Doubleday—R
Editorial Portavoz
Eerdmans Pub., Wm. B.—R
Ekklesia Press—R
(s)-Elderberry Press
Elijah Press
(s)-Essence—R
(s)-Fairway Press—R
FaithWalk
Fortress Press
Forward Movement
Founders Press
Geneva Press
Gollehon Press
Greenwood/Praeger
(s)-Hannibal Books—R
HarperOne
Hidden Brook Press—R
(s)-Holy Fire Publishing—R
(s)-IMD Press—R
InterVarsity Press—R
Intl. Awakening—R
Johns Hopkins—R
Judson Press
Kirk House
Kregel—R
Libros Liguori
Lift Every Voice—R
Lighthouse Publishing—R
Loyola Press
Lutheran Univ. Press
Lutterworth Press—R
Millennium III—R
Mission World Library—R
Monarch Books
Morehouse—R
NavPress Th1nk—R
New Canaan—R
New Seeds—R
New York Univ. Press
(s)-One World—R
Our Sunday Visitor—R
P & R Publishing—R
Pacific Press
Parsons Publishing—R
Pauline Books—R
Paulist Press
(s)-Pleasant Word—R
Presbyterian Pub.
(s)-Providence Pub.—R
Quintessential Books—R
Randall House
(s)-Reformation Publishers—R
Reformation Trust
Rose Publishing
Scepter Publishers—R
(s)-Selah Publishing—R
Sheed & Ward—R
Smyth & Helwys
St. Anthony Mess. Press—R
(s)-Star Bible Public.
(s)-Tate Publishing—R
(s)-Trafford Publishing—R
Trinity Foundation—R
Univ. of AR Press—R
Univ. Press of America—R
Westminster John Knox
WindRiver—R
(s)-WinePress—R
Wood Lake Books—R
(s)-Word Alive
World Publishing
Yale Univ. Press—R
(s)-Zoe Life Publishing
Zondervan

CHURCH LIFE

Abingdon Press
ACTA Publications
Ambassador-Emerald—R
(s)-American Binding—R
B & H Publishing
Baal Hamon—R
Baker Books
Baker's Plays—R
Bethany House
(s)-Black Forest/Tennessee—R
(s)-Booklocker.com—R
(s)-Brentwood—R
(s)-Brown Books—R
Chalice Press
CharismaKids
Christian Writer's Ebook—R
Continuum Intl.—R
(s)-Creation House—R
Crossroad Publishing—R
CSS Publishing—R
(s)-DCTS Publishing
Destiny Image—R
Discovery House—R
Doubleday—R
Educational Ministries
Eerdmans Pub., Wm. B.—R
(s)-Elderberry Press
(s)-Essence—R
(s)-Fairway Press—R
FaithWalk
FaithWords
Forward Movement
Friends United Press
Good News Pub.
Greenwood/Praeger
(s)-Hannibal Books—R
HarperOne
Harrison House
Hidden Brook Press—R
Hill Street Press—R
(s)-Holy Fire Publishing—R
Hope Publishing—R
Howard Books
(s)-IMD Press—R
(s)-Impact Christian—R
InterVarsity Press—R
Jubilant Press—R
Judson Press
Kirk House
Kregel—R
Libros Liguori
Lift Every Voice—R
Lighthouse Publishing—R
Mission World Library—R
Monarch Books
Morehouse—R
NavPress
NavPress Th1nk—R
(s)-One World—R
P & R Publishing—R
Pacific Press
Parson Place—R
Parsons Publishing—R
Pathway Press
Pauline Books—R
Pilgrim Press—R
(s)-Pleasant Word—R
Presbyterian Pub.
(s)-Providence Pub.—R
Quintessential Books—R
Randall House
(s)-Reformation Publishers—R
Reformation Trust
Regal
RiverOak
Rose Publishing
(s)-Scribe Book—R
(s)-Selah Publishing—R
Smyth & Helwys
St. Anthony Mess. Press—R
(s)-Star Bible Public.

Strang Book Group—R
(s)-Tate Publishing—R
Torch Legacy
Touch Publications—R
(s)-Trafford Publishing—R
(s)-VMI Publishers
W Publishing
Wesleyan Publishing
Westminster John Knox
(s)-WinePress—R
(s)-Winer Foundation—R
Wood Lake Books—R
Woodland Gospel
(s)-Word Alive
Youth Specialties
(s)-Zoe Life Publishing

CHURCH MANAGEMENT

Abingdon Press
(s)-American Binding—R
Baal Hamon—R
(s)-Black Forest/Tennessee—R
BMH Books
(s)-Booklocker.com—R
(s)-Brown Books—R
Chalice Press
Christian Heritage—R
CSS Publishing—R
Doubleday—R
(s)-Elderberry Press
(s)-Essence—R
(s)-Fairway Press—R
Gospel Publishing
Group Publishing
(s)-Hannibal Books—R
Hidden Brook Press—R
(s)-Holy Fire Publishing—R
Hope Publishing—R
(s)-IMD Press—R
InterVarsity Press—R
Judson Press
Kirk House
Kregel—R
Lighthouse Publishing—R
Lutheran Univ. Press
Mission World Library—R
Monarch Books
Morehouse—R
New Leaf
(s)-One World—R
Our Sunday Visitor—R
Parsons Publishing—R
(s)-Pleasant Word—R
Presbyterian Pub.
(s)-Providence Pub.—R
(s)-Reformation Publishers—R
Regal
St. Anthony Mess. Press—R
(s)-Star Bible Public.
(s)-Tate Publishing—R
(s)-Trafford Publishing—R
(s)-WinePress—R
(s)-Word Alive

CHURCH RENEWAL

Abingdon Press
ACTA Publications
(s)-American Binding—R
B & H Publishing
Baal Hamon—R
Baker Books
Bethany House
(s)-Booklocker.com—R
(s)-Brentwood—R
(s)-Brown Books—R
Canticle Books—R
Carey Library, Wm.—R
Chalice Press
CharismaKids
Christian Focus—R
Christian Writer's Ebook—R
(s)-Creation House—R
Crossroad Publishing—R
CSS Publishing—R
Destiny Image—R
Doubleday—R
Eerdmans Pub., Wm. B.—R
(s)-Elderberry Press
(s)-Essence—R
(s)-Fairway Press—R
FaithWalk
FaithWords
Forward Movement
Geneva Press
Greenwood/Praeger
(s)-Hannibal Books—R
HarperOne
Hidden Brook Press—R
Hill Street Press—R
(s)-Holy Fire Publishing—R
Hope Publishing—R
Howard Books
(s)-IMD Press—R
(s)-Impact Christian—R
InterVarsity Press—R
Intl. Awakening—R
Judson Press
Libros Liguori
Lighthouse Publishing—R
Lutheran Univ. Press
Magnus Press—R
Marshall Trumann
(s)-McDougal Publishing—R
MegaGrace Books
Mission World Library—R
Monarch Books
Morehouse—R
NavPress Th1nk—R
Nelson, Thomas
(s)-One World—R
Pacific Press
Parson Place—R
Parsons Publishing—R
Pauline Books—R
Pilgrim Press—R
(s)-Pleasant Word—R
Presbyterian Pub.
(s)-Providence Pub.—R
Quintessential Books—R
(s)-Reformation Publishers—R
Regal
Rose Publishing
Salvation Publisher—R
(s)-Scribe Book—R
(s)-Selah Publishing—R
(s)-Sermon Select Press
Smyth & Helwys
(s)-So. Baptist Press—R
St. Anthony Mess. Press—R
(s)-Star Bible Public.
Strang Book Group—R
(s)-Tate Publishing—R
(s)-Trafford Publishing—R
(s)-VMI Publishers
Wesleyan Publishing
Westminster John Knox
(s)-WinePress—R
(s)-Word Alive

CHURCH TRADITIONS

Abingdon Press
ACTA Publications
Alba House—R
Ambassador-Emerald—R
(s)-American Binding—R
Anglicans United—R
Atheneum/Yg Readers
B & H Publishing
Baal Hamon—R
Baker Books
Baker's Plays—R
(s)-Black Forest/Tennessee—R
(s)-Booklocker.com—R
(s)-Brown Books—R
Carey Library, Wm.—R
Catholic Answers—R
Chalice Press
Christian Family—R
Christian Heritage—R
Christian Writer's Ebook—R
Conciliar Press—R
Continuum Intl.—R
(s)-Creation House—R
Crossroad Publishing—R
CSS Publishing—R
Doubleday—R
Eerdmans Pub., Wm. B.—R
(s)-Elderberry Press
(s)-Essence—R
(s)-Fairway Press—R
FaithWalk
Forward Movement
Founders Press
Greenwood/Praeger
Hidden Brook Press—R

Hill Street Press—R
(s)-Holy Fire Publishing—R
(s)-IMD Press—R
Inkling Books—R
InterVarsity Press—R
Libros Liguori
Lift Every Voice—R
Lighthouse Publishing—R
Liturgy Training—R
Lutterworth Press—R
Mission World Library—R
Monarch Books
Morehouse—R
NavPress Th1nk—R
New York Univ. Press
(s)-One World—R
Our Sunday Visitor—R
Pacific Press
Parsons Publishing—R
Pauline Books—R
(s)-Pleasant Word—R
Presbyterian Pub.
(s)-Providence Pub.—R
Randall House
(s)-Reformation Publishers—R
Rose Publishing
St. Anthony Mess. Press—R
(s)-Star Bible Public.
(s)-Tate Publishing—R
(s)-Trafford Publishing—R
(s)-VMI Publishers
(s)-WinePress—R
Wood Lake Books—R
(s)-Word Alive

COFFEE-TABLE BOOKS

ACTA Publications
(s)-ACW Press—R
(s)-Black Forest/Tennessee—R
Bridge-Logos—R
(s)-Brown Books—R
Cistercian—R
FaithWords
GRQ—R
Harvest House
Hidden Brook Press—R
(s)-IMD Press—R
Kirk House
Liturgy Training—R
Lutheran Univ. Press
Monarch Books
New Leaf
Pelican Publishing—R
Players Press—R
(s)-Pleasant Word—R
(s)-Providence Pub.—R
(s)-Reformation Publishers—R
Reformation Trust
Salt Works
(s)-Synergy Publishers—R
(s)-Trafford Publishing—R
(s)-VMI Publishers
(s)-WinePress—R
(s)-Zoe Life Publishing

COMPILATIONS

(s)-American Binding—R
Baal Hamon—R
Baker's Plays—R
Barbour
(s)-Black Forest/Tennessee—R
(s)-Booklocker.com—R
(s)-Brentwood—R
(s)-Brown Books—R
Christian Heritage—R
Christian Writer's Ebook—R
(s)-Creation House—R
Doubleday—R
(s)-Elderberry Press
(s)-Essence—R
(s)-Fairway Press—R
GRQ—R
Hidden Brook Press—R
(s)-Holy Fire Publishing—R
Howard Books
Judson Press
Lighthouse Publishing—R
Monarch Books
(s)-One World—R
P & R Publishing—R
(s)-Pleasant Word—R
(s)-Providence Pub.—R
(s)-Reformation Publishers—R
Reformation Trust
Regal
RiverOak
Salt Works
(s)-Tate Publishing—R
(s)-Trafford Publishing—R
Univ. Press of America—R
(s)-VMI Publishers
WaterBrook Press—R
(s)-WinePress—R
Woodland Gospel
(s)-Word Alive

CONTROVERSIAL ISSUES

Aadeon Publishing—R
Ambassador-Emerald—R
(s)-American Binding—R
AMG Publishers—R
Atheneum/Yg Readers
B & H Publishing
Baal Hamon—R
Baker Books
Baker's Plays—R
(s)-Black Forest/Tennessee—R
Blue Dolphin
(s)-Booklocker.com—R
Boyds Mills Press—R
Branden Publishing—R
(s)-Brentwood—R
(s)-Brown Books—R
Canadian Inst. for Law—R
Catholic Answers—R
Chalice Press
Christian Family—R
Christian Writer's Ebook—R
Conciliar Press—R
Continuum Intl.—R
(s)-Creation House—R
(s)-Dean Press, Robbie—R
Destiny Image—R
Doubleday—R
Ekklesia Press—R
(s)-Elderberry Press
(s)-Essence—R
(s)-Fairway Press—R
FaithWalk
FaithWords
Fifth Estate—R
Gollehon Press
Green Key Books
Greenwood/Praeger
(s)-Hannibal Books—R
HarperOne
Haworth Pastoral—R
Hay House
Hidden Brook Press—R
Hill Street Press—R
(s)-Holy Fire Publishing—R
Hope Publishing—R
Howard Books
Inkling Books—R
Jireh Publishing
Jossey-Bass
Judson Press
Kregel—R
Life Journey Books
Lift Every Voice—R
Lighthouse Publishing—R
Lighthouse Trails—R
Lutterworth Press—R
Magnus Press—R
Marshall Trumann
Millennium III—R
Monarch Books
MountainView
NavPress Th1nk—R
(s)-One World—R
Parson Place—R
Pilgrim Press—R
(s)-Pleasant Word—R
(s)-Providence Pub.—R
(s)-Reformation Publishers—R
Regal
Regnery
RiverOak
Rose Publishing
Salt Works
(s)-Scribe Book—R
(s)-Selah Publishing—R
Still Waters Revival—R
Strang Book Group—R
(s)-Tate Publishing—R

(s)-Trafford Publishing—R
Virginia Pines Press
(s)-VMI Publishers
(s)-WinePress—R
(s)-Word Alive
(s)-Zoe Life Publishing

COOKBOOKS

ACTA Publications
Adams Media
(s)-American Binding—R
Ballantine
Barbour
(s)-Black Forest/Tennessee—R
(s)-Book Publishers—R
(s)-Booklocker.com—R
(s)-Brentwood—R
(s)-Brown Books—R
Christian Writer's Ebook—R
Countryman, J.
(s)-Creation House—R
(s)-CrossHouse—R
Cumberland House
Dabbling Mum Press
DiskUs Publishing
Dover Publications—R
(s)-Elderberry Press
(s)-Essence—R
Evergreen Press
Extreme Diva
(s)-Fairway Press—R
Guardian Angel
(s)-Hannibal Books—R
Hidden Brook Press—R
Hill Street Press—R
(s)-IMD Press—R
Journey Stone—R
(s)-Lifevest Publishing
Monarch Books
(s)-One World—R
One World/Ballantine
Pacific Press
(s)-Pleasant Word—R
(s)-Providence Pub.—R
Salt Works
Siloam
(s)-So. Baptist Press—R
(s)-Tate Publishing—R
(s)-TEACH Services—R
(s)-Trafford Publishing—R
(s)-WinePress—R
(s)-Word Alive
(s)-Zoe Life Publishing

COUNSELING AIDS

ACTA Publications
(s)-American Binding—R
B & H Publishing
Baal Hamon—R
Baker Books
(s)-Black Forest/Tennessee—R
Blue Dolphin
BMH Books
(s)-Booklocker.com—R
(s)-Brentwood—R
(s)-Brown Books—R
Carepoint Publishing—R
Chalice Press
Christian Family—R
Christian Writer's Ebook—R
(s)-Creation House—R
CSS Publishing—R
(s)-Dean Press, Robbie—R
Editorial Portavoz
(s)-Elderberry Press
(s)-Essence—R
Evergreen Press
Fair Havens—R
(s)-Fairway Press—R
FaithWalk
Fifth Estate—R
Good Book—R
Harcourt Religion
Harrison House
Haworth Pastoral—R
Hidden Brook Press—R
Hill Street Press—R
(s)-Holy Fire Publishing—R
Howard Books
InterVarsity Press—R
Judson Press
Kaleidoscope Press—R
Langmarc
Life Cycle Books—R
Life Journey Books
Lift Every Voice—R
Lighthouse Publishing—R
Marshall Trumann
(s)-McDougal Publishing—R
MegaGrace Books
Monarch Books
(s)-One World—R
P & R Publishing—R
Paradise Research—R
Pauline Books—R
Pilgrim Press—R
(s)-Pleasant Word—R
(s)-Providence Pub.—R
Quintessential Books—R
Randall House
(s)-Reformation Publishers—R
RiverOak
Rose Publishing
(s)-Sermon Select Press
(s)-So. Baptist Press—R
(s)-Star Bible Public.
(s)-Tate Publishing—R
(s)-Trafford Publishing—R
(s)-VMI Publishers
WindRiver—R
(s)-WinePress—R
(s)-Word Alive
Youth Specialties

CREATION SCIENCE

(s)-American Binding—R
Baal Hamon—R
(s)-Black Forest/Tennessee—R
Blue Dolphin
BMH Books
(s)-Booklocker.com—R
(s)-Brown Books—R
Christian Family—R
Christian Writer's Ebook—R
(s)-Creation House—R
Editorial Portavoz
(s)-Elderberry Press
(s)-Essence—R
Fair Havens—R
(s)-Fairway Press—R
Hidden Brook Press—R
Hill Street Press—R
(s)-Holy Fire Publishing—R
Hope Publishing—R
Inkling Books—R
Kaleidoscope Press—R
Lighthouse Publishing—R
Master Books
Millennium III—R
Monarch Books
NavPress Th1nk—R
New Leaf
(s)-One World—R
P & R Publishing—R
Pacific Press
Parsons Publishing—R
(s)-Path Publishing in Christ—R
(s)-Pleasant Word—R
(s)-Reformation Publishers—R
Rose Publishing
Salt Works
(s)-Star Bible Public.
(s)-Tate Publishing—R
(s)-Trafford Publishing—R
Whitaker House
(s)-WinePress—R
(s)-Word Alive
(s)-Zoe Life Publishing

CULTS/OCCULT

(s)-American Binding—R
B & H Publishing
Baker Books
Baker Trittin
Baker's Plays—R
(s)-Black Forest/Tennessee—R
(s)-Booklocker.com—R
Bridge-Logos—R
(s)-Brown Books—R
Catholic Answers—R
Christian Writer's Ebook—R
Conciliar Press—R

(s)-Creation House—R
Editorial Portavoz
(s)-Elderberry Press
(s)-Essence—R
(s)-Fairway Press—R
Greenwood/Praeger
HarperOne
Harrison House
Hidden Brook Press—R
Hill Street Press—R
(s)-Holy Fire Publishing—R
(s)-Impact Christian—R
Kregel—R
Lighthouse Publishing—R
Living Books for All
Monarch Books
New York Univ. Press
(s)-One World—R
P & R Publishing—R
Parson Place—R
(s)-Pleasant Word—R
(s)-Reformation Publishers—R
RiverOak
Rose Publishing
(s)-Selah Publishing—R
(s)-Star Bible Public.
(s)-Synergy Publishers—R
(s)-Tate Publishing—R
(s)-Trafford Publishing—R
Whitaker House
(s)-WinePress—R
(s)-Word Alive

CURRENT/SOCIAL ISSUES

Aadeon Publishing—R
Ambassador-Emerald—R
(s)-American Binding—R
AMG Publishers—R
Atheneum/Yg Readers
B & H Publishing
Baker Academic
Baker Books
Baker Trittin
Baker's Plays—R
Beacon Hill Press—R
(s)-Black Forest/Tennessee—R
Blue Dolphin
(s)-Booklocker.com—R
Boyds Mills Press—R
Branden Publishing—R
(s)-Brentwood—R
Bridge-Logos—R
(s)-Brown Books—R
Canadian Inst. for Law—R
Catholic Answers—R
Chalice Press
Christian Family—R
Christian Writer's Ebook—R
Conari Press
(s)-Creation House—R
Crossroad Publishing—R
Cumberland House
(s)-DCTS Publishing
Destiny Image—R
Doubleday—R
Editorial Portavoz
Eerdmans Pub., Wm. B.—R
(s)-Elderberry Press
(s)-Essence—R
(s)-Fairway Press—R
FaithWalk
FaithWords
Forward Movement
Georgetown Univ. Press
Gollehon Press
Good News Pub.
Greenwood/Praeger
(s)-Hannibal Books—R
HarperOne
Harrison House
Haworth Pastoral—R
Hidden Brook Press—R
Hill Street Press—R
(s)-Holy Fire Publishing—R
Howard Books
Inkling Books—R
InterVarsity Press—R
Jossey-Bass
Judson Press
Kregel—R
Life Cycle Books—R
Life Journey Books
Lighthouse Publishing—R
Loyola Press
Marshall Trumann
Millennium III—R
Monarch Books
NavPress Th1nk—R
Nelson, Thomas
New Canaan—R
New Hope—R
New York Univ. Press
(s)-One World—R
P & R Publishing—R
Parson Place—R
Pilgrim Press—R
(s)-Pleasant Word—R
(s)-Providence Pub.—R
(s)-Reformation Publishers—R
Regal
Regnery
RiverOak
Rose Publishing
Salt Works
(s)-Scribe Book—R
(s)-Selah Publishing—R
Sheed & Ward—R
Smyth & Helwys
(s)-Star Bible Public.
Still Waters Revival—R
Strang Book Group—R
(s)-Synergy Publishers—R
(s)-Tate Publishing—R
(s)-Trafford Publishing—R
Tyndale House—R
(s)-VMI Publishers
W Publishing
Whitaker House
(s)-WinePress—R
Wood Lake Books—R
(s)-Word Alive
Yale Univ. Press—R
(s)-Zoe Life Publishing

CURRICULUM

Augsburg—R
Baker Trittin
Big Idea
(s)-Brown Books—R
Carepoint Publishing—R
Christian Ed. Pub.
Christian Liberty Press
College Press—R
Concordia
Congregational Life
Cook, David C.
(s)-CrossHouse—R
(s)-Elderberry Press
(s)-Fairway Press—R
Gospel Light
Gospel Publishing
(s)-Hannibal Books—R
Harcourt Religion
Hidden Brook Press—R
Hill Street Press—R
(s)-IMD Press—R
Knight George Pub.
Lighthouse Publishing—R
Monarch Books
New Leaf
Northwestern
(s)-One World—R
Parsons Publishing—R
(s)-Providence Pub.—R
Randall House Digital
(s)-Reformation Publishers—R
Smyth & Helwys
Standard Publishing
(s)-Tate Publishing—R
(s)-Trafford Publishing—R
UMI Publishing—R
Univ. Press of America—R
W Publishing
(s)-WinePress—R
(s)-Word Alive
Youth Specialties
(s)-Zoe Life Publishing

DATING/SEX

Ambassador-Emerald—R
(s)-American Binding—R
Baal Hamon—R
Baker's Plays—R

Ballantine
Barbour
Bethany House
Blue Dolphin
(s)-Booklocker.com—R
(s)-Brown Books—R
Catholic Answers—R
Christian Writer's Ebook—R
Cook, David C.
(s)-Creation House—R
Crossroad Publishing—R
Doubleday—R
(s)-Elderberry Press
(s)-Essence—R
Evergreen Press
(s)-Fairway Press—R
FaithWalk
FaithWords
FamilyLife (books)—R
Fell, Frederick—R
Fifth Estate—R
Forward Movement
Greenwood/Praeger
HarperOne
Harrison House
Harvest House
Hidden Brook Press—R
(s)-Holy Fire Publishing—R
Howard Books
InterVarsity Press—R
Judson Press
Kregel—R
Life Journey Books
Lift Every Voice—R
Lighthouse Publishing—R
Marshall Trumann
Mission World Library—R
Monarch Books
NavPress Th1nk—R
(s)-One World—R
Parson Place—R
Pauline Books—R
Peter Pauper Press
(s)-Pleasant Word—R
(s)-Providence Pub.—R
Randall House
(s)-Reformation Publishers—R
Regal
Resource Public.
Rose Publishing
(s)-Scribe Book—R
Siloam
St. Anthony Mess. Press—R
(s)-Star Bible Public.
(s)-Tate Publishing—R
(s)-Trafford Publishing—R
(s)-VMI Publishers
Walk Worthy—R
WaterBrook Press—R
Whitaker House
(s)-WinePress—R
(s)-Word Alive
Youth Specialties
(s)-Zoe Life Publishing

DEATH/DYING

Abingdon Press
ACTA Publications
Ambassador-Emerald—R
(s)-American Binding—R
Augsburg—R
Baal Hamon—R
Baker Books
Baker's Plays—R
Bethany House
(s)-Black Forest/Tennessee—R
Blue Dolphin
(s)-Book Publishers—R
(s)-Booklocker.com—R
(s)-Brown Books—R
Chalice Press
Christian Family—R
Christian Writer's Ebook—R
Cook, David C.
(s)-Creation House—R
CSS Publishing—R
Discovery House—R
Doubleday—R
Editorial Portavoz
Eerdmans Pub., Wm. B.—R
Ekklesia Press—R
(s)-Elderberry Press
(s)-Essence—R
Evergreen Press
(s)-Fairway Press—R
FaithWalk
FaithWords
Fifth Estate—R
Forward Movement
Good News Pub.
Greenwood/Praeger
Guardian Angel
HarperOne
Harrison House
Harvest House
Haworth Pastoral—R
Hidden Brook Press—R
Hill Street Press—R
(s)-Holy Fire Publishing—R
Hope Publishing—R
Judson Press
Kregel—R
Life Cycle Books—R
Life Journey Books
Lift Every Voice—R
Lighthouse Publishing—R
Liturgy Training—R
Loyola Press
Marshall Trumann
Monarch Books
Nelson, Thomas
New Seeds—R
(s)-One World—R
Pacific Press
Parson Place—R
(s)-Path Publishing in Christ—R
Pauline Books—R
Paulist Press
Pilgrim Press—R
(s)-Pleasant Word—R
(s)-Providence Pub.—R
Randall House
(s)-Reformation Publishers—R
Regal
Resource Public.
RiverOak
Rose Publishing
Sheed & Ward—R
Siloam
Smyth & Helwys
St. Anthony Mess. Press—R
(s)-Star Bible Public.
(s)-Tate Publishing—R
(s)-Trafford Publishing—R
(s)-VMI Publishers
WaterBrook Press—R
Wesleyan Publishing
Whitaker House
(s)-WinePress—R
(s)-Word Alive
(s)-Zoe Life Publishing

DEVOTIONAL BOOKS

Abingdon Press
ACTA Publications
Ambassador Books
Ambassador-Emerald—R
(s)-American Binding—R
B & H Publishing
Baal Hamon—R
Baker Books
Baker Trittin
Barbour
Bethany House
(s)-Black Forest/Tennessee—R
(s)-Booklocker.com—R
(s)-Brentwood—R
Bridge-Logos—R
(s)-Brown Books—R
Canticle Books—R
Christian Family—R
Christian Focus—R
Christian Heritage—R
Christian Writer's Ebook—R
Congregational Life
Contemporary Drama
Continuum Intl.—R
Cook, David C.
Countryman, J.
(s)-Creation House—R
CSS Publishing—R
Dimensions for Living
Discovery House—R
Doubleday—R
Editorial Portavoz

(s)-Elderberry Press
(s)-Essence—R
Evergreen Press
Extreme Diva
(s)-Fairway Press—R
FaithWalk
FaithWords
Forward Movement
Founders Press
Friends United Press
(s)-FruitBearer Pub.
Gollehon Press
Good Book—R
Green Key Books
Greenwood/Praeger
GRQ—R
(s)-Hannibal Books—R
HarperOne
Harrison House
Harvest Day
Harvest House
HeartSpring Pub.—R
Hidden Brook Press—R
(s)-Holy Fire Publishing—R
Honor Books
Howard Books
(s)-IMD Press—R
(s)-Impact Christian—R
Inkling Books—R
(s)-J and J Publishing
Jireh Publishing
Judson Press
Knight George Pub.
Kregel—R
Legacy Press—R
Libros Liguori
Lift Every Voice—R
Lighthouse Publishing—R
(s)-Lightning Star Press—R
Liguori—R
Liturgy Training—R
Living Books for All
Magnus Press—R
Marshall Trumann
(s)-McDougal Publishing—R
MegaGrace Books
Messianic Jewish—R
Mission City Press
Mission World Library—R
Monarch Books
MOPS Intl.
Morehouse—R
Nelson, Thomas
New Seeds—R
(s)-One World—R
P & R Publishing—R
Paradise Research—R
Parson Place—R
Parsons Publishing—R
(s)-Path Publishing in Christ—R
Pauline Books—R
Pilgrim Press—R
(s)-Pleasant Word—R
(s)-Providence Pub.—R
Ragged Edge—R
Randall House
(s)-Reformation Publishers—R
Regal
RiverOak
Rose Publishing
Salvation Publisher—R
(s)-Selah Publishing—R
Smyth & Helwys
St. Anthony Mess. Press—R
Standard Publishing
(s)-Star Bible Public.
Starik Publishing
(s)-Synergy Publishers—R
(s)-Tate Publishing—R
(s)-TEACH Services—R
(s)-Trafford Publishing—R
Tsaba House
Tyndale House—R
(s)-VMI Publishers
W Publishing
WaterBrook Press—R
Wesleyan Publishing
White Stone Books—R
(s)-WinePress—R
(s)-Winer Foundation—R
(s)-Word Alive
World Publishing
Youth Specialties
(s)-Zoe Life Publishing

DISCIPLESHIP

Aadeon Publishing—R
Abingdon Press
Ambassador-Emerald—R
(s)-American Binding—R
Anglicans United—R
B & H Publishing
Baal Hamon—R
Baker Books
Baker Trittin
Baker's Plays—R
Barbour
Beacon Hill Press—R
Bethany House
(s)-Black Forest/Tennessee—R
BMH Books
(s)-Booklocker.com—R
(s)-Brentwood—R
Bridge-Logos—R
(s)-Brown Books—R
Canticle Books—R
Carey Library, Wm.—R
Chalice Press
CharismaKids
Christian Family—R
Christian Focus—R
Christian Heritage—R
Christian Writer's Ebook—R
College Press—R
Continuum Intl.—R
Cook, David C.
(s)-Creation House—R
Crossroad Publishing—R
CSS Publishing—R
(s)-DCTS Publishing
Discovery House—R
Doubleday—R
Editorial Portavoz
Educational Ministries
Ekklesia Press—R
(s)-Elderberry Press
(s)-Essence—R
Evergreen Press
(s)-Fairway Press—R
FaithWalk
FaithWords
Forward Movement
Founders Press
Foursquare Media
Good News Pub.
Gospel Publishing
Green Key Books
Group Publishing
HarperOne
Harrison House
Hensley Publishing
Hidden Brook Press—R
Hill Street Press—R
(s)-Holy Fire Publishing—R
Howard Books
(s)-IMD Press—R
Inkling Books—R
InterVarsity Press—R
Jebaire Publishing
Judson Press
Kregel—R
Lift Every Voice—R
Lighthouse Publishing—R
Living Books for All
Lutheran Univ. Press
Marshall Trumann
(s)-McDougal Publishing—R
MegaGrace Books
Messianic Jewish—R
Mission City Press
Mission World Library—R
Monarch Books
Moody Publishers
Morehouse—R
NavPress
NavPress Th1nk—R
Nelson, Thomas
New Hope—R
(s)-One World—R
P & R Publishing—R
Pacific Press
Parson Place—R
Parsons Publishing—R
Pathway Press
Pauline Books—R
Pilgrim Press—R

(s)-Pleasant Word—R
Pray! Books—R
(s)-Providence Pub.—R
Quintessential Books—R
Randall House
(s)-Reformation Publishers—R
Reformation Trust
Regal
RiverOak
Rose Publishing
Salvation Publisher—R
(s)-Scribe Book—R
Smyth & Helwys
(s)-So. Baptist Press—R
St. Anthony Mess. Press—R
Standard Publishing
(s)-Star Bible Public.
(s)-Synergy Publishers—R
(s)-Tate Publishing—R
Touch Publications—R
(s)-Trafford Publishing—R
(s)-VMI Publishers
W Publishing
WaterBrook Press—R
Wesleyan Publishing
Whitaker House
WindRiver—R
(s)-WinePress—R
(s)-Winer Foundation—R
(s)-Word Alive
World Publishing
Youth Specialties
(s)-Zoe Life Publishing

DIVORCE

Abingdon Press
ACTA Publications
Ambassador Books
(s)-American Binding—R
Baal Hamon—R
Baker Books
Baker's Plays—R
(s)-Black Forest/Tennessee—R
Blue Dolphin
(s)-Book Publishers—R
(s)-Booklocker.com—R
(s)-Brentwood—R
Bridge-Logos—R
(s)-Brown Books—R
Chalice Press
Christian Writer's Ebook—R
Cook, David C.
(s)-Creation House—R
CSS Publishing—R
Dabbling Mum Press
(s)-Dean Press, Robbie—R
Editorial Portavoz
(s)-Elderberry Press
(s)-Essence—R
(s)-Fairway Press—R
FaithWalk
FaithWords
Forward Movement
Greenwood/Praeger
GuidepostsBooks
Harvest House
Haworth Pastoral—R
Hidden Brook Press—R
Hill Street Press—R
(s)-Holy Fire Publishing—R
(s)-IMD Press—R
Life Journey Books
Lift Every Voice—R
Lighthouse Publishing—R
Marshall Trumann
Monarch Books
Nelson, Thomas
(s)-One World—R
Pacific Press
Parson Place—R
(s)-Pleasant Word—R
(s)-Providence Pub.—R
Randall House
(s)-Reformation Publishers—R
Regal
Regnery
RiverOak
Rose Publishing
(s)-So. Baptist Press—R
St. Anthony Mess. Press—R
(s)-Star Bible Public.
(s)-Synergy Publishers—R
(s)-Tate Publishing—R
(s)-Trafford Publishing—R
(s)-VMI Publishers
WaterBrook Press—R
(s)-WinePress—R
(s)-Word Alive
(s)-Zoe Life Publishing

DOCTRINAL

Abingdon Press
Ambassador-Emerald—R
(s)-American Binding—R
B & H Publishing
Baal Hamon—R
Baker Books
Baker's Plays—R
Beacon Hill Press—R
(s)-Black Forest/Tennessee—R
BMH Books
(s)-Booklocker.com—R
(s)-Brentwood—R
(s)-Brown Books—R
Canticle Books—R
Catholic Answers—R
Chalice Press
Chapter Two—R
Christian Family—R
Christian Focus—R
Christian Heritage—R
Christian Writer's Ebook—R
College Press—R
Concordia
Continuum Intl.—R
(s)-Creation House—R
(s)-DCTS Publishing
Doubleday—R
Editorial Portavoz
(s)-Elderberry Press
(s)-Essence—R
(s)-Fairway Press—R
Forward Movement
Friends United Press
Good News Pub.
Harrison House
Hidden Brook Press—R
Hill Street Press—R
(s)-Holy Fire Publishing—R
(s)-IMD Press—R
(s)-Impact Christian—R
InterVarsity Press—R
Intl. Awakening—R
Kregel—R
Libros Liguori
Lighthouse Publishing—R
Lighthouse Trails—R
Liturgical Press
Lutheran Univ. Press
Lutterworth Press—R
Magnus Press—R
MegaGrace Books
Millennium III—R
Monarch Books
Morehouse—R
(s)-One World—R
P & R Publishing—R
Pacific Press
Parson Place—R
Pauline Books—R
(s)-Pleasant Word—R
(s)-Providence Pub.—R
(s)-Reformation Publishers—R
Reformation Trust
RiverOak
Rose Publishing
Scepter Publishers—R
(s)-So. Baptist Press—R
St. Anthony Mess. Press—R
(s)-Star Bible Public.
Still Waters Revival—R
(s)-Tate Publishing—R
(s)-Trafford Publishing—R
Trinity Foundation—R
Tyndale House—R
UMI Publishing—R
WindRiver—R
(s)-WinePress—R
(s)-Word Alive
(s)-Zoe Life Publishing

DRAMA

(s)-American Binding—R

Baker Trittin
Baker's Plays—R
Big Idea
(s)-Black Forest/Tennessee—R
(s)-Brentwood—R
(s)-Brown Books—R
Contemporary Drama
(s)-Creation House—R
(s)-Elderberry Press
Eldridge Plays
(s)-Fairway Press—R
Group Publishing
Guardian Angel
Hidden Brook Press—R
Judson Press
Lighthouse Publishing—R
Lillenas
Meriwether
Monarch Books
New Hope—R
(s)-One World—R
(s)-Path Publishing in Christ—R
(s)-Path Publishing—R
Players Press—R
(s)-Pleasant Word—R
(s)-Providence Pub.—R
Randall House
(s)-Reformation Publishers—R
Salt Works
(s)-So. Baptist Press—R
(s)-Tate Publishing—R
(s)-Trafford Publishing—R
(s)-WinePress—R
(s)-Word Alive
Youth Specialties
(s)-Zoe Life Publishing

E-BOOKS

B & H Publishing
Blue Dolphin
(s)-Booklocker Jr.
(s)-Booklocker.com—R
Christian Writer's Ebook—R
College Press—R
Dabbling Mum Press
(s)-Dean Press, Robbie—R
Descant Publishing
DiskUs Publishing
E-Digital Books
Fair Havens—R
Fifth Estate—R
Guardian Angel
InterVarsity Press—R
Jireh Publishing
Jubilant Press—R
Life Changing Media
Lighthouse Publishing—R
(s)-Lightning Star Press—R
MoreThanNovellas
(s)-One World—R
Paradise Research—R
Parsons Publishing—R
(s)-Path Publishing in Christ—R
(s)-Path Publishing—R
Randall House Digital
Resource Public.
(s)-Selah Publishing—R
Smyth & Helwys
Sweetheart Romances
(s)-Trafford Publishing—R
Tyndale House—R
White Rose
White Stone Books—R
(s)-Word Alive
(s)-Xulon Press—R

ECONOMICS

(s)-American Binding—R
Baker Books
Baylor Univ. Press
(s)-Booklocker.com—R
(s)-Brentwood—R
(s)-Brown Books—R
Canadian Inst. for Law—R
Christian Writer's Ebook—R
(s)-Elderberry Press
(s)-Essence—R
(s)-Fairway Press—R
FaithWalk
Haworth Pastoral—R
Hidden Brook Press—R
Hill Street Press—R
(s)-Holy Fire Publishing—R
InterVarsity Press—R
Lift Every Voice—R
Lighthouse Publishing—R
Monarch Books
(s)-One World—R
Pilgrim Press—R
(s)-Pleasant Word—R
(s)-Providence Pub.—R
Quintessential Books—R
(s)-Reformation Publishers—R
Regnery
RiverOak
Salvation Publisher—R
Sheed & Ward—R
(s)-Star Bible Public.
(s)-Tate Publishing—R
(s)-Trafford Publishing—R
Trinity Foundation—R
Univ. Press of America—R
(s)-VMI Publishers
(s)-WinePress—R
(s)-Word Alive
Yale Univ. Press—R
(s)-Zoe Life Publishing

ENCOURAGEMENT

Ambassador-Emerald—R
(s)-American Binding—R
Baker's Plays—R
Barbour
Bethany House
(s)-Black Forest/Tennessee—R
BMH Books
(s)-Booklocker.com—R
Bridge-Logos—R
(s)-Brown Books—R
Carepoint Publishing—R
Christian Family—R
Christian Focus—R
(s)-Creation House—R
CSS Publishing—R
Discovery House—R
Doubleday—R
(s)-Elderberry Press
(s)-Essence—R
Fair Havens—R
(s)-Fairway Press—R
FaithWords
Good News Pub.
Guardian Angel
Harvest House
Hidden Brook Press—R
(s)-Holy Fire Publishing—R
Howard Books
(s)-IMD Press—R
(s)-J and J Publishing
Jebaire Publishing
Judson Press
Life Changing Media
Lift Every Voice—R
Lighthouse Publishing—R
Marshall Trumann
Monarch Books
NavPress Th1nk—R
(s)-One World—R
Parson Place—R
Parsons Publishing—R
(s)-Path Publishing—R
Pauline Books—R
Peter Pauper Press
(s)-Pleasant Word—R
(s)-Providence Pub.—R
Quintessential Books—R
Randall House
(s)-Reformation Publishers—R
Regal
Rose Publishing
Salvation Publisher—R
(s)-Scribe Book—R
(s)-Star Bible Public.
(s)-Synergy Publishers—R
(s)-Tate Publishing—R
(s)-Trafford Publishing—R
WaterBrook Press—R
Wesleyan Publishing
White Stone Books—R
(s)-WinePress—R
(s)-Word Alive
(s)-Zoe Life Publishing

ENVIRONMENTAL ISSUES

Abingdon Press
ACTA Publications
(s)-American Binding—R
Baker Books
Baker's Plays—R
(s)-Black Forest/Tennessee—R
Blue Dolphin
(s)-Booklocker.com—R
(s)-Brown Books—R
Christian Writer's Ebook—R
Dawn Publications
Doubleday—R
(s)-Elderberry Press
(s)-Essence—R
Facts on File
(s)-Fairway Press—R
FaithWalk
Forward Movement
Georgetown Univ. Press
Grupo Nelson
Haworth Pastoral—R
Hidden Brook Press—R
Hill Street Press—R
(s)-Holy Fire Publishing—R
InterVarsity Press—R
Johns Hopkins—R
Judson Press
Lift Every Voice—R
Lighthouse Publishing—R
Monarch Books
(s)-One World—R
Pilgrim Press—R
(s)-Pleasant Word—R
Quintessential Books—R
Ravenhawk Books—R
(s)-Reformation Publishers—R
RiverOak
Sheed & Ward—R
(s)-So. Baptist Press—R
Tarcher, Jeremy P.—R
(s)-Tate Publishing—R
(s)-Trafford Publishing—R
Univ. Press of America—R
(s)-VMI Publishers
(s)-WinePress—R
(s)-Word Alive

ESCHATOLOGY

Abingdon Press
Alba House—R
(s)-American Binding—R
Anglicans United—R
B & H Publishing
Baker Books
(s)-Black Forest/Tennessee—R
Blue Dolphin
BMH Books
(s)-Booklocker.com—R
(s)-Brown Books—R
Chalice Press
Chapter Two—R
Christian Family—R
Christian Heritage—R
Christian Writer's Ebook—R
College Press—R
Continuum Intl.—R
(s)-Creation House—R
CSS Publishing—R
(s)-DCTS Publishing
(s)-Elderberry Press
(s)-Essence—R
(s)-Fairway Press—R
FaithWords
Gospel Publishing
Grupo Nelson
Hidden Brook Press—R
Hill Street Press—R
(s)-Holy Fire Publishing—R
(s)-IMD Press—R
Kirk House
Kregel—R
Lighthouse Publishing—R
Lighthouse Trails—R
Lutheran Univ. Press
Lutterworth Press—R
Messianic Jewish—R
Millennium III—R
Monarch Books
New Seeds—R
(s)-One World—R
Pacific Press
Parson Place—R
Parsons Publishing—R
Pauline Books—R
(s)-Pleasant Word—R
(s)-Reformation Publishers—R
Rose Publishing
(s)-Scribe Book—R
(s)-Selah Publishing—R
(s)-Star Bible Public.
(s)-Strong Tower—R
(s)-Tate Publishing—R
(s)-Trafford Publishing—R
(s)-WinePress—R
(s)-Word Alive
World Publishing
(s)-Zoe Life Publishing

ETHICS

Aadeon Publishing—R
Abingdon Press
Alba House—R
(s)-American Binding—R
B & H Publishing
Baker Books
Baker's Plays—R
Bethany House
(s)-Black Forest/Tennessee—R
Blue Dolphin
(s)-Booklocker.com—R
(s)-Brentwood—R
Bridge-Logos—R
(s)-Brown Books—R
Catholic Answers—R
Chalice Press
Christian Heritage—R
Christian Writer's Ebook—R
Conciliar Press—R
Continuum Intl.—R
(s)-Creation House—R
Crossroad Publishing—R
Dover Publications—R
Eerdmans Pub., Wm. B.—R
(s)-Elderberry Press
(s)-Essence—R
(s)-Fairway Press—R
FaithWalk
Fortress Press
Forward Movement
Geneva Press
Georgetown Univ. Press
Greenwood/Praeger
Guardian Angel
(s)-Hannibal Books—R
Haworth Pastoral—R
Hidden Brook Press—R
Hill Street Press—R
(s)-Holy Fire Publishing—R
Howard Books
(s)-IMD Press—R
Inkling Books—R
InterVarsity Press—R
Judson Press
Kirk House
Kregel—R
Libros Liguori
Life Cycle Books—R
Lift Every Voice—R
Lighthouse Publishing—R
Lutheran Univ. Press
Lutterworth Press—R
Marshall Trumann
Monarch Books
NavPress Th1nk—R
(s)-One World—R
Our Sunday Visitor—R
P & R Publishing—R
Pacific Press
Paragon House—R
Parson Place—R
Parsons Publishing—R
Paulist Press
Pilgrim Press—R
(s)-Pleasant Word—R
Presbyterian Pub.
(s)-Providence Pub.—R
Quintessential Books—R
(s)-Reformation Publishers—R
Regnery
Resource Public.
RiverOak
Salt Works
(s)-Scribe Book—R
Sheed & Ward—R

Smyth & Helwys
St. Anthony Mess. Press—R
(s)-Star Bible Public.
Still Waters Revival—R
(s)-Synergy Publishers—R
T & T Clark—R
(s)-Tate Publishing—R
(s)-Trafford Publishing—R
Trinity Foundation—R
Univ. Press of America—R
(s)-VMI Publishers
Walk Worthy—R
Westminster John Knox
Whitaker House
(s)-WinePress—R
Wood Lake Books—R
(s)-Word Alive
World Publishing

ETHNIC/CULTURAL

Abingdon Press
ACTA Publications
(s)-Ali Literary, Alfred—R
(s)-American Binding—R
B & H Publishing
Baal Hamon—R
Baker Books
Baker Trittin
Baker's Plays—R
Bethany House
(s)-Black Forest/Tennessee—R
Blue Dolphin
(s)-Booklocker.com—R
Branden Publishing—R
(s)-Brown Books—R
Carey Library, Wm.—R
Chalice Press
Christian Writer's Ebook—R
College Press—R
Concordia
(s)-Creation House—R
(s)-Dean Press, Robbie—R
Doubleday—R
E-Digital Books
(s)-Elderberry Press
(s)-Essence—R
Facts on File
(s)-Fairway Press—R
FaithWalk
Fortress Press
Forward Movement
Friends United Press
Genesis Press—R
Georgetown Univ. Press
Good News Pub.
Greenwood/Praeger
Grupo Nelson
Guardian Angel
Guernica Editions—R
HarperOne
Haworth Pastoral—R
Hidden Brook Press—R
Hill Street Press—R
(s)-Holy Fire Publishing—R
(s)-IMD Press—R
InterVarsity Press—R
Judson Press
Kaleidoscope Press—R
Kirk House
Libros Liguori
Lift Every Voice—R
Lighthouse Publishing—R
Liguori—R
Liturgy Training—R
Living Books for All
Lutheran Univ. Press
Marshall Trumann
Messianic Jewish—R
Monarch Books
Moody Publishers
NavPress Th1nk—R
New Hope—R
New Seeds—R
New York Univ. Press
(s)-One World—R
One World/Ballantine
Oregon Catholic
P & R Publishing—R
Pacific Press
Paulist Press
Pilgrim Press—R
(s)-Pleasant Word—R
(s)-Providence Pub.—R
(s)-Reformation Publishers—R
Regal
Salt Works
(s)-Scribe Book—R
St. Anthony Mess. Press—R
Standard Publishing
(s)-Tate Publishing—R
Third World Press—R
Torch Legacy
(s)-Trafford Publishing—R
UMI Publishing—R
Univ. of AR Press—R
Univ. Press of America—R
(s)-VMI Publishers
Walk Worthy—R
Whitaker House
(s)-WinePress—R
(s)-Word Alive
Yale Univ. Press—R
(s)-Zoe Life Publishing

EVANGELISM/WITNESSING

Ambassador-Emerald—R
(s)-American Binding—R
Anglicans United—R
B & H Publishing
Baal Hamon—R
Baker Books
Baker Trittin
(s)-Black Forest/Tennessee—R
BMH Books
(s)-Booklocker.com—R
(s)-Brentwood—R
(s)-Brown Books—R
Carey Library, Wm.—R
Christian Family—R
Christian Focus—R
Christian Heritage—R
Christian Writer's Ebook—R
Church Growth Inst.
Cook, David C.
(s)-Creation House—R
CSS Publishing—R
(s)-DCTS Publishing
Discovery House—R
Earthen Vessel—R
Editorial Portavoz
(s)-Elderberry Press
(s)-Essence—R
Evergreen Press
Fair Havens—R
(s)-Fairway Press—R
Faith Alive
FaithWalk
Founders Press
Friends United Press
Gollehon Press
Good News Pub.
Gospel Publishing
Harrison House
Harvest Day
Hidden Brook Press—R
(s)-Holy Fire Publishing—R
(s)-IMD Press—R
(s)-Impact Christian—R
InterVarsity Press—R
Jebaire Publishing
Judson Press
Kregel—R
Lift Every Voice—R
Lighthouse Publishing—R
(s)-Lightning Star Press—R
Living Books for All
Lutheran Univ. Press
Lutterworth Press—R
Marshall Trumann
(s)-McDougal Publishing—R
MegaGrace Books
Messianic Jewish—R
Millennium III—R
Mission World Library—R
Monarch Books
Moody Publishers
NavPress Th1nk—R
Nelson Ignite
Nelson, Thomas
New Hope—R
New Leaf
(s)-One World—R
Pacific Press
Paradise Research—R
Parson Place—R
Parsons Publishing—R

Pilgrim Press—R
(s)-Pleasant Word—R
(s)-Providence Pub.—R
Randall House
(s)-Reformation Publishers—R
Reformation Trust
Regal
RiverOak
Rose Publishing
Salt Works
(s)-Selah Publishing—R
(s)-So. Baptist Press—R
St. Anthony Mess. Press—R
(s)-Star Bible Public.
Still Waters Revival—R
Strang Book Group—R
(s)-Tate Publishing—R
(s)-Trafford Publishing—R
Tyndale House—R
(s)-VMI Publishers
W Publishing
Wesleyan Publishing
WindRiver—R
(s)-WinePress—R
Woodland Gospel
(s)-Word Alive
World Publishing
(s)-Zoe Life Publishing

EXEGESIS

Abingdon Press
Ambassador-Emerald—R
(s)-American Binding—R
Baker Books
(s)-Black Forest/Tennessee—R
BMH Books
(s)-Booklocker.com—R
(s)-Brown Books—R
Catholic Answers—R
Christian Family—R
Christian Focus—R
Christian Writer's Ebook—R
Cistercian—R
College Press—R
Continuum Intl.—R
(s)-Creation House—R
CSS Publishing—R
Doubleday—R
Eerdmans Pub., Wm. B.—R
(s)-Elderberry Press
(s)-Essence—R
(s)-Fairway Press—R
Geneva Press
Greenwood/Praeger
Hidden Brook Press—R
(s)-Holy Fire Publishing—R
(s)-IMD Press—R
InterVarsity Press—R
Johns Hopkins—R
Kregel—R
Lighthouse Publishing—R
Lutheran Univ. Press
Lutterworth Press—R
(s)-McDougal Publishing—R
Monarch Books
New Leaf
(s)-One World—R
P & R Publishing—R
Parsons Publishing—R
Pauline Books—R
Paulist Press
(s)-Pleasant Word—R
(s)-Providence Pub.—R
(s)-Reformation Publishers—R
Reformation Trust
Rose Publishing
St. Anthony Mess. Press—R
(s)-Star Bible Public.
(s)-Tate Publishing—R
(s)-Trafford Publishing—R
(s)-VMI Publishers
Westminster John Knox
(s)-WinePress—R
(s)-Word Alive
World Publishing
(s)-Zoe Life Publishing

EXPOSÉS

Ambassador-Emerald—R
(s)-American Binding—R
Baker Books
(s)-Booklocker.com—R
(s)-Brentwood—R
Christian Writer's Ebook—R
(s)-Elderberry Press
(s)-Fairway Press—R
Greenwood/Praeger
Hidden Brook Press—R
(s)-Holy Fire Publishing—R
Lighthouse Publishing—R
Lighthouse Trails—R
(s)-One World—R
(s)-Reformation Publishers—R
(s)-So. Baptist Press—R
(s)-Star Bible Public.
(s)-Trafford Publishing—R
(s)-WinePress—R
(s)-Word Alive
(s)-Zoe Life Publishing

FAITH

Aadeon Publishing—R
Abingdon Press
ACTA Publications
Alba House—R
Ambassador Books
Ambassador-Emerald—R
(s)-American Binding—R
B & H Publishing
Baal Hamon—R
Baker Books
Baker Trittin
Baker's Plays—R
Barbour
Bethany House
(s)-Black Forest/Tennessee—R
(s)-Booklocker.com—R
Bridge-Logos—R
(s)-Brown Books—R
Canticle Books—R
Chalice Press
Christian Family—R
Christian Focus—R
Christian Heritage—R
Christian Writer's Ebook—R
Continuum Intl.—R
(s)-Creation House—R
(s)-DCTS Publishing
Destiny Image—R
Discovery House—R
Doubleday—R
Educational Ministries
Eerdmans Pub., Wm. B.—R
(s)-Elderberry Press
(s)-Essence—R
Evergreen Press
(s)-Fairway Press—R
Faith Communications
FaithWalk
FaithWords
Forward Movement
(s)-FruitBearer Pub.
Gollehon Press
Good News Pub.
Green Key Books
Greenwood/Praeger
Grupo Nelson
Guardian Angel
GuidepostsBooks
HarperOne
Harrison House
Hensley Publishing
Hidden Brook Press—R
Hill Street Press—R
(s)-Holy Fire Publishing—R
Howard Books
(s)-IMD Press—R
Jebaire Publishing
Jireh Publishing
Judson Press
Kregel—R
Legacy Publishers
Life Changing Media
Lift Every Voice—R
Lighthouse Publishing—R
Living Books for All
Loyola Press
Lutheran Univ. Press
Lutterworth Press—R
Magnus Press—R
Marshall Trumann
(s)-McDougal Publishing—R
MegaGrace Books

Mission City Press
Mission World Library—R
Monarch Books
Morehouse—R
NavPress Th1nk—R
Nelson, Thomas
New Seeds—R
(s)-One World—R
P & R Publishing—R
Pacific Press
Paradise Research—R
Parson Place—R
Parsons Publishing—R
(s)-Path Publishing in Christ—R
Pauline Books—R
Peter Pauper Press
Pilgrim Press—R
(s)-Pleasant Word—R
(s)-Providence Pub.—R
Quintessential Books—R
Randall House
(s)-Reformation Publishers—R
Reformation Trust
Regal
RiverOak
Rose Publishing
Salt Works
Salvation Publisher—R
Scepter Publishers—R
(s)-Scribe Book—R
(s)-Selah Publishing—R
St. Anthony Mess. Press—R
(s)-Star Bible Public.
(s)-Synergy Publishers—R
(s)-Tate Publishing—R
(s)-TEACH Services—R
(s)-Trafford Publishing—R
Tyndale House—R
UMI Publishing—R
Virginia Pines Press
(s)-VMI Publishers
W Publishing
WaterBrook Press—R
Wesleyan Publishing
Whitaker House
White Stone Books—R
WindRiver—R
(s)-WinePress—R
(s)-Word Alive
World Publishing
Youth Specialties
(s)-Zoe Life Publishing

FAMILY LIFE

Abingdon Press
ACTA Publications
Ambassador Books
Ambassador-Emerald—R
(s)-American Binding—R
Augsburg—R
B & H Publishing
Baal Hamon—R
Baker Books
Baker Trittin
Baker's Plays—R
Barbour
Beacon Hill Press—R
BelleBooks—R
Bethany House
Big Idea
(s)-Black Forest/Tennessee—R
BMH Books
(s)-Booklocker.com—R
Boyds Mills Press—R
(s)-Brentwood—R
Bridge-Logos—R
(s)-Brown Books—R
Carepoint Publishing—R
Chalice Press
Christian Family—R
Christian Focus—R
Christian Writer's Ebook—R
Cladach Publishing
College Press—R
Conari Press
Concordia
Cook, David C.
(s)-Creation House—R
Crossroad Publishing—R
Dabbling Mum Press
(s)-DCTS Publishing
Destiny Image—R
Dimensions for Living
Discovery House—R
E-Digital Books
Editorial Portavoz
(s)-Elderberry Press
(s)-Essence—R
Evergreen Press
Extreme Diva
(s)-Fairway Press—R
Faith Communications
FaithWalk
FaithWords
FamilyLife (books)—R
Focus on the Family
Forward Movement
(s)-FruitBearer Pub.
Good News Pub.
Greenwood/Praeger
Grupo Nelson
Guardian Angel
GuidepostsBooks
(s)-Hannibal Books—R
HarperOne
Harrison House
Harvest House
Haworth Pastoral—R
Health Commun.
Hensley Publishing
Hidden Brook Press—R
Hill Street Press—R
(s)-Holy Fire Publishing—R
Hope Publishing—R
Howard Books
Ideals/Children
(s)-IMD Press—R
(s)-J and J Publishing
Jebaire Publishing
Jireh Publishing
Judson Press
Kregel—R
Langmarc
(s)-Leading Lady
Legacy Press—R
Life Changing Media
Life Cycle Books—R
Life Journey Books
Lift Every Voice—R
Lighthouse Publishing—R
Liguori—R
Loyola Press
Marshall Trumann
(s)-McDougal Publishing—R
Mission World Library—R
Monarch Books
MOPS Intl.
MountainView
Nelson Ignite
Nelson, Thomas
New Hope—R
New Leaf
(s)-One World—R
Our Sunday Visitor—R
P & R Publishing—R
Pacific Press
Parson Place—R
Parsons Publishing—R
Pauline Books—R
Peter Pauper Press
Pflaum Publishing
Pilgrim Press—R
(s)-Pleasant Word—R
(s)-Providence Pub.—R
(s)-Quiet Waters
Quintessential Books—R
Randall House
(s)-Recovery Commun.
(s)-Reformation Publishers—R
Regal
RiverOak
Rose Publishing
Salvation Publisher—R
(s)-Scribe Book—R
(s)-Selah Publishing—R
Sheed & Ward—R
(s)-So. Baptist Press—R
St. Anthony Mess. Press—R
(s)-Star Bible Public.
Starik Publishing
Still Waters Revival—R
(s)-Synergy Publishers—R
(s)-Tate Publishing—R

Torch Legacy
(s)-Trafford Publishing—R
Tyndale House—R
(s)-VMI Publishers
W Publishing
WaterBrook Press—R
Whitaker House
White Stone Books—R
(s)-WinePress—R
Wood Lake Books—R
Woodland Gospel
(s)-Word Alive
World Publishing
(s)-Zoe Life Publishing

FICTION: ADULT/GENERAL

(s)-American Binding—R
Ballantine
Bethany House
Breakneck Books—R
(s)-Brown Books—R
Cladach Publishing
(s)-Essence—R
FaithWords
Fell, Frederick—R
Guernica Editions—R
Invisible College Press
Kregel—R
Lifesong Publishers
(s)-Lifevest Publishing
Multnomah
Nelson, Fiction, Thomas
One World/Ballantine
P & R Publishing—R
Parson Place—R
Power Publishing
(s)-Providence Pub.—R
Quintessential Books—R
Ravenhawk Books—R
Salt Works
(s)-Scribe Book—R
Sweetheart Romances
Whitaker House
White Stone Books—R
WindRiver—R

FICTION: ADULT/RELIGIOUS

(s)-ACW Press—R
Adams Media
Ambassador Books
Ambassador-Emerald—R
(s)-American Binding—R
American Book
B & H Publishing
Baal Hamon—R
Baker Books
Baker's Plays—R
Ballantine
Barbour
BelleBooks—R
Bethany House
(s)-Black Forest/Tennessee—R
Blue Dolphin
(s)-Book Publishers—R
(s)-Booklocker.com—R
Branden Publishing—R
Breakneck Books—R
Bridge Resources
(s)-Brown Books—R
Capstone Fiction—R
Christian Focus—R
Christian Liberty Press
Christian Writer's Ebook—R
Cladach Publishing
(s)-Creation House—R
Descant Publishing
Destiny Image—R
DiskUs Publishing
Doubleday—R
E-Digital Books
Eerdmans Pub., Wm. B.—R
Ekklesia Press—R
(s)-Elderberry Press
Elijah Press
Emerald Pointe Bks
(s)-Essence—R
Evergreen Press
(s)-Fairway Press—R
FaithWalk
FaithWords
Fifth Estate—R
Focus on the Family
Genesis Press—R
GuidepostsBooks
(s)-Hannibal Books—R
HarperOne
HeartQuest
Heartsong Presents
HeartSpring Pub.—R
Hidden Brook Press—R
Hill Street Press—R
(s)-Holy Fire Publishing—R
Howard Books
(s)-IMD Press—R
(s)-Insight Publishing—R
Invisible College Press
(s)-J and J Publishing
Jireh Publishing
Kregel—R
(s)-Lifevest Publishing
Lift Every Voice—R
Lighthouse Publishing—R
Lighthouse Trails—R
(s)-Lightning Star Press—R
Love Inspired
Love Inspired Historical
(s)-McDougal Publishing—R
Messianic Jewish—R
Moody Publishers
MountainView
Mt. Olive College Press
Multnomah
NavPress
Nelson, Fiction, Thomas
New Seeds—R
(s)-One World—R
One World/Ballantine
P & R Publishing—R
Pacific Press
Parson Place—R
Parsons Publishing—R
(s)-Pleasant Word—R
Port Hole Books
(s)-Providence Pub.—R
Quintessential Books—R
Randall House
(s)-Reformation Publishers—R
Revell
Salt Works
Scepter Publishers—R
(s)-Scribe Book—R
(s)-Selah Publishing—R
(s)-Self Publish Press—R
(s)-Star Bible Public.
Steeple Hill/Single Title
Strang Book Group—R
Sweetheart Romances
(s)-Tate Publishing—R
Treble Heart Books—R
Tsaba House
Vintage Romance
Virginia Pines Press
Vision Forum
(s)-VMI Publishers
Walk Worthy—R
WaterBrook Press—R
Whitaker House
White Rose
White Stone Books—R
WindRiver—R
(s)-WinePress—R
Wood Lake Books—R
(s)-Word Alive
(s)-Xulon Press—R

FICTION: ADVENTURE

(s)-ACW Press—R
Ambassador Books
Ambassador-Emerald—R
(s)-American Binding—R
Atheneum/Yg Readers
B & H Publishing
Baker Books
Baker Trittin
Baker's Plays—R
Barbour
(s)-Black Forest/Tennessee—R
(s)-Book Publishers—R
(s)-Booklocker.com—R
Boyds Mills Press—R
Breakneck Books—R
(s)-Brentwood—R
(s)-Brown Books—R
Christian Ed. Pub.
Christian Family—R

Christian Writer's Ebook—R
(s)-Creation House—R
DiskUs Publishing
E-Digital Books
Eerdmans/Yg Readers
(s)-Elderberry Press
(s)-Essence—R
Evergreen Press
(s)-Fairway Press—R
FaithWalk
FaithWords
Fifth Estate—R
Genesis Press—R
Hidden Brook Press—R
(s)-Holy Fire Publishing—R
Ideals Publications
(s)-Insight Publishing—R
Kaleidoscope Press—R
Knight George Pub.
(s)-Lifevest Publishing
Lift Every Voice—R
Lighthouse Publishing—R
(s)-Lightning Star Press—R
Mission City Press
MountainView
Multnomah
Nelson, Fiction, Thomas
(s)-One World—R
One World/Ballantine
Parson Place—R
Parsons Publishing—R
(s)-Pleasant Word—R
PREP Publishing—R
(s)-Providence Pub.—R
Quintessential Books—R
Randall House
Ravenhawk Books—R
(s)-Reformation Publishers—R
Salt Works
(s)-Scribe Book—R
(s)-Selah Publishing—R
(s)-Self Publish Press—R
(s)-So. Baptist Press—R
Starik Publishing
Steeple Hill/Single Title
(s)-Tate Publishing—R
Treble Heart Books—R
Virginia Pines Press
(s)-VMI Publishers
WaterBrook Press—R
White Stone Books—R
WindRiver—R
(s)-WinePress—R

FICTION: ALLEGORY

(s)-ACW Press—R
(s)-American Binding—R
Atheneum/Yg Readers
Baker Books
Baker Trittin
Baker's Plays—R
Barbour
Bethany House
(s)-Black Forest/Tennessee—R
Blue Dolphin
(s)-Booklocker.com—R
(s)-Brown Books—R
Capstone Fiction—R
Christian Family—R
Christian Writer's Ebook—R
(s)-Creation House—R
Ekklesia Press—R
(s)-Elderberry Press
(s)-Essence—R
Evergreen Press
(s)-Fairway Press—R
Hidden Brook Press—R
(s)-Insight Publishing—R
Knight George Pub.
(s)-Lifevest Publishing
Lighthouse Publishing—R
MountainView
Multnomah
New Seeds—R
(s)-One World—R
P & R Publishing—R
Parson Place—R
(s)-Pleasant Word—R
(s)-Providence Pub.—R
Randall House
Realms
(s)-Reformation Publishers—R
Reformation Trust
Salt Works
(s)-Scribe Book—R
(s)-Selah Publishing—R
Strang Book Group—R
(s)-Tate Publishing—R
(s)-VMI Publishers
White Stone Books—R
Wilshire Book—R
(s)-WinePress—R

FICTION: BIBLICAL

(s)-ACW Press—R
(s)-American Binding—R
Atheneum/Yg Readers
Baker Books
Baker Trittin
Baker's Plays—R
(s)-Black Forest/Tennessee—R
(s)-Booklocker.com—R
(s)-Brentwood—R
(s)-Brown Books—R
Capstone Fiction—R
CharismaKids
Christian Family—R
Christian Writer's Ebook—R
Cladach Publishing
College Press—R
(s)-Creation House—R
Destiny Image—R
Eerdmans Pub., Wm. B.—R
Eerdmans/Yg Readers
Ekklesia Press—R
(s)-Elderberry Press
(s)-Essence—R
Evergreen Press
(s)-Fairway Press—R
FaithWords
GuidepostsBooks
(s)-Hannibal Books—R
Hidden Brook Press—R
(s)-Holy Fire Publishing—R
(s)-IMD Press—R
(s)-Insight Publishing—R
(s)-J and J Publishing
(s)-Kindred Books—R
Knight George Pub.
Lifesong Publishers
(s)-Lifevest Publishing
Lift Every Voice—R
Lighthouse Publishing—R
Love Inspired Historical
Messianic Jewish—R
Mission City Press
Moody Publishers
MountainView
Mt. Olive College Press
Multnomah
NavPress
NavPress Th1nk—R
New Seeds—R
(s)-One World—R
Pacific Press
Parson Place—R
Parsons Publishing—R
(s)-Pleasant Word—R
PREP Publishing—R
(s)-Providence Pub.—R
Quintessential Books—R
Randall House
Realms
(s)-Reformation Publishers—R
Reformation Trust
Salt Works
(s)-Self Publish Press—R
(s)-So. Baptist Press—R
Steeple Hill/Single Title
Strang Book Group—R
(s)-Tate Publishing—R
(s)-VMI Publishers
Walk Worthy—R
WaterBrook Press—R
White Stone Books—R
WindRiver—R
(s)-WinePress—R

FICTION: CHICK LIT

(s)-ACW Press—R
Ambassador Books
Atheneum/Yg Readers
Baker's Plays—R
BelleBooks—R
Bethany House

(s)-Black Forest/Tennessee—R
(s)-Booklocker.com—R
(s)-Brown Books—R
By Grace Publications
Christian Writer's Ebook—R
(s)-Elderberry Press
(s)-Essence—R
FaithWords
Harvest House
HeartQuest
Hidden Brook Press—R
(s)-Insight Publishing—R
(s)-Lifevest Publishing
Lift Every Voice—R
Lighthouse Publishing—R
Love Inspired Suspense
MOPS Intl.
Multnomah
NavPress Th1nk—R
Nelson, Fiction, Thomas
(s)-One World—R
Parson Place—R
(s)-Pleasant Word—R
Randall House
Ravenhawk Books—R
(s)-Reformation Publishers—R
(s)-Scribe Book—R
Steeple Hill/Single Title
(s)-VMI Publishers
WaterBrook Press—R
Whitaker House
White Stone Books—R
(s)-WinePress—R

FICTION: CHILDREN'S PICTURE BOOKS*

Atheneum/Yg Readers
(s)-Black Forest/Tennessee—R
(s)-Booklocker.com—R
Boyds Mills Press—R
(s)-Brown Books—R
Eerdmans/Yg Readers
(s)-Essence—R
Guardian Angel
Heart to Heart
Ideals Publications
Illumination Arts
(s)-IMD Press—R
Journey Stone—R
Judson Press
Knight George Pub.
Kregel Kidzone
Legacy Press—R
(s)-Lifevest Publishing
P & R Publishing—R
Pauline Books—R
Pelican Publishing—R
(s)-Providence Pub.—R
Random Hs./Golden Bks
(s)-Reformation Publishers—R
Salt Works
Salty's Books
White Stone Books—R

FICTION: CONTEMPORARY

(s)-ACW Press—R
Ambassador Books
(s)-American Binding—R
Atheneum/Yg Readers
Avon Inspire
B & H Publishing
Baker Books
Baker Trittin
Baker's Plays—R
Ballantine
Barbour
BelleBooks—R
Bethany House
BJU/Journey Forth—R
(s)-Black Forest/Tennessee—R
(s)-Booklocker.com—R
Branden Publishing—R
(s)-Brentwood—R
(s)-Brown Books—R
Capstone Fiction—R
CharismaKids
Christian Ed. Pub.
Christian Writer's Ebook—R
Cladach Publishing
(s)-Creation House—R
Descant Publishing
Destiny Image—R
DiskUs Publishing
E-Digital Books
Eerdmans/Yg Readers
(s)-Elderberry Press
Emerald Pointe Bks
(s)-Essence—R
(s)-Fairway Press—R
FaithWalk
FaithWords
Fell, Frederick—R
Fifth Estate—R
Focus on the Family
Genesis Press—R
Harvest House
HeartQuest
Heartsong Presents
Hidden Brook Press—R
(s)-Holy Fire Publishing—R
(s)-Insight Publishing—R
Invisible College Press
(s)-J and J Publishing
Jireh Publishing
Knight George Pub.
Kregel—R
(s)-Lifevest Publishing
Lift Every Voice—R
Lighthouse Publishing—R
Love Inspired
(s)-McDougal Publishing—R
Mission City Press
Moody Publishers
MOPS Intl.
MountainView
Mt. Olive College Press
Multnomah
NavPress
NavPress Th1nk—R
Nelson, Fiction, Thomas
(s)-One World—R
One World/Ballantine
P & R Publishing—R
(s)-Pleasant Word—R
Putnam/Young Readers
Randall House
Ravenhawk Books—R
(s)-Reformation Publishers—R
Revell
Salt Works
(s)-Scribe Book—R
(s)-Self Publish Press—R
(s)-So. Baptist Press—R
Steeple Hill/Single Title
(s)-Tate Publishing—R
Third World Press—R
Treble Heart Books—R
Tyndale House—R
(s)-VMI Publishers
Walk Worthy—R
WaterBrook Press—R
Whitaker House
White Stone Books—R
(s)-WinePress—R

FICTION: ETHNIC

(s)-ACW Press—R
(s)-American Binding—R
Atheneum/Yg Readers
Baker Books
Baker Trittin
Baker's Plays—R
Ballantine
Bethany House
(s)-Black Forest/Tennessee—R
Blue Dolphin
(s)-Booklocker.com—R
Boyds Mills Press—R
Branden Publishing—R
(s)-Brown Books—R
Christian Writer's Ebook—R
(s)-Creation House—R
Destiny Image—R
DiskUs Publishing
E-Digital Books
(s)-Elderberry Press
(s)-Essence—R
Evergreen Press
(s)-Fairway Press—R
Focus on the Family
Genesis Press—R
Guernica Editions—R

Hidden Brook Press—R
(s)-Holy Fire Publishing—R
(s)-IMD Press—R
(s)-Insight Publishing—R
Kaleidoscope Press—R
(s)-Lifevest Publishing
Lift Every Voice—R
Lighthouse Publishing—R
Living Books for All
Messianic Jewish—R
MountainView
Multnomah
(s)-One World—R
One World/Ballantine
(s)-Pleasant Word—R
Putnam/Young Readers
(s)-Reformation Publishers—R
Salt Works
(s)-Tate Publishing—R
Third World Press—R
(s)-VMI Publishers
Walk Worthy—R
White Stone Books—R
(s)-WinePress—R

FICTION: FABLES/PARABLES

(s)-ACW Press—R
(s)-American Binding—R
Baker's Plays—R
(s)-Black Forest/Tennessee—R
(s)-Booklocker.com—R
(s)-Brown Books—R
(s)-Elderberry Press
(s)-Essence—R
HarperOne
Hidden Brook Press—R
(s)-Holy Fire Publishing—R
(s)-Lifevest Publishing
Lift Every Voice—R
Lighthouse Publishing—R
MountainView
(s)-One World—R
Parson Place—R
(s)-Pleasant Word—R
(s)-Providence Pub.—R
Quintessential Books—R
Randall House
(s)-Reformation Publishers—R
Resource Public.
Salt Works
(s)-Scribe Book—R
(s)-Tate Publishing—R
(s)-VMI Publishers
(s)-WinePress—R

FICTION: FANTASY

(s)-ACW Press—R
(s)-American Binding—R
American Book
AMG Publishers—R
Atheneum/Yg Readers
B & H Publishing
Baker Trittin
Baker's Plays—R
Ballantine
Barbour
BelleBooks—R
Bethany House
Big Idea
(s)-Black Forest/Tennessee—R
(s)-Book Publishers—R
(s)-Booklocker.com—R
Breakneck Books—R
(s)-Brown Books—R
Capstone Fiction—R
Christian Writer's Ebook—R
(s)-Creation House—R
Descant Publishing
Destiny Image—R
DiskUs Publishing
Dover Publications—R
E-Digital Books
Eerdmans Pub., Wm. B.—R
(s)-Elderberry Press
Evergreen Press
(s)-Fairway Press—R
Genesis Press—R
Hidden Brook Press—R
(s)-Insight Publishing—R
Invisible College Press
Knight George Pub.
(s)-Lifevest Publishing
Lift Every Voice—R
Lighthouse Publishing—R
Mission City Press
MountainView
Multnomah
NavPress Th1nk—R
Nelson, Fiction, Thomas
(s)-One World—R
P & R Publishing—R
(s)-Pleasant Word—R
Putnam/Young Readers
Ravenhawk Books—R
Realms
(s)-Reformation Publishers—R
(s)-Scribe Book—R
Starik Publishing
Strang Book Group—R
(s)-Tate Publishing—R
Treble Heart Books—R
(s)-VMI Publishers
WaterBrook Press—R
Whitaker House
(s)-WinePress—R

FICTION: FRONTIER

(s)-ACW Press—R
Ambassador-Emerald—R
(s)-American Binding—R
Atheneum/Yg Readers
Baker Books
Baker Trittin
Baker's Plays—R
(s)-Black Forest/Tennessee—R
(s)-Booklocker.com—R
(s)-Brentwood—R
(s)-Brown Books—R
Christian Writer's Ebook—R
Cladach Publishing
(s)-Elderberry Press
(s)-Essence—R
(s)-Fairway Press—R
Guardian Angel
Harvest House
Hidden Brook Press—R
(s)-Insight Publishing—R
Kaleidoscope Press—R
(s)-Lifevest Publishing
Lighthouse Publishing—R
Mission City Press
MountainView
Multnomah
(s)-One World—R
P & R Publishing—R
Parson Place—R
(s)-Pleasant Word—R
Randall House
Ravenhawk Books—R
(s)-Reformation Publishers—R
(s)-Self Publish Press—R
(s)-So. Baptist Press—R
(s)-Tate Publishing—R
(s)-VMI Publishers
Whitaker House
(s)-WinePress—R

FICTION: FRONTIER/ROMANCE

(s)-ACW Press—R
Ambassador-Emerald—R
(s)-American Binding—R
Baker Books
Baker's Plays—R
Barbour
(s)-Black Forest/Tennessee—R
(s)-Booklocker.com—R
(s)-Brentwood—R
(s)-Brown Books—R
Christian Writer's Ebook—R
(s)-Elderberry Press
(s)-Essence—R
(s)-Fairway Press—R
Heartsong Presents
Hidden Brook Press—R
(s)-Insight Publishing—R
(s)-Lifevest Publishing
Lighthouse Publishing—R
(s)-Lightning Star Press—R
Love Inspired Historical
MoreThanNovellas
MountainView

Multnomah
(s)-One World—R
Parson Place—R
(s)-Pleasant Word—R
PREP Publishing—R
Randall House
Ravenhawk Books—R
(s)-Reformation Publishers—R
(s)-Self Publish Press—R
(s)-So. Baptist Press—R
Sweetheart Romances
(s)-Tate Publishing—R
Vintage Romance
(s)-VMI Publishers
Whitaker House
White Rose
White Stone Books—R
(s)-WinePress—R

FICTION: HISTORICAL

(s)-ACW Press—R
Ambassador Books
Ambassador-Emerald—R
(s)-American Binding—R
Atheneum/Yg Readers
Avon Inspire
B & H Publishing
Baker Books
Baker Trittin
Baker's Plays—R
Ballantine
Bethany House
BJU/Journey Forth—R
(s)-Black Forest/Tennessee—R
Blue Dolphin
(s)-Booklocker.com—R
Boyds Mills Press—R
Branden Publishing—R
Breakneck Books—R
(s)-Brentwood—R
(s)-Brown Books—R
Capstone Fiction—R
CharismaKids
Christian Family—R
Christian Liberty Press
Christian Writer's Ebook—R
(s)-Creation House—R
DiskUs Publishing
Dove Inspirational
E-Digital Books
Eerdmans Pub., Wm. B.—R
Eerdmans/Yg Readers
(s)-Elderberry Press
Emerald Pointe Bks
(s)-Essence—R
(s)-Fairway Press—R
FaithKidz
Fifth Estate—R
Focus on the Family
(s)-Hannibal Books—R
HeartQuest
Hidden Brook Press—R
(s)-Holy Fire Publishing—R
(s)-Insight Publishing—R
Knight George Pub.
Kregel—R
(s)-Lifevest Publishing
Lift Every Voice—R
Lighthouse Publishing—R
Mission City Press
Moody Publishers
MountainView
Multnomah
NavPress
Nelson, Fiction, Thomas
New Canaan—R
(s)-One World—R
One World/Ballantine
P & R Publishing—R
Parson Place—R
(s)-Pleasant Word—R
(s)-Providence Pub.—R
Putnam/Young Readers
Quintessential Books—R
Randall House
Ravenhawk Books—R
Realms
(s)-Reformation Publishers—R
Reformation Trust
Revell
(s)-Scribe Book—R
(s)-Self Publish Press—R
(s)-So. Baptist Press—R
Steeple Hill/Single Title
Strang Book Group—R
(s)-Tate Publishing—R
Third World Press—R
Treble Heart Books—R
Vintage Romance
Vision Forum
(s)-VMI Publishers
WaterBrook Press—R
Whitaker House
White Stone Books—R
WindRiver—R
(s)-WinePress—R

FICTION: HISTORICAL/ROMANCE

(s)-ACW Press—R
Ambassador-Emerald—R
(s)-American Binding—R
B & H Publishing
Baker Books
Baker's Plays—R
Barbour
(s)-Black Forest/Tennessee—R
(s)-Book Publishers—R
(s)-Booklocker.com—R
(s)-Brentwood—R
(s)-Brown Books—R
Christian Writer's Ebook—R
(s)-Elderberry Press
Emerald Pointe Bks
(s)-Essence—R
(s)-Fairway Press—R
(s)-Hannibal Books—R
Harvest House
Heartsong Presents
Hidden Brook Press—R
(s)-Insight Publishing—R
(s)-Lifevest Publishing
Lift Every Voice—R
Lighthouse Publishing—R
Love Inspired Historical
MoreThanNovellas
MountainView
Multnomah
Nelson, Fiction, Thomas
(s)-One World—R
Parson Place—R
(s)-Pleasant Word—R
Putnam/Young Readers
Randall House
Ravenhawk Books—R
(s)-Reformation Publishers—R
(s)-Self Publish Press—R
(s)-So. Baptist Press—R
Steeple Hill/Single Title
Sweetheart Romances
(s)-Tate Publishing—R
Tyndale House—R
Vintage Romance
(s)-VMI Publishers
WaterBrook Press—R
Whitaker House
White Rose
White Stone Books—R
(s)-WinePress—R

FICTION: HUMOR

(s)-ACW Press—R
Ambassador Books
Ambassador-Emerald—R
(s)-American Binding—R
American Book
Atheneum/Yg Readers
Baker Books
Baker Trittin
Baker's Plays—R
Ballantine
BelleBooks—R
Bethany House
Big Idea
BJU/Journey Forth—R
(s)-Black Forest/Tennessee—R
(s)-Booklocker.com—R
Boyds Mills Press—R
(s)-Brown Books—R
Christian Focus—R
Christian Writer's Ebook—R
DiskUs Publishing

E-Digital Books
Eerdmans/Yg Readers
(s)-Elderberry Press
(s)-Essence—R
Evergreen Press
(s)-Fairway Press—R
FaithWords
Harvest House
Hidden Brook Press—R
(s)-Holy Fire Publishing—R
(s)-Insight Publishing—R
(s)-J and J Publishing
Kaleidoscope Press—R
Knight George Pub.
(s)-Lifevest Publishing
Lift Every Voice—R
Lighthouse Publishing—R
MountainView
Multnomah
NavPress Th1nk—R
(s)-One World—R
One World/Ballantine
P & R Publishing—R
Parson Place—R
(s)-Pleasant Word—R
Putnam/Young Readers
Quintessential Books—R
Randall House
Ravenhawk Books—R
(s)-Reformation Publishers—R
Salt Works
(s)-Scribe Book—R
(s)-Selah Publishing—R
(s)-Tate Publishing—R
Treble Heart Books—R
(s)-VMI Publishers
White Stone Books—R
WindRiver—R
(s)-WinePress—R

FICTION: JUVENILE (Ages 8-12)

(s)-ACW Press—R
Ambassador Books
Ambassador-Emerald—R
(s)-American Binding—R
Atheneum/Yg Readers
Avon Inspire
Baal Hamon—R
Baker Books
Baker Trittin
Barbour
BelleBooks—R
Bethany House
Big Idea
BJU/Journey Forth—R
(s)-Black Forest/Tennessee—R
Blue Dolphin
(s)-Booklocker.com—R
Boyds Mills Press—R
Branden Publishing—R
(s)-Brown Books—R
Carson-Dellosa
Christian Focus—R
(s)-Creation House—R
(s)-Dean Press, Robbie—R
DiskUs Publishing
Dover Publications—R
E-Digital Books
Eerdmans Pub., Wm. B.—R
Eerdmans/Yg Readers
(s)-Elderberry Press
(s)-Essence—R
Evergreen Press
(s)-Fairway Press—R
FaithKidz
Guardian Angel
Hidden Brook Press—R
(s)-Holy Fire Publishing—R
Ideals Publications
(s)-Insight Publishing—R
(s)-J and J Publishing
Journey Stone—R
Kaleidoscope Press—R
(s)-Kindred Books—R
Knight George Pub.
Kregel—R
Kregel Kidzone
Lifesong Publishers
(s)-Lifevest Publishing
Lift Every Voice—R
Lighthouse Publishing—R
(s)-Lightning Star Press—R
Mission City Press
Moody Publishers
New Canaan—R
(s)-One World—R
P & R Publishing—R
Pacific Press
Parson Place—R
Pauline Books—R
(s)-Pleasant Word—R
(s)-Providence Pub.—R
Putnam/Young Readers
(s)-Reformation Publishers—R
Reformation Trust
Salt Works
Salty's Books
(s)-Selah Publishing—R
(s)-Self Publish Press—R
Standard Publishing
Starik Publishing
(s)-Tate Publishing—R
Third World Press—R
Tyndale House—R
Vintage Romance
(s)-VMI Publishers
Walk Worthy—R
White Stone Books—R
WindRiver—R
(s)-WinePress—R
(s)-Word Alive

FICTION: LITERARY

(s)-ACW Press—R
Ambassador Books
Ambassador-Emerald—R
(s)-American Binding—R
Atheneum/Yg Readers
B & H Publishing
Baker Books
Baker's Plays—R
Ballantine
Bethany House
(s)-Black Forest/Tennessee—R
Blue Dolphin
(s)-Booklocker.com—R
Boyds Mills Press—R
Branden Publishing—R
(s)-Brown Books—R
Christian Writer's Ebook—R
Cladach Publishing
DiskUs Publishing
Dover Publications—R
E-Digital Books
Eerdmans Pub., Wm. B.—R
Eerdmans/Yg Readers
(s)-Elderberry Press
(s)-Essence—R
(s)-Fairway Press—R
FaithWalk
FaithWords
Focus on the Family
Guernica Editions—R
HarperOne
Hidden Brook Press—R
(s)-Insight Publishing—R
Invisible College Press
(s)-Lifevest Publishing
Lighthouse Publishing—R
Moody Publishers
Mt. Olive College Press
Multnomah
NavPress
Nelson, Fiction, Thomas
(s)-One World—R
One World/Ballantine
P & R Publishing—R
Pauline Books—R
(s)-Pleasant Word—R
PREP Publishing—R
Putnam/Young Readers
Quintessential Books—R
Ravenhawk Books—R
(s)-Reformation Publishers—R
Salt Works
(s)-Scribe Book—R
(s)-Self Publish Press—R
Skysong Press
Steeple Hill/Single Title
(s)-Tate Publishing—R
Third World Press—R
Virginia Pines Press
(s)-VMI Publishers

Walk Worthy—R
WaterBrook Press—R
White Stone Books—R
(s)-WinePress—R

FICTION: MYSTERY/ROMANCE

(s)-ACW Press—R
(s)-American Binding—R
Baker Books
Baker's Plays—R
Ballantine
Barbour
Bethany House
(s)-Black Forest/Tennessee—R
(s)-Book Publishers—R
(s)-Booklocker.com—R
(s)-Brentwood—R
(s)-Brown Books—R
Christian Writer's Ebook—R
Destiny Image—R
(s)-Elderberry Press
(s)-Essence—R
(s)-Fairway Press—R
FaithWords
Genesis Press—R
GuidepostsBooks
Harvest House
Heartsong/Mysteries
Hidden Brook Press—R
(s)-Insight Publishing—R
(s)-Lifevest Publishing
Lift Every Voice—R
Lighthouse Publishing—R
(s)-Lightning Star Press—R
Love Inspired Suspense
MoreThanNovellas
MountainView
Multnomah
Nelson, Fiction, Thomas
(s)-One World—R
Parson Place—R
(s)-Pleasant Word—R
PREP Publishing—R
(s)-Providence Pub.—R
Randall House
(s)-Reformation Publishers—R
(s)-Scribe Book—R
(s)-Selah Publishing—R
(s)-Self Publish Press—R
(s)-So. Baptist Press—R
Starik Publishing
Steeple Hill/Single Title
Sweetheart Romances
(s)-Tate Publishing—R
Vintage Romance
(s)-VMI Publishers
White Rose
White Stone Books—R
WindRiver—R
(s)-WinePress—R

FICTION: MYSTERY/SUSPENSE

(s)-ACW Press—R
Ambassador Books
Ambassador-Emerald—R
(s)-American Binding—R
American Book
Avon Inspire
B & H Publishing
Baker Books
Baker's Plays—R
Ballantine
Bethany House
(s)-Black Forest/Tennessee—R
(s)-Booklocker.com—R
Breakneck Books—R
(s)-Brown Books—R
Capstone Fiction—R
Christian Ed. Pub.
Christian Focus—R
Christian Writer's Ebook—R
Descant Publishing
DiskUs Publishing
E-Digital Books
Eerdmans/Yg Readers
(s)-Elderberry Press
(s)-Essence—R
(s)-Fairway Press—R
FaithWords
Focus on the Family
Genesis Press—R
GuidepostsBooks
Harvest House
HeartQuest
Hidden Brook Press—R
(s)-Holy Fire Publishing—R
Howard Books
(s)-Insight Publishing—R
Invisible College Press
Jireh Publishing
Kregel—R
(s)-Lifevest Publishing
Lift Every Voice—R
Lighthouse Publishing—R
Love Inspired Suspense
Mission City Press
Moody Publishers
MountainView
Mt. Olive College Press
Multnomah
Nelson, Fiction, Thomas
(s)-One World—R
One World/Ballantine
Parson Place—R
(s)-Pleasant Word—R
(s)-Providence Pub.—R
Putnam/Young Readers
Quintessential Books—R
Ravenhawk Books—R
(s)-Reformation Publishers—R
Revell
Salt Works
(s)-Scribe Book—R
(s)-Selah Publishing—R
(s)-Self Publish Press—R
Starik Publishing
(s)-Tate Publishing—R
Treble Heart Books—R
Tyndale House—R
(s)-VMI Publishers
WindRiver—R
(s)-WinePress—R

FICTION: NOVELLAS

(s)-ACW Press—R
(s)-American Binding—R
Atheneum/Yg Readers
Baker Books
Barbour
(s)-Black Forest/Tennessee—R
(s)-Booklocker.com—R
(s)-Brown Books—R
Christian Writer's Ebook—R
(s)-Elderberry Press
(s)-Essence—R
(s)-Fairway Press—R
Hidden Brook Press—R
(s)-Insight Publishing—R
Lift Every Voice—R
Lighthouse Publishing—R
Mission City Press
MoreThanNovellas
MountainView
(s)-One World—R
(s)-Pleasant Word—R
Quintessential Books—R
(s)-Reformation Publishers—R
Salt Works
White Stone Books—R

FICTION: PLAYS

A.D. Players Theater
(s)-American Binding—R
Baker's Plays—R
(s)-Brentwood—R
Bridge Resources
CSS Publishing—R
Dover Publications—R
Eldridge Plays
(s)-Essence—R
(s)-Fairway Press—R
Guardian Angel
(s)-Holy Fire Publishing—R
(s)-IMD Press—R
Lillenas
Meriwether
Mission City Press
Mt. Olive College Press
(s)-One World—R
(s)-Path Publishing in Christ—R
Players Press—R

(s)-Pleasant Word—R
Salt Works
(s)-So. Baptist Press—R
Third World Press—R

FICTION: ROMANCE

(s)-ACW Press—R
(s)-American Binding—R
American Book
B & H Publishing
Baker Books
Baker's Plays—R
Ballantine
Barbour
(s)-Black Forest/Tennessee—R
(s)-Booklocker.com—R
(s)-Brown Books—R
By Grace Publications
Capstone Fiction—R
Christian Writer's Ebook—R
DiskUs Publishing
E-Digital Books
(s)-Elderberry Press
(s)-Essence—R
(s)-Fairway Press—R
Genesis Press—R
(s)-Hannibal Books—R
Heartsong Presents
Hidden Brook Press—R
(s)-Insight Publishing—R
(s)-J and J Publishing
Jireh Publishing
(s)-Lifevest Publishing
Lift Every Voice—R
Lighthouse Publishing—R
(s)-Lightning Star Press—R
Love Inspired
Love Inspired Suspense
MoreThanNovellas
MountainView
Multnomah
Nelson, Fiction, Thomas
(s)-One World—R
One World/Ballantine
Parson Place—R
Parsons Publishing—R
(s)-Pleasant Word—R
PREP Publishing—R
Randall House
(s)-Reformation Publishers—R
(s)-Selah Publishing—R
Steeple Hill/Single Title
Sweetheart Romances
(s)-Tate Publishing—R
Treble Heart Books—R
Tyndale House—R
Vintage Romance
(s)-VMI Publishers
WaterBrook Press—R
Whitaker House
White Rose
White Stone Books—R
WindRiver—R
(s)-WinePress—R

FICTION: SCIENCE FICTION

(s)-ACW Press—R
(s)-American Binding—R
American Book
Atheneum/Yg Readers
Baker's Plays—R
Bethany House
(s)-Black Forest/Tennessee—R
(s)-Booklocker.com—R
Breakneck Books—R
(s)-Brown Books—R
Capstone Fiction—R
Christian Focus—R
Christian Writer's Ebook—R
Descant Publishing
Destiny Image—R
DiskUs Publishing
Dover Publications—R
(s)-Elderberry Press
Evergreen Press
(s)-Fairway Press—R
Fifth Estate—R
Genesis Press—R
Hidden Brook Press—R
(s)-Insight Publishing—R
Invisible College Press
(s)-Lifevest Publishing
Lift Every Voice—R
Lighthouse Publishing—R
(s)-Lightning Star Press—R
MountainView
(s)-One World—R
P & R Publishing—R
(s)-Pleasant Word—R
Putnam/Young Readers
Quintessential Books—R
Realms
(s)-Reformation Publishers—R
Skysong Press
Strang Book Group—R
(s)-Tate Publishing—R
Treble Heart Books—R
(s)-VMI Publishers
WaterBrook Press—R
WindRiver—R
(s)-WinePress—R

FICTION: SHORT STORY COLLECTION

(s)-ACW Press—R
(s)-American Binding—R
Atheneum/Yg Readers
Baker Books
Baker Trittin
Ballantine
BelleBooks—R
(s)-Black Forest/Tennessee—R
(s)-Booklocker.com—R
Branden Publishing—R
(s)-Brown Books—R
Christian Writer's Ebook—R
DiskUs Publishing
E-Digital Books
Eerdmans Pub., Wm. B.—R
Ekklesia Press—R
(s)-Elderberry Press
(s)-Essence—R
(s)-Fairway Press—R
Hidden Brook Press—R
(s)-Holy Fire Publishing—R
(s)-IMD Press—R
(s)-Insight Publishing—R
Kaleidoscope Press—R
Knight George Pub.
Lift Every Voice—R
Lighthouse Publishing—R
(s)-Lightning Star Press—R
MountainView
Mt. Olive College Press
(s)-One World—R
Parson Place—R
(s)-Pleasant Word—R
Quintessential Books—R
Randall House
(s)-Reformation Publishers—R
Salt Works
(s)-Scribe Book—R
(s)-Tate Publishing—R
Third World Press—R
Treble Heart Books—R
(s)-VMI Publishers
Walk Worthy—R
(s)-WinePress—R

FICTION: SPECULATIVE

(s)-ACW Press—R
(s)-American Binding—R
Baker Books
Baker's Plays—R
Bethany House
(s)-Black Forest/Tennessee—R
Blue Dolphin
(s)-Booklocker.com—R
Breakneck Books—R
(s)-Brown Books—R
Capstone Fiction—R
Christian Writer's Ebook—R
(s)-Elderberry Press
(s)-Essence—R
Fifth Estate—R
Hidden Brook Press—R
(s)-Holy Fire Publishing—R
(s)-Insight Publishing—R
(s)-Lifevest Publishing
Lighthouse Publishing—R
MountainView
Multnomah

(s)-One World—R
(s)-Pleasant Word—R
Realms
(s)-Reformation Publishers—R
Strang Book Group—R
(s)-Tate Publishing—R
(s)-VMI Publishers
(s)-WinePress—R

FICTION: TEEN/YOUNG ADULT

(s)-ACW Press—R
Ambassador Books
(s)-American Binding—R
American Book
AMG Publishers—R
Atheneum/Yg Readers
Baal Hamon—R
Baker Books
Baker Trittin
Barbour
BelleBooks—R
Bethany House
Big Idea
BJU/Journey Forth—R
(s)-Black Forest/Tennessee—R
Blue Dolphin
(s)-Book Publishers—R
(s)-Booklocker.com—R
Boyds Mills Press—R
(s)-Brown Books—R
Christian Focus—R
Christian Writer's Ebook—R
(s)-Creation House—R
DiskUs Publishing
E-Digital Books
Eerdmans/Yg Readers
(s)-Elderberry Press
(s)-Essence—R
Evergreen Press
(s)-Fairway Press—R
Faith Communications
Hidden Brook Press—R
(s)-Holy Fire Publishing—R
(s)-Insight Publishing—R
(s)-J and J Publishing
Kregel—R
Legacy Press—R
(s)-Lifevest Publishing
Lift Every Voice—R
Lighthouse Publishing—R
Lighthouse Trails—R
(s)-Lightning Star Press—R
Mission City Press
Moody Publishers
MountainView
Multnomah
NavPress
NavPress Th1nk—R
Nelson, Fiction, Thomas
New Canaan—R
(s)-One World—R
Parson Place—R
Pauline Books—R
(s)-Pleasant Word—R
Putnam/Young Readers
Randall House
Ravenhawk Books—R
(s)-Reformation Publishers—R
(s)-Selah Publishing—R
Starik Publishing
(s)-Tate Publishing—R
Third World Press—R
Vintage Romance
Virginia Pines Press
(s)-VMI Publishers
Walk Worthy—R
WaterBrook Press—R
WindRiver—R
(s)-WinePress—R
(s)-Word Alive

FICTION: WESTERNS

(s)-ACW Press—R
(s)-American Binding—R
B & H Publishing
Baker Books
Baker Trittin
Baker's Plays—R
BJU/Journey Forth—R
(s)-Black Forest/Tennessee—R
(s)-Booklocker.com—R
(s)-Brown Books—R
Christian Writer's Ebook—R
DiskUs Publishing
E-Digital Books
(s)-Elderberry Press
(s)-Essence—R
(s)-Fairway Press—R
Hidden Brook Press—R
(s)-Insight Publishing—R
(s)-Lifevest Publishing
Lighthouse Publishing—R
MountainView
Multnomah
(s)-One World—R
P & R Publishing—R
Parson Place—R
(s)-Pleasant Word—R
Quintessential Books—R
Randall House
Ravenhawk Books—R
(s)-Reformation Publishers—R
(s)-Tate Publishing—R
Treble Heart Books—R
Vintage Romance
(s)-VMI Publishers
Whitaker House
White Stone Books—R
(s)-WinePress—R

FORGIVENESS

Abingdon Press
ACTA Publications
Alba House—R
Ambassador-Emerald—R
(s)-American Binding—R
Baal Hamon—R
Baker Trittin
Baker's Plays—R
Barbour
Bethany House
(s)-Black Forest/Tennessee—R
(s)-Booklocker.com—R
Bridge-Logos—R
(s)-Brown Books—R
Carepoint Publishing—R
Chalice Press
Christian Family—R
Christian Focus—R
Christian Writer's Ebook—R
(s)-Creation House—R
CSS Publishing—R
(s)-DCTS Publishing
Discovery House—R
Doubleday—R
Editorial Portavoz
Eerdmans Pub., Wm. B.—R
(s)-Elderberry Press
(s)-Essence—R
Evergreen Press
(s)-Fairway Press—R
FaithWalk
FaithWords
Forward Movement
Good News Pub.
Green Key Books
Greenwood/Praeger
Guardian Angel
HarperOne
Harrison House
Hensley Publishing
Hidden Brook Press—R
(s)-Holy Fire Publishing—R
Howard Books
(s)-IMD Press—R
Jossey-Bass
Judson Press
Kregel—R
Life Journey Books
Lift Every Voice—R
Lighthouse Publishing—R
Living Books for All
Marshall Trumann
MegaGrace Books
Monarch Books
NavPress
NavPress Th1nk—R
Nelson, Thomas
New Leaf
(s)-One World—R
P & R Publishing—R
Pacific Press
Parson Place—R
Parsons Publishing—R
Pilgrim Press—R

(s)-Pleasant Word—R
(s)-Providence Pub.—R
Randall House
(s)-Reformation Publishers—R
Regal
Rose Publishing
Salt Works
Salvation Publisher—R
(s)-Scribe Book—R
St. Anthony Mess. Press—R
(s)-Star Bible Public.
Strang Book Group—R
(s)-Synergy Publishers—R
(s)-Tate Publishing—R
Torch Legacy
(s)-Trafford Publishing—R
(s)-VMI Publishers
Wesleyan Publishing
White Stone Books—R
WindRiver—R
(s)-WinePress—R
(s)-Word Alive
World Publishing
(s)-Zoe Life Publishing

GAMES/CRAFTS

Baker Books
Big Idea
(s)-Booklocker.com—R
Contemporary Drama
(s)-Elderberry Press
(s)-Essence—R
(s)-Fairway Press—R
Group Publishing
Guardian Angel
Harcourt Religion
Hidden Brook Press—R
(s)-Holy Fire Publishing—R
Jubilant Press—R
Kaleidoscope Press—R
Knight George Pub.
Legacy Press—R
Lighthouse Publishing—R
Mission City Press
Monarch Books
Morehouse—R
(s)-One World—R
Pflaum Publishing
Players Press—R
Rainbow Publishers—R
Salt Works
Standard Publishing
(s)-Tate Publishing—R
(s)-Trafford Publishing—R
Wood Lake Books—R
(s)-Zoe Life Publishing

GIFT BOOKS

ACTA Publications
Adams Media
Ambassador Books
(s)-American Binding—R
B & H Publishing
Baker Books
Ballantine
Barbour
Big Idea
(s)-Black Forest/Tennessee—R
Blue Mountain Arts
(s)-Book Publishers—R
(s)-Booklocker.com—R
(s)-Brown Books—R
Christian Writer's Ebook—R
Contemporary Drama
Cook, David C.
Countryman, J.
(s)-Creation House—R
Cumberland House
(s)-DCTS Publishing
(s)-Dean Press, Robbie—R
Dimensions for Living
Editorial Portavoz
Eerdmans Pub., Wm. B.—R
(s)-Elderberry Press
(s)-Essence—R
Evergreen Press
(s)-Fairway Press—R
Faith Communications
Gollehon Press
Green Key Books
GRQ—R
Guardian Angel
HarperOne
Hay House
Hidden Brook Press—R
Hill Street Press—R
(s)-Holy Fire Publishing—R
Honor Books
Howard Books
Illumination Arts
(s)-IMD Press—R
Kaleidoscope Press—R
Lift Every Voice—R
Lighthouse Publishing—R
Monarch Books
Mt. Olive College Press
New Leaf
New Seeds—R
(s)-One World—R
Our Sunday Visitor—R
Peter Pauper Press
(s)-Pleasant Word—R
(s)-Providence Pub.—R
Ravenhawk Books—R
(s)-Reformation Publishers—R
Regal
Rose Publishing
Salt Works
(s)-Tate Publishing—R
(s)-Trafford Publishing—R
(s)-VMI Publishers
White Stone Books—R
(s)-WinePress—R
Woodland Gospel
(s)-Word Alive

GRIEF*

Abingdon Press
ACTA Publications
(s)-American Binding—R
Anglicans United—R
(s)-Black Forest/Tennessee—R
(s)-Booklocker.com—R
(s)-Brown Books—R
Carepoint Publishing—R
Chalice Press
Crossroad Publishing—R
Dabbling Mum Press
Discovery House—R
(s)-Elderberry Press
(s)-Essence—R
Good News Pub.
Harvest House
(s)-IMD Press—R
Judson Press
Lighthouse Publishing—R
Lutterworth Press—R
Monarch Books
Parson Place—R
Pauline Books—R
(s)-Providence Pub.—R
Randall House
(s)-Reformation Publishers—R
Regal
Resource Public.
Salvation Publisher—R
(s)-Scribe Book—R
(s)-Star Bible Public.
Whitaker House

GROUP STUDY BOOKS

Abingdon Press
(s)-American Binding—R
AMG Publishers—R
Baker Books
Baker Trittin
BMH Books
(s)-Booklocker.com—R
(s)-Brentwood—R
Bridge Resources
Carepoint Publishing—R
Carey Library, Wm.—R
Chalice Press
Christian Writer's Ebook—R
(s)-Creation House—R
CSS Publishing—R
Educational Ministries
Emmaus Road—R
(s)-Essence—R
Evergreen Press
(s)-Fairway Press—R
Founders Press
Gospel Publishing
Group Publishing
GRQ—R
(s)-Hannibal Books—R

Hensley Publishing
Hidden Brook Press—R
Hill Street Press—R
(s)-IMD Press—R
Jubilant Press—R
Judson Press
Lift Every Voice—R
Lighthouse Publishing—R
Liturgy Training—R
Living Books for All
Marshall Trumann
Mission City Press
Monarch Books
NavPress Th1nk—R
New Hope—R
(s)-One World—R
P & R Publishing—R
Pacific Press
Paradise Research—R
Parson Place—R
Parsons Publishing—R
Pilgrim Press—R
(s)-Pleasant Word—R
(s)-Providence Pub.—R
Randall House
(s)-Reformation Publishers—R
Regal
Rose Publishing
(s)-Scribe Book—R
Smyth & Helwys
(s)-So. Baptist Press—R
St. Anthony Mess. Press—R
(s)-Star Bible Public.
(s)-Tate Publishing—R
(s)-Trafford Publishing—R
UMI Publishing—R
(s)-VMI Publishers
Wesleyan Publishing
WindRiver—R
(s)-WinePress—R
(s)-Word Alive
(s)-Zoe Life Publishing

HEALING

ACTA Publications
(s)-American Binding—R
Augsburg—R
Baal Hamon—R
Baker Books
Baker's Plays—R
(s)-Black Forest/Tennessee—R
Blue Dolphin
(s)-Book Publishers—R
(s)-Booklocker.com—R
(s)-Brentwood—R
Bridge-Logos—R
(s)-Brown Books—R
Canticle Books—R
Carepoint Publishing—R
Chalice Press
Christian Heritage—R
Christian Writer's Ebook—R
Cook, David C.
(s)-Creation House—R
CSS Publishing—R
Destiny Image—R
(s)-Elderberry Press
(s)-Essence—R
(s)-Fairway Press—R
FaithWalk
FaithWords
Forward Movement
Good Book—R
Gospel Publishing
Greenwood/Praeger
Harrison House
Haworth Pastoral—R
Hay House
Hidden Brook Press—R
Hill Street Press—R
(s)-Holy Fire Publishing—R
Hope Publishing—R
(s)-Impact Christian—R
Jireh Publishing
Life Changing Media
Life Journey Books
Lighthouse Publishing—R
(s)-Lightning Star Press—R
Living Books for All
Loyola Press
Magnus Press—R
Marshall Trumann
(s)-McDougal Publishing—R
Monarch Books
Northstone
(s)-One World—R
Pacific Press
Paradise Research—R
Parson Place—R
Parsons Publishing—R
(s)-Path Publishing in Christ—R
Pauline Books—R
Pilgrim Press—R
(s)-Pleasant Word—R
(s)-Providence Pub.—R
(s)-Recovery Commun.
(s)-Reformation Publishers—R
Regal
Revival Nation
RiverOak
Salvation Publisher—R
(s)-Scribe Book—R
(s)-Selah Publishing—R
Siloam
(s)-So. Baptist Press—R
(s)-Star Bible Public.
Strang Book Group—R
(s)-Synergy Publishers—R
(s)-Tate Publishing—R
(s)-Trafford Publishing—R
(s)-VMI Publishers
Wesleyan Publishing
Whitaker House
(s)-WinePress—R
Wood Lake Books—R
(s)-Word Alive
World Publishing
(s)-Zoe Life Publishing

HEALTH

Ambassador Books
(s)-American Binding—R
Baal Hamon—R
Baker Books
Baker's Plays—R
Ballantine
Blue Dolphin
(s)-Book Publishers—R
(s)-Booklocker.com—R
Branden Publishing—R
(s)-Brentwood—R
(s)-Brown Books—R
Chalice Press
Christian Writer's Ebook—R
Cladach Publishing
(s)-Creation House—R
(s)-Elderberry Press
(s)-Essence—R
Evergreen Press
Facts on File
(s)-Fairway Press—R
FaithWords
Forward Movement
Good Book—R
Greenwood/Praeger
GRQ—R
Grupo Nelson
Harrison House
Harvest House
Haworth Pastoral—R
Hay House
Health Commun.
Hidden Brook Press—R
Hill Street Press—R
(s)-Holy Fire Publishing—R
Hope Publishing—R
(s)-IMD Press—R
Judson Press
Kaleidoscope Press—R
Langmarc
Legacy Publishers
Life Changing Media
Life Cycle Books—R
Lift Every Voice—R
Lighthouse Publishing—R
Loyola Press
Marshall Trumann
Monarch Books
MountainView
Nelson, Thomas
New Hope—R
(s)-One World—R
Pacific Press
Paradise Research—R
Parson Place—R
Parsons Publishing—R

(s)-Path Publishing in Christ—R
(s)-Pleasant Word—R
(s)-Providence Pub.—R
Quintessential Books—R
(s)-Recovery Commun.
(s)-Reformation Publishers—R
Regal
Regnery
RiverOak
Salvation Publisher—R
Siloam
(s)-So. Baptist Press—R
(s)-Star Bible Public.
Strang Book Group—R
Tarcher, Jeremy P.—R
(s)-Tate Publishing—R
(s)-TEACH Services—R
Third World Press—R
(s)-Trafford Publishing—R
Treble Heart Books—R
(s)-VMI Publishers
(s)-WinePress—R
Wood Lake Books—R
(s)-Word Alive
(s)-Zoe Life Publishing

HISTORICAL

Aadeon Publishing—R
Ambassador Books
(s)-American Binding—R
American Book
Atheneum/Yg Readers
B & H Publishing
Baker Academic
Baker Books
Baker's Plays—R
(s)-Black Forest/Tennessee—R
Blue Dolphin
(s)-Book Publishers—R
(s)-Booklocker.com—R
Boyds Mills Press—R
Branden Publishing—R
(s)-Brentwood—R
(s)-Brown Books—R
Canadian Inst. for Law—R
Canticle Books—R
Carey Library, Wm.—R
Catholic Answers—R
Chalice Press
Chapter Two—R
Christian Family—R
Christian Heritage—R
Christian Writer's Ebook—R
College Press—R
Conciliar Press—R
Continuum Intl.—R
(s)-Creation House—R
Cumberland House
Custom Communications
Doubleday—R
E-Digital Books
Eerdmans Pub., Wm. B.—R
(s)-Elderberry Press
(s)-Essence—R
ETC Publications
Facts on File
(s)-Fairway Press—R
FaithWalk
FaithWords
Fordham Univ. Press—R
Founders Press
Foursquare Media
Friends United Press
Good Book—R
Greenwood/Praeger
HarperOne
Harvest Day
Hidden Brook Press—R
Hill Street Press—R
(s)-Holy Fire Publishing—R
(s)-IMD Press—R
(s)-Impact Christian—R
Inkling Books—R
Johns Hopkins—R
Jossey-Bass
Kirk House
(s)-Lifevest Publishing
Lift Every Voice—R
Lighthouse Publishing—R
Loyola Press
Lutheran Univ. Press
Lutterworth Press—R
Mercer Univ. Press—R
Monarch Books
Mt. Olive College Press
New Leaf
New Seeds—R
New York Univ. Press
Northstone
(s)-One World—R
One World/Ballantine
P & R Publishing—R
Paradise Research—R
Parson Place—R
Parsons Publishing—R
Pauline Books—R
(s)-Pleasant Word—R
(s)-Providence Pub.—R
Quintessential Books—R
Ragged Edge—R
(s)-Reformation Publishers—R
Regnery
RiverOak
Rose Publishing
Scepter Publishers—R
(s)-So. Baptist Press—R
St. Augustine's Press—R
(s)-Star Bible Public.
Still Waters Revival—R
(s)-Tate Publishing—R
Third World Press—R
(s)-Trafford Publishing—R
Trinity Foundation—R
Univ. of AR Press—R
Univ. Press of America—R
Virginia Pines Press
WindRiver—R
(s)-WinePress—R
(s)-Winer Foundation—R
Wood Lake Books—R
(s)-Word Alive
Yale Univ. Press—R

HOLIDAY/SEASONAL

ACTA Publications
Airleaf Publishing
Ambassador Books
(s)-American Binding—R
Augsburg—R
Baker Trittin
Baker's Plays—R
Barbour
(s)-Book Publishers—R
(s)-Booklocker.com—R
Boyds Mills Press—R
(s)-Brown Books—R
Chalice Press
Christian Writer's Ebook—R
Cook, David C.
(s)-Creation House—R
CSS Publishing—R
Cumberland House
Discovery House—R
Educational Ministries
(s)-Elderberry Press
Eldridge Plays
(s)-Essence—R
Evergreen Press
(s)-Fairway Press—R
FaithWords
FamilyLife (books)—R
Forward Movement
Good News Pub.
Greenwood/Praeger
Guardian Angel
GuidepostsBooks
HarperOne
Hidden Brook Press—R
(s)-Holy Fire Publishing—R
Howard Books
(s)-IMD Press—R
Judson Press
Lift Every Voice—R
Lighthouse Publishing—R
Liturgy Training—R
Meriwether
Messianic Jewish—R
Monarch Books
(s)-One World—R
Parson Place—R
Pelican Publishing—R
Peter Pauper Press
(s)-Pleasant Word—R
(s)-Providence Pub.—R
Randall House
Ravenhawk Books—R

(s)-Reformation Publishers—R
Regal
Salt Works
St. Anthony Mess. Press—R
Standard Publishing
(s)-Tate Publishing—R
(s)-Trafford Publishing—R
(s)-VMI Publishers
White Stone Books—R
(s)-WinePress—R
(s)-Word Alive

HOLINESS

Alba House—R
Ambassador-Emerald—R
(s)-American Binding—R
Baal Hamon—R
Bethany House
(s)-Black Forest/Tennessee—R
(s)-Booklocker.com—R
Bridge-Logos—R
(s)-Brown Books—R
Chalice Press
Christian Family—R
Christian Focus—R
Christian Heritage—R
(s)-Elderberry Press
(s)-Essence—R
FaithWords
Forward Movement
Good News Pub.
Gospel Publishing
GRQ—R
Hidden Brook Press—R
(s)-Holy Fire Publishing—R
(s)-IMD Press—R
Monarch Books
NavPress Th1nk—R
Parson Place—R
Parsons Publishing—R
Pauline Books—R
(s)-Providence Pub.—R
(s)-Reformation Publishers—R
Reformation Trust
Regal
Salvation Publisher—R
St. Anthony Mess. Press—R
(s)-Star Bible Public.
Strang Book Group—R
(s)-Synergy Publishers—R
(s)-Tate Publishing—R
(s)-Trafford Publishing—R
Wesleyan Publishing
WindRiver—R
(s)-Zoe Life Publishing

HOLY SPIRIT

Alba House—R
Ambassador-Emerald—R
(s)-American Binding—R
Baal Hamon—R
Baker Trittin
Baker's Plays—R
Baylor Univ. Press
(s)-Black Forest/Tennessee—R
(s)-Booklocker.com—R
Bridge-Logos—R
(s)-Brown Books—R
Canticle Books—R
Chapter Two—R
Christian Family—R
Christian Focus—R
Christian Heritage—R
Christian Writer's Ebook—R
(s)-Creation House—R
CSS Publishing—R
Destiny Image—R
(s)-Elderberry Press
(s)-Essence—R
(s)-Fairway Press—R
FaithWords
Forward Movement
(s)-FruitBearer Pub.
Gospel Publishing
Greenwood/Praeger
GRQ—R
Harrison House
Hidden Brook Press—R
(s)-Holy Fire Publishing—R
(s)-IMD Press—R
Judson Press
Kregel—R
Lighthouse Publishing—R
Living Books for All
Magnus Press—R
Marshall Trumann
Monarch Books
NavPress Th1nk—R
(s)-One World—R
P & R Publishing—R
Pacific Press
Parsons Publishing—R
Pathway Press
Pauline Books—R
Pilgrim Press—R
(s)-Pleasant Word—R
(s)-Providence Pub.—R
(s)-Reformation Publishers—R
Regal
Revival Nation
Rose Publishing
Salvation Publisher—R
St. Anthony Mess. Press—R
(s)-Star Bible Public.
Strang Book Group—R
(s)-Synergy Publishers—R
(s)-Tate Publishing—R
(s)-Trafford Publishing—R
(s)-VMI Publishers
Wesleyan Publishing
Westminster John Knox
Whitaker House
(s)-WinePress—R
(s)-Word Alive
(s)-Zoe Life Publishing

HOMESCHOOLING RESOURCES

(s)-American Binding—R
B & H Publishing
Baker Books
Big Idea
(s)-Black Forest/Tennessee—R
(s)-Book Publishers—R
(s)-Booklocker.com—R
(s)-Brentwood—R
Christian Focus—R
Christian Writer's Ebook—R
(s)-Creation House—R
Ekklesia Press—R
(s)-Elderberry Press
(s)-Essence—R
(s)-Fairway Press—R
Guardian Angel
(s)-Hannibal Books—R
Heart of Wisdom
Hidden Brook Press—R
(s)-Holy Fire Publishing—R
(s)-IMD Press—R
Judson Press
Lighthouse Publishing—R
Marshall Trumann
Master Books
McRuffy Press
Mission City Press
Monarch Books
New Canaan—R
New Leaf
(s)-One World—R
P & R Publishing—R
(s)-Providence Pub.—R
(s)-Reformation Publishers—R
Rose Publishing
Starik Publishing
(s)-Tate Publishing—R
(s)-Trafford Publishing—R
Virginia Pines Press
(s)-WinePress—R
(s)-Word Alive
(s)-Zoe Life Publishing

HOMILETICS

Abingdon Press
ACTA Publications
Alba House—R
Ambassador-Emerald—R
(s)-American Binding—R
B & H Publishing
Baker Books
(s)-Black Forest/Tennessee—R
(s)-Booklocker.com—R
(s)-Brown Books—R
Chalice Press

Christian Family—R
Christian Focus—R
Christian Writer's Ebook—R
(s)-Creation House—R
CSS Publishing—R
(s)-DCTS Publishing
Earthen Vessel—R
Eerdmans Pub., Wm. B.—R
(s)-Elderberry Press
(s)-Essence—R
(s)-Fairway Press—R
Hendrickson—R
Hidden Brook Press—R
(s)-Holy Fire Publishing—R
(s)-IMD Press—R
InterVarsity Press—R
Judson Press
Kregel—R
Lighthouse Publishing—R
Liturgy Training—R
Lutheran Univ. Press
Monarch Books
(s)-One World—R
P & R Publishing—R
Parsons Publishing—R
Pauline Books—R
(s)-Pleasant Word—R
Presbyterian Pub.
(s)-Providence Pub.—R
(s)-Reformation Publishers—R
Resource Public.
St. Anthony Mess. Press—R
(s)-Star Bible Public.
(s)-Tate Publishing—R
(s)-Trafford Publishing—R
(s)-VMI Publishers
Westminster John Knox
(s)-WinePress—R
Wood Lake Books—R
(s)-Word Alive
(s)-Zoe Life Publishing

HOW-TO

Adams Media
(s)-American Binding—R
American Book
B & H Publishing
Baker Books
Ballantine
(s)-Black Forest/Tennessee—R
Blue Dolphin
BMH Books
(s)-Book Publishers—R
(s)-Booklocker.com—R
(s)-Brentwood—R
(s)-Brown Books—R
Christian Writer's Ebook—R
Church Growth Inst.
(s)-Creation House—R
Cumberland House
Dabbling Mum Press
Descant Publishing
Destiny Image—R
DiskUs Publishing
Educational Ministries
(s)-Elderberry Press
(s)-Essence—R
Evergreen Press
Fair Havens—R
(s)-Fairway Press—R
FaithWalk
FaithWords
Fell, Frederick—R
Gospel Light
Greenwood/Praeger
GRQ—R
Guardian Angel
Harcourt Religion
Hidden Brook Press—R
Hill Street Press—R
(s)-Holy Fire Publishing—R
(s)-IMD Press—R
Inkling Books—R
Judson Press
Kaleidoscope Press—R
Kirk House
(s)-Lifevest Publishing
Lift Every Voice—R
Lighthouse Publishing—R
(s)-Lightning Star Press—R
Marshall Trumann
MegaGrace Books
Meriwether
Monarch Books
MountainView
Mt. Olive College Press
(s)-One World—R
One World/Ballantine
Our Sunday Visitor—R
Pacific Press
Parson Place—R
(s)-Path Publishing in Christ—R
(s)-Path Publishing—R
Perigee Books
Players Press—R
(s)-Pleasant Word—R
PREP Publishing—R
(s)-Providence Pub.—R
Quintessential Books—R
(s)-Recovery Commun.
(s)-Reformation Publishers—R
Regal
Revell
RiverOak
Rose Publishing
Salt Works
Salvation Publisher—R
(s)-So. Baptist Press—R
Standard Publishing
Still Waters Revival—R
Tarcher, Jeremy P.—R
(s)-Tate Publishing—R
(s)-Trafford Publishing—R
Treble Heart Books—R
(s)-VMI Publishers
Walk Worthy—R
Wilshire Book—R
(s)-WinePress—R
(s)-Winer Foundation—R
(s)-Word Alive
(s)-Zoe Life Publishing

HUMOR

Ambassador Books
(s)-American Binding—R
American Book
B & H Publishing
Baker Books
Baker's Plays—R
Ballantine
Barbour
BelleBooks—R
(s)-Black Forest/Tennessee—R
Blue Dolphin
(s)-Booklocker.com—R
Boyds Mills Press—R
(s)-Brentwood—R
(s)-Brown Books—R
Christian Writer's Ebook—R
Cook, David C.
Countryman, J.
(s)-Creation House—R
Crossroad Publishing—R
Cumberland House
(s)-Elderberry Press
(s)-Essence—R
Evergreen Press
(s)-Fairway Press—R
FaithWords
Forward Movement
Friends United Press
GRQ—R
GuidepostsBooks
Harvest House
Hidden Brook Press—R
Hill Street Press—R
(s)-Holy Fire Publishing—R
Ideals/Children
Kaleidoscope Press—R
Kirk House
Lighthouse Publishing—R
Living Books for All
Loyola Press
Meriwether
Monarch Books
MOPS Intl.
NavPress Th1nk—R
(s)-One World—R
One World/Ballantine
Pacific Press
Parson Place—R
Parsons Publishing—R
(s)-Path Publishing in Christ—R

(s)-Pleasant Word—R
(s)-Providence Pub.—R
Quintessential Books—R
(s)-Reformation Publishers—R
Regal
RiverOak
Rose Publishing
Salvation Publisher—R
(s)-Scribe Book—R
(s)-Selah Publishing—R
(s)-So. Baptist Press—R
(s)-Tate Publishing—R
(s)-Trafford Publishing—R
Treble Heart Books—R
(s)-VMI Publishers
Walk Worthy—R
Wesleyan Publishing
White Stone Books—R
WindRiver—R
(s)-WinePress—R
(s)-Word Alive
(s)-Zoe Life Publishing

INSPIRATIONAL

Aadeon Publishing—R
Abingdon Press
ACTA Publications
Adams Media
Alba House—R
(s)-Ali Literary, Alfred—R
Ambassador Books
(s)-American Binding—R
American Book
B & H Publishing
Baal Hamon—R
Baker Books
Baker Trittin
Baker's Plays—R
Barbour
Beacon Hill Press—R
Bethany House
(s)-Black Forest/Tennessee—R
Blue Dolphin
BMH Books
(s)-Book Publishers—R
(s)-Booklocker.com—R
(s)-Brentwood—R
Bridge-Logos—R
(s)-Brown Books—R
Canticle Books—R
Catholic Book
Chapter Two—R
CharismaKids
Christian Family—R
Christian Focus—R
Christian Writer's Ebook—R
Concordia
Continuum Intl.—R
Countryman, J.
(s)-Creation House—R
Crossroad Publishing—R
CSS Publishing—R
(s)-DCTS Publishing
Destiny Image—R
Dimensions for Living
Discovery House—R
Doubleday—R
(s)-Elderberry Press
(s)-Essence—R
Evergreen Press
(s)-Fairway Press—R
Faith Communications
FaithWalk
FaithWords
Forward Movement
Friends United Press
Gollehon Press
Green Key Books
GRQ—R
Grupo Nelson
Guardian Angel
Harrison House
Harvest House
Hay House
Health Commun.
HeartSpring Pub.—R
Hidden Brook Press—R
Hill Street Press—R
(s)-Holy Fire Publishing—R
Hope Publishing—R
Howard Books
Ideals/Children
Illumination Arts
(s)-IMD Press—R
(s)-Impact Christian—R
(s)-J and J Publishing
Jebaire Publishing
Journey Stone—R
Judson Press
Kaleidoscope Press—R
Kirk House
Langmarc
Life Changing Media
(s)-Lifevest Publishing
Lift Every Voice—R
Lighthouse Publishing—R
(s)-Lightning Star Press—R
Living Books for All
Loyola Press
Lutheran Univ. Press
Magnus Press—R
Marshall Trumann
(s)-McDougal Publishing—R
MegaGrace Books
Monarch Books
MountainView
NavPress Th1nk—R
Nelson, Thomas
New Leaf
New Seeds—R
(s)-One World—R
Pacific Press
Parson Place—R
Parsons Publishing—R
(s)-Path Publishing in Christ—R
(s)-Path Publishing—R
Pauline Books—R
Paulist Press
Pelican Publishing—R
Perigee Books
Peter Pauper Press
Pilgrim Press—R
(s)-Pleasant Word—R
(s)-Providence Pub.—R
Quintessential Books—R
Ragged Edge—R
Ravenhawk Books—R
(s)-Reformation Publishers—R
Regal
RiverOak
Salvation Publisher—R
(s)-Scribe Book—R
(s)-Selah Publishing—R
Smyth & Helwys
(s)-So. Baptist Press—R
St. Anthony Mess. Press—R
(s)-Star Bible Public.
Starik Publishing
Strang Book Group—R
(s)-Synergy Publishers—R
(s)-Tate Publishing—R
Tau-Publishing—R
(s)-TEACH Services—R
Torch Legacy
TowleHouse—R
(s)-Trafford Publishing—R
Tyndale House—R
(s)-VMI Publishers
W Publishing
WaterBrook Press—R
Wesleyan Publishing
Whitaker House
White Stone Books—R
(s)-WinePress—R
(s)-Winer Foundation—R
Wood Lake Books—R
Woodland Gospel
(s)-Word Alive
World Publishing
(s)-Zoe Life Publishing

LEADERSHIP

Abingdon Press
(s)-American Binding—R
B & H Publishing
Baal Hamon—R
Baker Books
Baker's Plays—R
Beacon Hill Press—R
(s)-Black Forest/Tennessee—R
BMH Books
(s)-Book Publishers—R
(s)-Booklocker.com—R

Bridge Resources
Bridge-Logos—R
(s)-Brown Books—R
Chalice Press
Christian Family—R
Christian Focus—R
Christian Writer's Ebook—R
Church Growth Inst.
College Press—R
Cook, David C.
(s)-Creation House—R
Crossroad Publishing—R
CSS Publishing—R
(s)-DCTS Publishing
Destiny Image—R
Editorial Portavoz
(s)-Elderberry Press
(s)-Essence—R
Evergreen Press
(s)-Fairway Press—R
Faith Alive
FaithWalk
FaithWords
Gospel Publishing
Greenwood/Praeger
Group Publishing
Grupo Nelson
Guardian Angel
Harrison House
Harvest House
Hidden Brook Press—R
Hill Street Press—R
(s)-Holy Fire Publishing—R
(s)-IMD Press—R
InterVarsity Press—R
Jossey-Bass
Jubilant Press—R
Judson Press
Kirk House
Kregel—R
Lift Every Voice—R
Lighthouse Publishing—R
Living Books for All
Lutheran Univ. Press
Marshall Trumann
(s)-McDougal Publishing—R
MegaGrace Books
Monarch Books
NavPress
NavPress Th1nk—R
Neibauer Press—R
Nelson, Thomas
New Hope—R
New Leaf
(s)-One World—R
Parson Place—R
Parsons Publishing—R
Pilgrim Press—R
(s)-Pleasant Word—R
Ponder Publishing
Power Publishing
(s)-Providence Pub.—R
Quintessential Books—R
Randall House
(s)-Reformation Publishers—R
Regal
Rose Publishing
Salvation Publisher—R
(s)-Scribe Book—R
(s)-Selah Publishing—R
Standard Publishing
(s)-Star Bible Public.
(s)-Synergy Publishers—R
(s)-Tate Publishing—R
(s)-Trafford Publishing—R
UMI Publishing—R
Univ. Press of America—R
(s)-VMI Publishers
WaterBrook Press—R
Wesleyan Publishing
Whitaker House
White Stone Books—R
WindRiver—R
(s)-WinePress—R
(s)-Winer Foundation—R
Wood Lake Books—R
(s)-Word Alive
Yale Univ. Press—R
(s)-Zoe Life Publishing

LIFESTYLE*

(s)-American Binding—R
(s)-Booklocker.com—R
(s)-Brown Books—R
Chalice Press
Dabbling Mum Press
Discovery House—R
(s)-Elderberry Press
(s)-Essence—R
Fair Havens—R
Howard Books
Judson Press
Lighthouse Publishing—R
Monarch Books
NavPress
NavPress Th1nk—R
Pauline Books—R
(s)-Providence Pub.—R
Ravenhawk Books—R
(s)-Reformation Publishers—R
Regal
Salvation Publisher—R
(s)-Scribe Book—R
(s)-Star Bible Public.

LITURGICAL STUDIES

ACTA Publications
(s)-American Binding—R
American Cath. Press—R
Baker Books
Baker's Plays—R
(s)-Booklocker.com—R
(s)-Brentwood—R
(s)-Brown Books—R
Catholic Answers—R
Catholic Book
Chalice Press
Christian Heritage—R
Christian Writer's Ebook—R
Cistercian—R
Conciliar Press—R
Continuum Intl.—R
CSS Publishing—R
Doubleday—R
Eerdmans Pub., Wm. B.—R
(s)-Elderberry Press
(s)-Fairway Press—R
Greenwood/Praeger
Hidden Brook Press—R
(s)-Holy Fire Publishing—R
Johns Hopkins—R
Lighthouse Publishing—R
Liturgy Training—R
Lutheran Univ. Press
Lutterworth Press—R
Monarch Books
Morehouse—R
New Seeds—R
(s)-One World—R
Oregon Catholic
Pauline Books—R
Pilgrim Press—R
(s)-Pleasant Word—R
(s)-Providence Pub.—R
(s)-Reformation Publishers—R
Resource Public.
(s)-So. Baptist Press—R
St. Anthony Mess. Press—R
(s)-Tate Publishing—R
(s)-Trafford Publishing—R
Univ. Press of America—R
(s)-WinePress—R
(s)-Word Alive

MARRIAGE

Abingdon Press
ACTA Publications
Ambassador Books
Ambassador-Emerald—R
(s)-American Binding—R
Anglicans United—R
B & H Publishing
Baal Hamon—R
Baker Books
Baker's Plays—R
Barbour
Beacon Hill Press—R
BelleBooks—R
Bethany House
(s)-Black Forest/Tennessee—R
Blue Dolphin
(s)-Booklocker.com—R
(s)-Brentwood—R

Bridge-Logos—R
(s)-Brown Books—R
Catholic Answers—R
Christian Family—R
Christian Writer's Ebook—R
College Press—R
Cook, David C.
(s)-Creation House—R
Crossroad Publishing—R
CSS Publishing—R
Dabbling Mum Press
(s)-Dean Press, Robbie—R
Destiny Image—R
Dimensions for Living
Discovery House—R
Doubleday—R
Dove Inspirational
Editorial Portavoz
Eerdmans Pub., Wm. B.—R
(s)-Elderberry Press
Emmaus Road—R
(s)-Essence—R
Evergreen Press
(s)-Fairway Press—R
FaithWalk
FaithWords
FamilyLife (books)—R
Focus on the Family
Forward Movement
Good News Pub.
Greenwood/Praeger
GuidepostsBooks
HarperOne
Harrison House
Harvest House
Haworth Pastoral—R
Hensley Publishing
Hidden Brook Press—R
Hill Street Press—R
(s)-Holy Fire Publishing—R
Hope Publishing—R
Howard Books
(s)-IMD Press—R
(s)-J and J Publishing
Judson Press
Kregel—R
Legacy Publishers
Life Changing Media
Life Journey Books
Lift Every Voice—R
Lighthouse Publishing—R
Living Books for All
Loyola Press
Marshall Trumann
(s)-McDougal Publishing—R
Millennium III—R
Mission World Library—R
Monarch Books
MOPS Intl.
Nelson Ignite
Nelson, Thomas
New Hope—R
(s)-One World—R
P & R Publishing—R
Pacific Press
Parson Place—R
Parsons Publishing—R
Pauline Books—R
Paulist Press
Pilgrim Press—R
(s)-Pleasant Word—R
(s)-Providence Pub.—R
(s)-Quiet Waters
Quintessential Books—R
Randall House
(s)-Reformation Publishers—R
Regal
Revell
RiverOak
Rose Publishing
Scepter Publishers—R
(s)-Selah Publishing—R
(s)-So. Baptist Press—R
St. Anthony Mess. Press—R
Standard Publishing
(s)-Star Bible Public.
Still Waters Revival—R
(s)-Synergy Publishers—R
(s)-Tate Publishing—R
(s)-TEACH Services—R
(s)-Trafford Publishing—R
Tyndale House—R
(s)-VMI Publishers
W Publishing
WaterBrook Press—R
Whitaker House
(s)-WinePress—R
(s)-Word Alive
World Publishing
(s)-Zoe Life Publishing

MEMOIRS

(s)-American Binding—R
Baal Hamon—R
Baker Books
Baker's Plays—R
Ballantine
BelleBooks—R
(s)-Black Forest/Tennessee—R
(s)-Book Publishers—R
(s)-Booklocker.com—R
(s)-Brown Books—R
Christian Heritage—R
Christian Writer's Ebook—R
Cladach Publishing
(s)-Creation House—R
Cumberland House
Descant Publishing
Doubleday—R
(s)-Elderberry Press
(s)-Fairway Press—R
FaithWalk
FaithWords
Forward Movement
(s)-FruitBearer Pub.
Greenwood/Praeger
Guernica Editions—R
GuidepostsBooks
HarperOne
Hidden Brook Press—R
Hill Street Press—R
(s)-Holy Fire Publishing—R
Ideals/Children
(s)-Leading Lady
(s)-Lifevest Publishing
Lighthouse Publishing—R
Lighthouse Trails—R
Lutterworth Press—R
Monarch Books
NavPress Th1nk—R
(s)-One World—R
One World/Ballantine
Pacific Press
Parson Place—R
(s)-Pleasant Word—R
(s)-Providence Pub.—R
Quintessential Books—R
Randall House
(s)-Reformation Publishers—R
Regal
Salvation Publisher—R
(s)-Scribe Book—R
Shoreline—R
(s)-Tate Publishing—R
TowleHouse—R
(s)-Trafford Publishing—R
Univ. Press of America—R
(s)-VMI Publishers
(s)-WinePress—R
(s)-Word Alive
(s)-Zoe Life Publishing

MEN'S BOOKS

Ambassador Books
(s)-American Binding—R
AMG Publishers—R
B & H Publishing
Baal Hamon—R
Baker Books
Barbour
Beacon Hill Press—R
Bethany House
(s)-Black Forest/Tennessee—R
Blue Dolphin
(s)-Booklocker.com—R
Bridge-Logos—R
(s)-Brown Books—R
Christian Writer's Ebook—R
College Press—R
(s)-Creation House—R
Dimensions for Living
Doubleday—R
Editorial Portavoz

(s)-Elderberry Press
Emmaus Road—R
(s)-Essence—R
Evergreen Press
(s)-Fairway Press—R
Faith Communications
FaithWalk
FaithWords
Green Key Books
GRQ—R
Hensley Publishing
Hidden Brook Press—R
Hill Street Press—R
(s)-Holy Fire Publishing—R
(s)-IMD Press—R
Inkling Books—R
(s)-J and J Publishing
Judson Press
Life Journey Books
Lift Every Voice—R
Lighthouse Publishing—R
Loyola Press
Marshall Trumann
(s)-McDougal Publishing—R
Monarch Books
NavPress Th1nk—R
Nelson, Thomas
New Leaf
(s)-One World—R
Pacific Press
Parson Place—R
Pilgrim Press—R
(s)-Pleasant Word—R
(s)-Providence Pub.—R
Quintessential Books—R
Randall House
(s)-Reformation Publishers—R
Regal
RiverOak
Rose Publishing
(s)-Selah Publishing—R
(s)-Star Bible Public.
(s)-Synergy Publishers—R
(s)-Tate Publishing—R
(s)-Trafford Publishing—R
(s)-VMI Publishers
W Publishing
WaterBrook Press—R
Wesleyan Publishing
Whitaker House
White Stone Books—R
(s)-WinePress—R
(s)-Word Alive
(s)-Zoe Life Publishing

MINIBOOKS

(s)-American Binding—R
Baal Hamon—R
(s)-Black Forest/Tennessee—R
(s)-IMD Press—R
Legacy Press—R
Lighthouse Publishing—R
Monarch Books
(s)-One World—R
(s)-Path Publishing in Christ—R
Peter Pauper Press
(s)-Tate Publishing—R

MIRACLES

(s)-American Binding—R
Baker Books
Baker's Plays—R
(s)-Black Forest/Tennessee—R
Blue Dolphin
(s)-Booklocker.com—R
(s)-Brentwood—R
(s)-Brown Books—R
Canticle Books—R
Christian Heritage—R
Christian Writer's Ebook—R
(s)-Creation House—R
Crossroad Publishing—R
CSS Publishing—R
(s)-Elderberry Press
(s)-Essence—R
Evergreen Press
(s)-Fairway Press—R
FaithWords
Friends United Press
Gollehon Press
Good Book—R
Greenwood/Praeger
GuidepostsBooks
HarperOne
Harrison House
Hidden Brook Press—R
(s)-Holy Fire Publishing—R
(s)-IMD Press—R
(s)-Impact Christian—R
Lighthouse Publishing—R
Loyola Press
Marshall Trumann
(s)-McDougal Publishing—R
Monarch Books
(s)-One World—R
Pacific Press
Parsons Publishing—R
(s)-Path Publishing in Christ—R
Pauline Books—R
(s)-Pleasant Word—R
(s)-Providence Pub.—R
(s)-Reformation Publishers—R
Revival Nation
Rose Publishing
Salvation Publisher—R
(s)-Selah Publishing—R
(s)-So. Baptist Press—R
St. Anthony Mess. Press—R
(s)-Star Bible Public.
Strang Book Group—R
(s)-Tate Publishing—R
(s)-Trafford Publishing—R
(s)-VMI Publishers
Whitaker House
(s)-WinePress—R
(s)-Word Alive
World Publishing
(s)-Zoe Life Publishing

MISSIONARY

Ambassador-Emerald—R
(s)-American Binding—R
Baker Books
Baker's Plays—R
(s)-Black Forest/Tennessee—R
(s)-Booklocker.com—R
(s)-Brentwood—R
(s)-Brown Books—R
Carey Library, Wm.—R
Christian Focus—R
Christian Heritage—R
Christian Writer's Ebook—R
(s)-Creation House—R
CSS Publishing—R
Discovery House—R
Ekklesia Press—R
(s)-Elderberry Press
(s)-Essence—R
Evergreen Press
(s)-Fairway Press—R
FaithWalk
Forward Movement
Friends United Press
Greenwood/Praeger
(s)-Hannibal Books—R
Harrison House
Harvest Day
Hidden Brook Press—R
(s)-Holy Fire Publishing—R
Hope Publishing—R
(s)-IMD Press—R
Lift Every Voice—R
Lighthouse Publishing—R
Lighthouse Trails—R
Living Books for All
Lutheran Univ. Press
Lutterworth Press—R
Marshall Trumann
(s)-McDougal Publishing—R
Mission World Library—R
Monarch Books
Morehouse—R
New Hope—R
(s)-One World—R
Pacific Press
Parsons Publishing—R
Pauline Books—R
(s)-Pleasant Word—R
(s)-Providence Pub.—R
(s)-Quiet Waters
Randall House
(s)-Reformation Publishers—R
Rose Publishing

Salt Works
(s)-So. Baptist Press—R
St. Anthony Mess. Press—R
(s)-Star Bible Public.
Strang Book Group—R
(s)-Tate Publishing—R
(s)-Trafford Publishing—R
(s)-VMI Publishers
Wesleyan Publishing
(s)-WinePress—R
(s)-Word Alive
(s)-Zoe Life Publishing

MONEY MANAGEMENT

(s)-American Binding—R
Baker Books
Barbour
Blue Dolphin
(s)-Booklocker.com—R
(s)-Brentwood—R
Bridge-Logos—R
(s)-Brown Books—R
Christian Writer's Ebook—R
Cook, David C.
(s)-Creation House—R
Dabbling Mum Press
Editorial Portavoz
(s)-Elderberry Press
(s)-Essence—R
Evergreen Press
(s)-Fairway Press—R
FaithWalk
FaithWords
Forward Movement
Good News Pub.
Greenwood/Praeger
GRQ—R
Grupo Nelson
(s)-Hannibal Books—R
Harrison House
Harvest House
Hensley Publishing
Hidden Brook Press—R
(s)-Holy Fire Publishing—R
(s)-IMD Press—R
Judson Press
(s)-Leading Lady
Legacy Publishers
Life Journey Books
Lift Every Voice—R
Lighthouse Publishing—R
Living Books for All
Marshall Trumann
Moody Publishers
MountainView
Nelson, Thomas
(s)-One World—R
Pacific Press
Parsons Publishing—R
(s)-Pleasant Word—R
Power Publishing
(s)-Providence Pub.—R
Quintessential Books—R
(s)-Reformation Publishers—R
Regnery
RiverOak
Rose Publishing
Salvation Publisher—R
(s)-Scribe Book—R
(s)-So. Baptist Press—R
(s)-Star Bible Public.
(s)-Synergy Publishers—R
(s)-Tate Publishing—R
(s)-Trafford Publishing—R
(s)-VMI Publishers
Walk Worthy—R
WaterBrook Press—R
(s)-WinePress—R
(s)-Winer Foundation—R
(s)-Word Alive
(s)-Zoe Life Publishing

MUSIC-RELATED BOOKS

Ambassador-Emerald—R
American Cath. Press—R
Baker Books
Blue Dolphin
(s)-Booklocker.com—R
Christian Writer's Ebook—R
Contemporary Drama
Countryman, J.
(s)-Essence—R
(s)-Fairway Press—R
FaithWalk
FaithWords
Guardian Angel
Hidden Brook Press—R
Hill Street Press—R
(s)-Holy Fire Publishing—R
Lighthouse Publishing—R
MegaGrace Books
Monarch Books
(s)-One World—R
Parsons Publishing—R
(s)-Providence Pub.—R
(s)-Reformation Publishers—R
Regal
Standard Publishing
(s)-Star Bible Public.
T & T Clark—R
(s)-Tate Publishing—R
(s)-Trafford Publishing—R
(s)-VMI Publishers
(s)-WinePress—R
(s)-Word Alive

NOVELTY BOOKS FOR KIDS

Atheneum/Yg Readers
Augsburg—R
Baker Books
Baker Trittin
Big Idea
(s)-Elderberry Press
(s)-Fairway Press—R
Guardian Angel
(s)-IMD Press—R
Journey Stone—R
Kregel Kidzone
Legacy Press—R
Lift Every Voice—R
Monarch Books
(s)-One World—R
Ravenhawk Books—R
Salt Works
Standard Publishing
(s)-Tate Publishing—R
(s)-Trafford Publishing—R
White Stone Books—R
(s)-Word Alive

PAMPHLETS

Chalice Press
Chapter Two—R
Christian Writer's Ebook—R
Concordia
Ekklesia Press—R
(s)-Essence—R
Forward Movement
Founders Press
(s)-FruitBearer Pub.
Good Book—R
Good News Pub.
Harvest House
(s)-IMD Press—R
InterVarsity Press—R
Intl. Awakening—R
Libros Liguori
Lift Every Voice—R
Liguori—R
Liturgy Training—R
Living Books for All
Neibauer Press—R
(s)-One World—R
Our Sunday Visitor—R
Paradise Research—R
Paulist Press
Rose Publishing
Salt Works
Trinity Foundation—R

PARENTING

ACTA Publications
Adams Media
Ambassador Books
(s)-American Binding—R
AMG Publishers—R
Augsburg—R
B & H Publishing
Baker Books
Baker Trittin
Baker's Plays—R
Ballantine
Barbour
Beacon Hill Press—R
Bethany House
(s)-Black Forest/Tennessee—R

Blue Dolphin
(s)-Book Publishers—R
(s)-Booklocker.com—R
(s)-Brentwood—R
(s)-Brown Books—R
Christian Family—R
Christian Writer's Ebook—R
College Press—R
Conari Press
Conciliar Press—R
Concordia
Cook, David C.
(s)-Creation House—R
Crossroad Publishing—R
Dabbling Mum Press
(s)-Dean Press, Robbie—R
Dimensions for Living
Discovery House—R
Editorial Portavoz
(s)-Elderberry Press
(s)-Essence—R
Evergreen Press
(s)-Fairway Press—R
FaithWords
Focus on the Family
Forward Movement
(s)-FruitBearer Pub.
Good News Pub.
Greenwood/Praeger
Grupo Nelson
Harrison House
Harvest House
Health Commun.
Hensley Publishing
Hidden Brook Press—R
Hill Street Press—R
(s)-Holy Fire Publishing—R
Howard Books
(s)-IMD Press—R
Judson Press
Kaleidoscope Press—R
Langmarc
(s)-Leading Lady
Life Changing Media
Life Journey Books
Lift Every Voice—R
Lighthouse Publishing—R
Liguori—R
Living Books for All
Marshall Trumann
(s)-McDougal Publishing—R
Mission City Press
Monarch Books
MOPS Intl.
Nelson, Thomas
New Hope—R
(s)-One World—R
Our Sunday Visitor—R
P & R Publishing—R
Pacific Press
Parson Place—R
Parsons Publishing—R
Pauline Books—R
Pflaum Publishing
(s)-Pleasant Word—R
(s)-Providence Pub.—R
Quintessential Books—R
Randall House
(s)-Reformation Publishers—R
Regal
Revell
RiverOak
Rose Publishing
Scepter Publishers—R
(s)-Selah Publishing—R
St. Anthony Mess. Press—R
Standard Publishing
(s)-Star Bible Public.
Still Waters Revival—R
Tarcher, Jeremy P.—R
(s)-Tate Publishing—R
Torch Legacy
(s)-Trafford Publishing—R
Tyndale House—R
(s)-VMI Publishers
W Publishing
Walk Worthy—R
WaterBrook Press—R
Whitaker House
(s)-WinePress—R
Wood Lake Books—R
(s)-Word Alive
World Publishing
(s)-Zoe Life Publishing

PASTORS' HELPS

Abingdon Press
(s)-American Binding—R
B & H Publishing
Baal Hamon—R
Baker Academic
Baker Books
Beacon Hill Press—R
BMH Books
(s)-Booklocker.com—R
(s)-Brentwood—R
Chalice Press
Christian Focus—R
Christian Writer's Ebook—R
Church Growth Inst.
(s)-Creation House—R
CSS Publishing—R
(s)-DCTS Publishing
Earthen Vessel—R
Editorial Portavoz
(s)-Elderberry Press
(s)-Essence—R
(s)-Fairway Press—R
Fortress Press
Gospel Publishing
Greenwood/Praeger
Group Publishing
Harcourt Religion
Harrison House
Haworth Pastoral—R
Hidden Brook Press—R
(s)-Holy Fire Publishing—R
(s)-IMD Press—R
Judson Press
(s)-Kindred Books—R
Kregel—R
Lift Every Voice—R
Lighthouse Publishing—R
Liturgy Training—R
Lutheran Univ. Press
Marshall Trumann
Monarch Books
Morehouse—R
Neibauer Press—R
(s)-One World—R
P & R Publishing—R
Parson Place—R
Parsons Publishing—R
Pathway Press
Pilgrim Press—R
(s)-Pleasant Word—R
(s)-Providence Pub.—R
Randall House
(s)-Reformation Publishers—R
Reformation Trust
Regal
Rose Publishing
(s)-Sermon Select Press
(s)-So. Baptist Press—R
St. Anthony Mess. Press—R
Standard Publishing
(s)-Star Bible Public.
(s)-Tate Publishing—R
Torch Legacy
(s)-Trafford Publishing—R
(s)-VMI Publishers
Wesleyan Publishing
(s)-WinePress—R
(s)-Winer Foundation—R
(s)-Word Alive
(s)-Zoe Life Publishing
Zondervan

PERSONAL EXPERIENCE

Ambassador-Emerald—R
(s)-American Binding—R
Baal Hamon—R
Baker Books
Baker's Plays—R
(s)-Black Forest/Tennessee—R
Blue Dolphin
(s)-Booklocker.com—R
(s)-Brentwood—R
(s)-Brown Books—R
Carepoint Publishing—R
Chicken Soup
Christian Family—R
Christian Writer's Ebook—R
(s)-Creation House—R
(s)-DCTS Publishing
Destiny Image—R

(s)-Elderberry Press
(s)-Essence—R
(s)-Fairway Press—R
FaithWalk
Friends United Press
(s)-FruitBearer Pub.
Greenwood/Praeger
GRQ—R
(s)-Hannibal Books—R
HarperOne
Hidden Brook Press—R
(s)-Holy Fire Publishing—R
(s)-IMD Press—R
Life Changing Media
Lift Every Voice—R
Lighthouse Publishing—R
Lighthouse Trails—R
Living Books for All
Marshall Trumann
(s)-McDougal Publishing—R
Monarch Books
NavPress Th1nk—R
(s)-One World—R
Pacific Press
Parsons Publishing—R
(s)-Path Publishing in Christ—R
(s)-Pleasant Word—R
Power Publishing
(s)-Providence Pub.—R
Randall House
(s)-Reformation Publishers—R
Regal
RiverOak
Salvation Publisher—R
(s)-Scribe Book—R
Shoreline—R
(s)-So. Baptist Press—R
(s)-Star Bible Public.
(s)-Tate Publishing—R
(s)-Trafford Publishing—R
(s)-VMI Publishers
W Publishing
(s)-WinePress—R
(s)-Winer Foundation—R
(s)-Word Alive
(s)-Zoe Life Publishing

PERSONAL GROWTH

Aadeon Publishing—R
ACTA Publications
(s)-Ali Literary, Alfred—R
Ambassador Books
Ambassador-Emerald—R
(s)-American Binding—R
B & H Publishing
Baal Hamon—R
Baker Books
Baker's Plays—R
Barbour
Bethany House
(s)-Black Forest/Tennessee—R
Blue Dolphin
BMH Books
(s)-Book Publishers—R
(s)-Booklocker.com—R
Bridge-Logos—R
(s)-Brown Books—R
Carepoint Publishing—R
CharismaKids
Christian Family—R
Christian Writer's Ebook—R
Conari Press
(s)-Creation House—R
Crossroad Publishing—R
Dabbling Mum Press
(s)-DCTS Publishing
Destiny Image—R
Discovery House—R
(s)-Elderberry Press
(s)-Essence—R
Evergreen Press
(s)-Fairway Press—R
FaithWalk
FaithWords
Forward Movement
(s)-FruitBearer Pub.
Greenwood/Praeger
GRQ—R
GuidepostsBooks
(s)-Hannibal Books—R
HarperOne
Hay House
Hensley Publishing
Hidden Brook Press—R
Hill Street Press—R
(s)-Holy Fire Publishing—R
(s)-IMD Press—R
(s)-J and J Publishing
Jebaire Publishing
Jossey-Bass
Judson Press
(s)-Kindred Books—R
Life Changing Media
Life Journey Books
Lift Every Voice—R
Lighthouse Publishing—R
Living Books for All
Marshall Trumann
(s)-McDougal Publishing—R
MegaGrace Books
Monarch Books
NavPress
NavPress Th1nk—R
Nelson, Thomas
New Seeds—R
(s)-One World—R
P & R Publishing—R
Pacific Press
Parson Place—R
Parsons Publishing—R
(s)-Path Publishing in Christ—R
(s)-Path Publishing—R
Pathway Press
Peter Pauper Press
Pilgrim Press—R
(s)-Pleasant Word—R
(s)-Providence Pub.—R
Quintessential Books—R
Randall House
(s)-Reformation Publishers—R
Regal
RiverOak
(s)-Scribe Book—R
(s)-Star Bible Public.
Strang Book Group—R
(s)-Synergy Publishers—R
(s)-Tate Publishing—R
(s)-TEACH Services—R
(s)-Trafford Publishing—R
Tyndale House—R
(s)-VMI Publishers
W Publishing
WaterBrook Press—R
White Stone Books—R
(s)-WinePress—R
(s)-Winer Foundation—R
(s)-Word Alive
World Publishing
(s)-Zoe Life Publishing

PERSONAL RENEWAL

(s)-Ali Literary, Alfred—R
(s)-American Binding—R
B & H Publishing
Baal Hamon—R
Baker Books
Baker's Plays—R
Barbour
Bethany House
(s)-Black Forest/Tennessee—R
(s)-Booklocker.com—R
Bridge-Logos—R
(s)-Brown Books—R
CharismaKids
Christian Writer's Ebook—R
Conari Press
(s)-Creation House—R
(s)-DCTS Publishing
Destiny Image—R
(s)-Elderberry Press
(s)-Essence—R
Evergreen Press
(s)-Fairway Press—R
FaithWalk
FaithWords
Forward Movement
Friends United Press
(s)-FruitBearer Pub.
Greenwood/Praeger
GRQ—R
(s)-Hannibal Books—R
HarperOne
Haworth Pastoral—R
Hensley Publishing
Hidden Brook Press—R
Hill Street Press—R

(s)-Holy Fire Publishing—R
(s)-IMD Press—R
(s)-Impact Christian—R
Intl. Awakening—R
Jebaire Publishing
Jossey-Bass
Judson Press
Kirk House
Life Changing Media
Life Journey Books
Lift Every Voice—R
Lighthouse Publishing—R
Living Books for All
Marshall Trumann
(s)-McDougal Publishing—R
MegaGrace Books
Monarch Books
NavPress
NavPress Th1nk—R
New Seeds—R
(s)-One World—R
P & R Publishing—R
Pacific Press
Parson Place—R
Parsons Publishing—R
(s)-Path Publishing in Christ—R
(s)-Path Publishing—R
Pilgrim Press—R
(s)-Pleasant Word—R
(s)-Providence Pub.—R
Randall House
(s)-Reformation Publishers—R
Regal
RiverOak
Rose Publishing
(s)-Scribe Book—R
(s)-Star Bible Public.
Strang Book Group—R
(s)-Synergy Publishers—R
(s)-Tate Publishing—R
(s)-Trafford Publishing—R
Tyndale House—R
(s)-VMI Publishers
(s)-WinePress—R
(s)-Winer Foundation—R
(s)-Word Alive
World Publishing
(s)-Zoe Life Publishing

PHILOSOPHY

Abingdon Press
Alba House—R
(s)-American Binding—R
Baal Hamon—R
Baker Books
Baker's Plays—R
Baylor Univ. Press
(s)-Black Forest/Tennessee—R
Blue Dolphin
(s)-Booklocker.com—R
(s)-Brentwood—R
(s)-Brown Books—R
Cambridge Univ. Press
Christian Writer's Ebook—R
Continuum Intl.—R
(s)-Creation House—R
Crossroad Publishing—R
Doubleday—R
Dover Publications—R
Eerdmans Pub., Wm. B.—R
(s)-Elderberry Press
(s)-Essence—R
(s)-Fairway Press—R
FaithWalk
Fifth Estate—R
Fordham Univ. Press—R
Friends United Press
Greenwood/Praeger
HarperOne
Hidden Brook Press—R
Hill Street Press—R
(s)-Holy Fire Publishing—R
(s)-IMD Press—R
Inkling Books—R
InterVarsity Press—R
Larson Publications—R
Lighthouse Publishing—R
Lutterworth Press—R
Mercer Univ. Press—R
Monarch Books
New Seeds—R
(s)-One World—R
One World/Ballantine
P & R Publishing—R
Paragon House—R
Pauline Books—R
(s)-Pleasant Word—R
Quintessential Books—R
(s)-Reformation Publishers—R
Regnery
Rose Publishing
Salt Works
St. Augustine's Press—R
(s)-Star Bible Public.
Still Waters Revival—R
Tarcher, Jeremy P.—R
(s)-Tate Publishing—R
Third World Press—R
(s)-Trafford Publishing—R
Trinity Foundation—R
Univ. Press of America—R
(s)-VMI Publishers
(s)-WinePress—R
(s)-Winer Foundation—R
(s)-Word Alive
Yale Univ. Press—R

PHOTOGRAPHS (FOR COVERS)

Abingdon Press
(s)-Ali Literary, Alfred—R
Ambassador Books
(s)-American Binding—R
Baal Hamon—R
(s)-Black Forest/Tennessee—R
(s)-Book Publishers—R
(s)-Booklocker.com—R
(s)-Brentwood—R
Bridge-Logos—R
(s)-Brown Books—R
Canadian Inst. for Law—R
Carepoint Publishing—R
Carey Library, Wm.—R
Catholic Answers—R
Christian Focus—R
Church Growth Inst.
Cistercian—R
Conciliar Press—R
Continuum Intl.—R
(s)-Creation House—R
(s)-Dean Press, Robbie—R
Dove Inspirational
(s)-Essence—R
ETC Publications
Fair Havens—R
FaithWalk
FamilyLife (books)—R
Fifth Estate—R
(s)-FruitBearer Pub.
Georgetown Univ. Press
Guardian Angel
Guernica Editions—R
Harcourt Religion
(s)-IMD Press—R
Intl. Awakening—R
Jebaire Publishing
Jireh Publishing
Journey Stone—R
Jubilant Press—R
Life Changing Media
Lift Every Voice—R
Lighthouse Publishing—R
(s)-Lightning Star Press—R
Living Books for All
Lutheran Univ. Press
MegaGrace Books
Monarch Books
MountainView
Neibauer Press—R
New Canaan—R
New Hope—R
(s)-One World—R
Oregon Catholic
Our Sunday Visitor—R
Parson Place—R
Parsons Publishing—R
Paulist Press
Pelican Publishing—R
Pilgrim Press—R
Players Press—R
(s)-Pleasant Word—R
Quintessential Books—R
Ravenhawk Books—R
(s)-Reformation Publishers—R
(s)-Scribe Book—R
(s)-Selah Publishing—R

Sheed & Ward—R
St. Anthony Mess. Press—R
(s)-Star Bible Public.
Strang Book Group—R
(s)-Synergy Publishers—R
T & T Clark—R
(s)-Tate Publishing—R
Tau-Publishing—R
(s)-TEACH Services—R
Touch Publications—R
TowleHouse—R
Trinity Foundation—R
Troitsa Books
United Methodist
Univ. of AR Press—R
Virginia Pines Press
Wilshire Book—R
(s)-WinePress—R
(s)-Xulon Press—R
(s)-Zoe Life Publishing

POETRY

(s)-American Binding—R
Atheneum/Yg Readers
Baal Hamon—R
Baker's Plays—R
(s)-Black Forest/Tennessee—R
Blue Dolphin
(s)-Book Publishers—R
(s)-Booklocker.com—R
Boyds Mills Press—R
(s)-Brentwood—R
(s)-Brown Books—R
Christian Writer's Ebook—R
(s)-Creation House—R
(s)-Dean Press, Robbie—R
Destiny Image (books)—R
DiskUs Publishing
E-Digital Books
(s)-Elderberry Press
(s)-Essence—R
(s)-Fairway Press—R
Fifth Estate—R
(s)-FruitBearer Pub.
Guernica Editions—R
Harvest Day
Hidden Brook Press—R
(s)-Holy Fire Publishing—R
(s)-J and J Publishing
(s)-Leading Lady
(s)-Lifevest Publishing
Lighthouse Publishing—R
(s)-Lightning Star Press—R
Marshall Trumann
MoreThanNovellas
Mt. Olive College Press
New Seeds—R
(s)-One World—R
(s)-Path Publishing in Christ—R
(s)-Path Publishing—R
(s)-Pleasant Word—R
(s)-Poems By Me—R
(s)-Poet's Cove Press
(s)-Reformation Publishers—R
(s)-Selah Publishing—R
(s)-So. Baptist Press—R
(s)-Tate Publishing—R
(s)-Trafford Publishing—R
(s)-WinePress—R
(s)-Word Alive
(s)-Zoe Life Publishing

POLITICAL

Aadeon Publishing—R
(s)-American Binding—R
AMG Publishers—R
Baker Books
Baker's Plays—R
Baylor Univ. Press
(s)-Black Forest/Tennessee—R
(s)-Booklocker.com—R
Branden Publishing—R
(s)-Brentwood—R
Bridge-Logos—R
(s)-Brown Books—R
Canadian Inst. for Law—R
Christian Writer's Ebook—R
(s)-Creation House—R
Cumberland House
Doubleday—R
Ekklesia Press—R
(s)-Elderberry Press
(s)-Essence—R
(s)-Fairway Press—R
Fordham Univ. Press—R
Georgetown Univ. Press
Gollehon Press
Greenwood/Praeger
HarperOne
Hidden Brook Press—R
Hill Street Press—R
(s)-Holy Fire Publishing—R
Inkling Books—R
InterVarsity Press—R
Invisible College Press
Lighthouse Publishing—R
Marshall Trumann
Mercer Univ. Press—R
Millennium III—R
New Canaan—R
(s)-One World—R
One World/Ballantine
Pilgrim Press—R
(s)-Pleasant Word—R
Ravenhawk Books—R
(s)-Reformation Publishers—R
Regal
Regnery
Still Waters Revival—R
Strang Book Group—R
(s)-Synergy Publishers—R
(s)-Tate Publishing—R
Third World Press—R
(s)-Trafford Publishing—R
Trinity Foundation—R
Univ. Press of America—R
(s)-VMI Publishers
(s)-WinePress—R
(s)-Word Alive
Yale Univ. Press—R

POST MODERNISM*

Abingdon Press
(s)-American Binding—R
(s)-Booklocker.com—R
(s)-Brown Books—R
Chalice Press
(s)-Elderberry Press
(s)-Essence—R
Fair Havens—R
Howard Books
InterVarsity Press—R
Jossey-Bass
Lighthouse Trails—R
Monarch Books
P & R Publishing—R
Paragon House—R
Ravenhawk Books—R
(s)-Reformation Publishers—R
Regal
Resource Public.
Salt Works
(s)-Scribe Book—R
(s)-Star Bible Public.

PRAYER

Abingdon Press
ACTA Publications
Alba House—R
Ambassador Books
Ambassador-Emerald—R
(s)-American Binding—R
American Cath. Press—R
Anglicans United—R
B & H Publishing
Baal Hamon—R
Baker Books
Baker Trittin
Baker's Plays—R
Barbour
Beacon Hill Press—R
Bethany House
(s)-Black Forest/Tennessee—R
BMH Books
(s)-Booklocker.com—R
(s)-Brentwood—R
Bridge-Logos—R
(s)-Brown Books—R
Catholic Book
Chapter Two—R
CharismaKids
Christian Family—R
Christian Focus—R

Christian Heritage—R
Christian Writer's Ebook—R
College Press—R
Continuum Intl.—R
Cook, David C.
(s)-Creation House—R
Crossroad Publishing—R
CSS Publishing—R
(s)-DCTS Publishing
Destiny Image—R
Discovery House—R
Doubleday—R
Eerdmans Pub., Wm. B.—R
(s)-Elderberry Press
(s)-Essence—R
Evergreen Press
(s)-Fairway Press—R
FaithWalk
FaithWords
Forward Movement
Friends United Press
(s)-FruitBearer Pub.
Good Book—R
Good News Pub.
Greenwood/Praeger
GRQ—R
GuidepostsBooks
Harcourt Religion
HarperOne
Harrison House
Harvest House
Hensley Publishing
Hidden Brook Press—R
Hill Street Press—R
(s)-Holy Fire Publishing—R
Hope Publishing—R
Howard Books
(s)-IMD Press—R
(s)-Impact Christian—R
InterVarsity Press—R
Intl. Awakening—R
Jireh Publishing
Judson Press
Kregel—R
Legacy Press—R
Libros Liguori
Lift Every Voice—R
Lighthouse Publishing—R
(s)-Lightning Star Press—R
Liguori—R
Liturgy Training—R
Living Books for All
Loyola Press
Lutheran Univ. Press
Marshall Trumann
(s)-McDougal Publishing—R
Messianic Jewish—R
Mission World Library—R
Monarch Books
Moody Publishers
Morehouse—R
NavPress Th1nk—R
New Hope—R
New Seeds—R
(s)-One World—R
Our Sunday Visitor—R
P & R Publishing—R
Pacific Press
Paradise Research—R
Parson Place—R
Parsons Publishing—R
(s)-Path Publishing in Christ—R
Pauline Books—R
Paulist Press
Peter Pauper Press
Pflaum Publishing
Pilgrim Press—R
(s)-Pleasant Word—R
Pray! Books—R
(s)-Providence Pub.—R
Quintessential Books—R
Randall House
(s)-Reformation Publishers—R
Reformation Trust
Regal
Revival Nation
RiverOak
Rose Publishing
Salvation Publisher—R
Scepter Publishers—R
(s)-Selah Publishing—R
Smyth & Helwys
(s)-So. Baptist Press—R
St. Anthony Mess. Press—R
Standard Publishing
(s)-Star Bible Public.
Still Waters Revival—R
Strang Book Group—R
(s)-Synergy Publishers—R
(s)-Tate Publishing—R
(s)-TEACH Services—R
(s)-Trafford Publishing—R
Tyndale House—R
(s)-VMI Publishers
W Publishing
Walk Worthy—R
WaterBrook Press—R
Wesleyan Publishing
Westminster John Knox
Whitaker House
White Stone Books—R
(s)-WinePress—R
(s)-Winer Foundation—R
Wood Lake Books—R
Woodland Gospel
(s)-Word Alive
World Publishing
(s)-Zoe Life Publishing

PRINT-ON-DEMAND

Aadeon Publishing—R
(s)-ACW Press—R
(s)-American Binding—R
Baal Hamon—R
(s)-Black Forest/Tennessee—R
Blue Dolphin
(s)-Booklocker Jr.
(s)-Booklocker.com—R
Breakneck Books—R
(s)-Brentwood—R
Bridge-Logos—R
Capstone Fiction—R
Christian Writer's Ebook—R
Continuum Intl.—R
Crossroad Publishing—R
CSS Publishing—R
(s)-Dean Press, Robbie—R
Editorial Portavoz
Ekklesia Press—R
(s)-Elderberry Press
Evergreen Press
Fifth Estate—R
Friends United Press
Georgetown Univ. Press
(s)-Hannibal Books—R
Hidden Brook Press—R
(s)-Holy Fire Publishing—R
(s)-Infinity Publishing
Inkling Books—R
(s)-Insight Publishing—R
(s)-Kindred Books—R
Lighthouse Publishing—R
(s)-Lightning Star Press—R
(s)-One World—R
Parson Place—R
Parsons Publishing—R
(s)-Path Publishing in Christ—R
Players Press—R
(s)-Pleasant Word—R
(s)-Poems By Me—R
Randall House Digital
Ravenhawk Books—R
(s)-Reformation Publishers—R
Salvation Publisher—R
(s)-Scribe Book—R
(s)-Self Publish Press—R
Sheed & Ward—R
(s)-Strong Tower—R
(s)-Synergy Publishers—R
(s)-Trafford Publishing—R
Univ. Press of America—R
(s)-Word Alive
(s)-Xulon Press—R

PROPHECY

(s)-American Binding—R
B & H Publishing
Baal Hamon—R
Baker Books
Baker's Plays—R
(s)-Black Forest/Tennessee—R
BMH Books
(s)-Booklocker.com—R

(s)-Brentwood—R
Bridge-Logos—R
(s)-Brown Books—R
Chapter Two—R
CharismaKids
Christian Writer's Ebook—R
(s)-Creation House—R
CSS Publishing—R
(s)-Elderberry Press
(s)-Essence—R
(s)-Fairway Press—R
FaithWalk
FaithWords
(s)-FruitBearer Pub.
Gospel Publishing
Greenwood/Praeger
Harrison House
Harvest House
Hidden Brook Press—R
(s)-Holy Fire Publishing—R
(s)-IMD Press—R
Lighthouse Publishing—R
Living Books for All
Lutheran Univ. Press
(s)-McDougal Publishing—R
Messianic Jewish—R
Millennium III—R
Monarch Books
(s)-One World—R
P & R Publishing—R
Pacific Press
Parson Place—R
Parsons Publishing—R
(s)-Path Publishing in Christ—R
(s)-Pleasant Word—R
(s)-Providence Pub.—R
Randall House
(s)-Reformation Publishers—R
Revival Nation
RiverOak
Rose Publishing
Salvation Publisher—R
(s)-Selah Publishing—R
(s)-So. Baptist Press—R
(s)-Star Bible Public.
Still Waters Revival—R
Strang Book Group—R
(s)-Synergy Publishers—R
(s)-Tate Publishing—R
(s)-Trafford Publishing—R
(s)-VMI Publishers
W Publishing
(s)-WinePress—R
(s)-Word Alive
(s)-Zoe Life Publishing

PSYCHOLOGY

Adams Media
(s)-American Binding—R
Baker Academic
Baker's Plays—R
Blue Dolphin
BMH Books
(s)-Book Publishers—R
(s)-Booklocker.com—R
(s)-Brentwood—R
(s)-Brown Books—R
Carepoint Publishing—R
Christian Writer's Ebook—R
(s)-Creation House—R
Eerdmans Pub., Wm. B.—R
(s)-Elderberry Press
(s)-Essence—R
Evergreen Press
(s)-Fairway Press—R
FaithWalk
Fifth Estate—R
Greenwood/Praeger
GRQ—R
Haworth Pastoral—R
Health Commun.
Hidden Brook Press—R
Hill Street Press—R
(s)-Holy Fire Publishing—R
Hope Publishing—R
(s)-IMD Press—R
InterVarsity Press—R
Larson Publications—R
Life Changing Media
Life Journey Books
Lift Every Voice—R
Lighthouse Publishing—R
Lutterworth Press—R
Marshall Trumann
Monarch Books
MountainView
(s)-One World—R
One World/Ballantine
Paradise Research—R
Paragon House—R
(s)-Pleasant Word—R
(s)-Providence Pub.—R
Quintessential Books—R
(s)-Recovery Commun.
(s)-Reformation Publishers—R
Religious Education
Rose Publishing
Siloam
(s)-So. Baptist Press—R
(s)-Star Bible Public.
Strang Book Group—R
Tarcher, Jeremy P.—R
(s)-Tate Publishing—R
Third World Press—R
(s)-Trafford Publishing—R
Treble Heart Books—R
Tyndale House—R
Univ. Press of America—R
(s)-VMI Publishers
Wilshire Book—R
(s)-WinePress—R
(s)-Winer Foundation—R
(s)-Word Alive
Yale Univ. Press—R

RACISM

(s)-Ali Literary, Alfred—R
(s)-American Binding—R
Atheneum/Yg Readers
Baker Books
Baker's Plays—R
(s)-Black Forest/Tennessee—R
Blue Dolphin
(s)-Booklocker.com—R
(s)-Brown Books—R
Chalice Press
Christian Writer's Ebook—R
(s)-Creation House—R
(s)-DCTS Publishing
Destiny Image—R
(s)-Elderberry Press
(s)-Essence—R
(s)-Fairway Press—R
FaithWalk
Forward Movement
Greenwood/Praeger
Hidden Brook Press—R
Hill Street Press—R
(s)-Holy Fire Publishing—R
InterVarsity Press—R
Judson Press
Kirk House
Lift Every Voice—R
Lighthouse Publishing—R
Marshall Trumann
Monarch Books
(s)-One World—R
Pilgrim Press—R
(s)-Pleasant Word—R
(s)-Reformation Publishers—R
Salt Works
(s)-Star Bible Public.
Strang Book Group—R
(s)-Tate Publishing—R
(s)-Trafford Publishing—R
Univ. Press of America—R
(s)-VMI Publishers
(s)-WinePress—R
(s)-Word Alive
Yale Univ. Press—R

RECOVERY BOOKS

Ambassador Books
(s)-American Binding—R
B & H Publishing
Baker Books
(s)-Black Forest/Tennessee—R
Blue Dolphin
(s)-Booklocker.com—R
(s)-Brown Books—R
Carepoint Publishing—R
Chalice Press

Christian Writer's Ebook—R
(s)-Creation House—R
CSS Publishing—R
(s)-Elderberry Press
(s)-Essence—R
Evergreen Press
(s)-Fairway Press—R
Faith Communications
FaithWalk
FaithWords
Good Book—R
Greenwood/Praeger
GRQ—R
(s)-Hannibal Books—R
HarperOne
Haworth Pastoral—R
Health Commun.
Hidden Brook Press—R
Hill Street Press—R
(s)-Holy Fire Publishing—R
Hope Publishing—R
(s)-IMD Press—R
Judson Press
Langmarc
Life Journey Books
Lift Every Voice—R
Lighthouse Publishing—R
Marshall Trumann
(s)-McDougal Publishing—R
Monarch Books
(s)-One World—R
Paradise Research—R
Pauline Books—R
(s)-Pleasant Word—R
Randall House
(s)-Recovery Commun.
(s)-Reformation Publishers—R
Regal
RiverOak
Rose Publishing
Siloam
(s)-Star Bible Public.
(s)-Tate Publishing—R
(s)-Trafford Publishing—R
Tyndale House—R
(s)-VMI Publishers
WaterBrook Press—R
Wilshire Book—R
(s)-WinePress—R
(s)-Word Alive
(s)-Zoe Life Publishing

REFERENCE BOOKS

Ambassador-Emerald—R
(s)-American Binding—R
B & H Publishing
Baker Academic
Baker Books
Barbour
BMH Books
(s)-Booklocker.com—R
Branden Publishing—R
(s)-Brentwood—R
Bridge-Logos—R
Christian Heritage—R
Christian Writer's Ebook—R
Cook, David C.
(s)-Creation House—R
Cumberland House
Doubleday—R
Dover Publications—R
Editorial Portavoz
Eerdmans Pub., Wm. B.—R
(s)-Elderberry Press
Facts on File
(s)-Fairway Press—R
FaithWalk
GRQ—R
Grupo Nelson
Guardian Angel
HarperOne
Hendrickson—R
Hidden Brook Press—R
Hill Street Press—R
(s)-Holy Fire Publishing—R
(s)-IMD Press—R
(s)-Impact Christian—R
InterVarsity Press—R
Intl. Awakening—R
Invisible College Press
Johns Hopkins—R
Kaleidoscope Press—R
Kregel—R
Life Cycle Books—R
Lighthouse Publishing—R
Lutterworth Press—R
MegaGrace Books
Millennium III—R
Monarch Books
New Leaf
(s)-One World—R
Our Sunday Visitor—R
(s)-Providence Pub.—R
Randall House
(s)-Reformation Publishers—R
Religious Education
Rose Publishing
(s)-Scribe Book—R
Sheed & Ward—R
(s)-So. Baptist Press—R
(s)-Star Bible Public.
Still Waters Revival—R
(s)-Synergy Publishers—R
(s)-Tate Publishing—R
Third World Press—R
(s)-Trafford Publishing—R
Tyndale House—R
Univ. Press of America—R
WindRiver—R
(s)-WinePress—R
(s)-Word Alive
World Publishing
Zondervan

RELATIONSHIPS

ACTA Publications
Adams Media
Ambassador Books
(s)-American Binding—R
Baal Hamon—R
Barbour
Bethany House
(s)-Black Forest/Tennessee—R
(s)-Book Publishers—R
(s)-Booklocker.com—R
(s)-Brown Books—R
Carepoint Publishing—R
Christian Focus—R
Church Growth Inst.
Cladach Publishing
Crossroad Publishing—R
Discovery House—R
(s)-Elderberry Press
(s)-Essence—R
Extreme Diva
FaithWords
FamilyLife (books)—R
Forward Movement
GRQ—R
(s)-Hannibal Books—R
Health Commun.
Hensley Publishing
Hidden Brook Press—R
(s)-Holy Fire Publishing—R
Howard Books
(s)-IMD Press—R
(s)-J and J Publishing
Judson Press
Life Changing Media
Lighthouse Publishing—R
Marshall Trumann
Monarch Books
MOPS Intl.
NavPress
NavPress Th1nk—R
Parson Place—R
Pauline Books—R
(s)-Providence Pub.—R
Quintessential Books—R
(s)-Reformation Publishers—R
Regal
(s)-Scribe Book—R
St. Anthony Mess. Press—R
(s)-Star Bible Public.
(s)-Tate Publishing—R
Torch Legacy
(s)-Trafford Publishing—R
Whitaker House
(s)-Zoe Life Publishing

RELIGION

Abingdon Press

ACTA Publications
Alba House—R
(s)-Ali Literary, Alfred—R
Ambassador Books
(s)-American Binding—R
Atheneum/Yg Readers
Augsburg—R
B & H Publishing
Baal Hamon—R
Baker Academic
Baker Books
Baker Trittin
Baker's Plays—R
Ballantine
Baylor Univ. Press
(s)-Black Forest/Tennessee—R
Blue Dolphin
(s)-Booklocker.com—R
Boyds Mills Press—R
(s)-Brentwood—R
Bridge-Logos—R
(s)-Brown Books—R
Cambridge Univ. Press
Catholic Answers—R
Chalice Press
Chelsea House—R
Christian Family—R
Christian Heritage—R
Christian Writer's Ebook—R
Church Growth Inst.
Concordia
Continuum Intl.—R
(s)-Creation House—R
Crossroad Publishing—R
CSS Publishing—R
Descant Publishing
Doubleday—R
E-Digital Books
Educational Ministries
Eerdmans Pub., Wm. B.—R
(s)-Elderberry Press
(s)-Essence—R
Facts on File
(s)-Fairway Press—R
FaithWalk
FaithWords
Fifth Estate—R
Fordham Univ. Press—R
Fortress Press
Forward Movement
Friends United Press
Georgetown Univ. Press
Good Book—R
Greenwood/Praeger
HarperOne
Hidden Brook Press—R
Hill Street Press—R
(s)-Holy Fire Publishing—R
Howard Books
(s)-Impact Christian—R
Invisible College Press
Johns Hopkins—R
Jossey-Bass
Kirk House
Larson Publications—R
Libros Liguori
Life Changing Media
Life Cycle Books—R
Lighthouse Publishing—R
Lillenas
Liturgy Training—R
Loyola Press
Lutheran Univ. Press
Lutterworth Press—R
(s)-McDougal Publishing—R
Mercer Univ. Press—R
Messianic Jewish—R
Millennium III—R
Monarch Books
Morehouse—R
Mt. Olive College Press
NavPress Th1nk—R
Nelson, Thomas
New Hope—R
New Seeds—R
New York Univ. Press
Northstone
(s)-One World—R
Oregon Catholic
Our Sunday Visitor—R
Pacific Press
Paradise Research—R
Pauline Books—R
Paulist Press
Pflaum Publishing
Pilgrim Press—R
(s)-Pleasant Word—R
Presbyterian Pub.
(s)-Providence Pub.—R
Quintessential Books—R
Ragged Edge—R
(s)-Reformation Publishers—R
Regnery
Religious Education
Revell
RiverOak
Rose Publishing
(s)-Scribe Book—R
Sheed & Ward—R
Smyth & Helwys
(s)-So. Baptist Press—R
St. Anthony Mess. Press—R
(s)-Star Bible Public.
Still Waters Revival—R
(s)-Synergy Publishers—R
T & T Clark—R
Tarcher, Jeremy P.—R
(s)-Tate Publishing—R
Tau-Publishing—R
Third World Press—R
Torch Legacy
(s)-Trafford Publishing—R
Treble Heart Books—R
Trinity Foundation—R
Tyndale House—R
Univ. of AR Press—R
Univ. Press of America—R
(s)-VMI Publishers
W Publishing
WaterBrook Press—R
Westminster John Knox
Whitaker House
WindRiver—R
(s)-WinePress—R
Wood Lake Books—R
(s)-Word Alive
World Publishing
Yale Univ. Press—R
(s)-Zoe Life Publishing

RELIGIOUS TOLERANCE

Abingdon Press
ACTA Publications
(s)-American Binding—R
Baal Hamon—R
Baker Books
Baker's Plays—R
Baylor Univ. Press
(s)-Black Forest/Tennessee—R
Blue Dolphin
(s)-Booklocker.com—R
(s)-Brown Books—R
Chalice Press
Christian Writer's Ebook—R
(s)-Elderberry Press
(s)-Essence—R
(s)-Fairway Press—R
FaithWalk
Forward Movement
Greenwood/Praeger
Hidden Brook Press—R
Hill Street Press—R
(s)-Holy Fire Publishing—R
Howard Books
Johns Hopkins—R
Judson Press
Lighthouse Publishing—R
Lutterworth Press—R
Monarch Books
New Canaan—R
New Seeds—R
(s)-One World—R
Paragon House—R
(s)-Pleasant Word—R
(s)-Providence Pub.—R
(s)-Reformation Publishers—R
Resource Public.
Rose Publishing
Salt Works
St. Anthony Mess. Press—R
(s)-Star Bible Public.
(s)-Tate Publishing—R
(s)-Trafford Publishing—R
(s)-VMI Publishers
Westminster John Knox

(s)-WinePress—R
(s)-Word Alive

RETIREMENT

(s)-American Binding—R
B & H Publishing
Baker Books
Baker's Plays—R
(s)-Black Forest/Tennessee—R
Blue Dolphin
(s)-Booklocker.com—R
(s)-Brown Books—R
Christian Writer's Ebook—R
College Press—R
(s)-Creation House—R
(s)-Elderberry Press
(s)-Essence—R
(s)-Fairway Press—R
FaithWords
Forward Movement
Greenwood/Praeger
Harvest House
Hidden Brook Press—R
Hill Street Press—R
(s)-Holy Fire Publishing—R
Judson Press
Kirk House
Life Journey Books
Lighthouse Publishing—R
Monarch Books
(s)-One World—R
(s)-Pleasant Word—R
(s)-Providence Pub.—R
(s)-Reformation Publishers—R
Regnery
Rose Publishing
(s)-So. Baptist Press—R
(s)-Star Bible Public.
(s)-Tate Publishing—R
(s)-Trafford Publishing—R
(s)-WinePress—R
(s)-Word Alive
(s)-Zoe Life Publishing

SCHOLARLY

(s)-American Binding—R
American Book
American Cath. Press—R
Baal Hamon—R
Baker Academic
Baker Books
Baker's Plays—R
Baylor Univ. Press
Blue Dolphin
(s)-Booklocker.com—R
(s)-Brown Books—R
Chalice Press
Christian Heritage—R
Christian Writer's Ebook—R
Cistercian—R
Continuum Intl.—R
Cook, David C.
(s)-Creation House—R
Crossroad Publishing—R
Doubleday—R
Eerdmans Pub., Wm. B.—R
(s)-Elderberry Press
(s)-Essence—R
(s)-Fairway Press—R
Fifth Estate—R
Fordham Univ. Press—R
Fortress Press
Georgetown Univ. Press
Gollehon Press
Gospel Publishing
Greenwood/Praeger
Guardian Angel
Haworth Pastoral—R
Hendrickson—R
Hidden Brook Press—R
Hill Street Press—R
(s)-Holy Fire Publishing—R
(s)-IMD Press—R
(s)-Impact Christian—R
Inkling Books—R
InterVarsity Press—R
Intl. Awakening—R
Kregel—R
Life Cycle Books—R
Lighthouse Publishing—R
Liturgy Training—R
Lutheran Univ. Press
Lutterworth Press—R
Master Books
Mercer Univ. Press—R
Millennium III—R
Mt. Olive College Press
New Leaf
New York Univ. Press
(s)-One World—R
P & R Publishing—R
Paragon House—R
Parsons Publishing—R
Pilgrim Press—R
(s)-Pleasant Word—R
(s)-Providence Pub.—R
(s)-Quiet Waters
Quintessential Books—R
(s)-Reformation Publishers—R
Religious Education
Smyth & Helwys
St. Augustine's Press—R
(s)-Star Bible Public.
T & T Clark—R
(s)-Tate Publishing—R
(s)-Trafford Publishing—R
Trinity Foundation—R
Univ. of AR Press—R
Univ. Press of America—R
(s)-VMI Publishers
Westminster John Knox
(s)-WinePress—R
(s)-Word Alive
Yale Univ. Press—R
Youth Specialties
(s)-Zoe Life Publishing
Zondervan

SCIENCE

(s)-American Binding—R
B & H Publishing
Baal Hamon—R
Baker Books
Baker's Plays—R
(s)-Black Forest/Tennessee—R
Blue Dolphin
(s)-Booklocker.com—R
Boyds Mills Press—R
(s)-Brown Books—R
Christian Family—R
Christian Writer's Ebook—R
Doubleday—R
(s)-Elderberry Press
(s)-Essence—R
Facts on File
(s)-Fairway Press—R
Fifth Estate—R
Fordham Univ. Press—R
Forward Movement
Greenwood/Praeger
Guardian Angel
Hidden Brook Press—R
Hill Street Press—R
(s)-Holy Fire Publishing—R
Inkling Books—R
InterVarsity Press—R
Jossey-Bass
Kaleidoscope Press—R
Lighthouse Publishing—R
Master Books
Millennium III—R
Monarch Books
New Leaf
(s)-One World—R
Parsons Publishing—R
(s)-Pleasant Word—R
Quintessential Books—R
(s)-Reformation Publishers—R
Regnery
Rose Publishing
(s)-Star Bible Public.
T & T Clark—R
(s)-Tate Publishing—R
(s)-Trafford Publishing—R
Trinity Foundation—R
Troitsa Books
(s)-WinePress—R
(s)-Word Alive
Yale Univ. Press—R

SELF-HELP

ACTA Publications
Adams Media
(s)-Ali Literary, Alfred—R
Ambassador Books
(s)-American Binding—R

B & H Publishing
Baal Hamon—R
Baker Books
Ballantine
(s)-Black Forest/Tennessee—R
Blue Dolphin
BMH Books
(s)-Book Publishers—R
(s)-Booklocker.com—R
Bridge-Logos—R
(s)-Brown Books—R
Carepoint Publishing—R
Christian Writer's Ebook—R
(s)-Creation House—R
Crossroad Publishing—R
(s)-DCTS Publishing
(s)-Dean Press, Robbie—R
Descant Publishing
Destiny Image—R
Dimensions for Living
(s)-Elderberry Press
(s)-Essence—R
Evergreen Press
Extreme Diva
(s)-Fairway Press—R
FaithWalk
FaithWords
Fell, Frederick—R
Fifth Estate—R
(s)-FruitBearer Pub.
Genesis Press—R
Gollehon Press
Good Book—R
GRQ—R
Grupo Nelson
GuidepostsBooks
HarperOne
Harvest House
Hay House
Health Commun.
Hidden Brook Press—R
Hill Street Press—R
(s)-Holy Fire Publishing—R
(s)-IMD Press—R
(s)-J and J Publishing
Judson Press
Langmarc
(s)-Leading Lady
Life Changing Media
Life Journey Books
Lighthouse Publishing—R
(s)-Lightning Star Press—R
Marshall Trumann
MegaGrace Books
Monarch Books
MountainView
Mt. Olive College Press
Nelson, Thomas
Northstone
(s)-One World—R
One World/Ballantine
Paradise Research—R
Parson Place—R
(s)-Path Publishing in Christ—R
(s)-Path Publishing—R
Pauline Books—R
Perigee Books
Peter Pauper Press
Pilgrim Press—R
(s)-Pleasant Word—R
PREP Publishing—R
(s)-Providence Pub.—R
Quintessential Books—R
Ragged Edge—R
(s)-Reformation Publishers—R
Revell
RiverOak
Salvation Publisher—R
(s)-Selah Publishing—R
(s)-Star Bible Public.
Starik Publishing
Strang Book Group—R
(s)-Synergy Publishers—R
Tarcher, Jeremy P.—R
(s)-Tate Publishing—R
(s)-TEACH Services—R
Third World Press—R
Torch Legacy
(s)-Trafford Publishing—R
Treble Heart Books—R
Tsaba House
Tyndale House—R
(s)-VMI Publishers
Walk Worthy—R
WaterBrook Press—R
Wilshire Book—R
WindRiver—R
(s)-WinePress—R
(s)-Winer Foundation—R
(s)-Word Alive

SENIOR ADULT CONCERNS

ACTA Publications
(s)-American Binding—R
Baker Books
Baker's Plays—R
(s)-Black Forest/Tennessee—R
Blue Dolphin
BMH Books
(s)-Book Publishers—R
(s)-Booklocker.com—R
(s)-Brown Books—R
Chalice Press
Christian Writer's Ebook—R
Cook, David C.
(s)-Creation House—R
Discovery House—R
Educational Ministries
(s)-Elderberry Press
(s)-Essence—R
Evergreen Press
Fair Havens—R
(s)-Fairway Press—R
Focus on the Family
Gollehon Press
Haworth Pastoral—R
Hidden Brook Press—R
Hill Street Press—R
(s)-Holy Fire Publishing—R
(s)-IMD Press—R
Judson Press
Langmarc
Life Journey Books
Lift Every Voice—R
Lighthouse Publishing—R
Monarch Books
(s)-One World—R
Parson Place—R
(s)-Path Publishing in Christ—R
Pauline Books—R
(s)-Pleasant Word—R
(s)-Providence Pub.—R
(s)-Reformation Publishers—R
Regal
Rose Publishing
(s)-So. Baptist Press—R
(s)-Star Bible Public.
(s)-Synergy Publishers—R
(s)-Tate Publishing—R
(s)-Trafford Publishing—R
(s)-VMI Publishers
(s)-WinePress—R
(s)-Word Alive
(s)-Zoe Life Publishing

SERMONS

Alba House—R
Ambassador-Emerald—R
(s)-American Binding—R
American Cath. Press—R
Baal Hamon—R
Baker Books
(s)-Black Forest/Tennessee—R
(s)-Booklocker.com—R
(s)-Brentwood—R
(s)-Brown Books—R
Chalice Press
Christian Family—R
Christian Focus—R
Christian Writer's Ebook—R
Church Growth Inst.
Continuum Intl.—R
(s)-Creation House—R
(s)-CrossHouse—R
CSS Publishing—R
(s)-DCTS Publishing
Editorial Portavoz
Educational Ministries
(s)-Elderberry Press
(s)-Fairway Press—R
Group Publishing
Hidden Brook Press—R
(s)-Holy Fire Publishing—R
(s)-IMD Press—R
Judson Press

Kregel—R
Lift Every Voice—R
Lighthouse Publishing—R
Liturgical Press
(s)-McDougal Publishing—R
Mission World Library—R
Monarch Books
Morehouse—R
MountainView
(s)-One World—R
P & R Publishing—R
Pacific Press
Parson Place—R
Parsons Publishing—R
(s)-Pleasant Word—R
(s)-Providence Pub.—R
(s)-Reformation Publishers—R
Reformation Trust
Salvation Publisher—R
(s)-Sermon Select Press
(s)-So. Baptist Press—R
(s)-Star Bible Public.
Still Waters Revival—R
(s)-Tate Publishing—R
Torch Legacy
(s)-Trafford Publishing—R
(s)-VMI Publishers
(s)-WinePress—R
(s)-Word Alive
(s)-Zoe Life Publishing

SINGLES ISSUES

Ambassador Books
(s)-American Binding—R
B & H Publishing
Baker Books
Baker's Plays—R
Barbour
Bethany House
(s)-Black Forest/Tennessee—R
(s)-Booklocker.com—R
(s)-Brentwood—R
Bridge-Logos—R
(s)-Brown Books—R
Christian Focus—R
Christian Writer's Ebook—R
Cook, David C.
(s)-Creation House—R
(s)-Dean Press, Robbie—R
Destiny Image—R
(s)-Elderberry Press
(s)-Essence—R
Evergreen Press
(s)-Fairway Press—R
FaithWalk
Green Key Books
Greenwood/Praeger
GRQ—R
Harrison House
Harvest House
Hensley Publishing
Hidden Brook Press—R
Hill Street Press—R
(s)-Holy Fire Publishing—R
(s)-IMD Press—R
(s)-J and J Publishing
Judson Press
Life Journey Books
Lift Every Voice—R
Lighthouse Publishing—R
Marshall Trumann
(s)-McDougal Publishing—R
Monarch Books
NavPress Th1nk—R
(s)-One World—R
Pacific Press
Parson Place—R
Pauline Books—R
Perigee Books
(s)-Pleasant Word—R
(s)-Providence Pub.—R
Quintessential Books—R
(s)-Reformation Publishers—R
Regal
Rose Publishing
(s)-Star Bible Public.
(s)-Synergy Publishers—R
(s)-Tate Publishing—R
(s)-Trafford Publishing—R
(s)-VMI Publishers
Walk Worthy—R
Whitaker House
(s)-WinePress—R
(s)-Word Alive
(s)-Zoe Life Publishing

SOCIAL JUSTICE ISSUES

Abingdon Press
ACTA Publications
(s)-American Binding—R
Atheneum/Yg Readers
B & H Publishing
Baker Books
Baker's Plays—R
(s)-Black Forest/Tennessee—R
(s)-Booklocker.com—R
(s)-Brentwood—R
Bridge-Logos—R
(s)-Brown Books—R
Canadian Inst. for Law—R
Chalice Press
Christian Writer's Ebook—R
(s)-Creation House—R
Crossroad Publishing—R
(s)-DCTS Publishing
Destiny Image—R
Eerdmans Pub., Wm. B.—R
(s)-Elderberry Press
(s)-Essence—R
(s)-Fairway Press—R
Forward Movement
Georgetown Univ. Press
Greenwood/Praeger
HarperOne
Haworth Pastoral—R
Hidden Brook Press—R
Hill Street Press—R
(s)-Holy Fire Publishing—R
Hope Publishing—R
Howard Books
Inkling Books—R
InterVarsity Press—R
Jossey-Bass
Judson Press
Libros Liguori
Life Cycle Books—R
Lift Every Voice—R
Lighthouse Publishing—R
Marshall Trumann
Monarch Books
NavPress
NavPress Th1nk—R
(s)-One World—R
Our Sunday Visitor—R
Paulist Press
Pilgrim Press—R
(s)-Pleasant Word—R
(s)-Providence Pub.—R
Quintessential Books—R
(s)-Reformation Publishers—R
Regal
Regnery
Rose Publishing
Sheed & Ward—R
St. Anthony Mess. Press—R
(s)-Star Bible Public.
Still Waters Revival—R
(s)-Synergy Publishers—R
(s)-Tate Publishing—R
(s)-Trafford Publishing—R
(s)-VMI Publishers
Wesleyan Publishing
(s)-WinePress—R
(s)-Word Alive
Youth Specialties

SOCIOLOGY

(s)-American Binding—R
Baker Books
Baker's Plays—R
(s)-Black Forest/Tennessee—R
Blue Dolphin
(s)-Booklocker.com—R
Branden Publishing—R
(s)-Brentwood—R
(s)-Brown Books—R
Carey Library, Wm.—R
Christian Writer's Ebook—R
Eerdmans Pub., Wm. B.—R
(s)-Elderberry Press
(s)-Essence—R
(s)-Fairway Press—R
FaithWalk
Fordham Univ. Press—R
Greenwood/Praeger

Haworth Pastoral—R
Hidden Brook Press—R
Hill Street Press—R
(s)-Holy Fire Publishing—R
(s)-IMD Press—R
InterVarsity Press—R
Life Cycle Books—R
Lighthouse Publishing—R
Marshall Trumann
(s)-McDougal Publishing—R
Monarch Books
New York Univ. Press
(s)-One World—R
(s)-Pleasant Word—R
(s)-Reformation Publishers—R
RiverOak
(s)-Star Bible Public.
Still Waters Revival—R
(s)-Tate Publishing—R
Third World Press—R
(s)-Trafford Publishing—R
Univ. Press of America—R
(s)-VMI Publishers
(s)-WinePress—R
(s)-Word Alive

SPIRITUAL GIFTS

Abingdon Press
ACTA Publications
Ambassador Books
(s)-American Binding—R
B & H Publishing
Baal Hamon—R
Baker Books
Baker's Plays—R
(s)-Black Forest/Tennessee—R
Blue Dolphin
(s)-Booklocker.com—R
Bridge-Logos—R
(s)-Brown Books—R
Canticle Books—R
Christian Writer's Ebook—R
(s)-Creation House—R
CSS Publishing—R
(s)-Dean Press, Robbie—R
Destiny Image—R
(s)-Elderberry Press
(s)-Essence—R
(s)-Fairway Press—R
FaithWalk
FaithWords
Forward Movement
Gospel Publishing
Greenwood/Praeger
Grupo Nelson
Guardian Angel
Harrison House
Hensley Publishing
Hidden Brook Press—R
Hill Street Press—R
(s)-Holy Fire Publishing—R
Howard Books
(s)-IMD Press—R
Jebaire Publishing
Lighthouse Publishing—R
Living Books for All
Lutheran Univ. Press
Magnus Press—R
Marshall Trumann
Mission World Library—R
Monarch Books
Nelson, Thomas
(s)-One World—R
Pacific Press
Paradise Research—R
Parson Place—R
Parsons Publishing—R
(s)-Path Publishing in Christ—R
Pauline Books—R
(s)-Pleasant Word—R
(s)-Providence Pub.—R
(s)-Reformation Publishers—R
Regal
RiverOak
Rose Publishing
Salvation Publisher—R
(s)-Selah Publishing—R
Shoreline—R
St. Anthony Mess. Press—R
(s)-Star Bible Public.
Strang Book Group—R
(s)-Synergy Publishers—R
(s)-Tate Publishing—R
Tau-Publishing—R
(s)-Trafford Publishing—R
(s)-VMI Publishers
W Publishing
Wesleyan Publishing
Whitaker House
WindRiver—R
(s)-WinePress—R
(s)-Word Alive
(s)-Zoe Life Publishing

SPIRITUALITY

Abingdon Press
ACTA Publications
Alba House—R
(s)-Ali Literary, Alfred—R
Ambassador Books
(s)-American Binding—R
American Book
Augsburg—R
B & H Publishing
Baal Hamon—R
Baker Books
Baker's Plays—R
Ballantine
Bethany House
(s)-Black Forest/Tennessee—R
Blue Dolphin
(s)-Book Publishers—R
(s)-Booklocker.com—R
(s)-Brentwood—R
Bridge-Logos—R
(s)-Brown Books—R
Canticle Books—R
Christian Heritage—R
Christian Writer's Ebook—R
Cistercian—R
Conari Press
Continuum Intl.—R
(s)-Creation House—R
Crossroad Publishing—R
CSS Publishing—R
Descant Publishing
Destiny Image—R
Discovery House—R
Doubleday—R
E-Digital Books
Educational Ministries
Eerdmans Pub., Wm. B.—R
(s)-Elderberry Press
Elijah Press
Emmaus Road—R
(s)-Essence—R
Evergreen Press
(s)-Fairway Press—R
Faith Communications
FaithWalk
FaithWords
Fell, Frederick—R
Fifth Estate—R
Forward Movement
Friends United Press
Greenwood/Praeger
GRQ—R
Guardian Angel
HarperOne
Hay House
Health Commun.
Hidden Brook Press—R
Hill Street Press—R
(s)-Holy Fire Publishing—R
Howard Books
(s)-IMD Press—R
(s)-Impact Christian—R
InterVarsity Press—R
Invisible College Press
Johns Hopkins—R
Jossey-Bass
Judson Press
Kirk House
Kregel—R
Larson Publications—R
Libros Liguori
Lighthouse Publishing—R
Liguori—R
Liturgy Training—R
Living Books for All
Loyola Press
Lutheran Univ. Press
Magnus Press—R
Marshall Trumann
Mission World Library—R
Monarch Books

Morehouse—R
Mt. Olive College Press
NavPress Th1nk—R
Nelson, Thomas
New Hope—R
New Seeds—R
Northstone
(s)-One World—R
P & R Publishing—R
Pacific Press
Paragon House—R
Parsons Publishing—R
(s)-Path Publishing in Christ—R
Pauline Books—R
Paulist Press
Perigee Books
Peter Pauper Press
Pflaum Publishing
Pilgrim Press—R
(s)-Pleasant Word—R
(s)-Providence Pub.—R
Quintessential Books—R
Ragged Edge—R
(s)-Reformation Publishers—R
Regal
Regnery
Resource Public.
RiverOak
Rose Publishing
(s)-Scribe Book—R
(s)-Selah Publishing—R
Sheed & Ward—R
Smyth & Helwys
(s)-So. Baptist Press—R
St. Anthony Mess. Press—R
(s)-Star Bible Public.
Strang Book Group—R
(s)-Synergy Publishers—R
(s)-Tate Publishing—R
Tau-Publishing—R
(s)-Trafford Publishing—R
Treble Heart Books—R
Tyndale House—R
(s)-VMI Publishers
W Publishing
WaterBrook Press—R
Wesleyan Publishing
WindRiver—R
(s)-WinePress—R
(s)-Winer Foundation—R
Wood Lake Books—R
(s)-Word Alive
(s)-Zoe Life Publishing

SPIRITUAL LIFE

Aadeon Publishing—R
Abingdon Press
ACTA Publications
Ambassador Books
(s)-American Binding—R
American Book
Anglicans United—R
Baal Hamon—R
Baker Trittin
Baker's Plays—R
Barbour
Bethany House
(s)-Black Forest/Tennessee—R
BMH Books
(s)-Booklocker.com—R
Bridge-Logos—R
(s)-Brown Books—R
Canticle Books—R
Chapter Two—R
Christian Family—R
Christian Focus—R
Christian Writer's Ebook—R
Church Growth Inst.
Continuum Intl.—R
(s)-Creation House—R
Crossroad Publishing—R
CSS Publishing—R
(s)-Elderberry Press
(s)-Essence—R
Evergreen Press
(s)-Fairway Press—R
FaithWalk
FaithWords
Forward Movement
Gospel Publishing
GRQ—R
Guardian Angel
HarperOne
Harrison House
Hidden Brook Press—R
(s)-Holy Fire Publishing—R
Howard Books
(s)-IMD Press—R
InterVarsity Press—R
(s)-J and J Publishing
Jossey-Bass
Judson Press
Kregel—R
Legacy Publishers
Life Changing Media
(s)-Lifevest Publishing
Lift Every Voice—R
Lighthouse Publishing—R
Liturgy Training—R
Living Books for All
Magnus Press—R
Marshall Trumann
MegaGrace Books
Mission World Library—R
Monarch Books
Morehouse—R
NavPress
NavPress Th1nk—R
New Hope—R
New Seeds—R
(s)-One World—R
P & R Publishing—R
Parson Place—R
Parsons Publishing—R
(s)-Path Publishing in Christ—R
Pathway Press
Pauline Books—R
Paulist Press
Pilgrim Press—R
(s)-Pleasant Word—R
(s)-Providence Pub.—R
Quintessential Books—R
Randall House
(s)-Reformation Publishers—R
Regal
Rose Publishing
Salvation Publisher—R
(s)-Scribe Book—R
St. Anthony Mess. Press—R
(s)-Star Bible Public.
Strang Book Group—R
(s)-Synergy Publishers—R
(s)-Tate Publishing—R
(s)-TEACH Services—R
(s)-Trafford Publishing—R
(s)-VMI Publishers
WaterBrook Press—R
Wesleyan Publishing
Whitaker House
(s)-WinePress—R
(s)-Word Alive
World Publishing
(s)-Zoe Life Publishing

SPIRITUAL WARFARE

Aadeon Publishing—R
(s)-American Binding—R
Anglicans United—R
B & H Publishing
Baal Hamon—R
Baker Books
Baker's Plays—R
(s)-Black Forest/Tennessee—R
(s)-Booklocker.com—R
Bridge-Logos—R
(s)-Brown Books—R
Carey Library, Wm.—R
Christian Family—R
Christian Focus—R
Christian Writer's Ebook—R
(s)-Creation House—R
Destiny Image—R
Editorial Portavoz
(s)-Elderberry Press
(s)-Essence—R
Evergreen Press
(s)-Fairway Press—R
FaithWalk
FaithWords
Good News Pub.
Gospel Publishing
Greenwood/Praeger
Grupo Nelson
Harrison House
Harvest House
Hensley Publishing

Hidden Brook Press—R
(s)-Holy Fire Publishing—R
(s)-IMD Press—R
(s)-Impact Christian—R
Jireh Publishing
Judson Press
Legacy Publishers
Lift Every Voice—R
Lighthouse Publishing—R
(s)-Lightning Star Press—R
Living Books for All
Marshall Trumann
(s)-McDougal Publishing—R
Mission World Library—R
Monarch Books
NavPress Th1nk—R
(s)-One World—R
P & R Publishing—R
Parson Place—R
Parsons Publishing—R
(s)-Path Publishing in Christ—R
(s)-Pleasant Word—R
(s)-Providence Pub.—R
Ravenhawk Books—R
(s)-Reformation Publishers—R
Regal
Rose Publishing
Salvation Publisher—R
(s)-Selah Publishing—R
St. Anthony Mess. Press—R
(s)-Star Bible Public.
Strang Book Group—R
(s)-Synergy Publishers—R
(s)-Tate Publishing—R
(s)-Trafford Publishing—R
Virginia Pines Press
W Publishing
Whitaker House
(s)-WinePress—R
(s)-Winer Foundation—R
(s)-Word Alive
World Publishing
(s)-Zoe Life Publishing

SPORTS/RECREATION

ACTA Publications
Ambassador Books
(s)-American Binding—R
Baker Books
Baker's Plays—R
Ballantine
(s)-Booklocker.com—R
Boyds Mills Press—R
(s)-Brown Books—R
Christian Writer's Ebook—R
Cumberland House
(s)-Elderberry Press
(s)-Essence—R
Evergreen Press
Facts on File
(s)-Fairway Press—R
Greenwood/Praeger
Guardian Angel
Hidden Brook Press—R
Hill Street Press—R
(s)-Holy Fire Publishing—R
Lift Every Voice—R
Lighthouse Publishing—R
Marshall Trumann
Monarch Books
(s)-One World—R
One World/Ballantine
(s)-Pleasant Word—R
Power Publishing
(s)-Providence Pub.—R
Ravenhawk Books—R
(s)-Reformation Publishers—R
Regal
(s)-Tate Publishing—R
TowleHouse—R
(s)-Trafford Publishing—R
(s)-VMI Publishers
(s)-WinePress—R
(s)-Word Alive
(s)-Zoe Life Publishing

STEWARDSHIP

(s)-American Binding—R
Baker Books
(s)-Black Forest/Tennessee—R
(s)-Booklocker.com—R
Bridge-Logos—R
(s)-Brown Books—R
Christian Focus—R
Christian Writer's Ebook—R
College Press—R
(s)-Creation House—R
CSS Publishing—R
Educational Ministries
(s)-Elderberry Press
(s)-Essence—R
Evergreen Press
(s)-Fairway Press—R
FaithWalk
Forward Movement
Geneva Press
Good News Pub.
Group Publishing
Harrison House
Hensley Publishing
Hidden Brook Press—R
Hill Street Press—R
(s)-Holy Fire Publishing—R
Hope Publishing—R
(s)-IMD Press—R
Judson Press
Kirk House
Lift Every Voice—R
Lighthouse Publishing—R
Lutheran Univ. Press
Marshall Trumann
(s)-McDougal Publishing—R
Monarch Books
Neibauer Press—R
(s)-One World—R
Our Sunday Visitor—R
Pacific Press
Parson Place—R
Pilgrim Press—R
(s)-Pleasant Word—R
Presbyterian Pub.
(s)-Providence Pub.—R
(s)-Reformation Publishers—R
Regal
RiverOak
Rose Publishing
Salvation Publisher—R
St. Anthony Mess. Press—R
(s)-Star Bible Public.
(s)-Synergy Publishers—R
(s)-Tate Publishing—R
(s)-Trafford Publishing—R
(s)-VMI Publishers
Wesleyan Publishing
Westminster John Knox
WindRiver—R
(s)-WinePress—R
(s)-Winer Foundation—R
(s)-Word Alive
World Publishing
(s)-Zoe Life Publishing

THEOLOGY

Abingdon Press
Alba House—R
Ambassador-Emerald—R
(s)-American Binding—R
American Cath. Press—R
B & H Publishing
Baal Hamon—R
Baker Books
Baker's Plays—R
Bethany House
Blue Dolphin
BMH Books
(s)-Booklocker.com—R
(s)-Brentwood—R
Bridge Resources
Bridge-Logos—R
(s)-Brown Books—R
Canticle Books—R
Catholic Answers—R
Chalice Press
Christian Family—R
Christian Focus—R
Christian Heritage—R
Christian Writer's Ebook—R
Cistercian—R
College Press—R
Conciliar Press—R
Concordia
Continuum Intl.—R
Cook, David C.

(s)-Creation House—R
Crossroad Publishing—R
CSS Publishing—R
Doubleday—R
Earthen Vessel—R
Eerdmans Pub., Wm. B.—R
(s)-Elderberry Press
(s)-Essence—R
(s)-Fairway Press—R
FaithWalk
Fifth Estate—R
First Fruits of Zion
Fortress Press
Forward Movement
Founders Press
Friends United Press
Geneva Press
Georgetown Univ. Press
Gollehon Press
Good News Pub.
Gospel Publishing
GRQ—R
HarperOne
Hidden Brook Press—R
Hill Street Press—R
(s)-Holy Fire Publishing—R
(s)-IMD Press—R
(s)-Impact Christian—R
Inkling Books—R
InterVarsity Press—R
Intl. Awakening—R
Judson Press
Kirk House
Kregel—R
Lighthouse Publishing—R
Liturgical Press
Liturgy Training—R
Lutheran Univ. Press
Lutterworth Press—R
Magnus Press—R
Mercer Univ. Press—R
Messianic Jewish—R
Millennium III—R
Mission World Library—R
Monarch Books
Multnomah
NavPress Th1nk—R
(s)-One World—R
P & R Publishing—R
Pacific Press
Parsons Publishing—R
Pauline Books—R
Paulist Press
Pilgrim Press—R
(s)-Pleasant Word—R
Presbyterian Pub.
(s)-Providence Pub.—R
Randall House
(s)-Reformation Publishers—R
Reformation Trust
Religious Education
Resource Public.
RiverOak
Rose Publishing
(s)-Scribe Book—R
Sheed & Ward—R
Smyth & Helwys
(s)-So. Baptist Press—R
St. Anthony Mess. Press—R
St. Augustine's Press—R
(s)-Star Bible Public.
Still Waters Revival—R
Strang Book Group—R
(s)-Synergy Publishers—R
T & T Clark—R
(s)-Tate Publishing—R
(s)-Trafford Publishing—R
Trinity Foundation—R
Tyndale House—R
UMI Publishing—R
Univ. Press of America—R
(s)-VMI Publishers
Westminster John Knox
(s)-WinePress—R
(s)-Word Alive
World Publishing
Yale Univ. Press—R
(s)-Zoe Life Publishing
Zondervan

TIME MANAGEMENT

(s)-American Binding—R
B & H Publishing
Baker Books
Barbour
(s)-Black Forest/Tennessee—R
(s)-Book Publishers—R
(s)-Booklocker.com—R
(s)-Brown Books—R
Christian Writer's Ebook—R
Cook, David C.
(s)-Creation House—R
(s)-DCTS Publishing
(s)-Elderberry Press
(s)-Essence—R
Evergreen Press
(s)-Fairway Press—R
FaithWords
Forward Movement
Good News Pub.
GRQ—R
Harvest House
Hensley Publishing
Hidden Brook Press—R
Hill Street Press—R
(s)-Holy Fire Publishing—R
Howard Books
(s)-IMD Press—R
Judson Press
Kirk House
Life Journey Books
Lift Every Voice—R
Lighthouse Publishing—R
Marshall Trumann
Monarch Books
Nelson, Thomas
(s)-One World—R
Parsons Publishing—R
Pauline Books—R
(s)-Pleasant Word—R
(s)-Providence Pub.—R
(s)-Reformation Publishers—R
Regal
RiverOak
Rose Publishing
Salvation Publisher—R
(s)-Star Bible Public.
(s)-Tate Publishing—R
(s)-Trafford Publishing—R
(s)-VMI Publishers
Walk Worthy—R
(s)-WinePress—R
(s)-Winer Foundation—R
(s)-Word Alive
(s)-Zoe Life Publishing

TRACTS

Chapter Two—R
Christian Writer's Ebook—R
Crossway Books
(s)-Essence—R
Forward Movement
(s)-FruitBearer Pub.
Good News Pub.
(s)-IMD Press—R
Intl. Awakening—R
Libros Liguori
Liguori—R
Living Books for All
Neibauer Press—R
(s)-One World—R
Randall House
Rose Publishing
Tract League
Trinity Foundation—R
(s)-Word Alive

TRAVEL

(s)-American Binding—R
Baker Books
Baker's Plays—R
Ballantine
(s)-Booklocker.com—R
(s)-Brentwood—R
(s)-Brown Books—R
Christian Heritage—R
Christian Writer's Ebook—R
Cumberland House
Destiny Image (books)—R
E-Digital Books
(s)-Elderberry Press
(s)-Essence—R
(s)-Fairway Press—R

FaithWalk
Greenwood/Praeger
Hidden Brook Press—R
Hill Street Press—R
(s)-Holy Fire Publishing—R
Hope Publishing—R
Ideals/Children
(s)-IMD Press—R
(s)-Lifevest Publishing
Lighthouse Publishing—R
Liguori—R
Monarch Books
(s)-One World—R
One World/Ballantine
Peter Pauper Press
(s)-Pleasant Word—R
(s)-Providence Pub.—R
(s)-Reformation Publishers—R
(s)-Tate Publishing—R
(s)-Trafford Publishing—R
(s)-WinePress—R
(s)-Word Alive

TWEEN BOOKS

Ambassador Books
(s)-American Binding—R
Atheneum/Yg Readers
Baker Trittin
Barbour
(s)-Black Forest/Tennessee—R
(s)-Booklocker.com—R
(s)-Brown Books—R
(s)-Elderberry Press
(s)-Essence—R
Hidden Brook Press—R
Journey Stone—R
(s)-Kindred Books—R
Kregel—R
Legacy Press—R
Lighthouse Publishing—R
Mission City Press
New Leaf
Pauline Books—R
(s)-Reformation Publishers—R
Starik Publishing
(s)-Tate Publishing—R
(s)-Trafford Publishing—R
White Stone Books—R
(s)-Zoe Life Publishing

WOMEN'S ISSUES

ACTA Publications
Adams Media
Ambassador Books
(s)-American Binding—R
AMG Publishers—R
B & H Publishing
Baker Academic
Baker Books
Baker's Plays—R
Ballantine
Barbour
Beacon Hill Press—R
BelleBooks—R
Bethany House
(s)-Black Forest/Tennessee—R
Blue Dolphin
BMH Books
(s)-Booklocker.com—R
Bridge-Logos—R
(s)-Brown Books—R
Chalice Press
Christian Writer's Ebook—R
College Press—R
Cook, David C.
(s)-Creation House—R
Crossroad Publishing—R
(s)-Dean Press, Robbie—R
Destiny Image—R
Discovery House—R
Doubleday—R
(s)-Elderberry Press
Emmaus Road—R
(s)-Essence—R
Evergreen Press
Facts on File
(s)-Fairway Press—R
Faith Communications
FaithWalk
FaithWords
FamilyLife (books)—R
Focus on the Family
Fortress Press
Green Key Books
Greenwood/Praeger
GRQ—R
Guernica Editions—R
HarperOne
Harrison House
Haworth Pastoral—R
Health Commun.
Hensley Publishing
Hidden Brook Press—R
Hill Street Press—R
(s)-Holy Fire Publishing—R
Hope Publishing—R
Howard Books
(s)-IMD Press—R
Inkling Books—R
(s)-J and J Publishing
Johns Hopkins—R
Jossey-Bass
Jubilant Press—R
Judson Press
Kirk House
Kregel—R
Langmarc
Legacy Publishers
Life Cycle Books—R
Life Journey Books
Lift Every Voice—R
Lighthouse Publishing—R
(s)-Lightning Star Press—R
Loyola Press
Marshall Trumann
(s)-McDougal Publishing—R
Monarch Books
Moody Publishers
NavPress
NavPress Th1nk—R
Nelson, Thomas
New Hope—R
New Leaf
New York Univ. Press
(s)-One World—R
One World/Ballantine
Parson Place—R
Parsons Publishing—R
Pauline Books—R
Pelican Publishing—R
Perigee Books
Pilgrim Press—R
(s)-Pleasant Word—R
(s)-Providence Pub.—R
Randall House
Ravenhawk Books—R
(s)-Reformation Publishers—R
Regal
Resource Public.
RiverOak
Rose Publishing
(s)-Scribe Book—R
(s)-Selah Publishing—R
Sheed & Ward—R
(s)-So. Baptist Press—R
St. Anthony Mess. Press—R
(s)-Star Bible Public.
Starik Publishing
Still Waters Revival—R
Strang Book Group—R
(s)-Synergy Publishers—R
Tarcher, Jeremy P.—R
(s)-Tate Publishing—R
Third World Press—R
(s)-Trafford Publishing—R
Treble Heart Books—R
Univ. of AR Press—R
(s)-VMI Publishers
W Publishing
Wesleyan Publishing
Whitaker House
White Stone Books—R
(s)-WinePress—R
(s)-Word Alive
(s)-Zoe Life Publishing

WORLD ISSUES

Aadeon Publishing—R
(s)-American Binding—R
AMG Publishers—R
Baker Books
Baker's Plays—R
(s)-Black Forest/Tennessee—R

Blue Dolphin
(s)-Booklocker.com—R
Boyds Mills Press—R
Bridge-Logos—R
(s)-Brown Books—R
Carey Library, Wm.—R
Chalice Press
Christian Writer's Ebook—R
(s)-Creation House—R
Doubleday—R
(s)-Elderberry Press
(s)-Essence—R
(s)-Fairway Press—R
FaithWalk
Fifth Estate—R
Georgetown Univ. Press
Greenwood/Praeger
Guernica Editions—R
HarperOne
Harrison House
Hidden Brook Press—R
Hill Street Press—R
(s)-Holy Fire Publishing—R
InterVarsity Press—R
Kirk House
Lift Every Voice—R
Lighthouse Publishing—R
Marshall Trumann
Monarch Books
NavPress
NavPress Th1nk—R
(s)-One World—R
Pilgrim Press—R
(s)-Pleasant Word—R
(s)-Providence Pub.—R
Quintessential Books—R
(s)-Reformation Publishers—R
Regal
Regnery
RiverOak
Rose Publishing
(s)-Scribe Book—R
(s)-Selah Publishing—R
(s)-Star Bible Public.
Still Waters Revival—R
Strang Book Group—R
(s)-Synergy Publishers—R
(s)-Tate Publishing—R
(s)-Trafford Publishing—R
Tyndale House—R
(s)-VMI Publishers
(s)-WinePress—R
(s)-Word Alive
(s)-Zoe Life Publishing

WORSHIP

Abingdon Press
ACTA Publications
Ambassador-Emerald—R
(s)-American Binding—R
American Cath. Press—R
Augsburg/Worship & Music
B & H Publishing
Baal Hamon—R
Baker's Plays—R
Barbour
Bethany House
(s)-Black Forest/Tennessee—R
BMH Books
(s)-Booklocker.com—R
Bridge-Logos—R
(s)-Brown Books—R
Chalice Press
Chapter Two—R
CharismaKids
Christian Focus—R
Christian Heritage—R
Christian Writer's Ebook—R
College Press—R
Continuum Intl.—R
Cook, David C.
(s)-Creation House—R
CSS Publishing—R
Destiny Image—R
Educational Ministries
(s)-Elderberry Press
(s)-Essence—R
(s)-Fairway Press—R
Faith Alive
FaithWalk
FaithWords
Forward Movement
Founders Press
Greenwood/Praeger
Group Publishing
Harrison House
Harvest Day
Hidden Brook Press—R
Hill Street Press—R
(s)-Holy Fire Publishing—R
(s)-IMD Press—R
InterVarsity Press—R
Judson Press
Kregel—R
Life Journey Books
Lift Every Voice—R
Lighthouse Publishing—R
Liturgy Training—R
Living Books for All
Lutheran Univ. Press
Mission World Library—R
Monarch Books
NavPress Th1nk—R
(s)-One World—R
Oregon Catholic
P & R Publishing—R
Pacific Press
Parson Place—R
Parsons Publishing—R
Pauline Books—R
Pilgrim Press—R
(s)-Pleasant Word—R
(s)-Providence Pub.—R
Randall House
(s)-Reformation Publishers—R
Reformation Trust
Regal
Resource Public.
Rose Publishing
Salt Works
(s)-Scribe Book—R
(s)-Selah Publishing—R
St. Anthony Mess. Press—R
(s)-Star Bible Public.
(s)-Synergy Publishers—R
(s)-Tate Publishing—R
(s)-Trafford Publishing—R
(s)-VMI Publishers
W Publishing
Wesleyan Publishing
Westminster John Knox
(s)-WinePress—R
(s)-Word Alive

WORSHIP RESOURCES

Abingdon Press
ACTA Publications
(s)-American Binding—R
Augsburg/Worship & Music
Baal Hamon—R
Baker Books
(s)-Black Forest/Tennessee—R
(s)-Booklocker.com—R
(s)-Brown Books—R
Catholic Book
Chalice Press
Christian Writer's Ebook—R
CSS Publishing—R
(s)-DCTS Publishing
(s)-Elderberry Press
(s)-Essence—R
(s)-Fairway Press—R
Faith Alive
FaithWalk
Forward Movement
Founders Press
Geneva Press
Greenwood/Praeger
Group Publishing
Harvest Day
Hidden Brook Press—R
Hill Street Press—R
(s)-Holy Fire Publishing—R
(s)-IMD Press—R
InterVarsity Press—R
Judson Press
Lighthouse Publishing—R
Liturgical Press
Liturgy Training—R
Monarch Books
(s)-One World—R
Our Sunday Visitor—R
Parsons Publishing—R

Pilgrim Press—R
(s)-Pleasant Word—R
Presbyterian Pub.
(s)-Providence Pub.—R
Randall House
(s)-Reformation Publishers—R
Resource Public.
Rose Publishing
Salt Works
Smyth & Helwys
Standard Publishing
(s)-Tate Publishing—R
(s)-Trafford Publishing—R
(s)-VMI Publishers
Wesleyan Publishing
Westminster John Knox
(s)-WinePress—R
Wood Lake Books—R
(s)-Word Alive
(s)-Zoe Life Publishing

WRITING HOW-TO

(s)-American Binding—R
(s)-Booklocker.com—R
(s)-Brown Books—R
Christian Writer's Ebook—R
Dabbling Mum Press
(s)-Elderberry Press
(s)-Essence—R
Evergreen Press
Fair Havens—R
(s)-Fairway Press—R
FaithWalk
Filbert Publishing—R
Hidden Brook Press—R
(s)-Holy Fire Publishing—R
Jubilant Press—R
Lighthouse Publishing—R
Mission City Press
(s)-One World—R
Parson Place—R
(s)-Pleasant Word—R
(s)-Providence Pub.—R
(s)-Reformation Publishers—R
(s)-Selah Publishing—R
(s)-Tate Publishing—R
(s)-Trafford Publishing—R
(s)-VMI Publishers
(s)-WinePress—R
(s)-Word Alive
Write Now—R

YOUTH BOOKS (Nonfiction)

Note: Listing denotes books for 8- to 12-year-olds, junior highs, or senior highs. If all three, it will say "all." If no age group is listed, they did not specify.

Ambassador Books (All)
(s)-American Binding—R (Jr./Sr. High)
Anglicans United—R (8-12/Jr. High)
Atheneum/Yg Readers (All)
B & H Publishing
Baker Books
Baker Trittin (All)
Barbour (8-12/Jr. High)
Bethany House (All)
Big Idea (8-12/Jr. High)
BJU/Journey Forth—R (8-12)
(s)-Black Forest/Tennessee—R (All)
(s)-Book Publishers—R (All)
(s)-Booklocker.com—R (All)
Boyds Mills Press—R (All)
(s)-Brown Books—R (All)
Carson-Dellosa (8-12)
CharismaKids (8-12/Jr. High)
Christian Ed. Pub.
Christian Focus—R (All)
Christian Writer's Ebook—R (All)
Conciliar Press—R (8-12)
Concordia (All)
Contemporary Drama
(s)-Creation House—R (All)
Dawn Publications (Jr. High)
Educational Ministries
Eerdmans Pub., Wm. B.—R (All)
Ekklesia Press—R (Sr. High)
(s)-Elderberry Press (All)
(s)-Essence—R (All)
Evergreen Press
Facts on File
Focus on the Family (Sr. High)
Friends United Press
Grupo Nelson (Jr. High)
Guardian Angel (8-12)
Harcourt Religion (Sr. High)
Harrison House (All)
Health Commun.
Hidden Brook Press—R (All)
(s)-Holy Fire Publishing—R (All)
(s)-IMD Press—R (All)
(s)-J and J Publishing (8-12/Jr. High)
Journey Stone—R (8-12/Jr. High)
(s)-Kindred Books—R (All)
Knight George Pub. (All)
Kregel—R (All)
Legacy Press—R (8-12)
Life Cycle Books—R (8-12)
Lift Every Voice—R (All)
Lighthouse Publishing—R (All)
Master Books (All)
McRuffy Press (8-12)
Meriwether (Jr./Sr. High)
Mission City Press (8-12)
Monarch Books (All)
Moody Publishers
NavPress (Sr. High)
NavPress Th1nk—R (Sr. High)
New Canaan—R (All)
New Leaf (All)
(s)-One World—R (All)
P & R Publishing—R (All)
Pacific Press
Parson Place—R (All)
(s)-Path Publishing—R
Pauline Books—R (All)
Peter Pauper Press (8-12)
Pflaum Publishing (8-12/Jr. High)
(s)-Pleasant Word—R (All)
Randall House (All)
Ravenhawk Books—R (All)
(s)-Reformation Publishers—R (All)
Salt Works (All)
Starik Publishing (All)
Strang Book Group—R (8-12)
(s)-Tate Publishing—R (All)
(s)-Trafford Publishing—R (All)
(s)-VMI Publishers (All)
WaterBrook Press—R (All)
White Stone Books—R (All)
(s)-WinePress—R (All)
(s)-Word Alive (All)
Youth Specialties (Jr./Sr. High)
(s)-Zoe Life Publishing

YOUTH PROGRAMS

Abingdon Press
(s)-American Binding—R
Baker Books
Carson-Dellosa
Christian Writer's Ebook—R
Church Growth Inst.
Contemporary Drama
Educational Ministries
(s)-Fairway Press—R
Faith Alive
Gospel Publishing
Group Publishing
Harcourt Religion
(s)-Holy Fire Publishing—R
(s)-IMD Press—R
Judson Press
Lift Every Voice—R
Mission City Press
Monarch Books
NavPress Th1nk—R
(s)-One World—R
Parson Place—R
Pflaum Publishing
Pilgrim Press—R
Ponder Publishing
(s)-Providence Pub.—R
Randall House Digital
(s)-Reformation Publishers—R
Rose Publishing
Salt Works
Standard Publishing
(s)-Tate Publishing—R

ALPHABETICAL LISTINGS OF BOOK PUBLISHERS

If you do not find the publisher you are looking for, check the General Index. See the introduction to that index for the codes used to identify the current status of each unlisted publisher. If you do not understand all the terms or abbreviations used in these listings, read the "How to Use This Book" section at the front of the book.

(+) A plus sign before a listing indicates it is a new listing this year.

AADEON PUBLISHING COMPANY, PO Box 223, Hartford CT 06141. Fax 206-666-5132. E-mail: submissions@aadeon.com. Website: www.aadeon.com. Submit to The Editor. Addresses social, cultural, and political issues related to the United States of America; must be insightful, historically and biblically accurate, and focused toward a Christian readership. Publishes 1 title/yr.; trade paperback. Accepts mss through agents. Does print-on-demand. Reprints books. Requires 160 pgs. or more. Royalty 8% on net; no advance. Average first printing 100-5,000. Publication within 1 yr. Considers simultaneous submissions. Requires accepted ms on disk in Microsoft Word. Responds in 1-4 mos. Requires NKJV. Guidelines on Website; no catalog.

Nonfiction: Proposal/3 chapters or complete ms; no phone/fax/e-query.

Photos/Artwork: Open to queries from freelance artists.

Tips: "We are particularly interested in manuscripts that challenge average people to confront and overcome the negative influences of an increasingly secular and godless society. Manuscripts must be well organized, professionally edited, easy to understand, biblically based, and scripturally supported (frequent quotations from the Bible—chapter and verse—to support writings). Manuscripts must clearly speak to both a Christian and non-Christian audience."

ABINGDON PRESS, 201—8th Ave. S., PO Box 801, Nashville TN 37202. (615)749-6301. Fax (615)749-6512. E-mail: (first initial and last name) @umpublishing.org. Website: www.abingdonpress.com. United Methodist Publishing House. Editors: Harriett Jane Olson, ed. dir.; Ron Kidd, gen. interest bks.; Robert Ratcliff, professional and academic bks.; John Kutsko, reference bks.; Joseph A. Crowe, gen. interest bks.; Marj Pon, children's bks.; Crys Zinkiewicz, youth bks. Books and church supplies directed primarily to a mainline religious market. Imprint: Dimensions for Living (see separate listing). Publishes 120 titles/yr.; hardcover, trade paperbacks. Receives 3,000 submissions annually. Less than 5% of books from first-time authors. Accepts mss through agents. No reprints. Prefers 144 pgs. Royalty 5-10% on retail; advance. Average first printing 3,500-4,000. Publication within 18 mos. Prefers no simultaneous submissions. Requires requested ms on disk. Responds in 8-12 wks. Prefers NRSV or a variety of which NRSV is one. Guidelines (also by e-mail); free catalog.

Nonfiction: Proposal/2 chapters; no phone/fax/e-query.

Ethnic Books: African American, Hispanic, Native American, Korean.

Photos/Artwork: Accepts freelance photos for book covers.

Tips: "We develop and produce materials to help more people in more places come to know and love God through Jesus Christ and to choose to serve God and neighbor."

ACTA PUBLICATIONS, 5559 W. Howard St., Skokie IL 60077-2621. Toll-free (800)397-2282. (847)676-2282. Fax (800)397-0079. (847)676-2287. E-mail: acta@actapublications.com. Website: www.actapublications.com. Catholic. Gregory F. Augustine Pierce, pres. & co-pub. Wants books that successfully integrate daily life and spirituality. Publishes 10 titles/yr.; hardcover, trade paperbacks, coffee-table books. Receives 100 submissions annually. 50% of books from first-time authors. Prefers 150-200 pgs. Royalty 10-12% of net; no advance. Average first printing 3,000. Publication within 1 yr. Responds in 2 mos. Prefers NRSV. Guidelines; catalog for 9x12 SAE/2 stamps.

Nonfiction: Query or proposal/1 chapter; no phone/fax/e-query.

Tips: "Most open to books that are useful to a large number of average Christians. Read our catalog and one of our books first."

ADAMS MEDIA CORP., 57 Littlefield St., Avon MA 02322. (508)427-7100. Fax (800)872-5628. E-mail: submissions@adamsmedia.com. Website: www.adamsmedia.com. Division of F + W Publications. Jill Alexander, sr. ed. Publishes 230 titles/yr. Receives 6,500 submissions annually. 40% of books from first-time authors. Accepts mss through agents. Royalty; variable advance; or outright purchase. Publication within 12-18 mos. Considers simultaneous submissions. Responds in 3 mos. No mss accepted by e-mail. Guidelines on Website; catalog for 9x12 SAE/5 stamps.

Nonfiction: Query first; no phone/fax/e-query.

Tips: General publisher that does some inspirational books.

A.D. PLAYERS THEATER, 2710 W. Alabama, Houston TX 77098. (713)439-0181, ext. 116. E-mail: lee@adplayers.org. Website: www.adplayers.org. Lee Walker, literary mngr. Produces full-length plays and musicals with Judeo-Christian world-view; interested only in scripts suitable for production. Payment negotiable. Guidelines available by e-mail or Website.

Fiction: Play scripts only/query first; phone/fax/e-query OK. "Send synopsis and/or brief scene or demo tape/CD. Include cast list."

Tips: "Our only consideration is whether the scripts are suitable for production in our theater—we don't publish them." They do not publish books, scripts, etc.

AIRLEAF PUBLISHING, LLC, 35 Industrial Dr., Ste. 104, Martinsville IN 46151. Toll-free (800)342-6068. Fax (765)342-7217. E-mail: Carl@airleaf.com. Website: www.airleaf.com. Carl Lau, pres.; Krystal Hatfield, author consultant. Incomplete topical listings.

ALBA HOUSE/ST. PAULS, 2187 Victory Blvd., Staten Island NY 10314-6603. (718)761-0047. Fax (718)761-0057. E-mail: Edmund_Lane@juno.com. Website: www.alba-house.com. Catholic/Society of St. Paul. Edmund C. Lane, SSP, ed-in-chief; Frank Sadowski, SSP, ed. Imprint: St. Pauls. Publishes 24 titles/yr.; trade paperbacks. Receives 450 submissions annually. 20% of books from first-time authors. No mss through agents. Reprints books. Prefers 124 pgs. Royalty 7-10% on retail; no advance. Average first printing 3,500. Publication within 9 mos. Prefers requested ms on disk. Responds in 1-2 mos. Free guidelines/catalog.

Nonfiction: Query.

Special Needs: Spirituality in the Roman Catholic tradition; lives of the saints.

AMBASSADOR BOOKS INC., 91 Prescott St., Worcester MA 01605-1702. (508)756-2893. Fax (508)757-7055. E-mail: info@ambassadorbooks.com, or through Website: www.ambassadorbooks.com. Catholic. Mr. Chris Driscoll, acq. ed. Books of intellectual and spiritual excellence. Publishes 9 titles/yr.; hardcover, trade paperbacks. Receives 2,100 submissions annually. 50% of books from first-time authors. Accepts mss through agents. No reprints. Royalty 8-10% of retail; no advance. Publication within 1 yr. Considers simultaneous submissions. Responds in 3-4 mos. Prefers NAB. Guidelines (also by e-mail/Website); free catalog (or on Website).

Nonfiction: Query; no phone/fax/e-query.

Fiction: Query. Juvenile, young adult, adult; picture books & board books.

Photos/Artwork: Accepts freelance photos for book covers.

Tips: "Most open to books that will have a positive impact on readers' lives. Must be well written and fit with our mission."

AMBASSADOR-EMERALD, INTL., 427 Wade Hampton Blvd., Greenville SC 29609. (864)235-2434. Fax (864)235-2491. E-mail: publisher@emeraldhouse.com. Website: www.emeraldhouse.com. European office: Ambassador Productions, Providence House, Ardenlee, Belfast BT6 8QJ, N. Ireland. Phone 028 90450010. Fax 028 90739659. E-mail: info@ambassador-productions.com. Emerald House Group Inc. Sam Lowry, ed. Dedicated to spreading the gospel of Christ and empowering Christians through the written word. Publishes 55 titles/yr.; hardcover, trade paperbacks. Receives 400 submissions annually. 15% of books from first-time authors. Accepts mss through agents. **SUBSIDY PUBLISHES 1%.** Reprints books. Prefers 150-200 pgs. Royalty 5-15% of net; advance $1,000. Average first printing 5,000. Publication within 1 yr. Considers simultaneous submissions. Prefers requested ms on disk or by e-mail. Responds in 3 mos. Prefers KJV. Guidelines (also by e-mail); free catalog.

Nonfiction: Query only; fax/e-query OK.

Fiction: Query only; fax/e-query OK. All ages.

Tips: "We're most open to nonfiction writing for women."

AMERICAN BOOK PUBLISHING. E-mail: acqeditor@american-book.com (submissions), or info@american-book.com (guidelines). Website: www.american-book.com. Open to inspirational, Christian spiritual, and wholesome books only. Guidelines by e-mail/Website.

Nonfiction/Fiction: E-query required; submission instructions on Website.

Tips: "We prefer to publish wholesome, inspirational, or educational books. We offer a variety of publishing options, which may include a contract with an advance for well-established authors; a contract with a refundable deposit of $780 for a promising new author. The deposit is returned to the author the first quarter after the book is released when minimum sales have been met."

AMERICAN CATHOLIC PRESS, 16565 State St., South Holland IL 60473-2025. (708)331-5485. Fax (708)331-5484. E-mail: acp@acpress.org. Website: www.acpress.org, or www.leafletmissal.com. Catholic worship resources. Father Michael Gilligan, ed. dir. Publishes 4 titles/yr.; hardcover. Receives 10 submissions annually. Reprints books. Pays $25-100 for outright purchases only. Average first printing 3,000. Publication within 1 yr. No simultaneous submissions. Responds in 2 mos. Prefers NAS. No guidelines; catalog for SASE.

Nonfiction: Query first; no phone/fax/e-query.

Tips: "We publish only materials on the Roman Catholic liturgy. Especially interested in new music for church services. No poetry or fiction."

AMG PUBLISHERS/LIVING INK BOOKS, 6815 Shallowford Rd. (37421), PO Box 22000, Chattanooga TN 37422. Toll-free (800)266-4977. (423)894-6060. Toll-free fax (800)265-6690 or (423)894-9511. E-mail: danp@amginternational.org. Website: www.amgpublishers.com. AMG International. Dan Penwell, dir. of product development/acquisitions; Dr. Warren Baker, sr. ed.; Richard Steele, assoc. ed. To provide biblically oriented books for reference, learning, and personal growth. Imprint: Living Ink Books. Publishes 30 titles/yr.; hardcover, trade paperbacks. Receives 2,500 submissions annually. 30% of books from first-time authors. Accepts mss through agents. Reprints books. Prefers 50,000 wds. or 175 pgs. Royalty 10-16% of net; advance $1,500 and up. Average first printing 3,000. Publication within 18 mos. Accepts simultaneous submissions. Prefers accepted ms by mail. Responds in 1-4 mos. Prefers KJV, NASB, NIV, NKJV, NLT. Guidelines (also by e-mail/Website); catalog for 9x12 SAE/5 stamps.

Nonfiction: Query letter first; e-query preferred. "Looking for well-written nonfiction. We have a broad interest in biblically oriented books."

Fiction: Teen fantasy.

Special Needs: Women's issues, men's issues, and other current issues—including Christian-political action books.

Also Does: Bible software, Bible audio cassettes, CD-ROMs.

Tips: "Most open to a book that is well thought out, clearly written, and finely edited. A professional proposal, following our specific guidelines, has the best chance of acceptance. Spend extra time in developing a good proposal. We are always looking for something new and different—with a niche. Write, and rewrite, and rewrite, and rewrite again."

****Note:** This publisher serviced by The Writer's Edge.

ANGLICANS UNITED/LATIMER PRESS, PO Box 763217, Dallas TX 75376. (972)293-7443. Fax (972)293-7559. E-mail: anglicansunited@sbcglobal.net. Website: www.anglicansunited.com; www.latimerpress.com. Episcopal Church USA. Cheryl M. Wetzel, ed. Provides educational materials for biblically orthodox Anglicans and Episcopalians. Publishes 4 titles/yr.; trade paperbacks, mass-market paperbacks. Receives 20 submissions annually. 90% of books from first-time authors. Accepts mss through agents. **SOME SUBSIDY.** Reprints books. Prefers up to 225 pgs. Outright purchase for $100-500. Average first printing 1,500-2,000. Publication within 6 mos. Considers simultaneous submissions. Prefers ms by disk or e-mail. Responds in 1 mo. Prefers NIV. Guidelines; catalog for #10 SAE/1 stamp.

Nonfiction: Query letter only first; no phone query; fax/e-query OK. "Looking for Anglican history and practice; adult education."

Ethnic Books: Beginning to translate classical Anglican books into Spanish for Latin American market.

Also Does: Booklets; Videos/DVDs.

Photos/Artwork: Open to queries from freelance artists.

Tips: "Most open to (1) a book (60-110 pages total), used in Christian education classes for adults and teens; (2) a book (60 pages) on baptism, marriage, grief, confirmation, or stewardship."

****Note:** This publisher serviced by The Writer's Edge.

ATHENEUM BOOKS FOR YOUNG READERS, 1230 Avenue of the Americas, New York NY 10020. (212)698-2715. Fax (212)698-2796. Website: www.simonsayskids.com. Imprint of Simon & Schuster. Submit to The Editor. Publishes books for pre-school through high school. Publishes in hardcover. Prefers mss through agents. Royalty; advance. Considers simultaneous submissions. Guidelines.

Nonfiction: Query only; no phone/fax/e-query. For children/young adult readers only.

Fiction: Query only. For children and teens.

Tips: "Most open to well-written, fast-paced, unique books for middle-grade readers. Subjects include religion."

AUGSBURG BOOKS, PO Box 1209, Minneapolis MN 55440-1209. (612)330-3300. E-mail: booksub@augsburgfortress.org. Website: www.augsburgbooks.com. Augsburg Fortress Publishers. Bill Huff, VP of Publishing; submit to Book Editor. Publishing house of the Evangelical Lutheran Church in America. Publishes trade paperbacks, mass-market paperbacks. Reprints books. Royalty. Guidelines on Website; catalog for 9x12 SAE/3 stamps.

Nonfiction: Query or proposal.

+AUGSBURG FORTRESS WORSHIP & MUSIC, Worship Submissions or Music Submissions, PO Box 1209, Minneapolis MN 55440-1209. E-mail: worshipsub@augsburgfortress.com, or musicsub@augsburgfortress.com. Website: www.augsburgfortress.com. Evangelical Lutheran Church in America. Submit to Worship Editor or Music Editor. Committed to the publication and distribution of worship and music resources representing high musical and liturgical quality in a variety of styles and genres, sound theological substance, pastoral sensitivity, Lutheran heritages, and ecumenical usefulness. Music Imprints: Augsburg Fortress Music and Chantry Press. Royalty 10% on music. Responds in 3 mos. Guidelines on Website.

Worship: Query or proposal by mail or e-mail. "Most done as work-for-hire, but proposals are welcomed."

Music: See Website for submission guidelines for music. Congregational song, choral music, and instrumental music.

Tips: "For music we have two publication dates, March 1 and October 1. Submissions need to arrive at least 9-12 months prior to those dates."

+AVON INSPIRE, HarperCollins, 10 E. 53rd St., New York NY 10022. (212)207-7000. Website: www.avonbooks.com. Published in partnership with HarperOne. Cynthia DiTiberio, ed.

Inspirational women's fiction. Publishes 6-10 titles/yr. Agented submissions only. Royalty and advance negotiable.

Fiction: Historical & contemporary for now; also planning suspense and children's novels.

+BAAL HAMON PUBLISHER, 28 Akinniranye St., PO Box 2338, Akure, Ondo State, Nigeria. Phone: +234 (0)34 216 339. E-mail: info@baalhamon.com. Website: www.baalhamon.com. Joy and Truth Christian Ministry. Submit to Acquisitions Editor (submissions@ baalhamon.com). Company is named for the biblical town in which Solomon had a vineyard that was kept for him by a husbandman; company motto is "the vineyard of life-changing words." Estab. 2006. Publishes 30-40 titles/yr.; hardcover, trade paperbacks. Receives 600 submissions annually. 75% of books from first-time authors. Accepts mss through agents. **SUBSIDY PUBLISHES 6-8%;** does print-on-demand. Reprints books. Prefers 40,000-60,000 wds., or 160-240 pgs. Royalty 10-20% on retail; seldom gives $2,000 advance. Average first printing 2,500. Publication within 3-6 mos. Considers simultaneous submissions. Responds in 1-3 wks. Prefers accepted mss by e-mail. Prefers NIV/GNB. Guidelines by e-mail.

Nonfiction: Proposal/1 chapter; unsolicited mss returned unopened; e-query OK.

Fiction: Proposal/1-2 chapters; unsolicited mss returned unopened; e-query OK. For all ages.

Ethnic Books: Black.

Photos: Accepts freelance photos for book covers; open to queries from freelance artists.

Contest: Short Story Contest. Guidelines by e-mail (info@baalhamon.com).

Tips: "Writers should aim at an international, multicultural audience."

BAKER ACADEMIC, PO Box 6287, Grand Rapids MI 49516-6287. (616)676-9185. Fax (616)676-2315. E-mail: submissions@bakeracademic.com. Website: www.bakeracademic .com. Imprint of Baker Publishing Group. Jim Kinney, ed. dir. Publishes religious academic books and professional books for students and church leaders. Publishes 50 titles/yr.; hardcover, trade paperbacks. 10% of books from first-time authors. Accepts mss through agents. Royalty; advance. Publication within 1 yr. Guidelines on Website; catalog for 10x13 SAE/3 stamps.

Nonfiction: No unsolicited queries.

BAKER BOOKS, Box 6287, Grand Rapids MI 49516-6287. (616)676-9185. Fax (616)676-9573. Website: www.bakerbooks.com. Imprint of Baker Publishing Group. Jack Kuhatschek, ed. dir. Ministry titles for the church. No unsolicited proposals. Guidelines; catalog for 10x13 SAE/3 stamps. Submit only through an agent, Writer's Edge, or ChristianManuscript Submissions.com.

BAKER'S PLAYS INC., 45 W. 25th St., Fl. 9, New York NY 10010-2035. (212)255-8085. Fax (212)627-7753. E-mail: editor@bakersplays.com. Website: www.bakersplays.com. Deirdre Shaw, mng. dir.; submit to Associate Editor. Publishes 2-8 titles/yr. Receives 800 submissions annually. 60% of plays from first-time authors. Accepts mss through agents. Reprints plays. Book royalty 10% on retail; performance royalty 50%; no advance. Average first printing 1,000. Publication within 6 mos. Considers simultaneous submissions. Accepts requested ms on disk. Responds in 6-8 mos. Guidelines on Website; separate section in their general catalog, $4.

Plays: Complete ms. "Most open to plays that involve biblical stories or skits on modern Christian life."

Tips: "We currently publish full-length plays, one-act plays for young audiences, theater texts and musicals, plays written by high schoolers, with a separate division which publishes religious plays. We consider plays year round." If your play has been produced, send copies of press clippings. If sending music, you must include a CD, tape, or sheet music.

BAKER TRITTIN PRESS, PO Box 277, Winona Lake IN 46590. (574)269-6100. Fax (574)269-6130. E-mail: info@btconcepts.com. Website: www.bakertrittinpress.com. Marvin G. Baker, ed-in-chief. Imprint: Tweener Press. Books for tweens and young adults 8- to 18-year-olds. Publishes 4-5 fiction titles/yr. 50% of books from first-time authors. Accepts mss through agents. No reprints. Prefers 20,000-40,000 wds. Royalty 7-10% on retail; no advance. Average first printing 2,500. Publication within 18 mos. No simultaneous submissions. Responds in 3 mos. Accepts mss on disk or by e-mail. Prefers NIV.

Nonfiction: Proposal/3 chapters; no phone query; fax/e-query OK.

Fiction: Proposal/3 chapters; no phone query; fax/e-query OK.

BALLANTINE PUBLISHING GROUP, 1745 Broadway, 18th Fl., New York NY 10019. (212)782-9000. Website: www.randomhouse.com/BB. A Division of Random House. Dan Smetanka, religion ed. General publisher that does a few religious books. Mss from agents only. No e-query. Royalty 8-15%; variable advances. Nonfiction & fiction. Guidelines on Website; no catalog.

B & H PUBLISHING GROUP, 127—9th Ave. N., Nashville TN 37234-0115. (615)251-2644. Fax (615)251-3752. E-mail: courtney.brooks@lifeway.com, or through Website: www.broadmanholman.com. Book and Bible division of LifeWay Christian Resources. Ray Clendenen, ed. dir.; Leonard Goss, sr. acq. ed.; Karen Ball, sr. acq. ed. for fiction. Imprints: Holman Bibles, Broadman Supplies, Holman Reference, and B & H Espanol (to come: B & H Books, B & H Academic, B & H Educational, and B & H Kids). Publishes books in the conservative, evangelical tradition by and for the larger Christian world. Publishes 90-100 titles/yr.; hardcover, trade paperbacks. Receives 3,000 submissions annually. 10% of books from first-time authors. Prefers 60,000-80,000 wds. Negotiable royalty on net; advance. Average first printing 5,000. Publication within 12-18 mos. Considers simultaneous submissions. Responds in 9-12 mos. Requires requested ms on disk. Prefers HCSB, NIV, NASB. Guidelines on Website; free catalog.

Nonfiction: Query first; no phone/fax query.

Fiction: Query first. Prefers religious adult contemporary.

Ethnic: Spanish translations.

Also Does: Rocket e-books.

Blog: www.holmantv.com. A series of weekly video episodes for high school and college students.

Tips: "Follow guidelines when submitting. Be informed about the market in general and specifically related to the book you want to write." Expanding into fiction, gift books, and children's books.

**Note: This publisher serviced by The Writer's Edge.

BANTAM BOOKS— See Doubleday Religion.

BARBOUR PUBLISHING INC., 1810 Barbour Dr., PO Box 719, Uhrichsville OH 44683. (740)922-6045. Fax (740)922-5948. E-mail: editors@barbourbooks.com. Website: www.barbourbooks.com. Paul Muckley (pmuckley@barbourbooks.com), sr. ed./nonfiction; Rebecca Germany (rgermany@barbourbooks.com), sr. ed./romance and women's fiction (novels & novellas); Kelly Williams (kwilliams@barbourbooks.com), mng. ed. and youth/children/gift acquisitions. To publish and distribute inspirational products offering exceptional value and biblical encouragement to the masses. Imprints: Barbour Books (fiction and nonfiction) and Heartsong Presents (romance: see separate listing). Publishes 100 titles/yr.; hardcover, trade paperbacks, mass-market paperbacks. Receives 2,000 submissions annually. 10% of books from first-time authors. Accepts mss through agents. No subsidy. Prefers 50,000 wds. (novels & nonfiction). Royalty 8-12% of net; outright purchases $500-5,000; advance $500-7,500. Average first printing 15,000-20,000. Publication within 12 mos. Considers simultaneous submissions. Responds in 3-6 mos. Prefers NIV, KJV. Guidelines (also by e-mail/Website); free catalog.

Nonfiction: Proposal/3 chapters; no phone/fax query; e-query OK.

Fiction: Proposal/3 chapters to Rebecca Germany, fiction ed. Novellas 20,000 wds. For all ages. "We are interested in a mystery/romance series." See separate listing for Heartsong Presents & Heartsong Presents—Mysteries.

Tips: "We seek solid, evangelical books with the greatest mass appeal. A good title on practical Christian living will go much farther with Barbour than will a commentary on Jude. Do your homework before sending us a manuscript; send material that will work well within our publishing philosophy."

****Note:** This publisher serviced by The Writer's Edge.

BARCLAY PRESS, 211 N. Meridian St., Ste. 101, Newberg OR 97132. (503)538-9775. Fax (503) 554-8597. E-mail: info@barclaypress.com. Website: www.barclaypress.com. Friends/ Quaker. Dan McCracken, gen. mngr. No unsolicited manuscripts.

****Note:** This publisher serviced by The Writer's Edge.

BAYLOR UNIVERSITY PRESS, One Bear Pl., #97363, Waco TX 76798-7308. (254)710-3164. Fax (254)710-3440. E-mail: Carey_Newman@baylor.edu. Website: www.baylorpress.com. Baptist. Dr. Carey C. Newman, dir., (254)710-3522, carey_newman@baylor.edu; Casey Blaine, acq. ed., (254)710-2846), casey_blaine@baylor.edu. Imprint: Markham Press Fund. Academic press producing scholarly books on religion and social sciences; church-state studies. Publishes 30 academic titles/yr.; hardcover, trade paperback. Receives 100+ submissions annually. 10% of books from first-time authors. Accepts mss through agents. No subsidy publishing. No reprints. Royalty 10% on net; no advance. Average first printing 1,000. Publication within 12 mos. Accepts simultaneous submissions. Responds in 2 mos. Guidelines on Website; free catalog.

Nonfiction: Query only first; no phone/fax query, e-query OK. "Looking for academic books; religion and public life."

BEACON HILL PRESS OF KANSAS CITY, PO Box 419527, Kansas City MO 64141. (816)931-1900. Fax (816)753-4071. E-mail: jap@bhillkc.com. Website: www.bhillkc.com. Nazarene Publishing House/Church of the Nazarene. Bonnie Perry, pub. dir.; Richard Buckner, ministry line ed.; Judi Perry, consumer ed. A Christ-centered publisher that provides authentically Christian resources that are faithful to God's Word and relevant to life. Imprint: Beacon Hill Books. Publishes 30 titles/yr.; hardcover, trade paperbacks. Accepts mss through agents. Reprints books. Prefers 30,000-60,000 wds. or 250 pgs. Royalty 12-14% of net; advance; some outright purchases. Average first printing 5,000. Publication within 1 yr. Considers simultaneous submissions. Responds in 3 mos. or longer. Free guidelines/ catalog.

Nonfiction: Proposal/2 chapters; no phone/fax query. "Looking for practical Christian living, felt needs, Christian care, spiritual growth, and ministry resources."

Tips: "Nearly all our titles come through acquisitions, and the number of freelance submissions has declined dramatically. If you wish to submit, follow guidelines above. You are always welcome to submit after sending for guidelines."

****Note:** This publisher serviced by The Writer's Edge.

+BELIEVE BOOKS, Washington DC, (703)318-0773. E-mail: BelieveBooks@gmail.com. Website: www.BelieveBooks.com. Elizabeth Stalcup, ed. Publishes inspirational life stories of people from around the world. E-query.

BELLEBOOKS, PO Box 67, Smyrna GA 30081. (770)384-1348. Fax (891)334-7705. E-mail: bellebooks@bellebooks.com. Website: www.bellebooks.com. Deborah Smith, ed. Publishes Southern, wholesome, feel-good fiction and nonfiction. Publishes 1 title/yr. Receives 25-40 submissions annually. 0% of books from first-time authors. Accepts mss through agents. Reprints books. Prefers 75,000 wds. or 300 pgs. Royalty; advance. Average first printing 3,000. Publication within 12 mos. Considers simultaneous submissions. Responds in 3 mos. No guidelines or catalog.

Nonfiction: Query by e-mail only; no unsolicited mss. "Looking for nondenominational books with an emphasis on general spirituality."

Fiction: Query by e-mail only "We only publish books with Southern (S.E. USA) settings."

Photos/Artwork: Open to queries from freelance artists.

Tips: "We publish humorous, nondenominational, general inspiration suitable for mainstream as well as Christian readers."

BETHANY HOUSE PUBLISHERS, 11400 Hampshire Ave. S., Bloomington MN 55438. (952)829-2500. Fax (952)996-1304 or (952)829-2768. Website: www.bethanyhouse.com. Baker Publishing Group. Submit to nonfiction, fiction, or juvenile ed. To publish books communicating biblical truth that will inspire and challenge people in both spiritual and practical areas of life. Publishes 90-120 titles/yr.; hardcover, trade paperbacks, mass-market paperback reprints. 2% of books from first-time authors. Accepts mss through agents. No reprints. Negotiable royalty on net; negotiable advance. Publication within 1 yr. Considers simultaneous submissions. Responds in 3 mos. Guidelines for fiction/nonfiction/juvenile on Website; catalog for 9x12 SAE/5 stamps.

Nonfiction: One-page fax query only; all unsolicited submissions returned unopened. "Seeking well-planned and developed books in the following categories: personal growth, deeper-life spirituality, contemporary issues, women's issues, reference, applied theology, and inspirational."

Fiction: One-page fax query only; all unsolicited submissions returned unopened. "We publish adult fiction in several genres, teen/young adult fiction, and children's fiction series (6-12 yrs.)."

Tips: "We do not accept unsolicited queries or proposals via telephone, regular mail, or e-mail, but will consider one-page queries sent by facsimile (fax) and directed to Adult Nonfiction, Adult Fiction, or Young Adult/Children."

****Note:** This publisher serviced by The Writer's Edge and ChristianManuscript Submissions.com.

BIG IDEA INC., 230 Franklin Rd., #2-A, Franklin TN 37064. Toll-free (800)295-0557. (615)224-2200. E-mail: customerservice@bigidea.com. Website: www.bigidea.com. Classic Media. Cindy Kenney, sr. mng. ed. To creatively impact the lives of children, ages 2 through 12, with stories that teach biblical values. Publishes 20 titles/yr.; hardcover. Receives 2,500 submissions annually. 5% of books from first-time authors. Accepts mss through agents. No reprints. Prefers 1,500-2,000 wds. Negotiable outright purchase (no royalties); no advance. Average first printing 10,000-20,000. Publication within 20 mos. Considers simultaneous submissions. Responds in 3-6 mos. Prefers NIV. No catalog (see online).

Nonfiction: Query first; complete ms for picture or board books; no phone/fax query; e-query OK.

Fiction: Query first; complete ms for picture books; no phone/fax query; e-query OK.

Tips: Not accepting unsolicited manuscripts for now.

BJU PRESS/JOURNEYFORTH, 1700 Wade Hampton Blvd., Greenville SC 29614. (864)370-1800, ext. 4350. Fax (864)298-0268, ext. 4324. E-mail: jb@bju.edu. Website: www.bjupress.com. Bob Jones University Press. Nancy Lohr, youth ed. Our goal is to publish excellent, trustworthy books for children. Publishes 10 titles/yr.; trade paperbacks. Receives 500 submissions annually. 30% of books from first-time authors. Accepts mss through agents. Reprints books. Royalty on net; outright purchases (for first-time authors). Average first printing 5,000. Publication within 12-18 mos. Considers simultaneous submissions. No submissions by disk or e-mail. Responds in 8-12 wks. Requires KJV. Guidelines (also by e-mail/Website); catalog for 9x12 SAE/3 stamps.

Nonfiction: Query only first; fax query OK.

Fiction: Proposal/5 chapters or complete ms. For children & teens. "We prefer overtly Christian or Christian world-view."

Photos/Artwork: Open to queries from freelance artists.

Tips: "Any of the topics indicated have a good chance, provided the writing is clear and compelling. Mediocre writing is not going to get past the first reader. Take time to learn about and hone your craft. The precollege, homeschool market welcomes print-rich, well-written books, and we welcome youth manuscripts that fit that bill. Respect the time and intelligence of the young reader. When we see a manuscript that is carefully plotted and developed with a solid theme, we'll take a hard look. No picture books, please, but compelling novels for early readers are always good for us. Biographies on the lives of Christian heroes and statesmen are also a good fit."

****Note:** This publisher serviced by The Writer's Edge.

BLUE DOLPHIN PUBLISHING INC., PO Box 8, Nevada City CA 95959. (530)477-1503. Fax (530)477-8342. E-mail: Bdolphin@bluedolphinpublishing.com. Website: www.bluedolphinpublishing.com. Paul M. Clemens, pub. Imprint: Pelican Pond (fiction & poetry), Papillon Publishing (juvenile), and Symposium Publishing (nonfiction). Books that help people grow in their social and spiritual awareness. Publishes 20-24 titles/yr. (includes 10-12 print-on-demand). Receives 4,800 submissions annually. 90% of books from first-time authors. Prefers about 60,000 wds. or 200-300 pgs. Royalty 10-15% of net; no advance. Average first printing 300, then on demand. Publication within 10 mos. Considers simultaneous submissions. Requires requested ms on disk. Responds in 3-6 mos. Guidelines (also on Website); catalog for 6x9 SAE/2 stamps.

Nonfiction: Query or proposal/1 chapter; no phone/e-query. "Looking for books that will increase people's spiritual and social awareness. We will consider all topics."

Fiction: Query/2-pg. synopsis. Pelican Pond Imprint. Will consider all genres for all ages, except children's board books or picture books.

Tips: "We look for topics that would appeal to the general market, are interesting, different, and will aid in the growth and development of humanity. See Website before submitting."

Note: This publisher also publishes books on a range of topics, including cross-cultural spirituality. They also may offer a co-publishing arrangement, not necessarily a royalty deal.

+BMH BOOKS, PO Box 544, Winona Lake IN 46590. (574)268-1122. Fax (574)268-5384. E-mail: tdwhite@bmhbooks.com. Website: www.BMHbooks.com. Fellowship of Grace Brethren Churches. Terry White, ed./pub. Solid theologically. Publishes 15-18 titles/yr.; hardcover, trade paperbacks. Receives 30 submissions annually. 50% of books from first-time authors. Accepts mss through agents. No subsidy or print-on-demand. Seldom reprints books. Prefers 50,000-75,000 wds., or 128-256 pgs. Royalty 8-10% on retail; rarely pays an advance. Average first printing 4,000. Publication within 1 yr. Prefers not to considers simultaneous submissions. Responds in 3 mos. Prefers KJV or NIV. Requires accepted mss by e-mail. Guidelines by e-mail; free catalog.

Nonfiction: Proposal/2 chapters; no phone/fax query; e-query OK.

Tips: "Most open to biblically based, timeless, discipleship material."

BOYDS MILLS PRESS, 815 Church St., Honesdale PA 18431. Website: www.boydsmillspress.com. General publisher. Submit to Editorial director. Publishes a wide range of literary children's titles, for preschool through young adult; very few religious. Publishes 80 titles/yr.; hardcover, trade paperbacks. Receives 15,000 submissions annually. 40% of books from first-time authors. Reprints books. Royalty 4-12% on retail; advances vary. Considers simultaneous submissions. Guidelines.

Nonfiction: Query/proposal package, outline, 3 sample chapters (expert review of manuscript recommended).

Fiction: Outline/synopsis/first 3 chapters for novels; complete ms for picture books. "We are always interested in multicultural settings."

Tips: "We look for a broad range of books with fresh voices for children and young adults. We publish very few specifically religious books that are not multicultural or otherwise of broad appeal. Please consult our Website for the types of books we publish before submitting your manuscript."

BRANDEN PUBLISHING CO., PO Box 812094, Wellesley MA 02482. (781)235-3634. Fax (781)790-1056. E-mail through Website: www.branden.com. Adolph Caso, ed. Books by or about women, children, military, Italian American or African American themes; religious fiction. Publishes 15 titles/yr.; hardcover, trade paperbacks. Receives 1,000 submissions annually. 80% of books from first-time authors. Accepts mss through agents. Reprints books. Royalty 5-10% of net; advance $1,000 max. Publication within 10 mos. Responds in 1 mo.

Nonfiction: Paragraph query only with author's vita & SASE; no phone/fax/e-query.

Fiction: Paragraph query only with author's vita & SASE. Ethnic, religious fiction.

+BREAKNECK BOOKS, PO Box 122, Barrington NH 03825. E-mail: info@breakneckbooks.com. Website: www.breakneckbooks.com. Charity Heller Hogge, ed.; submit to Submissions. Dedicated to bridging the gap between Christian and mainstream fiction by publishing non-CBA thrillers that appeal to both markets. Imprints: Breakneck Redo, Breakneck Classics. Estab. 2006. Publishes 2-3 titles/yr.; trade paperbacks. Receives 100 submissions annually. 80% of books from first-time authors. Accepts mss through agents. No subsidy. Does print-on-demand. Reprints books. Prefers 85,000-110,000 wds. Royalty 40% on net; no advance. Publication within 6-10 mos. Accepts simultaneous submissions. Responds in 3 mos. Guidelines on Website; catalog online.

Fiction: Query by e-mail first, including a cover letter with a 50 word summary of the book. Attach a 3-page synopsis and first two chapters (25 pages max.) For teens and adults. "No anti-Christian, pro-occult, gratuitous sex, over the top profanity, or hateful (against any race or religion) works."

Special Needs: "Currently looking for thrillers in all genres, creature features (monster stories), and non-CBA Christian thrillers (those too edgy or explicit for most Christian publishers)." Also open to reprinting classic novels in the public domain (published prior to 1923).

Tips: "Creature fiction (like Peretti's *Monster*) is our primary interest, but we're also highly interested in action-thrillers similar to those by top authors like James Rollin, Steve Alten, Lincoln Child, Matthew Reilly, Clive Cussler, Michael Crichton, etc., but from a Christian perspective. But if the book is well-written, compelling and imaginative, we're open to a lot."

BRIDGE-LOGOS, 5850 T. G. Lee Blvd., Ste. 300, Orlando FL 32822-4409. (407) 888-2131. Fax (407)888-2318. E-mail: editorial@bridgelogos.com, or sueteubner@bridgelogos.com. Website: www.bridgelogos.com. Sue Teubner, acq. ed. Purpose is to clearly define God's changeless Word to a changing world. Imprints: Logos, Bridge, Selah, Synergy. Publishes 40 titles/yr.; hardcover, trade paperbacks, mass-market paperbacks, coffee-table books. Receives 200 submissions annually. 90% of books from first-time authors. Accepts mss through agents. **SUBSIDY PUBLISHES 1%;** does print-on-demand. Reprints books. Prefers 200 pgs. Royalty on net or outright purchase; no advance. Average first printing 4,000. Publication within 12 mos. Considers simultaneous submissions. Responds in 12 mos. No disk; prefers accepted mss by e-mail. Guidelines on Website; free catalog.

Nonfiction: Proposal/5 chapters; no phone/fax/e-query. "Most open to evangelism, spiritual growth, self-help, and education."

Special Needs: Reference, biography, current issues, controversial issues, church renewal, women's issues, and Bible commentary.

Photos/Artwork: Accepts freelance photos for book covers.

Tips: "Have a great message, a well-written manuscript, and a specific plan and willingness to market your book. Looking for previously published authors with an active ministry who are experts on their subject."

****Note:** This publisher serviced by The Writer's Edge.

BRIDGE RESOURCES/WITHERSPOON PRESS, 100 Witherspoon St., Louisville KY 40202-1396. Toll-free (888)728-7228, ext. 5124. (502)569-5124. Fax (502)569-8329. E-mail through Website: www.pcusa.org/bridgeresources. Congregational Ministries Publishing/Presbyterian Church (USA). Sandra Albritton Moak, pub.; Martha S. Gilliss, ed. Publishes nonfiction works that help congregations fulfill their ministries and individuals more thoroughly understand the Presbyterian Church (USA); Bible studies, resources for children, youth and adults; bringing those with special needs into fuller participation; lay leadership. Reformed theology only. Responds in 6-8 wks. Prefers NRSV. Guidelines on Website. Incomplete topical listings.

Nonfiction: Complete ms or proposal/sample chapters. Manuscripts will not be returned. "Treatment/sample chapters required for consideration."

+BY GRACE PUBLICATIONS, PO Box 893, Brinkley AR 72021. E-mail: bygracepublishing@yahoo.com. Website: www.bygracepublishing.com. Blog: http://ue_authors.bravejournal.com. Division of Unique Enterprises. Sheila Holloway, sr. ed. Inspirational Romance, Tender Romance, and Chick-Lit—all in three different lengths: 30,000-40,000 wds., 45,000-55,000 wds., or 60,000-65,000 wds.; plus a few Special Releases (3/yr.) of 70,000-85,000 wds. Royalty 50% of net; no advance. Guidelines on Website.

Fiction: Proposal/1st 3 chapters by e-mail (uniqueenterprisessubmit@yahoo.com). Attach RTF files only.

CAMBRIDGE UNIVERSITY PRESS, 32 Avenue of the Americas, New York NY 10013-2473. Toll-free (800)872-7423. (212)924-3900 or (212)337-5941. Fax (212)691-3239. E-mail: information@cup.org. (Specific e-mails on Website.) Website: www.cup.org. University of Cambridge. Andrew Beck, religion ed. (abeck@cambridge.org). Editors for other topics listed on Website.

Nonfiction: Proposal; no complete mss. Scholarly nonfiction.

CANADIAN INSTITUTE FOR LAW, THEOLOGY & PUBLIC POLICY INC., 89 Douglasview Rise S.E., Calgary AB T2Z 2P5, Canada. (403)720-8714. Fax (403)720-4746. E-mail: ciltpp@cs.com. Website: www.ciltpp.com. Will Moore, pres. Integrating Christianity with the study of law and political science. Publishes 2-4 titles/yr.; trade paperbacks. Receives 4-5 submissions annually. 1% of books from first-time authors. Accepts mss through agents. Reprints books. Royalty 7% on retail; no advance. Average first printing 1,000. Publication within 12-24 mos. No simultaneous submissions. Responds in 6-12 mos. Prefers NIV. Guidelines (also by e-mail); free catalog.

Nonfiction: Proposal/1 chapter. "Looking for books integrating Christianity with law and political science."

Photos/Artwork: Accepts freelance photos for book covers.

CANDY CANE PRESS—See Ideals Publications.

CANTICLE BOOKS, PO Box 2666, Carlsbad CA 92018. (760)806-3743. Fax (760)806-3689. E-mail: magnuspres@aol.com. Website: www.magnuspress.com. Imprint of Magnus Press. Warren Angel, ed. dir. To publish biblical studies by Catholic authors which are written for the average person and which minister life to Christ's Church. Publishes 2 titles/yr.; trade paperbacks. Receives 60 submissions annually. 50% of books from first-time authors. Accepts mss through agents. Reprints books. Prefers 105-300 pgs. Royalty 6-12% on retail; no advance. Average first printing 2,500. Publication within 1 yr. Considers simultaneous submissions. Accepts requested ms on disk. Responds in 1 mo. Guidelines (also by e-mail); free catalog.

Nonfiction: Query or proposal/2-3 chapters; fax query OK. "Looking for spirituality, thematic biblical studies, unique inspirational/devotional books."

Tips: "Our writers need solid knowledge of the Bible and a mature spirituality that reflects a profound relationship with Jesus Christ. Most open to well-researched, popularly written biblical studies geared to Catholics, or personal experience books that share/emphasize a person's relationship with Christ."

+CAPSTONE FICTION GROUP, LLC, PO Box 8, Waterford VA 20197. (540)882-9062. Fax (540)882-3719. E-mail: inquiries@capstonefiction.com, or rtucker@capstonefiction.com. Website: www.capstonefiction.com. Jeff Nesbitt, mng. dir.; Ramona Tucker, ed. dir. To create opportunities for new, talented Christian writers, and to promote leading-edge fiction by established Christian authors; inspirational fiction only. Estab. 2006. Does print-on-demand. Reprints books. Royalty; no advance. Guidelines on Website.

Fiction: Submit by e-mail (attached file) in one Word file. For all ages.

CAREPOINT PUBLISHING, (formerly listed as CarePoint Ministries) 1154 Westchester Dr., Lilburn GA 30047. (404)625-9217. E-mail: info@carepointministry.com. Website: www.christiancarepoint.org. Independent Christian publisher. Dr. Scott Philip Stewart, ed. Publishes Christian care books and software to help 21st-century Christians and seekers and those who minister to them. Publishes 12 titles/yr.; trade paperbacks. Receives 100+ submissions annually. 75% of books from first-time authors. Accepts mss through agents. Reprints books. Royalty 10-15% of net; no advance. Publication within 6 mos. Considers simultaneous submissions, if notified. Accepts requested manuscript on disk or by e-mail. Responds in 4 wks. Guidelines on Website.

Nonfiction: Proposal/2-3 chapters; prefers e-mail query. "Looking for support-group resources."

Photos/Artwork: Accepts freelance photos for book covers.

Special Needs: Self-help, personal growth, counseling aids, resources for peer and professional Christian caregivers and counselors.

Also Does: Interactive multimedia; book/CD sets

Tips: "Most open to practical, grace-full support group resources that minister our Lord's healing love, grace, and mercy to the wounded among us. Encourage one another!"

WILLIAM CAREY LIBRARY PUBLISHERS & DISTRIBUTORS, 1605 E. Elizabeth St., Pasadena CA 91104. Toll-free (800)647-7466. (706)554-1594. E-mail: publishing@WCLBooks.com, or through Website: www.missionbooks.org. U.S. Center for World Mission. Suzanne Harlan, editorial mngr. Purpose is to publish the best in Evangelical Christian mission literature. Imprint: Mandate Press. Publishes 10-15 titles/yr.; trade paperbacks. Reprints books. Variable lengths. Royalty 10% on net; no advance. Publication time varies. Guidelines on Website; free catalog.

Nonfiction: Query only; e-query OK. Charges a processing fee. "As a specialized publisher, we do only books and studies of church growth, missions, world issues, and ethnic/cultural issues."

Special Needs: Anthropology and cross-cultural.

Photos/Artwork: Accepts freelance photos for book covers.

Tips: "We mostly publish books on missions, evangelization, and unreached people groups. We welcome books that missionaries and mission-minded people would find useful and encouraging. Please see the 'Manuscript Submissions Guidelines' on our Website for more information."

CARSON-DELLOSA CHRISTIAN EDUCATION, 7027 Albert Pick Rd., PO Box 35665, Greensboro NC 27425. (336)632-0084. Fax (336)808-3249. E-mail: clayton@carsondellosa.com.

Website: www.carsondellosa.com. Carson-Dellosa Publishing Inc. Carol Layton, ed. dir. Creates high quality children's products (interactive activities) that teach the Word of God, share His love and goodness, assist in faith development, and glorify His Son, Jesus Christ. Publishes 20 titles/yr.; soft-cover, reproducible, 8 1/2 x11, teacher resource books. Receives 200 submissions annually. 25% of books from first-time authors. No reprints. Prefers 64 pgs. Royalty & advance confidential. Publication within 18 mos. Considers simultaneous submissions. Responds in 12 wks. Prefers NIV. Guidelines on Website; free catalog.

Nonfiction: Proposal/2 chapters; hard copy only. "Looking for books that teach the Word of God to children in an engaging and fun way, particularly in a classroom setting."

Fiction: Proposal/2 chapters. "Fiction must be suited for classroom use."

Photos/Artwork: Accepts queries from freelance artists.

Also Does: Board games, teaching beach balls.

Tips: "Understand the type of books we publish and submit an engaging, well-written proposal. Most open to lesson and activity books that are fun for students and teachers."

CASCADIA PUBLISHING HOUSE LLC., 126 Klingerman Rd., Telford PA 18969. (215)723-9125. E-mail: editor@cascadiapublishinghouse.com. Website: www.cascadiapublishinghouse.com. Mennonite. Michael A. King, ed. Imprint: DreamSeeker Books. Open to freelance; uses little unsolicited. Some books are subsidized by interested institutions. Guidelines/catalog on Website. Not included in topical listings.

Nonfiction: Query only/vita; e-query OK.

CATHOLIC ANSWERS, PO Box 199000, 2020 Gillespie Way, El Cajon CA 92020. (619)387-7200. Fax (619)387-0042. E-mail: juerillo@catholic.com. Website: www.catholic.com. Karl Keating, pres.; Mary Jane O'Brien, submissions ed. Publishes 10 titles/yr. Receives 10-15 submissions annually. 1% of books from first-time authors. No mss through agents. No subsidy. Reprints books. Prefers 40,000 wds. Royalty on retail; negotiable advance. Average first printing 5,000. Publication within 12 mos. Accepts simultaneous submissions. Responds in 1-3 mos. Prefers RSV-Catholic edition. Guidelines by e-mail; free catalog.

Nonfiction: Query first; no phone/fax/e-query.

Photos/Artwork: Accepts freelance photos for book covers.

Tips: "Most open to Catholic apologetics and evangelization."

CATHOLIC BOOK PUBLISHING CO., 77 West End Rd., Totowa NJ 07512. (973)890-2400. Fax (973)890-2410. E-mail: info@catholicbookpublishing.com. Website: www.catholicbook publishing.com. Catholic. Anthony Buono, mng. ed. Inspirational books for Catholic Christians. Acquired Resurrection Press and World Catholic Press. Publishes 15-20 titles/yr. Receives 75 submissions annually. 30% of books from first-time authors. No mss through agents. Variable royalty or outright purchases; no advance. Average first printing 3,000. Publication within 12-15 mos. No simultaneous submissions. Responds in 2-3 mos. Catalog for 9x12 SAE/5 stamps.

Nonfiction: Query letter only; no phone/fax query.

Tips: "We publish mainly liturgical books, Bibles, Missals, and prayer books. Most of the books are composed in-house or by direct commission with particular guidelines. We strongly prefer query letters in place of full manuscripts."

CHALICE PRESS, 1221 Locust St., Ste. 670, St. Louis MO 63103. (314)231-8500. Fax (314)231-8524. E-mail: pubassist@cbp21.com. Website: www.cbp21.com. Christian Church (Disciples of Christ)/Christian Board of Publication. Cyrus N. White, ed. Books for a thinking, caring church; in Bible, theology, ethics, homiletics, pastoral care, Christian education, Christian living, and spiritual growth. Publishes 50 titles/yr.; hardcover, trade paperbacks, mass-market paperbacks. Receives 500 submissions annually. 15% of books from first-time authors. No mss through agents. Prefers 144-160 pgs. for general books, 160-300 pgs. for academic books. Royalty 14-18% of net. Average first printing 2,500-3,000. Publication within 1 yr.

Accepts simultaneous submissions. Requires requested proposal and ms by e-mail. Responds in 1-3 mos. Guidelines on Website; catalog for 9x12 SAE/2 stamps.

Nonfiction: Proposal/1 chapter; e-proposal preferred. "Looking for books on evangelism, leadership, and spiritual growth."

Also Does: Pamphlets.

CHAPTER TWO, Fountain House, Conduit Mews, London SE18 7AP, United Kingdom. Phone ++44 (0) 20 8316 5389. Fax ++44 (0) 20 8854 5963. E-mail: chapter2uk@aol.com. Website: www.chaptertwobooks.org.uk. Plymouth Brethren. Mr. E. Cross, ed. Publishing Plymouth Brethren titles and evangelistic materials. Publishes 20-30 titles/yr.; hardcover, trade paperbacks. No mss through agents. Reprints books. Royalty 0-10% on retail (most of their authors donate their work). Average first printing 3,000. Publication within 12 mos. No simultaneous submissions. Prefers KJV, NKJV. No guidelines; free catalog.

Nonfiction: Query first; phone/e-query OK.

Special Needs: Plymouth Brethren commentaries.

Tips: "Writer must be in a Plymouth Brethren assembly and have orthodox Christian doctrine."

CHARIOT BOOKS—See David C. Cook.

CHARIOT VICTOR PUBLISHING—See David C. Cook.

CHARISMAKIDS, 600 Rinehart Rd., Lake Mary FL 32746. (407)333-0600. Fax (407)333-7100. E-mail: Custsvc@strang.com. Website: www.charismakids.com. Strang Book Group. Submit to The Editor. Books to help children experience God's presence, find His purpose for their lives, and receive the power of the Holy Spirit. Publishes 12 titles/yr. Receives hundreds of submissions annually. 10% of books from first-time authors. Prefers mss through agents. No reprints. Prefers 2,400 wds. or 32 pgs. Royalty on net; advance. Average first printing 10,000. Publication within 1 yr. Considers simultaneous submissions. Responds in 6 mos. Guidelines & catalog on Website.

Nonfiction: Proposal/1 chapter; fax/e-query OK.

Fiction: Proposal/1 chapter. Charismatic children's books; for children 4-8 years.

Ethnic Books: Black, Charismatic.

Tips: "Most open to books with a Charismatic world-view for children."

+THE CHARLES PRESS, PUBLISHERS, 133 N. 21st St., Ste. 2, Philadelphia PA 19103. (212)561-2786. Fax (215)561-0191. E-mail: mailbox@charlespresspub.com. Website: www.charlespresspub.com. Lauren Metzler, ed. (lauren@charlespresspub.com). Responds in 4-16 wks. Guidelines on Website; catalog.

Nonfiction: Proposal (to 10 pgs.)

CHELSEA HOUSE PUBLISHERS, 132 W. 31st St., Fl. 17, New York NY 10001. Toll-free (800) 322-8755. Toll-free fax (800)678-3633. E-mail: editorial@factsonfile.com. Website: www.chelseahouse.com. Haights Cross Communications. Submit to Editorial Director. Publishes curriculum-based nonfiction books for middle school and high school students, including on religion. Publishes in hardcover. Reprints books. Considers simultaneous submissions. Guidelines on Website; catalog on Website.

Nonfiction: Query or proposal/ 2-3 chapters.

Photos/Artwork: Open to queries from freelance artists; send photocopies.

CHICKEN SOUP FOR THE SOUL BOOKS—See listing in Periodical section.

CHOSEN BOOKS, Division of Baker Publishing Group, 3985 Bradwater St., Fairfax VA 22031-3702. Toll-free (800)322-8755. (703)764-8250. Toll-free fax (800)678-3633. (703)764-3995. E-mail: chosenbooks@cox.net. Website: www.chosenbooks.com. Jane Campbell, editorial dir. Charismatic; Spirit-filled life titles. No unsolicited mss, but will respond to e-mails. Submit through Writer's Edge or ChristianManuscriptSubmissions.com.

CHRISTIAN ED. PUBLISHERS, Box 26639, San Diego CA 92196. (858)578-4700. Fax (858)578-2431 (for queries only). E-mail: Editor@cehouse.com. Website: www.ChristianEdWarehouse.com. Janet Ackelson, asst. ed. An evangelical publisher of Bible Club materials for ages two through high school, church special-event programs, and online Bible lessons. Publishes 80 curriculum titles/yr. Receives 150 submissions annually. 10% of books from first-time authors. No mss through agents. Outright purchases for .03/wd.; no advance. Publication within 1 yr. Accepts requested ms on disk or by e-mail. Responds in 3-5 mos. No simultaneous submissions or reprints. Prefers NIV, KJV. Guidelines (also by e-mail); catalog for 9x12 SAE/4 stamps.

Nonfiction: Query only; phone/fax/e-query OK. Children's Bible studies, curriculum, and take-home papers.

Fiction: Query only. Juvenile fiction for take-home papers. "Each story is about 900 wds. Write for an application; assignments only."

Photos/Artwork: Open to freelance illustrators. Send files in Adobe Illustrator.

Tips: "All writing done on assignment. Request our guidelines, then complete a writer application before submitting. Need Bible-teaching ideas for preschool through sixth grade. Also publishes Bible stories for preschool and primary take-home papers, 200 words."

CHRISTIAN FAMILY PUBLICATIONS, 185 Makarios Dr., Unit 4, St. Augustine FL 32080-8776. (904)471-4307. E-mail: christianfamily@mail.com. Website: www.christianfamilybooks.com. Gene Fedele, ed. Imprints: Christian Family Library, Great Christian Biographies. Publishes 1-3 titles/yr.; hardcover, trade paperbacks. Receives 20-30 submissions annually. 50% of books from first-time authors. No mss through agents. Reprints books. Prefers KJV or NKJV. Accepted mss on disk or by e-mail. Free catalog.

Tips: "Most open to books from a Reformed theological position."

CHRISTIAN FOCUS PUBLICATIONS, LTD., Geanies House, Fearn, Tain, Ross-shire IV20 1TW, Scotland, UK. Phone 01862 871011. Fax 01862 871699. E-mail: info@christianfocus.com. Website: www.christianfocus.com. Willie MacKenzie, adult editorial mngr.; Catherine MacKenzie, children's ed. Focuses on having strong biblical content. Imprints: Mentor, Christian Heritage, Christian Focus, Christian Focus 4 Kids. Publishes 90 titles/yr.; hardcover, trade paperbacks, mass-market paperbacks. Receives 300+ submissions annually. 10% of books from first-time authors. Accepts mss through agents. Reprints books. Royalty on net or outright purchase. Publication within 24 mos. Considers simultaneous submissions. Accepts requested ms on disk. Responds typically in 4 mos. Guidelines on Website; free catalog.

Nonfiction: Proposal/2 chapters; fax/e-query OK.

Fiction: Complete ms. For children and teens only. See guidelines for descriptions of children's fiction lines.

Photos/Artwork: Accepts freelance photos for book covers.

Tips: "We are 'reformed,' though we don't insist all our authors would consider themselves reformed." Most open to issues-based popular books, and children's fiction and biography. A prize-winning British publisher with good worldwide coverage.

+CHRISTIAN HERITAGE SOCIETY, Box 519, Baldwin Place NY 10505. Phone/fax (914)962-3287. E-mail: grkurian@aol.com. George Kurian, ed. Publishes 6 titles/yr.; hardcover, trade paperbacks. Receives 100 submissions annually. 50% of books from first-time authors. Prefers mss through agents. No subsidy. Reprints books. Prefers 120,000 wds. Royalty 10-15% on net; no advance. Average first printing 10,000. Publication within 1 yr. Considers simultaneous submissions. Responds in 3 mos. Guidelines; free catalog.

Nonfiction: Query; e-query OK. "Looking for Christian history, reference books, memoirs, devotionals, and evangelism."

CHRISTIAN LIBERTY PRESS, 502 W. Euclid Ave., Arlington Heights IL 60004. (847)259-4444. Fax (847)259-2941. E-mail: acquisitions@christianlibertypress.com, or larsj@christian libertypress.com. Website: www.christianlibertypress.com. Publishing arm of Christian Liberty Academy and Christian Liberty Academy School System (CLASS). Lars Johnson, admin. dir. Dedicated to publishing works that are consistent with the Word of God. Curriculum for kindergarten through high school.

Nonfiction: Proposal/2 chapters. A variety of enrichment and support books, including biographies, education resources, and Bible study materials.

Fiction: Proposal/2 chapters. Christian and historical.

CHRISTIAN WRITER'S EBOOK NET, PO Box 446, Ft. Duchesne UT 84026. (435)772-3429. E-mail: editor@writersebook.com. Website: www.writersebook.com. Nondenominational/Evangelical Christian. Linda Kay Stewart Whitsitt, ed-in-chief; Terry Gordon Whitsitt, asst. ed. Gives first-time authors the opportunity to bring their God-given writing talent to the Christian market. Publishes 15 titles/yr. Receives 100 submissions annually. 95% of books from first-time authors. Accepts mss through agents. **SUBSIDY PUBLISHES 25%.** Reprints books. Prefers 60+ pgs. Royalty 35-50%; no advance. E-Books only. Publication within 6 mos. Considers simultaneous submissions. Electronic queries and submissions only; mss need to be in electronic form (MS Word, WordPerfect, ASCII, etc.) to be published; send by e-mail (preferred). No mail submissions accepted without contact by e-mail first. Responds in 1-2 mos. Guidelines on Website.

Nonfiction: E-query only. Any topic.

Fiction: E-query only. Any genre.

Also Does: Booklets, pamphlets, tracts.

Tips: "Make sure your work is polished and ready for print. The books we publish are sold in our online store. If you are not sure what an e-book is, check out our Website's FAQ page."

CHURCH & SYNAGOGUE LIBRARY ASSN. INC., 2920 S.W. Dolph Ct., Ste. 3A, Portland OR 97219. (503)244-6919. Fax (503)977-3734. E-mail: csla@worldaccessnet.com. Website: www.cslainfo.org. Karen Bota, ed. An interfaith group established to help librarians set up and organize/reorganize their religious libraries. Publishes 6 titles/yr.; trade paperbacks. No mss through agents. No reprints. No royalty. Average first printing 750. Catalog.

CHURCH GROWTH INSTITUTE, PO Box 7, Elkton MD 21922-0007. (434)525-0022. Fax (434)525-0608. E-mail: cgimail@churchgrowth.org. Website: www.churchgrowth.org. Ephesians Four Ministries. Cindy G. Spear, resource development dir. Providing practical tools for leadership, evangelism, and church growth. Publishes 4 titles/yr.; trade paperbacks. Receives 40 submissions annually. 7% of books from first-time authors. No mss through agents. Prefers 64-160 pgs. Royalty 6% on retail or outright purchase; no advance. Average first printing 100. Publication within 1 yr. Considers simultaneous submissions. Responds in 3 mos. Requires requested ms on disk. Guidelines sent after query/outline is received; catalog for 9x12 SAE/4 stamps, or on Website.

Nonfiction: Query; no phone/fax query; e-query OK. "We prefer our writers to be experienced in what they write about, to be experts in the field."

Special Needs: Topics that help churches grow spiritually and numerically; leadership training; attendance and stewardship programs; new or unique ministries (how-to). Self-discovery and evaluation tools, such as our Spiritual Gifts Inventory and Spiritual Growth Survey.

Photos/Artwork: Accepts freelance photos for book covers.

Tips: "Most open to a practical manual or audio album (CDs/audiotapes and workbooks) for the pastor or other church leaders—something unique with a special niche. Must be practical and different from anything else on the same subject—or must be a topic/slant few others have published. Also very interested in evaluation tools as mentioned above. Please no devotionals, life testimonies, commentaries, or studies on books of the Bible."

CISTERCIAN PUBLICATIONS INC., WMU Station, 1903 W. Michigan Ave., Kalamazoo MI 49008-5415. (269)387-8920. Fax (269)387-8390. E-mail: cistpub@wmich.edu. Website: www.cistercianpublications.org. Catholic/Order of Cistercians of the Strict Observance. Dr. E. Rozanne Elder, ed. dir. Works of monastic tradition and studies that foster renewal, spirituality, and ongoing formation of monastics. Publishes 8-14 titles/yr.; hardcover, trade paperbacks, some coffee-table books. Receives 30 submissions annually. 50% of books from first-time authors. No mss through agents. Reprints books. Prefers 204-286 pgs. Royalty on net; no advance. Average first printing 1,500. Publication within 2-10 yrs. Requires requested ms on disk. Guidelines on Website; free style sheet/catalog.

Nonfiction: Query only; no phone query; fax query OK. History, spirituality, and theology.

Photos/Artwork: Accepts freelance photos for book covers.

Tips: "We publish only on the Christian Monastic Tradition. Most open to a translation of a monastic text, or study of a monastic movement, author, or subject."

CLADACH PUBLISHING, PO Box 336144, Greeley CO 80633. (970)371-9530. Fax (970)351-8240. E-mail: staff@cladach.com. Website: www.cladach.com. Independent Christian publisher. Catherine Lawton, pub. (cathyl@cladach.com); Hannah Lawton, ed. Seeks to influence those inside and outside the body of Christ by giving a voice to talented writers with a clear, articulate, and Christ-honoring vision. Publishes 2-3 titles/yr. Receives 200 submissions annually. 70% of books from first-time authors. Accepts proposals through agents. No reprints. Prefers 160-256 pgs. Royalty 7-10% on net; no advance. Average first printing 1,500. Publication within 1 yr. Considers simultaneous submissions. Accepted mss by e-mail. Responds in 3-6 mos. Guidelines on Website; free catalog.

Nonfiction: Query letter only first; phone/e-query OK. "Looking for nonfiction that helps people in their relationship with God."

Fiction: Query letter only first (1-2 pgs.); phone/e-query OK (copied into message). For adults. "Prefers gripping stories depicting inner struggles and real-life issues; well crafted. Would like to see Christian world-view, literary fiction."

Tips: "We want writing that shows God active in our world and that helps readers experience His presence and power in their lives."

COLLEGE PRESS PUBLISHING CO. INC., 223 W. Third St. (64801), PO Box 1132, Joplin MO 64802. Toll-free (800)289-3300. (417)623-6280. Fax (417)623-8250. E-mail: jmcclarnon@collegepress.com, or through Website: www.collegepress.com. Christian Church/Church of Christ. Submit to Acquisitions Ed. Christian materials that will help fulfill the Great Commission and promote unity on the basis of biblical truth and intent. Imprint: HeartSpring Publishing (see separate listing). Publishes 15-20 titles/yr.; hardcover, trade paperbacks. Receives 700 submissions annually. 25% of books from first-time authors. Accepts mss through agents. Reprints books. Prefers 250-300 pgs. (paperback) or 300-600 pgs. (hardback). Royalty 5-15% of net; no advance. Average first printing 3,000. Publication within 6 mos. Considers simultaneous submissions. Requires requested ms on disk; no e-mail submissions. Responds in 2-3 mos. Prefers NIV, NASB, NAS. Guidelines on Website; catalog for 9x12 SAE/5 stamps.

Nonfiction: Query only first, then proposal/2-3 chapters; no phone/fax query. "Looking for Bible study, reference, divorced leaders, blended families, and leadership." Expanding search for new authors, especially in women's ministry.

Ethnic Books: Reprints their own books in Spanish.

Also Does: E-books.

Tips: "We develop and supply Christian resources for use by individuals, churches, colleges/universities/seminaries, and small groups. We are interested in biblical studies and resources that come from an 'Arminian' view and/or 'amillennial' slant."

CONARI PRESS, 500 Third St., Ste. 230, San Francisco CA 94107. E-mail: info@redwheel weiser.com. Website: www.conari.com or www.redwheelweiser.com. An imprint of Red Wheel/Weiser, LLC. Ms. Pat Bryce, ed. Books on spirituality, personal growth, parenting, and social issues. Publishes 30 titles/yr. Responds in up to 3 mos. Guidelines and catalog on Website. Incomplete topical listings.

CONCILIAR PRESS, PO Box 76, Ben Lomand CA 95005. Toll-free (800)967-7377. (831)336-5118. Fax (831)336-8882. Website: www.conciliarpress.com. Antiochian Orthodox Christian Archdiocese of N.A., Father Thomas Zell, ed.; submit to Ginny Nieuwsma, acq. ed. (vhnieuwsma@ prodigy.net). Publishes 5-10 titles/yr. Receives 50 submissions annually. 20% of books from first-time authors. Accepts mss through agents. **SUBSIDY PUBLISHES 10%.** Reprints books. Royalty; no advance. Average first printing 5,000. Prefers e-mail submission. Responds in 3 mos. Prefers NKJV. Guidelines on Website; catalog for 9x12 SAE/5 stamps.

Nonfiction: Query/proposal with up to 50-60 pgs. of the manuscript (including first chapter); phone/e-query OK.

Photos/Artwork: Accepts freelance photos for book covers.

Children's Books: Send hard copy to Jane G. Meyer, children's book project mngr., Conciliar Press Ministries, 3112 Calle Rosales, Santa Barbara CA 93105.

CONCORDIA ACADEMIC PRESS, 3558 S. Jefferson Ave., St. Louis MO 63118-3968. (314)268-1098. Fax (314)268-1329. E-mail: mark.sell@cph.org. Website: www.concordiaacademic press.org. Lutheran Church/Missouri Synod. Imprint of Concordia Publishing House. Mark E. Sell, ed. Scholarly and professional books in biblical studies, 16th-century studies, historical theology, and theology and culture. Publication within 2 yrs. Responds in 8-12 wks. Guidelines on Website.

Nonfiction: Proposal/sample chapters.

Tips: "Freelance submissions are welcome. Prospective authors should consult the guidelines on the Website for an author prospectus and submissions guidelines."

CONCORDIA PUBLISHING HOUSE, 3558 S. Jefferson Ave., St. Louis MO 63118-3968. (314)268-1187. Fax (314)268-1329. Website: www.cph.org. Lutheran Church/Missouri Synod. Peggy Kuethe: children's resources, children's and family devotions, teaching resources, adult nonfiction, and devotionals; Mark Sell: academic books; Fred Baue: pastoral and congregational resources. Publishes 50 titles/yr.; hardcover, trade paperbacks. Receives 3,000 submissions annually. 10% of books from first-time authors. Royalty 2-12% on retail; some outright purchases; some advances $500-1,500. Average first printing 6,000-8,000. Publication within 2 yrs. Considers simultaneous submissions. Responds in 6 mos. Prefers accepted submissions on disk. Prefers NIV. Guidelines on Website; catalog for 9x12 SAE/4 stamps.

Nonfiction: Proposal/2 chapters; no phone/fax query. No poetry, personal experience, or biography.

Ethnic Books: Hispanic; Asian American.

Also Does: Pamphlets, booklets.

Tips: "Publishes Christ-centered resources for The Lutheran Church—Missouri Synod. Most open to family, devotional, and teaching resources. Any proposal should be Christ centered, Bible based, and life directed. It must be creative in its presentation of solid scriptural truths. Call for current needs."

****Note:** This publisher serviced by The Writer's Edge.

+CONGREGATIONAL LIFE AND LEARNING, Augsburg Fortress Canada, 500 Trillium Dr., Box 9940, Kitchener ON N2G 4Y4, Canada. E-mail: cllcub@augsburgfortress.com. Website: www.afcanada.com. Submit using online form. Works to provide congregations with materials and resources for group and individual use that nurture faith, foster learning, and promote spiritual renewal among children, youth, and adults. All material is work-for-hire. Responds in 4 mos. Guidelines at www.afcanada.com/company/submitcongregational.jsp.

Nonfiction: Query first; e-query OK. "Looking for Sunday school materials, Bible study materials, and devotionals."

CONTEMPORARY DRAMA SERVICE, Meriwether Publishing Co., 885 Elkton Dr., Colorado Springs CO 80907. E-mail: merPCDS@aol.com. Website: www.meriwetherpublishing.com. Publishes Christian plays for mainline churches. Also supplemental textbooks on theatrical subjects. Prefers comedy, but does publish some serious works. Accepts full-length or one-act plays—comedy or musical. General and Christian. Publishes 30 plays/yr. See the Meriwether Publishing listing for additional details.

CONTINUUM INTERNATIONAL PUBLISHING, 80 Maiden Lane, Rm. 704, New York NY 10038-4814. Toll-free (800)561-7704. (212)953-5858. Fax (212)953-5944. E-mail: info@continuum books.com. Website: www.continuumbooks.com. Robin J. Baird-Smith, pub. dir.; Thomas Kraft, assoc. pub. Imprints: T and T Clark; Burns & Oates. Publishes 60 titles/yr.; hardcover, trade paperbacks. Receives 500 submissions annually. 10% of books from first-time authors. Accepts mss through agents. **SUBSIDY PUBLISHES 5%.** Does print-on-demand. Reprints books. Royalty to 15%; advance. Prefers 60,000-120,000 wds. Publication within 9 mos. No simultaneous submissions. Responds in 1 mo. Guidelines by e-mail/Website; free catalog.

Nonfiction: Query, proposal/1 chapter, or complete ms; phone/fax/e-query OK.

Photos/Artwork: Accepts freelance photos for book covers.

Contest: Trinity Prize.

DAVID C. COOK, (formerly Cook Communications Ministry), 4050 Lee Vance View, Colorado Springs CO 80918. (719)536-0100. Fax (719)536-3269. Website: www.cookministries.com. Dan Rich, Sr. VP & pub.; Ingrid Beck, mng. ed. Discipleship is foundational; everything we publish needs to move the reader one step closer to maturity in Christ. Brands: David C. Cook (for teachers or program leaders who want Bible-based discipleship resources; Bible and study resources for serious Bible students; books for Christian families seeking biblical answers to life problems; books to equip kids—birth to age 12—for life); and Honor Books (devotional books that inspire and motivate, packaged as gift books). Publishes 85 titles/yr.; hardcover, trade paperbacks. 10% of books from first-time authors. Requires mss through agents. Publication within 1-2 yrs. Considers simultaneous submissions. Responds in 3-6 mos. Prefers requested ms by e-mail. Prefers NIV. Guidelines (also by e-mail/Website).

Nonfiction: Not currently accepting any unsolicited or unagented submissions.

Fiction: Not currently accepting any unsolicited or unagented submissions.

Note: Cook has eliminated all brands/imprints except David C. Cook and Honor Books—including NexGen, Victor, Life Journey, and FaithKidz.

****Note:** This publisher serviced by The Writer's Edge.

J. COUNTRYMAN, PO Box 141000, Nashville TN 37214-1000. (615)902-3134. Fax (615)902-3200. Website: www.jcountryman.com. Thomas Nelson Inc. Gift-book imprint. No longer accepting unsolicited manuscripts or proposals.

****Note:** This publisher serviced by The Writer's Edge.

THE CROSSROAD PUBLISHING CO., 16 Penn Plaza, Ste. 1550, New York NY 10001. (212)868-1801. Fax (212)868-2171. E-mail: ask@crossroadpublishing.com. Website: www.cpcbooks .com. Dr. John Jones, ed. dir. Books on religion, spirituality, and personal growth that speak to the diversity of backgrounds and beliefs; hopeful books that inform, enlighten, and heal; particular strengths in Catholic and Anglican titles as well as Christian spirituality and leadership. Imprints: see below. Publishes 50 titles/yr. Receives 1,200 submissions annually. 15% of books from first-time authors. Accepts mss through agents. **SUBSIDY PUBLISHES 5%** with institutions only. Does print-on-demand. Reprints books. Prefers 50,000-60,000 wds. or 160-176 pgs. Royalty 8-10-12% of net; small advance (more for established authors). Average first printing 4,000. Publication within 1 yr. Considers simultaneous submissions. Responds in 2-8 wks. Accepts requested ms on disk. Guidelines by e-mail/Website.

Nonfiction: Proposal/2 chapters; e-query OK. Books that explore and celebrate the Christian life.

Tips: "Most authors need some combination of (1) exceptional writing ability, (2) expertise or authority in a field, (3) an existing platform for sales (speaking engagements, etc.)."

Herder & Herder: 200 years of international publishing in the service of theology and church. Monographs, reference works, theological, and philosophical discourse. Special focus on younger and emerging theologians as well as the Christian spiritual disciplines.

CROSS TRAINING PUBLISHING, PO Box 1874, Kearney NE 68848. Toll-free (800)430-8588. Fax (308)338-2058. E-mail: gordon@crosstrainingpublishing.com. Website: www.crosstrainingpublishing.com. Gordon Thiessen, pub. Sports books for children and adults.

CROSSWAY BOOKS AND BIBLES, 1300 Crescent St., Wheaton IL 60187. (630)682-4300. Fax (630)682-4785. E-mail: editorial@gnpcb.org. Website: www.crosswaybooks.com. A publishing ministry of Good News Publishers. Allan Fisher, VP editorial; submit to Jill Carter, editorial administrator. Publishes books that combine the Truth of God's Word with a passion to live it out, with unique and compelling Christian content. Publishes 70 titles/yr.; hardcover, trade paperbacks. Receives 1,000 submissions annually. 1% of books from first-time authors. Accepts mss through agents. No reprints. Prefers 25,000 wds. & up. Royalty 10-21% of net; advance varies. Average first printing 5,000-10,000. Publication within 18 mos. Considers simultaneous submissions. Responds in 6-8 wks. Prefers ESV. Guidelines (also on Website); free catalog.

Nonfiction/Fiction: Currently not accepting unsolicited submissions.

Also Does: Tracts. See Good News Publishers.

****Note:** This publisher serviced by The Writer's Edge and ChristianManuscript Submissions.com.

**Recipient of five 2006 Silver Angel Awards from Excellence in Media.

CSS PUBLISHING GROUP INC., 517 S. Main St., Lima OH 45804. (419)227-1818. Fax (419)228-9184. E-mail: editor@csspub.com, or through Website: www.csspub.com. Rebecca Brandt, ed. Serves the needs of pastors, worship leaders, and parish program planners in the broad Christian mainline of the American church. Imprints: Fairway Press (subsidy—see separate listing); Academic Renewal Press (reprints textbooks for professors and colleges); B.O.D. (Books On Demand). Publishes 50 titles/yr. Receives 1,200-1,500 submissions annually. 50% of books from first-time authors. **SUBSIDY PUBLISHES 40%** through Fairway Press. Prefers 100-125 pgs. No royalty or advance. Average first printing 1,000. Publication within 6-10 mos. Considers simultaneous submissions. Requires requested mss (only) on disk. Responds in 3 wks. to 3 mos.; final decision within 6 mos. Accepts requested ms on disk. Prefers NRSV. Guidelines (also on Website); free catalog.

Nonfiction: Query or proposal/3 chapters; no e-mail submissions; complete ms for short works. "Looking for pastoral resources for ministry. Our material is practical in nature."

Fiction: Complete ms. Easy-to-perform dramas and pageants for all age groups. "Our drama interest primarily includes Advent, Christmas, Epiphany, Lent, and Easter. We do not publish long plays."

Tips: "Suggest what you can do to help promote the book."

CUMBERLAND HOUSE PUBLISHING, 431 Harding Industrial Dr., Nashville TN 37211. (615)832-1171. Fax (615)832-0633. E-mail: info@cumberlandhouse.com. Website: www.cumberlandhouse.com. Tilly Katz, acq. ed. Historical nonfiction, cooking, mystery, and Christian titles. Publishes 60 titles/yr. Receives 3,500 submissions annually. 30% of books from first-time authors. Accepts mss through agents. Royalty 10-15% on net; advance $500-5,000. Publication within 1 yr. Considers simultaneous submissions. Prefers accepted ms on disk; no e-mail submissions. Responds in 4-6 mos. Guidelines on Website; catalog for 8x10 SAE/4 stamps.

Nonfiction: Query/outline by mail; no phone/e-query. See guidelines for how to submit cookbooks.

Tips: "Most open to history or biography. In your cover letter, briefly describe the book and the market for the book. In a statement or two indicate who you are and why you have written or plan to write the book you are proposing."

CUSTOM COMMUNICATIONS SERVICES INC./SHEPHERD PRESS/CUSTOM BOOK, 77 Main St., Tappan NY 10983. Toll-free (800)631-1362. (845)365-0414. Fax (845)365-0864. E-mail: customusa@aol.com. Website: www.customstudios.com. Norman Shaifer, pres. Publishes 50-75 titles/yr. 50% of books from first-time authors. No mss through agents. Royalty on net; some outright purchases for specific assignments. Publication within 6 mos. Responds in 1 mo. Guidelines.

Nonfiction: Query/proposal/chapters. "Histories of individual congregations, denominations, or districts."

Tips: "Find stories of larger congregations (750 or more households) who have played a role in the historic growth and development of the community or region."

THE DABBLING MUM PRESS, 508 W. Main St., Beresford SD 57004. E-mail: dm@thedabblingmum.com. Website: www.thedabblingmum.com. Alyice Edrich, ed. E-book publisher. Publishes 12-24 titles/yr. Receives 6 submissions annually. 90% of books from first-time authors. No mss through agents. No subsidy publishing. No reprints. Prefers 150-300 pgs. Royalty 50% on retail; no advance. Offers a nonexclusive contract; author can sell e-book on other sites. Publication within 5 mos. No simultaneous submissions. Responds monthly. Prefers NIV. Guidelines on Website; no catalog.

Nonfiction: Proposal/1 chapter; no phone/fax query; e-query OK. "Any book that fits: parenting, recipes, home, small business, writing. Well researched, professionally edited, and with a hands-on approach."

Tips: "We like to focus on niches. Books that can't or won't be published by traditional publishers; books that need updating on a regular basis."

DAWN PUBLICATIONS, 12402 Bitney Springs Rd., Nevada City CA 95959. (530)274-7775. Fax (530)274-7778. Website: www.dawnpub.com. Glenn Hovemann, acq. ed. Dedicated to inspiring in children a sense of appreciation for all of life on earth. Publishes 6 titles/yr.; hardcover, trade paperbacks. Receives 3,000 submissions annually. 15% of books from first-time authors. Accepts mss through agents. No reprints. Royalty on net; advance. Publication within 1-2 yrs. Considers simultaneous submissions. Responds in 2 mos. Guidelines & catalog on Website.

Nonfiction: Complete manuscript.

Tips: "Most open to creative nonfiction. We look for nature awareness and appreciation titles that promote a relationship with the natural world and specific habitats, usually through inspiring treatment and nonfiction."

DESCANT PUBLISHING, PO Box 12973, Mill Creek WA 98082. (206)235-3357. Fax (646)365-7513. Bret Sable, nonfiction ed.; Alex Royal, fiction ed. General publisher that does books on religion and spirituality, and religious fiction. Publishes 10-12 titles/yr. Receives 1,200 submissions annually. 50% of books from first-time authors. Accepts mss through agents. Royalty 6-15%. Publication within 18 mos. Considers simultaneous submissions. Responds in 3 mos. Guidelines for SASE.

Nonfiction: For adults and children. Query by mail.

Fiction: For adults. Query by mail.

Also Does: Some e-books.

DESTINY IMAGE PUBLISHERS, PO Box 310, Shippensburg PA 17257. (717)532-3040. Fax (717)532-9291. E-mail: dlm@destinyimage.com, or through Website: www.destinyimage.com. Don Milam, ed. mngr. Publishes biblically sound prophetic words to strengthen the church as a whole. Imprints: Destiny Image, Revival Press, Treasure House, Fresh Bread. Publishes 36 titles/yr. Receives 1,500 submissions annually. 10% of books from first-time authors. Accepts mss through agents. **SUBSIDY PUBLISHES 1-2%.** Reprints books. Prefers 128-190 pgs. Royalty 10-15% on net; no advance. Average first printing 10,000. Publication within 9 mos. Considers simultaneous submissions. Send unsolicited mss via their online Manuscript Submission Form. Responds in up to 6 mos. Guidelines on Website; free catalog.

Nonfiction: Query or proposal/chapters; no e-query. Charges a $25 fee for unsolicited manuscripts (enclose with submission).

Fiction: Proposal. Adult. Biblical.

Tips: "Most open to books on the deeper life, Charismatic interest."

DIMENSIONS FOR LIVING, 201—8th Ave. S., Nashville TN 37203. Fax (615)749-6512. E-mail: sbriese@umpublishing.org. Website: www.abingdonpress.com. United Methodist Publishing House. Joseph A. Crowe, ed.; submit to Manuscript Submissions (by mail only). Books for the general Christian reader. Publishes 120 titles/yr. Receives 2,000 submissions annually. Less than 1% of books from first-time authors. No reprints. Prefers 144 pgs. Royalty 7.5% on retail; some outright purchases; no advance. Average first printing 3,000. Publication within 2 yrs. Requires requested ms on disk. Responds in 6-8 wks. Guidelines on Website; free catalog.

Nonfiction: Proposal/2 chapters; no phone query. Open to inspiration/devotion, self-help, home/family, special occasion gift books.

DISCOVERY HOUSE PUBLISHERS, PO Box 3566, Grand Rapids MI 49501. Toll-free (800)653-8333. (616)942-9218. Fax (616)974-2224. E-mail: books@dhp.org. Website: www.dhp.org. RBC Ministries. Carol Holquist, pub.; submit to Manuscript Review Editor. Publishes books that foster Christian growth and godliness. Publishes 12-18 titles/yr.; hardcover, trade paperbacks, mass-market paperbacks. Accepts mss through agents. Reprints books. Royalty 10-14% on net; no advance. Publication within 12-18 mos. Considers simultaneous submissions. Requires accepted mss on disk or by e-mail. Responds in 4-6 wks. Guidelines (also by e-mail/Website); free catalog.

Nonfiction: Query letter only; e-query OK.

****Note:** This publisher serviced by The Writer's Edge and ChristianManuscript Submissions.com.

DISKUS PUBLISHING, PO Box 43, Albany IN 47320. E-mail: editor@diskuspublishing.com. Submissions to: editor@diskuspublishing.com, or submissions@diskuspublishing.com. Website: www.diskuspublishing.com. Marilyn Nesbitt, ed-in-chief; Joyce McLaughlin, inspirational ed. E-book publisher. Publishes 50 titles/yr. Royalty 40%. Publication within 6-8 mos. Considers simultaneous submissions. Prefers manuscripts by e-mail. Guidelines (also on Website); catalog for #10 SAE.

Nonfiction: Complete ms or query by mail or e-mail.

Fiction: Complete ms or query by mail or e-mail. Includes religious fiction.

Tips: "Follow very specific guidelines on Website."

DOUBLEDAY RELIGION, 1745 Broadway, New York NY 10019. (212)782-9000. Fax (212)782-8338. E-mail: mrapkin@randomhouse.com, or tmurphy@randomhouse.com. Website: www.randomhouse.com. Imprint of Random House Inc. Michelle Rapkin, VP, Dir. of Religious Publishing; Bill Barry, VP and publisher; submit to Trace Murphy, editorial dir. Imprints: Image, Galilee, New Jerusalem Bible, Three Leaves Press, Anchor Bible Commentaries, Anchor Bible Reference Library. Publishes 45-50 titles/yr.; hardcover, trade paperbacks. Receives 1,500 submissions annually. 10% of books from first-time authors. Requires mss through agents. Reprints books. Royalty 7.5-15% on retail; advance. Average first printing varies. Publication within 8 mos. Considers simultaneous submissions. Responds in 4 mos. No disk. No guidelines; catalog for 9x12 SAE/3 stamps.

Nonfiction: Agented submissions only. Proposal/3 chapters; no phone query.

Fiction: Agented submissions only.

Ethnic Books: African American; Hispanic.

Tips: "Most open to a book that has a big and well-defined audience. Have a clear proposal, lucid thesis, and specified audience."

+DOVE INSPIRATIONAL PRESS, 1000 Burmaster St., Gretna LA 70053. (504)368-1175. Fax (504)368-1195. E-mail: editorial@pelicanpub.com. Website: www.pelicanpub.com. Nina Kooij, ed-in-chief. To publish books of quality and permanence that enrich the lives of those who read them. Imprint of Pelican Publishing. Publishes 2 titles/yr.; hardcover, trade paperbacks. Receives 250 submissions annually. No books from first-time authors. Accepts mss through agents. Reprints books. Prefers 200+ pgs. Royalty; some advances. Publication within 9-18 mos. No simultaneous submissions. Responds in 1 mo. on queries. Requires accepted ms on disk. Prefers KJV. Guidelines (also on Website); catalog for 9x12 SAE/6 stamps.

Nonfiction/Fiction: Proposal/2 chapters; no phone/fax/e-query.

Photos/Artwork: Accepts freelance photos for book covers; open to queries from freelance artists.

DOVER PUBLICATIONS INC., 31 E. 2nd St., Mineola NY 11501-3852. (516)294-7000, ext. 173. Fax (516)873-1401 or (516)742-6953. E-mail: mwaldrep@doverpublications.com. Website: www.doverpublications.com. M. C. Waldrep, ed-in-chief. Publishes some religious titles, reprints only. Makes outright purchases. Query. Free catalog online.

Nonfiction: Query. Religion topics.

EARTHEN VESSEL PUBLISHING, 289 Miller Ave., Mill Valley CA 94941. Phone/fax (415)381-6020. E-mail: kentphilpott@comcast.net. Website: www.earthenvessel.net. Reformed Baptist. Kent Philpott, ed. Publishes 2 titles/yr. Receives 1-3 submissions annually. 50% of books from first-time authors. No mss through agents. Reprints books. Outright purchases. Average first printing varies. Publication time varies. Considers simultaneous submissions. Responds soon. No guidelines or catalog.

Nonfiction: Accepts phone query.

Photos/Artwork: Open to queries from freelance artists.

E-DIGITAL BOOKS, LLC., 1155 S. Havana St., #11-364, Aurora CO 80012. E-mail: submissions@edigitalbooks.com. Website: www.edigitalbooks.com. T. R. Allen, ed-in-chief. Publishes 10-15 titles/yr. Receives 10 submissions annually. 50% of books from first-time authors. No mss through agents. Royalty 30-60% on retail. Publication within 6 mos. Considers simultaneous submissions. Responds in 6 mos. by e-mail. Guidelines/catalog by e-mail.

Nonfiction: Query by e-mail only. (Put "Nonfiction Query" in subject line.)

Fiction: Query by e-mail.

Tips: "Interested in Christian religious poetry with uplifting, positive, and inspirational themes. We have a family-oriented Christian audience." Also see: www.E-digitalCatholic.com.

EDITORIAL PORTAVOZ, PO Box 2607, Grand Rapids MI 49501-2607. Toll-free (800)733-2607. (616)451-4775. Fax (616)451-9330. E-mail: editor@portavoz.com. Website: www.portavoz.com. Spanish Division of Kregel Publishing. Submit to The Editor. To provide trusted, biblically based resources that challenge and encourage Spanish-speaking individuals in their Christian lives and service. Publishes 40+ titles/yr. 2-5% of books from first-time authors. Accepts mss through agents. Does print-on-demand. No reprints. Negotiable royalty on net; negotiable advance. Average first printing 5,000. Publication within 13 mos. Considers simultaneous submissions. Responds in 2-4 mos. Guidelines on Website.

Nonfiction: Send proposal by e-mail or CD-ROM, with 2-3 chapters. "Looking for original Spanish reference works."

Photos/Artwork: Purchases artwork outright.

EDITORIAL UNILIT, 1360 N.W. 88th Ave., Miami FL 33172-3093. Toll-free (800)767-7726. (305)592-6136. Fax (305)592-0087. Website: www.editorialunilit.com. Spanish House. Submit to The Editor. To glorify God by providing the church and Spanish-speaking people with the tools to communicate clearly the gospel of Jesus Christ and help them grow in their relationship with Him and His church.

EDUCATIONAL MINISTRIES, 165 Plaza Dr., Prescott AZ 86303. Toll-free (800)221-0910. (928)771-8601. Fax (928)771-8621. E-mail: edmin2@aol.com. Website: www.educationalministries.com. Linda Davidson, ed. Our liberal theology sets us apart—our books do not give pat answers. Periodical: Church Educator (see separate listing). Publishes 2-3 titles/yr. Receives 30 submissions annually. 15% of books from first-time authors. No mss through agents. No reprints. Outright purchases; no advance. Average first printing 500. Publication within 6 mos. Considers simultaneous submissions. Prefers accepted ms on disk. Responds in 2-3 mos. Guidelines; catalog for 9x12 SAE/3 stamps.

Nonfiction: Complete ms; phone query OK.

EERDMANS BOOKS FOR YOUNG READERS, 2140 Oak Industrial Dr. N.E., Grand Rapids MI 49505. Toll-free (800)253-7521. (616)459-4591. Fax (616)459-6540. E-mail: youngreaders@eerdmans.com. Website: www.eerdmans.com/youngreaders. Wm. B. Eerdmans Publishing. Shannon White, ed. dir. Produces books for general trade, school, and library markets. Publishes 6-7 titles/yr.; hardcover, trade paperbacks. Receives 5,000 submissions annually. 3% of books from first-time authors. Prefers mss through agents. Age-appropriate length. Royalty & advance vary. Average first printing varies. Publication within 36 mos. No simultaneous submissions (mark "Exclusive" on envelope). Responds in 3 mos. Guidelines (also by e-mail/Website); catalog for 9x12 SAE/4 stamps.

Fiction: Proposal/3 chapters for book length; complete ms for picture books. For children and teens.

Photos/Artwork: Please do not send illustrations with picture book manuscripts unless you are a professional illustrator. When submitting artwork, send color copies, not originals.

Tips: "Most open to thoughtful submissions that address needs in children's literature. We are not looking for retold Bible stories or Christmas stories at this time."

WM. B. EERDMANS PUBLISHING CO., 2140 Oak Industrial Dr. N.E., Grand Rapids MI 49505. Toll-free (800)253-7521. (616)459-4591. Fax (616)459-6540. E-mail: info@eerdmans.com. Website: www.eerdmans.com. Protestant/Academic/Theological. Jon Pott, ed-in-chief. Imprint: Eerdmans Books for Young Readers (see separate listing). Publishes 120-130 titles/yr.; hardcover, trade paperbacks. Receives 3,000-4,000 submissions annually. 10% of books from first-time authors. Accepts mss through agents. Reprints books. Royalty; occasional advance. Average first printing 4,000. Publication within 1 yr. Considers simultaneous submissions. Responds in 4 wks. to query; several months for mss. Guidelines on Website; free catalog.

Nonfiction: Proposal/2-3 chapters; no fax/e-query. "Looking for religious approaches to contemporary issues, spiritual growth, scholarly works."

Fiction: Proposal/chapter; no fax/e-query. "We are looking for adult novels with high literary merit."

Tips: "Most open to material with general appeal, but well-researched, cutting-edge material that bridges the gap between evangelical and mainline worlds."

****Note:** This publisher serviced by The Writer's Edge.

ELDRIDGE CHRISTIAN PLAYS & MUSICALS, PO Box 14367, Tallahassee FL 32317. Toll-free (800)95-CHURCH. Toll-free fax (800)453-5179. E-mail: info@95church.com. Website: www.95church.com. Independent Christian drama publisher. Susan Shore, religious ed. To provide superior religious drama to enhance preaching and teaching, whatever your Christian denomination. Publishes 12 plays and 1-2 musicals/yr. Receives 350-400 plays annually. 75% of plays from first-time authors. One-act to full-length plays. Outright purchases of $100-1,000 on publication; no advance. Publication within 1 yr. Considers simultaneous submissions. Responds in 1-3 mos. Requires requested ms on disk or by e-mail. Free guidelines (also by e-mail or Website)/catalog.

Plays: Complete ms; e-query OK. For children, teens, and adults.

Special Needs: Always looking for high quality Christmas and Easter plays but open to other holiday and "anytime" Christian plays too. Can be biblical or contemporary, for performance by all ages, children through adult.

Tips: "Have play produced at your church and others prior to submission, to get out the bugs. At least try a stage reading."

ELIJAH PRESS, Meadow House Communications Inc., PO Box 317628, Cincinnati OH 45231-7628. (513)521-7362. Fax (513)521-7364. Website: www.elijahpress.com. Publishes quality religious/spiritual fiction and nonfiction books and tapes on and related to Christian living, church history, and spiritual reflection. S. R. Davis, ed. Publishes 3-5 titles/yr. Prefers 50,000-100,000 wds. Responds in 1 mo. Guidelines on Website. Incomplete topical listings.

Nonfiction: One-page query; must have completed ms; no phone/e-query.

Fiction: Accepts fiction.

+EMERALD POINTE BOOKS, Box 35035, Tulsa OK 74153. Toll-free (800)888-4126. (918)523-5400. E-mail: customerservice@harrisonhouse.com. Website: www.harrison house.com. Evangelical/charismatic. Submit to Fiction Editor. Fiction imprint of Harrison House. No mss through agents. No reprints. Royalty on net or retail; no advance. Average first printing 5,000. Publication within 12-24 mos. Responds in 6 mos. Accepts requested ms by e-mail. No guidelines or catalog.

Fiction: Query. Adult. Contemporary and historical.

EMMAUS ROAD PUBLISHING, 827 N. Fourth St., Steubenville OH 43952. Toll-free (800)398-5470. (740)281-2404. Fax (740)283-4011. E-mail: shughes@emmausroad.org. Website: www.emmausroad.org. Catholics United for the Faith. Regis J. Flaherty, ed-in-chief. Guidelines on Website. Not accepting submissions at this time.

ETC PUBLICATIONS, 1456 Rodeo Rd., Palm Springs CA 92262. Toll-free (866)514-9969. (760)316-9695. Fax (760)316-9681. E-mail: etcbooks@earthlink.net. Website: www .etcpublications.com. Dr. Richard W. Hostrop, pub.; Lee Ona S. Hostrop, ed. dir. Publishes textbooks for the Christian and general markets at all levels of education. Publishes 6-12 titles/yr.; hardcover, trade paperbacks. Receives 50 submissions annually. 75% of books from first-time authors. Accepts mss through agents. No reprints. Prefers 128-256 pgs. Royalty 5-15% on net or retail; no advance. Average first printing 1,500-2,500. Publication within 9 mos. No simultaneous submissions. Responds in 10 days. No guidelines (use *Chicago Manual of Style*); catalog for #10 SAE/1 stamp.

Nonfiction: Complete ms; e-query OK. "We are interested only in Christian-oriented, state history textbooks to be used in Christian schools and by homeschoolers."

Photos/Artwork: Accepts freelance photos for book covers.

Tips: "Open only to state histories that are required at a specific grade level and are Christian oriented, with illustrations."

EVERGREEN PRESS, 6215 Rangeline Rd., Bldg. 111, Theodore AL 36582-5223. Toll-free (800) 367-8203. Fax (251)443-7090. E-mail: Brian@evergreenpress.com. Website: www.ever greenpress.com. Genesis Communications. Brian Banashak, pub.; Kathy Banashak, ed-in-chief. Publishes books that empower people for breakthrough living by being practical, biblical, and engaging. Imprints: Evergreen Press, Gazelle Press, Axiom Press (print-on-demand). Publishes 30 titles/yr. Receives 250 submissions annually. 40% of books from first-time authors. Accepts mss through agents. **SUBSIDY PUBLISHES 35%.** Does print-on-demand.

No reprints. Prefers 96-160 pgs. Royalty on net; no advance. Average first printing 4,000. Publication within 6 mos. Considers simultaneous submissions. Requires requested ms on disk or by e-mail. Responds in 4-6 wks. Guidelines on Website; free catalog.

Nonfiction: Complete ms; fax/e-query OK. Submission form on Website.

Fiction: For all ages. Complete ms; phone/fax/e-query OK. Submission form on Website.

Special Needs: Business, finance, personal growth, women's issues, family/parenting, relationships, prayer, humor, and angels.

Also Does: Booklets.

Tips: "Most open to books with a specific market (targeted, not general) that the author is qualified to write for and that is relevant to today's believers and seekers. Author must also be open to editorial direction."

EXTREME DIVA MEDIA INC. E-mail: query@extremedivamedia.com. Website: www.extreme divamedia.com. Jean Ann Duckworth, ed./pub. Publishes books in 4 areas: reducing stress, increasing joy, simplifying life, and enhancing relationships. Guidelines on Website.

Nonfiction: E-query only. Full manuscripts will be discarded unless requested.

Special Needs: Devotions to Go (30-day devotionals); Self Improvement; Cookbooks/ Entertainment Guides.

Tips: "Joy is a factor in everything we do."

FACTS ON FILE INC., 132 W. 31st St., 17th Fl., New York NY 10001. Toll-free (800)322-8755. (212)967-8800. Fax (212)967-9196. E-mail: llikoff@factsonfile.com, or editorial@factson file.com. Website: www.factsonfile.com. Laurie Likoff, ed. dir. School and library reference and trade books (for middle- to high-school students) tied to curriculum and areas of cross-cultural studies, including religion. Imprint: Checkmark Books. Publishes 3-5 religious titles/yr. Receives 10-20 submissions annually. 2% of books from first-time authors. Accepts mss through agents. No reprints. Prefers 224-480 pgs. Royalty 10% on retail; outright purchases of $2,000-10,000; advance $5,000-10,000. Some work-for-hire. Average first printing 3,000. Publication within 9-12 mos. Considers simultaneous submissions. Responds in 2 mos. Requires requested ms on disk. Guidelines (also on Website)/free catalog.

Nonfiction: Query or proposal/1 chapter; fax/e-query OK.

Tips: "Most open to reference books tied to curriculum subjects or disciplines."

FAIR HAVENS PUBLICATIONS, PO Box 1238, Gainesville TX 76241-1238. Toll-free (800)771-4861. (940)668-6044. Fax (940)668-6984. E-mail: info@fairhavenspub.com, or submit through Website: www.fairhavenspub.com. J. Ray Smith, chief ed.; D. Joan Smith, children's ed. Produces quality books, teaching and evangelistic literature, audiotapes and videotapes, CD-ROMs, dramas, and artworks that inspire faith and courage. Publishes 1-2 titles/yr.; hardcover, trade paperbacks. Receives 100 submissions annually. No first-time authors. Accepts mss through agents. **SUBSIDY PUBLISHES 25%**; does print-on-demand. Reprints books. Prefers 250-300 pgs. Royalty 10-20% on net; no advance. Average first printing 200-3,000. Publication within 8 mos. Considers simultaneous submissions. Responds in 12 or more wks. Requires requested ms on disk. Prefers NKJV. Guidelines on Website; no catalog.

Nonfiction: Proposal/3 chapters; no phone/fax/e-query. "We are interested in books based on original research based on compiled data, case studies, etc."

Special Needs: Nonfiction; personal experience; how-to books packed with practical information relating to a felt need.

Also Does: Booklets, audio & videotapes, CD-ROMs, dramas.

Photos/Artwork: Accepts freelance photos for book covers; open to queries from freelance artists.

Tips: "We are flexible and work closely with our authors. We will help authors to self-publish if we do not elect to publish their manuscripts."

FAITH ALIVE CHRISTIAN RESOURCES, 2850 Kalamazoo Ave. S.E., Grand Rapids MI 49560. Toll-free (800)333-8300. (616)224-0819. E-mail: editors@faithaliveresources.org. Website: www.faithaliveresources.org. CRC Publications/Christian Reformed Church. Leonard Vander Zee, ed-in-chief. Incomplete topical listings.

FAITH COMMUNICATIONS, 3201 S.W. 15th St., Deerfield Beach FL 33442. (954)360-0909. Fax (954)360-0034. Website: www.hcibooks.com. Christian imprint of Health Communications Inc. Submit to Editorial Committee. Dedicated to publishing exceptional products that cultivate the desire to pursue Christ, grow in faith, and share his love with others. No phone/e-queries. Guidelines on Website. Incomplete topical listings.

Nonfiction/Fiction: Proposal/2 chapters.

Tips: "Books should have a very clear Christian focus—fiction or nonfiction."

FAITHGIRLZ!/ZONDERKIDZ, 5300 Patterson S.E., Grand Rapids MI 49530-0002. (616)698-3400. Fax (616)698-3326. E-mail: zpub@zondervan.com. Website: www.zonderkidz.com. Zondervan/HarperCollins. Not currently accepting submissions for this line.

FAITHKIDZ BOOKS—No longer a separate brand; see David C. Cook.

FAITHWALK PUBLISHING, 333 Jackson St., Grand Haven MI 49417. Toll-free (800)335-7177. (616)846-9360. Fax (616)846-0072. E-mail: submissions@faithwalkpub.com. Website: www.faithwalkpub.com Dirk Wierenga, ed. Called to publish books which appeal to seekers and believers who might otherwise never purchase a religious book. Publishes 10 titles/yr. Receives 500+ submissions annually. 10% of books from first-time authors. Accepts mss through agents. No reprints. Prefers 160-356 pgs. Royalty 7-10% of retail; advance. Average first printing 5,000. Publication within 9-12 mos. Considers simultaneous submissions (if indicated). Does not respond to submissions unless interested (no SASE needed). Prefers NIV, NRSV. Guidelines (also by e-mail/Website); catalog.

Nonfiction: Proposal/1-2 chapters; no fax submissions; e-query OK. No children's or gift books.

Fiction: Proposal/1-2 chapters; e-query OK. Adult; adventure, contemporary, and literary.

Photos/Artwork: Accepts freelance photos for book covers.

FAITHWORDS, 10 Cadillac Dr., Ste. 220, Brentwood TN 37027. (615)221-0996. Fax (615)221-0962. Website: www.hachettebookgroupusa.com/christian/index.html. Hachette Book Group USA. Gary Terashita & Ann Goldsmith, eds. Accepts no unsolicited mss; unfamiliar packages returned unopened. Accepts submissions through agents or from contacts at writers' conferences.

FAMILYLIFE PUBLISHING, PO Box 7111, Little Rock AR 72223. Toll-free (800)358-6329. E-mail through Website: www.familylife.com. Campus Crusade for Christ. Margie Clark, product development mngr. Our uniqueness is creating/publishing connecting resources: marrying together truth, relationship, and experience. Publishes 10 titles/yr.; hardcover, trade paperbacks. Receives 100 submissions annually. 10% of books from first-time authors. Accepts mss through agents. Reprints books. Royalty 2-18% of net or outright purchase; advance. Average first printing 10,000. Publication within 12 mos. Considers simultaneous submissions. Requires submissions on disk or by e-mail. Responds in 6 mos. Prefers NASB, ESV, NIV. Guidelines (also by e-mail/Website); catalog on Website or for 9x12 SAE/4 stamps.

Nonfiction: Proposal/2 chapters; e-query OK. "Looking for books on marriage: intimacy, communication."

Also Does: Booklets; multipiece activity packs.

Photos/Artwork: Accepts freelance photos for book covers; open to queries from freelance artists.

Tips: "Most open to multipiece, interactive products. The query and proposal should be professional. Before you submit to us, be sure to read our writer's guidelines and The

Family Manifesto (both on Website). If you don't know who we are or what we do, please send your material elsewhere."

****Note:** This publisher serviced by ChristianManuscriptSubmissions.com.

FREDERICK FELL PUBLISHERS INC., 1403 Shoreline Way, Hollywood FL 33019. (954)925-5242. Fax (954)925-5244. E-mail: fellpub@aol.com. Website: www.fellpub.com. Barbara Newman, sr. ed. General publisher that publishes 2-4 religious titles/yr.; hardcover, trade paperbacks. Receives 4,000 submissions annually. 95% of books from first-time authors. Reprints books. Prefers 60,000 wds. or 200-300 pgs. Royalty 6-15% on retail; advance $500-10,000. Average first printing 7,500. Publication within 1 yr. Considers simultaneous submissions. Responds in 5-13 wks. Requires submissions by e-mail. Guidelines on Website.

Nonfiction: Proposal/3 chapters; no phone/fax/e-query. Looking for self-help and how-to books. Include a clear marketing and promotional strategy.

Fiction: Complete ms; no phone/fax/e-query. For adults; adventure and historical. "Looking for great story lines, with potential movie prospects."

Tips: "Spirituality, optimism, and a positive attitude have international appeal. Steer clear of doom and gloom; less sadness and more gladness benefits all." Also publishes New Age books. SASE required.

FIFTH ESTATE PUBLISHERS, PO Box 116, Blountsville AL 35031. Toll-free (888)734-2476. (205)625-5733. E-mail: admin@fifth-estate.net. Website: www.fifth-estate.net. Joyce Dujardin, exec. ed. Publishes 10 titles/yr.; hardcover, trade paperbacks, mass-market paperbacks. Receives 100+ submissions annually. 50% of books from first-time authors. Prefers mss through agents. Does print-on-demand. Reprints books. Prefers 104-730 pgs. Royalty on net; no advance. Publication within 6 mos. Considers simultaneous submissions. Responds in 1 mo. Requires accepted ms on disk or by e-mail. Guidelines (also by e-mail or Website); free catalog for SASE.

Nonfiction: Query only first; mail/phone/e-query OK. "Looking for spiritual and children's books."

Fiction: Query only first; e-query OK. For all ages.

Photos/Artwork: Accepts freelance photos for book covers; open to queries from freelance artists.

Tips: "When an author tells me their book is different, I usually find it is not. Find what is in demand; write about it; and write it well."

FILBERT PUBLISHING, Box 326, Kandiyohi MN 56251. (320)382-6662. E-mail: filbertpublishing@filbertpublishing.com. Website: www.filbertpublishing.com. Closed to submissions until further notice.

FIRST FRUITS OF ZION, PO Box 620099, Littleton CO 80162-0099. Fax (303)933-0997. Website: www.FFOZ.org. Hope Egan, ed. A nonprofit ministry devoted to strengthening the love and appreciation of the Body of Messiah for the land, people, and Scripture of Israel. Publishes 2-6 titles/yr.; trade paperbacks. No mss through agents. Royalty; no advance. Publication within 6 mos. Considers simultaneous submissions. Responds in 1 mo. Prefers NASB.

Nonfiction: Query first; no phone/fax/e-query.

Special Needs: Books on Jewish or Hebraic roots only.

Tips: "Be very familiar with our material before submitting to us."

FOCUS ON THE FAMILY BOOK PUBLISHING AND RESOURCE DEVELOPMENT, 8605 Explorer Dr., Colorado Springs CO 80920-1051. (719)531-3400. Fax (719)531-3448. Website: www.family.org. Submit to Acquisitions Assistant. Exists to support the family; all our products are about topics pertaining to families. Publishes 30-40 titles/yr.; hardcover, trade paperbacks, mass-market paperbacks (rarely). 12% of books from first-time authors. Rarely reprints books. Length depends on genre. Royalty or work-for-hire; advance varies. Average first printing varies. Publication within 12 mos. No longer considers unsolicited submissions. Responds in 1-3 mos. Prefers NIV (but accepts 7 others). Guidelines by e-mail; no catalog.

Nonfiction: Query Letter only through an agent or writer's conference contact with a Focus editor. "Most open to family advice topics. We look for excellent writing and topics that haven't been done to death—or that have a unique angle."

Fiction: Query Letter only through an agent or writer's conference contact with a Focus editor. Stories must incorporate traditional family values or family issues; from 1900 to present day. Also does Mom Lit.

Photos/Artwork: Open to queries from freelance artists (but not for specific projects).

****Note:** This publisher serviced by The Writer's Edge and ChristianManuscript Submissions.com.

FORDHAM UNIVERSITY PRESS, 2546 Belmont Ave., University Box L, Bronx NY 10458. (718)817-4795. Fax (718)817-4785. E-mail: tartar@fordham.edu. Website: www.fordham press.com. Helen Tartar, ed. dir. Publishes for both an academic and general audience; includes religion. Publishes hardcover & trade paperbacks. Reprints books. Guidelines on Website; catalog.

Nonfiction: Query; no e-query.

FORTRESS PRESS, Box 1209, Minneapolis MN 55440-1209. (612)330-3300. Fax (612)330-3215. E-mail: booksub@augsburgfortress.org. Website: www.fortresspress.com. J. Michael West, ed-in-chief. Publishes religious academic books. Publishes 60 titles/yr.; hardcover, trade paperbacks. Receives 1,000 submissions annually. 5-10% of books from first-time authors. Accepts mss through agents. No reprints. Royalty on retail. Publication within 2 yrs. Considers simultaneous submissions. Responds in 3 mos. Guidelines on Website; free catalog (call 1-800-328-4648).

Nonfiction: Query/sample pages. "Please study guidelines before submitting."

Ethnic Books: African American studies.

FORWARD MOVEMENT, 300 W. 4th St., Cincinnati OH 45202-2666. Toll-free (800)543-1813. (513)721-6659. Fax (513)721-0729. E-mail: rschmidt@forwarddaybyday.com. Website: www.forwardmovement.org. Episcopal. Submit to The Editor. Provides resources to support persons in their lives of prayer and faith. Publishes 2-3 books/yr., and 25 tracts & booklets. Receives 1,000 submissions annually. 50% of books from first-time authors. No mss through agents. No reprints. Prefers up to 200 pgs. One-time honorarium; no advance. Average first printing 5,000. Publication within 9 mos. Considers simultaneous submissions. Prefers requested ms on disk as an RTF file. Responds in 1-2 mos. Prefers NRSV. Guidelines; free catalog.

Nonfiction: Query for book, complete ms if short; no phone/fax/e-query. "Looking for books on prayer and spirituality, devotionals, Christian living, and spiritual life."

Ethnic Books: Black & Hispanic pamphlets.

Also Does: Booklets, 4-32 pgs.; pamphlets 4-8 pgs.; tracts.

Tips: "We sell primarily to a mainline Protestant audience. Most open to books that deal with the central doctrines of the Christian faith. Spirituality and Christian living."

FOUNDERS PRESS, PO Box 150931, Cape Coral FL 33915. (239)772-1400. Fax (239)772-1140. E-mail through Website: www.founders.org. Founders Ministries/Southern Baptist. Kenneth Puls, ed. Committed to producing and distributing books, pamphlets, and other materials that are consistent with the doctrines of grace and that speak from a historic Southern Baptist perspective. Responds in 4 mos. (or contact them). Guidelines on Website. Incomplete topical listings.

Nonfiction: Proposal, plus completed author information sheet (available on the Website).

Also Does: Pamphlets.

+FOURSQUARE MEDIA, 1910 W. Sunset Blvd., Ste. 200, Los Angeles CA 90026-0176. (213)989-4494. E-mail: media@foursquare.org. Website: www.foursquare.org/landing_pages/83,3.html. In partnership with Creation House (Strang Communications). Rick Wulfestieg, dir.; Larry Libby, sr. ed. To capture Foursquare history, vision, and values; for cell study groups, church ministry institutes, and pastoral-led congregational studies. Estab. 2006. Publishes 4+ titles/yr.

Nonfiction: E-query.

Also Does: Will host writers' conferences in the future to encourage ministry leaders in developing writing and publishing skills.

FRIENDS UNITED PRESS, 101 Quaker Hill Dr., Richmond IN 47374. (765)962-7573. Fax (765)966-1293. E-mail: friendspress@fum.org. Website: www.fum.org. Friends United Meeting (Quaker). Trish Edwards-Konic, ed. To gather persons into a fellowship where Jesus Christ is known as Lord and Teacher. Publishes 3 titles/yr. Receives 25 submissions annually. 50% of books from first-time authors. No mss through agents. Does print-on-demand. Prefers 150-200 pgs. Royalty 7.5% of net; no advance. Average first printing 1,000-1,500. Publication within 1 yr. Considers simultaneous submissions; e-mail submissions preferred. Responds in 3 mos. Prefers requested ms by e-mail. Guidelines (also by e-mail/Website); free catalog.

Nonfiction: Proposal/2 chapters; e-query preferred.

Ethnic Books: Howard Thurman Books (African American), Underground Railroad.

Tips: "Primarily open to Quaker authors. Looking for Quaker-related spirituality, or current faith issues/practice addressed from a Christian Quaker experience or practice."

GENESIS PRESS INC., PO Box 101, Columbus MS 39701. Toll-free (888)463-4461. (662)329-9927. Fax (662)329-9399. E-mail through Website: www.genesis-press.com. Angelique Justin, acq. ed. African American press; wants to approach romance with a classy, realistic, and fun, yet inspirational, Christian outlook. Imprints: Indigo Christian Romance; Indigo Glitz, and Indigo Vibe (all fiction); and Mount Blue (Christian living). Publishes 2 titles/yr.; hardcover, trade paperbacks. Receives 300+ submissions annually. 75% of books from first-time authors. Accepts mss through agents. **SOME SUBSIDY.** Reprints books. Prefers 85,000 wds. Royalty 6-8% of net; advance $750. Average first printing 15,000. Publication within 6 mos. Considers simultaneous submissions. Responds in 3-4 mos. Guidelines on Website; free catalog.

Nonfiction: Proposal/3 chapters; no phone/fax/e-query. Hard copy only.

Fiction: Query first; proposal/150 pgs.; no phone/fax/e-query. Hard copy only. Christian/inspirational romance. Prefers African American or cross-cultural fiction. Also does teen fiction for 12- to 18-year-olds, and fiction for 21- to 30-year-olds (under Indigo Vibe Imprint).

Ethnic Books: African American and multicultural romances.

Tips: "We are the largest privately owned African American publisher in the country, focusing on African American, Hispanic, Asian, and interracial fiction."

GENEVA PRESS—See Presbyterian Publishing Corporation.

GEORGETOWN UNIVERSITY PRESS, 3240 Prospect St. N.W., Washington DC 20007. (202)687-5889. Fax (202)687-6340. E-mail: reb7@georgetown.edu, or gupress@georgetown.edu. Website: www.press.georgetown.edu. Georgetown University. Richard Brown, dir. Scholarly books in religion, theology, ethics, and other fields, with an emphasis on cross-disciplinary and cross-cultural studies. Publishes 10 titles/yr. Receives 100 submissions annually. 10% of books from first-time authors. Accepts mss through agents. No reprints. Prefers 80,000 wds. Royalty 8-12% on net; negotiable advance. Average first printing 2,000-3,000. Publication within 9-10 mos. Considers simultaneous submissions. Requires requested ms on disk. Responds in 6-8 wks. Prefers NRSV. Does print-on-demand. Guidelines on Website; free catalog.

Nonfiction: Proposal/1 chapter; fax/e-query OK. "Should be thoroughly researched and original."

Special Needs: Work relations, theology, ethics—with scholarly bent.
Ethnic Books: Hispanic.
Also Does: CD-ROMs.
Photos/Artwork: Accepts freelance photos for book covers.

GOLLEHON PRESS INC., 6157—28th St. S.E., Grand Rapids MI 49546. (616)949-3515. Fax (616)949-8674. E-mail: john@gollehonbooks.com. Website: www.gollehonbooks.com. Becky Anderson, ed. Publishes 3-4 titles/yr.; hardcover, trade paperbacks. Receives 50-100 submissions annually. 90% of books from first-time authors. Accepts mss through agents. No subsidy publishing. No reprints. Prefers 50,000-80,000 wds., or 200-250 pgs. Royalty 6-8% on retail; advance to $1,000. Average first printing 5,000-10,000. Publication within 8-10 mos. Encourages simultaneous submissions. Responds in 1-2 mos., if interested. Prefers KJV. Guidelines pending; no catalog.
Nonfiction: Brief book proposal; if interested will request full ms. Do not send unsolicited mss. Unable to respond to all queries.
Tips: "Most open to inspirational, miracles, and from the heart. Also more scholarly books, such as the first century church."

GOOD BOOK PUBLISHING COMPANY, PO Box 837, Kihei HI 96753-0837. Phone/fax (808) 874-4876. E-mail: dickb@dickb.com. Website: www.dickb.com/index.shtml. Christian/Protestant/Bible Fellowship. Ken Burns, pres. Researches and publishes books on the biblical/Christian roots of Alcoholics Anonymous. Publishes 1 title/yr.; publishes trade paperbacks, mass-market paperbacks. Receives 8 submissions annually. 80% of books from first-time authors. No mss through agents. Reprints books. Prefers 250 pgs. Royalty 10%; no advance. Average first printing 3,000. Publication within 2 mos. Considers simultaneous submissions. Responds in 1 wk. No disk. Prefers KJV. No guidelines; free catalog.
Nonfiction: Proposal; no phone/fax/e-query. Books on the spiritual history and success of AA; 12-step spiritual roots; Bible study.
Also Does: Pamphlets, booklets.

GOOD NEWS PUBLISHERS, 1300 Crescent St., Wheaton IL 60187. (630)682-4300. Fax (630) 682-4785. E-mail: tracts@gnpcb.org. Website: www.goodnewspublishers.org. Kate Felinski, dir. of Literature Ministries. Tracts only; publishing the gospel message in an attractive and relevant format. Publishes 30 tracts/yr. Receives 500 submissions annually. 2% of tracts from first-time authors. Prefers 650-800 wds. Pays about $150 or a quantity of tracts. Average first printing 100,000. Publication within 16 mos. Considers simultaneous submissions. Responds in 12 wks. Prefers ESV. Guidelines; free tract catalog.
Tracts: Complete ms.
Also Does: Pamphlets.
Tips: "Most open to seasonal tracts—Easter, Halloween, or Christmas. Be concise, clear, and careful with Christian terms."

GOSPEL LIGHT, 1957 Eastman Ave., Ventura CA 93003. Toll-free (800)4-GOSPEL. (805)-644-9721, ext. 1223. Website: www.gospellight.com. Anita Griggs, ed. Accepts proposals for Sunday school and Vacation Bible School curriculum and related resources for children from birth through the preteen years; also teacher resources. Guidelines on Website.
Also Does: Sometimes has openings for readers of new curriculum projects. See Website for how to apply.
Tips: "All our curriculum is written and field-tested by experienced teachers; most of our writers are on staff."

GOSPEL PUBLISHING HOUSE, 1445 N. Boonville Ave., Springfield MO 65802. Toll-free (800)641-4310. (417)831-8000. E-mail: newproducts@gph.org. Website: www.gospel publishing.com. Assemblies of God. Julie Horner, ed. The majority of titles specifically address Pentecostal audiences in a variety of ministries in the local church. Publishes 5-10 titles/yr. Receives 250 submissions annually. 25% of books from first-time authors. Accepts mss through agents. No reprints. Royalty 5-10% of retail; no advance. Average first printing 5,000. Publication within 1 yr. Considers simultaneous submissions. Responds in 4 mos. Requires accepted mss on disk or by e-mail. Guidelines on Website; free catalog.

Nonfiction: Proposal/1 chapter; no phone query, e-query OK. "Looking for Holy Spirit; Pentecostal focus for pastors, local church lay leaders, and individuals; children's ministry programs and resources; small group resources."

Tips: "Most open to a new program or resource for small groups, children's ministry, compassion ministry, or evangelistic outreach, written by someone who is actively leading it at the local church."

GREEN KEY BOOKS, 2514 Aloha Pl., Holiday FL 34691. Toll-free (888)900-0197. (727)934-0927. Fax (727)934-4241. E-mail: acquisitions@greenkeybooks.com. Website: www.greenkeybooks.com. Christian publisher. Krissi Castor, mng. ed./acquisitions. Publishes 10-12 titles/yr.; hardcover, trade paperbacks. Receives 200-400 submissions annually. 10% of books from first-time authors. Accepts mss through agents. No reprints. Royalty; no advance. Average first printing 5,000. Publication within 9-12 mos. No simultaneous submissions. Accepts mss by e-mail. Responds in 16 wks. Guidelines on Website; free catalog.

Nonfiction: Query first; e-query OK. Query can include a synopsis or brief project outline. "Looking for men's devotionals, niche topics, books for military families."

Fiction: Not currently considering fiction or children's books.

Tips: "Most open to a book that is editorially tight (specifically grammar and punctuation) in adherence to the *Chicago Manual of Style.*"

****Note:** This publisher serviced by The Writer's Edge and ChristianManuscriptSubmissions.com.

GREENWOOD PUBLISHING GROUP/PRAEGER PUBLISHERS, 88 Post Road W., Westport CT 06881. (203)226-3571. Fax (203)222-1502. E-mail: suzanne.staszak-silva@greenwood.com. Website: www.Greenwood.com. Reed Elsevier Co. (USA). Suzanne Staszak-Silva, ed. List of editors by subject on Website. Imprints: Greenwood, Praeger, PSI. Publishes 5-30 titles/yr.; hardcover. Receives 40-60 submissions annually. No reprints. Prefers up to 100,000 wds. Variable royalty on net; some advances. Average first printing 1,500. Publication within 8-10 mos. Considers simultaneous submissions. Responds in 1-3 mos. Guidelines & catalog on Website.

Nonfiction: Book proposal/1-2 chapters or all chapters available; e-query preferred.

Special Needs: Religious studies (general interest); criminology (general interest); literary studies, science.

Ethnic Books: Black studies (general interest); Islamic studies; Jewish studies; Native American studies; Hispanic/Latino studies.

Tips: "Most open to general interest books."

GROUP PUBLISHING INC., 1515 Cascade Ave., Loveland CO 80539-0481. Toll-free (800)447-1070. (970)292-4243. Fax (970)622-4370. E-mail: kloesche@group.com. Website: www.group.com. Nondenominational. Kerri Loesche, ed. asst./copyright coordinator. Imprint: Group Books. To equip churches to help children, youth, and adults grow in their relationship with Jesus, with resources that are R.E.A.L. (relational, experiential, applicable, learner based). Publishes 40 titles/yr.; hardcover, trade paperbacks. Receives 1,000+ submissions annually. 5% of books from first-time authors. Accepts mss through agents. **SOME SUBSIDY**. No reprints. Prefers 128-250 pgs. Outright purchases of $25-3,000 or royalty of 6-10% of net; advance $1,500. Average first printing 5,000. Publication within 12-18 mos. Considers simultaneous submissions. Responds in 6 mos. Requires requested ms on disk. Prefers NIV. Guidelines on Website; catalog.

Nonfiction: Query or proposal/2 chapters/intro/cover letter/SASE; no phone/fax/e-query. "Looking for practical ministry tools for youth workers, C. E. directors, and teachers with an emphasis on active learning. Read *Unforgettable!* by Thom and Joani Schultz (available June 2008)."

Tips: "Most open to a practical resource that will help church leaders change lives. Tell our readers something they don't already know, in a way that they've not seen before."

****Note:** This publisher serviced by The Writer's Edge.

GRQ INC., PO Box 1067, Brentwood TN 37204. (615)776-3275. Fax (615)507-1709. E-mail: rzaloba@comcast.net. Robert Zaloba, pres. A book packager. Publishes 40-50 titles/yr.; hardcover, trade paperbacks, coffee-table books. Receives 200-300 submissions annually. 70% of books from first-time authors. Accepts mss through agents. **SUBSIDY PUBLISHES 5%.** Reprints books. Does mostly work-for-hire; rates depend on project; ranges from $1,500-$20,000; advance. Average first printing varies, 10,000-50,000. Publication within 10 mos. Considers simultaneous submissions. Response time varies. Requires accepted ms on disk. No guidelines or catalog.

Nonfiction: Query only first; no phone/fax query; e-query OK.

Tips: "We are a book packager who produces books that speak to the Christian market at large. Our books are found outside of the traditional CBA market. They are uniquely formatted and targeted for an 'average' reader. Most open to practical, unique self-help; unique devotions."

GRUPO NELSON, PO Box 141000, Nashville TN 37214. Toll-free (800)322-7423. (615)902-2372/2375. Fax (615)883-9376. E-mail: info@editorialcaribe.com. Website: www.grupo nelson.com. Thomas Nelson has reformed its Spanish division into Grupo Nelson, with five Spanish-language imprints listed below. Larry Downs, VP/Publisher. Targets the needs and wants of the Hispanic community. Publishes 65-80 titles/yr. Receives 50 submissions annually. 90% of books from first-time authors. No mss through agents. Prefers 192 pgs. Royalty on net; advance $500. Average first printing 4,000. Publication within 15 mos. Accepts e-mail submissions. No guidelines; free catalog.

Nonfiction: Query letter only; no phone/fax/e-query.

Ethnic Books: Hispanic imprints.

Also Does: Computer games.

Tips: "Most open to Christian books based on the Bible."

Editorial Diez Puntos: Specializes in parenting & family, personal finance, health and fitness, self-help, and popular culture.

Leader Latino: Business & leadership.

Editorial Caribe: Bibles, Bible reference, and electronic products.

Editorial Betania: Inspirational, popular religious, and children's.

Editorial Catolica: Catholic books and Bibles.

+GUARDIAN ANGEL PUBLISHING INC., 12430 Teeson Ferry Rd., #186, St. Louis MO 63128. (314)276-8482. Fax (314)843-8517. E-mail: publisher@guardianangelpublishing.com. Website: www.guardianangelpublishing.com. Lynda S. Burch, ed. Goal is to inspire children to learn and grow and develop character skills to instill a Christian and healthy attitude of learning, caring, and sharing. Imprints: Wings of Faith, Angel to Angel, Angelic Harmony, Littlest Angels, Academic Wings, Guardian Angel Pets. Publishes 6-12 titles/yr.; hardcover, trade paperbacks, coffee-table books. Receives 300-600 submissions annually. 75% of books from first-time authors. No subsidy; does print-on-demand. Prefers 100-5,000 wds. or 32 pgs. Royalty 30-50% on download; no advance. Average first printing 50. Publication within 3-6 mos. No simultaneous submissions. Responds in 1 wk.-1 mo. Accepted mss by disk or e-mail. Guidelines on Website; catalog as e-book PDF.

Nonfiction: Complete ms; no phone/fax query; e-query OK. "Looking for all kinds of kids' books."

Fiction: Complete ms; no phone/fax query; e-query OK.

Photos: Accepts freelance photos for book covers; open to queries from freelance artists.

Contest: Sponsors children's writing contest for schools.

Tips: "Most open to books that teach children to read and love books; to learn or grow from books."

GUERNICA EDITIONS, 11 Mount Royal Ave., Toronto ON M6H 2S2, Canada. (416)658-9888. Fax (416)657-8885. E-mail: guernicaeditions@cs.com. Website: www.guernicaeditions.com. Antonio D'Alfonso, ed. Interested in the next generation of writers. Publishes 1 religious title/yr.; trade paperbacks, mass-market paperbacks. Receives 100 submissions annually. 5% of books from first-time authors. No mss through agents. Reprints books. Prefers 100 pgs. Royalty 8-10% of retail; some outright purchases of $200-5,000; advance $200-2,000. Average first printing 1,500. Publication within 10 mos. Responds in 1-6 mos. Requires requested ms on disk; no e-mail. No guidelines (read one of our books to see what we like); catalog online.

Nonfiction: Query first; no phone/fax/e-query. "Looking for books on world issues."

Fiction: Query first. "Looking for short and profound literary works."

Ethnic Books: Concentration on other cultures. "We are involved in translations and ethnic issues."

Photos/Artwork: Accepts freelance photos for book covers.

Tips: "Know what we publish. We're interested in books that bridge time and space; works that fit our editorial literary policies."

GUIDEPOSTSBOOKS, 16 E. 34th St., 12th Fl., New York NY 10016-4397. (212)251-8143. Website: www.guidepostsbooks.com. Guideposts Inc. Marilyn Moore, VP/ed-in-chief; Andrew Attaway, sr. acq. ed. Focuses on inspirational fiction, memoirs, story collections, devotionals, and faith-based true stories. Publishes 20 titles/yr.

HARCOURT RELIGION PUBLISHERS, 6277 Sea Harbor Dr., Orlando FL 32887. Toll-free (800)922-7696. (407)345-3800. Fax (407)345-3798. E-mail: hrpwebmaster@harcourt .com. Website: www.harcourtreligion.com. Catholic. Craig O'Neil, sr. ed. Catholic educational market; high school curriculum. Publishes 50-100 titles/yr. Receives 100-300 submissions annually. Variable royalty or outright purchase; rarely pays advance. Average first printing 1,000-3,000. Publication within 1 yr. Considers simultaneous submissions. Responds in 6 mos. Free catalog.

Nonfiction: Complete ms. "Looking primarily for school and parish textbooks."

Photos/Artwork: Accepts freelance photos for book covers. Submit to Lynn Molony, production mngr.

HARPERONE, (formerly HarperSanFrancisco), 353 Sacramento St., #500, San Francisco CA 94111-3653. (415)477-4400. Fax (415)477-4444. E-mail: hcsanfrancisco@harper collins.com. Website: www.harpercollins.com. Religious division of HarperCollins. Michael G. Maudlin, ed. dir. Strives to be the preeminent publisher of the most important books across the full spectrum of religion and spiritual literature, adding to the wealth of the world's wisdom by respecting all traditions and favoring none; emphasis on quality Christian spirituality and literary fiction. Publishes 75 titles/yr.; hardcover, trade paperbacks. Receives 10,000 submissions annually. 5% of books from first-time authors. Prefers mss through agents. No reprints. Prefers 160-256 ms pgs. Royalty 7.5-15% on retail; advance $20,000-100,000. Average first printing 10,000. Publication within 18 mos. Considers simultaneous submissions. Responds in 3 mos. Requires requested ms on disk. No guidelines/catalog.

Nonfiction: Proposal/1 chapter; fax query OK.

Fiction: Complete ms; contemporary adult fiction, literary, fables & parables, spiritual.

Tips: "Agented proposals only."

HARRISON HOUSE PUBLISHERS, Box 35035, Tulsa OK 74153. Toll-free (800)888-4126. (918)523-5400. E-mail: customerservice@harrisonhouse.com. Website: www.harrison

house.com. Evangelical/charismatic. Julie Lechlider, mng. ed. To challenge Christians to live victoriously, grow spiritually, and know God intimately. Fiction imprint: Emerald Pointe Books (see separate listing). Publishes 20 titles/yr.; hardcover, trade paperbacks, mass-market paperbacks. 5% of books from first-time authors. No mss through agents. No reprints. Royalty on net or retail; no advance. Average first printing 5,000. Publication within 12-24 mos. Responds in 6 mos. Accepts requested ms by e-mail. No guidelines or catalog. Not currently accepting proposals or manuscripts.

Nonfiction: Query first; then proposal/table of contents/1 chapter; no phone/fax query; e-query OK.

+HARVEST DAY BOOKS, 10300 E. Leelanau Ct., Traverse City MI 49684. (231)929-1999. Fax (231)929-1993. E-mail: Info@bookmarketingsolutions.com. Website: www.BookMarketingSolutions.com. Imprint of Book Marketing Solutions LLC. Tom White, pres. (tom@BookMarketingSolutions.com). Publishes works of the Christian faith. Guidelines on Website.

Nonfiction: Submission form on Website.

Poetry: Also accepting submissions for a 5-book poetry series called "Of the Heart." Although not exclusively Christian, they are hoping for an excellent Christian representation. For details, see Website or contact Tom White.

HARVEST HOUSE PUBLISHERS, 990 Owen Loop N., Eugene OR 97402. (541)343-0123. E-mail: admin@harvesthousepublishers.com. Website: www.harvesthousepublishers.com. Evangelical. Books and products that affirm biblical values and help people grow spiritually strong. Publishes 170 titles/yr.; hardcover, trade paperbacks, mass-market paperbacks, coffee-table books. No longer accepting unsolicited submissions, proposals, queries, etc.

Nonfiction: Self-help; Christian living.

Fiction: Interesting women's fiction.

Tips: "Find a good agent."

****Note:** This publisher serviced by The Writer's Edge and ChristianManuscriptSubmissions.com.

THE HAWORTH PASTORAL PRESS, an imprint of The Haworth Press, 10 Alice St., Binghamton NY 13904-1580. Toll-free (800)429-6784. (607)722-5857. Fax (607)722-8465. E-mail: getinfo@haworthpress.com. Website: www.haworthpress.com. Rebecca Brown, project mngr. Publishes 10 titles/yr.; hardcover, trade paperbacks. Receives 100 submissions annually. 60% of books from first-time authors. Reprints books. Prefers up to 250 pgs. Royalty 7-15% of net; advance $500-1,000. Average first printing 1,500. Publication within 1 yr. No simultaneous submissions. Requires requested ms on disk. Responds in 6-8 wks. Guidelines; free catalog.

Nonfiction: Proposal/1-3 chapters; no phone/fax/e-query. "Looking for books on psychology/social work, etc., with a pastoral perspective."

HAY HOUSE INC., PO Box 5100, Carlsbad CA 92018-5100. (760)431-7695. Fax (760)431-6948. E-mail:editorial@hayhouse.com. Website: www.hayhouse.com. Jill Kramer, ed. dir.; Jessica Kelley, submissions ed. Books to help heal the planet. Publishes 1 religious title/yr.; hardcover, trade paperbacks. Receives 200 religious submissions annually. 5% of books from first-time authors. Agented submissions only. Prefers 70,000 wds. or 250 pgs. Royalty. Average first printing 5,000. Publication within 12-15 mos. Considers simultaneous submissions. Responds in 1-2 mos. Guidelines (also by e-mail); free catalog for SASE.

Nonfiction: Proposal/3 chapters; hard copy only. "Looking for self-help/spiritual with a unique ecumenical angle."

Also Does: Some gift books.

Tips: "We are looking for books with a unique slant, ecumenical, but not overly religious. We want an open-minded approach." Includes a broad range of religious titles, including New Age.

HEALTH COMMUNICATIONS INC., 3201 S.W. 15th St., Deerfield Beach FL 33442. Toll-free (800)441-5569. (954)360-0909 (no phone calls). Fax (954)360-0034. E-mail: editorial@hcibooks.com. Website: www.hci-online.com, or www.hcibooks.com. Amy Hughes, religion ed.; submit to Editorial Committee. Nonfiction that emphasizes self-improvement, personal motivation, psychological health, and overall wellness; recovery/addiction, self-help/psychology, soul/spirituality, inspiration, women's issues, relationships, and family. Imprint: HCI Teens. Publishes 50 titles/yr. 20% of books from first-time authors. Accepts mss through agents. Prefers 250 pgs. Royalty 15% of net. Publication within 9 mos. Considers simultaneous submissions. Responds in 3 mos. Follow guidelines for submission. Guidelines (also on Website); catalog for 9x12 SASE.

Nonfiction: Query/outline and 2 chapters; no phone/fax/e-query. Needs books for Christian teens.

HEART OF WISDOM PUBLISHERS, 146 Chriswood Ln., Stafford VA 22556-6601. (540)752-2593. E-mail: info@heartofwisdom.com. Website: www.heartofwisdom.com. Publishes a variety of academic materials to help Christian families bring up children with a heart's desire for and knowledge of the Lord. Robin Sampson, ed. Query only. Guidelines on Website.

Special Needs: Currently accepting queries for high-quality history, science, and life skills unit studies for grades 4-12. Not accepting any other titles.

Tips: "We market to home educators and Christian schools."

HEARTQUEST/TYNDALE HOUSE PUBLISHERS, PO Box 80, Wheaton IL 60189-0080. (630)668-8310. Fax (630)668-3245. Website: www.heartquest.com. Anne Goldsmith, sr. ed. To encourage and challenge readers in their faith journey and Christian walk. Accepts mss through agents or by request only. Prefers fiction 75,000-90,000 wds. (contemporary), and 100,000+ wds. (historical). Responds in 3 mos. Royalty on net; advance. Guidelines (also by e-mail).

HEARTSONG PRESENTS, Imprint of Barbour Publishing Inc., PO Box 721, 1810 Barbour Dr., Uhrichsville, OH 44683. E-mail: fictionsubmit@barbourbooks.com. Website: www.heartsongpresents.com. JoAnne Simmons, ed. Produces affordable, wholesome entertainment through a book club that also helps to enhance and spread the gospel. Publishes 52 titles/yr.; mass-market paperbacks. Receives 1,000 submissions annually. 10% of books from first-time authors. Accepts mss through agents. Prefers 45,000-50,000 wds. Royalty 8% of net; advance $2,200. Average first printing 20,000. Publication within 1 yr. Considers simultaneous submissions. Responds in 6-12 mos. Requires electronic submissions; no proposals via regular mail. Prefers KJV for historicals; NIV for contemporary. Guidelines (also by e-mail); no catalog.

Fiction: Proposal/3 chapters; electronic submissions only (fictionsubmit@barbourbooks.com). Adult. "We publish 2 contemporary and 2 historical romances every 4 weeks. We cover all topics and settings. Specific guidelines available."

Tips: "Romance only, with a strong conservative-Christian theme. Read our books and study our style before submitting."

****Note:** This publisher serviced by The Writer's Edge.

HEARTSONG PRESENTS/MYSTERIES, (was listed as Spy glass Lane Mysteries), Imprint of Barbour Publishing Inc., PO Box 721, 1810 Barbour Dr., Uhrichsville, OH 44683. (740)922-6045. Fax (740)922-5948. E-mail: acquisitions@barbourbooks.com. Website: www.barbourbooks.com. Susan Downs, ed. Produces affordable, wholesome entertainment through a book club that also helps to enhance and spread the gospel. Publishes 32 titles/yr.; mass-market paperbacks. 25% of books from first-time authors. Accepts mss through agents. No subsidy. Prefers 60,000 wds. Royalty or outright purchase; advance. Average first printing 15,000-20,000. Publication within 9-12 mos. Considers simultaneous submissions. Responds in 3-6 mos. Accepts mss by e-mail. Guidelines (also by e-mail/Website).

Fiction: Proposal/3 chapters; no phone/fax query; e-query OK. Accepts only cozy mysteries with a romance plot thread.

Tips: "Cozy mysteries should feature an amateur sleuth in a setting that has a small-town 'feel.' The inciting crime should occur in the first chapter or two so the majority of the plot focuses on solving the 'whodunit' of the mystery. Study our specific guidelines thoroughly prior to proposal submission."

****Note:** This publisher serviced by The Writer's Edge.

HEARTSPRING PUBLISHING, 223 W. Third St. (64801), PO Box 1132, Joplin MO 64802. Toll-free (800)289-3300. (417)623-6280. Fax (417)623-8250. E-mail: jmcclarnon@collegepress.com. Website: www.collegepress.com. Christian Church/Church of Christ. Submit to Acquisitions Editor. Nonacademic imprint of College Press Publishing Co. Publishes 15-20 titles/yr.; trade paperbacks. Receives 700 submissions annually. 25% of books from first-time authors. Accepts mss through agents. Reprints books. Prefers 250-300 pgs. Royalty 5-15% of net; no advance. Average first printing 3,000. Publication within 6 mos. Considers simultaneous submissions. Requires requested ms on disk; no e-mail submissions. Responds in 2-3 mos. Prefers NIV, NASB, NAS. Guidelines on Website; catalog for 9x12 SAE/5 stamps.

Nonfiction: Query only, then proposal/2-3 chapters; no phone/fax query.

Fiction: Christian fiction.

+HEART TO HEART CHRISTIAN BOOKS, 23 W. Center St., Madisonville KY 42431. (270)821-6741. Fax (270)825-9492. Editor: Pat Day-Bivins. Children's picture books.

HENDRICKSON PUBLISHERS, 140 Summit St., PO Box 3473, Peabody MA 01961. (978)532-6546. Fax (978)573-8276. E-mail: editorial@hendrickson.com. Website: www.hendrickson.com. Submit to: Editorial Dept./Book Proposals. To provide biblically oriented books for reference, learning, and personal growth, and resources for pastors. Publishes 25-35 titles/yr.; hardcover, trade paperbacks. Receives 500-600 submissions annually. 10% of books from first-time authors. Accepts mss through agents. Reprints books. Prefers 150-500 pgs. Royalty; some advances. Average first printing 2,000. Publication within 12-18 mos. No simultaneous submissions. Responds in 4-6 mos. Prefers accepted ms by e-mail; will accept on disk. Follow *Chicago Manual of Style.* Prefers NIV. Guidelines (also by e-mail/Website); catalog for 9x12 SAE/$2.13 postage (mark "Media Mail").

Nonfiction: Proposal/1-2 chapters; fax, e-query OK. "Looking for popular reference material." Also publishes academic books through their Academic Book Division. No fiction, devotionals, children's books, or poetry.

Tips: "Most open to books about current 'hot' topics in churches; books that help readers understand and explore Scripture and early church history; and books that encourage Bible study and application of theology in practical life. Best chance: Scholarly/academic, reference; Christian living (not devotionals). Submit proposal in accordance with our book proposal guidelines (available by mail, e-mail, or on our Website)."

****Note:** This publisher serviced by The Writer's Edge.

HENSLEY PUBLISHING, 6116 E. 32nd St., Tulsa OK 74135. (918)664-8520. Fax (918)664-8562. E-mail: editorial@hensleypublishing.com. Website: www.hensleypublishing.com. Terri Kalfas, dir. of publishing. Goal is to get people studying the Bible instead of just reading books about the Bible; Bible study only. Publishes 5-10 titles/yr.; trade paperbacks. Receives 800 submissions annually. 50% of books from first-time authors. No mss through agents. No reprints. Royalty on net; some outright purchases; no advance. Average first printing 2,500. Publication within 12-18 mos. Considers simultaneous submissions. Requires requested ms in MAC format. Responds in 2 mos. Guidelines & catalog on Website.

Nonfiction: Query first, then proposal/first 3 chapters; no phone/fax query. "Looking for Bible studies of varying length for use by small or large groups, or individuals."

Special Needs: Bible study workbooks for small or large groups, or individuals.
****Note:** This publisher serviced by The Writer's Edge.

HIDDEN BROOK PRESS, 109 Bayshore Rd., RR#4, Brighton ON K0K 1H0, Canada. (613)475-2368. E-mail: writers@hiddenbrookpress.com. Website: www.hiddenbrookpress.com. Richard M. Grove, ed./pub. Imprints: Hidden Brook Press, Arc Communications. Does hardcover, trade paperbacks, coffee-table books. Receives 1,000 submissions annually. 98% of books from first-time authors. Accepts mss through agents and authors directly. Does subsidy and print-on-demand, as well as royalty contracts. Reprints books. Royalty on retail or net; no advance. Average first printing 50-5,000. Accepts simultaneous submissions. Guidelines by e-mail.

Nonfiction: E-query or e-submissions. All topics.

Fiction: E-query or e-submissions. All genres.

HILL STREET PRESS, 191 E. Broad St., Ste. 216, Athens GA 30601-2848. (706)613-7200. Fax (706)613-7204. E-mail: editorial@hillstreetpress.com. Website: www.hillstreetpress.com. Judy Long (long@hillstreetpress.com), ed. Liberal, ecumenical, progressive. Imprint: Hill Street Classics. Publishes 1-2 titles/yr.; hardcover, trade paperbacks. Receives 75-100 submissions annually. 40% of books from first-time authors. Prefers mss through agents. Reprints books. Prefers 50,000-85,000 wds. Royalty; some advances. First printing varies. Publication within 12-15 mos. Considers simultaneous submissions. Responds in 1-3 mos. Guidelines/catalog on Website.

Nonfiction: Proposal/3 chapters/query letter/résumé; no phone/fax/e-query. "All electronic submissions are returned unread."

Fiction: Proposal/3 chapters/query letter/résumé; no phone/fax/e-query.

Ethnic Books: Jewish, black.

Tips: "Most open to a book that is short, ecumenical, and liberal."

HONOR BOOKS, 4050 Lee Vance View, Colorado Springs CO 80918. (719)536-0100. Fax (719)536-3269. Website: www.cookministries.com. Division of David C. Cook. Inspiration and motivation for the Seasons of Life (gift and devotional titles). For current policies and submission guidelines, visit their Website: www.cookministries.com/proposals. Devotional books that inspire and motivate, packaged as gift books. Not accepting unsolicited manuscripts at this time except through agents or from contacts made with their editors at writer's conferences.

HOPE PUBLISHING HOUSE, PO Box 60008, Pasadena CA 91106. (626)792-6123. Fax (626)792-2121. E-mail: hopepub@sbcglobal.net. Website: www.hope-pub.com. Southern California Ecumenical Council. Faith A. Sand, pub. Produces thinking books that challenge the faith community to be serious about their pilgrimage of faith. Imprint: New Paradigm Books. Publishes 6 titles/yr. Receives 40 submissions annually. 30% of books from first-time authors. No mss through agents. Reprints books. Prefers 200 pgs. Royalty 10% on net; no advance. Average first printing 3,000. Publication within 6 mos. No simultaneous submissions. Accepts mss by disk or e-mail. Responds in 3 mos. Prefers NRSV. No guidelines; catalog for 7x10 SAE/4 stamps.

Nonfiction: Query only first; no phone/fax query; e-query OK.

Tips: "Most open to a well-written manuscript, with correct grammar, that is provocative, original, challenging, and informative."

HOURGLASS BOOKS, 387 Northgate Rd., Lindenhurst IL 60046. E-mail: editor@hourglassbooks.org. Website: www.hourglassbooks.org/submissions.html. Gina Frangello and Molly McQuade, eds. Publishes anthologies of short stories assembled around a common theme. Accepts simultaneous submissions & reprints. Shared royalties for contributors to the anthologies. Guidelines on Website.

Fiction: Submit by e-mail (copied into message). Literary fiction only. Currently working on *Occupational Hazards: Stories from the World of Work.* No word limits, or fixed closing dates.

HOWARD BOOKS, 3117 N. 7th St., West Monroe LA 71291. (318)396-3122. Fax (318)397-1882. E-mail: dboultinghouse@howardpublishing.com. Website: www.howardpublishing.com. John Howard, pres.; Denny Boultinghouse, exec. ed.; submit to Manuscript Review Committee. A division of Simon & Schuster Inc. Imprint: Howard Kids/LSI. Publishes 65 titles/yr.; hardcover, trade paperbacks. Receives 1,000 submissions annually. 5% of books from first-time authors. Prefers 200-250 pgs. Negotiable royalty & advance. Average first printing 10,000. Publication within 16 mos. Considers simultaneous submissions. Accepted ms by e-mail. Responds in 6-8 mos. No disk. Prefers NIV. No guidelines/catalog.

Nonfiction: Accepting queries only, by e-mail; no phone queries.

Fiction: Accepting queries only, by e-mail. Adult; mystery suspense.

Tips: "Our authors must first be Christ-centered in their lives and writing, then qualified to write on the subject of choice. Public name recognition is a plus. Authors who are also public speakers usually have a ready-made audience."

****Note:** This publisher serviced by The Writer's Edge.

IDEALS CHILDREN'S BOOKS—See Ideals Publications.

IDEALS PUBLICATIONS, 535 Metroplex Dr., Ste. 250, Nashville TN 37211. E-mail: pschaefer@guideposts.org. Website: www.idealsbooks.com. A Guideposts company. Peggy Schaefer, pub.; submit to Candy Cane Press Submissions, or Ideals Children's Book submissions. Imprints: Candy Cane Press, Ideals Children's Books. Publishes 25-30 children's titles/yr. Variable payment structure. Publication within 24-36 mos. Considers simultaneous submissions. Responds in 3 mos. Accepts manuscripts by mail only. Guidelines (also on Website); no catalog.

ILLUMINATION ARTS PUBLISHING INC., PO Box 1865, Bellevue WA 98009. (425)644-7185. Fax (425)644-9274. E-mail: JThompson@Illumin.com. Website: www.Illumin.com. John M. Thompson, pres.; Ruth Thompson, ed. dir. Publishes high quality, enlightening children's picture books with enduring, inspirational, and spiritual values (inspirational, not religious). Publishes 1-4 titles/yr.; hardcover. Receives 2,000 submissions annually. 80% of books from first-time authors. Prefers 500-1,500 wds. Royalty on net; advance for artists. Responds in 3 mos. Guidelines (also on Website); catalog for 9x12 SASE.

Nonfiction: Complete ms/cover letter; no phone/fax/e-query.

Fiction: Complete ms/cover letter. Picture books under 1,000 wds. (preferred); 1,500 wds. max. No chapter books.

Special Needs: Picture books only.

Tips: "Our current preference is books for the youngest readers—4 to 6 years. Include a description of what makes your book special or different from others currently on the market."

INKLING BOOKS, 6528 Phinney Ave. N., Seattle WA 98103. (206)365-1624. E-mail: editor@inklingbooks.com. Website: www.InklingBooks.com. Michael W. Perry, pub. Publishes 6 titles/yr.; hardcover, trade paperbacks. No mss through agents. Reprints books. Prefers 150-400 pgs. No advance. Print-on-demand. Publication within 2 mos. No guidelines or catalog. Not currently accepting submissions.

INTERNATIONAL AWAKENING PRESS, 139 N. Washington, PO Box 232, Wheaton IL 60189. Phone/fax (630)653-8616. E-mail: internationalawakening@juno.com. Website: www.intl-awaken.com. Intl. Awakening Ministries Inc. Richard Owen Roberts, pres. Scholarly books on religious awakenings or revivals. Publishes 4 titles/yr. Receives 12 submissions annually. Reprints books. Royalty negotiated; no advance. Average first printing 3,000. Publication within 6 mos. Responds in 3 mos. Prefers requested ms on disk. Any translation; no paraphrases. No guidelines; free catalog.

Nonfiction: Query only; no phone/fax/e-query. "Looking for scholarly theology, especially Bible commentaries, church history, and revival-related material."

Also Does: Booklets, pamphlets, tracts.

Photos/Artwork: Accepts freelance photos for book covers.

Tips: "Most open to scholarly books."

INTERVARSITY PRESS, Box 1400, Downers Grove IL 60515-1426. Receptionist: (630)734-4000 or 4036. Fax (630)734-4200. E-mail: email@ivpress.com. Website: www.ivpress.com. InterVarsity Christian Fellowship. Andrew T. LePeau, ed. dir.; submit to David Zimmerman, assoc. ed. IVP books are characterized by a thoughtful, biblical approach to the Christian life that transforms the hearts, souls, and minds of readers in the university, church, and the world, on topics ranging from spiritual disciplines to apologetics, to current issues, to theology. Imprints: IVP Academic (Gary Deddo, ed.), IVP Connect (Cindy Bunch, ed.), IVP General (Al Hsu, ed.). Publishes 80-90 titles/yr.; hardcover, trade paperbacks, mass-market paperbacks. Receives 2,500 submissions annually. 15% of books from first-time authors. Accepts mss through agents. Reprints books. Prefers 50,000 wds. or 200 pgs. Negotiable royalty on retail or outright purchase; negotiable advance. Average first printing 5,000. Publication within 12 mos. Considers simultaneous submissions. Responds in 3 mos. Prefers NIV, NRSV. Accepts e-mail submissions after acceptance. Guidelines on Website; catalog for 9x12 SAE/5 stamps.

Nonfiction: Query only first, with detailed letter according to submissions guidelines, then proposal with 2 chapters: no phone/fax/e-queries.

Ethnic Books: Especially looking for ethnic writers (black, Hispanic, Asian American).

Also Does: Booklets, 5,000 wds.; pamphlets; e-books.

Blogs: www.ivpress.com/blogs/behindthebooks; www.ivpress.com/blogs/andyunedited; www.ivpress.com/blogs/addenda-errata.

Tips: "Most open to book written by pastors (though not collections of sermons) or other church staff, by professors, by leaders in Christian organizations. Authors need to bring resources for publicizing and selling their own books, such as a Website, an organization they are part of that will promote their books, speaking engagements, well-known people they know personally who will endorse and promote their book, writing articles for national publication, etc."

****Note:** This publisher serviced by The Writer's Edge and ChristianManuscript Submissions.com.

INVISIBLE COLLEGE PRESS, PO Box 209, Woodbridge VA 22194-0209. (703)590-4005. E-mail: submissions@invispress.com. Website: www.invispress.com. Dr. Phillip Reynolds, nonfiction ed.; Paul Mossinger, fiction ed. This publisher majors on the paranormal, science fiction, spiritual, religious, etc. Publishes 12 titles/yr.; trade paperbacks. Receives 150 submissions annually. 75% of books from first-time authors. Accepts mss through agents. No reprints. Prefers 70,000 wds. or more. Royalty 10-25% on net; $100 advance. Publication within 4 mos. Considers simultaneous submissions. Responds in 1-3 mos. Guidelines & catalog on Website.

Nonfiction: E-query preferred (copied into message), or query/SASE/proposal package/1 chapter. Reference, religion, spirituality.

Fiction: E-query preferred, or query/synopsis & 1 chapter.

JEBAIRE PUBLISHING, PO Box 843, Snellville GA 30078. (770)823-9017. E-mail: info@jebairepublishing.com. Website: www.jebairepublishing.com. Shannon Clark, acq. ed. Our mission is "to give gifted writers a voice and hungry souls a full meal." Publishes 2-4 titles/yr.; trade paperbacks. 50% of books from first-time authors. No mss through agents. No subsidy, print-on-demand, or reprints. Prefers 125-250 pgs. Royalty 12-15% on net; no advance. Average first printing 1,000. Publication within 12 mos. Considers simultaneous submissions. Responds in 4-6 week (to proposals). Requires accepted mss on disk. Guidelines (also by e-mail); no catalog.

Nonfiction: Proposal/2-3 chapters; no phone/fax query; e-query OK. "Looking for women's devotionals, Christian living, personal growth, and faith."

Photos: Accepts freelance photos for book covers; open to queries from freelance artists.

Contest: Sponsors an annual contest for youth, ages 9-16. Essays 700-1,200 words on specific topics. Submit between April 1 and June 15. Guidelines available. Submissions must be mailed to above address. Twenty winners will have their work published in a nonfiction anthology and receive a copy of the book.

Tips: "We look for writers who have an 'approachable' writing style. We want our readers to feel uplifted and encouraged rather than 'talked down to' or discouraged."

JIREH PUBLISHING CO., PO Box 1911, Suisun City CA 94585-1911. (425)645-0423. E-mail: jaholman@jirehpublishing.com. E-mail inquires first to: jireh_subms@jirehpublishing.com, or through Website: www.jirehpublishing.com. Janice Holman, ed. To spread the gospel and teach the Word of God throughout the world. Publishes 2-5 titles/yr. Receives 275 submissions annually. 95% of books from first-time authors. Accepts mss through agents. No reprints. Prefers 96+ pgs. Royalty 10-12% of net; no advance. Average first printing 500-1,000. Publication within 9-12 mos. Considers simultaneous submissions. Responds in 5-13 wks. Guidelines/catalog on Website.

Nonfiction: Proposal/3 chapters; fax/e-query OK. "Looking for manuscript which helps teach believers how to walk by faith and receive all the blessings that God has for them." Likes to see first and last chapter.

Fiction: Proposal/3 chapters. Adult only. Contemporary, mystery/romance, and mystery/suspense.

Also Does: E-books.

Photos/Artwork: Accepts freelance photos for book covers.

Tips: "We are looking for authors who would like to work with us to create e-books (initially fiction titles)." Responds only to accepted manuscripts.

JOHNS HOPKINS UNIVERSITY PRESS, 2715 N. Charles St., Baltimore MD 21218-4363. (410)516-6900. Fax (410)516-6968. E-mail: tcl@mail.press.jhu.edu. Website: www.press.jhu.edu. Nondenominational. Trevor Lipscombe, ed-in-chief. Publishes 4-6 religious titles/yr.; hardcover, trade paperbacks. Receives 50-75 submissions annually. 10-25% of books from first-time authors. Accepts mss through agents. Reprints books. Prefers 100,000 wds. Royalty. Publication within 1 yr. Considers simultaneous submissions only on proposals. Guidelines/catalog on Website.

Nonfiction: Query only; no phone/fax/e-query.

JOSSEY-BASS, a Wiley Imprint, 989 Market St., 5th Fl., San Francisco CA 94103-1741. (415)782-3145. Fax (415)433-0499. E-mail: Sfullert@jbp.com. Website: www.jossey-bass.com. John Wiley & Sons Inc. Sheryl Fullerton, exec. ed. Because of a nondenominational focus on Christian spirituality and general corporate ownership, they are able to reach the broadest range of markets and readership. Imprint: Religion and Spirituality. Publishes 40 titles/yr.; hardcover, trade paperbacks. Receives hundreds of submissions annually. Up to 20% of books from first-time authors. Accepts mss through agents. No reprints. Prefers 60,000 wds. or 250 pgs. Royalty negotiable on net; advance. Average first printing 10,000. Publication within 1 yr. Considers simultaneous submissions. Responds in 1 mo. Prefers NRSV, NIV. Guidelines (also by e-mail); free catalog.

Nonfiction: Proposal/2 chapters; e-query OK. "Looking for fresh, vital resources to deepen faith and Christian identity."

Tips: "Our mission is to provide innovative, thoughtful, and useful resources for people on their faith journeys. Authors with compelling ideas and an established audience (and/or track record) from which to promote and market themselves, as well as clearly relevant credentials and expertise will be enthusiastically received. We are not interested in books that would be considered 'more of the same,' nor in books that are narrow or marginal in their perspective. We are particularly interested in books for the emerging church and those that encourage a generous orthodoxy. Create an excellent proposal that clearly presents your idea in a way that is viable for its market and fully describes your platform."

JOURNEY STONE CREATIONS, 3533 Danbury Rd., Fairfield OH 45014. (513)860-5616. Fax (513)860-0176. E-mail: pat@jscbooks.com. Website: www.jscbooks.com. Patricia Stirnkorb, ed.; Janet Kelly, submissions ed.; Danelle Pickett, creative dir. Dedicated to producing excellent quality, excellent content, and excellent entertainment for children of all ages. Imprints: Little Gems, Little Nuggets, Chunky Board. Publishes 30+ titles/yr.; hardcover, trade paperbacks. Receives 2,400 submissions annually. 90% of books from first-time authors. Accepts mss through agents. No subsidy publishing. Reprints books. Prefers 1,500 wds. or less. Royalty 6% on net; some outright purchases negotiated; minimal advance. Average first printing 10,000-12,000. Publication within 12-24 mos. Considers simultaneous submissions. Responds in 60-90 days. Accepts full ms by e-mail if less than 20 pages (attachment). Guidelines (also by e-mail/Website); no catalog.

Nonfiction: Query first by e-query.

Photos/Artwork: Accepts freelance photos for book covers.

Tips: "We like 1,200 words or less: fiction or picture books for children 18 months to 12 years. We enjoy 'planting seeds' about Christ and God. No Bible doctrines. Be sure name and address is on each page."

JUBILANT PRESS: An Electronic & Print Publisher, PO Box 6421, Longmont CO 80501. E-mail: jubilantpress@aol.com. Website: www.JubilantPress.com. Supports Right to the Heart Ministries. Linda Shepherd, & Rebekah Montgomery, pubs. Publishes downloadable e-books with instant information to change your life. Publishes 10 e-titles/yr., plus 1 print bk. Acquires print & e-books by invitation only. 0% of books from first-time authors. Accepts mss through agents. Reprints books. Prefers 20-100 pgs. Pays for the right to publish, plus a percentage of author's online sales (author must have an active Web page); variable advance. Publication within 6 mos. Prefers NIV. Guidelines provided for specific projects.

Nonfiction: Brief e-mail query only; no phone/fax query.

Special Needs: Women's ministry helps, banquet-planning helps, speaking and writing helps.

Photos/Artwork: Accepts freelance photos for book covers.

Tips: "Submissions accepted by invitation only. Best to send a brief e-mail with description of your idea. Please see our Web page to best understand our publishing program. Most open to a how-to, informational book with a need-to-know marketability."

JUDSON PRESS, PO Box 851, Valley Forge PA 19482-0851. Toll-free (800)4-JUDSON. Fax (610)768-2441. E-mail: jpacquisitions@abc-usa.org. Website: www.judsonpress.com. American Baptist Churches USA/National Ministries. Rebecca Irwin-Diehl, ed. Publishers Christ-centered leadership resources for the transformation of persons, congregations, communities, and cultures. Publishes 12-15 titles/yr.; hardcover, trade paperbacks. Receives 800 submissions annually. 20% of books from first-time authors. Accepts mss through agents. No subsidy; print-on-demand rarely. Rarely reprints books. Prefers 100-200 pgs., or 30,000-75,000 wds. Royalty 10-15% on net; some work-for-hire agreements or outright purchases; occasional advance $300. Average first printing 4,500. Publication within 1 yr. Considers simultaneous submissions. Requires accepted submissions on disk or by e-mail. Responds in 4-6 mos. Prefers NRSV. Guidelines on Website; catalog for 9x12 SAE/4 stamps.

Nonfiction: Query or proposal/2-3 chapters; fax/e-query OK.

Fiction: Query or proposal. Rarely does children's picture books. Prefers multicultural children's books.

Ethnic Books: African American & Hispanic.

Photos/Artwork: Open to queries from freelance artists. Attn: Wendy Ronga, creative dir.

Tips: "Most open to books that are unique, compelling, and practical. Theologically and socially we are a moderate publisher. And we like to see a detailed marketing plan from an author committed to partnering with us."

****Note:** This publisher serviced by The Writer's Edge.

KIRK HOUSE PUBLISHERS, PO Box 390759, Minneapolis MN 55439. (952)835-1828. Fax (952)835-2613. E-mail: publisher@kirkhouse.com. Website: www.kirkhouse.com. Leonard Flachman, pub. Imprints: Lutheran University Press, Quill House Publishers. Publishes 6-8 titles/yr.; hardcover, trade paperbacks, coffee-table books. Receives hundreds of submissions annually. 95% of books from first-time authors. No mss through agents. No reprints. Royalty 10-15% on net; no advance. Average first printing 500-3,000. Publication within 6 mos. No simultaneous submissions. Requires disk or e-mail submission. Responds in 2-3 wks. No guidelines; free catalog.

Nonfiction: Proposal/1-2 chapters.

+KNIGHT GEORGE PUBLISHING HOUSE, LLC, 348 Bradley Ave., #131A, Flint MI 48503. (586)481-0466. E-mail: authors@knightgeorge.com. Website: www.KnightGeorge.com. Matt Jones, pres. A privately-owned, independent provider of innovative Christian educational materials. New publisher; hardcover, trade paperbacks. 16% of books from first-time authors. No mss through agents. No subsidy or print-on-demand. Royalty 2-15% of net; no advance. Considers simultaneous submissions. Responds in 1 mo. Accepted mss on disk. Guidelines (also by e-mail); no catalog.

Nonfiction: Proposal/2 chapters; no phone/fax query; e-query OK.

Fiction: Query only first. Children's stories and classroom reading books.

Special Needs: Classroom materials: textbooks, workbooks, hands-on learning aids. Innovative teaching methods and newest technology is preferred.

Also Does: Board games, computer games, all hands-on learning methods.

Photos/Artwork: Open to queries from freelance artists.

Tips: "We prefer books be submitted complete with original artwork. Most open to textbooks (teacher's editions should contain full student's edition within them), workbooks (as applicable), and projects, preferably as a package. Find new and creative ways to teach. We are a publishing house, but will consider any other products (within pricing limits) that educate. Of course, God should be at least implicit, but don't force biblical examples in your work."

KREGEL KIDZONE, PO Box 2607, Grand Rapids MI 49501-2607. (616)451-4775. Fax (616) 451-9330. Website: www.kregelpublications.com. Publishes books and collateral materials that target both the spiritual and educational development of children. Royalty; some outright purchases. Publication within 16 mos. Responds in 4 mos. Catalog for 9x12 SAE/3 stamps. No longer reviewing unsolicited queries, proposals, or manuscripts, except through agents, Writer's Edge or ChristianManuscriptSubmissions.com.

****Note:** This publisher serviced by The Writer's Edge and ChristianManuscript Submissions.com.

KREGEL PUBLICATIONS, PO Box 2607, Grand Rapids MI 49501-2607. (616)451-4775. Fax (616)451-9330. Website: www.kregelpublications.com. Evangelical/Conservative. Dennis R. Hillman, pub.; Jim Weaver, academic & professional books ed.; submissions policy on Website. To provide tools for ministry and Christian growth from a conservative, evangelical perspective. Imprints: Kregel Kidzone (see separate listing), Kregel Academic and Professional, Kregel Classics. Publishes 90 titles/yr.; hardcover, trade paperbacks. 20% of books from first-time authors. Reprints books. Royalty 8-16% of net; some outright purchases; advance $200-2,000. Average first printing 5,000. Publication within 16 mos. Responds in 4 mos. Guidelines on Website; catalog for 9x12 SAE/3 stamps. No longer reviewing unsolicited queries, proposals, or manuscripts, except through agents, Writer's Edge, or ChristianManuscript Submissions.com.

Nonfiction: "Most open to contemporary issues or academic works."

Fiction: For all ages. "Looking for high-quality contemporary fiction with strong Christian themes and characters."

Tips: "We are adding more fiction, but again, we are very selective. Strong story lines with an evident spiritual emphasis are required."

****Note:** This publisher serviced by The Writer's Edge and ChristianManuscript Submissions.com.

LANGMARC PUBLISHING, PO Box 90488, Austin TX 78709-0488. (512)394-0989. Fax (512)394-0829. E-mail: langmarc@booksails.com. Website: www.langmarc.com. Lutheran. Lois Qualben, pub. Focuses on spiritual growth of readers. Publishes 6 titles/yr.; hardcover, trade paperbacks. Receives 200 submissions annually. 50% of books from first-time authors. No mss through agents. No reprints. Prefers 150-300 pgs. Royalty 10-13% on net; no advance. Average first printing varies. Publication usually within 1 yr. Considers simultaneous submissions. Responds in 2-4 mos. Requires requested ms on disk. Prefers NIV. Guidelines (also by e-mail/Website); catalog for #10 SAE/1 stamp.

Nonfiction: Proposal/3 chapters; no phone query. "Most open to inspirational books."

LARSON PUBLICATIONS/PBPF, 4936 NYS Rte. 414, Burdett NY 14818-9729. (607)546-9342. Fax (607)546-9344. E-mail: larson@lightlink.com. Website: www.larsonpublications.org. Paul Cash, dir. Books cover philosophy, psychology, religion, and spirituality. Publishes 4-5 titles/yr.; hardcover, trade paperbacks. Receives 1,000 submissions annually. 5% of books from first-time authors. Some reprints. Variable royalty; rarely gives an advance. Publication within 1-2 yrs. Considers simultaneous submissions. Requires accepted mss on disk. Responds in 4-6 mos. Prefers NIV. No guidelines/catalog.

Nonfiction: Query by mail/outline & SASE; no phone/fax/e-query.

LEGACY PRESS, PO Box 261129, San Diego CA 92196. Toll-free (800)638-4428. Toll-free fax (800)331-0297. E-mail: editor@rainbowpublishers.com. Website: www.rainbowpublishers .com. Rainbow Publishers. Submit to The Editor. Publishes nondenominational nonfiction and fiction for children in the evangelical Christian market. Publishes 15 titles/yr. Receives 250 submissions annually. 50% of books from first-time authors. Reprints books. Prefers 150 pgs. & up. Royalty 8% & up on net; advance $500+. Average first printing 5,000. Publication within 2 yrs. Considers simultaneous submissions. Prefers requested ms on disk. Responds in 3 mos. Prefers NIV. Guidelines (also on Website); catalog for 9x12 SAE/2 stamps.

Nonfiction: Proposal/3-5 chapters; no e-queries. "Looking for nonfiction for girls and boys ages 2-12."

Fiction: Proposal/3 chapters. For ages 2-12 only. Must include an additional component beyond fiction (e.g., devotional, Bible activities, etc.)

Special Needs: Nonfiction for ages 10-12, particularly Christian twists on current favorites, such as cooking, jewelry making, games, etc.

Tips: "All books must offer solid Bible teaching in a fun, meaningful way that appeals to kids. Research popular nonfiction for kids in the general market, then figure out how to present those fun ideas in ways that teach the Bible. As a smaller publisher, we seek to publish unique niche books that stand out in the market."

LEGACY PUBLISHERS INTERNATIONAL, 1301 S. Clinton St., Denver CO 80247. (303)283-7480. Fax (303)283-7536. E-mail: dmiller@hccweb.org, or through Website: www.legacy publishersinternational.com. Michelle Leonard, acq. ed. To pass the Gospel of Jesus Christ on to future generations through the written word. Accepts some freelance. Catalog. Incomplete topical listings.

LIBROS LIGUORI, 1 Liguori Dr., Liguori MO 63057-9999. (636)464-2500. Fax (636)464-8449. E-mail: amedina@liguori.org. Website: www.liguori.org. Spanish division of Liguori Publications. Jose Antonio Medina [(636)223-1471)], ed. To spread the gospel in the Hispanic community by means of low-cost publications. Publishes 5 titles/yr. Receives 6-8 submissions annually. 5% of books from first-time authors. Prefers up to 30,000 wds. Royalty 8-10% of net or outright purchases of $450 (book and booklet authors get royalties; pamphlet authors get $400 on acceptance); advance. Average first printing 3,500-5,000. Publication within 18 mos. No simultaneous submissions. Requires accepted mss on electronic file. Responds in 4-8 wks. Free guidelines/catalog.

Nonfiction: Proposal/2 chapters; fax/e-query OK. "Looking for issues families face today—substance abuse, unwanted pregnancies, etc.; family relations; religion's role in immigrants' experiences, pastoral Catholic faith."

Ethnic Books: Focuses on Spanish-language products.

Also Does: Pamphlets, booklets, tracts, PC software, clip art.

Tips: "Contact us before writing. It's much easier to work together from the beginning of a project. We need books on the Hispanic experience in the U.S. Keep it concise, avoid academic/theological jargon, and stick to the tenets of the Catholic faith. Avoid abstract arguments."

LIFE CHANGING MEDIA, 10777 W. Sample Rd., Unit 302, Coral Springs FL 33065-3768. (954) 554-1921. E-mail: PaulGundotra@yahoo.com. Website: www.lifechangingmedia.net. Life Changing Publications. Paul Gundotra, pres.; Sindhu Roy, chief ed. Mass-market paperbacks. Royalty on retail; no advance. Average first print run varies. Publication within 3 mos. Considers simultaneous submissions (if indicated). Prefers accepted mss by e-mail. Responds in 30-60 days. Guidelines by e-mail/Website; no catalog.

Nonfiction: Query first; e-query OK. "Please include a description of the book project, brief bio including publishing history. Let us know if you have the ability for public speaking."

Photos/Artwork: Accepts freelance photos for book covers.

Tips: "Looking for books that entertain, inform, but most of all that are life changing."

LIFE CYCLE BOOKS, PO Box 1008, Niagara Falls NY 14304-1008. Toll-free (800)214-5849. (416)690-5860. Toll-free fax (888)690-8532. (416)690-8532. E-mail: paulb@lifecyclebooks.com. Website: www.lifecyclebooks.com. Paul Broughton, gen. mngr.; submit to The Editor. Specializes in pro-life material. Publishes 6 titles/yr. Receives 100 submissions annually. No mss through agents. 50% of books from first-time authors. Reprints books. Royalty 8-10% of net; outright purchase of brochure material, $250+; advance $250-1,000. **SUBSIDY PUBLISHES 10%.** Publication within 1 yr. No simultaneous submissions. Responds in 5 wks. Catalog on Website.

Nonfiction: Query or complete ms. "Our emphasis is on pro-life and pro-family titles."

Tips: "We are most involved in publishing leaflets of about 1,500 words, and we welcome submissions of manuscripts of this length."

LIFE JOURNEY BOOKS—No longer a separate brand; see David C. Cook.

LIFESONG PUBLISHERS, PO Box 183, Somis CA 93066. (805)655-5644. Fax (614)455-5030. E-mail: mailbox@lifesongpublishers.com. Website: www.lifesongpublishers.com. Laurie Donahue, pub. Provides Christian families with tools that will aid in spiritual development of family members. Publishes 1-4 titles/yr.; trade paperbacks. No mss through agents. No reprints. **WOULD CONSIDER SUBSIDY.** Royalty 10% on net; small advance. Publication within 12 mos. Considers simultaneous submissions. Responds in 2-4 wks. No guidelines; catalog for 9x12 SAE/2 stamps. Not included in nonfiction topical listings.

Nonfiction: Proposal/3 chapters; e-query OK. "Looking for an author with an existing ministry."

LIFT EVERY VOICE, 820 N. LaSalle Blvd., Chicago IL 60610. (312)329-2140. Fax (312)329-4157. E-mail: lifteveryvoice@moody.edu. Website: www.moodypublishers.com/LEV. African American imprint of Moody Publishers. Moody Bible Institute and Institute for Black Family Development. Cynthia Ballenger, ed. To advance the cause of Christ through publishing African American Christians who educate, edify, and disciple Christians. Publishes 6 titles/yr. Receives 50-60 submissions annually. 98% of books from first-time authors. Accepts mss through agents. No subsidy. Reprints books. Prefers 40,000+ wds., or 250+ pgs. Royalty on retail; advance. Average first printing 5,000. Publication within 12 mos. Considers simultaneous submissions. Responds biyearly. Accepts requested ms on disk or by e-mail. Prefers KJV. Guidelines (also by e-mail); free catalog.

Nonfiction: Proposal/2-3 chapters; e-query OK.

Fiction: Proposal/2-3 chapters; e-query OK. For all ages. Send for fiction writer's guidelines.

Special Needs: Devotions for the African American; family stories of unity and faith; uplifting and spiritual historical information on African Americans (living or deceased); fiction and nonfiction regarding African Americans.

Ethnic Books: African American imprint.

Photos/Artwork: Accepts freelance photos for book covers; open to queries from freelance artists.

Tips: "We're looking for Christian literature that will edify and uplift the African American community."

LIGHTHOUSE PUBLISHING, 5531 Dufferin Dr., Savage MN 55378. (952)447-8604. E-mail: AndyOverett@lighthousebooks.com. Website: www.lighthouseebooks.com, or www.lighthousechristianpublishing.com. Nondenominational. Andy Overett, ed.; submit to Sylvia Charvet. To distribute a wide variety of Christian media to vast parts of the globe, so people can hear about the gospel for free or very inexpensively (e-books, comics, movies, and online radio). Imprints: Lighthouse Publishing, Lighthouse Music Publishing. Publishes 20-30 titles/yr.; hardcover, trade paperbacks, mass-market paperbacks. Receives 50-60 submissions annually. 60% of books from first-time authors. Accepts mss through agents. **SUBSIDY PUBLISHES 15-20%.** Does print-on-demand. Reprints books. Any length, Royalty on net; no advance. Average first printing 60-100. Publication within 6 mos. Considers simultaneous submissions. Prefers submissions by e-mail. Responds in 6-8 wks. Prefers NAS. Guidelines by e-mail; catalog $10.

Nonfiction: Complete ms; e-query OK. Any topic. "Looking for children's books, Intelligent Design, and science."

Fiction: Complete ms; e-query OK. Any genre, for all ages.

Ethnic Books: Publishes books for almost all foreign language markets.

Also Does: Comics, animation on CD, music CDs, plans to do Christian computer games in the future.

Photos/Artwork: Accepts freelance photos for book covers; open to queries from freelance artists.

Tips: "Most open to children's books, comics, and graphic novels; scientific and academic works with a Christian perspective."

LIGHTHOUSE TRAILS PUBLISHING, PO Box 958, Silverton OR 97381. (503)873-9092. Fax (503)873-3879. E-mail: editors@lighthousetrails.com. Website: www.lighthousetrails.com. David Dombrowski, acq. ed. Books that bring clarity and light to areas of spiritual darkness or deception, and to preserving the integrity of God's Word in all our books. Publishes 2-4 titles/yr. Receives 50-100 submissions annually. 35% of books from first-time authors. Accepts mss through agents. No subsidy or print-on-demand. Reprints books. Prefers 160-300 pgs. Royalty 12-17% of net, or 20% of retail; advance $1,000. Average first printing

2,500. Publication within 6-9 mos. Considers simultaneous submissions. Requires accepted ms on disk or by e-mail. Responds in 6-8 wks. Prefers KJV, NKJV. Guidelines (also on Website); free catalog.

Nonfiction: Proposal/2 chapters; no phone/fax query; e-query OK.

Fiction: Proposal/2-3 chapters. For teens and adults. "We are looking for a fiction or fiction series that would include elements from our books exposing the emerging church and mystical spirituality.

Special Needs: Will look at autobiographies or biographies about people who have courageously endured through overwhelming circumstances (Holocaust survivors, child-abuse survivors, etc.) with a definite emphasis on the Lord's grace and faithfulness.

Photos/Artwork: Open to queries from freelance artists.

Tips: "No poetry at this time. Any book we consider will not only challenge the more scholarly reader, but also be able to reach young adults who may have less experience and comprehension. Our books will include human interest and personal experience scenarios as a means of getting the point across. Read a couple of our books to better understand the style of writing we are looking for. Also check our research Website for an in-depth look at who we are (www.lighthousetrailsresearch.com)."

LIGUORI PUBLICATIONS, 1 Liguori Dr., Liguori MO 63057-9999. Toll-free (800)325-9521. (636)464-2500. Fax (636)464-8449. E-mail: mkessler@liguori.org. Website: www.liguori.org. Catholic/Redemptorists. Harry Grile, pub.; submit to Daniel Michaels, acq. ed. Spreading the good news of the gospel by means of low-cost publications. Imprints: Libros Liguori (Spanish language), Liguori Books, Liguori/Triumph. Publishes 50 titles/yr.; trade paperbacks. Receives 20-30 submissions annually. 5% of books from first-time authors. Reprints books. Prefers up to 30,000 wds. for books; 40-100 pgs. for booklets; pamphlets 16-18 pgs. Royalty 8-10% of net (on trade books) or outright purchase of $450; book & booklet authors get royalties; pamphlet authors get $400 on acceptance; advance varies. Average first printing 3,500-5,000 on books & booklets, 10,000 on pamphlets. Publication within 18 mos. No simultaneous submissions. Requires requested ms by e-mail attachment. Responds in 4-8 wks. Requires NRSV. Guidelines on Website; free catalog.

Nonfiction: Proposal/2 chapters; fax/e-query OK. "Looking for issues families face today—substance abuse, unwanted pregnancies, etc.; family relations; pastoral Catholic faith."

Ethnic Books: Publishes books in Spanish. See separate listing for Libros Liguori.

Also Does: Booklets, pamphlets, tracts; books on Catholic faith.

Tips: "Contact us before writing. It's much easier to work together from the beginning of a project. Keep it concise, avoid academic/theological jargon, and stick to the tenets of the Catholic faith. Avoid abstract arguments. Manuscripts accepted by us must have strong, middle-of-the-road, practical spirituality."

LILLENAS PUBLISHING CO., Program Builder Series and Other Drama Resources, Box 419527, Kansas City MO 64141-6527. (816)931-1900. Fax (816)412-8390. E-mail: drama@lillenas.com. Website: www.lillenasdrama.com. Kimberly R. Messer, product line mngr. Imprint: Lillenas Drama Resources. Publishes 12+ titles/yr.; mass-market paperbacks or electronic versions. Accepts mss through agents. Royalty 10% of retail for drama resources; outright purchase of program builder material; no advance. No simultaneous submissions. Responds in 3-4 mos. Guidelines on Website; catalog.

Drama Resources: Query or complete ms; phone/fax/e-query OK. Accepts readings, one-act and full-length plays, program and service features, monologues, and sketch collections. Religion & life issues.

Special Needs: Sketch collections and plays; full-length and one-act plays for adults. Seasonal; children's or youth 5-minute sketches.

Tips: "Most open to biblically based sketches and plays that have small- to medium-size casts and are easy to stage; short sketches—4 to 8 minutes."

LION PUBLISHING, 4050 Lee Vance View, Colorado Springs CO 80918-7102. (719)536-3271. David C. Cook. Accepts no freelance submissions.

LITTLE SIMON INSPIRATIONS, 1230 Avenue of the Americas, New York NY 10020. Website: www.simonsayskids.com. Faith-based imprint of Simon & Schuster Children's Publishing Division. No unsolicited manuscripts.

THE LITURGICAL PRESS, PO Box 7500, St. John's Abbey, Collegeville MN 56321-7500. Toll-free (800)858-5450. (320)363-2213. Toll-free fax (800)445-5899 or (320)363-3299. E-mail: Sales@litpress.org. Website: www.litpress.org. St. John's Abbey (a Benedictine group). Imprints: Liturgical Press Books, Michael Glazier Books, Pueblo Books. Peter Dwyer, dir.; submit to Hans Christoffersen, ed. dir. (hchristoffe@csbsju.edu). Publishes 75 titles/yr. Prefers 100-300 pgs. Royalty 10% of net; some outright purchases; no advance. No simultaneous submissions. Responds in 3 mos. Guidelines (also on Website); free catalog.

Nonfiction: Query/proposal. Adult only.

Tips: "We publish liturgical, scriptural, and pastoral resources."

LITURGY TRAINING PUBLICATIONS, Archdiocese of Chicago, 1814 N. Hermitage Ave., Chicago IL 60622-1101. Toll-free (800)933-1800. (773)486-8970. Fax (773)486-7094. E-mail: editorialmanager@ltp.org. Website: www.LTP.org. Catholic/Archdiocese of Chicago. Donna M. Crilly, mng. ed.; Danielle Knott, ed. (dknott@ltp.org). Resources for liturgy in Christian life. Imprint: Hillenbrand Books (Kevin Thornton, ed.). Publishes 25 titles/yr.; hardcover, trade paperbacks, coffee-table books. Receives 150 submissions annually. 25% of books from first-time authors. Accepts mss through agents. No subsidy or print-on-demand. Reprints books. Variable royalty or work-for-hire; advance. Average first printing 2,000-5,000. Publication within 1 yr. Considers simultaneous submissions. Responds in 4-6 wks. Prefers NAB. Guidelines (also by e-mail/Website); free catalog.

Nonfiction: Proposal/1 chapter; no phone/fax/e-query.

Ethnic Books: Hispanic.

Photos/Artwork: Open to queries from freelance artists.

LIVING BOOKS FOR ALL, PO Box 98425 (TST), Kowloon, Hong Kong. Phone 852 2723 1525. Fax 852 2366 6519. E-mail: clchk@hkstar.com. Website: www.hkstar.com/~clchk. CLC Ministries International, Hong Kong. Mrs. Mare Allison, ed. Prefers books of interest to Asians or Western readers interested in Asia. Imprint: Bellman House (Chinese); Living Books for All (LBA) English. Publishes 1-5 titles/yr. Receives 20 submissions annually. Considers Chinese translations of English books and English translations of Chinese books. No mss through agents. Prefers up to 200 pgs. Royalty 5% on retail or payment in copies of book; no advance. Average first printing 3,000. Publication within 1 yr. Considers simultaneous submissions. Responds in 2 mos. Prefers requested ms on disk or by e-mail in Rich Text Format (RTF). Responds in 1-3 mos. Guidelines (by e-mail or Website, www.hkstar.com/~clchk/lbaguide .html.); free Chinese book catalog.

Nonfiction: Proposal with 3 chapters (up to 30 pages), or complete ms; e-query preferred. "Most open to practical, Christian living books relevant to English readers in Asia."

Fiction: "Fiction for adults in an Asian context. Must have a spiritual impact."

Special Needs: Biblically based material for teaching adults English and books to help Christian workers in China.

Ethnic Books: For Asian market.

Also Does: Pamphlets, booklets.

Tips: "Write in direct, personal, inclusive style; then simplify. No dissertations. We are looking for Chinese manuscripts." Prefers American spelling to English spelling. Accepts manuscripts in English or Chinese.

LIVING THE GOOD NEWS, 600 Grant St., Ste. 400, Denver CO 80203. Fax (303)832-4971. Division of the Morehouse Group. Not currently accepting submissions.

LOYOLA PRESS, 3441 N. Ashland Ave., Chicago IL 60657. Toll-free (800)621-1008. (773)281-1818. Fax (773)281-0152. E-mail: editorial@loyolapress.com. Website: www.loyolapress.org. Catholic. Joseph Durepos, acq. ed. (durepos@loyolapress.com). Publishes in the Jesuit and Ignatian Spirituality tradition. Publishes 20-30 titles/yr.; hardcover, trade paperbacks. Accepts mss through agents. Prefers 25,000-75,000 wds. or 150-300 pgs. Variable royalty on net; advance. Average first printing 7,500-10,000. Considers simultaneous submissions and first-time authors without agents. Responds in 10-12 wks. Prefers NRSV (Catholic Edition). Guidelines on Website.

Nonfiction: Query first; proposal/sample chapters; no phone query; e-query OK.

Tips: "Looking for books and authors that help make Catholic faith relevant and offer practical tools for the well-lived spiritual life."

LUTHERAN UNIVERSITY PRESS, PO Box 390759, Minneapolis MN 55439. (952)835-1828. Fax (972)835-2613. E-mail: publisher@lutheranupress.org. Website: www.lutheranupress.org. Karen Walhof, ed. Publishes 8-10 titles/yr.; hardcover, trade paperbacks, coffee-table books. Receives dozens of submissions annually. **SUBSIDY PUBLISHES 25%.** No print-on-demand or reprints. Royalty 10-15% of net; no advance. Average first printing 500-2,000. Publication within 6 mos. No simultaneous submissions. Responds in 3 wks. No guidelines; free catalog.

Nonfiction: Proposal/sample chapters in electronic format.

Photos/Artwork: Accepts freelance photos for book covers.

Tips: "We accept manuscripts only from faculty of Lutheran colleges, universities, seminaries, and Lutheran faculty from other institutions."

+LUTHERAN VOICES, Book Submissions, Augsburg Fortress, PO Box 1209, Minneapolis MN 55440-1209. E-mail: lutheranvoices@augsburgfortress.org. Website: www.augsburgfortress.com. Evangelical Lutheran Church in America. Develops quality, accessible books written primarily by ELCA authors that inform, teach, inspire, and renew. Series of books; 96 pgs. ea. Royalty. Responds in 8-12 wks. Guidelines on Website.

Nonfiction: Proposal.

Tips: "We are seeking prophets and preachers, politicians and pastors; educators and scientists; caregivers and counselors; professors and students; scholars and homemakers—people who have a story to tell, topics to illumine, and ideas to explore. It is expected that authors will write out of a foundational understanding of Lutheran theology and practice, though topics may be of interest to a wider Christian audience."

THE LUTTERWORTH PRESS/JAMES CLARKE & CO. LTD., PO Box 60, Cambridge CB1 2NT, England. Phone +44 (0)1223 350865. Fax +44 (0)1223 366951. E-mail: publishing@lutterworth.com. Website: www.lutterworth.com, or www.jamesclarke.co.uk. Adrian Brink, ed. Imprints: The Lutterworth Press (general); James Clarke & Co. (academic/reference). Publishes 25 titles/yr. (15 reprints, 10 new). Receives 100 submissions annually. 90% of books from first-time authors. Accepts mss through agents. Reprints books. **SUBSIDY PUBLISHES 2%.** Royalty on retail; some advances. Publication within 18 mos. No simultaneous submissions. Responds in 3 mos. Requested ms by mail. Guidelines on Website; free catalog.

Nonfiction: Proposal/2 chapters; e-query OK.

Tips: "For full author guidelines, visit our Website."

MACALESTER PARK PUBLISHING, 24558—546th Ave., Austin MN 55912. Toll-free fax (800)407-9078. (507)396-0135. E-mail: Macalesterpark@macalesterpark.com. Website: www.macalesterpark.com. Focuses on reprinting books. Sue Franklin, owner.

MAGNUS PRESS, PO Box 2666, Carlsbad CA 92018. (760)806-3743. Fax (760)806-3689. E-mail: magnuspres@aol.com. Website: www.magnuspress.com. Warren Angel, ed. dir. To publish biblical studies that are written for the average person and that minister life to Christ's church. Imprint: Canticle Books. Publishes 3 titles/yr.; trade paperbacks. Receives 60 submissions annually. 50% of books from first-time authors. Accepts submissions through agents. Reprints books. Prefers 105-300 pgs. Graduated royalty on retail; no advance. Average first printing 2,500. Publication within 1 yr. Considers simultaneous submissions. Accepts requested ms on disk. Responds in 1 mo. Guidelines (also by e-mail); free catalog.

Nonfiction: Query or proposal/2-3 chapters; fax query OK. "Looking for spirituality, thematic biblical studies, unique inspirational/devotional books, e.g. *Adventures of an Alaskan Preacher.*"

Tips: "Our writers need solid knowledge of the Bible and a mature spirituality that reflects a profound relationship with Jesus Christ. Most open to a popularly written biblical study that addresses a real concern/issue in the church at large today; or a unique inspirational book. Study the market; know what we do and don't publish."

****Note:** This publisher serviced by The Writer's Edge.

MARSHALL TRUMANN PUBLISHING, 3710 S. Calhoun St., Fort Wayne IN 46807. (260)744-0579. E-mail: jtolbert@wincoprint.com. Winco Printing. Submit to: submissions@marshall trumann.com. Website: www.marshalltrumann.com. James E. Tolbert, ed. We focus on family relationships (coaching men). Publishes 12 titles/yr.; hardcover, trade paperbacks. Receives about 50 submissions annually. 90+% of books from first-time authors. Accepts mss through agents. No subsidy publishing or reprints. Prefers 200-300 pgs. Royalty 10% on net; no advance. Average first printing 500-1,000. Publication within 9 mos. Considers simultaneous submissions. Accepts requested mss by e-mail only. Responds to queries in 60 days; mss in 90 days. Prefers NIV. No guidelines or catalog.

Nonfiction: Query letter only first; then proposal/2 chapters; no phone/fax queries; accepts e-queries as indicated above. Looking for devotionals, self-help, and Bible studies.

Photos/Artwork: Open to queries from freelance artists.

Tips: "Most open to authors with a strong promotional/marketing plan; an author who conducts lectures, seminars, or does guest speaking. We want to attract authors who find getting published to be a daunting task, but do not want to self-publish."

MASTER BOOKS, PO Box 726, Green Forest AR 72638. (870)438-5288. Fax (870)438-5120. E-mail: submissions@newleafpress.net. Website: www.masterbooks.net. Imprint of New Leaf Press. Amanda Price, ed. Publisher of creation science books; all books are completely evolution free. Publishes 15-20 titles/yr.; hardcover, trade paperbacks. Receives 1,200 submissions annually. 10% of books from first-time authors. Accepts mss through agents. No subsidy, print-on-demand, or reprints. Prefers 140-240 pgs. Variable royalty; rarely gives an advance. Average first printing 5,000. Publication within 12 mos. Considers simultaneous submissions. Responds in 3 mos. Guidelines (also by e-mail/Website); catalog for 9x12 SAE/5 stamps.

Nonfiction: Proposal/no chapters; no phone/fax query; e-query OK; submission form on Website. "Looking for biblical creationism, biblical science, creation/evolution debate material."

Special Needs: Creation science books, and books for the Christian Education/homeschool markets.

Tips: "Most open to books for education with lots of hands-on activities."

****Note:** This publisher serviced by The Writers' Edge.

MCRUFFY PRESS, PO Box 212, Raymore MO 64083. Toll-free (888)967-1200. Toll-free fax (888)967-1300. E-mail: brian@mcruffy.com. Website: www.mcruffy.com. Brian Davis, ed. Christian publisher of children's trade books, children's audio, and homeschool materials. Open to freelance. Requires e-query. Incomplete topical listings.

Tips: "Most open to seeing elementary educational materials, any subject area. Not currently accepting picture book manuscripts."

MEGAGRACE BOOKS, PO Box 80180, Las Vegas NV 89180-0180. E-mail: ds@scherf.com, or grace@megagrace.com. Websites: www.megagrace.com, or www.scherf.com/scherf books.htm. Dietmar Scherf, ed. Books that positively discuss and teach the pure grace message of the Bible. Imprint: Scherf Books. Publishes 2 titles/yr. Receives 500 submissions annually. 90% of books from first-time authors. No mss through agents. No reprints. Prefers 40,000-50,000 wds. (nonfiction), or 90,000-120,000 wds. (fiction). Royalty 5-10% of retail or outright purchase; no advance. Average first printing 2,000-5,000. Publication within 18 mos. Considers simultaneous submissions. No mss by disk or e-mail. Responds in 4-6 wks. Prefers KJV, NASB, or AMP. Guidelines and catalog on Website.

Nonfiction: Query first/SASE; no phone/fax/e-query. "Looking for Christian living and spiritual life books."

Also Does: Audio CDs on the pure grace of God.

Photos/Artwork: Accepts freelance photos for book covers.

Tips: "We like books that gently help folks discover the pure grace of God."

MERCER UNIVERSITY PRESS, 1400 Coleman Ave., Macon GA 31207-0003. (478)301-2880. Fax (478)301-2264. E-mail: jolley_ma@mercer.edu. Website: www.mupress.org. Baptist. Submit to Editor-in-Chief. Publishes 15 titles/yr. Receives 200 submissions annually. 75% of books from first-time authors. Accepts mss through agents. Some reprints. Royalty on net; no advance. Average first printing 800-1,200. Publication within 15 mos. Prefers requested ms on disk; no e-mail submissions. Responds in 3-4 mos.

Nonfiction: Proposal/2 chapters; fax/e-query OK. "We are looking for books on history, philosophy, theology, and religion, including history of religion, philosophy of religion, Bible studies, and ethics."

Fiction: No religious fiction, only Southern literary. Author information form on Website.

MERIWETHER PUBLISHING LTD./CONTEMPORARY DRAMA SERVICE, 885 Elkton Dr., Colorado Springs CO 80907. (719)594-4422. Fax (719)594-9916. E-mail: MerPCDS@aol.com. Website: www.meriwetherpublishing.com. Nondenominational. Arthur L. Zapel, exec. ed.; submit to Rhonda Wray, Christian ed. Publishes 30-45 plays & books/yr. Primarily a publisher of plays for Christian and general markets; must be acceptable for use in a wide variety of Christian denominations. Imprint: Contemporary Drama Service. Publishes 3 bks./25 plays/yr. Receives 1,200 submissions annually (mostly plays). 75% of submissions from first-time authors. Accepts mss through agents. No reprints. Prefers 225 pgs. Royalty 10% of net or retail; no advance. Average first printing of books 1,500-2,500, plays 500. Publication within 6 mos. Considers simultaneous submissions. No e-mail submissions. Responds in up to 2 mos. Any Bible version. Guidelines (also by e-mail); catalog for 9x12 SASE.

Nonfiction: Table of contents/1 chapter; fax/e-query OK. "Looking for creative worship books, i.e., drama, using the arts in worship, how-to books with ideas for Christian education." Submit books to Meriwether.

Fiction: Complete ms for plays. Plays only, for all ages. Always looking for Christmas and Easter plays (1 hr. maximum). Submit plays to Contemporary Drama.

Special Needs: Religious drama—or religious plays—mainstream theology. We prefer plays that can be staged during a worship service.

Tips: "Our books are on drama or any creative, artistic area that can be a part of worship. Writers should familiarize themselves with our catalog before submitting to ensure that their manuscript fits with the list we've already published." Contemporary Drama Service wants easy-to-stage comedies, skits, one-act plays, large-cast musicals, and full-length comedies for schools (junior high through college), and churches (including chancel dramas for Christmas and Easter). Most open to anything drama-related. "Study our catalog so you'll know what we publish and what would fit our list."

MESSIANIC JEWISH PUBLISHERS, PO Box 615; 6120 Day Long Ln., Clarksville MD 21029. (410)531-6644. Fax (410)531-9440. E-mail: guidelines@messianicjewish.net. Website: www.MessianicJewish.net. Lederer/Messianic Jewish Communications. Submit to The Editor. Books that build up the Messianic Jewish community, witness to unbelieving Jewish people, or help Christians understand their Jewish roots. Imprints: Lederer Books, Remnant Press (subsidy only). Publishes 6-12 titles/yr.; hardcover, trade paperbacks. Receives 100+ submissions annually. 50% of books from first-time authors. No mss through agents. Reprints books. Prefers 50,000-88,000 wds. Royalty 7-15% on net. Average first printing 5,000. Publication within 12-24 mos. No simultaneous submissions. Responds in 3-6 mos. Requires requested ms on disk. Prefers Complete Jewish Bible. Guidelines by e-mail; free catalog.

Nonfiction: Write or call for submission guidelines first; then query. Messianic Judaism, Jewish evangelism, or Jewish roots of Christian faith. "Must have Messianic Jewish theme and demonstrate familiarity with Jewish culture and thought."

Fiction: Write or call for submission guidelines first. For adults. Jewish themes only.

Special Needs: Messianic Jewish commentaries.

Ethnic Books: Jewish; Messianic Jewish.

Photos/Artwork: Open to queries from freelance artists.

Tips: "Must request guidelines before submitting book proposal; all submissions must meet our requirements. Looking for Messianic Jewish commentaries. Books must address one of the following: Jewish evangelism, Jewish roots of Christianity, or Messianic Judaism."

MILLENNIUM III PUBLISHERS, 174 N. Moore Rd., Simpsonville SC 29680. E-mail: willramsey@millenniatech.info. Willard A. Ramsey, sr. ed. Restoring our culture to a Christian world-view. Publishes 4-5 titles/yr. Receives 100+ submissions annually. 50% of books from first-time authors. Accepts mss through agents. Reprints books. Prefers 200-300 pgs. Royalty 10-15% on net; some advances. Publication within 10-12 mos. Considers simultaneous submissions. Responds in 6-8 wks. Prefers NKJV. Guidelines.

Nonfiction: Query; e-query OK.

Tips: "Most open to nonfiction books applying Christian solutions to contemporary cultural problems."

MISSION CITY PRESS, 202—2nd Ave. S., Franklin TN 37064-2650. (615)591-1007. Fax (615)591-1006. E-mail: info@missioncitypress.com. Website: www.missioncitypress.com, or www.alifeoffaith.com. Wendy Witherow, ed. coordinator. Provides role models, resources, and relationships designed to help 8- to 14-year-old girls understand, imagine, and experience what it means to live a life of faith; books & dolls for girls. Imprint: A Life of Faith. Publishes 5 titles/yr.; hardcover, trade paperbacks. 50% of books from first-time authors. Prefers mss through agents. No subsidy publishing or reprints. Prefers 50,000 wds./224 pgs.; or 25,000 wds./112 pgs. Outright purchases. Publication within 6 months. Free catalog.

Nonfiction: Query only first. All topics indicated are for children and youth only.

Fiction: Proposal/2 chapters. "Looking for youth/children's historical fiction (8- to 12-year-old readers). Must be fiction that truly disciples kids."

Also Does: Board games, dolls, and accessories.

Photos/Artwork: Open to queries from freelance artists.

Contest: Sponsors a contest (see Website).

Tips: "Spend a lot of time on our Website first and only pitch us things that fit our brand."

+MISSION WORLD LIBRARY INC., #187-23 Chunggok-dong, Kwangjin-ku, Seoul, Korea 143-901. Phone: (82)2-461-4194. Fax (82)2-462-5718. E-mail: openfamily@kore.com. Website: www.missionworld.co.kr. Sophia Park, ed. Publishes 30 titles/yr.; hardcover, trade paperbacks. Receives 50 submissions annually. 30% of books from first-time authors.

Accepts mss through agents. Reprints books. Prefers 250 pgs. Royalty 6-8%; advance. Average first printing 4,000. Publication within 1 mo. Considers simultaneous submissions. Guidelines by e-mail; free catalog.

Nonfiction: Query or proposal; e-query OK. Requires accepted mss by e-mail.

Tips: "Most open to books on family, church renewal, or Christian living."

+MONARCH BOOKS, 256 Banbury Rd., Oxford, UK, OX2 7DH. Phone (01144)(0)1865 302750. Fax (01144)(0)1865 302757. E-mail: enquiries@lionhudson.com. Website: www.lionhudson.com. Lion Hudson PLC. Tony Collins, editorial dir. The largest independent British publisher of books inspired by the Christian faith. Imprints: Monarch, Candle, Lion, Lion Children's. Publishes 160 titles/yr.; hardcover, trade paperbacks, mass-market paperbacks, coffee-table books. Receives 750 submissions annually. 20% of books from first-time authors. Accepts mss through agents. No subsidy, print-on-demand, or reprints. Prefers 30,000 wds. & up. Royalty 12.5-15% on net; advance. Average first printing 6,000. Publication within 9 mos. Considers simultaneous submissions. Prefers accepted mss by e-mail. Responds in 4-6 wks. Any Bible version. Guidelines by e-mail; free catalog (don't send U.S. stamps).

Nonfiction: Proposal/2 chapters; phone/fax/e-query OK.

Special Needs: Original, saleable books with integrity and Christian core.

Photos: Accepts freelance photos for book covers; open to queries from freelance artists.

Tips: "Most open to original, energetic, Spirit-filled books.

MOODY PUBLISHERS, 820 N. LaSalle Blvd., Chicago IL 60610. Fax (312)329-2144. Website: www.moodypublishers.org. Imprints: Northfield Publishing, Lift Every Voice (African American). Moody Bible Institute. Paul Santhouse, dir. of acquisitions; Jennifer Lyell, women's acq. ed.; Elizabeth Cody Newenhuyse, acq. ed. for family, lifestyle, and relationships; submit to Acquisitions Coordinator. To provide books that evangelize, edify the believer, and educate concerning the Christian life. Publishes 65-70 titles/yr.; hardcover, trade paperbacks, mass-market paperbacks. Receives 3,500 submissions annually. 1% of books from first-time authors. Accepts mss through agents. Royalty on net; advance $500-50,000. Average first printing 10,000. Publication within 1 yr. No simultaneous submissions. Requires requested ms on disk. Responds in 2-3 mos. Prefers NAS, NLT, NIV. Guidelines; catalog for 9x12 SASE/$2.13 postage (mark "Media Mail").

Nonfiction: Considers agented proposals only; no phone/fax/e-query. "For nonfiction, we review only those proposals that come from professional literary agents." Closed to all other unsolicited mss.

Fiction: Proposal/3-5 chapters; for all ages. "We are looking for stories that glorify God both in content and style. We believe that God gives some of his children the talents to write beautiful works of fiction, and we will seek out those artists and the stories they create. We wish to direct people toward God through beauty and truth." No picture books or romance genre fiction.

Ethnic Books: African American.

Tips: "Most open to books where the writer is a recognized expert and already has a platform to promote the book."

****Note:** This publisher serviced by The Writer's Edge.

MOPS INTERNATIONAL, 2370 S. Trenton Way, Denver CO 80231-3822. (303)733-5353. Fax (303)733-5770. E-mail: blagerborg@MOPS.org. Website: www.MOPShop.org. Publishes books dealing with the needs and interests of mothers with young children, who may or may not be Christians. Publishes 4-5 titles/yr. Catalog on Website.

Nonfiction: Query or proposal/3 chapters; by mail, fax, or e-mail.

Fiction: Mom fiction.

Tips: "Review existing titles on our Website to avoid duplication."

MOREHOUSE PUBLISHING CO., 4775 Linglestown Rd., Harrisburg PA 17112. (717)541-8130. Fax (717)541-8136. E-mail: morehouse@morehousegroup.com. Website: www.morehouse publishing.org. Episcopal/Church Publishing Inc. Nancy Fitzgerald, exec. ed. Publishes 35 titles/yr.; hardcover, trade paperbacks. Receives 750 submissions annually. 95% of books from first-time authors. Accepts mss through agents. No print-on-demand. Reprints books. Prefers 100-200 pgs. Royalty 10% of net; advance $1,000. Average first printing 3,000. Publication within 12 mos. Considers simultaneous submissions. Responds in 8 wks. Guidelines; for free catalog call (800)877-0012.

Nonfiction: Proposal/1 chapter; no phone/fax/e-query.

Special Needs: Spirituality, Episcopal oriented.

Tips: "We primarily accept books in our stated categories that are written by Episcopalians and written from an Anglican perspective. Not currently accepting children's book manuscripts."

+MORE THAN NOVELLAS.COM. E-mail: lizdelayne@hotmail.com. Website: www.MoreThan Novellas.com. Liz DeLayne, ed. To promote and build a library of family friendly fiction—with values that exemplify the teachings and walk of Christ—for people to read on the Web. Novellas online. No payment. Guidelines on Website.

Nonfiction: Some romantic poetry.

Fiction: Complete ms by e-mail (copied into the message).

WILLIAM MORROW, 10 E. 53rd St., New York NY 10022. (212)207-7000. Fax (212)207-7145. Website: www.harpercollins.com. Imprint of HarperCollins Publishers. General trade imprint; religious titles published by HarperOne. Submit to Acquisitions Editor. Royalty on retail; advance. Agented submissions only.

MOUNTAINVIEW PUBLISHING, 1284 Overlook Dr., Sierra Vista AZ 85635-5512. (520)458-5602. Fax (520)458-5618. E-mail: leeemory@earthlink.net. Website: www.trebleheart books.com. Christian division of Treble Heart Books. Ms. Lee Emory, ed./pub. Online Christian publisher. Receives 300 submissions annually. 10% of books from first-time authors. No word-length preference. Royalty 35% of net; no advance. Books are published electronically, and in trade-size print. Publication usually within 1 yr. No simultaneous submissions (a 90-day exclusive is required on all submissions). Responds in 3-4 mos. Guidelines on Website.

Nonfiction: Submissions to: 1thbsubmissions2@earthlink.net (e-mail submissions only). Submissions are now open only between the 1st and 14th of each month. Very much interested in seeking excellent nonfiction, inspirational books.

Fiction: E-mail submissions only. Historical romances; contemporary romances; novellas preferred. "Seeking high-quality manuscripts; not necessarily romances. Looking for good mainstream and traditional inspirationals in most categories; also mysteries, westerns, and historicals."

Photos/Artwork: Accepts some high quality freelance photos for book covers.

Tips: "All inspirational fiction should contain a faith element. Challenge the reader to think, to look at things through different eyes. Avoid head-hopping and clichés; avoid heavy-handed or evangelistic preaching. No sci-fi or fantasy or dark angel stories. Send consecutive chapters, not random. A well-developed marketing plan must accompany all submissions, and no submissions will be accepted for consideration unless guidelines are followed. Actively looking for more nonfiction."

MOUNT OLIVE COLLEGE PRESS, 634 Henderson St., Mount Olive NC 28365. (919)658-2502. Dr. Pepper Worthington, ed. Publishes 5 titles/yr. Receives 2,500 submissions annually. 75% of books from first-time authors. Prefers 220 pgs. Negotiated royalty. Average first printing 500. Publication within 1-3 yrs. No simultaneous submissions. Responds in 6-12 mos. No disk. Free guidelines/catalog.

Tips: Accepting no freelance for at least 1 year.

MULTNOMAH BOOKS, 12265 Oracle Blvd., Ste. 200, Colorado Springs CO 80921. (719)590-4999. E-mail: info@waterbrookpress.com. Websites: www.mpbooks.com. Part of Water-Brook Multnomah, a division of Random House Inc. Ken Petersen, VP/pub. dir. Imprint information listed below. Publishes 75 titles/yr.; hardcover, trade paperbacks. Royalty on net; advance. Publication within 2 yrs. Multnomah is currently not accepting unsolicited manuscripts, proposals, or queries; no proposals for biographies, poetry, or children's books. Queries will be accepted through literary agents and at writers' conferences at which a Multnomah representative is present.

Multnomah Books: Christian living and popular theology books.

Multnomah Fiction: Well-crafted fiction that uses truth to change lives.

****Note:** This publisher serviced by The Writer's Edge.

NATIONAL BLACK THEATRE INC., 2033 Fifth Ave., Harlem NY 10035. (212)722-3800. Fax (212)860-8004. E-mail: nbitca@aol.com. Website: www.nationalblacktheatre.org. Does drama, musicals, and children's plays. Scripts need to reflect an African or African American lifestyle. Especially open to historical or inspirational forms. Also holds workshops and readings.

NATIONAL DRAMA SERVICE, LifeWay Christian Resources, One Lifeway Plaza, Nashville TN 37234. E-mail: terry@lifeway.com. Website: www.lifeway.com. Publishes dramatic material for use in Christian ministry: drama in worship, puppet & clown scripts, Christian comedy, mime/movement scripts, readers theater, creative worship services, monologues. Open to scripts 2-10 minutes long. E-mail for specific submissions guidelines.

NAVPRESS, Box 35001, Colorado Springs CO 80935. Toll-free (800)366-7767. (719)531-3548. Website: www.navpress.com. Dan Benson, editorial dir.; Caleb Seeling, sr. acq. ed. ; Rod Morris, sr. fiction ed.; Rebekah Guzman, Th1nk sr. developmental ed. To advance the calling of the Navigators by publishing life-transforming products that are biblically rooted, culturally relevant, and which glorify the Gospel of Jesus Christ and His Kingdom. Lines: Th1nk, Deliberate. Publishes 85-95 titles/yr.; hardcover, trade paperbacks. Receives 400+ submissions annually. Less than 25% of books from first-time authors. Requires mss through agents. No subsidy or reprints. Escalating royalty; advance. Publication within 16 mos. Accepts simultaneous submissions through agents. Responds in 2-4 wks. on agented submissions. Guidelines on Website.

Nonfiction: Proposal/3 chapters; no phone/fax/e-query.

Fiction: Proposal/3 chapters. For teens & adults.

Tips: "We do not publish devotionals, children's books or gift books; YA/youth fiction, short stories, poetry, horror, or pure romance."

****Note:** This publisher serviced by The Writer's Edge and ChristianManuscript Submissions.com.

+NAVPRESS TH1NK, 3820 N. 30th St., Colorado Springs CO 80904. Fax (719)260-7223. E-mail: rebekah.guzman@navpress.com. Website: www.thinkbooks.com. NavPress Publishing. Rebekah Guzman, sr. ed. Books for the teen/YA market. Publishes 15-18 titles/yr.; hardcover, trade paperbacks. Receives 200-350 submissions annually. 40% of books from first-time authors. Accepts mss through agents. Reprints books. Variable royalty/advance. Average first printing varies. Publication within 12 mos. Considers simultaneous submissions. Responds in 2-4 wks. Prefers *The Message* (Bible version). Guidelines by e-mail/Website.

Nonfiction: Proposal/2 chapters; no phone/fax query; e-query OK. Prefers accepted mss by e-mail.

Fiction: Proposal/2 chapters; no phone/fax query; e-query OK. Prefers accepted mss by e-mail. "Must be suitable for teen/YA audience."

NAZARENE PUBLISHING HOUSE—See Beacon Hill Press of Kansas City.

NEIBAUER PRESS, 20 Industrial Dr., Warminster PA 18974. (215)322-6200, ext. 255. Fax (215)322-2495. E-mail: Nathan@Neibauer.com. Website: www.Neibauer.com. Nathan

Neibauer, ed. For Evangelical/Protestant clergy and church leaders. Publishes 8 titles/yr. Receives 100 submissions annually. 5% of books from first-time authors. No mss through agents. Reprints books. Prefers 200 pgs. Royalty on net; some outright purchases; no advance. Average first printing 1,500. Publication within 6 mos. Considers simultaneous submissions. Responds in 4 wks. Prefers e-mail submissions. Prefers NIV. No guidelines/catalog.

Nonfiction: Query or proposal/2 chapters; fax query OK.

Also Does: Pamphlets, tracts.

Photos/Artwork: Accepts freelance photos for book covers.

Tips: "Publishes only religious books on stewardship and church enrollment, stewardship and tithing, and church enrollment tracts."

TOMMY NELSON—See Thomas Nelson Publishers.

NELSON BOOKS—See Thomas Nelson Publishers.

THOMAS NELSON, FICTION (formerly WestBow Press), PO Box 141000, Nashville TN 37215. (615)889-9000. Website: www.ThomasNelson.com. Thomas Nelson Inc. Ami McConnell, sr. acq. ed.; Amanda Bostic, assoc. acq. ed. Fiction from a Christian world-view. Publishes less than 30 titles/yr.; hardcover, trade paperbacks, mass-market paperbacks. Requires mss through agents; does not accept unsolicited manuscripts. Prefers 80,000-100,000 wds. Royalty on net; advance. Publication within 12 mos. Accepts simultaneous submissions. Responds in about 60 days. Guidelines on Website; free catalog.

Fiction: Proposal/3 chapters. For teens and adults. All unsolicited manuscripts returned unopened.

Special Needs: Southern fiction.

NELSON IGNITE—See Thomas Nelson Publishers.

NELSON/NAKED INK—See Thomas Nelson Publishers.

THOMAS NELSON PUBLISHERS, (formerly listed as Nelson Books) PO Box 141000, Nashville TN 37214-1000. (615)902-2729. Fax (615)902-2745. Website: www.thomasnelson.com. Does not accept or review any unsolicited queries, proposals, or manuscripts.

****Note:** This publisher serviced by The Writer's Edge and ChristianManuscript Submissions.com.

NEW CANAAN PUBLISHING CO. INC., PO Box 752, New Canaan CT 06840. (203)966-3408. Fax (203)548-9072. E-mail: info@newcanaanpublishing.com. Website: www.newcanaan publishing.com. Kathy Mittelstadt, ed. Children's books with strong educational and moral content, for grades 1-9 (ages 5-16); also aggressively building its Christian titles list. Publishes 3-4 titles/yr.; hardcover, trade paperbacks. Receives 120 submissions annually. 50% of books from first-time authors. Accepts mss through agents. Reprints books. Prefers 20,000-50,000 wds. or 120-250 pgs. Royalty 8-10% of net; occasional advance. Average first printing 500-5,000. Publication within 1 yr. No simultaneous submissions. Responds in 3-4 mos. Requires requested ms on disk; no e-mail submissions. Guidelines and catalog on Website, or for #10 SASE.

Nonfiction: Proposal/2 chapters or complete ms; no e-query. Does not return submissions.

Fiction: Proposal/2 chapters or complete ms; no e-query. For children and teens, 6-14 yrs. "We want children's books with strong educational and moral content; 10,000-20,000 wds." Now accepts picture books.

Special Needs: Middle-school-level educational books.

Photos/Artwork: Accepts freelance photos for book covers.

Tips: "Looking for teen/youth fiction and religious instructional materials for teens/youth."

NEW HOPE PUBLISHERS, Box 12065, Birmingham AL 35202-2065. (205)991-8100. Fax (205)991-4015. E-mail: new_hope@wmu.org. Website: www.newhopepublishers.com. Division of WMU. Submit to Acquisitions Editor. Publishes Christian nonfiction for women and families, and books with a missional focus. Imprints: New Hope Impact (missional community, social, personal-commitment, church-growth, and leadership issues); New Hope Arise (inspiring women, changing lives); New Hope Grow (Bible-study & teaching resources). Publishes 20-28 titles/yr. Receives 350 submissions annually. 25% of books from first-time authors. Accepts mss through agents. Reprints books. Royalty on net. Average first printing 5,000-10,000. Publication within 2 yrs. Considers simultaneous submissions. Requires requested ms on disk or by e-mail. Guidelines; catalog for 9x12 SAE/3 stamps.

Nonfiction: No unsolicited submissions, prefers query & prospectus; no phone/fax/e-query. "We look for authors whose messages have a missional emphasis."

Photos/Artwork: Accepts freelance photos for book covers.

****Note:** This publisher serviced by The Writer's Edge.

NEW LEAF PUBLISHING GROUP, PO Box 726, Green Forest AR 72638-0726. (870)438-5288. Fax (870)438-5120. E-mail: submissions@newleafpress.net. Website: www.nlgp.com. Amanda Price, ed. Endeavors to bring the lost to Christ and understanding to the body of Christ. Imprints: New Leaf Press, Master Books, Balfour Books. Publishes 30-35 titles/yr.; hardcover, trade paperbacks, coffee-table books. Receives 1,200 submissions annually. 15% of books from first-time authors. Accepts mss through agents. No subsidy, print-on-demand, or reprints. Prefers 100-400 pgs. Variable royalty on net; rarely gives advance. Average first printing 5,000. Publication within 12 mos. Considers simultaneous submissions. Requires accepted ms on disk. Responds in 3 mos. Prefers KJV. Guidelines (also by e-mail/Website); catalog for 9x12 SAE/5 stamps.

Nonfiction: Proposal/no chapters; no phone/fax query; e-query OK. "Looking for books for the homeschool market, especially grades 1-8."

Tips: "The best way to submit to us is to fill out the Author's Proposal form available by e-mail or on our Website."

****Note:** This publisher serviced by The Writers' Edge.

NEW SEEDS BOOKS, 300 Massachusetts Ave., Boston MA 02115. (617)424-0030. Fax (617) 236-1563. E-mail: doneal@shambhala.com. Website: www.shambhala.com. Shambhala Publications Inc. David O'Neal, sr. ed.; Katie Keach, asst. ed. (kkeach@shambhala.com). A new imprint devoted to publishing works of the Christian contemplative traditions, cross-traditionally; also new and readable translations of classic texts. Publishes hardcover & trade paperbacks. Accepts mss through agents. Reprints books. Length open. Royalty; advance. Average first printing 10,000-30,000. Publication within 1 yr. Considers simultaneous submissions. Responds in 6 wks. Prefers accepted ms on disk or by e-mail. Guidelines; free catalog.

Nonfiction: Query, proposal/2 chapters, or complete ms; e-query OK.

NEW YORK UNIVERSITY PRESS, 838 Broadway, 3rd Fl., New York NY 10003-4812. (212)998-2575. Fax (212)995-3833. E-mail: information@nyupress.org. Website: www.nyupress.org. Jennifer Hammer, religion ed. Embraces ideological diversity. Publishes 100 titles/yr.; hardback, trade paperbacks. Receives 800-1,000 submissions annually. 30% of books from first-time authors. Few mss through agents. Royalty on net. Publication within 10-12 mos. Considers simultaneous submissions. Initial response usually within 1 mo. (peer reviewed). Guidelines on Website.

Nonfiction: Query or proposal/1 chapter.

Tips: "As a university press, we primarily publish works with a scholarly foundation written by PhDs affiliated with a university department. Our focus within religious studies is on religion in American history, culture, and politics. We do not publish liturgical studies, pastoral care, spiritual guides, or exegesis. If you are not a university or seminary-affiliated scholar (or a professional journalist) it is unlikely that your work will be appropriate for our list."

NEXGEN—No longer a separate brand; see David C. Cook.

NORTHFIELD PUBLISHING CO., 820 N. LaSalle Blvd., Chicago IL 60610. Fax (312)329-2019. Website: www.moodypublishers.org. Imprint of Moody Publishers. Submit to Acquisitions Coordinator. Books for non-Christians or those exploring the faith. Publishes 3-5 titles/yr.; hardcover, trade paperbacks, mass-market paperbacks. 1% of books from first-time authors. Royalty on net; advance $500-50,000. Publication within 1 yr. No simultaneous submissions. Responds in 2-3 mos. Guidelines (also on Website); catalog for 9x12 SAE/2 stamps. Incomplete topical listings.

Nonfiction: Proposal/2-3 chapters. "We decline all unsolicited proposals."

Fiction: For all ages.

NORTHSTONE PUBLISHING, 9590 Jim Bailey Rd., Kelowna BC V4V 1R2, Canada. Toll-free (800)299-2926. (250)766-2778. Toll-free fax (888)841-9991. Fax (250)766-2736. E-mail: acquisitions@woodlake.com. Website: www.woodlakebooks.com. Imprint of Wood Lake Books Inc. Michael Schwartzentruber, ed. To provide high quality products promoting positive social and spiritual values. Publishes 6 titles/yr. Receives 900 submissions annually. 30% of books from first-time authors. Prefers 192-256 pgs. Royalty 7.5-10% of retail; some advances $1,000. Average first printing 4,000. Publication within 18 mos. Considers simultaneous submissions. Prefers requested ms on disk or by e-mail. Guidelines (also by e-mail/Website); catalog $2.

Nonfiction: Proposal/2 chapters; phone/fax/e-query OK.

Tips: "Most open to truth-seeking, life-affirming books that promote positive social and spiritual values. Although we publish from a Christian perspective, we seek to attract a general audience. Our target audience is interested in spirituality and values, but may not even attend church (nor do we assume that they should)."

NORTHWESTERN PUBLISHING HOUSE, 1250 N. 113th St., Milwaukee WI 53226-3284. Toll-free (800)662-6022. Fax (414)475-7684. E-mail: braunj@nph.wels.net. Website: www.nph.net. Lutheran. Rev. John A. Braun, VP of publishing services. Open to freelance. Responds in 2-3 mos. Guidelines on Website (www.nph.net/cgi-bin/site.pl?aboutUs Manuscript). Incomplete topical listings.

Nonfiction: Complete ms/cover letter; or query letter/outline.

ONE WORLD/BALLANTINE BOOKS, 1745 Broadway, New York NY 10036. (212)782-9000. Fax (212)572-4949. Website: www.randomhouse.com. Submit to Senior Editor. Imprint of Ballantine Books. Novels that are written by and focus on African Americans, but from an American perspective. Publishes 24 titles/yr.; hardcover, trade paperbacks, mass-market paperbacks. Receives 850 submissions annually. 50% of books from first-time authors. Submissions from agents only. No reprints. Prefers 80,000 wds. Royalty 7.5-15% on retail; advance $40,000-200,000. Average first printing 10,000. Publication within 18 mos. Considers simultaneous submissions. Responds in 2 mos. No disk or e-mail. No guidelines/catalog. Note: No unsolicited submissions, proposals, manuscripts, or queries at this time.

Fiction: Proposal/3 chapters; no phone/fax/e-query. "Contemporary/ethnic novels only; for African American women."

Ethnic Books: All are ethnic books.

Tips: "You must understand African American culture and avoid time-worn stereotypes."

OREGON CATHOLIC PRESS, PO Box 18030, Portland OR 97218-0030. Toll-free (800)548-8749. (503)281-1191. Toll-free fax (800)462-7329. E-mail: submissions@ocp.org. Website: www.ocp.org. Submit to Regina Alilat. To enhance the worship in the Catholic Church in the United States. Imprint: Pastoral Press. Publishes 8 titles/yr. Receives 80 submissions annually. 5% of books from first-time authors. No mss through agents. No reprints. Prefers 192 pgs. Royalty 5-12% of net; no advance. Average first printing 500. Publication within 12 mos. Considers simultaneous submissions. Prefers requested ms on disk; no e-mail submissions. Responds in 3 mos. Prefers NAB. Free catalog; guidelines by e-mail/Website.

Nonfiction: Proposal/1 chapter; no phone/fax/e-query. "Looking for liturgical ministries."
Ethnic Books: Hispanic/Spanish language.
Photos/Artwork: Accepts freelance photos for book covers.
Tips: "Most open to Catholic liturgical works."

OUR SUNDAY VISITOR INC., 200 Noll Plaza, Huntington IN 46750-4303. Toll-free (800)348-2440. (219)356-8400. Fax (219)356-8472. E-mail: booksed@osv.com, or oursunvis@osv.com. Website: www.osv.com. Catholic. Submit to Acquisitions Editor. To assist Catholics to be more aware and secure in their faith and capable of relating their faith to others. Publishes 30-40 titles/yr.; hardcover, trade paperbacks. Receives 500+ submissions annually. 10% of books from first-time authors. Prefers not to work through agents. Reprints books. Royalty 10-12% of net; advance $1,500 average. Average first printing 5,000. Publication within 1-2 yrs. No simultaneous submissions. Responds in 3 mos. Requires requested ms on disk. Guidelines on Website; catalog for 9x12 SASE.
Nonfiction: Proposal/2 chapters; e-query OK. "Most open to devotional books (not first person), church history, heritage and saints, the parish, prayer, and family."
Also Does: Pamphlets, booklets.
Photos/Artwork: Occasionally accepts freelance photos for book covers.
Tips: "All books published must relate to the Catholic Church; unique books aimed at our audience. Give as much background information as possible on author qualification, why the topic was chosen, and unique aspects of the project. Follow our guidelines. We are expanding our religious education product line and programs."

PACIFIC PRESS PUBLISHING ASSN., Box 5353, Nampa ID 83653-5353. (208)465-2570. Fax (208)465-2531. E-mail: booksubmissions@pacificpress.com. Website: www.pacificpress.com. Seventh-day Adventist. David Jarnes, book ed.; submit to Tim Lale, acq. ed. Books of interest and importance to Seventh-day Adventists and other Christians of all ages. Publishes 30 titles/yr. Receives 500 submissions annually. 5% of books from first-time authors. Accepts mss through agents. Prefers 40,000-70,000 wds. or 128-256 pgs. Royalty 12-15% of net; advance $1,500. Average first printing 5,000. Publication within 12-24 mos. Considers simultaneous submissions. Responds in 3 mos. Requires requested ms on disk, or by e-mail. Guidelines at www.pacificpress.com/index/php?pgName=newsBookSub; free catalog.
Nonfiction: Query only; e-query OK.
Fiction: Query only; almost none accepted; adult/biblical. Children's books: "Must be on a uniquely Seventh-day Adventist topic. No talking animals."
Ethnic Books: Occasionally publishes for ethnic market.
Also Does: Booklets.
Tips: "Most open to spirituality, inspirational, Christian living, or gift books. Our Website has the most up-to-date information, including samples of recent publications. Do not send full manuscript unless we request it after reviewing your proposal."

P & R PUBLISHING CO., PO Box 817, Phillipsburg NJ 08865. (908)454-0505. Fax (908)454-0859. E-mail: editorial@prpbooks.com. Website: www.prpbooks.com. Marvin Padgett, editorial; Melissa Craig, acq. ed. Devoted to stating, defending, and furthering the gospel in the modern world. Publishes 40 titles/yr.; hardcover & trade paperbacks. Receives 400 submissions annually. 5% of books from first-time authors. Accepts mss through agents. Reprints books. Prefers 140-240 pgs. Royalty 10-14% of net; advance. Average first printing 4,000. Publication within 10-12 mos. Considers simultaneous submissions. Responds in 1-4 mos. Guidelines on Website; free catalog.
Nonfiction: E-query only.
Fiction: Query only. For children or teens.
Also Does: Booklets.

Tips: "Direct biblical/Reformed content. Clear, engaging, and insightful applications of reformed theology to life. Offer us fully developed proposals and polished sample chapters. All books must be consistent with the Westminster Confession of Faith."

****Note:** This publisher serviced by The Writer's Edge.

PARADISE RESEARCH PUBLICATIONS INC., PO Box 837, Kihei HI 96753-0837. Phone/fax (808)874-4876. E-mail: dickb@dickb.com. Website: www.dickb.com/index.shtml. Ken Burns, VP. Imprint: Tincture of Time Press. Publishes 5 titles/yr.; trade paperbacks. Receives 8 submissions annually. 80% of books from first-time authors. No mss through agents. Reprints books. Prefers 250 pgs. Royalty 10% of retail; no advance. Average first printing 5,000. Publication within 2 mos. Considers simultaneous submission. Responds in 1 wk. No disk. Prefers KJV. No guidelines; free catalog.

Nonfiction: Query only; no phone/fax/e-query. Books on the biblical/Christian history of early Alcoholics Anonymous.

Also Does: Pamphlets, booklets, e-books.

Tips: "Most open to the history of early AA Christian Fellowship Program; healing of alcoholism/addiction by power of God."

PARAGON HOUSE, 1925 Oakcrest Ave., Ste. 7, St. Paul MN 55113-2619. (651)644-3087. Fax (651)644-0997. E-mail: paragon@paragonhouse.com. Website: www.paragonhouse.com. Rosemary Yokoi, acq. ed. Serious nonfiction and texts with an emphasis on religion and philosophy. Imprints: New Era Books, Athena, Omega. Publishes 12-15 titles/yr.; hardcover, trade paperback. Receives 3,000 submissions annually. 20% of books from first-time authors. Accepts mss through agents. Reprints books. Prefers 250 pgs. Royalty 7-10% of net; advance $1,000. Average first printing 2,000-3,000. Publication within 10-18 mos. Considers few simultaneous submissions. Prefers requested ms as hard copy; accepts disk. Responds in 3 mos. Guidelines on Website; catalog available online.

Nonfiction: Query; proposal/2-3 chapters, or complete ms; no phone/fax/e-query. "Looking for scholarly overviews of religious teachers and movements; textbooks in philosophy; new information, theories, ecumenical subjects; and reference books."

PARSON PLACE PRESS LLC, 10701 Tanner Williams Rd., Mobile AL 36608-8846. E-mail: info@parsonplacepress.com. Website: www.parsonplacepress.com. Michael L. White, mng. ed. Devoted to giving both Christian authors and Christian readers a fair deal. Publishes 3-5 titles/yr.; hardcover, trade paperbacks. Receives 50 submissions annually. 75% of books from first-time authors. Accepts mss through agents. **SUBSIDY PUBLISHES 10-20%;** does print-on-demand. Reprints books. Prefers 104-200 pgs. Royalty 50% of net; no advance. Average first printing 4 (because of print-on-demand capabilities). Publication within 3 mos. No simultaneous submissions. Responds in 4-6 wks. Requested mss by e-mail (attached file). Prefers NASB. Guidelines on Website; no catalog.

Nonfiction: Proposal/2 chapters; e-query OK. Christian topic/content only.

Fiction: Proposal/2 chapters; e-query OK. For all ages.

Special Needs: In nonfiction, discipleship, encouragement, personal growth, pastoral ministry, church growth, development, leadership. In fiction, mystery, suspense, romance, serials.

Contests: Sponsors a poetry contest; guidelines on Website.

Photos/Artwork: Accepts freelance photos for book covers; open to queries from freelance artists.

Tips: "Most open to conservative, biblically-based content that ministers to Christians. Write intelligently, clearly, sincerely, and engagingly."

+PARSONS PUBLISHING HOUSE, PO Box 6428, Panama City FL 32404. (850)867-3061. Fax (850)784-9693. E-mail: darrell@parsonspublishinghouse.com. Website: www.parsons

publishinghouse.com. Nondenominational. Diane Parsons, chief ed. Exists to partner with authors to release their voice into their world. Publishes 15 titles/yr.; hardcover, trade paperbacks. Receives 15 submissions annually. 75% of books from first-time authors. Accepts mss through agents. **SUBSIDY PUBLISHES 25%;** does print-on-demand. Reprints books. Prefers 100-150 pgs. Royalty 10-20% on net; no advance. Average first printing 250. Publication within 2 mos. Considers simultaneous submissions. Responds in 30 days. Receives accepted mss by e-mail. Prefers KJV or NKJV. Guidelines by e-mail/Website; free catalog.

Nonfiction: Query; proposal/3 chapters; e-query OK.

Fiction: Query; proposal/3 chapters; e-query OK. For adults.

Ethnic Books: Hispanic.

Photos: Accepts freelance photos for book covers; open to queries from freelance artists.

PATHWAY PRESS, 1080 Montgomery Ave., Cleveland TN 37311. Toll-free (800)553-8506. (423)478-7592. Fax (423)478-7616. E-mail: wanda_griffith@pathwaypress.org. Website: www.pathwaypress.org. Church of God (Cleveland TN). Wanda Griffith, bk. ed. Publishes 20-24 titles/yr. Receives 150 submissions annually. 25% of books from first-time authors. Prefers 120-300 pgs. Royalty 10% of wholesale; no advance. Average first printing 2,500-5,000. Publication within 12-18 mos. Guidelines on Website (www.pathwaypress.org/Evangel).

Nonfiction: Proposal/1-3 chapters; no phone/fax/e-query. "Manuscripts returned only when accompanied by an SASE."

Tips: "Pathway markets to evangelical readers and publishes from a Pentecostal/Charismatic perspective. Acquisitions committee meets quarterly."

PAULINE BOOKS & MEDIA, Daughters of St. Paul, 50 Saint Pauls Ave., Jamaica Plain MA 02130-3491. (617)522-8911. Fax (617)524-9805. E-mail: editorial@paulinemedia.com. Website: www.pauline.org. Catholic. Sr. Maria Grace Dateno, FSP, ed.; Submit to Debra Lavelle, ed. asst. To help clarify Catholic belief and practice for the average reader. Imprint: Pauline Kids. Publishes 40 titles/yr.; hardcover, trade paperbacks. Receives 350-400 submissions annually. 10% of books from first-time authors. No ms through agents. No subsidy or print-on-demand. Reprints books. Prefers 10,000-60,000 wds. Royalty 8-12% on net; advance. Average first printing 4,000-10,000. Publication within 24 mos. Considers simultaneous submissions. Responds in 2 mos. Accepts requested ms by e-mail. Prefers NRSV. Guidelines (also by e-mail/Website); free catalog.

Nonfiction: Written query only/synopsis/2 chapters., e-query OK.

Fiction: Proposal/2 chapters. For children & teens only. No strictly nonreligious works considered.

Special Needs: "Spirituality (prayer/holiness of life/seasonal titles), faith formation (religious instruction/catechesis), family life (marriage/parenting issues), teacher resources (reproducibles, activities, games, crafts, etc.), biographies of the saints, prayer books, and a wide variety of children's books. Of particular interest is our faith and culture line, which includes titles that show how Christ is present and may be more fully embraced and proclaimed within our media culture."

Photos/Artwork: Open to queries from freelance artists. Sr. Mary Joseph Peterson, FSP, art director.

Tips: "Submissions are evaluated on adherence to Gospel values, harmony with the Catholic tradition, relevance of topic, and quality of writing."

PAULIST PRESS, 997 Macarthur Blvd., Mahwah NJ 07430. (201)825-7300. Fax (201)825-8345. E-mail: info@paulistpress.com. Website: www.paulistpress.com. Catholic. Lawrence Boadt, ed. dir. Catholic publisher that publishes books for a broad spiritual market with a particular focus on ecumenism, reconciliation, and dialog with people in search of faith. Imprints: Newman Press, HiddenSpring, Stimulus. Publishes 80 titles/yr. Receives 1,000 submissions annually. 15% of books from first-time authors. Accepts mss through agents. Prefers 150-250 pgs. Royalty 7-10% of net; advance $500-1,000. Average first printing 2,000-2,500. Publication within 18-24 mos. Considers simultaneous submissions (prefers 1st option). Requires requested ms on disk. Responds in 2 mos. Prefers NRSV. Guidelines (also by e-mail/Website); free catalog.

Nonfiction: Proposal/2 chapters or complete ms; e-query OK. "Looking for theology (Catholic and ecumenical Christian), popular spirituality, liturgy, and religious education texts." Children's books for 2-5, 5-8, 8-12, 9-14 years, as per guidelines; complete ms.

Ethnic Books: A few Hispanic.

Also Does: Booklets, pamphlets.

Photos/Artwork: Accepts freelance photos for book covers.

Tips: "Most open to good spirituality books that have solid input and a clear sense of tradition behind them. Demonstrate grounded convictions. Stay well read. Pay attention to contemporary social needs."

PELICAN PUBLISHING CO. INC., 1000 Burmaster St., Gretna LA 70053. (504)368-1175. Fax (504)368-1195. E-mail: editorial@pelicanpub.com. Website: www.pelicanpub.com. Nina Kooij, ed-in-chief. To publish books of quality and permanence that enrich the lives of those who read them. Imprints: Firebird Press, Jackson Square Press, Dove Inspirational Press (see separate listing). Publishes 3 titles/yr.; hardcover, trade paperbacks, coffee-table books. Receives 250 submissions annually. No books from first-time authors. Accepts mss through agents. Reprints books. Prefers 200+ pgs. Royalty; some advances. Publication within 9-18 mos. No simultaneous submissions. Responds in 1 mo. on queries. Requires accepted ms on disk. Prefers KJV. Guidelines (also on Website); catalog for 9x12 SAE/6 stamps.

Nonfiction: Proposal/2 chapters; no phone/fax/e-query. Children's picture books to 1,100 wds. (send complete ms); middle readers about Louisiana (ages 8 & up) at least 25,000 wds.; cookbooks at least 200 recipes.

Fiction: Complete ms. Children's picture books. For ages 5-8 only.

Photos/Artwork: Accepts freelance photos for book covers; open to queries from freelance artists.

Tips: "On inspirational titles we need a high-profile author who already has an established speaking circuit so books can be sold at these appearances."

PENGUIN PRAISE, 375 Hudson St., New York NY 10014. (212)366-2000. Website: www.penguin.com. Joel Fotinos, pub.; Denise Silvestro, exec. ed. Christian publishing imprint of Penguin Group (USA). Will publish books by top-tier Christian authors. Distribution handled by Strang Communications and Noble sales group.

PERIGEE BOOKS, 375 Hudson St., New York NY 10014. (212)366-2000. Fax (212)366-2365. Website: www.penguin.com. Penguin Group (USA) Inc. John Duff, pub.; Sheila Curry Oakes, exec. ed.; Michelle Howry, ed. (spirituality). Publishes 3-5 spirituality titles out of 55-60 titles/yr. Receives 300 submissions annually. 30% of books from first-time authors. Strongly prefers mss through agents (but accepts freelance). Prefers 60,000-80,000 wds. Royalty 6-7.5%; advance $5,000-150,000. Average first printing varies. Publication within 18 mos. Considers simultaneous submissions. Responds in 2 mos. Guidelines available with contract; free catalog.

Nonfiction: Query only; no phone/e-query; fax query OK. "Looking for spiritual, prescriptive, self-help, and women's issues; no memoirs or personal histories."

PETER PAUPER PRESS, 202 Mamaroneck Ave., Ste. 400, White Plains NY 10601-5376. Toll-free (800)833-2311. (914)681-0144. Fax (914)681-0389. E-mail: bpaulding@peterpauper.com. Website: www.peterpauper.com. Barbara Paulding, ed. dir. Does small-format, illustrated gift books. Imprint: Inspire Books (evangelical imprint). Publishes 2 religious titles/yr.

Receives 30 submissions annually. 0% of books from first-time authors. Accepts mss through agents. No reprints. Prefers 800-2,000 wds. Outright purchase only, $250-1,000. Average first printing 10,000. Publication within 1 yr. No simultaneous submissions. Requires requested ms on disk. Responds in 1 mo. Guidelines (request by e-mail that a copy be faxed); no catalog.

Nonfiction: Query by mail or e-mail. General inspirational themes.

Tips: "We want original aphorisms, 67-75 to a book. Title should be focused on a holiday or special occasion, or family such as mother, sister, graduation, new baby, wedding, etc."

PFLAUM PUBLISHING GROUP, 2621 Dryden Rd., Ste. 300, Dayton OH 45439. (935)293-1415. Fax (937)293-1310. E-mail: kcannizzo@pflaum.com, or jeanlarkin@pflaum.com. Website: www.pflaum.com. Peter Li Education Group/Catholic. Karen Cannizzo, ed. dir., or Jean Larkin, ed. dir. Weekly lectionary-based magazines for pre-K through 8; sacramental preparation programs for primary, junior high, and high school; catechetical resources for pre-K through 12, and religious educators. Publishes 20 titles/yr.; trade paperbacks. Receives 25 submissions annually. 10% of books from first-time authors. No reprints. Royalty on net or outright purchase; advance depends on author arrangement. Average first printing 2,000. Publication within 9 mos. No simultaneous submissions. Requires accepted ms on disk or by e-mail. Responds as soon as possible. Prefers NRSV. Free guidelines/catalog.

Nonfiction: Proposal with at least 1 chapter; e-query OK. "We like user-friendly resources."

Tips: "We are looking for user-friendly, field-tested resources, particularly related to sacramental preparation and lectionary-based catechesis. We specialize in consumable resources—one book per user—that need to be replaced every year, for example, for Lent and Advent."

THE PILGRIM PRESS, 700 Prospect Ave. E., Cleveland OH 44115-1100. (216)736-3755. Fax (216)736-2207. E-mail: ksadler@thepilgrimpress.com, or tstaveteig@thepilgrimpress.com. Website: www.thepilgrimpress.com. United Church of Christ. Timothy G. Staveteig, pub.; Kim Sadler, ed. dir. Church and educational resources. Publishes 55 titles/yr. Receives 500 submissions annually. 60% of books from first-time authors. Prefers mss through agents. Reprints books. Royalty 10% of net; or work-for-hire, one-time fee; negotiable advance. Average first printing 2,000. Publication within 18 mos. No simultaneous submissions. Responds in 13 wks. Accepts submissions on disk or by e-mail. Guidelines/catalog on Website.

Nonfiction: Query first. Proposal/2 chapters; e-query through Website.

Special Needs: Children's sermons, worship resources, youth materials, and religious materials for ethnic groups.

Ethnic Books: African American, Native American, Asian American, Pacific Islanders, and Hispanic.

Photos/Artwork: Accepts freelance photos for book covers.

Tips: "Most open to well-written manuscripts that address mainline Protestant-Christian needs and that use inclusive language and follow the *Chicago Manual of Style.*"

PLAYERS PRESS INC., PO Box 1132, Studio City CA 91614-0132. (818)789-4980. Players Press International. Robert W. Gordon, ed. To create is to live life's purpose. Publishes only dramatic works; prides themselves on high quality titles. Publishes 1-6 religious titles/yr.; hardcover, trade paperbacks, coffee-table books. Receives 600-1,200 submissions annually. 15-20% of books from first-time authors. Accepts mss through agents. No subsidy publishing. Does print-on-demand with older titles. Rarely reprints books. Variable length. Royalty on net; some advances. Average first printing 1,000-10,000. Publication within 12 mos. No simultaneous submissions. No submissions by disk or e-mail. Responds in 1-3 wks. on query; 3-12 mos. on ms. Guidelines by mail; catalog for 9x12 SAE/5 stamps.

Nonfiction/Plays: Query only; no phone/fax/e-query. "Technical theatre and/or film, plays, musicals, and theatre education. For all ages."

Fiction: Query only first.

Photos/Artwork: Accepts freelance photos for book covers; open to queries from freelance artists.

Tips: "Most open to plays, musicals, books on theatre, film, television, and supporting areas: cameras, lighting, costumes, etc."

+PONDER PUBLISHING, 15128 27B Ave., Surrey BC V4P 1P2, Canada. E-mail: connect@ponderpublishing.ca. Website: www.PonderPublishing.ca. Darian Kovacs, pub. Focuses on Canadian writers primarily, writing material for youth and youth workers.

PORT HOLE BOOKS, PO Box 205, Westlake OR 97493-0205. E-mail: porthole@digisys.net. Open to freelance. Novels.

+POWER PUBLISHING, 5641 W. 73rd St., Indianapolis IN 46278. (317)347-1051. Fax (317) 347-1068. E-mail: Janet@powerpublishinginc.com. Website: www.powerpublishinginc.com. Janet Schwind, ed.; submit by mail or through Website. To make a positive difference in the lives of our readers; captivating the power of the written word. Royalty publisher. **ALSO OFFERS CO-OP OR SUBSIDY PROGRAMS.** Guidelines & book list on Website. Incomplete topical listings.

Tips: "We are currently soliciting manuscripts. We seek inspiring/motivational and/or instructional/reference books across a wide variety of genres, including nonfiction, fiction, children's books, and textbooks."

+PRAY! BOOKS, PO Box 35004, Colorado Springs CO 80932. (719)531-3555. Website: www.navpress.com. NavPress. Lora Schrock, mng. ed. Publishes 5-10 titles/yr.; hardcover, trade paperbacks. 20% of books from first-time authors. Prefers mss through agents. No subsidy or print-on-demand. Reprints books. Royalty on net; advance $3,000. Average first printing 2,500. Publication within 9 mos. Considers simultaneous submissions. Responds in 6 wks. Prefers NIV. Guidelines on Website.

Nonfiction: Query; no phone query. "Looking for books on prayer—how to deepen your prayer life; and prayer classics.

PREP PUBLISHING, 1110 1/2 Hay St., Fayetteville NC 28305. (910)483-6611. Fax (910)483-2439. E-mail: preppub@aol.com. Website: www.prep-pub.com. PREP Inc. Anne McKinney, mng. ed. (mckinney@prep-pub.com); submit to Frances Sweeney (sweeney@prep-pub.com). Books to enrich people's lives and help them find joy in the human experience. Publishes 10 titles/yr.; hardcover, trade paperbacks. Receives 1,500+ submissions annually. 85% of books from first-time authors. Reprints books. Prefers 250 pgs. Royalty 6-10% of retail; advance. Average first printing 3,000-5,000. Publication within 18 mos. Considers simultaneous submissions. Responds in 1 mo. Guidelines (also on Website) & catalog for #10 SAE/2 stamps.

Nonfiction: Query only; no phone query.

Fiction: Query only (cover letter and up to 3-page synopsis). All ages. "We are attempting to grow our Judeo-Christian fiction imprint."

Tips: "Rewrite, rewrite, rewrite with your reader clearly in focus."

PRESBYTERIAN PUBLISHING CORP., 100 Witherspoon St., Louisville KY 40202-1396. Toll-free (800)523-1631. (502)569-5052. E-mail: customer_service@wjkbooks.com. Website: www.ppcbooks.com. Submit to The Editor. Addresses the needs of the Christian community by fostering religious and cultural dialog by contributing to the intellectual, moral, and spiritual nurture of the church and the broader human family. Imprints: Geneva Press, Westminster John Knox Press. Publishes 80 titles/yr.; hardcover, trade paperbacks. Receives 2,000 submissions annually. Less than 10% of books from first-time authors. No mss through agents. No subsidy. No reprints. Prefers 200-400 pgs. Royalty 7.5-9%; no advance. Average first printing 2,000. Publication within 24 mos. Reluctantly considers simultaneous submissions. Responds in 8-12 wks. Prefers NRSV. Guidelines (also by e-mail/Website); catalog for 9x12 SASE.

Nonfiction: Proposal/1-2 chapters; no phone/fax/e-query. Mailed submissions preferred.

G. P. PUTNAM'S SONS BOOKS FOR YOUNG READERS, 345 Hudson St., 14th Fl., New York NY 10014. (212)414-3610. Fax (212)366-2664. Website: www.penguinputnam.com. Submit to Children's Manuscript Editor. Imprint: Penguin Group USA. Publishes 45 titles/yr.; hardcover. Accepts mss through agents. No reprints. Variable royalty on retail; negotiable advance. Considers simultaneous submissions. No disk or e-mail submissions. Responds in 6 mos. Guidelines for SASE.

Nonfiction: Proposal/1-2 chapters. "We publish some religious/inspirational books and books for ages 2-18."

Fiction: For children or teens. Complete ms for picture books; proposal/3 chapters for novels. Primarily picture books or middle-grade novels.

QUINTESSENTIAL BOOKS, PO Box 8755, Kansas City MO 64114-0755. (816)561-1555. E-mail: support@quintessentialbooks.com. Website: www.quintessentialbooks.com. Laura C. Joyce, ed. dir. Books that will challenge people to think deeply and live passionately in accordance with sound principles. Publishes 5-10 titles/yr.; hardcover, trade paperbacks, mass-market paperbacks. Receives 150 submissions annually. 25% of books from first-time authors. Prefers mss through agents. Reprints books. Prefers 60,000-70,000 wds. or 224 pgs. Royalty on net; negotiable advance. Average first printing varies. Publication within 18 mos. Considers simultaneous submissions. Responds in 3-4 mos. Requires requested ms by e-mail. Prefers NIV or NLT. Guidelines (also on Website).

Nonfiction: Query only; no phone/fax/e-query. "Nonfiction books must address significant topics in a fresh way, must speak boldly on controversial issues, and must be clear and accurate. Manuscripts on medicine, mental health, and nutrition will only be accepted from credentialed health professionals."

Fiction: Query only; no phone/fax/e-query. For adults. "Fiction must exhibit an understanding of human hearts and relationships, must create a complete and credible world for the reader, and must have multifaceted characters and aesthetic depth."

Photos/Artwork: Accepts freelance photos for book covers; open to queries from freelance artists.

Tips: "We are interested in reaching an intelligent, widely read audience. Avoid submitting simplistic material."

****Note:** This publisher serviced by The Writer's Edge.

RAGGED EDGE PRESS, 73 W. Burd St., PO Box 708, Shippenburg PA 17257. (717)532-2237. Fax (717)532-6110. E-mail: marketing@whitemane.com, or editorial@whitemane.com. Website: www.whitemane.com. White Mane Publishing Co. Inc. Harold E. Collier, acq. ed. Christian, social science, and self-help books that make a difference in people's lives. Publishes 10-15 titles/yr. Receives 50-75 submissions annually. 50% of books from first-time authors. **SUBSIDY PUBLISHES 20%.** Reprints books. Prefers 200 pgs. Variable royalty on net; no advance. Average first printing 3,000. Publication within 12-18 mos. Considers simultaneous submissions. Responds in 30-90 days. Guidelines (also by e-mail); catalog online.

Nonfiction: Query only; fax/e-query OK.

Tips: "Most open to a Protestant book in the middle of the spectrum."

RAINBOW PUBLISHERS, PO Box 261129, San Diego CA 92196. Toll-free (800)323-7337. Toll-free fax (800)331-0297. E-mail: editor@rainbowpublishers.com. Website: www.rainbowpublishers.com. Submit to The Editor. Publishes Bible-teaching, reproducible books for children's teachers. Publishes 20 titles/yr. Receives 250 submissions annually. 50% of books from first-time authors. Reprints books. Prefers 96 pgs. Outright purchases $640 & up. Average first printing 2,500. Publication within 2 yrs. Considers simultaneous submissions. Responds in 3 mos. No disk or e-mail submissions. Prefers NIV. Guidelines (also on Website); catalog for 9x12 SAE/2 stamps.

Nonfiction: Proposal/2-5 chapters; no phone/e-query. "Looking for fun and easy ways to teach Bible concepts to kids, ages 2-12."

Special Needs: Creative puzzles and unique games.

Tips: "Request a catalog or visit your Christian bookstore to see what we have already published. We have over 100 titles and do not like to repeat topics, so a proposal needs to be unique for us but not necessarily unique in the market. Most open to writing that appeals to teachers who work with kids and Bible activities that have been tried and tested on today's kids. No preachy, old-fashioned methods."

+RANDALL HOUSE DIGITAL, 114 Bush RD.; PO Box 17306, Nashville TN 37217. Toll-free (800)877-7030. (615)361-1221. Fax (615)367-0535. E-mail: digital@randallhouse.com. Website: www.randallhouse.com. National Assn. of Free Will Baptists. Keith Fletcher, dir. Estab. 2006. Produces curriculum-on-demand via the Internet, and electronic resources to supplement existing printed curriculum. Guidelines by e-mail.

Nonfiction: Query first; e-query OK.

Special Needs: Teacher-training material (personal or group), elective Bible studies for adults, children's curriculum (other than Sunday school), and elective materials for teens.

Tips: "We are looking for writers with vision for worldwide ministry who would like to see their works help a greater section of the Body of Christ than served by the conventionally printed products."

RANDALL HOUSE PUBLICATIONS, 114 Bush Rd., Nashville TN 37217. Toll-free (800)877-7030. (615)361-1221. Fax (615)367-0535. E-mail: emily.white@randallhouse.com. Website: www.randallhouse.com. Free Will Baptist. Michelle Orr, acq. ed. Publishes Sunday school and Christian education materials to make Christ known, from a conservative perspective. Publishes 5-10 titles/yr.; hardcover, trade paperbacks, mass-market paperbacks. Receives 100-150 submissions annually. 50% of books from first-time authors. Accepts mss through agents. No reprints. Length flexible. Royalty 10-15% on net; rarely gives an advance. Average first printing 2,000-5,000. Publication within 12-14 mos. Considers simultaneous submissions. Accepts requested mss by e-mail. Responds in 10-12 wks. Guidelines (also by e-mail/Website); free catalog.

Nonfiction: Query; e-query OK; proposal/4 chapters. Must fill out book proposal form they provide.

Fiction: For teens & adults. Query first; e-query OK; proposal/6 chapters. Must fill out book proposal form they provide.

Photos/Artwork: Open to queries from freelance artists (andrea.young@randallhouse.com).

Tips: "We are expanding our book division with a conservative perspective. We have a very conservative view as a publisher."

RANDOM HOUSE/GOLDEN BOOKS, 1745 Broadway, New York NY 10019. (212)782-9000. Starting a new, aggressive Christian-interest publishing program through Golden Books. Website: www.randomhouse.com/golden.

RAVENHAWK BOOKS, 7739 E. Broadway Blvd., #95, Tucson AZ 85710. E-mail: ravenhawk6dof@yahoo.com. Website: www.ravenhawk.biz. The 6DOF Group. Hans B. Shepherd or Carl Lasky, eds.; Shelly Geraci, submissions ed. Publishes variable number of titles/yr.; hardcover, trade paperbacks. Receives 20-30 submissions annually. 70% of books from first-time authors. Print-on-demand. Reprints books. Royalty 40-50% on gross profits; no advance. Average first printing 2,500. Publication in up to 18 mos. Considers simultaneous submissions. Responds in 6 wks. Catalog on Website.

Nonfiction: Query first. "Looking for profitable books from talented writers."

Fiction: Query first. For all ages.

Photos/Artwork: Accepts freelance photos for book covers; open to queries from freelance artists.

Tips: "Most open to crisp, creative, entertaining writing that also informs and educates. Writing, as any creative art, is a gift from God. Not everyone has the innate talent to do it well. We are author-oriented. We don't play games with the numbers."

REALMS—See Strang Book Group.

REFERENCE SERVICE PRESS, 5000 Windplay Dr., Ste. 4, El Dorado Hills CA 95762. (916)939-9620. Fax (916)939-9626. E-mail: info@rspfunding.com. Website: www.rspfunding.com. Stuart Hauser, ed. Books related to financial aid and Christian higher education. Publishes 1 title/yr.; hardcover, trade paperbacks. Receives 3-5 submissions annually. Most books from first-time authors. No reprints. Royalty 10% of net; usually no advance. Publication within 5 mos. May consider simultaneous submissions. No guidelines; free catalog for 2 stamps.

Nonfiction: Proposal/several chapters.

Special Needs: Financial aid directories for Christian college students.

+REFORMATION TRUST PUBLISHING, Editorial Dept., 400 Technology Park, Lake Mary FL 32746. Toll-free (800)435-4343. (407)333-4244. Fax (407)333-4233. E-mail: gbailey@ligonier.org. Website: www.ligonier.org/publishing_reformationtrust.php. Imprint of Ligonier Ministries. Greg Bailey, dir. of publications. Exists to publish books true to the historic Christian faith from the best of today's pastors and scholars. Publishes 8-10 titles/yr.; hard cover, trade paperbacks, coffee-table books. Receives 100 submissions annually. Open to first-time authors. Accepts mss through agents. No subsidy or reprints. Prefers 40,000-80,000 wds. Royalty on net; no advance. Average first printing 5,000. Publication within 10 mos. Considers simultaneous submissions. Responds in 2 mos. Prefers ESV. Guidelines on Website; free catalog.

Nonfiction: Proposal/2 chapters; no complete mss. Accepted ms by disk or e-mail.

Fiction: Proposal/2 chapters. Children's fiction only. "As in all our titles, we want our children's books to touch the deep truths of the Christian faith."

Tips: "We are looking for books that teach the historic Christian faith in layman's language. Our books are not academic, but good scholarship is important. Above all, our books must be based on scripture. Our theological stance is Reformed/Calvinist."

REGAL PUBLISHING GROUP, 1957 Eastman Ave., Ventura CA 93003. (805)644-9721. Fax (805) 644-9728. E-mail: editors@gospellight.com. Website: www.regalbooks.com. Gospel Light. Submit to The Editor. To know Christ and to make Him known; publishing resources to create meaningful dialogue. Publishes 60+ titles/yr.; hardcover, trade paperbacks, mass-market paperbacks. Receives 1,000 submissions annually. 20% of books from first-time authors. Requires mss through agents. No subsidy, print-on-demand, or reprints. Royalty. Publication within 18 mos. Considers simultaneous submissions. Prefers NIV. No guidelines or catalog.

Nonfiction: All unsolicited mss returned unopened.

Tips: "Most open to books that are well-written; unique in some way. Work through an agent."

****Note:** This publisher serviced by The Writer's Edge.

REGNERY PUBLISHING, One Massachusetts Ave. N.W., Washington DC 20001. Toll-free (888)219-4747. (202)216-0600. Fax (202)216-0612. E-mail: submissions@regnery.com. Website: www.regnery.com. Eagle Publishing. Trade publisher that does conservative political and cultural books. Few books from first-time authors. Requires mss through agents. Prefers 250-500 pgs. Royalty 8-15% on retail; advances to $50,000. Average first printing 5,000. Publication within 1 yr. Responds in 3 mos.

Nonfiction: Accepts manuscripts through agents only. Proposal/1-3 chapters or query; no fax/e-query.

Tips: "Books should relate to politics, current affairs, biography, and public policy. Most open to a book that deals with a topical issue from a conservative point of view."

RELIGIOUS EDUCATION PRESS, 5316 Meadow Brook Rd., Birmingham AL 34242. (205)991-1000. Fax (205)991-9669. E-mail: releduc@ix.netcom.com. Website: www.bham.net/releduc. Unaffiliated. James Michael Lee, ed. Mission is specifically directed toward helping fulfill, in an interfaith and ecumenical way, the Great Commission. Publishes 5-6 titles/yr. Receives 500 submissions annually. 40% of books from first-time authors. Prefers 200-500 pgs. Royalty 5% of net; advance. Average first printing 2,000. Publication within 9 mos. Responds in 1 mo. Requires requested ms on disk. Guidelines; free catalog.

Tips: "We are not accepting manuscripts for the foreseeable future."

RESOURCE PUBLICATIONS INC., 160 E. Virginia St., Ste. 290, San Jose CA 95112-5876. (408)286-8505. Fax (408)287-8748. E-mail: info@rpinet.com. Website: www.rpinet.com. William Burns, pub. Publishes 10 titles/yr.; trade paperbacks. Receives 450 submissions annually. 30% of books from first-time authors. Prefers 50,000 wds. Royalty 8% of net; rare advance. Average first printing 3,000. Publication within 1 yr. Responds in 10 wks. Prefers requested ms on disk. Guidelines on Website; catalog on Website or for 9x12 SAE/$2.13 postage (mark "Media Mail").

Nonfiction: Proposal/1 chapter; phone/fax/e-query OK.

Fiction: Proposal/2-3 chapters. Adult. Only read-aloud stories for storytellers; fables and parables. "Must be useful in ministerial, counseling, or educational settings."

Also Does: Computer programs; aids to ministry or education. E-books.

Tips: "Know our market. We cater to ministers in Catholic and mainstream Protestant settings. We are not an evangelical house or general interest publisher. Looking for nonfiction ideas that save people time, save money, or help people do their jobs better. Most open to a book that will help a practicing minister understand and deal with a pressing problem he or she faces."

REVELL BOOKS, Fleming H. Revell, Box 6287, Grand Rapids MI 49516. Toll-free (800)877-2665. (616)676-9185. Toll-free fax (800)398-3111. (616)676-2315. Website: www.bakerbooks.com. Imprint of Baker Publishing Group. Publishes inspirational fiction and nonfiction for the broadest Christian market. Guidelines & catalog on Website. No unsolicited mss. Submit through Writer's Edge or ChristianManuscriptSubmissions.com.

REVIEW AND HERALD PUBLISHING ASSN., 55 W. Oak Ridge Dr., Hagerstown MD 21740-7390. (301)393-3000. Fax (301)393-4055. E-mail: editorial@rhpa.org. Website: www.rhpa.org. Seventh-day Adventist. Richard Coffen, VP/editorial; Jeannette Johnson, acq. ed. No freelance.

+REVIVAL NATION PUBLISHING, 1049 Finch Dr., Sarnia ON N7S 6A8, Canada. (519)330-6346. E-mail: publishing@revivalnation.com. Website: www.revivalnation.com. Revival Nation Evangelistic Ministries. Greg Holmes, pres. Publishes 10-12 titles/yr. Gives preference to Canadian authors but open to all. Accepts e-mail submissions (attached file in Word). Looking for revival, Holy Spirit, miracles, healing, prophecy, prayer, and the kingdom of God.

RIVEROAK PUBLISHING—See David C. Cook.

ROSE PUBLISHING, 4733 Torrance Blvd., #259, Torrance CA 90503. Toll-free (800)532-4278. (310)353-2100. Fax (310)353-2116. E-mail: rosepubl@aol.com. Website: www.rose-publishing.com. Nondenominational. Lynnette Pennings, acq./mng. ed. Publishes primarily Bible studies, apologetics; Sunday school wall charts and visual aids. Publishes 30-40 titles/yr. 2% of projects from first-time authors. No mss through agents. No reprints. Outright purchases. Publication within 18 mos. Considers simultaneous submissions. Requires accepted mss by disk or e-mail. Responds in 2-3 mos. Catalog for 9x12 SAE/4 stamps.

Nonfiction: Query or proposal. No books, mainly booklets/pamphlets, wall charts/posters, or PowerPoints.

Special Needs: Query with sketch of proposed chart or poster (nonreturnable); fax query OK; e-query OK if less than 100 wds. (copied into message). Open to material that makes difficult Bible topics or theological topics easier; wall charts, study guides and worksheets on sharing your faith and salvation with skeptics. Typical subjects include: cults, books of the Bible, church history, world religions, discipleship, angels, prayer, teens, hot topics.

Also Does: PowerPoint presentations for biblical subjects.

Photos/Artwork: Open to queries from freelance artists.

Tips: "Now accepting more freelance submissions. No fiction."

+THE SALT WORKS, PO Box 37, Roseville CA 95678. (916)784-0500. Fax (916)773-7421. E-mail: books@publishersdesign.com. Website: www.publishersdesign.com. Division of Publishers Design Group Inc. Robert Brekke, pub. Seeks to demonstrate through books that God is sovereign, just, and merciful in all He does. Imprint: Salty Books (children's—see separate listing). Publishes 2-5 titles/yr.; hard cover, trade paperbacks, coffee-table books. Receives 20-35 submissions annually. 70% of books from first-time authors. No mss through agents. **SUBSIDY PUBLISHES 35%;** no print-on-demand. Reprints few books. Prefers 85,000-120,000 wds. Royalty 5-12% on net/advance; co-publishing and subsidy publishing by agreement. Average first printing 7,500 for CBA (10,000 for ABA). Publication within 18 mos. Considers simultaneous submissions. Responds in 30-45 days. Prefers ESV/NASB/NKJV/NIV (in that order). Guidelines by mail (after initial phone interview); free catalog.

Nonfiction: E-query only; followed by proposal. Unsolicited mss returned unopened. "Looking for titles that communicate a biblical Christian world-view without promoting overly simplistic, idealistic, or theoretical solutions to life's questions; books that honestly show no timidity in addressing our humanness, and yet, do not sensationalize a subject."

Fiction: E-query only; followed by proposal. Unsolicited mss returned unopened. For adults and children. "Looking for titles that help believers in exploring and facing common issues surrounding God's sovereignty, His grace and forgiveness, their own sin and idolatry, and the areas where pop-culture has influenced the church. Characters are blatantly human."

Also Does: Board games and other specialty products: fitness products, art projects and products, interactive projects for children.

Photos: Open to queries from freelance artists.

Tips: "Most open to books that look at the Christian experience through a realistic biblical and reformed perspective. Books that address the Christian's real problems as a 'heart' problem—not a theological problem, not from a victim mindset, not a mental or logical one, not from a perspective of merely needing another program, pep-talk, or the latest re-hash of formulas for victorious living. Books that show the author understands that unless God changes the heart and brings a person to repentance, there are no real and lasting answers."

****Note:** This publisher serviced by The Writer's Edge and ChristianManuscript Submissions.com.

+SALTY'S BOOKS, PO Box 37, Roseville CA 95678. (916)784-0500. Fax (916)773-7421. E-mail: books@publishersdesign.com. Website: www.publishersdesign.com. Division of Publishers Design Group Inc. Robert Brekke, pub. Imprint for children's Christian books.

SCEPTER PUBLISHERS INC., PO Box 211, New York NY 10018. Toll-free (800)322-8773. (212)354-0670. Fax (212)354-0736. E-mail: info@scepterpublishers.org. Website: www.scepterpublishers.org. Catholic. John Powers, ed. Books on how to struggle to live faith and virtue in one's daily life. Publishes 20 titles/yr. 0-2% of books from first-time authors. Accepts mss through agents. Reprints books. Prefers 200-250 pgs. Royalty on net; advance $2,000-10,000. Average first printing 2,000. Publication within 24 mos. No simultaneous submissions. Responds after 12 mos. Guidelines on Website; free catalog.

Nonfiction: Query only first with a 1-2 pg. synopsis; no phone/fax/e-query. Does not return material.

Fiction: Query only first; no phone/fax/e-query.

Tips: "Looking for short, practical books addressing reader needs."

SCRIPTURE PRESS—See David C. Cook.

SHEED & WARD, 4501 Forbes Blvd., Ste. 200, Lanham MD 20706. Toll-free (800)462-6420. (301)459-3366. Fax (301)429-5747. Website: www.sheedandward.com. Imprint of Rowman & Littlefield Publishers Inc. Jon Sisk, pub. (jsisk@rowmanlittlefield.com); Ross Miller (rmiller@rowman.com) & John Loudon (jloudon@rowman.com), eds. Publishes books of contemporary impact and enduring merit in Catholic-Christian thought and action. Publishes 25-30 titles/yr.; hardcover, trade paperbacks. Receives 2,000 submissions annually. 25% of books from first-time authors. Does print-on-demand. Reprints books. Prefers 35,000-65,000 wds. Royalty 6-12% on retail; $500-2,000 advance. Average first printing 3,000. Publication within 8 mos. No simultaneous submissions. Responds in 1-2 mos. Requires requested ms on disk. Prefers NAB, NRSV (Catholic editions). Guidelines/catalog on Website.

Nonfiction: Proposal/1-2 chapters; phone/fax/e-query OK. "Looking for parish ministry (health care, spirituality, leadership, general trade books for mass audiences, sacraments, small group, or priestless parish facilitating books)."

Photos/Artwork: Considers photos/artwork as part of book package.

Tips: "Looking for general trade titles and academic titles (oriented toward the classroom) in areas of spirituality, parish ministry, leadership, sacraments, prayer, faith formation, church history, and scripture."

SHORELINE, 23 Ste-Anne, Ste-Anne-de-Bellevue QC H9X 1L1, Canada. Phone/fax (514)457-5733. E-mail: shoreline@sympatico.ca. Website: www.shorelinepress.ca. Judith Isherwood, ed. Supports first-time authors of books that show creativity, originality, and care in nonfiction or creative nonfiction; many are memoirs. Publishes trade paperbacks. Receives 50 submissions annually. No mss through agents. No subsidy. Reprints books. Prefers under 200 pgs. Royalty 10% on retail; no advance. Average first printing 500-1,000. Publication within 1 yr. Considers simultaneous submissions. Responds in 3 mos. Guidelines on Website; catalog for #10 SAE/2 Canadian stamps.

Nonfiction: Query only first; phone/fax/e-query OK.

Tips: "We publish first-time authors."

SILOAM—See Strang Book Group.

SKYSONG PRESS, 35 Peter St. S., Orillia ON L3V 5A8, Canada. E-mail: skysong@bconnex.net. Website: www.bconnex.net/~skysong. Steve Stanton, ed. Imprint: Dreams & Visions. Publishes 2 titles/yr. Guidelines on Website.

Fiction: Publishers of Christian or "spiritual" short stories under the imprint Dreams & Visions.

SMYTH & HELWYS PUBLISHING INC., 6316 Peake Rd., Macon GA 31210-3960. Toll-free (800)747-3016. (478)757-0564. Fax (478)757-1305. E-mail: Proposals@helwys.com. Website: www.helwys.com. Submit to Book Editor. Quality resources for the church, the academy, and individual Christians who are nurtured by faith and informed by scholarship. Publishes 25-30 titles/yr. Receives 600 submissions annually. 40% of books from first-time authors. Prefers 144 pgs. Royalty 7%. Considers simultaneous submissions. Responds in 3 mos. Free guidelines (also by e-mail/Website); free catalog.

Nonfiction: Query only; fax/e-query OK. "Manuscripts requested for topics appropriate for mainline church and seminary/university textbook market."

Also Does: E-books. Copies of print books and original books. Go to: www.nextsunday.com.

Tips: "Most open to books with a strong secondary or special market. Niche titles and short-run options available for specialty subjects."

STANDARD PUBLISHING, 8805 Governor's Hill Dr., Ste. 400, Cincinnati OH 45249. (513)931-4050. Fax (513)931-0950. E-mail: books@standardpub.com. Website: www.standard pub.com. Standex International Corp. Robin Stanley, children's acq. ed.; Bob Irvin, teen & young adult acq. ed.; Elaina Meyers, church resources & program books ed.; Dale Reeves, ad. acq. ed. An evangelical Christian publisher of books, curriculum, classroom resources. Following are the trade book departments for this company (see guidelines or Website for details): Children & Tween (ages birth-12), publishes 25 titles/yr.; hardcover, trade paperbacks. Imprint: Refuge. 25% freelance. Teen/Young Adult (ages 13-22). Adults. No reprints. Royalty & work-for-hire; advance. Average first printing 10,000 (depends on product). Publication within 12-18 mos. Considers simultaneous submissions. Responds in 2-3 mos. Guidelines on Website; catalog $2.

Nonfiction: Query for classroom resources; proposal/2 chapters.

Fiction: Proposal/2 chapters. For children.

Special Needs: Elaina Meyers is open to submissions for Christmas and Easter Program books. Guidelines on Website under: Quick Links, Information Desk, Writers' Guidelines, Church Ministry Resources.

Tips: "We provide true-to-the-Bible resources that inspire, educate, and motivate Christians to a growing relationship with Jesus Christ."

****Note:** This publisher serviced by The Writer's Edge.

ST. ANTHONY MESSENGER PRESS and **FRANCISCAN COMMUNICATIONS,** 28 W. Liberty St., Cincinnati OH 45202. Toll-free (800)488-0488. (513)241-5615, ext. 123. Fax (513)241-0399. E-mail: StAnthony@AmericanCatholic.org. Website: www.AmericanCatholic.org. Catholic. Lisa Biedenbach, ed. dir. (lisab@AmericanCatholic.org); Katie Carroll, Mary Hackett, & Abby Colich, book eds. Seeks to publish affordable resources for living a Catholic-Christian lifestyle. Imprints: Servant Books, Franciscan Communications, Fischer Productions, Ikonographics (videos). S.A.M.P. publishes 30-40 titles/yr.; Servant publishes 15 titles/yr.; hardcover, trade paperbacks (mostly). Receives 450 submissions annually. 5% of books from first-time authors. Accepts mss through agents. Reprints books (seldom). Prefers 25,000-50,000 wds. or 100-300 pgs. Royalty 10-12% on net; advance $1,000. Average first printing 5,000. Publication within 18 mos. No simultaneous submissions. Requires accepted ms on disk; e-mail OK. Responds in 5-9 wks. Prefers NRSV. Guidelines on Website; catalog for 9x12 SAE/4 stamps.

Nonfiction: Query only/500-wd. summary; fax/e-query OK. "Looking for family-based catechetical programs; living the Catholic-Christian life at home and in workplace; and Franciscan topics."

Special Needs: Catholic identity, spirituality, resources for new and inactive Catholics.

Ethnic Books: Hispanic, occasionally.

Tips: "Most open to books with sound Catholic doctrine that include personal experiences or anecdotes applicable to today's culture. Our books are decidedly Catholic."

STARIK PUBLISHING, PO Box 307, Slaton TX 79364. E-mail: submissions@starik publishing.com. Website: www.starikpublishing.com. Stacie Craig, exec. ed. A family-oriented publishing house seeking to improve families through literature. Publishes 1-3 titles/yr.; trade paperbacks. 30% of books from first-time authors. No books through agents. No subsidy or reprints. Prefers 100-400 pgs. Royalty; no advance. Considers simultaneous submissions. Responds in 6-8 wks. Guidelines (also by e-mail/Website); no catalog.

Nonfiction: Proposal/3 chapters & short author bio; e-query OK. Accepts disk or e-mail submissions.

Fiction: Proposal/3 chapters & short author bio; e-query OK. Teen/young adult & adult Christian fiction.

Photos/Artwork: Open to queries from freelance artists.

ST. AUGUSTINE'S PRESS, PO Box 2285, South Bend IN 46680. (574)291-3500. Fax (574)291-3700. E-mail: bruce@staugustine.net. Website: www.staugustine.net. A conservative, non-denominational (although mostly Catholic) scholarly publisher of academic titles, mainly in academic philosophy, theology, and cultural history. Bruce Fingerhut, pres. Publishes 20-40 titles/yr.; hardcover, trade paperbacks. Receives 100+ submissions annually. 5% of books from first-time authors. Accepts mss through agents. Reprints books. Royalty 6-15% of net; advance $1,000. Average first printing 1,000. Publication within 1 yr. Considers simultaneous submissions. Responds in 3 mos. No guidelines; free catalog.

Nonfiction: Query or proposal/chapters. "Most of our titles are philosophy." Cultural history.

Tips: "Most open to books on subjects or by authors similar to what/who we already publish."

STEEPLE HILL (Single Title), 233 Broadway, Ste. 1001, New York NY 10279-0001. (212)553-4200. Fax (212)277-8969. E-mail: Emily_Rodmell@harlequin.ca. Website: www.SteepleHill.com. Harlequin Enterprises. Submit to any of the following: Joan Marlow Golan, exec. ed.; Melissa Endlich, ed.; Krista Stroever, sr. ed.; Jessica Alvarez, asst. ed.; Emily Rodmell, ed. asst. Single title, trade paperback Christian women's fiction that will help women guide themselves and their families toward purposeful, faith-driven lives. Lines: Love Inspired (mass-market category romances), see separate listing; Love Inspired Suspense; Love Inspired Historical, see separate listing; Steeple Hill Café (women's fiction). Publishes 96-108 titles/yr.; trade paperbacks, mass-market paperbacks. Receives 500-1,000 submissions annually. 15% of books from first-time authors. Accepts mss through agents. No reprints. Prefers 80,000-125,000 wds. or 350-500 pgs. Royalty on retail; competitive advance. Publication within 12-24 mos. Considers simultaneous submissions for trade books, not for mass market. Requires accepted ms on disk/hard copy. Responds in 3 mos. Prefers KJV. Guidelines (also on Website): no catalog.

Fiction: Query letter for single titles or complete ms for series; no phone/fax/e-query.

Tips: "We want quality inspirational novels that focus on the more complex and thoughtfully developed stories, with many characters, subplots, and so on. They are mostly character-driven, depicting sympathetic protagonists as they learn important lessons about the power of faith. Subgenres include relationship novels, contemporary and historical romances, family dramas, Christian chick lit, romantic suspense, mysteries, and thrillers."

STEEPLE HILL LOVE INSPIRED, 233 Broadway, Ste. 1001, New York NY 10279-0001. (212) 553-4200. Fax (212)277-8969. E-mail: Emily_Rodmell@harlequin.ca. Website: www.SteepleHill.com. Harlequin Enterprises. Submit to any of the following: Joan Marlow Golan, exec. ed.; Krista Stroever, sr. ed.; Melissa Endlich, ed.; Jessica Alvarez, asst. ed.; Emily Rodmell, ed. asst. Mass-market Christian romance novels. Publishes 48 titles/yr.; mass-market paperbacks. Receives 500-1,000 submissions annually. 15% of books from first-time authors. Accepts mss through agents. No reprints. Prefers 60,000-65,000 wds. or 300-320 pgs. Royalty on retail; competitive advance. Publication within 12-24 mos. Requires ms on disk/hard copy. Responds in 3 mos. Prefers KJV. Guidelines (also on Website); no catalog.

Fiction: Query letter or 3 chapters and up to 5-page synopsis; no phone/fax/e-query.

Tips: "We want character-driven romance with an author voice that inspires."

STEEPLE HILL LOVE INSPIRED HISTORICAL, 233 Broadway, Ste. 1001, New York NY 10279-0001. (212)553-4200. Fax (212)227-8969. E-mail: Emily_Rodmell@harlequin.ca. Website: www.SteepleHill.com. Harlequin Enterprises. Submit to any of the following: Melissa Endlich, ed.; Diane Dietz, asst. ed.; Emily Rodmell, ed. asst. Mass-market Christian historical romance novels. Publishes 24 titles/yr.; mass-market paperbacks. Receives 500-1,000 submissions annually. 15% of books from first-time authors. Accepts mss through agents. No subsidy; no reprints. Prefers 70,000-75,000 wds. Royalty on retail; competitive advance. Publication within 12-24 mos. No simultaneous submissions. Responds in 3 mos. Prefers KJV. Guidelines by e-mail/Website; no catalog.

Fiction: Proposal/3 chapters. Biblical, frontier romance, or historical romance.

Tips: "We are looking for complex stories rich in historical detail, featuring Christian characters facing challenges of life and love."

STEEPLE HILL LOVE INSPIRED SUSPENSE, 233 Broadway, Ste. 1001, New York NY 10279-0001. (212)553-4200. Fax (212)277-8969. E-mail: Emily_Rodmell@harlequin.ca. Website: www.SteepleHill.com. Harlequin Enterprises. Submit to any of the following: Joan Marlow Golan, exec. ed.; Krista Stroever, sr. ed.; Melissa Endlich, ed.; Jessica Alvarez, asst. ed.; Elizabeth Mazer, ed. asst. Mass-market Christian romance novels. Publishes 48 titles/yr.; mass-market paperbacks. Receives 500-1,000 submissions annually. 15% of books from first-time authors. Accepts mss through agents. No reprints. Prefers 60,000-65,000 wds. or 300-320 pgs. Royalty on retail; competitive advance. Publication within 12-24 mos. Requires accepted ms on disk/hard copy. Responds in 3 mos. Prefers KJV. Guidelines (also on Website); no catalog.

Fiction: Query letter or 3 chapters and up to 5-page synopsis; no phone/fax/e-query.

Special Needs: "We are looking for edge-of-the-seat, contemporary romantic suspense tales of intrigue and romance featuring Christian characters facing challenges to their faith—and to their lives. Each story should have a compelling mystery or a suspenseful situation threatening the hero and the heroine, combined with an emotional, satisfying, and mature romance. An element of faith must be present in the books, and should be well integrated into the plot."

Tips: "We want character-driven fiction with an author voice that inspires, whether in a contemporary romance or contemporary romantic suspense."

STILL WATERS REVIVAL BOOKS, 4710—37A Ave., Edmonton AB T6L 3T5, Canada. (708)450-3730. Fax (708)468-1096. E-mail: swrb@swrb.com. Website: www.swrb.com. Covenanter Church. Reg Barrow, pres. Publishes 100 titles/yr. Receives few submissions. Very few books from first-time authors. Reprints books. Prefers 128-160 pgs. Negotiated royalty or outright purchase. Considers simultaneous submissions. Catalog for 9x12 SAE/2 stamps.

Nonfiction: Proposal/2 chapters.

Tips: "Only open to books defending the Covenanted Reformation, nothing else."

+ST. MICHAEL'S ABBEY PRESS, Farnborough, Hampshire, England GU17 7NQ. Phone 44(0)1252 546105. Fax 44(0)1252 372822. E-mail: abbeypress@farnboroughabbey.org or info@farnboroughabbey.org. Website: www.farnboroughabbey.org/press/index.php. Open to freelance submissions. Details on Website.

STRANG BOOK GROUP, 600 Rinehart Rd., Lake Mary FL 32746. (407)333-0600. Fax (407)333-7100. E-mail: creationhouse@strang.com. Website: www.strangbookgroup.com. Strang Communications. Submit to Acquisitions Assistant for specific imprint. To inspire and equip people to live a Spirit-led life and walk in the divine purpose for which they were called. This house has 8 imprints, which are listed below with descriptions/details. Publishes 100 titles/yr.; hardcovers, trade paperbacks. Receives 600-1,000 submissions annually. 20% of books (Charisma House) & 80% of books (Creation House) from first-time authors. Accepts mss through agents. Reprints books. Prefers 55,000 wds. Royalty on net; advance. Average first printing varies. Publication within 12 mos. Considers simultaneous submissions. Accepts requested ms on disk or on Website. Responds in 3-4 mos. Guidelines (also on Website); free catalog.

Nonfiction: Proposal or complete ms; by mail or e-query OK; no phone query. Book proposal application on Website. "Open to any books that are well written and glorify Jesus Christ."

Fiction: Proposal or complete ms; by mail or e-query OK; no phone query. Book proposal application on Website. "For all ages. Fiction must have a biblical world-view and point the reader to Christ."

Photos/Artwork: Accepts freelance photos for book covers.

Charisma House: Books on Christian living, mainly from a Charismatic/Pentecostal perspective. Topics: Christian living, work of the Holy Spirit, prophecy, prayer, Scripture, adventures in evangelism and missions, popular theology.

Siloam: Books about living in good health—body, mind, and spirit. Topics: alternative medicine; diet and nutrition; and physical, emotional, and psychological wellness.

FrontLine: Books on contemporary issues from a Christian perspective.

Creation House: Co-publishing imprint for a wide variety of Christian books. Author is required to buy a quantity of books from the first press run. This is not self-publishing or print-on-demand.

Realms: Christian fiction in the supernatural, speculative genre. Full-length adult novels, 80,000-120,000 wds. Will also consider historical or biblical fiction if supernatural element is substantial.

Charisma Kids (see separate listing): Children' s books. No 24- to 32-page picture books.

Casa Creacion: Publishes and translates books into Spanish. (800)987-8432. E-mail: casacreacion@strang.com. Website: www.casacreacion.com.

Publicaciones Casa: Publishes the same as Creation House and is for people who like to co-publish in Spanish. Contact info same as Casa Creacion.

+SWEETHEART ROMANCES.CO, PO Box 870, Oregon City OR 97045. (503)656-9663. E-mail: question@SweetheartRomances.com, or submissions@SweetheartRomances.com. Website: www.SweetheartRomances.com. Melanie Emry, ed. A Sweetheart Romance will leaves its readers feeling good when they finish the novel. E-book publisher. Prefers 40,000-75,000 wds. Royalty 25% of earnings from downloads (paid every other month); no advance. Responds in 3 mos. Guidelines on Website; no catalog.

Fiction: Proposal/chapter-by-chapter synopsis & 3 chapters (incl. 1st & last chapters).

Tips: "Can you tell a powerful love story without resorting to anatomy texts and clinical descriptions of love making? Can you avoid obscene language? Can you write a story that will leave readers a little better than they were? If you answered Yes to these questions, we invite you to try."

TAN BOOKS AND PUBLISHERS INC., PO Box 424, Rockford IL 61105. Toll-free (800)437-5876, ext. 205. (815)226-7777. Fax (815)226-7770. E-mail: taneditor@tanbooks.com. Website: www.TanBooks.com. Catholic. Thomas A. Nelson, ed. Not included in topical listings.

T & T CLARK INTERNATIONAL, PO Box 1321, Harrisburg PA 17108. (717)541-8130. Fax (717)541-8136. E-mail: hcarriga@continuum-books.com. Website: www.tandtclarkinternational.com. Continuum Publishing. Thomas Kraft, ed. A nondenominational, academic religious publisher. Imprints: Trinity Press International, Continuum. Publishes 50-60 titles/yr.; trade paperbacks. Receives 150-200 submissions annually. 3% of books from first-time authors. Accepts mss through agents. Reprints books. Royalty 10% of net; advance $500 & up. Average first printing 1,000. Publication within 9 mos. Considers simultaneous submissions. Responds in 4-6 wks. Prefers NRSV. Guidelines (also by e-mail); free catalog.

Nonfiction: Proposal/1 chapter, or complete ms; fax/e-query OK. "Looking for biblical studies, theology, religion, and music." No dissertations or essays.

Special Needs: Religion and film; American religious history; and religion and science.

Photos/Artwork: Accepts freelance photos for book covers.

Tips: "Most open to a book that is academic, to be used in undergraduate biblical studies, theology, or religious studies programs."

JEREMY P. TARCHER, 375 Hudson St., New York NY 10014. (212)366-2000. Fax (212)366-2670. Website: www.penguinputnam.com. Penguin Putnam Inc. Mitch Horowitz, exec. ed.; Sara Carder, sr. ed. Publishes ideas and works about human consciousness that are large enough to include matters of spirit and religion. Publishes 40-50 titles/yr.; hardcover, trade paperbacks. Receives 2,000 submissions annually. 20% of books from first-time authors. Accepts mss through agents. Reprints books. Royalty 5-8% of retail; advance. Considers simultaneous submissions. Free catalog.

Nonfiction: Query. Religion.

TAU-PUBLISHING, 1422 E. Edgemont Ave., Phoenix AZ 85006. (602)264-4828. Fax (602)248-9656. E-mail: phoenixartist@msn.com, or through Website: www.tau-publishing.org. Catholic. Jeffrey Campbell, pub. Imprint: Aleph-First. Publishes 3-4 titles/yr. Receives 25 submissions annually. 50% of books from first-time authors. Prefers mss through agents. **SOME SUBSIDY.** Reprints books. Prefers 25,000-50,000 wds. or 100-200 pgs. Royalty on net; no advance. Average first printing 3,000. Publication within 8 mos. Considers simultaneous submissions. Responds in 4-6 mos. Guidelines on Website; no catalog.

Nonfiction: Query; fax/e-query OK. "Looking for Catholic inspirational material; reflections and meditations."

Photos/Artwork: Accepts freelance photos for book covers.

THIRD WORLD PRESS, PO Box 19730, Chicago IL 60619. (773)651-0700. Fax (773)651-7286. E-mail: GwenMTWP@aol.com, or TWPress3@aol.com. Website: www.ThirdWorldPressInc.com. Bennett Johnson, ed. African American publisher. Publishes 20 titles/yr.; hard cover, trade paperbacks. Receives 400-500 submissions annually. 20% of books from first-time authors. Accepts mss through agents. Reprints books. Royalty on retail; advance varies. Publication within 18 mos. Considers simultaneous submissions. Responds in 5-6 mos. Guidelines; free catalog. Note: this company is open to submissions in July only.

Nonfiction/Fiction: Query by mail, or proposal/5 chapters.

Ethnic Books: African American.

Tips: "Submit complete manuscript for poetry; must be African American centered."

TORCH LEGACY PUBLICATIONS, PO Box 372573, Atlanta GA 30037; or PO Box 165046, Irving TX 75016. (877)TORCHLP. Fax (817)887-3089. E-mail: info@torchlegacy.com. Website: www.torchlegacy.com. Torch Ministries Intl. Daniel Whyte III, pres. Dedicated to publishing Bible-based books of all genres by and for African Americans and whosoever will. Publishes 7+ titles/yr. 80% of books from first-time authors. Royalty 10% of net; no advance. Average first printing 5,000. Publication within 12 mos. Considers simultaneous submissions. Responds in 2 mos.

Nonfiction: Query first; e-query OK. "We are especially interested in Christian self-help books for the African-American community for all age groups. Submissions in all categories are welcome."

Ethnic Books: African American.

Also Does: "We also handle the production and publishing of sermon books by local pastors for local churches, and we transcribe sermons for pastors."

Tips: "We are looking for books that are conservative and Bible based but at the same time are exciting and life changing. Our mission is to turn many from darkness to light in the Black community in America through presenting a clear, understandable presentation of the Gospel."

TOUCH PUBLICATIONS, 509 Garden Oaks Blvd., Houston TX 77018. Toll-free (800)735-5865. (713)896-7478. Fax (713)742-5998. E-mail: randall@touchusa.org, or from Website: www.touchusa.org. Touch Outreach Ministries. Randall Neighbour, dir. of publishing. To empower pastors, group leaders, and members to transform their lives, churches, and the world through basic Christian communities called cells. Publishes 8 titles/yr. Receives 25 submissions annually. 40% of books from first-time authors. Reprints books. Prefers 75-200 pgs. Royalty 10-15% of net; no advance. Average first printing 2,000. Guidelines (also by e-mail). Not in topical listings.

Nonfiction: Query only. "Must relate to cell church life."

Photos/Artwork: Accepts freelance photos for book covers.

Tips: "Our market is extremely focused. We publish books, resources, and discipleship tools for churches, using a cell group strategy."

TOWLEHOUSE PUBLISHING, 117 Township Ct., Hendersonville TN 37075-2909. (615)822-6405, or (615)338-0283. E-mail: vermonte@aol.com. Website: www.towlehouse.com. Mike

Towle, pres. A sports-oriented publisher—mostly golf, baseball, football, and basketball—interested in books with a Christian angle. Publishes 8-10 titles/yr.; hardcover, trade paperbacks, mass-market paperbacks. Receives 100-250 submissions annually. 75% of books from first-time authors. Accepts mss through agents. Reprints books. Prefers 25,000-30,000 wds. Royalty 8-20% of net; $500-2,000 advance. Average first printing 5,000. Publication within 9 mos. Considers simultaneous submissions. Responds in 4-6 mos. Prefers requested ms on disk. No guidelines; catalog for #10 SAE/2 stamps.

Nonfiction: Query or proposal/2 chapters; fax/e-query OK. "Looking for sports books, especially golf."

Photos/Artwork: Accepts freelance photos for book covers.

THE TRACT LEAGUE, 2627 Elmridge Dr., Grand Rapids MI 49544-1390. (616)453-7695. Fax (616)453-2460. E-mail: info@tractleague.com. Website: www.tractleague.com. Publishes very few tracts from outside writers, but willing to look at ideas. Submit to General Manager.

TREBLE HEART BOOKS, 1284 Overlook Dr., Sierra Vista AZ 85635. (520)458-5602. Fax (520)458-5618. E-mail: submissions@trebleheartbooks.com. Website: www.trebleheartbooks.com. Lee Emory, ed./pub. Imprint: MountainView (Christian division). Publishes 48 titles/yr. Receives 1,500 submissions annually. 30% of books from first-time authors. Prefers mss through agents. Reprints few books. Royalty 15-35% on net or retail. Publication within 8-12 mos. No simultaneous submissions. Responds in 1-4 mos. Guidelines on Website.

Nonfiction: Complete ms by e-mail only (no hard copies, even from agents).

Fiction: Complete ms; e-query OK.

Note: This publisher currently overstocked and accepting no submissions.

THE TRINITY FOUNDATION, PO Box 68, Unicoi TN 37692. (423)743-0199. Fax (423)743-2005. E-mail: jrob1517@aol.com. Website: www.trinityfoundation.org. John W. Robbins, pres. To promote the logical system of truth found in the Bible. Publishes 5 titles/yr.; hardcover, trade paperbacks. Receives 3 submissions annually. No books from first-time authors. No mss through agents. Reprints books. Prefers 200 pgs. Outright purchases up to $1,500; free books; no advance. Average first printing 2,000. Publication within 9 mos. No simultaneous submissions. Requires requested ms on disk. Responds in 2-3 mos. No guidelines; catalog on Website.

Nonfiction: Query letter only. Open to Calvinist/Clarkian books, Christian philosophy, economics, and politics.

Also Does: Pamphlets, booklets, tracts.

Photos/Artwork: Accepts freelance photos for book covers.

Tips: "Most open to doctrinal books that conform to the Westminster Confession of Faith; nonfiction, biblical, and well-reasoned books, theologically sound, clearly written, and well organized."

TROITSA BOOKS, 400 Oser Ave., Ste. 1600, Hauppauge NY 11788-3619. (631)231-7269. Fax (631)231-8175. E-mail: Novaeditorial@earthlink.net. Website: www.novapublishers.com. Religious imprint of Nova Science Publishers Inc. Submit to Editor-in-Chief. Publishes 5-20 titles/yr. Receives 50-100 submissions annually. No mss through agents. Various lengths. Royalty; no advance. Publication within 6-18 mos. Considers simultaneous submissions. Accepts requested ms on disk or by e-mail (prefers e-mail for all submissions and correspondence). Responds in 1 mo. Guidelines on Website; free catalog.

Nonfiction: Proposal/2 chapters by e-mail. Send to above e-mail with a copy to novascil@aol.com.

Fiction: Proposal/2 chapters by e-mail. For adults.

Photos/Artwork: Accepts freelance photos for book covers.

+TSABA HOUSE, 2252—12th St., Reedley CA 93654. (559)643-8575. E-mail: info@tsabahouse.com. Website: www.tsabahouse.com. Jodie Nazaroff, VP & sr. ed. Christian publishing company currently publishing fiction, nonfiction, self-help, teaching, and devotionals; no children's books or poetry. Estab. 2002. Accepts mss through agents. Royalty. Guidelines on Website.

Nonfiction/Fiction: Proposal/cover letter, chapter-by-chapter synopsis, 1 chapter, and word count; no e-query. Accepts during the month of January ONLY.

Tips: "Your manuscript must be completed. We offer contracts to authors with a 3 book option only. You must commit to publish one book at least every two years—annually is preferable."

TYNDALE ESPANOL, 351 Executive Dr., Carol Stream IL 60188. (630)784-5272. Fax (630)344-0943. E-mail: andresschwartz@tyndale.com. Website: www.tyndale.com. Andres Schwartz, dir. Spanish division of Tyndale House Publishers.

TYNDALE HOUSE PUBLISHERS, 351 Executive Dr., Carol Stream IL 60188. Toll-free (800)323-9400. (630)668-8300. Fax (800)684-0247. E-mail: manuscripts@tyndale.com. Website: www.tyndale.com. Submit to Manuscript Review Committee. Practical Christian books for home and family. Imprints: HeartQuest (see separate listing); Tyndale Espanol (Spanish imprint); Picket Fence Press (resources for women juggling multiple priorities in and outside the home). Publishes 225-250 titles/yr.; hardcover, trade paperbacks, mass-market paperbacks (reprints). 5% of books from first-time authors. Prefers mss through agents. Reprints books. Royalty negotiable; outright purchase of some children's books; advance negotiable. Average first printing 5,000-10,000. Publication within 9 mos. Considers simultaneous submissions. Responds in 3-6 mos. Prefers NLT. No unsolicited mss. Guidelines/catalog on Website.

Nonfiction: Query from agents or published authors only; no phone/fax query. No unsolicited mss.

Fiction: "We accept queries only from agents, Tyndale authors, authors known to us from other publishers, or other people in the publishing industry. Novellas, 25,000-30,000 wds.; novels 75,000-100,000 wds. All must have an evangelical Christian message."

Also Does: E-books.

****Note:** This publisher serviced by The Writer's Edge.

UMI PUBLISHING, 1551 Regency Court, Calumet IL 60409. Toll-free (800)860-8642. (708)868-7100. Fax (708)868-6759. E-mail: khall@urbanministries.com, or customerservice@urbanministries.com. Website: www.urbanministries.com. Urban Ministries Inc. Carl Jeffrey Wright, pub.; Kathryn Hall, mng. ed. Called of God to create, produce, and distribute quality Christian education products; to provide quality Christian educational services that will empower God's people, especially in the black community; to evangelize, disciple, and equip people for serving Christ, his Kingdom, and his church. Publishes 2-3 titles/yr.; trade paperbacks. Receives 25-40 submissions annually. 85% of books from first-time authors. Accepts mss through agents. Reprints books. Prefers 256 pgs. Royalty to 40%; no advance. Average first printing 2,500-5,000. Publication within 2 yrs. Acknowledges receipt within 4 wks.; accepts or rejects in 6-12 mos. No simultaneous submissions. Prefers accepted ms on disk. Prefers KJV or NIV. Guidelines by e-mail; free catalog.

Nonfiction: Query only; no unsolicited mss; no phone/fax/e-query.

Special Needs: Christian living, theology, Christian education, and Christian doctrine.

Ethnic Books: African American.

Tips: "Follow guidelines for submissions (strictly); send query letter first."

****Note:** This publisher serviced by The Writer's Edge.

UNITED CHURCH PRESS—No freelance; see Pilgrim Press.

UNITED METHODIST PUBLISHING HOUSE—See Abingdon Press or Dimensions for Living.

UNIVERSITY OF ARKANSAS PRESS, 201 Ozark Ave., Fayetteville AR 72701. Toll-free (800)626-0090. (479)575-3246. Fax (479)575-6044. E-mail: uapress@uark.edu. Website: www.uapress.com. Lawrence Malley, ed. (lmalley@uark.edu). Academic publisher. Publishes 30 titles/yr.; hardcover, trade paperbacks. Receives 1,000 submissions annually. 30% of books from first-time authors. Accepts mss through agents. Reprints books. Prefers 300 pgs. Royalty on net; no advance. Average first printing 1,000-2,000. Publication within 1 yr. Reluctantly considers simultaneous submissions. Responds in 3 mos. Requires accepted ms on disk. Guidelines on Website; free catalog.

Nonfiction: Query. "All our books are scholarly." Looking for regional books.

Photos/Artwork: Accepts freelance photos for book covers.

UNIVERSITY PRESS OF AMERICA, 4501 Forbes Blvd., Ste. 200, Lanham MD 20706. (301)459-3366. Fax (301)429-5748. E-mail: submitupa@univpress.com. Website: www.univpress.com. Rowman & Littlefield Publishing Group/Academic. Patti Belcher, acq. ed. (pbelcher@univpress.com). Publishes scholarly works in the social sciences and humanities; established by academics for academics. Imprint: Hamilton Books (biographies & memoirs). Publishes 75 religion titles/yr. Receives 700 submissions annually. 75% of books from first-time authors. Accepts mss through agents. **SOME SUBSIDY.** Does Digital Printing. Reprints books. Prefers 90-300 pgs. Royalty up to 12% of net; no advance. Average first printing 200-300. Publication within 4-6 mos. Considers simultaneous submissions. Accepts e-mail submissions. Responds in 2 wks. Accepts requested ms on disk or by e-mail. Guidelines on Website; free catalog.

Nonfiction: Proposal/3 chapters or complete ms; phone/fax/e-query OK. "Looking for scholarly manuscripts."

Ethnic Books: African studies; black studies.

Tips: "Most open to timely, thoroughly researched, and well-documented books. Moderately controversial topics. We publish academic and scholarly books only. Authors are typically affiliated with a college, university, or seminary."

VICTOR BOOKS—See David C. Cook.

VINTAGE ROMANCE PUBLISHING, LLC, PO Box 1164, Ladson SC 29456-1165. (843)225-9735. E-mail: editor@vrpublishing.com. Website: www.vrpublishing.com. Dawn Carrington, ed-in-chief. Old-fashioned romance fiction set anytime before the 1960s. Publishes 12+ titles/yr. Currently closed to submissions except by author referral or invitation by publisher, but actively seeking strong inspirational romances. Accepts mss through agents. No subsidy. Prefers 75,000 wds. Royalty 6% on retail; no advance. Average first printing 100+. Publication within 18 mos. Guidelines on Website.

Fiction: E-query only; no attachments; no phone/fax query. "Please include previous publication information. Authors should be familiar with marketing and promotions and be willing to submit a detailed marketing plan."

Tips: "We do not accept formulaic romances, nor do we accept inspirational romances which preach or teach readers about a certain type of religion. All our inspirational romances should weave faith into the story line seamlessly."

VIRGINIA PINES PRESS, 7092 Jewell-North, Kinsman OH 44428. (330)876-3504. Fax (209)882-5803. E-mail: virginiapines@nlc.net. Website: www.virginiapines.com. Helen C. Caplan, pub. Publishes fiction with a Christian viewpoint and creative nonfiction that helps document 21st-century America. Publishes 3-5 titles/yr. Receives 40-50 submissions annually. 90% of books from first-time authors. Accepts mss through agents. No reprints. Prefers 80,000-100,000 wds. Royalty 6-8% on net; some outright purchases; no advance. Average first printing 1,000. Publication within 8 mos. Considers simultaneous submissions. Prefers requested ms on disk. Responds in 1-10 mos. Prefers NKJV. Guidelines on Website; free catalog.

Nonfiction: Query, proposal, or complete ms; phone/fax/e-query OK. "We are always on the lookout for third-person, full-length, creative nonfiction works, to which we give top priority."

Fiction: Query, proposal, or complete ms; phone/fax/e-query OK. "Looking for excellent, full-length spiritual warfare works that teach by example of the characters within the story how to identify spiritual warfare in daily life and how to become victorious over these types of attacks on family, finances, business, and peace of mind."

Photos/Artwork: Accepts freelance photos for book covers.

Contest: Sponsors several cover design contests each year. See Website for details of current contest.

+THE VISION FORUM, 4719 Blanco Rd., San Antonio TX 78212. (210)340-5250. Fax (210) 340-8577. Website: www.visionforum.com. Douglas W. Phillips, pres. Dedicated to the restoration of the biblical family. Historical fiction.

WALK WORTHY PRESS, 33290 W. 14 Mile Rd., #482, West Bloomfield MI 48322. (248)737-1747. Fax (248)737-1766. E-mail: editor@walkworthypress.net. Website: www.walkworthypress.net. Denise Stinson, pub. Primarily fiction for the African American Christian. Publishes 10 titles/yr. Receives 200 submissions annually. 95% of books from first-time authors. Accepts mss through agents. Reprints books. Prefers 75,000-100,000 wds., or 300 pgs. Royalty 10-15% on retail; variable advance. Average first printing varies. Publication within 9 mos. Considers simultaneous submissions (if informed). No disk or e-mail submissions. Responds in 6-8 wks. Prefers KJV, NKJV, NIV, Amplified. Guidelines on Website; free catalog.

Nonfiction: Proposal/2 chapters; no phone/fax/e-query. "We do primarily fiction. Our nonfiction is generally from authors who have a high profile."

Fiction: Complete ms; no phone/fax/e-query. Seasoned fiction author may send proposal/3 chapters. For all ages. Contemporary, ethnic, fantasy, juvenile, literary, short-story collection. Big commercial fiction.

Ethnic Books: African American.

Tips: "Present a good package. Read our books first. Do a story synopsis, not book-jacket copy. We like manuscripts that explore little-explored areas of life in Christian books."

WATERBROOK PRESS, 12265 Oracle Blvd., Ste. 200, Colorado Springs CO 80921. Toll-free (800)603-7051. (719)590-4999. Fax (719)590-8977. Website: www.waterbrookpress.com. Random House Inc. Imprint: Shaw (Fisherman Bible Studyguides). Jeanette Thomason, ed. dir. Publishes 70 titles/yr. Receives 1,000 submissions annually. 15% of books from first-time authors. Prefers mss through agents. Reprints books. Royalty; advance. Publication in approximately 12 mos. Considers simultaneous submissions. Responds in 1-2 mos. No guidelines; catalog on Website.

Nonfiction/Fiction: Agented submissions only.

****Note:** This publisher serviced by ChristianManuscriptSubmissions.com.

WESLEYAN PUBLISHING HOUSE, PO Box 50434, Indianapolis IN 46250-0434. (317)774-3853. Fax (317)774-3860. E-mail: wph@wesleyan.org. Website: www.wesleyan.org/wph, or www.wesleyan.org/writer. The Wesleyan Church. Lawrence Wilson, ed. dir. Communicates the life-transforming message of holiness to the world. Publishes 15 titles/yr.; hardcover, trade paperbacks. Receives 150 submissions annually. 10-20% of books from first-time authors. Accepts mss through agents. No reprints. Prefers 25,000-40,000 wds. Royalty and advance. Average first printing 4,000. Publication within 9-12 mos. Considers simultaneous submissions. Accepts requested ms by e-mail. Responds in 2 mos. Prefers NIV. Guidelines on Website; free catalog.

Nonfiction: Proposal/2 chapters; no phone/fax/e-query. "Looking for books that help Christians understand the faith and apply it to their lives."

Tips: "Explain spiritual concepts simply and show readers how to make practical life change."

WESTBOW PRESS—See Thomas Nelson, Fiction.

WESTMINSTER JOHN KNOX PRESS—See Presbyterian Publishing Corporation.

WHITAKER HOUSE, 1030 Hunt Valley Cir., New Kensington PA 15068. (724)334-7000. (724)334-1200. E-mail: publisher@whitakerhouse.com. Website: www.whitakerhouse.com. Whitaker Corp. Tom Cox, sr. ed. To advance God's Kingdom by providing biblically based products that proclaim the power of the Gospel and minister to the spiritual needs of people around the world. Publishes 30-40 titles/yr.; hardcover, trade paperbacks, mass-market paperbacks. Receives 500 submissions annually. 25% of books from first-time authors. Accepts mss through agents. No subsidy, print-on-demand, or reprints. Prefers 50,000 wds. Royalty 6-15% on net; some variable advances. Average first printing 5,000. Publication within 6 mos. Considers simultaneous submissions. Prefers accepted ms by e-mail. Responds in 4 mos. Prefers NIV. Guidelines on Website; no catalog.

Nonfiction: Query only first; no phone/fax query; e-query OK.

Fiction: Proposal/3 chapters.

Special Needs: Charismatic & spiritual warfare.

Ethnic Books: Hispanic translations of current English titles.

Tips: "Looking for quality fiction and previously published authors with a national marketing platform. Most open to high-quality, well-thought-out, compelling pieces of work. Do the research and work required by our guidelines."

****Note:** This publisher serviced by The Writer's Edge.

+WHITE ROSE /THE WILD ROSE PRESS, PO Box 706, Adams Basin NY 14410. (336)793-6092. E-mail: admin@thewildrosepress.com. Website: www.thewildrosepress.com. Lori Graham, ed. To give writers a background and forum to perfect their craft; the "garden" is truly a place for new authors to grow and "bloom" along with giving experienced writers a place to gain some flexibility. White Rose imprint is devoted specifically to inspirational, Christian romances. This is a new line; 54 submitted last year & 7 in print. 50% of books from first-time authors. Accepts mss through agents. Does e-publishing for anything under 55,000 wds.; over that is print & e-publishing. Does print-on-demand. No reprints. Any length. Royalty 30% on download; 7% on POD. No advance. Publication within 6-8 mos. (usually). Considers simultaneous submissions. Responds quarterly. Prefers NIV. Guidelines on Website.

Fiction: E-query/synopsis to queryus@thewildrosepress.com; romance only. "We accept all romance but are actively pursuing inspirational romance." Accepts short stories as well as full-length manuscripts.

WHITE STONE BOOKS, 2761 E. Skelly Dr., Ste. 700-8, Tulsa OK 74105. (918)523-5411. Fax (918)523-5782. E-mail: info@whitestonebooks.com. Website: www.whitestonebooks.com. Christian books. Amanda Pilgrim, ed. Publishes 25 titles/yr.; hardcover, trade paperbacks, mass-market paperbacks. 30% of books from first-time authors. Accepts mss through agents. **SUBSIDY PUBLISHES OCCASIONALLY.** Reprints books. Publication within 18 mos. Considers simultaneous submissions. Guidelines (also by e-mail); free catalog.

Nonfiction: Proposal/1 chapter.

Fiction: Proposal/1 chapter. For all ages. "We prefer scripts with several connecting layers, with story lines that are compelling and thought provoking."

Special Needs: Adult & teen novels; seasonally appropriate for gift giving, especially for Mother's Day and Christmas.

Photos/Artwork: Open to queries from freelance artists.

Tips: "Most open to books that are seasonally appropriate, but not seasonally specific: Mothers/Mother's Day; Fathers/Father's Day."

****Note:** This publisher serviced by The Writers Edge and ChristianManuscript Submissions.com.

WILSHIRE BOOK COMPANY, 9731 Variel Ave., Chatsworth CA 91311-4315. (818)700-1522. Fax (818)700-1527. E-mail: mpowers@mpowers.com. Website: www.mpowers.com. A general publisher of motivational books. Melvin Powers, pres.; Marcia Powers, ed. Books that help you become who you choose to be tomorrow. Publishes 6 titles/yr. 80% of books from first-time authors. Accepts mss through agents. Reprints books. Prefers 30,000 wds. or 128-160 pgs. Royalty 5% on retail; variable advance. Average first printing 5,000. Publication within 6 mos. Considers simultaneous submissions. No disk or e-mail submissions. Responds in 2 mos. Guidelines (also by e-mail/Website)/catalog for SAE/2 stamps.

Nonfiction: Query or proposal/3 chapters; phone/e-query OK.

Fiction: Allegory for adults that teaches principles of psychological/spiritual growth.

Photos/Artwork: Accepts freelance photos for book covers; open to queries from freelance artists.

Tips: "We are looking for adult allegories such as *Illusions* by Richard Bach, *The Little Prince* by Antoine de Saint Exupery, and *The Greatest Salesman in the World* by Og Mandino. Analyze each one to discover what elements make it a winner. Duplicate those elements in your own style, using a creative, new approach and fresh material. We need 30,000-60,000 words."

WINDRIVER PUBLISHING INC., 72 N. WindRiver Rd., Silverton ID 83867-0446. (208)752-1836. Fax (208)752-1876. E-mail: info@windriverpublishing.com. Website: www.TrumpetMedia.com. Nondenominational. Gail Howick, ed-in-chief. To provide family entertainment and education that fulfills the admonition of Paul in Philippians 4:8. Imprint: Trumpet Media. Publishes 4 titles/yr.; hardcover, trade paperbacks. Receives 300 submissions annually. 90% of books from first-time authors. Accepts mss through agents. Reprints books. Prefers 100,000 wds. Royalty 10-15% of net; no advance. Average first printing 3,000. Publication within 14 mos. Considers simultaneous submissions. Requires accepted ms on disk; no e-mail submissions. Responds in 4-6 mos. Guidelines on Website; catalog online & free on request.

Nonfiction: Proposal/3 chapters; no phone/e-query; fax query OK.

Fiction: Proposal/3 chapters; no phone/e-query; fax query OK. For all ages.

Photos/Artwork: Open to queries from freelance artists.

WOOD LAKE BOOKS INC., 9025 Jim Bailey Rd., Kelowna BC V4V 1R2, Canada. Toll-free (800)299-2926. (250)766-2778. Toll-free fax (888)841-9991. (250)766-2736. E-mail: acquisitions@woodlake.com. Website: www.woodlakebooks.com. Ecumenical/mainline; Wood Lake Books Inc. Michael Schwartzentruber, series ed. Publishes quality resources that respond to the needs of the ecumenical church and promote spiritual growth and commitment to God. Imprint: Northstone Publishing. Publishes 3 titles/yr. Receives 300 submissions annually. 25% of books from first-time authors. Reprints books. Prefers 200-250 pgs. Royalty on net; compiler's fee (for compilations) $1,000-3,000; some advances $1,000. Average first printing 3,000-4,000. Publication within 18-24 mos. Considers simultaneous submissions. Prefers requested ms on disk. Responds in 6-12 wks. Guidelines; catalog $2.

Nonfiction: Query or proposal/2 chapters; fax/e-query OK. "Books with inclusive language and mainline, Protestant interest."

Tips: "Most open to books with inclusive language, mainline/liberal theology, truth seeking, life affirming, and those that deal positively with life and faith. We publish books, curriculum, and resources for the mainline church. All queries and submissions should reflect this in their theological approach."

WOODLAND GOSPEL PUBLISHING HOUSE, 118 Woodland Dr., Ste. 1101, Chapmanville WV 25508. (304)752-7500. Fax (304)752-9002. E-mail: info@woodlandpress.com, or from Website: www.woodlandpress.com. Woodland Press LLC. Cheryl Davis, ed; submit to Mike Collins. Publishes 7 titles/yr. Receives 150 submissions annually. 90% of books from first-time authors. Accepts mss through agents. No reprints. Prefers 60,000 wds. or 230 pgs. Royalty on net; no advance. Average first printing 2,000. Publication within 1 yr. No simultaneous submissions. Responds in 2 mos. No mss by disk or e-mail. No guidelines or catalog.

Nonfiction: Proposal/3 chapters; no phone/fax/e-query.

W PUBLISHING GROUP, PO Box 141000, Nashville TN 37214. (615)889-9000. Fax (615)902-2112. Website: www.Wpublishinggroup.com. Thomas Nelson Inc. David Moberg, pub.; Greg Daniel, assoc. pub. Publishes 75 titles/yr. Less than 3% of books from first-time authors. Prefers mss through agents. No reprints. Does not accept unsolicited manuscripts. Prefers 65,000-95,000 wds. Royalty. No guidelines.

Nonfiction: Query letter only first; no unsolicited ms. "Nonfiction dealing with the relationship and/or application of biblical principles to everyday life; 65,000-95,000 words."

****Note:** This publisher serviced by The Writer's Edge.

WRITE NOW PUBLICATIONS, PO Box 110390, Nashville TN 37222. Toll-free (800)21-WRITE. E-mail: RegAForder@aol.com. Website: www.writenowpublications.com. Reg A. Forder, exec. ed. To train and develop quality Christian writers; books on writing and speaking for writers and speakers. Royalty division of ACW Press. Publishes 1-2 titles/yr.; trade paperbacks. Receives 6 submissions annually. 0% from first-time authors. Accepts mss through agents. Reprints books. Royalty 10% of net. Average first printing 2,000. Publication within 12 mos. Considers simultaneous submissions. Requires requested ms on disk. No guidelines/catalog.

Nonfiction: Writing how-to only. Query letter only; e-query OK.

YALE UNIVERSITY PRESS, PO Box 209040, New Haven CT 06518-9040. (203)432-0960. Fax (203)432-0948. Website: www.yale.edu/yup. Christopher Rogers, exec. ed., history, current events, religion. Publishes scholarly and general-interest books, including religion. Publishes 10 religious titles/yr.; hardcover, trade paperbacks. Receives 200 submissions annually. 15% of books from first-time authors. Accepts mss through agents. Reprints books. Prefers up to 100,000 wds. or 400 pgs. Royalty from 0% to standard trade royalties; advance $0-100,000. Average first printing varies by field. Publication within 1 yr. Considers simultaneous submissions. Requires requested ms on disk; no e-mail submissions. Responds in 1-2 mos. Guidelines & catalog on Website (www.yalebooks.com).

Nonfiction: Query or proposal/sample chapters; fax query OK; no e-query. "Excellent and salable scholarly books."

Contest: Yale Series of Younger Poets competition. Open to poets under 40 who have not had a book of poetry published. Submit manuscripts of 48-64 pages by November 15. Entry fee $15. Send SASE for guidelines (also on Website). Send complete manuscript.

YOUTH SPECIALTIES, 5300 Patterson S.E., Grand Rapids MI 49530. (619)440-2333. Fax (619)440-0582. E-mail: jay@youthspecialties.com. Website: www.youthspecialties.com. Zondervan. Jay Howver, pub. Books for youth workers and teenagers. Imprint: Invert. Publishes 30 titles/yr. Accepts mss through agents. No reprints. Prefers 35,000 wds. Royalty on net or outright purchase of $3,000-8,000; advance. Publication within 18 mos. Considers simultaneous submissions. Responds in 4-6 wks. Prefers NIV. Guidelines by e-mail/Website; free catalog

Nonfiction: Proposal/2 chapters.

Tips: "We prefer books from youth workers who are in the trenches working with students."

ZONDERKIDZ, 5300 Patterson S.E., Grand Rapids MI 49530-0002. (616)698-3400. Fax (616) 698-3326. E-mail: zpub@zondervan.com. Website: www.zonderkidz.com. Zondervan/ HarperCollins. Bruce Nuffer, children's pub. Children's book line of Zondervan; ages 12 & under. Not currently accepting proposals for new products.

ZONDERVAN, General Trade Books; Academic and Professional Books, 5300 Patterson S.E., Grand Rapids MI 49530-0002. Toll-free (800)226-1122. (616)698-6900. E-mail: submis sions@zondervan.com. Website: www.zondervan.com. HarperCollins. Submit to Manuscript Proposal Review Editor. Seeks to meet the needs of people with resources that glorify Jesus Christ and promote biblical principles. Publishes 120 trade titles/yr.; hardcover, trade paperbacks, mass-market paperbacks. Receives 3,000+ submissions annually. 10% of books from first-time authors. Accepts mss through agents. No subsidy or reprints. Royalty 12-14% of net; variable advance. Average first printing 10,000. Publication within 12-18 mos. Considers simultaneous submissions. Requires requested ms by e-mail. Responds in 6-12 wks. Prefers NIV. See guidelines on Website for manuscripts they are currently accepting.

Nonfiction: Outline/1 chapter. "When submitting, proposal should include the book title; a table of contents (2 or 3 sentence description of each chapter); a brief description of the proposed book, including its unique contribution and why you feel it should be published; your intended reader; and your vita, including your qualifications to write the book. The proposal should be no more than 5 pages. If we're interested, we will respond within 6 weeks. E-mail your proposal to the Manuscript Proposal Review Editor."

Fiction: No fiction at this time; refer to Website for updates.

Children's Lines: ZonderKidz and Faithgirlz (not currently accepting new products).

Ethnic Books: Vida Publishers division: Spanish and Portuguese.

Tips: "Absolutely stellar prose that meets demonstrated needs of our market always receives a fair and sympathetic hearing. Great writing, great content always catch our attention." Accepts mss by e-mail only. "See guidelines on Website for types of manuscripts we are now accepting."

****Note:** This publisher serviced by ChristianManuscriptSubmissions.com.

SUBSIDY PUBLISHERS

In this section you will find publishers who do 50 percent or more subsidy publishing. For our purposes, I am defining a subsidy publisher as any publisher that requires the author to pay for any part of the publishing costs. They may call themselves by a variety of names, such as a book packager, a cooperative publisher, a self-publisher, or simply someone who helps authors get their books published. Note that some of these publishers do at least some royalty publishing, so they could be approached as any other royalty publisher. You just need to realize that they are likely to offer you a subsidy deal, so indicate in your cover letter that you are only interested in a royalty arrangement, if that is the case.

As technology makes book publishing more accessible, more subsidy publishers have sprung up, and there has been an increase in confusion over what type of subsidy publishing is legitimate, and what publishers fall in with what we call "vanity publishers." As many of the legitimate publishers (and even some questionable ones) try to distance themselves from the reputation of the vanity publisher, they have come up with a variety of names to try to form definite lines of distinction. Unfortunately, this has only served to confuse the authors who might use their services. It is my hope in offering this separate listing that I can help you understand what this side of publishing entails, what to look for in a subsidy publisher, and what to look out for. To my knowledge the following publishers are legitimate subsidy publishers and are not vanity publishers, but I cannot guarantee that. It is important that as a writer you understand that any time you are asked to send money for any part of the production of your book, you are entering into a nontraditional relationship with a publisher. In this constantly changing field it becomes a matter of buyer beware.

Realize, too, that some of these publishers will publish any book, as long as the author can afford to pay for it. Others are as selective about what they publish as a royalty publisher would be, or they publish only certain types of books. Fortunately I'm seeing more publishers who are being selective; consequently, the professional quality of subsidy books is improving overall. Many will publish only nonfiction—no novels or children's books. These distinctions will be important as you seek the right publisher for your project.

Because there is so much confusion about subsidy publishing, with many authors going into agreements with these publishers having little or no knowledge of what to expect or even what is typical in this situation, many have come away unhappy or disillusioned. For that reason I frequently get complaints from authors who feel they have been cheated or taken advantage of. (Of course, I sometimes get similar complaints about the royalty publishers listed in this book.) Each complaint brings with it an expectation that I should drop that publisher from this book. Although I am sensitive to their complaints, I also have come to the realization that I am not in a position to pass judgment on which publishers should be dropped. It has been my experience in publishing that for every complaint I get on a publisher, I can usually find several other authors who will sing the praises of the same publisher. For that reason, I feel I can serve the needs of authors better by giving them some insight into what to expect from a subsidy publisher and what kinds of terms should send up a red flag.

Because I am not an expert in this field and because of space limitations, I will keep this brief. Let me clarify first that unless you know your book has a limited audience or you have your own method of distribution (such as being a speaker who can sell your own books when you speak), I recommend that you try all the appropriate royalty publishers first. If you are unsuccessful with the royalty publishers but feel strongly about seeing your book published and have the financial resources to do so (or have your own distribution), one of the following publishers may be able to help you.

You can go to a local printer and take your book through all the necessary steps yourself, but a legitimate subsidy publisher has the contacts, know-how, and resources to make the task easier and often less expensive. It is always good to get more than one bid to determine whether the terms and services you are being offered are fair. Note that this listing is beginning to also include printers who offer the necessary services to help you complete the printing process yourself, so you will want to check out those as well.

As with any contract, have someone review it before signing anything. I do such reviews, as do a number of others listed in the Editorial Services section of this book. Be sure that any terms agreed upon are *in writing*. Verbal agreements won't be binding. A legitimate subsidy publisher will be happy to provide you with a list of former clients as references (if they aren't, watch out). Don't just ask for that list; follow through and contact more than one of those references. Get a catalog of their books or a list of books they have published, and find them or ask the publisher to send you a review copy of one or two books they have published. Use those to check the quality of their work, the bindings, etc. See if their books are available through Amazon.com or similar online services. Get answers to all your questions before you commit yourself to anything.

Keep in mind that the more copies of a book that are printed, the lower the cost per copy, but never let a publisher talk you into publishing more (or fewer) copies than you think is reasonable. Also, find out up front, and have included in the contract, whether and how much promotion the publisher is going to do. Some will do as much as a royalty publisher; others do none at all. If they are not doing promotion, and you don't have any means of distribution yourself, it may not be a good idea to pursue subsidy publication. You don't want to end up with a garage full of books you can't sell. Following this section I am including the names and addresses of Christian book distributors. Some of them have indicated that they will handle self-published books. For more help on self-publishing, go to: www.bookmarket.com/index.html.

LISTING OF SUBSIDY PUBLISHERS

Below is a listing of any publishers that do 50 percent or more subsidy publishing (in which the author pays some or all of the production costs). Before entering into dealings with any of these publishers, be sure to read the preceding section on what you need to know.

(+) A plus sign before a listing indicates it is a new listing this year or was not included last year.

ACW PRESS, American Christian Writers, PO Box 110390, Nashville TN 37222. Toll-free (800)21-WRITE. E-mail: Jim@JamesWatkins.com. Website: www.acwpress.com. Reg A. Forder, owner; Jim Watkins, editorial advisor. A self-publishing book packager. Imprint: Write Now Publications (see separate listing). Publishes 40 titles/yr.; hardcover, trade paperbacks, mass-market paperbacks, coffee-table books. Reprints books. **SUBSIDY PUBLISHES 95%;** does print-on-demand. Average first printing 2,500. Publication within 4-6 mos. Responds in 48-72 hrs. Request for estimate form available on Website. Not in topical listings; will consider any nonfiction or fiction topic. Guidelines by e-mail/Website.

Nonfiction/Fiction: All types considered.

Tips: "We offer a high quality publishing alternative to help Christian authors get their material into print. High standards, high quality. If authors have a built-in audience, they have the best chance to make self-publishing a success." Has a marketing program available to authors.

****Note:** This publisher serviced by The Writer's Edge and ChristianManuscriptSubmissions .com.

ALFRED ALI LITERARY WORKS INC., PO Box 582, Southfield MI 48076. (248)356-5111. Fax (248)356-1367. E-mail: AALiterary@aol.com. Website: www.AlfredAli.com. San Serif, ed. Spreading the word on how the Word of God can change and improve lives. Publishes 1 title/yr. Receives 5 submissions annually. 80% of books from first-time authors. Accepts mss through agents. Reprints books. **SUBSIDY PUBLISHES 70%.** Prefers 210 pgs. Royalty 25%

of retail; no advance. Average first printing 1,000-5,000. Publication within 9 mos. Accepts e-mail submissions. No guidelines; catalog $3.

Nonfiction: Query only; fax query OK.

Ethnic Books: Publishes for the African American market.

Photos/Artwork: Accepts freelance photos for book covers.

Tips: "Most open to books that are based on inspiration that leads to self-awareness."

AMERICAN BINDING & PUBLISHING CO., PO Box 60049, Corpus Christi TX 78466-0049. Toll-free (800)863-3708. (361)658-4221. E-mail: rmagner@grandecom.net, or info@americanbindingpublishing.com. Website: www.americanbindingpublishing.com. Rose Magner, pub. Publishes 60 titles/yr. Receives 200 submissions annually. 95% of books from first-time authors. No mss through agents. Reprints books. **SUBSIDY PUBLISHES 100%;** does print-on-demand. Prefers 200 pgs. Royalty 15% on retail; no advance. Publication within 2 wks. Considers simultaneous submissions. Requires requested ms on disk (Microsoft Word format). Responds in 2 wks. Any Bible version. Guidelines (also by e-mail); free catalog. Not included in topical listings.

Nonfiction: Complete ms; phone/e-query OK. Will consider any topic.

Fiction: Complete ms; phone/e-query OK. For all ages; all genres.

Ethnic Books: Black and Hispanic.

Photos/Artwork: Accepts freelance photos for book covers.

Tips: "We are print-on-demand; authors are responsible for their own marketing. We will consider any topic—nonfiction or fiction, but most open to fiction."

AMPELOS PRESS, 316 Blanchard Rd., Drexel Hill PA 19026. Phone/fax (610)626-6833. E-mail: mbagnull@aol.com. Website: www.writehisanswer.com. Marlene Bagnull, LittD, pub./ed. Services (depending on what is needed) include critiquing, editing, proofreading, typesetting, and cover design. Publishes 1-3 titles/yr. **SUBSIDY PUBLISHES 100%.** Query only. Not included in topical listings (see Tips).

Tips: "Our vision statement reads: 'Strongly, unashamedly, uncompromisingly Christ-centered. Exalting the name of Jesus Christ. Seeking to teach His ways through holding up the Word of God as the Standard.' (*Ampelos* is the Greek word for 'vine' in John 15:5.)"

BETHANY PRESS—CUSTOM SOLUTIONS, 6820 W. 115th St., Bloomington MN 55438. Toll-free (800)341-4192. (952)914-7400. Fax (952)914-7410. E-mail: customsolutions@bethanypress.com. Website: www.bethanypress.com. Janet Weaver Smith, marketing specialist/publishing coordinator (JWeaverSmith@Bethanypress.com). Exclusive-to-Christian-authors **SELF-PUBLISHING SERVICE** whose company profits go entirely to a Christian missionary-sending agency, Bethany International. Details on Website. Not included in topical listings. No questionnaire returned.

+BLACK FOREST PRESS/TENNESSEE PUBLISHING HOUSE, Belle Arden Run Estate, 488 Mountain View Dr., Mosheim TN 37818-3524. Phone/fax (423)422-4711(call ahead for fax). E-mail: dahkknox@embarqmail.com. Pentecostal Holiness. Dr. Dahk Knox, pub.; Dr. Jan Knox, CFO. Provides truthful information about an author's book; whether you publish with them or not, you get free help and advice. Imprints: Tennessee Publishing House, World Truth Publishing House. Publishes up to 25 titles/yr.; hardcover, trade paperbacks, mass-market paperbacks, coffee-table books. Receives 25 submissions annually. 50% of books from first-time authors. No mss through agents. **SUBSIDY PUBLISHES 50%;** does print-on-demand. Reprints books (with permission). Prefers up to 400 pgs. Royalty on net or retail (100% of sales, minus $1/bk., unless other arrangements made); no advance. Average first printing 1,000-2,000, or 100-500 POD. Publication within 6 wks. Considers simultaneous submissions. Requires accepted ms on disk. Responds in 2-3 days. Prefers NIV/NKJV. Guidelines by e-mail; free catalog.

Nonfiction: Query or complete ms; phone/fax query OK; e-query preferred.

Fiction: Complete ms. For all ages.

Photos/Artwork: Accepts freelance photos for book covers.

Tips: "Most open to a book that has something special to say, not the same old story told over and over with another suit of clothes on! Get something exciting, that moves and has considerable events taking place that keep a reader's interest. Be realistic, and don't expect a book about your life to be a bestseller—it just isn't going to happen. We are truthful and to the point."

BOOKLOCKER.COM INC., PO Box 2399, Bangor ME 04402-2399. (207)262-9696. Fax (207) 262-5544. E-mail: angela@booklocker.com. Website: www.booklocker.com. Angela Hoy, pub. We seek unique, eclectic, and different manuscripts. Publishes 40-50 titles/yr.; hard cover, trade paperbacks. 90% of books from first-time authors. No mss through agents. **SUBSIDY PUBLISHES 100%;** does print-on-demand. Reprints books. Prefers 48-740 pgs. Royalty 35% on retail (15% on wholesale orders; 35% on booklocker.com orders); no advance. Publication within 4-6 wks. Considers simultaneous submissions. Responds in less than a week. Bible version is author's choice. Guidelines on Website; no catalog

Nonfiction: Complete ms; e-query OK. "We're open to all ideas."

Fiction: Complete ms; e-query OK. All genres for all ages.

Ethnic Books: Publishes for all ethnic groups.

Photos/Artwork: Accepts freelance photos for book covers; open to queries from freelance artists.

Contest: The WritersWeekly.com 24-Hour Short Story Contest is held quarterly.

BOOKLOCKER JR, PO Box 2399, Bangor ME 04402-2399. Fax (207)262-5544. E-mail from Website: www.booklocker.com/getpublished/published.html. E-books or print-on-demand. Seeking submissions from young authors, under 18 years. Royalty varies according to product/price. Prices, terms, guidelines, and contract on Website.

BOOK PUBLISHERS NETWORK, PO Box 2256, Bothell WA 98041. (425)483-3040. Fax (425) 483-3098. E-mail: sherynhara@bookpublishersnetwork.com. Website: www.bookpublishers network.com. Sheryn Hara, ed. Publishes 5-8 titles/yr.; hardcover, trade paperbacks. Receives 20 submissions annually. 100% of books from first-time authors. Accepts mss through agents. **100% SUBSIDY.** Reprints books. No preference on length. No royalty/advance. Publication within 3 mos. Considers simultaneous submissions. Responds in 1 mo. Guidelines on Website; no catalog.

Nonfiction: Proposal or complete ms; phone/fax/e-query OK.

Fiction: Proposal or complete ms; phone/fax/e-query OK. For all ages.

Photos/Artwork: Accepts freelance photos for book covers.

BRENTWOOD CHRISTIAN PRESS, 4000 Beallwood Ave., Columbus GA 31904. Toll-free (800) 334-2828. (706)576-5787. Fax (706)317-5808. E-mail: Brentwood@aol.com. Website: www.BrentwoodBooks.com. Mainline. U. D. Roberts, exec. ed. Publishes 267 titles/yr. Receives 2,000 submissions annually. Reprints books. **SUBSIDY PUBLISHES 95%.** Offers InstaBooks and Just in Time publishing (print-on-demand). Average first printing 500. Publication within 1 mo. Considers simultaneous submissions. Responds in 2 days. Guidelines.

Nonfiction: Complete ms. "Collection of sermons on family topics, poetry, relation of Bible to current day."

Fiction: Complete ms. "Stories that show how faith helps overcome small, day-to-day problems."

Photos/Artwork: Accepts freelance photos for book covers.

Tips: "Keep it short; support facts with reference." This publisher specializes in small print runs of 300-1,000. Can best serve the writer who has a completed manuscript.

BROWN BOOKS PUBLISHING GROUP, 16200 N. Dallas Pkwy., Ste. 170, Dallas TX 75248. (972)381-0009. Fax (972)248-4336. E-mail: natalie@brownbooks.com. Website:

www.brownbooks.com. Milli A. Brown, pub.; submit to Kathryn Grant, sr. ed. (Kgrant@brownbooks.com). Publishes books in the areas of self-help, religion/inspirational, relationships, business, mind/body/spirit, and women's issues; we build relationships with our authors. Imprints: Personal Profiles, P3, Brown Books (trade imprint), Hispanic, Fine Books. Publishes 10-150 titles/yr.; hardcover, trade paperbacks, mass-market paperbacks, coffee-table books. Receives 1,200 submissions annually. 80% of books from first-time authors. Accepts mss through agents. **SUBSIDY PUBLISHES 100%** through Personal Profiles & P3 imprints. Accepts reprints. Royalty 100% of retail; no advance. Authors retain rights to their work. Average first printing 3,000. Publication in 2-3 mos. Accepts simultaneous submissions. Accepts mss on disk or by e-mail. Responds in 1 wk. Guidelines on Website.

Nonfiction: Complete ms; phone/fax/e-query OK.

Fiction: Complete ms; phone/fax/e-query OK. For all ages.

Photos/Artwork: Accepts freelance photos for book covers; open to queries from freelance artists.

+**CHRISTIAN SERVICES NETWORK,** 833 Broadway, Ste. 201, El Cajon CA 92021. Toll-free (866)484-6184. Website: www.csnbooks.com. Michael Wourms, ed. **SELF-PUBLISHING COMPANY**. Details on Website.

CREATION HOUSE, 600 Rinehart Rd., Lake Mary FL 32746-4872. (407)333-0600. Fax (407) 333-7100. E-mail: allen.quain@strang.com. Website: www.strang.com. Strang Communications Co. Allen Quain, mngr. To inspire and equip people to live a Spirit-led life and to walk in the divine purpose for which they were created. Imprints: Charisma House, Siloam Press, CharismaKids. Publishes 50-100 titles/yr. Receives 500 submissions annually. 80% of books from first-time authors. Accepts mss through agents. **CO-PUBLISHES 100%;** no print-on-demand. Reprints books. Prefers 25,000+ wds. or 100-200 pgs. Royalty 12-18% of net; no advance. Average first printing 6,000. Publication within 5 mos. Considers simultaneous submissions. Responds in 6-12 wks. Open to submissions on disk or by e-mail. Guidelines (also by e-mail/Website); free catalog.

Nonfiction: Proposal or complete ms; phone/fax/e-query OK. "Open to any books that are well written and glorify Jesus Christ."

Fiction: Proposal or complete ms; phone/fax/e-query OK. For all ages. "Fiction must have a biblical world-view and point the reader to Christ."

Photos/Artwork: Accepts freelance photos for book covers.

Tips: "We use the term 'co-publishing' to describe a hybrid between conventional royalty publishing and self or subsidy publishing, utilizing the best of both worlds. We produce a high quality book for our own inventory, market it, distribute it, and pay the author a royalty on every copy sold. In return, the author agrees to buy, at a deep discount, a portion of the first print run."

+**CROSSHOUSE,** PO Box 461592, Garland TX 75046. Toll-free (877)212-0933. Toll-free fax (888)252-3022. E-mail: crosshousepublishing@earthlink.net. Website: www.crosshousepublishing.org. Self-publishing branch of KLMK Communications. Katie Moore, pub. To achieve excellence in Christian self-publishing without sacrificing personal interest and care for customers. **SUBSIDY PUBLISHER.** Guidelines/price list on Website.

Tips: "We provide authors the opportunity to have their books distributed through a wide array of Christian and general bookstores. We aspire to offer the marketplace superior Christian literature that will impact reader's lives."

DCTS PUBLISHING, PO Box 40216, Santa Barbara CA 93140. Toll-free (800)965-8150. Fax (805)653-6522. E-mail: dennis@dctspub.com. Website: www.dctspub.com. Dennis Stephen Hamilton, ed. Books are designed to enrich the mind, encourage the heart, and empower the spirit. Publishes 5 titles/yr. Receives 25 submissions annually. 35% of books from first-time authors. No mss through agents. **SUBSIDY PUBLISHES 70%.** No reprints. Prefers 100-300 pgs. Royalty 17% of retail; no advance. Average first printing 3,500. Publication within 6-8 mos. No simultaneous submissions. Prefers KJV. Guidelines; free catalog & brochure.

Nonfiction: Query or proposal/2-3 chapters; e-query OK.

ROBBIE DEAN PRESS, 2910 E. Eisenhower Parkway, Ann Arbor MI 48108. (734)973-9511. Fax (734)973-9475. E-mail: Fairyha@aol.com. Website: www.RobbieDeanPress.com. Interested in works that are multiculturally appealing and that approach a topic in a unique manner. Dr. Fairy C. Hayes-Scott, owner. Publishes 1 title/yr. Receives 20 submissions annually. 100% of books from first-time authors. Accepts mss through agents. **SUBSIDY PUBLISHES 75%;** does print-on-demand. Reprints books. Length flexible. Royalty 10-20%; no advance. Average first printing 250. Publication within 6 mos. Considers simultaneous submissions. Responds in 2-6 wks. Guidelines by e-mail; free catalog.

Nonfiction: Query first. "We're open to new ideas."

Fiction: "We seldom do fiction." For children only.

Ethnic Books: Multicultural.

Also Does: Booklets; e-books; computer games.

Photos/Artwork: Accepts freelance photos for book covers.

Tips: "Most open to self-help, reference, senior adult topics, and parenting."

EKKLESIA PRESS, 6709 Francis St., Lincoln NE 68505. (402)465-5108. E-mail: tprice@kindgomcitizenship.org, or through Website: www.ekklesiapress.us. Timothy L. Price, ed. A ministry to help authors publish works not considered profitable by mainstream publishers; works that will impact and motivate followers of Christ to fulfill the Great Commission. Imprints: Trestle Press, Tamarin Press (kid's books). Publishes 10-12 titles/yr.; hardcover, trade paperbacks, audio books. Receives 10-12 submissions annually. 90% of books from first-time authors. No mss through agents. **SUBSIDY PUBLISHES 20%;** does print-on-demand. Reprints books. Prefers 40,000-75,000 wds., or 150-475 pgs.; will also do 51-149 pgs. Royalty 25-35% on retail; no advance. Average first printing 400; only 100 required. Publication within 6-8 mos. Accepts simultaneous submissions. Requires accepted mss on CD. Responds in 10-12 business days. Prefers NASB or any nonparaphrase. Guidelines (also by e-mail/Website); no catalog.

Nonfiction: Complete ms with submission coversheet (PDF downloadable on Website); phone/e-query OK. "Manuscript submissions must be in Microsoft Word document form, double-spaced, and justified."

Fiction: Complete ms with submission coversheet (PDF downloadable on Website); phone/e-query OK. For teens & adults. "Manuscript submissions must be in Microsoft Word document form, double-spaced, and justified."

Special Needs: "Anything that would help differentiate the Kingdom of God from just going to church; house church stuff; the church as an alternative to society."

Also Does: Pamphlets up to 50 pgs.

Photos/Artwork: Open to queries from freelance artists.

Tips: "Mainly I would like to have mss on the following: church-state relations; the church as ambassadors rather than activists/lobbyists; early church history; the church being an alternative society to the world; the high cost of following Christ; fellowshipping in the sufferings of Christ; and practical works on house church. I will look at other works as well." Does custom cover designs; designs Website to help promote author's book. Book distribution handled through Ingram Books.

ELDERBERRY PRESS INC., 1393 Old Homestead Rd., 2nd Fl., Oakland OR 97462. (541)459-6043. Fax (270)458-6043. E-mail: editor@elderberrypress.com. Website: www.elderberrypress.com. David W. St. John, exec. ed. Publishes 15 titles/yr. Receives 150-250 submissions annually. 90% of books from first-time authors. No mss through agents. **SUBSIDY PUBLISHES 50%;** does print-on-demand. Royalty 10-25%; no advance. Publication within 3 mos. Considers simultaneous submissions. Accepts disk or e-mail submissions. Responds in 1 mo. Guidelines on Website; free catalog.

Nonfiction: Complete ms; phone/fax/e-query OK. "We consider all topics."

Fiction: Complete ms; phone/fax/e-query OK. All genres for all ages.

ESSENCE PUBLISHING CO. INC., 20 Hanna Ct., Belleville ON K8P 5J2, Canada. (613)962-0234. Toll-free (800)238-6376. Fax (613)962-4711. E-mail: publishing@essencegroup.com. Website: www.essence-publishing.com. Essence Communications Group. Sherrill Brunton, acqs. mgr. Provides affordable, short-run book publishing to the Christian community. Publishes 100-150+ titles/yr. Receives 250+ submissions annually. 75% of books from first-time authors. **SUBSIDY PUBLISHES 90%.** Reprints books. Any length. Average first printing 500-1,000. Publication within 3-5 mos. Considers simultaneous submissions. Responds in 3-4 wks. Prefers requested ms on disk. Guidelines (also by e-mail/Website); catalog online (www.essencebookstore.com).

Nonfiction: Complete ms; phone/fax/e-query OK. Accepts all topics.

Fiction: Complete ms. All genres for all ages. Also picture books.

Also Does: Pamphlets, booklets, tracts.

Photos/Artwork: Accepts freelance photos for book covers.

FAIRWAY PRESS, subsidy division for CSS Publishing Company, 517 S. Main St., Box 4503, Lima OH 45802-4503. Toll-free (800)241-4056. (419)227-1818. Fax (419)228-9184. E-mail: editor@csspub.com. Website: www.fairwaypress.com. David Runk, ed. (david@csspub.com). Imprint: Express Press. Publishes 100 titles/yr. Receives 200-300 submissions annually. 80% of books from first-time authors. Reprints books. **SUBSIDY PUBLISHES 100%.** Royalty to 50%; no advance. Average first printing 500-1,000. Publication within 6-9 mos. Considers simultaneous submissions. Responds in up to 1 mo. Prefers requested ms on disk; no e-mail submissions. Prefers NRSV. Free guidelines (also on Website)/catalog for 9x12 SAE.

Nonfiction: Complete ms; phone/fax/e-query OK. All types. "Looking for manuscripts with a Christian theme, and seasonal material."

Fiction: Complete ms. For adults, teens, or children; all types. No longer producing anything in full color or with four-color illustrations.

FRUITBEARER PUBLISHING, PO Box 777, Georgetown DE 19947. (302)856-6649. Fax (302)856-7742. E-mail: candy.abbott@verizon.net. Website: www.fruitbearer.com. Branch of Candy's Creations. Candy Abbott, pres. Offers editing services and advice for self-publishers. Publishes 5-10 titles/yr. Receives 10-20 submissions annually. 90% of books from first-time authors. **SUBSIDY PUBLISHES 100%.** No reprints. Average first printing 30-5,000. Publication within 1-6 mos. Responds in 3 mos. Brochure for #10 SAE/1 stamp.

Nonfiction: Proposal/2 chapters; phone/fax/e-query OK.

Also Does: Pamphlets, booklets, tracts.

Photos/Artwork: Accepts freelance photos for book covers.

Tips: "Accepting limited submissions."

GESHER—See Winer Foundation.

HANNIBAL BOOKS, PO Box 461592, Garland TX 75046-1592. Toll-free (800)747-0738. Toll-free fax (888)252-3022. E-mail: hannibalbooks@earthlink.net. Website: www.hannibalbooks.com. KLMK Communications Inc. Louis Moore, pub. Evangelical Christian publisher specializing in missions, marriage and family, critical issues, and Bible-study curriculum. Publishes 8-10 titles/yr.; trade paperbacks, mass-market paperbacks. Receives 300 submissions annually. 80% of books from first-time authors. Accepts mss through agents. **SUBSIDY PUBLISHES 80%.** Some print-on-demand. Reprints books. Prefers 50,000-60,000 wds. Royalty on net or outright purchase; no advance. Average first printing 2,000-10,000. Publication within 3 mos. No simultaneous submissions. Responds in 3 mos. Prefers NIV. Guidelines; free catalog.

Nonfiction: Book Proposal/1-3 chapters; no phone/fax/e-query. "Looking for missionary, marriage restoration, homeschooling, and devotionals."

Fiction: Book Proposal/1-3 chapters; no phone/fax/e-query.

Tips: "We are looking for go-get-'em new authors with a passion to be published. Most open to missionary life and Bible studies. Obtain our guidelines and answer each question thoroughly."

HOLY FIRE PUBLISHING, 1525 Old Trolley Rd., #116, Summerville SC 29485-8928. (843)628-0319. E-mail: publisher@christianpublish.com. Website: www.christianpublish.com. Venessa Hensel, VP. A ministry helping the Christian author reach the world through the printed word. Publishes 100 titles/yr.; hardcover, trade paperbacks. Receives 2,000+ submissions annually. 50% of books from first-time authors. Accepts mss through agents. **ONLY DOES PRINT-ON-DEMAND.** Reprints books. Prefers 48-750 pgs. Royalty 50-100% on net; no advance. Publication within 2 mos. Prefers submissions on disk or by e-mail. Guidelines on Website; no catalog.

Nonfiction: Proposal/1 chapter; phone/fax/e-query OK. "Looking for Christian Living or Christian poetry."

Fiction: Proposal/1 chapter; phone/fax/e-query OK. For all ages.

Photos/Artwork: Open to queries from freelance artists.

+IMD PRESS, 7150 Hooker St., Ste. A, Westminster CO 80030. (303)482-1426. Fax (303)232-5009. E-mail: PaulV@IMDPress.com. Website: www.IMDPress.com. IMD International. Paul Varghese, exec. dir. A nonprofit printing ministry that uses the resources gained from printing to train pastors and plant churches around the world. Publishes 5-10 titles/yr.; hardcover, trade paperbacks, mass-market paperbacks, coffee-table books. Receives 5-10 submissions annually. 50% of books from first-time authors. Accepts mss through agents. **100% SUBSIDY**; no print-on-demand. Reprints books (with permission). Any length. Royalty or outright purchase; no advance. Average first printing 1,000. Publication within 2 mos. Considers simultaneous submissions. Responds within 1 mo. Prefers NIV. Guidelines; no catalog.

Nonfiction: Complete ms; requires e-mail submission.

Fiction: Complete ms. For all ages.

Ethnic Books: Indian, African.

Photos/Artwork: Accepts freelance photos for book covers; open to queries from freelance artists.

Tips: "We do not buy mss or retain your rights. Submit only completed mss. We do not edit." Also prints periodicals.

IMPACT CHRISTIAN BOOKS INC., 332 Leffingwell Ave., Ste. 101, Kirkwood MO 63122. (314)822-3309. Fax (314)822-3325. E-mail: info@impactchristianbooks.com. Website: www.impactchristianbooks.com. William D. Banks, pres. Books of healing, miraculous deliverance, and spiritual warfare, drawing individuals into a deeper walk with God. Publishes 20+ titles/yr. Receives 20-50 submissions annually. 50-70% of books from first-time authors. No mss through agents. **SUBSIDY PUBLISHES 50-70%.** Reprints books. Average first printing 5,000. Publication within 2 mos. Considers simultaneous submissions. Responds by prior arrangement in 30 days. Requires requested ms on disk. Guidelines; catalog for 9x12 SAE/5 stamps. Not in topical listings.

Nonfiction: Query only; phone/fax query OK. Outstanding personal testimonies and Christ-centered books.

INFINITY PUBLISHING, 1094 New Dehaven St., Ste. 100, West Conshohocken PA 19428-2713. Toll-free (877)BUY-BOOK. (610)941-9999. Fax (610)941-9959. E-mail: info@infinitypublishing.com. Website: www.infinitypublishing.com. **100% PRINT-ON-DEMAND.** Charges $400 up-front fee. First order of books is at 50% discount; additional orders 40% discount. Royalty 10%.

INSIGHT PUBLISHING GROUP, 8810 S. Yale, Ste. 410, Tulsa OK 74137. (918)493-1718. Fax (918)493-2219. E-mail: mail@freshword.com. Website: www.freshword.com. Christian Publisher. John Mason, ed. Owned by a best-selling author who established the company to serve authors. Publishes 50 titles/yr. Receives 50 submissions annually. 50% of books from first-time authors. Accepts mss through agents. **100% PRINT-ON-DEMAND.** Reprints books. Prefers 160 pgs. Royalty 15-17% on net; no advance. Average first printing 5,000. Publication within 6 mos. Considers simultaneous submissions. Requires disk or e-mail submission. Responds in 2 mos. Guidelines by e-mail/Website; no catalog. Will consider most fiction and nonfiction topics.

Nonfiction: Complete ms; phone/fax/e-query OK.

Fiction: Complete ms; phone/fax/e-query OK. Nondenominational Christian. For all ages.

Also Does: Booklets.

Tips: "We help people self-publish. To those authors we can offer a variety of services including distribution and small print runs. Most open to books that are unique, authentic, and relevant."

+J AND J PUBLISHING COMPANY, PO Box 291205, Columbia SC 29229. (803)968-5196. Fax (803)234-4071. E-mail: jjpublisher@yahoo.com. Website: www.jandjpublishingonline.com. Stephanie McKenny, ed. A self-publishing company that will assist the author throughout the lifetime of the book. Publishes 5 titles/yr.; trade paperbacks. 90% of books from first-time authors. No mss through agents. **100% SELF-PUBLISHING.** No reprints. Prefers 40 pgs. and up. Royalty 55-70%; no advance. Publication within 3-6 mos. Considers simultaneous submissions. Responds in 3-6 wks. Prefers KJV or AB. Guidelines by mail/e-mail; no catalog.

Nonfiction: Proposal/5 chapters.

Fiction: Proposal/5 chapters. For all ages. "No erotica or explicit language."

Special Needs: Christian novels, inspirational, women's issues, relationships, self-help.

Photos: Accepts freelance photos for book covers.

KINDRED BOOKS, 1310 Taylor Ave., Winnipeg MB R3M 3Z6, Canada. Toll-free (800)545-7322. (204)654-5765. Fax (204)654-1865. E-mail: kindred@mbconf.ca. Website: www.kindred productions.com. Mennonite Brethren/Imprint of Kindred Productions. Submit to: Attn. Manager. Publisher for the Mennonite Brethren Church in North America. Publishes 3-4 titles/yr.; hardcover, trade paperbacks. Receives 20 submissions annually. 95% of books from first-time authors. No mss through agents. **SUBSIDY PUBLISHES 100%;** does print-on-demand. Reprints books. Prefers 60,000 wds. or 200 pgs. Average first printing 1,000-2,000. Publication within 18 mos. Considers simultaneous submissions. Responds in 4 mos. Accepts requested ms by e-mail. Prefers NIV. Guidelines (by e-mail/Website); free catalog.

Nonfiction: Proposal/2-3 chapters; no phone query, fax/e-query OK. "Looking for Christian living and inspirational books."

Fiction: Proposal/2-3 chapters. For children & teens.

Tips: "Most open to Christian living or inspirational books that help everyday people grow in their relationship with Jesus. Books that help meet basic church needs. Material submitted should be in line with the Christian/evangelical faith."

LEADING LADY PUBLICATIONS, PO Box 35, Worton MD 21678. Toll-free (800)597-9428. E-mail: leadingladyenterprises@yahoo.com. Website: www.leadingladypublications.com. Anointed Word Media Group. Tamika Johnson, CEO & pub. Committed to publishing and promoting Christian works that equip, educate, and empower women to overcome their struggles in life and step into their destiny. **SUBSIDY PUBLISHER.** Details of their publishing program on their Website.

Nonfiction: Query first.

Fiction: Query first.

+LIFEVEST PUBLISHING INC., 4901 E. Dry Creek Rd., #170, Centennial CO 80122. Toll-free (877)843-1007. Website: www.lifevestpublishing.com. Ric Simmons, CEO. Specializes in children's books, educational literature, inspirational works, family/personal histories, and poetry. **100% SUBSIDY.** Submission form on Website.

LIGHTNING STAR PRESS, PO Box 730393, San Jose CA 95173. (408)270-0572. Fax (425)645-0423. E-mail: jessie@lightningstarpress.com, or info@lightningstarpress.com. Website: www.lightningstarpress.com. Submit to The Editor. Publishes 2-4 titles/yr. Receives 50 submissions annually. 99% of books from first-time authors. Accepts mss through agents. **99% SUBSIDY;** does print-on-demand. Reprints books. Prefers 32+ pgs. No royalty or advance. Average first printing 100+. Publication within 6 mos. Considers simultaneous submissions. Responds in 1-2 wks. Accepts e-mail submissions. Guidelines on Website; no catalog.

Nonfiction: Complete ms or proposal/2 chapters; phone/fax/e-query OK.

Fiction: Complete ms or proposal/3 chapters; phone/fax/e-query OK. For all ages.

Photos/Artwork: Accepts freelance photos for book covers.

MARKETING NEW AUTHORS.COM, 2910 E. Eisenhower Pkwy., Ann Arbor MI 48108. Toll-free (800)431-1579. (734)975-0028. Fax (734)973-9475. E-mail: info@marketingnewauthors.com, or MarketingNewAuth@aol.com. Website: www.MarketingNewAuthors.com. Imprint of Robbie Dean Press. To primarily serve authors who wish to self-publish. Dr. Fairy C. Hayes-Scott, owner. 100% of books from first-time authors. Accepts mss through agents. **SUBSIDY PUBLISHES 100%.** Reprints books. Length flexible. Publication within 6 mos. Considers simultaneous submissions. Responds in 2-6 wks. Guidelines by e-mail/Website. Offers 7 different marketing plans; see Website.

MCDOUGAL PUBLISHING, PO Box 3595, Hagerstown MD 21742. (301)797-6637. Fax (301) 733-2767. E-mail: publishing@mcdougal.org. Website: www.mcdougalpublishing.com. Pentecostal/Charismatic, nondenominational. Diane McDougal, pres.; Janet Durbin, mng. ed. Publishes books for the body of Christ. Imprints: McDougal Publishing, Fairmont Books, Parable Publishing, and Serenity Books. Publishes 15-20 titles/yr. Receives 150 submissions annually. 70% of books from first-time authors. Accepts mss through agents. **SUBSIDY PUBLISHES 20%.** Reprints books. Prefers 80-192 pgs. Royalty 10-15% of net; no advance. Requires all authors to buy 3,000 copies of their book. Average first printing 3,000-5,000. Publication within 6 mos. Considers simultaneous submissions. Responds in 2 mos. Guidelines (also on Website); free catalog.

Nonfiction: Proposal/1-2 chapters (preferred); phone/fax/e-query OK. "Looking for titles on all topics relevant to the Christian life."

Fiction: Complete ms. "Now considering adult fiction from authors with an established market; no romance."

Tips: "Know who your audience is, and write to that audience. Also, keep focused on one central theme."

+MEN OF STANDARD PUBLICATIONS, PO Box 35, Worton MD 21678. Toll-free (800)597-9428. E-mail: manuscripts@publishyourchristianbook.com. Website: www.publishyourchristianbook.com. Anointed Word Media Group. Tamika Johnson, CEO & pub. Committed to publishing and promoting works by Christian men. **SUBSIDY PUBLISHER.** Details of their publishing program on their Website. No questionnaire returned.

Nonfiction: Query first.

Fiction: Query first.

MILESTONES INTERNATIONAL PUBLISHERS, 140 Danika Dr. N.W., Huntsville AL 35806-2274. (256)830-0362. Fax (256)830-9206. E-mail: jimrill@milestoneintl.com, or milestoneintl@bellsouth.net. Website: www.milestonesintl.com. Jim Rill, pres. Bringing significance to life's journey. Author is asked to buy 3,000 books at $6/ea.

NEXT GENERATION PUBLISHING, 207 Paces Ct., Gainesville GA 30504. (687)897-8872. E-mail: ngpinfo@yahoo.com. Website: www.nextgenerationpublishers.com. Thresia D. Phillips, ed. **SUBSIDY PUBLISHER.** Open to religious submissions.

ONE WORLD PRESS, 1042 Willow Creek Rd., Prescott AZ 86301. Toll-free (800)250-8171. (928)445-2081. Fax (928)717-1779. E-mail: dasya@oneworldpress.com. Website: www.oneworldpress.com. Joe Zuccarello, operations mngr. Publishes many titles/yr. Receives 25-50 submissions annually. 50% of books from first-time authors. Accepts mss through agents. **SUBSIDY PUBLISHES 100%;** does print-on-demand. Reprints books. Average first printing up to author. Publication within 2 mos. Considers simultaneous submissions. Responds in 2-4 wks. No guidelines or catalog.

Nonfiction: Complete manuscript. All ages. "We publish about anything within decency and reason."

Also Does: Booklets, e-books, pamphlets, tracts.

+PATH PUBLISHING INC., 4302 W. 51st, #121, Amarillo TX 79109-6159. Phone/fax (806)322-7007 (call first for fax). E-mail: path2@pathpublishing.com. Website: www.pathpublishing.com. John Schmidt, ed. This imprint focuses on self-help and children's books. Has published 15 titles to date. Receives 40 submissions annually. 100% of books from first-time authors. Accepts mss through agents. Would reprint books. Prefers 80-120 pgs. **SUBSIDY PUBLISHES 80%.** Considers simultaneous submissions. Responds in days. Guidelines (also by e-mail/Website); flyer for #10 SASE, no catalog.

Nonfiction: Query letter only first; e-query preferred.

Also Does: Expanding into e-books, Christian music sales, Website design, and more.

Photos/Artwork: Open to queries from freelance artists.

Contest: Periodically sponsors contests.

Tips: "We also do lots of poetry books. Check our Website for 'Tips for Writers' and more."

PATH PUBLISHING IN CHRIST, 4302 W. 51st, #121, Amarillo TX 79109-6159. Phone/fax (806)322-7007. E-mail: path2@pathpublishing.com. Website: www.pathpublishing.com. Path Publishing Inc. John Schmidt, ed./pub. As a teaching ministry, we can take a reasonably rough manuscript and turn it into a finished book. Path Publishing, parent company, specializes in self-help, poetry, and general Christian nonfiction. Publishing 4-5 titles (trade paperback) & 2-3 e-books/yr. Receives 40 submissions annually. 100% of books from first-time authors. Accepts mss through agents. Would reprint books. **50% SUBSIDY**; could do print-on-demand. Prefers 100 pgs. (80-120 pgs.). Royalty 8-12% on net; no advance. Average first printing 500. Considers simultaneous submissions. Prefers accepted submissions on disk or by e-mail. Responds in 1 wk. Guidelines (also by e-mail/Website); flier for #10 SASE; no catalog.

Nonfiction: Query letter ONLY first; e-query preferred.

Special Needs: Looking for self-help books: original point of view, insightful, and aware of future trends; also devotionals.

Also Does: Christian music, CDs, chapbooks (72 pgs.), and CD-ROM books.

Photos/Artwork: Open to queries from freelance artists.

Contest: Periodically sponsors contests.

Tips: "Most open to a book people want. Do some market research first—not last or never! Authors who pay for editing and printing can get back 80% of sales. We are not a vanity publisher but are a great opportunity for some authors."

PLEASANT WORD, 1730 Railroad St., PO Box 428, Enumclaw WA 98022. Toll-free (800)326-4674. (360)802-9758. Fax (360)802-9992. E-mail: tammy@winepressgroup.com. Website: www.pleasantword.com. WinePress Publishing. Tammy Hopf, acq. ed. In an industry where print-on-demand publishers will print almost anything, Pleasant Word has high standards for both design and content of POD books. Publishes 300 titles/yr.; hardcover, trade paperbacks, coffee-table books. Receives 700+ submissions annually. 70% of books from first-time authors. Accepts mss through agents. **100% SUBSIDY;** print-on-demand division. Reprints books. Any length, 48-740 pgs.; 10,000-150,000 wds.; color picture books in soft cover only, 12-480 pgs. Royalty on net; no advance. Cost to print the book and fill the order is deducted from the payment by the customer, and the balance is paid to the author as a royalty. Substantial discounts to author regardless of quantity purchased. Average first printing 150. Publication within 3-4 mos.; longer with editing. Considers simultaneous submissions. Responds online. Accepted mss by e-mail or on disk. Guidelines (also by e-mail) & free catalog.

Nonfiction: Complete ms submitted online through Website; e-query OK. "We accept all topics except books that promote the prosperity doctrine, 'Toronto Blessing,' or women in leadership over men."

Fiction: Complete ms submitted online through Website; e-query OK. Fiction for all ages.

Ethnic Books: Black & Hispanic.

Also Does: Full-color children's books and full-color coffee-table books available on demand (soft-cover only).

Photos/Artwork: Accepts freelance photos for book covers.

Tips: "As the leader in quality print-on-demand publishing, we offer professional book packaging for Christian writers. We not only offer a full line of editorial, design, layout, and printing services, but full service order fulfillment and distribution as well. Our publicity department offers cutting edge and effective marketing, media contact, and promotional services. Our print-on-demand titles are fully returnable and have reasonable suggested retail prices. Our in-house team of professionals is committed to serving our authors with excellent customer service and honest advice. We don't purchase rights to books and choose not to partner with messages that promote name-it-claim-it or prosperity doctrines; sexually explicit material; anything that offends or denounces the deity of Jesus; or material that confuses gender roles."

****Note:** This publisher serviced by The Writer's Edge and ChristianManuscriptSubmissions .com.

POEMS BY ME, 4000 Beallwood Ave., Columbus GA 31904. Toll-free (800)334-2828. E-mail: Brentwood@aol.com. Website: www.PoemsByMe.com. Brentwood Christian Press. Joyce Warren, ed. Poetry that is spiritual, personal, emotional. Receives 80 submissions annually. 75% of books from first-time authors. Accepts mss through agents. **100% SUBSIDY;** does print-on-demand. Reprints books. Need at least 40 poems for a book. Same-week response.

POET'S COVE PRESS, 4000 Beallwood Ave., Columbus GA 31904. Toll-free (800)334-2828. (706) 576-5787. E-mail: Brentwood@aol.com. Website: www.BrentwoodBooks.com. Subsidiary of Brentwood Publishers Group. U. D. Roberts, exec. dir. Publishes 75 titles/yr. **SUBSIDY OR CUSTOM PUBLISHES 100%.** Specializes in self-publishing books of religious or inspirational poetry, in small press runs of under 500 copies. Publication in 45 days. Same-day response.

Tips: "Type one poem per page; include short bio and photo with first submission."

PROVIDENCE HOUSE PUBLISHERS, (formerly listed as Providence Publishing Corp.) 238 Seaboard Ln., Franklin TN 37174. Toll-free (800)321-5692. (615)771-2020. Fax (615)771-2002. E-mail: books@providencehouse.com. Website: www.providence-publishing.com. Nancy Wise, mng. ed.; submit to Acquisitions Editor. Seeks to publish beautiful, professional, university-press quality books; our heart is to publish life-changing Christian truth. Publishes 20+ religious titles/yr.; hardcover, trade paperbacks, coffee-table books. Receives 100+ submissions annually. 90% of books from first-time authors. No mss through agents. **SUBSIDY PUBLISHES 90%;** no print-on-demand. Reprints books. Prefers 96-512 pgs. Author receives 100% income from sales. Average first printing 3,000. Publication within 9-10 mos. Considers simultaneous submissions. Responds in up to 6 mos. Prefers accepted ms on disk. Prefers NIV, NKJV. Guidelines; no catalog.

Nonfiction: Complete ms; no phone/fax query; e-query OK. No full ms by e-mail.

Fiction: Complete ms. For all ages. "Looking for Christian suspense."

Special Needs: Biography, church histories, ministry histories, missionary memoirs.

Photos/Artwork: Open to queries from freelance artists.

Tips: "Most open to biblically based books; history or memoir; those with a speaking ministry tend to receive more attention. Well-written texts only."

QUIET WATERS PUBLICATIONS, PO Box 34, Bolivar MO 65613-0034. (417)326-5001. Fax (617)249-0256. E-mail: QWP@usa.net. Website: www.QuietWatersPub.com. Stephen Trobisch, ed. **SUBSIDY PUBLISHER.** Books on marriage, family, and missions.

RECOVERY COMMUNICATIONS INC., PO Box 19910, Baltimore MD 21211. (410)243-8352. Fax (410)243-8558. E-mail: tdrews3879@aol.com. Website: www.GettingThemSober.com. Toby R. Drews, ed. Publishes 4-6 titles/yr. No mss through agents. **SUBSIDY PUBLISHER.** Prefers 110 pgs. Co-op projects; no royalty or advance. Average first printing 5,000. Publication within 9 mos. Excellent nationwide distribution and marketing in bookstores. Send for their free information packet.

Nonfiction: Query only.

Tips: "Although technically we are a subsidy publisher, we are more of a hybrid publisher in that we give the author enough free books to sell in the back of the room to totally recoup all the money they have paid; plus we share 50/50 on net sales at bookstores. Over half of our authors have gotten their money back and made a great profit. We are also aggressive in our pursuit of catalog sales and foreign rights sales (we recently sold to a German publisher). We also individually coach all our authors, at no cost to them, to help them successfully obtain speaking engagements."

REFORMATION PUBLISHERS, 242 University Dr., Prestonburg KY 41653. (606)886-7222. Fax (606)886-8222. E-mail: rpublisher@aol.com. Website: www.reformationpublishers.com. Church of God (Anderson IN). To keep Church of God books in print. Steven V. Williams, ed./pub. Publishes 250 titles/yr.; hardcover, trade paperbacks, coffee-table books. Receives 10 submissions annually. 100% of books from first-time authors. Accepts mss through agents. **SUBSIDY PUBLISHES 5%;** does print-on-demand. Reprints books. Royalty 20% on retail; no advance. Average first printing 10. Publication within 1 mo. Considers simultaneous submissions. Prefers accepted ms on disk. Responds quarterly. No guidelines; free catalog.

Nonfiction: Complete ms; phone/fax/e-query OK. Open to all topics.

Fiction: Complete ms; phone/fax/e-query OK. All genres for all ages.

Photos/Artwork: Accepts freelance photos for book covers; open to queries from freelance artists.

Tips: "Most open to doctrinal books."

+SALVATION PUBLISHER AND MARKETING GROUP, PO Box 42429, Santa Barbara CA 93140. (805)682-0316. Fax (call first). E-mail: opalmaedailey@aol.com. Wisdom Today Ministries. Opal Mae Dailey, ed-in-chief. We encourage, inspire, and educate; author has the choice to be involved as much or little as desired—which gives the opportunity to control income. Publishes 5-7 titles/yr.; hardcover, trade paperbacks, mass-market paperbacks. 60% of books from first-time authors. No mss through agents. **SUBSIDY PUBLISHES 80%;** does print-on-demand. Reprints books. Prefers 96-224 pgs. Average first printing 1,000. Publication within 3-4 mos. No simultaneous submissions. Accepts requested ms on disk or by e-mail. Responds in 1 mo. Prefers KJV. Guidelines (also by e-mail).

Nonfiction: Query only first; phone/fax/e-query OK.

Tips: "Turning taped messages into book form for pastors is a specialty of ours. We do not accept any manuscript that we would be ashamed to put our name on."

SCRIBE BOOK COMPANY, 138 Old Liberty Pike, Franklin TN 37064. E-mail: info@scribebookcompany.com. Website: www.scribebookcompany.com. Angela DePriest, ed-in-chief; submit to Dan or Angela DePriest, acq. eds. Applies equilibrium theory to all publishing relationships: a shared goal of cooperation and success in the publishing process. Publishes 6-8 titles/yr.; hardcover, trade paperbacks, mass-market paperbacks. Receives 20-30 submissions annually. 25% of books from first-time authors. No mss through agents. **SUBSIDY PUBLISHES 75%;** does print-on-demand. Reprints books. Length open. Royalty 30-40% for royalty projects; no advance. Average first printing 10,000. Publication within 4-9 mos. Accepts simultaneous submissions. Responds in 6-8 wks. Any Bible version. No guidelines/catalog.

Nonfiction: Proposal/1 chapter; e-query OK. Prefers e-mail submissions.

Fiction: Proposal/1 chapter; e-query OK. For all ages.

Photos/Artwork: Accepts freelance photos for book covers; open to queries from freelance artists.

Tips: "We like books that fill an unsatisfied need or desire in the literary marketplace; books that provide fresh perspective on new and old controversy; books that writers write for the reader and not for themselves. We publish books that are truthful, innovative, and that elevate readers' imaginations and improve their lives. Most of our clients are ministries and organizations that have platforms conducive to private publishing. After production fees, their average return on investment is 400-600%."

SELAH PUBLISHING GROUP, LLC., 16238 W. Young St., Surprise AZ 85374-5744. Toll-free (877)616-6451. E-mail: garlen@selahbooks.com. Website: www.selahbooks.com. Garlen Jackson, pub. A publisher that does not water down the author's message. Publishes 45 titles/yr. Receives 20 submissions annually. 75% of books from first-time authors. Prefers mss through agents. Reprints books. Prefers 40,000 wds. or 144 pgs. **SUBSIDY PUBLISHER/BOOK PACKAGER.** Royalty 12-18% of net; no advance. Average first printing 2,500. Publication within 6 mos. No simultaneous submissions. Prefers requested ms on disk. Responds in 2 mos. Prefers ASV. Guidelines by e-mail; free catalog.

Nonfiction: Complete ms; no phone/fax/e-query.

Fiction: Complete ms; no phone/fax/e-query. For all ages.

Also Does: E-books.

Photos/Artwork: Accepts freelance photos for book covers.

Tips: "Most open to time-sensitive, current events, and controversial books. Writers should spend more time selling who they are in regard to character and integrity."

SELF PUBLISH PRESS, 4000 Beallwood Ave., Columbus GA 31904. Toll-free (800)334-2828. (706)576-5787. Fax (706)317-5808. E-mail: Brentwood@aol.com. Website: www.PublishMyBook.com. Brentwood Publishing Group. U. D. Roberts, exec. ed.; submit to Marie Warren, ed. All books must be family suitable. Receives 100 submissions annually. 98% of books from first-time authors. Accepts mss through agents. **SUBSIDY PUBLISHES 98%;** does print-on-demand. Offers InstaBooks and Just in Time publishing (print-on-demand). Reprints books. Prefers 64-300 pgs. Publication within 1 mo. Considers simultaneous submissions. Responds in 3 days. Guidelines on Website; no catalog.

Nonfiction: Complete ms/disk; no phone/fax/e-query. All religious—for family or youth.

Fiction: Complete ms/disk; no phone/fax/e-query. For all ages.

SERMON SELECT PRESS, 4000 Beallwood Ave., Columbus GA 31904. Toll-free (800)334-2828. (706)576-5787. Fax (706)317-5808. E-mail: Brentwood@aol.com. Website: www.BrentwoodBooks.com. Subsidiary of Brentwood Publishers Group. U. D. Roberts, exec. dir. **SUBSIDY OR CUSTOM PUBLISHES 100%.** Focus is on sermon notes, outlines, illustrations, plus news that pastors would find interesting. Publishes 100 copies. Cost of about $3-4/book. Publication in 45 days. Same-day response.

SOUTHERN BAPTIST PRESS, 4000 Beallwood, Columbus GA 31904. Toll-free (800)334-2828. (706)576-5787. E-mail: Brentwood@aol.com. Website: www.SouthernBaptistPress.com. U. D. Roberts, exec. ed. Publishes 25 books/yr. Receives 600 submissions annually. Reprints books. **SUBSIDY OR CUSTOM PUBLISHES 95%.** Average first printing 500. Publication within 2 mos. Considers simultaneous submissions. Responds in 1 week. Guidelines.

Nonfiction: Complete ms. "Collections of sermons on family topics; poetry; relation of Bible to current day."

Fiction: Complete ms. "Stories that show how faith helps overcome small, day-to-day problems."

Tips: "Keep it short; support facts with reference."

STAR BIBLE PUBLICATIONS, 1105 S. Airport Cir., Ste. C, Euless TX 76040. Toll-free (800)433-7507. (817)416-5889. Fax (682)334-0405. E-mail: publishing@starbible.com. Website: www.starbible.com. Church of Christ. Books that will be in harmony with New Testament principles and useful among general audience markets and among Churches of Christ. Publishes 10-15 titles/yr.; mass-market paperbacks. Receives 20-25 submissions annually. 50% of books from first-time authors. No mss through agents. **SUBSIDY PUBLISHES 80%.** No reprints. Prefers 110 pgs. Royalty on retail; no advance. Average first printing 1,000-1,500. Publication within 2 mos. No simultaneous submissions. Responds in 1 mo. Accepts mss on disk or by e-mail. Prefers ASV, KJV, NIV. Guidelines (also by e-mail/Website); catalog on Website.

Nonfiction: Complete ms; phone/fax/e-query OK.

Fiction: Complete ms. For adults.

Photos/Artwork: Accepts freelance photos for book covers.

Tips: "We are looking for general audience books that focus on the gospel and encourage readers to read the Bible, books that encourage people in their Christian walk, books on doctrine, studies on the Bible or specific books of the Bible, and topical studies."

STRONG TOWER PUBLISHING, PO Box 973, Milesburg PA 16853. E-mail: strongtowerpubs@aol.com. Website: www.strongtowerpublishing.com. Heidi L. Nigro, pub. Specializes in eschatology and books that challenge the reader to think more deeply about their faith and scriptural truths; must be biblically responsible, doctrinally defensible, and consistent with their statement of faith. Publishes 1-2 titles/yr.; trade paperbacks. 50% of books from first-time authors. No mss through agents. Reprints books. **PRINT-ON-DEMAND 100%.** Royalty 25% of net; no advance. Average first printing 50. Publication within 3-4 mos. Guidelines, information, and prices on Website.

Nonfiction: Query. Eschatology.

Tips: "We recommend that all first-time authors have their manuscript professionally edited. We will consider putting first-time authors into print, but by invitation only. That invitation comes only after the manuscript has been thoroughly evaluated and we have discussed the pros and cons of our unique on-demand publishing model with the author."

SYNERGY PUBLISHERS, 5850 T G Lee Blvd., Ste. 300, Orlando FL 32822-4409. (407)888-2131. Fax (407)888-2318. E-mail: sueteubner@bridgelogos.com. Website: www.bridgelogos.com. Sue Teubner, acq. ed. Imprint of Bridge-Logos. Pays for cost of production and royalties, but author is required to buy a certain number of books up-front. Publishes 5 titles/yr.; hardcover, trade paperbacks, mass-market paperbacks, coffee-table books. Receives 200 submissions annually. 90% of books from first-time authors. Accepts mss through agents. **SUBSIDY PUBLISHES 1%;** does print-on-demand. Reprints books. Prefers 200 pgs. Average first printing 4,000. Publication within 12 mos. Considers simultaneous submissions. Responds in 12 mos. No disk; prefers accepted ms by e-mail. Guidelines on Website; free catalog.

Nonfiction: Proposal/5 chapters; no phone/fax/e-query.

Special Needs: Reference, biography, current issues, controversial issues, church renewal, women's issues, and Bible commentary.

Photos/Artwork: Accepts freelance photos for book covers.

Tips: "Have a great message, a well-written manuscript, and a specific plan and willingness to market your book. Looking for previously published authors with an active ministry who are experts on their subject."

****Note:** This publisher serviced by The Writer's Edge.

TATE PUBLISHING & ENTERPRISES, LLC., Tate Publishing Bldg., 127 E. Trade Center Ter., Mustang OK 73064-4421. (405)376-4900. Fax (405)376-4401. E-mail: info@tatepublishing.com. Website: www.tatepublishing.com. David Dolphin, dir. of production; submit to acq. sr. ed. Owns and operates their own, state-of-the-art printing plant facility. Publishes 120 titles/yr.; hardcover, trade paperbacks, mass-market paperbacks. 80% of books from first-time authors. Prefers mss through agents. **PRIMARILY A SUBSIDY PUBLISHER** (most authors asked to contribute $3,985.50 toward cost of production). No print-on-demand. Accepts reprints. Prefers 115,000 wds. Royalty 15-40% of net; outright purchase negotiable; negotiable advance. Average first printing 5,000-10,000. Publication within 5 mos. Considers simultaneous submissions. Responds in 3-6 wks. Accepts submissions by disk or e-mail. Any Bible version. Guidelines (also by e-mail/Website); free catalog & brochure.

Nonfiction: Proposal with synopsis & any number of chapters, or complete ms; phone/fax/e-query OK. Any topic. "Looking for books that sell."

Fiction: Proposal with synopsis & any number of chapters or complete ms; phone/fax/e-query OK. For all ages.

Ethnic Books: For all ethnic markets.

Photos/Artwork: Has 10 full-time artists on staff.

Tips: "We invest resources in every work we accept, and accept first-time authors."

****Note:** This publisher serviced by The Writer's Edge.

TEACH SERVICES INC., 254 Donovan Rd., Brushton NY 12916. (518)358-3494. Fax (518)358-3028. E-mail: publishing@TEACHservices.com. Website: www.teachservices.com. Timothy Hullquist, pres.; submit to Wayne Reid, acq. ed. To publish uplifting books for the lowest price. Publishes 40-50 titles/yr. Receives 100 submissions annually. 35% of books from first-time authors. No mss through agents. **SUBSIDY PUBLISHES 75%** (author has to pay for first printing, then publisher keeps it in print). Reprints books. Prefers 45,000 wds. or 96 pgs. Royalty 10% of retail; no advance. Average first printing 2,000. Publication within 6 mos. Requires requested ms on disk. Responds in 2 wks. Prefers KJV. Guidelines (also by e-mail/Website)/catalog for #10 SAE/2 stamps.

Nonfiction: Query only; no phone/fax query. "Looking for books on nutrition."

Special Needs: Personal testimonies.

Photos/Artwork: Accepts freelance photos for book covers.

TRAFFORD PUBLISHING, 6E—2333 Government St., Victoria BC V8T 4P4, Canada. Toll-free (888)232-4444. (250)383-6864. Fax (250)383-6804. E-mail: info@trafford.com. Website: www.trafford.com. Gord Hooker, pres. Publishes 100-200 titles/yr.; hardcover, trade paperbacks. Receives thousands of submissions annually. 85% of books from first-time authors. Accepts mss through agents. **100% PRINT-ON-DEMAND.** Reprints books. Prefers less than 700 pgs. Royalty 60%. Average first printing 40. Publication within 4-6 wks. Considers simultaneous submissions. Responds immediately. Guidelines (also by e-mail/Website); no catalog.

Tips: "Authors choose the retail price for their books and their royalty is 60% of the gross margin."

VMI PUBLISHERS, 26306 Metolius Meadows Dr., Camp Sherman OR 97730. E-mail: bill@vmipublishers.com. Website: www.vmipublishers.com. Virtue Ministries Inc. Bill and Nancie Carmichael, pubs. Partnering with new authors. Publishes 8-12 titles/yr.; hardback, trade paperbacks, coffee-table books. Receives dozens of submissions annually. 95% of books from first-time authors. Accepts mss through agents. No reprints. Prefers 65,000+ wds., or 192-400 pgs. Royalty 12-18% of net; no advance. **CO-OP PUBLISHER; YOU PURCHASE BOOKS.**

Average first printing 2,500+. Publication within 6-12 mos. Considers simultaneous submissions. Requires accepted mss on disk or by e-mail. Responds in 2 mos. Guidelines on Website.

Nonfiction: Query first by e-mail only.

Fiction: Query first by e-mail only. For all ages. "Anything Christian or inspirational that is well written, especially from new authors."

Tips: "Go to our Website first, and read how we partner with new authors. Then, if you feel VMI would be a good fit for you, e-mail your proposal."

WINEPRESS PUBLISHING, PO Box 428, 1730 Railroad St., Enumclaw WA 98022. Toll-free (800)326-4674. (360)802-9758. Fax (360)802-9992. E-mail: athena@winepressgroup.com. Website: www.winepresspub.com. The WinePress Group. Athena Dean, acq. ed. Serves Christian authors with attentive service, quick responses, and honesty. Imprints: WinePress Publishing, WinePress Kids (children's books), Annotation Press (general market), UpWrite Books (writers resources), Pleasant Word (on demand—see separate listing). Publishes 75 titles/yr.; hardcover, trade paperbacks, mass-market paperbacks, coffee-table books. Receives 700+ submissions annually. 70% of books from first-time authors. Accepts mss through agents. **BOOK PACKAGERS 100%.** Reprints books. Lengths range from 10,000-150,000 wds. or 48-1,300 pgs. Author pays production costs, keeps all profit from sales. Average first printing 3,000 (2,500 min.). Publication in up to 6 mos. Considers simultaneous submissions. Responds in 48-72 hrs. Accepts requested ms on disk. Prefers NIV. Guidelines (also by e-mail)/free catalog. Not included in topical listings because they consider any topic or genre.

Nonfiction: Complete ms; e-query OK. Publishes any topic as long as it's biblical or glorifies God.

Fiction: Complete ms. All ages and all genres.

Also Does: Board books, music CDs packaged with books, DVD teaching packaged with manual, genuine leather Bibles, full-color children's books, board games & computer games.

Photos/Artwork: Accepts freelance photos for book covers.

Tips: "As the leader in quality custom publishing, we offer professional book packaging for Christian writers. We not only offer a full line of editorial, design, layout, and printing services, but full-service warehousing, order fulfillment, and distribution as well. Selected titles may be represented by exclusive sales force to the trade. Our publicity department offers cutting edge and effective marketing, media contact, promotional services. New division also offers audio books and other audio/video promotional products for our authors. Our in-house team of professionals is committed to serving our authors with excellent customer service and honest advice. We don't purchase rights to books and choose not to partner with messages that promote 'name-it-claim-it' or prosperity doctrine; sexually explicit material; anything that offends or denounces the deity of Jesus; or material that confuses gender roles. All manuscripts that do not have a reasonably good chance of selling at least 2,000 copies in the first 18 months are encouraged to take advantage of our print-on-demand services (see Pleasant Word listing)."

****Note:** This publisher serviced by The Writer's Edge and ChristianManuscriptSubmissions.com.

WINER FOUNDATION, PO Box 33373, Philadelphia PA 19142-3373. (215)365-3350. Fax (215)365-3325. E-mail: info@winerfoundation.org. Website: www.winerfoundation.org. Robert Winer, pres. Helping people walk in all that God intends for them. Publishes 4 titles/yr. **SUBSIDY PUBLISHES 90%.** Reprints books. Prefers 150-250 pgs. Royalty 3-10% of retail; advance $250-500. Average first printing 3,000-5,000. Publication within 6-8 mos. Considers simultaneous submissions. Requires requested ms on disk (Word, WordPerfect, or RTF format). Responds in 1-2 mos. Prefers NKJV. Guidelines (also by e-mail); no catalog.

Nonfiction: Proposal with 2-3 chapters; e-query OK. "Books on deeper spirituality to help people mature in the Lord."

Special Needs: Messianic Jewish in addition to general Christianity.

Tips: "Most open to books that fulfill our mission statement."

WORD ALIVE PRESS, 131 Cordite Rd., Winnipeg MB R3W 1S1, Canada. Toll-free (866)967-3782, ext. 203. (204)777-7100. Toll-free fax (800)352-9272. E-mail: Cschmidt@wordalive.ca. Website: www.wordalive.ca. C. Schmidt, ed. At least 6,000 wds. or 50 pgs. **100% PRINT-ON-DEMAND.** Guidelines and price list available. Request their Free Guide to Publishing brochure.

Nonfiction: "Looking for books on family, marriage, and character."

Fiction: For all ages.

XLIBRIS, 2 International Plz., Ste. 340, Philadelphia PA 19113-9902. Toll-Free (888)795-4274, ext. 278. E-mail: info@xlibris.com. Website: www.xlibris.com. Random House. Mercedes Bournias, publishing consultant. **100% SUBSIDY.** Can produce novels to 700 pgs. and picture books to 24 pgs. Basic Package is $499; up to Executive Package at $5,999. Open to any topic.

XULON PRESS INC., 2180 W. State Rd. 434, Ste. 2140, Longwood FL 32779. Toll-free (866)381-2665, ext. 103. Fax (407)339-9898. E-mail: kkochenburger@xulonpress.com, or acquisitions@xulonpress.com. Website: www.xulonpress.com. Division of Salem Communications. Tom Freiling, VP & gen. mngr; Karen Kochenburger, ed. Uses digital and print-on-demand technologies to help Christian authors get published. Publishes 1,500 titles/yr.; hardcover, trade paperbacks. Receives 2,500 submissions annually. 80% of books from first-time authors. **100% PRINT-ON-DEMAND.** Reprints books. Any length. Royalty 100% of net; no advance. Publication within 90 days. Considers simultaneous submissions. Responds in 1 mo. Not in topical listings; will consider all appropriate Christian topics. Guidelines on Website; free catalog.

Nonfiction/Fiction: Phone/fax/e-query OK.

Also Does: Booklets, e-books.

Photos/Artwork: Accepts freelance photos for book covers.

Tips: "We offer on-demand publishing, bookstore distribution, and publicity and promotional services. We also exhibit at the annual International Christian Retail Convention (ICRC). Please refer to the Website for information about how we promote and publicize books."

****Note:** This publisher (royalty division) serviced by The Writer's Edge.

ZOE LIFE PUBLISHING, PO Box 871066, Canton MI 48187. (734)547-7801. Fax (734)547-7805. E-mail: submissions@zoelifepub.com. Website: www.zoelifepub.com. Zoe Life Industries LLC. Sabrina Adams, ed. Imprints: Pen of a Ready Writer, Titus, Business Builders. Publishes 40 titles/yr.; hardcover, trade paperbacks, mass-market paperbacks, coffee-table books. 50+% of books from first-time authors. Prefers mss through agents. **SUBSIDY PUBLISHES 50%;** no print-on-demand or reprints. Length open. Royalty 5-25%; usually no advance. Average first printing 3,000. Publication within 6-12 mos. Responds in 21 days. Open on Bible version. Guidelines by e-mail/Website; free catalog.

Photos/Artwork: Accepts freelance photos for book covers.

DISTRIBUTORS

LISTING OF CHRISTIAN BOOK/MUSIC/GIFT DISTRIBUTORS

AIRLEAF PUBLISHING & BOOK SELLING, 35 Industrial Dr., Ste. 104, Martinsville IN 46151. Toll-free (800)342-6068. Fax (765)342-7217. Website: www.bookmanmarketing.com. Distributes self-published and print-on-demand books for authors (even from other publishers). Contact: Brien Jones.

ALLIANCE—MUSIC, 4250 Coral Ridge Dr., Coral Springs FL 33065-7615. (954)255-4600. Fax (954)255-4825. E-mail: custsvc@aent.com. Website: www.aent.com. Music.

AMAZON ADVANTAGE PROGRAM. Go to Amazon.com, scroll down to "Make Money" section in left-hand column, and click on "Advantage." Site to contact if you want Amazon to distribute your book.

ANCHOR-WHITAKER DISTRIBUTORS, 1030 Hunt Valley Cir., New Kensington PA 15068. Toll-free (800)444-4484. (724)334-7000. Fax (800)765-1960 or (724)334-1200. E-mail: purchasing@anchordistributors.com, or marketing@anchordistributors.com. Website: www.anchordistributors.com. Donna Bonarati, intl. sales mngr. (800)444-4484, ext. 246. Christian books, Bibles, music, and gifts. Distributes self-published books on a contract distribution basis. Mail a copy of the book and all pertinent information to John Whitaker.

B. BROUGHTON CO., LTD., 2105 Danforth Ave., Toronto ON M4C 1K1, Canada. Toll-free (800)268-4449 (Canada only). (416)690-4777. Fax (416)690-5357. E-mail: brian@bbroughton.com. Website: www.bbroughton.com. Brian Broughton, owner. Canadian distributor. Distributes books, DVDs, gifts, greeting cards. Does not distribute self-published books.

CAMPUS CRUSADE FOR CHRIST/NEW LIFE RESOURCES, 375 Hwy. 74 S., Ste. A, Peachtree City GA 30269. Toll-free (800)235-7255, or (800)827-2788. Fax (800)514-7072, or (770)631-9916. E-mail: pat.pearce@campuscrusade.org. Website: www.campuscrusade.org. Contact: Pat Pearce.

CBA MAILING LISTS OF CHRISTIAN BOOKSTORES, PO Box 62000, Colorado Springs CO 80962-2000. (719)265-9895. Fax (719)272-3510. E-mail: lpaquette@cbaonline.org. Website: www.cbaonline.org. Available for rental. Four different lists available, including nonmember stores, 5,000 addresses ($249); member stores, 1,400 addresses ($649); chainstore headquarters (39) plus largest independent stores 750 addresses ($449); or a combined list of all stores, 6,500 addresses ($699). Prices subject to change. Call toll-free (800)252-1950 for full details.

+CENTRAL SOUTH DISTRIBUTION, 3730 Vulcan Dr., Nashville TN 37211. (615)833-5960. Fax (615)331-2501. Website: www.centralsouthdistribution.com. Contact: Chuck Adams (cadams@csouth.com). Distributes Black music and devotionals.

CHRISTIAN BOOK DISTRIBUTORS, PO Box 7000, Peabody MA 01961-7000. Toll-free (800)247-4784. (978)977-5080. Fax (978)977-5010. E-mail: customer.service@christianbooks.com. Website: www.christianbooks.com.

CONSORTIUM BOOK SALES & DISTRIBUTION INC., 1045 Westgate Dr., Ste. 90, St. Paul MN 55114. Toll-free (800)283-3572. (651)221-9035. Fax (651)221-0124. Website: www.cbsd.com.

COOK COMMUNICATIONS CANADA, 55 Woodslee Ave., Box 98, Paris ON N3L 3E5, Canada. Toll-free (800)263-2664. Fax (800)461-8575. E-mail: custserv@davidcook.ca. Website: www.davidcook.ca. Can distribute only in Canada.

+CORNERSTONE FULFILLMENT SERVICE, LL, PO Box 102, 35 Beaver St., Bondville VT05340. (802)297-3771. Fax (802)297-3326. E-mail through Website. Website: www.CornerstoneFulFillmentService.com. Sue Leonard, owner. Distributes books, videos, DVDs, CDs, journals, consumer literature. Specializes in self-published books, videos, DVDs, CDs. Contact by phone or e-mail.

CROWN DISTRIBUTION, Toll-free (800)661-9467. (780)471-1417. Website: www.crowndistribution.com. Distributes Christian film & video in U.S., Canada, and around the world.

DDMDIRECT.COM, 1175 William St., Buffalo NY 14206. Toll-free (800)597-5605. (716)893-8671. Fax (877)632-9657. Website: www.ddmdirect.com. Distributes books, children's books.

DICKSONS, PO Box 368, Seymour IN 47274. (812)522-1308. Fax (812)522-1319. E-mail: marketing@dicksonsgifts.com. Website: www.dicksonsgifts.com. Distributes gift products only. Open to outside submissions for its product line. Website includes a list of additional distributors.

EFULFILLMENT SERVICE INC., 6893 Sullivan Rd., Grawn MI 49637. (231)276-5057, ext. 100. Fax (231)276-5074. E-mail: alc@efulfillmentservice.com, or info@efulfillmentservice.com. Website: www.efulfillmentservice.com. Jordan Lindberg, pres. Services include storage and order fulfillment.

FAITHWORKS, 129 Mobilization Dr., Waynesboro GA 30830. Toll-free (877)323-4550. Fax (877)323-4551. E-mail: lcarpenter@faithworksonline.com, or custserv@faithworksonline.com. Website: www.faithworksonline.com. Contact: Larry Carpenter. Christian products, including books, music, videos, audiotapes, and software.

FOUNDATION DISTRIBUTING INC., 9 Cobbledick St., PO Box 98, Orono ON L0B 1M0, Canada. (905)983-1188. Fax (905)983-1190. E-mail: info@fdi.ca. Website: www.fdi.ca. Canadian distributor.

GENESIS MARKETING, 770 Pelham Rd., Ste. 200, Greenville SC 29615-3254. Toll-free (800)627-2651. (864)233-2651. Toll-free fax (800)849-4363. E-mail: CustomerRelations@genesislink.com. Website: www.genesislink.com.

GL SERVICES, 1957 Eastman Ave., Ventura CA 93003. (805)677-6815. Fax (805)644-4729. E-mail: JeffMesinoff@GLServices.com. Website: www.GLServices.com. Contact: Jeff Mesinoff. A division of Gospel Light. Does not distribute books for individual authors.

GODSPEED COMPUTING'S DIGITAL DISTRIBUTION SYSTEM, #215, 603—11 Ave. S.W., Calgary AB T2R 0E1, Canada. Toll-free (866)463-7733. (403)274-6510. Fax (403)282-1238. E-mail: sales@godspeedcomputing.com, or info@godspeedcomputing.com. Website: www.godspeedcomputing.com. E-book distributor.

INGRAM BOOK GROUP/DISTRIBUTION, One Ingram Blvd., La Vergne TN 37086-1986. Toll-free (800)937-8000. (615)793-5000. Website: www.ingrambookgroup.com. The best way to have your book/product distributed by this company is to go through one of their trading partners. For a list of distributing partners and more information, visit their Website.

KEY MARKETING GROUP, PO Box 162, Jenks OK 74037. Toll-free (877)727-0697. (918)298-0232. Fax (918)299-5912. E-mail: info@keymarketinggroup.net. Website: www.keymarketinggroup.net. Bryan Norris, owner (bryan@keymarketinggroup.net).

LIGHTNING SOURCE INC., 1246 Heil Quaker Blvd., La Vergne TN 37086. (615)213-5815. Fax (615)213-4426. E-mail: inquiry@lightningsource.com. Website: www.lightningsource.com.

MALACO CHRISTIAN DISTRIBUTION, 3023 W. Northside Dr., Jackson MS 39213. Toll-free (877)462-3623. (601)982-4522. Fax (601)982-4528. E-mail: tgoodwin@malaco.com, or malaco@malaco.com. Website: www.malaco.com. Tony Goodwin, mng. dir. of sales. Music distributor.

MCBETH CORP, Fulfillment and Distribution Headquarters, PO Box 400, Chambersburg PA 17201. Toll-free (800)876-5112. (717)263-5600. Fax (717)263-5909. E-mail: mcbethcorp@supernet.com. Distributes Christian gift products.

R. G. MITCHELL FAMILY BOOKS INC., 565 Gordon Baker Rd., Willowdale ON M2H 2W2, Canada. Toll-free (800)268-3445. (416)499-4615. Toll-free fax (800)268-5696. Fax (416)499-6340. E-mail: info@rgm.ca. Website: www.rgm.ca. David Freeland, pres.

NEW DAY CHRISTIAN DISTRIBUTORS, 126 Shivel Dr., Hendersonville TN 37075. Toll-free (800)251-3633. (615)822-3633. Toll-free fax (800)361-2533. E-mail: service@newday christian.com. Website: www.newdaychristian.com. Contact: Jeff Stangenberg (jstangen berg@newdaychristian.com). Music (primarily), books, Bibles, gift items. Distributes self-published books. Contact by e-mail.

NOAH'S ARK DISTRIBUTION, 28545 Felix Valdez Ave., Ste. B4, Temecula CA 92590-1859. Toll-free (800)562-8093. (760)723-3101. Fax (951)693-2747. E-mail: slvanyo@msn.com. Website: www.christianbooksanddvds.com. Contact: Scott Vanyo, manager.

THE PARABLE GROUP, 3563 Empleo St., San Luis Obispo CA 93401. Toll-free (800)366-6031, ext. 525. (805)549-2500. Fax (800)543-2136. E-mail: info@parable.com, or through Website: www.parable.com. A marketing program for Christian bookstores. Chris Scotti, member services and sales director.

PUBLISHERS GROUP WEST, National Headquarters: 1700 Fourth St., Berkeley CA 94710. (510) 528-1444. Fax (510)528-3444. E-mail: info@pgw.com. Website: www.pgw.com. Send all inquiries to National Headquarters. Distribution Center: 7326 Winton Dr., Indianapolis IN 46268.

PUBLISHERS MARKETING ASSN., 627 Aviation Way, Manhattan Beach CA 90266-7107. (310)372-2732. Fax (310)374-3342. E-mail: info@pma-online.org. Website: www.pma-on line.org. Trade association of independent publishers. Provides cooperative marketing programs for books, e-books, and audio books. Jan Nathan, exec. dir. (jan@pma-online.org).

QUALITY BOOKS, 1003 W. Pines Rd., Oregon IL 61061. Toll-free (800)323-4241. (815)732-4450. Fax (815)732-4499. E-mail: info@quality-books.com Website: www.quality-books.com. Owner: Dawson Holdings PLC. Tiffani Griffin, mngr. of customer service & sales (tiffani.griffin@quality-books.com). Distributes small press books, videos, audios, DVDs, and CD-ROMs to public libraries. Asks for 1 copy of your book, plus 30 covers.

RANDOLF PRODUCTIONS INC., 18005 Sky Park Cir., Ste. K, Irvine CA 92614-6514. Toll-free (800)266-7741. (949)794-9109. Fax (949)794-9117. E-mail: sales@go2rpi.com. Website: www.go2rpi.com, and www.goccc.com. Distributor of Christian DVDs, books, and music. A subsidiary of Campus Crusade for Christ. Contact: Randy Ray, pres. (randy@go2rpi.com).

SPRING ARBOR DISTRIBUTORS, PO Box 3006, One Ingram Blvd., Mailstop 671, La Vergne TN 37086. Toll-free (800)395-4340. Toll-free fax (800)876-0186 or (615)213-5192. E-mail: custserv@springarbor.com. Website: www.springarbor.com. Contact: Karen K. Bishop, Director, National Sales. Books, music, Bibles; no gift items or church supplies.

STL/APPALACHIAN DISTRIBUTORS, PO Box 1573, 522 Princeton Rd., Johnson City TN 37601. Toll-free (800)289-2772. Fax (800)759-2779. Website: www.appalink.com. A full-service distributor with two locations. Includes the homeschool market and Catholic products.

+TRIUMPH MARKETING, LLC., 2450 Atlanta Hwy., Ste. 1803, Cumming GA 30040. Toll-free (877)494-0525. (678)947-5615. Fax (678)947-1490. Website: www.triumphmarketingllc .com. Stephen McGonigle, pres. (steve@triumphmarketingllc.com); Gary Costello, VP of sales, marketing, and acquisitions (gary@triumphmarketingllc.com). Submit books/products for consideration.

WINDFLOWER COMMUNICATIONS, 67 Flett Ave., Winnipeg MB R2K 3N3, Canada. Toll-free (800) 465-6564. (204)668-7475. Fax (204)661-8530. E-mail: windflower@brandtfamily .com. Website: www.brandtfamily.com. Brandt Family Enterprises. Gilbert Brandt, pres. Book distributor.

WORD ALIVE INC., 131 Cordite Rd., Winnipeg MB R3W 1S1, Canada. Toll-free (800)665-1468. (204)667-1400. Toll-free fax (800)352-9272. Fax (204)669-0947. E-mail: orderdesk@ wordalive.ca. Website: www.wordalive.ca. Distributes Christian books. Contact: Caroline Schmidt. Distributes self-published books. Contact by mail.

MARKET ANALYSIS

PUBLISHERS IN ORDER OF MOST BOOKS PUBLISHED PER YEAR

Adams Media 230
Tyndale House 225-250
United Methodist 175
Harvest House 170
Monarch Books 160
Cook Communications 125
Eerdmans 120-130
Abingdon Press 120
Zondervan 120
Nelson Books 100-150
Barbour Publishing 100
Hazelden Publishing 100
New York Univ. Press 100
Strang Book Group 100
Steeple Hill 96-108
Bethany House 90-100
Broadman & Holman 90-100
Christian Focus 90
NavPress 85-95
InterVarsity Press 80-90
Boyds Mills Press 80
Christian Ed. Publishers 80
Paulist Press 80
Presbyterian Publishing 80
Standard Publishing 75-100
HarperSanFrancisco 75
Liturgical Press 75
Multnomah 75
W Publishing Group 75
Love Inspired 72
Crossway 70
WaterBrook Press 70
Grupo Nelson 65-80
Moody Publishers 65-70
Honor Books 60+
Regal Publishing 60+
Continuum Intl. 60
Fortress Press 60
Kregel 60
Ambassador-Emerald 55
Pilgrim Press 55
Heartsong Presents 52
Harcourt Religion 50-100
Custom Commun. 50-75
Tommy Nelson 50-75
T & T Clark. 50-60
Holy Fire Publishing 50+
Chalice Press 50
Concordia 50
Crossroad Publishing 50
CSS Publishing 50
DiskUs Publishing 50
Liguori Publications 50
G. P. Putnam's Sons 50
University Press 50
ZonderKidz 50
Love Inspired Suspense 48
Treble Heart Books 48
Capall Bann 46
Howard Publishing 46
St. Anthony Mess. Press 45-55
Doubleday Religion 45-50
Editores Betania-Caribe 45
RiverOak 45
Faith Kids Books 40-50
GRQ 40-50
Peter Pauper Press 40-50
Jeremy P. Tarcher 40-50
Editorial Portavoz 40+
Bridge-Logos 40
Group Publishing 40
Health Communications 40
Jossey-Bass 40
Legacy Press 40
P & R Publishing 40
Pauline Books 40
Eldridge (plays) 35
Morehouse Publishing 35
Spyglass Lane Mysteries 32
Baal Hamon Publishers 30-40
FaithWords 30-40
Focus on the Family 30-40
Hendrickson 30-40
Our Sunday Visitor 30-40
New Leaf Press 30-35
AMG Publishers 30
Baylor Univ. Press 30
Beacon Hill Press 30
Christian Writer's Ebook 30
Cross Cultural 30
Genesis Communications 30
Good News Publishers (tracts) 30
Journey Stone Creations 30
Mission World Library 30
Thomas More 30
Pacific Press 30
Youth Specialties 30
Rose Publishing 25-30
Sheed & Ward 25-30
Smyth & Helwys 25-30
WestBow Press 25-30
Forward Movement 25
Libros Liguori 25
Liturgy Training 25
Lutterworth Press 25
Meriwether (plays) 25
Alba House 24
Love Inspired Historical 24
One World 24
St. Augustine's Press 20-40
Chapter Two 20-30
Lighthouse eBooks 20-30
Loyola Press 20-30
New Hope 20-28
Nelson Ignite 20-25
Blue Dolphin 20-24
Pathway Press 20-24
Carson-Dellosa Publishing 20
Pflaum Publishing 20
Rainbow Pub./Rainbow Books 20
Resource Publications 20
Scepter Publishers 20
Shining Star 20
Third World Press 20
Dimension Books 18
Big Idea 15-20
Catholic Book Publishing 15-20
College Press 15-20
Master Books 15-20
BMH Books 15-18
NavPress Th1nk, 15-18
Branden Publishing 15
Mercer Univ. Press 15
Parsons Publishing 15
Rainbow Pub./Legacy Press 15
Still Waters 15
Wesleyan Publishing House 15
Dabbling Mum Press 12-24
Discovery House 12-18
CarePoint 12-16
Judson Press 12-15
Paragon House 12-15
Vintage Romance 12+
Promise Press/Suspense 12
Marshall Trumann 12
Wm. Carey Library 10-15
E-Digital 10-15
Ragged Edge 10-15
Descant Publishing 10-12
Green Key 10-12
Lillenas 10-12
Starburst Publishers 10-12
ACTA Publications 10
BJU Press/Journey Forth 10
Catholic Answers 10
FaithWalk Publishing 10
FamilyLife Publishing 10
Fifth Estate Publishers 10
Georgetown University Press 10
Haworth Press 10
Jubilant Press 10 (e-books)
PREP Publishing 10
Walk Worthy Press 10
Yale Univ. Press 10
Ambassador Books 9
Cistercian Publications 8-14
Emmaus Road 8-10
Holy Cross Orthodox 8-10

Lutheran University Press 8-10
Millennium III 8-10
Reformation Trust 8-10
TowleHouse Publishing 8-10
Neibauer Press 8
Oregon Catholic Press 8
Touch Publications 8
Woodland Gospel 7
Guardian Angel Pub. 6-12
Messianic Jewish 6-12
Kirk House Publishers 6-8
Eerdmans/Young Readers 6-7
Americana Publishing 6
Christian Heritage 6
Church & Synagogue Libraries 6
Filbert Publishing 6
Hope Publishing 6
Inkling Books 6
Langmarc Publishing 6
Life Cycle Books 6
Lift Every Voice 6
Northstone Publishing 6
Square One Publishers 6
Wilshire Book Co. 6
Greenwood Publishing 5-30
Troitsa Books 5-20
Conciliar Press 5-10
Gospel Publishing House 5-10
Hensley Publishing 5-10
Pray! Books 5-10
Quintessential Books 5-10
Randall House 5-10
World Publishing 5-10
Perigee Books 5-8
Religious Education Press 5-6
ACU Press 5
Mission City Press 5
Mt. Olive College Press 5
Paradise Research 5
Synergy Publishers 5
Trinity Foundation 5
Friends United Press 4-6
Baker Trittin 4-5
Illumination Arts 4-5
Larson Publications 4-5
American Catholic Press 4
Anglicans United 4
Church Growth Institute 4
Iceagle Press 4
Intl. Awakening Press 4
WindRiver Publishing 4
Breakneck Books 3-5
Cerdic-Publications 3-5
Facts on File 3-5
Northfield Publishing 3-5
Parson Place Press 3-5
Virginia Pines Press 3-5
Gollehon Press 3-4
New Canaan 3-4
Tau-Publishing 3-4
ETC Publications 3
Magnus Press 3
Meriwether 3
Pelican Publishing 3
Wood Lake Books 3
Baker's Plays 2-8
First Fruits of Zion 2-6
Jireh Publishing 2-5
Salt Works 2-5
Canadian Institute for Law 2-4
Frederick Fell 2-4
Jebaire Publishing 2-4
Cladach Publishing 2-3
Daybreak Books/Rodale 2-3
Educational Ministries 2-3
UMI Press 2-3
Canticle Books 2
Earthen Vessel 2
Genesis Press 2
Read 'N Run Books 2
Skysong Press 2
Players Press 1-6
Barclay Press 1-5
Living Books for All 1-5
LifeSong Publishers 1-4
Christian Family 1-3
Starik Publishing 1-3
Fair Havens Publications 1-2
Hill Street Press 1-2
Write Now 1-2
Aadeon Publishing 1
BelleBooks 1
Gilgal Publications 1
Goetz 1
Good Book 1
Guernica Editions 1
Hay House 1
Noveledit 1

SUBSIDY PUBLISHERS

Xulon Press 1,500
Pleasant Word 300
Brentwood 267
Trafford Publishing 100-200
Essence Publishing 100-150+
Fairway Press 100
Poet's Cove Press 75
WinePress 75
American Binding 60
Insight Publishing Group 50
Selah Publishing 45
TEACH Services 40-50
ACW Press 40
Zoe Life 40
Black Forest Press 25
Southern Baptist Press 25
Impact Christian Books 20+
Providence House 20+
McDougal Publishing 15-20
Elderberry Press 15
Brown Books 10-15
Star Bible 10-15
Ekklesia Press 10-12
VMI Publishers 8-12
Hannibal Books 8-10
Scribe Book 6-8
Fruitbearer Publishing 5-10
IMD Press 5-10
Book Publishers 5-8
Salvation Publisher 5-7
DCTS Publishing 5
J and J Publishing 5
Recovery Communications 4-6
Path Publishing in Christ 4-5
Winer Foundation 4
Kindred Books 3-4
Lightning Star Press 2-4
Ampelos Press 1-3
Strong Tower Publishing 1-2
Alfred Ali Literary 1
Robbie Dean Press 1

BOOK TOPICS MOST POPULAR WITH PUBLISHERS

The numbers following the topics below indicate how many publishers said they were interested in seeing a book on that topic. To find the list of publishers interested in each topic, go to the Topical Listings for books (see Contents).

MISCELLANEOUS TALLIES:

Art-Freelance 52
Booklets 45
Canadian/Foreign 21
Coffee-table books 28
E-books 37
Minibooks 11
Photographs for covers 89
Print-on-demand 53
Tracts 19

TOPICS BY POPULARITY

1. Inspirational 149
2. Family Life 147
3. Prayer 146
4. Christian Living 145
5. Religion 142
6. Bible/Biblical Studies 139
7. Spirituality 135
8. Devotional Books 127
9. Women's Issues 127
10. Faith 126
11. Discipleship 124
12. Marriage 121
13. Theology 120
14. Fiction: Adult/Religious 118
15. Parenting 114
16. Biography 109
17. Church History 106
18. Self-help 106
19. Historical 105
20. Personal Growth 102
21. Evangelism/Witnessing 100
22. Spiritual Life 100
23. Current/Social Issues 99
24. Leadership 99
25. Church Life 98
26. Christian Education 95
27. Ethics 95
28. Ethnic/Cultural 93
29. Fiction: Contemporary 90
30. Forgiveness 90
31. How-to 89
32. Worship 88
33. Youth Books (nonfiction) 88
34. Fiction: Historical 87
35. Death/Dying 86
36. Personal Renewal 85
37. Bible Commentary 84
38. Church Renewal 84
39. Controversial Issues 84
40. Christ 83
41. Healing 83
42. Scholarly 82
43. Health 81
44. Doctrinal 80
45. Fiction: Juvenile (ages 8-12) 80
46. Christian Business 79
47. Spiritual Gifts 77
48. Apologetics 76
49. Spiritual Warfare 75
50. Men's Books 74
51. Fiction: Biblical 73
52. Fiction: Adventure 72
53. Humor 72
54. Pastors' Helps 72
55. Church Traditions 71
56. Fiction: Mystery/Suspense 71
57. Reference Books 71
58. Fiction: Teen/Young Adult 70
59. Social Justice Issues 70
60. Dating/Sex 69
61. Counseling Aids 68
62. Gift Books 68
63. Group Study Books 68
64. Holy Spirit 68
65. Psychology 67
66. Autobiography 66
67. Divorce 66
68. Missionary 66
69. Money Management 66
70. Philosophy 66
71. Stewardship 66
72. Fiction: Literary 65
73. Encouragement 64
74. Holiday/Seasonal 64
75. Personal Experience 63
76. Singles Issues 63
77. Children's Picture Books 62
78. Prophecy 62
79. Recovery Books 61
80. Fiction: Humor 60
81. Memoirs 60
82. World Issues 60
83. Eschatology 59
84. Fiction: Fantasy 59
85. Miracles 59
86. Sermons 59
87. Worship Resources 59
88. Christian Homeschooling 58
89. Exegesis 57
90. Fiction: Romance 57
91. Political 57
92. Archaeology 56
93. Relationships 55
94. Fiction: Mystery/Romance 54
95. Senior Adult Concerns 54
96. Time Management 54
97. Children's Easy Readers 53
98. Homiletics 53
99. Fiction: Ethnic 51
100. Fiction: Historical/Romance 50
101. Poetry 50
102. Science 50
103. Liturgical Studies 48
104. Church Management 47
105. Fiction: Allegory 47
106. Religious Tolerance 47
107. Christian School Books 46
108. Environmental Issues 46
109. Cookbooks 45
110. Fiction: Science Fiction 45
111. Charismatic 44
112. Cults/Occult 44
113. Fiction: Short Story Collection 44
114. Racism 44
115. Creation Science 43
116. Holiness 43
117. Sociology 43
118. Curriculum 42
119. Homeschooling Resources 42
120. Fiction: Frontier/Romance 41
121. Compilations 40
122. Economics 40
123. Retirement 40
124. Fiction: Frontier 39
125. Sports/Recreation 39
126. Fiction: Chick Lit 38
127. Drama 37
128. Fiction: Westerns 37
129. Travel 37
130. Celebrity Profiles 34
131. Grief 32
132. Music-related Books 32
133. Youth Programs 32
134. Fiction: Speculative 30
135. Games/Crafts 30
136. Pamphlets 29
137. Writing How-to 29
138. Fiction: Fables/Parables 28
139. Fiction: Adult/General 27
140. Fiction: Children's Picture Books 27
141. Fiction: Novellas 25
142. Fiction: Plays 25
143. Tween Books 25
144. Lifestyle 23
145. Novelty Books For Kids 22
146. Post Modernism 22
147. Exposés 21
148. Children's Board Books 13
150. Commentaries 7

SUMMARY OF INFORMATION ON CHRISTIAN BOOK PUBLISHERS FOUND IN THE ALPHABETICAL LISTINGS

Note: Following is some general information based on averages of the information supplied by the book publishers for this guide. This information will be valuable in determining if the contract offered by your publisher is in line with other publishers in some of these areas. For further help, check the section on editorial services to find those who offer contract evaluations, which are most valuable.

TOTAL MANUSCRIPTS RECEIVED

Christian book publishers receive a combined total of about 250,000 manuscripts during the year. That averages out to over 900 manuscripts per publisher, per year. The actual number of manuscripts received ranges from 5 to 10,000 per publisher.

NUMBER OF BOOKS PUBLISHED

Over 300 publishers will publish a combined total of almost 12,000 titles during a typical year. That is an average of 40 books per publisher. The actual number per publisher ranges from 1 to 1,000. If each publisher actually publishes the maximum estimate of books for the year, about 5 percent of the manuscripts submitted will be published.

AVERAGE FIRST PRINT RUN

The average first printing of a book for a new author is just under 4,700 books.

ROYALTIES

Of the almost 300 publishers who indicated that they paid royalties, about 23 percent pay on the retail price, 53 percent pay on the wholesale price or net, and the rest did not indicate which. The average royalty based on the retail price of the book was about 9 percent to 14 percent. Actual royalties on retail varied from 2 percent to 50 percent. The average royalty based on net varied from 10 percent to 15 percent. The average royalties in both categories are up this year. Actual royalties on net varied from 2 percent to 50 percent. The recommended royalty based on net is 18 percent, but only 14 percent of the Christian publishers counted here are paying 18 percent or higher.

ADVANCES

Not all publishers are willing to disclose whether they pay an advance, and if so, how much. For that reason it is hard to come up with accurate figures. Of those that answered the question about advances, 55 percent pay an advance, and 45 percent say they do not. Of those who indicated a specific amount, the average ranged from about $3,000 to $16,000. (Although one publisher indicated they pay up to a $1 million advance, we didn't include them in order to keep these averages realistic.) Most publishers pay more for established authors or potentially best-selling books. It is not unusual for a first-time author to get no advance or a small one. Once you have one or more books published, feel free to ask for an advance, and raise the amount for each book. Don't be afraid to ask for an advance, even on a first book, if you need the money to support you while you finish the manuscript.

REPORTING TIME

Waiting for a response from an editor is often the hardest part of the writing business. The average response is just over twelve weeks. However, since the times they actually gave ranged from one to fifty-two weeks, be sure to check the listing for the publisher you are interested in. Give them a two- to four-week grace period; then feel free to write a polite letter asking about the current status of your manuscript. Give them another month to respond, and if you don't hear anything, you can call as a last resort or ask for your manuscript to be returned.

E-MAIL AND WEBSITES

Almost every book publisher has both an e-mail and a Website, but some are reluctant to list their e-mail (because of concerns about spam) so they are requiring e-mail submissions to come through their Website.

PREFERRED BIBLE VERSION

Book publishers list their preferred Bible versions as NIV, KJV, NRSV, and NKJV, in that order. Each publisher's preference is indicated in the regular listings.

BOOK PUBLISHERS WITH THE MOST BOOKS ON THE BESTSELLER LIST FOR THE LAST YEAR

This tally is based on actual sales in Christian bookstores reported from July 2006 to June 2007 (most recent information available). Numbers behind the names indicate the number of titles each publisher had on that particular bestseller list during the year.

GENERAL INTEREST

1. Barbour 9
2. Zondervan 6
3. J Countryman 3
4. Standard 3
5. Nelson Books (Nelson Business) 2
6. Abingdon Press 1
7. Bethany House 1
8. Calvary Distribution 1
9. Concordia 1
10. Family Life 1
11. Harper/SanFrancisco 1
12. Harvest House 1
13. Hendrickson 1
14. Howard 1
15. Multnomah 1
16. Nelson Books 1
17. Regal (Gospel Light) 1
18. Revell 1
19. WaterBrook 1
20. W Publishing 1

BIBLICAL STUDIES

1. InterVarsity 11
2. Thomas Nelson 11
3. Nelson Reference 11
4. Zondervan 9
5. NavPress 4
6. AMG Publishers 3
7. Barbour 3
8. Harvest House 3
9. Shaw (WaterBrook) 3
10. WaterBrook 3
11. Nelson/Impact 2
12. Regal 2
13. Tyndale House 2
14. Victor (Cook) 2
15. B&H Publishing Group 1
16. Gospel Light 1
17. Hensley 1
18. Higley 1
19. Sampson Resources 1

CHRISTIAN LIVING

1. Thomas Nelson 20
2. Zondervan 15
3. Harvest House 8
4. FaithWords (Hachette) 6
5. WaterBrook 6
6. Multnomah 5
7. B&H Publishing 4
8. Integrity 3
9. Tyndale 3
10. Warner Faith 3
11. Bethany House 2
12. Charisma (Strang) 2
13. Moody 2
14. Moody (Northfield) 2
15. Revell 2
16. W Publishing (Nelson) 2
17. J Countryman 1
18. Green Key Books 1
19. HarperCollins (Zondervan) 1
20. Ideals 1
21. Life Journey (Cook) 1
22. Nelson/Impact 1

CHURCH & MINISTRY

1. Standard 13
2. Zondervan 7
3. Baker 1
4. Baker Academic 1
5. B&H Publishing Group 1
6. Catholic Book Publishing 1
7. Group Publishing 1
8. NavPress 1
9. Nelson Reference 1
10. New Leaf Press 1
11. Review & Herald Pub 1
12. Tyndale 1

INSPIRATIONAL

1. Barbour 15
2. J Countryman (Nelson) 10
3. Thomas Nelson 10
4. Zondervan 10
5. FaithWords (Hachette) 7
6. Tyndale 6
7. Integrity 3
8. B&H Publishing 2
9. Charisma (Strang) 2
10. Destiny Image 2
11. Frontline (Strang) 2
12. Howard 2
13. Master (New Leaf Press) 2
14. Whitaker House 2
15. Barbour (Discovery) 1
16. Crossway 1
17. Elm Hill (Nelson) 1
18. Harrison House 1
19. Harvest House 1
20. Honor (Cook) 1
21. Regal 1
22. Revell 1
23. Saltriver (Tyndale) 1
24. W Publishing 1
25. Zondervan (Inspirio) 1

THEOLOGY

1. Tyndale 4
2. Zondervan 3
3. InterVarsity 2
4. Thomas Nelson 2
5. B&H Publishing Group 1
6. Chosen (Baker) 1
7. Harper/SanFrancisco 1
8. Moody 1
9. Nelson Reference 1
10. Victor (Cook) 1

FICTION

1. Tyndale 21
2. Bethany House 17
3. Zondervan 10
4. Barbour 7
5. WestBow Press (Nelson) 7
6. Thomas Nelson 6
7. Harvest House 5
8. Multnomah (WaterBrook) 3
9. Viking Adult (Penguin) 2
10. WaterBrook 2
11. Center Street (Hachette) 1
12. HarperCollins 1
13. Putnam Adult (Penguin) 1

CHILDREN'S BOOKS

1. ZonderKidz 16
2. Tommy Nelson 13
3. Standard 12
4. Concordia 8
5. Barbour 3
6. FaithKidz (Cook) 3
7. Multnomah 3
8. B&H Publishing Group 2
9. Tyndale Kids 2
10. Zondervan 2
11. Abingdon Press 1
12. Baker 1
13. CHV 1
14. Crossway 1
15. Dalmatian Press 1
16. Ideals 1
17. Moody 1
18. Tyndale 1

YOUNG ADULT BOOKS

1. Revell 7
2. Harvest House 5
3. Tyndale 5
4. Barbour 4
5. Multnomah 3
6. Tommy Nelson 3
7. B&H Publishing Group 2
8. Bethany House 2
9. Howard 2
10. WaterBrook 2
11. Barbour (Discovery House) 1
12. Integrity 1
13. Living Ink Books (AMC) 1
14. NavPress 1
15. Tyndale Kids 1
16. Victory (Cook) 1
17. Zondervan 1

COMBINED BESTSELLER LISTS

1. Zondervan 63
2. Thomas Nelson 50
3. Tyndale House 43
4. Barbour 41
5. Standard 28
6. Harvest House 23
7. Bethany House 22
8. Tommy Nelson 16
9. ZonderKidz 16
10. Multnomah 15
11. J Countryman 14
12. WaterBrook 14
13. B&H Publishing Group 13
14. FaithWords 13
15. InterVarsity 13
16. Nelson Reference 13
17. Revell 11
18. Concordia 9
19. Integrity 7
20. WestBow/Nelson 7
21. NavPress 6
22. Howard 5
23. Charisma (Strang) 4
24. Moody Press 4
25. Victor (Cook) 4
26. W Publishing 4
27. AMG Publishers 3
28. Cook/FaithKidz 3
29. HarperSanFrancisco 3
30. Nelson/Impact 3
31. Regal 3
32. Shaw (WaterBrook) 3
33. Tyndale Kids 3
34. Warner Faith 3
35. Abingdon Press 2
36. Baker 2
37. Barbour (Discovery) 2
38. Crossway 2
39. Destiny Image 2
40. Frontline (Strang) 2
41. Ideals 2
42. Master Books 2
43. Moody (Northfield) 2
44. Nelson Business 2
45. Viking Adult (Penguin) 2
46. Whitaker House 2
47. Baker Academic 1
48. Calvary Distribution 1
49. Catholic Book Pub 1
50. Center Street (Hachette) 1
51. Chosen (Baker) 1
52. CHV 1
53. Dalmation 1
54. Elm Hill 1
55. Family Life 1
56. Gospel Light 1
57. Green Key Books 1
58. Group Publishing 1
59. HarperCollins 1
60. Harrison House 1
61. Hendrickson 1
62. Hensley Publishing 1
63. Higley 1
64. Honor (Cook) 1
65. Living Ink Books (AMC) 1
66. New Leaf Press 1
67. Putnam Adult (Penguin) 1
68. Regal (Gospel Light) 1
69. Review & Herald Pub 1
70. Saltriver (Tyndale) 1
71. Sampson Resources 1
72. Zondervan (Inspirio) 1

Top 50 Book Publishers

This list this year is based on which publishers had the most books on the list of the Top 50 books each month. It varies from the combined list above in that it tracks the top 50 sellers regardless of genre. It is interesting to note that there are only 33 publishers with books on this list during the year

1. Zondervan 32
2. Thomas Nelson 25
3. Tyndale House 22
4. Barbour 21
5. Harvest House 11
6. J. Countryman 7
7. FaithWords (Hachette) 7
8. WaterBrook 7
9. Bethany 6
10. Multnomah 6
11. Standard 6
12. Integrity 4
13. B&H Publishing Group 3
14. Tommy Nelson 3
15. WestBow (Nelson) 3
16. W Publishing (Nelson) 3
17. Charisma (Strang) 2
18. Frontline (Strang) 2
19. Moody 2
20. Revell 2
21. Warner Faith 2
22. Barbour (Discovery House) 1
23. Center Street (Hachette) 1
24. Concordia 1
25. Destiny Image 1
26. HarperCollins 1
27. Howard 1
28. Ideals 1
29. Life Journey (Cook) 1
30. Moody (Northfield) 1
31. Putnam Adult (Penguin) 1
32. Regal 1
33. Victor (Cook) 1

TOPICAL LISTINGS OF PERIODICALS

As soon as you have an article or story idea, look up that topic in the following topical listings (see table of contents for a full list of topics). Study the appropriate periodicals in the primary/alphabetical listings (as well as their writers' guidelines and sample copies) and select those that are most likely targets for the piece you are writing.

Note that most ideas can be written for more than one periodical if you slant them to the needs of different audiences. Have a target periodical and audience in mind before you start writing. Each topic is divided by age group/audience, so you can pick appropriate markets for your particular slant.

If the magazine prefers or requires a query letter, be sure to write that letter first and then follow any guidelines or suggestions they make if they give you a go-ahead.

R-Takes reprints
(*)-Indicates new topic this year
$-Indicates a paying market
($)-Indicates a market that sometimes pays

APOLOGETICS
ADULT/GENERAL
$-Arkansas Catholic—R
$-Aujourd'hui Credo—R
Bread of Life—R
$-Bridal Guides—R
$-Catholic Insight
CBN.com—R
$-Celebrate Life—R
Channels—R
Christian C. L. RECORD—R
Christian Online
Christian Ranchman
$-Christian Research
$-Christian Standard—R
$-Christianity Today—R
Church of England News
$-City Light News—R
Desert Call—R
$-Discipleship Journal—R
Encompass
Evangelical Advocate—R
$-Focus on the Family
$-HonorBound—R
$-Horizons (adult)—R
($)-Impact—R
$-Light & Life
$-Lookout
$-Montgomery's Journey
MovieGuide
$-National Catholic
$-On Mission
$-Our Sunday Visitor—R
Perspectives—R
Perspectives/Science
PrayerWorks—R
Priscilla Papers
Rare Jewel—R
$-Seek—R
Sight 360—R
$-Social Justice—R
Sword and Trumpet
Sword of the Lord—R
Three One Six—R
$-Today's Christian—R
Wisconsin Christian

CHILDREN
$-SHINEbrightly—R

DAILY DEVOTIONALS
Penned from the Heart—R

PASTORS/LEADERS
$-Catholic Servant
$-Christian Century—R
$-Lutheran Partners—R
$-Outreach—R
Pulpit Helps—R
Theological Digest—R
$-This Rock

TEEN/YOUNG ADULT
$-Boundless Webzine—R
$-Breakaway
$-Brio
$-CLEAR Direction
$-CLEAR Horizon
$-Ignite Your Faith
$-True Girl
$-Young Salvationist—R

WOMEN
$-Canticle
Right to the Heart—R

BIBLE STUDIES
ADULT/GENERAL
$-Advance
($)-AGAIN—R
$-Alive Now—R
$-Arlington Catholic
$-Aujourd'hui Credo—R
Bread of Life—R
Breakthrough Intercessor—R
$-Bridal Guides—R
$-Catholic Peace Voice—R
$-Catholic Yearbook—R
CBN.com—R
Choice Newspaper—R
Christian C. L. RECORD—R
Christian Computing—R
Christian Motorsports
Christian Online
Christian Ranchman
$-Christian Research
$-Christian Standard—R
Church Herald & Holiness—R
Connecting Point—R
Creation Care—R
$-Culture Wars—R
Desert Call—R
$-DreamSeeker—R
E-Quality
Eternal Ink—R
FaithWebbin—R
$-Gem—R
Heartlight—R
$-HonorBound—R
HopeKeepers—R
$-In Touch
$-Indian Life—R
$-Light & Life
$-Lutheran Journal—R
$-Mature Years—R
Methodist History
$-New Freeman—R
$-New Wineskins—R
$-Parabola—R
Perspectives—R

$-Positive Thinking—R
PrayerWorks—R
$-Precepts for Living
Priscilla Papers
Quaker Life—R
Reverent Submissions—R
SearchingWisdom.org—R
$-Seek—R
Sight 360—R
$-Social Justice—R
$-Spiritual Life
$-St. Anthony Messenger
Star of Zion
Sword and Trumpet
Sword of the Lord—R
Three One Six—R
Trumpeter—R
Victory Herald—R
$-War Cry—R
$-Way of St. Francis—R
Wisconsin Christian

CHILDREN
$-Primary Street
$-SHINEbrightly—R

CHRISTIAN EDUCATION/LIBRARY
Catholic Library
$-Children's Ministry
Congregational Libraries
$-Group
$-Preschool Playhouse (CE)
$-RTJ—R

MISSIONS
$-Glad Tidings (Canada)—R
Railroad Evangelist—R
Women of the Harvest

PASTORS/LEADERS
$-African American Pulpit
$-Catholic Servant
$-Let's Worship
Pulpit Helps—R
Sewanee Theo. Review
Sharing the Practice—R
$-Small Group Dynamics—R
Theological Digest—R
$-This Rock
$-Word & World

TEEN/YOUNG ADULT
$-Breakaway
$-Passageway.org—R
$-Sharing the VICTORY—R
TeensForJC—R
$-Young Christian—R

WOMEN
($)-Beyond the Bend—R
CelebrateMoms—R
$-Inspired Living—R
Precious Times—R
Proverbs 31 Sisters—R
Right to the Heart—R
($)-Simply Blessed—R
Together with God—R
Virtuous Woman—R
Women's Ministry

BOOK EXCERPTS

ADULT/GENERAL
($)-AGAIN—R
$-Alive Now—R
$-Associated Content—R
$-BGC World—R
Books & Culture
Breakthrough Intercessor—R
$-Catholic Digest—R
CBN.com—R
Channels—R
$-Charisma
$-Chicken Soup Books—R
Christian C. L. RECORD—R
$-Christian Journal—R
Christian Observer
$-Christian Renewal—R
$-Christian Retailing
$-Christianity Today—R
Church of England News
$-Culture Wars—R
First Call Hospice—R
$-Home Times—R
$-HonorBound—R
HopeKeepers—R
$-Indian Life—R
$-Interim—R
New Heart—R
$-New Wineskins—R
$-Parabola—R
Parents & Teens—R
$-Power for Living—R
$-Prairie Messenger—R
Priscilla Papers
$-Prism
Regent Global—R
Rock & Sling
Sacred Journey—R
Sight 360—R
SingleAgain.com—R
Spiritual Voice—R
Spirituality for Today
STEPS
$-Today's Christian—R
Trumpeter—R
$-United Church Observer—R
$-Upscale
Urban Kingdom—R
$-Vista
$-Wittenburg Door—R

CHRISTIAN EDUCATION/LIBRARY
Christian Early Ed.—R
$-Journal/Adventist Ed.—R

MISSIONS
Intl. Jour./Frontier—R

PASTORS/LEADERS
$-African American Pulpit
$-Christian Century—R
Jour./Amer. Soc./Chur. Growth—R
$-Ministry Today
$-Outreach—R
Rick Warren's Ministry—R

TEEN/YOUNG ADULT
$-Boundless Webzine—R
$-J.A.M.
$-Passageway.org—R
TeensForJC—R

WOMEN
($)-Beyond the Bend—R
CelebrateMoms—R
$-Godly Business Woman—R
$-Heart & Soul
$-Inspired Living—R
$-Link & Visitor—R
$-MOMsense—R
Proverbs 31 Sisters—R
Share
$-SpiritLed Woman
Virtuous Woman—R
Woman of Worth—R

WRITERS
$-Freelance Writer's Report—R
Money the Write Way—R
$-Writer

BOOK REVIEWS

ADULT/GENERAL
$-Abilities
$-Advance
African Voices—R
($)-AGAIN—R
$-America
$-Anglican Journal
$-Animal Trails—R
$-Arkansas Catholic—R
$-Arlington Catholic
$-Associated Content—R
$-Atlantic Catholic
$-Aujourd'hui Credo—R
Books & Culture
Bread of Life—R
Breakthrough Intercessor—R
$-Bridal Guides—R
byFaith
$-Cathedral Age—R
$-Catholic Insight
$-Catholic Peace Voice—R
$-CBA Retailers
CBN.com—R
Channels—R
$-Charisma
Charlotte World
Chocolate Pages

Choice Newspaper—R
Christian C. L. RECORD—R
$-Christian Citizen USA
Christian Computing—R
$-Christian Courier/CAN—R
$-Christian Herald—R
$-Christian Journal—R
Christian Media—R
Christian Observer
Christian Radio
Christian Ranchman
$-Christian Renewal—R
$-Christian Research
$-Christian Retailing
$-Christianity Today—R
Citizen USA—R
$-City Light News—R
Creation Care—R
$-Cresset
CrossHome.com
$-Culture Wars—R
Desert Voice
Diamond Dust
Divine Ascent
$-Dovetail—R
E-Quality
$-Episcopal Life—R
Eternal Ink—R
$-Eureka Street
Evangelical Advocate—R
$-Faith & Family
$-Faith & Friends—R
$-Faith Today
First Call Hospice—R
Founders Journal
Good News Journal—R
Good News Today
Good News!
Good News/S. Florida
$-Haruah—R
Heartland Gatekeeper—R
$-Home Times—R
$-HonorBound—R
HopeKeepers—R
$-Image/WA
Imagine
($)-Impact—R
$-Indian Life—R
Infuze
$-Inland NW Christian
$-Interim—R
$-Liguorian
($)-Mennonite Historian—R
Methodist History
$-Minnesota Christian—R
MovieGuide
($)-Mutuality—R
New Frontier
$-New Wineskins—R
$-Our Sunday Visitor—R
$-Parabola—R
Parents & Teens—R
Penwood Review
Perspectives/Science
$-Prairie Messenger—R
Presbyterian Outlook
Priscilla Papers
$-Prism
$-Pure Inspiration—R
Purpose Magazine—R
Radix—R
Regent Global—R
Reverent Submissions—R
Rock & Sling
Sacred Journey—R
$-Science & Spirit
Sight 360—R
$-Significant Living—R
Silver Wings—R
SingleAgain.com—R
$-Social Justice—R
$-Spiritual Life
Spiritual Voice—R
Star of Zion
Studio—R
$-Testimony—R
Time of Singing—R
Trumpeter—R
$-Upscale
Urban Kingdom—R
Victory Herald—R
$-Way of St. Francis—R
$-Weavings—R
$-Wireless Age—R
$-World & I—R
Xavier Review

CHILDREN

$-New Moon—R
$-SHINEbrightly—R
$-Sparkle—R

CHRISTIAN EDUCATION/LIBRARY

Catholic Library
Christian Early Ed.—R
Christian Librarian—R
Christian School Ed.—R
$-Church Libraries—R
Congregational Libraries
$-Group
Jour. of Christian Ed.
Jour. of Christianity—R
Jour./Ed. & Christian Belief—R
Jour./Research on Christian Ed.
$-Journal/Adventist Ed.—R
$-Momentum
$-Teachers of Vision—R

MISSIONS

$-Evangelical Missions—R
$-Glad Tidings (Canada)—R
Missiology
OpRev Equipper—R
Women of the Harvest

MUSIC

$-CCM Magazine
$-Creator—R
Hymn

PASTORS/LEADERS

$-African American Pulpit
$-Christian Century—R
Cross Currents
$-Diocesan Dialogue—R
$-Emmanuel
$-Enrichment—R
$-Interpreter
Jour./Amer. Soc./Chur. Growth—R
Jour./Pastoral Care—R
$-Leadership—R
$-Let's Worship
Lutheran Forum—R
$-Lutheran Partners—R
$-Ministry
Ministry in Motion—R
$-Ministry Today
Pulpit Helps—R
$-Reformed Worship—R
Sharing the Practice—R
$-Small Group Dynamics—R
Theological Digest—R
$-Willow—R
$-Word & World
$-Worship Leader
$-Your Church—R

TEEN/YOUNG ADULT

$-Boundless Webzine—R
Bubblemag
$-CLEAR Direction
$-CLEAR Horizon
$-Devo'Zine—R
$-J.A.M.
TeensForJC—R
$-True Girl

WOMEN

($)-Beyond the Bend—R
$-Esprit—R
$-Godly Business Woman—R
$-Heart & Soul
$-Herizons
$-Hope for Women
$-Horizons (women)—R
$-Inspired Living—R
$-inSpirit—R
Precious Times—R
Proverbs 31 Sisters—R
Right to the Heart—R
Share
($)-Simply Blessed—R
Virtuous Woman—R
Woman of Worth—R
Women's Ministry
$-WT Online—R

WRITERS
$-Adv. Christian Writer—R
Areopagus
$-Christian Communicator—R
$-Cross & Quill—R
$-Fellowscript—R
Money the Write Way—R
$-Novel Writer—R
NW Christian Author—R
Opinari—R
Poetic Voices—R
$-Spirit-Led Writer—R
$-Tickled by Thunder
$-WIN-Informer
Write Connection
$-Writer
$-Writers' Journal

CANADIAN/FOREIGN MARKETS
ADULT/GENERAL
$-Abilities
Anglican
$-Anglican Journal
$-Annals of St. Anne
$-Atlantic Catholic
$-Aujourd'hui Credo—R
$-Australian Catholics—R
$-B.C. Catholic—R
Bread of Life—R
$-Canada Lutheran—R
Canadian Lutheran
$-Canadian Mennonite—R
CanadianChristianity
$-Catholic Insight
Catholic Register
Challenge Weekly
$-Challenging Destiny—R
Channels—R
Christian Courier/WI—R
$-Christian Herald—R
Christian Outlook
$-Christian Renewal—R
$-ChristianWeek—R
Church of England News
$-City Light News—R
$-Common Ground—R
Creation
$-Dreams & Visions—R
$-Eureka Street
Evangelical Times
$-Faith & Friends—R
$-Faith Today
Fellowship
($)-Impact—R
$-Indian Life—R
$-Interim—R
Island Catholic
LifeSite News
$-Living Light—R
($)-Mennonite Historian—R
$-Messenger
$-Messenger, The
$-Messenger/Sacred Heart
$-Messenger/St. Anthony
Mosaic—R
$-New Freeman—R
$-Prairie Messenger—R
Rhubarb
Studio—R
$-Testimony—R
$-United Church Observer—R

CHRISTIAN EDUCATION/LIBRARY
$-Christian Educators—R
Jour. of Christian Ed.
Jour./Ed. & Christian Belief—R

MISSIONS
Catholic Missions/Canada
Glad Tidings
$-Glad Tidings (Canada)—R

PASTORS/LEADERS
$-Evangelical Baptist—R
Technologies for Worship—R
Theological Digest—R

WOMEN
Christian Women Today—R
$-Esprit—R
Life Tools for Women
$-Link & Visitor—R
Making Waves
Tapestry (Canada)
$-Tapestry/GA
Women Today—R
$-WT Online—R

WRITERS
Areopagus
$-Canadian Writer's Jour.—R
$-Fellowscript—R
$-Novel Writer—R
$-Tickled by Thunder
Writers Manual

CELEBRITY PIECES
ADULT/GENERAL
American Tract—R
$-Angels on Earth
$-Animal Trails—R
$-Arlington Catholic
$-Associated Content—R
$-Australian Catholics—R
Breakthrough
$-Catholic Digest—R
CBN.com—R
$-Celebrate Life—R
$-Challenging Destiny—R
$-Christian Citizen USA
$-Christian Herald—R
$-Christian Journal—R
Christian Motorsports
Christian Online
Christian Radio
Christian Ranchman
$-Christianity Today Movies—R
$-Chronicle Christian
Church of England News
Citizen USA—R
$-City Light News—R
($)-Community Spirit—R
$-Episcopal Life—R
Eternal Ink—R
$-Focus on the Family
$-Focus on Your Child
$-God Allows U-Turns—R
Good News Journal—R
$-Good News, Etc.—R
$-Great Mystery—R
$-Guideposts—R
Heartland Gatekeeper—R
Heartlight—R
$-Home Times—R
$-HonorBound—R
HopeKeepers—R
($)-Impact—R
$-In Touch
$-Indian Life—R
$-Light & Life
$-Living Light—R
Looking Up
$-Minnesota Christian—R
$-Montgomery's Journey
MovieGuide
($)-Mutuality—R
$-New Wineskins—R
$-Positive Thinking—R
$-Power for Living—R
$-Priority!—R
$-Prism
$-Pure Inspiration—R
Sacred Journey—R
Sight 360—R
$-Significant Living—R
Spiritual Voice—R
$-St. Anthony Messenger
$-Today's Christian—R
Tri-State Voice
Trumpeter—R
Urban Kingdom—R
$-Vibrant Life—R
$-War Cry—R
$-Wireless Age—R
$-Wittenburg Door—R

CHILDREN
$-American Girl—R
$-Cadet Quest—R
$-High Adventure—R
$-SHINEbrightly—R
$-Sparkle—R
$-Winner—R

MUSIC
$-Christian Music Today—R
Christian Music Weekly—R

PASTORS/LEADERS
$-Catholic Servant
$-Ministry Today

TEEN/YOUNG ADULT
$-Brio
Bubblemag
$-CLEAR Direction
$-CLEAR Horizon
$-Essential Connection
$-J.A.M.
$-Passageway.org—R
$-Sharing the VICTORY—R
$-Steelroots
$-TC Magazine
TeensForJC—R
$-Young Salvationist—R

WOMEN
($)-Beyond the Bend—R
$-Canticle
$-Godly Business Woman—R
$-Heart & Soul
$-Inspired Living—R
$-Journey
$-MOMsense—R
More to Life
Precious Times—R
Virtuous Woman—R
Woman of Worth—R

CHRISTIAN BUSINESS

ADULT/GENERAL
$-Angels on Earth
$-Animal Trails—R
$-Bridal Guides—R
$-CBA Retailers
CBN.com—R
Choice Newspaper—R
Christian Business
$-Christian Citizen USA
$-Christian Courier/CAN—R
$-Christian Journal—R
Christian Motorsports
Christian Online
$-Christian Retailing
$-ChristianWeek—R
$-Chronicle Christian
Citizen USA—R
$-City Light News—R
($)-Community Spirit—R
Desert Call—R
Disciple's Journal—R
Evangel/OR—R
$-Faith Today
$-Gem—R
Good News Journal—R
$-Gospel Today—R
$-Guideposts—R
Heartland Gatekeeper—R
Heartlight—R
Highway News—R
$-Home Times—R
$-HonorBound—R
$-In Touch
$-Indian Life—R
$-Light & Life
$-Living—R
Looking Up
$-Lookout
Marketplace
Men of the Cross
$-Minnesota Christian—R
$-Montgomery's Journey
$-New Freeman—R
Nostalgia—R
NRB Magazine—R
$-On Mission
$-Power for Living—R
$-Prism
Purpose Magazine—R
Regent Global—R
$-Science & Spirit
Sight 360—R
SingleAgain.com—R
Spiritual Voice—R
$-St. Anthony Messenger
$-Today's Christian—R
$-Together—R
Trumpeter—R
Urban Kingdom—R
Victory Herald—R
$-War Cry—R
$-Wireless Age—R
Wisconsin Christian

CHRISTIAN EDUCATION/LIBRARY
Christian School Ed.—R
$-Resource—R

MISSIONS
$-Evangelical Missions—R

MUSIC
Gospel Synergy

PASTORS/LEADERS
$-African American Pulpit
$-Catholic Servant
$-Clergy Journal—R
$-InSite—R
$-Interpreter
Ministry in Motion—R
Rick Warren's Ministry—R
Technologies for Worship—R
$-Today's Parish—R
$-Willow—R
$-Your Church—R

TEEN/YOUNG ADULT
$-Boundless Webzine—R
$-J.A.M.

WOMEN
($)-Beyond the Bend—R
Christian Women Today—R
$-Dabbling Mum—R
$-Godly Business Woman—R
$-Heart & Soul
$-Inspired Living—R
Precious Times—R
($)-Simply Blessed—R
Virtuous Woman—R
Women Today—R

WRITERS
Money the Write Way—R
Writing Corner—R

CHRISTIAN EDUCATION

ADULT/GENERAL
$-Advance
African Voices—R
$-America
$-Anglican Journal
$-Animal Trails—R
$-Arlington Catholic
$-Atlantic Catholic
$-Aujourd'hui Credo—R
$-B.C. Catholic—R
Breakthrough Intercessor—R
$-Bridal Guides—R
$-Canada Lutheran—R
$-Catholic Peace Voice—R
$-Celebrate Life—R
Channels—R
Christian C. L. RECORD—R
$-Christian Citizen USA
$-Christian Courier/CAN—R
$-Christian Examiner
$-Christian Home & School
$-Christian Journal—R
Christian Observer
Christian Online
Christian Ranchman
$-Christian Renewal—R
$-Christian Retailing
$-Christian Standard—R
$-Christianity Today—R
$-ChristianWeek—R
$-Chronicle Christian
$-City Light News—R
$-Columbia—R
($)-Community Spirit—R
$-Company—R
$-Covenant Companion—R
$-Cresset
$-Culture Wars—R
Desert Call—R
$-Direction
Encompass
Eternal Ink—R
Evangelical Advocate—R
$-Faith & Family
$-Faith Today
$-Family Digest—R
$-Gem—R
Good News Journal—R
$-Gospel Today—R

Heartlight—R
Highway News—R
$-Home Times—R
$-Homeschooling Today—R
$-HonorBound—R
$-In Touch
$-Indian Life—R
$-Inland NW Christian
$-Light & Life
$-Living Church
Looking Up
$-Lookout
$-Messenger/Sacred Heart
Methodist History
$-Minnesota Christian—R
$-Montgomery's Journey
Mosaic—R
MovieGuide
$-National Catholic
$-New Freeman—R
$-New Wineskins—R
Nostalgia—R
Penned from the Heart—R
Perspectives—R
PrayerWorks—R
$-Precepts for Living
Presbyterian Outlook
$-Presbyterians Today—R
$-Prism
$-Purpose—R
Reverent Submissions—R
$-Seek—R
Sight 360—R
SingleAgain.com—R
$-Social Justice—R
Spiritual Voice—R
Spirituality for Today
$-St. Anthony Messenger
Star of Zion
Sword and Trumpet
Sword of the Lord—R
$-Testimony—R
$-Together—R
Trumpeter—R
Urban Kingdom—R
Victory Herald—R
$-Vista
$-War Cry—R
$-Way of St. Francis—R
Wisconsin Christian

CHILDREN

$-Adventures
$-Guide—R
$-JuniorWay
$-Primary Street
$-Sparkle—R

CHRISTIAN EDUCATION/LIBRARY

$-Catechist
$-Children's Ministry
Christian Early Ed.—R
$-Christian Educators—R
Christian Librarian—R
Christian School Ed.—R
$-Group
Ideas Unlimited—R
Jour. of Christian Ed.
Jour. of Christianity—R
Jour./Ed. & Christian Belief—R
Jour./Research on Christian Ed.
$-Journal/Adventist Ed.—R
$-Kids' Ministry Ideas—R
$-Momentum
$-Preschool Playhouse (CE)
$-Resource—R
$-RTJ—R
$-Teach Kids!—R
$-Teachers of Vision—R
$-Today's Catholic Teacher—R
$-Youth & CE Leadership

MISSIONS

$-Evangelical Missions—R
$-Glad Tidings (Canada)—R

PASTORS/LEADERS

$-African American Pulpit
$-Catholic Servant
$-Christian Century—R
Christian Ed. Jour. (CA)—R
$-Clergy Journal—R
Cross Currents
$-Enrichment—R
$-Interpreter
Lutheran Forum—R
$-Lutheran Partners—R
$-Ministry Today
Pulpit Helps—R
$-RevWriter Resource
Rick Warren's Ministry—R
Technologies for Worship—R
$-This Rock
$-Today's Parish—R
$-Word & World
$-Youthworker

TEEN/YOUNG ADULT

$-Boundless Webzine—R
$-J.A.M.
TeensForJC—R
$-True Girl
$-Young Adult Today—R
$-Young Christian—R

WOMEN

CelebrateMoms—R
Christian Woman's Page—R
Crowned with Silver
$-Godly Business Woman—R
Hearts at Home—R
$-Horizons (women)—R
$-inSpirit—R
Just Between Us—R
Precious Times—R
Right to the Heart—R
Share
Together with God—R
Virtuous Woman—R
$-WT Online—R

CHRISTIAN LIVING

ADULT/GENERAL

$-Advance
($)-AGAIN—R
Alabama Baptist
$-Alive Now—R
$-America
American Tract—R
$-Angels on Earth
$-Animal Trails—R
$-Annals of St. Anne
$-Arkansas Catholic—R
$-Arlington Catholic
$-Atlantic Catholic
$-Aujourd'hui Credo—R
$-Australian Catholics—R
$-B.C. Catholic—R
$-BGC World—R
$-Bible Advocate—R
$-Brave Hearts—R
Bread of Life—R
Breakthrough Intercessor—R
$-Bridal Guides—R
$-Canada Lutheran—R
$-Cathedral Age—R
$-Catholic Digest—R
$-Catholic Forester—R
$-Catholic New York
$-Catholic Yearbook—R
CBN.com—R
$-Celebrate Life—R
$-CGA World—R
Channels—R
$-Charisma
$-Chicken Soup Books—R
Choice Newspaper—R
$-Christian Citizen USA
$-Christian Courier/CAN—R
Christian Courier/WI—R
$-Christian Examiner
$-Christian Journal—R
Christian Observer
Christian Online
Christian Radio
Christian Ranchman
$-Christian Research
$-Christian Standard—R
$-Christianity Today—R
$-ChristianWeek—R
$-Chronicle Christian
Church Herald & Holiness—R
Church of England News
$-City Light News—R
$-Columbia—R
($)-Community Spirit—R
Connecting Point—R

$-Covenant Companion—R
$-Culture Wars—R
Desert Call—R
$-Discipleship Journal—R
Divine Ascent
$-DreamSeeker—R
$-EFCA Today—R
$-En Confianza
Encompass
Eternal Ink—R
$-Evangel/IN—R
Evangel/OR—R
Evangelical Advocate—R
$-Faith & Family
$-Faith & Friends—R
$-Faith Today
FaithWebbin—R
$-Family Digest—R
Family Room
$-Focus on the Family
$-Gem—R
$-Gems of Truth—R
$-God Allows U-Turns—R
$-Good News—R
Good News Journal—R
$-Gospel Today—R
$-Guideposts—R
Halo Magazine
$-Haruah—R
Heartlight—R
Highway News—R
$-Home Times—R
$-Homeschooling Today—R
$-HonorBound—R
HopeKeepers—R
$-Horizons (adult)—R
$-Ideals—R
($)-Impact—R
$-In Touch
$-Indian Life—R
$-Inland NW Christian
Keys to Living—R
Leaves—R
$-Light & Life
$-Liguorian
$-Live—R
$-Living—R
$-Living Church
Looking Up
$-Lookout
$-Lutheran Digest—R
$-Lutheran Journal—R
$-Marian Helper
$-Mature Living
$-Mature Years—R
$-Men of Integrity—R
Men of the Cross
Mensajero ala Blanca
MESSAGE/Open Bible—R
$-Messenger/Sacred Heart
Methodist History
$-Minnesota Christian—R
$-Montgomery's Journey
Mosaic—R
($)-Mutuality—R
Nappaland.com
$-New Freeman—R
New Heart—R
$-New Wineskins—R
Nostalgia—R
$-On Mission
$-Over the Back Fence—R
$-Ozarks Senior Living—R
$-Parabola—R
Parents & Teens—R
Penned from the Heart—R
Perspectives—R
$-Positive Thinking—R
$-Power for Living—R
PrayerWorks—R
$-Presbyterians Today—R
$-Psychology for Living—R
$-Pure Inspiration—R
$-Purpose—R
Quaker Life—R
Regent Global—R
Reverent Submissions—R
$-Science & Spirit
SearchingWisdom.org—R
$-Seek—R
Sharing—R
Sight 360—R
Silver Wings—R
SingleAgain.com—R
$-Spiritual Life
Spiritual Voice—R
Spirituality for Today
$-St. Anthony Messenger
$-Standard—R
$-Storyteller—R
SW Kansas Faith
Sword and Trumpet
Sword of the Lord—R
$-Testimony—R
Three One Six—R
$-Today's Christian—R
$-Today's Pentecostal—R
$-Together—R
Trumpeter—R
$-U.S. Catholic
$-United Church Observer—R
Urban Kingdom—R
$-Vibrant Life—R
Victory Herald—R
$-Victory in Grace—R
$-Vision—R
$-Vista
$-War Cry—R
$-Way of St. Francis—R
$-Wesleyan Life—R
$-Whole
Wisconsin Christian

CHILDREN
$-Adventures
$-BREAD/God's Children—R
$-Cadet Quest—R
$-Courage—R
$-Discoveries—R
$-Focus/Clubhouse Jr.
$-Guide—R
$-High Adventure—R
$-JuniorWay
$-Partners—R
$-Passport—R
$-Pockets—R
$-Primary Pal/IL
$-Primary Street

CHRISTIAN EDUCATION/LIBRARY
Congregational Libraries
$-Group
$-Resource—R
$-Teachers of Vision—R
$-Youth & CE Leadership

DAILY DEVOTIONALS
Penned from the Heart—R

MISSIONS
$-Evangelical Missions—R
$-Glad Tidings (Canada)—R
Women of the Harvest

PASTORS/LEADERS
$-African American Pulpit
$-Barefoot—R
$-Catholic Servant
$-Christian Century—R
$-Interpreter
$-Net Results
$-Preaching Well—R
$-Proclaim—R
Pulpit Helps—R
$-Review for Religious
Rick Warren's Ministry—R
Technologies for Worship—R
$-Word & World

TEEN/YOUNG ADULT
$-Boundless Webzine—R
$-Brio
$-CLEAR Direction
$-CLEAR Horizon
$-Credo—R
$-Devo'Zine—R
$-Essential Connection
$-Ignite Your Faith
$-J.A.M.
$-Passageway.org—R
$-Real Faith in Life—R
$-Rock
$-Sharing the VICTORY—R
$-TC Magazine
TeensForJC—R
$-True Girl

$-Young Christian—R
$-Young Salvationist—R

WOMEN

$-At the Center—R
($)-Beyond the Bend—R
$-Canticle
CelebrateMoms—R
Christian Woman's Page—R
Crowned with Silver
$-Dabbling Mum—R
First Lady
$-Godly Business Woman—R
Handmaidens
Hearts at Home—R
$-Hope for Women
$-Horizons (women)—R
$-Inspired Living—R
$-inSpirit—R
$-Journey
Just Between Us—R
$-Link & Visitor—R
Lutheran Woman's Quar.
$-MOMsense—R
P31 Woman—R
Precious Times—R
Proverbs 31 Sisters—R
Right to the Heart—R
Share
($)-Simply Blessed—R
$-SpiritLed Woman
$-Today's Christian Woman—R
Together with God—R
Virtuous Woman—R
Woman of Worth—R
$-Women Alive!—R
Women of the Cross
Women Today—R
Women's Ministry
$-WT Online—R

CHURCH GROWTH

ADULT/GENERAL

($)-AGAIN—R
$-America
$-Animal Trails—R
$-Atlantic Catholic
Bread of Life—R
$-Bridal Guides—R
$-Catholic Peace Voice—R
Channels—R
$-Christian Examiner
$-Christian Journal—R
Christian News NW—R
Christian Online
$-Christian Standard—R
$-ChristianWeek—R
Church Herald & Holiness—R
Church of England News
$-City Light News—R
($)-Community Spirit—R
$-Covenant Companion—R
$-Culture Wars—R
Desert Call—R
Encompass
Eternal Ink—R
$-Evangel/IN—R
Evangelical Advocate—R
$-Faith & Family
$-Faith Today
$-Gem—R
$-Good News—R
$-Home Times—R
$-HonorBound—R
$-Indian Life—R
$-Light & Life
$-Living Church
Looking Up
$-Lookout
MESSAGE/Open Bible—R
$-Messenger/Sacred Heart
Mosaic—R
$-National Catholic
$-New Freeman—R
$-New Wineskins—R
$-On Mission
Penned from the Heart—R
Presbyterian Outlook
$-Presbyterians Today—R
$-Purpose—R
$-Seek—R
Sight 360—R
Spiritual Voice—R
Spirituality for Today
$-St. Anthony Messenger
Star of Zion
Sword and Trumpet
Sword of the Lord—R
$-Testimony—R
Three One Six—R
Trumpeter—R
$-U.S. Catholic
Urban Kingdom—R
$-Victory in Grace—R
$-Wesleyan Life—R
Wisconsin Christian

CHRISTIAN EDUCATION/LIBRARY

$-Children's Ministry
Congregational Libraries
$-Group
$-Youth & CE Leadership

MISSIONS

$-Evangelical Missions—R
Missiology
$-PIME World—R

MUSIC

$-Creator—R

PASTORS/LEADERS

$-African American Pulpit
$-Catholic Servant
$-Christian Century—R
Christian Ed. Jour. (CA)—R
$-Clergy Journal—R
$-Enrichment—R
$-Growth Points—R
$-Interpretation
$-Interpreter
Jour./Amer. Soc./Chur. Growth—R
$-Leadership—R
$-Let's Worship
$-Lutheran Partners—R
Ministry in Motion—R
$-Ministry Today
$-Net Results
$-Outreach—R
Pulpit Helps—R
$-RevWriter Resource
Rick Warren's Ministry—R
Sharing the Practice—R
Technologies for Worship—R
Theological Digest—R
$-This Rock
$-Willow—R
$-Worship Leader
$-Your Church—R

TEEN/YOUNG ADULT

$-CLEAR Direction
$-CLEAR Horizon
$-J.A.M.
$-Passageway.org—R
TeensForJC—R
$-Young Christian—R

WOMEN

($)-Beyond the Bend—R
$-Hope for Women
$-inSpirit—R
Just Between Us—R
Right to the Heart—R
Share
Together with God—R

CHURCH HISTORY

ADULT/GENERAL

African Voices—R
$-America
$-Animal Trails—R
$-Atlantic Catholic
$-Aujourd'hui Credo—R
Bread of Life—R
$-Bridal Guides—R
$-Catholic Digest—R
$-Catholic Insight
$-Catholic Peace Voice—R
$-Catholic Sentinel
$-Catholic Yearbook—R
CBN.com—R
Channels—R
Choice Newspaper—R
$-Christian History—R

Christian Online
Christian Ranchman
$-Christian Renewal—R
$-Christian Standard—R
Church Herald & Holiness—R
Church of England News
Citizen USA—R
$-City Light News—R
$-Columbia—R
$-Company—R
$-Covenant Companion—R
$-Cresset
Desert Call—R
Divine Ascent
Encompass
Evangelical Advocate—R
$-Family Digest—R
Founders Journal
Friends Journal—R
$-Home Times—R
$-HonorBound—R
$-Horizons (adult)—R
$-In Touch
$-Indian Life—R
Jour. of Church & State
$-Leben—R
$-Light & Life
$-Liguorian
$-Lookout
$-Lutheran Journal—R
($)-Mennonite Historian—R
$-Messiah
Methodist History
Mosaic—R
MovieGuide
$-National Catholic
$-New Wineskins—R
$-Our Sunday Visitor—R
$-Parabola—R
PrayerWorks—R
Presbyterian Outlook
$-Presbyterians Today—R
Priscilla Papers
$-Purpose—R
Rare Jewel—R
$-Science & Spirit
Sight 360—R
$-Social Justice—R
Spiritual Voice—R
Spirituality for Today
$-St. Anthony Messenger
Star of Zion
Sword and Trumpet
Sword of the Lord—R
Three One Six—R
Trumpeter—R
$-U.S. Catholic
Urban Kingdom—R
Victory Herald—R
$-Way of St. Francis—R
$-Wesleyan Life—R
Wisconsin Christian

CHILDREN

$-BREAD/God's Children—R
$-Guide—R
$-Primary Pal/IL

CHRISTIAN EDUCATION/LIBRARY

Catholic Library
$-Group

DAILY DEVOTIONALS

Penned from the Heart—R

MISSIONS

$-Evangelical Missions—R
Missiology
OpRev Equipper—R
Railroad Evangelist—R

PASTORS/LEADERS

$-African American Pulpit
$-Christian Century—R
$-Clergy Journal—R
Cross Currents
$-Leadership—R
$-Ministry & Liturgy—R
Pulpit Helps—R
Sharing the Practice—R
Theological Digest—R
$-This Rock

TEEN/YOUNG ADULT

$-Boundless Webzine—R
$-Breakaway
$-CLEAR Direction
$-CLEAR Horizon
$-Essential Connection
$-J.A.M.
$-Living My Faith
$-Passageway.org—R
$-Real Faith in Life—R
TeensForJC—R
$-Young Christian—R

WOMEN

($)-Beyond the Bend—R
($)-History's Women—R
$-Horizons (women)—R
$-Link & Visitor—R
Share

CHURCH LIFE

ADULT/GENERAL

($)-AGAIN—R
$-America
$-Animal Trails—R
$-Arkansas Catholic—R
$-Atlantic Catholic
$-Aujourd'hui Credo—R
$-Australian Catholics—R
Bread of Life—R
$-Bridal Guides—R
$-Cathedral Age—R
$-Catholic Digest—R
$-Catholic Insight
$-Catholic Sentinel
$-Catholic Yearbook—R
CBN.com—R
Channels—R
Choice Newspaper—R
Christian News NW—R
Christian Online
$-Christian Standard—R
$-Christianity Today—R
$-ChristianWeek—R
Church Herald & Holiness—R
Church of England News
Citizen USA—R
$-City Light News—R
$-Columbia—R
($)-Community Spirit—R
$-Company—R
$-Covenant Companion—R
Desert Call—R
$-DisciplesWorld
$-DreamSeeker—R
Encompass
Eternal Ink—R
$-Evangel/IN—R
Evangel/OR—R
Evangelical Advocate—R
$-Faith & Family
$-Faith Today
$-Family Digest—R
$-Gem—R
$-Good News—R
$-Home Times—R
$-HonorBound—R
$-Horizons (adult)—R
$-In Touch
Leaves—R
$-Light & Life
$-Liguorian
$-Live—R
$-Living Church
$-Lookout
$-Lutheran Journal—R
($)-Mennonite Historian—R
MESSAGE/Open Bible—R
$-Messenger/St. Anthony
$-Minnesota Christian—R
$-Montgomery's Journey
Mosaic—R
($)-Mutuality—R
$-National Catholic
$-New Freeman—R
$-New Wineskins—R
Nostalgia—R
$-On Mission
$-Our Sunday Visitor—R
$-Parabola—R
Penned from the Heart—R
$-Precepts for Living
Presbyterian Outlook
$-Presbyterians Today—R
Priscilla Papers

$-Purpose—R
Reverent Submissions—R
$-Seek—R
Sight 360—R
Silver Wings—R
Spiritual Voice—R
Spirituality for Today
$-St. Anthony Messenger
Star of Zion
Sword of the Lord—R
$-Testimony—R
Three One Six—R
$-Today's Christian—R
$-Today's Pentecostal—R
Trumpeter—R
$-U.S. Catholic
Urban Kingdom—R
Victory Herald—R
$-Way of St. Francis—R
$-Wesleyan Life—R

CHILDREN
$-Primary Street

CHRISTIAN EDUCATION/LIBRARY
$-Children's Ministry
$-Group
$-Resource—R
$-Youth & CE Leadership

DAILY DEVOTIONALS
Penned from the Heart—R

MISSIONS
$-Evangelical Missions—R
$-Glad Tidings (Canada)—R

PASTORS/LEADERS
$-African American Pulpit
$-Catholic Servant
$-Christian Century—R
$-Enrichment—R
$-Interpreter
$-Leadership—R
$-Ministry
Ministry in Motion—R
$-Ministry Today
$-Net Results
$-Priest
$-RevWriter Resource
Rick Warren's Ministry—R
Sharing the Practice—R
Technologies for Worship—R
$-Willow—R
$-Worship Leader
$-Youthworker

TEEN/YOUNG ADULT
$-Boundless Webzine—R
$-Breakaway
$-J.A.M.
$-Passageway.org—R
$-Young Christian—R

WOMEN
($)-Beyond the Bend—R
$-Canticle
Christian Woman's Page—R
Handmaiden—R
$-Hope for Women
$-Horizons (women)—R
$-inSpirit—R
Right to the Heart—R
Share
Together with God—R

CHURCH MANAGEMENT

ADULT/GENERAL
$-America
$-Animal Trails—R
$-Atlantic Catholic
$-Bridal Guides—R
Channels—R
Christian Computing—R
Christian News NW—R
Christian Online
$-Christian Standard—R
$-ChristianWeek—R
Church of England News
$-City Light News—R
($)-Community Spirit—R
$-Culture Wars—R
Disciple's Journal—R
Encompass
Evangelical Advocate—R
$-Faith Today
$-Gem—R
$-Good News, Etc.—R
$-Gospel Today—R
$-HonorBound—R
$-Living Church
$-Lookout
Mosaic—R
$-New Freeman—R
$-On Mission
Presbyterian Outlook
Priscilla Papers
Regent Global—R
Sight 360—R
Spiritual Voice—R
$-St. Anthony Messenger
Star of Zion
Sword of the Lord—R
Trumpeter—R
$-U.S. Catholic

CHRISTIAN EDUCATION/LIBRARY
$-Children's Ministry
$-Group
$-Resource—R
$-Youth & CE Leadership

DAILY DEVOTIONALS
Penned from the Heart—R

MISSIONS
$-Evangelical Missions—R

PASTORS/LEADERS
$-African American Pulpit
$-Catholic Servant
Christian Ed. Jour. (CA)—R
Christian Management—R
$-Clergy Journal—R
$-Enrichment—R
$-Growth Points—R
$-Interpretation
$-Interpreter
Jour./Amer. Soc./Chur. Growth—R
$-Leadership—R
$-Lutheran Partners—R
$-Ministry
Ministry in Motion—R
$-Ministry Today
$-Net Results
Pulpit Helps—R
$-RevWriter Resource
Rick Warren's Ministry—R
Sharing the Practice—R
Technologies for Worship—R
$-Word & World
$-Worship Leader
$-Your Church—R

TEEN/YOUNG ADULT
$-Young Christian—R

WOMEN
Just Between Us—R
Right to the Heart—R
Share
Women's Ministry

CHURCH OUTREACH

ADULT/GENERAL
($)-AGAIN—R
$-America
$-Animal Trails—R
$-Atlantic Catholic
Bread of Life—R
$-Bridal Guides—R
$-Catholic Sentinel
CBN.com—R
Channels—R
Choice Newspaper—R
Christian News NW—R
Christian Online
$-Christian Research
$-Christian Standard—R
$-ChristianWeek—R
Church of England News
$-City Light News—R
$-Columbia—R
($)-Community Spirit—R
$-Company—R
$-Covenant Companion—R
$-Culture Wars—R
Desert Call—R

$-DisciplesWorld
Encompass
$-Episcopal Life—R
Eternal Ink—R
$-Evangel/IN—R
Evangel/OR—R
Evangelical Advocate—R
$-Faith & Friends—R
$-Faith Today
First Call Hospice—R
$-Gem—R
$-Good News—R
Heartland Gatekeeper—R
$-Home Times—R
$-HonorBound—R
HopeKeepers—R
$-Light & Life
$-Living Church
$-Lookout
MESSAGE/Open Bible—R
$-Montana Catholic
Mosaic—R
$-National Catholic
Network
$-New Freeman—R
$-New Wineskins—R
$-On Mission
$-Our Sunday Visitor—R
$-Precepts for Living
Presbyterian Outlook
$-Presbyterians Today—R
$-Priority!—R
Priscilla Papers
$-Prism
$-Purpose—R
$-Science & Spirit
$-Seek—R
Sight 360—R
Spiritual Voice—R
$-St. Anthony Messenger
$-St. Joseph's Messenger—R
Sword of the Lord—R
$-Testimony—R
$-Today's Christian—R
Trumpeter—R
$-U.S. Catholic
Urban Kingdom—R
Victory Herald—R
$-Way of St. Francis—R
$-Wesleyan Life—R
Wisconsin Christian

CHILDREN

$-Primary Street

CHRISTIAN EDUCATION/LIBRARY

$-Children's Ministry
$-Group
$-Journal/Adventist Ed.—R
$-Kids' Ministry Ideas—R
$-Momentum
$-Resource—R
$-Teach Kids!—R
$-Youth & CE Leadership

MISSIONS

$-Evangelical Missions—R
$-Glad Tidings (Canada)—R
Missiology
$-PIME World—R
Railroad Evangelist—R

PASTORS/LEADERS

$-African American Pulpit
$-Catholic Servant
$-Christian Century—R
$-Clergy Journal—R
$-Cornerstone Youth—R
$-Enrichment—R
$-Growth Points—R
$-Interpreter
Jour./Amer. Soc./Chur. Growth—R
$-Leadership—R
$-Let's Worship
$-Lutheran Partners—R
$-Ministry
Ministry in Motion—R
$-Ministry Today
$-Net Results
$-Outreach—R
$-Rev. Magazine
$-RevWriter Resource
Rick Warren's Ministry—R
Sharing the Practice—R
Technologies for Worship—R
$-This Rock
$-Today's Parish—R
$-Willow—R
$-Word & World
$-Worship Leader
$-Youthworker

TEEN/YOUNG ADULT

$-CLEAR Direction
$-CLEAR Horizon
$-Credo—R
$-Passageway.org—R
TeensForJC—R
$-True Girl
$-Young Christian—R

WOMEN

Christian Woman's Page—R
$-Hope for Women
$-inSpirit—R
Just Between Us—R
Proverbs 31 Sisters—R
Right to the Heart—R
Share
Together with God—R
Virtuous Woman—R
Women's Ministry

CHURCH TRADITIONS

ADULT/GENERAL

($)-AGAIN—R
$-America
$-Animal Trails—R
$-Arkansas Catholic—R
$-Atlantic Catholic
$-Aujourd'hui Credo—R
$-Bridal Guides—R
$-Canada Lutheran—R
$-Catholic Digest—R
$-Catholic Yearbook—R
CBN.com—R
$-Celebrate Life—R
$-CGA World—R
Channels—R
$-Christian Examiner
$-Christian History—R
Christian Online
$-Christian Research
$-Christian Standard—R
Church of England News
$-City Light News—R
$-Columbia—R
$-Cresset
Desert Call—R
Encompass
Evangelical Advocate—R
$-Faith & Family
$-Faith Today
$-Family Digest—R
$-Gem—R
$-Gospel Today—R
$-HonorBound—R
$-Indian Life—R
$-Light & Life
$-Living Church
$-Lutheran Journal—R
($)-Mennonite Historian—R
Mosaic—R
$-National Catholic
$-New Freeman—R
$-New Wineskins—R
Nostalgia—R
$-Our Sunday Visitor—R
$-Parabola—R
Perspectives—R
PrayerWorks—R
$-Presbyterians Today—R
Priscilla Papers
$-Science & Spirit
Sight 360—R
$-Social Justice—R
Spiritual Voice—R
$-St. Anthony Messenger
$-Standard—R
Star of Zion
$-Testimony—R
Three One Six—R
$-Together—R

Trumpeter—R
$-U.S. Catholic
$-Way of St. Francis—R

CHRISTIAN EDUCATION/LIBRARY
$-Children's Ministry
$-Group
$-RTJ—R

DAILY DEVOTIONALS
Penned from the Heart—R

PASTORS/LEADERS
$-African American Pulpit
$-Barefoot—R
$-Christian Century—R
$-Clergy Journal—R
$-Interpreter
$-Leadership—R
$-Ministry & Liturgy—R
$-Ministry Today
Pulpit Helps—R
Rick Warren's Ministry—R
Sharing the Practice—R
Theological Digest—R
$-This Rock

TEEN/YOUNG ADULT
$-J.A.M.
$-Passageway.org—R
TeensForJC—R
$-True Girl
$-Young Christian—R

WOMEN
$-Canticle
Handmaiden—R
$-Horizons (women)—R
Share

CONTROVERSIAL ISSUES

ADULT/GENERAL
($)-AGAIN—R
$-America
American Tract—R
$-Animal Trails—R
$-Associated Content—R
$-Aujourd'hui Credo—R
$-Bible Advocate—R
Biblical Recorder
$-Bridal Guides—R
CanadianChristianity
$-Catholic Insight
$-Catholic Peace Voice—R
CBN.com—R
$-Celebrate Life—R
Challenge Weekly
Channels—R
Christian C. L. RECORD—R
$-Christian Citizen USA
$-Christian Courier/CAN—R
$-Christian Examiner
Christian Media—R
Christian Online
Christian Radio
$-Christian Renewal—R
$-Christian Response—R
$-Christian Standard—R
$-Christianity Today—R
$-Christianity Today Movies—R
$-ChristianWeek—R
$-Chronicle Christian
Church of England News
Citizen USA—R
$-City Light News—R
($)-Community Spirit—R
$-Creative Nonfiction
$-Culture Wars—R
Desert Christian
Desert Voice
$-Discipleship Journal—R
$-Dovetail—R
$-DreamSeeker—R
$-En Confianza
Encompass
Evangelical Advocate—R
Evangelical Times
$-Faith Today
$-God Allows U-Turns—R
$-Good News—R
Good News Today
Good News!
Good News/S. Florida
$-Gospel Today—R
Heartland Gatekeeper—R
$-Home Times—R
$-Homeschooling Today—R
$-HonorBound—R
($)-Impact—R
$-Interim—R
LarkNews.com
$-Light & Life
$-Live—R
$-Living Church
$-Lookout
$-Minnesota Christian—R
MovieGuide
($)-Mutuality—R
$-National Catholic
$-New Wineskins—R
$-Now What?—R
$-Our Sunday Visitor—R
$-Parabola—R
Perspectives—R
$-Prairie Messenger—R
Priscilla Papers
$-Prism
$-Psychology for Living—R
$-Purpose—R
Rare Jewel—R
Rock & Sling
Sacred Journey—R
$-Science & Spirit
Sight 360—R
SingleAgain.com—R
$-Social Justice—R
Spiritual Voice—R
$-St. Anthony Messenger
Sword of the Lord—R
Three One Six—R
$-Today's Christian—R
Tri-State Voice
Trumpeter—R
$-U.S. Catholic
Urban Kingdom—R
$-War Cry—R
$-Way of St. Francis—R
$-Whole
Wisconsin Christian
$-Wittenburg Door—R
$-World & I—R
World Net Daily
Xavier Review

CHILDREN
$-New Moon—R
Skipping Stones

CHRISTIAN EDUCATION/LIBRARY
Catholic Library
$-Group
$-Teachers of Vision—R
$-Today's Catholic Teacher—R

MISSIONS
$-Evangelical Missions—R
Intl. Jour./Frontier—R
OpRev Equipper—R

MUSIC
$-Christian Music Today—R
Hymn

PASTORS/LEADERS
$-African American Pulpit
Alpha News
$-Christian Century—R
$-Clergy Journal—R
Cross Currents
$-InSite—R
$-Interpreter
Jour./Pastoral Care—R
$-Let's Worship
$-Ministry & Liturgy—R
$-Ministry Today
$-Outreach—R
Pulpit Helps—R
$-This Rock
$-Word & World
$-Worship Leader

TEEN/YOUNG ADULT
$-Boundless Webzine—R
$-Brio
FOTF Dare 2 Dig Deeper

$-Ignite Your Faith
$-Insight—R
$-J.A.M.
$-Passageway.org—R
$-Sharing the VICTORY—R
$-TC Magazine
TeensForJC—R
$-True Girl
$-Young Christian—R
$-Young Salvationist—R

WOMEN
($)-Beyond the Bend—R
$-Canticle
$-Esprit—R
$-Godly Business Woman—R
$-Heart & Soul
$-Herizons
$-Hope for Women
$-Inspired Living—R
$-inSpirit—R
Precious Times—R
Right to the Heart—R
$-WT Online—R

WRITERS
Areopagus

CRAFTS

ADULT/GENERAL
$-Associated Content—R
$-Atlantic Catholic
$-CGA World—R
Christian Online
($)-Community Spirit—R
Diamond Dust
$-Faith & Family
Imagine
$-Living—R
$-Mature Living
$-Parabola—R
SearchingWisdom.org—R
Spiritual Voice—R
Sword of the Lord—R
Urban Kingdom—R
Victory Herald—R
$-World & I—R

CHILDREN
$-Adventures
$-American Girl—R
$-BREAD/God's Children—R
$-Cadet Quest—R
$-Celebrate
$-Courage—R
$-Discoveries—R
$-Focus/Clubhouse
$-Focus/Clubhouse Jr.
$-High Adventure—R
$-Junior Companion—R
$-JuniorWay
$-Passport—R
$-Pockets—R
$-Preschool Playhouse (child)
$-Primary Pal/IL
$-SHINEbrightly—R
$-Sparkle—R
$-Story Mates—R

CHRISTIAN EDUCATION/LIBRARY
$-Catechist
$-Children's Ministry
$-RTJ—R
$-Teach Kids!—R
$-Youth & CE Leadership

PASTORS/LEADERS
$-Interpreter

TEEN/YOUNG ADULT
$-Brio
$-J.A.M.
TeensForJC—R
$-True Girl

WOMEN
CelebrateMoms—R
Christian Woman's Page—R
Keeping Hearts & Home
$-MOMsense—R
P31 Woman—R
Proverbs 31 Sisters—R
Right to the Heart—R
Virtuous Woman—R
Woman of Worth—R
Women's Ministry

CREATION SCIENCE

ADULT/GENERAL
Answers
$-Bible Advocate—R
$-Bridal Guides—R
CBN.com—R
$-Christian Citizen USA
$-Christian Courier/CAN—R
$-Christian Examiner
Christian Observer
$-Christian Renewal—R
$-Christian Research
Citizen USA—R
$-City Light News—R
$-Faith Today
$-Haruah—R
$-Home Times—R
$-Homeschooling Today—R
$-HonorBound—R
$-Horizons (adult)—R
$-Living—R
$-Lookout
$-New Freeman—R
Perspectives/Science
Rare Jewel—R
$-Salvo
Sight 360—R
Spiritual Voice—R
$-St. Anthony Messenger
Sword and Trumpet
Sword of the Lord—R
Three One Six—R
Trumpeter—R
$-War Cry—R
Wisconsin Christian

CHILDREN
$-Courage—R
$-Guide—R
$-Nature Friend
$-Primary Pal/IL
$-Sparkle—R

CHRISTIAN EDUCATION/LIBRARY
$-Journal/Adventist Ed.—R

PASTORS/LEADERS
Cross Currents
Pulpit Helps—R
$-This Rock

TEEN/YOUNG ADULT
$-Boundless Webzine—R
$-Breakaway
$-J.A.M.
$-Passageway.org—R
$-Real Faith in Life—R
$-Young Christian—R
$-Young Salvationist—R

WOMEN
$-Godly Business Woman—R
Together with God—R

CULTS/OCCULT

ADULT/GENERAL
American Tract—R
CBN.com—R
Choice Newspaper—R
Christian C. L. RECORD—R
$-Christian Citizen USA
$-Christian Examiner
$-Christian Renewal—R
$-Christian Research
Citizen USA—R
$-City Light News—R
$-Creative Nonfiction
$-Culture Wars—R
$-Faith Today
$-HonorBound—R
$-Lookout
New Heart—R
$-Now What?—R
Sight 360—R
Spiritual Voice—R
Sword of the Lord—R
Three One Six—R
Trumpeter—R
Wisconsin Christian

MISSIONS
Intl. Jour./Frontier—R

PASTORS/LEADERS
$-Ministry Today
$-Word & World

TEEN/YOUNG ADULT
$-Boundless Webzine—R
$-CLEAR Direction
$-CLEAR Horizon
$-Passageway.org—R
$-Real Faith in Life—R
$-TC Magazine
TeensForJC—R
$-Young Salvationist—R

WOMEN
$-Journey
Together with God—R

CURRENT/SOCIAL ISSUES

ADULT/GENERAL
$-Advance
American Tract—R
$-Anglican Journal
$-Animal Trails—R
$-Apocalypse Chronicles—R
$-Arlington Catholic
$-Associated Content—R
$-Aujourd'hui Credo—R
$-B.C. Catholic—R
$-BGC World—R
$-Bible Advocate—R
Biblical Recorder
$-Bridal Guides—R
CanadianChristianity
$-Catholic Insight
$-Catholic New York
$-Catholic Peace Voice—R
CBN.com—R
Challenge Weekly
Channels—R
Christian C. L. RECORD—R
$-Christian Citizen USA
$-Christian Courier/CAN—R
Christian Courier/WI—R
$-Christian Examiner
Christian Observer
Christian Online
Christian Outlook
Christian Ranchman
$-Christian Renewal—R
$-Christian Research
$-Christian Standard—R
$-Christianity Today—R
$-Christianity Today Movies—R
$-ChristianWeek—R
$-Chronicle Christian
Church Herald & Holiness—R
Church of England News
Citizen USA—R
$-City Light News—R
$-Columbia—R
($)-Community Spirit—R
$-Covenant Companion—R
$-Creative Nonfiction
$-Cresset
$-Culture Wars—R
Desert Call—R
Desert Christian
Desert Voice
$-Discipleship Journal—R
$-DisciplesWorld
$-Dovetail—R
$-DreamSeeker—R
$-En Confianza
Encompass
$-Eureka Street
Evangel/OR—R
Evangelical Advocate—R
Evangelical Times
$-Faith Today
$-Focus on the Family
Friends Journal—R
$-Gem—R
$-God Allows U-Turns—R
$-Good News—R
Good News Connection
Good News Journal—R
Good News Today
Good News/S. Florida
Heartland Gatekeeper—R
Heartlight—R
$-Homeschooling Today—R
$-HonorBound—R
$-In Touch
$-Indian Life—R
$-Inland NW Christian
Island Catholic
Jour. of Church & State
LarkNews.com
$-Liberty
LifeSite News
$-Light & Life
$-Liguorian
$-Living—R
Looking Up
$-Lookout
$-Marian Helper
$-Mature Living
$-Men of Integrity—R
$-MESSAGE
MESSAGE/Open Bible—R
$-Messenger/St. Anthony
$-Minnesota Christian—R
$-Montgomery's Journey
Mosaic—R
MovieGuide
($)-Mutuality—R
$-National Catholic
$-New Freeman—R
New Heart—R
$-New Wineskins—R
$-Now What?—R
$-Our Sunday Visitor—R
$-Ozarks Senior Living—R
$-ParentLife
Perspectives—R
$-Priority!—R
Priscilla Papers
$-Prism
$-Psychology for Living—R
$-Purpose—R
Sacred Journey—R
$-Seek—R
Sight 360—R
Silver Wings—R
SingleAgain.com—R
$-Social Justice—R
Society/Prevention of Cruelty
$-Special Living—R
Spiritual Voice—R
$-St. Anthony Messenger
$-St. Joseph's Messenger—R
$-Storyteller—R
Sword of the Lord—R
Three One Six—R
$-Today's Christian—R
$-Together—R
Tri-State Voice
Trumpeter—R
$-U.S. Catholic
Urban Kingdom—R
$-Vista
$-War Cry—R
$-Way of St. Francis—R
West Wind Review
$-Whole
Wisconsin Christian
$-Wittenburg Door—R
$-World & I—R
World Net Daily

CHILDREN
$-JuniorWay
$-New Moon—R
$-SHINEbrightly—R
Skipping Stones
$-Sparkle—R

CHRISTIAN EDUCATION/LIBRARY
Catholic Library
$-Children's Ministry

DAILY DEVOTIONALS
Penned from the Heart—R

MISSIONS
$-New World Outlook
$-One
OpRev Equipper—R
$-PIME World—R
Women of the Harvest

MUSIC
$-CCM Magazine
$-Christian Music Today—R

PASTORS/LEADERS
$-African American Pulpit
Alpha News
$-Barefoot—R
$-Catholic Servant
$-Christian Century—R
Engage
$-InSite—R
$-Interpreter
$-Leadership—R
$-Lutheran Partners—R
$-Ministry Today
$-Outreach—R
Pulpit Helps—R
$-This Rock
$-Willow—R
$-Word & World

TEEN/YOUNG ADULT
$-Boundless Webzine—R
$-Breakaway
$-Brio
$-CLEAR Direction
$-CLEAR Horizon
$-Credo—R
$-Devo'Zine—R
FOTF Dare 2 Dig Deeper
$-J.A.M.
$-Passageway.org—R
$-Risen
$-Sharing the VICTORY—R
$-TC Magazine
TeensForJC—R
$-True Girl
$-Young Adult Today—R
$-Young Christian—R
$-Young Salvationist—R

WOMEN
($)-Beyond the Bend—R
Comfort Café
$-Esprit—R
$-Fullfill
$-Godly Business Woman—R
Handmaiden—R
$-Heart & Soul
$-Herizons
$-Hope for Women
$-Horizons (women)—R
$-Inspired Living—R
$-inSpirit—R
$-Link & Visitor—R
Making Waves
$-SpiritLed Woman
Together with God—R
Virtuous Woman—R
Women Today—R
$-WT Online—R

WRITERS
Areopagus

DEATH/DYING

ADULT/GENERAL
($)-AGAIN—R
$-America
American Tract—R
$-Arlington Catholic
$-Associated Content—R
$-Atlantic Catholic
$-Aujourd'hui Credo—R
$-BGC World—R
$-Bible Advocate—R
Bread of Life—R
CBN.com—R
$-Celebrate Life—R
Channels—R
$-Chicken Soup Books—R
$-Christian Journal—R
Christian Online
Christian Ranchman
$-Christianity Today—R
$-ChristianWeek—R
$-Chronicle Christian
Citizen USA—R
$-City Light News—R
($)-Community Spirit—R
$-Creative Nonfiction
Desert Call—R
$-Dovetail—R
Evangelical Advocate—R
$-Faith Today
First Call Hospice—R
$-Focus on the Family
$-Gem—R
$-God Allows U-Turns—R
$-Guideposts—R
Heartlight—R
$-Homeschooling Today—R
HopeKeepers—R
$-Horizons (adult)—R
$-In Touch
$-Liguorian
$-Live—R
Looking Up
$-Lookout
$-Mature Living
$-Men of Integrity—R
$-Messenger/Sacred Heart
$-National Catholic
$-New Freeman—R
New Heart—R
$-New Wineskins—R
$-Now What?—R
$-Positive Thinking—R
$-Prairie Messenger—R
PrayerWorks—R
Presbyterian Outlook
$-Presbyterians Today—R
$-Prism
$-Psychology for Living—R
Sacred Journey—R
SearchingWisdom.org—R
$-Seek—R
Sight 360—R
$-Significant Living—R
Silver Wings—R
SingleAgain.com—R
Spiritual Voice—R
$-St. Anthony Messenger
$-Storyteller—R
Sword of the Lord—R
$-Testimony—R
Three One Six—R
$-Today's Christian—R
Trumpeter—R
$-U.S. Catholic
Urban Kingdom—R
$-Vista
$-War Cry—R
$-Way of St. Francis—R
Wisconsin Christian

CHILDREN
$-New Moon—R
Skipping Stones
$-Sparkle—R

DAILY DEVOTIONALS
Penned from the Heart—R

PASTORS/LEADERS
$-Catholic Servant
$-Christian Century—R
$-Clergy Journal—R
$-InSite—R
$-Interpreter
Jour./Pastoral Care—R
$-Leadership—R
$-Lutheran Partners—R
$-RevWriter Resource
Sharing the Practice—R

TEEN/YOUNG ADULT
$-Boundless Webzine—R
$-Brio
$-J.A.M.
$-Passageway.org—R
TeensForJC—R
$-True Girl

WOMEN
($)-Beyond the Bend—R
$-Canticle
Comfort Café
$-Godly Business Woman—R
$-Hope for Women
$-inSpirit—R
Precious Times—R
Together with God—R
Virtuous Woman—R
Woman of Worth—R

Women Today—R
$-WT Online—R

DEVOTIONALS/ MEDITATIONS

ADULT/GENERAL

$-Advance
$-Alive Now—R
$-America
$-Animal Trails—R
$-Annals of St. Anne
$-Arlington Catholic
$-Aujourd'hui Credo—R
$-Australian Catholics—R
Bread of Life—R
$-Bridal Guides—R
$-Catholic Peace Voice—R
CBN.com—R
$-Chicken Soup Books—R
Choice Newspaper—R
$-Christian Journal—R
Christian Online
Christian Ranchman
Church Herald & Holiness—R
$-Covenant Companion—R
Creation Care—R
CrossHome.com
Desert Call—R
Diamond Dust
Divine Ascent
Eternal Ink—R
$-Evangel/IN—R
Evangelical Advocate—R
Evangelical Times
$-Faith & Family
$-Faith & Friends—R
FaithWebbin—R
First Call Hospice—R
Founders Journal
$-Gem—R
$-Good News—R
Good News Journal—R
$-Haruah—R
Heartlight—R
$-HonorBound—R
HopeKeepers—R
$-Ideals—R
Keys to Living—R
Leaves—R
LifeTimes Catholic
$-Liguorian
$-Live—R
$-Living Church
Looking Up
$-Lutheran Digest—R
$-Mature Living
Men of the Cross
$-Messenger/Sacred Heart
$-Messenger/St. Anthony
Mosaic—R
($)-Mutuality—R
$-National Catholic
$-New Freeman—R
New Heart—R
$-New Wineskins—R
$-Parabola—R
Penned from the Heart—R
Perspectives—R
$-Positive Thinking—R
PrayerWorks—R
$-Prism
$-Pure Inspiration—R
Quaker Life—R
Radix—R
Reverent Submissions—R
SearchingWisdom.org—R
Sight 360—R
Silver Wings—R
Spiritual Voice—R
$-Sports Spectrum
$-St. Anthony Messenger
$-Standard—R
Star of Zion
Sword of the Lord—R
Three One Six—R
$-Today's Christian—R
$-Today's Pentecostal—R
Trumpeter—R
$-U.S. Catholic
Urban Kingdom—R
Victory Herald—R
$-Victory in Grace—R
$-Vision—R
$-Vista
$-War Cry—R
$-Way of St. Francis—R
$-Weavings—R
$-Wesleyan Life—R

CHILDREN

$-Discoveries—R
$-Keys for Kids—R
$-Passport—R
$-Pockets—R
$-Primary Pal/IL
$-Sparkle—R

CHRISTIAN EDUCATION/LIBRARY

Congregational Libraries
$-Group

DAILY DEVOTIONALS

Anchor Devotional
CLEAR Living
$-Closer Walk
Daily Dev. for Deaf
$-Devotions
E-ncouragement
$-Forward Day by Day
Fruit of the Vine
$-InDeed
$-Light from the Word
$-My Daily Visitor
Our Journey
Penned from the Heart—R
$-Quiet Hour
$-Secret Place
$-These Days
$-Upper Room
$-Word in Season

MISSIONS

$-Glad Tidings (Canada)—R
$-One
Women of the Harvest

PASTORS/LEADERS

$-Catholic Servant
$-Emmanuel
$-Ministry Today
$-RevWriter Resource

TEEN/YOUNG ADULT

$-Acquire the Fire—R
$-Breakaway
$-Devo'Zine—R
$-J.A.M.
$-Passageway.org—R
$-Real Faith in Life—R
$-Take Five Plus
TeensForJC—R
$-True Girl
$-Young Adult Today—R
$-Young Christian—R

WOMEN

($)-Beyond the Bend—R
$-Canticle
CelebrateMoms—R
Christian Woman's Page—R
Comfort Café
$-Godly Business Woman—R
Handmaidens
Hearts at Home—R
$-Horizons (women)—R
$-Inspired Living—R
$-InspiredMoms—R
$-Journey
Keeping Hearts & Home
$-Melody of the Heart
Precious Times—R
Proverbs 31 Sisters—R
Right to the Heart—R
($)-Simply Blessed—R
$-SpiritLed Woman
Together with God—R
Virtuous Woman—R
Woman of Worth—R
$-Women Alive!—R
$-WT Online—R

WRITERS

ChristianWriters
$-Cross & Quill—R

$-Fellowscript—R
$-Shades of Romance—R
$-Spirit-Led Writer—R

DISCIPLESHIP

ADULT/GENERAL

$-Alive Now—R
$-Arlington Catholic
$-Aujourd'hui Credo—R
$-Bible Advocate—R
Bread of Life—R
$-Bridal Guides—R
$-Canada Lutheran—R
CBN.com—R
Choice Newspaper—R
Christian C. L. RECORD—R
$-Christian Journal—R
Christian Motorsports
Christian News NW—R
Christian Online
Christian Ranchman
$-Christian Research
$-Christian Standard—R
$-ChristianWeek—R
$-Chronicle Christian
Church of England News
$-City Light News—R
($)-Community Spirit—R
Creation Care—R
$-Decision
Desert Call—R
$-Discipleship Journal—R
$-DisciplesWorld
Eternal Ink—R
$-Evangel/IN—R
Evangelical Advocate—R
$-Faith & Family
$-Faith & Friends—R
$-Faith Today
$-Family Digest—R
$-Gem—R
$-Good News—R
Heartlight—R
Highway News—R
$-Homeschooling Today—R
$-HonorBound—R
$-Horizons (adult)—R
$-In Touch
$-Indian Life—R
$-Inland NW Christian
$-Light & Life
$-Live—R
Looking Up
$-Lookout
$-Men of Integrity—R
Men of the Cross
MESSAGE/Open Bible—R
$-Montgomery's Journey
Mosaic—R
MovieGuide
$-National Catholic
$-New Freeman—R
$-New Wineskins—R
NRB Magazine—R
$-On Mission
$-Parabola—R
Penned from the Heart—R
Perspectives—R
$-Precepts for Living
$-Prism
$-Purpose—R
Regent Global—R
Reverent Submissions—R
$-Seek—R
Sight 360—R
Spiritual Voice—R
$-St. Anthony Messenger
$-St. Joseph's Messenger—R
$-Stewardship—R
Sword of the Lord—R
Three One Six—R
$-Today's Christian—R
Trumpeter—R
$-U.S. Catholic
Urban Kingdom—R
Victory Herald—R
$-Vista
$-War Cry—R
$-Way of St. Francis—R
$-Wesleyan Life—R
$-Whole

CHILDREN

$-BREAD/God's Children—R
$-Primary Street
$-SHINEbrightly—R
$-Sparkle—R

CHRISTIAN EDUCATION/LIBRARY

$-Group
$-Resource—R
$-Youth & CE Leadership

DAILY DEVOTIONALS

Penned from the Heart—R

MISSIONS

$-Glad Tidings (Canada)—R
$-PIME World—R

PASTORS/LEADERS

$-African American Pulpit
$-Barefoot—R
$-Catholic Servant
$-Christian Century—R
Christian Ed. Jour. (CA)—R
$-Growth Points—R
$-InSite—R
$-Interpreter
Jour./Amer. Soc./Chur. Growth—R
$-Leadership—R
$-Lutheran Partners—R
$-Net Results
$-Proclaim—R
Pulpit Helps—R
$-Rev. Magazine
$-RevWriter Resource
$-Small Group Dynamics—R
Theological Digest—R
$-This Rock
$-Word & World

TEEN/YOUNG ADULT

$-Boundless Webzine—R
$-Breakaway
$-Brio
$-CLEAR Direction
$-CLEAR Horizon
$-Credo—R
$-Devo'Zine—R
$-J.A.M.
$-Passageway.org—R
$-Real Faith in Life—R
$-TC Magazine
TeensForJC—R
$-Young Christian—R
$-Young Salvationist—R

WOMEN

($)-Beyond the Bend—R
CelebrateMoms—R
Christian Woman's Page—R
Christian Women Today—R
$-Godly Business Woman—R
$-Horizons (women)—R
$-Inspired Living—R
$-inSpirit—R
$-Journey
Just Between Us—R
$-Link & Visitor—R
P31 Woman—R
Precious Times—R
Proverbs 31 Sisters—R
Right to the Heart—R
$-Today's Christian Woman—R
Together with God—R
Virtuous Woman—R
Woman of Worth—R
$-Women Alive!—R
Women of the Cross
$-WT Online—R

DIVORCE

ADULT/GENERAL

American Tract—R
$-Angels on Earth
$-Arlington Catholic
$-Associated Content—R
$-Aujourd'hui Credo—R
$-Bridal Guides—R
$-Catholic Digest—R
CBN.com—R
$-Christian Citizen USA
$-Christian Examiner
Christian Motorsports

Christian Online
Christian Ranchman
$-ChristianWeek—R
$-Chronicle Christian
Church of England News
Citizen USA—R
($)-Community Spirit—R
$-Culture Wars—R
$-Dovetail—R
Evangelical Advocate—R
$-Faith Today
Family Room
$-Family Smart E-tips—R
$-Focus on the Family
$-Gem—R
$-God Allows U-Turns—R
$-Guideposts—R
$-Home Times—R
$-Homeschooling Today—R
$-HonorBound—R
HopeKeepers—R
$-In Touch
$-Indian Life—R
$-Live—R
$-Living—R
$-Living Church
Looking Up
$-Lookout
$-Minnesota Christian—R
$-National Catholic
$-New Freeman—R
New Heart—R
$-New Wineskins—R
$-On Mission
$-Parabola—R
Parents & Teens—R
Perspectives—R
$-Positive Thinking—R
Priscilla Papers
$-Prism
$-Psychology for Living—R
$-Seek—R
Sight 360—R
SingleAgain.com—R
$-Social Justice—R
Spiritual Voice—R
$-St. Anthony Messenger
$-Storyteller—R
Three One Six—R
$-Today's Christian—R
Trumpeter—R
Urban Kingdom—R
$-War Cry—R
Wisconsin Christian
$-World & I—R

PASTORS/LEADERS
$-Christian Century—R
$-Interpreter
$-Lutheran Partners—R
$-Word & World

TEEN/YOUNG ADULT
$-CLEAR Horizon
$-J.A.M.
$-Listen—R
$-Passageway.org—R
$-Young Christian—R
$-Young Salvationist—R

WOMEN
($)-Beyond the Bend—R
CelebrateMoms—R
Comfort Café
$-Godly Business Woman—R
$-Hope for Women
$-Inspired Living—R
$-InspiredMoms—R
$-inSpirit—R
$-Journey
$-MOMsense—R
Precious Times—R
Virtuous Woman—R
Woman of Worth—R
Women Today—R
$-WT Online—R

DOCTRINAL

ADULT/GENERAL
($)-AGAIN—R
$-Anglican Journal
$-Atlantic Catholic
$-Aujourd'hui Credo—R
$-B.C. Catholic—R
$-Bridal Guides—R
$-Catholic Insight
CBN.com—R
Channels—R
Christian Media—R
Christian Online
$-Christian Research
$-Christian Standard—R
Church Herald & Holiness—R
($)-Community Spirit—R
$-Culture Wars—R
Evangelical Advocate—R
Evangelical Times
$-Faith & Family
$-Faith Today
Founders Journal
$-Homeschooling Today—R
$-HonorBound—R
$-Horizons (adult)—R
($)-Impact—R
$-Light & Life
$-Live—R
Looking Up
MESSAGE/Open Bible—R
MovieGuide
$-National Catholic
$-New Freeman—R
$-New Wineskins—R
Perspectives—R
Priscilla Papers
$-Social Justice—R
Spiritual Voice—R
$-St. Anthony Messenger
Sword and Trumpet
Sword of the Lord—R
Three One Six—R
Trumpeter—R
$-U.S. Catholic
Urban Kingdom—R
$-Wesleyan Life—R

CHRISTIAN EDUCATION/LIBRARY
Catholic Library

MISSIONS
Intl. Jour./Frontier—R
Missiology

PASTORS/LEADERS
$-Catholic Servant
$-Interpreter
$-Lutheran Partners—R
Sewanee Theo. Review
Sharing the Practice—R
Theological Digest—R
$-This Rock
$-Word & World
$-Worship Leader

TEEN/YOUNG ADULT
$-Essential Connection
$-J.A.M.
$-Passageway.org—R
$-Real Faith in Life—R

WOMEN
Virtuous Woman—R
$-WT Online—R

WRITERS
Opinari—R

ECONOMICS

ADULT/GENERAL
$-America
$-Associated Content—R
$-Aujourd'hui Credo—R
$-Bridal Guides—R
$-Catholic Peace Voice—R
$-CBA Retailers
CBN.com—R
Choice Newspaper—R
Christian Business
$-Christian Citizen USA
Christian Media—R
Christian Motorsports
Christian Online
Christian Ranchman
$-Christian Renewal—R
$-Christian Retailing
$-ChristianWeek—R
Citizen USA—R
$-City Light News—R
($)-Community Spirit—R

$-Covenant Companion—R
$-Creative Nonfiction
$-Culture Wars—R
Evangelical Advocate—R
$-Faith Today
Good News Journal—R
$-Home Times—R
$-Homeschooling Today—R
$-HonorBound—R
$-In Touch
$-Light & Life
$-Live—R
$-Living—R
Looking Up
MovieGuide
$-National Catholic
$-New Freeman—R
NRB Magazine—R
$-Parabola—R
Perspectives—R
$-Positive Thinking—R
$-Prism
Rare Jewel—R
Regent Global—R
Sight 360—R
$-Social Justice—R
Spiritual Voice—R
$-St. Anthony Messenger
Three One Six—R
Trumpeter—R
Urban Kingdom—R
Wisconsin Christian
$-World & I—R

PASTORS/LEADERS

$-Today's Parish—R
$-Word & World

TEEN/YOUNG ADULT

$-Boundless Webzine—R
$-J.A.M.
TeensForJC—R

WOMEN

$-Godly Business Woman—R
Together with God—R

ENCOURAGEMENT

ADULT/GENERAL

$-Animal Trails—R
$-BGC World—R
$-Brave Hearts—R
Bread of Life—R
Breakthrough Intercessor—R
$-Bridal Guides—R
$-Catholic Digest—R
$-Catholic Forester—R
CBN.com—R
Channels—R
$-Chicken Soup Magazine
Choice Newspaper—R
$-Christian Journal—R
Christian Online
Christian Ranchman
$-Christian Standard—R
$-Chronicle Christian
$-City Light News—R
($)-Community Spirit—R
$-Discipleship Journal—R
$-EFCA Today—R
Eternal Ink—R
$-Evangel/IN—R
Evangelical Advocate—R
$-Faith & Family
$-Faith & Friends—R
$-Faith Today
$-Family Digest—R
Family Room
First Call Hospice—R
$-Focus on the Family
$-Gems of Truth—R
$-God Allows U-Turns—R
Halo Magazine
$-Home Times—R
$-Homeschooling Today—R
$-HonorBound—R
HopeKeepers—R
$-Horizons (adult)—R
$-In Touch
$-Indian Life—R
Keys to Living—R
Leaves—R
$-Lifeglow—R
$-Light & Life
$-Liguorian
Looking Up
$-Lookout
$-Lutheran Digest—R
$-Mature Living
Men of the Cross
$-Minnesota Christian—R
Mosaic—R
($)-Mutuality—R
New Heart—R
$-New Wineskins—R
Nostalgia—R
$-Ozarks Senior Living—R
Penned from the Heart—R
PrayerWorks—R
$-Pure Inspiration—R
Regent Global—R
Reverent Submissions—R
Sacred Journey—R
SearchingWisdom.org—R
$-Seek—R
Sight 360—R
$-Significant Living—R
Silver Wings—R
Spiritual Voice—R
Spirituality for Today
$-St. Joseph's Messenger—R
$-Standard—R
$-Storyteller—R
Sword of the Lord—R
Three One Six—R
$-Today's Christian—R
$-Together—R
Urban Kingdom—R
Victory Herald—R
$-Victory in Grace—R
$-Vista
$-Wesleyan Life—R
$-Whole
Wisconsin Christian

CHILDREN

$-BREAD/God's Children—R
$-Cadet Quest—R
$-SHINEbrightly—R
Skipping Stones
$-Sparkle—R

CHRISTIAN EDUCATION/LIBRARY

$-Youth & CE Leadership

DAILY DEVOTIONALS

E-ncouragement
Penned from the Heart—R

MISSIONS

$-Glad Tidings (Canada)—R

PASTORS/LEADERS

$-Interpretation
Pulpit Helps—R

TEEN/YOUNG ADULT

$-Boundless Webzine—R
$-Breakaway
$-Brio
$-CLEAR Direction
$-CLEAR Horizon
$-J.A.M.
$-Rock
$-Young Christian—R
$-Young Salvationist—R

WOMEN

$-Canticle
CelebrateMoms—R
Crowned with Silver
First Lady
Hearts at Home—R
$-Hope for Women
$-Inspired Living—R
$-inSpirit—R
$-Journey
$-MOMsense—R
P31 Woman—R
Precious Times—R
Right to the Heart—R
($)-Simply Blessed—R
$-Today's Christian Woman—R
Together with God—R
Virtuous Woman—R
Woman of Worth—R

Women of the Cross
$-WT Online—R

WRITERS
$-Christian Communicator—R
$-Cross & Quill—R
$-Fellowscript—R
Opinari—R

ENVIRONMENTAL ISSUES

ADULT/GENERAL
$-America
$-Anglican Journal
$-Animal Trails—R
$-Associated Content—R
$-Aujourd'hui Credo—R
$-Bridal Guides—R
$-Cathedral Age—R
$-Catholic Peace Voice—R
$-Christian Citizen USA
$-Christian Courier/CAN—R
Christian Online
Christian Outlook
Christian Ranchman
$-ChristianWeek—R
$-Chronicle Christian
Citizen USA—R
$-City Light News—R
$-Common Ground—R
($)-Community Spirit—R
$-Covenant Companion—R
Creation Care—R
$-Creation Illust.—R
$-Creative Nonfiction
Desert Call—R
Evangelical Advocate—R
$-Faith Today
$-HonorBound—R
HopeKeepers—R
$-In Touch
$-Indian Life—R
LarkNews.com
$-Light & Life
$-Liguorian
$-Living—R
$-Living Church
Looking Up
$-Lookout
$-Minnesota Christian—R
$-National Catholic
$-New Freeman—R
$-New Wineskins—R
$-Parabola—R
Pegasus Review—R
Perspectives—R
Presbyterian Outlook
$-Prism
Ruminate
Sacred Journey—R
$-Science & Spirit
$-Seek—R
Sight 360—R
Spiritual Voice—R
$-St. Anthony Messenger
$-St. Joseph's Messenger—R
Three One Six—R
Trumpeter—R
Urban Kingdom—R
$-War Cry—R
$-Way of St. Francis—R
Wisconsin Christian
$-World & I—R

CHILDREN
$-New Moon—R
$-Pockets—R
$-SHINEbrightly—R
Skipping Stones
$-Sparkle—R

CHRISTIAN EDUCATION/LIBRARY
Jour./Research on Christian Ed.

PASTORS/LEADERS
$-Christian Century—R
$-InSite—R
$-Interpreter
$-RevWriter Resource
$-Word & World

TEEN/YOUNG ADULT
$-Boundless Webzine—R
$-Devo'Zine—R
$-J.A.M.
$-Passageway.org—R
$-TC Magazine
TeensForJC—R
$-Young Christian—R
$-Young Salvationist—R

WOMEN
$-Esprit—R
$-Godly Business Woman—R
$-Herizons
$-Horizons (women)—R
$-Inspired Living—R
$-inSpirit—R
Share

ESSAYS

ADULT/GENERAL
African Voices—R
$-America
$-Annals of St. Anne
$-Arlington Catholic
$-Associated Content—R
Books & Culture
$-Cathedral Age—R
$-Catholic Digest—R
$-Catholic Peace Voice—R
$-Chicken Soup Books—R
Christian C. L. RECORD—R
$-Christian Courier/CAN—R
Christian Online
$-Christian Renewal—R
$-Christianity Today—R
$-Company—R
Creation Care—R
$-Creative Nonfiction
$-Culture Wars—R
$-DisciplesWorld
$-Dovetail—R
$-Eureka Street
$-Faith Today
$-Gem—R
$-God Allows U-Turns—R
Heartland Gatekeeper—R
$-Home Times—R
HopeKeepers—R
Imagine
($)-Impact—R
$-In Touch
$-Lifeglow—R
$-Liguorian
$-Lutheran Digest—R
Men of the Cross
($)-Mutuality—R
$-National Catholic
$-New Wineskins—R
$-Ozarks Senior Living—R
$-Parabola—R
Pegasus Review—R
Penwood Review
$-Prism
$-Pure Inspiration—R
Reverent Submissions—R
Rock & Sling
$-Rose & Thorn
Ruminate
Sacred Journey—R
$-Science & Spirit
$-Seek—R
Sight 360—R
$-Significant Living—R
$-Social Justice—R
$-Spiritual Life
Spiritual Voice—R
$-St. Anthony Messenger
STEPS
$-Storyteller—R
$-This I Believe
Three One Six—R
Tiferet
Tri-State Voice
Trumpeter—R
$-U.S. Catholic
Urban Kingdom—R
$-War Cry—R
$-Way of St. Francis—R
$-Wittenburg Door—R
$-World & I—R
Xavier Review

CHILDREN
$-Nature Friend
$-New Moon—R
Skipping Stones

CHRISTIAN EDUCATION/LIBRARY
Catholic Library
$-Journal/Adventist Ed.—R

MISSIONS
$-Evangelical Missions—R
$-PFI World—R
$-PIME World—R
Railroad Evangelist—R

MUSIC
$-Creator—R

PASTORS/LEADERS
$-African American Pulpit
$-Catholic Servant
$-Christian Century—R
Cross Currents
Jour./Pastoral Care—R
$-Priest
Theological Digest—R
$-Torch Legacy Leader
$-Word & World
$-Youthworker

TEEN/YOUNG ADULT
$-Breakaway
$-InsideOut—R
$-Passageway.org—R
$-TC Magazine
TeensForJC—R

WOMEN
Christian Woman's Page—R
$-Godly Business Woman—R
Handmaidens
Hearts at Home—R
$-Herizons
$-Horizons (women)—R

WRITERS
$-Adv. Christian Writer—R
$-Christian Communicator—R
Money the Write Way—R
Once Upon a Time—R
Opinari—R
$-Spirit-Led Writer—R
$-Writer
$-Writer's Digest—R

ETHICS

ADULT/GENERAL
($)-AGAIN—R
$-America
$-Angels on Earth
$-Animal Trails—R
$-Associated Content—R
$-Aujourd'hui Credo—R
$-Bridal Guides—R
$-Canada Lutheran—R
$-Cathedral Age—R
$-Catholic Digest—R
$-Catholic Insight
$-Catholic Peace Voice—R
CBN.com—R
Channels—R
Christian C. L. RECORD—R
$-Christian Citizen USA
$-Christian Courier/CAN—R
$-Christian Examiner
Christian Media—R
Christian Observer
Christian Online
Christian Ranchman
$-Christian Renewal—R
$-Christian Research
$-Christian Standard—R
$-ChristianWeek—R
$-Chronicle Christian
Church of England News
$-City Light News—R
($)-Community Spirit—R
$-Creative Nonfiction
$-Cresset
$-Culture Wars—R
Desert Call—R
$-DisciplesWorld
$-Dovetail—R
Evangelical Advocate—R
$-Faith Today
$-Focus on the Family
$-God Allows U-Turns—R
Good News Journal—R
$-Home Times—R
$-Homeschooling Today—R
$-HonorBound—R
$-Horizons (adult)—R
$-Indian Life—R
$-Interim—R
Island Catholic
$-Light & Life
$-Liguorian
$-Live—R
$-Living Church
$-Lookout
$-Men of Integrity—R
$-Minnesota Christian—R
Missionwares
MovieGuide
$-National Catholic
$-New Freeman—R
New Heart—R
$-New Wineskins—R
NRB Magazine—R
$-Our Sunday Visitor—R
$-Parabola—R
Pegasus Review—R
Perspectives—R
Perspectives/Science
$-Positive Thinking—R
$-Prairie Messenger—R
Presbyterian Outlook
Priscilla Papers
$-Prism
$-Pure Inspiration—R
Regent Global—R
Sacred Journey—R
$-Science & Spirit
$-Seek—R
Sight 360—R
Silver Wings—R
$-Social Justice—R
Spiritual Voice—R
$-St. Anthony Messenger
Three One Six—R
Trumpeter—R
$-U.S. Catholic
Urban Kingdom—R
$-War Cry—R
$-World & I—R

CHILDREN
$-New Moon—R
Skipping Stones

CHRISTIAN EDUCATION/LIBRARY
Christian Librarian—R
Jour./Research on Christian Ed.

DAILY DEVOTIONALS
Penned from the Heart—R

PASTORS/LEADERS
$-Christian Century—R
$-Clergy Journal—R
Cross Currents
$-Interpreter
Jour./Pastoral Care—R
$-Lutheran Partners—R
$-Ministry Today
Sewanee Theo. Review
Sharing the Practice—R
Theological Digest—R
$-This Rock
$-Word & World

TEEN/YOUNG ADULT
$-Boundless Webzine—R
$-Devo'Zine—R
$-Passageway.org—R
$-Real Faith in Life—R
$-Risen
TeensForJC—R
$-Young Salvationist—R

WOMEN
$-Esprit—R
$-Godly Business Woman—R
Handmaiden—R
$-Inspired Living—R
Women Today—R

ETHNIC/CULTURAL PIECES

ADULT/GENERAL
$-Advance

African Voices—R
($)-AGAIN—R
$-America
$-Arlington Catholic
$-Associated Content—R
$-Aujourd'hui Credo—R
$-Bridal Guides—R
$-Catholic Digest—R
$-Catholic Peace Voice—R
$-CBA Retailers
CBN.com—R
$-Celebrate Life—R
Channels—R
Chocolate Pages
$-Christian Citizen USA
$-Christian Courier/CAN—R
Christian News NW—R
Christian Online
Christian Ranchman
$-ChristianWeek—R
$-Chronicle Christian
Citizen USA—R
$-City Light News—R
$-Columbia—R
$-Commonweal
($)-Community Spirit—R
Creation Care—R
$-Creative Nonfiction
Desert Call—R
$-Dovetail—R
$-En Confianza
$-Episcopal Life—R
Evangel/OR—R
Evangelical Advocate—R
$-Faith Today
$-Gem—R
$-Good News—R
Good News!
$-Gospel Today—R
$-Haruah—R
$-Home Times—R
$-Homeschooling Today—R
$-HonorBound—R
($)-Impact—R
$-Indian Life—R
$-Light & Life
$-Liguorian
$-Live—R
$-Lookout
$-Men of Integrity—R
Mensajero ala Blanca
$-MESSAGE
MESSAGE/Open Bible—R
$-Minnesota Christian—R
MovieGuide
($)-Mutuality—R
$-National Catholic
$-New Freeman—R
$-New Wineskins—R
$-Our Sunday Visitor—R
$-Parabola—R
Penned from the Heart—R
Priscilla Papers
$-Prism
Purpose Magazine—R
Sacred Journey—R
$-Salvo
$-Science & Spirit
$-Seek—R
Sight 360—R
$-Social Justice—R
Society/Prevention of Cruelty
Spiritual Voice—R
$-St. Anthony Messenger
Star of Zion
$-Today's Christian—R
$-Together—R
Trumpeter—R
$-U.S. Catholic
$-Upscale
Urban Kingdom—R
$-Vista
$-War Cry—R
$-Wesleyan Life—R
West Wind Review
Wisconsin Christian
$-World & I—R
Xavier Review

CHILDREN

$-Faces
$-New Moon—R
Skipping Stones
$-Sparkle—R

CHRISTIAN EDUCATION/LIBRARY

$-Momentum

DAILY DEVOTIONALS

Penned from the Heart—R

MISSIONS

$-Evangelical Missions—R
Missiology
OpRev Equipper—R
$-PIME World—R
Women of the Harvest

PASTORS/LEADERS

$-African American Pulpit
$-Barefoot—R
$-Christian Century—R
$-Interpreter
Jour./Pastoral Care—R
$-Lutheran Partners—R
$-Ministry Today
$-Net Results
Pulpit Helps—R
$-This Rock
$-Torch Legacy Leader
$-Worship Leader

TEEN/YOUNG ADULT

$-Boundless Webzine—R
$-Credo—R
$-Devo'Zine—R
$-Essential Connection
$-Passageway.org—R
$-Real Faith in Life—R
TeensForJC—R
$-Young Christian—R
$-Young Salvationist—R

WOMEN

$-Esprit—R
$-Godly Business Woman—R
$-Heart & Soul
$-Herizons
$-Horizons (women)—R
$-Inspired Living—R
$-inSpirit—R
$-Link & Visitor—R
Precious Times—R
$-SpiritLed Woman

EVANGELISM/WITNESSING

ADULT/GENERAL

$-America
American Tract—R
$-Anglican Journal
$-Animal Trails—R
$-Annals of St. Anne
$-Aujourd'hui Credo—R
$-BGC World—R
$-Bible Advocate—R
Bread of Life—R
$-Bridal Guides—R
$-Canada Lutheran—R
$-Catholic Telegraph
$-Catholic Yearbook—R
CBN.com—R
Channels—R
Choice Newspaper—R
Christian Courier/WI—R
Christian Online
Christian Ranchman
$-Christian Research
$-Christian Standard—R
$-Christianity Today—R
$-Chronicle Christian
Church Herald & Holiness—R
Church of England News
$-City Light News—R
($)-Community Spirit—R
Creation Care—R
$-Decision
$-Discipleship Journal—R
Encompass
$-Episcopal Life—R
Eternal Ink—R
$-Evangel/IN—R
Evangel/OR—R
Evangelical Advocate—R
$-Faith & Family
$-Faith Today
$-Gem—R
$-God Allows U-Turns—R
$-Good News—R

Good News Today
Halo Magazine
Heartbeat/CMA
$-HonorBound—R
$-Horizons (adult)—R
$-In Touch
$-Indian Life—R
$-Inland NW Christian Leaves—R
$-Light & Life
$-Liguorian
$-Live—R
$-Living Church
Looking Up
$-Lookout
$-Lutheran Journal—R
$-Mature Living
$-Men of Integrity—R
MESSAGE/Open Bible—R
$-Minnesota Christian—R
$-Montgomery's Journey
Mosaic—R
$-New Freeman—R
New Heart—R
$-New Wineskins—R
$-On Mission
Penned from the Heart—R
$-Power for Living—R
$-Priority!—R
$-Prism
$-Purpose—R
Regent Global—R
Reverent Submissions—R
SearchingWisdom.org—R
$-Seek—R
Sharing—R
Sight 360—R
Spiritual Voice—R
Spirituality for Today
$-St. Anthony Messenger
$-Standard—R
Sword of the Lord—R
$-Testimony—R
Three One Six—R
$-Today's Christian—R
Trumpeter—R
Urban Kingdom—R
Victory Herald—R
$-Vista
$-War Cry—R
$-Way of St. Francis—R
$-Wesleyan Life—R
$-Whole
Wisconsin Christian

CHILDREN

$-BREAD/God's Children—R
$-Courage—R
$-Focus/Clubhouse Jr.
$-Guide—R
$-JuniorWay
$-Primary Pal/IL
$-Sparkle—R

CHRISTIAN EDUCATION/LIBRARY

Catholic Library
$-Group
$-Kids' Ministry Ideas—R
$-Resource—R
$-RTJ—R
$-Teach Kids!—R
$-Youth & CE Leadership

DAILY DEVOTIONALS

Penned from the Heart—R

MISSIONS

$-Evangelical Missions—R
Intl. Jour./Frontier—R
$-Leaders for Today
Missiology
OpRev Equipper—R

MUSIC

Christian Music Weekly—R

PASTORS/LEADERS

$-Catholic Servant
$-Growth Points—R
$-Interpreter
Jour./Amer. Soc./Chur. Growth—R
$-Leadership—R
$-Let's Worship
$-Lutheran Partners—R
$-Ministry Today
$-Outreach—R
Pulpit Helps—R
$-RevWriter Resource
Rick Warren's Ministry—R
$-This Rock
$-Willow—R

TEEN/YOUNG ADULT

$-Boundless Webzine—R
$-Brio
$-CLEAR Direction
$-Credo—R
$-Devo'Zine—R
$-Essential Connection
$-J.A.M.
$-Passageway.org—R
$-Real Faith in Life—R
$-TC Magazine
TeensForJC—R
$-True Girl
$-Young Christian—R
$-Young Salvationist—R

WOMEN

$-At the Center—R
$-Canticle
$-Godly Business Woman—R
$-Inspired Living—R
$-inSpirit—R
$-Journey
Just Between Us—R
$-Link & Visitor—R
P31 Woman—R
Precious Times—R
Proverbs 31 Sisters—R
Share
$-SpiritLed Woman
Together with God—R
Virtuous Woman—R
$-Women Alive!—R
$-WT Online—R

EXEGESIS

ADULT/GENERAL

$-Alive Now—R
$-Aujourd'hui Credo—R
$-Bible Advocate—R
$-Bridal Guides—R
$-Catholic Insight
CBN.com—R
Channels—R
Christian Ranchman
$-Christian Standard—R
Evangelical Advocate—R
$-HonorBound—R
$-Light & Life
$-Living Church
$-National Catholic
$-New Freeman—R
Perspectives—R
Priscilla Papers
Regent Global—R
Reverent Submissions—R
$-Social Justice—R
$-St. Anthony Messenger
Sword and Trumpet
Sword of the Lord—R
Trumpeter—R
$-Wesleyan Life—R

PASTORS/LEADERS

$-Enrichment—R
Pulpit Helps—R
Theological Digest—R
$-This Rock

TEEN/YOUNG ADULT

$-Boundless Webzine—R
$-Passageway.org—R
$-Young Adult Today—R

WRITERS

Opinari—R

FAITH

ADULT/GENERAL

African Voices—R
$-America
$-Animal Trails—R
$-Arkansas Catholic—R
$-Aujourd'hui Credo—R
$-Believer's Bay
$-BGC World—R
$-Bible Advocate—R

$-Brave Hearts—R
Bread of Life—R
Breakthrough Intercessor—R
$-Bridal Guides—R
byFaith
$-Canada Lutheran—R
$-Catholic Digest—R
$-Catholic Insight
$-Catholic Peace Voice—R
$-Catholic Yearbook—R
CBN.com—R
Channels—R
Choice Newspaper—R
Christian C. L. RECORD—R
$-Christian Courier/CAN—R
$-Christian Journal—R
Christian Online
Christian Ranchman
$-Christian Research
$-Christian Retailing
$-Christian Standard—R
$-Christianity Today—R
$-ChristianWeek—R
$-Chronicle Christian
Church of England News
$-City Light News—R
$-Columbia—R
($)-Community Spirit—R
$-Covenant Companion—R
Desert Call—R
Disciple's Journal—R
$-Discipleship Journal—R
$-Dovetail—R
Encompass
Eternal Ink—R
Evangel/OR—R
Evangelical Advocate—R
$-Faith & Family
$-Faith & Friends—R
$-Faith Today
$-Family Digest—R
Family Room
$-Focus on the Family
$-Gem—R
$-God Allows U-Turns—R
Good News Journal—R
$-Haruah—R
Highway News—R
$-Home Times—R
$-HonorBound—R
HopeKeepers—R
$-Ideals—R
$-In Touch
Island Catholic
LifeTimes Catholic
$-Light & Life
$-Liguorian
$-Live—R
Looking Up
$-Lookout
$-Lutheran Digest—R
$-Lutheran Journal—R
$-Mature Living
$-Men of Integrity—R
Men of the Cross
$-Minnesota Christian—R
$-Montgomery's Journey
Mosaic—R
$-National Catholic
$-New Freeman—R
New Heart—R
$-New Wineskins—R
Nostalgia—R
$-Now What?—R
$-Our Sunday Visitor—R
$-Parabola—R
Parents & Teens—R
Pegasus Review—R
Penned from the Heart—R
$-Positive Thinking—R
$-Prairie Messenger—R
PrayerWorks—R
$-Precepts for Living
Priscilla Papers
$-Psychology for Living—R
$-Pure Inspiration—R
Quaker Life—R
Reverent Submissions—R
Sacred Journey—R
SearchingWisdom.org—R
$-Seek—R
Sight 360—R
$-Significant Living—R
$-Social Justice—R
Spiritual Voice—R
Spirituality for Today
$-St. Anthony Messenger
$-St. Joseph's Messenger—R
$-Standard—R
$-Storyteller—R
SW Kansas Faith
Sword and Trumpet
Sword of the Lord—R
$-Testimony—R
Three One Six—R
$-Today's Christian—R
$-Together—R
Trumpeter—R
$-U.S. Catholic
$-United Church Observer—R
Urban Kingdom—R
$-Victory in Grace—R
$-Vista
$-Way of St. Francis—R
$-Weavings—R
$-Wesleyan Life—R
$-World & I—R

CHILDREN

$-BREAD/God's Children—R
$-Courage—R
$-Focus/Clubhouse Jr.
$-JuniorWay
$-Our Little Friend—R
$-Primary Street
$-Primary Treasure—R
$-SHINEbrightly—R
$-Sparkle—R

CHRISTIAN EDUCATION/LIBRARY

Catholic Library
$-Children's Ministry
Christian Librarian—R
$-Group
$-Momentum
$-Teachers of Vision—R
$-Youth & CE Leadership

DAILY DEVOTIONALS

Penned from the Heart—R

MISSIONS

$-Glad Tidings (Canada)—R
$-PIME World—R

MUSIC

Christian Music Weekly—R

PASTORS/LEADERS

$-African American Pulpit
$-Interpreter
$-Ministry Today
$-Proclaim—R
$-RevWriter Resource
$-Worship Leader

TEEN/YOUNG ADULT

$-Boundless Webzine—R
$-Breakaway
$-Brio
$-CLEAR Direction
$-CLEAR Horizon
$-Credo—R
$-Devo'Zine—R
$-J.A.M.
$-Passageway.org—R
$-Risen
$-TC Magazine
TeensForJC—R
$-True Girl
$-Young Adult Today—R
$-Young Christian—R
$-Young Salvationist—R

WOMEN

($)-Beyond the Bend—R
$-Canticle
CelebrateMoms—R
Christian Woman's Page—R
Comfort Café
$-Esprit—R
$-Godly Business Woman—R
Hearts at Home—R
$-Hope for Women
$-Horizons (women)—R
$-Inspired Living—R
$-inSpirit—R

$-Journey
Just Between Us—R
Life Tools for Women
P31 Woman—R
Proverbs 31 Sisters—R
Right to the Heart—R
$-SpiritLed Woman
$-Today's Christian Woman—R
Virtuous Woman—R
Woman of Worth—R
$-Women Alive!—R
Women Today—R
$-WT Online—R

WRITERS

Areopagus
Opinari—R

FAMILY LIFE

ADULT/GENERAL

$-Abilities
$-Advance
African Voices—R
($)-AGAIN—R
Alabama Baptist
$-America
$-Angels on Earth
$-Animal Trails—R
$-Annals of St. Anne
Anointed Pages
$-Arkansas Catholic—R
$-Arlington Catholic
$-Associated Content—R
$-Atlantic Catholic
$-Aujourd'hui Credo—R
$-Australian Catholics—R
$-B.C. Catholic—R
$-Believer's Bay
$-BGC World—R
$-Bible Advocate—R
$-Brave Hearts—R
Bread of Life—R
$-Bridal Guides—R
byFaith
$-Canada Lutheran—R
$-Catholic Digest—R
$-Catholic Forester—R
$-Catholic Insight
CBN.com—R
Channels—R
$-Chicken Soup Books—R
$-Chicken Soup Magazine
Christian C. L. RECORD—R
$-Christian Courier/CAN—R
Christian Courier/WI—R
$-Christian Home & School
$-Christian Journal—R
Christian Online
Christian Ranchman
$-Christian Renewal—R
$-ChristianWeek—R
$-Chronicle Christian
Citizen USA—R
$-City Light News—R
$-Columbia—R
($)-Community Spirit—R
Connecting Point—R
$-Covenant Companion—R
$-Creative Nonfiction
$-Culture Wars—R
Desert Call—R
Disciple's Journal—R
$-Dovetail—R
$-EFCA Today—R
Eternal Ink—R
Evangelical Advocate—R
$-Faith & Family
$-Faith & Friends—R
$-Faith Today
FaithWebbin—R
$-Family Digest—R
Family Room
$-Family Smart E-tips—R
$-Focus on the Family
$-Focus on Your Child
$-Gem—R
$-God Allows U-Turns—R
Godly Places
Gold Country Families—R
Good News Journal—R
$-Grand
$-Guideposts—R
Heartlight—R
Highway News—R
$-Home Times—R
$-Homeschooling Today—R
$-HonorBound—R
$-Horizons (adult)—R
$-Ideals—R
$-In Touch
$-Indian Life—R
$-Inland NW Christian
Keys to Living—R
LifeSite News
LifeTimes Catholic
$-Light & Life
$-Liguorian
$-Live—R
$-Living—R
$-Living Church
$-Living Light—R
Looking Up
$-Lookout
$-Lutheran Digest—R
$-Marriage Partnership—R
$-Mature Living
$-Mature Years—R
$-Men of Integrity—R
Men of the Cross
($)-Mennonite Historian—R
$-Messenger/St. Anthony
$-Minnesota Christian—R
$-Montgomery's Journey
($)-Mutuality—R
Nappaland.com
$-New Freeman—R
$-New Wineskins—R
Nostalgia—R
$-Now What?—R
$-Our Sunday Visitor—R
$-Over the Back Fence—R
$-ParentLife
Parents & Teens—R
Pegasus Review—R
Penned from the Heart—R
$-Positive Thinking—R
$-Power for Living—R
$-Prairie Messenger—R
Priscilla Papers
$-Psychology for Living—R
$-Purpose—R
Reverent Submissions—R
Sacred Journey—R
$-Science & Spirit
SearchingWisdom.org—R
$-Seek—R
Sight 360—R
$-Significant Living—R
SingleAgain.com—R
$-Social Justice—R
$-Special Living—R
Spiritual Voice—R
Spirituality for Today
$-St. Anthony Messenger
STEPS
$-Storyteller—R
SW Kansas Faith
Sword and Trumpet
Sword of the Lord—R
$-Testimony—R
Three One Six—R
$-Today's Christian—R
$-Today's Pentecostal—R
$-Together—R
Trumpeter—R
$-U.S. Catholic
$-United Church Observer—R
Urban Kingdom—R
$-Vibrant Life—R
$-Victory in Grace—R
$-Vista
$-War Cry—R
$-Way of St. Francis—R
$-Wesleyan Life—R
West Wind Review
Wisconsin Christian
$-World & I—R

CHILDREN

$-BREAD/God's Children—R
$-Focus/Clubhouse
$-Focus/Clubhouse Jr.
$-Guide—R
$-JuniorWay
$-New Moon—R
$-Pockets—R

Skipping Stones
$-Sparkle—R

CHRISTIAN EDUCATION/LIBRARY

$-Children's Ministry
$-Group
$-Youth & CE Leadership

DAILY DEVOTIONALS

Penned from the Heart—R

MISSIONS

$-Glad Tidings (Canada)—R
Women of the Harvest

PASTORS/LEADERS

$-African American Pulpit
$-Catholic Servant
Engage
$-Enrichment—R
$-InSite—R
$-Interpreter
Jour./Pastoral Care—R
$-Ministry Today
$-Preaching Well—R
$-Rev. Magazine
$-RevWriter Resource
$-Today's Parish—R
$-Word & World

TEEN/YOUNG ADULT

$-Brio
$-Credo—R
$-J.A.M.
$-Listen—R
$-Passageway.org—R
$-Real Faith in Life—R
$-TC Magazine
TeensForJC—R
$-Young Adult Today—R
$-Young Christian—R
$-Young Salvationist—R

WOMEN

$-Canticle
CelebrateMoms—R
Christian Woman's Page—R
Comfort Café
Crowned with Silver
$-Dabbling Mum—R
$-Esprit—R
$-Godly Business Woman—R
Handmaiden—R
Hearts at Home—R
$-Hope for Women
$-Horizons (women)—R
$-Inspired Living—R
$-InspiredMoms—R
$-inSpirit—R
$-Journey
Just Between Us—R
Keeping Hearts & Home
Ladies First
Life Tools for Women
$-Link & Visitor—R
Lutheran Woman's Quar.
$-MOMsense—R
P31 Woman—R
Precious Times—R
Proverbs 31 Sisters—R
($)-Shalom Bayit
Share
$-Simple Joy
($)-Simply Blessed—R
$-SpiritLed Woman
$-Today's Christian Woman—R
Together with God—R
Virtuous Woman—R
Woman of Worth—R
$-Women Alive!—R
Women of the Cross
Women Today—R
$-WT Online—R

FILLERS: ANECDOTES

ADULT/GENERAL

$-Advance
$-Angels on Earth
$-Animal Trails—R
Breakthrough Intercessor—R
$-Bridal Guides—R
$-Catholic Digest—R
$-Catholic Yearbook—R
Channels—R
$-Chicken Soup Books—R
Christian Courier/WI—R
$-Christian Journal—R
Christian Motorsports
Christian Ranchman
$-Christian Response—R
$-Chronicle Christian
Church Herald & Holiness—R
$-City Light News—R
Desert Call—R
Disciple's Journal—R
$-DisciplesWorld
$-Faith & Family
$-Family Digest—R
$-Gem—R
$-God Allows U-Turns—R
Good News Journal—R
Heartlight—R
Highway News—R
$-Home Times—R
($)-Impact—R
$-Living—R
$-Lutheran Digest—R
$-Lutheran Journal—R
MovieGuide
New Heart—R
$-Now What?—R
$-Purpose—R
Reverent Submissions—R
$-Significant Living—R
SingleAgain.com—R
Spiritual Voice—R
Spirituality for Today
$-St. Anthony Messenger
Star of Zion
STEPS
Three One Six—R
$-Today's Pentecostal—R
Urban Kingdom—R
Victory Herald—R
$-War Cry—R
$-Way of St. Francis—R

CHILDREN

$-High Adventure—R
Skipping Stones

CHRISTIAN EDUCATION/LIBRARY

Christian Librarian—R
$-RTJ—R

MISSIONS

Railroad Evangelist—R

MUSIC

$-Creator—R

PASTORS/LEADERS

$-Barefoot—R
$-Leadership—R
$-Preaching Well—R
$-PreachingToday.com
Pulpit Helps—R
Sharing the Practice—R
$-Sunday Sermons—R

TEEN/YOUNG ADULT

$-InsideOut—R
$-Young Christian—R
$-Young Salvationist—R

WOMEN

($)-Beyond the Bend—R
CelebrateMoms—R
Christian Woman's Page—R
Hearts at Home—R
$-Inspired Living—R
Just Between Us—R
Proverbs 31 Sisters—R
Right to the Heart—R
$-Today's Christian Woman—R
Virtuous Woman—R
Woman of Worth—R
$-WT Online—R

WRITERS

$-Canadian Writer's Jour.—R
$-Cross & Quill—R
Money the Write Way—R
$-New Writer's Mag.
NW Christian Author—R
Once Upon a Time—R
$-Tickled by Thunder
Write Connection
$-Writers' Journal

FILLERS: CARTOONS

ADULT/GENERAL

$-Advance
African Voices—R
American Tract—R
$-Angels on Earth
$-Animal Trails—R
Breakthrough Intercessor—R
$-Bridal Guides—R
$-Catholic Digest—R
$-CBA Retailers
Channels—R
$-Chicken Soup Books—R
$-Christian Citizen USA
Christian Computing—R
$-Christian Herald—R
$-Christian Journal—R
Christian Motorsports
Christian Ranchman
$-Chronicle Christian
Citizen USA—R
$-City Light News—R
Connecting Point—R
$-Culture Wars—R
Disciple's Journal—R
$-DisciplesWorld
$-Eureka Street
$-Evangel/IN—R
Evangel/OR—R
$-Faith & Family
$-Faith & Friends—R
$-Gem—R
Good News Journal—R
$-Gospel Today—R
Heartlight—R
Highway News—R
$-Home Times—R
($)-Impact—R
$-Interchange
$-Interim—R
$-Liguorian
$-Lutheran Digest—R
$-Mature Years—R
MovieGuide
New Heart—R
Pegasus Review—R
$-Power for Living—R
$-Presbyterians Today—R
$-Purpose—R
Sight 360—R
$-Significant Living—R
$-Special Living—R
Spiritual Voice—R
$-St. Anthony Messenger
Star of Zion
STEPS
$-Storyteller—R
Three One Six—R
Trumpeter—R
$-United Church Observer—R
Urban Kingdom—R
$-Vista
$-Way of St. Francis—R
$-Wireless Age—R
$-Wittenburg Door—R

CHILDREN

$-Adventures
$-American Girl—R
$-Discoveries—R
$-Passport—R
$-SHINEbrightly—R
Skipping Stones

CHRISTIAN EDUCATION/LIBRARY

$-Children's Ministry
Christian Librarian—R
$-Group
$-Journal/Adventist Ed.—R
$-Teachers of Vision—R
$-Today's Catholic Teacher—R
$-Youth & CE Leadership

MISSIONS

Mission Frontiers
Railroad Evangelist—R

MUSIC

Christian Music Weekly—R
$-Creator—R
Tradition

PASTORS/LEADERS

$-Barefoot—R
$-Catholic Servant
$-Christian Century—R
Christian Management—R
$-Diocesan Dialogue—R
$-Enrichment—R
$-Leadership—R
$-Lutheran Partners—R
$-Priest
Pulpit Helps—R
$-Rev. Magazine
$-Sabbath School Leadership—R
Sharing the Practice—R
$-Small Group Dynamics—R
$-Your Church—R

TEEN/YOUNG ADULT

$-InsideOut—R
$-Listen—R
TeensForJC—R
$-Young Christian—R
$-Young Salvationist—R

WOMEN

Hearts at Home—R
Just Between Us—R
Proverbs 31 Sisters—R
($)-Simply Blessed—R
$-Today's Christian Woman—R

WRITERS

$-Canadian Writer's Jour.—R
$-Cross & Quill—R
$-New Writer's Mag.
Once Upon a Time—R
$-Writer
$-Writers' Journal

FILLERS: FACTS

ADULT/GENERAL

$-Animal Trails—R
$-Bible Advocate—R
Bread of Life—R
Breakthrough Intercessor—R
$-Bridal Guides—R
$-Catholic Digest—R
$-Catholic Yearbook—R
$-CBA Retailers
$-Chicken Soup Books—R
Christian Courier/WI—R
$-Christian Herald—R
Christian Motorsports
Christian Ranchman
$-Christian Response—R
$-Chronicle Christian
$-City Light News—R
Desert Call—R
Diamond Dust
Disciple's Journal—R
Eternal Ink—R
$-Gem—R
$-God Allows U-Turns—R
Good News Journal—R
Highway News—R
$-Home Times—R
$-Interchange
$-Lutheran Digest—R
$-Lutheran Journal—R
MESSAGE/Open Bible—R
MovieGuide
$-Now What?—R
PrayerWorks—R
Sight 360—R
$-Significant Living—R
SingleAgain.com—R
Spiritual Voice—R
$-St. Anthony Messenger
Sword and Trumpet
Sword of the Lord—R
$-Today's Pentecostal—R
Urban Kingdom—R
$-Vista
$-Way of St. Francis—R

CHILDREN

$-Adventures
$-High Adventure—R
$-Nature Friend

CHRISTIAN EDUCATION/LIBRARY

$-RTJ—R
$-Teachers of Vision—R
$-Today's Catholic Teacher—R

PASTORS/LEADERS

$-Interpreter

TEEN/YOUNG ADULT
$-Real Faith in Life—R
TeensForJC—R
$-True Girl
$-Young Christian—R
$-Young Salvationist—R

WOMEN
($)-Beyond the Bend—R
CelebrateMoms—R
Christian Woman's Page—R
Hearts at Home—R
$-Inspired Living—R
Proverbs 31 Sisters—R
($)-Simply Blessed—R
Virtuous Woman—R
Woman of Worth—R

WRITERS
Areopagus
$-Fellowscript—R
Money the Write Way—R
$-New Writer's Mag.
Write Connection
$-Writers' Journal

FILLERS: GAMES

ADULT/GENERAL
$-Catholic Yearbook—R
$-CGA World—R
$-Christian Citizen USA
$-Christian Herald—R
Christian Motorsports
Christian Ranchman
$-Chronicle Christian
Citizen USA—R
Connecting Point—R
$-Creation Illust.—R
Diamond Dust
Disciple's Journal—R
$-Faith & Friends—R
$-Family Smart E-tips—R
$-Gem—R
Good News Journal—R
Heartlight—R
$-Lutheran Journal—R
MovieGuide
Spiritual Voice—R
Star of Zion
Victory Herald—R

CHILDREN
$-Adventures
$-American Girl—R
$-Courage—R
$-Guide—R
$-Pockets—R
$-SHINEbrightly—R
$-Sparkle—R

CHRISTIAN EDUCATION/LIBRARY
Catholic Library
$-Group
$-RTJ—R

MISSIONS
$-Glad Tidings (Canada)—R

PASTORS/LEADERS
$-Barefoot—R

TEEN/YOUNG ADULT
$-Listen—R
TeensForJC—R
$-Young Salvationist—R

WOMEN
CelebrateMoms—R
Keeping Hearts & Home
Proverbs 31 Sisters—R

FILLERS: IDEAS

ADULT/GENERAL
$-Animal Trails—R
Breakthrough Intercessor—R
$-Bridal Guides—R
$-CBA Retailers
$-CGA World—R
$-Christian Home & School
Christian Motorsports
Christian Ranchman
$-Chronicle Christian
($)-Community Spirit—R
Diamond Dust
Disciple's Journal—R
Eternal Ink—R
Evangel/OR—R
$-Family Smart E-tips—R
$-Gem—R
$-God Allows U-Turns—R
Good News Journal—R
Heartlight—R
Highway News—R
$-Home Times—R
MovieGuide
Reverent Submissions—R
$-Seek—R
SingleAgain.com—R
Spiritual Voice—R
$-St. Joseph's Messenger—R
Urban Kingdom—R

CHRISTIAN EDUCATION/LIBRARY
$-Children's Ministry
Christian Librarian—R
Congregational Libraries
$-Group
$-Preschool Playhouse (CE)
$-RTJ—R
$-Teach Kids!—R
$-Youth & CE Leadership

MISSIONS
$-Evangelical Missions—R

MUSIC
$-Creator—R

PASTORS/LEADERS
$-Barefoot—R
$-Enrichment—R
$-Interpreter
$-Lutheran Partners—R
$-Pray!—R
$-Preaching Well—R
$-Rev. Magazine
$-RevWriter Resource
$-Small Group Dynamics—R

TEEN/YOUNG ADULT
$-Real Faith in Life—R
$-Young Christian—R

WOMEN
($)-Beyond the Bend—R
CelebrateMoms—R
Christian Woman's Page—R
Hearts at Home—R
$-Inspired Living—R
Just Between Us—R
P31 Woman—R
Proverbs 31 Sisters—R
Right to the Heart—R
Virtuous Woman—R
Woman of Worth—R
$-WT Online—R

WRITERS
Areopagus
$-Canadian Writer's Jour.—R
Dedicated Author
Money the Write Way—R
Once Upon a Time—R
$-Tickled by Thunder
Write Connection
$-Writers' Journal

FILLERS: JOKES

ADULT/GENERAL
$-Catholic Digest—R
$-Christian Journal—R
Christian Motorsports
Christian Ranchman
Citizen USA—R
$-City Light News—R
Disciple's Journal—R
Eternal Ink—R
$-Faith & Friends—R
$-Gem—R
Good News Journal—R
Heartlight—R
$-Home Times—R
($)-Impact—R
$-Interchange
$-Liguorian
$-Lutheran Digest—R
$-Mature Years—R
$-Miracles, Healings
MovieGuide

New Heart—R
PrayerWorks—R
Reverent Submissions—R
$-Significant Living—R
SingleAgain.com—R
Spiritual Voice—R
$-St. Anthony Messenger
Star of Zion

MUSIC
$-Creator—R

PASTORS/LEADERS
Churchlife Inspiration
$-Preaching Well—R
Pulpit Helps—R
Sharing the Practice—R

TEEN/YOUNG ADULT
TeensForJC—R

WOMEN
Proverbs 31 Sisters—R
Virtuous Woman—R

WRITERS
Write Connection
$-Writers' Journal

FILLERS: KID QUOTES

ADULT/GENERAL
$-Animal Trails—R
Breakthrough Intercessor—R
$-Bridal Guides—R
$-Chicken Soup Books—R
$-Christian Journal—R
$-Chronicle Christian
Citizen USA—R
$-City Light News—R
$-DisciplesWorld
Eternal Ink—R
Highway News—R
$-Home Times—R
$-Indian Life—R
MovieGuide
Reverent Submissions—R
SingleAgain.com—R
Spiritual Voice—R
$-Today's Christian—R
$-Upscale
Victory Herald—R

CHRISTIAN EDUCATION/LIBRARY
$-Children's Ministry

WOMEN
CelebrateMoms—R
Proverbs 31 Sisters—R

FILLERS: NEWSBREAKS

ADULT/GENERAL
$-Anglican Journal
$-Arkansas Catholic—R
$-B.C. Catholic—R
$-Canada Lutheran—R
$-Catholic Telegraph
$-CBA Retailers
Choice Newspaper—R
Christian Courier/WI—R
$-Christian Journal—R
Christian Motorsports
Christian Ranchman
$-Christian Renewal—R
$-Chronicle Christian
$-City Light News—R
Disciple's Journal—R
Evangel/OR—R
Friends Journal—R
$-Gem—R
$-God Allows U-Turns—R
Good News Journal—R
Heartlight—R
Highway News—R
$-Home Times—R
MovieGuide
NRB Magazine—R
Sight 360—R
Spiritual Voice—R
STEPS
Sword and Trumpet
Sword of the Lord—R
Urban Kingdom—R

CHRISTIAN EDUCATION/LIBRARY
Christian Librarian—R

MISSIONS
OpRev Equipper—R

PASTORS/LEADERS
$-Preaching Well—R

TEEN/YOUNG ADULT
$-Real Faith in Life—R

WOMEN
$-Hope for Women

WRITERS
Areopagus
$-New Writer's Mag.
$-Writers' Journal

FILLERS: PARTY IDEAS

ADULT/GENERAL
$-Animal Trails—R
$-Bridal Guides—R
Christian Ranchman
$-Chronicle Christian
Citizen USA—R
Disciple's Journal—R
Good News Journal—R
Highway News—R
MovieGuide
Spiritual Voice—R
Urban Kingdom—R
Victory Herald—R

CHILDREN
$-Adventures
$-Sparkle—R

CHRISTIAN EDUCATION/LIBRARY
$-Youth & CE Leadership

MUSIC
$-Creator—R

PASTORS/LEADERS
$-Barefoot—R

TEEN/YOUNG ADULT
TeensForJC—R
$-Young Christian—R

WOMEN
CelebrateMoms—R
Hearts at Home—R
$-Hope for Women
$-Inspired Living—R
Keeping Hearts & Home
P31 Woman—R
Proverbs 31 Sisters—R
Right to the Heart—R
Virtuous Woman—R
Woman of Worth—R

FILLERS: PRAYERS

ADULT/GENERAL
$-Angels on Earth
$-Animal Trails—R
Breakthrough Intercessor—R
$-Bridal Guides—R
$-Catholic Yearbook—R
$-CGA World—R
Channels—R
$-Christian Herald—R
$-Christian Journal—R
Christian Motorsports
Christian Online
Christian Ranchman
$-Chronicle Christian
Desert Call—R
Diamond Dust
Disciple's Journal—R
Eternal Ink—R
$-Family Digest—R
First Call Hospice—R
$-Gem—R
$-God Allows U-Turns—R
Good News Journal—R
Heartlight—R
Highway News—R
$-Home Times—R
LifeTimes Catholic
$-Mature Years—R
MovieGuide
PrayerWorks—R
Reverent Submissions—R
SingleAgain.com—R
Spiritual Voice—R

Spirituality for Today
Star of Zion
Three One Six—R
Urban Kingdom—R
Victory Herald—R
$-Way of St. Francis—R

CHILDREN
$-SHINEbrightly—R
$-Sparkle—R

CHRISTIAN EDUCATION/LIBRARY
$-RTJ—R

DAILY DEVOTIONALS
$-Word in Season

MISSIONS
$-Glad Tidings (Canada)—R

TEEN/YOUNG ADULT
TeensForJC—R
$-True Girl
$-Young Christian—R
$-Young Salvationist—R

WOMEN
CelebrateMoms—R
$-Inspired Living—R
Just Between Us—R
Keeping Hearts & Home
Proverbs 31 Sisters—R
Right to the Heart—R
($)-Simply Blessed—R
Virtuous Woman—R
Woman of Worth—R

WRITERS
$-Cross & Quill—R
$-Fellowscript—R
Write Connection
$-Writers' Journal

FILLERS: PROSE

ADULT/GENERAL
$-Animal Trails—R
$-Bible Advocate—R
Bread of Life—R
Breakthrough Intercessor—R
$-Bridal Guides—R
Christian Motorsports
Christian Online
Christian Ranchman
$-Chronicle Christian
$-Decision
Desert Call—R
Diamond Dust
Disciple's Journal—R
Eternal Ink—R
Evangel/OR—R
$-Faith & Family
First Call Hospice—R
$-Gem—R
$-God Allows U-Turns—R
Good News Journal—R
Heartlight—R
Highway News—R
$-Home Times—R
MovieGuide
$-Now What?—R
Pegasus Review—R
Reverent Submissions—R
SingleAgain.com—R
Spiritual Voice—R
Sword and Trumpet
Sword of the Lord—R
Three One Six—R
$-Today's Pentecostal—R
Urban Kingdom—R
Victory Herald—R
$-Way of St. Francis—R
$-Wireless Age—R

CHILDREN
$-Partners—R

MISSIONS
$-Glad Tidings (Canada)—R

PASTORS/LEADERS
$-Preaching Well—R

TEEN/YOUNG ADULT
$-Brio
$-Listen—R
$-Real Faith in Life—R
TeensForJC—R
$-Young Christian—R

WOMEN
CelebrateMoms—R
$-Melody of the Heart
$-Today's Christian Woman—R

WRITERS
Areopagus
$-Freelance Writer's Report—R
Write Connection
$-Writer
$-Writers' Journal

FILLERS: QUIZZES

ADULT/GENERAL
$-Animal Trails—R
$-Bridal Guides—R
$-Catholic Yearbook—R
Christian Motorsports
Christian Online
Christian Ranchman
$-Chronicle Christian
Church Herald & Holiness—R
Citizen USA—R
Diamond Dust
Disciple's Journal—R
Eternal Ink—R
$-Faith & Friends—R
$-Gem—R
Good News Journal—R
$-Home Times—R
($)-Impact—R
$-Lutheran Journal—R
MovieGuide
Sight 360—R
Spiritual Voice—R
Urban Kingdom—R
$-Wittenburg Door—R

CHILDREN
$-Cadet Quest—R
$-Focus/Clubhouse
$-Guide—R
$-Nature Friend
$-Partners—R
$-SHINEbrightly—R
Skipping Stones
$-Sparkle—R
$-Story Mates—R

MISSIONS
$-Glad Tidings (Canada)—R

TEEN/YOUNG ADULT
$-Listen—R
$-Real Faith in Life—R
TeensForJC—R
$-True Girl
$-Young Christian—R
$-Young Salvationist—R

WOMEN
CelebrateMoms—R
$-Melody of the Heart
Proverbs 31 Sisters—R
Virtuous Woman—R

WRITERS
Once Upon a Time—R
$-Writers' Journal

FILLERS: QUOTES

ADULT/GENERAL
$-Animal Trails—R
Bread of Life—R
Breakthrough Intercessor—R
$-Bridal Guides—R
$-Catholic Digest—R
$-Catholic Yearbook—R
$-Chicken Soup Books—R
Choice Newspaper—R
$-Christian Herald—R
$-Christian Journal—R
Christian Motorsports
Christian Ranchman
$-Christian Response—R
$-Chronicle Christian
Citizen USA—R
$-Culture Wars—R
Desert Call—R
Disciple's Journal—R
$-DisciplesWorld
Eternal Ink—R
$-Faith & Friends—R

$-Family Smart E-tips—R
First Call Hospice—R
$-Gem—R
$-God Allows U-Turns—R
Good News Journal—R
Heartlight—R
$-Home Times—R
$-Indian Life—R
$-Lutheran Journal—R
MESSAGE/Open Bible—R
MovieGuide
$-Now What?—R
Pegasus Review—R
PrayerWorks—R
Reverent Submissions—R
$-Seek—R
Spiritual Voice—R
Spirituality for Today
$-St. Anthony Messenger
$-Storyteller—R
Urban Kingdom—R

CHILDREN

$-Adventures
$-Partners—R
Skipping Stones

MISSIONS

Railroad Evangelist—R

PASTORS/LEADERS

Pulpit Helps—R
$-Rev. Magazine

TEEN/YOUNG ADULT

$-True Girl
$-Young Christian—R

WOMEN

($)-Beyond the Bend—R
CelebrateMoms—R
$-Inspired Living—R
Just Between Us—R
Proverbs 31 Sisters—R
Right to the Heart—R

WRITERS

$-Canadian Writer's Jour.—R
Money the Write Way—R
Write Connection
$-Writers' Journal

FILLERS: SERMON ILLUSTRATIONS

ADULT/GENERAL

Choice Newspaper—R
Urban Kingdom—R

PASTORS/LEADERS

Churchlife Inspiration
$-Preaching Well—R
$-PreachingToday.com
Pulpit Helps—R
$-RevWriter Resource
$-Sunday Sermons—R

WOMEN

($)-Beyond the Bend—R
Proverbs 31 Sisters—R

FILLERS: SHORT HUMOR

ADULT/GENERAL

$-Angels on Earth
$-Animal Trails—R
Breakthrough Intercessor—R
$-Bridal Guides—R
$-Cappers
$-Chicken Soup Books—R
$-Christian Citizen USA
$-Christian Journal—R
Christian Motorsports
Christian Online
Christian Ranchman
$-Chronicle Christian
Citizen USA—R
$-City Light News—R
Diamond Dust
Disciple's Journal—R
$-DisciplesWorld
Eternal Ink—R
$-Family Digest—R
Friends Journal—R
$-Gem—R
$-God Allows U-Turns—R
Good News Journal—R
Heartlight—R
Highway News—R
$-Home Times—R
($)-Impact—R
$-Indian Life—R
$-Leben—R
$-Living—R
$-Lutheran Digest—R
MESSAGE/Open Bible—R
MovieGuide
New Heart—R
PrayerWorks—R
$-Presbyterians Today—R
$-Purpose—R
Reverent Submissions—R
$-Rose & Thorn
$-Seek—R
$-Significant Living—R
SingleAgain.com—R
Spiritual Voice—R
STEPS
Three One Six—R
Urban Kingdom—R
Victory Herald—R
$-Vista
$-Wittenburg Door—R

CHILDREN

$-High Adventure—R
$-SHINEbrightly—R
$-Sparkle—R

CHRISTIAN EDUCATION/LIBRARY

Christian Librarian—R

MUSIC

Christian Music Weekly—R
$-Creator—R

PASTORS/LEADERS

$-Barefoot—R
$-Catholic Servant
Churchlife Inspiration
$-Enrichment—R
$-Interpreter
$-Leadership—R
$-Preaching Well—R
Pulpit Helps—R
Sharing the Practice—R

TEEN/YOUNG ADULT

$-InsideOut—R
$-Real Faith in Life—R
TeensForJC—R
$-Young Christian—R
$-Young Salvationist—R

WOMEN

($)-Beyond the Bend—R
CelebrateMoms—R
Christian Woman's Page—R
Hearts at Home—R
Just Between Us—R
Keeping Hearts & Home
$-Melody of the Heart
Proverbs 31 Sisters—R
Woman of Worth—R

WRITERS

Areopagus
$-Christian Communicator—R
$-New Writer's Mag.
Once Upon a Time—R
$-Tickled by Thunder
Write Connection
$-Writers' Journal

FILLERS: TIPS

ADULT/GENERAL

$-Animal Trails—R
$-Bridal Guides—R
Christian Ranchman
$-Chronicle Christian
Diamond Dust
Eternal Ink—R
Highway News—R
$-Home Times—R
MovieGuide
Reverent Submissions—R
SingleAgain.com—R
$-Special Living—R
$-Storyteller—R
Urban Kingdom—R
Victory Herald—R

CHILDREN
$-Adventures
$-Cadet Quest—R

CHRISTIAN EDUCATION/LIBRARY
$-Youth & CE Leadership

PASTORS/LEADERS
$-Barefoot—R
$-Sabbath School Leadership—R
$-Your Church—R

TEEN/YOUNG ADULT
TeensForJC—R
$-Young Christian—R

WOMEN
($)-Beyond the Bend—R
CelebrateMoms—R
Christian Woman's Page—R
$-Hope for Women
$-Inspired Living—R
$-MOMsense—R
Proverbs 31 Sisters—R
($)-Simply Blessed—R
Virtuous Woman—R
Woman of Worth—R
Women's Ministry

WRITERS
$-Fellowscript—R
$-Freelance Writer's Report—R
Money the Write Way—R
NW Christian Author—R
Once Upon a Time—R
Write Connection
$-Writers' Journal

FILLERS: WORD PUZZLES

ADULT/GENERAL
$-Animal Trails—R
$-Bridal Guides—R
$-Catholic Yearbook—R
$-CGA World—R
$-Christian Citizen USA
$-Christian Herald—R
$-Christian Journal—R
Christian Ranchman
$-Chronicle Christian
Citizen USA—R
Connecting Point—R
Diamond Dust
Disciple's Journal—R
$-Evangel/IN—R
$-Faith & Friends—R
Friends Journal—R
$-Gem—R
Good News Journal—R
$-Gospel Today—R
Heartlight—R
$-Home Times—R
$-Horizons (adult)—R
($)-Impact—R
$-Mature Years—R
MovieGuide
$-Power for Living—R
$-Significant Living—R
Spiritual Voice—R
$-Standard—R
Star of Zion
$-Vista

CHILDREN
$-Adventures
$-American Girl—R
$-Cadet Quest—R
$-Discoveries—R
$-Faces
$-Focus/Clubhouse
$-Guide—R
$-Nature Friend
$-Our Little Friend—R
$-Partners—R
$-Passport—R
$-Pockets—R
$-Primary Pal/IL
$-SHINEbrightly—R
Skipping Stones
$-Story Mates—R

CHRISTIAN EDUCATION/LIBRARY
$-RTJ—R
$-Youth & CE Leadership

MISSIONS
$-Glad Tidings (Canada)—R

TEEN/YOUNG ADULT
$-Real Faith in Life—R
TeensForJC—R
$-True Girl
$-Young Christian—R
$-Young Salvationist—R

WOMEN
CelebrateMoms—R
$-Melody of the Heart

WRITERS
$-Writers' Journal

FOOD/RECIPES

ADULT/GENERAL
$-Animal Trails—R
$-Associated Content—R
$-Bridal Guides—R
CBN.com—R
$-Chicken Soup Magazine
Choice Newspaper—R
Christian Online
Christian Ranchman
Citizen USA—R
Diamond Dust
$-Dovetail—R
$-Faith & Family
$-Home Times—R
HopeKeepers—R
$-Ideals—R
($)-Impact—R
$-Mature Living
$-Montgomery's Journey
Parents & Teens—R
SearchingWisdom.org—R
$-Significant Living—R
Spiritual Voice—R
$-St. Anthony Messenger
Urban Kingdom—R
Victory Herald—R
$-World & I—R

CHILDREN
$-Adventures
$-American Girl—R
$-Cadet Quest—R
$-Celebrate
$-Faces
$-Focus/Clubhouse
$-Focus/Clubhouse Jr.
$-Pockets—R
$-SHINEbrightly—R
$-Sparkle—R

MISSIONS
Women of the Harvest

TEEN/YOUNG ADULT
$-Boundless Webzine—R
$-Brio
$-J.A.M.
TeensForJC—R
$-Young Christian—R

WOMEN
($)-Beyond the Bend—R
CelebrateMoms—R
Christian Women Today—R
Crowned with Silver
$-Dabbling Mum—R
First Lady
$-Godly Business Woman—R
Hearts at Home—R
$-Hope for Women
$-Inspired Living—R
Keeping Hearts & Home
$-Melody of the Heart
Precious Times—R
Proverbs 31 Sisters—R
$-Simple Joy
Virtuous Woman—R
Woman of Worth—R
Women Today—R
$-WT Online—R

GRANDPARENTING*

ADULT/GENERAL
$-CGA World—R
Christian Ranchman
$-City Light News—R
Eternal Ink—R
$-Focus on the Family
$-Grand

$-Home Times—R
$-In Touch
$-Liguorian
$-Live—R
$-Lutheran Digest—R
PrayerWorks—R
$-Seek—R
$-Significant Living—R
$-Today's Pentecostal—R
$-Vista

WOMEN

Crowned with Silver
Hearts at Home—R

HEALING

ADULT/GENERAL

$-Advance
$-America
$-Angels on Earth
$-Animal Trails—R
Anointed Pages
$-Associated Content—R
Bread of Life—R
Breakthrough Intercessor—R
$-Bridal Guides—R
$-Canada Lutheran—R
CBN.com—R
$-Celebrate Life—R
Channels—R
Choice Newspaper—R
$-Christian Journal—R
Christian Motorsports
Christian Online
Christian Ranchman
$-ChristianWeek—R
$-Chronicle Christian
$-City Light News—R
($)-Community Spirit—R
Connecting Point—R
Evangelical Advocate—R
$-Faith Today
First Call Hospice—R
$-Gem—R
$-God Allows U-Turns—R
$-Good News—R
$-Guideposts—R
$-Home Times—R
$-HonorBound—R
HopeKeepers—R
$-Light & Life
$-Live—R
Looking Up
$-Miracles, Healings
$-National Catholic
New Heart—R
Nostalgia—R
Perspectives—R
$-Positive Thinking—R
Prayer Closet
$-Pure Inspiration—R
Sacred Journey—R
$-Seek—R
Sharing—R
Sight 360—R
$-Significant Living—R
SingleAgain.com—R
$-Sound Body—R
$-Spiritual Life
Spiritual Voice—R
$-St. Anthony Messenger
$-St. Joseph's Messenger—R
STEPS
$-Storyteller—R
$-Testimony—R
Three One Six—R
$-Today's Christian—R
Trumpeter—R
$-United Church Observer—R
Urban Kingdom—R
$-Vista
$-World & I—R

CHILDREN

$-BREAD/God's Children—R

DAILY DEVOTIONALS

Penned from the Heart—R

PASTORS/LEADERS

$-Word & World

TEEN/YOUNG ADULT

$-Boundless Webzine—R
$-J.A.M.
$-Young Christian—R

WOMEN

$-Canticle
Christian Woman's Page—R
$-Godly Business Woman—R
Hearts at Home—R
$-Hope for Women
$-Inspired Living—R
Precious Times—R
Share
$-SpiritLed Woman
$-WT Online—R

WRITERS

Areopagus

HEALTH

ADULT/GENERAL

$-Abilities
$-Angels on Earth
$-Anglican Journal
$-Animal Trails—R
Anointed Pages
$-Apocalypse Chronicles—R
$-Associated Content—R
$-Aujourd'hui Credo—R
$-B.C. Catholic—R
$-Brave Hearts—R
$-Bridal Guides—R
$-Canada Lutheran—R
$-Catholic Forester—R
CBN.com—R
$-Celebrate Life—R
$-CGA World—R
Channels—R
$-Chicken Soup Magazine
Choice Newspaper—R
$-Christian Courier/CAN—R
Christian Courier/WI—R
$-Christian Journal—R
Christian Online
Christian Ranchman
$-ChristianWeek—R
$-Chronicle Christian
Citizen USA—R
$-City Light News—R
$-Common Ground—R
($)-Community Spirit—R
Creation Care—R
$-Creative Nonfiction
Disciple's Journal—R
Evangelical Advocate—R
$-Faith Today
First Call Hospice—R
$-Gospel Today—R
$-Guideposts—R
$-Home Times—R
$-HonorBound—R
HopeKeepers—R
$-Inland NW Christian
Island Catholic
$-Lifeglow—R
$-Light & Life
Looking Up
$-Lookout
$-Mature Living
$-Mature Years—R
$-MESSAGE
$-Montgomery's Journey
New Heart—R
Nostalgia—R
$-Ozarks Senior Living—R
Penned from the Heart—R
$-Positive Thinking—R
$-Pure Inspiration—R
Purpose Magazine—R
Sacred Journey—R
SearchingWisdom.org—R
Sight 360—R
$-Significant Living—R
SingleAgain.com—R
$-Sound Body—R
$-Special Living—R
Spiritual Voice—R
$-St. Anthony Messenger
$-Testimony—R
$-Today's Christian—R
$-Today's Pentecostal—R
Trumpeter—R
$-Upscale
Urban Kingdom—R
$-Vibrant Life—R
$-Vista

$-War Cry—R
$-Whole
Wisconsin Christian
$-World & I—R

CHILDREN
$-American Girl—R
$-Guide—R
$-New Moon—R
$-Sparkle—R
$-Winner—R

CHRISTIAN EDUCATION/LIBRARY
$-Teachers of Vision—R

DAILY DEVOTIONALS
Penned from the Heart—R

PASTORS/LEADERS
$-Christian Century—R
$-InSite—R
$-Interpreter
$-Word & World

TEEN/YOUNG ADULT
$-Boundless Webzine—R
$-Breakaway
$-Brio
$-Devo'Zine—R
$-J.A.M.
$-Listen—R
TeensForJC—R
$-True Girl
$-Young Christian—R

WOMEN
$-At the Center—R
Christian Woman's Page—R
Christian Women Today—R
Comfort Café
$-Esprit—R
$-Godly Business Woman—R
$-Heart & Soul
Hearts at Home—R
$-Herizons
$-Horizons (women)—R
$-Inspired Living—R
$-InspiredMoms—R
$-inSpirit—R
$-Journey
Keeping Hearts & Home
Life Tools for Women
Lutheran Woman's Quar.
Precious Times—R
Share
($)-Simply Blessed—R
$-SpiritLed Woman
$-Today's Christian Woman—R
Together with God—R
Virtuous Woman—R
Woman of Worth—R
Women Today—R
$-WT Online—R

HISTORICAL

ADULT/GENERAL
($)-AGAIN—R
$-Angels on Earth
$-Animal Trails—R
$-Arlington Catholic
$-Associated Content—R
$-Bridal Guides—R
$-Cappers
$-Catholic Peace Voice—R
CBN.com—R
$-Celebrate Life—R
Channels—R
Choice Newspaper—R
$-Christian Courier/CAN—R
$-Christian History—R
Christian Motorsports
Christian Observer
Christian Online
Christian Ranchman
$-Christian Renewal—R
$-Chronicle Christian
Citizen USA—R
$-City Light News—R
$-Company—R
$-Dovetail—R
Evangelical Advocate—R
Evangelical Times
$-Faith Today
$-Haruah—R
$-Home Times—R
$-HonorBound—R
$-Indian Life—R
$-Leben—R
$-Lifeglow—R
$-Light & Life
Looking Up
$-Lutheran Digest—R
$-Mature Living
($)-Mennonite Historian—R
$-Messiah
Messianic Times
Methodist History
$-National Catholic
$-New Freeman—R
$-New Wineskins—R
Nostalgia—R
$-Parabola—R
Perspectives—R
$-Power for Living—R
Presbyterian Outlook
Priscilla Papers
Rare Jewel—R
Sharing—R
Sight 360—R
$-Social Justice—R
Spiritual Voice—R
$-St. Anthony Messenger
Star of Zion
$-Storyteller—R
Sword of the Lord—R
Three One Six—R
Trumpeter—R
$-U.S. Catholic
$-Upscale
Urban Kingdom—R
$-Way of St. Francis—R
$-Wesleyan Life—R
$-Wireless Age—R
Wisconsin Christian
$-World & I—R

CHILDREN
$-Faces
$-Focus/Clubhouse Jr.
$-Guide—R
$-High Adventure—R
$-New Moon—R
$-Sparkle—R

CHRISTIAN EDUCATION/LIBRARY
Catholic Library
$-Teachers of Vision—R

MISSIONS
$-One
Women of the Harvest

MUSIC
$-Creator—R
Hymn

PASTORS/LEADERS
$-Leadership—R
$-Ministry Today
$-Priest
Pulpit Helps—R
Sewanee Theo. Review
Theological Digest—R
$-This Rock
$-Today's Parish—R
$-Word & World

TEEN/YOUNG ADULT
$-Boundless Webzine—R
$-Breakaway
$-CLEAR Direction
$-CLEAR Horizon
$-InsideOut—R
$-J.A.M.
$-Listen—R
$-Passageway.org—R
$-Real Faith in Life—R
TeensForJC—R
$-Young Adult Today—R
$-Young Christian—R

WOMEN
($)-History's Women—R
Just Between Us—R
($)-Shalom Bayit
$-SpiritLed Woman

WRITERS
Areopagus
$-Tickled by Thunder

HOLIDAY/SEASONAL

ADULT/GENERAL

$-Advance
Alabama Baptist
$-Alive Now—R
American Tract—R
$-Angels on Earth
$-Animal Trails—R
$-Annals of St. Anne
$-Arlington Catholic
$-BGC World—R
$-Brave Hearts—R
$-Bridal Guides—R
$-Canada Lutheran—R
$-Cappers
$-Cathedral Age—R
$-Catholic Digest—R
$-Catholic New York
CBN.com—R
$-CGA World—R
Channels—R
$-Chicken Soup Books—R
$-Christian Courier/CAN—R
Christian Courier/WI—R
$-Christian Home & School
$-Christian Journal—R
Christian Online
Christian Ranchman
$-Christian Renewal—R
$-Christian Retailing
$-ChristianWeek—R
$-Chronicle Christian
Church Herald & Holiness—R
Citizen USA—R
$-City Light News—R
($)-Community Spirit—R
Connecting Point—R
$-Covenant Companion—R
Desert Call—R
Diamond Dust
$-Dovetail—R
Eternal Ink—R
Evangelical Advocate—R
$-Faith & Family
$-Faith Today
$-Family Digest—R
$-Family Smart E-tips—R
$-Focus on the Family
$-Gem—R
$-Gems of Truth—R
$-God Allows U-Turns—R
Good News Journal—R
$-Guideposts—R
Heartlight—R
$-Home Times—R
$-HonorBound—R
HopeKeepers—R
$-Horizons (adult)—R
$-Ideals—R
$-In Touch
$-Indian Life—R
$-Lifeglow—R
$-Light & Life
$-Liguorian
$-Live—R
$-Living—R
$-Living Church
$-Living Light—R
Looking Up
$-Lookout
$-Marriage Partnership—R
$-Mature Living
$-Mature Years—R
MESSAGE/Open Bible—R
$-Minnesota Christian—R
$-Miraculous Medal
$-Montana Catholic
$-Montgomery's Journey
$-National Catholic
Parents & Teens—R
Pegasus Review—R
Penned from the Heart—R
$-Positive Thinking—R
$-Power for Living—R
$-Psychology for Living—R
$-Pure Inspiration—R
$-Purpose—R
Quaker Life—R
Reverent Submissions—R
Sacred Journey—R
SearchingWisdom.org—R
$-Seek—R
Sharing—R
$-Significant Living—R
$-Special Living—R
Spiritual Voice—R
Spirituality for Today
$-St. Anthony Messenger
$-St. Joseph's Messenger—R
$-Standard—R
Star of Zion
$-Storyteller—R
Sword of the Lord—R
$-Today's Christian—R
$-Together—R
Trumpeter—R
$-U.S. Catholic
$-United Church Observer—R
Urban Kingdom—R
$-Vibrant Life—R
Victory Herald—R
$-Victory in Grace—R
$-Vista
$-War Cry—R
$-Wesleyan Life—R
$-World & I—R

CHILDREN

$-Courage—R
$-Focus/Clubhouse
$-Focus/Clubhouse Jr.
$-Guide—R
$-High Adventure—R
$-Junior Companion—R
$-JuniorWay
$-Nature Friend
$-Pockets—R
$-Primary Pal/IL
$-Primary Street
$-SHINEbrightly—R
$-Sparkle—R

CHRISTIAN EDUCATION/LIBRARY

$-Group
Ideas Unlimited—R
$-Resource—R
$-Teach Kids!—R
$-Teachers of Vision—R
$-Today's Catholic Teacher—R
$-Youth & CE Leadership

DAILY DEVOTIONALS

Penned from the Heart—R
$-These Days

MISSIONS

$-Glad Tidings (Canada)—R
Railroad Evangelist—R
Women of the Harvest

MUSIC

$-Creator—R

PASTORS/LEADERS

$-Catholic Servant
$-Enrichment—R
$-Interpreter
$-Preaching Well—R
Pulpit Helps—R
$-Sunday Sermons—R

TEEN/YOUNG ADULT

$-Boundless Webzine—R
$-Breakaway
$-Brio
$-CLEAR Direction
$-CLEAR Horizon
$-Credo—R
$-Essential Connection
$-J.A.M.
$-Listen—R
$-Real Faith in Life—R
TeensForJC—R
$-True Girl
$-Young Christian—R
$-Young Salvationist—R

WOMEN

($)-Beyond the Bend—R
$-Canticle
CelebrateMoms—R
Christian Women Today—R
$-Esprit—R
Handmaiden—R
Hearts at Home—R
($)-History's Women—R
$-Hope for Women

$-Inspired Living—R
$-InspiredMoms—R
$-inSpirit—R
$-Journey
Lutheran Woman's Quar.
$-MOMsense—R
P31 Woman—R
Precious Times—R
$-Today's Christian Woman—R
Together with God—R
Virtuous Woman—R
Woman of Worth—R
$-WT Online—R

WRITERS

Areopagus

HOLY SPIRIT*

ADULT/GENERAL

Bread of Life—R
$-Bridal Guides—R
Christian C. L. RECORD—R
$-Christian Journal—R
Christian Ranchman
Church Herald & Holiness—R
$-City Light News—R
Eternal Ink—R
$-Home Times—R
$-Live—R
$-Pure Inspiration—R
Reverent Submissions—R
$-Seek—R
Spirituality for Today
Three One Six—R
Urban Kingdom—R
Victory Herald—R
$-Vista

CHILDREN

$-BREAD/God's Children—R

PASTORS/LEADERS

$-Lutheran Partners—R
$-Ministry Today

TEEN/YOUNG ADULT

$-Boundless Webzine—R
$-Breakaway
$-Brio
$-Young Christian—R

WOMEN

Hearts at Home—R
$-Inspired Living—R

HOMESCHOOLING

$-Anglican Journal
$-Animal Trails—R
$-Arlington Catholic
$-CBA Retailers
CBN.com—R
Channels—R
Christian C. L. RECORD—R
Christian Computing—R
$-Christian Examiner
Christian Observer
Christian Online
$-ChristianWeek—R
$-Chronicle Christian
Citizen USA—R
$-City Light News—R
($)-Community Spirit—R
Creation Care—R
Disciple's Journal—R
$-Dovetail—R
$-Faith & Family
$-Faith Today
$-Family Smart E-tips—R
$-Focus on the Family
Good News Journal—R
$-Home Times—R
$-Homeschooling Today—R
$-Light & Life
$-Lookout
$-Minnesota Christian—R
Parents & Teens—R
$-Psychology for Living—R
Sight 360—R
$-Social Justice—R
Spiritual Voice—R
$-St. Anthony Messenger
Sword of the Lord—R
Trumpeter—R
Urban Kingdom—R
$-Vista
Wisconsin Christian
$-World & I—R

CHILDREN

$-BREAD/God's Children—R
$-New Moon—R
Skipping Stones

CHRISTIAN EDUCATION/LIBRARY

Jour./Ed. & Christian Belief—R

MISSIONS

Women of the Harvest

TEEN/YOUNG ADULT

$-Boundless Webzine—R
$-Brio
$-J.A.M.
$-Passageway.org—R
$-True Girl
$-Young Christian—R

WOMEN

$-Canticle
CelebrateMoms—R
Christian Woman's Page—R
Crowned with Silver
Hearts at Home—R
$-Hope for Women
$-InspiredMoms—R
$-inSpirit—R
$-Journey
($)-Shalom Bayit
Together with God—R
Virtuous Woman—R
Woman of Worth—R
Women of the Cross
$-WT Online—R

HOMILETICS

ADULT/GENERAL

CBN.com—R
Channels—R
Christian Ranchman
Evangelical Advocate—R
$-New Wineskins—R
Perspectives—R
Priscilla Papers
$-Social Justice—R
$-St. Anthony Messenger
$-Stewardship—R
$-Testimony—R
Trumpeter—R
$-Way of St. Francis—R
$-Wesleyan Life—R

PASTORS/LEADERS

$-African American Pulpit
$-Christian Century—R
$-Clergy Journal—R
$-Lutheran Partners—R
$-Ministry & Liturgy—R
Preaching—R
$-Preaching Well—R
$-Priest
$-Proclaim—R
$-Rev. Magazine
Sewanee Theo. Review

WOMEN

$-SpiritLed Woman

HOW-TO

ADULT/GENERAL

$-Associated Content—R
$-Bridal Guides—R
$-CBA Retailers
CBN.com—R
$-Celebrate Life—R
$-CGA World—R
Channels—R
$-Christian Journal—R
Christian Motorsports
Christian Observer
Christian Online
$-Christian Retailing
$-City Light News—R
Connecting Point—R
Creation Care—R
Diamond Dust
$-Direction
$-Discipleship Journal—R
$-Dovetail—R
$-Faith & Family

$-Faith Today
$-Family Digest—R
$-Family Smart E-tips—R
$-Focus on the Family
Good News Journal—R
$-Home Times—R
HopeKeepers—R
$-Inland NW Christian
$-Light & Life
$-Live—R
$-Living—R
$-Living Church
Looking Up
$-Mature Living
$-MESSAGE
$-Montgomery's Journey
($)-Mutuality—R
$-On Mission
$-Positive Thinking—R
$-Presbyterians Today—R
Regent Global—R
SearchingWisdom.org—R
Spiritual Voice—R
$-St. Anthony Messenger
$-Testimony—R
$-Today's Christian—R
Trumpeter—R
$-U.S. Catholic
Urban Kingdom—R
$-Vibrant Life—R
Victory Herald—R
Village Note Cards—R
$-Vista
$-World & I—R

CHILDREN
$-Sparkle—R

CHRISTIAN EDUCATION/LIBRARY
$-Catechist
Catholic Library
$-Christian Educators—R
Christian Librarian—R
$-Church Libraries—R
Congregational Libraries
$-Group
Ideas Unlimited—R
$-Journal/Adventist Ed.—R
$-Kids' Ministry Ideas—R
$-Preschool Playhouse (CE)
$-Resource—R
$-RTJ—R
$-Teachers of Vision—R
$-Today's Catholic Teacher—R
$-Youth & CE Leadership

MISSIONS
$-PFI World—R

PASTORS/LEADERS
$-African American Pulpit
$-Cornerstone Youth—R
$-Lutheran Partners—R
$-Ministry
$-Ministry Today
$-Net Results
$-Newsletter Newsletter
$-Outreach—R
$-RevWriter Resource
$-Sabbath School Leadership—R
$-Willow—R
$-Worship Leader
$-Your Church—R

TEEN/YOUNG ADULT
$-Breakaway
$-Brio
$-Insight—R
$-Listen—R
$-Real Faith in Life—R
TeensForJC—R
$-True Girl
$-Young Christian—R

WOMEN
($)-Beyond the Bend—R
CelebrateMoms—R
Christian Woman's Page—R
Christian Women Today—R
$-Dabbling Mum—R
Hearts at Home—R
$-Hope for Women
Just Between Us—R
$-Melody of the Heart
Precious Times—R
Proverbs 31 Sisters—R
$-Today's Christian Woman—R
Together with God—R
Virtuous Woman—R
Woman of Worth—R

WRITERS
Author-Me
$-Christian Communicator—R
$-Cross & Quill—R
$-Fellowscript—R
$-Freelance Writer's Report—R
Money the Write Way—R
$-Novel Writer—R
Once Upon a Time—R
Poetic Voices—R
$-Poets & Writers
$-Spirit-Led Writer—R
$-Writer's Digest—R

HOW-TO ACTIVITIES (JUV.)

ADULT/GENERAL
$-Animal Trails—R
$-Associated Content—R
$-Bridal Guides—R
Channels—R
$-Christian Home & School
Christian Online
$-City Light News—R
($)-Community Spirit—R
Creation Care—R
$-Dovetail—R
$-Faith & Family
$-Family Smart E-tips—R
Good News Journal—R
$-Homeschooling Today—R
$-Indian Life—R
Keys to Living—R
$-Light & Life
Spiritual Voice—R
$-St. Anthony Messenger
$-Vista
$-World & I—R

CHILDREN
$-Adventures
$-American Girl—R
$-BREAD/God's Children—R
$-Cadet Quest—R
$-Celebrate
$-Courage—R
$-Faces
$-Focus/Clubhouse
$-Focus/Clubhouse Jr.
$-Guide—R
$-High Adventure—R
$-Junior Companion—R
$-JuniorWay
$-Nature Friend
$-Pockets—R
$-Preschool Playhouse (CE)
$-Preschool Playhouse (child)
$-Primary Pal/IL
$-Seeds
$-SHINEbrightly—R
$-Sparkle—R
$-Winner—R

CHRISTIAN EDUCATION/LIBRARY
$-Children's Ministry
Christian Early Ed.—R
$-Group
$-Kids' Ministry Ideas—R
$-Preschool Playhouse (CE)
$-RTJ—R
$-Teach Kids!—R
$-Teachers of Vision—R

PASTORS/LEADERS
$-Interpreter

TEEN/YOUNG ADULT
$-Brio
$-True Girl
$-Young Christian—R

WOMEN
$-Godly Business Woman—R
Hearts at Home—R
Just Between Us—R

HUMOR

ADULT/GENERAL

American Tract—R
$-Angels on Earth
$-Associated Content—R
$-Bridal Guides—R
$-Catholic Digest—R
$-Catholic Forester—R
$-Catholic Peace Voice—R
CBN.com—R
$-CGA World—R
Channels—R
$-Chicken Soup Books—R
Christian Computing—R
$-Christian Courier/CAN—R
$-Christian Journal—R
Christian Online
Christian Radio
Christian Ranchman
$-Christianity Today—R
$-Chronicle Christian
$-City Light News—R
($)-Community Spirit—R
Connecting Point—R
$-Creative Nonfiction
Disciple's Journal—R
$-Dovetail—R
$-Faith & Family
$-Faith Today
$-Family Digest—R
$-Family Smart E-tips—R
$-Focus on the Family
$-Focus on Your Child
$-Gem—R
$-God Allows U-Turns—R
Good News Journal—R
$-Haruah—R
Highway News—R
$-Home Times—R
$-Homeschooling Today—R
HopeKeepers—R
$-Horizons (adult)—R
$-Ideals—R
$-In Touch
$-Indian Life—R
$-Inland NW Christian
$-Lifeglow—R
$-Light & Life
$-Live—R
$-Living—R
$-Living Church
$-Living Light—R
Looking Up
$-Lookout
$-Mature Living
$-Miracles, Healings
$-National Catholic
$-New Freeman—R
New Heart—R
$-New Wineskins—R
Nostalgia—R
$-Over the Back Fence—R
$-Ozarks Senior Living—R
$-Parabola—R
$-ParentLife
Pegasus Review—R
Penned from the Heart—R
$-Positive Thinking—R
PrayerWorks—R
$-Psychology for Living—R
Reverent Submissions—R
$-Rose & Thorn
Ruminate
Sacred Journey—R
$-Seek—R
$-Significant Living—R
Silver Wings—R
Spiritual Voice—R
$-St. Anthony Messenger
$-Storyteller—R
$-Testimony—R
Three One Six—R
$-Today's Christian—R
$-Together—R
Trumpeter—R
$-U.S. Catholic
Urban Kingdom—R
Victory Herald—R
$-Victory in Grace—R
$-Vista
$-War Cry—R
$-Weavings—R
$-Wildwood Reader—R
$-Wittenburg Door—R
$-World & I—R
Xavier Review

CHILDREN

$-Faces
$-Focus/Clubhouse Jr.
$-High Adventure—R
$-SHINEbrightly—R
$-Sparkle—R

CHRISTIAN EDUCATION/LIBRARY

$-Children's Ministry
$-Teachers of Vision—R

DAILY DEVOTIONALS

Penned from the Heart—R

MISSIONS

Women of the Harvest

MUSIC

Christian Music Weekly—R
$-Creator—R

PASTORS/LEADERS

$-Catholic Servant
Churchlife Inspiration
$-Enrichment—R
$-Leadership—R
$-Lutheran Partners—R
$-Preaching Well—R
$-Priest
$-Small Group Dynamics—R
$-Today's Parish—R
$-Willow—R

TEEN/YOUNG ADULT

$-Boundless Webzine—R
$-Breakaway
$-Brio
$-CLEAR Horizon
$-Essential Connection
$-Insight—R
$-Listen—R
$-Passageway.org—R
$-Real Faith in Life—R
$-TC Magazine
TeensForJC—R
$-Young Christian—R
$-Young Salvationist—R

WOMEN

($)-Beyond the Bend—R
CelebrateMoms—R
Crowned with Silver
$-Esprit—R
Hearts at Home—R
$-Hope for Women
$-Horizons (women)—R
$-Journey
Just Between Us—R
Keeping Hearts & Home
Lutheran Woman's Quar.
$-Melody of the Heart
$-MOMsense—R
($)-Simply Blessed—R
$-SpiritLed Woman
$-Today's Christian Woman—R
Together with God—R
Virtuous Woman—R
Woman of Worth—R
$-WT Online—R

WRITERS

Areopagus
Beginnings—R
$-ByLine
$-Christian Communicator—R
$-New Writer's Mag.
Once Upon a Time—R

INNER LIFE

ADULT/GENERAL

$-Bridal Guides—R
$-Catholic Digest—R
CBN.com—R
Channels—R
$-Christian Journal—R
Christian Ranchman
$-ChristianWeek—R
$-Chronicle Christian
Church Herald & Holiness—R
$-City Light News—R

($)-Community Spirit—R
$-Discipleship Journal—R
Divine Ascent
$-Faith & Family
$-Faith Today
$-Focus on the Family
Halo Magazine
$-Home Times—R
$-In Touch
LifeTimes Catholic
$-Light & Life
$-Live—R
$-Living—R
Looking Up
$-Mature Years—R
$-Men of Integrity—R
$-Minnesota Christian—R
Mosaic—R
$-National Catholic
$-New Wineskins—R
$-Now What?—R
$-Parabola—R
Penned from the Heart—R
$-Positive Thinking—R
$-Presbyterians Today—R
$-Pure Inspiration—R
Regent Global—R
Reverent Submissions—R
Rock & Sling
Sacred Journey—R
$-Seek—R
$-Significant Living—R
Silver Wings—R
Spiritual Voice—R
Spirituality for Today
$-Testimony—R
$-Together—R
Urban Kingdom—R
Victory Herald—R
$-Vista
$-Weavings—R
$-Whole
$-Wildwood Reader—R
$-World & I—R

CHRISTIAN EDUCATION/LIBRARY

$-Teachers of Vision—R

PASTORS/LEADERS

$-Interpreter
Jour./Pastoral Care—R
$-Lutheran Partners—R

TEEN/YOUNG ADULT

$-Boundless Webzine—R
$-Breakaway
$-TC Magazine
TeensForJC—R
$-Young Christian—R
$-Young Salvationist—R

WOMEN

$-Canticle
Christian Woman's Page—R
Crowned with Silver
$-Fullfill
$-Inspired Living—R
$-Journey
$-Today's Christian Woman—R
Woman of Worth—R
Women Today—R
$-WT Online—R

INSPIRATIONAL

ADULT/GENERAL

$-Advance
African Voices—R
$-Alive Now—R
$-Angels on Earth
$-Animal Trails—R
$-Annals of St. Anne
$-Arlington Catholic
$-Associated Content—R
$-Aujourd'hui Credo—R
$-Brave Hearts—R
Bread of Life—R
Breakthrough Intercessor—R
$-Bridal Guides—R
$-Canada Lutheran—R
$-Cappers
$-Catholic Forester—R
$-Catholic Peace Voice—R
CBN.com—R
$-Celebrate Life—R
$-CGA World—R
Channels—R
$-Chicken Soup Books—R
$-Christian Journal—R
Christian Motorsports
Christian Online
Christian Radio
Christian Ranchman
$-Chronicle Christian
Church Herald & Holiness—R
$-City Light News—R
($)-Community Spirit—R
Connecting Point—R
$-Covenant Companion—R
$-Decision
Diamond Dust
$-Discipleship Journal—R
$-DisciplesWorld
Divine Ascent
$-DreamSeeker—R
Eternal Ink—R
$-Evangel/IN—R
Evangelical Advocate—R
$-Faith & Family
$-Faith Today
$-Family Digest—R
Family Room
First Call Hospice—R
$-Focus on the Family
$-Gem—R
$-God Allows U-Turns—R
$-Good News—R
Good News Journal—R
$-Gospel Today—R
$-Guideposts—R
Halo Magazine
Heartlight—R
Highway News—R
$-Home Times—R
HopeKeepers—R
$-Ideals—R
$-In Touch
$-Indian Life—R
$-Inland NW Christian
Keys to Living—R
Leaves—R
$-Lifeglow—R
$-Light & Life
$-Liguorian
$-Live—R
$-Living—R
$-Living Church
Looking Up
$-Lookout
$-Lutheran Digest—R
$-Marian Helper
$-Mature Living
Men of the Cross
($)-Mennonite Historian—R
$-MESSAGE
MESSAGE/Open Bible—R
$-Messenger/Sacred Heart
$-Minnesota Christian—R
$-Montgomery's Journey
Mosaic—R
($)-Mutuality—R
$-National Catholic
$-New Freeman—R
New Heart—R
$-Now What?—R
Parents & Teens—R
Pegasus Review—R
Penned from the Heart—R
$-Positive Thinking—R
$-Power for Living—R
$-Prairie Messenger—R
$-Precepts for Living
$-Presbyterians Today—R
$-Priority!—R
$-Psychology for Living—R
$-Pure Inspiration—R
Quaker Life—R
Reverent Submissions—R
Sacred Journey—R
SearchingWisdom.org—R
$-Seek—R
Sight 360—R
$-Significant Living—R
Silver Wings—R
SingleAgain.com—R
Spiritual Voice—R
Spirituality for Today
$-St. Anthony Messenger

$-St. Joseph's Messenger—R
$-Standard—R
Star of Zion
$-Stewardship—R
$-Storyteller—R
SW Kansas Faith
Sword and Trumpet
Sword of the Lord—R
$-Testimony—R
Three One Six—R
$-Today's Christian—R
$-Together—R
Trumpeter—R
$-U.S. Catholic
$-United Church Observer—R
$-Upscale
Urban Kingdom—R
Victory Herald—R
$-Victory in Grace—R
$-Vision—R
$-Vista
$-War Cry—R
$-Way of St. Francis—R
$-Wesleyan Life—R
$-Whole
$-Wildwood Reader—R
$-World & I—R

CHILDREN

$-BREAD/God's Children—R
$-Cadet Quest—R
$-High Adventure—R
$-Partners—R
$-Passport—R
$-Primary Street
$-SHINEbrightly—R
Skipping Stones
$-Sparkle—R

CHRISTIAN EDUCATION/LIBRARY

Catholic Library
$-Children's Ministry
Congregational Libraries
$-Journal/Adventist Ed.—R
$-Resource—R
$-Teachers of Vision—R
$-Youth & CE Leadership

DAILY DEVOTIONALS

CLEAR Living
Penned from the Heart—R

MISSIONS

Women of the Harvest

MUSIC

$-Creator—R

PASTORS/LEADERS

$-African American Pulpit
$-Catholic Servant
Churchlife Inspiration
$-Interpreter
$-Let's Worship
$-Ministry Today
$-Preaching Well—R
$-Priest
Technologies for Worship—R

TEEN/YOUNG ADULT

$-Boundless Webzine—R
$-Breakaway
$-Brio
$-CLEAR Direction
$-CLEAR Horizon
$-Devo'Zine—R
$-InsideOut—R
$-J.A.M.
$-Passageway.org—R
TeensForJC—R
$-True Girl
$-Young Christian—R
$-Young Salvationist—R

WOMEN

($)-Beyond the Bend—R
CelebrateMoms—R
Christian Women Today—R
$-Esprit—R
$-Fullfill
$-Godly Business Woman—R
Handmaiden—R
Hearts at Home—R
$-Hope for Women
$-Horizons (women)—R
$-Inspired Living—R
$-InspiredMoms—R
$-inSpirit—R
$-Journey
Just Between Us—R
$-Link & Visitor—R
Lutheran Woman's Quar.
$-MOMsense—R
P31 Woman—R
Precious Times—R
Proverbs 31 Sisters—R
Share
($)-Simply Blessed—R
$-SpiritLed Woman
$-Today's Christian Woman—R
Together with God—R
Virtuous Woman—R
Woman of Worth—R
$-Women Alive!—R
$-WT Online—R

WRITERS

Areopagus
NW Christian Author—R
Once Upon a Time—R
Opinari—R
$-Writer's Digest—R

INTERVIEWS/PROFILES

ADULT/GENERAL

$-Abilities
($)-AGAIN—R
American Tract—R
Anglican
$-Anglican Journal
Anointed Pages
$-Arkansas Catholic—R
$-Arlington Catholic
$-Associated Content—R
$-Australian Catholics—R
Baptist Standard
Beacon/AL
Biblical Recorder
Books & Culture
Breakthrough Intercessor—R
CanadianChristianity
$-Cathedral Age—R
$-Catholic New York
$-Catholic Peace Voice—R
CBN.com—R
$-Celebrate Life—R
Challenge Weekly
$-Challenging Destiny—R
Channels—R
$-Charisma
Charlotte World
$-Chicken Soup Magazine
Christian Business
Christian Chronicle
$-Christian Citizen USA
Christian Courier/WI—R
$-Christian Herald—R
$-Christian Home & School
$-Christian Journal—R
Christian Motorsports
Christian News NW—R
Christian Observer
Christian Online
Christian Ranchman
$-Christianity Today—R
$-Christianity Today Movies—R
$-ChristianWeek—R
$-Chronicle Christian
Church of England News
$-City Light News—R
$-Columbia—R
($)-Community Spirit—R
Creation Care—R
$-Culture Wars—R
Desert Call—R
Desert Christian
Desert Voice
$-DisciplesWorld
Divine Ascent
$-Dovetail—R
$-EFCA Today—R
Encompass
$-Episcopal Life—R
Eternal Ink—R
$-Faith Today
$-Focus on the Family
$-Gem—R
$-God Allows U-Turns—R
$-Good News—R

Good News Connection
Good News Today
$-Good News, Etc.—R
Good News/S. Florida
$-Gospel Today—R
$-Great Mystery—R
$-Guideposts—R
Heartland Gatekeeper—R
Heartlight—R
$-Home Times—R
$-HonorBound—R
HopeKeepers—R
$-In Touch
$-Indian Life—R
$-Interim—R
$-Kindred Spirit—R
$-Lifeglow—R
LifeSite News
$-Light & Life
$-Liguorian
$-Living Church
Looking Up
$-Lookout
$-Mature Living
$-MESSAGE
$-Minnesota Christian—R
$-Montgomery's Journey
($)-Mutuality—R
$-National Catholic
New Heart—R
$-On Mission
$-Ozarks Senior Living—R
$-Parabola—R
$-Positive Thinking—R
$-Power for Living—R
$-Precepts for Living
Presbyterian Outlook
$-Priority!—R
$-Prism
$-Pure Inspiration—R
Rare Jewel—R
Regent Global—R
Rock & Sling
Sacred Journey—R
$-Science & Spirit
Sight 360—R
$-Significant Living—R
Spiritual Voice—R
$-St. Anthony Messenger
STEPS
$-Stewardship—R
$-Testimony—R
Three One Six—R
$-Today's Christian—R
Tri-State Voice
Trumpeter—R
$-United Church Observer—R
$-Upscale
Urban Kingdom—R
$-Vibrant Life—R
$-War Cry—R
$-Way of St. Francis—R
$-Weavings—R
$-Wireless Age—R
$-Wittenburg Door—R
$-World & I—R
World Net Daily

CHILDREN

$-American Girl—R
$-Faces
$-New Moon—R
$-Pockets—R
$-Primary Street
$-SHINEbrightly—R
$-Sparkle—R

CHRISTIAN EDUCATION/LIBRARY

$-Children's Ministry
Christian Librarian—R
$-Church Libraries—R
$-Teachers of Vision—R
$-Youth & CE Leadership

MISSIONS

$-Evangelical Missions—R
$-Leaders for Today
OpRev Equipper—R
$-PFI World—R

MUSIC

$-Christian Music Today—R

PASTORS/LEADERS

$-African American Pulpit
Alpha News
$-Catholic Servant
$-Christian Century—R
$-InSite—R
Ministry in Motion—R
$-Ministry Today
$-Outreach—R
$-Priest

TEEN/YOUNG ADULT

$-Boundless Webzine—R
$-Brio
Bubblemag
$-CLEAR Direction
$-CLEAR Horizon
$-Credo—R
$-Essential Connection
$-Insight—R
$-J.A.M.
$-Listen—R
$-Passageway.org—R
$-Risen
$-Spirit
$-TC Magazine
TeensForJC—R
$-True Girl
$-Young Salvationist—R
$-YouthWalk

WOMEN

CelebrateMoms—R
$-Esprit—R
$-Godly Business Woman—R
$-Herizons
$-Horizons (women)—R
$-Inspired Living—R
$-Journey
$-Link & Visitor—R
More to Life
Precious Times—R
Proverbs 31 Sisters—R
$-Today's Christian Woman—R
Virtuous Woman—R
Woman of Worth—R
$-WT Online—R

WRITERS

$-Adv. Christian Writer—R
Areopagus
$-Christian Communicator—R
$-Cross & Quill—R
$-Fellowscript—R
Money the Write Way—R
$-New Writer's Mag.
$-Novel Writer—R
Once Upon a Time—R
$-Poets & Writers
Write Connection
$-Writer
$-Writer's Digest—R
Writers Manual

LEADERSHIP

ADULT/GENERAL

$-Advance
African Voices—R
$-Angels on Earth
Bread of Life—R
$-Bridal Guides—R
CBN.com—R
Channels—R
Christian Business
Christian C. L. RECORD—R
$-Christian Courier/CAN—R
Christian Motorsports
Christian News NW—R
$-Christian Retailing
$-Christian Standard—R
$-ChristianWeek—R
$-Chronicle Christian
Church Herald & Holiness—R
$-City Light News—R
($)-Community Spirit—R
$-Culture Wars—R
Disciple's Journal—R
$-EFCA Today—R
Evangelical Advocate—R
$-Faith Today
$-Gem—R
$-Good News—R
Heartlight—R
$-Home Times—R
$-HonorBound—R

HopeKeepers—R
$-In Touch
$-Inland NW Christian
$-Light & Life
$-Living Church
Looking Up
$-Lookout
$-Men of Integrity—R
Men of the Cross
$-Minnesota Christian—R
Mosaic—R
($)-Mutuality—R
$-National Catholic
$-New Freeman—R
$-New Wineskins—R
NRB Magazine—R
$-On Mission
Presbyterian Outlook
Priscilla Papers
$-Prism
Regent Global—R
Reverent Submissions—R
Sacred Journey—R
Sight 360—R
Spiritual Voice—R
$-St. Anthony Messenger
$-Stewardship—R
$-Testimony—R
Three One Six—R
Trumpeter—R
$-United Church Observer—R
Urban Kingdom—R
Victory Herald—R
$-Way of St. Francis—R
$-Wireless Age—R
Wisconsin Christian
$-World & I—R

CHRISTIAN EDUCATION/LIBRARY

Catholic Library
$-Children's Ministry
Christian Early Ed.—R
Christian School Ed.—R
$-Group
Ideas Unlimited—R
Jour./Research on Christian Ed.
$-Momentum
$-Resource—R
$-Today's Catholic Teacher—R
$-Youth & CE Leadership

MISSIONS

$-Leaders for Today

PASTORS/LEADERS

$-African American Pulpit
$-Catholic Servant
$-Christian Century—R
Christian Ed. Jour. (CA)—R
Christian Management—R
$-Clergy Journal—R
$-Enrichment—R
$-Growth Points—R
$-InSite—R
$-Interpreter
Jour./Amer. Soc./Chur. Growth—R
$-Leadership—R
$-Lutheran Partners—R
$-Ministry
Ministry in Motion—R
$-Ministry Today
$-Net Results
$-Outreach—R
Pulpit Helps—R
Relevant Leader
$-Rev. Magazine
$-RevWriter Resource
Rick Warren's Ministry—R
$-Sabbath School Leadership—R
$-Small Group Dynamics—R
Theological Digest—R
$-Willow—R
$-Word & World
$-Worship Leader
$-Your Church—R

TEEN/YOUNG ADULT

$-Boundless Webzine—R
TeensForJC—R

WOMEN

($)-Beyond the Bend—R
$-Esprit—R
$-Godly Business Woman—R
$-Horizons (women)—R
Just Between Us—R
$-MOMsense—R
Precious Times—R
Proverbs 31 Sisters—R
Right to the Heart—R
Share
$-SpiritLed Woman
Tapestry (Canada)
Together with God—R
Virtuous Woman—R
Women Today—R
$-WT Online—R

WRITERS

$-Cross & Quill—R

LIFESTYLE ARTICLES

ADULT/GENERAL

Alabama Baptist
Anointed Pages
$-Bible Advocate—R
Boomer Babes Rock
Breakthrough
$-Bridal Guides—R
byFaith
$-Catholic Insight
CBN.com—R
$-Christian Journal—R
Christian Ranchman
$-ChristianWeek—R
$-Chronicle Christian
$-City Light News—R
($)-Community Spirit—R
Evangel/OR—R
$-Focus on the Family
$-Home Times—R
$-In Touch
$-Liguorian
$-Live—R
Looking Up
$-Lookout
$-Mature Living
Nostalgia—R
$-Priority!—R
$-Pure Inspiration—R
$-Seek—R
$-Significant Living—R
Spiritual Voice—R
$-Storyteller—R
Three One Six—R
Urban Kingdom—R
$-Vibrant Life—R
Victory Herald—R
$-Vista

TEEN/YOUNG ADULT

$-Boundless Webzine—R
$-Insight—R
$-TC Magazine
$-Young Christian—R

WOMEN

($)-Beyond the Bend—R
Christian Woman's Page—R
Crowned with Silver
$-Fullfill
$-Hope for Women
$-Inspired Living—R
Women Today—R
$-WT Online—R

LITURGICAL

ADULT/GENERAL

($)-AGAIN—R
$-Alive Now—R
$-Arlington Catholic
$-Aujourd'hui Credo—R
$-Cathedral Age—R
$-Catholic Yearbook—R
Channels—R
$-City Light News—R
$-Culture Wars—R
Divine Ascent
$-Dovetail—R
$-Episcopal Life—R
$-Family Digest—R
$-Living Church
$-Lutheran Journal—R
$-Messenger/Sacred Heart
$-National Catholic
$-New Wineskins—R
$-Parabola—R
Perspectives—R

Silver Wings—R
$-Social Justice—R
$-St. Anthony Messenger
$-Testimony—R
Urban Kingdom—R
$-Way of St. Francis—R

CHRISTIAN EDUCATION/LIBRARY
$-Momentum

PASTORS/LEADERS
$-African American Pulpit
$-Barefoot—R
$-Catholic Servant
$-Christian Century—R
$-Clergy Journal—R
Cross Currents
$-Diocesan Dialogue—R
$-Lutheran Partners—R
$-Ministry & Liturgy—R
$-Parish Liturgy—R
$-Preaching Well—R
$-Reformed Worship—R
Rick Warren's Ministry—R
Sewanee Theo. Review
$-This Rock
$-Today's Parish—R
$-Word & World

WOMEN
$-Horizons (women)—R

MARRIAGE

ADULT/GENERAL
$-Advance
$-Angels on Earth
Anointed Pages
$-Arlington Catholic
$-Associated Content—R
$-Atlantic Catholic
$-BGC World—R
$-Bible Advocate—R
Bread of Life—R
$-Bridal Guides—R
$-Canada Lutheran—R
$-Catholic Digest—R
CBN.com—R
$-Celebrate Life—R
Channels—R
Christian C. L. RECORD—R
$-Christian Courier/CAN—R
$-Christian Examiner
$-Christian Home & School
$-Christian Journal—R
Christian Motorsports
Christian Online
Christian Ranchman
$-Christian Research
$-Christian Standard—R
$-ChristianWeek—R
$-Chronicle Christian
Church Herald & Holiness—R
Citizen USA—R
$-City Light News—R
$-Columbia—R
($)-Community Spirit—R
$-Culture Wars—R
$-Decision
Disciple's Journal—R
$-Discipleship Journal—R
$-Dovetail—R
$-EFCA Today—R
$-Evangel/IN—R
Evangelical Advocate—R
$-Faith & Family
$-Faith Today
FaithWebbin—R
$-Family Digest—R
Family Room
$-Family Smart E-tips—R
$-Focus on the Family
$-Gem—R
$-God Allows U-Turns—R
Godly Places
Good News Journal—R
$-Guideposts—R
Heartlight—R
$-Home Times—R
$-Homeschooling Today—R
$-HonorBound—R
HopeKeepers—R
$-In Touch
$-Indian Life—R
$-Lifeglow—R
$-Light & Life
$-Liguorian
$-Live—R
$-Living—R
$-Living Church
$-Living Light—R
Looking Up
$-Lookout
$-Marriage Partnership—R
$-Mature Living
$-Men of Integrity—R
$-Minnesota Christian—R
$-Montgomery's Journey
Mosaic—R
($)-Mutuality—R
Nappaland.com
$-New Freeman—R
$-New Wineskins—R
$-On Mission
Pegasus Review—R
Penned from the Heart—R
Perspectives—R
$-Positive Thinking—R
$-Prairie Messenger—R
PrayerWorks—R
Priscilla Papers
$-Prism
$-Psychology for Living—R
$-Pure Inspiration—R
$-Purpose—R
SearchingWisdom.org—R
$-Seek—R
Sight 360—R
$-Significant Living—R
SingleAgain.com—R
$-Social Justice—R
Spiritual Voice—R
Spirituality for Today
$-St. Anthony Messenger
$-Standard—R
$-Storyteller—R
$-Testimony—R
Three One Six—R
$-Today's Christian—R
$-Together—R
Trumpeter—R
$-U.S. Catholic
Urban Kingdom—R
$-Vibrant Life—R
$-Vista
$-War Cry—R
$-Wesleyan Life—R
$-Whole
$-Wildwood Reader—R
Wisconsin Christian
$-World & I—R

DAILY DEVOTIONALS
Penned from the Heart—R

PASTORS/LEADERS
$-African American Pulpit
$-Catholic Servant
$-Christian Century—R
$-Interpreter
Jour./Pastoral Care—R
$-Lutheran Partners—R
$-Ministry Today
$-Preaching Well—R
$-Rev. Magazine
Theological Digest—R
$-Today's Parish—R
$-Word & World

TEEN/YOUNG ADULT
$-Boundless Webzine—R
TeensForJC—R
$-Young Adult Today—R
$-Young Christian—R

WOMEN
CelebrateMoms—R
Christian Woman's Page—R
Comfort Café
Crowned with Silver
First Lady
$-Godly Business Woman—R
$-Heart & Soul
Hearts at Home—R
$-Hope for Women
$-Horizons (women)—R
$-Inspired Living—R
$-inSpirit—R
$-Journey

Just Between Us—R
Ladies First
Lutheran Woman's Quar.
P31 Woman—R
Precious Times—R
Proverbs 31 Sisters—R
($)-Shalom Bayit
$-Simple Joy
($)-Simply Blessed—R
$-SpiritLed Woman
$-Today's Christian Woman—R
Together with God—R
Virtuous Woman—R
Woman of Worth—R
$-Women Alive!—R
Women Today—R
$-WT Online—R

MEN'S ISSUES

ADULT/GENERAL

$-Advance
$-Annals of St. Anne
$-Arlington Catholic
$-Associated Content—R
$-BGC World—R
$-Bible Advocate—R
Bread of Life—R
$-Bridal Guides—R
CBN.com—R
Channels—R
$-Chicken Soup Books—R
$-Christian Examiner
$-Christian Journal—R
Christian News NW—R
Christian Online
Christian Ranchman
$-ChristianWeek—R
$-Chronicle Christian
Citizen USA—R
$-City Light News—R
$-Columbia—R
($)-Community Spirit—R
$-Creative Nonfiction
Disciple's Journal—R
$-Dovetail—R
$-EFCA Today—R
$-Evangel/IN—R
$-Faith Today
Family Room
$-Family Smart E-tips—R
$-Focus on the Family
$-Gem—R
$-God Allows U-Turns—R
Godly Places
Good News Journal—R
Heartlight—R
Highway News—R
$-Home Times—R
$-Homeschooling Today—R
$-HonorBound—R
HopeKeepers—R
$-Indian Life—R
$-Inland NW Christian
$-Light & Life
$-Live—R
$-Living—R
Looking Up
$-Lookout
$-Men of Integrity—R
Men of the Cross
$-Minnesota Christian—R
$-Montgomery's Journey
Mosaic—R
($)-Mutuality—R
$-New Freeman—R
$-On Mission
Penned from the Heart—R
Perspectives—R
$-Positive Thinking—R
Presbyterian Outlook
Priscilla Papers
$-Prism
$-Psychology for Living—R
$-Purpose—R
Regent Global—R
Sight 360—R
$-Significant Living—R
SingleAgain.com—R
Spiritual Voice—R
$-St. Anthony Messenger
$-Standard—R
$-Testimony—R
Three One Six—R
$-Today's Christian—R
$-Together—R
Trumpeter—R
$-U.S. Catholic
$-United Church Observer—R
Urban Kingdom—R
$-Vibrant Life—R
$-Vista
$-Wesleyan Life—R
West Wind Review
Wisconsin Christian
$-World & I—R

PASTORS/LEADERS

$-African American Pulpit
$-Interpreter
$-Lutheran Partners—R
$-Word & World

TEEN/YOUNG ADULT

$-Boundless Webzine—R
$-Breakaway
TeensForJC—R

WOMEN

$-At the Center—R
$-Hope for Women

MIRACLES

ADULT/GENERAL

$-Angels on Earth
$-Animal Trails—R
Bread of Life—R
$-Bridal Guides—R
CBN.com—R
$-CGA World—R
Channels—R
$-Chicken Soup Books—R
$-Christian Journal—R
Christian Motorsports
Christian Online
Christian Ranchman
$-Chronicle Christian
Citizen USA—R
$-City Light News—R
($)-Community Spirit—R
Connecting Point—R
$-Culture Wars—R
Diamond Dust
Divine Ascent
Evangelical Advocate—R
$-Faith Today
$-Gem—R
$-God Allows U-Turns—R
$-Guideposts—R
$-Home Times—R
HopeKeepers—R
$-Lifeglow—R
$-Light & Life
$-Live—R
$-Miracles, Healings
$-New Freeman—R
New Heart—R
Nostalgia—R
Pegasus Review—R
Penned from the Heart—R
$-Positive Thinking—R
$-Pure Inspiration—R
Sight 360—R
Spiritual Voice—R
$-St. Anthony Messenger
$-Testimony—R
Three One Six—R
$-Today's Christian—R
Trumpeter—R
Urban Kingdom—R
$-Vista

CHILDREN

$-BREAD/God's Children—R
$-Guide—R

DAILY DEVOTIONALS

Penned from the Heart—R

PASTORS/LEADERS

$-Ministry Today
$-Word & World

TEEN/YOUNG ADULT

$-CLEAR Direction
$-CLEAR Horizon
$-Young Christian—R

WOMEN

$-Godly Business Woman—R

$-SpiritLed Woman
$-WT Online—R

MISSIONS

ADULT/GENERAL

($)-AGAIN—R
$-Anglican Journal
$-Aujourd'hui Credo—R
$-B.C. Catholic—R
$-Bridal Guides—R
$-Catholic Yearbook—R
CBN.com—R
Channels—R
Christian Online
Christian Ranchman
$-Christian Standard—R
$-Christianity Today—R
$-ChristianWeek—R
Church Herald & Holiness—R
Citizen USA—R
$-City Light News—R
($)-Community Spirit—R
Connecting Point—R
$-Culture Wars—R
$-Decision
Disciple's Journal—R
$-Discipleship Journal—R
$-Episcopal Life—R
Evangel/OR—R
Evangelical Advocate—R
$-Faith Today
$-Gem—R
Godly Places
$-Good News—R
$-Home Times—R
HopeKeepers—R
$-Horizons (adult)—R
$-In Touch
$-Light & Life
$-Live—R
$-Living Church
$-Lookout
$-Lutheran Journal—R
$-Men of Integrity—R
Men of the Cross
$-Minnesota Christian—R
$-Montgomery's Journey
Mosaic—R
$-National Catholic
$-New Freeman—R
New Heart—R
$-New Wineskins—R
Nostalgia—R
$-On Mission
Penned from the Heart—R
Perspectives—R
$-Power for Living—R
PrayerWorks—R
Presbyterian Outlook
$-Priority!—R
Priscilla Papers
$-Prism
$-Purpose—R
$-Seek—R
Sight 360—R
$-Significant Living—R
Silver Wings—R
Spirituality for Today
$-St. Anthony Messenger
$-Standard—R
Sword and Trumpet
Sword of the Lord—R
$-Testimony—R
$-Today's Christian—R
Trumpeter—R
Urban Kingdom—R
Victory Herald—R
$-Vista
$-Way of St. Francis—R
$-Wireless Age—R

CHILDREN

$-BREAD/God's Children—R
$-Guide—R
$-Sparkle—R

CHRISTIAN EDUCATION/LIBRARY

Catholic Library
$-Children's Ministry
Christian Librarian—R
$-Teach Kids!—R
$-Youth & CE Leadership

DAILY DEVOTIONALS

Penned from the Heart—R

MISSIONS

Catholic Missions/Canada
$-Evangelical Missions—R
$-Glad Tidings (Canada)—R
Intl. Jour./Frontier—R
$-Leaders for Today
Missiology
Mission Frontiers
$-New World Outlook
$-One
OpRev Equipper—R
$-PFI World—R
$-PIME World—R
Railroad Evangelist—R
Women of the Harvest

PASTORS/LEADERS

$-African American Pulpit
$-Clergy Journal—R
$-Enrichment—R
$-Interpreter
Jour./Amer. Soc./Chur. Growth—R
$-Lutheran Partners—R
$-Ministry Today
Pulpit Helps—R
$-RevWriter Resource
Rick Warren's Ministry—R
$-This Rock
$-Word & World

TEEN/YOUNG ADULT

$-Boundless Webzine—R
$-Brio
$-CLEAR Direction
$-CLEAR Horizon
$-Credo—R
$-Devo'Zine—R
$-Insight—R
$-Passageway.org—R
$-Real Faith in Life—R
$-Young Christian—R
$-Young Salvationist—R

WOMEN

$-Esprit—R
$-Godly Business Woman—R
Hearts at Home—R
$-Hope for Women
$-Horizons (women)—R
$-Inspired Living—R
$-Journey
Just Between Us—R
$-Link & Visitor—R
$-SpiritLed Woman
Together with God—R

WRITERS

Opinari—R

MONEY MANAGEMENT

ADULT/GENERAL

$-Anglican Journal
$-Animal Trails—R
$-Associated Content—R
$-Bridal Guides—R
byFaith
$-Catholic Forester—R
$-CBA Retailers
CBN.com—R
Channels—R
$-Christian Citizen USA
$-Christian Journal—R
Christian Motorsports
Christian Online
Christian Ranchman
$-ChristianWeek—R
$-Chronicle Christian
Citizen USA—R
$-City Light News—R
($)-Community Spirit—R
Connecting Point—R
$-Creative Nonfiction
Disciple's Journal—R
$-Discipleship Journal—R
Evangelical Advocate—R
$-Faith & Family
$-Faith Today

FaithWebbin—R
$-Family Smart E-tips—R
$-Focus on the Family
$-Gem—R
Heartlight—R
Highway News—R
$-Home Times—R
$-Homeschooling Today—R
$-HonorBound—R
$-In Touch
$-Inland NW Christian
$-Lifeglow—R
$-Light & Life
$-Live—R
Looking Up
$-Lookout
$-Mature Years—R
Men of the Cross
$-Montgomery's Journey
NRB Magazine—R
Parents & Teens—R
Penned from the Heart—R
Sight 360—R
$-Significant Living—R
SingleAgain.com—R
Spiritual Voice—R
$-St. Anthony Messenger
$-Testimony—R
$-Today's Christian—R
$-Together—R
Trumpeter—R
Urban Kingdom—R
$-War Cry—R
Wisconsin Christian
$-World & I—R

CHILDREN

$-SHINEbrightly—R

DAILY DEVOTIONALS

Penned from the Heart—R

PASTORS/LEADERS

$-African American Pulpit
Christian Management—R
$-Clergy Journal—R
$-Enrichment—R
$-Interpreter
$-Lutheran Partners—R
Rick Warren's Ministry—R
$-Today's Parish—R
$-Your Church—R

TEEN/YOUNG ADULT

$-Boundless Webzine—R
$-Breakaway
$-Brio
$-Real Faith in Life—R
$-Young Christian—R

WOMEN

CelebrateMoms—R
Christian Women Today—R
$-Godly Business Woman—R
$-Heart & Soul
Hearts at Home—R
$-Hope for Women
$-Horizons (women)—R
$-Inspired Living—R
$-InspiredMoms—R
$-Journey
Just Between Us—R
Life Tools for Women
More to Life
Precious Times—R
($)-Simply Blessed—R
$-Today's Christian Woman—R
Virtuous Woman—R
Woman of Worth—R
Women Today—R
$-WT Online—R

WRITERS

Money the Write Way—R

MOVIE REVIEWS

ADULT/GENERAL

$-Abilities
$-Associated Content—R
$-Atlantic Catholic
byFaith
CBN.com—R
Charlotte World
$-Christian Citizen USA
$-Christian Herald—R
$-Christian Journal—R
$-Christianity Today Movies—R
$-City Light News—R
$-Cresset
$-Faith & Friends—R
First Call Hospice—R
Good News Today
Good News/S. Florida
Heartland Gatekeeper—R
$-Home Times—R
Imagine
$-Interim—R
MovieGuide
$-Parabola—R
Perspectives—R
$-Prairie Messenger—R
Rock & Sling
Spiritual Voice—R
Urban Kingdom—R

CHILDREN

$-Sparkle—R

MUSIC

Hymn

TEEN/YOUNG ADULT

$-Breakaway
Bubblemag
$-Risen
$-TC Magazine

WOMEN

$-Herizons
$-Hope for Women
$-Inspired Living—R
Virtuous Woman—R
$-WT Online—R

MUSIC REVIEWS

ADULT/GENERAL

$-Advance
Alabama Baptist
$-Arlington Catholic
$-Associated Content—R
$-Atlantic Catholic
$-Aujourd'hui Credo—R
Breakthrough Intercessor—R
$-Catholic Peace Voice—R
$-CBA Retailers
CBN.com—R
Channels—R
$-Charisma
Charlotte World
$-Christian Citizen USA
$-Christian Herald—R
$-Christian Journal—R
Christian Media—R
Christian Radio
$-Christian Renewal—R
$-Christian Retailing
Citizen USA—R
$-City Light News—R
$-Cresset
Diamond Dust
$-Faith & Family
$-Faith Today
First Call Hospice—R
Good News/S. Florida
$-Haruah—R
Heartland Gatekeeper—R
Heartlight—R
Imagine
$-Indian Life—R
Infuze
$-Interim—R
$-Minnesota Christian—R
MovieGuide
$-Parabola—R
Parents & Teens—R
$-Prairie Messenger—R
$-Presbyterians Today—R
$-Prism
$-Pure Inspiration—R
Quaker Life—R
Rock & Sling
$-Rose & Thorn
Sight 360—R
Spiritual Voice—R

$-Testimony—R
Trumpeter—R
Urban Kingdom—R
$-Wireless Age—R
$-World & I—R

CHILDREN
$-Sparkle—R

CHRISTIAN EDUCATION/LIBRARY
Catholic Library
$-Church Libraries—R

MISSIONS
Women of the Harvest

MUSIC
$-CCM Magazine
$-Christian Music Today—R
Christian Music Weekly—R
$-Creator—R
Gospel Synergy
Tradition

PASTORS/LEADERS
$-Barefoot—R
$-Christian Century—R
$-Interpreter
$-Ministry Today
$-Reformed Worship—R
Technologies for Worship—R
$-Willow—R
$-Worship Leader

TEEN/YOUNG ADULT
$-Breakaway
Bubblemag
$-Credo—R
$-Devo'Zine—R
$-Risen
$-Sharing the VICTORY—R
$-TC Magazine
TeensForJC—R
$-True Girl

WOMEN
$-Godly Business Woman—R
$-Herizons
$-Hope for Women
$-Inspired Living—R
Precious Times—R
Proverbs 31 Sisters—R
Virtuous Woman—R
Woman of Worth—R
$-WT Online—R

NATURE

ADULT/GENERAL
$-Animal Trails—R
$-Associated Content—R
$-Aujourd'hui Credo—R
$-Bible Advocate—R
$-Bridal Guides—R
CBN.com—R
$-Christian Courier/CAN—R
$-Christian Renewal—R
$-Chronicle Christian
($)-Community Spirit—R
$-Covenant Companion—R
Creation
Creation Care—R
$-Creation Illust.—R
$-Creative Nonfiction
$-Gem—R
$-Ideals—R
$-In Touch
Keys to Living—R
$-Lifeglow—R
$-Light & Life
$-Lutheran Digest—R
$-Over the Back Fence—R
$-Parabola—R
Pegasus Review—R
Penned from the Heart—R
PrayerWorks—R
Ruminate
Sacred Journey—R
$-Salvo
$-Science & Spirit
$-Seek—R
Spiritual Voice—R
$-St. Anthony Messenger
$-Storyteller—R
$-Testimony—R
Trumpeter—R
Urban Kingdom—R
$-Wildwood Reader—R
Wisconsin Christian
$-World & I—R

CHILDREN
$-Cadet Quest—R
$-Focus/Clubhouse Jr.
$-Guide—R
$-Nature Friend
$-Partners—R
$-SHINEbrightly—R
Skipping Stones
$-Sparkle—R

PASTORS/LEADERS
$-Word & World

TEEN/YOUNG ADULT
$-Boundless Webzine—R
$-Devo'Zine—R
$-Young Christian—R

WOMEN
$-WT Online—R

NEWS FEATURES

ADULT/GENERAL
Alabama Baptist
Anglican
$-Animal Trails—R
$-Arkansas Catholic—R
$-Associated Content—R
$-Atlantic Catholic
Baptist Standard
Beacon/AL
Biblical Recorder
$-Bridal Guides—R
$-Canadian Mennonite—R
CanadianChristianity
$-Cathedral Age—R
$-Catholic Insight
$-Catholic New York
$-Catholic Peace Voice—R
$-Catholic Sentinel
CBN.com—R
Challenge Weekly
$-Charisma
Charlotte World
Choice Newspaper—R
Christian C. L. RECORD—R
Christian Chronicle
$-Christian Citizen USA
Christian Courier/WI—R
$-Christian Examiner
Christian News NW—R
Christian Radio
Christian Ranchman
$-Christian Renewal—R
$-Christian Research
$-Christian Response—R
$-Christian Retailing
$-Christianity Today Movies—R
$-ChristianWeek—R
$-Chronicle Christian
Church of England News
Citizen USA—R
$-City Light News—R
$-Commonweal
($)-Community Spirit—R
Compass Direct
Desert Christian
Desert Voice
$-Disaster News
$-Dovetail—R
Encompass
Evangel/OR—R
$-Faith Today
Founders Journal
Good News Connection
Good News Today
Good News!
Good News/S. Florida
Heartland Gatekeeper—R
$-Home Times—R
HopeKeepers—R
($)-Impact—R
$-Indian Life—R
$-Interchange
Island Catholic
LarkNews.com
$-Liberty
LifeSite News
$-Light & Life
$-Minnesota Christian—R

$-Montana Catholic
MovieGuide
$-National Catholic Network
$-Our Sunday Visitor—R
$-Priority!—R
Rare Jewel—R
$-Science & Spirit
Sight 360—R
Society/Prevention of Cruelty
Spiritual Voice—R
$-St. Anthony Messenger
Sword and Trumpet
$-Testimony—R
$-Today's Christian—R
Tri-State Voice
Trumpeter—R
$-Upscale
Urban Kingdom—R
$-War Cry—R
$-Wireless Age—R
Wisconsin Christian
Word News
$-World & I—R
World Net Daily

CHILDREN
$-Partners—R
$-Pockets—R

MISSIONS
$-Glad Tidings (Canada)—R
OpRev Equipper—R

MUSIC
$-Christian Music Today—R

PASTORS/LEADERS
Alpha News
$-Christian Century—R
$-Ministry Today
$-Pray!—R
Pulpit Helps—R
Rick Warren's Ministry—R

TEEN/YOUNG ADULT
$-Young Christian—R

WOMEN
$-Herizons
$-Hope for Women
$-Today's Christian Woman—R
$-WT Online—R

WRITERS
Money the Write Way—R
$-Poets & Writers

NEWSPAPERS/ TABLOIDS
Alabama Baptist
Alpha News
Anglican
$-Anglican Journal
$-Arkansas Catholic—R
$-Arlington Catholic
$-Atlantic Catholic
$-B.C. Catholic—R
Baptist Standard
Beacon/AL
Biblical Recorder
CanadianChristianity
$-Catholic New York
Catholic Register
$-Catholic Sentinel
$-Catholic Servant
$-Catholic Telegraph
Challenge Weekly
Charlotte World
Choice Newspaper—R
Christian Chronicle
$-Christian Citizen USA
$-Christian Courier/CAN—R
Christian Courier/WI—R
$-Christian Examiner
$-Christian Herald—R
$-Christian Journal—R
Christian Media—R
Christian News NW—R
Christian Observer
Christian Ranchman
$-Christian Renewal—R
$-ChristianWeek—R
$-Chronicle Christian
Church of England News
Citizen USA—R
$-City Light News—R
$-Common Ground—R
Desert Christian
Desert Voice
Disciple's Journal—R
$-Episcopal Life—R
Evangelical Times
Good News Connection
Good News Journal—R
Good News Today
Good News!
$-Good News, Etc.—R
Good News/S. Florida
Heartland Gatekeeper—R
Holy City Chronicle
$-Home Times—R
$-Indian Life—R
$-Inland NW Christian
$-Interchange
$-Interim—R
Island Catholic
$-Layman
LifeSite News
Light of the World
$-Living—R
$-Living Light—R
Living Stones
$-Messenger
Messianic Times
$-Minnesota Christian—R
$-Montana Catholic
Mosaic—R
$-National Catholic Network
$-New Freeman—R
New Frontier
$-Our Sunday Visitor—R
$-Ozarks Senior Living—R
Perspectives/Science
$-Prairie Messenger—R
PrayerWorks—R
Pulpit Helps—R
Senior Connection
Spiritual Voice—R
Star of Zion
SW Kansas Faith
Sword of the Lord—R
$-Together—R
Tri-State Voice
Wisconsin Christian
Word News
World Net Daily

NOSTALGIA

ADULT/GENERAL
$-Animal Trails—R
$-Associated Content—R
$-Bridal Guides—R
$-Catholic Forester—R
$-Chicken Soup Magazine
$-Chronicle Christian
$-City Light News—R
($)-Community Spirit—R
$-Home Times—R
$-In Touch
Looking Up
$-Lutheran Digest—R
$-Mature Living
Nostalgia—R
$-Over the Back Fence—R
$-Seek—R
Spiritual Voice—R
$-Storyteller—R
$-Testimony—R
Urban Kingdom—R
Victory Herald—R
$-Vista

CHILDREN
$-Faces
$-High Adventure—R

PASTORS/LEADERS
$-Priest

TEEN/YOUNG ADULT
$-InsideOut—R
$-Young Christian—R

WOMEN
Crowned with Silver
$-Journey
Woman of Worth—R
$-WT Online—R

ONLINE PUBLICATIONS

ADULT/GENERAL

$-Advance
$-America
$-Anglican Journal
Answers
$-Apocalypse Chronicles—R
$-Associated Content—R
$-Believer's Bay
Books & Culture
Breakthrough
CanadianChristianity
$-Catholic Digest—R
CBN.com—R
Challenge Weekly
$-Challenging Destiny—R
$-Charisma
Chocolate Pages
Christian C. L. RECORD—R
Christian Computing—R
$-Christian Examiner
$-Christian Home & School
$-Christian Journal—R
Christian Media—R
Christian Online
Christian Outlook
Christian Single Online
$-Christian Standard—R
$-Christianity Today—R
$-Christianity Today Movies—R
$-Chronicle Christian
$-Columbia—R
$-Company—R
Compass Direct
CrossHome.com
$-Decision
Diamond Dust
$-Disaster News
Disciple's Journal—R
Divine Ascent
$-Dragons, Knights & Angels—R
$-Drama Ministry—R
$-DreamSeeker—R
E-Quality
Eternal Ink—R
FaithWebbin—R
Family Room
$-Family Smart E-tips—R
First Call Hospice—R
Godly Places
Gold Country Families—R
Good News!
Haiku Hippodrome
$-Haruah—R
Heartlight—R
($)-Impact—R
Infuze
$-Interim—R
LarkNews.com
$-Layman
$-Leben—R
LifeSite News
LifeTimes Catholic
$-Lookout
$-Marian Helper
Men of the Cross
$-Messenger/St. Anthony
$-Minnesota Christian—R
Missionwares
Nappaland.com
$-National Catholic
$-New Wineskins—R
$-Now What?—R
NRB Magazine—R
$-On Mission
Parents & Teens—R
Perspectives—R
PrayerWorks—R
$-Priority!—R
Rare Jewel—R
Regent Global—R
$-Relevant
$-Rose & Thorn
Sacred Journey—R
Salt of the Earth
SearchingWisdom.org—R
SingleAgain.com—R
Society/Prevention of Cruelty
$-Sound Body—R
$-St. Anthony Messenger
$-Testimony—R
$-Today's Christian—R
$-Today's Pentecostal—R
Trumpeter—R
$-U.S. Catholic
Urban Kingdom—R
Victory Herald—R
$-World & I—R
World Net Daily

CHILDREN

$-American Girl—R
$-Focus/Clubhouse
$-Focus/Clubhouse Jr.
Girls Connection
$-Keys for Kids—R

CHRISTIAN EDUCATION/LIBRARY

Ideas Unlimited—R

DAILY DEVOTIONALS

$-Forward Day by Day

MISSIONS

Mission Frontiers
OpRev Equipper—R
Women of the Harvest

MUSIC

$-CCM Magazine
$-Christian Music Today—R
$-Creator—R

PASTORS/LEADERS

$-Barefoot—R
Engage
$-InSite—R
$-Interpretation
$-Interpreter
$-Leadership—R
$-Lutheran Partners—R
Ministry in Motion—R
$-Net Results
$-Newsletter Newsletter
Preaching—R
$-PreachingToday.com
Pulpit Helps—R
$-Reformed Worship—R
Relevant Leader
$-Rev. Magazine
$-RevWriter Resource
Rick Warren's Ministry—R
$-Small Group Dynamics—R
Technologies for Worship—R
$-Willow—R
$-Youthworker

TEEN/YOUNG ADULT

$-Boundless Webzine—R
Connected
Journalism Online
$-Passageway.org—R
Student Life
TeensForJC—R
$-Young Salvationist—R

WOMEN

$-At the Center—R
CelebrateMoms—R
Christian Woman's Page—R
Christian Women Today—R
Comfort Café
$-Dabbling Mum—R
Handmaidens
($)-History's Women—R
$-Hope for Women
$-InspiredMoms—R
Life Tools for Women
$-Melody of the Heart
Proverbs 31 Sisters—R
Right to the Heart—R
($)-Shalom Bayit
$-Simple Joy
Virtuous Woman—R
Women of the Cross
Women Today—R
Women's Ministry
$-WT Online—R

WRITERS

Author-Me
ChristianWriters
Dedicated Author
$-Freelance Writer's Report—R
Money the Write Way—R

Poetic Voices—R
$-Shades of Romance—R
$-Spirit-Led Writer—R
Teachers & Writers
WriteToInspire
Writing Corner—R

OPINION PIECES

ADULT/GENERAL

Anglican
$-Animal Trails—R
$-Annals of St. Anne
$-Arkansas Catholic—R
$-Arlington Catholic
$-Associated Content—R
$-B.C. Catholic—R
$-Bridal Guides—R
$-Catholic New York
$-Catholic Peace Voice—R
CBN.com—R
Christian C. L. RECORD—R
$-Christian Courier/CAN—R
$-Christian Examiner
$-Christian Journal—R
$-Christian Renewal—R
$-Christian Research
$-Christianity Today—R
$-Christianity Today Movies—R
$-ChristianWeek—R
$-Chronicle Christian
Church of England News
Citizen USA—R
$-Culture Wars—R
$-DisciplesWorld
$-Episcopal Life—R
$-Faith Today
Good News Journal—R
$-Home Times—R
HopeKeepers—R
$-Indian Life—R
$-Inland NW Christian
$-Interim—R
Island Catholic
$-Light & Life
$-Living Church
$-Lookout
$-Minnesota Christian—R
Mosaic—R
MovieGuide
$-National Catholic
$-New Freeman—R
NRB Magazine—R
Perspectives—R
$-Prairie Messenger—R
Presbyterian Outlook
Regent Global—R
$-Salvo
SearchingWisdom.org—R
Sight 360—R
Spiritual Voice—R
$-St. Anthony Messenger
$-Testimony—R
Three One Six—R
Trumpeter—R
$-U.S. Catholic
$-United Church Observer—R
Urban Kingdom—R
$-Way of St. Francis—R
$-Whole
$-Wittenburg Door—R
$-World & I—R

CHILDREN

$-New Moon—R
Skipping Stones

CHRISTIAN EDUCATION/LIBRARY

Catholic Library
$-Group
Jour. of Christianity—R
$-Teachers of Vision—R

MISSIONS

$-Evangelical Missions—R
OpRev Equipper—R

MUSIC

$-Christian Music Today—R

PASTORS/LEADERS

$-Catholic Servant
$-Ministry Today
$-Priest
$-Word & World
$-Worship Leader

TEEN/YOUNG ADULT

$-Listen—R
TeensForJC—R
$-Young Christian—R

WOMEN

($)-Beyond the Bend—R
Crowned with Silver
$-Esprit—R
$-Hope for Women

WRITERS

$-Adv. Christian Writer—R
Areopagus
Money the Write Way—R
$-New Writer's Mag.
Opinari—R

PARENTING

ADULT/GENERAL

$-Advance
Alabama Baptist
American Tract—R
$-Angels on Earth
$-Annals of St. Anne
$-Arkansas Catholic—R
$-Arlington Catholic
$-Associated Content—R
$-Atlantic Catholic
$-BGC World—R
$-Bible Advocate—R
Bread of Life—R
$-Bridal Guides—R
$-Canada Lutheran—R
$-Catholic Digest—R
$-Catholic Yearbook—R
CBN.com—R
$-Celebrate Life—R
$-Chicken Soup Books—R
$-Christian Courier/CAN—R
$-Christian Home & School
$-Christian Journal—R
Christian Motorsports
Christian Observer
Christian Ranchman
$-Christian Renewal—R
$-Christian Research
$-ChristianWeek—R
$-Chronicle Christian
Church Herald & Holiness—R
Citizen USA—R
$-City Light News—R
$-Columbia—R
($)-Community Spirit—R
Creation Care—R
$-Culture Wars—R
Disciple's Journal—R
$-Discipleship Journal—R
$-Dovetail—R
Evangelical Advocate—R
$-Faith & Family
$-Faith Today
FaithWebbin—R
$-Family Digest—R
Family Room
$-Family Smart E-tips—R
$-Focus on the Family
$-Focus on Your Child
$-Gem—R
Gold Country Families—R
Good News Journal—R
Heartlight—R
Highway News—R
$-Home Times—R
$-Homeschooling Today—R
$-HonorBound—R
HopeKeepers—R
$-Indian Life—R
$-Light & Life
$-Live—R
$-Living—R
$-Living Light—R
Looking Up
$-Lookout
$-Lutheran Journal—R
$-Marriage Partnership—R
$-Men of Integrity—R
$-Minnesota Christian—R
$-Montgomery's Journey

Mosaic—R
MovieGuide
($)-Mutuality—R
Nappaland.com
$-New Freeman—R
$-New Wineskins—R
$-ParentLife
Parents & Teens—R
Pegasus Review—R
Penned from the Heart—R
$-Positive Thinking—R
$-Power for Living—R
$-Prairie Messenger—R
$-Psychology for Living—R
$-Seek—R
Sight 360—R
SingleAgain.com—R
$-Special Living—R
Spiritual Voice—R
Spirituality for Today
$-St. Anthony Messenger
$-Standard—R
SW Kansas Faith
$-Testimony—R
$-Today's Christian—R
$-Today's Pentecostal—R
$-Together—R
Trumpeter—R
$-U.S. Catholic
Urban Kingdom—R
$-Vibrant Life—R
Victory Herald—R
$-Vista
$-War Cry—R
$-Way of St. Francis—R
$-Wesleyan Life—R
$-Whole
Wisconsin Christian
$-World & I—R

CHILDREN
$-Adventures

CHRISTIAN EDUCATION/LIBRARY
$-Children's Ministry

DAILY DEVOTIONALS
Penned from the Heart—R

PASTORS/LEADERS
$-Catholic Servant
Engage
$-Interpreter

WOMEN
$-At the Center—R
$-Canticle
CelebrateMoms—R
Christian Woman's Page—R
$-Dabbling Mum—R
$-Esprit—R
$-Godly Business Woman—R
Handmaiden—R
$-Heart & Soul
Hearts at Home—R
$-Hope for Women
$-Inspired Living—R
$-InspiredMoms—R
$-inSpirit—R
$-Journey
Just Between Us—R
Keeping Hearts & Home
$-Link & Visitor—R
Lutheran Woman's Quar.
$-MOMsense—R
P31 Woman—R
Precious Times—R
Proverbs 31 Sisters—R
($)-Shalom Bayit
$-Simple Joy
($)-Simply Blessed—R
$-SpiritLed Woman
$-Today's Christian Woman—R
Together with God—R
Virtuous Woman—R
Woman of Worth—R
$-Women Alive!—R
Women Today—R
$-WT Online—R

PEACE ISSUES

ADULT/GENERAL
$-Animal Trails—R
$-Associated Content—R
$-Aujourd'hui Credo—R
$-Bridal Guides—R
$-Cathedral Age—R
CBN.com—R
$-Christian Citizen USA
Christian Ranchman
$-ChristianWeek—R
$-City Light News—R
($)-Community Spirit—R
$-Home Times—R
$-Living—R
$-Lookout
($)-Mennonite Historian—R
Mosaic—R
$-National Catholic
$-Parabola—R
Penned from the Heart—R
Perspectives—R
$-Prairie Messenger—R
$-Pure Inspiration—R
$-Purpose—R
Quaker Life—R
Sacred Journey—R
$-Seek—R
Silver Wings—R
Spiritual Voice—R
$-St. Joseph's Messenger—R
$-Testimony—R
Three One Six—R
$-Together—R
$-U.S. Catholic
Urban Kingdom—R
$-Vista

CHILDREN
$-New Moon—R
$-Pockets—R
Skipping Stones

CHRISTIAN EDUCATION/LIBRARY
Catholic Library

MISSIONS
$-Glad Tidings (Canada)—R

PASTORS/LEADERS
$-African American Pulpit
$-Christian Century—R
$-Clergy Journal—R
$-Interpreter
$-Lutheran Partners—R

TEEN/YOUNG ADULT
$-True Girl
$-Young Christian—R

WOMEN
$-Esprit—R
$-Herizons
$-Horizons (women)—R
$-Inspired Living—R
Women Today—R

PERSONAL EXPERIENCE

ADULT/GENERAL
African Voices—R
($)-AGAIN—R
$-Alive Now—R
$-Angels on Earth
$-Animal Trails—R
$-Annals of St. Anne
$-Associated Content—R
$-Australian Catholics—R
$-B.C. Catholic—R
$-Bible Advocate—R
$-Brave Hearts—R
Bread of Life—R
Breakthrough
Breakthrough Intercessor—R
$-Bridal Guides—R
$-Catholic Digest—R
$-Catholic New York
$-Catholic Peace Voice—R
$-Catholic Yearbook—R
CBN.com—R
$-Celebrate Life—R
$-CGA World—R
Channels—R
$-Chicken Soup Books—R
$-Chicken Soup Magazine
$-Christian Courier/CAN—R
$-Christian Home & School
$-Christian Journal—R
Christian Motorsports
Christian Observer

Christian Online
Christian Ranchman
$-Christianity Today—R
$-ChristianWeek—R
$-City Light News—R
$-Commonweal
($)-Community Spirit—R
$-Creative Nonfiction
$-Decision
Diamond Dust
$-DisciplesWorld
$-Dovetail—R
$-EFCA Today—R
Eternal Ink—R
$-Evangel/IN—R
Evangelical Advocate—R
$-Faith Today
First Call Hospice—R
$-Focus on the Family
$-Gem—R
$-God Allows U-Turns—R
Good News Journal—R
$-Guideposts—R
Halo Magazine
Highway News—R
$-Home Times—R
HopeKeepers—R
$-Horizons (adult)—R
$-Ideals—R
$-In Touch
$-Indian Life—R
$-Inland NW Christian
Keys to Living—R
Leaves—R
$-Lifeglow—R
$-Light & Life
$-Liguorian
$-Live—R
$-Living—R
$-Living Church
Looking Up
$-Lookout
$-Lutheran Journal—R
$-Marian Helper
$-Marriage Partnership—R
$-Mature Living
Men of the Cross
$-MESSAGE
$-Miracles, Healings
($)-Mutuality—R
$-New Freeman—R
New Heart—R
$-New Wineskins—R
Nostalgia—R
$-Now What?—R
$-On Mission
$-Ozarks Senior Living—R
$-Parabola—R
Parents & Teens—R
Penned from the Heart—R
$-Positive Thinking—R
$-Power for Living—R
$-Psychology for Living—R
$-Pure Inspiration—R
$-Purpose—R
Reverent Submissions—R
Ruminate
Sacred Journey—R
SearchingWisdom.org—R
$-Seek—R
Sharing—R
Sight 360—R
Silver Wings—R
$-Spiritual Life
Spiritual Voice—R
$-St. Anthony Messenger
$-Standard—R
$-Storyteller—R
$-Testimony—R
Three One Six—R
$-Today's Christian—R
$-Together—R
Trumpeter—R
$-Upscale
Urban Kingdom—R
Victory Herald—R
$-Victory in Grace—R
$-Vision—R
$-Vista
$-War Cry—R
$-Way of St. Francis—R
$-Wesleyan Life—R
$-Whole
$-Wittenburg Door—R
$-World & I—R

CHILDREN

$-Faces
$-Guide—R
$-High Adventure—R
$-New Moon—R
$-Partners—R
$-Sparkle—R

CHRISTIAN EDUCATION/LIBRARY

$-Children's Ministry
$-Group
$-Journal/Adventist Ed.—R
$-Teachers of Vision—R

DAILY DEVOTIONALS

CLEAR Living
Penned from the Heart—R

MISSIONS

$-Evangelical Missions—R
$-PIME World—R
Railroad Evangelist—R
Women of the Harvest

PASTORS/LEADERS

$-Catholic Servant
Jour./Pastoral Care—R
$-Lutheran Partners—R
$-Priest
$-Rev. Magazine
$-Sabbath School Leadership—R
$-Today's Parish—R
$-Worship Leader
$-Youthworker

TEEN/YOUNG ADULT

$-Boundless Webzine—R
$-Breakaway
$-Brio
$-CLEAR Direction
$-CLEAR Horizon
$-Devo'Zine—R
$-Ignite Your Faith
$-InsideOut—R
$-Insight—R
$-Listen—R
$-Passageway.org—R
$-Real Faith in Life—R
$-Spirit
$-TC Magazine
TeensForJC—R
$-True Girl
$-Young Christian—R
$-Young Salvationist—R

WOMEN

CelebrateMoms—R
Christian Woman's Page—R
Comfort Café
$-Dabbling Mum—R
$-Esprit—R
$-Godly Business Woman—R
Handmaiden—R
Hearts at Home—R
$-Herizons
$-Hope for Women
$-Inspired Living—R
$-Journey
Just Between Us—R
$-Melody of the Heart
$-MOMsense—R
Precious Times—R
($)-Simply Blessed—R
$-SpiritLed Woman
$-Today's Christian Woman—R
Virtuous Woman—R
Woman of Worth—R
$-Women Alive!—R
Women Today—R
$-WT Online—R

WRITERS

Areopagus
Money the Write Way—R
$-New Writer's Mag.
NW Christian Author—R
Once Upon a Time—R

PERSONAL GROWTH

ADULT/GENERAL

$-Alive Now—R
$-Animal Trails—R
$-Annals of St. Anne

$-Associated Content—R
$-Bible Advocate—R
$-Brave Hearts—R
Bread of Life—R
Breakthrough Intercessor—R
$-Bridal Guides—R
$-Catholic Digest—R
$-Catholic Forester—R
$-Catholic Peace Voice—R
CBN.com—R
Channels—R
$-Christian Courier/CAN—R
$-Christian Journal—R
Christian Online
Church Herald & Holiness—R
$-City Light News—R
$-Common Ground—R
($)-Community Spirit—R
$-Decision
$-Discipleship Journal—R
Divine Ascent
$-Dovetail—R
Eternal Ink—R
$-Evangel/IN—R
Evangelical Advocate—R
$-Faith & Family
$-Faith & Friends—R
$-Faith Today
Family Room
First Call Hospice—R
$-Focus on the Family
$-Gem—R
$-God Allows U-Turns—R
Good News Journal—R
$-Home Times—R
HopeKeepers—R
$-Horizons (adult)—R
$-Ideals—R
$-In Touch
$-Indian Life—R
Keys to Living—R
Leaves—R
$-Light & Life
$-Liguorian
$-Live—R
$-Living—R
$-Living Church
Looking Up
$-Lookout
$-Lutheran Digest—R
$-Mature Living
$-Mature Years—R
$-Men of Integrity—R
Men of the Cross
Mosaic—R
($)-Mutuality—R
New Heart—R
$-New Wineskins—R
$-Now What?—R
Parents & Teens—R
Penned from the Heart—R
$-Positive Thinking—R
$-Psychology for Living—R
$-Pure Inspiration—R
$-Purpose—R
Regent Global—R
Reverent Submissions—R
Sacred Journey—R
$-Seek—R
Sight 360—R
SingleAgain.com—R
Spiritual Voice—R
Spirituality for Today
$-St. Anthony Messenger
$-Standard—R
STEPS
$-Stewardship—R
$-Testimony—R
Three One Six—R
$-Today's Christian—R
$-Together—R
Trumpeter—R
Urban Kingdom—R
Victory Herald—R
$-Victory in Grace—R
$-Vista
$-War Cry—R
$-Way of St. Francis—R
$-Wildwood Reader—R
Wisconsin Christian
$-World & I—R

CHILDREN

$-Guide—R
$-Sparkle—R
$-Winner—R

CHRISTIAN EDUCATION/LIBRARY

$-Children's Ministry
Christian Early Ed.—R
$-Resource—R
$-Youth & CE Leadership

DAILY DEVOTIONALS

Penned from the Heart—R

MISSIONS

Women of the Harvest

PASTORS/LEADERS

Christian Management—R
$-Ministry Today

TEEN/YOUNG ADULT

$-Boundless Webzine—R
$-Breakaway
$-Brio
$-Listen—R
$-Passageway.org—R
TeensForJC—R
$-True Girl
$-Young Adult Today—R
$-Young Christian—R
$-Young Salvationist—R

WOMEN

CelebrateMoms—R
Christian Woman's Page—R
$-Esprit—R
$-Fullfill
$-Godly Business Woman—R
Hearts at Home—R
$-Hope for Women
$-Horizons (women)—R
$-Inspired Living—R
$-inSpirit—R
$-Journey
Just Between Us—R
$-MOMsense—R
P31 Woman—R
Precious Times—R
($)-Simply Blessed—R
$-SpiritLed Woman
$-Today's Christian Woman—R
Together with God—R
Virtuous Woman—R
Woman of Worth—R
$-Women Alive!—R
Women of the Cross
Women Today—R
$-WT Online—R

WRITERS

Areopagus
Opinari—R

PHOTO ESSAYS

ADULT/GENERAL

$-Animal Trails—R
$-Associated Content—R
$-Brave Hearts—R
$-Bridal Guides—R
$-Cathedral Age—R
$-Christian Journal—R
Christian Motorsports
Citizen USA—R
$-Faith & Family
$-Home Times—R
Imagine
$-In Touch
Men of the Cross
Nostalgia—R
$-Ozarks Senior Living—R
$-Parabola—R
$-Priority!—R
Rock & Sling
Sacred Journey—R
$-Salvo
Sight 360—R
Spiritual Voice—R
$-St. Anthony Messenger
$-Today's Christian—R
Urban Kingdom—R
$-Way of St. Francis—R
$-Wildwood Reader—R
$-World & I—R

CHILDREN

$-Faces
Skipping Stones

CHRISTIAN EDUCATION/LIBRARY

$-Journal/Adventist Ed.—R

PASTORS/LEADERS

$-Ministry & Liturgy—R
$-Outreach—R
$-Priest
$-Youthworker

TEEN/YOUNG ADULT

$-Credo—R
$-Insight—R
$-Passageway.org—R
TeensForJC—R
$-Young Christian—R

WOMEN

Christian Woman's Page—R
$-Horizons (women)—R

PHOTOGRAPHS

Note: "Reprint" indicators (R) have been deleted from this section and "B" for black & white glossy prints or "C" for color transparencies inserted. An asterisk (*) before a listing indicates they buy photos with articles only.

ADULT/GENERAL

Advance
African Voices—B
Alive Now—B/C
American Tract
Ancient Paths—B
Anglican Journal—B/C
*Animal Trails—B/C
*Annals of St. Anne—B/C
*Arkansas Catholic—C
Arlington Catholic—B
Associated Content—C
BGC World—C
Bible Advocate—C
Brave Hearts—B/C
Breakthrough Intercessor—B/C
*Bridal Guides—B/C
Canada Lutheran—B
*Catholic Digest—B/C
Catholic Forester—B/C
*Catholic Insight
Catholic New York—B
Catholic Peace Voice—B/C
Catholic Sentinel—B/C
Catholic Telegraph—B
Catholic Yearbook—C
CBA Retailers—C
*Celebrate Life—C
*Charisma—C
*Christian Citizen USA—C
*Christian Courier/CAN—B
*Christian Examiner—C
Christian Herald—C
*Christian History—B/C
Christian Home & School—C
*Christian Motorsports—B
*Christian Online
Christian Radio
Christian Retailing—C
*Christian Standard—B/C
*Christianity Today—C
ChristianWeek—B/C
Chronicle Christian—B/C
*Church of England News
Citizen USA—C
City Light News—B/C
*Commonweal—B/C
Connecting Point—B
Cornerstone Christian
Covenant Companion—B/C
Culture Wars—B/C
Decision
*DisciplesWorld
Divine Ascent—B
Dovetail—B
Episcopal Life—B
Eureka Street
*Evangel/IN—B
*Evangel/OR—B/C
Evangelical Advocate—C
Faith & Family—C
*Faith & Friends—C
*Faith Today—C
Focus on the Family—B/C
Good News Journal
Gospel Today
*Guideposts—B/C
Highway News—B
Holy House Ministries—B
*Home Times—B/C
Homeschooling Today—B/C
HonorBound—C
*HopeKeepers—B/C
*Horizons (adult)
*Impact—C
*In Touch
*Indian Life—C
Inland NW Christian—B
Interchange—B
*Interim—B/C
Island Catholic
*Layman—B
Leaves—B/C
*Leben—C
Liberty—B/C
*Lifeglow—B/C
Light & Life—B/C
*Liguorian—C
*Live—B/C
Living—B/C
Living Church—B/C
*Living Light—B/C
Lookout—B/C
*Lutheran Journal—C
Marian Helper—B/C
*Mature Living
*Mature Years—C
Messenger—B
*Minnesota Christian—B/C
*Miracles, Healings
Montana Catholic
Montgomery's Journey
*Mosaic—B/C
Mutuality—B/C
*New Heart—C
New Wineskins—B/C
Nostalgia—B/C
On Mission—B/C
Our Sunday Visitor—B/C
Over the Back Fence—C
*Parabola—B
*Perspectives—B
Power for Living—B
Presbyterian Outlook—B/C
*Presbyterians Today—B/C
*Prism—B/C
*Psychology for Living—C
*Purpose—B
Quaker Life—B/C
Rhubarb—B
Rock & Sling—B/C
Sacred Journey—B/C
Salvo—C
*Seek—C
Sight 360—B/C
*Special Living—B/C
Spiritual Life—B
Spiritual Voice—B/C
Sports Spectrum—C
*St. Anthony Messenger—B/C
Standard—B
*Star of Zion
*Storyteller—B
*Testimony—B/C
Three One Six—B
Tiferet
*Today's Christian—B/C
Today's Pentecostal—B/C
*Together—B/C
*United Church Observer—B/C
Upscale
Urban Kingdom—C
*Vibrant Life—C
Vision—B/C
*War Cry—B/C
Way of St. Francis—B
West Wind Review—B
White Wing—C
*World & I—B/C

CHILDREN

American Girl—C

Celebrate—C
*Focus/Clubhouse—C
*Focus/Clubhouse Jr.—C
Nature Friend—B/C
*Pockets—B/C
Primary Pal/IL
SHINEbrightly—C
Skipping Stones
*Winner—C

CHRISTIAN EDUCATION/LIBRARY

*Christian Early Ed.—C
Christian Librarian—B
*Church Libraries—B/C
Journal/Adventist Ed.—B
RTJ—C
Teach Kids!—B/C
*Teachers of Vision—C
*Today's Catholic Teacher—C
*Youth & CE Leadership—C

DAILY DEVOTIONALS

Our Journey—C
Secret Place—B/C
Upper Room

MISSIONS

Evangelical Missions
Glad Tidings (Canada)—C
Intl. Jour./Frontier
*New World Outlook—C
*One—C
OpRev Equipper—B/C
PFI World
*PIME World—B/C

MUSIC

Christian Music Weekly—B
*Creator—B/C

PASTORS/LEADERS

Catholic Servant
Christian Century—B/C
Christian Management—C
*InSite—C
*Leadership—B
Lutheran Forum—B
*Lutheran Partners—B
Ministry—B
Priest
Rev. Magazine—C
*This Rock—B/C
Today's Parish—B/C
Willow—C
*Worship Leader—C
*Your Church—C
*Youthworker

TEEN/YOUNG ADULT

Breakaway—C
Brio—C
*CLEAR Direction—B/C
Credo—B/C
Essential Connection—B/C
Ignite Your Faith—C
*InsideOut
Listen—B/C
Passageway.org—B/C
*Real Faith in Life—B
*Sharing the VICTORY—C
*Spirit
Take Five Plus—B/C
Young Adult Today—B
*Young Christian—B/C

WOMEN

At the Center—C
Beyond the Bend—B/C
*Canticle
*Esprit—B
Handmaidens
Hearts at Home—B/C
Herizons
*Link & Visitor—B
*Precious Times—C
Proverbs 31 Sisters—B/C
Right to the Heart

WRITERS

*New Writer's Mag.
*Once Upon a Time
*Poets & Writers
Tickled by Thunder
Write Connection—B
*Writer's Digest—B
Writers Notes—C

POETRY

ADULT/GENERAL

African Voices—R
$-Alive Now—R
$-America
$-Ancient Paths—R
Angel Face—R
$-Associated Content—R
$-Aujourd'hui Credo—R
$-Bible Advocate—R
$-Brave Hearts—R
Bread of Life—R
Breakthrough Intercessor—R
$-Bridal Guides—R
$-Cappers
$-Catholic Forester—R
$-Catholic Peace Voice—R
$-Catholic Yearbook—R
Channels—R
$-Christian Courier/CAN—R
$-Christian Journal—R
Christian Motorsports
Christian Ranchman
$-Christian Research
$-Commonweal
Connecting Point—R
$-Covenant Companion—R
Creation Care—R
$-Creation Illust.—R
$-Cresset
CrossHome.com
$-Culture Wars—R
$-Decision
Desert Call—R
Diamond Dust
$-DisciplesWorld
$-Dovetail—R
$-Dragons, Knights & Angels—R
Eternal Ink—R
$-Eureka Street
$-Evangel/IN—R
Evangel/OR—R
First Call Hospice—R
Friends Journal—R
$-Gem—R
Good News Journal—R
$-Great Mystery—R
Haiku Hippodrome
Halo Magazine
$-Haruah—R
Highway News—R
$-Home Times—R
$-Ideals—R
$-Image/WA
($)-Impact—R
$-Indian Life—R
Infuze
Island Catholic
Keys to Living—R
Leaves—R
$-Liberty
LifeTimes Catholic
$-Light & Life
$-Live—R
Looking Up
$-Lutheran Digest—R
$-Lutheran Journal—R
$-Mature Living
$-Mature Years—R
Men of the Cross
$-Miraculous Medal
New Heart—R
$-New Wineskins—R
Pegasus Review—R
Penned from the Heart—R
Penwood Review
Perspectives—R
Perspectives/Science
$-Poetry Scout
$-Prairie Messenger—R
Priscilla Papers
$-Pure Inspiration—R
$-Purpose—R
Quaker Life—R
Radix—R
Relief Journal
Reverent Submissions—R
Rock & Sling
$-Rose & Thorn
Ruminate
Sacred Journey—R
SearchingWisdom.org—R

Sharing—R
Silver Wings—R
SingleAgain.com—R
Spiritual Voice—R
$-St. Anthony Messenger
$-St. Joseph's Messenger—R
$-Standard—R
Star of Zion
$-Storyteller—R
Studio—R
Sword and Trumpet
Sword of the Lord—R
$-Testimony—R
Three One Six—R
Tiferet
Time of Singing—R
To God Be the Glory!
$-U.S. Catholic
Urban Kingdom—R
Victory Herald—R
$-Vision—R
$-Vista
$-Way of St. Francis—R
$-Weavings—R
West Wind Review
$-Wittenburg Door—R
$-World & I—R
Xavier Review

CHILDREN

$-Adventures
$-American Girl—R
$-Faces
$-Focus/Clubhouse Jr.
$-Partners—R
$-Pockets—R
$-SHINEbrightly—R
Skipping Stones
$-Story Mates—R

CHRISTIAN EDUCATION/LIBRARY

$-Teachers of Vision—R
$-Today's Catholic Teacher—R

DAILY DEVOTIONALS

Penned from the Heart—R
$-Secret Place
$-These Days

MISSIONS

$-Glad Tidings (Canada)—R
Railroad Evangelist—R

PASTORS/LEADERS

$-Catechumenate
$-Christian Century—R
Cross Currents
$-Emmanuel
Jour./Pastoral Care—R
$-Lutheran Partners—R
$-Preaching Well—R
$-Review for Religious
Sharing the Practice—R

TEEN/YOUNG ADULT

$-Credo—R
$-Devo'Zine—R
$-Essential Connection
$-Ignite Your Faith
$-InsideOut—R
$-Insight—R
$-Take Five Plus
TeensForJC—R
$-Young Christian—R
$-Young Salvationist—R

WOMEN

Christian Woman's Page—R
$-Esprit—R
Handmaiden—R
Handmaidens
Hearts at Home—R
$-Link & Visitor—R
$-Melody of the Heart
$-MOMsense—R
Proverbs 31 Sisters—R
Virtuous Woman—R
Woman of Worth—R
Women of the Cross

WRITERS

Areopagus
$-ByLine
$-Canadian Writer's Jour.—R
$-Christian Communicator—R
ChristianWriters
$-Cross & Quill—R
$-New Writer's Mag.
NW Christian Author—R
Once Upon a Time—R
Poetic Voices—R
$-Tickled by Thunder
Write Connection
$-Writer's Digest—R
$-Writers Notes
$-Writers' Journal

POLITICAL

ADULT/GENERAL

African Voices—R
$-Anglican Journal
$-Arlington Catholic
$-Associated Content—R
$-Cathedral Age—R
$-Catholic Insight
$-Catholic Peace Voice—R
CBN.com—R
$-Challenging Destiny—R
Christian Business
Christian C. L. RECORD—R
$-Christian Citizen USA
$-Christian Courier/CAN—R
Christian Courier/WI—R
$-Christian Examiner
Christian Media—R
Christian Ranchman
$-Christian Renewal—R
$-Christianity Today—R
$-ChristianWeek—R
$-Chronicle Christian
Church of England News
Citizen USA—R
$-City Light News—R
$-Commonweal
($)-Community Spirit—R
Creation Care—R
$-Creative Nonfiction
$-Cresset
Desert Voice
$-DisciplesWorld
Evangel/OR—R
$-Faith Today
Good News/S. Florida
$-Home Times—R
$-Inland NW Christian
Jour. of Church & State
$-Light & Life
$-Minnesota Christian—R
MovieGuide
$-National Catholic Network
$-New Wineskins—R
Perspectives—R
Presbyterian Outlook
$-Prism
Sight 360—R
$-Social Justice—R
Spiritual Voice—R
$-St. Anthony Messenger
$-Testimony—R
Three One Six—R
Tri-State Voice
Trumpeter—R
Urban Kingdom—R
$-World & I—R

CHILDREN

$-New Moon—R

MISSIONS

$-One

PASTORS/LEADERS

$-Christian Century—R
$-Interpreter
$-Lutheran Partners—R
$-Word & World

TEEN/YOUNG ADULT

$-Boundless Webzine—R
$-InTeen—R
$-Young Christian—R

WOMEN

$-Esprit—R
$-Herizons
$-inSpirit—R

PRAYER

ADULT/GENERAL

$-Advance
African Voices—R
($)-AGAIN—R
$-Alive Now—R
$-Angels on Earth
$-Animal Trails—R
$-Annals of St. Anne
$-Believer's Bay
$-BGC World—R
$-Bible Advocate—R
Bread of Life—R
Breakthrough Intercessor—R
$-Bridal Guides—R
$-Canada Lutheran—R
$-Cathedral Age—R
$-Catholic Digest—R
$-Catholic Peace Voice—R
$-Catholic Yearbook—R
CBN.com—R
$-Celebrate Life—R
$-CGA World—R
Christian C. L. RECORD—R
$-Christian Journal—R
Christian Online
Christian Ranchman
$-Christian Research
$-Christian Standard—R
$-Christianity Today—R
$-ChristianWeek—R
$-Chronicle Christian
Church Herald & Holiness—R
$-City Light News—R
$-Columbia—R
($)-Community Spirit—R
Connecting Point—R
$-Covenant Companion—R
Creation Care—R
$-Culture Wars—R
$-Decision
Desert Call—R
$-Discipleship Journal—R
Divine Ascent
$-Dovetail—R
$-Episcopal Life—R
Eternal Ink—R
$-Evangel/IN—R
Evangelical Advocate—R
$-Faith & Family
$-Faith Today
$-Family Digest—R
$-Gem—R
$-God Allows U-Turns—R
$-Good News—R
Good News Journal—R
Heartlight—R
Holy House Ministries—R
$-Home Times—R
HopeKeepers—R
$-Horizons (adult)—R
$-In Touch
$-Inland NW Christian Leaves—R
$-Lifeglow—R
$-Light & Life
$-Liguorian
$-Live—R
$-Living Church
Looking Up
$-Lookout
$-Lutheran Digest—R
$-Lutheran Journal—R
$-Marian Helper
$-Mature Years—R
$-Men of Integrity—R
$-Miracles, Healings
$-Montgomery's Journey
Mosaic—R
$-National Catholic
$-New Freeman—R
$-New Wineskins—R
$-Now What?—R
$-On Mission
$-Parabola—R
Pegasus Review—R
Penned from the Heart—R
Perspectives—R
$-Positive Thinking—R
Prayer Closet
PrayerWorks—R
$-Precepts for Living
Presbyterian Outlook
$-Presbyterians Today—R
$-Priority!—R
$-Pure Inspiration—R
Reverent Submissions—R
Sacred Journey—R
$-Seek—R
Sight 360—R
Silver Wings—R
$-Spiritual Life
Spiritual Voice—R
Spirituality for Today
$-St. Anthony Messenger
$-St. Joseph's Messenger—R
Sword of the Lord—R
$-Testimony—R
Three One Six—R
$-Today's Christian—R
$-Today's Pentecostal—R
Trumpeter—R
$-U.S. Catholic
Urban Kingdom—R
Victory Herald—R
$-Vista
$-War Cry—R
$-Way of St. Francis—R
$-Wesleyan Life—R
$-Whole
Wisconsin Christian

CHILDREN

$-BREAD/God's Children—R
$-Guide—R
$-Primary Street
$-Sparkle—R

CHRISTIAN EDUCATION/LIBRARY

Catholic Library
$-Children's Ministry
$-Group
$-Resource—R
$-RTJ—R
$-Teach Kids!—R
$-Teachers of Vision—R
$-Youth & CE Leadership

DAILY DEVOTIONALS

Penned from the Heart—R

MISSIONS

Intl. Jour./Frontier—R
$-PFI World—R
Railroad Evangelist—R

MUSIC

$-Creator—R

PASTORS/LEADERS

$-Catholic Servant
$-Clergy Journal—R
$-Diocesan Dialogue—R
$-Emmanuel
$-Enrichment—R
$-Interpreter
$-Leadership—R
$-Lutheran Partners—R
$-Ministry Today
$-Pray!—R
$-Proclaim—R
$-Reformed Worship—R
$-Review for Religious
Rick Warren's Ministry—R
Sewanee Theo. Review
Theological Digest—R
$-Today's Parish—R
$-Word & World
$-Worship Leader

TEEN/YOUNG ADULT

$-Boundless Webzine—R
$-Breakaway
$-Brio
$-CLEAR Direction
$-CLEAR Horizon
$-Devo'Zine—R
$-InTeen—R
$-J.A.M.
$-Passageway.org—R
$-Real Faith in Life—R
TeensForJC—R
$-True Girl
$-Young Christian—R

$-Young Salvationist—R

WOMEN
($)-Beyond the Bend—R
$-Canticle
CelebrateMoms—R
Christian Woman's Page—R
Crowned with Silver
$-Hope for Women
$-Horizons (women)—R
$-Inspired Living—R
$-InspiredMoms—R
$-inSpirit—R
$-Journey
Just Between Us—R
Lutheran Woman's Quar.
P31 Woman—R
Precious Times—R
Proverbs 31 Sisters—R
Right to the Heart—R
$-SpiritLed Woman
$-Today's Christian Woman—R
Together with God—R
Virtuous Woman—R
Woman of Worth—R
$-Women Alive!—R
Women Today—R
$-WT Online—R

WRITERS
Areopagus
Opinari—R

PROPHECY

ADULT/GENERAL
$-Advance
$-Apocalypse Chronicles—R
$-Believer's Bay
$-Bible Advocate—R
Bread of Life—R
$-Bridal Guides—R
CBN.com—R
Christian Media—R
Christian Online
Christian Ranchman
$-Christian Research
$-Chronicle Christian
Evangelical Advocate—R
Godly Places
$-Home Times—R
$-Live—R
Midnight Call
$-New Freeman—R
Sight 360—R
SingleAgain.com—R
Spiritual Voice—R
$-St. Anthony Messenger
Sword of the Lord—R
$-Testimony—R
Three One Six—R
Trumpeter—R
Urban Kingdom—R

PASTORS/LEADERS
$-Ministry Today
Rick Warren's Ministry—R
$-Word & World

TEEN/YOUNG ADULT
$-InTeen—R
$-Real Faith in Life—R
TeensForJC—R
$-Young Christian—R
$-Young Salvationist—R

WOMEN
$-Inspired Living—R
$-SpiritLed Woman

PSYCHOLOGY

ADULT/GENERAL
$-Animal Trails—R
$-Associated Content—R
$-Aujourd'hui Credo—R
$-Bridal Guides—R
$-Catholic Peace Voice—R
CBN.com—R
$-Christian Courier/CAN—R
Christian Online
($)-Community Spirit—R
$-Creative Nonfiction
$-Dovetail—R
Evangelical Advocate—R
First Call Hospice—R
$-Gem—R
$-Home Times—R
$-Light & Life
$-Parabola—R
$-Psychology for Living—R
$-Science & Spirit
Sight 360—R
$-Spiritual Life
Spiritual Voice—R
$-St. Anthony Messenger
$-Testimony—R
Trumpeter—R
Urban Kingdom—R
$-Vibrant Life—R
$-World & I—R

CHILDREN
$-New Moon—R

PASTORS/LEADERS
Jour./Pastoral Care—R
$-Word & World

TEEN/YOUNG ADULT
$-Young Christian—R

WOMEN
($)-Beyond the Bend—R

PUPPET PLAYS

$-Children's Ministry
Christian Creative Arts
Christian Early Ed.—R
Imagine
$-Parabola—R
$-Teach Kids!—R
Victory Herald—R

RACISM

ADULT/GENERAL
$-Aujourd'hui Credo—R
$-Catholic Peace Voice—R
CBN.com—R
$-Christian Citizen USA
$-Christianity Today—R
$-ChristianWeek—R
$-City Light News—R
($)-Community Spirit—R
$-Creative Nonfiction
$-Discipleship Journal—R
$-Dovetail—R
$-Faith Today
$-Home Times—R
$-Light & Life
$-Live—R
$-Lookout
$-Men of Integrity—R
$-Minnesota Christian—R
($)-Mutuality—R
$-New Wineskins—R
$-Our Sunday Visitor—R
$-Parabola—R
Perspectives—R
$-Prairie Messenger—R
Priscilla Papers
$-Purpose—R
Sight 360—R
Spiritual Voice—R
$-St. Anthony Messenger
$-Testimony—R
$-Today's Christian—R
$-Together—R
Trumpeter—R
$-U.S. Catholic
$-Upscale
Urban Kingdom—R
$-World & I—R

CHILDREN
$-Guide—R
$-New Moon—R
$-Our Little Friend—R
$-Primary Treasure—R
Skipping Stones
$-Sparkle—R

PASTORS/LEADERS
$-Clergy Journal—R
Cross Currents
Jour./Pastoral Care—R
$-Ministry Today

TEEN/YOUNG ADULT
$-Boundless Webzine—R
$-Ignite Your Faith

$-Passageway.org—R
TeensForJC—R
$-True Girl
$-Young Salvationist—R

WOMEN

$-Horizons (women)—R
Making Waves
$-SpiritLed Woman
Together with God—R
$-WT Online—R

WRITERS

Teachers & Writers

RECOVERY

ADULT/GENERAL

$-Animal Trails—R
$-Bridal Guides—R
CBN.com—R
$-Christian Citizen USA
$-Christian Journal—R
Christian Ranchman
$-Chronicle Christian
$-City Light News—R
($)-Community Spirit—R
$-Creative Nonfiction
Evangelical Advocate—R
$-Focus on the Family
$-Home Times—R
HopeKeepers—R
$-Liguorian
$-Live—R
Looking Up
$-Lookout
$-Men of Integrity—R
$-Now What?—R
$-Priority!—R
Reverent Submissions—R
Ruminate
$-Seek—R
Sight 360—R
Spiritual Voice—R
Spirituality for Today
STEPS
Urban Kingdom—R
$-Vista
$-Wildwood Reader—R

PASTORS/LEADERS

Jour./Pastoral Care—R
$-Ministry Today

TEEN/YOUNG ADULT

$-Boundless Webzine—R
$-Young Christian—R

WOMEN

($)-Beyond the Bend—R
Comfort Café
$-inSpirit—R
Right to the Heart—R
Together with God—R
Virtuous Woman—R
Women Today—R
$-WT Online—R

RELATIONSHIPS

ADULT/GENERAL

$-Advance
$-Angels on Earth
$-Animal Trails—R
$-Annals of St. Anne
Anointed Pages
$-Associated Content—R
$-Aujourd'hui Credo—R
$-BGC World—R
$-Bible Advocate—R
Boomer Babes Rock
$-Brave Hearts—R
Bread of Life—R
$-Bridal Guides—R
$-Canada Lutheran—R
$-Canadian Mennonite—R
$-Catholic Digest—R
$-Catholic Forester—R
CBN.com—R
$-Celebrate Life—R
Channels—R
$-Chicken Soup Books—R
$-Christian Journal—R
Christian Online
Christian Ranchman
$-ChristianWeek—R
$-Chronicle Christian
Church Herald & Holiness—R
$-City Light News—R
($)-Community Spirit—R
$-Creative Nonfiction
Desert Call—R
$-Discipleship Journal—R
$-Dovetail—R
$-Evangel/IN—R
Evangel/OR—R
Evangelical Advocate—R
$-Faith Today
Family Room
$-Family Smart E-tips—R
First Call Hospice—R
$-Focus on the Family
$-Gem—R
$-Gems of Truth—R
$-God Allows U-Turns—R
Good News Journal—R
$-Gospel Today—R
$-Guideposts—R
Heartlight—R
Highway News—R
$-Home Times—R
$-Homeschooling Today—R
$-HonorBound—R
HopeKeepers—R
$-Horizons (adult)—R
$-In Touch
Keys to Living—R
$-Lifeglow—R
$-Light & Life
$-Liguorian
$-Live—R
$-Living—R
Looking Up
$-Lookout
$-Marriage Partnership—R
$-Mature Living
$-Mature Years—R
$-Men of Integrity—R
$-Minnesota Christian—R
$-Montgomery's Journey
($)-Mutuality—R
New Heart—R
$-New Wineskins—R
$-On Mission
$-Our Sunday Visitor—R
$-Parabola—R
Parents & Teens—R
Pegasus Review—R
Penned from the Heart—R
Perspectives—R
$-Positive Thinking—R
$-Prairie Messenger—R
Priscilla Papers
$-Pure Inspiration—R
Reverent Submissions—R
Sacred Journey—R
$-Science & Spirit
$-Seek—R
Sight 360—R
Silver Wings—R
SingleAgain.com—R
$-Special Living—R
Spiritual Voice—R
Spirituality for Today
$-St. Anthony Messenger
$-Standard—R
STEPS
$-Storyteller—R
$-Testimony—R
Three One Six—R
$-Today's Christian—R
$-Today's Pentecostal—R
$-Together—R
Trumpeter—R
$-Upscale
Urban Kingdom—R
$-Vibrant Life—R
$-Vision—R
$-Vista
$-War Cry—R
$-Wesleyan Life—R
$-Whole
$-Wildwood Reader—R
Wisconsin Christian
$-World & I—R

CHILDREN

$-BREAD/God's Children—R
$-Cadet Quest—R
$-Guide—R

$-New Moon—R
$-Passport—R
$-SHINEbrightly—R
$-Sparkle—R

CHRISTIAN EDUCATION/LIBRARY

$-Group
$-Resource—R
$-Teachers of Vision—R
$-Youth & CE Leadership

PASTORS/LEADERS

$-Leadership—R
$-Small Group Dynamics—R
$-Word & World

TEEN/YOUNG ADULT

$-Boundless Webzine—R
$-Breakaway
$-Brio
$-Credo—R
$-Ignite Your Faith
$-Insight—R
$-Listen—R
$-Passageway.org—R
$-Real Faith in Life—R
$-Rock
$-TC Magazine
TeensForJC—R
$-True Girl
$-Young Christian—R
$-Young Salvationist—R

WOMEN

$-At the Center—R
($)-Beyond the Bend—R
$-Canticle
CelebrateMoms—R
Christian Woman's Page—R
Comfort Café
Crowned with Silver
First Lady
$-Heart & Soul
Hearts at Home—R
$-Herizons
$-Hope for Women
$-Inspired Living—R
$-InspiredMoms—R
$-inSpirit—R
$-Journey
Just Between Us—R
Life Tools for Women
$-Link & Visitor—R
Lutheran Woman's Quar.
$-MOMsense—R
P31 Woman—R
Precious Times—R
Proverbs 31 Sisters—R
Right to the Heart—R
$-Simple Joy
($)-Simply Blessed—R
$-SpiritLed Woman
$-Today's Christian Woman—R
Together with God—R
Virtuous Woman—R
Woman of Worth—R
$-Women Alive!—R
Women of the Cross
Women Today—R
$-WT Online—R

RELIGIOUS FREEDOM

ADULT/GENERAL

$-Animal Trails—R
$-Arlington Catholic
$-Aujourd'hui Credo—R
$-Bridal Guides—R
$-Catholic Peace Voice—R
CBN.com—R
Channels—R
Christian C. L. RECORD—R
$-Christian Citizen USA
Christian Courier/WI—R
$-Christian Examiner
Christian News NW—R
Christian Observer
Christian Online
Christian Ranchman
$-Christian Response—R
$-Christianity Today—R
$-ChristianWeek—R
$-Chronicle Christian
Church of England News
Citizen USA—R
$-City Light News—R
$-Columbia—R
$-Commonweal
($)-Community Spirit—R
Compass Direct
Connecting Point—R
Desert Voice
$-Dovetail—R
$-Episcopal Life—R
Eternal Ink—R
Evangelical Advocate—R
$-Faith Today
$-Gem—R
Good News Today
Good News/S. Florida
$-Home Times—R
$-In Touch
$-Interim—R
Jour. of Church & State
$-Liberty
$-Lifeglow—R
$-Light & Life
$-Live—R
Looking Up
$-Lookout
MESSAGE/Open Bible—R
$-Minnesota Christian—R
$-National Catholic
$-New Freeman—R
$-New Wineskins—R
$-Our Sunday Visitor—R
$-Parabola—R
Pegasus Review—R
Perspectives—R
$-Prairie Messenger—R
Presbyterian Outlook
$-Prism
$-Pure Inspiration—R
Rare Jewel—R
$-Salvo
$-Science & Spirit
$-Seek—R
Sight 360—R
$-Social Justice—R
$-Spiritual Life
Spiritual Voice—R
$-St. Anthony Messenger
$-Standard—R
$-Testimony—R
Three One Six—R
Trumpeter—R
Urban Kingdom—R
Victory Herald—R
Wisconsin Christian
$-World & I—R

CHILDREN

$-Guide—R
$-New Moon—R
Skipping Stones

CHRISTIAN EDUCATION/LIBRARY

$-Teachers of Vision—R

MISSIONS

$-Evangelical Missions—R
OpRev Equipper—R

PASTORS/LEADERS

$-Catholic Servant
$-Christian Century—R
Cross Currents
$-This Rock
$-Word & World

TEEN/YOUNG ADULT

$-Boundless Webzine—R
$-InTeen—R
$-Passageway.org—R
TeensForJC—R
$-Young Christian—R

WOMEN

$-SpiritLed Woman
$-WT Online—R

RELIGIOUS TOLERANCE

ADULT/GENERAL

$-Animal Trails—R
$-Aujourd'hui Credo—R
Bread of Life—R
$-Bridal Guides—R
$-Catholic Peace Voice—R
CBN.com—R
Channels—R

Christian C. L. RECORD—R
$-Christian Citizen USA
$-Christian Examiner
Christian Online
$-Christianity Today—R
$-ChristianWeek—R
Church of England News
$-City Light News—R
$-Columbia—R
($)-Community Spirit—R
$-Dovetail—R
Evangelical Advocate—R
$-Faith Today
$-Home Times—R
$-Interim—R
Jour. of Church & State
$-Light & Life
$-Live—R
Looking Up
$-Lookout
$-Minnesota Christian—R
$-National Catholic
$-New Wineskins—R
$-Our Sunday Visitor—R
$-Parabola—R
Perspectives—R
$-Prairie Messenger—R
$-Pure Inspiration—R
Rare Jewel—R
$-Science & Spirit
$-Seek—R
Sight 360—R
Spiritual Voice—R
Spirituality for Today
$-St. Anthony Messenger
Star of Zion
$-Testimony—R
Three One Six—R
Trumpeter—R
Urban Kingdom—R
$-World & I—R

CHILDREN

$-New Moon—R
$-Primary Treasure—R
Skipping Stones

MISSIONS

OpRev Equipper—R

PASTORS/LEADERS

$-Christian Century—R
$-Clergy Journal—R
Cross Currents

TEEN/YOUNG ADULT

$-Boundless Webzine—R
$-Ignite Your Faith
$-Passageway.org—R
TeensForJC—R
$-Young Christian—R

WOMEN

$-Esprit—R
$-Hope for Women
Together with God—R
$-WT Online—R

WRITERS

Teachers & Writers

REVIVAL

ADULT/GENERAL

$-Animal Trails—R
$-BGC World—R
$-Bible Advocate—R
$-Bridal Guides—R
CBN.com—R
$-Christian Citizen USA
Christian Ranchman
$-Chronicle Christian
Church Herald & Holiness—R
$-City Light News—R
($)-Community Spirit—R
Diamond Dust
Evangelical Advocate—R
$-Home Times—R
$-Live—R
$-Lookout
$-Parabola—R
Reverent Submissions—R
Spiritual Voice—R
Urban Kingdom—R
Victory Herald—R
$-Vista

PASTORS/LEADERS

Jour./Amer. Soc./Chur. Growth—R
$-Ministry Today

TEEN/YOUNG ADULT

$-Boundless Webzine—R
$-Young Christian—R

WOMEN

$-Hope for Women
Right to the Heart—R
$-WT Online—R

SALVATION TESTIMONIES

ADULT/GENERAL

American Tract—R
$-Believer's Bay
$-BGC World—R
$-Bible Advocate—R
Bread of Life—R
Breakthrough Intercessor—R
$-Bridal Guides—R
CBN.com—R
Channels—R
Choice Newspaper—R
$-Christian Citizen USA
$-Christian Journal—R
Christian Motorsports
Christian Online
Christian Ranchman
$-Christian Research
$-City Light News—R
($)-Community Spirit—R
Connecting Point—R
$-Decision
E-Quality
Eternal Ink—R
$-Evangel/IN—R
Evangelical Advocate—R
$-Faith Today
$-Gem—R
$-Guideposts—R
Heartbeat/CMA
Highway News—R
$-Home Times—R
Leaves—R
$-Lifeglow—R
$-Light & Life
$-Live—R
Looking Up
$-Men of Integrity—R
$-MESSAGE
$-New Freeman—R
New Heart—R
$-Now What?—R
$-On Mission
Parents & Teens—R
$-Power for Living—R
PrayerWorks—R
$-Priority!—R
Reverent Submissions—R
$-Seek—R
Sight 360—R
Silver Wings—R
Spiritual Voice—R
$-St. Anthony Messenger
Sword of the Lord—R
$-Testimony—R
Three One Six—R
$-Today's Christian—R
$-Together—R
Trumpeter—R
Urban Kingdom—R
Victory Herald—R
$-Vista
$-War Cry—R
$-Wesleyan Life—R
Wisconsin Christian

CHILDREN

$-Guide—R
$-Sparkle—R

CHRISTIAN EDUCATION/LIBRARY

Catholic Library
$-Group

MISSIONS

Railroad Evangelist—R

PASTORS/LEADERS

$-This Rock

TEEN/YOUNG ADULT

$-Boundless Webzine—R

$-Breakaway
$-CLEAR Direction
$-CLEAR Horizon
$-InTeen—R
$-Passageway.org—R
TeensForJC—R

WOMEN
CelebrateMoms—R
$-Godly Business Woman—R
($)-History's Women—R
$-Hope for Women
$-Inspired Living—R
$-Journey
Precious Times—R
$-SpiritLed Woman
Together with God—R
Virtuous Woman—R
Women Today—R
$-WT Online—R

WRITERS
Areopagus

SCIENCE

ADULT/GENERAL
$-Animal Trails—R
Answers
$-Associated Content—R
$-Aujourd'hui Credo—R
$-Bridal Guides—R
CBN.com—R
$-Christian Citizen USA
$-Christian Courier/CAN—R
Citizen USA—R
$-City Light News—R
($)-Community Spirit—R
Creation
$-Creation Illust.—R
$-Creative Nonfiction
$-Faith Today
$-Home Times—R
$-Light & Life
Men of the Cross
$-National Catholic
$-New Freeman—R
$-Parabola—R
Perspectives—R
Perspectives/Science
Rare Jewel—R
$-Salvo
$-Science & Spirit
Sight 360—R
$-St. Anthony Messenger
$-Testimony—R
Trumpeter—R
Urban Kingdom—R
$-World & I—R

CHILDREN
$-Nature Friend
$-New Moon—R
$-Sparkle—R

MISSIONS
Intl. Jour./Frontier—R

PASTORS/LEADERS
$-Lutheran Partners—R
$-Word & World

TEEN/YOUNG ADULT
$-InTeen—R
$-Passageway.org—R
TeensForJC—R
$-Young Christian—R

SELF-HELP

ADULT/GENERAL
$-Animal Trails—R
$-Associated Content—R
$-Bridal Guides—R
$-Catholic Digest—R
CBN.com—R
$-CGA World—R
$-Christian Journal—R
$-Chronicle Christian
$-City Light News—R
($)-Community Spirit—R
Disciple's Journal—R
$-Dovetail—R
$-Family Smart E-tips—R
$-Home Times—R
HopeKeepers—R
$-Lifeglow—R
$-Light & Life
$-Liguorian
Looking Up
$-Lookout
$-Marriage Partnership—R
$-Pure Inspiration—R
Reverent Submissions—R
SearchingWisdom.org—R
$-Seek—R
Sight 360—R
$-Significant Living—R
SingleAgain.com—R
$-Special Living—R
Spiritual Voice—R
$-St. Anthony Messenger
$-Standard—R
$-Testimony—R
Three One Six—R
Trumpeter—R
Urban Kingdom—R
$-Vibrant Life—R
Victory Herald—R
$-Vista
$-World & I—R

CHILDREN
$-Winner—R

MISSIONS
Women of the Harvest

PASTORS/LEADERS
$-Interpreter

TEEN/YOUNG ADULT
$-Brio
$-CLEAR Direction
$-Listen—R
TeensForJC—R
$-Young Christian—R

WOMEN
CelebrateMoms—R
Christian Woman's Page—R
$-Fullfill
$-Inspired Living—R
$-Journey
$-Today's Christian Woman—R
$-WT Online—R

WRITERS
Money the Write Way—R

SENIOR ADULT ISSUES

ADULT/GENERAL
$-Angels on Earth
$-Anglican Journal
$-Annals of St. Anne
$-Arkansas Catholic—R
$-Associated Content—R
$-B.C. Catholic—R
$-BGC World—R
byFaith
$-Canada Lutheran—R
$-Catholic Forester—R
CBN.com—R
$-CGA World—R
Christian Ranchman
$-Christian Standard—R
$-ChristianWeek—R
$-Chronicle Christian
$-City Light News—R
($)-Community Spirit—R
$-Dovetail—R
$-Evangel/IN—R
Evangel/OR—R
Evangelical Advocate—R
$-Family Smart E-tips—R
First Call Hospice—R
$-Focus on the Family
$-Gem—R
$-Home Times—R
$-Homeschooling Today—R
HopeKeepers—R
$-Lifeglow—R
$-Light & Life
$-Liguorian
$-Live—R
Looking Up
$-Mature Living
$-Mature Years—R
$-New Freeman—R
$-On Mission
$-Ozarks Senior Living—R
Penned from the Heart—R
$-Power for Living—R
PrayerWorks—R

Reverent Submissions—R
$-Seek—R
Senior Connection
Sight 360—R
$-Significant Living—R
SingleAgain.com—R
Spiritual Voice—R
$-St. Anthony Messenger
Star of Zion
$-Testimony—R
$-Today's Christian—R
Trumpeter—R
$-U.S. Catholic
$-Vista
$-War Cry—R
$-Wesleyan Life—R

CHRISTIAN EDUCATION/LIBRARY

$-Resource—R
$-Youth & CE Leadership

DAILY DEVOTIONALS

Penned from the Heart—R

PASTORS/LEADERS

$-Diocesan Dialogue—R
$-Interpreter
$-Word & World

WOMEN

$-inSpirit—R
($)-Simply Blessed—R
$-Today's Christian Woman—R
$-WT Online—R

SERMONS

ADULT/GENERAL

$-Arlington Catholic
$-Catholic Yearbook—R
Choice Newspaper—R
Christian Ranchman
Church Herald & Holiness—R
($)-Community Spirit—R
Creation Care—R
Evangelical Advocate—R
$-Lutheran Journal—R
Pegasus Review—R
Sight 360—R
$-St. Anthony Messenger
Star of Zion
$-Stewardship—R
Sword of the Lord—R
$-Testimony—R
Three One Six—R
Trumpeter—R
Urban Kingdom—R
Victory Herald—R
$-Way of St. Francis—R
$-Weavings—R

PASTORS/LEADERS

$-African American Pulpit
$-Clergy Journal—R
$-Enrichment—R
$-Interpretation
$-Ministry Today
Preaching—R
$-Preaching Well—R
$-Proclaim—R
Pulpit Helps—R
Sharing the Practice—R
$-Sunday Sermons—R
$-Today's Parish—R
$-Torch Legacy Leader

SHORT STORY: ADULT/GENERAL

$-Ancient Paths—R
$-Bridal Guides—R
CBN.com—R
Christian C. L. RECORD—R
Desert Call—R
Diamond Dust
$-DisciplesWorld
$-Esprit—R
Handmaidens
$-Haruah—R
Imagine
$-Liguorian
$-Ministry & Liturgy—R
$-Miraculous Medal
$-New Writer's Mag.
Perspectives—R
$-Preaching Well—R
Relief Journal
Ruminate
$-Seek—R
$-Storyteller—R
Three One Six—R
Tiferet
Urban Kingdom—R
$-Wildwood Reader—R
$-Writers Notes

SHORT STORY: ADULT/RELIGIOUS

African Voices—R
$-Ancient Paths—R
$-Angels on Earth
$-Annals of St. Anne
Areopagus
$-Associated Content—R
$-Aujourd'hui Credo—R
$-Breakaway
$-Bridal Guides—R
$-Canadian Writer's Jour.—R
$-Catholic Forester—R
$-Catholic Yearbook—R
CBN.com—R
$-CGA World—R
$-Christian Century—R
$-Christian Courier/CAN—R
$-Christian Educators—R
$-Christian Home & School
$-Christian Journal—R
Christian Online
Christian Radio
$-Christian Renewal—R
$-Christian Research
Christian Woman's Page—R
Connecting Point—R
$-Covenant Companion—R
Cross Currents
Diamond Dust
$-DisciplesWorld
$-Dragons, Knights & Angels—R
$-Dreams & Visions—R
$-Esprit—R
$-Eureka Street
$-Evangel/IN—R
$-Faith & Family
First Call Hospice—R
$-Gem—R
$-Gems of Truth—R
$-Glad Tidings (Canada)—R
Good News Journal—R
Handmaidens
$-Haruah—R
Heartlight—R
Hearts at Home—R
$-Horizons (adult)—R
$-Horizons (women)—R
$-Ideals—R
$-Image/WA
Imagine
($)-Impact—R
$-Indian Life—R
Infuze
$-inSpirit—R
$-Liguorian
$-Live—R
$-Lutheran Journal—R
Lutheran Woman's Quar.
$-Mature Living
$-Mature Years—R
$-Melody of the Heart
$-Messenger/Sacred Heart
$-Messenger/St. Anthony
$-Miraculous Medal
$-National Catholic
$-New Wineskins—R
$-On Mission
Pegasus Review—R
Perspectives—R
PrayerWorks—R
Precious Times—R
Presbyterian Outlook
$-Proclaim—R
$-Purpose—R
Railroad Evangelist—R
Relief Journal
Reverent Submissions—R
Rock & Sling
Ruminate
Seeds of Hope
$-Seek—R
$-Shades of Romance—R

$-Sharing the VICTORY—R
($)-Simply Blessed—R
Spiritual Voice—R
$-St. Anthony Messenger
$-St. Joseph's Messenger—R
$-Standard—R
$-Storyteller—R
Studio—R
$-Testimony—R
Three One Six—R
$-Tickled by Thunder
Tiferet
$-U.S. Catholic
Urban Kingdom—R
Victory Herald—R
$-Vision—R
$-Vista
$-War Cry—R
$-Wesleyan Life—R
West Wind Review
$-Whole
$-Women Alive!—R

SHORT STORY: ADVENTURE

ADULT

$-Angels on Earth
$-Animal Trails—R
$-Annals of St. Anne
$-Associated Content—R
Beginnings—R
$-Bridal Guides—R
$-Cappers
CBN.com—R
Christian Radio
$-Dreams & Visions—R
$-Gem—R
$-Haruah—R
Heartlight—R
Infuze
$-Liguorian
$-Rose & Thorn
$-Standard—R
$-Storyteller—R
Studio—R
Urban Kingdom—R
Victory Herald—R
$-Vision—R
$-Vista
$-Weavings—R
$-Writers Notes

CHILDREN

$-American Girl—R
$-Animal Trails—R
Beginnings—R
$-BREAD/God's Children—R
Connecting Point—R
$-Courage—R
Eternal Ink—R
$-Focus/Clubhouse Jr.
$-High Adventure—R
$-Junior Companion—R
$-Kids' Ark
$-New Moon—R
$-Partners—R
$-Passport—R
$-Primary Pal/IL
$-SHINEbrightly—R
Skipping Stones
$-Sparkle—R
Spiritual Voice—R
Sword of the Lord—R
$-Young Christian—R

TEEN/YOUNG ADULT

$-Animal Trails—R
Beginnings—R
$-BREAD/God's Children—R
$-Breakaway
$-Brio
$-Cadet Quest—R
$-CLEAR Direction
$-CLEAR Horizon
$-Credo—R
$-InsideOut—R
$-InTeen—R
$-Partners—R
$-SHINEbrightly—R
Spiritual Voice—R
Sword of the Lord—R
TeensForJC—R
$-Young Adult Today—R
$-Young Christian—R
$-Young Salvationist—R

SHORT STORY: ALLEGORY

ADULT

$-Animal Trails—R
$-Associated Content—R
$-Bridal Guides—R
CBN.com—R
Christian C. L. RECORD—R
$-Christian Journal—R
Christian Woman's Page—R
$-Covenant Companion—R
$-Dragons, Knights & Angels—R
$-Dreams & Visions—R
$-Esprit—R
$-Gem—R
Heartlight—R
$-Home Times—R
$-Ideals—R
$-Indian Life—R
Infuze
$-Liguorian
$-New Wineskins—R
Railroad Evangelist—R
Reverent Submissions—R
Studio—R
Three One Six—R
Victory Herald—R
$-Vision—R
$-Vista

CHILDREN

$-Animal Trails—R
$-Dragons, Knights & Angels—R
$-Nature Friend
Spiritual Voice—R
Sword of the Lord—R
$-Young Christian—R

TEEN/YOUNG ADULT

$-Animal Trails—R
$-Breakaway
$-CLEAR Direction
$-CLEAR Horizon
$-Dragons, Knights & Angels—R
$-Home Times—R
Spiritual Voice—R
Sword of the Lord—R
$-Young Christian—R
$-Young Salvationist—R

SHORT STORY: BIBLICAL

ADULT

$-Animal Trails—R
$-Annals of St. Anne
$-Aujourd'hui Credo—R
Bread of Life—R
$-Bridal Guides—R
$-Catholic Yearbook—R
CBN.com—R
$-CGA World—R
Christian C. L. RECORD—R
$-Christian Journal—R
Christian Online
Christian Ranchman
Christian Woman's Page—R
Congregational Libraries
Connecting Point—R
Crowned with Silver
Desert Call—R
$-Dreams & Visions—R
$-Evangel/IN—R
$-Gem—R
$-Haruah—R
Heartlight—R
Hearts at Home—R
$-Home Times—R
$-Horizons (women)—R
$-Ideals—R
$-Lutheran Journal—R
Lutheran Woman's Quar.
$-National Catholic
$-New Wineskins—R
PrayerWorks—R
$-Purpose—R
Railroad Evangelist—R
Reverent Submissions—R
$-Seek—R
Spirituality for Today
Studio—R
Three One Six—R
Urban Kingdom—R
Victory Herald—R

$-Vista
$-War Cry—R
$-Wesleyan Life—R
$-Whole

CHILDREN

$-Adventures
$-Animal Trails—R
$-BREAD/God's Children—R
Christian Ranchman
$-Discoveries—R
Eternal Ink—R
$-Focus/Clubhouse
$-Kids' Ark
$-Nature Friend
$-Passport—R
$-Pockets—R
$-Sparkle—R
Spiritual Voice—R
Sword of the Lord—R
$-Teach Kids!—R
$-Young Christian—R

TEEN/YOUNG ADULT

$-Animal Trails—R
$-BREAD/God's Children—R
$-Breakaway
Christian Ranchman
$-CLEAR Direction
$-CLEAR Horizon
Crowned with Silver
$-Essential Connection
$-Home Times—R
$-InTeen—R
$-Rock
Spiritual Voice—R
Spirituality for Today
Sword of the Lord—R
TeensForJC—R
$-Young Adult Today—R
$-Young Christian—R

SHORT STORY: CONTEMPORARY

ADULT

African Voices—R
$-Ancient Paths—R
$-Angels on Earth
$-Animal Trails—R
$-Annals of St. Anne
$-Associated Content—R
$-Aujourd'hui Credo—R
Beginnings—R
$-Bridal Guides—R
$-ByLine
$-Canada Lutheran—R
CBN.com—R
$-Christian Century—R
$-Christian Courier/CAN—R
Christian Radio
$-Christian Renewal—R
Christian Woman's Page—R
Connecting Point—R
$-Covenant Companion—R
Diamond Dust
$-DisciplesWorld
$-Dreams & Visions—R
$-Esprit—R
$-Evangel/IN—R
$-Gem—R
$-Haruah—R
Heartlight—R
$-Home Times—R
$-Horizons (adult)—R
Imagine
$-Indian Life—R
Infuze
$-Liguorian
$-Mature Living
$-National Catholic
$-New Wineskins—R
$-New Writer's Mag.
Perspectives—R
Precious Times—R
Railroad Evangelist—R
Relief Journal
Reverent Submissions—R
Ruminate
$-Seek—R
$-Shades of Romance—R
($)-Simply Blessed—R
$-St. Joseph's Messenger—R
$-Standard—R
$-Storyteller—R
Studio—R
$-Teach Kids!—R
Tiferet
$-U.S. Catholic
Urban Kingdom—R
$-Vision—R
$-Vista
$-War Cry—R
West Wind Review
$-Whole
$-Wildwood Reader—R
Xavier Review

CHILDREN

$-Adventures
$-American Girl—R
$-Animal Trails—R
Beginnings—R
$-Cadet Quest—R
$-Discoveries—R
$-Focus/Clubhouse
$-Focus/Clubhouse Jr.
$-Kids' Ark
$-New Moon—R
$-Partners—R
$-Passport—R
$-Pockets—R
$-SHINEbrightly—R
$-Sparkle—R
Spiritual Voice—R
$-Story Mates—R
$-Teach Kids!—R
$-Winner—R
$-Young Christian—R

TEEN/YOUNG ADULT

$-Animal Trails—R
Beginnings—R
$-Breakaway
$-Brio
$-Cadet Quest—R
$-CLEAR Direction
$-CLEAR Horizon
$-Essential Connection
$-Home Times—R
$-Ignite Your Faith
$-InsideOut—R
$-Living My Faith
$-Partners—R
$-Real Faith in Life—R
$-Spirit
Spiritual Voice—R
TeensForJC—R
$-Young Christian—R
$-Young Salvationist—R

SHORT STORY: ETHNIC

ADULT

African Voices—R
$-Animal Trails—R
$-Associated Content—R
$-Bridal Guides—R
$-CGA World—R
$-DisciplesWorld
$-Dreams & Visions—R
$-Gem—R
$-Haruah—R
$-Indian Life—R
$-Purpose—R
$-Seek—R
Studio—R
$-U.S. Catholic
Urban Kingdom—R
Xavier Review

CHILDREN

$-American Girl—R
$-Animal Trails—R
$-Focus/Clubhouse
$-New Moon—R
Skipping Stones
$-Sparkle—R
Spiritual Voice—R
$-Young Christian—R

TEEN/YOUNG ADULT

$-Animal Trails—R
$-Breakaway
$-InsideOut—R
$-SHINEbrightly—R
Spiritual Voice—R
TeensForJC—R
$-Young Christian—R

SHORT STORY: FANTASY

ADULT

$-Associated Content—R
$-Challenging Destiny—R
Connecting Point—R
$-Dragons, Knights & Angels—R
$-Dreams & Visions—R
$-Gem—R
($)-Impact—R
Infuze
$-Rose & Thorn
$-Storyteller—R
Studio—R
$-Tickled by Thunder

CHILDREN

$-Dragons, Knights & Angels—R
$-Focus/Clubhouse
$-New Moon—R
$-SHINEbrightly—R
$-Sparkle—R
Spiritual Voice—R
Sword of the Lord—R

TEEN/YOUNG ADULT

$-CLEAR Direction
$-CLEAR Horizon
$-Credo—R
$-Dragons, Knights & Angels—R
$-InTeen—R
$-SHINEbrightly—R
Spiritual Voice—R
Sword of the Lord—R
TeensForJC—R
$-Young Adult Today—R

SHORT STORY: FRONTIER

ADULT

$-Animal Trails—R
$-Associated Content—R
$-Bridal Guides—R
$-Cappers
Connecting Point—R
$-Gem—R
$-Haruah—R
$-Home Times—R
$-Indian Life—R
Infuze
$-Storyteller—R
Studio—R

CHILDREN

$-Animal Trails—R
Eternal Ink—R
$-High Adventure—R
$-Kids' Ark
$-New Moon—R
$-SHINEbrightly—R
Sword of the Lord—R
$-Young Christian—R

TEEN/YOUNG ADULT

$-Breakaway
$-Credo—R
$-Home Times—R
Spiritual Voice—R
Sword of the Lord—R
$-Young Christian—R

SHORT STORY: FRONTIER/ROMANCE

$-Associated Content—R
$-Bridal Guides—R
$-Cappers
Connecting Point—R
$-Dreams & Visions—R
$-Gem—R
$-Haruah—R
$-Shades of Romance—R
$-Storyteller—R
Studio—R
Urban Kingdom—R

SHORT STORY: HISTORICAL

ADULT

$-Ancient Paths—R
$-Animal Trails—R
$-Associated Content—R
$-Aujourd'hui Credo—R
$-Bridal Guides—R
$-Cappers
CBN.com—R
Christian Ranchman
$-Christian Renewal—R
Connecting Point—R
$-Gem—R
$-Haruah—R
Heartlight—R
$-Home Times—R
$-Indian Life—R
Infuze
Lutheran Woman's Quar.
$-National Catholic
$-New Writer's Mag.
$-Parabola—R
$-Purpose—R
Railroad Evangelist—R
$-Rose & Thorn
$-Seek—R
Spirituality for Today
$-Storyteller—R
Studio—R
Urban Kingdom—R
$-Vista

CHILDREN

$-American Girl—R
$-Animal Trails—R
$-BREAD/God's Children—R
Christian Ranchman
$-Courage—R
$-Focus/Clubhouse
$-Focus/Clubhouse Jr.
$-High Adventure—R
$-Home Times—R
$-Kids' Ark
$-Nature Friend
$-New Moon—R
$-Partners—R
$-Primary Pal/IL
$-SHINEbrightly—R
Skipping Stones
$-Sparkle—R
Spiritual Voice—R
Sword of the Lord—R
$-Young Christian—R

TEEN/YOUNG ADULT

$-Animal Trails—R
$-BREAD/God's Children—R
$-Breakaway
Christian Ranchman
$-Credo—R
$-Home Times—R
$-InsideOut—R
$-InTeen—R
$-Partners—R
$-SHINEbrightly—R
Spiritual Voice—R
Spirituality for Today
Sword of the Lord—R
$-Young Adult Today—R
$-Young Christian—R

SHORT STORY: HISTORICAL/ROMANCE

African Voices—R
Areopagus
$-Associated Content—R
$-Bridal Guides—R
$-Cappers
CBN.com—R
Connecting Point—R
$-Dreams & Visions—R
$-Gem—R
$-Haruah—R
$-Home Times—R
$-Liguorian
$-Shades of Romance—R
$-Storyteller—R
Studio—R
Urban Kingdom—R

SHORT STORY: HUMOROUS

ADULT

African Voices—R
$-Ancient Paths—R
$-Animal Trails—R
$-Associated Content—R
Beginnings—R
$-Bridal Guides—R
$-Canada Lutheran—R
$-Catholic Forester—R
CBN.com—R
$-CGA World—R
$-Christian Courier/CAN—R
$-Christian Journal—R

Christian Radio
Christian Ranchman
Congregational Libraries
Connecting Point—R
$-Covenant Companion—R
$-Dreams & Visions—R
$-Esprit—R
$-Gem—R
$-Haruah—R
Heartlight—R
Hearts at Home—R
$-Home Times—R
$-Horizons (adult)—R
Infuze
$-Liguorian
$-Mature Living
$-Mature Years—R
$-Miraculous Medal
$-National Catholic
$-New Writer's Mag.
$-Over the Back Fence—R
PrayerWorks—R
Presbyterian Outlook
Reverent Submissions—R
$-Seek—R
Spiritual Voice—R
$-Storyteller—R
Studio—R
$-Tickled by Thunder
$-U.S. Catholic
Urban Kingdom—R
Victory Herald—R
West Wind Review

CHILDREN

Beginnings—R
$-Cadet Quest—R
Christian Ranchman
Congregational Libraries
Eternal Ink—R
$-Focus/Clubhouse
$-High Adventure—R
$-Home Times—R
$-New Moon—R
$-SHINEbrightly—R
Skipping Stones
$-Sparkle—R
Spiritual Voice—R
$-Story Mates—R
Sword of the Lord—R
$-Young Christian—R

TEEN/YOUNG ADULT

$-Animal Trails—R
Beginnings—R
$-Breakaway
$-Brio
$-Cadet Quest—R
Christian Ranchman
$-CLEAR Direction
$-CLEAR Horizon
$-Credo—R
$-Essential Connection
$-Home Times—R
$-Ignite Your Faith
$-InsideOut—R
$-InTeen—R
Spiritual Voice—R
Sword of the Lord—R
TeensForJC—R
$-Young Adult Today—R
$-Young Christian—R
$-Young Salvationist—R

SHORT STORY: JUVENILE

$-Adventures
$-American Girl—R
$-Animal Trails—R
Areopagus
$-Associated Content—R
$-Beginner's Friend—R
$-Bridal Guides—R
$-Brio
$-Cadet Quest—R
$-Catholic Forester—R
CBN.com—R
Christian Ranchman
$-Christian Renewal—R
Church Herald & Holiness—R
Congregational Libraries
$-Courage—R
$-Discoveries—R
$-Faces
$-Faith & Family
$-Focus/Clubhouse
$-Focus/Clubhouse Jr.
$-High Adventure—R
$-Indian Life—R
$-Junior Companion—R
$-Keys for Kids—R
$-Kids' Ark
$-Nature Friend
$-New Moon—R
$-Partners—R
$-Passport—R
$-Pockets—R
$-Primary Pal/IL
$-Primary Pal/KS—R
$-Seek—R
$-SHINEbrightly—R
$-Sparkle—R
$-Story Mates—R
$-Teach Kids!—R
TeensForJC—R
$-United Church Observer—R
Victory Herald—R
$-War Cry—R
$-Winner—R

SHORT STORY: LITERARY

ADULT

African Voices—R
$-Ancient Paths—R
$-Associated Content—R
Beginnings—R
$-ByLine
$-Christian Courier/CAN—R
$-Covenant Companion—R
$-Dreams & Visions—R
$-Gem—R
Handmaidens
$-Haruah—R
$-Home Times—R
$-Horizons (adult)—R
Imagine
$-National Catholic
$-New Wineskins—R
Perspectives—R
Reverent Submissions—R
Rock & Sling
$-Rose & Thorn
Ruminate
$-Seek—R
Spirituality for Today
$-Standard—R
$-Storyteller—R
Studio—R
Three One Six—R
$-Tickled by Thunder
Tiferet
$-U.S. Catholic
Urban Kingdom—R
Victory Herald—R
$-War Cry—R
West Wind Review
$-Wildwood Reader—R
Xavier Review

CHILDREN

Beginnings—R
$-New Moon—R
Spiritual Voice—R

TEEN/YOUNG ADULT

Beginnings—R
$-CLEAR Direction
$-CLEAR Horizon
$-Home Times—R
Spiritual Voice—R
Spirituality for Today

SHORT STORY: MYSTERY/ROMANCE

$-Associated Content—R
Beginnings—R
$-Bridal Guides—R
$-Brio
$-ByLine
$-Cappers
Connecting Point—R
$-Dreams & Visions—R
$-Gem—R
$-Great Mystery—R
$-Haruah—R
$-Shades of Romance—R
$-Storyteller—R
Studio—R

TeensForJC—R
Urban Kingdom—R

SHORT STORY: MYSTERY/SUSPENSE

ADULT
$-Animal Trails—R
$-Associated Content—R
Beginnings—R
$-Bridal Guides—R
$-ByLine
$-Cappers
CBN.com—R
Christian Radio
Connecting Point—R
$-Dreams & Visions—R
$-Gem—R
$-Great Mystery—R
$-Haruah—R
Heartlight—R
$-Indian Life—R
Infuze
$-Storyteller—R
Studio—R
$-Tickled by Thunder
$-Writers Notes

CHILDREN
$-American Girl—R
$-Animal Trails—R
Beginnings—R
$-High Adventure—R
$-Kids' Ark
$-New Moon—R
$-SHINEbrightly—R
$-Sparkle—R
Spiritual Voice—R
Sword of the Lord—R
$-Young Christian—R

TEEN/YOUNG ADULT
$-Animal Trails—R
Beginnings—R
$-Breakaway
$-Brio
$-Cadet Quest—R
$-CLEAR Direction
$-CLEAR Horizon
$-Credo—R
$-InTeen—R
$-SHINEbrightly—R
Spiritual Voice—R
Sword of the Lord—R
TeensForJC—R
$-Young Adult Today—R
$-Young Christian—R

SHORT STORY: PARABLES

ADULT
$-Animal Trails—R
$-Annals of St. Anne
$-Associated Content—R
$-Bridal Guides—R
$-Catholic Yearbook—R
$-Christian Courier/CAN—R
$-Christian Journal—R
$-Covenant Companion—R
$-Dreams & Visions—R
$-Esprit—R
$-Gem—R
Heartlight—R
$-Home Times—R
Imagine
($)-Impact—R
$-Indian Life—R
$-Liguorian
$-Lutheran Journal—R
$-Ministry & Liturgy—R
$-New Wineskins—R
Perspectives—R
$-Preaching Well—R
Railroad Evangelist—R
Reverent Submissions—R
$-Seek—R
$-St. Joseph's Messenger—R
Studio—R
$-Testimony—R
Urban Kingdom—R
Victory Herald—R

CHILDREN
$-Animal Trails—R
Eternal Ink—R
$-Faces
$-Focus/Clubhouse Jr.
Skipping Stones
$-Sparkle—R
Spiritual Voice—R
$-Young Christian—R

TEEN/YOUNG ADULT
$-Animal Trails—R
$-Brio
$-CLEAR Direction
$-CLEAR Horizon
$-Home Times—R
$-InTeen—R
$-SHINEbrightly—R
Spiritual Voice—R
TeensForJC—R
$-Testimony—R
$-Young Adult Today—R
$-Young Christian—R
$-Young Salvationist—R

SHORT STORY: PLAYS

Areopagus
Christian Creative Arts
$-Drama Ministry—R
$-Faces
$-Focus/Clubhouse Jr.
Imagine
$-J.A.M.
$-New Wineskins—R
$-RTJ—R
$-SHINEbrightly—R
Studio—R
TeensForJC—R
Urban Kingdom—R

SHORT STORY: ROMANCE

ADULT
$-Ancient Paths—R
$-Animal Trails—R
$-Associated Content—R
$-Bridal Guides—R
$-Cappers
CBN.com—R
Connecting Point—R
$-Dreams & Visions—R
$-Gem—R
$-Haruah—R
Precious Times—R
$-Rose & Thorn
$-Shades of Romance—R
$-Storyteller—R
Studio—R
Urban Kingdom—R
$-Wildwood Reader—R

TEEN/YOUNG ADULT
$-Animal Trails—R
Spiritual Voice—R
TeensForJC—R
$-Young Christian—R

SHORT STORY: SCIENCE FICTION

ADULT
African Voices—R
$-Associated Content—R
$-Challenging Destiny—R
Connecting Point—R
$-Dragons, Knights & Angels—R
$-Dreams & Visions—R
$-Gem—R
$-Home Times—R
Infuze
$-Rose & Thorn
$-Storyteller—R
Studio—R
$-Tickled by Thunder

CHILDREN
$-Dragons, Knights & Angels—R
$-New Moon—R
$-SHINEbrightly—R
$-Sparkle—R
Spiritual Voice—R
Sword of the Lord—R

TEEN/YOUNG ADULT
$-Breakaway
$-Credo—R
$-Dragons, Knights & Angels—R
$-Home Times—R
$-InTeen—R

$-J.A.M.
$-SHINEbrightly—R
Spiritual Voice—R
Sword of the Lord—R
$-Young Adult Today—R

SHORT STORY: SENIOR ADULT FICTION

ADULT

First Call Hospice—R
$-Glad Tidings (Canada)—R
$-Liguorian
$-Live—R
$-Mature Living
PrayerWorks—R
Reverent Submissions—R
$-Seek—R
$-St. Anthony Messenger

SHORT STORY: SKITS

$-Associated Content—R
Crowned with Silver
$-Drama Ministry—R
$-New Wineskins—R
Studio—R
Urban Kingdom—R

CHILDREN

$-Focus/Clubhouse Jr.
$-SHINEbrightly—R
Sword of the Lord—R

TEEN/YOUNG ADULT

Crowned with Silver
$-J.A.M.
$-SHINEbrightly—R
Sword of the Lord—R
TeensForJC—R

SHORT STORY: SPECULATIVE

ADULT

$-Associated Content—R
Bread of Life—R
$-Dreams & Visions—R
$-Home Times—R
Infuze
$-National Catholic
Reverent Submissions—R
Studio—R
Three One Six—R
$-Tickled by Thunder
Urban Kingdom—R

CHILDREN

$-New Moon—R
Spiritual Voice—R

TEEN/YOUNG ADULT

$-Home Times—R
Spiritual Voice—R
TeensForJC—R
$-Young Salvationist—R

SHORT STORY: TEEN/YOUNG ADULT

Beginnings—R
$-BREAD/God's Children—R
$-Breakaway
$-Bridal Guides—R
$-Brio
$-Canada Lutheran—R
$-Catholic Forester—R
CBN.com—R
Christian Ranchman
$-CLEAR Direction
$-CLEAR Horizon
$-Credo—R
Crowned with Silver
Diamond Dust
$-Essential Connection
$-Home Times—R
$-Ignite Your Faith
$-Indian Life—R
$-InsideOut—R
$-InTeen—R
$-J.A.M.
$-Living My Faith
$-New Moon—R
Precious Times—R
$-Real Faith in Life—R
$-Rock
$-Seek—R
$-Sharing the VICTORY—R
Skipping Stones
$-Spirit
Spirituality for Today
TeensForJC—R
$-Testimony—R
Tiferet
Urban Kingdom—R
Victory Herald—R
$-War Cry—R
West Wind Review
$-Young Adult Today—R
$-Young Salvationist—R
$-Youth Compass—R

SHORT STORY: WESTERNS

ADULT

$-Animal Trails—R
$-Associated Content—R
$-Bridal Guides—R
$-Cappers
Christian Ranchman
$-Dreams & Visions—R
Infuze
$-Storyteller—R
Studio—R
$-Tickled by Thunder

CHILDREN

$-Animal Trails—R
Christian Ranchman
$-High Adventure—R
$-Kids' Ark
$-Sparkle—R
Spiritual Voice—R
Sword of the Lord—R
$-Young Christian—R

TEEN/YOUNG ADULT

$-Animal Trails—R
Christian Ranchman
$-Credo—R
Spiritual Voice—R
Sword of the Lord—R
$-Young Christian—R

SINGLES ISSUES

ADULT/GENERAL

$-Advance
African Voices—R
$-Animal Trails—R
$-Annals of St. Anne
Anointed Pages
$-Associated Content—R
$-BGC World—R
$-Bible Advocate—R
Bread of Life—R
$-Bridal Guides—R
CBN.com—R
Channels—R
$-Christian Examiner
$-Christian Journal—R
Christian Online
Christian Ranchman
$-Christian Single
Christian Single Online
$-ChristianWeek—R
$-Chronicle Christian
$-City Light News—R
($)-Community Spirit—R
Disciple's Journal—R
$-Dovetail—R
$-Evangel/IN—R
Evangelical Advocate—R
$-Faith Today
$-Family Smart E-tips—R
$-Focus on the Family
$-Gem—R
Godly Places
Good News Journal—R
Heartlight—R
$-Home Times—R
$-Homeschooling Today—R
$-HonorBound—R
HopeKeepers—R
$-In Touch
$-Indian Life—R
$-Light & Life
$-Liguorian
$-Live—R
Looking Up
$-Lookout
Men of the Cross
$-Minnesota Christian—R

$-Montgomery's Journey
($)-Mutuality—R
Penned from the Heart—R
$-Power for Living—R
Priscilla Papers
$-Psychology for Living—R
$-Seek—R
Sight 360—R
SingleAgain.com—R
Spiritual Voice—R
$-St. Anthony Messenger
$-Testimony—R
Three One Six—R
$-Today's Christian—R
$-Together—R
Trumpeter—R
$-U.S. Catholic
Urban Kingdom—R
$-Vibrant Life—R
$-Vista
$-War Cry—R
$-Wesleyan Life—R
$-Wildwood Reader—R
Wisconsin Christian
$-World & I—R

CHRISTIAN EDUCATION/LIBRARY

$-Youth & CE Leadership

DAILY DEVOTIONALS

Penned from the Heart—R

MISSIONS

Women of the Harvest

PASTORS/LEADERS

$-Interpreter
$-Ministry Today
$-Word & World

TEEN/YOUNG ADULT

$-Boundless Webzine—R
$-Breakaway
$-InsideOut—R
$-InTeen—R
$-Passageway.org—R
$-TC Magazine
TeensForJC—R
$-Young Salvationist—R

WOMEN

$-At the Center—R
$-Canticle
CelebrateMoms—R
Christian Woman's Page—R
Christian Women Today—R
$-Godly Business Woman—R
$-Hope for Women
$-Inspired Living—R
$-inSpirit—R
Ladies First
($)-Shalom Bayit
($)-Simply Blessed—R
$-SpiritLed Woman
$-Today's Christian Woman—R
Together with God—R
Virtuous Woman—R
Women Today—R
$-WT Online—R

SMALL GROUP HELPS*

ADULT/GENERAL

$-Animal Trails—R
$-Bridal Guides—R
$-Christian Standard—R
$-City Light News—R
Evangel/OR—R
Reverent Submissions—R
$-Seek—R
Urban Kingdom—R
Victory Herald—R

PASTORS/LEADERS

$-Ministry Today
Pulpit Helps—R

TEEN/YOUNG ADULT

$-Boundless Webzine—R
$-Young Christian—R

SOCIAL JUSTICE

ADULT/GENERAL

$-Advance
$-Animal Trails—R
$-Arkansas Catholic—R
$-Arlington Catholic
$-Associated Content—R
$-Aujourd'hui Credo—R
$-Bridal Guides—R
$-Catholic Peace Voice—R
CBN.com—R
Channels—R
$-Christian Citizen USA
$-Christian Courier/CAN—R
Christian Online
$-Christian Response—R
$-Christian Standard—R
$-Christianity Today—R
$-ChristianWeek—R
$-Chronicle Christian Citizen USA—R
$-City Light News—R
$-Commonweal
($)-Community Spirit—R
$-Company—R
$-Covenant Companion—R
$-Creative Nonfiction
$-Cresset
$-Culture Wars—R
Desert Call—R
$-Dovetail—R
Evangelical Advocate—R
$-Faith & Family
$-Faith Today
$-Gem—R
$-Home Times—R
$-In Touch
$-Inland NW Christian
Island Catholic
$-Light & Life
$-Liguorian
Looking Up
$-Lookout
$-Men of Integrity—R
$-Minnesota Christian—R
Mosaic—R
($)-Mutuality—R
$-National Catholic
$-New Wineskins—R
$-Our Sunday Visitor—R
$-Parabola—R
Penned from the Heart—R
Perspectives—R
$-Prairie Messenger—R
Priscilla Papers
$-Prism
Rare Jewel—R
Salt of the Earth
$-Salvo
$-Science & Spirit
$-Seek—R
Sight 360—R
Silver Wings—R
$-Social Justice—R
Society/Prevention of Cruelty
$-Spiritual Life
Spiritual Voice—R
$-St. Anthony Messenger
$-St. Joseph's Messenger—R
$-Testimony—R
Three One Six—R
$-Today's Christian—R
$-Together—R
Trumpeter—R
$-U.S. Catholic
$-United Church Observer—R
Urban Kingdom—R
$-Way of St. Francis—R
$-World & I—R

CHILDREN

$-Pockets—R
Skipping Stones

CHRISTIAN EDUCATION/LIBRARY

Catholic Library
$-Journal/Adventist Ed.—R
$-Momentum
$-RTJ—R

MISSIONS

$-Glad Tidings (Canada)—R
Missiology

PASTORS/LEADERS

$-African American Pulpit
$-Barefoot—R
$-Christian Century—R
$-Clergy Journal—R
$-Interpreter

Jour./Pastoral Care—R
Sharing the Practice—R
Theological Digest—R
$-Torch Legacy Leader

TEEN/YOUNG ADULT
$-Boundless Webzine—R
$-Devo'Zine—R
$-Passageway.org—R
$-Spirit
$-TC Magazine
TeensForJC—R
$-True Girl
$-Young Christian—R
$-Young Salvationist—R

WOMEN
$-Esprit—R
$-Herizons
$-Horizons (women)—R
$-inSpirit—R
Making Waves

SOCIOLOGY

ADULT/GENERAL
$-Anglican Journal
$-Associated Content—R
$-Catholic Peace Voice—R
$-Christian Citizen USA
$-Christian Courier/CAN—R
Christian Online
$-Chronicle Christian
($)-Community Spirit—R
$-Creative Nonfiction
$-Culture Wars—R
$-Dovetail—R
Evangelical Advocate—R
$-Faith Today
$-Gem—R
Jour. of Church & State
$-Light & Life
$-Montgomery's Journey
$-National Catholic
$-Parabola—R
Perspectives—R
Priscilla Papers
$-Salvo
$-Science & Spirit
Sight 360—R
$-Social Justice—R
Spiritual Voice—R
$-St. Anthony Messenger
$-Testimony—R
Trumpeter—R
Urban Kingdom—R
$-World & I—R

PASTORS/LEADERS
Engage
Jour./Amer. Soc./Chur. Growth—R
$-Torch Legacy Leader
$-Word & World

TEEN/YOUNG ADULT
$-Boundless Webzine—R
$-InTeen—R
TeensForJC—R

WOMEN
($)-Beyond the Bend—R

SPIRITUAL GIFTS

ADULT/GENERAL
African Voices—R
$-Animal Trails—R
$-Bible Advocate—R
Bread of Life—R
$-Bridal Guides—R
CBN.com—R
Channels—R
Christian Motorsports
Christian Online
Christian Ranchman
$-Christian Standard—R
$-Christianity Today—R
$-ChristianWeek—R
$-Chronicle Christian
$-City Light News—R
$-Covenant Companion—R
$-Dovetail—R
Evangelical Advocate—R
$-Faith & Family
$-Faith & Friends—R
$-Faith Today
$-Home Times—R
HopeKeepers—R
$-Light & Life
$-Liguorian
$-Live—R
$-Mature Years—R
$-Men of Integrity—R
Mosaic—R
($)-Mutuality—R
$-New Freeman—R
$-New Wineskins—R
$-On Mission
Penned from the Heart—R
$-Positive Thinking—R
PrayerWorks—R
Priscilla Papers
Regent Global—R
Reverent Submissions—R
Sacred Journey—R
$-Seek—R
Sight 360—R
Silver Wings—R
Spiritual Voice—R
$-St. Anthony Messenger
$-Stewardship—R
Sword and Trumpet
$-Testimony—R
$-Today's Christian—R
$-Together—R
Trumpeter—R
Urban Kingdom—R
$-Vista
$-Way of St. Francis—R

CHILDREN
$-BREAD/God's Children—R
$-Our Little Friend—R
$-Primary Treasure—R
$-Sparkle—R

DAILY DEVOTIONALS
Penned from the Heart—R

PASTORS/LEADERS
$-Interpreter
Ministry in Motion—R
$-Ministry Today
$-RevWriter Resource
$-Worship Leader

TEEN/YOUNG ADULT
$-Breakaway
$-Passageway.org—R
$-TC Magazine
TeensForJC—R
$-Young Christian—R

WOMEN
($)-Beyond the Bend—R
Christian Woman's Page—R
$-Godly Business Woman—R
$-Hope for Women
$-Inspired Living—R
$-inSpirit—R
$-Journey
Just Between Us—R
P31 Woman—R
Precious Times—R
Proverbs 31 Sisters—R
$-SpiritLed Woman
Together with God—R
Virtuous Woman—R
Woman of Worth—R
Women Today—R
$-WT Online—R

WRITERS
Opinari—R

SPIRITUALITY

ADULT/GENERAL
African Voices—R
($)-AGAIN—R
$-Alive Now—R
American Tract—R
$-Angels on Earth
$-Animal Trails—R
$-Annals of St. Anne
Anointed Pages
$-Arkansas Catholic—R
$-Arlington Catholic
$-Associated Content—R
$-Atlantic Catholic
$-Aujourd'hui Credo—R
$-Bible Advocate—R

Bread of Life—R
Breakthrough Intercessor—R
$-Bridal Guides—R
$-Catholic Digest—R
$-Catholic Peace Voice—R
CBN.com—R
$-CGA World—R
Channels—R
Christian C. L. RECORD—R
$-Christian Courier/CAN—R
$-Christian Journal—R
Christian Online
Christian Ranchman
$-Christianity Today—R
$-ChristianWeek—R
$-Chronicle Christian
Church of England News
$-City Light News—R
$-Common Ground—R
($)-Community Spirit—R
$-Covenant Companion—R
$-Culture Wars—R
Desert Call—R
$-Discipleship Journal—R
Divine Ascent
$-Dovetail—R
$-Episcopal Life—R
Evangelical Advocate—R
$-Faith & Family
$-Faith & Friends—R
$-Faith Today
$-Family Digest—R
First Call Hospice—R
$-Gem—R
$-God Allows U-Turns—R
$-Good News—R
Good News Journal—R
$-Guideposts—R
Heartlight—R
$-Home Times—R
$-Horizons (adult)—R
Imagine
$-Inland NW Christian
Island Catholic
Leaves—R
$-Lifeglow—R
LifeTimes Catholic
$-Light & Life
$-Liguorian
$-Live—R
$-Living Church
Looking Up
$-Lookout
$-Mature Years—R
$-Men of Integrity—R
Men of the Cross
$-Messenger/Sacred Heart
$-Messenger/St. Anthony
$-Minnesota Christian—R
$-National Catholic
$-New Freeman—R
New Heart—R
$-New Wineskins—R
$-On Mission
$-Our Sunday Visitor—R
$-Parabola—R
Parents & Teens—R
Pegasus Review—R
Penned from the Heart—R
Penwood Review
$-Positive Thinking—R
$-Prairie Messenger—R
Presbyterian Outlook
$-Presbyterians Today—R
Priscilla Papers
$-Prism
$-Pure Inspiration—R
Sacred Journey—R
$-Seek—R
SingleAgain.com—R
$-Spiritual Life
Spiritual Voice—R
Spirituality for Today
$-St. Anthony Messenger
$-St. Joseph's Messenger—R
$-Standard—R
Star of Zion
$-Stewardship—R
Sword and Trumpet
$-Testimony—R
Three One Six—R
$-Today's Christian—R
$-Together—R
Trumpeter—R
$-U.S. Catholic
Urban Kingdom—R
Victory Herald—R
$-War Cry—R
$-Way of St. Francis—R
$-Weavings—R
$-Whole
$-Wittenburg Door—R
$-World & I—R

CHILDREN

$-BREAD/God's Children—R
$-New Moon—R
Skipping Stones

CHRISTIAN EDUCATION/LIBRARY

Catholic Library
$-Children's Ministry
Jour./Ed. & Christian Belief—R
Jour./Research on Christian Ed.
$-Momentum
$-RTJ—R

DAILY DEVOTIONALS

Penned from the Heart—R

MISSIONS

$-Evangelical Missions—R
Missiology

PASTORS/LEADERS

$-Christian Century—R
$-Diocesan Dialogue—R
$-Emmanuel
$-Interpreter
Jour./Pastoral Care—R
$-Leadership—R
$-Lutheran Partners—R
$-Ministry Today
$-Proclaim—R
$-Review for Religious
$-RevWriter Resource
Rick Warren's Ministry—R
Sharing the Practice—R
Theological Digest—R
$-Today's Parish—R
$-Word & World
$-Worship Leader

TEEN/YOUNG ADULT

$-Boundless Webzine—R
$-Breakaway
$-CLEAR Direction
$-CLEAR Horizon
$-InTeen—R
$-Passageway.org—R
$-TC Magazine
TeensForJC—R
$-True Girl
$-Young Adult Today—R
$-Young Christian—R

WOMEN

($)-Beyond the Bend—R
$-Canticle
CelebrateMoms—R
Christian Woman's Page—R
$-Godly Business Woman—R
Handmaiden—R
$-Heart & Soul
$-Herizons
$-Hope for Women
$-Horizons (women)—R
$-Inspired Living—R
$-inSpirit—R
$-Journey
Just Between Us—R
Lutheran Woman's Quar.
Precious Times—R
$-SpiritLed Woman
$-Today's Christian Woman—R
Women Today—R
$-WT Online—R

WRITERS

Areopagus

SPIRITUAL LIFE

ADULT/GENERAL

$-Animal Trails—R
$-Arkansas Catholic—R
$-Associated Content—R
$-Atlantic Catholic

$-Aujourd'hui Credo—R
$-Bible Advocate—R
Bread of Life—R
Breakthrough Intercessor—R
$-Bridal Guides—R
$-Cathedral Age—R
$-Catholic Digest—R
$-Catholic Peace Voice—R
$-Catholic Yearbook—R
CBN.com—R
Channels—R
$-Christian Examiner
$-Christian Journal—R
Christian Online
Christian Ranchman
$-Christian Research
$-ChristianWeek—R
$-Chronicle Christian
Church Herald & Holiness—R
$-City Light News—R
($)-Community Spirit—R
$-Discipleship Journal—R
Divine Ascent
$-En Confianza
Eternal Ink—R
Evangel/OR—R
Evangelical Advocate—R
$-Faith & Family
$-Faith & Friends—R
$-Faith Today
$-Family Digest—R
$-Focus on the Family
$-God Allows U-Turns—R
$-Home Times—R
$-Homeschooling Today—R
$-Horizons (adult)—R
$-In Touch
$-Indian Life—R
$-Light & Life
$-Liguorian
$-Live—R
Looking Up
$-Lookout
$-Lutheran Journal—R
$-Mature Living
$-Men of Integrity—R
$-Minnesota Christian—R
$-Montgomery's Journey
Mosaic—R
$-National Catholic
New Heart—R
$-New Wineskins—R
$-On Mission
$-Parabola—R
Penned from the Heart—R
Perspectives—R
PrayerWorks—R
$-Presbyterians Today—R
Priscilla Papers
$-Pure Inspiration—R
$-Purpose—R
Regent Global—R
Reverent Submissions—R
Ruminate
Sacred Journey—R
$-Science & Spirit
$-Seek—R
Sight 360—R
$-Significant Living—R
Silver Wings—R
SingleAgain.com—R
Spiritual Voice—R
Spirituality for Today
$-St. Anthony Messenger
$-Stewardship—R
Sword and Trumpet
$-Testimony—R
Three One Six—R
$-Today's Christian—R
$-Together—R
$-U.S. Catholic
Urban Kingdom—R
Victory Herald—R
$-Vista
$-Weavings—R
$-Whole
$-Wildwood Reader—R

CHILDREN
$-BREAD/God's Children—R
Skipping Stones
$-Sparkle—R

CHRISTIAN EDUCATION/LIBRARY
$-Momentum
$-Youth & CE Leadership

DAILY DEVOTIONALS
Penned from the Heart—R

MISSIONS
$-Glad Tidings (Canada)—R

PASTORS/LEADERS
$-African American Pulpit
$-Barefoot—R
Christian Ed. Jour. (CA)—R
$-Interpreter
Jour./Pastoral Care—R
$-Leadership—R
$-Ministry
$-Ministry Today
$-Review for Religious
$-RevWriter Resource
$-Willow—R

TEEN/YOUNG ADULT
$-Boundless Webzine—R
$-Breakaway
$-Brio
$-InsideOut—R
$-Insight—R
$-TC Magazine
$-True Girl
$-Young Christian—R
$-Young Salvationist—R

WOMEN
$-Canticle
CelebrateMoms—R
Christian Woman's Page—R
First Lady
$-Fullfill
$-Hope for Women
$-Horizons (women)—R
$-Inspired Living—R
$-inSpirit—R
$-Journey
More to Life
P31 Woman—R
Precious Times—R
($)-Simply Blessed—R
Together with God—R
Virtuous Woman—R
Woman of Worth—R
$-Women Alive!—R
Women Today—R
$-WT Online—R

SPIRITUAL RENEWAL

ADULT/GENERAL
$-Animal Trails—R
$-Arkansas Catholic—R
$-Associated Content—R
$-BGC World—R
$-Bible Advocate—R
Bread of Life—R
Breakthrough Intercessor—R
$-Bridal Guides—R
CBN.com—R
$-Christian Journal—R
Christian Online
Christian Ranchman
$-ChristianWeek—R
$-Chronicle Christian
Church Herald & Holiness—R
$-City Light News—R
($)-Community Spirit—R
Encompass
$-Evangel/IN—R
Evangel/OR—R
Evangelical Advocate—R
$-Home Times—R
$-HonorBound—R
$-Indian Life—R
$-Liguorian
$-Live—R
$-Lookout
$-Men of Integrity—R
Mosaic—R
$-New Wineskins—R
$-On Mission
$-Parabola—R
PrayerWorks—R
$-Pure Inspiration—R
Reverent Submissions—R

Sacred Journey—R
$-Seek—R
Spiritual Voice—R
Spirituality for Today
Sword and Trumpet
$-Testimony—R
Three One Six—R
$-Today's Christian—R
$-Today's Pentecostal—R
Urban Kingdom—R
Victory Herald—R
$-Vista
$-Wildwood Reader—R

CHILDREN
$-BREAD/God's Children—R
$-Sparkle—R

MISSIONS
$-Glad Tidings (Canada)—R

PASTORS/LEADERS
$-African American Pulpit
$-Christian Century—R
Christian Ed. Jour. (CA)—R
$-Interpreter
$-Leadership—R
$-Lutheran Partners—R
$-Ministry Today
$-RevWriter Resource
Theological Digest—R

TEEN/YOUNG ADULT
$-Boundless Webzine—R
$-Breakaway
$-CLEAR Direction
$-CLEAR Horizon
$-TC Magazine
$-True Girl
$-Young Christian—R
$-Young Salvationist—R

WOMEN
$-Canticle
CelebrateMoms—R
Christian Woman's Page—R
Hearts at Home—R
$-Hope for Women
$-Horizons (women)—R
$-Inspired Living—R
$-inSpirit—R
$-Journey
Precious Times—R
Proverbs 31 Sisters—R
Together with God—R
Virtuous Woman—R
Woman of Worth—R
$-Women Alive!—R
Women Today—R
$-WT Online—R

SPIRITUAL WARFARE

ADULT/GENERAL
($)-AGAIN—R
$-Angels on Earth
$-Animal Trails—R
$-Associated Content—R
$-Believer's Bay
$-Bible Advocate—R
Bread of Life—R
Breakthrough Intercessor—R
$-Bridal Guides—R
CBN.com—R
$-Celebrate Life—R
$-CGA World—R
Channels—R
Christian C. L. RECORD—R
$-Christian Citizen USA
$-Christian Journal—R
Christian Online
Christian Ranchman
$-Christian Research
$-Christianity Today—R
$-ChristianWeek—R
$-Chronicle Christian
$-City Light News—R
($)-Community Spirit—R
$-Discipleship Journal—R
Eternal Ink—R
Evangelical Advocate—R
$-Faith & Friends—R
$-Faith Today
$-Gem—R
$-Good News—R
Heartlight—R
$-Home Times—R
Leaves—R
$-Light & Life
$-Live—R
$-Lookout
$-Men of Integrity—R
Men of the Cross
Mosaic—R
$-New Freeman—R
New Heart—R
$-New Wineskins—R
Penned from the Heart—R
Prayer Closet
$-Purpose—R
Reverent Submissions—R
$-Seek—R
Spiritual Voice—R
$-St. Anthony Messenger
Sword and Trumpet
Sword of the Lord—R
$-Testimony—R
Three One Six—R
Trumpeter—R
Urban Kingdom—R
Wisconsin Christian

CHILDREN
$-BREAD/God's Children—R

DAILY DEVOTIONALS
Penned from the Heart—R

MISSIONS
Railroad Evangelist—R

PASTORS/LEADERS
$-Growth Points—R
$-Let's Worship
$-Ministry Today
$-Pray!—R
Rick Warren's Ministry—R

TEEN/YOUNG ADULT
$-Breakaway
$-CLEAR Direction
$-CLEAR Horizon
$-Passageway.org—R
TeensForJC—R
$-Young Christian—R
$-Young Salvationist—R

WOMEN
$-Godly Business Woman—R
Handmaiden—R
$-Hope for Women
$-Inspired Living—R
$-inSpirit—R
$-Journey
Just Between Us—R
Precious Times—R
($)-Simply Blessed—R
Together with God—R
Virtuous Woman—R
Women Today—R
$-WT Online—R

SPORTS/RECREATION

ADULT/GENERAL
$-Abilities
$-Angels on Earth
$-Animal Trails—R
$-Arlington Catholic
$-Associated Content—R
$-Bridal Guides—R
CBN.com—R
Christian Courier/WI—R
Christian Radio
$-Christian Renewal—R
$-Chronicle Christian
$-City Light News—R
($)-Community Spirit—R
Connecting Point—R
Diamond Dust
Eternal Ink—R
$-Faith Today
$-Family Smart E-tips—R
$-Gem—R
$-Gospel Today—R
$-Grand
$-Guideposts—R
Heartbeat/CMA
Heartland Gatekeeper—R
$-Home Times—R
$-HonorBound—R
$-In Touch

$-Lifeglow—R
$-Light & Life
$-Living Light—R
$-Lookout
$-Minnesota Christian—R
$-New Freeman—R
$-Parabola—R
Reverent Submissions—R
Sight 360—R
Spiritual Voice—R
$-Sports Spectrum
$-St. Anthony Messenger
$-Storyteller—R
$-Testimony—R
$-Today's Christian—R
Urban Kingdom—R
$-Vibrant Life—R
$-World & I—R

CHILDREN
$-American Girl—R
$-Cadet Quest—R
$-SHINEbrightly—R
$-Sparkle—R

PASTORS/LEADERS
$-Cornerstone Youth—R

TEEN/YOUNG ADULT
$-Boundless Webzine—R
$-Brio
$-Credo—R
$-InTeen—R
$-Listen—R
$-Passageway.org—R
$-Real Faith in Life—R
$-Sharing the VICTORY—R
$-Steelroots
$-TC Magazine
TeensForJC—R
$-Young Christian—R
$-Young Salvationist—R

WOMEN
$-Hope for Women

STEWARDSHIP

ADULT/GENERAL
$-Angels on Earth
$-Bible Advocate—R
Bread of Life—R
$-Bridal Guides—R
$-Catholic Yearbook—R
CBN.com—R
$-Celebrate Life—R
Channels—R
$-Christian Courier/CAN—R
$-Christian Journal—R
Christian Online
Christian Ranchman
$-Christian Standard—R
$-ChristianWeek—R
$-Chronicle Christian
Church Herald & Holiness—R
$-City Light News—R
($)-Community Spirit—R
$-Covenant Companion—R
Creation Care—R
$-Discipleship Journal—R
$-Evangel/IN—R
Evangelical Advocate—R
$-Faith Today
$-Family Digest—R
$-Focus on the Family
$-Gem—R
Highway News—R
$-Lifeglow—R
$-Light & Life
$-Live—R
$-Living Church
Looking Up
$-Lookout
$-Lutheran Journal—R
NRB Magazine—R
$-Our Sunday Visitor—R
Penned from the Heart—R
Perspectives—R
$-Positive Thinking—R
$-Power for Living—R
Presbyterian Outlook
$-Prism
Regent Global—R
$-Seek—R
Spiritual Voice—R
$-St. Anthony Messenger
$-Stewardship—R
$-Testimony—R
$-Today's Christian—R
Trumpeter—R
$-U.S. Catholic
$-United Church Observer—R
Urban Kingdom—R
$-Wesleyan Life—R
$-Wireless Age—R

CHILDREN
$-Guide—R
$-SHINEbrightly—R
$-Sparkle—R

CHRISTIAN EDUCATION/LIBRARY
$-Momentum

DAILY DEVOTIONALS
Penned from the Heart—R

MISSIONS
$-Glad Tidings (Canada)—R

PASTORS/LEADERS
Christian Management—R
$-Clergy Journal—R
$-InSite—R
$-Interpreter
$-Let's Worship
Ministry in Motion—R
$-Ministry Today
$-Net Results
$-Preaching Well—R
$-RevWriter Resource
Sharing the Practice—R
$-Your Church—R

TEEN/YOUNG ADULT
$-Boundless Webzine—R
$-Passageway.org—R
$-TC Magazine
TeensForJC—R
$-Young Christian—R
$-Young Salvationist—R

WOMEN
Crowned with Silver
$-Esprit—R
$-Godly Business Woman—R
$-Hope for Women
$-Horizons (women)—R
$-Inspired Living—R
$-Journey
Just Between Us—R
P31 Woman—R
Precious Times—R
$-Today's Christian Woman—R
Together with God—R
Virtuous Woman—R
$-WT Online—R

WRITERS
Opinari—R

TAKE-HOME PAPERS

ADULT/GENERAL
$-Evangel/IN—R
$-Gem—R
$-Gems of Truth—R
$-Horizons (adult)—R
$-Live—R
$-Power for Living—R
$-Purpose—R
$-Seek—R
$-Standard—R
$-Vision—R
$-Vista

CHILDREN
$-Adventures
$-Beginner's Friend—R
$-Celebrate
$-Courage—R
$-Discoveries—R
$-Good News—R
$-Good News (child)
$-Junior Companion—R
$-JuniorWay
$-Our Little Friend—R
$-Partners—R
$-Passport—R
$-Preschool Playhouse (child)
$-Primary Pal/IL
$-Primary Pal/KS—R

$-Primary Street
$-Primary Treasure—R
$-Promise
$-Seeds
$-Story Mates—R
$-Venture

TEEN/YOUNG ADULT
$-Insight—R
$-Living My Faith
$-Rock
Visions
$-Youth Compass—R

TEACHER HELPS*

ADULT/GENERAL
$-Animal Trails—R
$-City Light News—R
$-Home Times—R
$-Seek—R
Victory Herald—R

CHRISTIAN EDUCATION/LIBRARY
Christian Early Ed.—R

PASTORS/LEADERS
Christian Ed. Jour. (CA)—R
$-Ministry Today
Pulpit Helps—R

TEEN/YOUNG ADULT
$-Young Christian—R

THEOLOGICAL

ADULT/GENERAL
($)-AGAIN—R
$-Alive Now—R
$-America
$-Anglican Journal
$-Annals of St. Anne
$-Arkansas Catholic—R
$-Arlington Catholic
$-Atlantic Catholic
$-Aujourd'hui Credo—R
$-B.C. Catholic—R
$-Bible Advocate—R
byFaith
$-Cathedral Age—R
$-Catholic Peace Voice—R
$-Catholic Yearbook—R
CBN.com—R
Channels—R
$-Christian Courier/CAN—R
$-Christian Journal—R
Christian Online
Christian Ranchman
$-Christian Renewal—R
$-Christian Research
$-Christian Standard—R
$-Christianity Today—R
$-Chronicle Christian
Church Herald & Holiness—R
Church of England News
($)-Community Spirit—R
Creation Care—R
$-Cresset
$-Culture Wars—R
Divine Ascent
$-Dovetail—R
Encompass
$-Episcopal Life—R
$-Eureka Street
Evangelical Advocate—R
Evangelical Times
$-Faith Today
Founders Journal
$-Good News—R
$-Horizons (adult)—R
$-Light & Life
$-Live—R
$-Living Church
$-Lookout
$-Lutheran Journal—R
$-Messenger/Sacred Heart
$-Minnesota Christian—R
MovieGuide
$-National Catholic
$-New Freeman—R
$-New Wineskins—R
$-Parabola—R
Perspectives—R
$-Prairie Messenger—R
Presbyterian Outlook
Priscilla Papers
Purpose Magazine—R
$-Science & Spirit
$-Social Justice—R
$-Spiritual Life
Spiritual Voice—R
$-St. Anthony Messenger
Star of Zion
$-Testimony—R
Three One Six—R
Trumpeter—R
$-U.S. Catholic
$-United Church Observer—R
Urban Kingdom—R
$-Way of St. Francis—R

CHRISTIAN EDUCATION/LIBRARY
Jour. of Christianity—R

DAILY DEVOTIONALS
Penned from the Heart—R

MISSIONS
Missiology

PASTORS/LEADERS
$-African American Pulpit
$-Catechumenate
$-Christian Century—R
$-Clergy Journal—R
Cross Currents
$-Diocesan Dialogue—R
$-Growth Points—R
$-Interpretation
Jour./Amer. Soc./Chur. Growth—R
Jour./Pastoral Care—R
Lutheran Forum—R
$-Lutheran Partners—R
$-Ministry & Liturgy—R
$-Parish Liturgy—R
$-Preaching Well—R
$-Proclaim—R
$-Reformed Worship—R
$-RevWriter Resource
Rick Warren's Ministry—R
Sewanee Theo. Review
Sharing the Practice—R
$-This Rock
$-Today's Parish—R
$-Word & World
$-Worship Leader

TEEN/YOUNG ADULT
$-Boundless Webzine—R
$-Breakaway
$-CLEAR Direction
$-CLEAR Horizon
$-InTeen—R
$-Passageway.org—R
TeensForJC—R
$-Young Salvationist—R

WOMEN
$-Canticle
$-Esprit—R
$-Godly Business Woman—R
$-Horizons (women)—R
Making Waves

THINK PIECES

ADULT/GENERAL
$-Alive Now—R
$-Animal Trails—R
$-Annals of St. Anne
$-Associated Content—R
Baptist Standard
$-Bridal Guides—R
$-Catholic Forester—R
$-Catholic Peace Voice—R
$-CGA World—R
$-Christian Courier/CAN—R
Christian Online
$-Christianity Today—R
$-ChristianWeek—R
$-Chronicle Christian
$-City Light News—R
($)-Community Spirit—R
Creation Care—R
Desert Call—R
$-Dovetail—R
$-Episcopal Life—R
Evangelical Advocate—R
$-Faith Today
First Call Hospice—R
$-Gem—R

Good News Journal—R
$-Haruah—R
Heartlight—R
$-Home Times—R
$-In Touch
$-Lifeglow—R
$-Light & Life
Looking Up
$-Lookout
$-Minnesota Christian—R
$-New Wineskins—R
$-On Mission
$-Parabola—R
Pegasus Review—R
Penned from the Heart—R
Penwood Review
$-Positive Thinking—R
Presbyterian Outlook
Purpose Magazine—R
Reverent Submissions—R
$-Science & Spirit
$-Seek—R
Spiritual Voice—R
$-St. Anthony Messenger
$-Stewardship—R
$-Testimony—R
Three One Six—R
$-Today's Christian—R
Trumpeter—R
$-U.S. Catholic
Urban Kingdom—R
$-Way of St. Francis—R
$-Whole
$-Wittenburg Door—R
$-World & I—R

CHILDREN
$-Courage—R
Skipping Stones

CHRISTIAN EDUCATION/LIBRARY
$-Children's Ministry

PASTORS/LEADERS
Alpha News
$-Catholic Servant
$-Ministry Today
Rick Warren's Ministry—R
$-Word & World

TEEN/YOUNG ADULT
$-Boundless Webzine—R
$-Passageway.org—R
$-Real Faith in Life—R
$-TC Magazine
TeensForJC—R
$-Young Christian—R
$-Young Salvationist—R

WOMEN
CelebrateMoms—R
Crowned with Silver
$-Godly Business Woman—R

WRITERS
Areopagus
Money the Write Way—R
Opinari—R

TIME MANAGEMENT

ADULT/GENERAL
$-Animal Trails—R
$-Associated Content—R
$-Bridal Guides—R
$-Catholic Forester—R
$-CBA Retailers
CBN.com—R
Christian Business
$-Christian Journal—R
Christian Online
$-ChristianWeek—R
$-Chronicle Christian
$-City Light News—R
($)-Community Spirit—R
Disciple's Journal—R
Evangelical Advocate—R
$-Focus on the Family
$-Gem—R
Good News Journal—R
$-Home Times—R
$-Homeschooling Today—R
$-HonorBound—R
HopeKeepers—R
$-In Touch
LarkNews.com
$-Lifeglow—R
$-Light & Life
$-Live—R
$-Living Light—R
$-Lookout
Men of the Cross
Missionwares
NRB Magazine—R
$-Our Sunday Visitor—R
Parents & Teens—R
Penned from the Heart—R
$-Positive Thinking—R
Regent Global—R
Sight 360—R
Spiritual Voice—R
$-St. Anthony Messenger
$-Stewardship—R
$-Testimony—R
$-Today's Christian—R
$-Together—R
Trumpeter—R
Urban Kingdom—R
$-Victory in Grace—R
$-Wireless Age—R
$-World & I—R

CHRISTIAN EDUCATION/LIBRARY
Catholic Library
Christian Early Ed.—R
Christian Librarian—R
$-Resource—R
$-Youth & CE Leadership

DAILY DEVOTIONALS
Penned from the Heart—R

PASTORS/LEADERS
Christian Management—R
$-Enrichment—R
$-Interpreter
Ministry in Motion—R
Rick Warren's Ministry—R
$-Willow—R
$-Your Church—R

TEEN/YOUNG ADULT
$-Boundless Webzine—R
$-Brio
TeensForJC—R
$-True Girl
$-Young Christian—R

WOMEN
CelebrateMoms—R
Christian Woman's Page—R
$-Godly Business Woman—R
Hearts at Home—R
$-Hope for Women
$-Inspired Living—R
$-InspiredMoms—R
$-inSpirit—R
$-Journey
Just Between Us—R
Life Tools for Women
P31 Woman—R
Precious Times—R
Proverbs 31 Sisters—R
$-Simple Joy
$-Today's Christian Woman—R
Together with God—R
Virtuous Woman—R
Woman of Worth—R
$-Women Alive!—R
Women Today—R
$-WT Online—R

WRITERS
$-Adv. Christian Writer—R
$-Christian Communicator—R
$-Fellowscript—R
Money the Write Way—R
Opinari—R
Write Connection
$-Writer
$-Writers' Journal

TRAVEL

ADULT/GENERAL
$-Abilities
$-Angels on Earth
$-Animal Trails—R
$-Arlington Catholic
$-Associated Content—R
$-Bridal Guides—R

$-Cappers
CBN.com—R
$-Chicken Soup Magazine
$-Chronicle Christian
$-City Light News—R
$-Common Ground—R
($)-Community Spirit—R
$-Creative Nonfiction
$-DisciplesWorld
Evangelical Advocate—R
$-Family Digest—R
$-Gem—R
Gold Country Families—R
Good News Journal—R
$-Grand
$-Home Times—R
HopeKeepers—R
$-In Touch
$-Lifeglow—R
$-Mature Living
$-Mature Years—R
MovieGuide
$-Over the Back Fence—R
$-Ozarks Senior Living—R
$-Parabola—R
Sacred Journey—R
$-Seek—R
Sight 360—R
SingleAgain.com—R
$-Special Living—R
Spiritual Voice—R
$-Storyteller—R
$-Testimony—R
$-Today's Christian—R
$-Upscale
Urban Kingdom—R
$-World & I—R

CHILDREN

$-Faces
$-SHINEbrightly—R
Skipping Stones
$-Sparkle—R

MISSIONS

$-PIME World—R

TEEN/YOUNG ADULT

$-Boundless Webzine—R
TeensForJC—R
$-Young Christian—R

WOMEN

$-Dabbling Mum—R
$-Godly Business Woman—R
$-Hope for Women
$-Inspired Living—R
$-InspiredMoms—R
Precious Times—R

WRITERS

Money the Write Way—R

TRUE STORIES

ADULT/GENERAL

$-Advance
African Voices—R
$-Angels on Earth
$-Animal Trails—R
Baptist Standard
Beacon/AL
$-Bible Advocate—R
Biblical Recorder
Boomer Babes Rock
Breakthrough Intercessor—R
$-Bridal Guides—R
byFaith
$-Catholic Digest—R
CBN.com—R
Challenge Weekly
Channels—R
Charlotte World
$-Christian Citizen USA
$-Christian Journal—R
Christian Observer
Christian Online
Christian Ranchman
$-Chronicle Christian
$-City Light News—R
($)-Community Spirit—R
Creation Care—R
$-Creative Nonfiction
$-Culture Wars—R
$-Dovetail—R
$-En Confianza
Evangel/OR—R
Evangelical Advocate—R
Evangelical Times
$-Faith & Family
First Call Hospice—R
$-Focus on the Family
$-Gem—R
$-Gems of Truth—R
$-God Allows U-Turns—R
Good News Journal—R
Good News Today
$-Guideposts—R
$-Haruah—R
Heartland Gatekeeper—R
Heartlight—R
Highway News—R
$-Home Times—R
$-HonorBound—R
HopeKeepers—R
$-Horizons (adult)—R
$-In Touch
$-Lifeglow—R
$-Light & Life
$-Live—R
$-Lutheran Digest—R
$-Marriage Partnership—R
$-Mature Living
Men of the Cross
MESSAGE/Open Bible—R
$-Minnesota Christian—R
New Heart—R
$-New Wineskins—R
Nostalgia—R
$-Now What?—R
Parents & Teens—R
Penned from the Heart—R
$-Power for Living—R
PrayerWorks—R
$-Priority!—R
$-Pure Inspiration—R
Reverent Submissions—R
Sacred Journey—R
$-Science & Spirit
$-Seek—R
Sight 360—R
Spiritual Voice—R
$-St. Anthony Messenger
$-St. Joseph's Messenger—R
$-Storyteller—R
$-Testimony—R
Three One Six—R
$-Today's Christian—R
$-Today's Pentecostal—R
Tri-State Voice
Trumpeter—R
Urban Kingdom—R
Victory Herald—R
$-Victory in Grace—R
$-Vista
$-War Cry—R
World Net Daily

CHILDREN

$-Cadet Quest—R
$-Courage—R
$-Focus/Clubhouse Jr.
$-Guide—R
$-High Adventure—R
$-Nature Friend
$-New Moon—R
$-Our Little Friend—R
$-Partners—R
$-Pockets—R
$-Primary Treasure—R
$-SHINEbrightly—R
Skipping Stones
$-Sparkle—R
$-Story Mates—R
$-Winner—R

CHRISTIAN EDUCATION/LIBRARY

$-Children's Ministry

MISSIONS

$-Glad Tidings (Canada)—R
$-Leaders for Today

PASTORS/LEADERS

$-Leadership—R
$-Preaching Well—R
Sharing the Practice—R

TEEN/YOUNG ADULT
$-Boundless Webzine—R
$-Breakaway
$-Brio
$-CLEAR Direction
$-CLEAR Horizon
$-Credo—R
$-Essential Connection
$-Ignite Your Faith
$-Insight—R
$-Listen—R
$-Passageway.org—R
$-Real Faith in Life—R
$-Sharing the VICTORY—R
$-Spirit
$-TC Magazine
TeensForJC—R
$-True Girl
$-Young Christian—R
$-Young Salvationist—R
$-YouthWalk

WOMEN
$-Canticle
CelebrateMoms—R
$-Godly Business Woman—R
Hearts at Home—R
($)-History's Women—R
$-Hope for Women
$-Inspired Living—R
$-Journey
Just Between Us—R
Precious Times—R
($)-Simply Blessed—R
Together with God—R
Virtuous Woman—R
Women of the Cross
Women Today—R
$-WT Online—R

WRITERS
Areopagus

VIDEO REVIEWS

ADULT/GENERAL
$-Advance
$-Arlington Catholic
$-Atlantic Catholic
Breakthrough Intercessor—R
$-Catholic Peace Voice—R
$-CBA Retailers
CBN.com—R
Channels—R
Charlotte World
$-Christian Citizen USA
$-Christian Journal—R
Christian Radio
Christian Ranchman
$-Christian Renewal—R
$-Christianity Today Movies—R
Citizen USA—R
$-City Light News—R
Desert Call—R
$-Dovetail—R
Eternal Ink—R
$-Eureka Street
$-Faith & Family
First Call Hospice—R
Good News/S. Florida
Heartland Gatekeeper—R
$-Interim—R
$-Minnesota Christian—R
MovieGuide
$-Parabola—R
Parents & Teens—R
$-Presbyterians Today—R
$-Prism
$-Pure Inspiration—R
Quaker Life—R
$-Rose & Thorn
Sight 360—R
SingleAgain.com—R
Spiritual Voice—R
$-Testimony—R
Trumpeter—R
Urban Kingdom—R
$-Wireless Age—R

CHILDREN
$-Sparkle—R

CHRISTIAN EDUCATION/LIBRARY
$-Church Libraries—R
Congregational Libraries
Jour. of Christianity—R

MUSIC
$-Christian Music Today—R

PASTORS/LEADERS
$-Christian Century—R
$-Interpreter
$-Ministry Today
Technologies for Worship—R
$-Willow—R
$-Worship Leader

TEEN/YOUNG ADULT
Bubblemag
$-Credo—R
$-Devo'Zine—R
TeensForJC—R
$-True Girl

WOMEN
Christian Woman's Page—R
$-Hope for Women
$-Inspired Living—R
Precious Times—R
Proverbs 31 Sisters—R
Woman of Worth—R

WEBSITE REVIEWS

ADULT/GENERAL
$-Atlantic Catholic
$-Catholic Peace Voice—R
CBN.com—R
Charlotte World
$-Christian Home & School
$-Christian Journal—R
$-Christianity Today—R
Citizen USA—R
$-Dovetail—R
Eternal Ink—R
First Call Hospice—R
Good News/S. Florida
Heartland Gatekeeper—R
HopeKeepers—R
$-Minnesota Christian—R
$-New Wineskins—R
NRB Magazine—R
$-Parabola—R
SingleAgain.com—R
Spiritual Voice—R
$-Upscale
Urban Kingdom—R
$-Wireless Age—R
$-World & I—R

CHRISTIAN EDUCATION/LIBRARY
Christian Early Ed.—R
Christian Librarian—R

MISSIONS
OpRev Equipper—R

PASTORS/LEADERS
$-Interpreter

TEEN/YOUNG ADULT
Bubblemag
$-CLEAR Direction
$-CLEAR Horizon
$-Ignite Your Faith
TeensForJC—R
$-True Girl

WOMEN
$-Hope for Women
$-Today's Christian Woman—R
$-WT Online—R

WRITERS
Money the Write Way—R
NW Christian Author—R
$-Writers' Journal

WOMEN'S ISSUES

ADULT/GENERAL
$-Abilities
$-Advance
$-Alive Now—R
$-Anglican Journal
$-Annals of St. Anne
$-Arlington Catholic
$-Associated Content—R
$-BGC World—R
$-Bible Advocate—R
Boomer Babes Rock
Bread of Life—R
$-Bridal Guides—R

$-Catholic Forester—R
$-Catholic Peace Voice—R
$-CBA Retailers
CBN.com—R
$-Celebrate Life—R
$-CGA World—R
$-Chicken Soup Books—R
$-Chicken Soup Magazine
$-Christian Courier/CAN—R
$-Christian Examiner
$-Christian Journal—R
Christian News NW—R
Christian Online
Christian Ranchman
$-ChristianWeek—R
$-Chronicle Christian
Church of England News
Citizen USA—R
$-City Light News—R
$-Columbia—R
($)-Community Spirit—R
$-Creative Nonfiction
Disciple's Journal—R
$-Dovetail—R
$-EFCA Today—R
$-Episcopal Life—R
$-Evangel/IN—R
Evangel/OR—R
Evangelical Advocate—R
$-Faith & Family
$-Faith Today
Family Room
$-Family Smart E-tips—R
$-Gem—R
$-God Allows U-Turns—R
Godly Places
Good News Journal—R
$-Gospel Today—R
Heartlight—R
Holy House Ministries—R
$-Home Times—R
$-Homeschooling Today—R
HopeKeepers—R
$-In Touch
$-Indian Life—R
$-Light & Life
$-Liguorian
$-Live—R
Looking Up
$-Lookout
$-Minnesota Christian—R
$-Montgomery's Journey
Mosaic—R
($)-Mutuality—R
$-National Catholic
$-New Freeman—R
$-New Wineskins—R
$-On Mission
Penned from the Heart—R
Perspectives—R
$-Prairie Messenger—R
Presbyterian Outlook
Priscilla Papers
$-Psychology for Living—R
$-Purpose—R
Purpose Magazine—R
Reverent Submissions—R
$-Seek—R
Sight 360—R
Spiritual Voice—R
Spirituality for Today
$-St. Anthony Messenger
$-St. Joseph's Messenger—R
$-Storyteller—R
$-Testimony—R
Three One Six—R
$-Today's Christian—R
$-Together—R
Trumpeter—R
$-U.S. Catholic
$-United Church Observer—R
Urban Kingdom—R
$-Vibrant Life—R
Victory Herald—R
$-Vista
$-War Cry—R
$-Wesleyan Life—R
West Wind Review
$-Whole
Wisconsin Christian
$-World & I—R

CHILDREN

$-New Moon—R

CHRISTIAN EDUCATION/LIBRARY

$-Resource—R
$-Teachers of Vision—R

DAILY DEVOTIONALS

Penned from the Heart—R

MISSIONS

$-Glad Tidings (Canada)—R
Women of the Harvest

PASTORS/LEADERS

$-African American Pulpit
$-Enrichment—R
$-Interpreter
Ministry in Motion—R
$-Word & World

TEEN/YOUNG ADULT

$-Boundless Webzine—R
$-Brio
TeensForJC—R
$-True Girl

WOMEN

$-At the Center—R
($)-Beyond the Bend—R
$-Canticle
CelebrateMoms—R
Christian Woman's Page—R
Christian Women Today—R
Crowned with Silver
$-Esprit—R
First Lady
$-Fullfill
$-Godly Business Woman—R
Handmaiden—R
Handmaidens
$-Heart & Soul
Hearts at Home—R
$-Herizons
$-Hope for Women
$-Horizons (women)—R
$-Inspired Living—R
$-inSpirit—R
$-Journey
Just Between Us—R
Keeping Hearts & Home
Ladies First
Life Tools for Women
$-Link & Visitor—R
Lutheran Woman's Quar.
Making Waves
$-Melody of the Heart
$-MOMsense—R
More to Life
P31 Woman—R
Precious Times—R
Proverbs 31 Sisters—R
Right to the Heart—R
($)-Shalom Bayit
Share
$-Simple Joy
($)-Simply Blessed—R
$-SpiritLed Woman
Tapestry (Canada)
$-Tapestry/GA
$-Today's Christian Woman—R
Together with God—R
Virtuous Woman—R
Woman of Worth—R
$-Women Alive!—R
Women of the Cross
Women Today—R
Women's Ministry
$-WT Online—R

WORKPLACE ISSUES

ADULT/GENERAL

$-Animal Trails—R
$-Associated Content—R
$-BGC World—R
$-Bible Advocate—R
$-Bridal Guides—R
byFaith
CBN.com—R
Channels—R
Christian Business
$-Christian Examiner
$-Christian Journal—R
Christian News NW—R
Christian Online
$-Christian Retailing

$-ChristianWeek—R
$-Chronicle Christian
Citizen USA—R
$-City Light News—R
($)-Community Spirit—R
Desert Voice
$-Discipleship Journal—R
$-Evangel/IN—R
Evangelical Advocate—R
$-Faith & Friends—R
$-Faith Today
Good News Today
Good News/S. Florida
$-Gospel Today—R
Highway News—R
$-Home Times—R
$-HonorBound—R
HopeKeepers—R
$-In Touch
LarkNews.com
$-Light & Life
$-Liguorian
$-Live—R
Looking Up
$-Lookout
$-Men of Integrity—R
Men of the Cross
$-Minnesota Christian—R
Missionwares
$-Montana Catholic
$-Montgomery's Journey
New Heart—R
$-On Mission
Penned from the Heart—R
Perspectives—R
$-Positive Thinking—R
$-Purpose—R
Purpose Magazine—R
Regent Global—R
Reverent Submissions—R
$-Seek—R
Sight 360—R
Spiritual Voice—R
$-Storyteller—R
$-Testimony—R
Three One Six—R
$-Today's Christian—R
$-Together—R
$-U.S. Catholic
Urban Kingdom—R
Victory Herald—R
$-Vista
$-Wireless Age—R
$-World & I—R
World Net Daily

CHRISTIAN EDUCATION/LIBRARY

Catholic Library
Christian Librarian—R
$-Group
$-Teachers of Vision—R
$-Today's Catholic Teacher—R

PASTORS/LEADERS

Alpha News
$-Interpreter
$-Your Church—R

TEEN/YOUNG ADULT

$-Boundless Webzine—R

WOMEN

$-Fullfill
$-Herizons
$-Hope for Women
$-Inspired Living—R
$-InspiredMoms—R
$-Journey
Life Tools for Women
Making Waves
More to Life
$-Today's Christian Woman—R
Together with God—R
Virtuous Woman—R
Women Today—R
$-WT Online—R

WRITERS

$-Adv. Christian Writer—R

WORLD ISSUES

ADULT/GENERAL

($)-AGAIN—R
American Tract—R
$-Animal Trails—R
$-Annals of St. Anne
$-Arlington Catholic
$-Associated Content—R
$-Aujourd'hui Credo—R
Baptist Standard
Beacon/AL
$-Bible Advocate—R
Biblical Recorder
$-Bridal Guides—R
CanadianChristianity
$-Catholic Peace Voice—R
Catholic Register
CBN.com—R
$-CGA World—R
Challenge Weekly
Charlotte World
Christian C. L. RECORD—R
Christian Chronicle
$-Christian Examiner
Christian Observer
Christian Online
Christian Ranchman
$-Christian Renewal—R
$-ChristianWeek—R
$-Chronicle Christian
Citizen USA—R
$-City Light News—R
($)-Community Spirit—R
Compass Direct
Creation Care—R
$-Creative Nonfiction
$-Culture Wars—R
Desert Christian
Desert Voice
$-Dovetail—R
$-Evangel/IN—R
Evangelical Advocate—R
Evangelical Times
$-Faith Today
Friends Journal—R
$-Gem—R
Good News Connection
Good News Journal—R
Good News Today
Good News/S. Florida
Heartland Gatekeeper—R
Heartlight—R
$-Home Times—R
$-In Touch
$-Inland NW Christian
$-Liberty
LifeSite News
$-Light & Life
$-Liguorian
$-Living Church
$-Lookout
$-Minnesota Christian—R
$-Montgomery's Journey
MovieGuide
($)-Mutuality—R
$-New Freeman—R
$-New Wineskins—R
Penned from the Heart—R
Perspectives—R
$-Prairie Messenger—R
Presbyterian Outlook
$-Purpose—R
Purpose Magazine—R
Quaker Life—R
Rare Jewel—R
Sacred Journey—R
$-Salvo
SearchingWisdom.org—R
$-Seek—R
Sight 360—R
$-Social Justice—R
Spiritual Voice—R
$-St. Anthony Messenger
$-Testimony—R
Three One Six—R
$-Today's Christian—R
Tri-State Voice
Trumpeter—R
$-United Church Observer—R
Urban Kingdom—R
$-Vista
$-War Cry—R
West Wind Review
$-Wireless Age—R
Word News

$-World & I—R
World Net Daily

CHILDREN
$-New Moon—R
Skipping Stones

CHRISTIAN EDUCATION/LIBRARY
Catholic Library

MISSIONS
$-Glad Tidings (Canada)—R
Intl. Jour./Frontier—R
$-Leaders for Today
Missiology
Mission Frontiers
$-New World Outlook
$-One
OpRev Equipper—R
$-PFI World—R
$-PIME World—R

PASTORS/LEADERS
Alpha News
$-Christian Century—R
$-Ministry Today
$-Word & World

TEEN/YOUNG ADULT
$-Boundless Webzine—R
$-CLEAR Direction
$-CLEAR Horizon
$-Passageway.org—R
$-TC Magazine
TeensForJC—R
$-True Girl
$-Young Christian—R

WOMEN
$-Canticle
$-Esprit—R
$-Hope for Women
$-Horizons (women)—R
$-Inspired Living—R
$-SpiritLed Woman

WRITERS
Areopagus

WORSHIP

ADULT/GENERAL
$-Advance
($)-AGAIN—R
$-Angels on Earth
$-Animal Trails—R
$-Annals of St. Anne
$-Arlington Catholic
$-Aujourd'hui Credo—R
$-BGC World—R
$-Bible Advocate—R
Bread of Life—R
Breakthrough Intercessor—R
$-Bridal Guides—R
$-Catholic Yearbook—R
CBN.com—R
$-CGA World—R
Channels—R
$-Christian Examiner
$-Christian Journal—R
Christian Online
Christian Ranchman
$-Christian Standard—R
$-Christianity Today—R
$-ChristianWeek—R
$-Chronicle Christian
Church Herald & Holiness—R
$-City Light News—R
$-Columbia—R
($)-Community Spirit—R
Creation Care—R
$-Culture Wars—R
$-Dovetail—R
Eternal Ink—R
$-Evangel/IN—R
Evangelical Advocate—R
$-Faith Today
$-Family Digest—R
$-HonorBound—R
HopeKeepers—R
Imagine
$-Lifeglow—R
$-Light & Life
$-Liguorian
$-Live—R
$-Living Church
Looking Up
$-Lookout
$-Lutheran Journal—R
$-Minnesota Christian—R
$-Montgomery's Journey
Mosaic—R
$-New Freeman—R
$-New Wineskins—R
$-Parabola—R
Penned from the Heart—R
Perspectives—R
$-Power for Living—R
PrayerWorks—R
Presbyterian Outlook
$-Presbyterians Today—R
Priscilla Papers
Purpose Magazine—R
Reverent Submissions—R
$-Seek—R
Silver Wings—R
$-Spiritual Life
Spiritual Voice—R
$-St. Anthony Messenger
$-Stewardship—R
Sword and Trumpet
Sword of the Lord—R
$-Testimony—R
Three One Six—R
Time of Singing—R
$-Today's Christian—R
Trumpeter—R
$-United Church Observer—R
Urban Kingdom—R
Victory Herald—R
$-War Cry—R
$-Way of St. Francis—R
$-Wesleyan Life—R
$-World & I—R

CHILDREN
$-BREAD/God's Children—R
$-Promise
$-Sparkle—R

CHRISTIAN EDUCATION/LIBRARY
$-Group
$-RTJ—R
$-Teach Kids!—R
$-Youth & CE Leadership

DAILY DEVOTIONALS
Penned from the Heart—R

MISSIONS
$-Glad Tidings (Canada)—R

MUSIC
$-Creator—R

PASTORS/LEADERS
$-African American Pulpit
$-Barefoot—R
$-Clergy Journal—R
$-Enrichment—R
$-Growth Points—R
$-Interpretation
$-Interpreter
Jour./Amer. Soc./Chur. Growth—R
$-Leadership—R
$-Let's Worship
$-Lutheran Partners—R
$-Ministry & Liturgy—R
$-Ministry Today
$-Pray!—R
Preaching—R
Pulpit Helps—R
$-Reformed Worship—R
$-Rev. Magazine
$-RevWriter Resource
Rick Warren's Ministry—R
Sharing the Practice—R
Theological Digest—R
$-Today's Parish—R
$-Word & World
$-Worship Leader
$-Your Church—R

TEEN/YOUNG ADULT
$-Boundless Webzine—R
$-Breakaway
$-CLEAR Direction
$-CLEAR Horizon
$-Passageway.org—R
$-TC Magazine

TeensForJC—R
$-True Girl
$-Young Christian—R

WOMEN
CelebrateMoms—R
Christian Woman's Page—R
$-Godly Business Woman—R
$-Hope for Women
$-Horizons (women)—R
$-Inspired Living—R
$-Journey
Together with God—R
Virtuous Woman—R
Women Today—R
$-WT Online—R

WRITING HOW-TO

ADULT/GENERAL
$-Animal Trails—R
$-Associated Content—R
$-Bridal Guides—R
$-CBA Retailers
CBN.com—R
Christian Observer
Christian Online
($)-Community Spirit—R
Good News Journal—R
$-Haruah—R
$-Home Times—R
HopeKeepers—R
Parents & Teens—R
Penwood Review
Reverent Submissions—R
SingleAgain.com—R
Spiritual Voice—R
$-St. Anthony Messenger
$-Storyteller—R
Urban Kingdom—R
Victory Herald—R
Village Note Cards—R
$-World & I—R

CHRISTIAN EDUCATION/LIBRARY
Christian Librarian—R
$-Group

PASTORS/LEADERS
$-Newsletter Newsletter

TEEN/YOUNG ADULT
$-Boundless Webzine—R
TeensForJC—R
$-Young Christian—R

WOMEN
$-Dabbling Mum—R
$-Godly Business Woman—R
$-Hope for Women
Just Between Us—R
Precious Times—R
Right to the Heart—R

WRITERS
$-Adv. Christian Writer—R
Areopagus
Author-Me
Beginnings—R
$-ByLine
$-Christian Communicator—R
$-Cross & Quill—R
$-Fellowscript—R
$-Freelance Writer's Report—R
Money the Write Way—R
$-New Writer's Mag.
NW Christian Author—R
Once Upon a Time—R
Opinari—R
$-Poets & Writers
$-Shades of Romance—R
$-Spirit-Led Writer—R
Teachers & Writers
$-Tickled by Thunder
$-WIN-Informer
Write Connection
$-Writer
$-Writer's Digest—R
Writers Manual
$-Writers Notes
$-Writers' Journal
WriteToInspire
Writing Corner—R

YOUNG WRITER MARKETS

Note: These publications have indicated they will accept submissions from children or teens (C or T).

ADULT/GENERAL
African Voices
$-Ancient Paths (T)
$-Animal Trails
$-Aujourd'hui Credo (C or T)
Breakthrough Intercessor (C or T)
$-Bridal Guides (C or T)
$-Catholic Peace Voice (T)
$-Catholic Yearbook (C or T)
CBN.com (T)
$-Celebrate Life (C or T)
Channels (T)
Choice Newspaper (T)
$-Christian Citizen USA (T)
$-Christian Herald (T)
$-Christian Journal (C or T)
Christian Online (C or T)
$-ChristianWeek (T)
Church Herald & Holiness (C or T)
Citizen USA (C or T)
$-City Light News (T)
$-Creative Nonfiction (T)
Diamond Dust
$-Dragons, Knights & Angels (C or T)
$-Drama Ministry (T)
$-DreamSeeker (C or T)
Eternal Ink (C or T)
Family Room (T)
Friends Voice
Gold Country Families (C or T)
$-Gospel Today
$-Haruah (T)
Holy House Ministries (C or T)
$-Home Times (T)
$-HonorBound (T)
HopeKeepers (T)
$-Interchange (C or T)
$-Leben (T)
LifeTimes Catholic (T)
$-Light & Life (C or T)
$-Lutheran Journal (C or T)
$-Mature Living
Men of the Cross (T)
Missionwares (T)
$-Montgomery's Journey (T)
Mosaic (T)
$-ParentLife (C)
Parents & Teens (T)
Pegasus Review (T)
Penned from the Heart (C or T)
$-Priority! (C or T)
$-Pure Inspiration (C or T)
Purpose Magazine (C or T)
Quaker Life (C or T)
Rare Jewel (T)
Reverent Submissions (C or T)
Silver Wings (C or T)
Spiritual Voice (C or T)
$-Storyteller (C or T)
Three One Six (T)
Urban Kingdom (T)
Victory Herald (C or T)
$-Vista (C or T)

CHILDREN
$-American Girl
$-Courage (C)
$-Focus/Clubhouse (C)
$-New Moon (C or T)
$-Pockets (C)

CHRISTIAN EDUCATION/LIBRARY
Catholic Library
$-Children's Ministry (C or T)
Jour. of Christian Ed. (C or T)

DAILY DEVOTIONALS
Penned from the Heart (C or T)

MISSIONS
Glad Tidings
$-PIME World (T)

PASTORS/LEADERS
$-Cornerstone Youth
$-Let's Worship
$-RevWriter Resource (T)

TEEN/YOUNG ADULT
$-Breakaway (T)
$-CLEAR Direction (T)
$-Credo (T)
$-Essential Connection
$-Ignite Your Faith (T)
$-Insight (T)
$-Listen
$-Steelroots (T)
$-Take Five Plus (T)
$-TC Magazine (T)
TeensForJC (T)
$-True Girl (T)
$-Young Christian (C or T)

WOMEN
CelebrateMoms (C or T)
$-Dabbling Mum (C or T)
($)-History's Women (T)
Precious Times (T)
Proverbs 31 Sisters
Together with God (T)
Women of the Cross (T)
Women Today (T)

WRITERS
Beginnings (C or T)
$-Canadian Writer's Jour.
$-Fellowscript (T)
$-Merlyn's Pen
Money the Write Way
$-Novel Writer (C or T)
NW Christian Author (T)
Poetic Voices (C or T)
$-Spirit-Led Writer (T)
$-Tickled by Thunder (C or T)
Write Connection (T)
$-Writers' Journal (T)

YOUTH ISSUES

ADULT/GENERAL
$-Abilities
Alabama Baptist
American Tract—R
$-Animal Trails—R
$-Annals of St. Anne
Anointed Pages
$-Arlington Catholic
$-Associated Content—R
$-Atlantic Catholic
$-Aujourd'hui Credo—R
$-BGC World—R
$-Bible Advocate—R
Bread of Life—R
$-Bridal Guides—R
$-Catholic Forester—R
$-Catholic Peace Voice—R
CBN.com—R
Channels—R
$-Chicken Soup Books—R
$-Christian Citizen USA
$-Christian Examiner
$-Christian Home & School
$-Christian Journal—R
Christian Motorsports
Christian News NW—R
Christian Online
$-Christian Renewal—R
$-ChristianWeek—R
$-Chronicle Christian
Citizen USA—R
$-City Light News—R
($)-Community Spirit—R
$-Culture Wars—R
$-Dovetail—R
$-EFCA Today—R
Evangelical Advocate—R
$-Faith & Family
$-Faith Today
$-Family Smart E-tips—R
Godly Places
Good News Journal—R
$-Home Times—R
$-Homeschooling Today—R
$-In Touch
$-Indian Life—R
LifeTimes Catholic
$-Light & Life
$-Living Church
Looking Up
$-Lookout
MESSAGE/Open Bible—R
$-Montgomery's Journey
Mosaic—R
$-New Freeman—R
Parents & Teens—R
Penned from the Heart—R
$-Prairie Messenger—R
Presbyterian Outlook
$-Prism
SearchingWisdom.org—R
$-Seek—R
Sight 360—R
SingleAgain.com—R
Spiritual Voice—R
Spirituality for Today
$-St. Anthony Messenger
Sword of the Lord—R
$-Testimony—R
$-Today's Christian—R
Trumpeter—R
$-U.S. Catholic
Urban Kingdom—R
Victory Herald—R
$-Vista
$-Wesleyan Life—R
Wisconsin Christian
$-World & I—R

CHILDREN
$-American Girl—R
$-BREAD/God's Children—R
$-Cadet Quest—R
$-High Adventure—R
$-New Moon—R
$-SHINEbrightly—R
Skipping Stones
$-Sparkle—R
$-Winner—R

CHRISTIAN EDUCATION/LIBRARY
Catholic Library
$-Group
$-Journal/Adventist Ed.—R
$-Momentum
$-Resource—R
$-RTJ—R
$-Teachers of Vision—R
$-Youth & CE Leadership

PASTORS/LEADERS
$-Barefoot—R
$-Catholic Servant
$-Cornerstone Youth—R
Engage
$-Enrichment—R
$-InSite—R
$-Interpreter
$-Lutheran Partners—R
$-Word & World
$-Youthworker

TEEN/YOUNG ADULT
$-Boundless Webzine—R
$-Breakaway
$-Brio
Bubblemag
$-CLEAR Direction
$-CLEAR Horizon
Connected
$-Credo—R
FOTF Dare 2 Dig Deeper
$-InsideOut—R
$-Insight—R
$-Risen
$-Rock
$-Sharing the VICTORY—R
$-Spirit
Student Life
$-TC Magazine
$-True Girl
Visions
$-Young Christian—R
$-Young Salvationist—R
$-YouthWalk

WOMEN
$-Esprit—R
$-Godly Business Woman—R
Hearts at Home—R
Just Between Us—R
P31 Woman—R
($)-Shalom Bayit
Together with God—R

ALPHABETICAL LISTINGS OF PERIODICALS AND E-ZINES

Following are the listings of periodicals arranged alphabetically by type of periodical (see table of contents for a list of types). Nonpaying markets are indicated in bold letters within those listings, e.g. **NO PAYMENT**. Paying markets are indicated with a $ in front of the listing.

It is important that freelance writers request writer's guidelines and a recent sample copy before submitting to any publication. If you do not find the publication you are looking for, look in the General Index. See the introduction of that index for the codes used to identify the current status of each unlisted publication.

For a detailed explanation of how to understand and get the most out of these listings, as well as solid marketing tips, see the "How to Use This Book" section at the front of this book. Unfamiliar terms are explained in the Glossary at the back of the book.

(+) A plus sign means it is a new listing.
($) A dollar sign before a listing indicates a paying market.
(\$) A dollar sign in parentheses before a listing indicates they sometimes pay.

ADULT/GENERAL MARKETS

$ABILITIES MAGAZINE, 401—340 College St., Toronto ON M5T 3A9, Canada. (416)923-1885. Fax (416)923-9829. E-mail: ray@abilities.ca. Website: www.abilities.ca. Canadian Abilities Foundation; general. Raymond Cohen, ed-in-chief. Canada's foremost cross-disabilities lifestyle magazine. Open to freelance. Query; e-query preferred. Pays $50-350 Cdn. for 1st rts. Articles 500-2,000 wds. No simultaneous submissions. Requires disk. Kill fee 50%. Guidelines & theme list on Website. (Ads)

Tips: "Ensure your query is strongly Canadian and includes strategies, news, or ideas on living with a disability."

$ADVANCE, 1910 W. Sunset Blvd., Ste. 200, Los Angeles CA 90026-0176. Toll-free (888)635-4234. (213)989-4230. Fax (213)989-4590. E-mail: comm@foursquare.org, bshepson@foursquare.org, or through Website: www.foursquarechurch.org/advance. International Church of the Foursquare Gospel. Submit to Editorial Director. Quarterly mag. with bonus missions issue & online version; 32 pgs.; circ. 30,000. Subscription free. 100% assigned. Query (no complete mss); e-query OK. No full mss by e-mail. Payment negotiated individually. Pays on publication for all rts. Articles 2,000-3,000 wds.; book/music/video reviews 150 wds. Responds in 4 wks. No simultaneous submissions or reprints. Requires e-mail submissions (attached file). Kill fee negotiable. Regularly uses sidebars. Prefers NKJV. Guidelines (also by e-mail/Website); free copy on request. (No ads)

Tips: "Query only via e-mail on relevant real-life topics."

**2004 EPA Award of Excellence—Most Improved Publication; 2006, 2005 Award of Merit—Denominational.

AFRICAN VOICES, 270 W. 96th St., New York NY 10025. (212)865-2982. Fax (212)316-3335. E-mail: africanvoices@aol.com, or general@africanvoices.com. Website: www.africanvoices.com. African Voices Communications Inc. Carolyn A. Butts, mng. ed.; Kim Horne, fiction ed.; Debbie Officer, book review ed. Publishes original fiction, nonfiction, and poetry by artists of color. Quarterly mag.; 48 pgs.; circ. 20,000. Subscription $12. 75% unsolicited freelance; 25% assigned. Query/clips; e-query OK. **PAYS IN COPIES** for 1st rts. Articles 500-2,500 wds. (25/yr.); fiction 500-2,000 wds. (20/yr.); book reviews 500-1,200 wds. Responds in 16 wks. Seasonal 4 mos. ahead. Accepts simultaneous submissions & reprints (tell when/where appeared). Requires accepted submissions by e-mail (copied into message). Uses some sidebars. Guidelines; copy $5/9x12 SAE/$2.13 postage (mark "Media Mail"). (Ads)

Poetry: Layding Kalbia, poetry ed. Accepts 75-80/yr. Avant-garde, free verse, light verse, haiku, traditional; to 3 pgs. Submit max. 3 poems.

Fillers: Accepts 10/yr. Cartoons.

($)AGAIN MAGAZINE, 10090-A Hwy 9, PO Box 76, Ben Lomond CA 95005. Toll-free (800)967-7377. (831)336-5118. Fax (831)336-8882. E-mail: dsalibi@conciliarpress.com. Website: www.conciliarpress.com. Antiochian Orthodox Archdiocese of North America/Conciliar Press. Submit to Managing Editor. Historic Eastern Orthodox Christianity applied to our modern times. Quarterly mag.; 32 pgs.; circ. 5,000. Subscription $16. 1% unsolicited freelance; 99% assigned. Query; e-query OK. **USUALLY PAYS IN COPIES.** Articles 1,500-2,500 wds. (4/yr.); book reviews 800-1,000 wds. Responds in 6-8 wks. Seasonal 4-6 mos. ahead. Serials 2 parts. Accepts reprints (tell when/where appeared). Prefers requested ms on disk or by e-mail (copied into message). Uses some sidebars. Prefers NKJV. Guidelines (also by e-mail); copy for 9x12 SAE/4 stamps. (No ads)

Tips: "We are Orthodox in orientation, and interested in thoughtful, intelligent articles dealing with church history, Protestant/Orthodox dialog, relations between Protestants and Orthodox in foreign countries, also in modern ethical dilemmas—no fluff."

ALABAMA BAPTIST, 3310 Independence Dr., Birmingham AL 35209-5602. (205)870-4720. Fax (205)870-8957. E-mail: news@thealabamabaptist.org. Website: www.thealabamabaptist.org. Baptist. Dr. Bob Terry, ed. To share news and information relevant to the members of Baptist churches in Alabama. Weekly (50x) newspaper.; circ. 109,000. Subscription $18. Accepts unsolicited freelance. Query. Articles & reviews.

Tips: "Most open to feature stories, lifestyle area. Submit sample story for review."

$ALIVE NOW, PO Box 340004, Nashville TN 37203-0004. (615)340-7218. Fax (615)340-7267. E-mail: alivenow@upperroom.org. Website: www.alivenow.org. The Upper Room. JoAnn Evans Miller, ed. Short, theme-based writings in attractive graphic setting for reflection and meditation. Bimonthly mag.; 64 pgs.; circ. 70,000. Subscription $14.95. 30% unsolicited freelance; 70% assigned. Complete ms/cover letter; e-query OK. Pays $40-150 on acceptance for newspaper, periodical, or electronic rts. Articles 350-600 wds. (25/yr.). Responds 13 wks. before issue date. Seasonal 6-8 mos. ahead. Accepts simultaneous submissions & reprints (tell when/where appeared). Accepts e-mail submissions (copied into message). Uses some sidebars. Prefers NRSV. Guidelines/theme list (also on Website); copy for 6x9 SAE/4 stamps.

Poetry: Avant-garde, free verse, traditional; to 40 lines or one page; $25-100. Submit max. 5 poems. On issue's theme.

Tips: "Write for our theme list and make your submission relevant to the topic. Avoid the obvious and heavy-handed preachiness."

$AMERICA, 106 W. 56th St., New York NY 10019-3893. (212)581-4640. Fax (212)399-3596. E-mail: articles@americamagazine.org. Website: www.americamagazine.org. Catholic. Submit to Editor-in-Chief. For thinking Catholics and those who want to know what Catholics are thinking. Weekly mag. & online version; 32+ pgs.; circ. 46,000. Subscription $48. 100% unsolicited freelance. Complete ms/cover letter; fax/e-query OK. Pays $100-200 on acceptance. Articles 1,500-2,000 wds. Responds in 6 wks. Seasonal 3 mos. ahead. Does not use sidebars. Guidelines (also on Website); copy for 9x12 SAE. (Ads) Incomplete topical listings.

Poetry: Buys avant-garde, free verse, light verse, traditional; 20-35 lines; $2-3/line.

AMERICAN TRACT SOCIETY, Box 462008, Garland TX 75046. (972)276-9408. Fax (972)272-9642. E-mail: PBatzing@ATSTracts.org. Website: www.ATStracts.org. Peter Batzing, tract ed. Majority of tracts written to win unbelievers. New tract releases bimonthly; 40 new titles produced annually. 5% unsolicited freelance; 2% assigned. Complete ms/cover letter; e-query OK. **PAYS IN COPIES** on publication for exclusive tract rts. Tracts 600-1,200 wds. Responds in 6-8 wks. Seasonal 1 yr. ahead. Accepts simultaneous submissions & reprints (tell when/where appeared). Accepts requested ms on disk or by e-mail (attached or copied into message). Prefers NIV, KJV. Guidelines (also by e-mail)/free samples for #10 SAE/1 stamp. (No ads)

Special Needs: Youth issues, African American, cartoonists, critical issues.

Tips: "Read our current tracts; submit polished writing; relate to people's needs and experiences. Follow guidelines—almost no one does."

$ANCIENT PATHS, PO Box 7505, Fairfax Station VA 22039. E-mail: ssburris@msn.com. Website: www.editorskylar.com. Christian/nondenominational. Skylar Hamilton Burris, ed. For a literate Christian audience, or non-Christians open to and moved by traditional-themed poetry and fiction. Biennial literary mag; 80+ pgs.; circ. 175. Subscription $10. 100% unsolicited freelance. Complete ms only; no queries. Pays $6 for prose & $6 for artwork on publication for one-time, reprint, & optional electronic rts. Not copyrighted. No nonfiction. Fiction to 2,500 wds. (5/yr.). Responds in 5 wks. No seasonal. Accepts simultaneous submissions & reprints (tell when/where appeared). Accepts e-mail submissions only from outside U.S. No kill fee. Does not use sidebars. Prefers KJV. Also accepts submissions from teens (but must compete with adults). Guidelines (also on Website); copy $5 (make check to Skylar Burris). (Ads—1/2 pg. $30)

Poetry: Buys 30-40/yr. Free verse, traditional; 4-60 lines; pays $2 & 1 copy. Submit max. 5 poems.

Tips: "Looking for shorter fiction (under 2,000 wds.). Visit the Website and read sample literature or order a copy. Read the great Christian writers—O'Connor, Lewis, Hopkins, Donne, Herbert, Tennyson, etc. Send your best work, even if it's been previously published (we're open to reprints). Stir your reader's emotions; make your reader think and feel without being too obvious."

ANGEL FACE, PO Box 102, Huffman TX 77336. E-mail: MaryAnkaPress@cs.com. Website: www.maryanka.com. MaryAnka Press/Catholic. Mary Agnes Dalrymple, pub. Religious or general poetry based on the rosary, birth, rebirth, joy, light, sorrow, epiphany, hope, Jesus, Mary, the seasons of nature and the cycles of life, the search for God in everyday life, etc. (but open to all denominations). Annual literary mag.; 50 pgs.; circ. 100. Subscription $14. 10% unsolicited freelance. Complete ms/cover letter; no phone/fax/e-query. **PAYS 1 COPY** for one-time rts. Poetry only. Responds in 1-6 mos. Accepts simultaneous submissions & reprints (tell when/where appeared). No submissions by e-mail or on disk. Guidelines (also on Website); copy $7.

Poetry: Accepts 35/yr. Free-verse, 60-65 lines. Submit max. 5 poems (typed).

Tips: "I am open to all viewpoints and have published poems by non-Christians as well as Catholic and protestant writers. Send your best work even if you are not sure it fits the rosary pattern. Info on the rosary and sample poems from past issues can be found on my Website."

$ANGELS ON EARTH, 16 E. 34th St., New York NY 10016. (212)251-8100. Fax (212)684-1311. E-mail: submissions@angelsonearth.com. Website: www.angelsonearth.com. Guideposts. Colleen Hughes, ed-in-chief; Meg Belviso, depts. ed. for features and fillers. Presents true stories about God's angels and humans who have played angelic roles on earth. Bimonthly mag.; 75 pgs.; circ. 550,000. Subscription $19.95. 90% unsolicited freelance. Complete ms/cover letter; no phone/fax/e-query. Pays $25-400 on publication for all rts. Articles 100-2,000 wds. (100/yr.); all stories must be true. Responds in 13 wks. Seasonal 6 mos. ahead. E-mail submissions from Website. Guidelines on Website (www.angelsonearth.com/writers_Guidelines.asp); copy for 7x10 SAE/4 stamps.

Fillers: Buys many. Anecdotal shorts of similar nature (angelic); 50-250 wds.; $50-100.

Columns/Departments: Buys 50/yr. Messages (brief, mysterious happenings), $25. Earning Their Wings (good deeds), 150 wds., $50. Only Human? (human or angel?/mystery), 350 wds.; $100. Complete ms.

Tips: "We are not limited to stories about heavenly angels. We also accept stories about human beings doing heavenly duties."

THE ANGLICAN, 135 Adelaide St. E., Toronto M5C 1L8, Canada. Toll-free (800)668-8932, ext. 247. (416)363-6021. Fax (416)363-7678. E-mail: smann@toronto.anglican.ca. Website: www.toronto.anglican.ca. Anglican Diocese of Toronto. Stuart Mann, ed. Provides timely news, in-depth features, and challenging opinions to Anglicans in this diocese. Monthly (10X) tabloid; circ. 300. Subscription $8. Open to unsolicited freelance. Not included in topical listings. (Ads)

$ANGLICAN JOURNAL, 80 Hayden St., Toronto ON M4Y 2J6, Canada. (416)924-9199, ext. 306. Fax (416)921-4452. E-mail: editor@national.anglican.ca. Website: www.anglicanjournal.com. Anglican Church of Canada. Leanne Larmondin, ed.; Josie De Lucia, ed. asst. (jdelucia@national.anglican.ca). National newspaper of the Anglican Church of Canada; informs Canadian Anglicans about the church at home and overseas. Newspaper (10x/yr.) & online; 12-16 pgs.; circ. 200,000. Subscription $10 Cdn., $17 U.S. & foreign. 10% unsolicited freelance. Query only; fax/e-query OK. Pays $50-300 or .23/wd. Cdn., on acceptance for 1st & electronic rts. Articles 600 wds. (12-15/yr.). Responds in 2 wks. Seasonal 2 mos. ahead. No reprints. Guidelines (also by e-mail). (Ads)

Tips: "Select subject matter that would be of interest to a national audience."

$ANIMAL TRAILS, 2660 Peterborough St., Herndon VA 20171. E-mail: animaltrails@yahoo.com. Tellstar Publishing. Shannon Bridget Murphy, ed. Keeping animal memories alive through writing. Quarterly mag. 85% unsolicited freelance. Complete ms/cover letter; e-query OK. Pays .02-.05/wd. on acceptance for 1st, one-time, reprint, or simultaneous rts. Articles to 2,000 wds.; fiction to 2,000 wds. Responds in 2-8 wks. Seasonal 3 mos. ahead. Accepts simultaneous submissions & reprints (tell when/where appeared). Accepts disk or e-mail submissions (attached or copied into message.). No kill fee. Regularly uses sidebars. Prefers KJV. Guidelines by e-mail. (No ads)

Poetry: Buys variable number. Avant-garde, free verse, haiku, light verse, traditional; any length. Pays variable rates. Submit any number.

Fillers: Buys most types, to 1,000 wds.

Tips: "Most open to articles, stories, poetry and fillers that explain the value of animals and their relationship with God. The value of animals is the mission of Animal Trails. Include a scripture reference."

$THE ANNALS OF SAINT ANNE DE BEAUPRE, 9795 St. Anne Blvd., St. Anne de Beaupre QC G0A 3C0, Canada. (418)827-4538. Fax (418)827-4530. E-mail: mag@revuesteannedebeaupre.ca (for subscriptions only). Catholic/Redemptorist Fathers. Fr. Bernard Mercier, C.Ss.R., ed.; submit to Fr. R. Theberge, C.Ss.R., interim mng. ed. Promotes Catholic family values. Monthly mag.; 32 pgs.; circ. 30,000. Subscription $18.50 U.S. 80% unsolicited freelance. Complete ms/cover letter; no phone/fax/e-query. Pays .03-.04/wd. on acceptance for 1st N.A. serial rts. only. Articles 500-1,150 wds. (350/yr.), & fiction 500-1,500 wds. (200/yr.). Responds in 4-5 wks. Seasonal 6 mos. ahead. No simultaneous submissions or reprints. No disk or e-mail submission. Does not use sidebars. Prefers NRSV. Guidelines; copy for 9x12 SAE/IRC. (No ads)

Tips: "Writing must be uplifting and inspirational, clearly written, not filled with long quotations. We tend to stay away from extreme controversy and focus on the family, good family values, devotion, and Christianity. Write a well-researched, current story with 'across the board' appeal." Rights must be clearly stated. Typed manuscripts only.

+ANOINTED PAGES MAGAZINE, (414)517-8876 or (414)759-4959. Website: www.anointedpages.com. Interdenominational. Marvin Ivy, pub. (marvinivy@anointedpages.com); Jodine Ivy, editorial administrator (jodineive@anointedpages.com). To profile religious and community leaders and the lives that they are changing within their ministry and community, and to meet the needs of people with articles on the holistic lifestyle. Bimonthly mag. Subscription $19.99. Estab. 2007. Open to unsolicited freelance. Query. Articles. Also accepts submissions from teens.

ANSWERS MAGAZINE & ANSWERSMAGAZINE.COM, PO Box 510, Hebron KY 41048. (859)727-2222. Fax (859)727-2291. E-mail: admin@answersingenesis.org. Website: www.answersmagazine.com. Answers in Genesis. Dale Mason, exec. ed. Bible-affirming, creation-based. Quarterly mag. Articles to 300 wds. Responds in 30 days. Details on Website.

$THE APOCALYPSE CHRONICLES, Box 448, Jacksonville OR 97530. Phone/fax (541)899-8888. E-mail: James@ChristianMediaNetwork.com. Website: www.Christianmedia.tv. Christian Media. James Lloyd, ed./pub. Deals with the apocalypse exclusively. Quarterly & online newsletter; circ. 2,000-3,000. Query; prefers phone query. Payment negotiable for reprint rts. Articles. Responds in 3 wks. Requires KJV. No guidelines; copy for #10 SAE/2 stamps.

Tips: "It's helpful if you understand your own prophetic position and are aware of its name, i.e., Futurist, Historicist, etc."

$ARKANSAS CATHOLIC, PO Box 7417, Little Rock AR 72217. (501)664-0125. Fax (501)664-6572. E-mail: mhargett@dolr.org. Website: www.arkansas-catholic.org. Catholic Diocese of Little Rock. Malea Hargett, ed.; Tara Little, assoc. ed. Statewide newspaper for the local diocese. Weekly tabloid; 16 pgs.; circ. 7,700. Subscription $18. 1% unsolicited freelance; 10% assigned. Query/clips; e-query OK. Pays $3/inch on publication for 1st rts. Articles 1,000 wds. Accepts simultaneous submissions & reprints. Accepts requested ms on disk or by e-mail. Uses some sidebars. Prefers Catholic Bible. Guidelines (also by e-mail); copy for 9x12 SAE/2 stamps. (Ads)

Columns/Departments: Tara Little, ed. Buys 2/yr. Seeds of Faith (education). Complete ms. Pays $20.

Tips: "All stories and columns must have an Arkansas and Catholic connection."

$ARLINGTON CATHOLIC HERALD, 200 N. Glebe Rd., Ste. 600, Arlington VA 22203. (703)841-2590. Fax (703)524-2782. E-mail: editorial@catholicherald.com. Website: www.catholicherald.com/index.htm. Catholic Diocese of Arlington. Michael F. Flach, ed. Regional, for the local diocese. Weekly newspaper; 28 pgs.; circ. 53,000. Subscription $14. 10% unsolicited freelance. Query; phone/fax/e-query OK. Pays $50-150 on publication for one-time rts. Articles 500-1,500 wds. Responds in 2 wks. Seasonal 3 mos. ahead. Accepts simultaneous submissions. Prefers accepted ms on disk. Regular sidebars. Guidelines (also on Website); copy for 11x17 SAE. (Ads)

Columns/Departments: Sports; School News; Local Entertainment; 500 wds.

Tips: "All submissions must be Catholic related. Avoid controversial issues within the church."

$ASSOCIATED CONTENT, 88 Steele St., Ste. 250, Denver CO 80206-5714. (720)255-9185. E-mail: miguel@associatedcontent.com. Website: www.associatedcontent.com. Associated Content. Miguel Chacon, submissions mngr. Weekly e-zine; 1000+ pgs. Free online. Estab. 2004. 100% unsolicited freelance. Query online. Pays $3-20 on acceptance for nonexclusive, electronic rts. Articles 500-5,000 wds. (1,000+/yr.); fiction 500-5,000 wds. (1,000+/yr.). Responds in 2 wks. Seasonal 1 mo. ahead. Accepts simultaneous submissions & reprints (tell when/where appeared). Accepts submissions online only. Guidelines on Website; copy online.

Poetry: Avant-garde, free verse, haiku, light verse, traditional.

Tips: "Look over Website and see what the other writers are doing. Sign up, fill out a profile, and submit your work."

**This periodical was #6 on the 2007 Top 50 Christian Publishers list (#7 in 2006).

$ATLANTIC CATHOLIC, 88 College St., Antigonish NS B2G 2L7, Canada. (902)863-4370. Fax (902)863-1943. E-mail: atlanticcatholic@thecasket.ca. The Casket Printing and Publishing Co. Ken Sims, pub.; Brian Lazzuri, mng. ed. Reports religious news that will inform, educate, and inspire Catholics. Biweekly tabloid; circ. 2,000. Subscription $28. Open to unsolicited freelance. Pays $25/story. Articles to 800 wds. Accepts e-mail submissions of mss up to 800 wds. (Ads)

Tips: "Most open to book and movie reviews, less than 700 words; also celebrity profiles, less than 700 words."

$AUJOURD'HUI CREDO, 1332 Victoria, Longueuil QC J4V 1L8, Canada. (450)466-7733. Fax (450)466-2664. E-mail: davidfines@egliseunie.org. Website: www.united-church.ca. United Church of Canada. David Fines, dir. The only French Reformed magazine in North America. Monthly mag.; 28 pgs.; circ. 250. Subscription $25 Cdn. 20% unsolicited freelance. Complete ms; fax/e-query OK. Pays $50 on publication for nonexclusive rts. Not copyrighted. Articles 1,500 wds. (10/yr.); fiction 800 wds. (6/yr.); reviews 100 wds. Responds in 4 wks. Seasonal 2 mos. ahead. Accepts simultaneous submissions & reprints (tell when/where appeared). Requires e-mail submissions (attached or copied into message). No kill fee. Uses some sidebars. Also accepts submissions from children/teens. Prefers TOB. Guidelines/theme list by e-mail; free copy. (Ads)

Poetry: Accepts free verse.

Tips: "Most likely to break in by being inclusive and intelligent. Contact director. Must write in French."

$+AUSTRALIAN CATHOLICS, PO Box 553, Richmond 3121, Victoria, Australia. (613)9421 9666. E-mail: auscaths@jespub.jesuit.org.au. Website: www.australiancatholics.com.au. Jesuit Communications. Michael McVeigh, ed. Stories of faith and living for a contemporary Catholic audience. Mag. published 5X/yr.; 36 pgs.; circ. 200,000. Open to unsolicited freelance. Query; e-query OK. Payment by negotiation on publication for 1st rts. Articles 800-1,200 wds. Seasonal 4 mos. ahead. Accepts reprints (tell when/where appeared). Uses some sidebars.

Tips: "We generally prefer articles on people, either as interviews or reflections on personal experiences. We generally don't consider an overseas submission, unless it can be made relevant for an Australian audience.

THE BAPTIST STANDARD, PO Box 660267, Dallas TX 75266-0267. (214)630-4571. Fax (214)638-8535. E-mail: marvknox@baptiststandard.com. Website: www.baptiststandard.com/postnuke/index.php. Marv Knox, ed. The Texas Baptist news journal. Biweekly newspaper. Subscription $20.50. Incomplete topical listings.

$B.C. CATHOLIC, 150 Robson St., Vancouver BC V6B 2A7, Canada. (604)683-0281. Fax (604)683-8117. E-mail: bcc@rcav.bc.ca. Website: http://bcc.rcav.org. Roman Catholic Archdiocese of Vancouver. Paul Schratz, ed. News, education, and inspiration for Canadian Catholics. Weekly (48X) newspaper; 20 pgs.; circ. 20,000. Subscription $32. 20% unsolicited freelance. Query; phone query OK. Pays .15/wd. on publication for 1st rts. Photos $30. Articles 500-1,000 wds. Responds in 6 wks. Seasonal 4 wks. ahead. Accepts simultaneous submissions & reprints. Prefers e-mail submission (copied into message). Guidelines on Website; free copy. (Ads)

Tips: "Items of relevance to Catholics in British Columbia are preferred."

THE BEACON, 980 Hwy 331, Columbiana AL 35051. (205)664-7417. Fax (205)663-0794. E-mail: publisher@newsbeacon.com. Website: www.newsbeacon.com. Angela Carraway, ed. (editor@newsbeacon.com). Weekly newspaper. Incomplete topical listings.

BEHIND THE HAMMER, 1018 Main St., Akron PA 17501. (717)859-2201. E-mail: communications@mds.mennonite.net. Website: www.mds.mennonite.net. Mennonite Disaster Services. Scott Sundberg, ed. Quarterly & online mag. Subscription free. Open to freelance. Complete ms/cover letter. **NO PAYMENT.** Articles. Guidelines on Website; free copy. Not in topical listings.

Tips: "By sharing our stories we hope to encourage and motivate one another to continue expressing the love of God through MDS activity."

BELIEVE! MAGAZINE, PO Box 24333, Richmond VA 23224. Phone/fax (757)273-1602. E-mail: editor@believemag.net. Website: www.believemag.net. Emily Thomas, pub. To provide an avenue of excellence in which to spread the Gospel of our Lord and Savior Jesus Christ in order to promote Christian unity and a godly lifestyle. Monthly mag.; circ. 20,000. Subscription free. Open to unsolicited freelance. Complete ms by e-mail (submissions@believe mag.net). Articles. Not in topical listings. (Ads)

BELIEVER'S BAY, PO Box 6362, Clearwater FL 33758. Toll-free (888)564-3534. E-mail: editor@BelieversBay.com. Website: www.BelieversBay.com. Tim Russ (tim@BelieversBay .com), pub.; Kevin Molloy, ed. To unite the body of Christ through communication, exhortation, and edification while focusing on ministries in the body of Christ. Monthly online mag. Mostly freelance. Complete ms by e-mail only; e-query OK. **NO PAYMENT** for 1st & electronic rts. (keeps posted for 3 mos. & archives with permission). Articles 300-500 wds. Guidelines/monthly topical themes listed on Website submissions page.

Columns/Departments: Columns to 500 wds. Looking for writers who focus on prophecy. Pays $15.

Special Needs: Focuses on prayer every month.

Tips: "We need all submissions via e-mail."

$BGC WORLD, 2002 S. Arlington Heights Rd., Arlington Heights IL 60005-4102. Toll-free (800)323-4215. (847)228-0200. Fax (847)228-5376. E-mail: bputman@baptistgeneral .org. Website: www.bgcworld.org. Baptist General Conference. Bob Putman, ed. Almost exclusively for, about, and by the people and ministries of the Baptist General Conference. Monthly (10X) mag.; 16 pgs.; circ. 46,000. Subscription free. Estab. 2003. 35% unsolicited freelance; 65% assigned. Query/clips; e-query preferred. Pays $60-280 on publication for 1st, reprint, electronic rts. Articles 300-1,400 wds. (20-30/yr.). Responds in 5-9 wks. Seasonal 6 mos. ahead. Accepts simultaneous submissions & reprints (tell when/where appeared). Prefers accepted mss by e-mail (attached file). Kill fee 50%. Uses some sidebars. Prefers NIV. Guidelines/theme list (also by e-mail); free copy for #10 SAE. (Ads)

Columns/Departments: Buys 30/yr. New Life (first-person transformation story), 750-1,200 wds.; Profile (third-person story of key leader), 750 wds.; Around the BGC (short news blurb of happenings in churches), 75-200 wds.; Good Ideas (ministries working in BGC churches), 250-400 wds.; $15-20.

Tips: "Report on interesting happenings/ministry in BGC churches close to you for our 'Around the BGC' or 'Good Ideas' columns. Or query on a theme-related article."

**2007 EPA Award of Excellence—Denominational. This periodical was #50 on the 2007 Top 50 Christian Publishers list.

$BIBLE ADVOCATE, Box 33677, Denver CO 80233. (303)452-7973. Fax (303)452-0657. E-mail: bibleadvocate@cog7.org. Website: www.cog7.org/BA. Church of God (Seventh-day). Calvin Burrell, ed.; Sherri Langton, assoc. ed. Adult readers; 50% not members of the denomination. Monthly (8X) mag.; 32 pgs.; circ. 13,500. Subscription free. 25-35% unsolicited freelance. Complete ms/cover letter; no phone/fax/e-query. Pays $25-55 on publication for 1st, one-time, reprint, electronic, simultaneous rts. Articles 1,000-1,500 wds. (10-20/yr.). Responds in 4-8 wks. Seasonal 9 mos. ahead (no Christmas or Easter pieces). Accepts simultaneous submissions & reprints (tell when/where appeared). Accepts requested ms by e-mail (copied into message). Regularly uses sidebars. Prefers NIV, NKJV. Guidelines/theme list (also on Website); copy for 9x12 SAE/3 stamps. (No ads)

Poetry: Buys 6-10/yr. Free verse, traditional; 5-20 lines; $20. Submit max. 5 poems.

Fillers: Buys 5-10/yr. Facts, prose; 100-400 wds.; $20.

Special Needs: Articles centering on upcoming themes (ask for theme list).

Tips: "If you write well, all areas are open to freelance, especially personal experiences that tie in with the monthly themes. Articles that run 650-700 words are more likely to get in. Also, fresh writing with keen insight is most readily accepted. Writers may submit sidebars that fit our theme for each issue."

**This periodical was #28 on the 2003 Top 50 Christian Publishers list.

BIBLICAL RECORDER, PO Box 18808, Raleigh NC 27619. (919)847-2127. E-mail: editor@biblicalrecorder.org. Website: www.biblicalrecorder.org. Baptist. Tony W. Cartledge, ed. Newspaper. Subscription $13.40. Incomplete topical listings.

BOOKS & CULTURE, 465 Gundersen Dr., Carol Stream IL 60188. (630)260-6200. Fax (630)260-8428. E-mail: bceditor@booksandculture.com, or jwilson@christianitytoday.com. Website: www.booksandculture.com. Christianity Today Intl. John Wilson, ed. To edify, sharpen, and nurture the evangelical intellectual community by engaging the world in all its complexity from a distinctly Christian perspective. Bimonthly & online newsletter.; circ. 12,000. Subscription $24.95. Open to freelance. Query. Articles & reviews. Incomplete topical listings. (Ads)

**2004 & 2003 EPA Award of Merit—General. 2001 EPA Award of Excellence—General.

$BRAVE HEARTS, 1503 S.W. 42nd St., Topeka KS 66609-1265. Toll-free (800)678-5779, ext. 4345. (785)274-4300. Fax (785)274-4305. Website: www.braveheartsmagazine.com. Ogden Publications/Grit Magazine. K. C. Compton, exec. ed; Jean Teller and Traci Smith, mng. eds.; submit to Brave Hearts Editorial. Written by ordinary people who have an inspirational message to share. Quarterly mag.; 48 pgs.; circ. 1,000. Subscription $9.95. 100% unsolicited freelance. Complete ms/cover letter; no phone/fax/e-query. No full mss by e-mail. Pays $5-12 on publication for all rts. Articles 300-900 wds. (100/yr.). Responds in 6 mos. Seasonal 6 mos. ahead. No simultaneous submissions; accepts reprints (tell when/where appeared). No kill fee. Does not use sidebars. Guidelines/theme list (also on Website); copy for $4.95/6x9 SAE.

Poetry: Buys 20-25/yr. Free verse, light verse, traditional, 14-16 lines. Submit max. 5 poems. Pays $10.

Tips: "All departments open to freelancers. Send submissions that correspond with each issue's theme."

THE BREAD OF LIFE, 35—5100 S. Service Rd., PO Box 127, Burlington ON L7R 3X5, Canada. (905)634-5433. E-mail: steeners@cyberus.ca. Website: www.thebreadoflife.ca. Catholic. Fr. Peter Coughlin, ed. Catholic Charismatic; to encourage spiritual growth in areas of renewal in the Catholic Church today. Bimonthly mag.; 32 pgs.; circ. 2,500. Subscription $30. 5% unsolicited freelance. Complete ms/cover letter; fax query OK. **NO PAYMENT.** Articles 1,100-1,300 wds.; biblical fiction; book reviews 250 wds. Responds in 4-6 wks. Seasonal 6 mos. ahead. Accepts reprints (tell when/where appeared). No disk. Does not use sidebars. Prefers NAB, NJB. Guidelines; copy for 9x12 SAE/$2.13 postage (mark "Media Mail"). (Some ads)

Poetry: Accepts little.

Fillers: Accepts 10-12/yr. Facts, prose, quotes; to 250 wds.

Tips: "Most open to testimonies; contact managing editor. We do appreciate poetry submissions and shorter articles, 750 words. It is best if a writer includes a 2-3 line biography and photo for publication."

THE BREAKTHROUGH INTERCESSOR, PO Box 121, Lincoln VA 20160-0121. (540)338-5522. Fax (540)338-1934. Website: www.intercessors.org. Nondenominational. Nicole Arnold-Bik, mng. ed. Preparing and equipping people who pray; encouraging in prayer and faith. Quarterly mag.; 32 pgs.; circ. 7,000. Subscription $18. 100% unsolicited freelance. Complete ms/cover letter or query; phone/fax/e-query OK. Accepts full mss by e-mail. **NO PAYMENT** for 1st, reprint rts. Articles 1,000 wds. (50/yr.); book reviews 300-600 wds.; music/video reviews 300 wds. Responds in 3 weeks. Seasonal 6 mos. ahead. Accepts simultaneous submissions. Accepts requested ms by e-mail (copied into message). Uses some sidebars. Also accepts submissions from children/teens. Any Bible version. Guidelines (also by e-mail/Website); copy for 6x9 SAE/3 stamps. (No ads)

Poetry: Accepts 4/yr. Free verse, traditional, 4-32 lines. Submit any number (as long as they're about prayer).

Fillers: Accepts 8/yr. Anecdotes, cartoons, facts, ideas, kid quotes, prayers, prose, quotes, short humor; to 300 wds.

Special Needs: International stories emphasizing how God is at work through prayer across the globe.

Contest: Pays $25 for article with most reader impact, plus one free subscription.

Tips: "Break in by submitting true articles/stories about prayer and its miraculous results, and articles that teach about an aspect of prayer using scripture to support each point." Manuscripts acknowledged but not returned.

+BREAKTHROUGH MAGAZINE, (517)882-3595. E-mail: editor@breakthroughonlinemag.com. Website: www.breakthroughonlinemag.com. Baraka Miller, ed. "Every struggle endures a breakthrough, every breakthrough endures a struggle." Showcases those who have made their breakthrough in life and who are impacting their communities; sharing the joy of life, family, success, and above all Christ, the one who gives us strength to "Breakthrough." Webzine.

$BRIDAL GUIDES, 2660 Peterborough St., Herndon VA 20171. E-mail: bridalguides@yahoo.com. Tellstar Publishing. Shannon Bridget Murphy, ed. Theme-based wedding/reception ideas and planning for Christian wedding planners. Quarterly mag. 85% unsolicited freelance. Complete ms/cover letter; e-query OK. Pays .02-.05/wd. on acceptance for 1st, one-time, reprint, & simultaneous rts. Articles to 2,000 wds.; fiction to 2,000 wds. Responds in 2-8 wks. Seasonal 3 mos. ahead. Accepts simultaneous submissions & reprints (tell when/where appeared). Accepts disk or e-mail submissions (attached or copied into message.). No kill fee. Regularly uses sidebars. Also accepts submissions from children/teens. Prefers KJV. Guidelines by e-mail. (No ads)

Poetry: Buys variable number. Avant-garde, free verse, haiku, light verse, traditional; any length. Pays variable rates. Submit any number.

Fillers: Buys most types, to 1,000 wds.; .02-.05/wd.

Special Needs: "Most open to wedding and planning articles that show readers how to successfully complete plans for their events. Illustrations and art either with or without manuscript packages. Romance fiction related to weddings, travel, and home."

BYFAITH (byFaith), 1700 N. Brown Rd., Ste. 105, Lawrenceville GA 30043. (678)825-1000. Fax (678)825-1001. E-mail: editor@byfaithonline.com. Website: www.byfaithonline.com. Presbyterian Church in America (PCA). Dick Doster, ed. (ddoster@byfaithonline.com). Provides news of the PCA; connects members, guests, and staff members to the denomination. Bimonthly mag.; 54 pgs. Subscription $19.95. Open to unsolicited freelance. Complete ms by e-mail ("Editorial Submission" in subject line). **NO MENTION OF PAYMENT.** Articles 500-3,000 wds. Guidelines on Website. Incomplete topical listings.

Tips: "We publish in 5 areas: stories that provoke thinking and creativity; very practical theology; articles that help readers understand the arts and culture; sensible, down-to-earth information; and PCA news."

**2007 EPA Award of Merit—Denominational; 2006 EPA Award of Excellence—Denominational.

$CANADA LUTHERAN, 302—393 Portage Ave., Winnipeg MB R3B 3H6, Canada. Toll-free (888)786-6707. (204)984-9172. Fax (204)984-9185. E-mail: editor@elcic.ca, or canaluth@elcic.ca. Website: www.elcic.ca/clweb. Evangelical Lutheran Church in Canada. Ida Reichardt Backman, ed. Denominational. Monthly (8X) mag.; 42 pgs.; circ. 14,000. Subscription $35 U.S. 40% unsolicited freelance; 60% assigned. Query or complete ms/cover letter; fax/e-query OK. Pays $40-110 (.10/wd.) Cdn. on publication for one-time rts. Articles 700-1,200 wds. (15/yr.); fiction 850-1,200 wds. (4/yr.). Responds in 5 wks. Seasonal 10 mos. ahead. Accepts simultaneous submissions & reprints. Prefers e-mail submission (copied into message). Uses some sidebars. Prefers NRSV. Guidelines (also by e-mail). (Ads)

Tips: "Canadians/Lutherans receive priority here; others considered but rarely used. Want material that is clear, concise, and fresh. Articles that talk about real life experiences of faith receive our best reader response."

CANADIANCHRISTIANITY.COM, #200-20316—56 Ave., Langley BC V3A 3Y7, Canada. Toll-free (888)899-3777. E-mail: editor@canadianchristianity.com. Website: www.CanadianChristianity .com. A ministry of the Christian Info Society. Flyn Ritchie, ed. Online newspaper. Incomplete topical listings.

THE CANADIAN LUTHERAN, 3074 Portage Ave., Winnipeg MB R3K 0Y2, Canada. Toll-free (800)588-4226. (204)895-3433. Fax (204)897-4319. E-mail: communications@lutheran church.ca. Website: www.lutheranchurch.ca. Lutheran Church-Canada. Ian Adnams, ed. Monthly (10X) mag. Subscription $20. Open to unsolicited freelance. Not in topical listings. (Ads)

$CANADIAN MENNONITE, 490 Dutton Dr., Unit C5, Waterloo ON N2L 6H7, Canada. Toll-free (800)378-2524. (519)884-3810. Fax (519)884-3331. E-mail: submit@canadianmennonite .org. Website: www.canadianmennonite.org. Canadian Mennonite Publishing Service. Ross W. Muir, mng. ed. Seeks to promote covenantal relationships within the Mennonite Church Canada constituency (guided by Hebrews 10:23-25). Biweekly mag.; circ. 16,500. Subscription $32.50 Cdn.; $52.50 U.S. Open to unsolicited freelance. Pays .10/wd.; .05/wd. for reprints. Guidelines on Website. Not in topical listings. (Ads)

Tips: "We provide channels for sharing accurate and fair information, faith profiles, inspirational and educational materials, news, and analysis of issues facing the church."

$CAPPERS, 1503 S.W. 42nd St., Topeka KS 66609. (785)274-4300. Fax (785)274-4305. E-mail: cappers@cappers.com. Website: www.cappers.com. Ogden Publications. K. C. Kompton, ed-in-chief. Timely news-oriented features with positive messages. Biweekly mag.; 40-56 pgs.; circ. 150,000. Subscription $14.95. 40% unsolicited freelance. Complete ms/cover letter by mail only. Pays about $2.50/printed inch for nonfiction on publication, pays $100-400 for fiction on acceptance for one-time rts. Articles to 1,000 wds. (50/yr.); fiction to 2,000 wds., serials to 25,000 wds. (20/yr.). Responds in 2-6 mos. Seasonal 6 mos. ahead. No simultaneous submissions or reprints. Prefers requested ms on CD (Mac). Uses some sidebars. Guidelines (also on Website); copy $4/9x12 SASE/4 stamps. (Ads)

Poetry: Attn: Poetry Editor. Buys 50/yr. Free verse, light verse, traditional; 4-16 lines. Pays $10-15 on acceptance. Submit max. 5 poems.

Fillers: Attn: Fillers Dept. Buys 50/yr. Short humor (humorous or thought-provoking one-liners); 10-50 wds. No payment.

Columns/Departments: Buys 26/yr. Garden Path (gardens/gardening), 500-1,000 wds. Payment varies. This column most open.

Tips: "Our publication is all original material either written by our readers/freelancers or occasionally by our staff. Every department, every article is open. Break in by reading at least 6 months of issues to know our special audience. Most open to nonfiction features and garden stories." Submissions are not acknowledged or status reports given.

$CATHEDRAL AGE, 3101 Wisconsin Ave. N.W., Washington DC 20016. (202)537-5681. Fax (202)364-6600. E-mail: Cathedral_Age@cathedral.org. Website: www.cathedralage.org. Protestant Episcopal Cathedral Foundation. Craig W. Stapert, pub. mngr. News from Washington National Cathedral and stories of interest to friends and supporters of WNC. Quarterly & online mag.; 36 pgs.; circ. 36,000. Subscription $15. 50% assigned freelance. Query; e-query OK. Pays to $750 on publication for all rts. Articles 1,200-1,500 wds. (10/yr.); book reviews 600 wds., ($250). Responds in 6 wks. Seasonal 6 mos. ahead. Requires requested ms on disk or by e-mail (attached file). Kill fee 50%. Uses some sidebars. Prefers NRSV. No guidelines; copy $5/9x12 SAE/5 stamps. (No ads)

Special Needs: Art, architecture, music.

Tips: "We assign all articles, so query with clips first. Always write from the viewpoint of an individual first, then move into a more general discussion of the topic. Human-interest angle important."

$CATHOLIC DIGEST, PO Box 180, Mystic CT 06355. (860)536-2611. Fax (860)536-5600. E-mail: catholicdigest@bayard-inc.com. Submissions to: cdsubmissions@bayardpubs.com. Website: www.CatholicDigest.com. Catholic/Bayard Publications. Dan Connors, ed-in-chief. Readers have a stake in being Catholic and a wide range of interests: religion, family, health, human relationships, good works, nostalgia, and more. Monthly & online mag.; 128 pgs.; circ. 400,000. Subscription $18.95. 15% unsolicited freelance; 20% assigned. Complete ms (for original material)/cover letter, tear sheets for reprints; no e-query. Pays $200-400 ($100 for reprints) on acceptance for one-time rts. Online-only articles receive $100, plus half of any traceable revenue. Articles 750-2,000 wds. (60/yr.). Responds in 6-8 wks. Seasonal 5 mos. ahead. Accepts reprints (tell when/where appeared). Accepts requested ms on disk or by e-mail (copied into message). Regularly uses sidebars. Prefers NAB. Guidelines (also on Website: www.catholicdigest.org/stops/info/writers.html); copy for 7x10 SAE/2 stamps. (Ads)

Fillers: Fillers Editor. Buys 200/yr. Anecdotes, cartoons, facts, jokes, quotes; 1 line to 300 wds.; $2/published line on publication.

Columns/Departments: Buys 75/yr. Open Door (personal stories of conversion to Catholicism); 200-500 wds.; $2/published line. See guidelines for full list.

Special Needs: Family and career concerns of Baby Boomers who have a stake in being Catholic.

Contest: See Website for current contest, or send an SASE.

Tips: "We favor the anecdotal approach. Stories must be strongly focused on a definitive topic that is illustrated for the reader with a well-developed series of true-life, interconnected vignettes."

**This periodical was #37 on the 2007 Top 50 Christian Publishers list (#31 in 2006, #48 in 2005).

$CATHOLIC FORESTER, Box 3012, Naperville IL 60566-7012. (630)983-3381. Toll-free fax (800)811-2140. E-mail: magazine@catholicforester.com. Website: www.catholicforester.com. Catholic Order of Foresters. Mary Anne File, ed. For mixed audience, primarily parents and grandparents between the ages of 30 and 80+. Quarterly mag.; 40 pgs.; circ. 100,000. Free/membership. 10% unsolicited freelance. Complete ms/cover letter; no phone/fax/e-query. Pays .30/wd. on acceptance for 1st or one-time rts. Articles 1,000-1,500 wds. (12-16/yr.); fiction for all ages 500-1,500 wds. (12-16/yr.). Responds in 12-16 wks. Seasonal 4-6 mos. ahead. Accepts simultaneous submissions & reprints (tell when/where appeared). Accepts requested ms by e-mail. Uses some sidebars. Prefers Catholic Bible. Guidelines (also on Website); copy for 9x12 SAE/4 stamps. (No ads)

Poetry: Buys 3/yr. Light verse, traditional; to 15 lines. Pay .30/wd. Submit max. 5 poems.

Tips: "Looking for informational, inspirational articles on finances and health. Writing should be energetic with good style and rhythm. Most open to general interest and fiction."

**This periodical was #26 on the 2007 Top 50 Christian Publishers list (#19 in 2006, #36 in 2005, #37 in 2004, #15 in 2003).

$CATHOLIC INSIGHT, PO Box 625, Adelaide Sta., 31 Adelaide St. E., Toronto ON M5C 2J8, Canada. (416)204-9601. Fax (416)204-1027. E-mail: reach@catholicinsight.com. Website: www.catholicinsight.com. Life Ethics Information Center. Fr. Alphonse de Valk, ed./pub. News, analysis, and commentary on social, ethical, political, and moral issues from a Catholic perspective. Monthly (11X) mag.; 44 pgs.; circ. 3,700. Subscription $35 Cdn., $55 U.S., International $65. 2% unsolicited freelance; 98% assigned. Query preferred; phone/fax/e-query OK. Pays $200 for 1,500 wds. ($250 for 2,000 wds.) on publication for 1st rts. Articles 750-1,500 wds. (20-30/yr.); book reviews 750 wds. ($85). Responds in 6-8 wks. Seasonal 2 mos. ahead. Accepts requested ms on disk. Uses some sidebars. Prefers RSV (Catholic). Guidelines (also by e-mail); copy $4 Cdn./9x12 SAE/$2 Cdn. postage or IRC. (Ads)

Tips: "We are interested in intelligent, well-researched, well-presented commentary on a political, religious, social, or cultural matter from the viewpoint of the Catholic Church."

$CATHOLIC NEW YORK, 1011—1st Ave., Rm. 1721, New York NY 10022. (212)688-2399. Fax (212)688-2642. E-mail: cny@cny.org. Website: www.cny.org. Catholic. John Woods, ed-in-chief. To inform New York Catholics. Biweekly newspaper; 40 pgs.; circ. 135,000. Subscription $24. 2% unsolicited freelance. Query or complete ms/cover letter. Pays $15-100 on publication for one-time rts. Articles 500-800 wds. Responds in 5 wks. Copy $3.

Tips: "Most open to columns about specific seasons of the Catholic Church, such as Advent, Christmas, Lent, and Easter."

$CATHOLIC PEACE VOICE, 532 W. 8th, Erie PA 16502-1343. (814)453-4955. Fax (814)452-4784. E-mail: info@paxchristiusa.org. Website: www.paxchristiusa.org. Dave Robinson, ed. (Dave@paxchristiusa.org). For members of Pax Christi USA, the national Catholic Peace Movement. Bimonthly newsmag.; 16-20 pgs.; circ. 23,000. Subscription $20, free to members. 15-20% unsolicited freelance; 25-30% assigned. Complete ms; phone/fax/e-query OK. Pays $50-75 on publication for all & electronic rts. Articles 500-1,500 wds. (10-15/yr.); reviews 750 wds., $50. Responds in 1-2 wks. Accepts simultaneous submissions & reprints (tell when/where appeared). Accepted ms on disk or by e-mail (attached or copied into message). Uses some sidebars. Also accepts submissions from teens. Guidelines (also by e-mail); copy for 9x12 SAE/2 stamps. (Ads)

Poetry: Accepts 1-5/yr. Avant-garde, free verse, haiku, light verse, traditional. Submit max. 2 poems. No payment.

Tips: "Most open to features and news, as well as reviews and resources. E-mailing us and pitching a story is the best way to break into our publication. Emphasis is on nonviolence. No sexist language."

THE CATHOLIC REGISTER, 1155 Yonge St., #401, Toronto ON M4T 1W2, Canada. (416)934-3410. Fax (416)934-3409. E-mail: editor@catholicregister.org, or news@catholicregister.org, or through Website: www.catholicregister.org. Michey Conlon, mng. ed. To provide reliable information about the world from a Catholic perspective. Weekly (47X) tabloid; circ. 33,000. Subscription $37.20. Open to unsolicited freelance. Not in topical listings. (Ads)

$CATHOLIC SENTINEL, 5536 N.E. Hassalo St., Portland OR 97213. (503)281-1191. Fax (503)460-5496. E-mail: sentinel@ocp.org. Website: www.sentinel.org. Oregon Catholic Press. Bob Pfohman, ed. Weekly tabloid; 20 pgs.; circ. 16,000. Subscription $28. 2% unsolicited freelance; 0% assigned. Query/clips. Payment negotiable on publication for one-time rts. Articles 600-1,500 wds. Responds in 4 wks. Seasonal 2 mos. ahead. Accepts requested ms on disk or by e-mail (copied into message). Uses some sidebars. Prefers NAS. Incomplete topical listings. Guidelines on Website; copy for 9x12 SAE/3 stamps. (Ads)

Tips: "We're most open to local church news and feature articles."

$CATHOLIC TELEGRAPH, 100 E. 8th St., Cincinnati OH 45202. (513)421-3131. Fax (513)381-2242. E-mail: doconnor@catholiccincinnati.org. Website: www.catholiccincinnati.org. Dennis O'Connor, mng. ed. Diocese newspaper for Cincinnati area (all articles must have a Cincinnati or Ohio connection). Weekly newspaper; 24-28 pgs.; circ. 100,000. Limited unsolicited freelance; mostly assigned. Send résumé and writing samples for assignment. Pays varying rates on publication for all rts. Articles. Responds in 2-3 wks. Kill fee. No guidelines; copy $2/#10 SASE.

Fillers: Newsbreaks (local).

Special Needs: Personality features for "Everyday Evangelists" section. These are feature stories that offer a slice of life of a person who is making a difference as a Roman Catholic Christian in their community. Prefer to have a tie within the Archdiocese of Cincinnati;

must be an Ohioan. Complete ms; 800 wds.; pays $40 (extra for photos of individual interviewed).

Tips: "Most likely to accept an article about a person, event, or ministry with an Ohio connection—Cincinnati-Dayton area."

$THE CATHOLIC YEARBOOK, 7010—6th St. N., Oakdale MN 55128. (651)702-0086. Fax (651)702-0074. E-mail: catholic2@msn.com. Apostolic Publishing Co. Inc. Roger Jensen, ed. Family magazine of articles and prayers, promoting the sharing of Christian fellowship among Catholics. Annual mag.; 68-72 pgs.; circ. 400,000. 60% unsolicited freelance; 40% assigned. Complete ms/cover letter. Pays $5-50 on publication for 1st rts. Articles 750-1,500 wds. (20/yr.). Response time varies. No simultaneous submissions; accepts reprints. Accepts articles on disk or by e-mail (attached file). No kill fee. Uses some sidebars. Prefers NIV. Also accepts submissions from children/teens. Guidelines. (Ads)

Poetry: Buys 10/yr. Light verse, traditional; 15-50 wds., up to 150 wds. Pays $8-30. Submit max. 3 poems.

Fillers: Buys 5-10/yr. Anecdotes, facts, games, prayers, quizzes, quotes, and word puzzles; 50-300 wds. Pays $5-30.

$CBA RETAILERS+RESOURCES (formerly Aspiring Retail), 9240 Explorer Dr., Colorado Springs CO 80920. Toll-free (800)252-1950. (719)272-3555. Fax (719)272-3510. E-mail: publications@cbaonline.org. Website: www.cbaonline.org. Christian Booksellers Assn. Submit to The Editor; Carrie Erickson, music/video ed. (cerickson@cbaonline.org). To provide Christian bookstore owners and managers with professional retail skills, product information, and industry news. Monthly trade journal (also in digital edition); 110-260 pgs.; circ. 8,000. Subscription $59.95 (for nonmembers). 0% unsolicited freelance; 30% assigned. Query/clips; fax/e-query OK. Pays .20-.30/wd. on acceptance for all rts. Articles 800-2,000 wds. (30/yr. assigned); book/music/video reviews, 150 wds., $30-35. Responds in 8 wks. Seasonal 4-5 mos. ahead. Prefers requested ms on disk. Regularly uses sidebars. Accepts any modern Bible version. Theme list; copy $5/9x12 SAE/$2.13 postage (mark "Media Mail"). (Ads/Carlton Dunn & Assoc./856-582-0690)

Fillers: Buys 12/yr. Cartoons ($100), retail facts, ideas, trends, newsbreaks.

Columns/Departments: Buys 10-20/yr. Industry Watch; Music News; Gift News; Video & Software News; Book News; Kids News; Spanish News; all 100-500 wds. Pays .16-.25/wd. Query.

Special Needs: Trends in retail, consumer buying habits, market profiles. By assignment only.

Tips: "Looking for writers who have been owners/managers/buyers/sales staff in Christian retail stores. All our articles are by assignment and focus on producing and selling Christian products or conducting retail business. Send cover letter, including related experience and areas of interest, plus samples. We also assign reviews of books, music, videos, Spanish products, kids products, and software. Ask for calendar for product news and market-segment features."

CBN.COM (CHRISTIAN BROADCASTING NETWORK), 977 Centerville Turnpike, Virginia Beach VA 23463. (757)226-3557. Fax (757)226-3575. E-mail: chris.carpenter@cbn.org. Website: www.CBN.com. Christian Broadcasting Network. Chris Carpenter, dir. of internal programming; Belinda Elliott, books ed. Online mag.; 1.6 million users/mo. Free online. Open to unsolicited freelance. E-mail submissions (attached as a Word document). Query/clips; e-query OK. **NO PAYMENT.** Devotions 500-700 wds.; Spiritual Life Teaching, 700-1,500 wds.; Living Features (Family, Entertainment, Health, Finance), 700-1,500 wds.; Movie/TV/Music Reviews, 500-1,000 wds.; Hard News, 300-700 wds.; News Features, 700-1,500 wds.; News Interviews, 1,000-2,000 wds; fiction. Accepts reprints (tell when/where appeared). Also accepts submissions from teens. Prefers NLT/NASB/NKJV. Guidelines by e-mail; copy online. (No ads)

Special Needs: Adoption stories/references, world religions from Judeo/Christian perspective.

Tips: "In lieu of payment, we link to author's Website and provide a link for people to purchase the author's materials in our Web store."

$CELEBRATE LIFE, PO Box 1350, Stafford VA 22555. (540)659-4171. Fax (540)659-2586. E-mail: CLMag@all.org. Website: www.clmagazine.org. American Life League. Anita Crane, ed. A pro-life, pro-family magazine. Bimonthly mag.; 48 pgs.; circ. 65,000. Subscription $12.95. 50% unsolicited freelance; 50% assigned. E-query preferred. Pays on publication according to quality of article for one-time or reprint rts. Articles 400-1,600 wds. Seasonal 4 mos. ahead. Accepts few reprints. Prefers e-mail submissions. No kill fee. Also accepts submissions from children/teens. Prefers Jerusalem Bible (Catholic). Guidelines/theme list on Website. (No ads)

Special Needs: Personal experience about abortion, post-abortion stress/healing, adoption, activism/young people's involvement, death/dying, euthanasia, eugenics, special needs children, personhood, chastity, large families, stem cell science, and other right-to-life topics.

Tips: "We are no-exceptions pro-life in keeping with the Catholic Church. Photos are preferred for personal stories. No fiction or poetry."

**This periodical was #43 on the 2007 Top 50 Christian Publishers list.

$CGA WORLD, PO Box 249, Olyphant PA 18447. (570)586-1091. Fax (570)586-7721. E-mail: cgaemail@aol.com. Website: www.catholicgoldenage.org. Catholic Golden Age. Barbara Pegula, mng. ed. For Catholics 50+. Bimonthly mag.; 8 pgs.; circ. 100,000. Subscription/membership $12. Query. Pays .10/wd. on publication for 1st, one-time, or reprint rts. Articles 600-1,000 wds.; fiction 600-1,000 wds. Responds in 6 wks. Seasonal 6 mos. ahead. Accepts reprints (tell when/where appeared). Accepts requested ms on disk. Guidelines; copy for 9x12 SAE/3 stamps. (Ads)

CHALLENGE WEEKLY, PO Box 68-800, Newton, Auckland, New Zealand 1032. Phone (64-9)378 4052, or +64 027 271 2849. Fax (64-9)376-3855. E-mail: editor@challengeweekly.co.nz. Website: www.challengeweekly.co.nz. Challenge Publishing Society. Garth George, ed. Proclaiming the good news that Jesus is the Christ. Weekly online newspaper. Subscription $68. Incomplete topical listings.

$CHALLENGING DESTINY, RR #6, St. Marys ON N4X 1C8, Canada. E-mail: csp@golden.net. Website: http://challengingdestiny.com. Crystalline Sphere Publishing. David M. Switzer, ed. Canadian science fiction and fantasy short story magazine, with reviews and interviews with Canadian authors. Quarterly online mag; circ. 200. 80% unsolicited freelance. Complete ms; e-query OK. Pays .01/wd. (Cdn.) on publication for electronic rts. for 6 mos. Fiction 2,000-10,000 wds./18/yr. (considers shorter or longer stories). Responds in 2-6 wks. Accepts simultaneous submissions & sometimes reprints (tell when/where appeared). Send stories by mail; no e-mail submissions. Guidelines (also on Website); copy $6.50. (No ads)

Tips: "Not currently accepting stories."

CHANNELS, 3819 Bloor St. W., Toronto ON M9P 1K7, Canada. Phone/fax (519)651-2232. E-mail: cbbrown@rogers.com. Website: http://renewalfellowship.presbyterian.ca. The Renewal Fellowship/Presbyterian (P.C.C.). Calvin Brown, ed. For Presbyterians seeking spiritual renewal and biblical orthodoxy. Quarterly mag.; 20 pgs.; circ. 2,000. Subscription $12. 10% unsolicited freelance; 90% assigned. Query; e-query OK. **PAYS IN COPIES** for one-time rts. Articles 1,000-1,500 wds. (15/yr.); book reviews 300 wds. Responds in 4 wks. Seasonal 4-6 mos. ahead. Accepts reprints (tell when/where appeared). Prefers mss by e-mail (attached file/RTF). Regularly uses sidebars. Also accepts submissions from teens. No guidelines; copy for #10 SAE/3 stamps. (Ads)

Poetry: Accepts 3/yr. Free verse, haiku, light verse, traditional; 3 lines & up. Submit max. 6 poems.

Fillers: Accepts 4/yr. Anecdotes, cartoons, prayers.; 6-100 wds.

$CHARISMA & CHRISTIAN LIFE, 600 Rinehart Rd., Lake Mary FL 32746. (407)333-0600. Fax (407)333-7133. E-mail: charisma@strang.com. Website: www.charismamag.com. Strang Communications. J. Lee Grady, exec. ed.; Jimmy Stewart, mng. ed.; submit to Adrienne S. Gaines, assoc. ed. Primarily for the Pentecostal and Charismatic Christian community. Monthly & online mag.; 100+ pgs.; circ. 250,000. Subscription $24.97. 80% assigned freelance. Query only; no phone query, e-query OK. Pays up to $1,000 (for assigned) on publication for all rts. Articles 2,000-3,000 wds. (40/yr.); book/music reviews, 200 wds., $20-35. Responds in 8-12 wks. Seasonal 5 mos. ahead. Kill fee $50. Prefers accepted ms by e-mail. Regularly uses sidebars. Guidelines on Website; free copy. (Ads)

Tips: "Most open to news section, reviews, or features. Query (published clips help a lot)."
**#1 Best-selling magazine in Christian retail stores.

THE CHARLOTTE WORLD, 201 S. College St., Ste. 2010, Charlotte NC 28244. (704)295-7906. Fax (704)295-7919. E-mail: warren.smith@thecharlotteworld.com. Website: www.thecharlotteworld.com. World Newspaper Publishing. Warren Smith, ed. To report unreported, under-reported, or badly reported news, from a Christian perspective. Biweekly newspaper; circ. 20,000. Subscription $36. Open to unsolicited freelance. Query preferred. Articles; reviews. Incomplete topical listings. (Ads)

**2007 EPA Award of Merit—Newspaper; 2006 EPA Award of Excellence—Newspaper.

$CHICKEN SOUP FOR THE SOUL BOOK SERIES, PO Box 30880, Santa Barbara CA 93130. (805)563-2935. Fax (805)563-2945. E-mail: webmaster@chickensoupforthesoul.com. Website: www.chickensoup.com. Barbara LoMonaco, story acquisitions (blomonaco@chickensoupforthesoul.com). Inspirational anthologies to open your heart and rekindle your spirit; audience is open to all ages, races, etc. Quarterly trade paperback books; 385 pgs.; circ. 60 million. $14.95/book. 98% unsolicited freelance. Make submissions via Website. Pays $200 on publication for reprint, simultaneous, & electronic rts. Articles 1,200 wds. max. Seasonal anytime. Accepts simultaneous submissions & reprints (tell when/where appeared). Accepts e-mail submissions: stories@chickensoupforthesoul.com (attached file/Word). No kill fee. Guidelines/themes on Website; free sample. (No ads)

Fillers: Anecdotes, cartoons, facts, kid quotes, quotes, short humor; 10-200 wds. Pays.

Special Needs: See Website for a list of upcoming titles.

Contest: See Website for list of current contests.

Tips: "Visit our Website and be familiar with our book series. Send in stories via mail or e-mail, complete with contact information. Submit story typed, double spaced, max. 1,200 words, in a Word document."

$CHICKEN SOUP FOR THE SOUL MAGAZINE, PO Box 770458, Memphis TN 38177. (901) 312-7711. E-mail: staff@chickensoupmagazine.com. Website: www.chickensoupmagazine.com. Modern Media/Chicken Soup for the Soul Enterprises. Mignonne Wright, ed-in-chief. Bimonthly mag. Subscription $15. Pays $50 on publication for stories 500-1,000 wds. (from readers). Freelancers should send a query/writing samples by e-mail. Does not return submissions. Guidelines on Website. Acknowledges submissions only if made through Website. Incomplete topical listings. (Ads)

CHOCOLATE PAGES ONLINE MAGAZINE, 33011 Tall Oaks St., Farmington Hills MI 48336-4551. (248)249-2320. E-mail: pamperry@ministrymarketingsolutions.com. Website: www.ministrymarketingsolutions.com. Ministry Marketing Solutions. Pam Perry, pub. About current books targeting the African American Christian market; goes to bookstores, book clubs, black media, Christian media, church reading groups, and writer's clubs. Books for review accepted via mail and press kits via e-mail.

CHOICE NEWSPAPER, PO Box 111, Stevens PA 17578-0111. (215)825-7613. Fax (717)336-7670. E-mail: choicenews@gmail.com. Website: www.choicenews.org. Sergey V. Plotnikov, ed./pub. Provides opportunity to everyone to choose life through Jesus Christ, and encourage and strengthen them through editorials, sermons, testimonies, and news. Monthly newspaper published in Russian; 20 pgs.; circ. 8,000. Subscription $30. Open to freelance. Complete ms; e-query OK. Accepts full ms by e-mail. **NO PAYMENT** for nonexclusive rts. Not copyrighted. Accepts simultaneous submissions & reprints. Requires e-mail submission (attached file). Uses some sidebars. Also accepts submissions from teens. No guidelines; free copy. (Ads)

Fillers: Newsbreaks, quotes, sermon illustrations.

Tips: "Write by e-mail—preferably in Russian."

CHRISTIAN BUSINESS DAILY.COM (formerly Business Reform Magazine), c/o Selling Among Wolves LLC, 379 Interstate Blvd., Sarasota FL 34240. (941)377-9384. Fax (941)371-6211. E-mail: articles@christianbusinessdaily.com. Website: www.christianbusinessdaily.com. Business Reform Foundation. Lyle Becker, mng. ed. Business news from a Christian world-view. Bimonthly mag. Open to freelance. Query. Articles. Guidelines by e-mail. Incomplete topical listings. (Ads)

THE CHRISTIAN CHRONICLE, 2501 E. Memorial Rd., Edmond OK 73013. (405)425-5070. Fax (405)425-5076. E-mail: bailey.mcbride@oc.edu. Website: www.christianchronicle.org. Churches of Christ. Bobby Ross, mng. ed. An international newspaper for members of the Church of Christ. Monthly newspaper & online. Subscription $20 (one-time fee). Incomplete topical listings.

$CHRISTIAN CITIZEN USA, 250 N. Cassel Rd., Dayton OH 45377-9451. (937)233-6227. Fax (937)233-6231. E-mail: editor@ccn-usa.net. Website: www.citizenusa.us. Christian Media Group Inc. Pendra Snyder, ed. Only Judeo-Christian newspaper in Ohio; news features, current events presented from Judeo-Christian world-view. Monthly newspaper; circ. 60,000. Subscription $50/52 issues. 10% unsolicited freelance; 75% assigned. Query/clips; phone/fax/e-query OK. Accepts full mss by e-mail. Pay $25-50 (or no pmt.) on publication for all (if assigned) or 1st rts. Articles to 800 wds.; book reviews, 500-600 wds.; music reviews, 200-300 wds.; video reviews, 500 wds. (pays $20-25). Responds in 4 wks. Seasonal 2-3 mos. ahead. Prefers e-mail submissions (copied into message). No kill fee. Uses some sidebars. Also accepts submissions from teens. Prefers KJV. (Ads)

Fillers: Buys 4/yr. Cartoons, games, short humor, word puzzles. Pays $20-25.

Columns/Departments: Buys 4/yr. News features, under 800 wds., $20-50 or no payment. E-query.

Tips: "Most open to reviews and news features."

THE CHRISTIAN CIVIC LEAGUE OF MAINE RECORD, 70 Sewall St., Augusta ME 04330. (207)622-7634. Fax (207)621-0035. E-mail: email@cclmaine.org. Website: www.leaguerecord.com (online version of magazine). Michael Hein, administrator. Focuses on public policy, political action, some church and public service. Monthly newsletter; 4 pgs.; circ. 4,600. Subscription free. Some freelance. Query; phone/fax/e-query OK. **NO PAYMENT** for one-time rts. Articles 800-1,200 wds. (10-12/yr.). Responds in 4-8 wks. Accepts simultaneous query & reprints. Guidelines by e-mail/Website; free copy. (No ads)

Tips: "Most open to opinion pieces and news item commentary."

CHRISTIAN COMPUTING MAGAZINE, PO Box 319, Belton MO 64012. Toll-free phone/fax (800)456-1868. (816)331-8142. E-mail: steve@ccmag.com. Website: www.ccmag.com. Steve Hewitt, ed-in-chief. For Christian/church computer users. Monthly (11X) & online mag.; 2 pgs.; circ. 30,000. Subscription $14.95, or free digital version. 40% unsolicited freelance. Query/clips; fax/e-query OK. **NO PAYMENT** for all rts. Articles 1,000-1,800 wds. (12/yr.). Responds in 4 wks. Seasonal 2 mos. ahead. Accepts reprints. Requires requested ms on disk. Regularly uses sidebars. Guidelines; copy for 9x12 SAE.

Fillers: Accepts 6 cartoons/yr.

Columns/Departments: Accepts 12/yr. Telecommunications (computer), 1,500-1,800 wds.

Special Needs: Articles on Internet, DTP, computing.

$CHRISTIAN COURIER (Canada), 1 Hiscott St., St. Catherines ON L2R 1C7, Canada. (U.S. address: Box 110, Lewiston NY 14092-0110). Toll-free (800)969-4838. (905)682-8311. Fax (905)682-8313. E-mail: editor@christiancourier.ca. Website: www.christiancourier.ca. Reformed Faith Witness. Harry Der Nederlanden, ed. To present Canadian and international news, both religious and general, from a Reformed Christian perspective. Biweekly tabloid; 24-28 pgs.; circ. 4,000. Subscription $40 Cdn.; $32, U.S. 20% unsolicited freelance; 80% assigned. Complete ms/cover letter; fax/e-query OK. Pays $75-120 U.S., up to .10/wd. for assigned ($50-100 for unsolicited); 30 days after publication for one-time, reprint, or simultaneous rts. Not copyrighted. Articles 700-1,200 wds. (40/yr.); fiction to 1,200-2,500 wds. (6/yr.); book reviews 800-1,200 wds. Responds in 1-3 wks. Seasonal 3 mos. ahead. Accepts simultaneous submissions & reprints (tell when/where appeared). Prefers accepted ms by e-mail (attached file). No kill fee. Uses some sidebars. Prefers NIV. Guidelines/deadlines on Website; no copy. (Ads)

Poetry: Buys 12/yr. Avant-garde, free verse, light verse, traditional; 10-30 lines; $20-30. Submit max. 5 poems.

Tips: "Suggest an aspect of the theme which you believe you could cover well, have insight into, could treat humorously, etc. Show that you think clearly, write clearly, and have something to say that we should want to read. Have a strong biblical world-view and avoid moralism and sentimentality." Responds only if material is accepted.

CHRISTIAN COURIER (WI), 1933 W. Wisconsin Ave., Milwaukee WI 53233. (414)345-3545. Fax (414)345-3544. E-mail: christiancourier@juno.com. ProBuColls Assn. John M. Fisco Jr., pub.; Don Conklin, ed. To propagate the gospel of Jesus Christ in the Midwest. Monthly newspaper; circ. 10,000. 10% freelance. Query; phone/fax/e-query OK. **PAYS IN COPIES,** for one-time rts. Not copyrighted. Articles 300-1,500 wds. (6/yr.). Responds in 4-8 wks. Seasonal 2 mos. ahead. Accepts reprints. Guidelines; free copy. (Ads)

Fillers: Anecdotes, facts, newsbreaks; 10-100 wds.

Tips: "We are always in need of seasonal feature/filler type of articles: Christmas, Easter, 4th of July, etc."

$CHRISTIAN EXAMINER, PO Box 2606, El Cajon CA 92021. (619)668-5100. Fax (619)668-1115. E-mail: info@christianexaminer.com. Website: www.christianexaminer.com. Keener Communications. Lori Arnold, ed. To report on current events from an evangelical Christian perspective, particularly traditional family values and church trends. Monthly & online newspaper; 24-36 pgs.; circ. 180,000. Subscription $19.95. 5% assigned. Query/clips. Pays .10/wd., on publication for 1st & electronic rts. Articles 600-900 wds. Responds in 4-5 wks. Seasonal 3 mos. ahead. No simultaneous submissions or reprints. Prefers e-mail submissions (copied into message). No kill fee. Uses some sidebars. Guidelines by e-mail; copy $1.50/9x12 SAE. (Ads)

Tips: "We prefer news stories."

**2005, 2004 EPA Award of Merit—Newspaper.

$THE CHRISTIAN HERALD, PO Box 68526, Brampton ON L6R 0J8, Canada. (905)874-1731. Fax (905)874-1781. E-mail: info@christianherald.ca. Website: www.christianherald.ca. Covenant Communications. Fazal Karim Jr., ed-in-chief. A Canadian-Christian tabloid with a focus on Christian arts and entertainment. Monthly tabloid; 24 pgs.; circ. 31,000. Subscription free, or $26.75 if mailed. 5% unsolicited freelance; 95% assigned. Query; fax/e-query OK. Pays $20-100 or .10/wd. on publication for 1st rts. Articles 500-1,500 wds.; reviews 150-200 wds. (no payment). Responds in 4 wks. Seasonal 3 mos. ahead. Accepts simultaneous submissions & reprints (tell when/where appeared). Prefers e-mail submissions (attached file). No kill fee. Uses some sidebars. Also accepts submissions from teens. Prefers ESV, KJV, NLT. Guidelines (also by e-mail); copy for 9x12 SAE/$2 Canadian postage. (Ads)

Fillers: Accepts 10/yr. Cartoons, facts, games, jokes, prayers, quotes, and word puzzles; 20-100 wds. No payment.

Columns/Departments: Interviews (Christian newsmakers/personalities), 900 wds., $20-50.

Tips: "Most open to articles/columns with specific reference to Canadians, with Canadian quotes, relevance, etc."

$CHRISTIAN HISTORY & BIOGRAPHY, 465 Gundersen Dr., Carol Stream IL 60188. (630)260-6200. Fax (630)480-2004. E-mail: CHeditor@christianhistory.net. Website: www.christianhistory.net. Christianity Today Intl. David Neff, exec. ed.; Jennifer Trafton, mng. ed.; submit to Jennifer Golossanov, asst. ed. To teach Christian history to educated readers in an engaging manner. Quarterly mag. & newsletter; 52 pgs.; circ. 50,000. Subscription $19.95. 5% unsolicited freelance; 95% assigned. Query only. Pays .10-.25/wd. on publication for 1st rts. Articles 500-3,000 wds. (1/yr.). Responds in 2 mos. Accepts reprints (tell when/where appeared). Prefers accepted ms by e-mail (attached or copied into message). Kill fee 50%. Regularly uses sidebars. Prefers NIV. Guidelines/theme list (also by e-mail); copy for 9x12 SASE. (Ads)

Tips: "Let us know your particular areas of specialization and any books or articles you have published in the area of Christian history. Theme-related articles are usually assigned. Most open to nonthemed departments: Story Behind; People Worth Knowing; Turning Point. Please familiarize yourself with our magazine before querying."

**2005 EPA Award of Merit—General.

$CHRISTIAN HOME & SCHOOL, 3350 East Paris Ave. S.E., Grand Rapids MI 49512. (616)957-1070, ext. 239. Fax (616)957-5022. E-mail: RogerS@CSIonline.org, or GBordewyk@CSIonline.org. Website: www.CSIonline.org. Christian Schools Intl. Gordon L. Bordewyk, exec. ed.; Roger Schmurr, sr. ed. Focuses on parenting and Christian education; for parents who send their children to Christian schools. Quarterly & online mag.; 32 pgs.; circ. 67,000. Subscription $13.95. 95% unsolicited; 5% assigned. Complete ms or query, prefers e-query. Pays $175-250 on publication for 1st rts. Articles 1,000-2,000 wds. (30/yr.); Christmas fiction 1,000-2,000 wds. (5/yr.); book reviews $25 (assigned). Responds in 1 mo. Seasonal 4 mos. ahead. Accepts simultaneous query. Accepts requested ms on disk (clean copy they can scan); prefers e-mail submission (attached file). Regularly uses sidebars. Prefers NIV. Guidelines/theme list (also on Website); copy for 9x12 SAE/4 stamps. (Ads)

Fillers: Parenting ideas; 100-250 wds.; $25-40.

Tips: "Most open to feature articles. Include a mature. biblical perspective—not just a Bible verse tacked on. Looking for articles on teens, and single parenting. Ask to be assigned to do a book review, or send an article on speculation."

**2007 EPA Award of Merit—Organizational. This periodical was #44 on the 2007 Top 50 Christian Publishers list (#32 in 2006, #44 in 2005, #38 in 2004, #33 in 2003).

$CHRISTIANITY TODAY, 465 Gundersen Dr., Carol Stream IL 60188-2498. (630)260-6200. Fax (630)260-8428. E-mail: cteditor@christianitytoday.com. Website: www.christianitytoday.com/ctmag. Christianity Today Inc. David Neff, ed. For evangelical Christian thought leaders who seek to integrate their faith commitment with responsible action. Monthly & online mag.; 65-120 pgs.; circ. 155,000. Subscription $24.95. 80% freelance (mostly assigned). Query only; fax/e-query OK. Pays .20-.30/wd. on publication for 1st rts. Articles 1,000-4,000 wds. (60/yr.); book reviews 800-1,000 wds. (pays per-page rate). Responds in 13 wks. Seasonal 8 mos. ahead. Accepts reprints (tell when/where appeared—payment 25% of regular rate). Kill fee 50%. Does not use sidebars. Prefers NIV. Guidelines on Website; copy for 9x12 SAE/3 stamps. (Ads)

Tips: "Read the magazine." Does not return unsolicited manuscripts.

**#8 Best-selling Magazine in Christian retail stores. 2006, 2005 EPA Award of Excellence—General. 2006, 2005, 2004 EPA Award of Merit—Online (for ChristianityToday Online).

$CHRISTIANITY TODAY MOVIES, 465 Gundersen Dr., Carol Stream IL 60188. (630)260-6200. Fax (630)260-8428. E-mail: CTmovies@christianitytoday.com. Website: www.Christianity TodayMovies.com. Christianity Today Intl. Mark Moring, ed. To inform and equip Christian moviegoers to make discerning choices about films, through timely coverage, insightful reviews and interviews, educated opinion, and relevant news, all from a Christian world-view. Weekly e-zine. Subscription free. 10% unsolicited freelance; 90% assigned. Query; fax/e-query OK. Accepts full mss by e-mail. Pays $75-125 on acceptance for 1st rts. Articles 500-2,000 wds. (150/yr.) & movie reviews 700-1,000 wds. ($100). Responds in 2 wks. No seasonal. Sometimes accepts simultaneous submissions and reprints (tell when/where appeared). Prefers e-mail submissions (attached file). Some kill fees 50%. Uses some sidebars. Prefers NIV. No guidelines; copy online. (Ads)

Tips: "Study our Website; know what we're doing. Always looking for commentaries and/or news pieces on trends in the industry, especially as they relate to a Christian audience.

**2007 EPA Award of Merit—Online.

$THE CHRISTIAN JOURNAL, 1032 W. Main, Medford OR 97501. (541)773-4004. Fax (541)773-9917. E-mail: Chad@liftingthecross.com. Website: www.liftingthecross.com/journal-guidelines.php. Lifting the Cross Ministries. Chad McComas, ed. Dedicated to sharing encouragement with the body of Christ in Southern Oregon and Northern California. Monthly & online newspaper; 16-24 pgs.; circ. 15,000. Subscription $20; most copies distributed free. 50% unsolicited freelance; 50% assigned. Complete ms; phone/fax query OK. Pays .01/wd. on publication for one-time rts. Articles & fiction 600-800 wds; reviews 300-500 wds.; children's stories 600 wds. Prefers articles by e-mail to info@thechristianjournal.org (attached file). Also accepts submissions from children or teens. Guidelines/theme list by mail or on Website; copy $1.20/9x12 SAE/3 stamps. (Ads)

Poetry: Accepts 12-20/yr. Free verse, haiku, light verse, traditional; 4-12 lines. Submit max. 2 poems.

Fillers: Accepts 50/yr. Anecdotes, cartoons, jokes, kid quotes, newsbreaks, prayers, quotes, short humor, or word puzzles; 100-300 wds.

Columns/Departments: Accepts 6/yr. Youth, 600-800 wds; Seniors, 600-800 wds.; Children's stories, 600 wds.

Tips: "Send articles on themes; each issue has a theme. Theme articles get first choice."

CHRISTIAN MEDIA, Box 448, Jacksonville OR 97530. (541)899-8888. E-mail: James@Christian MediaNetwork.com. Website: www.ChristianMediaDaily.com, or www.ChristianMediaNetwork .com. James Lloyd, ed./pub. Updates on world conditions, politics, economics, in the light of prophecy. Quarterly & online tabloid; 24 pgs.; circ. 25,000. Query; prefers phone query. **NO PAYMENT** for negotiable rts. Articles; book & music reviews, 3 paragraphs. Accepts simultaneous submissions & reprints. Prefers requested ms on disk. Requires KJV. Copy for 9x12 SAE/2 stamps.

Special Needs: Particularly interested in stories that expose dirty practices in the industry—royalty rip-offs, misleading ads, financial misconduct, etc. No flowery pieces on celebrities; wants well-documented articles on abuse in the media.

CHRISTIAN MOTORSPORTS ILLUSTRATED, PO Box 929, Bristow OK 74010-0929. (607)742-3407. E-mail: cpo7@loving-hearts.org. Website: www.christianmotorsports.com. CPO Publishing. Roland Osborne, pub. Covers Christians involved in motorsports. Bimonthly mag.; 64 pgs.; circ. 40,000. Subscription $38/2 yrs. 50% unsolicited freelance. Complete ms; no phone/fax/e-query. **NO PAYMENT.** Articles 500-2,000 wds. (30/yr.). Seasonal 4 mos. ahead. Requires requested ms on disk. Regularly uses sidebars. No guidelines; free copy. (Ads)

Poetry: Accepts 10/yr. Any type. Submit max. 10 poems.

Fillers: Accepts 100/yr. Anecdotes, cartoons, facts, games, ideas, jokes, newsbreaks, prayers, prose, quizzes, quotes, short humor.

Columns/Departments: Accepts 10/yr.

Tips: "Most open to personal experiences of God's miraculous presence in lives: healing, salvation, deliverance from alcohol, drugs, pornography, etc., with some sort of motorsports as a background. Send a story on a Christian involved in motorsports: cars, tractors, motorcycles, airplanes, go-carts, lawnmowers, etc."

CHRISTIAN NEWS NORTHWEST, PO Box 974, Newberg OR 97132. Phone/fax (503)537-9220. E-mail: cnnw@cnnw.com. Website: www.cnnw.com. John Fortmeyer, ed./pub. News of ministry in the evangelical Christian community in western and central Oregon and southwest Washington; distributed primarily through evangelical churches. Monthly newspaper; 32-44 pgs.; circ. 33,000. Subscription $20. 10% unsolicited freelance; 5% assigned. Query; phone/fax/e-query OK. **NO PAYMENT.** Not copyrighted. Articles 300-400 wds. (100/yr.). Responds in 4 wks. Seasonal 3 mos. ahead. Accepts reprints (tell when/where appeared). Accepts e-mail submissions. Regularly uses sidebars. Guidelines (also by e-mail); copy $1.50. (Ads)

Tips: "Most open to ministry-oriented features. Our space is always tight, but stories on lesser-known, Northwest-based ministries are encouraged. Keep it very concise. Since we focus on the Pacific Northwest, it would probably be difficult for anyone outside the region to break into our publication."

**2006 EPA Award of Merit—Newspaper.

THE CHRISTIAN OBSERVER, 9400 Fairview Ave., Ste. 200, Manassas VA 22110. (703)335-2844. Fax (703)368-4817. E-mail: editor@christianobserver.org. Website: www.ChristianObserver.org. Christian Observer Foundation; Presbyterian Reformed. Dr. Edwin P. Elliott, mng. ed. To encourage and edify God's people and families; print version of *Presbyterians-Week*. Monthly newspaper; 32 pgs.; circ. 2,000. Subscription $27. 10% unsolicited freelance; 90% assigned. Query; phone/e-query OK. **NO PAYMENT.** Accepts e-mail submissions. (Ads)

CHRISTIAN ONLINE MAGAZINE. E-mail: submissions@christianmagazine.org. Website: www.ChristianMagazine.org. Darlene Osborne, pub. Strictly founded on the Word of God, this magazine endeavors to bring you the best Christian information on the net. Monthly e-zine. Subscription free. 10% unsolicited freelance; 90% assigned. E-query. Articles 500-700 wds. Responds in 1 wk. Seasonal 2 mos. ahead. Prefers accepted ms by e-mail (attached file). **NO PAYMENT.** Regularly uses sidebars. Also accepts submissions from children/teens. Prefers KJV. Guidelines on Website. (Ads)

Fillers: Accepts 50/yr. Prayers, prose, quizzes, short humor; 500 wds.

Columns/Departments: Variety Column, 700-1,000 wds. Query.

Tips: "Most open to solid Christian articles founded on the Word of God."

THE CHRISTIAN OUTLOOK, 492 Hob Moor Rd., Yardley, Birmingham B25 8UB, United Kingdom. Phone +44 (0)870 383 0197. Fax +44 (0)870 199 2302. E-mail through Website: www.thechristianoutlook.net. Nondenominational. Issues on life and living from a Christian perspective. E-zine. Free online. Open to unsolicited freelance. Submit through Website. Incomplete topical listings.

Tips: "We also maintain forums for online interaction among Christians, and between Christians and non-Christians."

THE CHRISTIAN RANCHMAN/COWBOYS FOR CHRIST, 504 "D" F.M. 718, Newark TX 76071. (817)236-0023. Fax (817)236-0024. E-mail: cwb4christ@cowboysforchrist.net. Website: www.CowboysforChrist.net. Interdenominational. Ted Pressley, ed. Monthly tabloid; 20 pgs.; circ. 43,800. No subscription. 85% unsolicited freelance. Complete ms/cover letter. **NO PAYMENT** for all rts. Articles 350-1,000 wds.; book/video reviews (length open). Does not use sidebars. Guidelines on Website; sample copy.

Poetry: Accepts 40/yr. Free verse. Submit max. 3 poems.

Fillers: Accepts all types.

Tips: "We're most open to true-life Christian stories, Christian testimonies, and Christian or livestock news. Contact us with your ideas first."

$CHRISTIAN RENEWAL, Box 770, Lewiston NY 14092-0770, or PO Box 777, Jordan Sta., ON L0R 1S0, Canada. (905)562-5059. Fax (905)562-1368. E-mail: JVANDYK@aol.com, or christian renewal@hotmail.com. Website: www.crmag.com. Reformed (Conservative). John Van Dyk, ed. Church-related and world news for members of the Reformed community of churches in North America. Biweekly newspaper; 24 pgs.; circ. 4,000. Subscription $39 U.S./$42 Cdn. (christianrenewal@hotmail.com). 5% unsolicited freelance; 20% assigned. Query/clips; e-query OK. Pays $25-100 for one-time rts. Articles 500-3,000 wds.; fiction 2,000 wds. (6/yr.); book reviews 50-200 wds. Seasonal 3 mos. ahead. Accepts simultaneous submissions & reprints. Prefers e-mail submission (copied into message). Uses some sidebars. Prefers NIV, ESV. No guidelines; copy $2. (Ads: christianrenewal@hotmail.com)

Tips: "Most open to stories written from a reformed, biblical perspective."

$CHRISTIAN RESEARCH JOURNAL, PO Box 8500, Charlotte NC 28271. (704)887-8200. E-mail: submissions@equip.org. Website: www.equip.org. Christian Research Institute. Elliot Miller, ed-in-chief. Probing today's religious movements, promoting doctrinal discernment and critical thinking, and providing reasons for Christian faith and ethics. Quarterly mag.; 64 pgs.; circ. 30,000. Subscription $30. 75% freelance. Query or complete ms/cover letter; fax query OK; e-query & submissions OK. Pays .16/wd. on publication for 1st rts. Articles to 4,200 wds. (25/yr.); book reviews 1,100-2,500 wds. Responds in 4 mos. Accepts simultaneous submissions. Kill fee to 50%. Guidelines (also by e-mail—guidelines@equip.org); copy $6. (Ads)

Columns/Departments: Effective Evangelism, 1,700 wds.; Viewpoint, 875 wds.; News Watch, to 2,500 wds.

Special Needs: Viewpoint on Christian faith and ethics, 1,700 wds.; news pieces, 800-1,200 wds.

Tips: "Be familiar with the Journal in order to know what we are looking for. We accept freelance articles in all sections (features and departments). E-mail for writer's guidelines."

**2003 EPA Award of Excellence—Organizational.

$THE CHRISTIAN RESPONSE, PO Box 125, Staples MN 56479-0125. (218)894-1165. E-mail: hapco2@brainerd.net. Website: www.brainerd.net/~hapco2. HAPCO Industries. Hap Corbett, ed./pub. Exposes anti-Christian bias in America and encourages readers to write letters against such bias. Bimonthly newsletter; 6 pgs. Subscription $13. 10% unsolicited freelance. Complete ms/cover letter; e-query OK. Accepts full mss by e-mail after acceptance. Pays $5-20 on acceptance for one-time rts. Articles 50-700 wds. (4-6/yr.). Responds in 2 wks. Seasonal 6 mos. ahead. Accepts simultaneous submissions & reprints. Does not use sidebars. Guidelines; copy for $1 or 3 stamps. (Ads—classified only)

Fillers: Buys 2-3/yr. Anecdotes, facts, quotes; up to 150 wds.; $5-10.

Special Needs: Articles on anti-Christian bias; tips on writing effective letters to the editor; pieces on outstanding accomplishments of Christians in the secular media.

Tips: "The best way to break in is to uncover an instance of a Christian being denied civil rights by any public unit or government agency because of being a Christian and writing a concise 500-700 word article about it."

$CHRISTIAN RETAILING, 600 Rinehart Rd., Lake Mary FL 32746. (407)333-0600. Fax (407)333-7133. E-mail: Christian.Retailing@strang.com. Website: www.christianretailing.com. Strang Communications. Andy Butcher, ed. (andy.butcher@strang.com). For Christian product industry manufacturers, distributors, retailers. Trade journal published

18X/yr.; circ. 10,500. Subscription $75. 75% assigned. Query/clips; no phone/fax/e-query. Pays .25/wd. on publication. Articles; book reviews. No simultaneous submissions. Accepts requested mss by e-mail (attached file). Kill fee. Uses some sidebars. Prefers NIV. Guidelines on Website. (Ads)

Tips: "Book reviews should focus on what the book contains and how it might help them in their walk with Christ." Also publishes 2 supplements: The Church Bookstore (8x/yr.) and Inspirational Gift Trends (4X/yr.).

$CHRISTIAN SINGLE and CHRISTIAN SINGLE ONLINE, One Lifeway Plaza, Nashville TN 37234. (615)251-2230. Fax (615)251-5008. E-mail: christiansingle@lifeway.com, or christiansingle@bssb.com. Website: www.christiansingle.com. Monthly mag. Print & online versions. No freelance.

**2003 EPA Award of Merit—General.

$CHRISTIAN STANDARD, 8805 Governor's Hill Dr., Ste. 400, Cincinnati OH 45249. (513)931-4050. Fax (513)931-0950. E-mail: christianstd@standardpub.com. Website: www.christian standard.com. Standard Publishing/Christian Churches/Churches of Christ. Mark A. Taylor, ed. Devoted to the restoration of New Testament Christianity, its doctrines, its ordinances, and its fruits. Weekly & online mag.; 16 pgs.; circ. 48,000. Subscription $31.99. 40% unsolicited freelance; 60% assigned. Complete ms; no phone/fax/e-query. Pays $20-160 on publication for one-time, reprint, & electronic rts. Articles 800-1,600 wds. (200/yr.). Responds in 9 wks. Seasonal 8-12 mos. ahead. Accepts reprints (tell when/where appeared). Guidelines & copy on Website. (Ads)

Tips: "We would like to hear ministers and elders tell about the efforts made in their churches. Has the church grown? Developed spiritually? Overcome adversity? Succeeded in missions?"

**2004 EPA Award of Merit—Most Improved Publication.

$CHRISTIANWEEK, Box 725, Winnipeg MB R3C 2K3, Canada. Toll-free (800)263-6695. (204)982-2060. Fax (204)947-5632. E-mail: editor@christianweek.org. Website: www.christianweek.org. Fellowship for Print Witness. Doug Koop, edit. dir. Canada's leading Christian news source; telling the stories of God and His people in Canada. Biweekly tabloid newspaper (25X/yr.); 12-16 pgs.; circ. 4,000. Subscription $44.95 (Cdn.), $65.95 (U.S.). Query; phone/fax/e-query OK. Pays $30-100 on publication for 1st rts. News articles 300-600 wds. Responds in 1-3 wks. Seasonal 6 mos. ahead. Might accept simultaneous submissions or reprints (tell when/where appeared). Prefers accepted ms by e-mail (attached or copied into message). Uses some sidebars. Prefers NRSV. Also accepts submissions from teens. Guidelines/theme list (also by e-mail/Website). (Ads)

Tips: "Most open to general news, profiles, and features. Writers are encouraged to query first with ideas about people or news events in their own community (Canadian angles, please) or denomination that would be of interest to readers in other denominations or in other areas of the country."

**2004 EPA Award of Excellence—Newspaper.

$THE CHRONICLE CHRISTIAN NEWSPAPER—KANSAS EDITION, PO Box 492, Newton KS 67114-0492. (316)282-0300. Fax (316)283-6090. E-mail: Jackie@thechronicleonline.net. Website: www.thechronicleonline.net. Big Picture Media Group Inc. Jackie Jones, ed. To inform the public of issues that affect our decision-making, to encourage and build up the body of Christ, to be a tool to bring others to a life-changing decision for Christ, and to give back to our community. Monthly tabloid & online newspaper; 32-36 pgs.; circ. 50,000. Subscription $25.50. 10% unsolicited freelance; 15% assigned. Query/clips or complete ms/cover letter; phone/fax/e-query OK. Accepts full mss by e-mail. Pays on publication for all rts. Responds in 2 wks. Seasonal 2-3 mos. ahead. Prefers e-mail submissions (attached file). Uses some sidebars. (Ads)

Fillers: Anecdotes, cartoons, facts, games, ideas, kid quotes, newsbreaks, party ideas, prayers, prose, quizzes, quotes, short humor, tips, and word puzzles.

Tips: "Always looking for great news (from a Christian perspective, of course)." See Website for editions from different cities.

CHURCH HERALD AND HOLINESS BANNER, 7407 Metcalf, Overland Park KS 66212. Fax (913)722-0351. E-mail: HBeditor@juno.com. Website: www.heraldandbanner.com. Church of God (Holiness)/Herald and Banner Press. Mark D. Avery, ed. Offers the conservative holiness movement a positive outlook on their church, doctrine, future ministry, and movement. Monthly mag.; 24 pgs.; circ. 1,100. Subscription $12.50. 5% unsolicited freelance; 5% assigned. Query; e-query OK. Accepts full mss by e-mail. **NO PAYMENT** for one-time, reprint, or simultaneous rts. Not copyrighted. Articles 500-1,200 wds. (3-5/yr.). Responds in 9 wks. Seasonal 6 mos. ahead. Accepts simultaneous submissions & reprints (tell when/where appeared). Accepts requested ms on disk or by e-mail (attached file). Uses some sidebars. Prefers KJV. Also accepts submissions from children/teens. Guidelines (also by e-mail); copy for 9x12 SAE/2 stamps. (No ads)

Fillers: Anecdotes, quizzes; 150-400 wds.

Tips: "Most open to short inspirational/devotional articles. Must be concise, well written, and get one main point across; 200-600 wds. Be well acquainted with the Wesleyan/Holiness doctrine and tradition. Articles which are well written and express this conviction are very likely to be used."

CHURCH OF ENGLAND NEWSPAPER, Religious Intelligence Ltd., 4th Fl., Central House, 142 Central St., London, England EC1V 8AR. Phone 020 7417 5800. Fax 020 7216 6410. E-mail: colin.blakely@churchnewspaper.com. Website: www.churchnewspaper.com. Religious Intelligence LTD. Colin Blakely, ed. Weekly newspaper; circ. 25,000. Subscription 60 pounds (UK); 85 pounds (U.S.). Query: phone/e-query OK. Accepts e-mail submissions (attached file). Uses some sidebars. Guidelines by e-mail. (Ads)

Tips: "Most open to news reports and general features."

CITIZEN USA, 3651 Wrightway Rd., Dayton OH 45424. (937)233-6227. Fax (937)233-6231. E-mail: editor@CCN-USA.net. Website: www.citizenusa.us. Citizens Media Group Inc. Pendra Lee Snyder, pub.; submit to Editor-in-Chief. General interest newspaper from a Judeo-Christian editorial perspective. Biweekly newspaper; 20 pgs.; circ. 30,000. Subscription $50/52 issues. 1% unsolicited freelance; 90% assigned. Query/clips; phone/fax/e-query OK. **NO PAYMENT** for all rts. (on assignments). Articles 600-800 wds.; book reviews 500 wds.; music/video reviews 300-400 wds. Accepts requested mss by e-mail (attached file or copied into message). Responds in 4 wks. Seasonal 3 mos. ahead. Accepts reprints (tell when/where appeared). Uses some sidebars. Prefers KJV. Also accepts submissions from children/teens. Guidelines/theme list by e-mail; copy. (Ads)

Fillers: Accepts 6/yr. Cartoons, games, jokes, kid quotes, party ideas, quizzes, quotes, short humor, and word puzzles; 300-500 wds.

$CITY LIGHT NEWS, 9827E Horton Rd. S.W., Calgary AB T2V 2X5, Canada. (403)640-2011. Fax (403)640-2000. E-mail: editor@calgarychristian.com. Website: www.calgarychristian.com. CLN Productions. John Syratt, ed. A Christian newspaper serving the church audience in Central and Southern Alberta and Southeastern BC. Monthly newspaper; 20-32 pgs.; circ. 12,000. Subscription $24.95 Cdn. 10% unsolicited freelance; 60% assigned. Query; e-query OK. Pays .10/wd. Cdn., on publication for 1st rts.; $20/photo. Articles 550 wds. (12/yr.); reviews 150 wds. ($15). Responds in 2 wks. No simultaneous submissions; accepts reprints (tell when/where appeared). Prefers e-mail submissions (attached file). No kill fee. Uses some sidebars. Also accepts submissions from teens. Guidelines/theme list on Website; copy for 10x13 SAE/$3 postage. (Ads)

Fillers: Buys 12/yr. Anecdotes, cartoons, facts, jokes, kid quotes, newsbreaks, short humor; $30-50.

Tips: "Most open to articles of interest to general church audience; news or gripping stories—lighthearted or tragic; and good news stories."

$COLUMBIA, PO Box 1670 (06507-0981), 1 Columbus Plaza, New Haven CT 06510-3326. (203)752-4398 or 4303. Fax (203)752-4109. E-mail: columbia@kofc.org, or through Website: www.kofc.org. Knights of Columbus. Tim S. Hickey, ed. Geared to a general Catholic family audience. Monthly & online mag.; 32 pgs.; circ. 1.6 million. Subscription $6; foreign $8. 25% unsolicited freelance; 75% assigned. Query; fax/e-query OK. Pays $250-600 on acceptance for 1st & electronic rts. Articles 500-1,500 wds. (12/yr.). Responds in 2 wks. Seasonal 3 mos. ahead. Occasional reprint (tell when/where appeared). Prefers e-mail submission (copied into message). Kill fee. Regularly uses sidebars. Free guidelines (also by e-mail)/copy. (No ads)

Special Needs: Essays on spirituality, personal conversion. Catholic preferred. Query first.

Tips: "We welcome contributions from freelancers in all subject areas. An interesting or different approach to a topic will get the writer at least a second look from an editor. Most open to feature writers who can handle church issues, social issues from an orthodox Roman Catholic perspective. Must be aggressive, fact-centered writers for these features." **This periodical was #45 on the 2007 Top 50 Christian Publishers list (#45 in 2006, #49 in 2005).

$COMMON GROUND, #204—4381 Fraser St., Vancouver BC V6V 4G4, Canada. (604)733-2215. Fax (604)733-4415. E-mail: editor@commonground.ca. Website: www.commonground.ca. Common Ground Publishing. Joseph Roberts, sr. ed. Covers health, environment, spirit, creativity, and wellness. Monthly tabloid; circ. 70,000. Subscription $60; U.S. $50. 10% unsolicited freelance. Query by e-mail. Pays .10/wd. (Cdn.) on publication (although most articles are donated) for one-time or reprint rts. Articles 600-1,500 wds. (to 2,500 wds.), (12/yr.). Responds in 6-13 wks. (returns material only if clearly specified). Seasonal 3 mos. ahead. Accepts simultaneous submissions & reprints. Requires requested ms by e-mail. Guidelines on Website; copy $5. Incomplete topical listings. (Ads)

Tips: "Donated articles are given priority over paid articles. Once an article has been published, we will contact you with the final word count, after which you may submit an invoice."

$COMMONWEAL, 475 Riverside Dr., Rm. 405, New York NY 10115-0499. (212)662-4200. Fax (212)662-4183. E-mail: editors@commonwealmagazine.org. Website: www.commonweal magazine.org. Commonweal Foundation/Catholic. Paul Baumann, ed. A review of public affairs, religion, literature, and the arts, for an intellectually engaged readership. Biweekly jour.; 32 pgs.; circ. 20,000. Subscription $47. 20% unsolicited freelance. Query/clips; phone query OK. Pays $75-100 on publication for all rts. Articles 2,000-2,500 wds. (30/yr.). Responds in 9 wks. Seasonal 2 mos. ahead. Prefers requested ms by e-mail. Kill fee 2%. Uses some sidebars. Guidelines on Website; free copy. (Ads)

Poetry: Rosemary Deen, poetry ed. Buys 20/yr. Free verse, traditional; to 75 lines; .75/line. Submit max. 5 poems. Submit October-May.

Columns/Departments: Upfronts (brief, newsy facts and information behind the headlines), 750-1,000 wds.; The Last Word (commentary based on insight from personal experience or reflection), 700 wds.

Tips: "Most open to meaningful articles on social, political, religious, and cultural topics; or columns."

($)COMMUNITY SPIRIT, 8835 S. Memorial, Tulsa OK 74133. (918)307-2323. Fax (918)307-1221. E-mail: tara@mccloudmedia.com. Website: www.communityspiritmagazine.com. McCloud Media. Tom McCloud, pub.; Tara Lynn Thompson, mng. ed. To glorify God by telling stories of individual Christians whose good works testify to God's active presence in Oklahoma. Monthly mag.; circ. 50,000. Subscription free. 40% unsolicited freelance; 60% assigned. Prefers e-query. Accepts full mss by e-mail. Pays for assignments only on publication for all rts. Articles 800 wds. Accepts reprints (tell when/where appeared). Accepts requested mss by e-mail (attached file). Regularly uses sidebars. (Ads)

Fillers: Ideas.

$COMPANY: The World of Jesuits and Their Friends, PO Box 60790, Chicago IL 60660. (773)761-9432. Fax (773)761-9443. E-mail: editor@companymagazine.org. Website: www.companymagazine.org. Martin McHugh, ed.; Maureen Ryan, asst. ed. For people interested in or involved with Jesuit ministries. Quarterly & online mag.; 32 pgs.; circ. 120,000. Free subscription. 40% unsolicited freelance; 60% assigned. Complete ms/cover letter; e-query OK. Pays $250-450 on publication for one-time rts. Articles 1,500 wds. Responds in 6 wks. Seasonal 3 mos. ahead. Accepts simultaneous submissions & reprints (tell when/where appeared). Prefers e-mail submission (attached file). Prefers NRSV, NAB, NJB. Guidelines (also by e-mail); copy for 9x12 SAE/4 stamps. (No ads)

Columns/Departments: Books with a Jesuit connection; Minims and Maxims (short items of interest to Jesuit world), 100-150 wds./photo; Letters to the Editor; Obituaries. No payment (usually).

Tips: "We welcome manuscripts as well as outlines of story ideas and indication of willingness to accept freelance assignments (please include résumé and writing samples with the latter two). Articles must be Jesuit-related, and writers usually have some prior association with and/or knowledge of the Jesuits. Looking for feature articles (Jesuit-related), historical, essays, or ministry-related articles."

COMPASS DIRECT NEWS, PO Box 27250, Santa Ana CA 92799. (949)862-0304. Fax (949)752-6536. E-mail: info@compassdirect.org. Website: www.compassdirect.org. Compass Direct. Jeff M. Sellers, mng. ed. To raise awareness of and encourage prayer for Christians worldwide who are persecuted for their faith. Online news source; circ. 730. E-mail subscription $25; for reprint rights $40. Uses little unsolicited freelance. Articles 800-1,200 wds.; no reviews. Query only. (No ads)

Tips: "An international journalist could submit an article query on a current/specific instance of Christian persecution in a country with religious liberty restrictions."

CONNECTING POINT, PO Box 685, Cocoa FL 32923. (321)632-0130. Fax (321)632-5540. E-mail: lhoward@specialgatherings.com, or info@specialgatherings.com. Linda G. Howard, ed. For and by the mentally challenged (mentally retarded) community; primarily deals with spiritual and self-advocacy issues. Monthly mag.; 12 pgs.; circ. 1,000. Free. 75% unsolicited freelance. Complete ms; phone/fax/e-query OK. **NO PAYMENT** for 1st rts. Articles (24/yr.) & fiction (12/yr.), 250-300 wds. Responds in 3-6 wks. Seasonal 3 mos. ahead. Accepts simultaneous submissions & reprints. Guidelines (also by e-mail); copy for 9x12 SAE/$2.13 postage (mark "Media Mail").

Poetry: Accepts 4/yr. Any type; 4-30 lines. Submit max. 10 poems.

Fillers: Accepts 12/yr. Cartoons, games, word puzzles; 50-250 wds.

Columns/Departments: Accepts 24/yr. Devotion Page, 250 wds.; Bible Study, 250 wds. Query.

Special Needs: Self-advocacy, integration/normalization, justice system.

Tips: "All manuscripts need to be in primary vocabulary."

$THE COVENANT COMPANION, 5101 N. Francisco Ave., Chicago IL 60625. (773)907-3328. Fax (773)784-4366. E-mail: communication@covchurch.org. Website: www.covchurch.org. Evangelical Covenant Church. Donald Meyer, ed.; Bob Smietana, features ed. Informs, stimulates thought, and encourages dialog on issues that affect the denomination. Monthly mag.; 40 pgs.; circ. 16,000. Subscription $19.95. 10-15% unsolicited freelance; 35% assigned.

Query or complete ms/cover letter; fax/e-query OK. Pays $50-100 after publication (within 3 wks.) for one-time or simultaneous rts. Articles 1,200-1,800 wds. (40/yr.). Prefers e-mail submission. Responds in 4 wks. Seasonal 4 mos. ahead. Accepts simultaneous submissions & reprints (tell when/where appeared). Some kill fees. Regularly uses sidebars. Prefers NRSV. Guidelines (also by e-mail/Website); copy for 9x12 SAE/5 stamps or $2.50. (Ads)

CREATION, PO Box 4545, Eight Mile Plains QLD 4113, Australia. Phone 07 3840 9888. Fax 07 3840 9889. E-mail: mail@creation.info. Website: www.creationontheweb.com. Creation Ministries Intl. Carl Wieland, managing dir. A family, nature, science magazine focusing on creation/evolution issues. Quarterly mag.; 56 pgs.; circ. 55,000. Subscription $25. 30% unsolicited freelance. Query; phone/fax/e-query OK. **NO PAYMENT** for all rts. Articles to 1,500 wds. (20/yr.). Responds in 2-3 wks. Prefers requested ms on disk or by e-mail (attached file). Regularly uses sidebars. Guidelines (also by e-mail); copy $6.95. (No ads)

Tips: "Get to know the basic content/style of the magazine and emulate. Send us a copy of your article, or contact us by phone."

CREATION CARE, 4485 Tench Rd., Ste. 850, Suwanee GA 30024. (678)541-0747 (office), or (404)414-7906 (direct). E-mail: een@creationcare.org. Website: www.creationcare.org/magazine. Evangelical Environmental Network. Rusty Prichard, PhD, ed. For Christians who care about stewardship of natural resources, environmental responsibility, sustainability, and simplicity. Quarterly mag.; 36 pgs.; circ. 6,000. Subscription $25 (free to supporters). 90% unsolicited freelance. Query; fax/e-query OK. **NO PAYMENT.** Articles 700-1,600 wds. (20/yr.); book reviews 250 wds. Responds in 6-8 wks. Seasonal 4 mos. ahead. No simultaneous submissions. Accepts reprints (tell when/where appeared). Prefers accepted ms by e-mail. Regularly uses sidebars. Prefers NRSV, NIV. Guidelines on Website. (Ads)

Tips: "Significant redesign in Summer 2007. Articles, essays, art, poetry sought. Past issues on our Website."

$CREATION ILLUSTRATED, PO Box 7955, Auburn CA 95604. (530)269-1424. Fax (530)269-1428. E-mail: creation@foothill.net, or ci@creationillustrated.com. Website: www.creation illustrated.com. Tom Ish, ed./pub. An uplifting, Bible-based Christian nature magazine that glorifies God; for ages 9-99. Quarterly mag.; 68 pgs.; circ. 20,000. Subscription $19.95. 60% unsolicited freelance; 40% assigned. Query or query/clips; fax/e-query OK. Pays $75-125 within 30 days of publication for 1st rts. (holds rts. for 6 mos.). Articles 1,000-2,000 wds. (20/yr.). Responds in 2 mos. Seasonal 6 mos. ahead. Accepts simultaneous submissions & reprints (tell when/where appeared). Prefers e-mail submission (copied into message). Kill fee 25%. Some sidebars. Prefers NKJV. Guidelines/theme list (also on Website); copy $3/9x12 SAE/$2.13 postage (mark "Media Mail"). (Some ads)

Poetry: Buys 4/yr. Light verse, traditional; 10-20 lines; $15. Submit max. 4 poems.

Fillers: Games, 100-200 wds. Pays variable rates.

Tips: "Most open to an experience with nature/creation that brought you closer to God and will inspire the reader to do the same. Include spiritual lessons and supporting scriptures—at least 3 or 4 of each."

$CREATIVE NONFICTION, 5501 Walnut St., Ste. 202, Pittsburgh PA 15232. (412)688-0304. Fax (412)688-0262. E-mail: information@creativenonfiction.org. Website: www.creativenon fiction.org. Lee Gutkind, ed. Publishes compelling nonfiction stories with a strong narrative and research element. Triannual jour.; 150 pgs.; circ. 5,000. Subscription $29.95 for 4 issues. 80% unsolicited freelance; 20% assigned. Complete ms/cover letter; no phone/fax/e-query. Pays $10/published page on publication for all rts. Articles to 5,000 wds. (30/yr.). Responds in 3-5 mos. Accepts simultaneous submissions; no reprints. No e-mail submissions. No kill fee. Does not use sidebars. Also accepts submissions from teens. Guidelines (also by e-mail/Website); copy $10/7x10 SAE/$2.13 postage (mark "Media Mail"). (Ads)

Contests: Sometimes sponsor contests; see Website for details.

$THE CRESSET: A Review of Arts, Literature & Public Affairs, 1409 Chapel Dr., Valparaiso IN 46383-9998. (219)464-6089. E-mail: cresset@valpo.edu. Website: www.valpo.edu/cresset. Valparaiso University/Lutheran. James Paul Old, ed. (tom.kennedy@valpo.edu). For college-educated, professors, pastors, laypeople; serious review essays on religious-cultural affairs. Mag. published 5X/yr.; 60 pgs.; circ. 4,500. Subscription $20. 10% unsolicited freelance; 90% assigned. Query; e-query OK. Pays $100-500 on publication for all rts. Articles 2,000-4,500 wds. (2/yr.); book/music reviews, 1,000 wds. ($150). Responds in 15 wks. No simultaneous submissions or reprints. Prefers requested ms by e-mail (attached or copied into message). Regularly uses sidebars. Prefers NRSV. Guidelines on Website; copy $4. (No ads)

Poetry: John Ruff, poetry ed. Buys 20/yr. Avant-garde, free verse, light verse, traditional; to 40 lines; $15-25. Submit max. 4 poems.

Columns/Departments: Buys 20/yr. Books; Music; Science & Technology; World Views; all 1,000 wds., $100-250. Query.

CROSSHOME.COM: Your Christian Home on the Net! E-mail: webmaster@crosshome.com. Website: www.crosshome.com. Online mag. Open to solicited freelance. Complete ms by e-mail; e-query OK. **NO PAYMENT** for one-time rts. Articles 300-1,000 wds.; devotionals 300-1,000 wds. (prefers 350-650 wds.); book reviews 300-800 wds. Responds in 1-3 wks. (if accepted). Requires accepted ms by e-mail (attached file in Word). Prefers KJV, NKJV, NIV, NASB. Guidelines on Website (www.crosshome.com/guidelines.shtml); copy online. (Ads)

Poetry: Accepts free verse, traditional; 30-50 wds.

Columns/Departments: Open to submissions for regular columns, or ideas for new ones. (See guidelines.)

Special Needs: See Website/guidelines for list of channels where your writing might fit.

Tips: "We do archive all writing, but any submissions can be deleted by request of the author by e-mail."

$CULTURE WARS, 206 Marquette Ave., South Bend IN 46617-1111. (574)289-9786. Fax (574)289-1461. E-mail: jones@culturewars.com, or letters@culturewars.com, or fidelitypress@sbcglobal.net. Website: www.culturewars.com. Ultramontagne Associates Inc. Dr. E. Michael Jones, ed. Issues relating to Catholic families and issues affecting America that affect all people. Monthly (11X) mag.; 48 pgs.; circ. 3,500. Subscription $30. 20% unsolicited freelance. Complete ms/cover letter; fax/e-query OK. Pays $100 & up on publication for all rts. Articles (25/yr.); book reviews $50. Responds in 12-24 wks. Query about reprints. Prefers requested ms on disk. Uses some sidebars. Developing guidelines; copy for 9x12 SAE/5 stamps.

Poetry: Buys 15/yr. Free verse, light verse, traditional; 10-50 lines; $25. Submit max. 2 poems.

Fillers: Buys 15/yr. Cartoons, quotes; 25 wds. & up; payment varies.

Columns/Departments: Buys 25/yr. Commentary, 2,500 wds.; Feature, 5,000 wds.; $100-250.

Tips: "All fairly open except cartoons. Single-spaced preferred; photocopies must be legible."

$DECISION/DECISION ONLINE, 1 Billy Graham Pkwy., Charlotte NC 28201-0001. (704)401-2432. Fax (704)401-3009. E-mail: submissions@bgea.org. Website: www.decisionmag.org. Billy Graham Evangelistic Assn. Bob Paulson, ed. Evangelism/Christian nurture; all articles must have connection to BGEA. Monthly (11X) & online mag.; 44 pgs.; circ. 400,000. Subscription $12. 5% unsolicited freelance; written mostly in-house. Query preferred; no phone/fax/e-query. Pays $200-400 on publication for all, 1st, or electronic rts. Articles 400-1,000 wds. (8/yr.). Response time varies. Seasonal 3-5 mos. ahead. Accepts ms by e-mail (attached file). Kill fee. Uses some sidebars. Prefers NIV. Guidelines (also by e-mail/Website); copy for 10x13 SAE/3 stamps. (No ads)

Poetry: Buys 6/yr. Free verse, light verse, traditional; 4-16 lines. Pays $1/wd. Submit max. 7 poems.

Columns/Departments: Buys 11/yr. Finding Jesus (people who have become Christians through Billy Graham ministries), 500-600 wds.; $200. Complete ms.

Special Needs: Personal experience articles telling how a Billy Graham ministry helped you live out your faith.

Tips: "Nearly all of our articles have some connection with a ministry of the Billy Graham Evangelistic Assn.—through the author's participation in the ministry or through the author's being touched by the ministry."

**2005, 2003 EPA Award of Merit—Organizational.

DESERT CALL: Contemplative Christianity and Vital Culture, Box 219, Crestone CO 81131. (719)256-4778. Fax (719)256-4719. E-mail: nada@fone.net. Website: www.spirituallife institute.org. Spiritual Life Institute/Catholic. Submit to The Editor. Practical spirituality and contemplative prayer; interfaith/interreligious dialog, the arts and culture, fiction. Quarterly mag.; 32 pgs.; circ. 2,000. Subscription $20. 15% unsolicited freelance; 10% assigned. Complete ms/cover letter; no phone/fax/e-query. **PAYS 3 COPIES** for 1st rts. Articles 1,000-2,500 wds. (4/yr.); some fiction. Responds in 15 wks. Seasonal 8 mos. ahead. Accepts reprints (tell when/where appeared). No disk or e-mail submissions. Uses some sidebars. No guidelines; copy $2.50/10x13 SAE. (No ads)

Poetry: Accepts 3/yr. Free verse, haiku, traditional; to 25 lines.

Fillers: Accepts 3/yr. Anecdotes, facts, prayers, prose, quotes; 50-250 wds.

DESERT CHRISTIAN NEWS, PO Box 4196, Palm Desert CA 92261. (760)772-2027. E-mail: smiller@desertchristiannews.org. Website: www.desertchristiannews.org. Susan Miller, ed. To encourage communication and unity amongst Christians in the Coachella Valley by sharing inspiring local news stories, feature articles, and information. Monthly newspaper; weekly TV/radio programs. Subscription $35. Open to freelance. Query preferred. Articles; reviews. (Ads) Incomplete topical listings.

THE DESERT VOICE, PO Box 567, Imperial CA 92251. (760)337-9200. Fax (760)355-0197. E-mail: editor@desertvoice.info. Website: www.desertvoice.info. Witness Publishing Inc. Alex Arroyave, ed. To reach the lost, and to provide family-friendly news not found elsewhere by bias or neglect, or simply because they don't feel it's important. Monthly newspaper; circ. 7,000. Subscription $20. Open to freelance. Complete ms. Articles; reviews. Incomplete topical listings. (Ads)

+DIAMOND DUST, E-mail: DiamondEditor@yahoo.com. Website: www.freewebs.com/diamond dustmagazine/writersguidelines.htm. Laura & Stephanie Rutlind, eds. To empower adults and teens in their Christian walk. Bimonthly Website and e-newsletter. Free online. Open to unsolicited freelance. Query or complete ms/cover letter. **NO PAYMENT** for one-time electronic rts. Articles 200-1,000 wds.; fiction to 1,200 wds.; devotionals 100-500 wds.; book/music reviews 200-700 wds. Responds in 4 wks. Seasonal 3 mos. ahead. Requires e-mail submissions (copied into message). Also accepts submissions from teens. Guidelines/theme list on Website; copy online.

Poetry: Accepts all types; under 30 lines. Submit max. 3 poems.

Fillers: Accepts facts, games, ideas, prayers, prose, quizzes, short humor, tips, and word puzzles; to 500 wds.

Special Needs: Fillers, seasonal mss, and general interest articles related to themes.

Tips: "We do not require submissions to be explicitly Christian, but we ask that they include good morals and clean content."

$DIRECTION, PO Box 436987, Chicago IL 60643. (708)868-7100, ext. 236. Fax (708)868-6759. E-mail: cywilson@urbanministries.com. Website: www.urbanministries.com. Urban Ministries Inc. Submit to Cheryl Willson, asst. ed. An adult-level Sunday School quarterly publication consisting of student book and teacher's guide. Quarterly mag; 64 pgs.; $18.45 (student) and $33.54 (teacher). 100% assigned. Query or query/clips; phone/fax/e-query OK. Accepts full manuscripts by e-mail. Pays to $200 ($300 for lessons) on acceptance, for all rts. Articles 1,500-3,500 wds. Responds in 4 wks. Seasonal 12 mos. ahead. No simultaneous submissions or reprints. Requires accepted ms on disk or by e-mail (attached or copied into message). Kill fee 50%. Does not use sidebars. Prefers KJV. Guidelines by e-mail; copy for SASE. (No ads)

Tips: "Send query with a writing sample, or attend our annual conference on the first weekend in November each year."

$DISASTER NEWS NETWORK, 9195C Red Branch Rd., Columbia MD 21045. Toll-free (888)384-3028. (410)884-7350. Fax (410)884-7353. E-mail: info@villagelife.org. Website: www.disasternews.net. Village Life Co. P. J. Heller, news ed. Online; an interactive daily news site on the World Wide Web. Query; phone/fax OK; e-query preferred. Pays $100-150 after publication for all rts. Articles 1,000 wds. Requires accepted ms by e-mail. Guidelines on Website. Not in topical listings.

Tips: "Most open to 'people stories' related to faith-based disaster response and/or mitigation. Also, faith-based response to incidents of public violence. Authors are expected to have an e-mail submission address. Check our Website." Authors must be DNN pre-approved contractor writers.

$DISCIPLESHIP JOURNAL, Box 35004, Colorado Springs CO 80935. (719)548-9222. Fax (719)598-7128. E-mail: djwriters@navpress.com. Website: www.discipleshipjournal.com. NavPress/The Navigators. Sue Kline, sr. ed./pub.; Connie Willems, ed.; Dianne Bundt, DJ Plus ed. For motivated, maturing Christians desiring to grow spiritually and to help others grow; biblical and practical. Bimonthly mag.; 84+ pgs.; circ. 100,000. Subscription $23.97. 65% unsolicited freelance; 35% assigned. Query/clips; fax/e-query OK. Accepts full mss by e-mail, if requested. Pays .25/wd. (.05/wd. for reprints) on acceptance for 1st, plus 10% for electronic rts. Articles 1,200-2,800 wds. (60/yr.). Responds in 6-8 wks. Seasonal 9 mos. ahead. No simultaneous submissions; accepts reprints (tell when/where appeared). Prefers requested ms by e-mail (attached or copied into message). Kill fee 50%. Regularly uses sidebars. Prefers NIV. Guidelines (also by e-mail/Website); copy for 9x12 SAE/$2.64 postage. (Ads)

Columns/Departments: Buys 60+/yr. DJ Plus (ministry how-to on missions, evangelism, serving, discipling, teaching, and small groups), under 400 wds. Complete manuscript. Pays .25/wd.

Special Needs: Small groups; discipling/one-on-one mentoring; biblical teaching.

Tips: "Most open to feature articles and DJ Plus. Our articles focus on biblical passages or topics. Articles should derive main principles from a thorough study of Scripture, should illustrate each principle, should show how to put each principle into practice, and should demonstrate with personal illustrations and vulnerability that the author has wrestled with the subject in his or her life."

**The #4 Best-selling magazine in Christian retail stores. This periodical was #2 on the 2007 Top 50 Christian Publishers list (#4 in 2006, #3 in 2005, #3 in 2004, #3 in 2003). 2006, 2005 EPA Award of Merit—General. 2004 EPA Award of Excellence—General.

DISCIPLE'S JOURNAL, 10 Fiorenza Dr., Wilmington MA 01887-4421. Toll-free (800)696-2344. (978)657-7373. Fax (978)657-5411. E-mail: dddj@disciplesdirectory.com, or info@disciplesdirectory.com. Website: www.disciplesdirectory.com. Kenneth A. Dorothy, ed. To strengthen, edify, inform, and unite the body of Christ. Monthly & online newspaper; 24-32 pgs.; circ. 8,000. Subscription $14.95. 5% unsolicited freelance. Query; fax/e-query OK. **NO PAYMENT** for one-time rts. Articles 400 wds. (24/yr.); book/music/video reviews 200 wds. Responds in 2 wks. Seasonal 2 mos. ahead. Accepts simultaneous submissions & reprints (tell when/where appeared). Prefers requested ms on disk or by e-mail (attached file). Uses some sidebars. Prefers NIV. Guidelines/theme list (also by e-mail); copy for 9x12 SAE/$2.13 postage (mark "Media Mail"). (Ads)

Fillers: Accepts 12/yr. All types; 100-400 wds.

Columns/Departments: Financial; Singles; Men; Women; Business; Parenting; all 400 wds.

Tips: "Most open to men's, women's, or singles' issues; missions; or homeschooling. Send sample of articles for review."

$DISCIPLESWORLD, 6325 Guilford Ave., Ste. 213, Indianapolis IN 46220-1992. (317)375-8846. Fax (317)375-8849. E-mail: editor@disciplesworld.com. Website: www.disciples world.com. Christian Church (Disciples of Christ). Sherri Wood Emmons, mng. ed. The journal of news, opinion, and mission for this denomination in North America. Monthly (10X) mag.; 48 pgs.; circ. 14,000. Subscription $25. 30% unsolicited freelance; 70% assigned. Complete ms/cover letter or query with/without clips; e-query OK. Pays .15/wd. on publication for 1st rts. Articles 500-1,200 wds. (40/yr.); fiction 150-1,500 wds. (8-10/yr.); reviews 600 wds. (no payment). Responds in 1 mo. Seasonal 3 mos. ahead. Accepts simultaneous submissions; no reprints. Requires submissions by disk or e-mail (attached file). No kill fee. Uses some sidebars. Prefers NRSV. Guidelines/theme list on Website; copy for #10 SASE. (Ads)

Poetry: Buys 6-10/yr. Free verse, light verse; 12-30 lines. Pays $10-50. Submit max. 3 poems.

Fillers: Buys 20/yr. Anecdotes, cartoons, kid quotes, quotes, short humor; 25-400 wds. Pays $0-100.

Columns/Departments: Buys 12-15/yr. Speak Out (opinion on an issue), 600 wds.; Disciples Go (travel to places relevant to Disciples), 600 wds., plus photos; $100. Quotable Quotes, 200 wds. (no pay).

Tips: "Looking for humorous short-shorts (200 wds.). Our readers are mostly college-educated, active in their churches, proud of their Disciples heritage, and all over the board politically and theologically. We like things with a Disciples connection."

**This periodical was #40 on the 2007 Top 50 Christian Publishers list (#46 in 2006, #45 in 2005).

DIVINE ASCENT: A Journal of Orthodox Faith, PO Box 439, 21770 Ponderosa Way, Manton CA 96059. (530)474-5964. Fax (530)474-3564. E-mail: office@monasteryofstjohn.org. Website: www.monasteryofstjohn.org. Monastery of St. John of Shanghai & San Francisco/ Orthodox Church in America. Fr. Jonah Paffhausen, Abbot & ed-in-chief. Focuses on contemporary Orthodox spirituality as seen in the lives and writings of saints, and holy men and women of our own time. Semi-annual & online jour.; 150 pgs. Subscription $25/2 yrs. 20% unsolicited freelance; 65% assigned. Query. **NO PAYMENT** for all rts. Articles (6/yr.); book reviews 500 wds. Responds in 4-8 wks. No reprints. Prefers disk or e-mail submissions (attached file). Does not use sidebars. Prefers RSV, KJV, NKJV. Guidelines by e-mail. (Ads, from Orthodox Christian businesses)

Tips: "Nothing Protestant."

$DOVETAIL: A Journal by and for Jewish/Christian Families, 775 Simon Greenwell Ln., Boston KY 40107. (502)549-5499. Fax (549)540-3543. E-mail: di-ifr@bardstown.com. Website: www.dovetailinstitute.org. Dovetail Institute for Interfaith Family Resources. Mary Helene Rosenbaum, ed. Offers balanced, nonjudgmental articles for interfaith families and the professionals who serve them. Bimonthly mag.; 12-16 pgs.; circ. 1,000. Subscription/ membership $39.95. 80% unsolicited freelance; 20% assigned. Query or complete ms; phone/fax/e-query OK. Pays $25 on publication for all rts. Articles 800-1,000 wds. (18-20/yr.); book reviews 500 wds., ($15). Responds in 2-6 wks. Seasonal 4 mos. ahead. Accepts simultaneous submissions & reprints (tell when/where appeared). Prefers requested ms on disk or by e-mail (copied into message). Uses some sidebars. Prefers RSV. Guidelines/theme list only by e-mail/Website; copy online PDF only. (Ads)

Poetry: Buys 1-2/yr. Traditional; $15. Submit max. 4 poems.

Columns/Departments: Buys 3-6/yr. Food & Family (Jewish & Christian), 500 wds.; Parent's Page, and Reviews; $15. Complete ms.

Special Needs: "We have expanded our scope to include other types of interfaith marriages, especially those involving a Muslim partner. Also soliciting stories for children and young adults for notebook publication. Author retains copyright. Stories must directly relate to interfaith family theme."

Tips: "Demonstrate real, concrete, practical knowledge of the challenges facing Jewish and Christian partners in a marriage. Do not send pieces of Christian interest only. No proselytizing." Show respect for the religious traditions of their Jewish staff and readers.

$DRAGONS, KNIGHTS, AND ANGELS: The Magazine of Christian Fantasy and Science Fiction, 9618 Misty Brook Cv., Cordova TN 38016. Toll-free (866)888-9671. (901) 213-3768. Fax (901)213-3878. E-mail: selena@dkamagazine.com. Website: www.dkamagazine.com. Double-Edged Publishing Inc./nondenominational. Selena Thomason, mng. ed. A family-friendly magazine of Christian fantasy and science fiction. Monthly e-zine; 600 hits/mo. Free online. 100% unsolicited freelance. Complete ms; e-query OK. Pays .005/wd. ($5-25 max.) on acceptance for one-time electronic rts. Fiction 1,000-5,000 wds., prefers under 3,000 wds. (36-48/yr.). Responds in 4 wks. Seasonal 3 mos. ahead. Rarely accepts reprints (tell when/where appeared). Accepted mss via online form only. Does not use sidebars. Also accepts submissions from children/teens. Guidelines/copy on Website. (No ads)

Poetry: Accepts 36-48/yr. Free verse, light verse, traditional; to 50 lines. Pays $1. Submit max. 5 poems.

Tips: "Please visit our Website and read our guidelines and vision statement before submitting."

$DRAMA MINISTRY, PO Box 681866, Franklin TN 37068-1866. Toll-free (866)859-7622. Fax (615)373-8502. E-mail: service@dramaministry.com, or through Website: www.dramaministry.com. Belden Street Music Company. Regi Stone, ed. Mag. published 8X/yr. & online; page count varies. 50% unsolicited freelance; 50% assigned. Complete ms/cover letter for scripts; query for articles; e-query OK. Pays $100-150 for scripts on publication for one-time rts. Articles 500-700 wds. (10/yr.); scripts 2-10 minutes (80/yr.). Responds in 6-8 wks. Seasonal 6 mos. ahead. Accepts simultaneous submissions & reprints (tell when/where appeared). Requires submissions by e-mail (attached file). No kill fee. Does not use sidebars. Also accepts submissions from teens. Any Bible version. Guidelines/theme list on Website. (No ads)

Tips: "If your script is well written and you have a true understanding of what works within the church drama ministry, then you will break into our publication easily. Please adhere to and read writer's guidelines thoroughly (see Website). We do not respond unless we choose to publish your script."

$DREAMS & VISIONS: Spiritual Fiction, 35 Peter St. S., Orillia ON L3V 5A8, Canada. Phone/fax (705)329-1770. E-mail: skysong@bconnex.net. Website: www.bconnex.net/~skysong. Skysong Press. Steve Stanton, ed. An international showcase for short literary fiction written from a Christian perspective. Semiannual jour.; 56 pgs.; circ. 300. Subscription $12. 100% unsolicited freelance. Complete ms; e-query OK. Pays .01/wd. on publication for 1st rts. Fiction 2,000-6,000 wds. (12/yr.). Responds in 3-9 wks. No seasonal. Accepts simultaneous submissions & reprints (tell when/where appeared). Guidelines on Website; copy $45.95 (4 back issues to writers $12).

$DREAMSEEKER MAGAZINE, 126 Klingerman Rd., Telford PA 18969. (215)723-9125. E-mail: DSM@CascadiaPublishingHouse.com, or editor@CascadiaPublishingHouse.com. Website: www.CascadiaPublishingHouse.com. Cascadia Publishing House. Submit to The Editor. For readers committed to exploring from the heart, with passion, depth, and flair, their own visions and issues of the day. Quarterly print & online mag.; 52 pgs.; circ. 1,000 (including online). Subscription $14.95. 10% unsolicited freelance; 90% assigned. Query; e-query OK. Accepts full mss by e-mail. Pays $5 or .01/wd. on publication for 1st or one-time rts. Articles 750-1,500 wds. (10/yr.). Responds in 8 wks. No seasonal. No simultaneous submissions; rarely buys reprints (tell when/where appeared). Prefers submissions on disk or by e-mail (attached file). No kill fee. Does not use sidebars. Also accepts submissions from children/teens. Guidelines on Website; copy online. Incomplete topical listings.

$EFCA TODAY, 418 Fourth St. N.E., PO Box 315, Charlottesville VA 22902. (434)961-2500. Fax (434)961-2507. E-mail: Today@EFCA.org, or DianeMc@journeygroup.com. Website: www.efca.org/today. Evangelical Free Church of America/Journey Communications. Diane McDougall, ed. Denominational. Quarterly mag.; 32 pgs.; circ. 44,000. Subscription $10. 30% unsolicited freelance; 70% assigned. Query (preferred) or complete ms/cover letter; fax/e-query OK. Pays .23/wd. or $75-325 for assigned/$46-250 for unsolicited; on acceptance for 1st and subsidiary (free use on EFCA Website or church bulletins) rts. Articles 300-1,000 wds. (6/yr.). Responds in 6 wks. Seasonal 6 mos. ahead. Accepts simultaneous submissions & reprints (tell when/where appeared). Prefers e-mail (attached file) or hard copy. Kill fee 50%. Regularly uses sidebars. Guidelines (also by e-mail); copy $1/10x13 SAE/$2.13 postage (mark "Media Mail"). (Ads)

Columns/Departments: Buys 6/yr. Home Base (topics affecting women's, men's, and youth ministries, as well as families); Cover-Theme Section (variety of topics applicable to church leadership), 500-1,000 wds.; pays $46-250.

Special Needs: Stories of EFCA churches in action.

Tips: "Have a unique story about a Free Church in action. The vast majority of articles are geared to sharing the Free Church at work."

**2007, 2006 EPA Award of Merit—Denominational. 2005, 2003 EPA Award of Excellence-Denominational. This periodical was #41 on the 2007 Top 50 Christian Publishers list (#50 in 2006, #44 in 2004).

$+EL HERALDO CRISTIANO (THE CHRISTIAN HERALD), PO Box 15040, Tampa FL 33687. (813)333-6999. Fax (813)333-9968. E-mail: info@elheraldocristiano.org. Website: www.elheraldocristiano.org. Pentecostal/published in Spanish. Joseph Diaz, ed./pub. Embracing the family for Christ. Estab. 2007; 36 pgs. Distributed in Tampa Bay area but nationwide eventually. Pays. Call or e-mail. Incomplete topical listings.

ENCOMPASS, 2296 Henderson Mills Rd. N.E., Ste. 406, Atlanta GA 30345. (770)414-1515. Fax (770)414-1518. E-mail: jabel@americananglican.org. Website: www.americananglican.org. The American Anglican Council. Jennifer Abel, ed. To provide news and information regarding the Episcopal Church and worldwide Anglican Communion; to provide inspirational articles for the spread of Christ's kingdom; to offer encouragement and challenge to the larger church. Monthly newsletter; 4-6 pgs.; circ. 45,000. Subscription free. Open to freelance. Query preferred; phone/e-query OK. **NO PAYMENT.** Articles 200-2,000 wds. Responds in 2 wks. Accepts articles by e-mail (attached file). Uses some sidebars. No guidelines; copy for 9x12 SAE/2 stamps.

Tips: "Most open to features or aspects of important people in the Anglican scene in America; commentary on current events in the Anglican community from the orthodox point of view."

$EN CONFIANZA, 8675 Explorer Dr., Colorado Springs CO 80920. (719)548-4660. Fax (719) 531-3383. E-mail: ardilama@fotf.org. Website: www.enfoqualafamilia.com. Focus on the Family. Marta Ardila, ed. To provide family-friendly material to our domestic Spanish constituents and inform the Hispanic community of culturally relevant issues that affect their families. Bimonthly mag.; circ. 30,000. Subscription free. Open to freelance. Complete ms/cover letter. Articles; no reviews. Incomplete topical listings. (No ads)

$EPISCOPAL LIFE and EPISCOPAL LIFE ONLINE, 815—2nd Ave., New York NY 10017. Toll-free (800)334-7626, ext. 6009. (212)716-6009. Fax (212)949-8059. E-mail: jhames@episcopalchurch.org.; mdavies@episcopalchurch.org. Website: www.episcopal-life.org. Episcopal Church. Jerrold F. Hames, newspaper ed.; Matthew Davies, online ed. Denominational. Monthly newspaper; 32 pgs.; circ. 280,000. Subscription $16.95. 10% assigned. Query/clips or complete ms/cover letter; phone query on breaking news only; e-query OK. Pays $50-300 on publication for 1st, one-time, or simultaneous rts. Articles 250-1,200 wds. (12/yr.); assigned book reviews 400 wds. ($35). Responds in 5 wks. Seasonal 4 mos. ahead. Accepts simultaneous submissions & reprints. Accepts e-mail submission. Kill fee 50%. Guidelines (by e-mail); free copy. (Ads)

Columns/Departments: Nan Cobbey, column ed. (ncobbey@dfms.org). Buys 36/yr. Commentary on political/religious topics; 300-600 wds.; $35-75. Query.

Tips: "All articles must have Episcopal Church slant or specifics. We need topical/issues, not devotional stuff. Most open to feature stories about Episcopalians—clergy, lay, churches, involvement in local efforts, movements, ministries."

E-QUALITY, 122 W. Franklin Ave., Ste. 218, Minneapolis MN 55404. (612)872-6898. Fax (612)872-6891. E-mail: cbe@cbeinternational.org. Website: www.cbeinternational.org. Christians for Biblical Equality. Submit to E-Quality editor. Geared to serve those who are exploring biblical equality. Quarterly online jour. Subscription free. Open to freelance. Wants 1st, reprint, and electronic rts. Articles 1,300-3,000 wds. Responds in 4+ wks. Seasonal 4-6 mos. ahead. No simultaneous submissions. Guidelines; copy. Not in topical listings. (Ads)

Tips: "Most articles we publish fall into these three categories—all related to biblical equality: personal testimonies, teaching on relevant Bible passages, or reviews of books on biblical equality."

ETERNAL INK, 4706 Fantasy Ln., Alton IL 62002. E-mail: meginrose@charter.net. Website: www.eternal-ink.com. Nondenominational. E-mail publication with a Website; open to any serious effort or submission. Mary-Ellen Grisham (meggy88@iwon.com), ed-in-chief; Carl Phillips, features ed. (CarlPhil10@aol.com); Jennifer Devlin, devotions ed. Biweekly e-zine; circ. 440+. Subscription free. 40% unsolicited freelance. Complete ms/cover letter; e-query OK. **NO PAYMENT** for 1st or reprint rts. Articles 300-1,500 wds. (26/yr.); reviews 400 wds. Responds in 6 wks. Seasonal 3 mos. ahead. Accepts reprints (tell when/where appeared). Accepts e-mail submissions (copied into message). Does not use sidebars. Prefers KJV. Also accepts submissions from children and teens. Guidelines/copy on Website. (Ad swaps)

Poetry: Accepts 26/yr. Free verse, traditional, inspirational; 20-30 lines. Submit max. 3 poems.

Fillers: Accepts 26/yr. Facts, ideas, jokes, kid quotes, prayers, prose, quizzes, quotes, short humor, and tips; 100-250 wds.

Columns/Departments: Accepts many/yr. See information on Website. Query.

Contest: See Website.

Tips: "We are earnestly praying to add someone else to our staff to write Bible Studies for the Website in conjunction with the writers we already have. Please contact Mary-Ellen Grisham for details. Any other queries can be answered on the Website."

$EUREKA STREET: An Online Magazine of Public Affairs, the Arts and Theology, PO Box 553, Richmond VIC 3121, Australia. Phone +613 9421 9666. Fax +613 9421 9600. E-mail: eureka@jespub.jesuit.org.au, or letters@eurekastreet.com. Website: www.eurekastreet.com.au. Jesuit Publications. Michael Mullins, ed. Mag. published every 2 wks.; circ. 20,000. Subscription $45. Accepts freelance. Complete ms by e-mail (attached file). Pays $100 U.S./800 wds. for one-time rts. No reprints. Guidelines online (www.eurekastreet.com.au/ab_write.html). Incomplete topical listings.

$EVANGEL (IN), Box 535002, Indianapolis IN 46253-5002. (317)244-3660. E-mail: evangeleditor@fmcna.org. Free Methodist/Light and Life Communications. Julie Innes, ed. For young to middle-aged adults; encourages spiritual growth. Weekly take-home paper (published quarterly); 8 pgs.; circ. 11,000. Subscription $9. 100% unsolicited freelance. Complete ms/cover letter; no e-query. Pays .04/wd. ($10 min.) on publication for one-time rts. Articles 1,200 wds. (100/yr.); fiction 1,200 wds. (100/yr.). Responds in 6-8 wks. Seasonal 12-15 mos. ahead. Accepts some simultaneous submissions & reprints (tell when/where appeared). Accepts requested mss by e-mail. Some sidebars. Prefers NIV. Guidelines (also by e-mail); copy for #10 SAE/1 stamp. (No ads)

Poetry: Buys 40+/yr. Free verse, light verse, traditional; 3-16 lines; $10. Submit max. 5 poems. Rhyming poetry not usually taken seriously.

Fillers: Buys 20/yr. Cartoons, crypto-word puzzles; to 100 wds; $10.

Tips: "Bring fresh insight to a topic. Submit material appropriate for the market and audience. Although we will cover a specific issue of concern to men or to women, we prefer that the problem be addressed universally. Don't ramble; stick to one thesis. A returned manuscript isn't always because of poor writing. Can also use short devotional material, 600 words or less."

EVANGEL (OR), 19532 N.E. Glisan St., Portland OR 97230. (503)492-4216. Fax (503)492-8965. E-mail: office@pnmc.org. Website: www.pnmc.org. Mennonite Church USA. Susan M. Palmer, ed. Official publication of the Pacific Northwest Mennonite Conference, featuring news and features about the churches, organizations, and people of the Mennonite Church USA in WA, OR, ID, AK, and W. MT. Quarterly mag.; 8 pgs.; circ. 3,000. Subscription free. 10% unsolicited freelance; 10% assigned. Query; phone/e-query OK. Accepts full mss by e-mail. **PAYS IN COPIES** for one-time rts. Not copyrighted. Articles 500-1,000 wds. (4/yr.). Responds in 2-4 wks. Seasonal 4 mos. ahead. No simultaneous submissions; accepts reprints (tell when/where appeared). Accepts requested mss on disk or by e-mail (attached file). Uses some sidebars. Guidelines (also by e-mail); copy for 9x12 SAE/.80 postage. (No ads)

Poetry: Accepts 1/yr. Free verse, haiku, traditional; 4-10 lines. Submit max. 4 poems.

Fillers: Accepts 2-4/yr. Cartoons, ideas, newsbreaks, prose, 50-150 wds.

Special Needs: Features on local congregational activities most open to freelancers.

Tips: "Become familiar with the views, beliefs of Mennonite Church USA. Visiting www.mennoniteusa.org is a good place to start. Please address issues from a Mennonite perspective."

THE EVANGELICAL ADVOCATE, Box 30, 1426 Lancaster Pike, Circleville OH 43113. (740)474-8856. Fax (740)477-7766. E-mail: directordoc@cccuhq.org. Website: www.cccuhq.org. Churches of Christ in Christian Union. Ralph Hux, dir. of communications. Provides news, information, and features which emphasize current events and world-view, appealing to the needs of our constituency, emphasizing fundamental evangelical holiness. Bimonthly mag.; 32-36 pgs.; circ. 4,000. Subscription $12. 15% unsolicited freelance; 15% assigned. Query (preferred) or complete ms/cover letter; fax/e-query OK. **NO PAYMENT.** Articles 500-1,000 wds. (15-20/yr.). Seasonal 2-3 mos. ahead. Accepts simultaneous submissions & reprints (tell when/where appeared). Prefers e-mail submissions (attached file). Regularly uses sidebars. Prefers KJV, NIV, NRSV. Theme list/Guidelines by e-mail; copy for 9x12 SAE. (No ads)

Poetry: Accepts 6-12/yr. Traditional.

Tips: "Best way to break in is to submit material for review by e-mail."

EVANGELICAL TIMES, Faverdale North Industrial Estate, Darlington DL3 0PH, United Kingdom. Phone +44 1325 380232. E-mail: office@evangelical-times.org. Website: www.evangelical-times.org. For churches who hold a biblical, Christ-centered theology and the doctrines of grace; circulated worldwide. Monthly newspaper; 32 pgs.; circ. 40,000. Subscription $25 (surface), $42 (airmail). Incomplete topical listings.

Tips: "Our paper offers UK and world news, Christian comment, and a wide variety of articles (biblical, devotional, practical, topical, doctrinal, and historical), with a strong missionary dimension."

$FAITH & FAMILY: The Magazine of Catholic Living, 432 Washington Ave., North Haven CT 06473. (203)230-3800. Fax (203)230-3838. E-mail: editor@faithandfamilymag.com. Website: www.faithandfamilymag.com. Catholic/Circle Media Inc. Tom & April Hoopes, eds.; submit to Robyn Lee, ed. asst. Features writing for Catholics and/or Christian families of all ages. Quarterly mag.; 100 pgs.; circ. 32,000. Subscription $14.95. 10% unsolicited freelance; 90% assigned. Query/clips; e-query OK. Pays .33/wd. on acceptance for 1st rts. Articles 700-3,000 wds. (35/yr.); brief reviews. Responds in 6-8 wks. Seasonal 6-9 mos. ahead. No reprints. Prefers e-mail submission (attached file). Kill fee. Regularly uses sidebars. Accepts illustrations from children. Prefers NAB. Guidelines (also on Website); copy $4.50/10x13 SAE. (Ads)

Fillers: Buys 10/yr. Anecdotes, cartoons, prose (brief).

Columns/Departments: Buys 75/yr. The Home Front (news); The Insider; Flair; The Season; Life Lessons; Faith & Folklore; Celebrations; Entertainment; The Where & How Guide; Spiritual Directions; and Back Porch; 600-1,200 wds. Query.

Tips: "Most open to well-written feature articles employing good quotations, anecdotes, and transitions about an interesting aspect of family life; departments; news items. To break in, submit ideas for The Home Front." Only wants Catholic theme-related material.

**This periodical was #33 on the 2007 Top 50 Christian Publishers list (#21 in 2005, #5 in 2004).

$FAITH & FRIENDS, 2 Overlea Blvd., Toronto ON M4H 1P4, Canada. (416)422-6226. Fax (416)422-6120. E-mail: faithandfriends@can.salvationarmy.org. Website: www.faithandfriends.ca. The Salvation Army. Geoffrey Moulton, mng. ed.; Ken Ramstead, assoc. ed. Monthly mag.; 32 pgs.; circ. 50,000. Subscription $16.50 Cdn. 90% assigned. Query/clips; e-query OK. Pays up to $200 Cdn. on publication for one-time rts. Articles 500-1,000 wds. Responds in 2 wks. Seasonal 6 mos. ahead. Accepts simultaneous submissions & reprints (tell when/where appeared). Prefers accepted ms by e-mail (attached file). Uses some sidebars. Prefers TNIV. Guidelines (also on Website); free copy. (No ads)

Fillers: Buys 10/yr. Cartoons, games, jokes, quizzes, quotes, word puzzles; 50 wds.; $25.

Columns/Departments: God in My Life (how Christians in the workplace find faith relevant), 600 wds.; Words to Live By (simple Bible studies/discussions of faith), 600 wds.; Faith Builders (Movie & TV reviews from a spiritual and faith perspective), 750-1,000 wds.; Between the Lines (book reviews), 500 wds.; Someone Cares.

$FAITH TODAY: To Connect, Equip and Inform Evangelical Christians in Canada, M.I.P. Box 3745, Markham ON L3R 0Y4, Canada. (905)479-5885. Fax (905)479-4742. E-mail: fteditor@efc-canada.com. Website: www.faithtoday.ca. Evangelical Fellowship of Canada. Gail Reid, mng. ed.; Bill Fledderus, sr. ed.; Karen Stiller, assoc. ed. A general-interest publication for Christians in Canada; almost exclusively about Canadians, including Canadians abroad. Bimonthly mag.; 56 pgs.; circ. 18,000. Subscription $25.08 Cdn. 20% unsolicited freelance; 80% assigned. Query only; fax/e-query preferred. Pays $80-500 (.20-.25 Cdn./wd.) on publication for 1st & electronic rts.; reprints .15/wd. Features 800-1,700 wds. (75/yr.); cover stories 2,000 wds.; essays 650-1,200 wds.; profiles 900 wds; reviews 300 wds. Responds in 6 wks. Prefers e-mail submission. Kill fee 30-50%. Regularly uses sidebars. Any Bible version. Guidelines on Website; copy for 9x12 SAE/$2.05 in Canadian funds. (Ads)

Tips: "Most open to short, colorful items, statistics, stories, profiles for Kingdom Matters department. Must be Canadian." Unsolicited manuscripts will not be returned.

**This periodical was #42 on the 2006 Top 50 Christian Publishers list (#37 in 2005).

FAITHWEBBIN, PO Box 8732, Columbia SC 29202. Fax (775)908-9660. E-mail: editor@faithwebbin.net. Website: www.faithwebbin.net. Tywebbin Creations. Mrs. Tyora Moody, ed. For Christian families. Monthly online mag. 100% unsolicited freelance. Complete ms by e-mail only; e-query OK. **NO PAYMENT.** Any Bible version. Articles 800-1,000 wds. (15-20/yr.). Responds in 1-2 wks. Seasonal 2 mos. ahead. Accepts reprints (tell when/where appeared). Requires e-mail submission (attached file). Regularly uses sidebars. Guidelines/theme list on Website. (No ads)

Columns/Departments: Accepts 12/yr. Seek (original Bible study lessons and devotions), 1,000-1,200 wds.; Grow (Christian living: family, finance, marriage, etc.), 800-1,000 wds.

Tips: "The two areas exclusively open to freelancers are Seek and Grow. Articles are normally accepted if they meet the length requirement and are not similar to what is already included on the site. Looking for fresh articles; love testimonial type devotions or articles that encourage and motivate the reader."

$THE FAMILY DIGEST, PO Box 40137, Fort Wayne IN 46804. Catholic. Corine B. Erlandson, manuscript ed. Dedicated to the joy and fulfillment of Catholic family life and its relationship to the Catholic parish. Bimonthly mag.; 48 pgs.; circ. 150,000. Distributed through parishes. 95% unsolicited freelance. Complete ms/cover letter; no phone/fax/e-query. Pays $40-60, 4-9 wks. after acceptance, for 1st rts. Articles 700-1,200 wds. (60/yr.). Responds in 4-9 wks. Seasonal 7 mos. ahead. Occasionally buys reprints (tell when/where appeared). No disk. Does not use sidebars. Prefers NAB. Guidelines & copy for 6x9 SAE/2 stamps. (No ads)

Fillers: Buys 18/yr. Anecdotes drawn from experience, prayers, short humor; 25-100 wds.; pays $25.

Tips: "Prospective freelance writers should be familiar with the types of articles we accept and publish. We are looking for upbeat articles which affirm the simple ways in which the Catholic faith is expressed in daily life. Articles on family life, parish life, seasonal articles, how-to pieces, inspirational, prayer, spiritual life, and church traditions will be gladly reviewed for possible acceptance and publication."

+THE FAMILY JOURNAL MAGAZINE, PO Box 1005, Springfield OH 45501. (937)399-9612. Fax (937)342-8797. E-mail: editor@familyjournalmagazine.org. Website: www.familyjournalmagazine.org. The Nuz News. Carolyn Hayes, ed. Christ-centered publication, advertiser-supported and free to readers; provides help for the young Christian and may also serve to introduce readers to Jesus Christ. Bimonthly mag.; circ. 4,500. Subscription $10. Open to unsolicited freelance. Complete ms. Articles & reviews. Not in topical listings. (Ads)

THE FAMILY ROOM, 5800 Ranch Dr., Little Rock AR 72223. (501)223-2629. Fax (501)224-2529. E-mail: yourfeedback@familylife.com. Website: www.familylife.com/familyroom. FamilyLife. Sabrina Beasley, Web ed. Primary audience is married couples, but also publishes parenting articles. Monthly e-zine.; circ. 180,000. Free online. 5% unsolicited freelance; 95% assigned. Complete ms/cover letter; fax/e-query OK. Accepts full mss by e-mail. **NO PAYMENT** for one-time rts. Articles 750-1,100 wds. (10/yr.) Responds in 4-6 wks. Seasonal 2 mos. ahead. Prefers e-mail submissions (attached file). Does not use sidebars. Also accepts submissions from teens. Prefers NASB. No guidelines; copy online. (No ads)

Tips: "We like fantastic and unusual true stories. It also needs to be biblical and backed with scripture."

$FAMILY SMART E-TIPS (formerly Smart Families), PO Box 1125, Murrieta CA 92564-1125. (858)513-7150. Fax (951)461-3526. E-mail: plewis@smartfamilies.com. Website: www.smartfamilies.com. Smart Families Inc. Paul Lewis, ed./pub. Christian parenting, with strong crossover to general families. E-newsletter. 20% unsolicited freelance. Complete ms preferred; fax/e-query OK. Pays $50-250 on publication for 1st rts. Articles 200-1,000 wds. Responds in 1-3 wks. Seasonal 4 mos. ahead. Accepts simultaneous submissions & reprints. Prefers e-mail submission (attached file). Uses some sidebars. Prefers NIV. No guidelines or copy. (No ads)

Fillers: Games, ideas, quotes.

Tips: "We are not a typical 'magazine' and have tight length requirements. Because of crossover audience, we do not regularly print Scripture references or use traditional God-word language."

FELLOWSHIP MAGAZINE, PO Box 412, 1109 Garner Ave., Fenwick ON L0S 1C0, Canada. Toll-free (800)678-2607. E-mail: minister@pelhamcommunitychurch.com. Website: www.fellowshipmagazine.org. Fellowship Publications/United Church of Canada/general lay audience. Rev. Dr. Diane Walker, ed. To provide a positive voice for orthodoxy and uphold the historic Christian faith within the denomination. Quarterly mag.; circ. 9,000. Subscription free for donation. Open to unsolicited freelance. No payment. Not in topical listings. (Ads)

FIRST CALL HOSPICE.COM, 9852 Business Park Dr., Ste. I, Sacramento CA 95827. (916)369-0508. Fax (916)369-1156. E-mail: fchospice@pacbell.net. Website: www.firstcallhospice.com. First Call Systems Inc. Rev. Paul V. Scholl, ed. First Call Hospice has offered patients comprehensive hospice care in the Sacramento area for the last 12 years. E-zine updated regularly & bimonthly newsletter. Open to freelance. Complete ms/cover letter; e-query OK. **NO PAYMENT** for 1st rts. Articles 500-1,000 wds.; fiction to 1,000 wds.; reviews 250 wds. Responds in 4 wks. Seasonal 3 mos. ahead. Accepts simultaneous submissions & reprints (tell when/where appeared). Requires e-mail submissions (attached file in Word format only). Does not use sidebars. Guidelines on Website; copy of newsletter; e-zine online. (Ads)

Poetry: Accepts several/yr. Avant-garde, free verse, haiku, light verse, traditional; any length. Submit max. 4 poems.

Fillers: Accepts several/yr. Prayers, prose, quotes.

$FOCUS ON THE FAMILY MAGAZINE, 8605 Explorer Dr., Colorado Springs CO 80920. (719)531-3400. Fax (719)531-3499. Website: www.family.org. Focus on the Family. Andrea Vinley Jewell, mng. ed.; Erin Prater, ed. asst.; Deb Landers, Midlife & Single-Parent ed.; Michael Ridgeway, Couples & Parents ed. To help families use Christian principles to strengthen marriages, improve child rearing, purposefully embrace midlife, hold a biblical world-view, and deal with the problems of everyday life. Monthly mag.; 32 pgs., 4 customized versions (young couples, parents, midlife, and single parents); circ. 1,500,000. Free subscription. 5% unsolicited freelance; 80% assigned; 15% staff written. Query; no phone/e-query; fax query OK. Accepts full mss by e-mail. Pays $100-300 on acceptance for 1st & electronic rts. Articles 750-1,100 wds. Responds in 4 wks. Seasonal 7 mos. ahead. Accepts simultaneous submissions; no reprints. Accepts purchased or assigned articles by e-mail (attached file in text or Word). Uses some sidebars. Prefers NIV. Guidelines (also by e-mail); copy for 9x12 SAE/2 stamps. (No ads)

Tips: "This magazine is 90% generated from within our ministry. It's very hard to break in. Midlife and single-parent areas most open to freelance. We look for unique angles and personal stories on common family-life topics. Writing must be concise, compelling, and accurate."

**2005 EPA Award of Merit—Most Improved Publication.

$+FOCUS ON YOUR CHILD NEWSLETTERS, (Early Stages, Discovery Years, Tween Ages, Teen Phases), 8605 Explorer Dr., Colorado Springs CO 80920. (719)531-3400. Fax (719)531-3499. E-mail: foycnewsletters@family.org. Website: www.focusonyourchild.com. Focus on the Family. Sheila Seifert, mng. ed. Four-color, segmented Christian parenting newsletters: *Early Stages* for parents of 0- to3-year-olds; *Discovery Years* for parents of 4- to 7-year-olds; *Tween Ages* for parents if 8- to12-year-olds; and *Teen Phases* for parents of 13- to 18-year-olds. Newsletter published 8X/yr.; 12 pages. ea.; circ. 25,000. Subscription $2/mo. 5-10% unsolicited freelance; 80% assigned. Complete ms/cover letter. Accepts full mss by e-mail. Pays .25-.30/wd. on acceptance for nonexclusive rts. Articles 350-600 wds. (over 500/yr.); no reviews. Responds in 8 wks. Seasonal 7 mos. ahead. Accepts simultaneous submissions; no reprints. Accepts e-mail submissions (copied into message). No kill fees. Uses some sidebars. Prefers NIV. Guidelines by e-mail; copies online. (No ads—but those interested could contact Derek Hanson regarding the possibility)

Fillers: Short parenting humor, 20-350 wds. Pays .25-.30/wd.

Special Needs: Dramatic narratives of true stories, or humor in regard to parenting.

Tips: "The editors are always interested in reviewing humorous personal experience, parenting ideas that focus on children—how a child was parented and NOT the parent's journey or a memory about a parent's childhood. The humorous, true story should contain at least one hands-on, parenting insight about how to raise children, and be focused on an individual child. Do not preach, moralize, or explain your point. The story should lend itself to your point."

THE FOUNDERS JOURNAL, PO Box 150931, Cape Coral FL 33915. (239)772-1400. Fax (239)772-1140. E-mail from Website: www.founders.org. Founders Ministries/Southern Baptist. Thomas K. Ascol, ed. Consistent with the doctrines of grace that speak from a historic Southern Baptist perspective. Quarterly jour. Complete ms/cover letter and completed author information form from Website. Articles & book reviews. Responds in 4 mos. or you may contact them. Guidelines on Website. Incomplete topical listings.

FRIENDS JOURNAL, Quaker Thought and Life Today, 1216 Arch St., #2A, Philadelphia PA 19107-2835. (215)563-8629. Fax (215)568-1377. E-mail: info@friendsjournal.org. Website: www.friendsjournal.org. Quaker. Robert Dockhorn, sr. ed. Reflects Quaker life with commentary on social issues, spiritual reflection, Quaker history, and world affairs. Monthly mag.; circ. 8,000. Subscription $29. 70% freelance. Complete ms by e-mail preferred; e-query OK. **NO PAYMENT.** Articles to 2,500 wds.; news items 50-200 wds.; reports of Quaker events 450 wds. Responds in 3-16 wks. Accepts simultaneous submissions or reprints, if notified. Also accepts disk. Guidelines on Website; free copy. Incomplete topical listings.

Poetry: To 25 lines.

Fillers: Games, short humor, newsbreaks, and word puzzles.

THE FRIENDS VOICE, 2748 E. Pikes Peak Ave., Colorado Springs CO 80909. (719)632-5721. E-mail: thevoice@evangelicalfriends.org. Website: www.evangelicalfriends.org. Evangelical Friends International/North America. Becky Towne, ed. Denominational newsletter intended for EFI-NA households. Triannual newsletter; 12 pgs.; circ. 21,000. Subscription $10. 25% unsolicited freelance from EFI-NA households. Query. **NO PAYMENT** for exclusive rts. Articles 450-900 wds. Accepted mss by e-mail (attached file). Uses some sidebars. Guidelines/theme list by e-mail; catalog. (No ads) Not included in topical listings.

Tips: "You must attend an EFI-NA church or meeting."

$THE GEM, 700 E. Melrose Ave., Box 926, Findlay OH 45839-0926. (419)424-1961. Fax (419)424-3433. E-mail: communications@cggc.org. Website: www.cggc.org. Churches of God, General Conference. Rachel Foreman, ed. To encourage and motivate people in their Christian walk. Monthly (13X) take-home paper for adults; 8 pgs.; circ. 6,000. Subscription $14. 80% unsolicited freelance; 20% assigned. Complete ms/cover letter; phone/fax/e-query OK. Payment made after publication for one-time rts. Articles 300-1,600 wds. (125/yr.); fiction 2,000 wds. (125/yr.); book/music reviews, 750 wds., $10. Responds in 12 wks. Seasonal 3 mos. ahead. Accepts simultaneous submissions & reprints (tell when/where appeared). Accepts requested ms on disk or by e-mail. Uses some sidebars. Prefers NIV. Guidelines (also by e-mail)/copy for #10 SAE/2 stamps. (No ads)

Poetry: Buys 100/yr. Any type, 3-40 lines; $5-15. Submit max. 3 poems.

Fillers: Buys 100/yr. All types, except party ideas; 25-100 wds; $5-15.

Special Needs: Missions and true stories. Be sure that fiction has a clearly religious/Christian theme.

Tips: "Most open to real-life experiences where you have clearly been led by God. Make the story interesting and Christian."

**This periodical was #9 on the 2007 Top 50 Christian Publishers list (#37 in 2006, #24 in 2005, #30 in 2004, #35 in 2003).

$GEMS OF TRUTH, PO Box 4060, Overland Park KS 66204. (913)432-0331. Fax (913)722-0351. E-mail: sseditor1@juno.com. Church of God (Holiness)/Herald & Banner Press. Arlene McGehee, Sunday school ed. Denominational. Weekly adult take-home paper; 8 pgs.; circ. 14,000. Subscription $2.25. Complete ms/cover letter; phone/fax/e-query OK (prefers mail or e-mail). Pays .005/wd. on publication for 1st rts. Fiction 1,000-2,000 wds. Seasonal 6-8 mos. ahead. Accepts simultaneous submissions & reprints (tell when/where appeared). Prefers KJV. Guidelines/theme list; copy. Not in topical listings. (No ads)

GLAD TIDINGS, 102 Westwood Ln., Springdale AR 72762. E-mail: glad_tidings@sbcglobal.net. Orthodox Anglican. Holly Michael, ed. Seeks a variety of articles pertaining to the orthodox Christian faith. Magazine. Not included in topical listings.

$GOD ALLOWS U-TURNS BOOK SERIES, c/o God Allows U-Turns, PO Box 717, Faribault, MN 55021-0717. Fax (507)334-6464. E-mail: editor@godallowsuturns.com. Website: www.godallowsuturns.com. Blog: www.godallowsuturns.blogspot.com. Submit to Editor. See Special Needs below for current volumes in development. For a complete list of books open to submissions, as well as related opportunities, visit Website. Timelines vary, so send stories any time, as they may fit another volume. Each book in the series will contain up to 100 true short stories written by contributors from all over the world. 98% unsolicited freelance. Includes byline and short bio. Stories 500-1,500 wds. Pays $25-50 on publication, plus 1 copy of book, for one-time or reprint rts. Accepts simultaneous submissions & reprints (tell when/where appeared). Online submissions only, via e-mail or Website. Submit story typed, double spaced, in an attached Word document only. No poetry. Guidelines and sample story available on Website. (No ads)

Special Needs: True short stories. Three volumes in production for 2008/2009 with release dates in 2008/2009/2010: *Parents Setting Boundaries; Boomers Speak Out; and Writers Speak Out.* See Website for details on these, as well as other topics in development. Open to well-written, personal inspirational pieces showing how faith in God can inspire, encourage, and heal. Hope should prevail. Human-interest stories with a spiritual application, affirming ways in which faith is expressed in daily life. These true stories must touch the emotions. Our contributors are a diverse group with no limits on age or denomination.

Tips: "Show us how your faith choices have changed your life. Read prior volumes, or see the sample story on our Website. Show, don't tell. Keep it real. Ordinary people doing extraordinary things with God's help. We publish the nitty-gritty issues of life—few subjects are taboo. Focus on timeless, universal themes like love, forgiveness, salvation, healing, hope, faith, etc. Be able to tell a good story with drama, description, and dialog. Avoid moralisms and preachy tone. Read niche volume synopses for specific guidelines. When possible, show how the choice you made, either through a change of heart, attitude, thought, and/or behavior occurred that clearly describes moving closer to God. Using a 'U-turn' lesson/analogy within the story is a plus."

Deadline: Deadlines vary; this is an ongoing book series. Check Website for frequent series updates.

GODLY PLACES.COM, 4010 Cherryhill Ct., Arlington TX 76016. E-mail: admin@godlyplaces.com. Website: www.GodlyPlaces.com. Brian Howard, founder. Focuses on various types of ministry. Online publication. Go to Website, click on "Contact Us/Author Application," fill out application, and then submit directly to site.)

Special Needs: Men's ministry, women's ministry, couple's ministry, family ministry, singles' ministry, teens' ministry, kids' ministry, online ministry, prophetic ministry, international missions, miscellaneous ministries, etc.

GOLD COUNTRY FAMILIES, PO Box 723, Meadow Vista CA 95722. (530)878-8353. E-mail: info@goldcountryfamilies.com. Website: www.goldcountryfamilies.com. Blessed Mom Publishing. Victoria Beninga, ed./pub. A free, online magazine and e-mail newsletter of Sierra Nevada Gold Country; family-friendly local activities and travel destinations. Monthly e-magazine & e-newsletter; circ. 450 for mag. Subscription free. Estab. 2003. 100% unsolicited freelance. Query; e-query OK. Accepts full mss by e-mail. **NO PAYMENT** for 1st rts. Articles 300-2,000 wds. (60/yr.). Responds in 1 wk. Seasonal 2 mos. ahead. Accepts simultaneous submissions & reprints (tell when/where appeared). Accepts e-mail submissions (copied into message or attached file). Uses some sidebars. Also accepts submissions from children/teens. No guidelines; copy online. (Ads)

Tips: "Most open to family-friendly travel destinations, getaways for parents. Need more travel articles outside California."

$GOOD NEWS, PO Box 150, Wilmore KY 40390. (859)858-4661. Fax (859)858-4972. E-mail: steve@goodnewsmag.org. Website: www.goodnewsmag.org. United Methodist/Forum for Scriptural Christianity Inc. Steve Beard, ed. Focus is evangelical renewal within the denomination. Bimonthly mag.; 44 pgs.; circ. 100,000. Subscription $20. 20% unsolicited freelance. Query first; no phone/fax/e-query. Pays $100-150 on publication for one-time rts. Articles 1,500-1,850 wds. (25/yr.). Responds in 24 wks. Seasonal 4-6 mos. ahead. Accepts simultaneous submissions & reprints (tell when/where appeared). Accepts requested ms on disk. Kill fee. Regularly uses sidebars. Prefers NIV. Guidelines (also on Website); copy $2.75/9x12 SAE. (Ads)

Tips: "Most open to features."

GOOD NEWS! 440 W. Nyack Rd., West Nyack NY 10994. (845)620-7438. Fax (845)620-7723. E-mail: warren_maye@use.salvationarmy.org. Website: www.sagoodnews.com. The Salvation Army. Warren Maye, ed. Monthly & online newspaper; 16 pgs.; circ. 30,000. 5% unsolicited freelance; 20% assigned.

GOOD NEWS CONNECTION, 105 Harris Ave., Portland ME 04103. Toll-free (800)357-0203. (207)797-4915. E-mail: goodnewsmaine@aol.com. Website: www.go-gnc.com. Jim Duran, pub. Enriching thousands of families, in Maine and New Hampshire, through churches, bookstores, numerous retail outlets, and on the Web. Monthly & online newspaper; circ. 6,000. Subscription $16.95. Query preferred. Articles; no reviews. Incomplete topical listings.

$GOOD NEWS, ETC., PO Box 2660, Vista CA 92085. (760)724-3075. E-mail: rmonroe@goodnewsetc.com. Website: www.goodnewsetc.com. Good News Publishers Inc. of California. Rick Monroe, ed. Feature stories and local news of interest to Christians in San Diego County. Monthly tabloid; 24-32 pgs.; circ. 42,000. Subscription $25. 5% unsolicited freelance; 5% assigned. Query; e-query OK. Pays $40 on publication for all, 1st, one-time, or reprint rts. Articles 500-700 wds. (15/yr.). Responds in 2 wks. Seasonal 2 mos. ahead. Accepts simultaneous submissions & reprints (tell when/where appeared). Prefers accepted ms on disk. Regularly uses sidebars. Prefers NIV. Guidelines; copy for 9x12 SAE/4 stamps. (Ads)

Tips: "Most open to local (San Diego), personality-type articles. A San Diego connection is needed."

**2005 EPA Award of Merit—Newspaper.

GOOD NEWS IN SOUTH FLORIDA, PO Box 101328, Ft. Lauderdale FL 33310. (954)564-5378. Fax (954)453-9291. E-mail: grif@goodnewsfl.org. Website: www.goodnewsfl.org. Calvary Chapel/Ft. Lauderdale. Grif Blackstone, ed. To report news with a biblical perspective, share life-changing stories and encouraging words from people in the community. Monthly & online newspaper; circ. 64,000. Subscription $19.95. Open to freelance. Query preferred. Articles; reviews. Incomplete topical listings. (Ads)

**2007 EPA Award of Merit—Newspaper.

GOOD NEWS JOURNAL, 9701 Copper Creek Dr., Austin TX 78729-3543. (512)249-6535. Fax (512)249-0018. E-mail: goodnews98@aol.com. Website: www.thegoodsnewsjournal.net.

Evelyn W. Davison, pub. Christian paper for national circulation by subscription, and Central Texas by free distribution. Monthly newspaper; 24 pgs.; circ. 60,000. Subscription $29.95. 40% unsolicited freelance; 60% assigned. Query; fax/e-query OK. **NO PAYMENT** for one-time rts. Articles 200-600 wds. Accepts reprints. Prefers accepted ms by e-mail. Guidelines (also by e-mail/Website); copy for 9x12 SAE/2 stamps. (Ads)

Poetry: Accepts 4-6/yr. Traditional.

Fillers: Accepts many. All types; 10-50 wds.

Tips: "Most open to short helps, funnies, inspirations, and current issues."

THE GOOD NEWS TODAY, (formerly Good News in RI), PO Box 2558, Providence RI 02906. Phone/fax (401)619-0418. E-mail: larry@goodnewsinri.org, or larry@thegoodnews today.org. Website: www.thegoodnewstoday.org. Good News Outreach. Lawrence Lepore, ed. To evangelize the lost and unite the body of Christ in Rhode Island and S.E. Massachusetts. Monthly newspaper; circ. 16,000. Subscription $20. Open to unsolicited freelance. Complete ms. Articles; book & movie reviews. Starting a new Boston edition. Incomplete topical listings. (Ads)

$GOSPEL TODAY MAGAZINE, 286 Highway 314, Ste. C, Fayetteville GA 30214. (770)719-4825. Fax (770)716-2660. E-mail: Gospeltodaymag@aol.com. Website: www.gospeltoday.com. Horizon Concepts Inc. Teresa Hairston, pub. Ministry/Christian lifestyle directed toward urban marketplace. Bimonthly (8X) mag.; 64-80 pgs.; circ. 200,000. (drhairstongt@aol .com). Subscription $14.97. 5% unsolicited freelance; 90% assigned. Query; e-query OK. Pays $75-250 on publication for all rts. Articles 1,000-3,500 wds. (4/yr.). Responds in 2 wks. Seasonal 3 mos. ahead. Accepts simultaneous submissions & reprints (tell when/where appeared). Prefers accepted ms by e-mail (attached file). Kill fee 15%. Uses some sidebars. Prefers NKJV. Guidelines on Website; copy $3.50. (Ads)

Fillers: Accepts 2-3/yr. Cartoons, word puzzles. No payment.

Columns/Departments: Precious Memories (historic overview of renowned personality), 1,500-2,000 wds.; From the Pulpit (issue-oriented observation from clergy), 2,500-3,000 wds.; Life & Style (travel, health, beauty, fashion tip, etc.), 1,500-2,500 wds.; Broken Chains (deliverance testimony), 1,200 wds. Query. Pays $50-75.

Tips: "Looking for great stories of great people doing great things to inspire others."

$GRAND, 4791 Baywood Point Dr., St. Petersburg FL 33711. Toll-free (800)810-0260. E-mail: editor@grandmagazine.com. Website: www.grandmagazine.com. General. Submit to The Editor. Celebrates the vital spirit and active lifestyle of today's grandparents. Bimonthly mag. Subscription $9.95. Open to unsolicited freelance. Query/clips; e-query OK. Pays $100-500, 30 days after acceptance. Articles 800-2,500 wds. Kill fee 25%. Guidelines on Website (www.grand magazineonline.com/template_WritersGuidelines.html). Incomplete topical listings. (Ads)

Columns/Departments: Departments, 650 wds., $100-200. Also buys shorter pieces for up-front section, "For Starters."

Special Needs: Topics of interest to grandparents only.

Tips: "Pay close attention to ethnic and socioeconomic balance."

$GREAT MYSTERY AND SUSPENSE MAGAZINE, PO Box 8008, St. Joseph MO 64508-8008. E-mail: editor@greatmysteryandsuspense.com. Website: www.greatmysteryandsuspense .com. Vicki Lipira, ed./pub. Quarterly mag; 50 pgs. Subscription $25. 90% unsolicited freelance; 10% assigned. Complete ms/cover letter. Accepts full mss by e-mail (no attachments). Pays $25-50 on acceptance for 1st & electronic rts. Fiction 750-2,500 wds. (40-50/yr.); interviews 400 wds. (4/yr.). Responds in 2-3 mos. Seasonal 6 mos. ahead. No simultaneous submissions; accepts reprints (tell when/where appeared). Accepts e-mail submissions (copied into message). Kill fee 50%. Does not use sidebars. Guidelines (also by e-mail/ Website); copy for $6/9x12 SAE. (Ads—mystery related only)

Poetry: Buys 5-10/yr. Free verse, traditional; any length. Pays $5. Submit max. 2 poems.

Columns/Departments: Buys 4/yr., 400 wds., $25. Profiles of well-known mystery/suspense writers or famous mystery fans.

Tips: "We are open to anyone—published or not—who can write a good mystery."

$GUIDEPOSTS, 16 E. 34th St., 21st Fl., New York NY 10016-4397. (212)251-8100. Website: www.guideposts.com. Interfaith. James McDermott, articles ed. Personal faith stories showing how faith in God helps each person cope with life in some particular way. Monthly mag.; 52 pgs.; circ. 3 million. Subscription $13.94. 40% unsolicited freelance; 20% assigned. Complete ms/cover letter, by mail only; no electronic submissions. Pays $250-500 on publication for all rts. Articles 750-1,500 wds. (40-60/yr.), shorter pieces 250-750 wds ($100-250.). Responds only to mss accepted for publication in 2 mos. Seasonal 6 mos. ahead. Accepts simultaneous submissions & reprints. Kill fee 20%. Uses some sidebars. Free guidelines on Website)/copy. (Ads)

Columns/Departments: Christopher Davis, column ed. Buys 24/yr. His Mysterious Ways (divine intervention), 250 wds.; What Prayer Can Do, 250 wds.; Angels Among Us, 400 wds.; Divine Touch (tangible evidence of God's help), 400 wds. ("This is our most open area. Write in 3rd person."); $100.

Contest: Writers Workshop Contest held on even years with a late June deadline. Winners attend a week-long seminar in New York (all expenses paid) on how to write for Guideposts. Also Young Writers Contest; $36,000 in college scholarships; best stories to 1,200 wds.; deadline November 29.

Tips: "Be able to tell a good story, with drama, suspense, description, and dialog. The point of the story should be some practical spiritual help that subjects learned through their experience. Use unique spiritual insights, strong and unusual dramatic details." First person only.

+HAIKU HIPPODROME, PO Box 2340, Clovis CA 93613-2340. (559)347-0194. E-mail: cloviswings@aol.com. Poetry on Wings. Jackson Wilcox, ed. Bimonthly mag. & e-zine; 8 pgs.; circ. 100. Subscription by donation. Estab. 2005. 100% unsolicited freelance. Complete ms/cover letter; phone query OK; some e-queries. No full mss by e-mail. **PAYS 1 COPY & SUBSCRIPTION** on publication for 1st rts. Haiku 3 lines. Responds in 4 wks. Seasonal 3+ mos. ahead. No simultaneous submissions or reprints. Also accepts submissions from children/teens. Prefers KJV. Guidelines by mail; copy for #10 SAE/1 stamp. (Ads)

Poetry: Accepts 225/yr. Haiku; 3 lines. Submit max. 3 poems.

Contest: Every issue includes a Hippodrome Tanka: 3 lines (5-7-5) which are given. The contestant then provides 2 lines or 7 syllables each. Prize for best 3 is publication in next issue.

Tips: "We accept a broad range of what many call English Haiku: (3 lines—often 5-7-5 syllables). However we encourage the style of the early haiku poets—seizing the actuality of the moment in nature and expressing it in the purity of a word or phrase."

HALO MAGAZINE, PO Box 1402, Sterling VA 20167. (540)877-3568. Fax (540)877-3535. E-mail: halomag@aol.com. Website: www.halomag.com. Marian Newman Braxton, ed. Designed to minister to the unsaved and encourage the Christian; reaches a wide audience, including churches, hospitals, and prison ministries across many states. Magazine. Open to unsolicited freelance. Complete ms by mail or e-mail. **NO PAYMENT FOR NOW.** Incomplete topical listings.

Poetry: Accepts original poems.

$HARUAH: Breath of Heaven, 9618 Misty Brook Grove, Memphis TN 38016. (901)213-3878. E-mail: editor@haruah.com. Website: www.haruah.com. Double-Edge Publishing. Steve Forstner, ed. A magazine dedicated to the art of writing; wanting to inspire and encourage our readers to think in new ways. Monthly e-zine & literary mag.; circ. 9,000. Subscription free online. Estab. 2006. 75% unsolicited freelance; 25% assigned. Complete ms/cover letter; no phone/fax query; e-query OK. No full mss by e-mail; use online submission form on Website. Pay $5 for one-time & electronic rts. No length limitations on articles (20+/yr.) or fiction (60+/yr.); reviews 500 wds. Responds in 4-6 wks. Seasonal several mos. ahead. No simultaneous submissions; some reprints (tell when/where appeared). Submit through their online submissions system. Does not use sidebars. Also accepts submissions from teens (students). Any Bible version. Guidelines on Website; copy online. (No ads)

Poetry: Rochita Loenen-Ruiz, poetry ed. Accepts 24+/yr. Free verse, light verse, traditional, literary; any number of lines. Submit max. 3 poems.

Tips: "Your story doesn't have to mention God, but we would prefer it to point to Him in one way or another. We have a family atmosphere and love to help emerging writers. But be aware that we keep our expectations for our publication high, and do not settle just to fill space. If you are thinking of submitting and aren't sure if your submission fits our guidelines, always feel free to e-mail a query. We have wonderful forums to mingle with the staff. Take advantage of those and get to know us."

HEARTBEAT/CMA, PO Box 9, Hatfield AR 71945. (870)389-6196. Fax (870)389-6199. E-mail: wendy@cmausa.org. Website: www.cmausa.org. Christian Motorcyclists Assn. Wendy McDaniel, ed. To encourage members and give them a tool when they are witnessing in the general world. Monthly; circ. 18,000. Subscription $12. Open to freelance. Complete ms/cover letter. Articles; no reviews. (Ads) Incomplete topical listings.

THE HEARTLAND GATEKEEPER, PO Box 241956, Omaha NE 68124. (402)926-2633. Fax (402)391-8744. E-mail: publisher@heartlandgatekeeper.org, or through Website: www.heartlandgatekeeper.org. Faith Missions Intl./nondenominational. Irene Jensen, ed./pub. To promote unity in the body of Christ, to encourage spiritual growth, to testify to the goodness of God through reporting from a Christian perspective, to reach those who have yet to know Jesus; for Omaha/Council Bluffs region. Monthly newspaper; circ. 10,000. Subscription $24. Open to freelance. Prefers query; e-query OK. **NO PAYMENT** for one-time or reprint rts. Articles 150-300 wds., 300-700 wds., or feature articles 500-1,000 wds. Accepts reprints (tell when/where appeared). E-mail submissions only. Guidelines on Website. Incomplete topical listings. (Ads)

HEARTLIGHT INTERNET MAGAZINE, PO Box 7044, Abilene TX 79608. E-mail: phil@heartlight.org. Website: www.heartlight.org. Westover Hills Church of Christ. Phil Ware, ed. Offers positive Christian resources for living in today's world. Weekly online mag.; 20+ pgs.; circ. 70,000+. Subscription free. 20% unsolicited freelance. E-query. **NO PAYMENT** for electronic rts. Articles 300-450 wds. (25-35/yr.); fiction 500-700 wds. (12-15/yr.). Responds in 3 wks. Seasonal 2 mos. ahead. Accepts simultaneous submissions & reprints (tell when/where appeared). Prefers e-mail submission. Regularly uses sidebars. Prefers NIV. Copy available on the Internet.

Fillers: Accepts 12/yr. Anecdotes, cartoons, games, ideas, jokes, newsbreaks, prayers, prose, quotes, short humor, word puzzles; to 350 wds.

Tips: "Most open to feature articles, Just for Men or Just for Women, or Heartlight for Children."

HIGHWAY NEWS AND GOOD NEWS, 1525 River Rd., Marietta PA 17547. (717)426-9977. Fax (717)426-9980. E-mail: tfcio@transportforchrist.org. Website: www.transportforchrist.org. Transport for Christ. Jennifer Landis, ed. For truck drivers and their families; evangelistic, with articles for Christian growth. Monthly mag.; 16 pgs.; circ. 35,000. Subscription $30 or donation. 60% unsolicited freelance. Complete ms/cover letter; fax query OK; e-query preferred. **PAYS IN COPIES** for rights offered. Articles 600 or 1,500 wds. Seasonal 4 mos. ahead. Accepts simultaneous submissions & reprints (tell when/where appeared). Prefers requested ms by e-mail (attached or copied into message). Uses some sidebars. Prefers NIV. Guidelines/theme list; free copy for 9x12 SAE. (No ads)

Poetry: Accepts 2/yr.; any type; 3-20 lines. Submit max. 5 poems.

Fillers: Accepts 12/yr. Anecdotes, cartoons, facts, ideas, prayers, prose, short humor, tips; to 100 wds.

Tips: "Looking for items affecting the trucking industry. Need pieces (any length) on health, marriage, and fatherhood. Most open to features and true stories about truckers. Send pictures."

HOLY CITY CHRONICLE, PO Box 1878, Mt. Pleasant SC 29465. Toll-free (888)641-1954. (843)270-3137. Fax (843)849-6713. E-mail: mail@holycitychronicle.com. Website: www.holycitychronicle.com. Alex Radin, ed. (alex@holycitychronicle.com). Monthly newspaper; circ. 20,000. Subscription free. Open to freelance. Query preferred. Articles; no reviews. (Ads) Not included in topical listings.

HOLY HOUSE MINISTRIES NEWSLETTER, 9641 Tujunga Canyon Blvd., Tujunga CA 91042. (818)249-3477. Fax (818)249-3131. E-mail: Holy House9@aol.com. Website: http://holy houseministries.tripod.com. Rev. Kimberlie Zakarian, pres. Ministers to the unity of families by writing to individual members. Bimonthly newsletter; 6 pgs. Subscription free. 20% unsolicited freelance; 80% assigned. Query; e-query OK. Prefers accepted ms by e-mail. **PAYS 5 COPIES** for one-time rts. Articles 300 wds. (50/yr.). Responds in 2 wks. Seasonal 3 mos. ahead. Accepts reprints (tell when/where appeared). Uses some sidebars. Also accepts submissions from children/teens. No guidelines; copy for $1.25. Incomplete topical listings.

Tips: "Most open to women's issues and prayer tips."

HOMECOMING. Contact by e-mail from their Website: www.gaithernet.com/home.php. Click on "Magazine." Bill & Gloria Gaither, pubs.; Joy MacKenzie, ed-at-large; Roberta Croteau, ed-in-chief. Estab. 2003. Open to submissions to several columns.

$HOMESCHOOLING TODAY, PO Box 244, Abingdon VA 24212. (276)628-7730. Fax (208)692-5505. E-mail: management@homeschooltoday.com. Website: www.homeschoolingtoday .com. Nehemiah Four LLC. Jim Bob Howard, ed-in-chief. Practical articles, encouragement, news, and lessons for homeschoolers. Bimonthly mag.; 72 pgs.; circ. 30,000. Subscription $21.99. 40% unsolicited freelance; 60% assigned. Complete ms by e-mail (attached file) or disk; fax/e-query OK. Pays .08/published wd. on publication for 1st rts. Feature articles 2,000-2,500 wds.; articles 800-1,200 wds. (30/yr.); book reviews 800 wds. Responds in 5-9 wks. Seasonal 1 yr. ahead. Accepts simultaneous submissions; no reprints. Requires requested ms by e-mail (attached file). Kill fee 25%. Uses some sidebars. KJV, NKJV, ESV, or 1599 Geneva. Guidelines/theme list on Website; free copy. (Ads)

Columns/Departments: Buys 20-24/yr. Abacus (teaching math), 700-950 wds.; Living Literature (unit study with Living Books), 1,100-1,350 wds.; Thinking (biblical worldview), 850-1,000 wds.; Hearth and Homeschool (encouraging words for moms), 1,200-1,5,00 wds. (See guidelines for additional departments.) Query. Pays .08/wd.

$HOME TIMES FAMILY NEWSPAPER, PO Box 22547, West Palm Beach FL 33416-2547. (888) 439-3509. Fax (561)249-4932. E-mail: publisher@myconservative.com. Website: www .hometimes.org. Neighbor News Inc. Dennis Lombard, ed./pub. Conservative, pro-Christian community newspaper. Monthly tabloid; 24-28 pgs.; circ. 8,000. Subscription $24. 20% unsolicited freelance; 15% assigned. Complete ms only/cover letter; no phone/fax/e-query. Pays $5-50 on acceptance for one-time rts. Articles 100-1,500 wds. (15/yr.); fiction 300-1,500 wds. (3/yr.); book reviews 200 wds. ($5-10). Responds in 2-3 wks. Seasonal 2 mos. ahead. Accepts simultaneous submissions & reprints (tell when/where appeared). Accepts requested ms by e-mail. No kill fee. Regularly uses sidebars. Also accepts submissions from teens. Any Bible version. Guidelines; 3 issues $3. (Ads)

Poetry: Buys 3-4/yr. Free verse, traditional; 2-16 lines; $5-10. Submit max. 3 poems.

Fillers: Uses 20-30/yr. Anecdotes, cartoons, facts, ideas, jokes, kid quotes, newsbreaks, prayers, prose, quizzes, quotes, short humor, tips, word puzzles; to 100 wds.; pays 3-6 copies.

Columns/Departments: Buys 30/yr. See guidelines for departments, to 600 wds.; $5-15.

Special Needs: Good short stories (creative nonfiction, or fiction). More faith, miracles, and personal experiences.

Tips: "Most open to personal stories or home/family pieces. Very open to new writers, but study guidelines and sample first; we are different. Published by Christians, but not religious. Looking for more positive articles and stories. Now seeking stringers in multiple viable markets to write local people features with photos. Journalism experience is preferred. E-mail query for more info with your name, brief background, and your address to hometimes2@aol.com."

$HONORBOUND, 1445 N. Boonville Ave., Springfield MO 65802. (417)862-1447. Fax (417)831-8230. E-mail: honorbound@ag.org. Website: www.honorbound.com. Assemblies of God. Andrew Templeton, dir. (atempleton@ag.org). Targeting men, ages 25-60; Christian/Pentecostal distinctive. Quarterly mag.; 32-40 pgs.; circ. 22,000. Subscription $11.95. 10% unsolicited freelance; 90% assigned. Query or complete ms; phone/fax/e-query OK. Pays $50-200 for 1st rts. Articles 1,200 wds. (5/yr.); book reviews ($50). Responds in 1 wk. Seasonal 5 mos. ahead. Accepts simultaneous submissions & reprints (tell when/where appeared). Prefers e-mail submissions (attached file). Regularly uses sidebars. Prefers NIV. Also accepts submissions from teens. Guidelines/theme list (also by e-mail); copy for 9x12 SAE/3 stamps. (Ads)

Tips: "Most open to topics on family and fathering."

**This periodical was #25 on the 2006 Top 50 Christian Publishers list.

HOPEKEEPERS MAGAZINE, PO Box 502928, San Diego CA 92150. Toll-free (888)751-7378. (858)486-4685. Toll-free fax (800)933-1078. E-mail: rest@restministries.org. Website: www.hopekeepersmagazine.com. Rest Ministries Inc. Lisa Copen, ed. For people who live with chronic illness or pain; offers encouragement, support, and hope dealing with everyday issues. Quarterly mag.; 64 pgs. Subscription $17.97. Estab. 2004. 40% unsolicited freelance; 60% assigned. Query; fax/e-query OK. **PAYS IN COPIES;** or to be determined for articles with extensive research; on publication. Articles 375-1,500 wds.; book reviews 300 wds. Responds in 6-8 wks. Seasonal 6 mos. ahead. Accepts simultaneous submissions & reprints. Prefers e-mail submissions (attached or copied into message). Regularly uses sidebars. Also accepts submissions from teens. Guidelines (also by e-mail/Website); free copy (call or see Website). (Ads)

Fillers: Accepts 25/yr. Facts, newsbreaks, tips; 40-90 wds.

Columns/Departments: Accepts 4/yr. Refreshments (devotional-style/journal writing), 350 wds.

Tips: "Topics should be 'attention grabbers' about specific emotions (Is it okay to be mad at God?), or experiences (parenting with a chronic illness), or helpful (5 things you should know about illness on the job). Most open to upbeat topical articles that give reader motivation to change/reflect; should be balanced with personal experience, others' experiences, facts, and scripture." Fiction is considered, but not used frequently.

$HORIZONS, 1300 N. Meacham Rd., Schaumburg IL 60173-4888. (847)843-1600. Fax (847)843-3757. E-mail: takehomepapers@garbc.org. Website: www.RegularBaptistPress.org. General Assn. of Regular Baptist Churches/Regular Baptist Press. Joan E. Alexander, ed. For adults associated with fundamental Baptist Churches. Weekly take-home paper that supports the adult curriculum by assisting adults in being grounded and growing Christians; 4 pgs. weekly. Open to freelance. Complete ms/cover letter including personal testimony; no phone/fax/e-query. Pays .05/wd. and up, on acceptance (usually) for 1st rts. Articles 800-1,000 wds. (if over 600 wds., use subheads); fiction 1,000-1,200 wds. Responds in 8-12 wks. Seasonal 1 yr. ahead. No simultaneous submissions; some reprints. Some sidebars. Prefers KJV. Guidelines/theme list on Website. Incomplete topical listings. (No ads)

Fillers: Buys 10-15/yr. Word puzzles.

Tips: "We are especially happy to meet competent writers who are using RBP materials in church, or are well acquainted with churches in which our materials are used. We recommend that prospective contributors purchase and study a full quarter of issues before submitting. We look for personal experience stories (both first person and as-told-to), articles with a story element to them, and well-written fiction that helps readers know more of God's character and ways. Check Website quarterly for updates concerning needs, themes, etc. We're planning one year in advance."

$IDEALS MAGAZINE, Ideals Publishing Inc., 535 Metroplex Dr., Ste. 250, Nashville TN 37211. (615)333-0478, ext. 433. Website: www.idealsbooks.com. Guideposts Inc. Melinda Rathjen, ed. Seasonal, inspirational, nostalgic magazine for mature men and women of traditional values. Soft-cover book/4X/yr.; 64 pgs. 40% unsolicited freelance. Complete ms/cover letter by mail only; no phone/fax/e-query. Pays .10/wd. on publication for one-time rts. Articles 800-900 wds. (20/yr.); fiction 600-800 wds. Responds in 6-8 wks. Seasonal 8 mos. ahead. Accepts simultaneous submissions & reprints (tell when/where appeared). No disk. Does not use sidebars. Prefers KJV. Guidelines; copy $4.

Poetry: Buys 100+/yr. Free verse, light verse, traditional; 12-50 lines; $10. Submit max. 15 poems.

Tips: "Most open to poetry or essays appropriate for current features. Each issue has a particular theme: Easter, Mother's Day, Thanksgiving, and Christmas. Check current issue for themes."

$IMAGE, 3307 Third Ave. W., Seattle WA 98119. (206)281-2988. Fax (206)281-2335. E-mail: image@imagejournal.org. Website: www.imagejournal.org. Gregory Wolfe, pub./ed. Publishes the best literary fiction, poetry, nonfiction, and visual arts that engages the Judeo-Christian tradition. Quarterly jour.; 128 pgs.; circ. 5,200. Subscription $12/issue. 50% unsolicited freelance; 50% assigned. Queries preferred; phone/fax/e-query OK. Pays $10/pg. on acceptance for 1st rts. Articles/essays 4,000-6,000 wds. (8/yr.); fiction 4,000-6,000 wds. (4/yr.); book reviews 2,000 wds. Responds in 1-2 mos. No seasonal. Accepts simultaneous submissions; no reprints. No kill fees. Does not use sidebars. Any Bible version. Guidelines (also on Website); copy $16 (postpaid). (Ads)

Poetry: Buys 30/yr. Good poetry. Pays $2/line (up to $150). Submit max. 5 poems.

Tips: "Read the journal to understand what we publish. We're always thrilled to see high quality literary work in the unsolicited freelance pile, but we really can't typify what we're looking for other than good writing that's honest about faith and the life of faith. No genre fiction."

+IMAGINE: Arts Ministry Journal for IMAGO DEI, (913)549-0043. Fax (913)385-7775. E-mail: lori@churcharts.org. Website: www.churcharts.org. IMAGO DEI: Friends of Christianity and the Arts. Terry Hoyland, sr. ed. For Christians interested in a broad view of the arts. Annual mag.; 100 pgs. 100% unsolicited freelance. Complete ms/cover letter; no phone/fax/e-query. No full mss by e-mail. Pays $25 on publication for one-time rts. Articles/fiction to 2,500 wds. Responds in 6 wks. Accepts simultaneous submissions; no reprints. Prefers disk. No kill fee. Does not use sidebars. Any Bible version. Guidelines (also on Website); copy $9.95/10x13 SAE/$3 postage. (Ads)

Poetry: Marie Asner, poetry ed. Buys several/yr. Free verse, traditional; to 40 lines. Pays $25. Submit max. 3 poems.

Special Needs: Arts ministry; drama ministry; visual arts; dance ministry.

($)IMPACT MAGAZINE, 301 Geylang Rd., #0304 Geylang Centre, Singapore 389 344. Phone 65 6748 1244. Fax 65 748 3744. E-mail: editor@impact.com.sg. Website: www.impact.com.sg. Impact Christian Comm. Ltd. Andrew Goh, ed.; Loy Chin Fen, copy ed. To help young working adults apply Christian principles to contemporary issues. Bimonthly & online mag.; 56 pgs.; circ. 6,000. Subscription $18. 10% unsolicited freelance. Query or complete ms/cover letter; phone/fax/e-query OK. Accepts full ms by e-mail. Ranges from no payment up to $40/pg., for all rts. Articles 1,200-1,500 wds. (12/yr.) & fiction (6/yr.); 1,000-2,000 wds. Seasonal 2 mos. ahead. Accepts reprints. Prefers e-mail submission (attached file). Uses some sidebars. Prefers NIV. Guidelines (also by e-mail); copy for $4/$3 postage (surface mail). (Ads)

Poetry: Accepts 2-3 poems/yr. Free verse, 20-40 lines. Submit max. 3 poems.

Fillers: Accepts 6/yr. Anecdotes, cartoons, jokes, quizzes, short humor, and word puzzles.

Columns/Departments: Closing Thoughts (current social issues), 600-800 wds.; Testimony (personal experience), 1,500-2,000 wds.; Parenting (Asian context), 1,000-1,500 wds.; Faith Seeks Understanding (answers to tough questions of faith/Scripture), 80-1,000 wds.

Tips: "We're most open to fillers and testimonies."

$INDIAN LIFE, PO Box 3765, Redwood Post Office, Winnipeg MB R2W 3R6, Canada. U.S. address: PO Box 32, Pembina ND 58271. (204)661-9333. Fax (204)661-3982. E-mail: ilm@indianlife.org. Website: www.indianlife.org. Indian Life Ministries/nondenominational. Viola Jones, ed. An evangelistic publication for English-speaking aboriginal people in North America. Bimonthly tabloid newspaper; 16 pgs.; circ. 22,000. Subscription $12. 3% unsolicited freelance; 5% assigned. Query (query or complete ms for fiction); fax/e-query OK. Pays .10/wd (to $150) on publication for 1st rts.; Internet rts. negotiable. Articles 200-500 wds. (20/yr.); reviews, 100 wds. Responds in 8 wks. Seasonal 4 mos. ahead. Accepts simultaneous submissions & reprints (tell when/where appeared). Accepts requested ms by e-mail (attached or copied into message). No kill fee. Uses some sidebars. Prefers New Life Version, NIV. Guidelines (also by e-mail); copy for 9x12 SAE/$2 postage (check or money order). (Ads)

Poetry: Buys 2 poems/yr.; free verse, light verse, traditional, to 100 wds.; pays $20. Submit max. 3 poems.

Fillers: Kid quotes, quotes, short humor, 50-200 wds.; $10-25.

Special Needs: Celebrity pieces must be aboriginal only. Looking for legends.

Tips: "Most open to testimonies from Native Americans/Canadians—either first person or third person—news features, or historical fiction with strong and accurate portrayal of Native American life from the Indian perspective. A writer should have understanding of some Native American history and culture. We suggest reading some Native American authors. Native authors preferred, but some others are published. Aim at a 10th-grade reading level; short paragraphs; avoid multisyllable words and long sentences."

**2003 Award of Excellence—Newspaper.

INFUZE MAGAZINE: Art, Entertainment and Faith, 607 Ladford Ln., High Point NC 27265. (336)687-0157. E-mail: creative@infuzemag.com, or through Website: www.infuzemag.com. Mr. Robin Parrish, ed./pub. Online mag. Open to unsolicited freelance. **NO PAYMENT;** nonprofit organization. Fiction 2,000 wds. & up. Guidelines on Website.

Poetry: Accepts poetry. "We prefer poetry about people and what they feel, think, or experience." No length requirements.

Special Needs: Original artwork short films and comic books. See guidelines.

Tips: "No preachy fiction—a thought-provoking moral to the story is enough for us. This publication is unique. Be sure to download guidelines before submitting."

$INLAND NORTHWEST CHRISTIAN NEWS, 222 W. Mission, Ste. 132, Spokane WA 99201. (509)328-0820. Fax (509)326-4921. E-mail: inldnwchrist@spocom.com. John McKelvey, ed. To inform, motivate, and encourage evangelical Christians in Spokane and the Inland Northwest. Monthly newspaper; 12 pgs.; circ. 10,000. Subscription $16.95. 30% freelance. Query; phone query OK. Pays $1/column-inch on publication for 1st rts. upon agreement. Articles 350 wds. Responds in 9 wks. (Ads)

$INTERCHANGE, 412 Sycamore St., Cincinnati OH 45202-4179. (513)421-0311. Fax (513)421-0315. E-mail: richelle_thompson@episcopal-dso.org, or through Website: www.episcopal-dso.org. Episcopal Diocese of Southern Ohio. Richelle Thompson, dir. of communications. Regional paper for the Episcopal and Anglican Church in southern Ohio. Monthly (11X) tabloid; 16 pgs.; circ. 12,000. Free. 20% unsolicited freelance. Query or complete ms/cover letter. Pays $50-150 on acceptance for all rts. Articles 500-2,000 wds. (8-10/yr.). Responds in 4 wks. Accepts simultaneous submissions. Prefers requested ms on disk/CD. Regularly uses sidebars. Also accepts submissions from children or teens. Copy for 9x12 SASE.

Fillers: Cartoons, facts, jokes.

Tips: "Most open to features, especially with a local angle."

$THE INTERIM, 104 Bond St., Toronto ON M5B 1X9, Canada. (416)204-1687. Fax (416)204-1027. E-mail: interim@lifesite.net. Website: www.lifesite.net. The Interim Publishing Co. Paul Tuns, ed. Abortion, euthanasia, pornography, feminism, and religion from a pro-life perspective; Catholic and evangelical Protestant audience. Monthly & online newspaper; 24 pgs.; circ. 20,000. Subscription $35 Cdn. or U.S. 60% unsolicited freelance. Query; phone/e-query OK. Pays $50-150 Cdn., on publication. Articles 400-750 wds.; book, music, video reviews, 500 wds. ($50-75 Cdn.). Responds in 2 wks. Seasonal 2 mos. ahead. Accepts simultaneous submissions & reprints (tell when/where appeared). Prefers e-mail submission (copied into message). Kill fee. Uses some sidebars. Prefers RSV & others. No guidelines; catalog. (Ads)

Fillers: Cartoons.

Tips: "We are most open to news on life, family, and moral issues; informative commentary."

$+IN TOUCH, 3836 DeKalb Technology Pkwy., Atlanta GA 30340. (770)451-1001. E-mail: writers@intouch.org. Website: www.intouch.org. In Touch Ministries. Tonya Stoneman, ed. Publishing arm of Dr. Charles Stanley's international ministry. Monthly mag.; 48 pgs.; circ. 1 million. Subscription free. 25% unsolicited freelance; 25% assigned. Query, e-query OK. No full mss by e-mail. Pays varying rates on acceptance for 1st, electronic, nonexclusive rts. Articles 800-2,000 wds. (60/yr.). Responds in 6-8 wks. Seasonal 6 mos. ahead. No simultaneous submissions or reprints. Prefers e-mail submissions (attached or copied into message). Kill fee 50%. Uses some sidebars. Prefers NASB. Guidelines by e-mail/Website; copy for 6x9 SAE. (No ads)

Columns/Departments: Mighty in Spirit (exegetical), 1,200 wds.; Family Room (family topics), 800-1,200 wds.; By Faith (profiles), 800-1,200 wds.; Solving Problems (life issues), 800-1,200 wds. Payment varies.

**2007 EPA Award of Merit—Devotional.

ISLAND CATHOLIC NEWS, PO Box 5424 LCD9, Victoria BC V8R 6S8, Canada. (250)727-9429. E-mail: icn@islandnet.com. Website: www.islandnet.com/~icn. Island Catholic News Society. Patrick Jamieson, mng. ed.; Larry Rumsby, chairman of board. News and features about spirituality, social justice, health, ethical and poverty issues from a faith perspective. Monthly tabloid; circ. 3,000. Subscription $30 Cdn.; $40 U.S./foreign. Open to unsolicited freelance. E-mail for editorial submissions and ads (e-mail sample for price estimate); lbeinhau@telus.net.

JOURNAL OF CHURCH AND STATE, Baylor University, One Bear Pl., #97308, Waco TX 76798-7308. (254)710-1510. Fax (254)710-1571. E-mail: Pat_Cornett@Baylor.edu. Website: www.baylor.edu/~church_state. J. M. Dawson Institute of Church-State Studies/Baylor University. Wallace L. Daniel, ed. Provides a forum for the critical examination of the interaction of religion and government worldwide. Quarterly jour.; 225 pgs.; circ. 1,700. Subscription $25 (indiv.); $39 (institution). 75% unsolicited freelance; 25% assigned. Complete ms (3 copies)/cover letter (also by e-mail); phone/fax query OK; no e-query. **NO PAYMENT** for all rights. Articles 25-30 pgs./footnotes (24/yr.). Responds in 9-18 wks. Prefers requested ms on disk, e-mail submission OK. Does not use sidebars. Prefers KJV. Guidelines (also by e-mail); copy $8/$2.81 postage (mark "Media Mail"). (Ads)

Special Needs: Church-state issues, philosophy, religion.

Tips: "Open to feature articles only. Send three copies of essay and cover letter. Follow writers' guidelines."

KEYS TO LIVING, 105 Steffens Rd., Danville PA 17821. (570)437-2891. E-mail: owcam@verizon.net. Connie Mertz, ed./pub. Educates, encourages, and challenges readers through devotional and inspirational writings; also nature articles, focusing primarily on wildlife in eastern U.S. Quarterly newsletter; 12 pgs. Subscription $10. 20% unsolicited freelance (needs freelance). Complete ms/cover letter; prefers e-mail submissions; no phone query. **PAYS 2 COPIES** for one-time or reprint rts. Articles 350-500 wds. Responds in 4 wks. Accepts reprints. No disk; e-mail submission OK (copied into message). Prefers NIV. Guidelines/theme list; copy for 7x10 SAE/2 stamps. (No ads)

Poetry: Accepts if geared to family, nature, personal living, or current theme. Traditional with an obvious message.

Special Needs: More freelance submissions on themes only.

Tips: "We are a Christ-centered family publication. It's best to request a sample copy. Submissions must focus on our current theme, which is included with Writers' Guidelines. No holiday material. Stay within word count. We are a ministry."

$KINDRED SPIRIT, 3909 Swiss Ave., Dallas TX 75204. (214)841-3556. Fax (972)222-1544. E-mail: sglahn@dts.edu. Website: www.dts.edu/ks. Dallas Theological Seminary. Sandra Glahn, ed-in-chief. Publication of Dallas Theological Seminary. Quarterly mag.; 16-20 pgs.; circ. 30,000. Subscription free. 75% unsolicited freelance. Query/clips; fax/e-query OK. Pays $350 flat fee on publication for 1st & electronic rts. Articles 1,100 wds. Responds in 6 wks. Seasonal 8 mos. ahead. No simultaneous submissions; accepts reprints. Requires accepted mss by e-mail (attached or copied into message). Regularly uses sidebars. Prefers NIV. Guidelines on Website; copy. (No ads)

Special Needs: Profiles/interviews of DTS grads and faculty.

Tips: "Any news or profiles or expositions of Scripture with a link to DTS will receive top consideration."

$+LARK NEWS.COM, E-mail: editor@larknews.com. Website: www.larknews.com. Flatiron Community Church. Joel Kilpatrick, pub.; Karen Hopkins, story ed. To publish cutting edge news on topics of interest to Christians. Online newsletter; circ. 45,000. Free online. Open to unsolicited freelance ideas. Submission form on Website. Pays $35 for ideas; no finished articles. Responds in 90 days, if interested. Guidelines on Website. Incomplete topical listings.

$THE LAYMAN, 136 Tremont Park Dr., PO Box 2210, Lenoir NC 28645. (828)758-8716. Fax (828)758-0920. E-mail: laymanletters@layman.org. Website: www.layman.org. Presbyterian Lay Committee. Parker T. Williamson, CEO; Craig M. Kibler, dir. of publications. For members of the Presbyterian Church (USA). Bimonthly & online newspaper; 24 pgs.; circ. 450,000. No subscriptions. 10% unsolicited freelance. Query. Pays negotiable rates on publication for 1st rts. Articles 800-1,200 wds. (12/yr.). Responds in 2 wks. Seasonal 2 mos. ahead. Prefers requested ms on disk. Regularly uses sidebars. Copy for 9x12 SAE/3 stamps. (No ads)

LEAVES, PO Box 87, Dearborn MI 48121-0087. (313)561-2330. Fax (313)561-9486. E-mail: leaves-mag@juno.com. Website: www.rc.net/detroit/mariannhill/leaves.htm. Catholic/Mariannhill Mission Society. Jacquelyn M. Lindsey, ed. For all Catholics; promotes devotion to God and His saints and publishes readers' spiritual experiences, petitions, and thanksgivings. Bimonthly mag.; 24 pgs.; circ. 50,000. Subscription free. 50% unsolicited freelance. Complete ms/cover letter; phone/fax/e-query OK. **NO PAYMENT** for 1st or reprint rts. Not copyrighted. Articles 500 wds. (6-12/yr.). Responds in 4 wks. Seasonal 4 mos. ahead. Accepts reprints. Accepts e-mail submissions (copied into message). Does not use sidebars. Prefers NAB, RSV (Catholic edition). No guidelines or copy. (No ads)

Poetry: Accepts 6-12/yr. Traditional; 8-20 lines. Submit max. 4 poems.

Special Needs: Testimonies of conversion or reversion to Catholicism.

Tips: "Besides being interestingly and attractively written, an article should be confidently and reverently grounded in traditional Catholic doctrine and spirituality. The purpose of our magazine is to edify our readers."

$+LEBEN, 2150 River Plaza Dr., Ste. 150, Sacramento CA 95833. (916)473-8866, ext. 4. E-mail: editor@Leben.us. Website: www.Leben.us. City Seminary Press. Wayne Johnson, ed. Focuses on Protestant Christian history and biography. Quarterly & online mag.; 24 pgs.; circ. 5,000. Subscription $9.95. Estab. 2005. 20% unsolicited freelance; 80% assigned. Complete ms; e-query OK. Accepts full mss by e-mail. Pays $25-200 (copies & subscription) on acceptance for 1st & electronic rts. Articles 500-3,000 wds. (4/yr.). Responds in 2 wks. Accepts simultaneous submissions & reprints (tell when/where appeared). Prefers e-mail submissions (attached file). Uses some sidebars. Also accepts submissions from teens. Prefers KJV. Guidelines on Website; copy for 9x12 SASE/$2 postage. (Ads)

Fillers: Buys 4-6/yr. Short humor. Pays $5-10.

Special Needs: Reprints from old publications; historical, humor, etc.

Tips: "We feature stories that are biographical, historically accurate, and interesting—about Protestant martyrs, patriots, missionaries, etc., with a 'Reformed' slant."

$LIBERTY, Dept. of Public Affairs and Religious Liberty, 12501 Old Columbia Pike, Silver Springs MD 20904-1608. (301)680-6690. Fax (301)680-6695. E-mail: steeli@nad.adventist.org. Website: www.libertymagazine.org. Seventh-day Adventist. Lincoln Steed, ed. (lincoln.steed@nad.adventist.org). Deals with religious liberty issues for government officials, civic leaders, and laymen. Bimonthly mag.; 32 pgs.; circ. 200,000. Subscription $6.95. 95% unsolicited freelance. Query/clips; phone/fax/e-query OK. Pays $250 & up on acceptance for 1st rts. Articles & essays 1,000-2,500 wds. Responds in 5-13 wks. Requires requested ms on disk or by e-mail. Guidelines; copy.

$LIFEGLOW, Box 6097, Lincoln NE 68506. (402)448-0981. Fax (402)488-7582. Website: www.christianrecord.org. Christian Record Services Inc. Gaylena Gibson, ed. For sight-impaired adults over 25; interdenominational Christian audience; inspirational/devotional articles. Bimonthly mag.; 65 pgs. (lg. print); circ. 34,000. Free to sight-impaired. 95% unsolicited freelance. Complete ms; no phone/e-query. Pays .04-.05/wd. on acceptance for one-time rts. Articles & true stories 750-1,400 wds. Responds in 52 wks. Seasonal anytime. Accepts simultaneous submissions & reprints. Accepts requested ms on disk. Does not use sidebars. Guidelines; copy for 7x10 SAE/5 stamps. (No ads) Note: Due to an overabundance of manuscripts, this publication will not be accepting manuscripts until 2009.

LIFESITE NEWS.COM, Canadian address: 104 Bond St. E., Third Fl., Toronto ON M5B 1X9, Canada. U.S. address: LPO Box 1008, Niagara Falls NY 14304-1008. Toll-free (866)787-9947. E-mail: editor@lifesitenews.com, or lsn@lifesite.net. Website: www.lifesitenews.com. An originally written online daily news service covering life, faith, family, and freedom. John-Henry Westen, ed. 20 million page views a yr. Free subscription at (www.lifesite.net/ldn/subscribe). Incomplete topical listings.

Tips: "Highly regarded as a leader in the field of pro-life and pro-family news."

LIFETIMES CATHOLIC eZINE. (810)743-2051. E-mail: bjubar@parishwebmaster.com (see guidelines for e-mail address for each department). Website: www.ParishWebmaster.com. Catholic. Brandon Jubar, ed. Designed to spread the Good News and minister to people online. Weekly online publication. Open to submissions. Query first. **NO PAYMENT.** Articles 300-600 wds. (300/yr.). Also accepts submissions from teens. Guidelines on Website.

Columns: Weekly Reflection; Catholic Catechism; Faith & Spirituality; Family; Self-Improvement; Teen Issues; Teen 2 Teen.

$LIGHT & LIFE, Box 535002, Indianapolis IN 46253-5002. (317)244-3660. Fax (317)244-1247. E-mail: LLMeditor@fmcna.org. Website: www.freemethodistchurch.org/Magazine.

Free Methodist Church of North America. Doug Newton, ed.; Cynthia Schnereger, mng. ed.; submit to Margie Newton, ms manager. Interactive magazine for maturing Christians; contemporary-issues oriented, thought-provoking; emphasizes spiritual growth, discipline, holiness as a lifestyle. Bimonthly mag.; 32 pgs. (plus pull-outs); circ. 13,000. Subscription $16. 95% unsolicited freelance. Query first; e-query OK. Pays .15/wd. on acceptance for 1st rts. Articles 500-1,700 wds. (24/yr.). Responds in 8-12 wks. Seasonal 12 mos. ahead. No simultaneous submissions. Prefers e-mail submission (attached file) after acceptance. No kill fee. Uses some sidebars. Prefers NIV. Also accepts submissions from children or teens. Guidelines on Website; copy $4. (Ads)

Tips: "Best to write a query letter. We are emphasizing contemporary issues articles, well researched. Ask the question, 'What topics are not receiving adequate coverage in the church and Christian periodicals?' Seeking unique angles on everyday topics."

+LIGHT OF THE WORLD NEWSPAPER, 177-34 Troutville Rd., Jamaica NY 11434. (718)938-7966. Fax (718)504-3814. E-mail: Christislight@aol.com. Julius Ogunnaya, ed. Monthly newspaper. Open to unsolicited freelance. Complete ms or query. Articles.

$LIGUORIAN, One Liguori Dr., Liguori MO 63057-9999. Toll-free (800)464-2555. (636)464-2500. Toll-free fax (800)325-9526. (636)464-8449. E-mail: liguorianeditor@liguori.org. Website: www.liguorian.org. Catholic/Liguori Publications. Rick Potts, C.Ss.R., ed-in-chief; Cheryl Plass, mng. ed. To help Catholics of all ages better understand the gospel and church teachings and to show how these teachings apply to life and the problems confronting them as members of families, the church, and society. Monthly (10X) mag.; 40 pgs.; circ. 120,000. Subscription $20. 30-40% unsolicited freelance; 60% assigned. Query, query/clips, or complete ms; phone/fax/e-query OK. Pays .12-.15/wd. on acceptance for 1st rts. Articles 1,500-1,800 wds. (30-50/yr.); fiction 2,000 wds. (10/yr.); book reviews 250 wds. No simultaneous submissions or reprints. Responds in 8-12 wks. Seasonal 6-8 mos. ahead. Prefers requested ms by e-mail (attached file). Uses some sidebars. Prefers NRSV. Guidelines (also by e-mail/Website); copy for 9x12 SAE/3 stamps. (Ads)

Fillers: Buys 10/yr. Cartoons, jokes.

Tips: "Most open to 1,000 word meditations; 1,800 word fiction; or 1,500 word personal testimonies. Send complete manuscript for fiction. Polish your own manuscript."

**This periodical was #16 on the 2007 Top 50 Christian Publishers list (#22 in 2006, #6 in 2005, #42 in 2004, #39 in 2003).

$LIVE, 1445 N. Boonville Ave., Springfield MO 65802-1894. (417)862-2781. Fax (417)862-6059. E-mail: rl-live@gph.org. Website: www.gospelpubling.com. Assemblies of God/Gospel Publishing House. Richard Bennett, adult ed. Inspiration and encouragement for adults. Weekly take-home paper; 8 pgs.; circ. 54,500. Subscription $14.80. 100% unsolicited freelance. Complete ms/cover letter; no phone/fax query; e-query OK. Pays .10/wd. (.07/wd. for reprints) on acceptance for 1st, one-time, simultaneous, or reprint rts. Articles 400-1,200 wds. (80-90/yr.); fiction 400-1,200 wds. (20/yr.). Responds in 4-6 wks. Seasonal 18 mos. ahead. Accepts simultaneous submissions & reprints (tell when/where appeared). Accepts e-mail submissions (attached file). No kill fees. Few sidebars. Prefers NIV, KJV. Guidelines (also by e-mail); copy for #10 SAE/1 stamp. (No ads)

Poetry: Buys 15/yr. Free verse, light verse, traditional; 12-20 lines; $60 ($35 for reprints) when scheduled. Submit max. 3 poems.

Tips: "We are often in need of good shorter stories (400-600 wds.), especially true stories or based on true stories. Often need holiday stories that are not 'how-to' stories, particularly for patriotic or nonreligious holidays. All areas open to freelance—human interest, inspirational, and difficulties overcome with God's help. Fiction must be especially good with biblical application. Follow our guidelines. Most open to well-written personal experience with biblical application. Send no more than two articles in the same envelope and send an SASE."

**This periodical was #1 on the 2007 Top 50 Christian Publishers list (#8 in 2006, #19 in 2005, #6 in 2004, #5 in 2003).

$LIVING, 1251 Virginia Ave., Harrisonburg VA 22802. Toll-free (888)833-3333. (540)433-5351. Fax (540)434-0247. E-mail: Tgether@aol.com. Website: www.churchoutreach.com. Shalom Foundation Inc. Melodie M. Davis, ed. A positive, practical, and uplifting publication for the whole family; mass distribution. Quarterly tabloid; 32 pgs.; circ. 50,000. Subscription free. 95% unsolicited freelance. Query or complete ms/cover letter; e-query OK. Pays $35-60 after publication for one-time rts. Articles 500-1,200 wds. (40-50/yr.). Responds in 13-18 wks. Seasonal 4 mos. ahead. Accepts simultaneous submissions & reprints (tell when/where appeared). Accepts requested ms by e-mail (copied into message; include e-mail address in message). Uses some sidebars. Prefers NIV. Guidelines (also by e-mail); copy for 9x12 SAE/4 stamps. (Ads)

Fillers: Buys 4-8/yr. Anecdotes, short humor; 100-200 wds.; $20-25.

Tips: "We are directed toward the general public, many of whom have no Christian interests, and we're trying to publish high-quality writing on family issues/concerns from a Christian perspective. That means religious language must be low key. Too much of what we receive is directed toward a Christian reader. We get far more than we can use, so something really has to stand out. Please carefully consider before sending. Need more articles of interest to men. Our articles need to have a family slant or fit the descriptor 'encouragement for families.'" When submitting by e-mail, put title of magazine and title of your piece in subject line. Also include your e-mail address in body of message.

$THE LIVING CHURCH, PO Box 514036, Milwaukee WI 53203-3436. Toll-free (800)211-2771. (414)276-5420. Fax (414)276-7483. E-mail: tlc@livingchurch.org. Website: www.livingchurch.org. Episcopal/The Living Church Foundation Inc. John Schuessler, mng. ed. Independent news coverage of the Episcopal Church for clergy and lay leaders. Weekly mag.; 24+ pgs.; circ. 9,000. Subscription $42.50. Open to freelance. Query; phone/fax/e-query OK. Pays $25-100 (for solicited articles, nothing for unsolicited) for one-time rts. Articles 1,000 wds. (10/yr.). Responds in 2-4 wks. Seasonal 2 mos. ahead. Prefers requested ms by e-mail (attached or copied into message). Uses some sidebars. Guidelines (by e-mail); free copy. (Ads)

Columns/Departments: Accepts 5/yr. Benediction (devotional/inspirational), 200 wds. Complete ms. No payment.

Tips: "Most open to features, as long as they have something to do with the Episcopal Church."

$LIVING LIGHT NEWS, #200, 5306—89th St., Edmonton AB T6E 5P9, Canada. (780)468-6397. Fax (780)468-6872. E-mail: shine@livinglightnews.org. Website: www.livinglightnews.org. Living Light Ministries. Jeff Caporale, ed. To motivate and encourage Christians; witnessing tool to the lost. Bimonthly tabloid; 36 pgs.; circ. 65,000. Subscription $24.95 U.S. 40% unsolicited freelance; 60% assigned. Query; e-query OK. Pays $20-125 (.05-.10/wd. Cdn. or .08/wd. U.S.) on publication for all, 1st, one-time, simultaneous, or reprint rts. Articles 350-700 wds. (75/yr.). Responds in 4 wks. Seasonal 3-4 mos. ahead. Accepts simultaneous submissions & reprints (tell when/where appeared). Guidelines by e-mail/Website; copy for 9x12 SAE/$2.50 Cdn. postage or IRCs (no U.S. postage). (Ads)

Columns/Departments: Buys 20/yr., 450-600 wds., $10-30 Cdn. Parenting; relationships. Query.

Special Needs: Celebrity interviews/testimonials of well-known personalities. Fun or informative articles (250-700 wds.) for Christian education supplement.

Tips: "Most open to a timely article about someone who is well known in North America, in sports or entertainment, and has a strong Christian walk."

**This periodical was #34 on the 2007 Top 50 Christian Publishers list (#38 in 2006, #34 in 2005, #25 in 2004, #14 in 2003).

LIVING STONES NEWS, 2031 E. First St., Duluth MN 55812. Phone/fax (218)728-4945. E-mail: corinne@livingstonesnews.com, or editor@livingstonesnews.com. Website: www.livingstonesnews.com. Corinne E. Scott, ed. To glorify God, to reach out to the unsaved, and to bring hope, encouragement, peace, and the unconditional love of Jesus Christ to our readers. Monthly newspaper; circ. 7,000. Subscription $18. Open to freelance. Query preferred. Articles. (Ads) Not included in topical listings.

LOOKING UP MAGAZINE, PO Box 24, Leavittsburg OH 44430. (330)647-4849. Fax (330)898-0687 (call first). E-mail: LookingUpMag@aol.com. Website: www.lookingupmagazine.com. Jeannie Schmucker, ed-in-chief. Sharing God's grace one page at a time. Bimonthly mag. Subscription $19 (includes 2 tickets to June writers' award banquet). **PAYS ONE COPY.** Salvation testimonies, articles, and devotions to 700 wds. Guidelines/theme list on Website.

Poetry: Accepts poetry; free verse, light verse, traditional.

Tips: "All topics and article types accepted—whatever God places on your heart."

$THE LOOKOUT, 8805 Governor's Hill Dr., Ste. 400, Cincinnati OH 45249. (513)931-4050. Fax (513)931-0950. E-mail: lookout@standardpub.com. Website: www.lookoutmag.com. Standard Publishing. Shawn McMullen, ed. For adults who are interested in learning more about applying the gospel to their lives. Weekly & online mag.; 16 pgs.; circ. 70,000. Subscription $26.99, plus $5 postage. 30% unsolicited freelance; 70% assigned. Query for theme articles; complete ms for others; e-query OK. Pays .11-.17/wd. on acceptance. Articles 500-1,600 wds. (200/yr.). Responds in 10 wks. Seasonal 6 mos. ahead. Accepts simultaneous submissions; no reprints. No disks or e-mail submissions. Kill fee 50%. Regularly uses sidebars. Prefers NIV. Guidelines/theme list (also by e-mail/Website: www.lookoutmag.com/write/default.asp); copy for #10 SAE/$1 postage. (No ads)

Columns/Departments: Buys 24/yr. Outlook (personal opinion); Salt & Light (innovative ways to reach out into the community); Faith Around the World; all 800 wds.; .11/wd. Query.

Tips: "Most open to feature articles according to our theme list. Get a copy of our theme list and query about a theme-related article at least six months in advance. Request sample copies of our magazine to familiarize yourself with our publishing needs (also available online). Send samples of published material."

**This periodical was #10 on the 2007 Top 50 Christian Publishers list (#30 in 2006, #4 in 2005, #2 in 2004, #24 in 2003).

$THE LUTHERAN DIGEST, Box 4250, Hopkins MN 55343. (952)933-2820. Fax (952)933-5708. E-mail: tldi@lutherandigest.com. Website: www.lutherandigest.com. Lutheran. David L. Tank, ed. Blend of general and light theological material used to win nonbelievers to the Lutheran faith. Quarterly mag.; 64 pgs.; circ. 105,000. Subscription $14. 100% unsolicited freelance. Query/clips or complete ms/cover letter; no phone/fax query. Pays $25-50 on acceptance for one-time rts. Articles to 1,000 wds. (25-30/yr.). Responds in 4-9 wks. Seasonal 6-9 mos. ahead. Accepts reprints (70% is reprints). No disk. Uses some sidebars. Guidelines (also on Website); copy $3.50/6x9 SAE/3 stamps. (Ads)

Poetry: Accepts 45-50/yr. Light verse, traditional; any length; no payment. Submit max. 3 poems.

Fillers: Anecdotes, cartoons, facts, jokes, short humor; to 100 wds.; no payment.

Tips: "We prefer real-life stories over theoretical essays. We need well-thought-out, well-written, professional articles. More nature pieces. Compose well-written, short pieces that would be of interest to middle-aged and senior Christians—and also acceptable to Lutheran church pastors. (The word 'hope' is frequently associated with our publication.) So much of the material we receive is poorly written and we spend too much time trying to clean it up. Research your market first. To catch our attention, the topic has to be catchy or stand out from the usual and must be well written. Write concisely. We are more likely to use short articles because of our small page size."

$THE LUTHERAN JOURNAL, 7010—6th St. N., PO Box 28158, Oakdale MN 55128. (651)702-0086. Fax (651)702-0074. E-mail: christianad2@msn.com. Roger Jensen, ed. Family magazine for, by, and about Lutherans, and God at work in the Lutheran world. Annual mag.; 40-48 pgs.; circ. 150,000. Subscription $6. 60% unsolicited freelance; 40% assigned. Complete ms/cover letter; fax query OK. Pays $5-50 on publication for 1st rts. Articles 750-1,500 wds. (20/yr.). Response time varies. Seasonal 4-5 mos. ahead. Accepts reprints. Uses some sidebars. Prefers NIV, NAS, KJV. Accepts requested ms on disk. Also accepts submissions from children or teens. Guidelines; copy for 9x12 SAE/3 stamps. (Ads)

Poetry: Buys 10/yr. Light verse, traditional; 50-150 wds.; $5-30. Submit max. 3 poems.

Fillers: Buys 5-10/yr. Anecdotes, facts, games, prayers, quizzes, quotes; 50-300 wds.; $5-30.

Columns/Departments: Buys 40/yr. Apron Strings (short recipes); About Books (reviews), 50-150 wds.; $5-25.

Tips: "Most open to Lutheran lifestyles or Lutherans in action."

$MARIAN HELPER, Marian Helpers Center, Eden Hill, Stockbridge MA 01263. (413)298-3691. Fax (413)298-3583. E-mail: came@marian.org, or amh@marian.org. Website: www.marian.org. Catholic/Marians of the Immaculate Conception. Dave Came, exec. ed.; Steve LaChance, review ed. Quarterly & online mag.; circ. 500,000. Rarely uses unsolicited; 25% assigned freelance. Query/clips or complete ms/cover letter. Pays $250 for 1,000-1,200 wds. (2-page feature), for 1st rts. Articles 500-900 wds. Responds in 6 wks. Seasonal 6 mos. ahead. Kill fee 30%. Guidelines/copy for #10 SAE. (No ads)

Tips: "Write about God's mercy touching people's everyday lives, or about devotion to the Blessed Virgin Mary in a practical, inspirational, or fresh way."

MARKETPLACE, 12900 Preston Rd., Ste. 1215, Dallas TX 75230-1328. Toll-free (800)775-7657. (972)385-7657. Fax (972)385-7307. E-mail: art.stricklin@marketplaceministries.com. Website: www.marketplaceministries.com. Marketplace Ministries. Art Stricklin, ed. Focus is on working in the corporate workplace. Triannual mag.; 12 pgs.; circ. 16,000. Subscription free. 10% assigned. Query or complete ms; e-query OK. **NO PAYMENT** for all rts. Articles. Prefers e-mail submission. No copy. Incomplete topical listings. (No ads)

Tips: "We are attempting to cut back on freelance and use only assigned stories."

$MARRIAGE PARTNERSHIP, 465 Gundersen Dr., Carol Stream IL 60188. (630)260-6200. Fax (630)260-0114. E-mail: mp@marriagepartnership.com. Website: www.marriagepartnership.com, or www.christianitytoday.com/marriage. Christianity Today Intl. Ginger Kolbaba, ed. To promote and strengthen Christian marriages. Quarterly mag.; 74 pgs.; circ. 60,000. Subscription $19.95. 50% unsolicited freelance; 50% assigned. Query only; fax/e-query OK. Pays .15-.25/wd. on acceptance for 1st rts. Articles 500-2,000 wds. Responds in 8-10 wks. Seasonal 9 mos. ahead. Accepts reprints (tell when/where appeared). Prefers accepted ms by e-mail (copied into message). Sometimes pays kill fee. Regularly uses sidebars. Prefers NIV. Guidelines (also on Website); copy $5/9x12 SAE. (Ads)

Columns/Departments: Buys 4/year/department. Work It Out (working out a marriage problem); Back from the Brink (real-life story of a marriage in recovery), 1,800 wds.; Starting Out (views from the early years, married 5 years or less), 900 wds., pays $150; That Thing We Do (unique hobby you share as a couple), 400 wds. Query with ideas.

Tips: "Please, only articles on marriage. If it's a parenting piece, it needs to be how that topic affects marriage. Know the magazine. Read a few issues to get the correct tone and feel. Most open to the departments listed above. Be fresh, creative, and have a thorough, well-crafted query."

$MATURE LIVING, One Lifeway Plaza, MSN 175, Nashville TN 37234-0175. (615)251-5677. E-mail: rene.holt@lifeway.com (to request guidelines only). Website: www.lifeway.com. LifeWay Christian Resources/ Southern Baptist. David T. Seay, ed-in-chief; submit to Rene Holt, ed. Christian leisure reading for senior adults (50+) characterized by human interest and Christian warmth. Monthly mag.; 52 pgs.; circ. 318,000. Subscription $21.95. 90% unsolicited freelance; 10% assigned. Complete ms/cover letter; no phone/fax/e-query. Accepts full mss by e-mail only after acceptance. Pays $75-105 on acceptance for all rts. Articles 600-1,200 wds. (85/yr.); senior adult fiction 600-1,200 wds. (12/yr.). Responds in 8-10 wks. Seasonal 8 mos. ahead. No simultaneous submissions or reprints. No kill fee. Uses some sidebars. Prefers KJV, HCSB. Guidelines (also by e-mail); copy for 9x12 SAE/4 stamps. (Ads)

Poetry: Buys 24/yr. Traditional; 8-16 lines; $25. Submit max. 3 poems.

Columns/Departments: Buys 300+/yr. Cracker Barrel, 4-line verse, $15; Grandparent's Brag Board, 50-100 wds., $15; Over the Garden Fence (gardening), 300-350 wds.; Communing with God (devotional), 125-200 wds.; Fun 'n Games (wordsearch/crossword puzzles), 300-350 wds.; Crafts; Recipes; $15-50. Complete ms. See guidelines for full list.

Tips: "Almost all areas open to freelancers, except medical and financial matters. Study the magazine for its style. Write for our readers' pleasure and inspiration."

**This periodical was #13 on the 2007 Top 50 Christian Publishers list (#10 in 2006, #47 in 2004, #46 in 2003).

$MATURE YEARS, Box 801, Nashville TN 37202. (615)749-6292. Fax (615)749-6512. E-mail: matureyears@umpublishing.org. United Methodist. Marvin W. Cropsey, ed. To help persons in and nearing retirement years understand and appropriate the resources of the Christian faith in dealing with specific problems and opportunities related to aging. Quarterly mag.; 112 pgs.; circ. 55,000. Subscription $21. 60% unsolicited freelance; 40% assigned. Complete ms/cover letter; fax/e-query OK. Pays .05/wd. on acceptance for one-time rts. Articles 900-2,000 wds. (60/yr.); fiction 1,200-2,000 wds. (4/yr.). Responds in 9 wks. Seasonal 14 mos. ahead. Accepts reprints. Prefers accepted ms by e-mail (copied into message). Regularly uses sidebars. Prefers NRSV, NIV. Guidelines (also by e-mail); copy $5. (No ads)

Poetry: Buys 24/yr. Free verse, haiku, light verse, traditional; 4-16 lines; .50-1.00/line. Submit max. 6 poems.

Fillers: Buys 20/yr. Anecdotes (to 300 wds.), cartoons, jokes, prayers, word puzzles (religious only); to 30 wds.; $5-25.

Columns/Departments: Buys 20/yr. Health Hints, 900-1,200 wds.; Modern Revelations (inspirational), 900-1,100 wds.; Fragments of Life (true-life inspirational), 250-600 wds.; Going Places (travel), 1,000-1,500 wds.; Money Matters, 1,200-1,800 wds.

Special Needs: Articles on crafts and pets. Fiction on older adult situations. All areas open except Bible studies.

**This periodical was #30 on the 2007 Top 50 Christian Publishers list (#35 in 2006, #31 in 2005, #35 in 2004, #43 in 2003).

($)MENNONITE HISTORIAN, 600 Shaftesbury Blvd., Winnipeg MB R3P 0M4, Canada. (204)888-6781. E-mail: aredekopp@mennonitechurch.ca. Website: www.mennonitechurch.ca/programs. Mennonite Church Canada/Canadian Conference of Mennonite Brethren Churches. Alf Redekopp, ed. Gathers and shares historical material related to Mennonites; focus on North America, but also beyond. Quarterly newsletter; 8 pgs.; circ. 2,600. Subscription $12. 40% unsolicited freelance; 20% assigned. Complete ms/cover letter; phone/e-query OK. **NO PAYMENT EXCEPT BY SPECIAL ARRANGEMENT** for 1st rts. Articles 250-1,000 wds. (6/yr.). Responds in 3 wks. Seasonal 3 mos. ahead. Accepts simultaneous submissions & reprints (tell when/where appeared). Prefers e-mail submission (attached file). Does not use sidebars. Guidelines (also by e-mail); copy $1/9x12 SAE. (Ads)

Tips: "Must be Mennonite related (i.e., related to the life and history of the denomination, its people, organizations, and activities). Most open to lead articles. Write us with your ideas. Also genealogical articles."

$MEN OF INTEGRITY, 465 Gundersen Dr., Carol Stream IL 60188. (630)260-6200. Fax (630)260-0114. E-mail: mail@menofintegrity.net. Website: www.MenofIntegrity.net. Christianity Today Inc. Harry Genet, mng. ed. Uses narrative to apply biblical truth to specific gritty issues men face. Bimonthly pocket-size mag.; 64 pgs.; circ. 95,000. Subscription $19.95. 10% unsolicited freelance. Complete ms. Pays $50 on acceptance for one-time & electronic rts. Articles 225 wds. (15/yr.). Responds in 6 wks. Accepts simultaneous submissions & reprints (tell when/where appeared). Accepts requested ms on disk or e-mail (attached file or copied into message). Does not use sidebars. Prefers NLT. Guidelines/theme list (also by e-mail); copy $4/#10 SAE. (Ads)

**2006 EPA Award of Merit—Devotional

MEN OF THE CROSS, 920 Sweetgum Creek, Plano TX 75023. (972)517-8553. E-mail: info@menofthecross.com. Website: www.menofthecross.com. Greg Paskal, content mngr. (greg@gregpaskal.com). Encouraging men in their walk with the Lord; strong emphasis on discipleship and relationship. Online community. 50% unsolicited freelance. Query by e-mail. **NO PAYMENT.** Not copyrighted. Articles 500-1,000 wds. (10/yr.). Responds in 2-4 wks. Seasonal 3 mos. ahead. Accepts simultaneous submissions; no reprints. Prefers e-mail submissions (attached or copied into message). Uses some sidebars. Prefers NIV, NKJV, NASB. Also accepts submissions from teens. Guidelines by e-mail; copy online. (No ads)

Poetry: Accepts 1/yr. Avant-garde, free verse; 50-250 lines. Submit max. 1 poem.

Special Needs: Christian living in the workplace.

Tips: "Appropriate topic could be a real, first-hand account of how God worked in the author's life. We are looking for humble honesty in hopes it will minister to those in similar circumstances. View online forums for specific topics."

MENSAJERO ALA BLANCA, PO Box 2910, Cleveland TN 37320-2910. (423)559-5223. Fax (423)449-5231. E-mail: mensajeroalablanca@wwph.com. Website: www.mensajeroalablanca.com (in Spanish). Church of God of Prophecy. Diana M. Garcia, ed. To provide up-to-date and relevant material in the Spanish language in order to equip, educate, and edify the saints in the kingdom. Bimonthly mag.; circ. 4,000. Subscription $10. Open to freelance. Query preferred. Articles & reviews. (No ads) Incomplete topical listings.

$MESSAGE, Review and Herald Pub. Assn., 55 W. Oak Ridge Dr., Hagerstown MD 21740. (301)393-4099. Fax (301)393-4103. E-mail: message@RHPA.org, or ronsmith@rhpa.org. Website: www.messagemagazine.org. Review & Herald/Seventh-day Adventist. Pat Harris, asst. ed. (pharris@rhpa.org). For African Americans and all people seeking practical Christian guidance on current events and a better lifestyle. Bimonthly mag.; 32 pgs.; circ. 70,000. Subscription $14.95. Most articles assigned. Query or complete ms/cover letter; fax/e-query OK. Pays $50-250 on acceptance for 1st rts. Articles 700-1,200 wds.; fiction for children (ages 5-8), 500 wds. Responds in 6-10 wks. Seasonal 6 mos. ahead. Prefers requested ms by e-mail. Regularly uses sidebars. Prefers KJV. Guidelines (also on Website); copy for 9x12 SAE/2 stamps. (Ads)

Columns/Departments: Buys for each issue. Healthspan (health issues), 700 wds.; MESSAGE Jr. (biblical stories or stories with clear-cut moral for ages 5-8), 500 wds.; $50-300.

Tips: "As with any publication, writers should have a working knowledge of *Message*. They should have some knowledge of our style and our readers."

MESSAGE OF THE OPEN BIBLE, 2020 Bell Ave., Des Moines IA 50315-1096. (515)288-6761. Fax (515)288-2510. E-mail: message@openbible.org. Website: www.openbible.org. Open

Bible Standard Churches. Andrea Johnson, ed. To inspire, inform, and educate the Open Bible family. Bimonthly mag.; 16 pgs.; circ. 3,000. Subscription $9.95. 3% unsolicited freelance; 3% assigned. Query or complete ms/cover letter; e-query OK. **PAYS 5 COPIES.** Not copyrighted. Articles 750 wds. (2/yr.). Responds in 4 wks. Seasonal 4 mos. ahead. Accepts simultaneous submissions & reprints (tell when/where appeared). Accepts requested ms on disk or by e-mail. Regularly uses sidebars. Prefers NIV. Guidelines/theme list (also by e-mail); copy for 9x12 SAE/2 stamps. (No ads)

Fillers: Accepts 6/yr. Facts, quotes, short humor; 50 wds.

Tips: "A writer can best break in by giving us material for an upcoming theme, or something inspiring, specifically as it would relate to an Open Bible lay person."

$MESSENGER, Box 15550, Covington KY 41015-0550. Fax (859)283-6226. Catholic. Diane Reder, news ed. Diocese paper of Covington KY. Weekly (45X) newspaper; 24 pgs.; circ. 16,000. Subscription $18. 40% unsolicited freelance. Query/clips. Pays $1.25/column inch on publication for 1st rts. Articles 500-800 wds. Responds in 1 wk. Seasonal 1 mo. ahead. Accepts simultaneous submissions. Guidelines; free copy. (Ads)

$THE MESSENGER, 440 Main St., Steinbach MB R5G 1Z5, Canada. (204)326-6401. Fax (204)326-1613. E-mail: emcmessenger@mts.net Website: www.emconf.ca/Messenger. Evangelical Mennonite Conference. Terry M. Smith, ed. Serves Evangelical Mennonite Conference members and general readers. Mag. published 22X/yr.; 16-24 pgs. Uses little freelance, but open. Query preferred; phone/fax/e-query OK. Accepts full mss by e-mail. Pays $30-100 on publication for 1st rts. only. Articles. Not included in topical listings.

$THE MESSENGER OF SAINT ANTHONY, Via Orto Botanico 11, 35123 Padova, Italy (U.S. address: Anthonian Assn., 101 Saint Anthony Dr., Mt. Saint Francis IN 47146). (812)923-6356 or 049 8229924. Fax (812)923-3200 or 049 8225651. E-mail: m.conte@santantonio.org (editor); or messenger@santantonio.org (ed. sec.). Website: www.saintanthonyofpadua.net. Catholic/Provincia Padovana F.M.C. Fr. Mario Conte OFM, ed.; Corrado Roeper, ed. sec. For middle-aged and older Catholics in English-speaking world; articles that address current issues. Monthly & online mag.; 50 pgs.; circ. 45,000. Subscription $25 U.S. 10% unsolicited freelance; 90% assigned. Query (complete ms for fiction); phone/fax/e-query OK. Pays $40/pg. (600 wds./pg.) for one-time rts. Articles 600-2,400 wds. (40/yr.); fiction 900-1,200 wds. (11/yr.). Responds in 8-10 wks. Seasonal 3 mos. ahead. Prefers e-mail submission (attached file or copied into message). Regularly uses sidebars. Prefers NEB (Oxford Study Edition). Guidelines (also by e-mail); free copy. (No ads)

Columns/Departments: Buys 50-60/yr. Documentary (issues), 600-2,000 wds.; Spirituality, 600-2,000 wds.; Church Life, 600-2,000 wds.; Saint Anthony (devotional), 600-1,400 wds.; Living Today (family life), 600-1,400 wds.; $55-200. Complete ms.

Special Needs: Short story of a moral or religious nature; St. Anthony.

Tips: "Most open to short stories; Saint Anthony, and devotional articles on parishes named after Saint Anthony, local feasts/shrines in Saint Anthony's honour. All writers should bring a uniquely Catholic perspective to their articles."

$MESSENGER OF THE SACRED HEART, 661 Greenwood Ave., Toronto ON M4J 4B3, Canada. (416)466-1195. Catholic/Apostleship of Prayer. Rev. F. J. Power, S.J., ed. Help for daily living on a spiritual level. Monthly mag.; 32 pgs.; circ. 11,000. Subscription $14. 20% freelance. Complete ms; no phone query. Pays .06/wd. on acceptance for 1st rts. Articles 750-1,500 wds. (30/yr.); fiction 750-1,500 wds. (12/yr.). Responds in 5 wks. Seasonal 5 mos. ahead. No disk. Does not use sidebars. Guidelines; copy $1/9x12 SAE. (No ads)

Tips: "Most open to inspirational stories and articles."

$MESSIAH MAGAZINE, PO Box 649, Marshfield MO 65706. (417)468-2741. Fax (417)468-2745. E-mail: amber@ffoz.org, or through Website: www.ffoz.org. First Fruits of Zion. Boaz Michael, ed. Dedicated to the study, exploration, and celebration of our righteous and sinless

Torah-observant King—Yeshua of Nazareth. Mag. published 5X/yr.; 34 pgs.; circ. 10,000. Subscription for donation. Open to freelance. Query; fax query OK. Pays on acceptance for all rts. Articles (15-20/yr.). Responds in 3 wks. Seasonal 6 mos. ahead. Accepts simultaneous submissions; no reprints. Requires e-mail submissions (attached file). Does not use sidebars. Prefers NASB. Copy for $4/9x12 SAE/5 stamps. Incomplete topical listings. (No ads)

Tips: "F.F.O.Z. is a nonprofit ministry devoted to strengthening the love and appreciation of the Body of the Messiah for the land, people, and scriptures of Israel. Since our focus is unique, please be very familiar with our magazine before submitting your query. Our Torah Testimony column is always open, as are some of the others. Looking for something on Hebrew roots."

MESSIANIC LIVING, 11742 Layton St., Leesburg FL 34788. (321)214-0026. Toll-free fax (866)793-4252. E-mail: info@messianicliving.com. Website: www.messianicliving.com. Messianic Living Press. Jeffrey Clarke, ed. Magazine. Open to freelance. Guidelines (guidelines@messianicliving.com). Not included in topical listings.

THE MESSIANIC TIMES, PO Box 2190, Niagara Falls NY 14302. (905)685-4072. Fax (905)685-7371. E-mail: mteditor@bellsouth.net, or through Website: www.messianictimes.com. Times of the Messiah Ministries. Paul Liberman, pub. To unify the Messianic Jewish community around the world, to serve as an evangelistic tool to the Jewish community, and to educate Christians about the Jewish roots of their faith. Bimonthly newspaper; circ. 35,000. Subscription $18. Accepts freelance. Query preferred. Articles & reviews. Not in topical listings. (Ads)

METHODIST HISTORY, PO Box 127, Madison NJ 07940. (973)408-3189. Fax (973)408-3909. E-mail: RWilliams@gcah.org. Website: www.gcah.org. United Methodist. Robert J. Williams, ed. History of the United Methodism and Methodist/Wesleyan churches. Quarterly jour.; 64 pgs.; circ. 800. Subscription $20. 100% unsolicited freelance. Query; phone/fax/e-query OK. **PAYS IN COPIES** for all rts. Historical articles to 5,000 wds. (15/yr.); book reviews 500 wds. Responds in 8 wks. Requires requested ms on disk. Does not use sidebars. Guidelines (also on Website); no copy. (Ads)

Special Needs: United Methodist church history.

MIDNIGHT CALL MAGAZINE, PO Box 280008, Columbia SC 29228. Toll-free (800)845-2420. (803)755-0733. Fax (803)755-6002. E-mail: info@midnightcall.com. Website: www.midnightcall.com. Arno Froese, ed. The world's only international voice of prophecy regarding end-time events. Subscription $24.50.

$MINNESOTA CHRISTIAN CHRONICLE, 623 N. Lilac Dr., Ste. A, Golden Valley MN 55422. (763)746-2468, ext. 213. Fax (763)746-2469. E-mail: editor@mcchronicle.com. Website: www.mcchronicle.com. Keener Communications Group. Bryan Malley, ed. Local news and features of interest to the Christian community. Monthly newsletter; 24-40 pgs.; circ. 35,000. Subscription $29.95. 20% unsolicited freelance; 80% assigned. Query; phone/fax/e-query OK. Prefers e-mail submissions (attached file). Pays $20-200 one month after publication for all rts. Articles 250-1,000 wds. (50-100/yr.); reviews 400 wds. Responds in 5 wks. Seasonal 2 mos. ahead. Rarely accepts simultaneous submissions or reprints (tell when/where appeared). No kill fee. Regularly uses sidebars. Guidelines by e-mail; copy $2. (Ads)

Tips: "Looking for church trend stories. We most often use freelancers in our local news and feature article sections. Stories with a strong Minnesota hook will be accepted. Unique ministries, events, and/or people interest our readers the most. We also encourage participation in communities."

**2007 EPA Award of Excellence—Newspaper; 2006, 2005 EPA Award of Merit—Newspaper.

$+MIRACLES, HEALINGS, & THE UNEXPLAINED, Solid Gold Publications, PO Box 30418, Portland OR 97294. (503)793-3026. Fax (503)256-0418. E-mail: info@miracles-magazine.com. Website:www.miracles-magazine.com. Sue Wade, ed./pub. Showing through the overwhelming evidence of miracles that Jesus is healing and revealing himself to people every day. Estab. 2007. Complete ms by e-mail/fax/or through Website. Pays $5-25 on publication. Guidelines & sample copy on Website. Incomplete topical listings.

$THE MIRACULOUS MEDAL, 475 E. Chelten Ave., Philadelphia PA 19144-5785. (215)848-1010. Fax (215)848-1014. Website: www.cammonline.org. Catholic. Rev. James O. Kiernan, C.M., ed. Fiction and poetry for Catholic adults, mostly women. Quarterly mag.; 36 pgs.; circ. 200,000. Subscription free to members. 40% unsolicited freelance. Query by mail only. Pays .03/wd. and up, on acceptance, for 1st rts. Religious fiction 1,000-2,000 wds.; some 1,000-1,500 wds. (6/yr.). Responds in 13 wks. Seasonal anytime. Accepts simultaneous submissions. Guidelines (also by e-mail); copy for 6x9 SAE/2 stamps. (No ads) Incomplete topical listings.

Poetry: Buys 6/yr. Free verse, traditional; to 20 lines; $1 & up/line. Send any number. "Must have religious theme, preferably about the Blessed Virgin Mary."

Tips: "Most open to good short stories, 1,500-2,500 wds., or poetry, with light religious theme."

MISSIONWARES.COM, 920 Sweetgum Creek, Plano TX 75023. (972)517-8553. E-mail: info@missionwares.com. Website: www.missionwares.com. Greg Paskal, owner. Website targeted toward Christian technologists. E-zine. 50% unsolicited freelance. Complete ms; e-query OK. Accepts full mss by e-mail. **NO PAYMENT** for one-time rts. Not copyrighted. Articles 1,500-5,000 wds. (3-5/yr.). Responds in 3-4 wks. No seasonal. No simultaneous submissions or reprints. Accepts e-mail submissions (attached file in Word or PDF). Does not use sidebars. Also accepts submissions from teens. Prefers NIV, NKJV, NLT. No guidelines; copy online. (No ads)

Special Needs: Technical White Papers. Best practices in technology as outlined by biblical precedence.

Tips: "We are looking for skilled and talented Christian technologists to write on biblical best practices as applied to their work life. Please see Website for examples."

$THE MONTANA CATHOLIC, PO Box 1729, Helena MT 59624. (406)442-5820. Fax (406)442-5191. E-mail: rstmartin@diocesehelena.org. Website: www.diocesehelena.org. Catholic Diocese of Helena. Renee St. Martin Wizeman, ed. Publishes news and features from a Catholic perspective, particularly as they pertain to the church in western Montana. Monthly tabloid; 20 pgs.; circ. 9,200. 5% freelance. Query or complete ms; e-query OK. Pays .05-.10/wd. on acceptance for 1st, one-time or simultaneous rts. Articles 400-1,200 wds. (5/yr.). Responds in 5 wks. Accepts simultaneous submissions. Kill fee 25%. Guidelines on Website. Incomplete topical listings.

Tips: "Most open to seasonal pieces or articles with a tie to western Montana. Must have a Catholic angle."

$MONTGOMERY'S JOURNEY, 555 Farmington Rd., Montgomery AL 36109-4609. (334)213-7940. Fax (334)213-7990. E-mail: reachout@montgomerysjourney.com. Website: www.watsonmedia.com. Keep Sharing LLC. DeAnne Watson, pub. For protestant Christians and Christian families. Monthly mag.; 60-72 pgs.; circ. 18,000. Subscription $20. Open to freelance. Complete ms by e-mail. Pays $25 on publication for one-time or reprint rts. Articles 1,800-2,000 wds. Seasonal 3 mos. ahead. Accepts requested ms on disk or by e-mail (attached file). No kill fee. Regularly uses sidebars. Also accepts submissions from teens. No guidelines or copy. (Ads)

Tips: "Mainly open to feature stories."

MOSAIC, 4315 Village Centre Ct., Mississauga ON L4Z 1S2, Canada. (905)848-2600. Fax (905) 848-2603. E-mail: howdenl@fmc-canada.org. Website: www.fmc-canada.org. Free Methodist Church in Canada. Lisa Howden, mng. ed. Reflecting the diversity of ministry expression within the Free Methodist family. Bimonthly tabloid; 8 pgs.; circ. 4,000. Open to unsolicited freelance. Query; phone/e-query OK. **NO PAYMENT.** Articles 800-1,200 wds. Responds in 2 wks. Seasonal 4 mos. ahead. Accepts reprints (tell when/where appeared). Accepts e-mail submissions (attached file). Guidelines/theme list by e-mail/Website; no sample copy. (Ads)

Tips: "Most open to inspirational pieces."

MOVIEGUIDE, 1151 Avenida Acaso, Camarillo CA 93012. Toll-free (800)577-6684. (770)825-0084. Fax (805)383-4089. E-mail through Website: www.movieguide.org. Good News Communications/Christian Film & Television Commission. Dr. Theodore Baehr, pub. Family guide to media entertainment from a biblical perspective. Monthly mag.; 32 pgs.; circ. 2,500. Subscription $40. 40% unsolicited freelance. Query/clips. **PAYS IN COPIES** for all rts. Articles 1,200 wds. (100/yr.); book/music/video/movie reviews, 1,200 wds. Responds in 6 wks. Seasonal 6 mos. ahead. Accepts requested ms on disk. Regularly uses sidebars. Guidelines/theme list; copy for SAE/4 stamps. (Ads)

Fillers: Accepts 1,000/yr.; all types; 20-50 wds.

Columns/Departments: MovieGuide; TravelGuide; VideoGuide; CDGuide, etc.; 1,200 wds.

Contest: Scriptwriting contest for movies with positive Christian content. go to: www.kairosprize.com.

Tips: "Most open to articles on movies and entertainment, especially trends, media literacy, historical, and hot topics."

($)MUTUALITY, 122 W. Franklin Ave., Ste. 218, Minneapolis MN 55404-2451. (612)872-6898. Fax (612)872-6891. E-mail: cdearmond@cbeinternational.org, or cbe@cbeinternational.org. Website: www.cbeinternational.org. Christians for Biblical Equality. Chelsea DeArmond, ed. Seeks to provide inspiration, encouragement, and information about equality within the Christian church around the world. Quarterly mag.; 32 pgs.; circ. 1,900. Subscription $30/free to members & donors. 80% assigned freelance. Query/clips; fax/e-query OK. **PAYS A GIFT CERTIFICATE TO THEIR BOOKSTORE** on publication for 1st or electronic rts. Articles 1,300-2,500 wds. (12/yr.); book reviews 650-1,200 wds. Responds in 6 wks. Accepts reprints (tell when/where appeared). Accepts requested ms on disk or by e-mail (attached file). Regularly uses sidebars. Prefers NRSV, NIV, TNIV. Guidelines (also on Website); copy for 9x12 SAE/3 stamps. (Ads)

+NAPPALAND.COM, 367 Hawthorn Dr., Loveland CO 80538. E-mail though Website: www.nappaland.com. Nappaland Communications Inc. Mike Nappa, pub. Webzine. The Internet magazine for families; always written from a Christian world-view. Free online. Open to unsolicited freelance. Query using online contact page; no attachments. Responds only to acceptances—not rejections. **NO PAYMENT.** Articles. Responds in 30 days. Guidelines on Website; copy online. Not in topical listings.

$NATIONAL CATHOLIC REPORTER, 115 E. Armour Blvd., Kansas City MO 64111-1203. (816)531-0538. Fax (816)968-2280. E-mail: tmalcolm@ncronline.com, or through Website: www.natcath.org. Catholic. Thomas Fox, pub.; Tom Roberts, ed-in-chief. Independent. Weekly (44X) & online newspaper; 44-48 pgs.; circ. 120,000. Subscription $24.95 print; $34.95 online. Query/clips. Pays .20/wd. on publication, or varying rates by agreement. Articles & short stories, varying lengths. Responds in up to 6 wks. Accepts simultaneous submissions. Guidelines (also by e-mail/Website); copy on Website.

Columns/Departments: Query with ideas for columns.

NETWORK, PO Box 131165, Birmingham AL 35213-6165. (205)328-7112. Website: www.networknewspaper.org. Interdenominational. Dolores Milazzo Hicks, ed./pub. (dolores@networknewspaper.org). To encourage and nurture dialog, understanding, and unity in Christian communities. Monthly tabloid; 12-16 pgs.; circ. 10,000. Subscription $17.50. 50% unsolicited freelance. Phone/fax/e-query OK. **NO PAYMENT.** Not copyrighted. Articles to 500 wds. Accepts simultaneous submissions. Articles and news.

Tips: "Most open to feature stories that express the unity of the body of Christ and articles that encourage and uplift our readers. We also cover state, local, national, and international news."

$THE NEW FREEMAN, One Bayard Dr., Saint John NB E2L 3L5, Canada. (506)653-6806. Fax (506)653-6818. E-mail: tnf@nbnet.nb.ca. Roman Catholic Diocese of St. John. Margie

Trafton, mng. ed. Weekly tabloid; 16 pgs.; circ. 7,500. Subscription $21.93 Cdn., $35 U.S. 70% unsolicited freelance; 30% assigned. Query/clips; phone/fax/e-query OK. Pays variable rates on publication. Not copyrighted. Articles about 200 wds. Seasonal 2 mos. ahead. Accepts simultaneous submissions & reprints (tell when/where appeared). Accepts requested ms on disk or by e-mail (attached/TXT format or copied into message). Kill fee. Uses some sidebars. No guidelines/copy. (Ads)

Tips: "We are very open to all sorts of freelance possibilities."

NEW FRONTIER, 180 E. Ocean Blvd., 4th Fl., Long Beach CA 90802. (562)491-8343. Fax (562)491-8791. E-mail: New_frontier@usw.salvationarmy.org. Website: www.salvation army.usawest.org/newfrontier. Salvation Army Western Territory. Robert L. Docter, ed. To share the good news of the gospel and the work of The Salvation Army in the western territory with salvationists and friends. Biweekly newspaper; circ. 25,500. Subscription $12. Open to freelance. Prefers query. Articles & reviews. Not in topical listings. (Ads)

A NEW HEART, PO Box 4004, San Clemente CA 92674-4004. (949)496-7655. Fax (949)496-8465. E-mail: HCFUSA@juno.com. Website: www.HCFUSA.com. Aubrey Beauchamp, ed. For Christian healthcare givers; information regarding medical/Christian issues. Quarterly mag.; 16 pgs.; circ. 5,000. Subscription $25. 20% unsolicited freelance; 10% assigned. Complete ms/cover letter; phone/fax/e-query OK. **PAYS 2 COPIES** for one-time rts. Not copyrighted. Articles 600-1,800 wds. (20-25/yr.). Responds in 2-3 wks. Accepts simultaneous submissions & reprints. Accepts e-mail submission. Does not use sidebars. Guidelines (also by fax); copy for 9x12 SAE/3 stamps. (Ads)

Poetry: Accepts 1-2/yr. Submit max. 1-3 poems.

Fillers: Accepts 3-4/yr. Anecdotes, cartoons, facts, jokes, short humor; 100-120 wds.

Columns/Departments: Accepts 20-25/yr. Chaplain's Corner, 200-250 wds.; Physician's Corner, 200-250 wds.

Tips: "Most open to real-life situations which may benefit and encourage healthcare givers and patients. True stories with medical and evangelical emphasis."

$NEW WINESKINS, PO Box 41028, Nashville TN 37204-1028. (615)292-2940. Fax (615)292-2931. E-mail: gtaylor@woodmont.org, or info@wineskins.org. Website: www.wineskins.org. The ZOE Group Inc. Greg Taylor, mng. ed. Combines biblical and cultural scholarly focus with popular-level articles and art for a powerful journal/magazine hybrid. Bimonthly e-zine; 15-20 articles/mo. Subscription $19.95 (online). 40% unsolicited freelance; 60% assigned. Query; e-query preferred. Pays $50-100 for online 2-3 mos. after publication for one-time and electronic rts. Articles 800-2,500 wds. (100/yr.); fiction 1,000-2,500 wds. (10/yr.); book reviews 800-1,200 wds. ($50-100). Responds in 1-2 mos. Seasonal 6 mos. ahead. Accepts simultaneous submissions & reprints (tell when/where appeared). Prefers e-mail submissions (attached or copied into message). No kill fee. Sometimes uses sidebars. Accept submissions from children or teens. Prefers NIV or NRSV. Guidelines by e-mail/Website; copy on Website. (Ads)

Poetry: Buys 4-5/yr. Avant-garde, free verse, light verse; 100-2,000 wds. Pays $50. Submit max. 1 poem.

Tips: "Best way to break in is by reviewing books, specifically ones we request. Also by writing well-shaped and well-researched pieces that are more than just opinions."

NOSTALGIA, 1703 N. Normandie St., Spokane WA 99205. (509)323-2086. Fax (509)323-2096. E-mail: editor@NostalgiaMagazine.net. Website: www.nostalgiamagazine.net. King's Publishing Group Inc. Mark Carter, ed. We provide a forum for baby boomers and before to share photos and stories of yesterday that enrich life today; we use exclusively dated images/photos. Bimonthly mag.; 48 pgs. Subscription $18.95. Estab. 2004. 90% unsolicited freelance; 10% assigned. Complete ms/cover letter; e-query OK. **PAYS COPIES** on publication for 1st, one-time, reprint, simultaneous, or electronic rts. Articles 400-1,500 wds. (150/yr.). Responds in up to 1 yr. Seasonal 4 mos. ahead. Accepts simultaneous submissions & reprints (tell when/where appeared). Prefers e-mail submissions (attached or copied into message). No kill fee. Regularly uses sidebars. Guidelines (also by e-mail); query for themes/topics; copy $5/9x12 SAE. (Ads)

Special Needs: Photos and family memories from 1940s, 1950s, and 1960s.

Tips: "Looking for personal family memories with interesting photos: traveling, camping, working together. Specific episodes are better than generalities (400-2,000 wds., 1 photo/400 wds.). Dig out a great fun photo showing people engaged in life, write a caption, submit. No genealogies. Send us a first-person account showing everyday life from the years 1950-1968, with great photos."

$NOW WHAT? Box 33677, Denver CO 80233. (303)452-7973. Fax (303)452-0657. E-mail: bibleadvocate@cog7.org. Website: http://nowwhat.cog7.org. Church of God (Seventh-day). Sherri Langton, assoc. ed. Articles on salvation, Jesus, social issues, life problems that are seeker sensitive. Monthly online mag.; available only online. 100% unsolicited freelance. Complete ms/cover letter; no query. Pays $25-55 on publication for first, one-time, electronic, simultaneous, or reprint rts. Articles 1,000-1,500 wds. (20/yr.). Responds in 4-8 wks. Accepts simultaneous submissions & reprints (tell when/where appeared). Accepts requested ms by e-mail (copied into message). Regularly uses sidebars. Prefers NIV. Guidelines (also on Website); copy of online article for #10 SAE/1 stamp. (No ads)

Fillers: Buys 5-10/yr. Anecdotes, facts, prose, quotes; 50-100 wds.; $20.

Special Needs: "Personal experiences must show a person's struggle that either brought him/her to Christ or deepened faith in God. The entire *Now What?* site is built around a personal experience each month."

Tips: "The whole e-zine is open to freelance. Think how you can explain your faith, or how you overcame a problem, to a non-Christian. It's a real plus for writers submitting a personal experience to also submit an objective article related to their story. Or they can contact Sherri Langton for upcoming personal experiences that need related articles."

NRB MAGAZINE, 9510 Technology Dr., Manassas VA 20110-4167. (703)330-7000. Fax (703) 330-7100. E-mail: vfraedrich@nrb.org, or info@nrb.org. Website: www.nrb.org. National Religious Broadcasters. Valerie D. Fraedrich, ed. Topics relate to Christian radio, television, satellite, church media, Internet, and all forms of communication; promoting access and excellence in Christian communications. Monthly (9X) & online mag.; 52 pgs.; circ. 9,300. Subscription $24; Canadians add $6 U.S.; foreign add $24 U.S. 70% unsolicited freelance. Complete ms/cover letter; fax/e-query OK. **PAYS 6 COPIES** ($100-200 for assigned) on publication for 1st or reprint rts. Articles 1,000-2,000 wds. (30/yr.). Responds in 6 wks. Seasonal 6 mos. ahead. Accepts simultaneous submissions & reprints (tell when/where appeared). Prefers accepted ms by e-mail. Regularly uses sidebars. Prefers NAS. Guidelines/theme list (also by e-mail); free copy. (Ads)

Columns/Departments: Valerie Fraedrich, asst. ed. Accepts 9/yr. Trade Talk (summary paragraphs of news items/events in Christian broadcasting), 50 wds.; Opinion (social issues), 750 wds. Columns coordinated in-house, 500 wds.

Special Needs: Electronic media; education. All articles must relate in some way to broadcasting: radio, TV, programs on radio/TV, or Internet.

Tips: "Most open to feature articles relevant to Christian communicators. Become acquainted with broadcasters in your area and note their struggles, concerns, and victories. Find out what they would like to know, research the topic, then write about it." Contact assistant editor for guidelines, reprint permission, classified ads, additional copies, etc.

$ON MISSION, 4200 North Point Pkwy., Alpharetta GA 30022-4176. (770)410-6382. Fax (770)410-6105. E-mail: onmission@namb.net. Website: www.onmission.com. North American Mission Board, Southern Baptist. Carol Pipes, ed. Helping readers share Christ in the real world. Quarterly & online mag.; 64 pgs.; circ. 100,000. Subscription $14.95. 1-5% unsolicited freelance; 50-60% assigned. Query/clips (complete ms for fiction); no phone/fax query; e-query OK. Pays .25/wd. on acceptance for 1st rts. Articles 600-1,800 wds. (20/yr.). Responds in 8 wks. Seasonal 8 mos. ahead. Accepts simultaneous submissions; no reprints. Accepts e-mail submission (attached and copied into message). Kill fee. Regularly uses sidebars. Prefers NIV. Guidelines (also on Website); copy for 9x12 SAE/$1.95 postage. (Ads)

Special Needs: Needs articles on these topics: sharing Christ, starting churches, volunteering in missions, sending missionaries.

Tips: "We are primarily a Southern Baptist publication reaching out to Southern Baptist pastors and lay people, equipping them to share Christ, start churches, volunteer in missions, and impact the culture. Write a solid, 750-word, how-to article geared to 20- to 40-year-old men and women who want fresh ideas and insight into sharing Christ in the real world in which they live, work, and play. Send a résumé, along with your best writing samples. We are an on-assignment magazine, but occasionally a well-written manuscript gets published."

**2007, 2006 EPA Award of Merit—Missionary; 2005 EPA Award of Merit—Most Improved Publication.

$OUR SUNDAY VISITOR, 200 Noll Plaza, Huntington IN 46750. Toll-free (800)348-2440. (260)356-8400. Fax (260)359-9117. E-mail: oursunvis@osv.com. Website: www.osv.com. Catholic. Gerald Korson, ed.; Joyce Durika & Sarah Hayes, article eds. Vital news analysis, perspective, spirituality for today's Catholic. Weekly newspaper; 24 pgs.; circ. 68,000. 10% unsolicited freelance; 90% assigned. Query or complete ms; fax/e-query OK. Pays $100-300 within 4 wks. of acceptance for 1st & electronic rts. Articles to 1,100 wds. (25/yr.). Responds in 4-6 wks. Seasonal 2 mos. ahead. No simultaneous submissions; rarely accepts reprints (tell when/where appeared). Kill fee. Regularly uses sidebars. Prefers RSV. Guidelines (also by e-mail/Website); copy for $2/10x13 SASE/.93 postage. (Ads)

Columns/Departments: Faith; Family; Trends; Profile; Heritage; Media; Q & A. See guidelines for details.

Tips: "Our mission is to examine the news, culture, and trends of the day from a faithful and sound Catholic perspective—to see the world through the eyes of faith."

**This periodical was #48 on the 2006 Top 50 Christian Publishers list (#14 in 2005).

$OVER THE BACK FENCE, PO Box 756, Chillicothe OH 45601. (740)772-2165. Fax (740)773-7626. E-mail: SarahW@longpointmedia.com Website: www.backfencemagazine.com. Long Point Media. Sarah Williamson, mng. ed. Positive news about Southern Ohio. Quarterly mag.; 64 pgs.; circ. 15,000. Subscription $12.95. 60% unsolicited freelance. Query/clips; fax/e-query OK. Pays .10-.20/wd. on publication for one-time rts. Articles 750-1,000 wds. (9-12/yr.); fiction 300-850 wds. (4/yr.). Responds in 12 wks. Seasonal 1 yr. ahead. Accepts simultaneous submissions & reprints (tell when/where appeared). Requires requested ms on disk or by e-mail (copied into message). Regularly uses sidebars. Guidelines (also on Website); copy $4/9x12 SAE, or on Website. (Ads)

Columns/Departments: Buys 10-20/yr. Profiles from the Past (interesting history that never made the headlines), 800-1,000 wds.; Heartstrings (touching essays), 800 wds.; Shorts (humorous essays), 800 wds. Complete ms. Pays $80-120.

Special Needs: Think upbeat and positive. Articles on nature, history, travel, nostalgia, and family.

Tips: "We need material for our columns most often—Humorous Shorts, Profiles from the Past, and Heartstrings. It is best for writers to send things with appeal for Midwest readers and be generally positive. We do not publish articles that criticize or create a negative feeling about a geographical area or people."

$OZARKS SENIOR LIVING NEWSPAPER, 2010 S. Steward, Springfield MO 65804. (417)862-0852. Fax (417)862-9079. E-mail: elefantwalk@msn.com. Website: www.slnewspaper.net.

Metropolitan Radio Group Inc. Joyce Yonker O'Neal, mng. ed. Positive, upbeat paper for people 55+; includes religious articles. Monthly newspaper; 40 pgs.; circ. 40,000. 25-50% unsolicited freelance. Query or complete ms/cover letter; no phone/fax/e-query. Pays $20-35 for assigned; $5-35 for unsolicited; 30 days after publication for 1st, reprint, electronic rts. Articles 600 wds. (65/yr.). Responds in 2-5 wks. Seasonal 4 mos. ahead. Guidelines; copy for 9x12 SAE/5 stamps.

$PARABOLA: Myth, Tradition, and the Search for Meaning, 135 E. 15th St., New York NY 10003-3557. (212)505-6200. Fax (212)979-7325. E-mail: editors@parabola.org. Website: www.parabola.org. The Society for the Study of Myth and Tradition. Robert Doto, mng. ed. Devoted to the exploration of the search for meaning as expressed in the myths, symbols, rituals, and art of the world's religious traditions. Quarterly jour.; 128 pgs.; circ. 40,000. Subscription $24. 20% unsolicited freelance; 80% assigned. Query; fax/e-query OK. Pays $150-400 on publication for 1st, one-time, electronic, or reprint rts. Articles 1,000-3,000 wds. (40/yr.); book/music/video reviews 500-700 wds., $100. Responds in 12 wks. Accepts simultaneous submissions & reprints (tell when/where appeared). Accepts e-mail submissions after query (attached or copied into message). Kill fee varies. Uses some sidebars. Also accepts submissions from children & teens. Prefers KJV. Guidelines/theme list (also by e-mail/Website); no copy. (Ads)

Columns/Departments: Buys 40/yr. Reviews (books, audios, videos, software), to 700 wds.; Epicycles (retellings of traditional stories), to 1,500 wds.; $75-150. Query.

Tips: "All submissions must relate to themes. We look for well-researched, well-written, and authentic material that strikes a balance between the personal and the objective. No journalistic or self-improvement articles, evangelism, or profiles of specific persons or organizations. No witnessing, no pieces solely focused on Christianity as the only religious truth. We are a multifaith journal and seek reflections on the truths that underlie all forms of religious and spiritual search. Visit our hints page at www.parabola.org/hints.html, for suggestions."

$PARENTLIFE, One Lifeway Plaza, Nashville TN 37234-0172. (615)251-2021. Fax (615)277-8142. E-mail: parentlife@lifeway.com. Website: www.lifeway.com/magazines. LifeWay Christian Resources. William Summey, ed-in-chief; Jodi Skulley, ed. (jodi.skulley@lifeway.com). A child-centered magazine for parents of children 12 and under. Monthly mag.; 52 pgs.; circ. 70,000. Subscription $29.65. 5% unsolicited freelance; 95% assigned. Query; e-query OK. Pays $150-400 on acceptance for nonexclusive rts. Articles 1,000 wds. Responds in 6 mos. Seasonal 1 yr. ahead. Accepts simultaneous submissions; no reprints. Prefers e-mail submissions (attached file). No kill fee. Regularly uses sidebars. Also accepts submissions from children. Prefers HCSB. Guidelines/theme list (also by e-mail/Website); copy for 10x13 SASE.

Columns/Departments: Buys 60/yr. The Funny Life (funny family stories), 100 wds.; $20. Family Life (family activities), 100-250 wds.; $50. Complete ms.

Tips: "Most open to a feature article with cutting edge approach to current issues affecting parents/children. E-mail a creative, concise query to Jodi Skulley."

PARENTS & TEENS. E-mail: submissions@parentsandteens.com. Website: www.parentsandteens.com. Lyn Gregory, ed./pub. (lyngregory@ntlworld.com). To help parents connect with their teens. Biweekly e-zine; 20 pgs.; circ. 10,000. Subscription free. 10% unsolicited freelance. E-mail submissions only. Accepts full ms by e-mail. **PAYS IN COPIES AND LINK TO YOUR WEBSITE/BIO OR E-BOOKS** for 1st, one-time, reprint, or electronic rts. Articles 400-1,200 wds. (12/yr.); reviews 500 wds. ($5). Responds in 1-2 wks. Seasonal 3 mos. ahead. Accepts simultaneous submissions & reprints (tell when/where appeared). Prefers e-mail submission (copied into message). Does not use sidebars. Also accepts submissions from teens. Guidelines on Website; copy on site archive. (Ads)

Special Needs: Parenting teens and frugal living. Also articles from dads of teens.

Tips: "Query by e-mail."

THE PEGASUS REVIEW, PO Box 88, Henderson MD 21640-0088. (410)482-6736. E-mail: bounds1@comcast.net. Art Bounds, ed. Theme-oriented poetry, short fiction, and essays; not necessarily religious; in calligraphy format. Quarterly mag.; 12-14 pgs.; circ. 150. Subscription $12. 100% unsolicited freelance. Query or complete ms/cover letter (include background); e-query OK. No complete mss by e-mail. **PAYS 2 COPIES** for one-time rts. Fiction 2.5 pgs. is ideal, single-spaced (6-10/yr.); also one-page essays. Responds in 4 wks. Accepts simultaneous submissions & reprints (tell when/where appeared). No disk or e-mail submissions. Does not use sidebars. Also accepts submissions from teens. Prefers KJV. Guidelines/theme list; copy $2.50. (No ads)

Poetry: Accepts 40-50/yr. Any type; 4-24 lines (shorter the better; pay attention to line length). Theme oriented. Submit max. 3 poems.

Fillers: Accepts 20/yr. Cartoons, prose, quotes; 100-150 wds.

Special Needs: 2008 themes: Jan—Courage; Apr—Family; July—Genius & Talent; October—Memories.

Tips: "Continue to persevere. No one ever said it would be easy, but the end result is worth the wait."

PENTECOSTAL MESSENGER, PO Box 850, Joplin MO 64802. Toll-free (800)444-4674. (417)624-7050. Toll-free fax (800)982-5687. (417)624-7102. E-mail: johnm@pcg.org. Website: www.pcg.org. Pentecostal Church of God. John Mallinak, ed. Denominational publication. Monthly (11X) mag.; circ. 5,000. Subscription $12. Accepts freelance. Prefers query. Complete ms. Articles. Copy $1.50. Not in topical listings. (Ads)

THE PENWOOD REVIEW, PO Box 862, Los Alamitos CA 90720-0862. E-mail: submissions@penwoodreview.com. Website: www.penwoodreview.com. Lori Cameron, ed. Poetry, plus thought-provoking essays on poetry, literature, and the role of spirituality and religion in the literary arts. Biannual jour.; 40+ pgs.; circ. 80-100. Subscription $12. 100% unsolicited freelance. Complete ms; no e-query. **NO PAYMENT** ($2 off subscription & 1 free copy), for one-time and electronic rts. Articles 2 pgs. Responds in 9-12 wks. Accepts requested ms by e-mail (copied into message). Guidelines (also by e-mail/Website); copy $6.

Poetry: Accepts 120-160/yr. Any type, including formalist; to 2 pgs. Submit max. 5 poems.

Special Needs: Faith and the literary arts; religion and literature. Needs essays (up to 2 pgs., single spaced).

Tips: "We publish poetry almost exclusively and are looking for well-crafted, disciplined poetry, not doggerel or greeting-card-style poetry. Poets should study poetry, read it extensively, and send us their best, most original work. Visit our Website or buy a copy for an idea of what we publish."

PERSPECTIVES: A Journal of Reformed Thought, 517 Peterson St., Alta IA 51002. (616)392-8555. Fax (616)392-7717. E-mail: perspectives@rca.org. Website: www.perspectivesjournal.org. Reformed Church Press. Dr. Scott Hoezee & Dr. James Bratt, eds. To express the Reformed faith theologically; to engage issues that Reformed Christians meet in personal, ecclesiastical, and societal life; and thus to contribute to the mission of the church of Jesus Christ. Monthly (10X) & online mag.; 24 pgs.; circ. 3,000. Subscription $30. 75% unsolicited freelance; 25% assigned. Complete ms/cover letter or query; fax/e-query OK. **PAYS 6 COPIES** for 1st rts. Articles (10/yr.) and fiction (3/yr.), 2,500-3,000 wds.; reviews 1,000 wds. Responds in 20 wks. Seasonal 10 mos. ahead. Accepts reprints (tell when/where appeared). Prefers requested ms by e-mail (attached file). Uses some sidebars. Prefers NRSV. Guidelines on Website; no copy. (Ads)

Poetry: Rhoda Janse, poetry ed. (Perspectives, Dept. of English, Hope College, Holland MI 49422-9000). Accepts 2-3/yr. Traditional. Submit max. 3 poems. Hard copy only.

Columns/Departments: Accepts 12/yr. As We See It (editorial/opinion), 750-1,000 wds.; Inside Out (biblical exegesis), 750 wds. Complete ms.

Tips: "Most open to feature-length articles. Must be theologically informed, whatever the topic. Avoid party-line thinking and culture-war approaches. I would say that a reading of past issues and a desire to join in a contemporary conversation on the Christian faith would help you break in here."

PERSPECTIVES ON SCIENCE & CHRISTIAN FAITH, 55 Market St., Ipswich MA 01938. (978)356-5656. Fax (978)356-4375. E-mail: asa@asa3.org. Website: www.asa3.org. American Scientific Affiliation. Submit to Roman J. Miller, ed. (4956 Singer Glen Rd., Harrisonburg VA 22802; millerrj@rica.net; 540-432-4412). Quarterly newspaper; 88 pgs.; circ. 1,300+. Subscription $35/yr. 75% unsolicited freelance; 25% assigned. E-query. Accepts full mss by e-mail. **NO PAYMENT.** Articles 6,000 wds. (20/yr.). Responds in 2 wks. Seasonal 4 mos. ahead. No simultaneous submissions or reprints. Accepts submissions by disk or e-mail (attached file). Regularly uses sidebars. Guidelines on Website.

Poetry: Submit to Richard Ruble, 212 Weston Hills Dr., Siloam Springs AR 72761, richardanne@cox-internet.com.

Special Needs: Science and faith; bioethics.

$POETRY SCOUT: Inspirational Poetry, (formerly Thomas-Ink), 3413 Peerless Rd. N.W., #3, Cleveland TN 37312. (423)339-9755. E-mail: director@poetryscout-centreministry.com. Website: www.poetryscout-centreministry.com. Poetry Scout—Centre Ministry. Tommy Lee Means, dir. Seeking Christian inspirational poetry writers to share in a partnership book publishing contract. Poetry only. (Ads only as Website links)

Poetry: Accepts 10 pages per poet per publishing contract; ten pages of theme-oriented poetry, quotes, and elaborating thoughts. Free verse or traditional (theme oriented); up to 32 lines/poem. Payment is based on contractual agreement with affiliated publisher, and within a partnership cost-share plan.

+PORTRAIT OF ACHIEVEMENT, PO Box 938711, Margate FL 33093. (954)485-0062. Website: www.poamagazine.org. Sharon Blackwood, pub. To deliver inspiring, provocative, and informative stories about our children's greatest achievements. Magazine. Subscription $15.99. Open to unsolicited freelance. Query or complete ms. **NO PAYMENT.** Articles. Also accepts submissions from children/teens. Guidelines on Website. Not in topical listings. (Ads)

Special Needs: Articles related to the health or welfare of children.

Tips: "Provide encouragement for children and parents."

$POSITIVE THINKING: Finding Joy & Fulfillment Every Day, 66 E. Main St., Pauling NY 12564. (212)251-8100. Fax (845)855-1036. E-mail: awong@guideposts.org. Website: www.guideposts.org. Guideposts. Amy Wong, ed. Spiritually oriented, based on positive thinking and faith. Bimonthly mag.; 36 pgs.; circ. 400,000. Subscription $15. 30% unsolicited freelance. Query preferred; phone/fax/e-query OK. Pays $75/pg. on publication for one-time rts. Articles 500-2,300 wds. (8/yr.). Responds in 3-4 wks. Seasonal 6 mos. ahead. Accepts reprints. Accepts submissions by e-mail. Does not use sidebars. Guidelines; copy for #10 SAE/1 stamp.

Special Needs: Contemporary heroes; overcoming (addiction, etc.) through faith. (1) Life-changing experiences that bring about faith in Jesus Christ. (2) Ways to improve prayer and spiritual life. (3) How positive thinking and faith provide answers to life's problems.

Tips: "Most open to true stories of finding faith through difficult circumstances. Avoid preachiness. How-tos (if applicable), stories (nonfiction only) that touch the heart and soul. Have a deep, living knowledge of Christianity. Our audience is 65-70% female, average age is 55."

$POWER FOR LIVING, MS #205—Manuscript Submission, 4050 Lee Vance View, Colorado Springs CO 80918. Toll-free (800)708-5550. (719)536-0100. Fax (719)535-2928. Website: www.cookministries.org. Cook Communications/Scripture Press Publications. Don Alban Jr., ed. To expressly demonstrate the relevance of specific biblical teachings to everyday life via reader-captivating profiles of exceptional Christians. Weekly take-home paper; 8 pgs.; circ. 250,000. Subscription $12. 15% unsolicited freelance; 85% assigned. Complete ms; no phone/fax/e-query. Pays up to .15/wd. (reprints up to .10/wd.) on acceptance for one-time rts. Profiles 700-1,500 wds. (20/yr.). Responds in 10 wks. Seasonal 1 yr. ahead. Accepts simultaneous submissions & reprints (tell when/where appeared). Accepts requested ms on disk. Kill fee. Requires KJV. Guidelines/copy for #10 SAE/1 stamp (Use address above, but change to MS #205—Sample Request). (No ads)

Special Needs: Third-person profiles of truly out-of-the-ordinary Christians who express their faith uniquely. We use very little of anything else.

Tips: "Most open to vignettes, 450-1,500 wds., of prominent Christians with solid testimonies or profiles from church history. Focus on the unusual. Signed releases required."

$PRAIRIE MESSENGER: Catholic Journal, PO Box 190, Muenster SK S0K 2Y0, Canada. (306)682-1772. Fax (306)682-5285. E-mail: pm.canadian@stpeterspress.ca. Website: www.stpeters.sk.ca/prairie_messenger. Catholic/Benedictine Monks of St. Peter's Abbey. Peter Novecosky, OSB, ed.; Maureen Weber, assoc. ed. For Catholics in Saskatchewan and Manitoba, and Christians in other faith communities. Weekly tabloid (46X); 20 pgs.; circ. 6,900. Subscription $29.50 Cdn. 10% unsolicited freelance; 90% assigned. Complete ms/cover letter; phone/fax/e-query OK. Pays $50-60 ($2.75/column inch for news items) on publication for 1st, one-time, simultaneous, and reprint rts. Not copyrighted. Articles 800-900 or 2,500 wds. (15/yr.). Responds in 9 wks. Seasonal 3 mos. ahead. Accepts simultaneous submissions & reprints. Regularly uses sidebars. Guidelines (also by e-mail/Website); copy for 9x12 SAE/$1 Cdn./$1.29 U.S. (Ads)

Poetry: Accepts 30/yr. Avant-garde, free verse, haiku, light verse; 4-30 lines. Pays $20 Cdn.

Columns/Departments: Accepts 5/yr. Pays $50 Cdn.

Special Needs: Ecumenism; social justice; native concerns.

Tips: "Comment/feature section is most open; send good reflection column of about 800 words; topic of concern or interest to Prairie readership. It's difficult to break into our publication."

THE PRAYER CLOSET, PO Box 278, Hickory, MS 39332. (601)646-2295. E-mail: prayer@prayerclosetministries.org. Website: www.prayerclosetministries.org. Dr. Kevin Meador, ed. Challenges and equips believers in the area of prayer, fasting, spiritual warfare, journaling, and healing. Monthly newsletter; circ. 3,000. Free subscription online. **PAYS IN COPIES.** Prefers NKJV. Guidelines.

Tips: "We are looking for sound, biblically based articles concerning the above-listed topics."

PRAYERWORKS, PO Box 301363, Portland OR 97294. (503)761-2072. E-mail: VannM1@aol.com. Website: www.prayerworksnw.org. The Master's Work. V. Ann Mandeville, ed. For prayer warriors in retirement centers; focuses on prayer. Weekly newspaper and online (soon); 4 pgs.; circ. 1,000. Subscription free. 100% unsolicited freelance. Complete ms. **PAYS IN COPIES/SUBSCRIPTION** for one-time rts. Not copyrighted. Articles (30-40/yr.) & fiction (30/yr.); 300-500 wds. Responds in 3 wks. Seasonal 2 mos. ahead. Accepts simultaneous submissions & reprints. Does not use sidebars. Guidelines; copy for #10 SAE/1 stamp. (No ads)

Poetry: Accepts 20-30/yr. Free verse, haiku, light verse, traditional. Submit max. 10 poems.

Fillers: Accepts up to 50/yr. Facts, jokes, prayers, quotes, short humor; to 50 wds.

Tips: "Write tight and well. Half our audience is over 70, but 30% is young families. Subject matter isn't important as long as it is scriptural and designed to help people pray. Have a strong, catchy takeaway."

$PRECEPTS FOR LIVING UMI, Annual Sunday School Commentary, PO Box 436987, Chicago IL 60643. (708)868-7100, ext. 362. Fax (708)868-6759. E-mail: cywilson@urbanministries.com. Website: www.urbanministries.com. Urban Ministries Inc. K. Hall, mng. ed; submit to Cheryl Wilson, asst. ed. *Precepts for Living* is a verse-by-verse Sunday School commentary geared toward an African American adult audience. Word studies are presented in the original Greek and Hebrew languages to further illuminate understanding of the text. KJV Scriptures. 500 pgs. $16.95 complete with an enhanced CD-ROM Bible study tool for interactive learning. The CD-ROM contains electronic versions of the New Living Translation Bible, Strong's Concordance, Strong's Greek and Hebrew Dictionary, and other helpful resources including a video tutorial feature. Strict adherence to guidelines. Query/clips; fax/e-query OK. Pays $200 per Bible Study lesson and $250 per verse-by-verse commentary which includes Greek and Hebrew word studies, 120 days after acceptance, for all rts. Requires accepted ms on disk.

THE PRESBYTERIAN OUTLOOK, Box 85623, Richmond VA 23285-5623. Toll-free (800)446-6008. (804)359-8442. Fax (804)353-6369. E-mail: editor@pres-outlook.org. Website: www.pres-outlook.com. Presbyterian Church (USA)/Independent. Jack Haberer, ed.; Randy Harris, book review ed. For ministers, members, and staff of the denomination. Weekly (43X) mag.; 16-40 pgs.; circ. 10,000. Subscription $42.95. 5% unsolicited freelance; 95% assigned. Query; phone/fax/e-query OK. **NO PAYMENT** for all rts. Not copyrighted. Articles/fiction to 1,000 wds.; book reviews 1 pg. Responds in 1-2 wks. Seasonal 2 mos. ahead. Accepts e-mail submissions. Uses some sidebars. Prefers NRSV. Guidelines (also by e-mail); free copy. (Ads)

Tips: "Correspond (mail or e-mail) with editor regarding current needs; most open to features. Most material is commissioned; anything submitted should be of interest to Presbyterian church leaders."

$PRESBYTERIANS TODAY, 100 Witherspoon St., Louisville KY 40202-1396. Toll-free (888)728-7228, ext. 5637. (502)569-5637. Fax (502)569-8632. E-mail: today@pcusa.org. Website: www.pcusa.org/today. Presbyterian Church (USA). Eva Stimson, ed.; John Sniffen, assoc. ed. Denominational; not as conservative or evangelical as some. Monthly (10X) mag.; 48 pgs.; circ. 58,000. Subscription $19.95. 25% freelance. Query or complete ms/cover letter; phone/fax/e-query OK. Pays $75-300 on acceptance for 1st rts. Articles 800-2,000 wds. (prefers 1,000-1,500). (20/yr.). Also uses short features 250-600 wds. Responds in 2-5 wks. Seasonal 3 mos. ahead. Few reprints. Accepts requested ms on disk or by e-mail. Kill fee 50%. Prefers NRSV. Guidelines on Website: www.pcusa.org/today/guidelines/guidelines.htm); free copy. (Ads)

Fillers: Cartoons, $25; and short humor to 150 wds., no payment.

Tips: "Most open to feature articles about Presbyterians—individuals, churches with special outreach, creative programs, or mission work. Do not often use inspirational or testimony-type articles."

**This periodical was #40 on the 2006 Top 50 Christian Publishers list (#32 in 2005, #32 in 2004, #27 in 2003).

$PRIORITY! 440 W. Nyack Rd., West Nyack NY 10994. (845)620-7450. Fax (845)620-7223. E-mail: linda_johnson@use.salvationarmy.org. Website: www.prioritypeople.org. The Salvation Army. Linda D. Johnson, ed.; Robert Mitchell, assoc. ed. Quarterly & online mag.; 48-56 pgs.; circ. 28,000. Subscription $6.95. 50% assigned. Query/clips; e-query OK. Pays $200-800 on acceptance for 1st rts. Articles 400-1,700 wds. (8-10/yr.). All articles assigned. Responds in 2 wks. Occasionally buys reprints (tell when/where appeared). Prefers accepted ms by e-mail (in Word or copied into message). Kill fee 50%. Regularly uses sidebars. Prefers NIV. Occasionally buys submissions from children/teens. Guidelines/theme list by e-mail; copy $1/9x12 SAE. (Ads from nonprofits only)

Columns/Departments: Buys 5-10/yr. Prayer Power (stories about answered prayer, or harnessing prayer power); Who's News (calling attention to specific accomplishments or missions); Q & A (answers to current questions); My Take (unpublished writer's view); all 400-700 wds.; $200-400. Query.

Special Needs: All articles must have a connection to The Salvation Army. Can be from any part of the U.S. Looking especially for freelancers with Salvation Army connections; Christmas recollections; people/program features.

Tips: "Most open to features on people. Every article, whether about people or programs, tells a story and must feature the Salvation Army. Stories focus on evangelism, holiness, prayer. The more a writer knows about The Salvation Army, the better. We are interested in finding a group of freelancers we can assign to specific features."

PRISCILLA PAPERS, 122 W. Franklin Ave., Ste. 218, Minneapolis MN 55404-2451. (612)872-6898. Fax (612)872-6891. E-mail: aspencer@gcts.edu. Website: www.cbeinternational.org. Christians for Biblical Equality. William David Spencer, ed. Addresses biblical interpretation and its relationship to gender, race/ethnicity, economic class, and age issues in the society, the Christian community, and the family. Quarterly jour.; 32 pgs.; circ. 2,000. Subscription $40 (includes subscription to *Mutuality*). 85% unsolicited freelance; 15% assigned. Query preferred; fax/e-query OK. **PAYS 3 COPIES, PLUS A FREE BOOK** for 1st & electronic rts. Articles 600-5,000 wds.; book review 600 wds (free book). Responds in 4 wks. Seasonal 3 mos. ahead. Prefers accepted ms on disk or by e-mail (attached file). No kill fee. Uses some sidebars. Prefers NIV, TNIV, NRSV. Guidelines on Website; copy for 9x12 SAE/$1.99 postage. (Ads)

Poetry: Accepts 1/yr. Avant-garde, free verse, traditional; pays a free book.

Tips: "All sections are open to freelancers. Any article presenting a solid exegetical and hermeneutical approach to biblical equality will be considered for publication."

$PRISM: America's Alternative Evangelical Voice, 6 E. Lancaster Ave., Wynnewood PA 19096-3495. (610)645-9391. Fax (610)649-8090. E-mail: prism@esa-online.org, or kristyn@esa-online.org. Website: www.esa-online.org. Evangelicals for Social Action. Kristyn Komarnicki, ed. For Christians who are interested in the social and political dimensions of the gospel. Bimonthly mag.; 40 pgs.; circ. 5,000. Subscription $35. 50% unsolicited freelance. Complete ms/cover letter; e-query OK. Accepts full mss by e-mail. Pays $25-300 on publication for 1st rts. Articles 500-3,000 wds. (10-12/yr.); no fiction; book/video reviews, 500 wds., $0-100. Responds in 5-9 wks. Seasonal 6 mos. ahead. No reprints. Prefers requested ms on disk. Regularly uses sidebars. Prefers NRSV. Guidelines; copy $3. (Ads)

Tips: "Looking for analysis on religious right; social justice. Understand progressive evangelicals and E.S.A. Read Tony Campolo, Ron Sider, and Richard Foster. Most open to features. We don't assign work to writers we haven't published before, so send a full manuscript."

$PSYCHOLOGY FOR LIVING, 250 W. Colorado Blvd., Ste. 200, Arcadia CA 91007. (626)821-8400. Fax (626)821-8409. E-mail: editor@ncfliving.org. Website: www.ncfliving.org. Narramore Christian Foundation. Robert & Melanie Whitcomb, eds. Addresses issues of everyday life from a Christian and psychological viewpoint. Quarterly mag.; 8 pgs. (one issue 24 pgs.); circ. 7,000. Subscription for $20 donation. Open to freelance. Complete ms/cover letter; fax OK, e-query preferred. Pays $75-200, plus a subscription, on publication for 1st, one-time, or reprint rts. Articles 1,000-1,700 wds. Responds in 2-4 wks. Seasonal 4 mos. ahead. Accepts reprints (tell when/where appeared). Prefers accepted ms by e-mail (attached file). Uses some sidebars. Prefers NIV. Guidelines (also by e-mail); free copy. (No ads)

Tips: "Tell a story or illustration that shows how a psychological/emotional problem was dealt with in a biblical and psychologically sound manner. Not preachy."

$+PURE INSPIRATION, 7 Waterloo Rd., Stanhope NJ 07874. (973)347-6900. Fax (973)347-6909. E-mail: marnold@lightstreampublishing.com. Website: www.pureinspirationmag.com. Lightstream Publishing LLC. Marie Arnold, mng. ed. Inspires people to live positive, healthier lives—spiritually and emotionally—emphasizing our similarities, not our differences; readership is 75% women. Quarterly mag.; 100 pgs.; circ. 25,000. Subscription $19.97. Estab. 2006. 50% unsolicited freelance; 25% assigned. Query, query/clips, or complete ms/cover letter; fax/e-query OK. Pays $100-125/pg. on publication for 1st rts. Articles 1,500-2,000 wds. (25-30/yr.). Responds in 2-3 wks. Seasonal 6 mos. ahead. No simultaneous submissions; reprints negotiable (tell when/where appeared). Prefers e-mail submissions (attached file). Some kill fees. Some sidebars. Also accepts submissions from children & teens. Guidelines (also by e-mail/Website); copy for 9x12 SAE/$2 postage. (Ads)

Poetry: Only inspirational poems.

Columns/Departments: Buys 10-12/yr. Share Your Story (true personal stories of inspiration), 1,000-1,500 wds., $100.

Tips: "Most open to any topic which is helpful to our readers, such as those that will help to improve their lives spiritually and inspire them."

$PURPOSE, 616 Walnut Ave., Scottdale PA 15683-1999. (724)887-3111. E-mail: Horsch@mph.org. Website: www.mph.org. Mennonite Publishing Network. James E. Horsch, ed. Denominational, for older youth & adults. Weekly take-home paper; 8 pgs.; circ. 8,900. Subscription $22. 85% unsolicited freelance; 15% assigned. Complete ms (only)/cover letter; e-mail submissions preferred. Pays up to .07/wd. on acceptance for one-time rts. Articles & fiction, to 600 wds. (60/yr.). Responds in 6 mos. Seasonal 9 mos. ahead. Accepts simultaneous submissions & reprints (tell when/where appeared). Regularly uses sidebars. Guidelines (also by e-mail); copy $2/6x9 SAE/2 stamps. (No ads)

Poetry: Buys 140/yr. Free verse, light verse, traditional; 3-12 lines; up to $2/line ($7.50-20). Submit max. 5 poems.

Fillers: Buys 70/yr. Anecdotes, cartoons, short stories; 300-600 wds.; up to .06/wd.

Tips: "All areas are open. Articles must carry a strong story line. First person is preferred. Don't exceed maximum word length, send no more than 3 works at a time."

**This periodical was #38 on the 2007 Top 50 Christian Publishers list (#43 in 2006, #50 in 2005, #28 in 2004, #48 in 2003).

PURPOSE MAGAZINE, PO Box 906, Temple Hills MD 20757. (614)418-1785. Fax (614) 253-2283. E-mail: purpose@iwaynet.net; ella@iwaynet.net. Website: www.purposemagazine.com. Ellavation Enterprises Inc. Ella Coleman, pub./ed-in-chief. Christian magazine for a predominately African American audience; personal and family empowerment to inspire, motivate, and educate readers to live their God-given purpose. Bimonthly mag.; 32-40 pgs.; circ. 5,000. Subscription $25. 25% unsolicited freelance; 75% assigned. Query/clips; e-query OK. **PAYS A SUBSCRIPTION & PROMOTION.** Articles. Accepts reprints (tell when/where appeared). Prefers e-mail submissions (attached file in Word). Regularly uses sidebars. Also accepts submissions from children & teens. Prefers NKJV. Guidelines on Website; copy for 9x12 SASE. (Ads)

Poetry: Accepts very few; 30-40 lines. Submit max. 20 poems.

Fillers: Most types; 200-500 wds.

Columns/Departments: Financial wisdom. Complete ms.

Contests: Occasionally sponsors a contest.

QUAKER LIFE, 101 Quaker Hill Dr., Richmond IN 47374. (765)962-7573. Fax (765)962-1293. E-mail: quakerlife@fum.org. Website: www.fum.org. Friends United Meeting. Trish Edwards-Konic, ed. For Christian Quakers, focusing on news around the world, peace and justice, simplicity, and inspiration. Bimonthly mag.; 36 pgs.; circ. 4,000. Subscription $24. 50% unsolicited freelance; 50% assigned. Query; fax/e-query OK. Accepts full ms by e-mail. **PAYS 3 COPIES** on publication for 1st rts. Articles to 1,500 wds. (40/yr.); book reviews 300 wds.; music/video reviews, 200 wds. Responds in 4 wks. Seasonal 4 mos. ahead. Accepts some reprints (tell when/where appeared). Accepts e-mail submissions (attached in Word or copied into message). No kill fee. Uses some sidebars. Prefers RSV. Also accepts submissions from children or teens. Guidelines/theme list (also by e-mail); copy for 9x12 SAE. (Ads)

Poetry: Accepts 2/yr.

Columns/Departments: Turning Point (first-person spiritual experiences); Ideas That Work (ideas from churches); Peace Notes (peace and justice news and ideas); each 750 wds. Query or complete ms.

Special Needs: Leadership, church growth, personal experience.

Tips: "Write on current issues or a personal spiritual experience from a Christian perspective. Be more practical than academic. For general readers who are Christian Quakers."

RADIX MAGAZINE, PO Box 4307, Berkeley CA 94704. (510)548-5329. E-mail: RadixMag@aol.com. Website: www.RadixMagazine.com. Sharon Gallagher, ed.; Luci Shaw, poetry ed. Features in-depth articles for thoughtful Christians who are interested in engaging the culture. Quarterly mag.; 32 pgs. Subscription $15. 10% unsolicited freelance; 90% assigned. E-queries only. **PAYS IN COPIES** for 1st rts. Meditations, 300-500 wds. (2/yr.); book reviews 700 wds. Responds in 6 wks. to e-mail only. Seasonal 6 mos. ahead. No simultaneous submissions or reprints. Accepted submissions by e-mail (attached file). Uses some sidebars. Prefers NRSV. Guidelines by e-mail; copy $5. (Ads)

Poetry: Accepts 12/yr. Avant-garde, free verse, haiku, traditional; 4-30 lines. Submit max. 1 poem.

Tips: "Most open to poetry, book reviews, meditations. Familiarity with the magazine is key."

RARE JEWEL ONLINE MAGAZINE, PO Box 2895, Rome GA 30164. (706)936-6457. E-mail: tim@rarejewelmag.com. Website: www.rarejewelmag.com. Rare Jewel Ministries. Tim Ewing, pub.; Rick Marschall, mng. ed. Empowering Christians to exercise a biblical world-view (Proverbs 20:15). Monthly e-zine. Estab. 2004. 20% unsolicited freelance; 80% assigned. Query/clips; e-query only. Accepts full mss by e-mail. **NO PAYMENT** for nonexclusive rts. Articles to 500 wds. (6/yr.). Responds in 4 wks. Seasonal 3 mos. ahead. Accepts simultaneous submissions & reprints (tell when/where appeared). Requires e-mail submissions (copied into message). Does not use sidebars. Prefers NIV. Also accepts submissions from teens. Guidelines by e-mail; copy online.

Columns/Departments: Rich Marschall, columns ed. Buys 12/yr.

Tips: "Most open to news and news commentary: Important cultural and political issues in America and around the world—analyzed from a biblical world-view."

REGENT GLOBAL BUSINESS REVIEW (formerly Regent Business Review), 1000 Regent University Dr., Virginia Beach VA 23464. (757)226-4074. E-mail: rgbr@regent.edu. Website: www.regent.edu/rgbr. Regent University—School of Global Leadership & Entrepreneurship. Julianne R. Cenac, ed. (Jcenac@regent.edu). For Christian leaders and managers who take their faith seriously and who give genuine thought to how to live out that faith in the workplace and everywhere else. Bimonthly e-zine; 30 pgs.; circ. 10,000. Free online. 25% unsolicited freelance; 75% assigned. Query/clips by e-mail only. **NO PAYMENT** for electronic rts. Feature articles 1,200-2,500 wds.; case studies 2,500-4,000 wds. (not including any data appendices); Tool Kit/Executive Summaries 250-500 wds. Responds in 2 wks. Seasonal 6 mos. ahead. No simultaneous submissions; accepts reprints. Requires accepted mss by e-mail (attached file). Regularly uses sidebars. Prefers NIV. Guidelines on Website.

Columns/Departments: Tool Kit (tips and resources) 250-500 wds.; Research Translations, 1,000-1,500 wds.

Tips: "If you are interested in contributing to the exploration and advancement of global business, we are interested in hearing from you. We seek articles from contributors who are recognized experts in their field or who have requisite experience and credentials to be qualified to speak authoritatively on the subject matter."

$RELEVANT & RELEVANTMAGAZINE.COM, 1220 Alden Rd., Orlando FL 32803-2546. Toll-free (877)538-4417. (407)660-1411. Fax (407)401-9100. E-mail: adam@relevantmediagroup.com. Website: www.RelevantMagazine.com. Relevant Media Group. Adam Smith, mng. ed. (ext. 603). Targets culture-savvy twentysomethings who are looking for purpose, depth, and spiritual truth. Bimonthly & online mag.; 100 pgs. Subscription $10. 80% freelance. Send a one-paragraph query/clips; prefers e-mail; no phone/fax query. Pays .10/wd. within 45 days of publication for 1st rts. & all electronic rts. for 6 mos.; nonexclusive rts. thereafter. Features 600-1,000 wds.; reviews 400-600 wds. Prefers submissions as Word attachments. Guidelines on Website (www.relevantmagazine.com/editorial); copy $2.98.

($)+RELIEF JOURNAL, 60 W. Terra Cotta, Ste. B, Unit 156, Crystal Lake IL 60014-3548. E-mail: editor@reliefjournal.com. Website: www.reliefjournal.com. Kimberly Culbertson, ed-in-chief. Open to unsolicited freelance. Use online submissions system only; no mail or e-mail submissions. Complete ms. **NO REGULAR PAYMENT; CASH PRIZES FOR BEST IN EACH GENRE.** Articles to 8,000 wds.; fiction to 10,000 wds. Accepts simultaneous submissions. Guidelines on Website. Incomplete topical listings.

Poetry: Accepts poetry that is well-written and makes sense; to 1,000 wds. Submit max. 5 poems.

REVERENT SUBMISSIONS JOURNAL, #2835, 1420 N.W. Gilman Blvd., Ste. 2, Issaquah WA 98027. (425)255-8825. E-mail: reverentsubmissions@comcast.net. J. D. O'Conor and Bev Fowler, co-pubs. A theme-based journal for Christians of all faiths, seeking to provide experience, exposure, and credibility for Christian writers while encouraging others in their daily life and spiritual walk. Quarterly newsletter; 12 pgs.; circ. 85. Subscription $12. Estab. 2005. 100% unsolicited freelance. Query; e-query OK. Accepts full mss by e-mail. **PAYS 2 COPIES** for 1st, one-time, reprint rts. Not copyrighted. Articles & fiction to 600 wds. (up to 48/yr. for ea.); book reviews to 600 wds. Responds in 12 wks. Seasonal 3 mos. ahead. Accepts simultaneous submissions and reprints (tell when/where appeared). Prefers e-mail submissions (attached file). Does not use sidebars. Also accepts submissions from children or teens. Prefers NIV. Guidelines/theme list (also by e-mail); copy for 9x12 SAE/2 stamps. (No ads)

Poetry: Accepts 12-15/yr. Free verse, haiku, light verse, traditional; up to 400 wds. Submit max. 1 poem.

Fillers: Buys as needed. Anecdotes, ideas, jokes, kid quotes, prayer, prose, quotes, short humor, tips; up to 100 wds.

Tips: "Christian-focused articles/fiction/poetry on the theme of each issue, with bio, contact information, and correct word count. Order upcoming theme list. Manuscripts will not be returned."

RHUBARB, 606—100 Arthur St., Winnipeg MB R3B 1H3, Canada. E-mail: rhubarb@mts.net. Website: www.mennolit.com. Mennonite Literary Society. Submit to The Editor. Designed to provide an outlet for the (loosely defined) Mennonite voice, reflecting the changing face of the Mennonite community, promoting dialog, and encouraging the Anabaptist tradition of reformation and protest. Quarterly mag. Subscription $25 Cdn., $20 U.S. Open to unsolicited freelance. Query for nonfiction; e-query OK. **NO REFERENCE TO PAYMENT.** Articles/fiction to 2,500 wds. Guidelines/theme list on Website.

ROCK & SLING: A Journal of Literature, Art and Faith, PO Box 30865, Spokane WA 99223. Fax (509)276-7833. E-mail: editors@rockandsling.org. Website: www.rockandsling.org. Susan Cowger, Kris Christensen, Laurie Klein, eds. Ardent, edgy, vibrant explorations of faith and experience. Semiannual jour.; 140 pgs. Subscription $18. 70% unsolicited freelance; 30% assigned. Complete ms/cover letter; no phone/fax/e-query. **PAYS 2 COPIES** for 1st rts. Essays & fiction 5,000-7,000 wds.; book reviews assigned based on clips. Responds in 6 wks. (or up to 4 mos. if held for consideration). Accepts simultaneous submissions (if indicated);

no reprints. Reads year round. Any Bible version. Guidelines on Website; copy $10. Incomplete topical listings.

Poetry: Accepts poetry to 60 lines (longer if exceptional). Avant-garde, free verse. Submit max. 5 poems.

Contest: Virginia Brendemuehl Poetry Prize: $1,000, plus publication. Finalists published. Postmark deadline July 31. Send SASE and $10, payable to *Rock & Sling,* for 1-3 poems. No simultaneous submissions for contest.

Photos: Accepts color for cover; B & W for journal. See guidelines.

Tips: "Read widely. First read *R & S* to understand the kind of essays, memoirs, and reviews we publish. Then read the great essayists and poets, both historical and contemporary. We look for work that explores faith's tensions as well as joys, work rich with complexity of thought and emotion. Send your best. We do not publish genre writing, didacticism, devotionals, or testimonies."

$THE ROSE & THORN: A Literary E-zine. E-mail: BAQuinn@aol.com. Website: www.theroseandthornezine.com. General. B. A. Quinn, ed. Showcases short fiction, poetry, essays, and anything of a literary nature; no children's or juvenile stories. Quarterly online literary mag. Open to freelance. Complete ms. Pays $5 and will provide a link to your Website. One-time nonexclusive rts. Articles/fiction to 2,000 wds. Requires submissions by e-mail (copied into message). Guidelines on Website.

Poetry: Now accepting poetry. Submit max. 3 poems; prefers shorter poems. E-mail to poetryeditor@hotmail.com.

Special Needs: Fiction, vignettes, and flash fiction; creative essays, perspective, humor.

Tips: "We have eclectic tastes, so go ahead and give us a shot."

+RUMINATE, Faith in Literature and Art, 140 N. Roosevelt Ave., Fort Collins CO 80521. (970)449-2726. E-mail: editor@ruminatemagazine.com. Website: www.ruminatemagazine.com. Brianna Van Dyke, ed.; submit to submissions@ruminatemagazine.com. An intimate and hip publication of faith literature and art; publishes work with both subtle and overt associations to the Christian faith as well as work that has no direct association. Quarterly mag.; 70 pgs.; circ. 600. Subscription $28. Estab. 2006. 100% unsolicited freelance. Complete ms/cover letter by e-mail only. **PAYS 3 COPIES OR SUBSCRIPTION** for 1st rts. Articles to 5,000 wds. (4-8/yr.); fiction to 5,000 wds. (8-12/yr.). Responds in 16 wks. Accepts simultaneous submissions; no reprints. Requires disk or e-mail submissions (attached file). Does not use sidebars. Guidelines/theme list on Website; order a copy on Website ($8). (Ads)

Poetry: Lacee Perrin, poetry ed. (poetry@ruminatemagazine.com). Accepts 50/yr. Avant-garde, free verse, traditional; to 50 lines. Submit max. 5 poems.

Contest: Annual poetry & fiction contest. Entry fee: $15. Deadline: June 1. Prizes: $300 1st prize; $150 to runner-up. Details on Website.

Tips: "We are looking for writers and artists who are interested in the process of creating quality work that reveals the nature of Christ."

+SACRED JOURNEY: The Journal of Fellowship in Prayer, 291 Witherspoon St., Princeton NJ 08542. (609)924-6863. Fax (609)924-6910. E-mail: submissions@sacredjourney.org. Website: www.sacredjourney.org. Fellowship in Prayer Inc. Submit to The Editor. Multifaith spirituality. Bimonthly jour. & e-zine; 48 pgs.; circ. 4,500. Subscription $18. 75% unsolicited freelance; 25% assigned. Complete ms/cover letter; phone/fax/e-query OK. **PAYS 5 COPIES & SUBSCRIPTION** for 1st & electronic rts. Articles to 1,500 wds. (30/yr.); reviews 500 wds. Responds in 9 wks. Seasonal 4 mos. ahead. Accepts simultaneous submissions & reprints (tell when/where appeared). Requires requested ms on disk or by e-mail. Does not use sidebars. Guidelines (also by e-mail/Website); copy $1.70/6x9 SAE. (No ads)

Poetry: Accepts 6-8/yr. Free verse, haiku, light verse, traditional; 10-35 lines. Submit max. 3 poems.

Columns/Departments: Accepts 30/yr. A Transforming Experience (personal experience of spiritual significance); Pilgrimage (journey taken for spiritual growth or service); Spirituality and the Family; Spirituality and Aging; to 1,500 wds.

Special Needs: Meditation and service to others.

Tips: "Write about your own spiritual experience and we'll consider it. Most open to a transforming experience feature."

SALT OF THE EARTH: Your Online Resource for Social Justice, 205 W. Monroe St., Chicago IL 60606. Toll-free (800)328-6515. (312)236-7782. Fax (312)236-8201. E-mail: clarkek @claretianpubs.org. Website: http://salt.claretianpubs.org. The Claretians/Catholic. Kevin Clarke, mng. ed. Monthly online mag.

$+SALVO MAGAZINE, 4125 W. Newport Ave., Chicago IL 60641. (773)4811090. Fax (773)481-1095. E-mail: editor@salvomag.com. Website: www.salvomag.com. Fellowship of St. James. Bobby Maddex, ed. Geared toward young adults, 25-45, who want to free themselves from the false world-views emanating from Hollywood, the media, and the Academy. Quarterly mag.; 96 pgs.; circ. 2,800. Subscription $25.99. Estab. 2006. 25% unsolicited freelance; 75% assigned. Query/clips; no phone/fax query, e-query OK. Accepts full mss by e-mail. Pays .20/wd. on publication for 1st rts. Articles 600-2,000 wds. (16/yr.). Responds in 4 wks. No seasonal. No simultaneous submissions or reprints. Prefers e-mail submissions (attached file). Kill fee $100. Regularly uses sidebars. No Bible references. Guidelines/theme list on Website; copy $6.99. (Ads)

Columns/Departments: Buys 12/yr. Dispatches (features) 2,000 wds.; The Trenches (tales of academic bias) 1,200 wds.; Random Flak (mini-features) 1,200 wds.; .20/wd.

Tips: "We are most open for features on science, sex, and society—anything that deconstructs false ideology and world-views, using reason and logic alone."

$SCIENCE & SPIRIT MAGAZINE, 1319 Eighteenth St. N.W., Washington DC. (202)296-6267. E-mail: JWilson@science-spirit.org. Website: www.science-spirit.org. Science & Spirit Resources Inc./Heldref Publications. Jamie Wilson, assoc. ed. Well-researched and reported articles on the intersection of science and religion in health, environment, human relationships, technology, and ethics. Bimonthly mag; 66 pgs.; circ. 7,500. Subscription $23.95. 20% freelance. Query by e-mail. Pays .20-.75/wd. for assigned, .20-.50/wd. for unsolicited for articles on acceptance for all rts. Makes work-for-hire assignments. No reprints. Articles 1,200-2,500 wds. (40/yr.) Responds in 1 mo. Seasonal 6 mos. ahead. Guidelines by e-mail; copy on Website.

Columns/Departments: Interlude (social/science environmental topic), 1,200-1,600 wds.; Critical Mass (news briefs covering all areas of science—physics, gender, space, psychology, etc.); pays $200-300. See Website for samples of departments.

Tips: "Common mistakes include shallow reporting, lack of in-depth writing, lack of diversity in religious perspectives. We're looking for well-researched articles that include interviews with scientists, theologians, and everyday people. The best articles include citations for recent research and current books. Thoughtful leads, transitions, and conclusions based on the writer's research and insight are a must."

+SEARCHING WISDOM.ORG EZINE, PO Box 1812, Smithfield NC 27577. E-mail: biblestudies@searchingwisdom.org. Website: www.SearchingWisdom.org. Donna Shepard, ed. Focus is on beginners and nonbeginners in God's Word, giving them a hunger for knowledge of His Word. Monthly e-zine.; 2-5 pgs. Subscription free online. Estab. 2007. 100% unsolicited freelance. Query or complete ms/cover letter; e-query OK. Accepts full mss by e-mail. **NO PAYMENT** for 1st, one-time, reprint, electronic rts. Articles 200-2,000 wds. Responds in 12-16 wks. Seasonal 4-6 mos. ahead. No simultaneous submissions; accepts reprints (tell when/where appeared). Requires accepted mss by e-mail. Does not use sidebars. Prefers KJV. No guidelines; copy by e-mail or online. (No ads)

Poetry: Accepts free verse, light verse, traditional; 8-30 lines. Submit max. 5 poems.

Special Needs: Chapter Bible studies; various topical studies.

Tips: "We like Bible studies that align with God's Word and are nondenominational. We like poetry that encourages one and reminds one of God's love for them. We believe the antichrist comes first before the true Christ returns and all will be here at that time. We do not believe in secular Easter and Christmas traditions, but teach the true meaning of those holidays."

SEEDS OF HOPE: Hope for the Healing of Hunger and Poverty, 602 James Ave., Waco TX 76706-1476. (254)755-7745. Fax (254)753-1909. E-mail: SeedsHope@aol.com. Website: www.seedspublishers.org. Seeds of Hope Publishers. Katie Cook, ed. Committed to the healing of hunger and poverty in our world. Quarterly worship packet; 20 pgs. of camera-ready resources. Subscription $120. Individual packet $50. Back issues less expensive. Also quarterly newsletter, *Hunger News & Hope,* published through denominational offices of national churches. E-query OK. **NO PAYMENT.**

$SEEK, 8805 Governor's Hill Dr., Ste. 400, Cincinnati OH 45249. E-mail: seek@standardpub.com. Website: www.Standardpub.com. Standard Publishing. Margaret K. Williams, ed. Light, inspirational, take-home reading for young and middle-aged adults. Weekly take-home paper; 8 pgs.; circ. 29,000. Subscriptions $14.69 (sold only in sets of 5). 75% unsolicited freelance; 25% assigned. Complete ms; no phone/fax/e-query. Pays .07/wd. on acceptance for 1st rts., .05/wd. for reprints. Articles 500-1,200 wds. (150-200/yr.); fiction 500-1,200 wds. Responds in 18 wks. Seasonal 1 yr. ahead. Accepts reprints (tell when/where appeared). Prefers submissions by e-mail (attached file). Uses some sidebars. Guidelines/theme list (also on Website); copy for 6x9 SAE/2 stamps. (No ads)

Fillers: Buys 50/yr. Ideas, short humor; $15.

Tips: "We now work with a theme list. Only articles tied to these themes will be considered for publication. Check Website for theme list and revised guidelines."

**This periodical was #7 on the 2007 Top 50 Christian Publishers list (#26 in 2006, #27 in 2005, #20 in 2004, #49 in 2003).

+SEEK (BIC), 431 Grantham Rd., PO Box A, Grantham PA 17027. (717)697-2634. Fax (717) 697-7714. E-mail: seek@messiah.edu. Website: www.BIC-church.org/seek. Denominational/ Brethren in Christ Church. Dulcimer Hope Brubake, ed. Highlights the spiritual journeys and writings of our members. Quarterly magazine. Subscription free to members. Open to unsolicited freelance. Query preferred. **NO PAYMENT.** Articles & reviews. Not in topical listings.

SENIOR CONNECTION, PO Box 38, Dundee IL 60118. (847)428-0205. E-mail: churchpb@flash.net. Website: www.seniorconnectionnewspaper.com. Churchill Publications/Catholic. Peter Rubino, ed. For Catholics ages 50 and up with ties to the Chicago area. Monthly newspaper; circ. 190,000. Subscription $18.95. Open to unsolicited freelance. Articles. Incomplete topical listings.

SHARING: A Journal of Christian Healing, 6807 Forest Haven, San Antonio TX 78240. (210)681-5146. Fax (210)681-5146. E-mail: Marjorie.George@dwtx.org. Website: www.orderofstluke.org. Order of St. Luke the Physician. Marjorie George, ed. For Christians interested in spiritual and physical healing. Monthly (10X) jour.; 16 pgs.; circ. 9,000. Subscription $20. 100% unsolicited freelance. Complete ms/cover letter. **NO PAYMENT** for one-time or reprint rts. Articles 750-900 wds. (50/yr.). Responds in 3 wks. Seasonal 2 mos. ahead. Accepts simultaneous submissions & reprints (tell when/where appeared). Prefers ms by e-mail. Some sidebars. Prefers RSV. Guidelines; copy for 8x10 SAE/2 stamps.

Poetry: Accepts 10-12/yr. Free verse, traditional; 6-14 lines.

Tips: "We're looking for crisp, clear, well-written articles on the theology of healing and personal witness of healing. We are totally open; best to send manuscript. We do not return manuscripts or poems, nor do we reply to inquiries regarding manuscript status."

+SIGHT 360, 415 Kosciuszko St, South Bend IN 46619-3507. (574)234-6967. E-mail: sight360@sbcglobal.net. J. Findley May Jr. Media. J. Findley May Jr., pub. Our audience is the public as a whole, focusing on tough minority and Christian issues. Bimonthly mag.; 40 pgs.; circ. 5,000. Subscription $14.99. Open to freelance. Query, query/clips, or complete ms; e-query OK. **PAYS IN COPIES** for one-time, reprint, electronic rts. Articles 1,000-6,000 wds. Responds in 3 wks. Seasonal 2 mos. ahead. Accepts simultaneous submissions & reprints (tell when/where appeared). Prefers disk or e-mail submissions (attached file). Also accepts submissions from teens. No guidelines except to subscribers; copy for $5 postage. (Ads)

Fillers: Accepts unlimited number. Cartoons, facts, newsbreaks, quizzes; 10-15 wds.

Columns/Departments: Accepts unlimited number. World Events (telling the side the media doesn't cover); Personal Experience (life stories of survival over difficult circumstances); Judicial (telling the other side of the police, courts and prison); all 1,000-6,000 wds. Complete ms.

Tips: "Contact us with powerful articles, dealing with real-life situations."

$+SIGNIFICANT LIVING: Maximizing Life After 50, 2800 Vision Ct., Aurora IL 60506. (630)801-3838. Fax (630)801-3839. E-mail: pshort@TLN.com. Website: www.significantliving.org. Peg Short, ed-in-chief. Dedicated to serving adults in the second half of life (boomers to seniors), empowering them to live with Christ-like vitality, and inspiring them to serve others, so that our nation may be strengthened and God may be honored. Bimonthly mag.; 40 pgs.; circ. 25,000. Subscription by membership only $19.95. Estab. 2007. 5-10% unsolicited freelance; 90-95% assigned. Query; e-query OK. Accepts full mss by e-mail. Pays .20-.30/wd. on acceptance for all rts. Articles 1,000-1,200 wds. Responds in up to 2-3 wks. Seasonal 6 mos. ahead. Accepts simultaneous submissions & reprints (tell when/where appeared). Prefers e-mail submissions (attached file). Kill fee $25. Uses some sidebars. Guidelines by e-mail/Website; free copy. (Ads)

Fillers: For boomers & seniors. Anecdotes, cartoons, facts, jokes, short humor, word puzzles.

Tips: "Most open to features—role model stories that reflect issues for boomers and seniors. Open to celebrity and athlete stories, and features that are issue-oriented to boomers and seniors. Human interest and role-model stories of middle and senior adult issues."

SILVER WINGS, PO Box 2340, Clovis CA 93613-2340. (559)347-0194. E-mail: cloviswings@aol.com. Poetry on Wings/Evangelical. Jackson Wilcox, ed. Christian understanding and uplift through poetry. Bimonthly mag.; 16 pgs.; circ. 300. Subscription free with donation. 100% unsolicited freelance. Query or complete ms; phone query OK. **PAYS ONE COPY** for articles for 1st rts.; book reviews 200 wds. Not copyrighted. Poetry only. Responds in 3 wks. Seasonal 3-12 mos. ahead. Sometimes accepts simultaneous submissions & reprints (tell when/where appeared). No disk or e-mail submissions. Does not use sidebars. Prefers KJV. Also accepts submissions from children/teens. Guidelines; copy for 6x9 SAE/2 stamps. (No ads)

Poetry: Accepts 175/yr. Free verse, haiku, light verse, traditional; 3-20 lines. Submit max. 3 poems. No payment. "Any poetry that conforms to Christian conduct, teaching, and morality. No profanity or mention of alcoholic beverages."

Fillers: Original sayings. No payment.

Contest: Annual poetry contest on a theme (December 31 deadline); send SASE for details. Winners published in March. $325 in prizes. $3 entry fee.

Tips: "We like poems with clear Christian message, observation, or description. Poetry should be easy to read and understand. Short poems get best attention. We are open to topics and material making a point that agrees with Christian teaching. We will even consider views that vary within the Christian community."

SINGLE AGAIN.COM WEBZINE & NEWSLETTER, 1237 Crescendo Dr., Roseville CA 95678-5165. (916)773-7337. E-mail: editor@singleagain.com. Website: www.singleagain.com.

Christian. Rev. Paul Scholl, pub. Caters to people trying to put their lives back together after divorce, separation, or death of a significant other. Quarterly & online newsletter; 8-10 pgs. Subscription $12. Open to freelance. Complete ms/cover letter by mail or e-mail (preferred). **NO PAYMENT** for simultaneous rts. Articles 500 wds. and up (50-75/yr.). Responds in 6 wks. Accepts simultaneous submissions & reprints (tell when/where appeared). Accepts requested mss by e-mail (attached file in Word only). Does not use sidebars. Guidelines on Website. Incomplete topical listings. (Ads)

Poetry: Accepts 6-12/yr. Any type to 24 lines. Submit max. 6 poems.

Fillers: Accepts 15-12/yr. Anecdotes, facts, ideas, jokes, kid quotes, prayers, prose, short humor, tips.

Tips: "Write from your heart first. Don't worry about your article being perfect. We will help you with any final editing."

$SOCIAL JUSTICE REVIEW, 3835 Westminster Pl., St. Louis MO 63108-3472. (314)371-1653. Fax (314)371-0889. E-mail: centbur@sbcglobal.net. Website: www.socialjusticereview.org. Central Bureau of the Catholic Central Verein. Rev. Edward Krause, C.S.C., ed. For those interested in the social teaching of the Catholic Church. Bimonthly mag.; 32 pgs.; circ. 5,000. Subscription $20. 90% unsolicited freelance. Query or complete ms/cover letter; no phone/fax/e-query. Pays .02/wd. on publication for one-time rts. Not copyrighted. Articles to 3,000 wds. (80/yr.); book reviews 500 wds. (no payment). Responds in 1 wk. Seasonal 3 mos. ahead. Accepts reprints (tell when/where appeared). Prefers submissions on disk. No kill fee. Does not use sidebars. No guidelines; copy for 9x12 SAE/3 stamps. (No ads)

Columns/Departments: Virtue; Economic Justice (Catholic views); variable length. Query or complete ms. Pays .02/wd.

Tips: "Articles and reviews open to freelancers. Fidelity to papal teaching and clarity and simplicity of style; thoughtful and thought-provoking writing."

+SOCIETY FOR PREVENTION OF CRUELTY TO HUMANS (SPCH), 12900 S.E. Nixon, Portland OR 97222. (503)659-2974. E-mail: scbaldwin@preventcrueltytohumans.com. Website: www.preventcrueltytohumans.com. Stan Baldwin, pub. To encourage personal acts of decency and kindness; to challenge and change the prevailing culture of cruelty. Mostly online publication. Open to unsolicited freelance. Submit by e-mail. **NO PAYMENT; CREDIT LINE & COPIES** for nonexclusive rts. Articles of variable length. Guidelines/copy on Website. (No ads)

Columns/Departments: Divisions of the Society include: Children, Seniors, the Workplace, Schools, Politics, Religion, Public Life (including media), Health Care, and others.

Tips: "Articles will be well-researched and offer hard data related to the damaging effects of meanness and cruelty. The writer will cite credible sources such as studies that have been done, professionals who have spoken, reliable statistics that have been compiled. Put a human face on the data with compelling anecdotes and examples."

$SOUND BODY, Box 448, Jacksonville OR 97530. Phone/fax (541)899-8888. E-mail: James@ChristianMediaNetwork.com. Websites: www.SoundBody.tv. Christian Media. James Lloyd, ed./pub. A health newsletter with an alternative slant. Quarterly & online newsletter. Query; prefers phone query. Payment negotiable for reprint rts. Articles. Responds in 3 wks. Requires KJV. No guidelines; copy for #10 SAE/2 stamps.

SOUTHWEST KANSAS FAITH AND FAMILY, PO Box 1454, Dodge City KS 67801. (620)225-4677. Fax (620)225-4625. E-mail: stan@swkfaithandfamily.org, or info@swkfaithandfamily.org. Website: www.swkfaithandfamily.org. Independent. Stan Wilson, pub. Dedicated to sharing the Word of God and news and information that honors Christian beliefs, family traditions, and values that are the cornerstone of our nation. Monthly newspaper; circ. 5,000. Subscription $18. Accepts freelance. Prefers e-query; complete ms OK. Articles; no reviews. Incomplete topical listings. (Ads)

$SPECIAL LIVING, PO Box 1000, Bloomington IL 61702. (309)66109277. E-mail: gareeb@aol.com. Website: www.specialiving.com. Betty Garee, pub./ed. For and about physically disabled adults, mobility impaired individuals. Quarterly mag.; 88 pgs.; circ. 12,000. Subscription $12. 90% unsolicited freelance; 5% assigned. Query; phone/fax/e-query OK. Pays .10/wd. on publication for 1st rts. Articles 300-800 wds. (50/yr.). Responds in 3 wks. Seasonal 6 mos. ahead. Accepts simultaneous submissions & reprints (tell when/where appeared). Prefers requested ms on disk. No kill fee. Uses some sidebars. No guidelines; copy $2. (Ads)

Fillers: Buys 20/yr. Cartoons, tips.

Tips: "Query with a specific idea. Have good photos to accompany your article. Most open to mobility impaired concerns and successes."

SPIRITUALITY FOR TODAY, PO Box 7466, Greenwich CT 06836. (203)316-9394. Fax (203)316-9396. E-mail: Clemons10@aol.com. Website: www.spirituality.org. Clemons Productions Inc. Dorothy Riera, asst. ed. Adults' spiritual renewal with articles that challenge reflection. Monthly mag.; 13-15 pgs.; circ. 495,000. Subscription free. Open to freelance. E-query OK. **NO PAYMENT.** Articles & short stories 1.5 pgs. Incomplete topical listings. (Ads)

Fillers: Accepts anecdotes, prayers, quotes.

Tips: "Most open to human interest pertaining to the church (2 pages); and human values. Submit an e-mail with article attached. We always respond to our e-mails." Spanish page included.

$SPIRITUAL LIFE, 2131 Lincoln Rd. N.E., Washington DC 20002-1199. Toll-free (888)616-1713. (202)832-5505. Fax (202)832-8967. E-mail: edodonnell@aol.com. Website: www.Spiritual-Life.org. Catholic. Edward O'Donnell, O.C.D., ed. Essays on Christian spirituality with a pastoral application to everyday life. Quarterly jour.; 64 pgs.; circ. 12,000. Subscription $20. 80% unsolicited freelance. Complete ms/cover letter; phone/fax/e-query OK. Pays $50-250 ($50/pg.) on acceptance for 1st rts. Articles/essays 3,000-5,000 wds. (20/yr.); book reviews 1,500 wds. ($15). Responds in 9 wks. Seasonal 9 mos. ahead. Accepts simultaneous submissions. Requires requested ms on disk. Does not use sidebars. Prefers NAB. Guidelines; copy for 7x10 SAE/5 stamps.

Tips: "No stories of personal healing, conversion, miracles, etc."

SPIRITUAL VOICE NEWS, PO Box 45, Kennett Square PA 19348. (610)347-6766. Fax (610) 347-6765. E-mail: spiritualvoicenews@verizon.net. Regional news. Linda T. Eckman, ed./pub. For backslidden Christians or the unsaved; available free at convenience stores, restaurants, etc. Quarterly newspaper; 16 pgs.; circ. 10,000. Subscription free. 100% unsolicited freelance. Complete ms/cover letter (by e-mail); phone/fax/e-query OK. **PAYS IN COPIES** for one-time, reprint, or simultaneous rts. Not copyrighted. Articles (all types if less than 750 wds.); all genres of fiction (less than 750 wds.); book/music/movie reviews. Responds in 1 wk. Seasonal 2 wks. to 1 mo. ahead. Accepts simultaneous submissions & reprints. E-mail submissions should be sent in Word Pad; no hard copies. Uses some sidebars. Also accepts submissions from children/teens. Guidelines/theme list (also by e-mail); copy for 6x9 SAE/3 stamps. (Ads)

Poetry: Accepts 30/yr. Any type. Send any number. No payment. Needs more.

Fillers: Accepts many. Any type. No payment. Needs more.

Special Needs: Column writers; more puzzles. Editor looking for a column linking physical and spiritual health.

Tips: "This paper is very open to new writers. Know how to write for nonbelievers (95% of our audience). If you have a heart for those who have been far from God or hurt by the 'religious authority,' your work will get published."

$SPORTS SPECTRUM, 105 Corporate Blvd., Ste. 2, Indian Trail NC 28105. (704)821-2971. Fax (704)821-2669. E-mail: dbranon@rbc.org. Website: www.sportsspectrum.com. Sports Spectrum Publishing. Dave Branon, mng. ed. Designed to feature sports people and issues as a way of introducing the gospel to non-Christian sports fans and encouraging Christian sports fans. Bimonthly mag.; 48 pgs.; circ. 20,000. Subscription $27.52. 80% assigned. Query/clips; e-query OK. Pays .21/wd. on acceptance for all rts. Not copyrighted. Articles 1,200-2,000 wds. (40/yr.). Responds in 3-4 wks. Requires accepted ms by e-mail (attached file). Kill fee 30-50%. Regularly uses sidebars. Prefers NIV. Guidelines (also by e-mail/Website); no sample copy. (Ads)

Tips: "The best thing a writer can do is to be aware of the special niche Sports Spectrum has developed in sports ministry. Then find athletes who fit that niche and who haven't been covered in the magazine."

**2007, 2006, 2005, 2004, 2003 EPA Award of Merit—General.

$STANDARD, 2923 Troost, Kansas City MO 64109. (816)931-1900. Fax (816)412-8306. E-mail: clyourdon@wordaction.com. Website: www.wordaction.com. Nazarene. Rev. Charlie Yourdon, ed. Examples of Christianity in everyday life for adults, college-age through retirement. Weekly take-home paper; 8 pgs.; circ. 150,000. 100% unsolicited freelance. Complete ms. Pays .035/wd. (.02/wd. for reprints) on acceptance for one-time rts. Articles (20/yr.) or fiction (200/yr.) 700-1,500 wds. Responds in 12 wks. Seasonal 6-9 mos. ahead. Accepts simultaneous submissions & reprints (tell when/where appeared). No disk; accepts e-mail submissions (attached). Does not use sidebars. Prefers NIV. Guidelines (also by e-mail); copy for #10 SAE/2 stamps. (No ads)

Poetry: Buys 30/yr. Free verse, haiku, traditional; to 30 lines; .25/line. Submit max. 5 poems.

Fillers: Buys 50/yr. Word puzzles; $20.

Tips: "Fiction or true-experience stories must demonstrate Christianity in action. Show us, don't tell us. Action in stories must conform to Wesleyan-Arminian theology and practices." Themes follow the Christian year, not celebrating national holidays.

**This periodical was #24 on the 2007 Top 50 Christian Publishers list (#27 in 2006, #38 in 2003).

$ST. ANTHONY MESSENGER, 28 W. Liberty St., Cincinnati OH 45202-6498. (513)241-5615. Fax (513)241-0399. E-mail: StAnthony@AmericanCatholic.org. Website: www.AmericanCatholic.org. Fr. Pat McCloskey, O.F.M., ed. For Catholic adults & families. Monthly & online mag.; 64 pgs.; circ. 305,000. Subscription $28. 55% unsolicited freelance. Query/clips (complete ms for fiction); e-query OK. Pays .20/wd. on acceptance for 1st, reprint (right to reprint), and electronic rts. Articles 1,500-3,000 wds., prefers 1,500-2,500 (35-50/yr.); fiction 1,500-2,500 wds. (12/yr.); book reviews 500 wds., $50. Responds in 3-9 wks. Seasonal 6 mos. ahead. Kill fee. Uses some sidebars. Prefers NAB. Guidelines on Website; copy for 9x12 SAE/4 stamps. (Ads)

Poetry: Christopher Heffron, poetry ed. Buys 20/yr. Free verse, haiku, traditional; 3-25 lines; $2/line ($20 min.) Submit max. 2 poems.

Fillers: Cartoons.

Tips: "Many submissions suggest that the writer has not read our guidelines or sample articles. Most open to articles, fiction, profiles, interviews of Catholic personalities, personal experiences, and prayer. Writing must be professional; use Catholic terminology and vocabulary. Writing must be faithful to Catholic belief and teaching, life, and experience. Our online writers' guidelines indicate the seven categories of articles. Texts of articles reflecting each category are linked to the online writers' guidelines for nonfiction articles."

**This periodical was #22 on the 2007 Top 50 Christian Publishers list (#33 in 2006, #40 in 2005, #40 in 2004, #45 in 2003).

STAR OF ZION, PO Box 26770, Charlotte NC 28221-6770. (704)599-4630, ext. 318. Fax (704)688-2546. E-mail: editor@starofzion.org. Submissions to jasnead@amezhqtr.org. Website: www.starofzion.org. African Methodist Episcopal Zion Church. Mike Lisby, ed. Religious denominational newspaper for A.M.E. Zion church members, pastors, and national officers. Bimonthly newspaper; 16 pgs.; circ. 9,200. Subscription $38. 10% unsolicited freelance; 75% assigned. Query/clips; fax/e-query OK. **NO PAYMENT; SUBSCRIPTION FOR ESTABLISHED COLUMNS** for 1st rts. Articles to 750 wds.; book reviews 500-750 wds. Responds in 4 wks. Seasonal 2 mos. ahead. Accepts simultaneous submissions. Prefers e-mail submissions (attached file or copied into message). No kill fee. Uses some sidebars. Copy of 9x12 SAE/$2.13 postage (mark "Media Mail"). (Ads)

Poetry: Accepts 12-24/yr. African American themes; traditional. Submit max. 12 poems.

Fillers: Accepts 24/yr. Anecdotes, cartoons, games, jokes, prayers, & word puzzles; 25-175 wds.

Columns/Departments: Accepts 24/yr. Motivational Message (sermon text), 500-1,000 wds.; 5-Minute Sermon (brief lesson), 500-750 wds.; From the Pulpit (pastor recollections and anecdotes). Query.

Contest: Annual essay contest: What Zion Means to Me.

Tips: "Most open to columns, black history articles, religious poems, humor, church (A.M.E. Zion) histories, and pastor biographies." This publication currently undergoing a complete makeover.

STEPS: A Magazine of Hope and Healing for Christians in Recovery, PO Box 215, Brea CA 92822-0215. (714)529-6227. Fax (714)529-1120. E-mail: barbaram@christianrecovery.com. Website: www.nacronline.com. National Assn. for Christian Recovery. Barbara Milligan, assoc. ed. Serves a broad audience of individuals, families, couples, ministry leaders, pastors, support-group leaders, and mental-health professionals. Quarterly mag. Subscription with $30 membership. Open to freelance. E-query only (see guidelines first on Website); no complete mss. Pays a small honorarium, plus a 1-year subscription. Articles to 1,000 wds. Uses some sidebars.

Fillers: Anecdotes, cartoons, newsbreaks, short humor; to 350 wds. All on a recovery theme.

Special Needs: The recovery church (news items from recovery churches in the U.S. and around the world); Twelve Step practice for Christians (practical, hands-on articles, as well as articles relating Twelve Step practice to Christian history and teaching); Twelve Step history and the history of drug and alcohol treatment, global perspectives (profiles of people in recovery around the world); theology of recovery (thoughtful reflections on the theological meaning of Twelve Step principles or on themes in Christian theology as they relate to Christians in recovery).

Tips: "Read back issues to get an idea of our tone and style. You'll find some articles on our Website by going to the NACR Library. If you'd like to tell someone's story of recovery (not yours), interview them and write a profile. Focus on specific ways that person's relationship with God has affected their recovery; be specific about their ongoing struggles." Accepts no poetry.

$STEWARDSHIP, PO Box 1561, New Canaan CT 06840. Toll-free (888)320-5576. (203)966-6470. Fax (203)966-4654. E-mail: guy@parishpublishing.org, or info@parishpublishing.org. Website: www.parishpublishing.org. Parish Publishing LLC. Guy Brossy, principal. Inspires parishioners to give to their church—abilities, time, and monies. Monthly newsletter; 4 pgs.; circ. 1 million. 50% unsolicited freelance; 50% assigned. Fax/e-query with cover letter. Pays $50 on acceptance for all & reprint rts. Articles 160, 200, or 250 wds. (50/yr.) Responds in 2 wks. Seasonal 3 mos. ahead. Accepts simultaneous submissions & reprints. Accepts e-mail submissions (attached or copied into message). Regularly uses sidebars. Free guidelines/copy. (No ads)

Tips: "Write articles that zero in on stewardship—general, time, talent, or treasure—as it relates to the local church."

$ST. JOSEPH'S MESSENGER AND ADVOCATE OF THE BLIND, PO Box 288, Jersey City NJ 07303-0288. (201)798-4141. Catholic/Sisters of St. Joseph of Peace. Sister Mary Kuiken, CSJP, ed. For older Catholics interested in supporting ministry to the aged, young, blind, and needy. Biannual mag.; 12-16 pgs.; circ. 14,000. Subscription $5. 30% unsolicited freelance. Complete ms. Pays $20-30 on acceptance for 1st rts. Articles 800-1,000 wds. (24/yr.); fiction 800-1,000 wds. (30/yr.). Responds in 5 wks. Seasonal 3 mos. ahead. Accepts simultaneous submissions & reprints (tell when/where appeared). Does not use sidebars. Guidelines; copy for 9x12 SAE/2 stamps. (No ads)

Poetry: Buys 25/yr. Light verse, traditional; 4-16 lines; $5-15 on publication. Submit max. 4 poems.

Fillers: Buys 20/yr. Ideas, 50-100 wds.; $5-10.

Tips: "Most open to contemporary fiction. No Christmas issue."

$THE STORYTELLER, 2441 Washington Rd., Maynard AR 72444. (870)647-2137. Fax (870) 847-2454. E-mail: storyteller1@hightowercom.com. Website: www.freewebs.com/fossil creek. Fossil Creek Publishing. Regina Cook Williams, ed./pub.; Ruthan Riney, review ed. Family audience; geared to (but not limited to) new writers. Quarterly mag.; 72 pgs.; circ. 600. Subscription $20. 100% unsolicited freelance. Complete ms/cover letter; phone/e-query OK. Pays .0025/wd. on publication for 1st rts. Articles 2,500 wds. (60/yr.); fiction 2,500 wds. (100-125/yr.). Responds in 1 wk. Seasonal 3 mos. ahead. Accepts simultaneous submissions & reprints (tell when/where appeared). Responds in 1-2 wks. No disk or e-mail submissions. Does not use sidebars. Also accepts submissions from children or teens. Guidelines (also on Website); copy $6/9x12 SAE/5 stamps. (Ads)

Poetry: Accepts 100/yr. Free verse, haiku, light verse, traditional; 3-40 lines. Submit max. 3 poems. Pays $1/poem.

Fillers: Accepts 10-20/yr. Cartoons, quotes, tips; 25-50 wds. Writing-related only.

Special Needs: Original artwork. Funny or serious stories about growing up as a pastor's child or being a pastor's wife. Also westerns and mysteries.

Contest: Offers 1 or 2 paying contests per year, along with People's Choice Awards, and Pushcart Prize nominations. Go to www.storyteller1.UPCsites.org, for announcements of all forthcoming contests for the year (contest site only).

Tips: "All sections of the magazine are open but how-to. Would consider how-to if you have the credentials to back it up. Send polished copy. We understand a mistake here and there, but figure that if you're too lazy to correct misspellings and obvious mistakes, you're too lazy to write a good story."

**This periodical was #42 on the 2007 Top 50 Christian Publishers list.

STUDIO: A Journal of Christians Writing, 727 Peel St., Albury NSW 2640, Australia. Phone/fax +61 2 6021 1135. E-mail: studio00@bigpond.net.au. Submit to Studio Editor. Quarterly jour.; 36 pgs.; circ. 300. Subscription $60 AUS. 90% unsolicited freelance; 10% assigned. Query. **PAYS IN COPIES** for one-time rts. Articles 3,000 wds. (15/yr.); fiction 3,000 wds. (50/yr.); book reviews 300 wds. Responds in 3 wks. Accepts simultaneous submissions & reprints (tell when/where appeared). No disks; e-mail submissions OK. Does not use sidebars. Guidelines (send IRC); copy for $10 AUS. (Ads)

Poetry: Accepts 200/yr. Any type; 4-100 lines. Submit max. 3 poems.

Contest: See copy of journal for details.

Tips: "We accept all types of fiction and literary article themes."

THE SWORD AND TRUMPET, PO Box 575, Harrisonburg VA 22803-0575. Phone/fax (540)867-9419. E-mail: swandtrump@verizon.net. Website: www.swordandtrumpet.org. Mennonite. Paul Emerson, ed. Primarily for conservative Bible believers. Monthly mag.; 37 pgs.; circ. 3,300. Subscription $15. **NO PAYMENT.** Articles. Prefers KJV. (No ads)

SWORD OF THE LORD NEWSPAPER, PO Box 1099, Murfreesboro TN 37133. Toll-free (800)247-9673. (615)893-6700. Fax (615)895-7447. E-mail: guyking@swordofthelord.com, or through Website: www.swordofthelord.com. Independent Baptists and other fundamentalists. Dr. Shelton Smith, pres./ed.; submit to Guy King. Revival and soul-winning. Biweekly newspaper; 24 pgs.; circ. 70,000. Subscription $15. Open to freelance. Query; phone/fax/e-query OK. **NO PAYMENT.** Articles 500-1,000 wds.; fiction for 4-7 & 8-12 yrs. and teenagers. Responds in 13 wks. Seasonal 3 mos. ahead. Accepts simultaneous submissions & reprints (tell when/where appeared). Accepts disk or e-mail submissions (attached file). No kill fee. Does not use sidebars. Requires KJV. Guidelines (also by e-mail); no copy. (Ads)

Poetry: Accepts variable number. Free verse, light verse, traditional; any length.

Fillers: Accepts variable number. Facts, newsbreaks, prose.

Columns/Departments: Accepts variable number. Kid's Korner (children's stories); Teen Talk (teen issues); both 500-700 wds.

Tips: "Most open to Bible study, soul-winning material, Christian growth, and youth character building that does not stress graphic portrayals of 'what's really going on out there.' Only works from a fundamentalist viewpoint and using the KJV are considered." Does not reprint articles from Mennonite, Lutheran, or Catholic publications.

$TESTIMONY, 2450 Milltower Ct., Mississauga ON L5N 5Z6, Canada. (905)542-7400. Fax (905)542-7313. E-mail: testimony@paoc.org. Website: www.paoc.org/testimony. The Pentecostal Assemblies of Canada. Steve Kennedy, ed. To encourage a Christian response to a wide range of issues and topics, including those that are peculiar to Pentecostals. Monthly & online mag.; 24 pgs.; circ. 14,000. Subscription $24 U.S./$19.05 Cdn. (includes GST). 10% unsolicited freelance; 90% assigned. Query; fax/e-query OK. Pays $20-75 on publication for 1st rts. (no pay for reprint rts.). Articles 700-900 wds. Responds in 6-8 wks. Seasonal 4 mos. ahead. Accepts reprints (tell when/where appeared). Prefers e-mail submission (copied into message). Regularly uses sidebars. Prefers NIV. Guidelines/theme list (also by e-mail/Website); copy $2/9x12 SAE. (Ads)

Tips: "View theme list on our Website and query us about a potential article regarding one of our themes. Our readership is 98% Canadian. We prefer Canadian writers or at least writers who understand that Canadians are not Americans in long underwear. We also give preference to members of this denomination, since this is related to issues concerning our fellowship."

$+THIS I BELIEVE ESSAYS, Website: www.npr.org/thisibelieve/guide.html. National Public Radio (NPR). Write and submit your own story of personal belief; those accepted will be recorded and read on the air. Guidelines & contract included on the Website. Complete ms. submitted through Website. Pays $200, 30 days after your essay is recorded. Personal essay 350-500 wds. Details on Website.

+THREE ONE SIX: A Journal of Christian Thinking, PO Box 79, Westville NJ 08093. E-mail: threeonesix@comcast.net. Website: www.the316journal.com. Nondenominational. Bill Dowis, ed./pub. Our goal is to provide provoking writing and artwork that ignites thought and discussion among everyone. Quarterly jour.; 150-200 pgs.; estab. 2007. 90% unsolicited freelance; 10% assigned. Complete ms/cover letter; e-query OK. **PAYS IN COPIES (plus a bonus based on sales)** for one-time rts. Articles to 10,000 wds.; fiction to 8,000 wds. Responds in 4-6 wks. Seasonal 6 mos. ahead. Accepts simultaneous submissions & reprints (tell when/where appeared). Accepts disk or e-mail submissions (attached or copied into message). Some sidebars. Prefers NIV or KJV. Also accepts submissions from teens. Guidelines on Website. (Ads)

Poetry: Accepts 40-60/yr. Avant-garde, free verse, haiku, light verse, traditional; to 30 lines. Submit max. 10 poems.

Fillers: Anecdotes, cartoons, prayers, prose, short humor.

Tips: "The entire journal is written by freelancers and we encourage anyone who has something to share to submit. Make sure you have something to say and the ability to say it well. Credentials are not important; good writing and thought-provoking topics are key."

+TIFERET: A Journal of Spiritual Literature, 21 Dryden Rd., Bernardsville NJ 07924-1108. (908)432-2149. E-mail: editors@tireretjournal.com. Website: www.tiferetjournal.com. Mary Mitchell, ed. Publishes writings from authors of many faiths. Semiannual literary mag.; 200 pgs. Open to unsolicited freelance. Complete ms/cover letter by mail or e-mail. **NO PAYMENT** for 1st rts. Articles; fiction. Responds in 4 mos. Accepts simultaneous submissions & rarely reprints. Prefers e-mail submissions (attached file). Guidelines on Website.

Poetry: Renee Ashley, poetry ed. Accepts poetry. Submit max. 6 poems.

Special Needs: Accepts photographic artwork.

TIME OF SINGING: A Magazine of Christian Poetry, PO Box 149, Conneaut Lake PA 16316. E-mail: timesing@zoominternet.net. Website: www.timeofsinging.bizland.com. Lora Zill, ed. We try to appeal to all poets and lovers of poetry. Quarterly booklet; 44 pgs.; circ. 250. Subscription $17. 95% unsolicited freelance; 5% assigned. Complete ms; e-query OK. **PAYS IN COPIES** for 1st, one-time, or reprint rts. Poetry only (some book reviews by assignment). Responds in 12 wks. Seasonal 6 mos. ahead. Accepts simultaneous submissions & reprints (tell when/where appeared). Accepts e-mail submission (attached file). Guidelines for SASE (also by e-mail/Website); copy $4 ea. or 2/$6.

Poetry: Accepts 150-200/yr. Free verse, haiku, light verse, traditional; 3-60 lines. Submit max. 5 poems. Always need form poems (sonnets, villanelles, triolets, etc.) with Christian themes. Fresh rhyme. "Cover letter not needed; your work speaks for itself."

Contest: Sponsors 1-2 annual poetry contests on specific themes or forms ($2 entry fee/poem) with cash prizes (send SASE for rules).

Tips: "Study poetry, read widely—both Christian and non-Christian. Work at the craft. Be open to suggestions and critique. If I have taken time to comment on your work, it is close to publication. If you don't agree, submit elsewhere. I appreciate poets who take chances, who write outside the box. *Time of Singing* is a literary poetry magazine, so I'm not looking for greeting card verse or sermons that rhyme."

$TODAY'S CHRISTIAN, 465 Gundersen Dr., Carol Stream IL 60188-2498. (630)260-6200. Fax (630)480-2004. E-mail: tceditor@christianitytoday.com. Website: www.todays-christian.com. Christianity Today Intl. Ed Gilbreath, ed. A Christian *Reader's Digest* that uses both reprints and original material. Bimonthly & online mag.; 64 pgs.; circ. 75,000. Subscription $17.95. 35% unsolicited freelance; 20% assigned. Complete ms/cover letter; phone/fax/e-query OK. Pays .10/wd. on acceptance for 1st, reprint & electronic rts. Articles 500-1,500 wds. (50/yr.). Responds in 6-8 wks. Seasonal 9 mos. ahead. Accepts reprints ($50-100, tell when/where appeared). Accepts e-mail submissions (copied into message). Kill fee. Sidebars, 150-300 wds. Prefers NIV. Guidelines/theme list (also on Website); copy for 6x9 SAE/4 stamps. (Ads)

Columns/Departments: Cynthia Thomas, columns ed. Buys 150/yr. Lite Fare (adult church humor); Kids of the Kingdom (kids say and do funny things); all to 250 wds.; $35.

**This periodical was #17 on the 2007 Top 50 Christian Publishers list (#16 in 2006, #18 in 2005, #16 in 2004, #6 in 2003).

$TODAY'S PENTECOSTAL EVANGEL, 1445 N. Boonville, Springfield MO 65802-1894. (417)862-2781. Fax (417)862-0416. E-mail: tpe@ag.org. Website: www.tpe.ag.org. Assemblies of God. Hal Donaldson, ed-in-chief; Ken Horn, ed.; submit to Scott Harrup, sr. assoc. ed. Denominational; Pentecostal. Weekly & online mag.; 32 pgs.; circ. 200,000. Subscription $28.99. 5% unsolicited freelance; 95% assigned. Complete ms/cover letter; no phone/fax/e-query. Accepts full mss by e-mail. Pays .06/wd. (.04/wd. for reprints) on acceptance for 1st

& electronic rts. Articles 500-1,200 wds. (10-15/yr.); testimonies 200-300 wds. Responds in 6-8 wks. Seasonal 6-8 mos. ahead. No simultaneous submissions; accepts reprints (tell when/where appeared). Kill fee 100%. Prefers e-mail submissions (attached file). Uses some sidebars. Prefers NIV, KJV. Guidelines (also by e-mail/Website); copy for 9x12 SAE/$1.31 postage. (No ads)

Fillers: Anecdotes, facts, personal experience, testimonies; 250-500 wds. Practical, how-to pieces on family life, devotions, evangelism, seasonal, current issues, Christian living; 250 wds.; pays about $25.

Tips: "True, first-person inspirational material is the best bet for a first-time contributor. We reserve any controversial subjects for writers we're familiar with. Positive family-life articles work well near Father's Day, Mother's Day, and holidays."

**2003 EPA Award of Merit—Denominational.

$TOGETHER, 1251 Virginia Ave., Harrisonburg VA 22802. Toll-free (888)833-3333. (540)433-5351. Fax (540)434-0247. E-mail: Tgether@aol.com. Website: www.churchoutreach.com. Shalom Foundation Inc. Melodie Davis, ed. An outreach magazine distributed by churches to attract the general public to Christian faith and life. Quarterly tabloid; 8 pgs.; circ. 50,000. Free. 90% unsolicited freelance. Complete ms/cover letter or query; e-query OK. Pays $35-60 after publication for 1st & electronic rts. Articles 500-1,200 wds. (16/yr.). Responds in 9-17 wks. Seasonal 6 mos. ahead. Accepts simultaneous submissions & reprints. Accepts requested ms on disk or by e-mail (copied into message). Uses some sidebars. Prefers NIV. Guidelines/theme list (also by e-mail/Website); copy on Website. (No ads)

Tips: "Deal with contemporary themes with fresh style. We need a variety of salvation testimonies from all racial/ethnic groups, with excellent photos available (don't submit photos until requested)." When submitting by e-mail, put title of magazine and title of your piece in subject line. Also include your e-mail address in body of message.

TO GOD BE THE GLORY! PUBLICATIONS, PO Box 171, Bangor MI 49013-0171. (269)906-5944. E-mail: CHRISTSANNOINTEDONE@yahoo.com. Website: www.TheLordSavedMe.com. M. J. Reynolds, owner/CEO. Devoted to lifting up the name of our precious Lord and Savior Jesus Christ. Mostly online mag.; offers a yearly poetry anthology with names/poems of contest winners. 100% unsolicited freelance. Query; no phone/fax/e-query. **NO PAYMENT** for 1st rts. Not copyrighted. Poetry only. Prefers KJV. Guidelines; copy $4. (Ads)

Poetry: Accepts a large number/yr. Traditional; mainly about Jesus Christ, but also accepts poems of the positive nature and even those that may be 'dark' (not too 'dark'), but tell a story or display a concept to help others.

Contest: Holds a few poetry contests throughout the year.

Tips: "We're open to all freelancers. This ministry also offers many other publishing avenues besides poetry. Go to the Website or write for guidelines and information. Please follow rules and guidelines."

+TOUCHED BY THE HAND OF GOD. Website: www.touchedbythehandofgod.com. Barrett Batson, ed. People share stories of how God has opened doors, hearts, or minds for them in remarkable ways and at just the right time. Website. Free online. Open to unsolicited freelance. Complete ms. Use submission form on Website. **NO PAYMENT** for one-time or reprint rts. Personal stories to 600 wds. Guidelines on Website.

+TRINITY TRIBUNE, PO Box 433, Santa Rosa CA 95402. (707)545-2203. Fax (707)545-7714. E-mail: hermsmeyer@gmail.com. Josh Hermsmeyer, ed. Newspaper. Open to unsolicited freelance. Query. Articles.

TRI-STATE VOICE, PO Box 110282, Nutley NJ 07110. (973)235-0776. Fax (973)235-1688. E-mail: tristatevoice@aol.com. Website: www.tristatevoice.com. Tom Campisi, ed. To be a voice to the Christian community in Greater NYC. Monthly newspaper; circ. 22,000. Subscription $24. Open to freelance. Query preferred. Articles; no reviews. Incomplete topical listings. (Ads)

THE TRUMPETER, 7757 S.W. 86th St., Ste. C-109, Miami FL 33143. (305)274-4880. Fax (302)370-1485. E-mail: martiele@thetrumpeter.com. Website: www.thetrumpeter.com. Swanko Communications. Martiele Swanko, ed-in-chief. Unites all South Florida Christian denominations, ethnic groups, and cultures. Bimonthly & online mag.; 80+ pgs.; circ. 20,000. Subscription $19.95. 90% unsolicited freelance. Query; fax/e-query OK. **NO PAYMENT** for one-time rts. Features & sports, 900-1,000 wds.; articles 500-1,200 wds.; book/music/video reviews, 100 wds. Responds in 4 wks. Accepts reprints (tell when/where appeared). Requires requested ms on disk or by e-mail. Regularly uses sidebars. Prefers KJV. Guidelines/theme list (also by e-mail/Website). (Ads)

Fillers: Cartoons.

Columns/Departments: Accepts 100/yr. Around Town (local talk), 100-125 wds.; Arts & Entertainment, 400 wds.; Legal, 450 wds.; Political/Viewpoint, 100-125 wds.

Tips: "Call us for a special feature assignment. Be a good writer. Know how to effectively write a paragraph by the rules and use active verbs instead of adjectives."

$THE UNITED CHURCH OBSERVER, 478 Huron St., Toronto ON M5R 2R3, Canada. (416)960-8500. Fax (416)960-8477. E-mail: dwilson@ucobserver.org. Website: www.ucobserver.org. United Church of Canada. David Wilson, ed. To voice hope for individual Christians, for the United Church, for God's world. Monthly (11X) mag.; circ. 70,000. Subscription $14. 20% freelance written; uses a limited amount of material from non-United Church freelancers. Pays variable rates for 1st rts. (sometimes all rts.). Articles to 1,200 wds. Accepts reprints (tell when/where appeared). (Ads)

$UPSCALE MAGAZINE: Exposure to the World's Finest, 600 Bronner Brothers Way S.W., Atlanta GA 30310. (404)758-7467. Fax (404)755-9892. E-mail: features@upscalemag.com (department editors listed on Website). Website: www.upscalemagazine.com. Upscale Communications Inc. Joyce E. Davis, sr. ed. To inspire, inform, and entertain African Americans. Monthly mag.; circ. 250,000. Subscription $20. 75-80% unsolicited freelance. Query; fax/e-query OK. Pays $100 & up on publication for 1st rts. Articles (135/yr.); novel excerpts. Seasonal 6 mos. ahead. Accepts simultaneous submissions. Responds in 5-9 wks. Kill fee 25%. Guidelines on Website; copy online.

Columns/Departments: Buys 6-10/yr. News & Business (factual, current); Lifestyle (travel, home, wellness, etc.); Beauty & Fashion (tips, trends, upscale fashion, hair); Arts & Entertainment. Query. Payment varies. These columns most open to freelance.

Tips: "We are open to queries for exciting and informative nonfiction." Uses inspirational and religious articles.

+URBAN KINGDOM MAGAZINE.COM, PO Box 77622, Washington DC 20013-8622. Toll-free (800)346-5589. E-mail: info@urbankingdommagazine.com. Website: www.urbankingdommagazine.com. Urban Kingdom Media Group LLC. Vashti Dominique, pub. & ed-in-chief. Characterizes the contemporary lifestyle of Christian young men and young women; a media source of realism and truth, encouragement, and entertainment. Webzine; circ. 3,000. Open to freelance. Query/2 clips by e-mail to: writers@urbankingdommagazine.com; phone/e-query OK. **NO PAYMENT.** Articles to 1,000 wds.; fiction length varies; book reviews 500 wds. Responds in 3 wks. Seasonal 3 mos. ahead. Accepts simultaneous submissions & reprints (tell when/where appeared). Requires e-mail submissions (attached file). Uses some sidebars. Also accepts submissions from teens. Guidelines/theme list by e-mail/Website; copy online. (Ads)

Poetry: Uses regularly. All types; any length.

Fillers: Uses regularly. Anecdotes, cartoons, facts, ideas, newsbreaks, party ideas, prayers, prose, quizzes, quotes, sermon illustrations, short humor, tips; 200-300 wds. or 350-500 wds.

Columns: Has a number of columns in these areas: Music, Urban Mode, Arts & Entertainment, Health, Beauty & Grooming, Community, News & Political Commentary/Current Event, Sports, Business/Finance/Technology, Lifestyle, Testimony, Book Reviews.

Special Needs: Music; style; arts & entertainment; community; business, finance & technology; health, beauty & grooming; home & living; travel. "We would like to give a more balanced focus to men's issues and interest in fashion, sports, etc."

Tips: "Writer must be a good writer and spiritually active. We appeal to a very contemporary, nontraditional Christian market. Most open to Music; Arts & Entertainment; Book Review; Fashion; Boy's Lounge."

$U.S. CATHOLIC, 205 W. Monroe St., Chicago IL 60606. (312)236-7782. Fax (312)236-8207. E-mail: editors@uscatholic.org. Website: www.uscatholic.org. The Claretians. Meinrad Schrer Emunds, ed. dir.; Heidi Schlumpf, mng. ed.; Rev. John Molyneau C.M.F., ed. Devoted to starting and continuing a dialog with Catholics of diverse lifestyles and opinions about the way they live their faith. Monthly & online mag.; 52 pgs.; circ. 40,000. Subscription $22. 95% unsolicited freelance. Complete ms/cover letter; phone/fax/e-query OK. Pays $250-600 (fiction $300-400) on acceptance for all rts. Articles 2,500-4,000 wds.; fiction 2,500-3,500 wds. Responds in 5 wks. Seasonal 6 mos. ahead. Accepts requested ms on disk or by e-mail. Regularly uses sidebars. Guidelines; copy for 10x13 SASE. (Ads: Tom Toussaint, 312-236-7782, ext. 854)

Poetry: Submit poetry (and fiction) to literaryeditor@uscatholic.org. All types except light verse, to 50 lines; $75.

Columns/Departments: (See guidelines first.) Sounding Board, 1,100-1,300 wds., $250; Practicing Catholic, 750 wds., $150.

Tips: "Most open to features and essays. All manuscripts (except for fiction or poetry) should have an explicit religious dimension that enables readers to see the interaction between their faith and the issue at hand. Fiction should be well written, creative, with solid character development."

**This periodical was #23 on the 2007 Top 50 Christian Publishers list (#23 in 2006, #22 in 2005, #33 in 2003).

$VIBRANT LIFE, 55 W. Oak Ridge Dr., Hagerstown MD 21740-7390. (301)393-4019. Fax (301)393-4055. E-mail: vibrantlife@rhpa.org. Website: www.vibrantlife.com. Seventh-day Adventist/Review & Herald. Charles Mills, ed. Total health publication (physical, mental, and spiritual); plus articles on family and marriage improvement; ages 30-50. Bimonthly mag.; 32 pgs.; circ. 30,000. Subscription $20.95. 50% unsolicited freelance; 30% assigned. Query/clips; fax/e-query OK. Pays $75-300 on acceptance for 1st, one-time, reprint, or electronic rts. Articles 600-1,500 wds. (50-60/yr.). Responds in 5 wks. Seasonal 9 mos. ahead. Accepts simultaneous submissions & reprints (tell when/where appeared). Accepts e-mail submissions (attached file). Kill fee 50%. Regularly uses sidebars. Prefers NIV. Guidelines on Website; copy $1/9x12 SAE. (Ads)

Tips: "Articles need to be very helpful, practical, and well documented. Don't be preachy. Sidebars are a real plus." Not accepting submissions until end of year; see Website.

**This periodical was #7 on the 2005 Top 50 Christian Publishers list (#7 in 2004, #4 in 2003).

VICTORY HERALD, Box 190, Tipton OK 73570. Phone/fax (580)667-4178. E-mail:dsmith@pldi.net. Website: www.victoryherald.com. To promote and encourage writers to submit works of inspirational content and purpose that will reach out and touch the hearts of readers. Donna Smith, ed. Monthly e-zine. Estab. 2005. 70% unsolicited freelance; 30% assigned. Complete ms; e-query OK. Accepts full mss by e-mail. **NO PAYMENT** for one-time rts. Articles 500-750 wds.; fiction 750-1,200 wds. Responds in 2 wks. Seasonal 2 mos. ahead. Accepts simultaneous submissions & reprints (tell when/where appeared). Prefers submissions by e-mail (attached file or copied into message). Uses some sidebars. Also accepts submissions from children/teens. Guidelines on Website; copy online. (No ads)

Poetry: Accepts 24-36/yr. Free verse, haiku, light verse, traditional; 40-45 lines max. Submit max. 3 poems.

Fillers: Accepts 24-36/yr. Anecdotes, games, kid quotes, party ideas, prayers, prose, short humor, tips; 50-150 wds.

Columns/Departments: Complete ms; no payment.

Tips: "More open to inspirational works. Goal is to encourage writers to reach out to encourage others—to inspire others."

$VICTORY IN GRACE, 60 Quentin Rd., Lake Zurich IL 60047. (847)438-4494. Fax (847)438-4232. E-mail: ddarling@victoryingrace.org, or julie@victoryingrace.org. Website: www.victoryingrace.org. Teaching and print ministry of Dr. James Scudder. Dan Darling, mng. ed. Serves to help and inspire viewers and listeners of Victory in Grace with Dr. James Scudder. Monthly mag.; 38 pgs.; circ. 15,000. Subscription $20. 5% unsolicited freelance; 95% assigned/in-house. E-query only. Pays .15/wd. on publication for 1st rts. Not copyrighted. Articles 1,200-1,500 wds. (20/yr.). Responds in 4-6 wks. Seasonal 6 mos. ahead. Accepts simultaneous submissions & reprints (tell when/where appeared). Prefers e-mail submissions (attached file). Sometimes pays kill fee. Regularly uses sidebars. Prefers KJV. Guidelines (also by e-mail); copy for 6x9 SAE (sign up on Website for 3 free issues).

Special Needs: True stories of how someone's life has changed through the ministry of *Victory in Grace.*

Tips: "Most open to a strong story about how God helps His people to cope with or overcome obstacles."

$+VILLAGE NOTE CARDS, 742 Elmhurst Cir., Claremont CA 91711. (909)437-0808. Fax (206)339-3765. E-mail: cards@villagenotecards.com. Website: www.villagenotecards.com. Diane Cooley, owner. A fine-art note card publisher seeking how-to-write articles for their Website. Estab. 2007. 100% unsolicited freelance. Complete ms; e-query OK. Accepts full mss by e-mail. Pays $5-25 on publication for electronic, nonexclusive rts. Articles 500-1,500 wds. Responds in 4-6 wks. Accepts reprints. Guidelines on Website.

Special Needs: How-to-write articles—sympathy note, thank-you note; I'm sorry note, etc. (any topic).

Tips: "We are open to new writers."

$THE VISION, 8855 Dunn Rd., Hazelwood MO 63042-2299. (314)837-7300. Fax (314)837-1803. E-mail: WAP@upci.org. Website: www.upci.org/wap. United Pentecostal Church. Richard M. Davis, ed.; submit to Karen Myers, administrative aide. Denominational. Weekly take-home paper; 4 pgs.; circ. 10,000. Subscription $1.85/quarter. 95% unsolicited freelance. Complete ms/cover letter; no e-query. Pays $8-25 on publication for 1st rts. Articles 500-1,600 wds. (to 120/yr.); fiction 1,200-1,600 wds. (to 120/yr.); devotionals 350-400 wds. Seasonal 9 months ahead. Accepts simultaneous submissions & reprints. Guidelines (also by e-mail); free copy/SASE. (No ads)

Poetry: Buys 30/yr.; $3-12.

Tips: "Most open to fiction short stories, real-life experiences, and short poems. Whether fiction or nonfiction, we are looking for stories depicting everyday life situations and how Christian principles are used to solve problems, resolve issues, or enhance one's spiritual growth. Be sure manuscript has a pertinent, spiritual application. Best way to break into our publication is to send a well-written article that meets our specifications."

$+VISTA, PO Box 50434, Indianapolis IN 46250-0434. (317)774-7900. E-mail: submissions@wesleyan.org. Website: www.wesleyan.org/wph. Wesleyan Publishing House. Mark Moore, ed. Weekly take-home paper; 8 pgs. 62% unsolicited freelance; 38% assigned. Complete ms; e-query OK. Accepts full mss by e-mail. Pays $25-35 on publication for one-time and reprint rts. Articles 500-600 wds.; fiction 1,000-1,200 wds. Seasonal 9 mos. ahead. No simultaneous submissions or reprints. Requires e-mail submission (attached or copied into message); on disk is 2nd choice. No kill fee. Regularly uses sidebars. Also accepts submissions from children & teens. Prefers NIV. Guidelines (also by e-mail/Website); copy for 9x12 SASE. (No ads)

Poetry: Buys many/yr. Free verse, haiku, light verse. Pays $10-20. Submit max. 5 poems.

Fillers: Buys many/yr. Cartoons, facts, short humor, and word puzzles, 60-175 wds.

Special Needs: Book excerpts from WPH products.

Tips: "Great market for beginning writers."

$WAR CRY, 615 Slaters Ln., Alexandria VA 22314. (703)684-5500. Fax (703)684-5539. E-mail: War_cry@USN.salvationarmy.org. Website: www.salvationarmypublications.org. The Salvation Army. Maj. Ed Forster, ed-in-chief; Jeff McDonald, mng. ed.; Major Christina Tyson, ed. Pluralistic readership reaching all socioeconomic strata and including distribution in institutions. Biweekly mag.; 24 pgs.; circ. 250,000. Subscription $10. 5% unsolicited freelance. Complete ms/brief cover letter; no phone/fax query; e-query OK. Accepts full mss by e-mail. Pays .15/wd. on acceptance for 1st, one-time, reprint rts. Articles 500-1,000 wds. (10/yr.); no fiction. Responds in 4-6 wks. Seasonal 1 yr. ahead. Accepts simultaneous submissions and reprints (tell when/where appeared). Prefers accepted ms by e-mail (attached or copied into message). No kill fee. Uses some sidebars. Prefers NIV. Guidelines (also by e-mail); copy for 9x12 SASE. (No ads)

Fillers: Buys 10/yr. Anecdotes (inspirational), 200-500 wds.; .15/wd.

**This periodical was #17 on the 2006 Top 50 Christian Publishers list (#33 in 2005, #21 in 2004, #23 in 2003).

$THE WAY OF ST. FRANCIS, 1500—34th Ave., Oakland CA 94601. (916)443-5717, ext. 16. Fax (916)443-2019. E-mail: ofmcadev@worldnet.att.net. Website: www.sbfranciscans.org. Franciscan Friars of California/Catholic. Sharon Melberg, mng. ed. For those interested in the message of St. Francis of Assisi as lived out by contemporary people. Bimonthly mag.; 48 pgs.; circ. 5,000. Subscription $15; $17 foreign. 25% unsolicited freelance; 75% assigned. Complete ms/cover letter; no phone/fax query; e-query OK. Pays $25-100 (or copy & subscription) on publication for 1st rts. Articles 500-1,500 wds. (4-6/yr.). Responds in 8 wks. (manuscripts are not returned). Seasonal 3 mos. ahead. Accepts simultaneous submissions & reprints (tell when/where appeared). Prefers requested ms on disk or by e-mail (attached file). Regularly uses sidebars. Any Bible version. Guidelines/theme list (also by e-mail); copy for 6x9 SAE/$2.13 postage (mark "Media Mail"). (No ads)

Poetry: Accepts poetry; pays $25-50.

Fillers: Anecdotes, cartoons, facts, prayers, prose; to 100 wds.; $25-50.

Columns/Departments: Buys 6/yr. First Person (opinion/issue), to 900 wds.; Portrait (interview or personality), to 1,200 wds.; Inspirations (spiritual), to 1,200 wds.; $25-50.

Contest: Annual Simon Scanlon Writing Awards. Articles 1,500-2,000 wds. Prizes: $250-1,000. Deadline October 4. Details on Website.

Tips: "Make direct connection to Franciscan spirituality, theology, history, or mission, or to St. Francis, St. Clare, or a recognizable aspect of their life and vision."

$WEAVINGS, 1908 Grand Ave., PO Box 340004, Nashville TN 37203-0004. (615)340-7200. E-mail: weavings@upperroom.org. Website: www.upperroom.org. The UpperRoom. Submit to The Editor. For clergy, lay leaders, and all thoughtful seekers who want to deepen their understanding of, and response to, how God's life and human lives are being woven together. Bimonthly mag. Subscription $28. Open to freelance. Complete ms. Pays .12/wd. & up on acceptance. Articles 1,250-2,500 wds.; sermons & meditations 500-2,500 wds.; stories (short vignettes or longer narratives) to 2,500 wds.; book reviews 750 wds. Responds within 13 wks. Accepts reprints. Accepts requested ms on disk or by e-mail. Guidelines/theme list on Website; copy for 7.5 x 10.5 SAE/5 stamps. Incomplete topical listings.

Poetry: Pays $75 & up.

Tips: "All contributions should reflect simplicity, authenticity, and inclusiveness."

$WESLEYAN LIFE, Box 50434, Indianapolis IN 46250-0434. (317)774-7909. Fax (317)774-7913. E-mail: communications@wesleyan.org. Website: www.wesleyan.org. The Wesleyan

Church Corp. Dr. Norman G. Wilson, gen. ed.; Jerry Brecheisen, mng. ed. Denominational. Quarterly mag.; 34 pgs.; circ. 50,000. Subscription controlled. 10% freelance. E-mail submissions only. Pays $50-80 for unsolicited on publication for 1st or simultaneous rts. Articles 400-500 wds. (50/yr.). Responds in 2 wks. Seasonal 6 mos. ahead. Accepts simultaneous submissions & reprints (tell when/where appeared). Guidelines (also by e-mail/Website); copy $2. (Ads—limited)

Tips: "Most open to 400-500 word articles. Must be submitted electronically. No poetry."

WEST WIND REVIEW, 1250 Siskiyou Blvd., Ashland OR 97520. (541)552-6518. E-mail: cwright@sou.edu, or WestWind@students.sou.edu. Website: www.sou.edu/English/west wind. Southern Oregon University. Student editor changes each year; Craig Wright, advisor. Strives to bring well-written, insightful stories and poems to the public. Annual anthology; 100-200 pgs.; circ. 250-500. 100% unsolicited freelance. Complete ms/cover letter & bio; no phone/e-query. **PAYS 1 COPY OF ANTHOLOGY** for 1st rts. Not copyrighted. Fiction (8-15/yr.). Accepts mss from May 15 through December 1. Responds in 5-10 wks. No simultaneous submissions or reprints. Does not use sidebars. No e-mail submissions. Guidelines on Website; copy $3. (No ads)

Poetry: Any type; any length. Submit max. 5 poems. Pays one copy of the anthology.

Special Needs: Poetry or short stories that reflect moving, human interest—in a tasteful manner. Fiction should be thoughtful, literary, and contemporary.

Tips: "We accept all submissions for consideration, and observe no borders in order to encourage original creativity. We accept all forms of poetry, prose, short story, and black & white photos. No erotica, sci-fi/fantasy, or racial bias."

WHITE WING MESSENGER, PO Box 2970, Cleveland TN 37320-2970. (423)559-5129. Fax (423)559-5121. E-mail: jenny@cogop.org. Website: www.cogop.org. Church of God of Prophecy/White Wing Publishing House. Virginia Chatham, mng. ed. Official voice of the denomination. Monthly mag.; 32 pgs.; circ. 7,000. Subscription $18. Open to freelance. Query; phone/fax/e-query OK. **NO PAYMENT.** Articles 500-1,000 wds.; no reviews. Responds in 3-4 wks. Not in topical listings. (No ads)

$WHOLE MAGAZINE, PO Box 414, Scott AR 72142. (501)612-0694. E-mail: publisher@wholemagazine.com. Website: www.wholemagazine.com. L. Marie Trotter, pub. A Christian living publication focusing on "wholeness" for the body of Christ: witness, health, opinion, lifestyle, and evangelism topics for the entire family of God. Quarterly mag; 64 pgs.; circ. 10,000. Subscription $20. 50% unsolicited freelance; 50% assigned. Complete ms/cover letter; e-query OK. Payment unknown. Articles 1,000-3,000 wds.; fiction 1,200-2,000 wds. Responds in 4 wks. Seasonal 4 mos. ahead. Uses some sidebars. Guidelines; copy for 9x12 SAE/3 stamps.

Tips: "Looking for in-depth and feature-length articles on a multitude of topics. Do your Bible and current-events homework. Christian short stories must be very well written and polished. Don't be afraid to address controversial issues, but be ready to 'wrap it up' with a clear, uncompromised Christian perspective."

$+THE WILDWOOD READER, PO Box 55-0898, Jacksonville FL 32255. (904)705-6806. E-mail: gonz2171@bellsouth.net. Timson Edwards Co. Alex Gonzalez, pub. Focus is on adult, literary short fiction that is uplifting and motivational for living life in wellness and spirit. Biweekly jour.; 16 pgs.; circ. 100. Subscription $12. Estab. 2006. 100% unsolicited freelance. Query; e-query OK. Pays $10-75, 60 days after publication for one-time rts. Fiction 800-2,400 wds. (18/yr.). Responds in 6 wks. Seasonal 4 mos. ahead. Accepts simultaneous submissions & reprints (tell when/where appeared). Requires CD by mail. Guidelines; no copy. (Ads)

Contest: Sponsors regular contests with winners being published. Readers pick the best of the year for an annual.

Tips: "Most open to good, solid, ready-to-print short stories that follow the indications above. I prefer new and emerging writers; we are not a high end publication yet, but working our way there. Your work must be edited and ready to publish."

$WIRELESS AGE: The Information Source for Christian Media, 5350 N. Academy Blvd., Ste. 200, Colorado Springs CO 80918. (719)536-9000. Fax (719)598-7461. E-mail: wmg@wpa.net, or westar@westarmediagroup.com. Website: www.westarmediagroup.com. Westar Media Group Inc. Dave Koch, pub./ed. For Christian media professionals working in the industry—especially those in radio. Quarterly mag.; 48 pgs.; circ. 4,000. 15% unsolicited freelance; 85% assigned. Query; fax/e-query OK. Pays variable rates for 1st rts. Articles 300-2,500 wds.; book reviews 150-250 wds. Responds in 2 wks. Accepts simultaneous submissions & reprints (tell when/where appeared). Prefers accepted ms by e-mail (attached or copied into message). Regularly uses sidebars. Prefers NIV. Guidelines (also by e-mail); copy for 10x13 SAE/$2.13 postage (mark "Media Mail"). (Ads)

Fillers: Buys 3/yr. Cartoons, prose, 50-300 wds.; pay varies.

Columns/Departments: Buys 48-55/yr. TV/Film (Christian TV/film issues/concerns); Radio (Christian broadcasting issues/concerns); Internet (using the Internet effectively); Programming/Production (radio program and production development); Music (profiles, reviews, news); Publishing (publishing concerns/issues); Technology (reviews, technology issues); Ministry (highlights, development of); plus others; all 800 wds., payment varies.

Special Needs: Technology pieces, affecting the way Christians communicate the gospel.

WISCONSIN CHRISTIAN NEWS, PO Box 756, 1007 W. Arlington St., Marshfield WI 54449. (715)486-8066. E-mail: christiannews@charter.net. Website: www.wisconsinchristiannews.com. Rob E. Pue, ed. Regional Christian newspaper for all of Wisconsin; nondenominational/evangelical. Monthly newspaper; 48 pgs.; circ. 10,000. Subscription $25. Open to freelance. Query; e-query OK. **NO PAYMENT.** Articles up to 1,000 wds. Responds in 1 wk. Seasonal 2 mos. ahead. Accepts e-mail submissions (copied into message). Uses some sidebars. Also accepts submissions from children/teens. No guidelines; copy $2. (Ads)

$THE WITTENBURG DOOR, 5620 Columbia Ave., Dallas TX 75214, or PO Box 1444, Waco TX 76703-1444. (214)827-2625. Fax (254)827-7938. E-mail (submissions): dooreditor@earthlink.net. Website: www.wittenburgdoor.com. Trinity Foundation. Robert Darden, sr. ed. Satire of evangelical church, plus issue-oriented interviews. Bimonthly mag.; 50 pgs.; circ. 7,500. Subscription $29.95. 90% unsolicited freelance; 10% assigned. Complete ms; e-query OK. Pays $50-250 on publication for 1st rts. Articles to 750 wds., prefers 500-750 wds. (45-50/yr.). Responds in 13 wks. Accepts simultaneous submissions & reprints (if from noncompeting markets; tell when/where appeared). Guidelines (also by e-mail); copy $5.95. (Ads)

Tips: "We look for biting satire/humor—*National Lampoon* not *Reader's Digest.* Write something funny and insightful about the state of the modern church. Read more than one issue to understand our 'wavelength.' We see religious humor and satire as a redemptive tool, not a weapon. We desperately need genuinely funny articles with a smart, satiric bent. Write funny stuff about religion. Interview interesting people with something to say about faith and/or religion."

WORD & WAY, 3236 Emerald Ln., Ste. 400, Jefferson City MO 65109-3700. (573)635-5939, ext. 205. Fax (573)635-1774. E-mail: vbrown@wordandway.org, or wordandway@wordandway.org. Website: www.wordandway.org. Baptist. Bill Webb, ed. (bwebb@wordandway.org/ext. 206). Biweekly. Subscription $15. To glorify God.

THE WORD NEWS, 1272 Delaware Ave., Buffalo NY 14209. Toll-free (866)469-9673. (585)723-9329. Fax (877)225-0423. E-mail: submissions@wordmagazine.net, or editor@wordmagazine.net. Website: www.wordmagazine.net. David R. McCleary, exec. ed. (davemc@wordmagazine.net). To publish the news from a godly perspective. Monthly newspaper. Open to unsolicited freelance. Query or complete ms by e-mail. Articles. Incomplete topical listings.

Tips: "It is our purpose to share information and educate the general public on community and civic issues, and to promote dialogue and stimulate individuals to critical thinking on such matters."

$THE WORLD & I ONLINE: The Magazine for Lifelong Learners, 3600 New York Ave. N.E., Washington DC 20002-1947. (202)635-4054. Fax (202)832-5780. E-mail: editors@worldandi.com. Website: www.worldandi.com. Washington Times Corp. Charles Kim, pub. Scholarly and encyclopedic. Monthly & online journal.; 350 pgs.; print circ. 30,000. Subscription rates on Website. 5-8% unsolicited freelance; 85% assigned. Query/clips; e-query OK. Pays $400-800 on publication for all rts. Articles 1,000-5,000 wds. (1,200/yr.); book reviews 2,000-2,500 wds. ($400-500). Responds in 6-10 wks. Seasonal 5 mos. ahead. Accepts reprints (tell when/where appeared). Prefers requested ms on disk. Kill fee 20%. Uses some sidebars. Guidelines on Website; copy $5/9x12 SAE/$2.13 postage (mark "Media Mail"). (Ads)

Poetry: Buys 4-6/yr. Haiku (Asian translation); $30-75. Submit max. 5 poems.

Columns/Departments: Buys 60/yr., plus 12 photo essays. Seven different columns, various lengths. See sample copy.

Tips: "Life and Culture areas most open to freelancers. Offer a great/original idea (with established background as a writer), and writing samples. We especially appreciate scholarly contributions."

**This periodical was #32 on the 2007 Top 50 Christian Publishers list (#41 in 2006, #49 in 2004, #31 in 2003).

WORLD NET DAILY, PO Box 1627, Medford OR 97501. (541)474-1776. Fax (541)474-1770. Website: www.worldnetdaily.com. WorldNetDaily.Com Inc. Joseph Farrah, ed. A fiercely independent news site committed to hard-hitting investigative reporting of government waste, fraud, and abuse. Daily news-zine. Incomplete topical listings.

XAVIER REVIEW, 1 Drexel Dr., Box 110C, Xavier University of Louisiana, New Orleans LA 70125. (504)520-7549 or (504)520-7303. Fax (504)520-7944. E-mail: rskinner@xula.edu. Website: www.xula.edu. Robert Skinner, ed. Publishes nondogmatic, thought-provoking, and sometimes humorous and even irreverent work on religious subject matters. Semiannual literary jour; 75 pgs.; circ. 300. Subscription $10 (individuals), $15(institutions). 90% unsolicited freelance; 10% assigned. Complete ms/cover letter; e-query OK. **PAYS IN COPIES** for 1st rts. Articles 250-5,000 wds. (3/yr.); fiction 250-5,000 wds. (6/yr.); book reviews 250-750 wds. Responds in 4 wks. Accepts simultaneous submissions; no reprints. Prefers accepted mss by e-mail (attached). No kill fee. Does not use sidebars. Guidelines by e-mail; copy for $2/7x10 SAE/3 stamps. (No ads)

Poetry: Accepts 20/yr. Avant-garde, free verse, traditional; 5-60 lines. Submit max. 5 poems.

+YOUR BACKYARD, 1392 Mapleash Ave., Columbia TN 38401. (931)334-3794. E-mail: yourbackyard@bellsouth.net. Website: being redesigned. Gabriel Publishing. Shelah Bayuk, ed./pub. (shelah@bellsouth.net). Jesus said to go into the highways and byways and compel them to come in; also to encourage each other—in love. Monthly/bimonthly mag. & online; 44 pgs.; circ. 250+. Subscription $30. Estab. 2005. 50% unsolicited freelance; 50% assigned. Complete ms/cover letter, query, or query/clips; no phone/fax query; e-query OK. **PAYS IN COPIES FOR NOW** for any rts. Articles 350-700 wds. (20/yr.); fiction 350-700 wds. (6/yr.). Responds in 4-6 wks. Seasonal 3 mos. ahead. Accepts simultaneous submissions & reprints (tell when/where appeared). Accepts e-mail submission (attached file). Uses some sidebars. Accepts submissions from children & teens. Prefers NKJV. Guidelines (also on Website); copy for #10/2 stamps & $2.50. (Ads)

Poetry: Accepts 24/yr. Avant-garde, free verse, light verse, traditional; 4-32 lines. Submit max. 3 poems.

Fillers: Accepts 50/yr. Anecdotes, cartoons, facts, games, ideas, jokes, kid quotes, newsbreaks, party ideas, prayers, prose, quizzes, quotes, short humor, tips, and word puzzles, 12-150 wds.

Columns/Departments: Accepts 12-20/yr. CheckPoints (human interest), 350-500 wds.; Teen Troubles/Challenges, 250-400 wds. Has an Opinion Column. Query or complete ms.

Special Needs: Humor, how-tos, photos, cartoons, greeting cards, mission experiences.

Contests: Coloring; poetry; article; and recipe.

Tips: "Write from the heart—share in love. Research and be professional. Do as if for the Lord."

CHILDREN'S MARKETS

$ADVENTURES, 2923 Troost Ave., Kansas City MO 64109-1538. (816)931-1900. Fax (816)412-8306. E-mail: jns@wordaction.com, or through Website: www.wordaction.com. Julie Smith, ed. For 6- to 8-yr.-olds (1st & 2nd graders); emphasis on principles, character building. Weekly take-home paper; 4 pgs.; circ. 40,000. Subscription $11.96 ($2.99/child/quarter). 45% unsolicited freelance. Query; e-query OK. Pays $15 on publication for all rts. Biblical or Christian contemporary fiction 100 wds. Responds in 4-6 wks. Accepts simultaneous submissions; no reprints. Accepts requested ms by e-mail (attached file). Prefers NIV. Guidelines/theme list (also by e-mail); copy for #10 SAE/1 stamp. (No ads)

Poetry: Buys free verse, light verse, traditional; 4-8 lines; $15. Submit any number.

Fillers: Buys cartoons, facts, games, party ideas, quotes, tips, word puzzles. Pays $15 for cartoons; $15 for 4-panel strip.

Special Needs: Rebus stories; interesting facts/trivia; trivia puzzles; recipes and crafts; activities.

Tips: "We accept a limited amount of material."

$AMERICAN GIRL, 8400 Fairway Pl., Middleton WI 53562. (608)836-4848. Fax (608)831-7089. E-mail: im_agmag_editor@pleasantco.com. Website: www.americangirl.com. Pleasant Company Publications. Kristi Thom, ed.; Barbara E. Stretchberry, mng. ed. General market; for girls ages 8-12 to recognize and celebrate girls' achievements yesterday and today, inspire their creativity, and nurture their hopes and dreams. Bimonthly & online mag.; 50 pgs.; circ. 700,000. Subscription $22.95. 5% unsolicited freelance; 10% assigned. Query (complete ms for fiction); no e-query. Pays $1/wd. ($300 minimum) on acceptance for 1st or all rts. Articles 150-1,000 wds. (10/yr.); fiction to 2,300 wds. (6/yr.; $500 min.). Responds in 13 wks. Seasonal 6 mos. ahead. Accepts simultaneous submissions & reprints. Kill fee 50%. Uses some sidebars. Guidelines on Website; copy $3.95 (check)/9x12 SAE/$2.13 postage (mark "Media Mail"). (No ads)

Poetry: All poetry is by children.

Fillers: Cartoons, puzzles, word games; $50.

Columns/Departments: Buys 10/yr. Girls Express (short profiles on girls), to 150 wds. (query); Giggle Gang (visual puzzles, mazes, word games, math puzzles, seasonal games/puzzles), send complete ms. Pays $50-200.

Contest: Contests vary from issue to issue.

Tips: "Girls Express offers the most opportunities for freelancers. We're looking for short profiles of girls who are doing great and interesting things. Key: a girl must be the 'star' and the story written from her point of view. Be sure to include the ages of the girls you are pitching to us. Write for 8- to 12-year-olds—not teenagers."

$BEGINNER'S FRIEND, PO Box 4060, Overland Park KS 66204. (913)432-0331. Fax (913)722-0351. E-mail: sseditor1@juno.com. Church of God (Holiness)/Herald and Banner Press.

Arlene McGehee, Sunday school ed. Denominational; for young children. Weekly take-home paper; 4 pgs.; circ. 2,700. Subscription $1.50. Complete ms/cover letter; phone/fax/e-query OK (prefers mail or e-mail). Pays .005/wd. on publication for 1st rts. Fiction 500-800 wds. Seasonal 6-8 mos. ahead. Accepts simultaneous submissions & reprints (tell when/where appeared). Prefers KJV. Guidelines/theme list; copy. Not in topical listings.

$BREAD FOR GOD'S CHILDREN, Box 1017, Arcadia FL 34265-1017. (863)494-6214. Fax (863)993-0154. E-mail: BREAD@sunline.net. Website: www.breadministries.org. Bread Ministries Inc. Judith M. Gibbs, ed. A family magazine for serious Christians who are concerned about their children or grandchildren. Bimonthly mag.; 32 pgs.; circ. 10,000. Subscription free. 20-25% unsolicited freelance. Complete ms; no e-query. Pays $25 ($40-50 for fiction) on publication for 1st rts. Not copyrighted. Articles 600-800 wds. (6/yr.); fiction & true stories 600-900 wds. for 4-10 yrs., 900-1,500 wds. for teens 14 and up (6/yr.). Responds in 8-12 wks. (may hold longer). Uses some simultaneous submissions & reprints (tell when/where appeared). Some sidebars. Prefers KJV. Guidelines (also by e-mail); 3 magazine copies for 9x12 SAE/5 stamps; 1 copy 3 stamps. (No ads)

Columns/Departments: Buys 5-8/yr. Let's Chat (discussion issues facing children), 500-800 wds.; Teen Page (teen issues), 600-900 wds.; and Idea Page (object lessons or crafts for children), 300-800 wds.; $10-30.

Tips: "Our child and youth fiction can always use a well-written piece about living out godly principles. We need good stories for the younger children—ages 4-10 years. Most open to fiction or real-life stories of overcoming through faith in Jesus Christ. No tag endings or adult solutions coming from children. Create realistic characters and situations. No 'sudden inspiration' solutions. Open to any areas of family life related from a godly perspective."

$CADET QUEST, PO Box 7259, Grand Rapids MI 49510. (616)241-5616. Fax (616)241-5558. E-mail: submissions@CalvinistCadets.org. Website: www.CalvinistCadets.org. Calvinist Cadet Corps. G. Richard Broene, ed. To show boys ages 9-14 how God is at work in their lives and in the world around them. Mag. published 7X/yr.; 24 pgs.; circ. 8,000. 35% unsolicited freelance. Complete ms/cover letter. Pays .04-.06/wd. on acceptance for 1st, one-time, or reprint rts. Articles 500-1,000 wds. (7/yr.); fiction 900-1,500 wds. (14/yr.). Responds in 4-6 wks. Accepts simultaneous submissions & reprints (tell when/where appeared). Accepts ms by e-mail (copied into message). Uses some sidebars. Prefers NIV. Guidelines, theme list (also on Website); copy for 9x12 SAE/4 stamps. (Ads—limited)

Fillers: Buys several/yr. Quizzes, tips, puzzles; 20-200 wds.; $5 & up.

Tips: "Most open to fiction or fillers tied to themes; request new theme list in January of each year (best to submit between January and April each year). Also looking for simple projects/crafts, and puzzles (word, logic)."

$CELEBRATE, 2923 Troost Ave., Kansas City MO 64109. (816)931-1900. Fax (816)412-8312. E-mail through Website: www.wordaction.com. Word-Action Publishing Co./Church of the Nazarene. Donna Fillmore, ed. Weekly activity/story paper connects Sunday school learning to life for preschoolers (3 & 4), kindergartners (5 & 6), and their families. Weekly take-home paper; 4 pgs.; circ. 40,000. Subscription $10. 50% unsolicited freelance. Query or complete ms/cover letter; e-query OK. Pays $15 or .25/line on acceptance for multiple-use rts. Responds in 4-6 wks. No seasonal. Accepts simultaneous submissions; no reprints. Accepts e-mail submissions (attached file). Prefers NIV. Guidelines (also by e-mail)/theme list/copy for #10 SAE/1 stamp. (No ads)

Special Needs: Activities, recipes, poems, piggyback songs, and crafts for 3- to 6-year-olds.

Tips: "We accept a limited amount of material."

$COURAGE, 1300 N. Meacham Rd., Schaumburg IL 60173-4806. Toll-free (888)588-1600. (847)843-1600. Fax (847)843-3757. E-mail: takehomepapers@garbc.org. Website:

www.garbc.org/rbp. General Assn. of Regular Baptist Churches/Regular Baptist Press. Joan Alexander, ed. For children, 9-11, in Sunday school. Weekly take-home paper; 4 pgs. Subscription $2.49/quarter. Complete ms/cover letter including personal testimony; no phone/fax/e-query. Pays .05/wd. and up, on acceptance for first and reprint rts. (needs multiple reprint rights so they can reprint 2-3 times until next revision). Lead stories 600-650 wds. (40/yr.). Fiction & true stories (40-50/yr.); some serials. Responds in 8-12 wks. Seasonal 1 yr. ahead. No simultaneous submissions; occasionally accepts reprints (tell when/where appeared). No mss by e-mail. Uses some sidebars. Also accepts submissions from children. Requires KJV. Guidelines/theme list on Website (go to RBP site map; site index; About Us; Write for RBP); copy for 9x12 SAE/3 stamps. (No ads)

Fillers: Accepts 15-25/yr. Puzzles & projects. "Not word puzzles; we're looking for logic puzzles, visual puzzles, and other innovative approaches to solving problems." Pays for fillers.

Special Needs: Looking for well-written stories that show the truth about God (related to the weekly Sunday school lesson) as it comes to bear in the lives of children today. Need stories for boys, or that have both boy and girl characters.

Tips: ""We are especially happy to meet competent writers who are using RBP materials in church, or are well acquainted with churches in which our materials are used. We recommend that prospective contributors purchase and study a full quarter of issues before submitting—and after new guidelines are posted on the Web. Check Website quarterly for updates concerning needs, themes, etc.: www.RegularBapristPress.org. This periodical will be revised in 2008 to correlate more closely with the new Middler department curriculum."

$DISCOVERIES, 2923 Troost Ave., Kansas City MO 64109. (816)931-1900. Fax (816)412-8306. E-mail: vlfolsom@wordaction.com, or kdadams@wordaction.com. Website: www.wordaction.com. Nazarene/Word Action Publishing. Virginia Folsom, ed.; submit to Kimberly Adams, asst. ed. For 8- to 10-yr.-olds, emphasizing Christian values and holy living; follows theme of Sunday school curriculum. Weekly take-home paper; 4 pgs.; circ. 30,000. 80% unsolicited freelance; 20% assigned. Query; phone/fax/e-query OK. Accepts full mss by e-mail. Guidelines/theme list (also by e-mail); copy for #10 SASE.

Fillers: Cartoons, word puzzles.

Tips: "Request our theme list and samples. Send a sample of your material that you think would be appropriate for our publication. Most open to relevant, real-life stories; creative puzzles, and cartoons."

**This periodical was #41 on the 2004 Top 50 Christian Publishers list (#44 in 2003).

$FACES, 30 Grove St., Ste. C, Peterborough NH 03458. Toll-free (800)821-0115. (603)924-7209. Fax (603)924-7380. E-mail: facesmag@yahoo.com. Website: www.cobblestonepub.com. Cobblestone Publishing/general. Elizabeth Crooker, ed. Introduces young readers (ages 9-14) to different world cultures, religion, geography, government, and art. Monthly mag.; circ. 15,000. Subscription $29.95. 90-100% freelance. Query only; e-query OK. Pays .20-.25/wd. on publication for all rts. Articles 300-800 wds. (45-50/yr.); fiction to 800 wds. (retold folktales, legends, plays; related to theme). Responds in 4 wks. to 4 mos. Accepts simultaneous submissions. Prefers disk or hard copy. Kill fee 50%. Guidelines/themes (also on Website); copy $4.95/9x12 SAE/$2 postage; also online.

Poetry: Any type to 100 wds.

Fillers: Activities, 100-600 wds.; .20-.25/wd.

$FOCUS ON THE FAMILY CLUBHOUSE, 8605 Explorer Dr., Colorado Springs CO 80920. (719)531-3400. Website: www.clubhousemagazine.com. Focus on the Family. Jesse Florea, ed.; Suzanne Hadley, assoc. ed. For children 8-12 years who desire to know more about God and the Bible. Monthly & online mag.; 24 pgs.; circ. 101,100. Subscription $18. 15% unsolicited freelance; 25% assigned. Complete ms/cover letter; no phone/fax/e-query. Pays

.15-.25/wd. for articles, up to $200 for fiction on acceptance for 1st, one-time, electronic rts. Articles to 800 wds. (5/yr.); fiction 500-1,800 wds. (30/yr.). Responds in 8 wks. Seasonal 6 mos. ahead. Accepts simultaneous submissions; no reprints. No disk or e-mail submissions. Kill fee. Uses some sidebars. Prefers NIV. Also accepts submissions from children. Guidelines; copy (call 1-800-232-6459). (No ads)

Fillers: Buys 6-8/yr. Quizzes, word puzzles, recipes; 200-800 wds.; .15-.25/wd.

Tips: "Most open to fiction, biblical fiction, and how-to pieces with a theme. Avoid stories dealing with boy-girl relationships, poetry, and contemporary, middle-class family settings (current authors meet this need). We look for fiction in exciting settings with ethnic characters. Creatively retold Bible stories and historical fiction are easy ways to break in. Send manuscripts with list of credentials. Read past issues."

**2006, 2005, 2004 EPA Award of Merit—Youth.

$FOCUS ON THE FAMILY CLUBHOUSE JR., 8605 Explorer Dr., Colorado Springs CO 80920. (719)531-3400. Fax (719)531-3499. E-mail: joanna.lutz@fotf.org. Website: www.clubhousemagazine.com. Focus on the Family. Annette Bourland, ed.; Suzanne Hadley, assoc. ed. For 4- to 8-year-olds growing up in a Christian family. Monthly (18X) & online mag.; 24 pgs.; circ. 79,800. Subscription $18. 25% unsolicited freelance; 50% assigned. Complete ms/cover letter; no phone/fax/e-query. Pays $25-200 ($50-100 for fiction) on acceptance for 1st, one-time, electronic rts. Articles 100-500 wds. (1-2/yr.); fiction 250-1,000 wds. (10/yr.); Bible stories 250-800 wds.; one-page rebus stories to 200 wds. Responds in 4-6 wks. Seasonal 5-6 mos. ahead. Kill fee 25%. Uses some sidebars. Guidelines; copy (call 1-800-232-6459). (No ads)

Poetry: Buys 4-8/yr. Traditional; 10-25 lines (to 250 wds.); $50-100.

Fillers: Buys 4-8/yr. Recipes/crafts; 100-500 wds.; $50-100.

Special Needs: Bible stories, rebus, fiction, and crafts.

Tips: "Most open to short, nonpreachy fiction, beginning reader stories, and read-to-me. Be knowledgeable of our style and try it out on kids first. Looking for stories set in exotic places; nonwhite, middle-class characters; historical pieces; humorous quizzes; and craft and recipe features are most readily accepted."

**2007 EPA Award of Merit—Youth; 2004 EPA Award of Excellence—Youth.

+GIRLS CONNECTION (formerly Club Connection), 1445 N. Boonville Ave., Springfield MO 65802-1894. Website: http://mgc.ag.org/connection. Missionettes Girls Clubs/Assemblies of God. A program for winning girls to Jesus Christ through love and acceptance. Webzine.

$GOOD NEWS (child), 2621 Dryden Rd., Moraine OH 45439. (937)293-1415. Fax (937)293-1310. E-mail: service@pflaum.com. Website: www.pflaum.com. Catholic. Joan Mitchell CSJ, ed. For children in grades 2 and 3. Weekly (32X) take-home paper. Not in topical listings.

$GUIDE, 55 W. Oak Ridge Dr., Hagerstown MD 21740. (301)393-4037. Fax (301)393-4055. E-mail: Guide@rhpa.org. Website: www.guidemagazine.org. Seventh-day Adventist/Review and Herald Publishing. Randy Fishell, ed.; Rachel Whitaker, asst. ed. A Christian journal for 10- to 14-yr.-olds, presenting true stories relevant to their needs. Weekly mag.; 32 pgs.; circ. 30,000. Subscription $49.95/yr. 90% unsolicited freelance; 10% assigned. Complete ms/cover letter; fax/e-query OK. Pays .06-.12/wd. ($25-125) on acceptance for 1st rts., reprint rts. True stories 750-1,500 wds. (300/yr.). Responds in 5 wks. Seasonal 8 mos. ahead. Accepts reprints (tell when/where appeared; pays 50% of standard rate). Prefers requested ms by e-mail (attached file). Uses some sidebars. Prefers NIV. Guidelines on Website; copy for 6x9 SAE/2 stamps. (No ads)

Fillers: Buys 75/yr. Games, quizzes, word puzzles on a spiritual theme; 20-50 wds.; $25-40. Accepting very few games, only the most unusual concepts.

Special Needs: "Most open to true action/adventure, Christian humor, and true stories showing God at work in a 10- to 14-year-old's life. Stories must have energy and a high level of intrinsic interest to kids. Put it together with dialog and a spiritual slant, and you're on the 'write' track for our readers. School life."

Tips: "We use only true stories, including school situations, humorous circumstances, adventure, short historical and biographical stories, and almost any situation relevant to 10- to 14-year-olds. Stories must have a spiritual point or implication."

**This periodical was #27 on the 2007 Top 50 Christian Publishers list (#44 in 2006, #25 in 2005, #34 in 2004, #19 in 2003).

$HIGH ADVENTURE, 1445 N. Boonville Ave., Springfield MO 65802-1894. (417)862-2781, ext. 4181. Fax (417)831-8230. E-mail: Rangers@ag.org. Website: www.royalrangers.com, or http://royalrangers.ag.org. Assemblies of God. Rev. Jerry Parks, ed. For the Royal Rangers, middle/upper elementary-age boys. Quarterly mag.; 16 pgs.; circ. 87,000. 25% unsolicited freelance; 60% assigned. Complete ms/cover letter; fax/e-query OK. Pays .06/wd. on publication for all, 1st, one-time rts., electronic rts. Articles 200-1,000 wds. (30/yr.); fiction 200-1,000 wds. (15/yr.). Responds in 4-26 wks. Seasonal 3 mos. ahead. Accepts simultaneous submissions & reprints (tell when/where appeared). Regularly uses sidebars. Prefers NIV. Guidelines (also by e-mail); copy for 9x12 SAE/2 stamps. (No ads)

Fillers: Buys 25-30/yr. Cartoons, jokes, short humor; 25-100 wds., $25-30; quizzes, word puzzles, $12-15.

Tips: "Both fiction and nonfiction are open to freelancers. Space is a major issue. We look for writers who are precise in their descriptions of events, but who can still meet the word count."

$JUNIOR COMPANION, PO Box 4060, Overland Park KS 66204. (913)432-0331. Fax (913)722-0351. E-mail: sseditor1@juno.com. Church of God (holiness)/Herald and Banner Press. Arlene McGehee, Sunday school ed. Denominational; for 4th-6th graders. Weekly take-home paper; 4 pgs.; circ. 3,500. Subscription $1.50. Complete ms/cover letter; phone/fax/e-query OK (prefers mail or e-mail). Pays .005/wd. on publication for 1st rts. Fiction 500-1,200 wds. Seasonal 6-8 mos. ahead. Accepts simultaneous submissions & reprints (tell when/where appeared). Prefers KJV. Guidelines/theme list; copy. Not in topical listings.

$JUNIORWAY, PO Box 436987, Chicago IL 60643. Fax (708)868-6759. Website: www.urban ministries.com. Urban Ministries Inc. K. Steward, ed. Sunday school take-home paper for 4th-6th graders. Open to freelance. Query/clips; fax/e-query OK. Pays $150, 120 days after acceptance, for all rts. Articles. Responds in 4 wks. Seasonal 6 mos. ahead. Accepts simultaneous submissions. Requires accepted ms on disk. Prefers NIV. Guidelines; copy for #10 SASE. (No ads) Incomplete topical listings.

Tips: "Send query with a writing sample. Looking for those with educational or Sunday school teaching experience."

$KEYS FOR KIDS, PO Box 1001, Grand Rapids MI 49501-1001. (616)647-4500. Fax (616)647-4950. E-mail: Hazel@cbhministries.org, or geri@cbhministries.org. Website: www.cbh ministries.org. CBH Ministries. Hazel Marett, ed.; Geri Walcott, ed. A daily devotional booklet for children (8-14) or for family devotions. Bimonthly booklet & online version; 80 pgs.; circ. 100,000. Subscription free. 100% unsolicited freelance. Complete ms; e-query OK. Accepts full mss by e-mail. Pays $25 on acceptance for 1st, reprint, or simultaneous rts. Not copyrighted. Devotionals (includes short fiction story) 375-425 wds. (60-70/yr.). Responds in 4-6 wks. Seasonal 4-5 mos. ahead. Accepts simultaneous submissions & reprints. Prefers NKJV. Guidelines (also by e-mail); copy for 6x9 SAE. (No ads)

Tips: "We want children's devotions. If you are rejected, go back to the sample and study it some more. We use only devotionals, but they include a short fiction story. Any appropriate topic is fine."

$THE KIDS' ARK, PO Box 3160, Victoria TX 77903. Toll-free (800)455-1770. (361)485-1770. E-mail: editor@thekidsark.com. Website: http://thekidsark.com. Interdenominational. Joy

Mygrants, sr. ed. To give kids, 6-12, a biblical foundation on which to base their choices in life. Quarterly mag. (soon to be online); 24 pgs.; circ. 8,000. 100% unsolicited freelance. Query or complete ms; e-query OK. Accepts full ms by e-mail. Pays $100 on publication for 1st, reprint ($25), electronic, world-wide rts. Fiction 600 wds. (12/yr.) Responds in 3-4 wks. No reprints. Prefers accepted submissions by e-mail (attached file). Kill fee 15%. Uses some sidebars. Also accepts submissions from children/teens. Prefers NIV. Guidelines/theme list by e-mail; copy for $1 postage. (Ads)

Tips: "Most open to fiction. Think outside the box! Must catch children's attention and hold it; be biblically based and related to theme. We want to teach God's principles in an exciting format. Every issue contains the Ten Commandments and the plan of salvation."

$NATURE FRIEND, Helping Children Explore the Wonders of God's Creation, 4253 Woodcock Ln., Dayton VA 22821. (540)867-0764. Fax (540)867-9516. E-mail: editor@naturefriendmagazine.com. Website: www.naturefriendmagazine.com. Dogwood Ridge Outdoors. Kevin Shank, ed. For ages 6-16. Monthly mag.; 24 pgs.; circ. 10,000. Subscription $30. 20% unsolicited freelance; 80% assigned. Complete ms/cover letter; no phone/fax/e-query. Pays .05/wd. on publication for 1st rts. Articles 250-750 wds. (50/yr.); or fiction 500-750 wds. (40/yr.). Responds in 12-13 wks. Seasonal 4 mos. ahead. Accepts simultaneous submissions; no reprints. Submit accepted articles on disk (Word format) or by e-mail. Uses some sidebars. KJV only. Guidelines $5 (www.dogwoodridgeoutdoors.com/v.php?pg=15); copy $3/9x12 SAE/$2 postage. (No ads)

Fillers: Buys 12/yr. Quizzes, word puzzles; 100-500 wds.; $10-15.

Tips: "We're looking for detailed science experiments that are nature/wildlife-related. Also need accompanying high quality photographs. We would also like to see project-based activities that are nature/wildlife-related. Please don't submit material unless you have seen our guidelines and a sample copy. We are very conservative in our approach. Everything must be nature-related (including fiction). Write on a child's level—stories, facts, puzzles about animals, and nature topics. No evolution."

$NEW MOON: The Magazine for Girls and Their Dreams, 2 W. First St., #101, Duluth MN 55802. (218)728-5507. Fax (218)728-0314. E-mail: girl@newmoon.org. Website: www.newmoon.org. New Moon Publishing. Submit to Editorial Dept. A feminist publication for girls 8-14 years of age; we value diversity and take girls seriously. Bimonthly mag.; 48 pgs.; circ. 30,000. Subscription $34.95. 40% unsolicited freelance; 50% assigned. Query or complete ms/cover letter; e-query OK. Accepts full mss by e-mail. Pays .06/wd. on publication for all rts. Articles 600-1,200 wds. (12/yr.); fiction 1,200-1,500 wds. (6/yr.); book reviews 300 wds. Responds in 24 wks. No seasonal/holiday. Accepts simultaneous submissions & reprints (tell when/where appeared). Prefers accepted articles by e-mail (copied into message). No kill fee. Regularly uses sidebars. Also accepts submissions from girls and teens. Guidelines & theme list on Website; copy $7/9x12 SAE. (No ads)

Poetry: Buys 12/yr. Poetry from girls 8-14 only. Pays $10. Submit any number/any length.

Columns/Departments: Buys 18/yr. Herstory (women from history), 600 wds.; Women's Work (women in careers), 600 wds.; Body Language (health & puberty issues for girls), 600 wds.; pays .06/wd.

Tips: "We accept work from girls and women only. Girls can submit to any department. Adults must limit their submissions to fiction and the columns listed above."

$OUR LITTLE FRIEND, Box 5353, Nampa ID 83653-5353. (208)465-2580. Fax (208)465-2531. E-mail: ailsox@pacificpress.com. Website: www.pacificpress.com. Seventh-day Adventist. Aileen Andres Sox, ed. To help children understand their infinite value to their Creator and Redeemer; learn how to respond to God; show love to their family and friends; serve others in their world; find fulfillment participating in the Seventh-day Adventist Church. Weekly take-home paper for 0- to 5-yr.-olds; 8 pgs. 25% unsolicited freelance (or reprints); 50%

assigned. Complete ms by e-mail. Pays $25-40 on acceptance for one-time or reprint rts. True stories 450-550 wds. (52/yr.); no articles. Responds in 26 wks. Seasonal 7 mos. ahead. Accepts simultaneous submissions & reprints; no serials. Prefers e-mail submissions (attached file). Guidelines (also on Website); copy for 9x12 SAE/2 stamps. (No ads)

$PARTNERS, Christian Light Publications Inc., Box 1212, Harrisonburg VA 22803-1212. (540)434-0768. Fax (540)433-8896. E-mail: partners@clp.org. Website: www.clp.org. Mennonite. Etta Martin, ed. Helping 9- to 14-yr.-olds to build strong Christian character. Weekly take-home paper; 4 pgs.; circ. 6,519. Subscription $10.40. 99% unsolicited free-lance; 1% assigned. Complete ms; e-query OK. Pays up to .03-.05/wd. on acceptance for 1st, multiuse, or reprint rts. Articles 200-1,000 wds. (100/yr.); fiction & true stories 1,000-1,600 wds. (200/yr.); serial stories up to 1,600 wds./installment; short-short stories to 400 wds. Responds in 6 wks. Seasonal 6 mos. ahead. Accepts reprints only 5 yrs. or more after last publication (tell when/where appeared); serials 2 parts. Prefers e-mail submissions (attached or copied into message). No kill fee. Requires KJV. Guidelines/theme list (also by e-mail); copy for 9x12 SAE/3 stamps. (No ads)

Poetry: Buys 250/yr. Traditional, story poems; 4-24 lines; .50-.70/line. Submit max. 6 poems.

Fillers: Buys 275/yr. Prose, quizzes, quotes, word puzzles (Bible-related); 200-800 wds.; .03-.05/wd. Must be theme-related.

Columns/Departments: Character Corner; Cultures & Customs; Historical Highlights; Maker's Masterpiece; Missionary Mail; Torches of Truth; or Nature Nook; all 200-800 or 1,000 wds.

Tips: "Most open to character-building articles and stories that teach a spiritual lesson. Please ask for our guidelines before submitting manuscripts. Someone who has experi-enced a genuine spiritual 'rebirth' has a much better chance of receiving an acceptance. Write in a lively way (showing, not telling) and on a child's level of understanding (ages 9-14). We do not require that you be Mennonite, but we do send a questionnaire for you to fill out if you desire to write for us."

**This periodical was #14 on the 2007 Top 50 Christian Publishers list (#15 in 2006, #15 in 2005, #12 in 2004, #21 in 2003).

$PASSPORT, 2923 Troost Ave., Kansas City MO 64109. (816)931-1900. Fax (816)412-8306. E-mail: rrpettit@wordaction.com, or kdadams@wordaction.com. Website: www.wordaction.com. Word Action/Nazarene Publishing House. Ryan Pettit, ed.; submit to Kimberly Adams, asst. ed. For preteens, 10- to 12-year-olds; supports the Sunday school lesson and provides an exciting way to learn about God and life. Weekly take-home paper; 4 pgs.; circ. 18,000. 30% unsolicited freelance. Accepts reprints.

Tips: "Most open to creative, true-to-life stories, or creative puzzles and cartoons."

$POCKETS, PO Box 340004, Nashville TN 37203-0004. (615)340-7333. Fax (615)340-7267. E-mail: pockets@upperroom.org. Website: www.pockets.org. United Methodist. Submit to Lynn W. Gilliam, ed. Devotional magazine for children (6-11 yrs.). Monthly (11X) mag.; 48 pgs.; circ. 67,000. Subscription $19.95. 75% unsolicited freelance. Complete ms/brief cover letter; no phone/fax/e-query. Pays .14/wd. on acceptance for one-time rts. Articles 400-800 wds. (10/yr.) & fiction 600-1,400 wds. (40/yr.). Responds in 6 wks. Seasonal 1 yr. ahead. Accepts reprints (tell when/where appeared). No mss by e-mail. Uses some sidebars. Prefers NRSV. Also accepts submissions from children through age 12. Guidelines/theme list (also by e-mail/Website); copy for 9x12 SAE/4 stamps. (No ads)

Poetry: Buys 25/yr. Free verse, haiku, light verse, traditional; 4-24 lines; $2/line. Submit max. 7 poems.

Fillers: Buys 50/yr. Games, word puzzles; $25 & up.

Columns/Departments: Buys 40/yr. Kids Cook; Pocketsful of Love (ways to show love in your family), 200-300 wds.; Peacemakers at Work (children involved in environmental, community, and peace/justice issues; include action photos and name of photographer), to 600 wds.; Pocketsful of Prayer, 400-600 wds.; Someone You'd Like to Know (preferably a child whose lifestyle demonstrates a strong faith perspective), 600 wds.

Special Needs: Two-page stories for ages 5-7, 600 words max. Need role model stories, retold Biblical stories, Someone You'd Like to Know, and Peacemakers at Work.

Contest: Fiction-writing contest; submit between 3/1 & 8/15 every year. Prize $1,000 and publication in Pockets. Length 1,000-1,600 wds. Must be unpublished and not historical fiction. Previous winners not eligible. Send to Pockets Fiction Contest at above address, and include an SASE for return of manuscript and response. Write "Fiction Contest" on envelope and on title/first page of manuscript.

Tips: "Well-written fiction that fits our themes is always needed. Make stories relevant to the lives of today's children and show faith as a natural part of everyday life. All areas open to freelance. Nonfiction probably easiest to sell for columns (we get fewer submissions for those). Read, read, read and study. Be attentive to guidelines, themes, and study past issues."

**This periodical was #11 on the 2007 Top 50 Christian Publishers list (#12 in 2006, #10 in 2005, #4 in 2004, #1 in 2003).

$PRESCHOOL PLAYHOUSE, 1551 Regency Ct., Calumet City IL 60409. (708)868-7100. Fax (708)868-7105. E-mail: jhull@urbanministries.com. Website: www.urbanministries.com. Urban Ministries. Dr. Judy Hull, ed. Sunday school magazine with activities for 2- to 5-year-olds with accompanying teacher's manual. Quarterly magazine for teachers; take-home paper for students; 96 pgs. Subscription $4.85 (teacher) and $2.85 (student). 80% assigned. Query/clips; fax/e-query OK. Pays $150, 120 days after acceptance, for all rts. Articles 6,000 characters for teacher, 2,900 characters for student (4/yr.). Responds in 4 wks. Seasonal 6 mos. ahead. Accepts simultaneous submissions. Requires accepted ms on disk. Prefers NIV. Guidelines; copy $2.25/#10 SASE. (No ads)

Tips: "By assignment only. Send a query with writing samples."

$PRIMARY PAL (IL), 1300 N. Meacham Rd., Schaumburg IL 60173-4806. (847)843-1600. Fax (847)843-3757. E-mail: takehomepapers@garbc.org. Website: www.garbc.org/rbp. General Assn. of Regular Baptist Churches/Regular Baptist Press. Joan Alexander, ed. For ages 6-7 (grades 1 & 2); fundamental, conservative. Weekly take-home paper. Complete ms/cover letter including personal testimony; no phone/fax/e-query; no unsolicited e-submissions. Pays .05/wd. & up, on acceptance for all rts. Lead stories 400-450 wds. (40+/yr. during revision cycle). Requires KJV. Currently in a reprint cycle. (No ads)

Fillers: Word puzzles; one page (include copy of solution). "We need items with a bit of visual puzzling. Writers also need to set the puzzle in a 'frame,' writing something to help child anticipate the challenge in solving the puzzle and receiving a takeaway in finding the solution." Generally connected to Bible lesson or lead story.

Special Needs: Lead stories should clearly support the Bible lesson children will be receiving in Sunday school. In fiction, we want mainstream stories of daily life for children of this age. May have elements of suspense, adventure, or humor, but pointed toward an understanding of God's character and ways as they apply to today.

Tips: "We are especially interested in writers who are using our materials or are acquainted with churches that do. We recommend that others buy and study a full quarter of issues before submitting. We also use crafts and service projects. In fiction, we want mainstream stories of daily life for children of this age. Check Website quarterly for updates concerning needs, themes, etc. (go to RBP site map: "About Us: Write for RBP"). Scheduled for major revision starting with fall 2008."

$PRIMARY PAL (KS), PO Box 4060, Overland Park KS 66204. (913)432-0331. Fax (913)722-0351. E-mail: sseditor1@juno.com. Church of God (holiness)/Herald and Banner Press.

Arlene McGehee, Sunday school ed. Denominational; for 1st-3rd graders. Weekly take-home paper; 4 pgs.; circ. 2,900. Subscription $1.50. Complete ms/cover letter; phone/fax/e-query OK (prefers mail or e-mail). Pays .005/wd. on publication for 1st rts. Fiction 500-1,000 wds. Seasonal 6-8 mos. ahead. Accepts simultaneous submissions & reprints (tell when/where appeared). Prefers KJV. Guidelines/theme list; copy. Not in topical listings.

$PRIMARY STREET, 1551 Regency Ct., Calumet City IL 60409. (708)868-7100. Fax (708)868-7105. E-mail: Jhull@urbanmisnistries.com. Website: www.urbanministries.com. Urban Ministries Inc. Dr. Judith Hull, sr. ed. Sunday school curriculum for African American children, ages 6-8. Quarterly mag./take-home paper (teacher 2 pgs./student 4 pgs.); circ. 20,000. Subscription $16.45 (student); $26.45 (teacher). 20% assigned. Query/clips; phone/e-query OK. Pays $150/lesson, 60 days from assignment date, for all rts. Teacher's material: 5,800 characters. Assignments only. No simultaneous submissions or reprints. Requires requested material on disk or by e-mail (attached file). No kill fee or sidebars. Prefers NIV. No guidelines; free copy (no envelope). (No ads)

Tips: "Writer may submit a résumé, testimony, and writing sample to be considered for an assignment."

$PRIMARY TREASURE, Box 5353, Nampa ID 83653-5353. (208)465-2500. Fax (208)465-2531. E-mail: ailsox@pacificpress.com. Website: www.pacificpress.com. Seventh-day Adventist. Aileen Andres Sox, ed. To help children understand their infinite value to their Creator and Redeemer; learn how to respond to God; show love to their family and friends; serve others in their world; find fulfillment participating in the Seventh-day Adventist Church. Weekly take-home paper for 6- to 9-yr.-olds (1st-4th grades); 16 pgs. 50% freelance (assigned), 25% reprints or unsolicited. Complete ms by e-mail preferred. Pays $25-50 on acceptance for one-time or reprint rts. True stories 900-1,000 wds. (52/yr.); articles used rarely (query). Responds in 13 wks. Seasonal 7 mos. ahead. For simultaneous submissions & reprints see guidelines; serials to 10 parts (query). E-mail submission preferred (attached file). Guidelines (also on Website); copy for 9x12 SAE/2 stamps. (No ads)

Tips: "We need true adventure stories with a spiritual slant; positive, lively stories about children facing modern problems and making good choices. We always need strong stories about boys and stories featuring dads. We need a spiritual element that frequently is missing from submissions."

$PROMISE, 2621 Dryden Rd., Moraine OH 45439. (937)293-1415. Fax (937)293-1310. E-mail: service@pflaum.com. Website: www.pflaum.com. Catholic. Joan Mitchell CSJ, ed. For kindergarten and grade 1; encourages them to participate in parish worship. Weekly (32X) take-home paper. Not in topical listings.

$SEEDS, 2621 Dryden Rd., Moraine OH 45439. (937)293-1415. Fax (937)293-1310. E-mail: service@pflaum.com. Website: www.pflaum.com. Catholic. Joan Mitchell CSJ, ed. Prepares children to learn about God; for preschoolers. Weekly (32X) take-home paper; 4 pgs. Not in topical listings.

$SHINE BRIGHTLY, Box 7259, Grand Rapids MI 49510. (616)241-5616, ext. 3034. Fax (616)241-5558. E-mail: servicecenter@gemsgc.org. Website: www.gemsgc.org. GEMS Girls Clubs. Sara Hilton, ed. To show girls ages 9-14 that God is at work in their lives and in the world around them. Monthly (9X) mag.; 24 pgs.; circ. 13,000. Subscription $13.25. 80% unsolicited freelance; 20% assigned. Complete ms; no e-query. Pays .03-.05/wd. on publication for 1st or reprint rts. Articles 100-400 wds. (10/yr.); fiction 400-900 wds. (30/yr.). Responds in 4-6 wks. Seasonal 10 mos. ahead. Accepts simultaneous submissions & reprints. Accepts requested ms on disk. Regularly uses sidebars. Prefers NIV. Guidelines/theme list (also by e-mail/Website); copy $1/9x12 SAE/3 stamps. (No ads)

Fillers: Buys 10/yr. Cartoons, games, party ideas, prayers, quizzes, short humor, word puzzles; 50-200 wds.; $5-10.

Special Needs: Craft ideas that can be used to help others. Articles on how words can help build others up or tear people down.

Tips: "Be realistic—we get a lot of fluffy stories with Pollyanna endings. We are looking for real-life-type stories that girls relate to. We mostly publish short stories but are open to short reflective articles. Know what girls face today and how they cope in their daily lives. We need angles from home life and friendships, peer pressure, and the normal growing-up challenges girls deal with."

SKIPPING STONES: A Multicultural Magazine, PO Box 3939, Eugene OR 97403. (541)342-4956. E-mail: editor@skippingstones.org. Website: www.skippingstones.org. Interfaith/multicultural. Arun N. Toké, exec. ed.; Nina Forsberg, asst. ed. A multicultural awareness and nature appreciation magazine for young people 7-17, worldwide. Bimonthly (5X) mag.; 36 pgs.; circ. 2,500. Subscription $25. 85% unsolicited freelance; 15% assigned. Query or complete ms/cover letter; no phone query; e-query/submissions OK. **PAYS IN COPIES** for 1st, electronic, and nonexclusive reprint rts. Articles (15-25/yr.) 750-1,000 wds.; fiction for teens, 750-1,000 wds. Responds in 9-13 wks. Seasonal 2-4 mos. ahead. Accepts simultaneous submissions. Accepts ms on disk or by e-mail. Regularly uses sidebars. Guidelines/theme list (also by e-mail/Website); copy $5/4 stamps. (No ads)

Poetry: Only from kids under 18. Accepts 100/yr. Any type; 3-30 lines. Submit max. 4-5 poems.

Fillers: Accepts 10-20/yr. Anecdotes, cartoons, games, quizzes, short humor, word puzzles; to 250 wds.

Columns/Departments: Accepts 10/yr. Noteworthy News (multicultural/nature/international/social, appropriate for youth), 200 wds.

Special Needs: Stories and articles on your community and country, peace, nonviolent communication, compassion, kindness, spirituality, tolerance, and giving.

Contest: Annual Book Awards for published books and authors (deadline February 1); Annual Youth Honor Awards for students 7-17 (deadline June 25). Send SASE for guidelines.

Tips: "Most of the magazine is open to freelance. We're seeking submissions by minority, multicultural, international, and/or youth writers. Do not be judgmental or preachy; be open or receptive to diverse opinions."

$SPARKLE, 1333 Alger S.E., Grand Rapids MI 49510. (616)241-5616. Fax (616)241-5558. E-mail: sarahv@gemsgc.org, or servicecenter@gemsgc.org. Website: www.gemsgc.org. GEMS Girls' Clubs (nondenominational). Sarah Vanderaa, mng. ed. To prepare girls, grades 1-3, to live out their faith and become world changers; to help girls make a difference in the world. Published 6x/yr. (October-March). Subscription $10.25. 80% unsolicited freelance; 20% assigned. Complete ms; no e-query. Pays .03/wd. on publication for 1st, reprint, or simultaneous rts. Articles 200-400 wds. (10/yr.); fiction 200-400 wds (6/yr.). Responds in 6 wks. Seasonal 10 mos. ahead. Accepts simultaneous submissions & reprints. Accepts requested ms on disk. Regularly uses sidebars. Prefers NIV. Guidelines/theme list (also by e-mail/Website); copy $1/9x12 SAE/3 stamps. (No ads)

Fillers: Buys 10/yr. Games, party ideas, prayers, quizzes, short humor; 50-200 wds.; $5-15.

Tips: "Send in pieces that teach girls how to be world-changers for Christ, or that fit our annual theme. We also are always looking for games, crafts, and recipes. Keep the writing simple. Keep activities short. Engage a 3rd grader, while being easy enough for a first-grader to understand."

$STORY MATES, Box 1212, Harrisonburg VA 22803-1212. (540)434-0768. Fax (540)433-8896. E-mail: StoryMates@clp.org. Website: www.clp.org. Mennonite/Christian Light Publications Inc. Crystal Shank, ed. For 4- to 8-yr.-olds. Weekly take-home paper; 4 pgs.; circ. 6,250. Subscription $10.40. 90% unsolicited freelance. Complete ms. Pays up to .04/wd. on acceptance for 1st rts. (.05/wd. for 1st rts., plus reprint rts.). Realistic or true stories, 800-900 wds. (50-75/yr.); picture stories 120-150 wds. Responds in 6 wks. Seasonal 6 mos. ahead. Accepts simultaneous submissions & reprints (tell when/where appeared). No disk. Requires KJV. Guidelines/theme list (also by e-mail); copy for 9x12 SAE/3 stamps. Will send questionnaire to fill out. (No ads)

Poetry: Buys 25/yr. Traditional, any length. Few story poems. Pays up to .50/line.

Fillers: Quizzes, word puzzles, craft ideas. "Need fillers that correlate with theme list; Bible related." Pays about $7.

Special Needs: True or true-to-life stories the children can relate to.

Tips: "Carefully read our guidelines and understand our conservative Mennonite applications of Bible principles." Very conservative.

**This periodical was #49 on the 2007 Top 50 Christian Publishers list.

$VENTURE, 2621 Dryden Rd., Moraine OH 45439. (937)293-1415. Fax (937)293-1310. E-mail: service@pflaum.com. Website: www.pflaum.com. Catholic. Joan Mitchell CSJ, ed. For grades 4-6. Weekly (32X) take-home paper. Not in topical listings.

$WINNER MAGAZINE, 55 W. Oak Ridge Dr., Hagerstown MD 21740. (301)393-4017. Fax (301)393-4055. E-mail: jschleifer@rhpa.org. Website: www.winnermagazine.org. The Health Connection. Jan Schleifer, ed. For elementary school children, grades 4-6; Saying No to Drugs, and Yes to Life. Monthly (during school year) mag.; 16 pgs.; circ. 9,000. Subscription $18.25. 20% unsolicited freelance; 80% assigned. Complete ms. Accepts full mss by e-mail. Pays $80 on acceptance for 1st rts. Articles 600-650 wds. (25-30/yr.); fiction 600-650 wds. (18/yr.) Responds in 4-13 wks. Seasonal 6-8 mos. ahead. Accepts simultaneous submissions & reprints (tell when/where appeared). Prefers e-mail submission (attached file). Kill fee 50%. Guidelines (also on Website); copy $2/9x12 SAE/3 stamps. (No ads)

Tips: "*Winner* is a positive lifestyle magazine. Most open to self-help stories, factuals on tobacco, alcohol, and other drugs—in story format (include sources), with a catchy ending. Each article needs at least three questions relating to the story and a puzzle/activity. We use celebrity pieces about drug-free young people who would be good role models. Need health articles on nutrition and exercise (have enough on sleep and drinking water). Articles on the dangers of using alcohol, tobacco, and drugs." Do not use Bible verses because magazine used in public schools.

CHRISTIAN EDUCATION/LIBRARY MARKETS

$CATECHIST, 2621 Dryden Rd., 3rd Fl., Dayton OH 45439. (937)847-5900. Fax (314)638-6812. E-mail: kdotterweich@peterli.com. Website: www.catechist.com. Catholic; Peter Li Education Group. Kass Dotterweich, ed. For Catholic school teachers and parish volunteer catechists. Mag. published 7X/yr.; 52 pgs.; circ. 52,000. Subscription $26.95. 30% unsolicited freelance; 70% assigned. Query (preferred) or complete ms. Pays $25-150 on publication. Articles 1,200 wds. Responds in 9-18 wks. Guidelines (also on Website); copy $3.

Tips: "Most open to short features, how-to lesson plans, and crafts."

CATHOLIC LIBRARY WORLD, Alumnae Library, Elm College, 291 Springfield St., Chicopee MA 01013-2839. (413)265-2354. Fax (413)594-7418. E-mail: gallagherm@elms.edu. Website: www.cathla.org. Catholic Library Assn. Sr. Mary E. Gallagher SSJ, gen. ed. For libraries at all levels—preschool to postsecondary to academic, parish, public, and private. Quarterly jour.; 80 pgs.; circ. 1,000. Subscription $60/$85 foreign. 90% unsolicited freelance; 10% assigned. Query or complete ms; phone/fax/e-query OK. **PAYS 1 COPY.** Articles; book/video reviews, 300-500 wds. Accepts requested ms on disk. Uses some sidebars. No guidelines; copy for 9x12 SAE. (Ads)

Special Needs: Topics of interest to academic libraries, high school and children's libraries, parish and community libraries, archives, and library education. Reviewers cover areas such as theology, spirituality, pastoral, professional, juvenile books and material, and media.

Tips: "Review section considers taking on new reviewers who are experts in field of librarianship, theology, and professional studies. No payment except a free copy of the book or materials reviewed. Query us by mail or e-mail."

$CHILDREN'S MINISTRY MAGAZINE, 1515 Cascade Ave., Loveland CO 80539. Toll-free (800)447-1070. Fax (970)292-4360. E-mail: jhooks@cmmag.com. Website: www.childrens ministry.com. Group Publishing/nondenominational. Christine Yount, exec. ed.; submit to Jennifer Hooks, mng. ed. (jhooks@cmmag.com). The leading resource for adults who work with children (ages 0-12) in the church. Bimonthly mag.; 140 pgs.; circ. 60,000. Subscription $24.95. 40% unsolicited freelance; 60% assigned. Complete ms/cover letter; e-query OK. Pays $25-400 on acceptance for all & electronic rts. Articles 50-1,800 wds. (250-300/yr.). Responds in 8-10 wks. Seasonal 6-9 mos. ahead. No simultaneous submissions or reprints. Accepts requested ms by e-mail (attached or copied into message). Regularly uses sidebars. Also accepts submissions from children & teens. Sometimes pays kill fee. Prefers NLT. Guidelines (also by e-mail/Website); copy $2/9x12 SAE/$2.13 postage (mark Media Mail). (Ads)

Fillers: Buys 25-50/yr. Cartoons, kid quotes; 25-50 wds.; $25-60.

Columns/Departments: Submit to Carmen Kamrath (ckamrath@cmmag.com). Buys 200+/yr. Age-level insights (age-appropriate ideas); Family Ministry (family ideas); Reaching Out (outreach ideas); 150-250 wds. Teacher Telegram (ideas for teachers); For Parents Only (parenting ideas); 150-300 wds.; $40-150. Complete ms.

Special Needs: Seasonal ideas, outreach ideas, volunteer management, and family ministry. Always looking for new ideas, crafts, games, and activities.

Tips: "All areas open to freelancers. Start small—ideas, activities, and personal essays. Or go big—wow us with a profoundly inspiring article that fits the magazine's makeup. We're looking for stand-out ideas and the very latest in this important ministry area. If you're in the trenches, we want to hear from you. We seek features from experts in practice or in theory. No poetry or fiction."

**This periodical was #8 on the 2007 Top 50 Christian Publishers list (#5 in 2006, #1 in 2005, #14 in 2004).

CHRISTIAN EARLY EDUCATION, PO Box 65130, Colorado Springs CO 80962-5130. (719)528-6906. Fax (719)531-0631. E-mail: earlyeducation@acsi.org. Website: www.acsi.org. Assn. of Christian Schools Intl. D'Arcy Maher, sr. ed. Equips individuals serving children ages 0-5 from a biblical perspective. Quarterly mag.; 40 pgs.; circ. 5,500. Subscription $14. 10% unsolicited freelance; 90% assigned. Query; phone/fax/e-query OK. **PAYS IN COPIES.** Not copyrighted. Articles 600-1,800 wds. (12-15/yr.). Responds in 4 wks. Seasonal 10 mos. ahead. Accepts reprints (tell when/where appeared). Prefers e-mail submissions (attached file). Does not use sidebars. Prefers NIV. Guidelines/theme list (also by e-mail); copy $1.50/9x12 SAE. (Ads)

Columns/Departments: Accepts up to 10/yr. Staff Training (training for teachers of young children, to use in staff meeting), 400 wds.; Parents' Place (material suitable for parents of young children), 400 wds. Complete ms.

Tips: "Most open to Unique Perspectives, Footprints in Development, Professional Edge, Resource Review, Heart 2 Heart, and Field Trip." (These appear to be columns.)

$CHRISTIAN EDUCATORS JOURNAL, 73 Highland Ave., St. Catherines ON L2R 4H9, Canada. Phone/fax (905)684-3991. E-mail: bert.witvoet@sympatico.ca. Website: www.CEJonline .com. Christian Educators Journal Assn. Bert Witvoet, mng. ed. For educators in Christian day schools at the elementary, secondary, and college levels. Quarterly jour.; 36 pgs.; circ. 4,200. Subscription $7.50 (c/o James Rauwerda, 2045 Boston St. S.E., Grand Rapids MI 49506,

616-243-2112). 50% unsolicited freelance; 50% assigned. Query; phone/e-query OK. Pays $30 on publication for one-time rts. Articles 750-1,500 wds. (20/yr.); fiction 750-1,500 wds. Responds in 5 wks. Seasonal 4 mos. ahead. Accepts simultaneous submissions & reprints. Guidelines/theme list; copy $1.50 or 9x12 SAE/4 stamps. (Limited ads)

Poetry: Buys 6/yr. On teaching day school; 4-30 lines; $10. Submit max. 5 poems.

Tips: "No articles on Sunday school, only Christian day school. Most open to theme topics and features."

THE CHRISTIAN LIBRARIAN, Ryan Library, PLNU, 3600 Lomaland Dr., San Diego CA 92106. (619)849-2208. Fax (619)849-7024. E-mail: apowell@pointloma.edu. Website: www.acl .org. Assn. of Christian Librarians. Anne-Elizabeth Powell, ed-in-chief. Geared toward academic librarians of the Christian faith. Quarterly (3X) jour.; 40 pgs.; circ. 800. Subscription $30. 50% unsolicited freelance; 50% assigned. E-mail; fax/e-query OK. **NO PAYMENT** for one-time rts. Not copyrighted. Articles 1,000-3,500 wds.; research articles to 5,000 wds. (6/yr.); reviews 150-300 wds. Responds in 5 wks. Accepts simultaneous submissions & reprints (tell when/where appeared). Prefers accepted ms by e-mail (attached file). Uses some sidebars. Guidelines (also by e-mail/Website); copy $5. (No ads)

Fillers: Anecdotes, ideas, short humor; 25-300 wds.

Special Needs: Articles dealing with the intersection of faith and professional duties in libraries. Interviews with library leaders, profiles of Christian academic libraries, international librarianship. Deal with all topics as they can be applied to librarianship.

Tips: "Reviews are a good way to gain publication. Write a tight, well-researched article about a current 'hot topic' in librarianship as it is defined in a Christian setting; or ethics of librarianship. Articles on 'how we did it right' are good entry publications."

CHRISTIAN SCHOOL EDUCATION, PO Box 65130, Colorado Springs CO 80962-5130. (719)528-6906. Fax (719)531-0631. E-mail: cse@acsi.org. Website: www.acsi.org. Association of Christian Schools, Intl. Steven C. Babbitt, ed. To provide accurate information as well as provoke thought and reflection about the ministry of Christian school education worldwide. 5X/yr. mag.; 56 pgs.; circ. 70,000. Subscription $16. 2% unsolicited freelance; 98% assigned. Query preferred; phone query OK. **NO PAYMENT.** Asks for photocopy permission for member schools. Articles 600-2,400 wds.; book reviews 600 wds. Responds in 12 wks. No seasonal material. Accepts simultaneous submissions & reprints (tell when/where appeared). Requires submissions by disk or e-mail (attached file). Regularly uses sidebars. Prefers NIV, NKJV. Guidelines by e-mail/Website. Incomplete topical listings. (Ads)

Tips: "Most articles for publication are solicited, therefore freelancers 'breaking into publication' is highly unlikely."

$CHURCH LIBRARIES, 9118 W. Elmwood Dr., #1G, Niles IL 60714-5820. (847)296-3964. Fax (847)296-0754. E-mail: linjohnson@ECLAlibraries.org. Website: www.ECLAlibraries.org. Evangelical Church Library Assn. Lin Johnson, mng ed. To assist church librarians in setting up, maintaining, and promoting church libraries and media centers. Quarterly mag.; 32-36 pgs.; circ. 450. Subscription $35. 25% unsolicited freelance. Complete ms or queries by e-mail only. Pays .05/wd. on acceptance for 1st or reprint rts. Articles 500-1,000 wds. (24-30/yr.); book/music/DVD reviews by assignment, 75-150 wds., free product. Responds in 4-6 wks. Seasonal 6 mos. ahead. Accepts reprints (tell when/where appeared). Requires e-mail submission. Regularly uses sidebars. Prefers NIV. Guidelines (also by e-mail/Website); copy for 9x12 SAE/4 stamps. (Ads)

Tips: "Talk to church librarians or get involved in library or reading programs. Most open to articles and promotional ideas; profiles of church libraries; roundups on best books in a category (query on topic first). Book reviews assigned; need for reviewers fluctuates; if interested e-mail for availability."

CONGREGATIONAL LIBRARIES TODAY (formerly Church & Synagogue Libraries), 2920 S.W. Dolph Ct., Portland OR 97219-4055. (503)244-6919. Fax (503)977-3734. E-mail: csla@worldaccessnet.com. Website: www.cslainfo.org. Church and Synagogue Library Assn. Judith Janzen, exec. dir. To help librarians run congregational libraries. Bimonthly; 24 pgs.; circ. 3,000. Subscription $35, $40 Cdn., $45 foreign. Query; no e-query. **NO PAYMENT.** Requires accepted ms on disk. Articles. Book & video reviews 1-2 paragraphs. Guidelines; copy available. (Ads)

Fillers: Ideas.

$GROUP MAGAZINE, Box 481, Loveland CO 80539. (970)669-3836. Fax (970)292-4373. E-mail: rlawrence@grouppublishing.com, or croberts@grouppublishing.com. Website: www.grouppublishing.com, or www.groupmag.com. Rick Lawrence, ed.; Chris Roberts, asst. ed. For leaders of Christian youth groups; to supply ideas, practical help, inspiration, and training for youth leaders. Bimonthly mag.; 85 pgs.; circ. 55,000. Subscription $29.95. 50% unsolicited freelance; 50% assigned. Query; fax/e-query OK. Pays $150-350 on acceptance for all rts. Articles 175-2,000 wds. (100/yr.). Responds in 6-9 wks. Seasonal 5 mos. ahead. No simultaneous submissions or reprints. Accepts e-mail submissions (copied into message). No kill fee. Uses some sidebars. Any Bible version. Guidelines on Website; copy $2/9x12 SAE/3 stamps. (Ads)

Fillers: Buys 5-10/yr. Cartoons, games, ideas; $40.

Columns/Departments: Buys 30-40/yr. Try This One (youth group activities), to 300 wds.; Hands-on-Help (tips for leaders), to 175 wds.; Strange But True (profiles remarkable youth ministry experience), 500 wds. Pays $50. Complete ms.

Special Needs: Articles geared toward working with teens; programming ideas; youth ministry issues.

Tips: "We're always looking for effective youth ministry ideas, especially those tested by youth leaders in the field. Most open to Hands-On-Help column (use real-life examples, personal experiences, practical tips, scripture, and self-quizzes or checklists). We buy the idea, not the verbatim submission."

**This periodical was #36 on the 2007 Top 50 Christian Publishers list.

IDEAS UNLIMITED FOR EFFECTIVE CHILDREN'S MINISTRY, PO Box 12624, Roanoke VA 24027. (540)342-7511. E-mail: ccmbbr@juno.com. Website: www.CreativeChristianMinistries.com. Betty Robertson, ed. For anyone ministering to children. Monthly e-zine; circ. 4,200. Subscription free. 25% unsolicited freelance; 75% assigned. E-query or e-submissions only. **NO PAYMENT** for 1st, one-time, or simultaneous rts. Not copyrighted. Articles 100-600 wds. Responds in 3 wks. Seasonal 6 mos. ahead. Accepts simultaneous submissions & reprints. Guidelines by e-mail.

$THE JOURNAL OF ADVENTIST EDUCATION, 12501 Old Columbia Pike, Silver Spring MD 20904-6600. (301)680-5075. Fax (301)622-9627. E-mail: rumbleb@gc.adventist.org. Website: http://education.gc.adventist.org/jae. General Conference of Seventh-day Adventists. Beverly J. Robinson-Rumble, ed. For Seventh-day teachers teaching in the church's school system, kindergarten to university. Bimonthly (5X) jour.; 48 pgs.; circ. 10,800. Selected articles are translated into French, Spanish, and Portuguese for a twice-yearly International Edition. Subscription $17.25 (add $1 outside U.S.). Percentage of freelance varies. Query or complete ms; phone/fax/e-query OK. Pays $25-300 on publication for 1st North American and translation rts., and permission to post on Website. Articles 1,000-2,000 wds. (2-20/yr.). Responds in 6-17 wks. Seasonal 6 mos. ahead. Accepts reprints (tell when/where appeared). Accepts requested ms on disk. Regularly uses sidebars. Guidelines e-mail/Website; copy for 10x12 SAE/5 stamps.

Fillers: Cartoons only, no payment.

Special Needs: "All articles in the context of parochial schools (not Sunday school tips); professional enrichment and teaching tips for Christian teachers. Need feature articles."

JOURNAL OF CHRISTIAN EDUCATION, PO Box 602, Epping NSW 1710, Australia. Phone/fax 61 2 9868 6644. E-mail: business@acfe.org.au, submit to editor@acfe.org.au. Website: http://jce.acfe.org.au. Australian Christian Forum on Education Inc. Dr. Grant Maple & Dr. Ian Lambert, eds. To consider the implications of the Christian faith for the entire field of education. Triannual jour.; 80 pgs.; circ. 400. Subscription $50 AUS, $45 U.S. for individuals; $64 AUS, $60 U.S. for institutions. 40% unsolicited freelance; 60% assigned. Complete ms/cover letter; phone/fax/e-query OK. **NO PAYMENT** for one-time rts. Articles 3,000-5,000 wds. (6/yr.); book reviews 400-600 wds. Responds in 4 wks. Seasonal 6 mos. ahead. Accepts requested ms on disk or by e-mail (attached file). Does not use sidebars. Also accepts submissions from children & teens. Free guidelines (also on Website) & copy. (No ads)

Tips: "Send for a sample copy, study guidelines, and submit manuscript. Most open to articles or book reviews. Open to any educational issue from a Christian perspective."

JOURNAL OF CHRISTIANITY AND FOREIGN LANGUAGES, Dept. of Germanic and Asian Languages, Calvin College, 3201 Burton St. S.E., Grand Rapids MI 49546. (616)957-8609. Fax (616)526-8583. E-mail: dsmith@calvin.edu. Website: www.spu.edu/orgs/NACFLA. North American Christian Foreign Language Assn. Dr. David Smith, ed. Scholarly articles dealing with the relationship between Christian belief and the teaching of foreign languages and literatures; mainly for college faculty. Annual jour.; 100 pgs.; circ. 100. Subscription $16 (indiv.), $27 (library). Open to freelance. Complete ms/cover letter; phone/fax/e-query OK. **PAYS IN COPIES/OFFPRINTS.** Articles 2,000-4,000 wds. (6/yr.); book/video reviews, 750 wds. Responds in 12-16 wks. Rarely accepts reprints (tell when/where appeared). Requires requested ms on disk or by e-mail (attached file). Does not use sidebars. Guidelines (also on Website); no copy. (Ads)

Columns/Departments: Accepts 1-3/yr. Forum (position papers, pedagogical suggestions), 1,000-1,500 wds.

Tips: "Most open to Forum column; see www.spu.edu/orgs/nacfla/for guidelines. Also see Website for abstracts and samples. Book reviews and opinion pieces must be related to Christianity and education in foreign languages and literature."

JOURNAL OF EDUCATION & CHRISTIAN BELIEF, Dept. of Germanic Languages, Calvin College, 3201 Burton St. S.E., Grand Rapids MI 49546. (616)957-8609. Fax (616)526-8583. E-mail: jecb@stapleford-centre.org. Website: www.jecb.org. Association of Christian Teachers. Editors: Dr. David Smith (use above address) & Dr. John Shortt, 1 Kiteleys Green, Leighton Buzzard, Beds LU7 3LD, United Kingdom. Phone +44 0 1525 379709. Semiannual jour.; 80 pgs.; circ. 400. Subscription $41.40. 80% unsolicited freelance; 20% assigned. Complete ms/cover letter; e-query OK. **NO PAYMENT** for 1st rts. Articles 5,000 wds. (12/yr.). Responds in 4-8 wks. Accepts reprints (tell when/where appeared). Prefers requested ms on disk or by e-mail (attached file). Does not use sidebars. Guidelines by e-mail; no copy. (No ads)

Tips: "Most open to reviews of books related to education and Christian belief; should be expert reviews addressed to an academic audience. Must address Christian education in competent, scholarly manner."

JOURNAL OF RESEARCH ON CHRISTIAN EDUCATION, Andrews University, Information Services Bldg., Ste. 101, Berrien Springs MI 49104. (269)471-6080. Fax (269)471-6224. E-mail: jrce@andrews.edu. Website: www.andrews.edu/jrce. Andrews University. Larry D. Burton, ed.; Janet Mallory, book rev. ed. Research related to Christian schooling (all levels) within the Protestant tradition. Biannual jour.; 150+ pgs.; circ. 400. Subscription $60. 100% unsolicited freelance. Complete ms/cover letter; phone/fax/e-query OK. **NO PAYMENT.** Articles

13-26, double-spaced pgs. (12-18/yr.); book reviews, 2-5 pgs. Responds in 1 wk.; decision within 6 mos. (goes through review board). No simultaneous submissions. Requires requested ms on disk. Does not use sidebars. Guidelines (also by e-mail). (No ads)

Tips: "This is a research journal. All manuscripts should conform to standards of scholarly inquiry. Manuscripts are submitted to a panel of 3 experts for their review. Publication decision is based on recommendation of reviewers. Authors should submit manuscripts written in scholarly style and focused on Christian schooling. Submit 5 copies along with a 100-word abstract and 30-word bio-sketch indicating institutional affiliation."

$KIDS' MINISTRY IDEAS, 55 W. Oak Ridge Dr., Hagerstown MD 21740. (301)393-4082. Fax (301)393-3209. E-mail: KidsMin@rhpa.org. Seventh-day Adventist. Candy DeVore, ed. For adults leading children (birth-8th grade) to Christ. Quarterly mag.; 32 pgs.; circ. 2,500. Complete ms/cover letter; e-query OK. Accepts full ms by e-mail. Guidelines on request.

$MOMENTUM, 1077—30th St. N.W., Ste. 100, Washington DC 20007-3852. (202)337-6232. Fax (202)333-6706. E-mail: momentum@ncea.org. Website: www.ncea.org. National Catholic Educational Assn. Brian Gray, ed. Features outstanding programs, issues, and research in Catholic education. Quarterly jour.; 96 pgs.; circ. 23,000. Subscription $20 (free to members). 50% unsolicited freelance; 30% assigned. Query or complete ms; phone/e-query OK. Pays $50-100 on publication for 1st rts. Articles 500-1,500 wds. (25-30/yr.); book reviews 400 wds. ($50). No simultaneous submissions. Accepts full mss by e-mail. Regularly uses sidebars. Guidelines/theme list (also by e-mail/Website); copy $5/9x12 SAE/$2.13 postage (mark "Media Mail"). (Ads)

Columns/Departments: From the Field (success ideas that can be used by other Catholic schools); DRE Directions (guidance for directors of religious education programs); both 700 wds.

Special Needs: Religious education; teaching methods; Catholic school administration.

Tips: "Always interested in parish-based religious education programs, especially for adolescents or whole-family catecheses. Good opportunity for freelancers because they are close to the sources."

$PRESCHOOL PLAYHOUSE, PO Box 436987, Chicago IL 60643. (708)868-7100. Fax (708)868-7105. Website: www.urbanministries.com. Urban Ministries Inc. K. Steward, ed. Sunday school magazine with activities for 2- to 5-year-olds with accompanying teacher's manual. Quarterly mag. for teachers; take-home paper for students; 96 pgs. Subscription $4.99 (teacher/64 pgs.) and $2.85 (student). 80% assigned. Query/clips; fax/e-query OK. Pays $150, 120 days after acceptance, for all rts. Articles 6,000 characters for teacher, 2,900 characters for student (4/yr.). Responds in 4 wks. Seasonal 6 mos. ahead. Accepts simultaneous submissions. Requires requested ms on disk. Prefers NIV. Guidelines; copy $2.25/#10 SASE. (No ads)

$RESOURCE, 6401 The Paseo, Kansas City MO 64131. (816)333-7000, ext. 2343. Fax (816)363-7092. E-mail: ssmith@nazarene.org. Website: www.nazarene.org. Church of the Nazarene. Shirley Smith, ed. asst. To provide information, training, and inspiration to those who are involved in ministering within the Christian Life and Sunday school departments of the local church. Quarterly mag.; 32 pgs.; circ. 25,000. Subscription $6.25. 95% unsolicited freelance; 5% assigned. Complete ms; phone/fax/e-query OK. Pays .05/wd. on publication for all, one-time, reprint, or simultaneous rts. Articles 1,000-2,000 wds. (150/yr.). Seasonal 9-12 mos. ahead. Accepts simultaneous submissions & reprints. Accepts requested ms on disk or by e-mail (attached or copied into message). Uses some sidebars. Prefers NIV, NRSV. Guidelines/theme list (also by e-mail); copy for 9x12 SAE/2 stamps. (No ads)

Tips: "Focus on issues, skills, concerns central to a particular age group; how-tos, examples, illustrations; skill development; roles of teachers/leaders; organizational tips."

$RTJ: The Magazine for Catechist Formation, PO Box 6015, New London CT 06320. Toll-free (800)321-0411. Fax (860)437-6246. E-mail: nwagner@twentythirdpublications.com. Website: www.twentythirdpublications.com. Catholic Publishers/Bayard. Nick Wagner, ed. For volunteer religion teachers who need practical, hands-on information as well as spiritual and theological background for teaching religion to kindergarten through high school. 7X/yr. mag.; 40 pgs.; circ. 32,000. Subscription $22.95. 40% unsolicited freelance; 60% assigned. Complete ms/cover letter; fax/e-query OK. Pays $50-125 on acceptance for 1st rts. Articles to 1,300 wds. (40/yr.); plays. Responds in 2-4 wks. Seasonal 6 mos. ahead. Accepts simultaneous submissions & rarely accepts reprints (tell when/where appeared). Prefers requested ms on disk or by e-mail (attached file). No kill fee. Regularly uses sidebars. Prefers NRSV (Catholic edition). Guidelines/theme list (also by e-mail); copy for 9x12 SAE/3 first class stamps. (Ads)

Fillers: Buys 20-30/yr. Anecdotes (about teaching), games, ideas, quizzes, crafts, successful class activities (especially seasonal); 50-300 wds.; $20-50.

Special Needs: Partnering with families; teaching the sacraments; prayer and prayer services; celebrating the seasons; spiritual formation for religion teachers/catechists; successful faith formation programs.

Tips: "Most open to articles on teaching skills; successful activity ideas/lessons; involving parents in religious education, especially in sacrament preparation; celebrating Advent and Lent; spiritual formation. Looking for clear, concise articles written from experience, for catechists and religion teachers (K-12). Articles should help readers move from theory/doctrine to concrete application." Unsolicited manuscripts not returned without an SASE.

**This periodical was #46 on the 2007 Top 50 Christian Publishers list (#49 in 2006, #43 in 2005, #43 in 2004, #22 in 2003).

$TEACHERS OF VISION MAGAZINE, 227 N. Magnolia Ave., Ste. 2, Anaheim CA 92801. E-mail: tov@ceai.org. Website: www.ceai.org. Christian Educators Assn., Intl. Judy Turpen, contributing ed.; F. L. Turpen, editorial dir.; Denise Trippett, mng. ed. To encourage, equip, and empower Christian educators serving in public and private schools. Quarterly mag.; circ. 10,000. Subscription $20. 50% unsolicited freelance; 50% assigned. Query; prefers e-query. Pays $40 ($30 for reprints) on publication for 1st or reprint rts. Articles 600-2,500 wds. (15-20/yr.); mini-features 400-750 wds., $25; very few book reviews 50 wds., (pays copies). Responds in 4-12 wks. Seasonal 4 mos. ahead. Accepts simultaneous submissions & reprints (tell when/where appeared). Accepts requested ms on disk or by e-mail (attached or copied into message). Regularly uses sidebars. Any Bible version. Guidelines/theme list on Website; copy for 9x12 SAE/4 stamps. (Ads)

Poetry: Accepts 2-3/yr. Free verse, haiku, light verse, traditional; 4-16 lines. Submit max. 3 poems.

Fillers: Educational only.

Special Needs: Legal and other issues in public education. Interviews; classroom resource reviews; living out your faith in your work.

Tips: "Know public education; write from a positive perspective as our readers are involved in public education by calling and choice. Most open to tips for teachers for living out their faith in the classroom in legally appropriate ways. All topics covered must be public-education related."

$TEACH KIDS! PO Box 348, Warrenton MO 63383-0348. (636)456-4321. Fax (636)456-9935. E-mail: editor@teachkidsmag.com. Website: www.teachkidsmag.com. Child Evangelism Fellowship. Elsie C. Lippy, ed. To equip Christians to lead the world's children (ages 4-11) to Christ and disciple them in the Word of God. Bimonthly mag.; 64 pgs.; circ. 12,000. Subscription $24. 25% unsolicited freelance; 75% assigned. Complete ms; no phone/fax query;

e-query OK. Pays $75-100 or up to .15/wd. for articles; $75-85 for fiction within 60 days of acceptance for all, first, reprint, or electronic rts. Articles 600 wds. (24/yr.); fiction 800-850 wds. (12/yr.). Responds in 4-6 wks. Seasonal 1 yr. ahead. Accepts few reprints (tell when/where appeared). Disk or e-mail submission OK. Kill fee 30%. Prefers NIV. Guidelines (also by e-mail/Website); copy $3/9x12 SAE. (Ads)

Easy Ideas: Complete ms, 250-300 wds.; $35-50 for teaching tips, object lessons, missions incentives, seasonal ideas, crafts with spiritual focus, attendance boosters, verse drills, and lesson reviews that teachers can use with children ages 4-11.

Special Needs: "Short (100-400 words) creative teaching tips and easy-to-prepare ideas for evangelizing and discipling kids, ages 4-11. We need teachers to share true incidents from the classroom that will encourage and motivate other teachers in their children's ministry."

Tips: "Fictional read-aloud stories and Easy Ideas are good areas to break into. A writer should be actively working with children in order to gain fresh anecdotes and insight to share with the readers. Fiction should be written at the third- to fourth-grade level. Feature contemporary settings with scriptural solutions to problems faced by children."

**This periodical was #31 on the 2007 Top 50 Christian Publishers list (#46 in 2005, #45 in 2004).

$TODAY'S CATHOLIC TEACHER, 2621 Dryden Rd., Dayton OH 45439. (937)293-1415. Fax (937)293-1310. E-mail: mnoschang@peterli.com. Website: www.catholicteacher.com. Catholic; Peter Li Education Group. Mary C. Noschang, ed. Directed to personal and professional concerns of teachers and administrators in K-12 Catholic schools. Monthly mag. (6X during school yr.); 60 pgs.; circ. 45,000. Subscription $14.95. 30% unsolicited freelance; 30% assigned. Query; phone/fax/e-query OK. Pays $100-250 on publication for 1st rts. Articles 600-800, 1,000-1,200, or 1,200-1,500 wds. (40-50/yr.). Responds in 18 wks. Seasonal 3 mos. ahead. Accepts simultaneous submissions & reprints (tell when/where appeared). Prefers requested ms by e-mail (attached file). Regularly uses sidebars. Guidelines/theme list (also on Website); copy $3/9x12 SAE. (Ads)

Special Needs: Activity pages teachers can copy and pass out to students to work on. Try to provide classroom-ready material teachers can use to supplement curriculum.

Tips: "Looking for material teachers in grades 3-9 can use to supplement curriculum material. Most open to articles or lesson plans."

**This periodical was #35 on the 2007 Top 50 Christian Publishers list.

$YOUTH AND CHRISTIAN EDUCATION LEADERSHIP, 1080 Montgomery Ave., Cleveland TN 37311. (423)478-7597. Fax (423)478-7616. E-mail: wanda_griffith@pathwaypress.org. Website: www.pathwaypress.org. Church of God/Pathway Press. Wanda Griffith, ed. To inform, equip, and inspire Christian education teachers and leaders. Quarterly mag.; 32 pgs.; circ. 10,000. Subscription $8. 10% unsolicited freelance; 90% assigned. Complete ms/cover letter; phone/e-query OK. Accepts full mss by e-mail. Pays $25-50 on publication for 1st or one-time rts. Articles 500-1,000 wds. (20/yr.). Responds in 2 wks. Seasonal 4 mos. ahead. Accepts simultaneous submissions; no reprints. Accepts requested ms on disk or by e-mail (attached file). No kill fee. Uses some sidebars. Prefers NIV. Guidelines (also by e-mail/Website); copy $1/9x12 SAE. (No ads)

Fillers: Buys 4/yr. Cartoons, ideas, party ideas, tips, word puzzles; 250-300 wds. Pays $35.

Special Needs: Most open to how-to articles relating to Christian education. Local church ministry stories; articles on youth ministry, children's ministry, Christian education, and Sunday school.

**2004 EPA Award of Excellence—Denominational.

DAILY DEVOTIONAL MARKETS

Due to the nature of the daily devotional market, the following market listings give a limited amount of information. Because most of these markets assign all material, they do not wish to be listed in the usual way.

If you are interested in writing daily devotionals, send to the following markets for guidelines and sample copies, write up sample devotionals to fit each one's particular format, and send to the editor with a request for an assignment. **DO NOT** submit any other type of material to these markets unless indicated.

ANCHOR DEVOTIONAL, PO Box 79997, Riverside CA 92513-1997. Toll-free (800)65HAVEN. Fax (951)710-1115. E-mail: ministry@haventoday.org. Website: www.haventoday.org/anchor.php. Haven Ministries. Joyce Gibson, ed. Monthly devotional mag. Devotions 200 wds. Assigns one month of devotions on a theme (author picks theme). Query first for theme.

CLEAR LIVING, 114 Bush Rd., Nashville TN 37217. (615)361-1221. Fax (615)367-0535. E-mail: dianne@randallhouse.com, or through Website: www.randallhouse.com. Randall House Publications. Dianne Sargent, ed. For adults 35-55 that encourages application of Scripture through devotions and experience, instructional, and inspirational articles. Quarterly mag.; circ. 28,000. Subscription $20. Open to freelance. Query preferred. Devotionals.

$CLOSER WALK, 4201 N. Peachtree Rd., Atlanta GA 30341. (770)458-9300. Fax (770)454-9313. E-mail: pubsinfo@walkthru.org. Website: www.walkthru.org. Walk Thru the Bible. Read through the New Testament in a year. Monthly mag. Requires NKJV.

DAILY DEVOTIONS FOR THE DEAF, 21199 Greenview Rd., Council Bluffs IA 51503-4190. (712)322-5493. Fax (712)322-7792. E-mail: JoKrueger@deafmissions.com. Website: www.deafmissions.com. Jo Krueger, ed. Quarterly. Circ. 26,000. Prefers to see completed devotionals; 225-250 wds. **NO PAYMENT.** E-mail submissions OK.

$DEVOTIONS, 8805 Governor's Hill Dr., Ste. 400, Cincinnati OH 45249-3319. (513)931-4050. Fax (513)931-0904. E-mail: gwilde1@cfl.rr.com. Website: www.standardpub.com. Gary Allen, ed. Assigned by work-for-hire contract to previously published writers only. Query by e-mail only. Pays $20/devotion. Send list of credits rather than a sample.

+E-NCOURAGEMENT/HEART-TO-HEART, PO Box 312, Champlin MN 55316. E-mail: e-encouragement@e-ncouragement.com, or e-ncouragement316@cfaith.com. Website: www.e-ncouragement.com. Chris & Jennie Courtney, eds. Twice weekly e-zine or daily devotional called *Heart-to-Heart.* Subscription free online. Open to unsolicited freelance. Complete ms; submit via e-mail (e-ncouragement316@cfaith.com). **NO PAYMENT.** Short articles and devotionals. No guidelines; copy online.

Tips: "We ask that contributors sign up for a free subscription to *E-ncouragement.*"

$FORWARD DAY BY DAY, 300 W. Fourth St., Cincinnati OH 45202-2665. Toll-free (800)543-1813. (513)721-6659. Fax (513)721-0729. E-mail: rschmidt@forwarddaybyday.com. Website: www.forwardmovement.org. Richard H. Schmidt, ed./dir. Also online version. Send a couple of samples and request an assignment. Likes author to complete an entire month's worth of devotions. No e-mail submissions. Length: 215 wds. Pays $300 for a month of devotions. Accepts reprints. (No ads)

FRUIT OF THE VINE, Barclay Press, 211 N. Meridian St., #101, Newberg OR 97132. (503)538-9775. Fax (503)554-8597. E-mail: info@barclaypress.com. E-mail submissions accepted at phampton@barclaypress.com. Website: www.barclaypress.com. Editorial team: Susan Fawver, Sherry Macy, Paula Hampton. Subscription $17. Send samples and request assignment. Prefers 250-290 wds. **PAYS FREE SUBSCRIPTION & 6 COPIES.** Guidelines.

$INDEED, 4201 N. Peachtree Rd., Atlanta GA 30341. (770)454-9300. Fax (770)454-9313. E-mail: indeed@walkthru.org. Website: www.walkthru.org. Walk Thru the Bible. Chris Tiegreen, ed. Devotional readings for adults. Bimonthly mag.; circ. 26,000. By assignment only. (No ads)

**2007 EPA Award of Merit—Devotional; 2005, 2004 EPA Award of Excellence-Devotional.

$LIGHT FROM THE WORD, PO Box 50434, Indianapolis IN 46250-0434. (317)774-7900. E-mail: submissions@wesleyan.org. Website: www.wesleyan.org/wph. Wesleyan. Mark Moore, ed. Devotions 215 wds. Pays $100 for seven devotions. Electronic submissions only. Send a couple of sample devotions to fit their format and request an assignment. No reprints.

MUSTARD SEED MINISTRIES DEVOTIONALS (formerly Pointing the World to Jesus Christ), 4854 W. 350S, Berne IN 46711. (260)334-5552. Fax (260)334-5993. E-mail: jema@only internet.net. Website: www.mustardseedministries.org. MustardSeed Ministries Inc. Robert Sutter, ed. Devotional mag. 100% unsolicited freelance. Complete ms; e-mail submissions preferred. **PAYS A UNIQUE, ATTRACTIVE PLAQUE.** Devotions 225-275 wds. Guidelines on Website.

Tips: "We do not return any submissions and prefer that they are e-mailed to us. We are looking for submissions that are biblically based. Most of us have a story to tell about how Christ touched our life in some situation that others in this world would benefit from; please send this to us."

$MY DAILY VISITOR, 200 Noll Plaza, Huntington IN 46750. (260)356-8400. Fax (260)356-8472. E-mail: mdvisitor@osv.com. Website: www.osv.com. Catholic. Submit to The Editor. Scripture meditations based on the day's Catholic Mass readings. Bimonthly devotional booklet. Open to freelance. Query by mail or e-mail/clips. Pays $500 for a month's devotions (28-31 days), plus 5 copies, on acceptance for one-time rts. Not copyrighted. Devotions 125-135 wds. ea. (assigns a full month at a time).

+OUR DAILY BREAD, PO Box 2222, Grand Rapids MI 49501-2222. Canadian address: Box 1622, Windsor ON N9A 6Z7, Canada. (616)974-2210. Website: www.rcb.net. RCB Ministries. Daily devotions.

OUR JOURNEY, PO Box 308, Grand Rapids MI 49501. (616)974-2663. Fax (616)957-5741. E-mail: articles@ourjourneyonline.org. Website: www.ourjourneyonline.org. RBC Ministries. Tom Felton, ed. (tfelten@rbc.org). Devotionals for today's young adult; features meditations on God's leading through life and community participation. Monthly devotional; 64 pgs. Subscription $5 or for donation. Open to unsolicited freelance. Complete ms (as a Word attachment). **PAYS 10 COPIES.** Articles/devotions 325-350 wds. Guidelines on Website. (No ads)

Special Needs: Art and photographs. See guidelines.

Tips: "Submit one article at a time, once a month."

PENNED FROM THE HEART, 55 W. Connelly Blvd., #612, Sharon PA 16146. (724)981-0963. E-mail: fjpratt@verizon.net. Website: www.gloriaclover.com. Son-Rise Publications (toll-free 800-358-0777). Fran Pratt, ed. Annual daily devotional book; about 240 pgs.; 5,000 copies/yr. 100% unsolicited freelance. Complete ms/cover letter; phone/e-query OK. **PAYS ONE COPY OF THE BOOK + A DISCOUNT TO RESELL BOOKS.** One-time rts. Devotions up to 250 wds. (365/yr.). Responds in 9-13 wks. Considers simultaneous submissions; accepts reprints (tell when/where appeared). Prefers mss by e-mail (attached). Also accepts submissions from children/teens. Guidelines (www.gloriaclover.com/guidelines.html) & copy on Website. (No ads)

Poetry: Accepts little; prefers rhyming; to 24 lines. Pays one copy.

Tips: "Devotions must be biblically based, and something with an unexpected 'punch' is preferred. Build faith, encourage, and glorify God. No New Age material. Follow guidelines, specifically 250 words or less."

$THE QUIET HOUR, 4050 Lee Vance View, Colorado Springs CO 80919. (719)536-0100. Fax (407)359-2850. E-mail: schmidtd@cookministries.org. Website: www.cookministries.com.

Cook Communications Ministries. Gary Wilde, ed; Doug Schmidt, mng. ed. 100% freelance (makes 13 assignments/yr.). Pays $15-35/devotional on acceptance. Send list of credits only, rather than a sample. Accepts e-mailed sample devotional. Responds in 3 mos.

$THE SECRET PLACE, Box 851, Valley Forge PA 19482-0851. (610)768-2434. Fax (610)768-2441. E-mail: thesecretplace@abc-usa.org. Website: www.judsonpress.com. Kathleen Hayes, sr. ed. Prefers to see completed devotionals, 200 wds. (use unfamiliar Scripture passages). 64 pgs. Circ. 150,000. 100% freelance. Pays $15 for 1st rts. Accepts poetry and buys photos (color & B & W). Prefers e-mail submissions. Guidelines.

$THESE DAYS, 100 Witherspoon St., Louisville KY 40202-1396. (502)569-5102. Fax (502)569-5113. E-mail: vpatton@presbypub.com. Website: www.ppcpub.com. Presbyterian Publishing Corp. Vince Patton, ed. Quarterly booklet; circ. 200,000. Subscription $6.95. Query/samples. 95% unsolicited freelance. Pays $14.25/devotion on acceptance for 1st and nonexclusive reprint rts. (makes work-for-hire assignments); 200 wds. (including key verse and short prayer). Wants short, contemporary poetry ($15) on church holidays and seasons of the year—overtly religious (15 lines, 33-character/line maximum). Query for their two feature segments (short articles): "These Moments" and "These Times." Guidelines; copy for 6x9 SAE/3 stamps.

$THE UPPER ROOM, PO Box 340004, Nashville TN 37203-0004. (615)340-7252. Fax (615)340-7267. E-mail: TheUpperRoomMagazine@upperroom.org. Website: www.upperroom.org. Mary Lou Redding, ed. dir. 95% unsolicited freelance. Pays $25/devotional on publication. 72 pgs. This publication wants freelance submissions and does not make assignments. Phone/fax/e-query OK. Send devotionals up to 250 wds. Buys explicitly religious art, in various media, for use on covers only (transparencies/slides requested); buys one-time, worldwide publishing rts. Accepts e-mail submissions (copied into message). Guidelines (also on Website); copy for 5x7 SAE/2 stamps. (No ads)

Tips: "We do not return submissions. Accepted submissions will be notified in 6-9 wks. Follow guidelines. Need meditations from men." Always include postal address with e-mail submissions.

+THE WORD AMONG US, 9639 Doctor Perry Rd., #126, Ijamsville MD 21754. Toll-free (800)775-9673. (301)831-1262. Fax (301)831-1188. E-mail: lrz@wau.org. Website: www.wau.org. Catholic. Leo Zanchettin, ed. Daily meditations based on the Mass readings; inspirational essays; and stories of the saints and other heroes of the faith.

$THE WORD IN SEASON, PO Box 1209, Minneapolis MN 55440-1209. Fax (612)330-3215. E-mail: rochelle@liferhymecoaching.com. Website: www.augsburgfortress.org. Augsburg Fortress. Rev. Rochelle Y. Melander, ed./mngr. 96 pgs. Devotions to 200 wds. Pays $20/devotion; $75 for prayers. Accepts e-mail submissions (copied into message) after reading guidelines. Guidelines for #10 SAE/2 stamps; copy for 9x12 SAE/4 stamps.

Tips: "We prefer that you write for guidelines. We will send instructions for preparing sample devotions. We accept new writers based on the sample devotions we request and make assignments after acceptance."

MISSIONS MARKETS

+ACTION MAGAZINE: Men for Missions Intl., 941 Fry Rd., Greenwood IN 46142. (317)881-6752. Fax (317)865-1076. E-mail: mfmi@omsinternational.org. Website: www.mfmi.org. Gene Bertolet, ed. Informs the public of ministry opportunities, as well as reporting on the various OMS mission teams. Quarterly mag. Open to unsolicited freelance. Complete ms. Articles.

CATHOLIC MISSIONS IN CANADA, 1155 Yonge St., #201, Toronto ON M4T 1W2, Canada. Toll-free (866)YESCMIC (937-2642). (416)934-3424. Fax (416)934-3425. E-mail: magazine@cmic.info. Website: www.cmic.info. Catholic Missions In Canada. Patria C. Rivera, ed. To share the faith journeys of missionaries as they share the love of Jesus in needy Catholic missions across Canada. Quarterly digest-size mag.; circ. 25,000. Subscription free to donors. Open to unsolicited freelance. Incomplete topical listings. (No ads)

EAST-WEST CHURCH & MINISTRY REPORT, Southern Wesleyan University, Box 1020, Central SC 29630. (864)644-5221. Fax (864)644-5902. E-mail: melliott@swu.edu. Website: www.eastwestreport.org. Dr. Mark R. Elliott, ed. Encourages Western Christian ministry in Central and Eastern Europe and the former Soviet Union that is effective, culturally sensitive, and cooperative. Quarterly literary magazine; 16 pgs.; circ. 430. Print subscription $44.95; e-mail subscription $19.95. 25% unsolicited freelance; 75% assigned. Query; phone/fax/e-query OK. **PAYS IN COPIES** for all rts. Articles 1,500-2,000 wds. (4/yr.); book reviews, 400 wds. Responds in 4 wks. Prefers requested ms on disk or by e-mail. Regularly uses sidebars. Any Bible version. Guidelines (also by e-mail/Website); copy $11.95. (No ads)

Tips: "All submissions must relate to Central and Eastern Europe or the former Soviet Union."

$EVANGELICAL MISSIONS QUARTERLY, PO Box 794, Wheaton IL 60189. (630)752-7158. Fax (630)752-7155. E-mail: emq@wheaton.edu. Website: www.emqonline.com. Evangelism and Missions Information Service (EMIS). A. Scott Moreau, ed.; Laurie Fortunak, mng. ed. For missionaries and others interested in missions trends, strategies, issues, problems, and resources. Quarterly jour.; 136 pgs.; circ. 7,000. Subscription $24.95. 67% unsolicited; 33% assigned. Query; phone/fax/e-query OK. Pays $100 on publication for all & electronic rts. Articles 3,000-3,500 wds. (30/yr.); book reviews 400 wds. (query/pays $25). Responds in 2 wks. Accepts few reprints (tell when/where appeared). Prefers requested ms on disk or by e-mail (copied into message). Uses some sidebars. Kill fee negotiable. Prefers NIV. Guidelines on Website; free copy. (Ads)

Columns/Departments: Buys 8/yr. In the Workshop (tips to increase missionary effectiveness), 800-2,000 wds.; Perspectives (opinion), 800 wds. Pays $50-100.

Tips: "We consider all submissions. It is best to check our Website for examples and guidelines. Present an article idea and why you are qualified to write it. All articles must target evangelical, cross-cultural missionaries. 'In the Workshop' is most open to freelancers. Most authors have a credible connection to and experience in missions."

$GLAD TIDINGS, 50 Wynford Dr., Toronto ON M3C 1J7, Canada. Toll-free (800)619-7301. (416)441-1111. Fax (416)441-2825. E-mail: shenderson@presbyterian.ca. Website: www.presbyterian.ca/wms/index.html. Women's Missionary Society/Presbyterian Church in Canada. Sonya Henderson, ed. To challenge concerned Christians to reflect on their faith through articles and reports related to mission and social justice issues; encourages readers to become informed, inspired, and motivated to action. Bimonthly mag.; 48 pgs.; circ. 5,000. Subscription $12 Cdn. 100% unsolicited freelance. Complete ms/cover letter; phone/fax/e-query OK. Accepts full mss by e-mail. Pays $15-50 on publication for one-time or reprint rts. Articles or fiction 300-1,500 wds.; book reviews 300 wds. (no payment). Responds in 2 wks. Seasonal 4-5 mos. ahead. Prefers e-mail submissions. Uses some sidebars. Also accepts submissions from teens. Guidelines by e-mail; free copy. (Ads)

Poetry: Buys 6-8/yr. Avant-garde, free verse, haiku, light verse, traditional; any length. Pays $15. Submit any number.

Fillers: Buys 6-8/yr. Games, prayers, prose, quizzes, word puzzles; $15-25.

Tips: "Send in samples of your work and we will respond."

INTERNATIONAL JOURNAL OF FRONTIER MISSIONS, 1539 E. Howard St., Pasadena CA 91104. (626)398-2108. Fax (626)398-2185. E-mail: ijfm@wciu.edu. Website: www.ijfm.org. William Carey Intl. University. Rory Clark, mng. ed. Dedicated to frontiers in missions. Quarterly jour.; 48 pgs.; circ. 500. Subscription $15. 75% unsolicited freelance. Complete ms/cover letter; phone/fax/e-query OK. **NO PAYMENT** for one-time rts. Articles 2,000-6,000 wds. Seasonal 3 mos. ahead. Accepts simultaneous submissions & reprints. Accepts e-mail submissions. Does not use sidebars. Guidelines/theme list (also by e-mail/Website); copy $2/10x13 SAE. (Ads)

Special Needs: Contextualization, church in missions, training for missions, mission trends and paradigms, de-westernization of the gospel and missions from the Western world, biblical world-view development, mission theology, Animism, Islam, Buddhism, Hinduism, nonliterate peoples, tent making, mission member care, reaching nomadic peoples, mission history, new religious movements and missions, science and missions, etc.

Tips: "Writers on specific issues we cover are always welcome. Although the circulation is small, the print run is 2,000 and used for promotional purposes. Highly recommended for mission schools, libraries, and mission executives."

$LEADERS FOR TODAY, Box 13, Atlanta GA 30370. (770)449-8869. Fax (770)449-8457. E-mail: rolandm@haggai-institute.com. Website: www.haggai-institute.com. Haggai Institute. Roland G. Moody, exec. production. Primarily for donors to ministry; focus is alumni success stories. Quarterly mag.; 16 pgs.; circ. 7,500. Subscription free. 100% assigned to date. Query; fax query OK. Pays .10-.25/wd. on acceptance for all rts. Articles 1,000-2,000 wds. Responds in 2-3 wks. Requires requested ms on disk or by e-mail (attached file). Kill fee 100%. Regularly uses sidebars. Prefers NIV. Guidelines/theme list; copy for 9x12 SAE/4 stamps. (No ads)

Tips: "If traveling to a developing country, check well in advance regarding the possibility of doing an alumni story. All articles are preassigned; query first."

**2005 EPA Award of Merit—Missionary.

MISSIOLOGY: An International Review, 204 N. Lexington Ave., Wilmore KY 40390. (859)858-2216. Fax (859)858-2375. E-mail: missiology@asburyseminary.edu. Website: www.asmweb.org. American Society of Missiology/Asbury Theological Seminary. Terry C. Muck, ed. A scholarly journal for those who study and practice missions worldwide. Quarterly jour.; 128-136 pgs.; circ. 1,500. Subscription $24. 60% unsolicited freelance; 40% assigned. Complete ms/cover letter. **PAYS 20 COPIES** for 1st rts. Articles 3,000-4,000 wds. (20/yr.); book reviews 400 wds. Responds in 12 wks. No seasonal. No simultaneous submissions or reprints. Prefers requested ms by e-mail (attached file) or on disk. Uses some sidebars. Any Bible version. Guidelines (also by e-mail); copy for 6x9 SAE/$2.81 postage ($6 foreign). (Ads)

MISSION FRONTIERS, 1605 Elizabeth St., Pasadena CA 91104. (626)797-1111. Fax (626) 398-2263. E-mail: mission.frontiers@uscwm.org. Website: www.missionfrontiers.org. U.S. Center for World Mission. Dr. Ralph Winter, ed.; Darrell Dorr, mng. ed. To stimulate a movement to establish indigenous churches where still needed around the world. Bimonthly & online mag.; 24 pgs.; circ. 100,000. Subscription free for donation. No unsolicited freelance; 100% assigned. Query. **NO PAYMENT.** Articles & reviews. Rarely responds. Accepts requested ms on disk or by e-mail (copied into message). Regularly uses sidebars. No guidelines; free copy. Incomplete topical listings. (Ads)

Fillers: Cartoons.

Tips: "Be a published missionary or former missionary. Be on the cutting edge of a strategic breakthrough or methods of reaching an unreached ethnic group." Looking for true-life, short sidebars of Muslims accepting Jesus, or impact of prayer in missions.

$NEW WORLD OUTLOOK, 475 Riverside Dr., Rm. 1476, New York NY 10115-0122. (212)870-3765. Fax (212)870-3940. E-mail: nwo@gbgm-umc.org. Website: http://gbgm-umc.org/nwo. United Methodist. Christie R. House, ed. Denominational missions. Bimonthly mag.; 48 pgs.; circ. 24,000. Subscription $15. 20% unsolicited freelance. Query; fax/e-query OK. Pays $50-300 on publication for all & electronic rts. Articles 500-2,000 wds. (24/yr.); book reviews 200-500 wds. (assigned). No guaranteed response time. Seasonal 4 mos. ahead. Kill fee 50% or $100. Prefers e-mail submission (Word Perfect 6.1 or 8.1 in attached file). Regularly uses sidebars. Prefers NRSV. Guidelines; copy $3. (Ads)

Tips: "Ask for a list of United Methodist mission workers and projects in your area. Investigate them, propose a story, and consult with the editors before writing. Most open to articles and/or color photos of U.S. or foreign mission sites visited as a stringer, after consultation with the editor."

$ONE, 1011 First Ave., New York NY 10022-4195. Toll-free (800)442-6392. (212)826-1480. Fax (212)826-8979. E-mail: cnewa@cnewa.org, or through Website: www.cnewa.org. Catholic Near East Welfare Assn. Michael La Civita, exec. ed. Interest in cultural, religious, and human rights development in Middle East, N.E. Africa, India, or Eastern Europe. Bimonthly mag.; 40 pgs.; circ. 100,000. Subscription $12. 50% unsolicited freelance; 50% assigned. Query/clips; fax query OK. Pays .20/edited wd. ($200) on publication for all rts. Articles 1,200-1,800 wds. (15/yr.). Responds in 9 wks. Accepts requested ms on disk. Kill fee $200. Prefers NAS. Guidelines (also by e-mail); copy for 8x11 SAE/2 stamps.

Tips: "We strive to educate our readers about the culture, faith, history, issues, and people who form the Eastern Christian churches. Anything on people in Palestine/Israel, Eastern Europe, or India. Material should not be academic. Include detailed photographs with story or article."

OPREV EQUIPPER, PO Box 3488, Monument CO 80132-3488. (719)572-5908. Fax (775)248-8147. E-mail: bside@oprev.org. Website: www.oprev.org. Mission To Unreached Peoples. Bruce T. Sidebotham, dir. Provides information to equip U.S. military Christians for cross-cultural ministry. Quarterly & online newsletter; 8 pgs.; circ. 1,500. Subscription free. 40% unsolicited freelance; 60% assigned. Query; phone/e-query OK. **PAYS IN COPIES** for one-time rts. Not copyrighted. Articles 250-1,000 wds. (4/yr.). Responds in 4 wks. Seasonal 4 mos. ahead. Accepts simultaneous submissions & reprints (tell when/where appeared). Accepts requested ms on disk. Regularly uses sidebars. Prefers NIV. No guidelines; copy .50/9x12 SAE/4 stamps. (No ads)

Fillers: Accepts 4/yr. Newsbreaks, to 150 wds.

Columns/Departments: Accepts 4/yr. Agency Profile (describes a mission agency's history and work), 200-300 wds.; Area Profile (describes spiritual landscape of a military theater of operations), 300-750 wds., Resource Review (describes a cross-cultural ministry tool), 100-200 wds. Query.

Special Needs: Ministry in Afghanistan and Iraq. World news and analysis; cross-cultural communication; area profiles and people profiles on military theaters of operation.

Tips: "We need insights for military personnel on understanding and relating the gospel to Muslims."

$PFI WORLD REPORT, Box 17434, Washington DC 20041. (703)481-0000. Fax (703)481-0003. E-mail: info@pfi.org, or chris@pfi.org. Website: www.pfi.org. Prison Fellowship Intl. Christopher P. Nicholson, ed. Targets issues and needs of prisoners, ex-prisoners, justice officials, victims, families, PFI staff, and volunteers in 75 countries. Bimonthly newsletter; 4-8 pgs.; circ. 4,750. Subscription free. 10% unsolicited freelance. Query; fax/e-query OK. Pays $100-350 on acceptance for all rts. Articles 500-750 wds. (4/yr.). Responds in 2 wks. Seasonal 4 mos. ahead. Accepts simultaneous submissions & reprints (tell when/where appeared). Accepts requested ms on disk. Kill fee. Regularly uses sidebars. Guidelines (also on Website); copy for #10 SAE/1 stamp. (No ads)

Special Needs: Prison issues, justice issues, anything that relates to international prison ministry.

Tips: "Looking for personal profiles of people active in prison ministry (preferably PFI officials); ex-prisoner success stories; how-to articles about various aspects of prison ministry. Avoid American slant."

$PIME WORLD, 17330 Quincy St., Detroit MI 48221-2765. (313)342-4066. Fax (313)342-6816. E-mail: pimeworld@pimeusa.org. Website: www.pimeusa.org. Pontifical Inst. for Foreign Missions/Catholic. Rick Schulte, ed. For those interested in and supportive of foreign missions. Published 5X/yr., plus newsletter supplement; 24 pgs.; circ. 16,000. Subscription $15. 10% unsolicited freelance. Complete ms; e-query OK. Pays $15-25 on publication for one-time rts. Photos $10. Articles 500-1,000 wds. Responds in 2 wks. Seasonal 4 mos. ahead. Accepts reprints (tell when/where appeared). Prefers e-mail submission (attached file). Uses some sidebars. Prefers NAB. Also accepts submissions from teens. Guidelines/theme list; copy for 6x9 SAE/2 stamps. (No ads)

Tips: "Features are open to freelancers. Needs missionary profiles; articles on PIME missionaries; interfaith dialog/experiences; and missions in Africa, especially Ivory Coast, Guinea Bissau, and Cameroon. Also issues like hunger, human rights, women's rights, peace, and justice as they are dealt with in developing countries by missionaries and locals alike."

THE RAILROAD EVANGELIST, PO Box 5026, Vancouver WA 98668-5026. (360)699-7208. E-mail: rrjoe@comcast.net. Website: www.railroadevangelist.com. Railroad Evangelistic Assn. Joe Spooner, ed. For railroad and transportation employees and their families. Tri-annual mag.; 16 pgs.; circ. 2,500. Subscription $8. 100% unsolicited freelance. Complete ms/no cover letter; phone query OK. **NO PAYMENT.** Articles 100-700 wds. (10-15/yr.); railroad-related fiction only, for children 5-12 yrs. Seasonal 4 mos. ahead. Accepts simultaneous submissions & reprints. Accepts e-mail submissions. Does not use sidebars. Guidelines (also by e-mail); copy for 9x12 SAE/2 stamps. (No ads)

Poetry: Accepts 4-8/yr. Traditional, any length. Send any number.

Fillers: Accepts many. Anecdotes, cartoons, quotes; to 100 wds.

Tips: "We need 400- to 700-word railroad-related salvation testimonies; or railroad-related human-interest stories; or model railroads. Since we publish only three times a year, we are focusing on railroad-related articles only. Just write and tell us or send us what you have. We'll let you know if we can use it or not."

WOMEN OF THE HARVEST, PO Box 151297, Lakewood CO 80215-9297. Toll-free (877)789-7778. (303)985-2148. Fax (303)989-4239. E-mail: editor@womenoftheharvest.com. Website: www.womenoftheharvest.com. Women of the Harvest Ministries Intl. Inc. Cindy Blomquist, ed. To support and encourage women serving in cross-cultural missions. Bimonthly e-zine; 35 pgs.; circ. 4,000. Free online. 90% unsolicited freelance; 10% assigned. Complete ms; e-query OK. Accepts full ms by e-mail. **NO PAYMENT** for one-time & electronic rts. Articles 300-800 wds. Responds in 2 wks. Seasonal 3 mos. ahead. No simultaneous submissions or reprints. Prefers requested ms by e-mail (copied into message or attached file). Uses some sidebars. Guidelines/theme list on Website; copy online. (No ads)

Tips: "This is a magazine designed especially for women serving cross-culturally. We need articles, humor, and anecdotes related to this topic. Best way to break in is by having a cross-cultural missions experience or to be heading to the mission field."

**2006 EPA Award of Merit—Online. 2004 EPA Award of Merit—Christian Ministries.

MUSIC MARKETS

$CCM MAGAZINE, 104 Woodmont Blvd., Ste. 300, Nashville TN 37205-2245. (615)386-3011. Fax (615)385-4112. E-mail: feedback@ccmmagazine.com, or through Website: www.ccmmagazine.com. Salem Communications Inc. Jay Schwartzendruber, ed. Encourages spiritual growth through contemporary music; provides news and information about the Christian music market. Monthly & online mag.; 80 pgs.; circ. 70,000. Subscription $21.95. 75% unsolicited freelance. Query/clips; phone/fax query OK. Pays .20/wd. for short pieces, or

$100/published pg. for features, on publication for all rts. Articles 500-2,500 wds.; music reviews 250-350 wds. Responds slowly. Seasonal 3 mos. ahead. Kill fee 50%. Prefers requested ms on disk or by e-mail (copied into message). Regularly uses sidebars. Guidelines; copy for 9x12 SAE/$4. (Ads)

**The #2 Best-selling Magazine in Christian retail stores.

$CHRISTIAN MUSIC TODAY, 465 Gundersen Dr., Carol Stream IL 60188. (630)620-6200. Fax (630)260-8428. E-mail: music@christianitytoday.com. Website: www.ChristianMusicToday.com. Christianity Today Intl. Russ Breimeier, mng. ed. To inspire and inform readers about today's Christian music, artists, and industry trends through timely coverage, relevant news, insightful reviews and interviews, and educated opinion, all from a Christian world-view. Weekly e-zine. 5% unsolicited freelance; 95% assigned. Query; fax/e-query OK. Accepts full mss by e-mail. Pays $50-200 on acceptance for 1st rts. Articles 400-2,000 wds (200/yr.); music reviews, 300-700 wds., payment varies. Responds in 2 wks. Occasionally accepts simultaneous submissions & reprints (tell when/where appeared). Prefers e-mail submissions (attached file). Sometimes pays kill fee 50%. Uses some sidebars. Prefers NIV. No guidelines; copy online. (Ads)

Columns/Departments: Buys 6-8/yr. Query. Glimpses of God (spiritual leanings in secular music), 1,000 wds. pays $75-100.

Special Needs: Reviews of music videos.

Tips: "Most open to Glimpses of God, news/trends, interviews, and commentaries."

CHRISTIAN MUSIC WEEKLY, 7057 Bluffwood Ct., Brownsburg IN 46112-8650. (317)892-5031. Fax (317)892-5034. Canadian address: 775 Pam Cres, Newmarket ON L3Y 5B7, Canada. E-mail through Website: www.ChristianMusicWeekly.com. Joyful Sounds. Rob Green, ed. Trade paper for Worship, Inspirational, Adult Contemporary, and Southern Gospel Music radio formats. Weekly trade paper; 12 pgs.; circ. 300-1,200. Subscription $104 (paper) or $52 (PDF via e-mail). 25% unsolicited freelance; 75% assigned. Query by e-mail only. **PAYS IN COPIES** (will publish photo of writer and tiny bio). Articles 600-2,000 wds.; music reviews, 100-300 wds. Responds in 2 wks. Seasonal 2 mos. ahead. Accepts reprints. Requires requested ms on disk (DOS-ASCII), prefers e-mail submission. Guidelines by e-mail; copy for 9x12 SAE/2 stamps. (Ads)

Fillers: Cartoons, short humor (particularly radio or music related).

Columns/Departments: Insider (artist interview); Programming 101 (radio technique); retail, inspirational, especially for musicians and radio people; 600-2,000 wds.

Special Needs: Songwriting and performance.

Tips: "Most open to artist interviews. Must be familiar with appropriate music formats."

CHRISTIAN RADIO & RETAIL WEEKLY: The Information Source for Christian Radio, 5350 N. Academy Blvd., Ste. 200, Colorado Springs CO 80918. (719)536-9000, ext. 101. Fax (719)598-7461. E-mail: dave@christianradioweekly.com. Website: www.christianradioweekly.com. Westar Media Group. David Koch, ed. For Christian media professionals working in radio and Christian music industry; Christian music charts, radio and retail music related news. Weekly mag.; 12 pgs.; circ. 500. Subscription $199. Open to freelance. Complete ms; e-query OK. **NO PAYMENT.** Articles & fiction 800 wds.

$CREATOR MAGAZINE, PO Box 3538, Pismo Beach CA 93448. Toll-free (800)777-6713. (707)837-9071. E-mail: creator@creatormagazine.com. Website: www.creatormagazine.com. Rod Ellis, ed. For interdenominational music ministry; promoting quality, diverse music programs in the church. Bimonthly & online mag.; 48-56 pgs.; circ. 6,000. Subscription $32.95. 35% unsolicited freelance. Query or complete ms/cover letter; fax/e-query OK. Pays $30-75 for assigned, $30-60 for unsolicited, on publication for 1st, one-time, reprint rts. Articles 1,000-10,000 wds. (20/yr.); book reviews ($20). Responds in 4-12 wks. Seasonal 4 mos. ahead. Accepts simultaneous submissions & reprints (tell when/where appeared). Prefers requested ms on disk. Regularly uses sidebars. Prefers NRSV. Guidelines/theme list; copy for 9x12 SAE/5 stamps. (Ads)

Fillers: Buys 20/yr. Anecdotes, cartoons, ideas, jokes, party ideas, short humor; 10-75 wds.; $5-25.

Special Needs: Articles on worship; staff relationships.

+GOSPEL SYNERGY MAGAZINE: For The Good News—God's Word and Gospel Music, PO Box 286261, Chicago IL 60628. (708)272-6640. E-mail: alcarter@gospelsynergy.com. Website: www.gospelsynergy.com. Andre Carter, pub. To provide information such as promotions, advertising, and record deals to help grow gospel music ministries and the independent gospel artists. Monthly magazine. (Ads)

Tips: "There is a wealth of information that many ministries and artists are not taking advantage of. My assignment is to provide that information with articles, entertainment, and more."

THE HYMN: A Journal of Congregational Song, School of Theology, Boston University, 745 Commonwealth Ave., Boston MA 02215-1401. Toll-free (800)THE-HYMN. Fax (617)353-7322. E-mail: hymneditor@aol.com. Website: www.bu.edu/sth/hymn, or www.hymnsociety.org. Hymn Society in the U.S. & Canada. Beverly A. Howard, ed. (5423 Via Alberca, Riverside CA 92507-6477). For church musicians, hymnologists, scholars; articles related to the congregational song. Quarterly jour.; 60 pgs.; circ. 3,000. Subscription $65. 85% unsolicited freelance; 15% assigned. Query; phone/e-query OK. **NO PAYMENT** for all rts. Articles any length (12/yr.); book and music reviews any length. Responds in 6 wks. Seasonal 4 mos. ahead. Prefers requested ms on disk or by e-mail. Regularly uses sidebars. Any Bible version. Guidelines (also on Website); free copy. (Ads)

Special Needs: Articles on history of hymns or practical ways to teach or use hymns. Controversial issues as related to hymns and songs. Contact editor. Articles on Charles Wesley or Paul Gerhardt.

Contest: Hymn text and tune contests for special occasions or themes.

Tips: "Focus all articles on congregational song. No devotional material."

+I AM MAGAZINE, 13055 Riverdale Dr. N.W., Ste. 500-222, coon Rapids MN 55448. (651)248-9671, or (763)221-7119. E-mail: jerrvals2003@yahoo.com. Website: www.myspace.com/iammagazine. Jerrvals Records. Jerry Griffis, pub.; Val Griffis, ed. To reach gospel music listeners in the urban communities through genres such as gospel, traditional, contemporary, rap, and gospel hip-hop; as well as giving independent and national gospel artists and record companies an opportunity to gain exposure. Quarterly mag. Subscription $12. Open to unsolicited freelance. Query or complete ms. Articles. Guidelines on Website. Not in topical listings. (Ads)

TRADITION MAGAZINE, PO Box 492, Anita IA 50020. Phone/fax (712)762-4363. E-mail: bobeverhart@yahoo.com. Website: www.oldtimemusic.bigstep.com. National Traditional Country Music Assn. Inc. Bob Everhart, pres./ed. Bimonthly mag.; 56 pgs.; circ. 3,500. Subscription $25. 30% unsolicited freelance; 70% assigned. Query. **PAYS IN COPIES** for one-time rts. Articles 1,000-2,000 wds. (4/yr.). Responds in 6-8 wks. Uses some sidebars. Prefers KJV. Guidelines; copy for 9x12 SAE/2 stamps. (Ads)

Fillers: Cartoons.

Columns/Departments: Accepts 4-6/yr. Query.

Tips: "Most articles need to deal with traditional or old-time music."

Note: Also see "Resources: Songwriting" in the Resources section in the front of this book.

PASTOR/LEADERSHIP MARKETS

$THE AFRICAN AMERICAN PULPIT, PO Box 381587, Germantown TN 38183. Toll-free (800)509-8227. Phone/fax (412)364-1688. E-mail: Info@theafricanamericanpulpit.com, or through Website: www.TheAfricanAmericanPulpit.com. Hope for Life Intl. Inc. Martha Simmons, pub.; Katara Washington & Eugene L. Gibson Jr., co-eds. The only journal focused exclusively on the art of black preaching. Quarterly jour.; 96 pgs.; circ. 4,000. Subscription $40 ($59 to libraries). 50% unsolicited freelance; 50% assigned. Complete ms/cover letter; phone/e-query OK. Pays $50 (flat fee) on publication for all rts. Articles 1,500 wds., sermons 2,500 wds. Responds in 13-26 wks. Seasonal 6-9 mos. ahead. Requires requested ms on disk or by e-mail. Does not use sidebars. Any Bible version. Guidelines (also by e-mail/Website); copy. (Ads)

Special Needs: Any type of sermon by African American preachers, and related articles or essays.

Contest: Sponsors contest occasionally; advertised in the magazine.

Tips: "The entire journal is open to freelancers. We strongly encourage freelancers to submit to us (as many pieces as you can), and freelancers can call anytime with questions. We are always looking for how-to articles, sermon helps, homiletic-method essays, seminarian pieces, and practical pieces."

ALPHA NEWS, 74 Trinity Pl., 9th Fl., New York NY 10006-2001. (212)406-5269. Fax (212)406-7521. E-mail: info@alphausa.org. Website: www.Alphausa.org. Alpha North America. Claudia Roux, ed. To keep church leaders informed about the Alpha course. Newspaper & online; circ. 195,000. Subscription free. Open to unsolicited freelance. Query preferred. Not in topical listings. (Ads)

$BAREFOOT, 2923 Troost Ave., Kansas City MO 64109-1593. Toll-free (866)355-9933. (816) 931-1900. Fax (816)412-812. E-mail: bfeditor@barefootministries.com, or through Website: www.barefootministries.com. Bo Cassell, ed. Dedicated to resourcing and equipping youth workers. 10% unsolicited freelance; 90% assigned. E-query preferred; fax query OK. Pays $50-100 on publication for all rts. Articles for youth workers 1,000-2,000 wds. (20-25/yr.); reviews 500 wds. ($25). Responds in 8 wks. Seasonal 6 mos. ahead. Accepts reprints (tell when/where appeared). Accepts e-mail submissions (attached or copied into message). Some kill fees. Does not use sidebars. Prefers NIV. Guidelines by e-mail; copy online. (No ads)

Fillers: Buys 20-40/yr. Anecdotes, cartoons, games, ideas, party ideas, short humor, and tips, 100-200 wds.; $20-40.

Special Needs: Youthworker and youth issues.

Tips: "We are most open to freelancers in the areas of product, music, and entertainment reviews. Where youth ministry articles and curricular pieces are concerned, we usually assign those to established youth ministry professionals."

$CATECHUMENATE: A Journal of Christian Initiation, 1800 N. Hermitage Ave., Chicago IL 60622-1101. Toll-free (800)933-1800. (773)486-8970. Toll-free fax (800)933-7094. E-mail: editors@ltp.org. Website: www.LTP.org. Catholic. Victoria M. Tufano, ed. For clergy and laity who work with those who are planning to become Catholic. Bimonthly jour.; 48 pgs.; circ. 5,600. Subscription $20. Complete ms/cover letter; phone/fax/e-query OK. Pays $100-250 on publication for all rts. Articles 1,500-3,000 wds. (10/yr.). Responds in 2-6 wks. Accepts simultaneous submissions. Prefers requested ms on disk. Kill fee. Does not use sidebars. Guidelines; copy for 6x9 SAE/4 stamps.

Poetry: Buys 6/yr. Free verse, traditional; 5-20 lines; $75. Submit max. 5 poems. One-time rts.

Columns/Departments: Buys 12/yr. Sunday Word (Scripture reflection on Sunday readings, aimed at catechumen); 450 wds.; $200-250. Query for assignment.

Special Needs: Christian initiation; reconciliation.

Tips: "It helps if the writer has experience working with Christian initiation. Approach is that this is something we are all learning together through experience and scholarship."

$THE CATHOLIC SERVANT, 3204 E. 43rd St., Minneapolis MN 55406. (612)729-7321. Cell (612)275-0431. Fax (612)724-8695. E-mail: jcsondag@mninter.net. Catholic. John Sondag, ed./pub. For Catholic evangelization, catechesis, and apologetics. Monthly tabloid; 12 pgs.; circ. 41,000 (during school yr.; 33,000 summer). Query/clips; fax query OK. Pays $60 on publication. Articles 750-1,000 wds. (12/yr.). Responds in 4 wks. Seasonal 3 mos. ahead. Requested mss by e-mail only. Uses some sidebars. (Ads)

Fillers: Cartoons & short humor.

Columns/Departments: Opinion column, 500-750 wds.

Tips: "We buy features or column only." Be sure to indicate "Ms for Catholic Servant" in subject line of e-mail.

$THE CHRISTIAN CENTURY, 104 S. Michigan Ave., Ste. 700, Chicago IL 60603. (312)263-7510. Fax (312)263-7540. E-mail: main@christiancentury.org. Website: www.christiancentury.org. Christian Century Foundation. Submit to: Attention Manuscripts. For ministers, educators, and church leaders interested in events and theological issues of concern to the ecumenical church. Biweekly mag.; 48 pgs.; circ. 30,000. Subscription $49. 20% unsolicited freelance; 80% assigned. Query (complete ms for fiction); phone/fax query OK. Pays $125 on publication for all or one-time rts. Articles 1,500-3,000 wds. (150/yr.); fiction 1,000-3,000 wds. (3/yr.); book reviews, 800-1,500 wds.; music or video reviews 1,000 wds.; pays $0-75. Responds in 1-9 wks. Seasonal 4 mos. ahead. No simultaneous submissions. Accepts reprints (tell when/where appeared). No kill fee. Regularly uses sidebars. Prefers NRSV. Guidelines/theme list (also by e-mail/Website); copy $5. (Ads)

Poetry: Poetry Editor. Buys 50/yr. Any type (religious but not sentimental); to 20 lines; $50. Submit max. 10 poems.

Special Needs: Film, popular culture commentary; news topics and analysis.

Tips: "Keep in mind our audience of sophisticated readers, eager for analysis and critical perspective that goes beyond the obvious. We are open to all topics if written with appropriate style for our readers."

CHRISTIAN CREATIVE ARTS ASSN., 5950 Lakehurst Dr., Ste. 290, Orland FL 32819. E-mail: info@ccaaonline.org. Website: www.ccaaonline.org. Conservative, evangelical dramas for stage, street, and sanctuary. Open to freelance. E-mail if interested. **NO PAYMENT.** Looking for any-length scripts for drama, puppetry, clowning, mime, interpretive movement, and comedy.

CHRISTIAN EDUCATION JOURNAL (CA), 13800 Biola Ave., LaMirada CA 90639. (562)903-6000, ext. 5528. Fax (562)906-4502. E-mail: editor.cej@biola.edu. Website: www.biola.edu/cej. Talbot School of Theology, Biola University. Kevin E. Lawson, ed. Academic journal on the practice of Christian education; for students, professors, and thoughtful ministry leaders in Christian education. Semiannual jour.; 200-250 pgs.; circ. 750. Subscription $28. Open to freelance. Query; e-query OK. Accepts full mss by e-mail. **NO PAYMENT** for 1st rts. Articles 3,000-6,000 wds. (20/yr.); book reviews 2-5 pgs. Responds in 4-6 wks. No seasonal. Might accept simultaneous submissions & reprints (tell when/where appeared). Requires e-mail submissions (attached file in Word format). Does not use sidebars. Any Bible version. Guidelines on Website; no copy. (Ads)

Tips: "Focus on foundations and/or research with implications for the conception and practice of Christian education." Book reviews must be preassigned and approved by the editor; guidelines on Website.

CHRISTIAN MANAGEMENT REPORT, PO Box 4090, San Clemente CA 92674-4090. Toll-free (800)727-4CMA. (877)487-0900. Fax (877)595-7649. E-mail: DeWayne@CMAonline.org, or cma@cmaonline.org. Website: www.CMAonline.org. Christian Management Assn. DeWayne Herbrandson, exec. ed. Management resources and leadership training for Christian nonprofit organizations and growing churches. Bimonthly jour.; 56-72 pgs.; circ. 3,500+. Subscription $39.95. 100% assigned. Complete ms; e-query encouraged. **PAYS 10 COPIES** for all, 1st, one-time, reprint, or electronic rts. Articles 770-1,500 wds./bio; book reviews 100-200 wds. Responds in 4 wks. Seasonal 6 mos. ahead. No simultaneous submissions; limited reprints. CMA members first choice. Prefers accepted ms by e-mail (attached file). Regularly uses sidebars. Prefers NIV, NLT. Guidelines (also by e-mail); free copy. (Ads)

Fillers: Cartoons.

Columns/Departments: Accepts 6/yr. General leadership issues, CEOs & senior team issues, general management issues, board governance, church leadership, church financial management, information technology, tax & legal trends; all 250-2,000 wds.

Special Needs: Evangelical Calendar of Events.

Tips: "All areas open. Submit a synopsis of article idea dealing with leadership and management issues relevant to megachurches or parachurch organizations. Send by e-mail (attached file)."

CHURCHLIFE INSPIRATION & HUMOR, 12372 W. 107th Terr., Overland Park KS 66210. Toll-free (888)638-7439. (719)302-3777. Fax (719)623-0251. Website: www.churchlife newsletter.com. Logos Media Network. Submit to The Editor. Humor and inspiration for pastors and church leaders. E-newsletter; circ. 65,000. Incomplete topical listings.

Fillers: Jokes, sermon illustrations, short humor.

$THE CLERGY JOURNAL, 6160 Carmen Ave. E., Inver Grove Heights MN 55076-4422. (651)451-9945. Fax (651)457-4617. E-mail: sfirle@logosstaff.com. Website: www.logos productions.com. Logos Productions Inc. Sharon Firle, mng. ed. Directed mainly to clergy—a practical guide to church leadership and personal growth. Monthly (9X) mag.; 56 pgs.; circ. 6,000. Subscription $44.95. 5% unsolicited freelance; 95% assigned. Complete ms/cover letter; fax/e-query OK. Pays $75-150 on publication for 1st rts. Articles 1,000-1,500 wds. (25/yr.). Responds in 4 wks. Seasonal 8 mos. ahead. Accepts simultaneous submissions & reprints (tell when/where appeared). Prefers requested ms by e-mail (attached file). No kill fee. Uses some sidebars. Prefers NRSV. Guidelines/theme list (also by e-mail/Website); copy for 9x12 SAE/4 stamps. (Ads—struran@logosstaff.com)

Columns/Departments: Ministry Issues; Preaching & Worship; Personal Issues; $75-150.

Special Needs: Church technology issues.

Tips: "Our greatest need is sermon writers who can write on assigned texts. Instructions sent on request. Our readers are mainline Protestant. We are interested in meeting the personal and professional needs of clergy in areas like worship planning, church and personal finances, and self-care—spiritual, physical, and emotional."

$CORNERSTONE YOUTH RESOURCE, 55 W. Oak Ridge Dr., Hagerstown MD 21740. E-mail: iyr_editor@yahoo.com. Seventh-day Adventist. Patricia Humphrey, ed. For Christian youth leaders; a practical resource filled with ideas for creative youth ministry and programming. Quarterly mag.; 48 pgs.; circ. 2,200. 5% unsolicited freelance; 95% assigned. Query/clips; fax query OK; best to e-mail, as editor lives in Texas. Pays $25-350 on acceptance for 1st rts. Articles 700-900 wds. (16/yr.). Responds in 8-12 wks. Seasonal 12 mos. ahead. Accepts reprints (tell when/where appeared). Accepts e-mail submissions (attached file in Microsoft Word). No kill fee. Regularly uses sidebars. Prefers KJV, NKJV, NIV. Also accepts submissions from teens. Guidelines (also by e-mail); copy for 9x12 SAE/$2.13 postage (mark "Media Mail"). (Ads)

Columns/Departments: Outreach Ideas (service activity ideas for teens), 800-1,000 wds.; Super Social Suggestions (social activities and games for teen groups), 800-1,000 wds.; Program Ideas (creative youth programming ideas), variable lengths.

Special Needs: Articles dealing with understanding and teaching youth. Innovative concepts in youth ministry.

Tips: "Areas most open to freelancers are the Super Social and Outreach Ideas. We are always looking for creative activity ideas that teen leaders can do with youth, ages 14-18. The activities should be fun to do and well written with clear, easy-to-follow instructions. Ideas that are tested and have worked well with your own youth group are preferred."

CROSS CURRENTS, 475 Riverside Dr., Ste. 1945, New York NY 10015. (212)870-2544. Fax (212)870-2539. E-mail: careym@crosscurrents.org, or ChasHenderson@mindspring.com. Website: www.crosscurrents.org. Association for Religion and Intellectual Life. Submit to Managing Editor. For thoughtful activists for social justice and church reform. Quarterly mag.; 144 pgs.; circ. 5,000. Subscription $30. 25% unsolicited freelance; 75% assigned. Mostly written by academics. Complete ms/cover letter; e-query OK. **PAYS IN COPIES** for all rts. Articles 3,000-5,000 wds.; fiction 3,000 wds.; book reviews 1,000 wds. Responds in 4-8 wks. Seasonal 6 mos. ahead. No simultaneous submissions or reprints. Prefers requested ms on disk or by e-mail (attached file). Does not use sidebars. Guidelines on Website; no copy. (Ads)

Poetry: Beverly Coyle, poetry ed. Accepts 12/yr. Any type or length; no payment. Submit max. 5 poems.

Tips: "Looking for focused, well-researched articles; creative fiction and poetry. Send two double-spaced copies; SASE; use *Chicago Manual of Style* and nonsexist language."

$DIOCESAN DIALOGUE, 16565 S. State St., South Holland IL 60473. (708)331-5485. Fax (708)331-5484. E-mail: acp@acpress.org. Website: www.americancatholicpress.org. A Mexican Catholic Press. Fr. Michael Gilligan, editorial dir. Targets Latin-Rite dioceses in the U.S. that sponsor a mass broadcast on TV or radio. Annual newsletter; 8 pgs.; circ. 750. Free. 20% unsolicited freelance. Complete ms/cover letter; no phone/fax/e-query. Articles 200-1,000 wds. Pays variable rates on publication for all rts. Responds in 10 wks. Accepts simultaneous submissions & reprints. Uses some sidebars. Prefers NAB (Confraternity). No guidelines; copy $3/9x12 SAE/2 stamps. (No ads)

Fillers: Cartoons, 2/yr.

Tips: "Writers should be familiar with TV production of the Mass and/or the needs of senior citizens, especially shut-ins."

$EMMANUEL, 5384 Wilson Mills Rd., Cleveland OH 44143. (440)442-6311. Fax (440)449-3862. E-mail: ssscommunications@blessedsacrament.com. Website: www.blessedsacrament.com. Catholic. Rev. Paul Bernier SSS, ed. (pbernier@earthlink.net); Patrick Riley, book review ed. Eucharistic spirituality for priests and others in church ministry. Bimonthly mag.; 96 pgs.; circ. 3,000. Subscription $26; $31 foreign. 30% unsolicited freelance. Query or complete ms/cover letter; e-query OK. Pays $75-150 for articles, $50 for meditations, on publication for all rts. Articles 2,000-2,750 wds.; meditations 1,000-1,250 wds.; book reviews 500-750 wds. Responds in 2 wks. Seasonal 4 mos. ahead. Accepts manuscripts on disk or as e-mail attachments. Guidelines (also by e-mail)/theme list. (Ads)

Poetry: Buys 15/yr. Free verse, light verse, traditional; 8 lines & up; $35. Submit max. 3 poems.

Tips: "Most open to articles, meditations, poetry oriented toward Eucharistic spirituality, prayer, and ministry."

ENGAGE: The Journal of Youth Culture from CPYU (formerly YouthCulture@Today), PO Box 414, Elizabethtown PA 17022-0414. (717)361-8429. Fax (717) 361-8964. E-mail: cpyu@cpyu.org. Website: www.cpyu.org. Center for Parent/Youth Understanding. Walt Mueller, pres. To equip parents, teens, and youth workers with analysis and commentary on youth culture and cross-generational ministry. Quarterly & online mag.; 24 pgs.; circ. 10,000. Subscription for $20 donation. 100% assigned. (No ads)

**2003 EPA Award of Merit—Newsletter.

$ENRICHMENT: A Journal for Pentecostal Ministry, 1445 N. Boonville Ave., Springfield MO 65802. (417)862-2781, ext. 4095. Fax (417)862-0416. E-mail: enrichmentjournal@ag.org. Website: www.enrichmentjournal.ag.org. Assemblies of God. Gary R. Allen, exec. ed.; Rick Knoth, mng. ed. (rknoth@ag.org). Enriching and encouraging Pentecostal ministers to equip and empower Spirit-filled believers for effective ministry. Quarterly jour.; 128-144 pgs.; circ. 33,000. Subscription $24; foreign add $18. 15% unsolicited freelance. Complete ms/cover letter. Pays up to .10/wd. ($75-175) on acceptance for 1st rts. Articles 1,000-3,000 wds. (25/yr.); book reviews, 250 wds. ($25). Responds in 8-12 wks. Seasonal 1 yr. ahead. Accepts simultaneous submissions & reprints (tell when/where appeared). Requires requested ms on disk or by e-mail (copied into message). Kill fee 50%. Regularly uses sidebars. Prefers NIV. Guidelines/theme list; copy for $7/10x13 SAE. (Ads)

Fillers: Cartoon; $50-75.

Columns/Departments: Buys many/yr. For Women in Ministry (leadership ideas), Associate Ministers (related issues), Managing Your Ministry (how-to), Financial Concepts (church stewardship issues), Family Life (minister's family), When Pews Are Few (ministry in smaller congregation); Worship in the Church; Leader's Edge; Preaching That Connects; all 1,200-1,500 wds.; $125-150.

Tips: "Open to sermon outlines."

**2007 EPA Award of Merit—Denominational. This periodical was #47 on the 2006 Top 50 Christian Publishers list.

$THE EVANGELICAL BAPTIST, 18 Louvigny, Lorraine QC J6Z 1T7, Canada. (450)621-3248. Fax (450)621-0253. E-mail: eb@fellowship.ca. Website: www.fellowship.ca. Fellowship of Evangelical Baptist Churches in Canada. Ginette Cotnoir, mng. ed. To enhance the life and ministry of pastors and leaders in local churches. Quarterly mag. Subscription $12. Query preferred. Pays .05/wd. on publication for one-time rts. Articles 800-2,400 wds.; book reviews 200-500 wds. Guidelines on Website.

$GROWTH POINTS, PO Box 892589, Temecula CA 92589-2589. Phone/fax (951)506-3086. E-mail: cgnet@earthlink.net. Website: www.churchgrowthnetwork.com. Dr. Gary L. McIntosh, ed. For pastors and church leaders interested in church growth. Monthly newsletter; 2 pgs.; circ. 8,000. Subscription $16. 10% unsolicited freelance; 90% assigned. Query; fax/e-query OK. Pays $25 for one-time rts. Not copyrighted. Articles 1,000-2,000 wds. (2/yr.). Responds in 4 wks. Accepts simultaneous submissions & reprints. Accepts requested ms on disk. Does not use sidebars. Guidelines; copy for #10 SAE/1 stamp. (No ads)

Tips: "Write articles that are short (1,200 words), crisp, clear, with very practical ideas that church leaders can put to use immediately. All articles must have a pro church-growth slant, be very practical, have how-to material, and be very tightly written with bullets, etc."

$INSITE, PO Box 62189, Colorado Springs CO 80962-2189. (719)260-9400. Fax (719)260-6398. E-mail: editor@ccca.org. Website: www.ccca.org. Christian Camp and Conference Assn. Alison Phillips, ed. To inform and inspire professionals serving in the Christian camp and conference community. Bimonthly mag.; 40 pgs.; circ. 8,750. Subscription $29.95. 15% unsolicited freelance; 85% assigned. Query; e-query OK. Pays .16/wd. on publication for 1st and electronic rts. Cover articles 1,500-2,000 wds. (12/yr.); features 1,200-1,500 wds. (30/yr.); sidebars 250-500 wds. (15-20/yr.) Responds in 4 wks. Seasonal 6 mos. ahead. Accepts simultaneous submissions & reprints (tell when/where appeared). Prefers e-mail submission (attached file). Kill fee. Regularly uses sidebars. Prefers NIV. Guidelines (also by e-mail); copy $4.95/10x13 SAE/$1.65 postage. (Ads)

Special Needs: Outdoor setting; purpose and objectives; administration and organization; personnel development; camper/guest needs; programming; health and safety; food service; site/facilities maintenance; business/operations; marketing and PR; relevant spiritual issues; and fund-raising.

Tips: "Most open to profiles and how-to pieces; get guidelines, then query first. Don't send general camping-related articles. We print stories specifically related to Christian camp and conference facilities; innovative programs or policies; how a Christian camp or conference experience affected a present-day leader. Review several issues so you know what we're looking for."

**2007 EPA Award of Excellence—Christian Ministries; 2006 EPA Award of Merit—Most Improved Publication; 2006, 2005, 2004 EPA Award of Merit—Christian Ministries.

$INTERPRETATION, 3401 Brook Rd., Richmond VA 23227. Toll-free (877)522-7799. (804)254-8062. E-mail through Website: www.interpretation.org. Union Theological Seminary and Presbyterian School of Christian Education. James A. Brashler, ed. Teachers and pastors receive scholarly guidance for teaching and preaching. Quarterly & online jour.; 112 pgs.; circ. 4,500. Subscription $27. 100% assigned. Query; no phone/fax/e-query. Does not accept full mss by e-mail. Pays $250 on publication. (Ads)

$INTERPRETER and INTERPRETER ONLINE, PO Box 320, Nashville TN 37202-0320. (615)742-5407. Fax (615)742-5460. E-mail: knoble@umcom.org, or through Website: www.InterpreterMagazine.org. United Methodist Church. Kathy Noble, ed. For lay leaders and pastors of the United Methodist Church; focus on ministry ideas and resources, spiritual growth issues, with a practical slant. Bimonthly & online mag.; 44+ pgs.; circ. 225,000. Subscription $12. Some assigned freelance. Query/clips. Pays on acceptance for all rts. Articles 500-1,000 wds. (6 print/yr.; some Web exclusive). Seasonal 6 mos. ahead. No simultaneous submissions or reprints. Use submission form on Website. No kill fee. Uses some sidebars. Prefers NRSV. Guidelines on Website; copy for 9x12 SAE/4 stamps. (Ads)

Fillers: Buys several/yr. Facts, ideas, short humor; 50-75 wds.

Columns/Departments: Buys 10/yr. Youth (how parents/church can reach and serve); Worship (new ideas/special days); Evangelism (new ideas for); Relationships (strengthening); Jumpstart Your Ministry (ideas for ministry/missions); Living Your Faith in the Real World (practical discipleship); all to 200 wds.; payment varies.

Tips: "All articles must have a specific and prominent United Methodist connection. Very difficult for unsolicited freelancers to break in, as we have an excellent pool and depend on them for referrals."

**This periodical was #19 on the 2005 Top 50 Christian Publishers list (#31 in 2004, #42 in 2003).

THE JOURNAL OF PASTORAL CARE & COUNSELING, 1068 Harbor Dr. S.W., Calabash NC 28467. Phone/fax (910)579-5084. E-mail: editor@jpcp.org. Website: www.jpcp.org. Dr. Orlo Strunk Jr., mng. ed. For chaplains/pastors/professionals involved with pastoral care and counseling in other than a church setting. Quarterly jour.; 116 pgs.; circ. 10,000. Subscription $35. 95% unsolicited freelance; 5% assigned. Query; phone/fax/e-query OK. **PAYS 10 COPIES** for 1st rts. Articles 5,000 wds. or 20 pgs. (30/yr.); book reviews 5 pgs. Responds in 8 wks. Accepts requested ms on disk. Does not use sidebars. Guidelines (also on Website); no copy. (Ads)

Poetry: Accepts 16/yr. Free verse; 5-16 lines. Submit max. 3 poems.

Special Needs: "We publish brief (500-600 wds.) 'Personal Reflections,' but they need to deal with clinical experiences that have led the writer to reflect on the religious and/or theological meaning generated."

Tips: "Most open to poems and personal reflections. Readers are highly trained clinically, holding professional degrees in religion/theology. Writers need to be professionals on topics covered."

JOURNAL OF THE AMERICAN SOCIETY FOR CHURCH GROWTH, c/o Dr. Gary L. McIntosh, ed., Talbot School of Theology, 13800 Biola Ave., LaMirada CA 90639. (562)944-0351. Fax (562)906-4502. E-mail: gary.mcintosh@biola.edu. Website: www.ascg.org. American Society for Church Growth. Dr. Gary L. McIntosh, ed. Targets professors, pastors, denominational executives, and seminary students interested in church growth and evangelism. Quarterly jour. (3X—fall, winter, spring); 100 pgs.; circ. 400. Subscription $24. 66% unsolicited freelance; 33% assigned. Complete ms/cover letter; phone/fax/e-query OK. **PAYS IN COPIES** for one-time rts. Not copyrighted. Articles 15 pgs. or 4,000-5,000 wds. (10/yr.); book reviews 750-2,000 wds. Responds in 8-12 wks. Accepts simultaneous submissions & reprints (tell when/where appeared). Prefers requested ms on disk or by e-mail. Does not use sidebars. Any Bible version. Guidelines (also in journal)/theme list; copy $10. (Ads)

Tips: "Provide well-researched and tightly written articles related to some aspect of church growth. Articles should be academic in nature, rather than popular in style. We're open to new writers at this time."

$LEADERSHIP, 465 Gundersen Dr., Carol Stream IL 60188. (630)260-6200. Fax (630)480-2004. E-mail: LJEditor@LeadershipJournal.net. Website: www.leadershipjournal.net. Christianity Today Intl. Marshall Shelley, ed. Practical help for pastors/church leaders, covering the spectrum of subjects from personal needs to professional skills. Quarterly & online jour.; 124 pgs.; circ. 55,000. Subscription $24.95. 20% unsolicited freelance; 80% assigned. Query or complete ms/cover letter; fax/e-query OK. Accepts full mss by e-mail. Pays .15-20/wd. on acceptance for 1st & electronic rts. Articles 500-3,000 wds. (10/yr.).; book reviews 100 wds. (pays $25). Responds in 6 wks. Seasonal 6 mos. ahead. Accepts reprints (tell when/where appeared). Accepts requested ms by e-mail (copied into message). Kill fee 30%. Regularly uses sidebars. Prefers NIV. Guidelines on Website; copy for 9x12 SAE/$1.50 postage. (Ads)

Fillers: Buys 80/yr. Cartoons, short humor; to 150 wds.; $25-50.

Columns/Departments: Skye Jetuani, ed. Buys 25/yr. Tool Kit (Practical stories or resources for preaching, worship, outreach, pastoral care, spiritual formation, and administration); 100-700 wds. Complete ms. Pays $50-250.

Tips: "*Leadership* is a practical journal for pastors. Tell real-life stories of church life—defining moments—dramatic events. What was learned the hard way—by experience. We look for articles that provide practical help for problems church leaders face, not essays expounding on a topic, editorials arguing a position, or homilies explaining biblical principles. We want 'how-to' articles based on first-person accounts of real-life experiences in ministry in the local church."

**2006 Award of Excellence—Christian Ministries; 2007, 2004, 2003 EPA Award of Merit—Christian Ministries. This periodical was #15 on the 2007 Top 50 Christian Publishers list (#14 in 2006, #8 in 2005, #8 in 2004, #12 in 2003).

$LET'S WORSHIP, One Lifeway Plaza, MSN 175, Nashville TN 37234-0170. (615)251-3775. Fax (615)251-2795. E-mail: craig.adams@lifeway.com. Website: www.lifeway.com. Southern Baptist/LifeWay Christian Resources. Craig Adams, ed-in-chief. Resources for pastors and worship leaders; countering the norm with contagious ideas. Quarterly mag.; 96 pgs.; circ. 5,500. Subscription $14.95. 10% unsolicited freelance; 90% assigned. Complete ms by e-mail only. Pays .105/wd. on acceptance for all, 1st, or one-time rts. Articles 1,500 wds. (50/yr.); book reviews 300 wds. ($50). Responds in 10 wks. Seasonal 10 mos. ahead. Accepts simultaneous submissions. Requires ms by e-mail (attached file or copied into message). Regularly uses sidebars. Prefers HCSB. No guidelines/copy. (No ads)

Columns/Departments: Wednesday Words (4-week Bible study with listening sheets); Bible study, 625 wds.; listening sheet, 200 wds.; Drama (original scripts), 900 wds.

Special Needs: Offer testimonials: How we do drama, start a drama ministry, use mime, transition worship, etc. in our church. Offer original scripts for short drama or reader's theater.

Tips: "Most open to short dramas, dramatic readings, dramatic monologues/dialogs."

LUTHERAN FORUM, PO Box 327, Delhi NY 13753-0327. (607)746-7511. E-mail: dkralpb@aol.com. Website: www.alpb.org. American Lutheran Publicity Bureau. Sarah Hinlicky Wilson, ed. For church leadership—clerical and laity. Quarterly jour.; 64 pgs.; circ. 3,200. Subscription $26.45. 80% unsolicited freelance. Complete ms/cover letter. **NO PAYMENT.** Articles 1,000-3,000 wds. Responds in 26-32 wks. Accepts simultaneous submissions & reprints. Requires requested ms on disk. Guidelines; copy for 9x12 SAE/$2 postage. (Ads)

$LUTHERAN PARTNERS, 8765 W. Higgins Rd., Chicago IL 60631-4101. Toll-free (800)638-3522, ext. 2884. (773)380-2884. Fax (773)380-2829. E-mail: Lutheran.Partners@ecla.org or LUTHERAN_PARTNERS@ecunet.org. Website: www.elca.org/lutheranpartners. Evangelical Lutheran Church in America. William A. Decker, ed. To encourage and challenge rostered leaders in the ELCA, including pastors and lay ministers. Bimonthly & online mag.; 40 pgs.; circ. 20,000. Subscription $13 (free to leaders), $19.50 outside North America. 10-15% unsolicited freelance; 85-90% assigned. Query; phone/fax/e-query OK. Pays $125-170 on publication for one-time rts. Articles 500-1,500 wds. (12-15/yr.). Responds in 16 wks. Seasonal 6-12 mos. ahead. Accepts simultaneous submissions & reprints (tell when/where appeared). Kill fee (rare). Prefers requested ms on disk or by e-mail (attached file). Regularly uses sidebars. Prefers NRSV. Guidelines/theme list (also by e-mail/Website); copy $2/9x12 SAE/5 stamps. (Ads)

Poetry: Buys 6/yr. Free verse, traditional; $50-75. Keep concise. Submit max. 6 poems.

Fillers: Buys 4-5/yr. Cartoons; ideas for parish ministry; to 500 wds.; $25.

Special Needs: Book reviews. Query the editor. Uses books predominately from mainline denominational and some evangelical publishers. Payment is copy of book. Youth and family issues, rural and urban ministry issues, men's issues. More articles from women and ethnic authors (especially if ordained or are in official lay-ministry leadership roles).

Tips: "Query me with ideas which show you know our audience, can feel their heartbeats, and walk in their shoes. First, we are a leadership publication. Our audience includes pastors and lay church staff. Your articles must answer concerns that leadership has. Secondly, understand Lutheran Church theology and ELCA congregational life. Pertinent topics include preaching, Christian education, youth and family issues, Lutheran identity, worship, Scripture and theology, and social issues."

**This periodical was #48 on the 2007 Top 50 Christian Publishers list.

$MINISTRY & LITURGY, 160 E. Virginia St., #290, San Jose CA 95112. (408)286-8505. Fax (408)287-8748. E-mail: mleditor@rpinet.com. Website: www.rpinet.com/ml. Resource Publications Inc. Donna M. Cole, ed. dir. To help liturgists and ministers make the imaginative connection between liturgy and life. Monthly (10X) mag.; 50 pgs.; circ. 20,000. Subscription $50. 5% unsolicited freelance; 5% assigned. Query only; fax/e-query OK. Pays a stipend on publication for 1st rts. Articles & fiction 1,500 wds. (30/yr.). Responds in 4 wks. Seasonal 6 mos. ahead. Accepts reprints (tell when/where appeared). Requires requested ms on disk. Regularly uses sidebars. Guidelines/theme list; copy $4/11x14 SAE/2 stamps. (Ads)

Special Needs: The practice of ministry: music ministry, youth ministry, pastoral ministry, and liturgical ministry.

Contest: Visual Arts Awards.

Tips: "Writers need to be able to help our reader do his or her job better. Be familiar enough with contemporary issues in ministry to provide perceivable value to the reader. Provide new insight or valuable insight into issues of concern to members of a ministry team. Credibility (training and experience in ministry) is important."

MINISTRY IN MOTION E-ZINE, 11335 Rosewood Ave., Athens OH 45701. (740)797-4023. E-mail: customerservice@ministryinmotion.net. Website: www.ministryinmotion.net. Nondenominational. Thomas Hanover, ed. We seek to equip lay and clergy leaders for ministry in the 21st century through the resources of publications, coaching, consulting, and other Website tools. Bimonthly e-zine; circulation 700+. Subscription free online. 25% unsolicited freelance; 75% assigned. Query/published clips; e-query OK. Accepts full mss by e-mail. **NO PAYMENT** for one-time & electronic rts. Articles 700-1,000 wds. (25/yr.); book reviews 250 wds. Responds in 4 wks. Seasonal 2 mos. ahead. Accepts simultaneous submissions & reprints (tell when/where appeared). Prefers submissions by e-mail (attached file). Uses some sidebars. Prefers NIV or NRSV. Guidelines by e-mail/Website; copy online or e-mailed. (Ads)

Fillers: Short humor.

Columns/Departments: Ministry Employment (how to find employment in ministry field); Women's Ministries (how to lead effective women's ministries); 700-1,000 wds. Complete ms.

Tips: "Share leadership tips and insights. The more practical and how-to, the better. No theology or heavily scholastic articles; we are for the everyday church worker. Avoid church culture terms and lingo related to your own denomination. If no experience, send us some samples. We'll work with you."

$MINISTRY MAGAZINE: International Journal for Pastors, 12501 Old Columbia Pike, Silver Spring MD 20904. (301)680-6510. Fax (301)680-6502. E-mail: MinistryMagazine@gc.adventist.org. Website: www.ministrymagazine.org. Seventh-day Adventist. Nikolaus Satelmajer, ed.; Willie E. Hucks II, assoc. ed. For pastors. Monthly jour.; 32 pgs.; circ. 19,000. Subscription $30.50. 90% unsolicited freelance. Query; fax/e-query OK. Pays $50-300 on acceptance for all rts. Articles 1,000-1,500 wds.; book reviews 100-150 wds. ($25). Responds within 13 wks. Prefers requested ms by e-mail. Uses some sidebars. Guidelines (also on Website)/theme list; copy for 9x12 SAE/5 stamps. (Ads)

$MINISTRY TODAY, 600 Rinehart Rd., Lake Mary FL 32746. (407)333-0600. Fax (407)333-7133. E-mail: ministrytoday@strang.com. Website: www.ministrytodaymag.com. Strang Communications. Submit to The Editor. Helps for pastors and church leaders, primarily in Pentecostal/charismatic churches. Bimonthly mag.; 70 pgs.; circ. 30,000. Subscription $24.95. 60-80% freelance. Query; fax/e-query preferred. Pays $50 or $500-800 on publication for all rts. Articles 1,800-2,500 wds. (25/yr.); book/music/video reviews, 300 wds., $25. Responds in 4 wks. Prefers accepted ms by e-mail. Kill fee. Regularly uses sidebars. Prefers NIV. Guidelines; copy $6/9x12 SAE. (Ads)

Columns/Departments: Buys 36/yr.

Tips: "Most open to columns. Write for guidelines and study the magazine. Please correspond with editor before sending an article proposal."

$NET RESULTS, PO Box 3930, Lubbock TX 79452-3930. (806)726-8094, ext. 198. Fax (806)762-8873. E-mail: netresults@netresults.org. Website: www.netresults.org. Net Results Inc. Bill Tenny-Brittian, sr. ed. (bill@hcna.us). Offers Christian church leaders practical, ministry vitalization ideas and methods. Monthly (10X) & online mag.; 32 pgs.; circ. 12,000. Subscription $29.95. 20% unsolicited freelance; 80% assigned. Query; fax/e-query OK. Accepts full ms through e-mail. Now pays a small amount on publication for one-time rts. Articles 1,000-2,000 wds. (20/yr.). Response time varies. Seasonal 6 mos. ahead. No simultaneous submissions or reprints. Requires accepted ms by e-mail (attached file). No kill fee. Regularly uses sidebars. Prefers NRSV. Copy for 9x12 SAE. (Limited ads)

Tips: "We prefer practical, how-to articles on ideas that have worked in a local church setting."

$THE NEWSLETTER NEWSLETTER, PO Box 36269, Canton OH 44735. Toll-free (800)992-2144. E-mail: jburns@comresources.com, or through Website: www.newsletternews

letter.com. Communication Resources. John Burns, ed. To help church secretaries and church newsletter editors prepare their newsletter. Monthly & online newsletter; 14 pgs. Subscription $49.95. 70% assigned. Complete ms; e-query OK. Pays $50-150 on acceptance for all rts. Articles 800-1,000 wds. (12/yr.). Responds in 4 wks. Seasonal 8 mos. ahead. Accepts simultaneous submissions. Requires requested ms on disk; accepts e-mail submissions. Kill fee. Regular sidebars. Guidelines (also by e-mail); copy for 9x12 SAE/3 stamps.

Tips: "Most open to how-to articles on various aspects of newsletter production—writing, graphics, layout and design, postal, printing, etc."

$OUTREACH MAGAZINE, 2230 Oak Ridge Way, Vista CA 92081. Fax (760)597-2314. E-mail: llowry@outreach.com. Website: www.outreachmagazine.com. Lindy Lowry, ed. Tells the ideas, insights, and stories of today's outreach-focused churches and is designed to inspire, challenge, and equip churches to connect with their communities and show the love of God to people both locally and globally. Bimonthly mag.; 130 pgs.; circ. 35,000. Subscription $29.95. Estab. 2003. 20% unsolicited freelance; 80% assigned. Query/clips; e-query OK. Pays $400 for articles; $700-1,000 for feature articles; on publication for 1st rts. Articles 1,200-2,000 wds. Responds in 6-8 wks. Seasonal 6 mos. ahead. No simultaneous submissions; rarely accepts reprints (tell when/where appeared). Prefers submissions by e-mail (attached file). Sometimes pays kill fee. Regularly uses sidebars. Guidelines on Website; free copy. (Ads)

Columns/Departments: Accepts fewer than 10/yr. Pulse (tight and bright stories about churches finding unique ways to outreach), 50-250 wds.; From the Frontline (profile of one church and the unique way it's reaching its community), 800 wds.; SoulFires (as-told-to pieces from interview with someone doing outreach), 950 wds.; .30/wd. or flat fee. Query.

Special Needs: Interviews with non-Christians.

Tips: "Most open to interviews/profiles (Soulfires, Frames, The Outreach Interview); church stories (Pulse, Idea Bank, From the Front Line); outreach ideas from churches (Idea Bank, Connections, Big Idea).

$PARISH LITURGY, 16565 S. State St., South Holland IL 60473. (708)331-5485. Fax (708)331-5484. E-mail: acp@acpress.org. Website: www.americancatholicpress.org. Catholic. Father Michael Gilligan, ed. dir. A planning tool for Sunday and holy day liturgy. Quarterly mag.; 40 pgs.; circ. 1,200. Subscription $24. 5% unsolicited freelance. Query; no phone/e-query. Pays variable rates for all rts. Articles 400 wds. Responds in 4 wks. Seasonal 4 mos. ahead. Accepts simultaneous submissions & reprints (tell when/where appeared). Uses some sidebars. Prefers NAB. No guidelines; copy available. (No ads)

Tips: "We only use articles on the liturgy—period. Send us well-informed articles on the liturgy."

$PRAY! PO Box 35004, Colorado Springs CO 80935-3504. (719)531-3585. Fax (719)598-7128. E-mail: pray.mag@navpress.com. Website: www.navpress.com/magazines/Pray! The Navigators. Cynthia Bezek, ed. A magazine entirely about prayer for believers who want to grow in their relationship with Christ through prayer and intercession—whether new to prayer, seasoned prayer warriors, or prayer leaders. Bimonthly mag.; 56-64 pgs.; circ. 41,000. Subscription $19.97. 70% unsolicited freelance; 30% assigned. Complete ms or query; e-query OK. Accepts full mss by e-mail. Pays .20/wd. (.05/wd. for reprints), plus a subscription, on acceptance for 1st, one-time, reprint, or electronic rts. Articles 800-1,500 wds., or 500 wds. or less. (30/yr.). Responds in 8-12 wks. No seasonal. Accepts simultaneous submissions & reprints (tell when/where appeared). Prefers e-mail submission (attached file). Kill fee 50%. Regularly uses sidebars. Prefers NIV. Guidelines/theme list (also by e-mail/Website); copy for 9x12 SAE/$2.69 postage. (Ads)

Fillers: Buys 25/yr. Ideas on prayer (no prayers or poetry); 100-450 wds.; .20/wd.

Columns/Departments: Buys 8/yr. Prayer Journeys (tells a personal story of a breakthrough, milestone, epiphany, or even setback you experienced in your prayer journey, which can teach others and draw them closer to Jesus through prayer); 800 wds. Prayer Ideas (short, practical articles that offer fresh and helpful ideas for readers to try in either personal or corporate prayer), 150-500 wds. Prayer News (using journalistic style, tells of a prayer event, preferably interdenominational and city- or region-wide, to encourage or inspire others), 200-400 wds.; complete ms; .20/wd.

Special Needs: Especially needs articles that move readers beyond praying for personal needs and toward praying for neighborhoods, churches, cities, and the nation.

Tips: "Please note that any topics indicated in the topical listings must be closely related to prayer (no general articles on those topics). Most open to prayer journeys, prayer ideas, non-theme features. Make sure you move people toward prayer as a relationship with Jesus and not just into more religious forms and structures. Be personal, vulnerable, biblical, and passionate. Keep in mind that our readers already pray, are highly motivated to pray. Be fresh and practical in your approach."

**#9 Best-Selling Magazine in Christian Retail Stores. This periodical was #4 on the 2007 Top 50 Christian Publishers list (#11 in 2006, #42 in 2005, #36 in 2004, #37 in 2003).

PREACHING, PREACHING ON-LINE & PREACHING NOW, 104 Woodmont Blvd., Ste. 300, Nashville TN 37205. (615)386-3011. Fax (615)312-4277. E-mail: editor@preaching.com. Website: www.preaching.com. Salem Communications. Dr. Michael Duduit, ed. Bimonthly; circ. 9,000. Subscription $39.95. 50% unsolicited freelance; 50% assigned. Query; fax/e-query OK. **PAYS A SUBSCRIPTION** for one-time & electronic rts. Responds in 4-8 wks. Seasonal 10-12 mos. ahead. Reprints from books only. Prefers requested ms by e-mail (attached file). Uses some sidebars. Guidelines on Website; copy online. (ads). *Preaching Online* is a professional resource for pastors that supplements *Preaching Magazine.* Includes all content from magazine, plus additional articles and sermons. **NO PAYMENT** for material used only online. *Preaching Now* is a weekly e-mail/e-zine; circ. 19,000. No freelance submissions; accepts books for review. (Ads)

$PREACHINGTODAY.COM, 465 Gundersen Dr., Carol Stream IL 60188-2498. (630)260-6200. Fax (630)260-0451. E-mail: blarson@christianitytoday.com. Website: www.preachingtoday.com. Christianity Today Intl. Brian Larson, ed. Open to fresh sermon illustrations from various sources for preachers (no recycled illustrations from other illustration sources). E-mail submissions only. Articles 250-500 wds. Responds in 1 mo. Guidelines on Website. Sermon illustrations only.

$PREACHING WELL, PO Box 3102, Margate NJ 08402. Toll-free (800)827-9401. (609)822-9401. Fax (609)822-1638. E-mail: techsupport@voicings.com. Website: www.voicings.com. Voicings Publications. James Colaianni Jr., pub. Sermon illustration resource for professional clergy. Monthly newsletter, 8 pgs. Subscription $47. 5% unsolicited freelance. Complete ms; e-query OK. Pays .10/wd. on publication for any rts. Illustrations/anecdotes 50-250 wds. Responds in 6 wks. Seasonal 4 mos. ahead. Accepts reprints. Prefers requested ms on disk or by e-mail. Guidelines/topical index (also by e-mail); copy for 9x12 SAE. (Ads)

Poetry: Light verse, traditional; 50-250 lines; .10/wd. Submit max. 3 poems.

Fillers: Various; sermon illustrations; 50-250 wds.; .10/wd.

Tips: "All sections open."

$THE PRIEST, 200 Noll Plaza, Huntington IN 46750-4304. (260)356-8400. Fax (260)356-8472. E-mail: tpriest@osv.com. Website: www.osv.com. Catholic/Our Sunday Visitor Inc. Msgr. Owen F. Campion, ed.; submit to Murray Hubley, assoc. ed. For Catholic priests, deacons, and seminarians; to help in all aspects of ministry. Monthly jour.; 48 pgs.; circ. 6,500. Subscription $39.95. 40% unsolicited freelance. Query (preferred) or complete ms/cover letter; phone/fax/e-query OK. Pays $50-250 on acceptance for 1st rts. Articles 1,500-5,000 wds. (96/yr.); some 2-parts. Responds in 5-13 wks. Seasonal 4 mos. ahead. Uses some sidebars. Prefers disk or e-mail submissions (attached file). Prefers NAB. Free guidelines/copy. (Ads)

Fillers: Murray Hubley, fillers ed. Cartoons; $35.

Columns/Departments: Buys 36/yr. Viewpoint, to 1,000 wds.; $75.

Tips: "Write to the point, with interest. Most open to nuts-and-bolts issues for priests, or features. Keep the audience in mind; need articles or topics important to priests and parish life. Include Social Security number."

$PROCLAIM, PO Box 1561, New Canaan CT 06840. Toll-free (888)320-5576. Fax (203)966-4654. E-mail: meg@parishpublishing.org, or info@parishpublishing.org. Website: www.parishpublishing.org. Parish Publishing LLC. Meg Brossy, ed. The leading inspirational preaching resource for church leaders. Weekly newsletter; 4 pgs. Subscription $59.95. Also available digitally at www.proclaimsermons.com, which includes archives of sermons. 20% unsolicited freelance; 80% assigned. Query/clips. Pays to $100 on publication or acceptance for reprint rts. Articles or fiction. Responds in 2 wks. Seasonal 3 mos. ahead. Prefers accepted mss by e-mail (attached file). (No ads)

Tips: "Proclaim follows the Catholic Lectionary and the Revised Common Lectionary (RCL). Writers are usually priests and ministers, or in seminary."

PULPIT HELPS, 6815 Shallowford Rd., Chattanooga TN 37421. Toll-free (800)251-7206. (423)894-6060. Fax (423)510-8074. E-mail: publisher@pulpithelps.com. Website: www.pulpithelps.com. AMG International. Justin Lonas, pub. Primarily reaches Bible-believing Christian pastors and functions as their primary source for information for sermon preparation and news from the Christian world. Monthly & online tabloid; 28 pgs.; circ. 25,000. Subscription $22.99. 10% unsolicited freelance; 70% assigned. Complete ms/cover letter; e-query OK. Accepts full mss by e-mail. **NO PAYMENT.** Articles 800 wds. (50-75/yr.); book reviews 250 wds. Responds in 2-4 wks. Seasonal 2-3 mos. ahead. Accepts simultaneous submissions & reprints (tell when/where appeared). Requires e-mail submission (attached file). Uses some sidebars. Prefers NAS (others accepted). Guidelines (also by e-mail/Website); copy for 9x12 SAE/2 stamps. (Ads)

Fillers: Accepts 50-100/yr. Anecdotes, cartoons, jokes, quotes, sermon illustrations, short humor, word puzzles; 25-150 wds.

Columns/Departments: Ted Kyle, mng. ed. (editor@pulpithelps.com) Accepts 2-4/yr. Missions Spotlight (innovative approaches to reaching the lost for Christ around the world); 800-1,200 wds.

Tips: "Most open to Sermon Starters—sermon outlines designed to give a busy pastor a leg up; any good missions-focused pieces; any good essays reflecting thoughtful Christian scholarship."

$REFORMED WORSHIP, 2850 Kalamazoo S.E., Grand Rapids MI 49560-0001. Toll-free (800)777-7270. (616)224-0763. Fax (616)224-0834. E-mail: info@reformedworship.org. Website: www.reformedworship.org. Faith Alive Christian Resources. Rev. Joyce Borger, ed. To provide worship leaders and committees with practical assistance in planning, structuring, and conducting congregational worship in the Reformed tradition. Quarterly & online mag.; 48 pgs.; circ. 4,600. Subscription $25.95. 30% unsolicited freelance; 70% assigned. Query; e-query OK. Accepts full mss by e-mail. Pays .05/wd. on publication for 1st & electronic rts. Articles 1,400 wds.; book reviews 200 wds. Responds in 4 wks. Seasonal 6 mos. ahead. Rarely accepts reprints (tell when/where appeared). Prefers e-mail submission (attached file). Uses some sidebars. Also accepts submissions from children/teens. Prefers TNIV. Guidelines on Website; copy for 9x12 SAE/$2.13 postage (mark "Media Mail"). (No ads)

Columns/Departments: Songs for the Season (music and background notes, usually 3 songs), 2,000 wds.; Worship Technology (intersection of worship and technology), 900 wds. Query.

Tips: "You need to understand and focus on the Reformed tradition of worship."

**2004 EPA Award of Merit—General.

RELEVANT LEADER & RELEVANT NETWORK.COM, 1220 Alden Rd., Orlando FL 32803. Toll-free (866)512-1108. (407)660-1411. Fax (407)401-9100. E-mail: adam@relevantmediagroup.com. Website: www.RelevantNetwork.com. Relevant Media Group. Adam Smith, mng. ed. Targets culture-savvy, relevant-minded ministers and leaders of 18- to 34-year-olds. Bimonthly & online mag.; 36 pgs. 80% freelance. Send a one-paragraph query/clips; prefers e-mail; no phone/fax query. **NO PAYMENT** for print or online contributions for 1st rts. & all electronic rts. Print features 1,500 wds.; Website features 800-1,200 wds; reviews 400-600 wds. Responds in 4-6 wks. Prefers submissions as Word attachments. Guidelines on Website. Incomplete topical listings.

$REVIEW FOR RELIGIOUS, 3601 Lindell Blvd., St. Louis MO 63108-3393. (314)633-4610. Fax (314)633-4611. E-mail: review@slu.edu. Website: www.reviewforreligious.org. Catholic/Jesuits of Missouri Province. Rev. David L. Fleming, S.J., ed. A forum for shared reflection on the lives and experience of all who find that the church's rich heritages of spirituality support their personal and apostolic Christian lives. Quarterly mag.; 112 pgs.; circ. 5,000. Subscription $24. 100% unsolicited freelance. Complete ms/cover letter; no phone/fax/e-query. Accepts full ms by e-mail. Pays $6/pg. on publication for 1st rts. Articles 1,500-5,000 wds. (50/yr.). Responds in 9 wks. Seasonal 8 mos. ahead. Accepts requested ms on disk. Does not use sidebars. Prefers RSV, NAB. Guidelines (also by e-mail); copy for 10x13 SAE/5 stamps. (No ads)

Poetry: Buys 10/yr. Light verse, traditional; 3-12 lines; $6. Submit max. 4 poems.

Tips: "Read the journal. Do not submit an article without reading at least one issue. Submit an article based on our guidelines."

$REV. MAGAZINE, PO Box 481, Loveland CO 80539-0481. (970)669-3836. Fax (970)679-4392. E-mail: lsparks@group.com, or info@group.com. Website: www.revmagazine.com. Group Publishing Inc. Lee Sparks, ed. For pastors; partnering with pastors. Bimonthly & online mag.; 104 pgs.; circ. 45,000. Subscription $19.95. 25% unsolicited freelance; 75% assigned. Complete ms/cover letter; e-query OK. Pays $300-400 on acceptance for all rts.; makes work-for-hire assignments. Articles 1,000-3,000 wds. (18-24/yr.) Responds in 9 wks. Seasonal 8 mos. ahead. Prefers requested ms on disk or by e-mail (attached file). Regularly uses sidebars. Guidelines on Website; copy $2/9x12 SAE/5 stamps. (Ads)

Fillers: Buys 3/yr. Cartoons, ideas, sermon illustrations; $50.

Columns/Departments: Ministry (preaching, worship, discipleship, outreach, family); Life (personal growth, health beat, home front); Leadership (church business, team work, leadership); Insight (today's trends, current culture, in the know); all 200-400 wds; $35-50.

Tips: "We are most open to short (250 word) practical articles for our departments. Write articles that deal with personal and professional topics for pastors."

$THE REVWRITER RESOURCE, PO Box 81, Perkasie PA 18944. (215)453-5066. Fax (215) 453-8128. E-mail: editor@revwriter.com. Website: www.revwriter.com. Nondenominational/RevWriter Resources LLC. Rev. Susan M. Lang, ed. An electronic newsletter for busy lay and clergy congregational leaders. Monthly e-zine.; circ. 500. Subscription free. 90% unsolicited freelance; 10% assigned. Query; e-query preferred. Pays $20 on publication for 1st electronic rts. & one-year archival rts.; $10 for devotions. Articles 800-1,000 wds.; questions or exercises for group use, 250-500 wds. No simultaneous submissions or reprints. Also accepts submissions from teens. Guidelines on Website; copy online. (Ads)

Fillers: Buys 10/yr. Ministry ideas; Ministry Resources List to accompany article; 250-400 wds. These are usually written by the feature-article writer. Also Practical Wisdom section.

Contest: Read current issues of the magazine to learn about new contests they are running. There are often drawings for free books.

Tips: "I'm always looking for articles for the Practical Wisdom section which focuses on program or ministry ideas that worked for you. This is an easy area to break into. They are short pieces, usually 250-400 words. Articles should be practical how-tos for busy church leaders—materials they can use in their ministry settings. Be sure to read archived issues for previous formats and ministry resources already covered. Looking for a new approach to stewardship. Most open to devotion writing in Lent and Advent, and the monthly articles and discussion questions. Send me an e-query detailing the article you'd like to write and include your expertise in this area. The material must be practical and applicable to life as a busy congregational leader. They want information they can use."

$SABBATH SCHOOL LEADERSHIP, 55 W. Oak Ridge Dr., Hagerstown MD 21740. (301)393-4095. Fax (301)393-4055. E-mail: fcrumbly@rhpa.org, or SabbathSchoolLeadership@rhpa.org. Website: www.Sabbathschool.com. Seventh-day Adventist/Review & Herald. Faith Crumbly, ed. Nurtures, educates, and supports adult Bible study and program leaders by providing training in leadership and interpersonal skills, plus programs. Monthly mag.; 32 pgs.; circ. 8,100. Subscription $34.95 (add $6 for addresses outside U.S., Canada, and Bermuda). 10% unsolicited freelance; 90% assigned. Complete ms. Pays $25-100 on acceptance for 1st rts. Articles 600-1,200 wds. (120-150/yr.). Responds in 1-2 wks. Seasonal 6-8 mos. ahead. Accepts reprints (tell when/where appeared). Prefers accepted ms by e-mail (attached file). Uses some sidebars. Guidelines/theme list on Website; copy. (For ads, contact: Margie Tooley at margie.tooley@rhpa.org.)

Fillers: Cartoons; $70-100.

Columns/Departments: Buys 5/yr. Leadership Tips (interpersonal skills, organization, mentoring, training), 600-800 wds. Query. Pays $70-100.

SEWANEE THEOLOGICAL REVIEW, University of the South, 335 Tennessee Ave., Sewanee TN 37383-0001. (931)598-1475. E-mail: STR@sewanee.edu. Website: www.sewanee.edu/theology/str/strhome. Anglican/Episcopal. Jim D. Jones, mng. ed. For Anglican/Episcopal clergy and interested laity. Quarterly jour.; 120 pgs. Subscription $24. Open to freelance. Complete ms/cover letter; no e-query. **NO PAYMENT** for all rts. Articles (24/yr.). Responds in 9-26 wks. Seasonal 24 mos. ahead. No simultaneous submissions or reprints. Prefers requested ms on disk or by e-mail (attached file). Prefers NRSV. No guidelines; copy $8. Incomplete topical listings. (Ads)

Special Needs: Anglican and Episcopal theology, religion, history, doctrine, ethics, homiletics, liturgies, hermeneutics, biography, prayer, practice.

SHARING THE PRACTICE, 100 S. Chestnut St., Kent OH 44240-3402. (330)678-0187. E-mail: journal@apclergy.org. Website: www.apclergy.org. Academy of Parish Clergy/Ecumenical/Interfaith. Rev. Dr. Robert Cornwall, ed-in-chief (drbobcornwall@msn.com); Dr. Forrest V. Fitzhugh, book rev. ed. (bond007@texas.net). Growth toward excellence through sharing the practice of parish ministry. Quarterly international jour.; 40 pgs.; circ. 250 (includes 80 seminary libraries & publishers). Subscription $25/yr. (send to APC, 2249 Florinda St., Sarasota FL 34231-1414). 100% unsolicited freelance. Complete ms/cover letter; e-query OK; query/clips for fiction. **NO PAYMENT** for 1st, reprint, simultaneous, or electronic rts. Articles 500-2,500 wds. (25/yr.); reviews 200 wds. Responds in 2 wks. Seasonal 6 mos. ahead. Accepts simultaneous submissions & reprints (tell when/where appeared). Prefers e-mail submissions (copied into message). Uses some sidebars. Prefers NRSV. Guidelines/theme list (also by e-mail); free copy. (No ads)

Poetry: Accepts 12/yr. Any type; 25-35 lines. Submit max. 2 poems.

Fillers: Accepts 6/yr. Anecdotes, cartoons, jokes, short humor; 50-100 wds.

Columns/Departments: Academy News; President's; Dean of Studies; and Church Health.

Contest: Book of the Year Award ($100+), Top Ten Books of the Year list, Parish Pastor of the Year Award ($200+). Inquire by e-mail to DIELPADRE@aol.com.

Tips: "We desire articles and poetry by practicing clergy of all kinds who wish to share their practice of ministry. Join the Academy."

$SMALL GROUP DYNAMICS, PO Box 621, Zionville IN 46077. (317)769-0945. E-mail: office@smallgroups.com. Website: http://smallgroups.com. Small Group Network. Dan Lentz, dir. How-to for small groups. Online e-zine/newsletter. Query; e-query OK. Pays $40-60 for all rts. Articles 500-1,000 wds. Seasonal 2-3 mos. ahead. Prefers requested ms by e-mail (attached file). Accepts reprints. Guidelines/theme list: http://smallgroups.com/pages/Theme_List.

Fillers: Small group cartoons.

Special Needs: Brief testimonies of how God has worked in your group; humor in groups; icebreaker ideas, etc.

Tips: "Follow our themes. We use mostly practical, how-to oriented articles."

$SUNDAY SERMONS, PO Box 3102, Margate NJ 08402. Toll-free (800)827-9401. (609)822-9401. Fax (609)822-1638. E-mail: techsupport@voicings.com. Website: www.voicings.com. Voicings Publications. James Colaianni Jr., pub. Full-text sermon resource serving professional clergy since 1970. Bimonthly booklet; 60 pgs. Subscription $62 or $89. 5% unsolicited freelance. Complete ms; e-query OK. Pays .10/wd. on publication for any rts. Complete sermon manuscripts 1,200-1,500 wds.; illustrations/anecdotes 50-250 wds. Responds in 6 wks. Seasonal 4 mos. ahead. Accepts reprints. Prefers requested ms on disk or by e-mail. Guidelines/topical index (also by e-mail); copy for 9x12 SAE. Incomplete topical listings.

Fillers: Various; sermon illustrations; 50-250 wds.; .10/wd.

Tips: "Submit complete sermon, 1,200-1,500 words. Read sample sermons on our Website."

TECHNOLOGIES FOR WORSHIP, 3891 Holborn Rd., Queensville ON L0G 1R0, Canada. (905)473-9822. Fax (905)473-9928. E-mail: krc@tfwm.com, or info@tfwm.com. Website: www.tfwm.com. ITC Inc. Kevin Rogers Cobus, ed. Bimonthly & online mag.; 92+ pgs.; circ. 35,000. Subscription $14.95. 100% unsolicited freelance. Query; phone/fax/e-query OK. **NO PAYMENT** for one-time rts. Articles 700-1,200 wds. Responds in 2 wks. Seasonal 2 mos. ahead. Accepts simultaneous submissions & reprints (tell when/where appeared). Prefers accepted ms by e-mail (attached or copied into message). Uses some sidebars. Free guidelines/theme list (also on Website)/copy. (Ads)

Special Needs: Website streaming resources for churches and ministries; technologies: audio, video, music, computers, broadcast, lighting, and drama; 750-2,500 wds.

Tips: "Call/fax/e-mail the editor to discuss idea for article or column. The publication is open to technical, educational articles that can benefit the church, providing hints, tips, guidelines, examples, studies, tutorials, etc. on new technology and new uses for it in the church."

THEOLOGICAL DIGEST & OUTLOOK, 415 Linwell Rd., St. Catherines ON L2M 2P3, Canada. (905)935-5369. Fax (905)935-7134. E-mail: p-d@niagara.com, or paul@firstgrantham.org. Website: www.ITCanada.com/~theology. United Church of Canada. Rev. Paul Miller, ed. For clergy and informed laity; evangelical/orthodox slant within denomination. Semiannual mag.; 32 pgs.; circ. 400. Subscription $15 Cdn., $19 U.S. 100% unsolicited freelance. Complete ms; phone/fax/e-query OK. **NO PAYMENT.** Articles 1,500-5,000 wds. (6-8/yr.). Responds in 2 wks. Accepts reprints (tell when/where appeared). Prefers disk or e-mail submissions. Does not use sidebars. Any Bible version. No guidelines. (No ads)

Tips: "Just submit."

$THIS ROCK, 2020 Gillespie Way, El Cajon CA 92020. (619)387-7200. Fax (619)387-0042. cpeacock@catholic.com. Website: www.catholic.com/magazines.asp. Catholic Answers. Cherie Peacock, ed. Deals with doctrine, evangelization, and apologetics. Monthly (10X) mag.; 48 pgs. Subscription $39.95. 10% unsolicited freelance; 90% assigned. Complete ms/cover letter; e-query OK. Pays $200-500 on acceptance for 1st & electronic rts. Articles 1,500-3,000 wds. (80/yr.). Responds in 4 wks. Seasonal 9 mos. ahead. Prefers RSV (Catholic version). No simultaneous submissions or reprints. Prefers e-mail submissions (attached file). Kill fee sometimes. Regularly uses sidebars. Guidelines (also by e-mail/Website); copy for 9x12 SAE/$2.13 postage (mark "Media Mail"). (No ads)

Columns/Departments: Buys 10/yr. Damascus Road (personal conversion story), 1,800-3,000 wds. Complete ms. Pays $200.

Tips: "Most open to Damascus Road—stories of conversion to Catholic Church."

$TODAY'S PARISH, 1 Montauk Ave., Ste. 200, New London CT 06320. Toll-free (800)321-0411, ext. 188 (editor). (860)536-2611. Fax (860)536-5674. E-mail: NWagner@twentythirdpublications.com. Websites: www.todaysparish.com, or www.twentythirdpublications.com. Catholic/Twenty-Third Publications. Nick Wagner, ed. Practical ideas and issues relating to parish life, management, and ministry. Mag. published 7X/yr.; 40 pgs.; circ. 14,800. Subscription $24.95. Very little unsolicited freelance. Query or complete ms. Pays $75-100 on publication for 1st rts. Articles 800-1,800 wds. (15/yr.). Responds 13 wks. Seasonal 6 mos. ahead. Guidelines; copy for 9x12 SASE.

$TORCH LEGACY LEADER, PO Box 372573, Atlanta GA 30037, or PO Box 165046, Irving TX 75016. (877)867-2457. Fax (817)887-3089. E-mail: info@torchlegacy.com. Website: www.torchlegacy.com. Torch Ministries Intl. Daniel Whyte, pres./ed. A biblically based journal for black church leaders and community leaders. Online jour. 60% unsolicited freelance; 40% assigned. Complete ms/cover letter; e-query OK. Pays $50 (flat fee) on publication for 1st rts. Best Black Sermon of the quarter receives $100 on publication. Articles 1,500 wds. Responds in 12 wks. Seasonal 6 mos. ahead. Requires requested ms on disk. Uses some sidebars. Prefers KJV. Guidelines (also by e-mail/Website). Incomplete topical listings.

Special Needs: Sermons; articles; essays on the spiritual, social, and moral crisis facing the black community in America, with biblically based solutions.

Tips: "We are looking for sound, biblically based material that can be used by God to help lift up black America to where it needs to be in every area of life."

RICK WARREN'S MINISTRY TOOLBOX, (formerly Pastors.com), 1 Saddleback Pkwy., Lake Forest CA 92630-8700. Toll-free (866)829-0300. (949)609-8703. E-mail: Tobinp@saddleback.net. Website: www.pastors.com (archive: www.pastors.com/Legacy/RWMT/MTAchive.asp). Tobin Perry, ed. dir. To mentor pastors worldwide. Weekly e-zine; circ. 177,000. Free e-mail newsletter. 10% unsolicited freelance; 90% assigned. Query; e-query OK. **NO PAYMENT** for one-time, reprint, simultaneous, & electronic rts. Will link readers to your site or book on Amazon in exchange for article. Articles 800-1,000 wds. (250/yr.). Responds in 6-8 wks. Seasonal 4 mos. ahead. Accepts simultaneous submissions & reprints (tell when/where appeared). Prefers accepted ms by e-mail (attached file). Uses some sidebars. Guidelines & copy by e-mail. (No ads)

Special Needs: Issues facing pastors and other ministry leaders. Time management, conflict resolution, facilitating change, communication and preaching, stewardship, worship, lay ministry, temptation, spiritual vitality, family matters, finances, creative ideas for ministry, vision, power, authority, encouragement, ministry and missions mobilization, small group leadership, facilitating spiritual growth, missions (specifically battling spiritual lostness, egocentric leadership, poverty, disease, and illiteracy locally and globally). Uses a lot of church leadership and pastoral book excerpts and articles adapted from books. The key is that the submission relates to church leaders, specifically pastors.

Tips: "We're very open to freelance contributions. Although we are unable to pay, this is a worldwide ministry to pastors."

$WILLOW, PO Box 3188, Barrington IL 60011-5046. (847)765-0070. Fax (847)765-5046. E-mail: Paulb@willowcreek.org. Website: www.willowcreek.com. Willow Creek Assn. Paul Braoudakis, mng. ed. To educate, inform, and inspire pioneering, innovative church leaders with ministry breakthroughs from churches all around the world. Quarterly & online newsletter; 40 pgs.; circ. 10,000. Subscription $39. 10% unsolicited; 25-30% assigned. Query/clips or complete ms; phone/fax/e-query OK. Pays .25/wd. on publication for all rts. Articles 500-1,000 wds.; book/music reviews 500 wds., video reviews 300 wds. Responds in 2 wks. Seasonal 2 mos. ahead. Accepts simultaneous submissions & reprints (tell when/where appeared). Requires requested ms on disk or by e-mail (attached file). Some sidebars. Prefers NIV, NLT. Free copy. (No ads)

Columns/Departments: News From the Frontlines (creative ministries within the church), 50-100 wds.; Strategic Trends (trends from growing churches), 200-250 wds.; .25/wd. Complete ms.

Tips: "Submit articles that will help other churches do what they do better. Any articles that pertain to doing a seeker-sensitive type of ministry will be considered. Also leadership issues in the church, outreach ideas, and effective evangelism."

**2007 EPA Award of Excellence—General; 2006 EPA Award of Merit—Most Improved Publication.

$WORD & WORLD: Theology for Christian Ministry, 2481 Como Ave., St. Paul MN 55108. (651)641-3210. Fax (651)641-3354. Website: www.luthersem.edu/word&world. E.L.C.A./ Luther Theological Seminary. Frederick J. Gaiser, ed. (fgaiser@luthersem.edu); Mark Thronveit, book rev. ed. (mthrontv@luthersem.edu). Addresses ecclesiastical and general issues from a theological perspective and addresses pastors and church leaders with the best fruits of theological research. Quarterly jour.; 104 pgs.; circ. 2,500. Subscription $24. 10% unsolicited freelance. Complete ms/cover letter; phone query OK. Pays $50 on publication for all rts. Articles 3,500 wds. Responds in 2-8 wks. Guidelines/theme list on Website; copy $7.

Tips: "Most open to general articles. We look for serious theology addressed clearly and interestingly to people in the practice of ministry. Creativity and usefulness in ministry are highly valued."

$WORSHIP LEADER, 32234 Paseo Adelanto, Ste. A, San Juan Capistrano CA 92675-3622. Toll-free (888)881-5861. (949)240-9339. Fax (949)240-0038. E-mail: editor@wlmag.com, or ybui@wlmag.com. Website: www.worshipleader.com. The Worship Leader Partnership. Julie Reid, exec. ed. A resource for current trends, theological insights, and planning programs for all those involved in church worship. Bimonthly (8X) mag.; 64-72 pgs.; circ. 50,000. Subscription $19.95. 20% unsolicited freelance; 80% assigned. Query/clips or complete ms by fax/e-mail OK. Pays $200-800 for assigned, $200-500 for unsolicited, on publication for all or 1st rts. Articles 1,200-2,000 wds. (15-30/yr.); reviews 300 wds. Responds in 6-13 wks. Seasonal 6 mos. ahead. Accepts e-mail submissions (attached file—MS Word). Kill fee 50%. Uses some sidebars. Prefers NIV. Guidelines/theme list on Website; copy $5. (Ads)

Tips: "Read our magazine. Become familiar with our themes. Submit a detailed and well-thought-out idea that fits our vision."

**2003 EPA Award of Merit—Christian Ministries.

$YOUR CHURCH, 465 Gundersen Dr., Carol Stream IL 60188. (630)260-6200. Fax (630)260-0114. E-mail: YCEditor@yourchuch.net. Website: www.yourchurch.net. Christianity Today Intl. Submit to Mike Schreiter, mng. ed. We give pastors and church leaders practical information to help them in managing the business side of the church. Bimonthly trade journal; 68+ pgs.; circ. 75,000. Subscription free to church administrators. 10% unsolicited freelance; 90% assigned. Query/clips; phone/fax/e-query OK. Accepts full mss by e-mail. Pays .20/wd. on acceptance for 1st & electronic rts. Articles 1,000-2,000 wds. (10/yr.). Responds in 2 wks. Seasonal 6 mos. ahead. Accepts simultaneous submissions & reprints (tell when/where appeared). Prefers e-mail submission (attached file). Accepts full manuscripts by e-mail. Kill fee 50%. Regularly uses sidebars. Prefers NIV. Guidelines/theme list by e-mail; copy for 9x12 SASE. (Ads: 630-260-6202)

Fillers: Buys 18/yr. Cartoons, $125.

Columns/Departments: Query. Church Makeover (recent remodeling project), 500-700 wds, plus several high-resolution photos, before/after project; Ask the Experts (Q & A), 100-300 wds.; $50-200.

Special Needs: Church management articles; audio/visual equipment; books/curriculum resources; music equipment; church products; furnishings; office equipment; computers/software; transportation (bus, van); video projectors; church architecture/construction.

Tips: "Write and ask to be considered for an assignment; tell of your background, experience, strengths, and writing history. All areas are open to freelancers—articles on every topic we cover. Writers who can research a topic, interview experts, and present clear, concise writing should persistently and consistently ask for assignments. It might take several months to get an assignment."

**This periodical was #12 on the 2007 Top 50 Christian Publishers list (#13 in 2006, #16 in 2005, #46 in 2004, #50 in 2003).

$YOUTHWORKER JOURNAL, 104 Woodmont Blvd., Ste. 300, Nashville TN 37205. (615)312-4250. Fax (615)385-4112. E-mail: proposals@youthworker.com, or Steve@Youthworker.com. Website: www.Youthworker.com. Salem Communications. Steve & Lois Rabey, eds. For youth workers/church and parachurch. Bimonthly & online jour.; 72 pgs.; circ. 20,000. Subscription $39.95. 100% unsolicited freelance. Query or complete ms (only if already written); e-query preferred. Pays $50-300 on publication for 1st/perpetual rts. Articles 250-3,000 wds. (30/yr.); length may vary. Responds in 26 wks. Seasonal 6 mos. ahead. No reprints. Kill fee $50. Guidelines/theme list on Website: www.youthworker.com/editorial_guidelines.php; copy $5/10x13 SAE. (Ads)

Columns/Departments: Buys 10/yr. International Youth Ministry, and Technology in Youth Ministry.

Tips: "Read *Youthworker;* imbibe its tone (professional, though not academic; conversational, though not chatty). Query me with specific, focused ideas that conform to our editorial style. It helps if the writer is a youth minister, but it's not required. Check Website for additional info, upcoming themes, etc."

**2003 Award of Merit—Most Improved Publication, & 2003 Award of Excellence—Christian Ministries.

TEEN/YOUNG ADULT MARKETS

$ACQUIRE THE FIRE, David C. Cook, Attn: Freelance/Independent Contracts, 4050 Lee Vance View, Colorado Springs CO 80918. A new devotional magazine for teens seeking authors to write/submit articles for publication. Submit résumé and unreturnable samples of your work to the address above.

$BOUNDLESS WEBZINE, 8605 Explorer Dr., Colorado Springs CO 80920. (719)531-5181. Fax (719)531-3349. E-mail: editor@boundless.org. Website: www.boundless.org. Focus on the Family. Ted Slater, ed. For Christian singles up to their mid-30s. Weekly e-zine; 200,000 visitors/mo.; 130 page views/mo. on blog. Free online. 5% unsolicited freelance; 95% assigned. Query/clips; e-query OK. Accepts full ms by e-mail. Pays .30/wd. on acceptance for nonexclusive rts. Articles 1,200-1,800 wds. (140/yr.). Responds in 4 wks. Seasonal 4 mos. ahead. Accepts simultaneous submissions & reprints (tell when/where appeared). Requires e-mail submission (attached—preferred—or copied into message). No kill fee. Does not use sidebars. Also accepts submissions from teens. Prefers ESV, NIV. Guidelines (on Website); copy online. (No ads)

Tips: "See author guidelines on our Website. Most open to conversational, winsome, descriptive, and biblical."

**This periodical was #25 on the 2007 Top 50 Christian Publishers list (#24 in 2006, #23 in 2005, #22 in 2004, #32 in 2003).

$BREAKAWAY, 8605 Explorer Dr., Colorado Springs CO 80921. (719)548-5838. Fax (719)531-3499. E-mail: erin.prater@fotf.org. Website: www.breakawaymag.com. Focus on the Family. Michael Ross, ed.; submit to Erin Prater, ed. asst. The 15-year-old unchurched teen (boy) in the public school is our target; boys 12-17 yrs. Monthly mag.; 32 pgs.; circ. 96,000. Subscription $18. 25% unsolicited freelance; 75% assigned. Query or complete ms/cover letter; no phone/fax/e-query. Pays .12-.15/wd. (.15-.20/wd. for fiction) on acceptance for 1st, one-time, or electronic rts. Articles 400-1,000 wds. (6/yr.); fiction to 2,000 wds. (3-4/yr.). Responds in 8-10 wks. Seasonal 6 mos. ahead. No simultaneous submissions or reprints. Kill fee $25. Uses some sidebars. Also accepts submissions from teens. Prefers NIV. Guidelines by e-mail/Website; copy for $1.50/9x12 SAE/3 stamps. (No ads)

Columns/Departments: Buys 2-3/yr. Epic Truth (devotional); 800 wds.

Tips: "Most open to nontypical, historical, and biblical fiction. Need strong lead. Brevity and levity a must. Have a teen guy or two read it. Make sure the language is up to date, but not overly hip." Needs drama-in-life stories involving boys.

**2007 EPA Award of Excellence—Youth; 2005, 2004, 2003 EPA Award of Merit—Youth. This periodical was #7 on the 2003 Top 50 Christian Publishers list.

$BRIO/BRIO & BEYOND, 8605 Explorer Dr., Colorado Springs CO 80920. (719)531-3400, ext. 1768. Fax (719)531-3499. E-mail: freelance@fotf.org. Website: www.briomag.com. Focus on the Family. Susie Shellenberger, ed.; submit to Mrs. Marty Kasza, assoc. ed. *Brio* is for teen girls, 12-15 yrs.; *Brio & Beyond* for teen girls, 16-19 years. Monthly mag.; 40 pgs.; circ. 142,500. Subscription $22. 25-50% unsolicited freelance; 50-75% assigned. Complete ms/cover letter; e-query OK. Pays .15-.35/wd. on acceptance for 1st rts. Articles 800-1,000 wds. (10/yr.); fiction 1,200-2,000 wds. (10/yr.). Accepts requested ms by e-mail or disk. Responds in 2-4 wks. Seasonal 8 mos. ahead. Rare kill fee $100. Uses some sidebars. Guidelines/theme list (also by e-mail); copy $2. (No ads)

Special Needs: All topics of interest to female teens are welcome: boys, makeup, dating, weight, ordinary girls who have extraordinary experiences, female adjustments to puberty, etc. Also teen-related female fiction.

Tips: "Study at least 3 issues of *Brio* before submitting. We're looking for a certain fresh, hip-hop, conversational style. Most open to fiction, articles, and quizzes."

**The #5 best-selling magazine in Christian retail stores. 2007 EPA Award of Merit—Youth (Brio & Beyond); 2006 EPA Award of Merit—Youth (*Brio*). This periodical was #50 on the 2004 Top 50 Christian Publishers list.

BUBBLEMAG, 8367 Lemon Ave., La Mesa CA 91941. E-mail: info@bubblemag.com. Website: www.bubblemag.com. Cross Cultural Entertainment. Nino Camilo, ed-in-chief. Entertainment lifestyle publication for Christian youth ages 13-20. Bimonthly mag.; circ. 50,000. Estab. 2006. No information yet on openness to freelance. Articles. Copy on Website. (Ads)

Tips: "In cartoons and comic books, the dream of a character is often revealed in a bubble floating over the character's head. Bubbles show what goes on inside our heads—our dreams, our feelings, and our goals. Our purpose is to encourage young disciples and potential disciples of Jesus to grow in their faith and to passionately pursue their God-given dreams, using their God-given talents."

$CLEAR DIRECTION, PO Box 17306, Nashville TN 37217. (615)361-1221. Fax (615)367-0535. E-mail: clearmag@randallhouse.com. Website: www.randallhouse.com. Randall House Publications. Tanya Shallahamer, ed. asst. Bringing junior high students to a closer relationship with Christ through devotionals, relevant articles, and pertinent topics. Quarterly mag.; 52 pgs.; circ. 5,300. Estab. 2004. Open to freelance. Complete ms/cover letter; query for fiction. Accepts full mss by e-mail. Pays $35-150 on publication for 1st rts. Articles 600-1,500 wds. (35/yr.); book reviews 600-800 wds. ($35). Responds in 6 wks. Seasonal 9 mos. ahead. Accepts simultaneous submissions; no reprints. Prefers e-mail submissions (attached file). No kill fee. Regularly uses sidebars. Also accepts submissions from teens. Prefers KJV. Guidelines (also by e-mail); copy for 9x12 SAE. (No ads)

Columns/Departments: Buys 10/yr. Changing Lanes (describe how God is changing you), 600-800 wds.; Between the Lines (review of book selected by Randall House), 600-800 wds.; $35-50.

Tips: "We are open to freelancers by way of articles and submissions to 'Changing Lanes' (600-800 wds.) and for feature articles (1,200-1,500 wds.) All articles should be about an aspect of the Christian life or contain a spiritual element, as the purpose of this magazine is to bring junior high students closer to Christ."

$CLEAR HORIZON, PO Box 17306, Nashville TN 37217. (615)361-1221. Fax (615)367-0535. E-mail: clearmag@randallhouse.com. Website: www.randallhouse.com. Randall House Publications. Emily D. White, ed. asst. Bringing high school students to a closer relationship with Christ through devotionals, relevant articles, and pertinent topics. Quarterly mag.; 52 pgs. Estab. 2004. Open to freelance. Complete ms/cover letter; query for fiction. Accepts full mss by e-mail. Pays $35-150 on publication for 1st rts. Articles 600-1,500 wds. (35/yr.); book reviews 600-800 wds. ($35). Responds in 6 wks. Seasonal 9 mos. ahead. Accepts simultaneous submissions; no reprints. Prefers e-mail submissions (attached file). No kill fee. Regularly uses sidebars. Also accepts submissions from teens. Prefers KJV. Guidelines (also by e-mail); copy for 9x12 SAE. (No ads)

Columns/Departments: Buys 10/yr. Changing Lanes (describe how God is changing you), 600-800 wds.; Between the Lines (review of book selected by Randall House), 600-800 wds.; $35-50.

Tips: "We are open to freelancers by way of articles and submissions to 'Changing Lanes' (600-800 wds.) All articles should be about an aspect of the Christian life or contain a spiritual element, as the purpose of this magazine is to bring high school students closer to Christ."

+CONNECTED, Box 6097, Lincoln NE 68506. (402)488-0981. E-mail: info@christianrecord.org. Website: http://connected.christianrecord.org. Christian Record Services Inc. Gaylena Gibson, ed. For sight-impaired young adults, 12-25 yrs.; for interdenominational Christian audience. E-zine. Not included in topical listings.

$CREDO MAGAZINE, PO Box 419527, Kansas City MO 64141. (816)931-1900. Fax (816)412-8312. E-mail: credomag@barefootministries.com. Website: www.credomagazine.com. Barefoot Ministries/Nazarene Publishing House. Stefanie Hendrickson, ed. A cutting-edge devotional magazine that also challenges teens in their spiritual walk with relevant articles dealing with the issues they are facing. Monthly mag.; 48 pgs.; circ. 15,000. Subscription $23.40. Estab. 2005. 20-30% unsolicited freelance; 70-80% assigned. Query. Pays $40-60 for articles; $60 for fiction; on acceptance for all rts. Articles 500-800 wds. (20-30/yr.); fiction 700-800 wds. (10-15/yr.); reviews 500 wds. ($25). Responds in 4-6 wks. Seasonal 4-6 mos. ahead. No simultaneous submissions; accepts reprints (tell when/where appeared). Requires e-mail submission (attached or copied into message). Kill fee. Uses some sidebars. Prefers NIV. Encourages submissions from teens. Guidelines/theme list (also by e-mail/Website); copy for 6x9 SAE/$1 postage (additional copies $1.95 ea.). (No ads)

Poetry: Accepts 10-15/yr. Any type. Will be used in the magazine or on the Web. No payment. Submit any number.

Columns/Departments: Buys 30-40/yr. Real Deal (life issues/relationships), 700-850 wds.; Kung Pao (features student's creative work—poetry, lyrics, short stories, essays, art, photos. etc.), 100-500 wds.; Unreal (fiction piece—looking for 4-6 part series with each part able to stand on its own), 800 wds.; Tune-Up (interviews/profiles/news on Christian artists and bands), 800-850 wds.; Life Zone (articles about youth God is using in cool ways), 800 wds.; $40-60.

Special Needs: All topics must be geared to teens.

Tips: "We are most open to freelancers in the areas of Kung Pao, Tune-Up, Life Zone, Unreal (fiction), and seasonal/fun articles written for teens. Also to music and entertainment reviews."

**This periodical was #18 on the 2007 Top 50 Christian Publishers list (#9 in 2006).

$DEVO'ZINE, PO Box 340004, Nashville TN 37203-0004. (615)340-7247. Fax (615)340-1783. E-mail: devozine@upperroom.org, or smiller@upperroom.org. Website: www.devozine.org. Upper Room Ministries. Sandy Miller, ed. Devotional; to help teens (12-18) develop and maintain their connection with God and other Christians. Bimonthly mag.; 64 pgs.; circ. 100,000. Subscription $20. 85% unsolicited freelance; 15% assigned. Query; phone/fax/e-query OK. Pays $25 for meditations, $100 for feature articles (assigned) on acceptance for these one-time rts.: newspaper, periodical, electronic, and software-driven rts., and the right to use in future anthologies. Meditations 150-250 wds. (350/yr.); articles 350-500 wds.; book/music/video reviews 350-500 wds., $100. Responds in 16 wks. Seasonal 6-8 mos. ahead. Accepts occasional reprints (tell when/where appeared). Accepts requested ms by e-mail or online submission. Regular sidebars. Prefers NRSV, NIV, CEV. Guidelines/theme list on Website; copy/7x10 SASE. (No ads)

Poetry: Buys 25-30/yr. Free verse, light verse, haiku, traditional; to 150 wds. or 10-20 lines; $25. Submit max. 1 poem/theme, 9 themes/issue.

Tips: "E-mail with ideas for weekend features related to specific themes."

**This periodicals was #3 on the 2007 Top 50 Christian Publishers list (#1 in 2006, #2 in 2005, #1 in 2004, #2 in 2003).

$ESSENTIAL CONNECTION (EC), One Lifeway Plaza, Nashville TN 37234-0174. (615)251-2008. Fax (615)277-8271. E-mail: ec@lifeway.com. Website: www.lifeway.com. LifeWay Christian Resources of the Southern Baptist Convention. Mandy Crow, ed. Christian leisure reading and devotional guide for 7th-12th graders. Monthly mag.; 60 pgs.; circ. 120,000. Subscription $24.95. 10% unsolicited freelance; 90% assigned. Query; e-query OK. Pays $80-120 on acceptance for all rts. Articles 800-1,200 wds. (12/yr.); fiction 1,200 wds. (12/yr.). Responds in 10 wks. Seasonal 9 mos. ahead. No simultaneous submissions or reprints. Prefers e-mail submission (attached file or copied into message). No kill fee. Uses some sidebars. Prefers NIV. Guidelines (also by e-mail); free copy. (No ads)

Poetry: Accepts 36/yr. All types. From teens only.

Special Needs: Always in search of Christian humor; sports profiles. Most open to fiction (send complete ms).

Tips: "We generally prefer writers to complete the writer process at www.lifeway.com/people."

$+FOCUS ON THE FAMILY DARE 2 DIG DEEPER SERIES, Youth Culture Dept., 8605 Explorer Dr., Colorado Springs CO 80920-1051. (719)531-3400. Fax (719)531-3448. Website: www.family.org. Submit to Acquisitions Editor. A series of small booklets that deal with hard topics that teens (ages 12-18) are struggling with. Query editor with your ideas to be sure they haven't already covered the topic.

$IGNITE YOUR FAITH, 465 Gundersen Dr., Carol Stream IL 60188. (630)260-6200. Fax (630) 480-2004. E-mail: Iyf@igniteyourfaith.com. Website: www.IgniteYourFaith.com. Christianity Today Intl. Christopher Lutes, ed. Dedicated to creatively engaging and empowering teens to become fully devoted followers of Jesus Christ. Bimonthly (plus 4 special Christian-college issues) mag.; 68-94 pgs.; circ. 100,000. Subscription $19.95. 20% assigned. Query or query/clips; fax/e-query OK. Pays .20-.25/wd. on acceptance for one-time & electronic rts. Articles 1,000-1,500 wds. (5-10/yr.); fiction 1,000-1,500 wds. (1-5/yr.). Responds in 4-6 wks. Seasonal 6 mos. ahead. Accepts simultaneous submissions; no reprints. Kill fee 50%. Uses some sidebars. Accepts queries from teens. Guidelines (also on Website); copy $3.95/9x12 SAE. (Ads)

Poetry: Buys 1-5/yr. Free verse; 5-20 lines; $25-50. Submit max. 2 poems. Rarely purchase.

Tips: "Most open to as-told-to stories. Interview students and get their stories."
**2007, 2003 EPA Award of Merit—Youth; 2006 EPA Award of Excellence—Youth.

$INSIDEOUT, 8855 Dunn Rd., Hazelwood MO 63042-2299. (314)837-7300. Fax (314)837-4503. E-mail: youth@upci.org. Website: www.pentecostalyouth.org. United Pentecostal Church Intl. Shay Mann, ed.; submit to Tamra Schultz (tschultz@upci.org). Addresses the spiritual concerns of youth 12-21 years. Bimonthly mag.; 20 pgs.; circ. 6,000. 80% freelance. Complete ms by e-mail only (attached file). Pays .065/wd. on publication for one-time rts. Articles 250-1,250 wds. (18/yr.); fiction 250-1,250 wds. Responds in 9 wks. Seasonal 4 mos. ahead. Accepts simultaneous submissions & reprints. Guidelines/themes on Website; copy for 9x12 SAE/3 stamps.

Poetry: Buys 2-4/yr. Traditional; $15. Submit max. 5 poems.

Fillers: Buys 4/yr. Anecdotes, cartoons, short humor; 100 wds.; $15.

Columns/Departments: Buys 6-10/yr. Complete ms.

Tips: "Our primary objective is inspiration—to portray happy, victorious living through faith in God."

$INSIGHT, 55 W. Oak Ridge Dr., Hagerstown MD 21740-7301. (301)393-4038. Fax (301)393-4055. E-mail: insight@rhpa.org. Website: www.insightmagazine.org. Review and Herald Publishing Assn./Seventh-day Adventist. Dwain Esmond, ed. A magazine of positive Christian living for Seventh-day Adventist high school students, ages 13-19. Weekly take-home mag.; 16 pgs.; circ. 20,000. Subscription $49.95. 80% unsolicited freelance. Complete ms/cover letter; fax/e-query OK. Pays $25-150 for assigned, $25-125 for unsolicited, on publication for 1st rts. Not copyrighted. Articles 500-1,500 wds. (120/yr.). Responds in 5 wks. Seasonal 6 mos. ahead. Accepts reprints (tell when/where appeared). Prefers e-mail submission (attached file). Kill fee. Regularly uses sidebars. Prefers NIV. Also accepts submissions from teens. Guidelines on Website; copy $2/#10 SASE. (No ads)

Poetry: Buys to 36/yr. All types; to 1 pg.; $10. By high school and college students only.

Columns/Departments: Buys 50/yr. On the Edge (drama in real life), 800-1,500 wds., $50-100; It Happened To Me (personal experience in first person), 600-900 wds., $50-75; Big Deal (big topics, such as prayer, premarital sex, knowing God's will, etc.) with sidebar, 1,200-1,700 wds., $75 + $25 for sidebar; So I Said (first-person opinion), 300-500 wds., $25-125. Complete ms.

Contest: Sponsors a nonfiction and poetry contest; includes a category for students under 21. Prizes to $250. June deadline (varies). Send SASE for rules.

Tips: "We are desperately in need of true, dramatic stories involving Christian young people. Also need stories by male authors, particularly some humor. Also profiles of Seventh-day Adventist teenagers who are making a notable difference."
**This periodical was #28 on the 2006 Top 50 Christian Publishers list (#28 in 2005, #19 in 2004, #20 in 2003).

$INTEEN, PO Box 436987, Chicago IL 60643. (708)868-7100, ext. 362. Fax (708)868-6759. E-mail: acarr@urbanministries.com. Website: www.urbanministries.com. Urban Ministries Inc. Aja Carr, ed. Teen curriculum for ages 15-17 (student and teacher manuals). Quarterly booklet; 32 pgs.; circ. 20,000. Subscription $11.25. 1% unsolicited freelance; 99% assigned. Query/clips; phone query OK; no e-query. Pays $75-150 on acceptance for all rts. Articles & fiction 1,200 wds. Responds in 4 wks. Seasonal 9 mos. ahead. Accepts some reprints (tell when/where appeared). Accepts requested ms on disk or by e-mail (copied into message). Prefers NIV. Free guidelines/theme list/copy for 10x13 SAE. (No ads)

Poetry: Buys 4/yr. Free verse; variable length; $25-60.

Tips: "Write in with sample writings and be willing and ready to complete an assignment. We prefer to make assignments. Most open to Bible study guides applicable and interesting for teens. Writers who can accurately explain scriptures to teens are always welcome."

$J.A.M.: JESUS AND ME, PO Box 436987, Chicago IL 60643. (708)868-7100, ext. 362. Fax (708)868-6759. E-mail: ksteward@urbanministries.com. Website: www.urbanministries.com. Urban Ministries Inc. C. Kathy Steward, ed. Magazine for 12- to 14-year-olds. Open to freelance. Query/clips; fax/e-query OK. Pays up to $150, 120 days after acceptance, for all rts. Articles 200-400 wds. Responds in 4 wks. Seasonal 6 mos. ahead. Accepts simultaneous submissions. Requires accepted ms on disk. Prefers NIV. Guidelines; copy for #10 SASE. (No ads)

Tips: "Send query with a writing sample, or attend our annual conference on the first weekend in November each year. Manuscripts are evaluated at the conference."

$LISTEN MAGAZINE, 55 W. Oak Ridge Dr., Hagerstown MD 21740. (301)393-4019. E-mail: editor@listenmagazine.org. Website: www.listenmagazine.org. The Health Connection. Celeste Perrino-Walker, ed. Positive lifestyle magazine for teens/young adults; emphasizes values in a general tone. Monthly mag. (September-May); 32 pgs.; circ. 20,000/exposure 100,000. Subscription $26.95. 50% unsolicited freelance; 50% assigned. Query or complete ms; phone/fax/e-query OK. Pays .06-.10/wd. ($50-150) on acceptance for 1st or reprint rts. Articles 800-1,000 wds. (30-50/yr.); true stories 800 wds. (15/yr.). Responds in 2 wks. to 3 mos. Seasonal 1 yr. ahead. Accepts simultaneous submissions & reprints (tell when/where appeared). Accepts requested ms on CD or by e-mail (attached file). Regularly uses sidebars. Guidelines/theme list (also on Website); copy $2/9x12 SAE/2 stamps. (No ads)

Fillers: Uses 500-word quizzes based on topic in our theme list.

Special Needs: Anti-drug, tobacco, alcohol; positive role models. For true stories, needs stories dealing with everyday problems: peer pressure, decision making, friendship, family conflict, self-discipline, divorce, abuse, anorexia/bulimia, and making positive choices.

Tips: "Need good true stories and celebrity features. We've stopped using fiction. While it isn't always possible, we like to feature stories about individuals who overcome the temptation to experiment with drugs and alcohol, and/or who find a creative way to deal with a bad situation."

**This periodical was #29 on the 2007 Top 50 Christian Publishers list (#20 in 2006, #13 in 2005, #11 in 2004, #9 in 2003).

$LIVING MY FAITH, 1300 N. Meacham Rd., Schaumburg IL 60173-4888. (847)843-1600. Fax (847)843-3757. E-mail: livingmyfaith@garbc.org. Website: www.rbpstudentministries.org. Regular Baptist Press. Mel Walker, dir. of student ministries. For junior high youth (12-14); conservative/fundamental. Weekly devotional booklet; 8 pgs. Complete ms; no e-query. Pays .04/wd. and up, on acceptance. Lead stories 450-550 wds; articles 300-800 wds.; true & fiction stories to 800 wds. Requires KJV. Check Website for guidelines before submitting at www.rbpstudentministries.org/contribute.

Tips: "Check Website quarterly for updates concerning needs, themes, etc. This is written chiefly by assignment."

$PASSAGEWAY.ORG, 1 Billy Graham Pkwy., Charlotte NC 28201. (612)338-0500. E-mail: ed@passageway.org. Website: www.passageway.org. Billy Graham Evangelistic Assn. Steve Knight, sr. ed.; Blaine Howard, asst. ed. Online publication for teens, 15-17 yrs. Biweekly e-zine. Subscription free. 10% unsolicited freelance; 90% assigned. Complete ms/cover letter; no phone query/e-query OK. Pays $100-250 on publication for all, electronic, or reprint rts. Articles 500-1,000 wds. (52/yr.); no fiction or reviews. Responds in 6-8 wks. Seasonal 2 mos. ahead. Accepts simultaneous submissions & reprints (tell when/where appeared). Prefers e-mail submission (attached or copied into message). Some kill fees 50%. Uses some sidebars. Prefers NIV. Guidelines on Website (www.passageway.org/guidelines); copy online. (No ads)

Columns/Departments: Grow and Pop Culture sections.

Tips: "Most open to a well-written article for the Grow section; it is the best way to break in. Also open to unique Pop Culture features that are relevant to teens. This is a youth Website, and writing that does not work for youth or the Web will not be considered."
**2004 EPA Award of Merit—Online.

$REAL FAITH IN LIFE, 1300 N. Meacham Rd., Schaumburg IL 60173-4888. (847)843-1600. Fax (847)843-3757. E-mail: realfaith@garbc.org. Website: www.rbpstudentministries.org. Regular Baptist Press. Mel Walker, dir. of student ministries. For senior high youth (15-18); conservative/fundamental. Quarterly devotional planner; 96 pgs. Complete ms; no e-query. Pays .04/wd. and up, on acceptance for first (preferred) or one-time rts. Articles 400-800 wds. (if more than 600 wds., include subheads). Using mostly assignment writers who are using the RBP student ministries materials or are familiar with churches who do. Some reprints. Guidelines (also on Website: www.rbpstudentministries.org/contribute); copy.

Tips: "Check Website quarterly for updates concerning needs, themes, etc. Written chiefly by assignment."

$RISEN MAGAZINE: The Art & Soul of Pop Culture 11772 Sorrento Valley Rd., Ste. 152, San Diego CA 92121. (858)481-5650. Fax (858)481-5660. E-mail: michaels@risenmagazine .com. Website: www.risenmagazine.com (online version of the magazine). Risen Media LLC. Steve Beard, ed-in-chief; Regina Goodman, mng. ed. Audience is 18- to 35-year-old seekers and new believers; original photos and one-on-one interviews cut to the heart of today's cultural icons. Estab. 2004. Bimonthly mag.; 34 pgs.; circ. 45,000+. Subscription $19.99. Open to freelance. Query; phone/e-query OK. Pays $150-700. Articles. (Ads)

$THE ROCK, 4050 Lee Vance View, Colorado Springs CO 80918-7100. (719)536-0100. Fax (719)536-3270. E-mail: gail.rolfing@davidccook.com. Website: www.CookMinistries.com. Cook Communications Ministries. Gail Rohlfing, children's curriculum ed. Take-home paper and in-class Bible study for middle-schoolers. Quarterly take-home paper; 104 pgs.; circ. 50,000. 15% assigned. Not accepting unsolicited mss at this time; no phone/fax/e-query. Pays on acceptance for all rts. Articles & fiction. Responds in 16 wks. Prefers NIV. Guidelines on Website; no copy available. (No ads)

Tips: "Check Website for writer needs."

$SHARING THE VICTORY, 8701 Leeds Rd., Kansas City MO 64129-1680. Toll-free (800)289-0909. (816)921-0909. Fax (816)921-8755. E-mail: stv@fca.org. Website: www.SharingThe Victory.com (online version of the magazine). Fellowship of Christian Athletes (Protestant and Catholic). Jill Ewert, ed. Equipping and encouraging athletes and coaches to take their faith seriously, in and out of competition. Monthly (9X—double issues in Jan., Jun. & Aug.) mag.; 40 pgs.; circ. 80,000. Subscription $19.95. 10% unsolicited freelance; 40% assigned. Query only/clips; e-query OK. Pays $150-400 on publication for 1st rts. Articles 500-1,000 wds. (5-20/yr.). Responds in 13 wks. Seasonal 6 mos. ahead. Accepts reprints, pays 50% (tell when/where appeared). Accepts requested ms on disk or by e-mail (attached or copied into message). Kill fee .05%. Uses some sidebars. Prefers HCSB. Guidelines on Website; copy $1/9x12 SAE/3 stamps. (Ads)

Special Needs: Articles on FCA camp experiences. All articles must have an athletic angle. Need stories featuring Christian female professional athletes with a FCA connection.

Tips: "FCA angle important; pro and college athletes and coaches giving solid Christian testimony; we run stories according to athletic season. Need articles on Christian pro athletes—all sports. It is suggested that writer actually look at the magazine for general style and presentation."

$SPIRIT, 1884 Randolph Ave., St. Paul MN 55105-1700. (651)690-7010. Fax (651)690-7039. E-mail: jmcsj9@aol.com. Catholic/Good Ground Press. Joan Mitchell, CSJ, ed. Religious education for Catholic high schoolers. Weekly newsletter; circ. 20,000. 50% freelance written.

Complete ms/cover letter or query; fax/e-query OK. Pays $250-300 on publication for all rts. Articles 1,000-1,200 wds. (4/yr.); fiction 1,000-1,200 wds. (10/yr.; $125-300). Responds in 5 wks. Seasonal 6 mos. ahead. Accepts simultaneous submissions. Free guidelines/copy.

Tips: "No born-again pieces. Articles about teens must be written from their point of view."

$STEELROOTS MAGAZINE, 7910 Crescent Executive Dr., 5th Fl., Charlotte NC 28217. (704)561-7602. Fax (704)561-7863. E-mail: info@steelroots.com. Website: www.steelroots.com. Inspiration Network. Carter J. Theis, mng. ed. Provides a look into the lives of professional skaters, snowboarders, and surfers through articles written about and by athletes; intended for Christian and general audience. Quarterly mag.; 152 pgs.; circ. 30,000. Query/clips; phone/e-query OK. Accepts full ms by e-mail. Pays .15-.25/wd. for all rts. Articles 500-4,000 wds.; book/music reviews, 50 wds. Also accepts submissions from teens. Copy $5. Incomplete topical listings. (Ads)

Columns/Departments: Buys 12/yr. Evangelism Feature (explaining Jesus to those who don't know him), 2,000 wds.; Discipleship Feature (hitting a topic that's different, but important in Christianity), 2,000 wds.; Final Feature (lies that kids have bought into about Jesus/Bible), 1,000 wds.

Tips: "Send a sample—have some street credibility." Distributed through Christian bookstores, specialty shops, and at youth events.

STUDENT LIFE PUBLISHING, PO Box 36040, Birmingham AL 35236. Toll-free (888)811-9934. Fax (205)503-5460. E-mail: emily@studentlife.net. Website: www.studentlife.net. Andy Blanks, exec. ed. Bible study curriculum intended to take jr. high and sr. high school students through the Bible in 6 years. Ty Gullick, exec. ed. for new Bible study curriculum for adult learners. Weekly online. Subscriptions on a sliding scale. Open to freelance. Complete ms/cover letter. (No ads)

$TAKE FIVE PLUS YOUTH DEVOTIONAL GUIDE, 1445 N. Boonville Ave., Springfield MO 65802-1894. (417)862-2781, ext. 4359. Fax (417)862-6059. E-mail: rl-take5plus@gph.org. Website: www.youth.ag.org/discipleship. Assemblies of God. Glen Ellard, sr. ed. Devotional for teens. By assignment only. Send 2 sample devotions and return a completed pastoral endorsement form available on their Website. Accepts e-mail submissions. Pays $25/devotion or $120 for a set of 6. Devotions exactly 210-235 wds. (not over that). Guidelines on Website.

Poetry: Accepts poetry from teens; no more than 25 lines.

Tips: "The sample devotions need to be based on a scripture reference listed on the Website. You will not be paid for the sample devotions." Also accepts digital photos.

$TC MAGAZINE, 915 E. Market, Ste. 10750, Searcy AR 72149. (501)279-4660. Fax (501)279-4931.E-mail: editor@tcmagazine.org. Website: www.tcmagazine.org. Institute for Church & Family. Laura Kaiser, ed. To help teenagers discover style in faith and love. Quarterly mag.; 52 pgs.; circ. 8,000. Subscription $14.95. Estab. 2006. 10% unsolicited freelance; 40% assigned. Complete ms; fax or e-query OK. Accepts full mss by e-mail. Pays variable rates on publication for one-time, reprint, electronic rts. Articles 500-1,200 wds. (10/yr.); no fiction. Responds only if chosen for publication. Seasonal 6 mos. ahead. No simultaneous submissions or reprints. No kill fee. Uses some sidebars. Also accepts submissions from teens. Guidelines by e-mail/Website; copy $3.95/9x12 SAE. (Ads—e-mail to request rate book & media kit)

Columns/Departments: Buys 5/yr. Complete ms. College (college prep for high schoolers), 800-1,000 wds.; Humor (funny article in first person), 800 wds.

Tips: "We really look for teen writers. First-person articles about personal experience are desired. No fiction at this time."

TEENS FOR JC.COM, 2855 Lawrenceville-Suwanee Rd., Ste. 760-355, Suwanee GA 30024. Phone/fax (770)831-8622. E-mail: uvaldes@aol.com. Website: www.teensforjc.com. PLGK Communications Inc. Quentin Plair, pres./CEO. Salutes the fun and exhilaration of being a Christian teen. Monthly e-zine. 90% unsolicited freelance; 10% assigned. Complete ms/cover letter; no phone/fax/e-query. Accepts requested ms on disk or by e-mail (attached file). **NO PAYMENT** for one-time rts. Not copyrighted. Articles 100-5,000 wds. (15/yr.) & fiction 100-5,000 wds. (12/yr.); reviews 200 wds. Responds in 12 weeks. Seasonal 4 mos. ahead. Accepts simultaneous submissions & reprints (tell when/where appeared). No kill fee. Uses some sidebars. Also accepts submissions from teens. Guidelines (also on Website). (Ads)

Poetry: Accepts many; any type; 1-200 lines.

Fillers: Accepts many; cartoons, facts, games, jokes, party ideas, prayers, prose, quizzes, short humor, tips, word puzzles; 10-750 wds.

Columns/Departments: Accepts 36/yr. School tips (teen tips for scholarly excellence); Scoop (current info); Music (music reviews/stories); Speak Out (opinion articles by teens); all 100-500 wds.

Tips: "Provide information teens need to lay a foundation for a successful life. Looking for great stories."

$TRUE GIRL, The Magazine for Catholic Teens, 703 Michigan Ave., Ste. 2, LaPorte IN 46352. (219)324-2780. E-mail: editor@truegirlonline.com. Website: www.truegirlonline.com. Catholic. Brandi Lee, ed-in-chief. For teenage girls; covers faith, life, and fashion. Bimonthly mag.; 32 pgs.; circ. 3,500. Subscription $18.95. Estab. 2005. Open to freelance. E-query preferred; no phone/fax query. Accepts full mss by e-mail. Pays .15-.20/wd. for 1st & electronic rts. Articles 800-1,200 wds.; no fiction; reviews 50-100 wds. ($25). Responds in 4-6 wks. Seasonal 12 mos. ahead. No simultaneous submissions or reprints. Some kill fees. Regularly uses sidebars. Also accepts submissions from teens (no pay). Prefers NAB or NRSV (Catholic editions only). Guidelines (also by e-mail); copy $4.99/7x10 SAE. (Ads)

Fillers: Buys Unlimited number. Facts, prayers, quizzes, quotes, word puzzles.

Columns/Departments: Social Justice; Health/Hygiene/Beauty; Teen Issues; Life Plan; Entertainment; Make-It-Your-Own; True Girl Saint. Pays by the word.

Tips: "Our feature articles are most open to freelancers. Reading back issues is imperative to understanding our mission, style, tone, and audience. A firm grasp of our reader's needs for educational, spiritual, and entertainment resources will help guide submissions."

VISIONS, 2621 Dryden Rd., Moraine OH 45439. (937)293-1415. Fax (937)293-1310. E-mail: service@pflaum.com. Website: www.pflaum.com. Catholic. Joan Mitchell CSJ, ed. For grades 7 & 8. Weekly (32X) take-home paper. Not in topical listings.

$YOUNG ADULT TODAY, PO Box 436987, Chicago IL 60643. (708)868-7100, ext. 362. Fax (708) 868-6759. E-mail: acarr@urbanministries.com. Website: www.urbanministries.com. Urban Ministries Inc. C. Aja Carr, ed. Magazine for 18- to 24-year-olds. Open to freelance. Query/clips; fax/e-query OK. Pays $75-150, 120 days after acceptance for all rts. Articles 200-400 wds. Responds in 4 wks. Seasonal 6 mos. ahead. Accepts simultaneous submissions. Accepts requested ms on disk. Prefers NIV. Free guidelines/theme list/copy for #10 SASE. (No ads)

Poetry: Buys 4/yr. Free verse; variable length; $25-60.

Tips: "Send query with a writing sample, or attend our annual conference on the first weekend in November each year. Manuscripts are evaluated at the conference."

$YOUNG CHRISTIAN, 2660 Petersborough St., Herndon VA 20171. E-mail: youngchristianmagazine@yahoo.com. Website: http://groups.yahoo.com/group/youngchristianmagazine. Tellstar Publishing. Shannon Bridget Murphy, ed. Christian writing with the Lord's message for children and teens. Quarterly mag. 85% unsolicited freelance. Complete ms/cover letter;

e-query OK. Pays .02-.05/wd. on acceptance for 1st or one-time rts. Articles 500-2,000 wds.; fiction 500-2,000 wds.; book/tape reviews. Responds in 2-8 wks. Seasonal 3-6 mos. ahead. Accepts simultaneous submissions & reprints (tell when/where appeared). Accepts disk; prefers e-mail submissions (attached or copied into message). No kill fee. Regularly uses sidebars. Prefers KJV. Guidelines by e-mail. (No ads)

Poetry: Buys variable number. Avant-garde, free verse, haiku, light verse, traditional; any length; variable rates. Submit any number.

Fillers: Buys anecdotes, cartoons, facts, ideas, kid quotes, party ideas, prayers, prose, quizzes, quotes, short humor, tips, and word puzzles; to 1,000 wds.

Tips: "Most open to nonfiction, fiction, poetry, and fillers written by children and teens. Include a scripture reference. *Young Christian* will provide information to teachers and educational employees on request. Accepts books, CDs, or tapes to be reviewed, but no written reviews."

$YOUNG SALVATIONIST, PO Box 269, Alexandria VA 22313-0269. (703)684-5500. Fax (703) 684-5539. E-mail: ys@usn.salvationarmy.org. Website: http://publications.salvationarmyusa.org. The Salvation Army. Curtiss A. Hartley, ed. (Curtiss_Hartley@USN.Salvationarmy.org). For teens and young adults in the Salvation Army. Monthly (10X) & online mag.; 24 pgs.; circ. 48,000. Subscription $4.50. 80% unsolicited freelance; 20% assigned. Complete ms preferred; e-query OK. Pays .15/wd. (.10/wd. for reprints) on acceptance for 1st, one-time, or reprint rts. Articles (60/yr.) & fiction (10/yr.), 600-1,200 wds.; short evangelistic pieces, 350-600 wds. Responds in 9 wks. Seasonal 6 mos. ahead. Accepts reprints (tell when/where appeared). Accepts requested ms on disk or by e-mail. Uses some sidebars. Prefers NIV. Guidelines/theme list (also on Website); copy for 9x12 SAE/3 stamps. (No ads)

Contest: Sponsors a contest for fiction, nonfiction, poetry, original art, and photography. Send SASE for details.

Tips: "Our greatest need is for nonfiction pieces that are relevant to the readers and offer clear application to daily life. We are most interested in topical pieces on contemporary issues that affect a teen's daily life, and pieces that work with the day-to-day challenges of faith. Although we use fiction and poetry, they are a small percentage of the total content of each issue."

**This periodical was #5 on the 2007 Top 50 Christian Publishers list (#3 in 2006, #12 in 2005, #9 in 2004, #10 in 2003).

$YOUTH COMPASS, PO Box 4060, Overland Park KS 66204. (913)432-0331. Fax (913)722-0351. E-mail: sseditor1@juno.com. Church of God (holiness)/Herald and Banner Press. Arlene McGehee, Sunday school ed. Denominational; for teens. Weekly take-home paper; 4 pgs.; circ. 4,800. Subscription $1.50. Complete ms/cover letter; phone/fax/e-query OK (prefers mail or e-mail). Pays .005/wd. on publication for 1st rts. Fiction 800-1,500 wds. Seasonal 6-8 mos. ahead. Accepts simultaneous submissions & reprints (tell when/where appeared). Prefers KJV. Guidelines/theme list; copy. Not in topical listings.

$YOUTHWALK, 4201 N. Peachtree Rd., Atlanta GA 30341. (770)451-9300. Fax (770)454-9313. E-mail: LMakohon@walkthru.org. Website: www.ywspace.org. Walk Thru the Bible Ministries. Laurin Makohon, ed. To help students navigate their Bibles, connect with God, and their own faith. Monthly devotional mag.; circ. 30,000. Subscription $18. 5% unsolicited freelance; 25% assigned. Complete ms. Pays $50-250. Articles 600-1,500 wds.; no reviews. Requires NIV. (No ads)

Tips: "We accept freelance for feature articles only; no devotionals. Submit a complete manuscript of a real-life teen story."

**2007 EPA Award of Excellence—Devotional; 2006 EPA Award of Merit—Devotional.

WOMEN'S MARKETS

$AT THE CENTER, PO Box 100, Morgantown PA 19543. Toll-free (800)588-7744. (610)856-6830, ext. 707. Fax (610)856-6831. E-mail: publications@rightideas.us, or elaine@right ideas.us. Website: www.atcmag.com. Scepter Institute/Right Ideas Inc. Jerry Thacker, ed.; submit to Elaine Williams, asst. ed. Designed to help staff, volunteers, and board members of Crisis Pregnancy Centers/Pregnancy Care Centers with relevant information and encouragement. Triannual & online mag.; 24 pgs.; circ. 30,000. Subscription free. 20% unsolicited freelance; 80% assigned. Complete ms; phone/fax query OK; e-query preferred. Pays $150 on publication for 1st, reprint, or simultaneous rts. Articles 800-1,000 wds. (15/yr.). Responds in 8-10 wks. Seasonal 6-8 mos. ahead. Accepts simultaneous submissions & reprints. Accepts e-mail submissions (attached or copied into message). No kill fee. Uses some sidebars. Prefers KJV, ESV. Guidelines/idea list (also by e-mail); copy for 9x12 SAE/3 stamps. (Ads: elaine@rightideas.us)

Special Needs: Articles that give ideas for other centers in the areas of recruiting and retaining volunteers, ways to reach abortion-minded clients, and creative fund-raising ideas.

Tips: "Looking for practical articles of help and encouragement for those involved in the work of CPC/PCC ministry. If someone has been involved in crisis pregnancy work, their insight into many areas of the ministry can be helpful to staff and board. Need good techniques for counseling abortion-minded clients."

($)BEYOND THE BEND, 22 Williams St., Batavia NY 14020. (585)343-2810. Fax (585)343-3245. E-mail: submissions@beyondthebend.com, or info@beyondthebend.com. Website: www.beyondthebend.com. PC Publications. Patti Chadwick, ed. (Patti@beyondthebend .com). For women in midlife. Estab. 2006. Monthly e-zine. Subscription free online. 50% unsolicited freelance; 50% assigned. Complete ms/cover letter or query; e-query OK. **PAYS IN FREE BOOKS OR $10/ARTICLE IF BUDGET PERMITS** for one-time and reprint rts. Articles 500-1,000 wds. (25/yr.); reviews 500 wds. Responds in 1 wk. Seasonal 6 mos. ahead. Accepts simultaneous submissions & reprints (tell when/where appeared). Prefers e-mail submissions (attached or copied into message). Uses some sidebars. Guidelines on Website; copy online. (Ads)

Fillers: Accepts 20/yr. Anecdotes, facts, ideas, quotes, sermon illustrations, short humor, and tips; 25-50 wds.

Tips: "Just e-mail me with a good story."

$+BOOMER BABES ROCK BOOK SERIES, c/o God Allows U-Turns, PO Box 717, Faribault, MN 55021-0717. Fax (507)334-6464. E-mail: storyeditor@boomerbabesrock.com. Website: www.boomerbabesrock.com, or www.godallowsuturns.com. Blog: www.godallowsuturns .blogspot.com. Submit to Editor. See Special Needs for current volumes in development. For a complete list of *Boomer Babes Rock* books open to submissions, as well as related opportunities, visit Website. Timelines vary, so send stories any time, as they may fit another volume. Each book in the series will contain up to 100 true short stories written by contributors from all over the world. 98% unsolicited freelance. Includes byline and short bio. Stories 500-1,500 wds. Pays $25-50 on publication, plus 1 copy of book, for one-time or reprint rts. Accepts simultaneous submissions & reprints (tell when/where appeared). Online submissions only, via e-mail or Website. Submit story typed, double spaced, in an attached Word document only. No poetry. Guidelines and sample story available on Website. (No ads)

Special Needs: True short stories by, for, and about baby boomer women. Multiple volumes in production for 2008/2009 with release dates in 2008/2009/2010: *Making Dreams Come True; Boomers Babes Rock; Moving Mountains;* and *Relationship Revelations.* See

Website for details on these, as well as other topics in development. Open to well-written, personal inspirational pieces showing how faith in God can inspire, encourage, and heal. Hope should prevail. Human-interest stories with a spiritual application, affirming ways in which faith is expressed in daily life. These true stories must touch the emotions. Our contributors are a diverse group with no limits on age or denomination.

Tips: "Show us how your faith choices have changed your life as a baby-boomer woman. New book series, see the sample story on our Website. Show, don't tell. Keep it real. Ordinary people doing extraordinary things with God's help. We publish the nitty-gritty issues of life—few subjects are taboo. Focus on timeless, universal themes like love, forgiveness, salvation, healing, hope, faith, etc. Be able to tell a good story with drama, description, and dialog. Avoid moralisms and preachy tone. Read niche volume synopses for specific guidelines. When possible, show how the choice you made, either through a change of heart, attitude, thought, and/or behavior occurred that clearly describes moving closer to God. Using a 'U-turn' lesson/analogy within the story is a plus."

Deadline: Deadlines vary; this is an ongoing book series. Check Website for frequent series updates.

+BREATHE AGAIN MAGAZINE, 222 W. 21st St., Ste. F126, Norfolk VA 23517. (757)404-1582. Fax (757)626-1669. E-mail: info@breatheagain.org. Website: www.breatheagainmagazine.com. Nicole Cleveland, ed./pub. (editor@breatheagain.org). Stirring stories about overcoming adversity and living triumphant, successful lives encourage and motivate women not only to endure but to overcome life's most challenging moments. Monthly online mag. Open to stories of overcoming.

$CANTICLE, 325 Scarlet Blvd., Oldsmar FL 34677. (734)429-2952. E-mail: heidi_saxton2002@yahoo.com. Website: www.canticlemagazine.com. Women of Grace/Catholic. Heidi Saxton, ed. Dedicated solely to the woman's vocation within the church. Bimonthly jour.; 32 pgs.; circ. 4,000. Subscription $29.95. 75% unsolicited freelance; 25% assigned. Query or complete ms; e-query OK. Pays $50-150 on publication for 1st rts. Articles 600 or 1,200 wds. Responds in 4-6 wks. Seasonal 4 mos. ahead. Requires e-mail submissions in attached file after acceptance. No kill fee. Regularly uses sidebars. Prefers NAB or RSV (Catholic version). Guidelines/theme list on Website; copy online. (Ads)

Columns/Departments: Buys 6/yr. Send complete ms. Solitary Genius (singles, widows; religious perspective), 600 wds.; pays $50-75. List of columns in guidelines; 500-750 wds.; $75 for assigned, less for unsolicited.

Contest: Check "Silent Canticle" blog for details (see below).

Tips: "Read guidelines and theme list, and read regularly our Catholic Writers' blog, the 'Silent Canticle' at http://heidihesssaxton.blogspot.com."

CELEBRATEMOMS.ORG, PO Box 570, Theodore AL 36590-0570. Toll-free (866)324-2893. E-mail: mhowell@celebratemoms.org. Website: www.celebratemoms.org. Nondenominational. Melissa Howell, co-founder/ed. Online conference and retreat center for moms. Interactive Website; continually updated. Estab. 2006. 20% unsolicited freelance; 80% assigned. Query/published clips; e-query OK. Accepts full mss by e-mail. **NO PAYMENT; BYLINE & LINK TO WEBSITE** for one-time & electronic rts. Articles. Responds in 6 wks. Seasonal 3 mos. ahead. Accepts simultaneous submissions & reprints (tell when/where appeared). Requires e-mail submission (attached file). Uses some sidebars. Also accepts submissions from children/teens. Any Bible version. Guidelines by e-mail; copy online. (No ads)

Fillers: Accepts several/yr. Anecdotes, facts, games, ideas, kid quotes, party ideas, prayers, prose, quizzes, quotes, short humor, tips, word puzzles.

Tips: "All areas open to freelancers. Read submission guidelines carefully and follow them. Be patient waiting for replies."

CHRISTIAN WOMAN'S PAGE. E-mail: editor@christianwomanspage.org. Website: www.christianwomanspage.org. Nondenominational. Janel Messenger, ed./pub. Strives to provide women with the whys and hows to live Christianity lovingly and practically in day-to-day life. Quarterly e-zine & weekly blog. Carries 12-16 articles/issue; 90,000 unique visitors/yr. 98% unsolicited freelance; 2% assigned. Complete ms/cover letter by e-mail only. **NO PAYMENT** for 1st, one-time, reprint, simultaneous, nonexclusive rts. Articles 1,200-1,700 wds.; devotions no less than 700 wds.; larger articles can be broken into parts; reviews 500-700 wds.; fiction 1,800 wds. Responds in 3-5 wks. Seasonal 2 mos. ahead. Accepts simultaneous submissions & reprints (tell when/where appeared). Requires e-mail submissions (attached or copied into message—preferred). Uses some sidebars. Prefers NIV. Guidelines/needs list on Website; copy online. (No ads)

Poetry: Accepts 3-5/yr. Light verse, traditional. Submit max. 3 poems.

Fillers: Accepts several/yr. Anecdotes, facts, ideas, short humor, and tips.

Columns/Departments: No columns, but open to them.

Tips: "We are an excellent new writer's market. We will use almost every well-written article submitted if it fits with our mission—encouraging women to live with passion and love for Jesus Christ."

CHRISTIAN WOMEN TODAY, Box 300, Sta. A, Vancouver BC V6C 2X3, Canada. (604)514-2000. Fax (604)514-2124. E-mail: editor@christianwomentoday.com. Website: www.christianwomentoday.com. French Website: www.chretiennes.com. Campus Crusade for Christ, Canada. Karen Schenk, pub.; Stacy Wiebe, ed. For Christian women, 20-60 yrs. Monthly online mag.; 2 million hits/mo. 30% unsolicited freelance. Query first; e-query preferred. **NO PAYMENT.** Lifestyle articles 200-500 wds.; features 500-1,000 wds.; life stories 500 wds. Seasonal 4 mos. ahead. Accepts simultaneous submissions & reprints (tell when/where appeared). Prefers e-mail submission (attached file). Guidelines/theme list on Website (www.christianwomentoday.com/volunteer/submissions.html). (Ads)

Tips: "The writer needs to have a global perspective, have a heart to build women in their faith, and help develop them to win others to Christ. Text should be written for online viewing with subheads and bullets in the body of the article."

CHURCHWOMAN, 475 Riverside Dr., Ste. 1626A, New York NY 10115. Toll-free (800)298-5551. (212)870-2347. Fax (212)870-2338. E-mail: cwu@churchwomen.org. Website: www.churchwomen.org. Church Women United. Julie Drews, ed. Shares stories of women acting on their faith and engaging in the work for peace and justice around the world. Quarterly mag.; 28 pgs.; circ. 3,000. Subscription $10. 1% unsolicited freelance. Query. **PAYS IN COPIES.** Articles to 3 pgs. Prefers accepted ms by e-mail (copied into message). Guidelines; copy $1.

COMFORT CAFÉ. E-mail: info@comfortcafe.net. Website: www.comfortcafe.net. Ruth Wood, ed. Women's publication. Online mag. Open to freelance. Complete ms/cover letter; e-query OK. **NO PAYMENT** for one-time electronic rts. Articles 800-1,200 wds.; devotions 300-500 wds. Responds in 4-6 wks. Guidelines & copy on Website.

Tips: "We minister to women facing difficult life challenges. Your submission should offer hope, help, and healing, allowing readers to see and experience the reality of God's love and provision in our lives. Write in first-person narrative."

CROWNED WITH SILVER, PO Box 10, Masonville CO 80541. E-mail: crownedwithsilver@yahoo.com. Website: www.crownedwithsilver.com. Submit to The Editor. Return to biblical femininity; Christian homemaking encouragement regarding home schooling, etiquette, marriage, womanhood, and nostalgic wisdom from the past. Quarterly mag. Subscription free. Articles & fiction.

Tips: "Send your article via e-mail and follow the topics indicated. Write 500 words—no longer—not shorter."

$THE DABBLING MUM, 508 W. Main St., Beresford SD 57004. (605)763-2549. E-mail: dm@thedabblingmum.com. Website: www.thedabblingmum.com. Nondenominational. Alyice Edrich, ed. Balance your life while you glean from successful entrepreneurs, parents, and Christians—just like you. Weekly e-zine; circ. 40,000. Subscription free online. 90% unsolicited freelance; 10% assigned. Complete ms submitted online; e-query OK. Accepts full mss by e-mail. Pays $20-40 (reprints $5-10) on acceptance for 1st, reprint, electronic & nonexclusive archival rts. Articles 500-1,500 wds. (96/yr.). Responds in 4-8 wks. Seasonal 1 mo. ahead. No simultaneous submissions; accepts reprints (tell when/where appeared). Accepts e-mail submissions (copied into message). No kill fee or sidebars. Also accepts submissions from children & teens, if it fits the topic. Prefers KJV or NAS. Guidelines/editorial calendar/copy on Website. (Ads)

Contest: Every 2-3 months they have an essay contest (http://thedabblingmum.com/contests/index.htm).

Tips: "We have a 'most wanted' section in our writers' guidelines to update writers on our current needs. It's imperative you study the style of the publication. We need business ideas, marketing, advertising, direct sales, hosting a writing event, niche writing, and fiction-writing articles."

**This periodical was #39 on the 2007 Top 50 Christian Publishers list.

$ESPRIT, Evangelical Lutheran Women, 302-393 Portage Ave., Winnipeg MB R3B 3H6, Canada. (204)984-9160. Fax (204)984-9162. E-mail: esprit@elcic.ca. Website: www.elw.ca. Evangelical Lutheran Church in Canada. Catherine Pate, ed. For Christian women. Quarterly mag.; 36 pgs.; circ. 5,000. Subscription $18 Cdn., $27 U.S. 65% unsolicited freelance; 35% assigned. Complete ms/cover letter; phone/fax/e-query OK. Pays $18/pg. Cdn. on publication for 1st or one-time rts. Articles & fiction 350-1,300 wds. Responds in 2-4 wks. Seasonal 4 mos. ahead. Accepts simultaneous submissions & reprints (tell when/where appeared). Prefers accepted mss by e-mail (attached). Uses some sidebars. Requires NRSV. Guidelines (also on Website); copy for #10 SAE/$1.50 Cdn. postage or $2 U.S. (Limited ads)

Poetry: Light verse, traditional; 8-100 lines; $18. Submit max. 3 poems.

Columns/Departments: Buys 4/yr., 325 wds. Family Matters.

Tips: "Most open to social justice, world issues, and women's issues (justice, violence). We are currently focusing on topical, well-researched articles with a particular eye on world events. Any submissions should emphasize this research-based approach."

**This periodical was #20 on the 2007 Top 50 Christian Publishers list (#34 in 2006, #30 in 2005, #18 in 2004, #34 in 2003).

+EXTREME WOMAN, PO Box 1562, Clemmons NC 27012. Rochelle L. Valasek, ed. Magazine. Articles.

+FIRST LADY, PO Box 1233, Mableton GA 30126. Website: www.FirstLadyMagazine.com. Tracey L. Smith, pub. To educate, encourage, and inspire women about many aspects of life from a Christian viewpoint. Quarterly mag.; circ. 20,000. Estab. 2005. Subscription $10. Articles.

$+FULLFILL, 2370 S. Trenton Way, Denver CO 80231-3822. E-mail: info@fullfill.org. Website: www.fullfill.org. MOPS Intl. Liz Selzer, exec. ed.; Carla Foote, ed. Encourages women in all seasons of life to realize, utilize, and maximize their influence. Quarterly mag. & online community. Open to unsolicited freelance. Complete ms preferred; considers queries. Pays varying amounts on publication. Articles 1,000-1,500 wds. Requires e-mail submissions (attached or copied into message—write@fullfill.org). Guidelines/themes on Website (click on "About Us," then "Write"). Incomplete topical listings.

Columns/Departments: Coaching Corner (coaching on personal growth, life management, professional growth), 650 wds.

$THE GODLY BUSINESS WOMAN. Toll-free (800)560-1090. (407)696-2805. Fax (407)695-8033. E-mail: kathleen@godlybusinesswoman.com. Website: www.godlybusinesswoman

.com. Kathleen B. Jackson, pub; Tracey Davison, mng. ed. Our goal is to educate, inspire, and encourage women to be all they can be through Jesus Christ; to be a resource that will shed light on God's view of the responsibilities we have been given. Quarterly mag.; 48 pgs.; circ. 25,000. Subscription $15.99. 45% unsolicited freelance; 55% assigned. Query; prefers e-queries. Pays $20 & up on acceptance for one-time rts. Articles 400-1,200 wds. Accepts reprints. Regularly uses sidebars. Guidelines on Website; free copy. (Ads)

Columns/Departments: Women on the Move; Missions Hall of Fame; Mind; 250-650 wds. Query. No payment.

Tips: "Our goal is to encourage educated decision making and harmony in women's lives, whether they are in or out of the workplace."

THE HANDMAIDEN, PO Box 76, Ben Lomond CA 95005. (831)336-5118. Fax (831)336-8882. E-mail: czell@conciliarpress.com. Website: www.conciliarpress.com/handmaiden. Antiochian Orthodox Archdiocese of North America. Carla Zell, ed. For women serving God within the Eastern Orthodox tradition. Quarterly jour.; 64 pgs.; circ. 3,000. Subscription $16.50. 5% unsolicited freelance; 95% assigned. Query; e-query OK. **PAYS IN COPIES/SUBSCRIPTION.** Articles 1,000-2,000 wds. (8/yr.). Responds in 6-8 wks. Seasonal 6 mos. ahead. Accepts reprints (tell when/where appeared). Prefers hard copy or e-mail submissions (copied into message). Uses some sidebars. Prefers NKJV. Guidelines (also by e-mail)/theme list; copy for 7x10 SAE/4 stamps. (No ads)

Poetry: Catherine Grace Bond, poetry ed. Accepts 4-8/yr. Free verse, light verse, traditional. Submit max. 3 poems.

Columns/Departments: Heroines of the Faith (lives of women saints within Orthodox tradition), 1,000-2,000 wds.

Tips: "Most open to theme features, sidebars, and poetry."

+HANDMAIDENS. E-mail: iona@handmaidens.org. Website: www.handmaidens.org. Iona Hoeppner, ed. For women of all (or no) denominations; consider the sensitivities of those whose theology may differ from your own. E-zine. Open to unsolicited freelance. Complete ms. **NO PAYMENT** for one-time rts. Articles; fiction. Requires e-mail submissions (copied into message). Guidelines on Website.

Poetry: Accepts poetry.

Tips: "We welcome your art, photos, poetry, essays, articles, short stories, devotional material, links, almost anything of interest to Christian women."

$HEART & SOUL, 2514 Maryland Ave., Baltimore MD 21218. Toll-free (800)834-8813, ext. 105. (410)576-9199. Fax (410)662-4596. E-mail: eavent@heartandsoul.com. Website: www.heartandsoul.com. General. Edwin V. Avent, pub. The African American woman's ultimate guide to total well-being (body, mind, and spirit). Bimonthly mag.; 88-96 pgs.; circ. 300,000. Subscription $18. Open to unsolicited freelance. Query preferred. Pays on acceptance. Articles 800-1,500 wds. (Ads) Incomplete topical listings.

HEARTS AT HOME, 1509 N. Clinton Blvd., Bloomington IL 61701-1813. (309)828-MOMS. E-mail: hearts@hearts-at-home.org. Website: www.hearts-at-home.org. Connected to annual conferences by the same name (held in Normal IL, Grand Rapids MI, and Rochester MN). Rachel Kitson, ed-in-chief. To encourage and educate mothers at home. Bimonthly mag.; 26 pgs.; circ. 1,500. Subscription $10. Open to unsolicited freelance. Complete ms by e-mail; e-query OK. **PAYS 5 COPIES** for one-time rts. Articles 300-720 wds. (40-50/yr.); fiction to 720 wds.; devotionals to 720 wds. Accepts reprints (tell when/where appeared). Prefers e-mail submissions (attached Word file to mag@hearts-at-home.org). Uses some sidebars. Any Bible version. Guidelines/theme list (also by e-mail/Website); copy $2/6x9 SAE/2 stamps. (No ads)

Poetry: Light verse, traditional; 10-25 lines (to 250 wds.).

Fillers: Anecdotes, cartoons, facts, ideas, party ideas, short humor; 25-100 wds.

Columns/Departments: Motherhood; Parenting; Marriage; Personal Growth; Spiritual Growth; Family Management; to 720 wds.

Special Needs: Articles that challenge mothers in their growth as a parent; uplift spouses in relationship with each other and children; encourage spiritual growth; educate mothers on networking, finding time for themselves, or overcoming personal challenges; tips on saving time and money; and using personal experiences to better parent kids.

Tips: "Submit a well-written, balanced, positive article which will encourage, educate, and/or entertain our audience. Personal stories of the triumphs and trials of being a mom are preferred. This publication is designed to be by moms and for moms. Please include a short biography to go with your article."

$+HERIZONS, PO Box 128, Winnipeg MB R3C 2G1, Canada. (204)774-6225. Fax (204)786-8038. E-mail: editor@herizons.ca. Website: www.herizons.ca. Herizons Magazine Inc. Submit to The Editor. Focuses on empowering women in their relationships, work, culture, health, social justice, spirituality, and family by incorporating current research and feminist theory in articles, essays, and interviews that inspire, inform, and engage readers. Quarterly mag. Open to unsolicited freelance. Query or complete ms; no e-query. Pays $200 Cdn. ($130 U.S.)/1,000 wds. on publication for nonexclusive 1st N.A. rts. Articles 1,000-3,000 wds.; news 500-800 wds.; reviews 400 wds. Responds in 12 wks. Prefers e-mail submissions (copied into message). Guidelines on Website (www.herizons.ca/writers.html). (Ads)

Tips: "With reviews, preference is given to Canadian authors, filmmakers, musicians. Articles in which the writer is engaged with the material she writes about work best; personal experiences, journalism-style articles, interviews, articles which bring in current research and a clear feminist perspective are all things we look for."

($)HISTORY'S WOMEN, 22 Williams St., Batavia NY 14020. (585)343-2810. Fax (585)343-3245. E-mail: submissions@historyswomen.com. Website: www.historyswomen.com. PC Publications. Patti Chadwick, ed. (patti@historyswomen.com). Online magazine highlighting the extraordinary achievements of women throughout history. Weekly e-zine; 20 pgs.; circ. 21,000. Subscription free. 20% unsolicited freelance. E-query/e-submissions only. **PAYS IN COPIES & FREE E-BOOKS** (occasionally pays $10, if budget permits) for 1st, one-time, reprint, or electronic rts. Articles 400-1,200 wds. (20/yr.). Responds in 1-2 wks. Seasonal 3 mos. ahead. Accepts simultaneous submissions & reprints (tell when/where appeared). Prefers e-mail submission (copied into message). Does not use sidebars. Also accepts submissions from teens. Guidelines on Website; copy on site archive. (Ads)

Columns/Departments: Buys 10-20/yr. Women to Admire, in these columns: Women of Faith; First Women (pioneers in their field); Social Reformers; Amazing Moms; Women Who Ruled (women rulers); Early America; all 500-1,000 wds., $10. Query or complete ms.

$HOPE FOR WOMEN MAGAZINE, PO Box 3241, Muncie IN 47307. Toll-free fax (800)936-2214. E-mail: admin@hopeforwomenmag.org. Website: www.hopeforwomenmag.org. Virtuous Publications Inc. Submit to Publisher. Quarterly mag.; 72 pgs.; circ. 10,000. Subscription $14.95. 95% unsolicited freelance; 5% assigned. Query/clips; e-query OK. Accepts full mss by e-mail. Pays .10/wd. on publication for 1st rts. Articles 500-2,000 wds.; reviews 300 wds. Responds in 4-6 wks. Seasonal 2-3 mos. ahead. No simultaneous submissions or reprints. Accepts e-mail submissions (attached file). Guidelines/theme list (also by e-mail); copy for #10 SASE. (Ads)

Fillers: Newsbreaks, party ideas, tips; .10/wd.

Columns/Departments: Relationships (nurturing and maintaining positive relationships), 800-1,200 wds.; Light (tough issues usually kept quiet in the church), 800-1,000 wds.; Journey (helps for a woman's life journey), 500-800 wds.; .10-.15/wd. Query. Additional columns listed on Website.

Tips: "Each issue features at least one interview with a woman of faith—often a celebrity—who has come through a difficult time and grown stronger in her faith because of it."

$HORIZONS, 100 Witherspoon St., Louisville KY 40202-1396. (502)569-5688. Fax (502)569-8085. E-mail: yhileman@ctr.pcusa.org. Website: www.pcusa.org/horizons. Presbyterian Church (USA)/Presbyterian Women. Yvonne Hileman, asst. ed. Justice issues and spiritual life for Presbyterian women. Bimonthly mag. & annual Bible study; 40 pgs.; circ. 25,000. Subscription $18. 10% unsolicited freelance; 90% assigned. Complete ms preferred; fax/e-query OK. Pays $50/600 wds. on publication for all rts. Articles 600-1,800 wds. (10/yr.) & fiction 800-1,200 wds. (5/yr.); book reviews 100 wds. ($25). Responds in 3 mos. Seasonal 6 mos. ahead. Accepts simultaneous submissions & reprints (tell when/where appeared). Accepts requested ms on disk or by e-mail (attached file or copied into message). Kill fee. Regularly uses sidebars. Prefers NRSV. Guidelines/theme list (also by e-mail/Website); copy $4/9x12 SAE. (No ads)

Poetry: Buys 5/yr. All types; $50-100. Submit max. 5 poems.

Fillers: Cartoons, church-related graphics; $50.

Tips: "Most open to devotionals, mission stories, justice and peace issues. Writer should be familiar with constituency of Presbyterian women and life in the Presbyterian Church (USA)."

**This periodical was #6 on the 2006 Top 50 Christian Publishers list (#11 in 2005, #10 in 2004, #8 in 2003).

+$INSPIRED LIVING MAGAZINE and INSPIRED LIVING MAGAZINE ONLINE, 3717 S. La Brea Ave., Ste. 111, Los Angeles CA 90016. (323)293-7100. Fax (323)293-7200. E-mail: editor@inspiredlivingmag.com. Website: www.inspiredlivingmag.com. Nicola Renee Moore, ed.; Tracy L. Williams, nonfiction/columns ed. A lifestyle resource designed to inspire women to know what God is saying NOW in every aspect of life—home, health, family, work, and beyond (for women 25-45). Quarterly mag.; 54 pgs.; circ. 20,000. Subscription $11.95. Estab. 2004. 40% unsolicited freelance; 60% assigned. Query/clips; e-query OK. Accepts full mss by e-mail. Pays $25-50 on publication for nonexclusive rts. Articles 750-1,000 wds. (60/yr.); book reviews 125 wds.; music & video reviews 100 wds. Responds in 6-8 wks. (to acceptances only). Seasonal 5 mos. ahead. Accepts simultaneous submissions & reprints (tell when/where appeared). Accepted mss on disk or by e-mail (attached file). Regularly uses sidebars. Accepts submissions from teens. Prefers NKJV or The Message. Guidelines/theme list (also by e-mail); copy for 9x12 SAE/$1.96 postage. (Ads)

Fillers: Accepts 20/yr. Anecdotes, facts, ideas, party ideas, prayers, quotes, tips; 10-45 wds.; no payment.

Columns/Departments: Accepts 6/yr. Women Who Inspire (true stories), 150-250 wds; Your Spirit NOW (spiritual growth/development); Relationships NOW (healthy relationships); Style & Beauty NOW (fashion, accessories/cosmetics, makeovers, products); Fitness & Health NOW (nutrition, exercise, recipes); Business & Wealth NOW (career); Home & Travel NOW (décor, lifestyle, vacations); all 500-750 wds.

Tips: "Lifestyle columns are most open to freelancers. Also original celebrity interviews, highlighting faith and Christian lifestyles."

$INSPIREDMOMS.COM, PO Box 293477, Lewisville TX 75077. (972)979-7438. E-mail: editor@inspiredmoms.com. Website: www.inspiredmoms.com. Inspired Life Ministries Inc. Wendy Stewart-Hamilton, site ed. Bimonthly e-zine (3 mo. summer edition & 1 mo. Christmas edition). Majority of content provided by staff writers, guest writers, and podcast speakers by assignment. Open to unsolicited freelance. Complete ms/bio; e-query OK. Pays $10/published article or podcast. Articles to 1,200 wds.; podcasts in MP3 format up to 10 minutes in length. Accepts reprints. Responds in 2-3 wks. Guidelines/theme list on Website.

Tips: "Staff writers are selected yearly for the upcoming publication season. Send résumé and two sample articles for moms for future assignment consideration by August 1 of current year. We need authors who can write for work-at-home and homeschool moms."

$INSPIRIT MAGAZINE, 5101 N. Francisco Ave., Chicago IL 60625. (773)907-3332. Fax (773) 784-4366. E-mail: wmc@covchurch.org. Website: www.covchurch.org/women. Dept. of Women Ministries. Ruth Hill, ed-in-chief. To inform and inspire women across the Evangelical Covenant denomination. Quarterly mag.; 50 pgs.; circ. 2,500. Subscription $10. 40% unsolicited freelance; 60% assigned. Complete ms/cover letter; phone/fax/e-query OK. Must include e-mail contact address. Pays $25-35 on publication. Articles about 750 wds. (4/yr.); fiction 750-800 wds. (4/yr.). Seasonal 2.5 mos. ahead. Accepts simultaneous submissions & reprints (tell when/where appeared). Prefers e-mail submissions (attached file). Uses some sidebars. Prefers TNIV or NIV. Guidelines/theme list on Website; copy for 6x9 SAE/$2.50. (Ads)

Tips: "Follow themes printed in issues and guidelines posted on our Website."

$JOURNEY: A Woman's Guide to Intimacy with God, One Lifeway Plaza, Nashville TN 37234-0175. (615)251-5659. E-mail: journey@lifeway.com. Website: www.lifeway.com. LifeWay Christian Resources. Articles to: Manuscript Submissions at address above. Devotional submissions to: Susan Nelson, Walk Through the Bible, 4201 N. Peachtree Rd., Atlanta GA 30341. Pamela Nixon, lead ed.; Tammy Drolsum, ed. Devotional magazine for women 30-50 years old. Monthly mag.; 44 pgs.; circ. 215,000. 15% unsolicited freelance; 85% staff or assigned. Subscription $22.05. Query/clips or complete ms/cover letter; no phone/fax/e-query or e-submissions. Pays $50-100 on acceptance for all rts. Articles 350-1,000 wds. (10-12/yr.). Responds in 8 wks. Seasonal 6-7 mos. ahead. Regularly uses sidebars. Prefers HCSB. Accepts requested ms on disk. Guidelines; copy for 6x9 SAE/2 stamps.

Special Needs: Strong feature articles, 750-1,000 words (including sidebars) on topics of interest to women 30-50 years old ranging from practical applications of faith to spiritual growth, as well as profiles of Christian women in leadership positions.

Tips: "Most open to feature articles that are well written with a thorough understanding of our magazine and target audience. Strong sample devotionals written in *Journey* style may be considered for assignment of a devotional."

JUST BETWEEN US, 777 S. Barker Rd., Brookfield WI 53045. Toll-free (800)260-3342. (262)786-6478. Fax (262)796-5752. E-mail: jbu@elmbrook.org. Website: www.justbetweenus.org. Elmbrook Church Inc. Shelly Esser, ed. Ideas, encouragement, and resources for wives of evangelical ministers and women in leadership. Quarterly mag.; 32 pgs.; circ. 8,000. Subscription $19.95. 85% unsolicited freelance; 15% assigned. Query; phone/fax/e-query OK. **NO PAYMENT** for one-time rts. Articles 250-500 wds. or 1,200-1,500 wds. (50/yr.). Responds in 8 wks. Accepts simultaneous submissions & reprints. Regularly uses sidebars. Prefers NIV. Guidelines (also by e-mail/Website); copy $4/9x12 SAE. (Ads)

Fillers: Accepts 15/yr. Anecdotes, cartoons, ideas, prayers, quotes, short humor; 50-250 wds.

Columns/Departments: Accepts 12/yr. Hospitality; Keeping Your Kids Christian; Women's Ministry (program ideas); all 700-900 wds.

Tips: "Most open to feature articles addressing the unique needs of women in leadership (Bible-study leaders, women's ministry directors, pastor's wives, missionary wives, etc.). Some of these needs would include relationship with God, staff, leadership skills, ministry how-tos, balancing ministry and family, and marriage. The best way to break in is to contact the editor directly."

KEEPING HEARTS & HOME, PO Box 278, Lincolnshire IL 60069-0278. E-mail: articles@keepinghearts.org. Website: www.keepinghearts.org. Jocelyn Zichterman, ed./pub. Sarah Burton, asst. ed. Uplifting and heartwarming; to encourage and inspire women in every stage of life. Quarterly mag.; 30 pgs. Subscription $14. Estab. 2003. Open to freelance. Complete ms by e-mail. **NO PAYMENT.** Articles 1,000-1,200 wds. Prefers e-mail submissions. Guidelines on Website. Incomplete topical listings. (Ads)

Fillers: Accepts games, household tips, party plans, prayers, short humor.

Columns/Departments: Has several columns.

Tips: "We prefer testimony-type articles—not necessarily instructional."

+LADIES FIRST MAGAZINE, For Women Who Choose to Put God First, 4370 Hwy. 6 N., Ste. 211, Houston TX 77084. (281)440-2770. Fax (281)440-2772. E-mail: info@ladiesfirstmagazine.com. Website: www.LadiesFirstMagazine.com. The Master Orchestrator Marketing firm. Connie Stewart, ed. (editor@ladiesfirstmagazine.com; www.myspace.com/pastorconniestewart). Articles and information tailored for women who are single, married, professionals, stay-at-home moms, pastors, First Ladies, students, or business owners. Quarterly mag. Articles. Incomplete topical listings.

LIFE TOOLS FOR WOMEN: Online Women's Lifestyle Magazine, 40 MacEwan Park Rise, N.W., Calgary AB T3K 3Z9, Canada. (403)295-1932. Fax (403)291-2515. E-mail: editor@lifetoolsforwomen.com. Website: www.lifetoolsforwomen.com. Judy Rushfeldt, ed. Equipping women to reach their potential. Monthly online mag. Monthly page views: 45,000. Articles 500-1,200 wds. **NO PAYMENT.** Provides a byline and up to 50-word bio, including e-mail & Website link. Prefers e-query & e-submission (attached file). Guidelines on Website.

$THE LINK & VISITOR, 100-304 The East Mall, Etobicoke ON M9B 6E2, Canada. (416)651-8967. E-mail: rjames@baptistwomen.com. Website: www.baptistwomen.com. Baptist Women of Ontario and Quebec. Renee James, ed. A positive, practical Baptist magazine for Canadian women who want to reach others for Christ. Bimonthly mag.; 24 pgs.; circ. 4,000. Subscription $16 Cdn., $16 U.S. 50% freelance. Complete ms; e-query OK. Pays .06-.10/wd. Cdn., on publication for one-time or simultaneous rts.; some work-for-hire. Articles 750-1,800 wds. (30-35/yr.). Responds in 16 wks. Seasonal 4 mos. ahead. Accepts simultaneous submissions & reprints (tell when/where appeared). Requires e-mail submission (copied into message). No kill fee. Uses some sidebars. Prefers NIV (inclusive language), NRSV, NLT. Guidelines/theme list on Website; copy for 9x12 SAE/2 Cdn. stamps. (Ads—limited/Canadian)

Poetry: Buys 3/yr. Free verse; 12-32 lines; pays $10-20. Submit max. 3 poems.

Tips: "Feature writers who know our magazine and our readers will know what topics and types of stories we are looking for. Canadian writers only, please."

LUTHERAN WOMAN'S QUARTERLY, PO Box 411993, St. Louis MO 63141-1993. Toll-free (800)252-5965. Fax (314)268-1532. E-mail: editor@lwml.org. Website: www.lwml.org. Lutheran Women's Missionary League. Nancy Graf Peters, ed-in-chief. For women of the Lutheran Church—Missouri Synod. Quarterly mag.; 44 pgs.; circ. 200,000. Subscription $5.50. 25% unsolicited freelance; 75% assigned. Complete ms/cover letter. **NO PAYMENT.** Not copyrighted. Articles 750-1,200 wds. (4/yr.); fiction 750-1,200 wds. (4/yr.). Responds in 2 wks. Seasonal 5 mos. ahead. Regularly uses sidebars. Prefers NIV. Guidelines/theme list (also by e-mail); no copy.

Tips: "Most open to articles. Must reflect the Missouri Synod teachings. Most of our writers are from the denomination. We set themes two years ahead. Contact us for themes and guidelines."

MAKING WAVES, 47 Queen's Park Cr. E., Toronto ON M5S 2C3, Canada. (416)929-5184. Fax (416)929-4064. E-mail: barfoot@wicc.org. Website: www.wicc.org. Women's Inter-Church Council of Canada. Gillian Barfoot, ed. A Christian feminist journal committed to addressing issues related to women, justice, and theology from an ecumenical faith perspective. Triannual mag.; circ. 1,400. Subscription for $35 donation. Open to unsolicited queries. Prefers e-mail submissions. Articles 500-800 wds., or 800-1,500 wds. Incomplete topical listings. Guidelines on Website. (No ads)

Tips: "We are connected to a wider network of women and men working to free church and society from racism, ageism, and sexism, and from the teachings and practices that discriminate against women."

$MELODY OF THE HEART E-ZINE: Reconciling Hearts; Offering Hope, 8409 S. Elder Glenwood St., Broken Arrow OK 74011-8286. (918)451-4017. Cell (918)695-4528. E-mail: editor1@epistleworks.com (do not e-mail directly; use submission form at site). Website: http://epistleworks.com/HeartMelody. No fax or postal submissions. EpistleWorks Creations. JoAnn Reno Wray, owner, ed./pub. For women, 30-60+ yrs. Vivid writing with scriptural accuracy to bring a practical and joyful approach to life. Quarterly e-zine; 130,000 hits a month. Open to freelance. Query only, using the online form. Pays $15-20 for articles, $20-25 for fiction, on publication for 1st or reprint electronic rts. Contracts issued for work used (archived for one issue only/3 mos.; exclusive for 1 month then may market elsewhere). Articles 500-900 wds.; short fiction 600-900 wds. Tries to respond but normally can't unless the queries meet editorial needs. Seasonal 6 mos. ahead. Guidelines/theme list/submission form on Website. PDF guidelines available online to download.

Poetry: Music of the Poet Department—poems on theme of targeted issue. Buys 8+/yr.; 4-24 lines. Submit max. 2 poems; theme-related. Complete ms. Pays $6.00-8.50. First or one-time electronic rts. "Avoid overused rhymes; try forms other than iambic pentameter; use words to paint vivid images and scenes to help readers see scriptural truths. More poetry is rejected than any other type of writing due to telegraphed end rhymes, or overused, tired ideas or inappropriate content. Use online form for poetry submissions."

Fillers: Buys 15-30 fillers/yr. Short humor, news, kids' sayings, anecdotes, husband/wife shorts, animal antics, interesting facts, health info, household tips, devotions. Needs more of these. Send complete ms via online form. Under 200 wds.; prefers under 150. Pays $3-10.

Columns/Departments: Life Steps (illustrates the work of God in your life in some way), 500-900 wds.; How Do I? (how-to), 500-750 wds.; Just Do It! (what you do that ministers God's love to others), 500-900 wds.; It's the Little Things (lessons learned or insights gained from the seemingly insignificant), 500-750 wds.; Teen Quest (teen interest), 500-750 wds.; Crafting Love (instructions for craft projects), 900 wds.; Cooking with Taste (recipes), 900 wds. Book Reviews (new and about-to-be-released books), 350-800 wds. New and needed: Quiet Heart Profiles (true stories of those in community who are quietly doing work of the Lord). Query only via online form. Pays $15-25. Open to new column proposals from writers. If accepted, they become staff columnists. Must include 2 sample columns and commit to 4/yr. Use online form. Pays $30 per column.

Tips: This publication temporarily on hold. Check Website for current status.

$MOMSENSE, 2370 S. Trenton Way, Denver CO 80231. (303)733-5353. Fax (303)733-5770. E-mail: MOMsense@mops.org. Website: www.MOMsense.com, or www.mops.org. MOPS Intl. Inc. (Mothers of Preschoolers). Mary Darr, ed. Nurtures mothers of preschoolers from a Christian perspective with articles that both inform and inspire on issues relating to womanhood and motherhood. Bimonthly mag.; 32 pgs.; circ. 120,000. Subscription $20. 20% unsolicited freelance; 30% assigned. Complete ms/cover letter & bio; e-query OK. Accepts full mss by e-mail. Pays .15/wd. on acceptance for 1st & reprint rts. Articles 600-1,200 wds. (15/yr.). Responds in 10-12 wks. Seasonal 6 mos. ahead. Accepts simultaneous submissions & reprints (tell when/where appeared). Prefers requested ms by e-mail (attached file or copied into message). Kill fee 10%. Uses some sidebars. Prefers NIV. Guidelines/theme list (also by e-mail/Website—Mom Resources/Writers Guidelines); copy for 9x12 SAE/$1.35 postage. (Ads)

Poetry: Buys 10/yr. Any type to 400 wds. Pays .15/wd. Submit max. 6 poems.

Fillers: Tips. No payment.

Contest: Sponsors several contests per year for writing and photography. Check Website for details on current contests.

Tips: "Most open to theme-specific features. Writers are more seriously considered if they are a mother with some connection to MOPS (but not required). Looking for original content ideas that appeal to Christian and non-Christian readers."

**This periodical was #21 on the 2007 Top 50 Christian Publishers list.

MORE TO LIFE (MTL), 415 Second St., Indian Rocks Beach FL 33785. (727)596-7625. Fax (727)593-3523. E-mail: info@munce.com. The Munce Group. Submit to The Editor. Lifestyle magazine for women who are discovering their spiritual core and true purpose. 8X/yr. mag.; 36-72 pgs.; circ. 250,000-2 million. Incomplete topical listings. (Ads)

Tips: "This magazine will draw attention to the quality, variety, and relevance of Christian products for everyday living and guide the readers back to Christian retail stores."

PRECIOUS TIMES, PO Box 2866, Costa Mesa CA 92628. Toll-free (800)299-0696. (714)564-3949. E-mail: senioreditor@precioustimesmag.com, or bookrevieweditor@precioustimes mag.com. Website: www.precioustimesmag.com. Independent. Pamela Caldwell, sr. ed.; Sandra Jowers, bk. rev. ed To help black women (ages 20-60) grow in their relationship with God, self, and others; biblical, but not preachy. Quarterly mag.; 76 pgs.; circ. 350,000. Subscription $18. 90% unsolicited freelance; 10% assigned. Complete ms; e-query OK. **PAYS 5 COPIES** for 1st rts. Personal testimonies, 1,800-2,000 wds.; everyday-life information, 1,200-2,400 wds.; health/fitness/beauty, 1,200 wds.; celebrity/personality interviews, 1,800-2,400 wds.; book reviews, 250-300 wds.; music reviews, 200-500 wds; fiction, 2,400-3,200. (20 articles/yr.; 4 fiction). Responds in 12 wks. Seasonal 10 mos. ahead. Accepts simultaneous submissions & reprints (tell when/where appeared). Requires e-mail submissions (attached or copied into message in Word only). Uses some sidebars. Prefers NIV. Also accepts submissions from teens. Guidelines (also by e-mail/Website); copy $5/9x12 SAE. (Ads)

Columns/Departments: Business, Health, Beauty, Finance; 600 wds.

Tips: "Provide practical theology for contemporary issues. All articles should have a personal perspective, be relevant, and use real life anecdotes. We prefer a black woman's perspective on life issues."

PROVERBS 31 SISTERS, 594 Ivy Hill, Harlan KY 40831. (606)573-6506. E-mail: submissions@ avirtuouswoman.org. Website: www.proverbs31sisters.org. Melissa Ringstaff, dir./ed. A group of women who want to minister in their local communities. Monthly/bimonthly newsletter/ e-zine. 90% unsolicited freelance. Complete ms/cover letter; e-query OK. Accepts full mss by e-mail. **NO PAYMENT** for first, reprint, electronic & anthology rts. Articles 500-1,000 wds. (36/yr.); reviews 500 wds. Responds in 4-6 wks. Seasonal 3-6 mos. ahead. No simultaneous submissions; accepts reprints (tell when/where appeared). Prefers e-mail submissions (attached file in DOC or TXT). Regularly uses sidebars. Also accepts submissions from teens. Prefers KJV, NIV, NLT. Guidelines/theme list (also on Website); copy for $1.50/#10 SASE/1 stamp.

Poetry: Accepts 5/yr. Free verse, traditional. Submit max. 1 poem.

Fillers: Accepts 24+/yr. Anecdotes, cartoons, facts, games, ideas, jokes, kid quotes, party ideas, prayers, quizzes, quotes, sermon illustrations, short humor, and tips; to 250 wds.

Special Needs: Devotional themes, Bible studies, Christian scrapbooking ideas/ layouts/devotions, icebreaker ideas, crafts, and group ministry materials.

Tips: "Submissions should be fresh, fun, faith filled, and well written. We appreciate creativity. Food and health articles should deal with vegetarian lifestyle."

P31 WOMAN, 616-G Matthews-Mint Hill Rd., Matthews NC 28105. (704)849-2270. Fax (704)849-7267. E-mail: editor@proverbs31.org. Website: www.proverbs31.org. Proverbs 31 Ministries. Glynnis Whitwer, ed.; submit to Janet Burke, asst. ed. (janet@proverbs

31.org). Seeks to offer a godly woman's perspective on life. Monthly mag.; 16 pgs.; circ. 10,000. Subscription for donation. 50% unsolicited freelance; 50% assigned. Complete ms; e-query OK. **PAYS IN COPIES** for one-time rts. Not copyrighted. Articles 200-1,000 wds. (40/yr.). Responds in 4-6 wks. Seasonal 3 mos. ahead. Accepts simultaneous submissions & reprints (tell when/where appeared). Prefers accepted ms by e-mail (attached file or copied into message). Uses some sidebars. Prefers NIV. Guidelines/theme list (also on Website); copy on Website. (No ads)

Fillers: Accepts 12/yr. Ideas, party ideas, prose; to 100 wds.

Tips: "Looking for articles that encourage women and offer practical advice as well."

RIGHT TO THE HEART OF WOMEN E-ZINE, 2217 Lake Park Dr., Longmont CO 80503. (303)772-2035. Fax (303)678-0260. E-mail: Rebekah@rebekahmontgomery.com. Website: www.righttotheheartofwomen.com. Rebekah Montgomery, ed. Encouragement and helps for women in ministry. Weekly online e-zine; 5 pgs.; circ. 15,000. Subscription free. 10% unsolicited freelance; 90% assigned. Query; e-query OK. **NO PAYMENT** for nonexclusive rts. Articles 100-800 wds. (20/yr.). Responds in 2 wks. Seasonal 2 mos. ahead. Accepts simultaneous submissions & reprints (tell when/where appeared). Requires accepted mss by e-mail (copied into message). Does not use sidebars. No guidelines; copy on Website. (Ads)

Fillers: Accepts 12/yr. Anecdotes, ideas, party ideas, prayers, quotes; 50-200 wds.

Columns/Departments: Accepts 10/yr. Women Bible Teachers; Profiles of Women in Ministry; Women's Ministry Tips; Author's and Speaker's Tips; 100 wds. Query.

Special Needs: Book reviews must be in first person, by the author. Looking for women's ministry event ideas.

Tips: "For free subscription, subscribe at Website above; also view e-zine. We want to hear from those involved in women's ministry or leadership. Also accepts manuscripts from AWSAs (see www.awsawomen.com). Query with your ideas."

($)SHALOM BAYIT: Peace in the Home, PO Box 23, West Charleston VT 05872. E-mail: puritanstore@aol.com. Website: www.thepuritanlight.com. The Puritan Light Ministry. Sharon White, ed. For old-fashioned keepers at home. Quarterly e-zine. Subscription $4. 20% unsolicited freelance; 80% assigned. Complete ms/cover letter; e-query OK (no attachments). Pays $10 for assigned articles only. Articles 400-1,500 wds. (16/yr.). Responds in 2 mos. Seasonal 6 mos. ahead. No simultaneous submissions or reprints. Accepts e-mail submissions (copied into message). Does not use sidebars. Guidelines on Website.

Columns/Departments: Memories of Grandmother (nostalgic stories of grandmother), 500-1,000 wds.; Dear Daughter (letter to a future keeper at home), 800 wds.; Etiquette (share how ladies behaved long ago), 400 wds.; Education at Home (helpful and thrifty tips for homeschooling your children), 500 wds.; Fashion and Home (stories and ideas for homemaking and modest apparel), 300-600 wds. Complete ms.

Tips: "The magazine is geared to very old-fashioned homemakers who strive to be devoutly religious, gentle-spirited mothers, and loving wives. The editor owns and operates a country store in rural Vermont. We focus on home business, home schooling, tender mothering, peaceful/lifelong marriage, and old-fashioned living. Order a sample issue, study it, consider if this is a good fit for your style of writing, then submit your work. You must be willing to make changes quickly and professionally and alter your work to meet our publishing goals. Be patient waiting for responses. If you are looking for assignments, submit constantly and regularly. If we continue to print your work, we will eventually begin to trust you and assign paid work."

SHARE, 10 W. 71st St., New York NY 10023-4201. (212)877-3041. Fax (212)724-5923. E-mail: CDofANatl@aol.com. Website: www.catholicdaughters.org. Catholic Daughters of the Americas. Peggy O'Brien, exec. dir.; submit to Peggy Eastman, ed. For Catholic women. Quarterly mag.; circ. 95,000. Free with membership. Most articles come from membership, but is open. **NO PAYMENT.** Buys color photos & covers. Guidelines/copy. (Ads)

Tips: "We use very little freelance material unless it is written by Catholic Daughters."

$SIMPLE JOY. E-mail: submission@simplejoy.org. Website: www.simplejoy.org. Jean Ann Duckworth, pub.; submit to The Editor. For women (target age 30-55) interested in a simpler way of life; general. Monthly online mag. Open to freelance. Complete mss; e-query OK. Pays $10 honorarium on publication for articles to 1,000 wds. (72-120/yr.); within 60 days of publication; for one-time rts. Seasonal 4 mos. ahead. Prefers e-mail (attached file in Word format). Guidelines on Website. Incomplete topical listings.

Special Needs: Focuses on 4 specific areas: reducing stress, enhancing joy, simplifying life, and building/strengthening relationships.

Tips: "Read the current issue to better understand our mission and market. We like working with first-time authors."

($)+SIMPLY BLESSED CHRISTIAN WOMEN'S MAGAZINE, PO Box 291205, Columbia SC 29229. (803)968-5196. Fax (803)234-4071. E-mail: jjpublisher@yahoo.com. Website: www.jandjpublishingonline.com. J and J Publishing Co. Stephanie McKenny, ed./pub. For all women 25-55, focusing on encouraging and empowering them to perform in their roles at a greater capacity along with sharing information that will assist them in their day-to-day lifestyles. Bimonthly mag.; 40+ pgs. Subscription $18. Estab. 2007. 60% unsolicited freelance; 40% assigned. Query/clips; e-query OK. Accepts full mss by e-mail. **PAYS A 1/2 PAGE AD WORTH $150** for nonexclusive rts. Not copyrighted. Articles 800-1,000 wds. (3/yr.); fiction 800-1,000 wds. (3/yr.); reviews 500 wds. Responds in 2 wks. Seasonal 3 mos. ahead. Accepts reprints (tell when/where appeared). Accepts e-mail submissions (attached file). Uses some sidebars. Prefers KJV or AMP. Guidelines (also by e-mail); copy for $2/9x12 SAE. (Ads)

Fillers: Accepts 6/yr. Cartoons, facts, prayers, tips; 200-300 wds.

Columns/Departments: Accepts 6-10/yr. Seasoned Sisters (women 50+); Pastor's Wives Corner (encouragement for pastor's wives); Health Awareness; Single & Satisfied; all 500-800 wds. Query.

Tips: "Most open to health, marriage, singles, wealth, and business."

$SPIRITLED WOMAN, 600 Rinehart Rd., Lake Mary FL 32746. (407)333-0600. Fax (407)333-7100. E-mail: spiritledwoman@strang.com. Website: www.spiritledwoman.com. Strang Communications. Brenda J. Davis, ed. To call women, ages 20-60, into intimate fellowship with God so He can empower them to fulfill His purpose for their lives. Bimonthly mag.; 100 pgs.; circ. 100,000. Subscription $17.95. 1% unsolicited freelance; 99% assigned. Query (limit to 500 wds.); e-query OK. Pays to $300 ($50 for humor, $75 for testimonies) on publication for 1st and all electronic rts. Articles 1,200-2,000 wds. Responds in 18-26 wks. No simultaneous submissions. Guidelines (also by e-mail); copy. (Ads)

Columns/Departments: Testimonies; Final Fun (funny stories or embarrassing moments, to 200 wds.); cartoons; $25-50.

Tips: "Most of our articles are commissioned. Mainly we want high-impact feature articles that depict a practical and spiritual application of scriptural teachings. Need brief testimonies of 350 words or less (open to all); profiles of women in ministry. Articles need to deal with the heart issues that hold a woman back. Also humorous anecdotes and book excerpts."

**2007 EPA Award of Merit—Most Improved Publication.

TAPESTRY (Canada), 2816 Calder Ave., Saskatoon SK S7J 1W1, Canada. (306)343-7396. E-mail: tapestry@lutheranwomen.ca. Lutheran Women's Missionary League—Canada. Marion Hollinger, ed-in-chief. To encourage women as they live out their faith in Jesus Christ in their daily lives. Quarterly mag.; circ. 3,200. Subscription $7. Open to unsolicited freelance. Incomplete topical listings. (Ads)

$TAPESTRY: A Woman's Guide to Intimacy with God, 4201 N. Peachtree Rd., Atlanta GA 30341. (770)458-9300. Fax (770)454-9313. E-mail: pubsinfo@walkthru.org. Website: www.walkthru.org. Walk Thru the Bible. Susan Nelson, ed. Monthly mag. Subscription $16.95. Requires NIV.

**2007, 2005 Award of Merit—Devotional; 2004 EPA Award of Excellence—Christian Ministries.

$TODAY'S CHRISTIAN WOMAN, 465 Gundersen Dr., Carol Stream IL 60188-2498. (630)260-6200. Fax (630)260-0114. E-mail: TCWedit@christianitytoday.com. Website: www.TodaysChristianWoman.com. Blog: http://blog.todayschristianwoman.com/editors. Christianity Today Intl. Camerin Courtney, mng.ed.; Jane Johnson Struck, ed. To help Christian women (20-49 yrs.) grow in their relationship to God by providing practical, biblical perspectives on marriage, sex, parenting, work, health, friendship, single life, and self. Bimonthly mag.; 80-150 pgs.; circ. 250,000. Subscription $17.95. 25% unsolicited freelance; 75% assigned. Query only; fax/e-query OK. Pays .20/published wd. on acceptance for 1st & electronic rts. Articles 1,000-1,500 wds. (6-12/yr.); no fiction. Responds in 8 wks. Seasonal 6 mos. ahead. Accepts reprints (tell when/where appeared); no simultaneous submissions. Accepts e-mail submission (copied into message). Regularly uses sidebars. Prefers NIV. Guidelines; copy $5. (Ads)

Columns/Departments: Camerin Courtney, ed. of My Story. Buys 6/yr. My Story (dramatic story of overcoming a difficult situation), 1,500 wds., $300.

Special Needs: Articles slanted for mature Christians that deal with spiritual life topics; short humor pieces.

Tips: "Break in by submitting to My Story. Make sure your writing has a fresh approach to a relational topic and that it has a personal tone and anecdotal approach. Please query first."

**The #3 best-selling magazine in Christian retail stores.

TOGETHER WITH GOD (formerly CoLaborer), PO Box 5002, Antioch TN 37011. Toll-free (877)767-7662. (615)731-6812. Fax (615)731-0771. E-mail: twg@wnac.org. Website: www.wnac.org. Women Nationally Active for Christ of National Assn. of Free Will Baptists. Sarah Fletcher, ed. A women's magazine with emphasis on fulfilling the Great Commission. Bimonthly mag.; 32 pgs.; circ. 7,500. Subscription $12. Estab. 2007. 25% unsolicited freelance; 75% assigned. Complete ms/cover letter. Accepts full ms by e-mail. **PAYS IN COPIES** for 1st rts. Articles 750-1,200 wds. (10/yr.). Responds in 8 wks. Seasonal 12 mos. ahead. No simultaneous submissions; accepts reprints (tell when/where appeared). Prefers e-mail submissions (attached file). Regularly uses sidebars. Also accepts submissions from teens. Prefers KJV. Guidelines/theme list by e-mail; copy for 10x13 SAE/$1. (No ads)

Columns/Departments: Young Woman (teen girl issues); Active for Christ (helps, issues, evangelism); 500-700 wds.

Special Needs: Prayer & Christian life.

Contest: Annual Creative Arts Contest. March 1 deadline. Categories include Programs, Articles, Poetry, Plays/Skits, Devotionals, Art/Photography. Open to our subscribers, Women Active for Christ, or any woman active in the Free Will Baptist Church.

Tips: "Most open to articles. Most of our material comes from our Active for Christ or Free Will Baptist writers."

A VIRTUOUS WOMAN, 594 Ivy Hill, Harlan KY 40831. (606)573-6506. E-mail: submissions@avirtuouswoman.org. Website: www.avirtuouswoman.org. Melissa Ringstaff, dir./ed. Strives to provide practical articles for women ages 20-60 years; based on Proverbs 31. Monthly e-zine; circ. 20,000+ online. 50% unsolicited freelance; 50% assigned. Complete ms/cover letter; e-query OK. Accepts full mss by e-mail. **NO PAYMENT** for first, reprint, electronic rts. Articles 500-1,000 wds. (150+/yr.); reviews 500 wds. Responds in 6 wks. Seasonal 3-6 mos. ahead. No simultaneous submissions; accepts reprints (tell when/where appeared). Prefers e-mail submissions (attached file in DOC or TXT). Regularly uses sidebars. Prefers KJV, NIV, NLT. Guidelines/theme list on Website; copy online. (Ads)

Poetry: Accepts 5/yr. Free verse, traditional. Submit max. 2 poems.

Fillers: Accepts 12/yr. Anecdotes, facts, ideas, jokes, party ideas, prayers, quizzes, and tips; to 200 wds.

Tips: "Write practical articles that appeal to the average woman—articles that women can identify with. Do not preach."

A WOMAN OF WORTH, 594 Ivy Hill, Harlan KY 40831. (606)573-6506. E-mail: submissions@avirtuouswoman.org. Website: www.avirtuouswoman.org. Melissa Ringstaff, dir. Strives to provide practical articles for women ages 20-60 years; based on Proverbs 31. Quarterly mag.; 16 pgs.; circ. 100+. Subscription $18. 90% unsolicited freelance. Complete ms/cover letter; e-query OK. Accepts full mss by e-mail. **PAYS IN COPIES** for first, reprint, electronic, & anthology rts. Articles 500-1,000 wds. (60+/yr.); reviews 500 wds. Responds in 4-6 wks. Seasonal 3-6 mos. ahead. No simultaneous submissions; accepts reprints (tell when/where appeared). Prefers e-mail submissions (attached file in DOC or TXT). Uses some sidebars. Prefers KJV, NIV, NLT. Guidelines/theme list (also on Website); copy for $1.50/6x9 SAE/2 stamps.

Poetry: Accepts 5/yr. Free verse, traditional. Submit max. 1 poem.

Fillers: Accepts 6/yr. Anecdotes, facts, ideas, party ideas, prayers, short humor, and tips; to 250 wds.

Tips: "Articles should be practical and encourage women to grow in their faith. Food and health articles should deal with vegetarian lifestyle."

$WOMEN ALIVE! PO Box 480052, Kansas City MO 64148. (816)268-8928. E-mail: pamenderby@gmail.com. Website: www.womenaliveministries.org. Pam Enderby, mng. ed. To encourage women to live holy lives by applying Scripture to their daily lives. Bimonthly mag.; 20 pgs.; circ. 4,000. Subscription $13.95. 50% unsolicited freelance; 2% assigned. Complete ms/no cover letter or query; no phone/fax query; e-query OK. Accepts full mss by e-mail. Pays $25-50 on publication for one-time, simultaneous, or reprint rts. Articles 500-1,200 wds. (30/yr.). Responds in 4-6 wks. Seasonal 6 mos. ahead. Accepts reprints (tell when/where appeared) . Uses some sidebars. Prefers e-mail submissions (attached file). Prefers NIV. Guidelines/theme list (also by e-mail); copy for $2/9x12 SAE/3 stamps. (No ads)

Special Needs: Looking for keys to building healthy relationships between mothers/daughters and mothers/sons with a spiritual emphasis; caring for elderly parents; and loving your husband God's way.

Tips: "We look for articles that draw women into a deeper spiritual life—articles on surrender, prayer, Bible study—yet written with personal illustrations."

WOMEN OF THE CROSS, 920 Sweetgum Creek, Plano TX 75023. (972)517-8553. Greg Paskal, content mngr. (greg@gregpaskal.com). Encouraging women in their walk with the Lord; strong emphasis on discipleship and relationship. Online community. 50% unsolicited freelance. Complete ms by e-mail; e-query OK. **NO PAYMENT.** Articles 500-1,500 wds. (10/yr.). Responds in 2-4 wks. Seasonal 3 mos. ahead. Accepts simultaneous submissions; no reprints. Prefers e-mail submissions (attached or copied into message). Uses some sidebars. Prefers NIV, NKJV, NASB. Also accepts submissions from teens. Guidelines by e-mail. (No ads)

Poetry: Accepts 2/yr. Avant-garde, free verse, haiku, or light verse; 50-250 lines. Submit max. 1 poem.

Columns/Departments: Accepts 10/yr. Features (Christian living, encouragement); Article (to other women); all 500-1,500 wds.

Special Needs: Personal stories of growing in the Lord; faith-stretching stories about international adoption.

Tips: "Appropriate topics could be first-hand accounts of how God worked in the author's life through a personal or family experience. View online forum for specific topics."

WOMEN'S MINISTRY MAGAZINE, 4319 S. National Ave., #303, Springfield MO 65810-2607. (417)888-2067. Fax (417)888-2095. E-mail: publisher@womensministry.net. Website: www.womensministry.net, or www.jenniferrothschild.com. Jennifer and Philip Rothschild, pubs. Where more than 25,000 women's ministry leaders find news, events, and tips for women's ministry in the local church. Online newsletter. Subscription free. Open to freelance. Guidelines by e-mail.

Special Needs: Punchy, practical tips and ideas related to leading effective women's ministry.

WOMEN TODAY MAGAZINE, Box 300, Sta. A, Vancouver BC V6C 2X3, Canada. Toll-free (800)563-1106, ext. 252. (604)514-2000 (no phone calls). Fax (604)514-2002. E-mail: editor@womentodaymagazine.com. Website: www.womentodaymagazine.com. Campus Crusade for Christ, Canada. Karen Schenk, pub.; Claire Colvin, sr. ed. For the professional, pre-seeking woman, 20-60 years; provides quality information that leads into a discussion of spiritual things and a presentation of the gospel. Monthly e-zine; 1.5 million hits/mo.; 100,000 unique visitors/mo. 60% unsolicited freelance; up to 10% assigned. Use online submission system on Website; e-query OK. Accepts full ms by e-mail. **NO PAYMENT** for one-time or reprint rts. Articles 300-1,000 wds. (12-24/yr.). Responds in 8-12 wks. to accepted material only. Seasonal 4 mos. ahead. Accepts simultaneous submissions & reprints. Requires online submission. Does not use sidebars. Also accepts submissions from teens. Guidelines/theme list on Website. (Ads)

Columns/Departments: Columns tend toward how-to; 600-1,000 wds. Beauty & Fashion; Health & Fitness; Food & Cooking; Advice.

Tips: "Write on a topic from the theme list 4-5 months in advance. Beauty/fashion, relationships, and self-esteem are big draws on our site, and we can always use more great content. To break in, make your article approachable to an unchurched audience, avoid Christian jargon, and speak the truth plainly."

$WT ONLINE, 1445 N. Boonville Ave., Springfield MO 65802-1894. (417)862-2781. Fax (417) 862-0503. E-mail: womanstouch@ag.org. Website: www.wtonline.ag.org. Assemblies of God Women's Ministries Dept. Darla J. Knoth, mng. ed. Inspirational online magazine for women. Monthly Webzine. 20% unsolicited freelance. Query only; fax/e-query OK. Articles 500-800 wds. (20/yr.). Responds in 13 wks. Seasonal 10 mos. ahead. Accepts simultaneous submissions & reprints (tell when/where appeared). Accepts e-mail submission. Kill fee. Regularly uses sidebars. Prefers NIV. Guidelines/theme list (also by e-mail); copy for 9x12 SAE/3 stamps. (Ads)

Columns/Departments: Buys 30/yr. The Single Woman (never married, widowed, divorced), 400 wds.; Family Matters (single or married moms); I Still Do! (marriage), 400 wds.

Tips: "Request guidelines and theme list for guidance on types of articles needed."

**2005 EPA Award of Merit—General; 2003 EPA Award of Excellence—Most Improved Publication.

WRITERS' MARKETS

$ADVANCED CHRISTIAN WRITER, 9118 W. Elmwood Dr., #1G, Niles IL 60714-5820. (847) 296-3964. Fax (847)296-0754. E-mail: ljohnson@wordprocommunications.com. Website: www.ACWriters.com. American Christian Writers/Reg Forder, Box 110390, Nashville TN 37222. Toll-free (800)21-WRITE. E-mail: ACWriters@aol.com (for samples, advertising, and subscriptions). Lin Johnson, mng. ed. A professional newsletter for published writers. Bimonthly newsletter; 8 pgs.; circ. 500. Subscription $19.95. 60% unsolicited freelance. Query, correspondence, & mss by e-mail only. Pays $20 on publication for 1st or reprint rts. Articles 500-1,000 wds. (18/yr.). Responds in 4-6 wks. Seasonal 6 mos. ahead. Accepts reprints (tell when/where appeared). Uses some sidebars. Requires e-mail submission. Prefers NIV. Guidelines (also by e-mail); copy for #10 SAE/1 stamp. (Ads)

Special Needs: Behind the scenes look at a publishing house (how it started, how editorial operates, current needs, submission procedures); how-to; profiles; opinion pieces; time management; workplace issues.

Tips: "We accept articles only from professional, well-published writers and from editors. We need manuscripts about all aspects of being a published freelance writer and how to increase sales and professionalism; on the advanced level; looking for depth beyond the basics."

AREOPAGUS MAGAZINE. E-mail for UK: editor@areopagus.org.uk. E-mail from U.S.: editor@areopagus.org.uk. Website: www.areopagus.org.uk. Areopagus Publications. Julian Barritt, ed. For amateur Christian writers, producing both general and Christian writing. Quarterly mag.; 32 pgs.; circ. 100. Subscription $21. 100% unsolicited freelance. Complete ms/cover letter (if subscriber); e-query OK. **NO PAYMENT.** Articles 1,800 wds. (6/yr.); fiction 1,800 wds. (5/yr.); book reviews 300 wds. Responds in 1 mo. Seasonal 4 mos. ahead. Accepts e-mail submissions (attached or copied into message). Does not use sidebars. Any Bible version. Guidelines; copy on Website.

Poetry: Accepts 40/yr.; any type; to 60 lines. Submit max. 3 poems.

Fillers: Accepts 10/yr. Facts, ideas, newsbreaks, prose, short humor, to 200 wds.

Contest: Sponsors a quarterly, subscribers-only, writing competition (fiction, nonfiction, or poetry) with prizes of 28 pounds (UK only).

Tips: "Items are selected by merit from subscribers only. If not accepted, a recommendation for re-submission is given if there is potential."

AUTHOR-ME.COM. E-mail: Peachy2@prodigy.net. Website: www.Author-Me.com. Independent. Bruce L. Cook, pub.; Adam W. Smith, ed. dir. (awsmith@patriot.net); Winona Rasheed, mng. ed. (mzcoffeecake2001@yahoo.com). Endeavors to encourage and nurture new writers in their craft. Accepts freelance. Complete ms. **NO PAYMENT.** No submissions from writers under age 14. Edit manuscripts before submitting. Requires e-mail submissions from Website form. Guidelines on Website.

Poetry: Submit max. 4 poems.

BEGINNINGS: A Magazine for Novice Writers, PO Box 214, Bayport NY 11705. E-mail: jenineb@optonline.net. Website: www.scbeginnings.com. Beginnings Publishing Inc. Jenine Killoran, ed/pub. The only magazine that caters exclusively to the new writer. Triannual mag.; 48 pgs.; circ. 1,500. Subscription $14. 95% unsolicited freelance; 5% assigned. Charges a reading fee of $10 if you send more than one ms or 5 poems at a time. Complete ms/cover letter. **PAYS IN COPIES** for one-time rts. Articles any length (10/yr.); short stories to 3,000 wds. (27-30/yr.). Responds in 14-16 wks. Accepts simultaneous submissions & reprints (tell when/where appeared). Requested ms by mail only. Uses some sidebars. Guidelines (also by e-mail/Website: www.scbeginnings.com/guidelines.htm); copy for 10x13 SAE/$2.13 postage (mark "Media Mail"). (Ads)

Poetry: Freada Dillon, poetry ed. Accepts 60/yr. Any type; reasonable length. Submit only by mail. Submit max. 2 poems.

Fillers: Cartoons.

Special Needs: Short stories, poetry, or artwork by children. Written work: ages 5-12. Or same material from young adults: 13-19 yrs. Artwork must be on plain, unruled white paper.

Contest: Sponsors poetry and short story contests, 4 contests for each season. See Website for current contests and details.

Tips: "Read a sample copy! See Website!" Fiction for 5- to 12-year-olds.

$BYLINE, PO Box 111, Albion NY 14411-0111. E-mail: robbi@bylinemag.com. Website: www.BylineMag.com. General market. Robbi Hess, ed. Offers practical tips, motivation, and encouragement to freelance writers and poets. Monthly (11X) mag.; 36 pgs.; circ. 3,000+. Subscription $24. 80% unsolicited freelance. Query or complete ms; e-query OK. Pays $100 for features; $75 for fiction; less for shorts, on acceptance for 1st rts. Articles 1,500-1,800 wds. (75/yr.); personal essays 700 wds.; fiction 2,000-3,000 wds. (11/yr.). Responds in 3 mos. Seasonal 6 mos. ahead. Accepts simultaneous submissions. No full mss by e-mail. Encourages sidebars. Guidelines on Website; copy $5. (Ads)

Poetry: Donna Marbach, poetry ed. Buys 50-100/yr. Any type; to 30 lines; $10. Writing themes only. Submit max. 3 poems.

Fillers: Anecdotes, prose, short humor for humor page; 50-400 wds.; $15-25. Must pertain to writing.

Columns/Departments: Buys 50-60/yr. End Piece (personal essay on writing theme), 550 wds., $35; First Sale accounts, 300 wds., $20; Only When I Laugh (writing humor), short, $15-25. Complete ms.

Contests: Sponsors many year round; details included in magazine, on Website, or send SASE for flier.

Special Needs: Accepts articles only about writing and selling; likes mainstream fiction.

Tips: "All areas except our regular columns are open to freelancers. We get much more fiction than nonfiction. Always looking for instructive, well-written articles."

$CANADIAN WRITER'S JOURNAL, White Mountain Publications, Box 1178, New Liskeard ON P0J 1P0, Canada. Canada-wide toll-free (800)258-5451. (705)647-5424. Fax (705)647-8366. E-mail: editor@cwj.ca. For submissions: submissions@cwj.ca. Website: www.cwj.ca. Deborah Ranchuk, ed./pub. How-to articles for writers. Bimonthly mag.; 64 pgs.; circ. 350. Subscription $35. 75% unsolicited freelance; 15% assigned. Complete ms/cover letter or query; phone/fax/e-query OK. Pays $7.50 Cdn./published pg. (about 450 wds.) on publication (2-9 mos. after acceptance) for one-time rts. Articles 400-2,000 wds. (200/yr.); fiction to 1,200 wds (see contest below); book/music/video reviews 250-500 wds. ($7.50). Responds in 9 wks. Seasonal 3 mos. ahead. Accepts simultaneous submissions & reprints (tell when/where appeared). Prefers e-mail submission (copied into message only). Some sidebars. Prefers KJV. Also accepts submissions from teens. Guidelines (also by e-mail/Website); copy $9. (Ads)

Poetry: Buys 40-60/yr. All types; to 40 lines; $2-5. Submit max. 10 poems.

Fillers: Buys 15-20/yr. Anecdotes, cartoons, ideas, quotes; 20-200 wds.; $3-5.

Contest: Sponsors semiannual short fiction contest (March 31 and September 30 deadlines); to 1,200 wds. Entry fee $5. Prizes $100, $50, $25. All fiction needs are filled by this contest. E-mail: cwc-calendar@cwj.ca.

Tips: "Send clear, complete, concise how-to-write articles with a sense of humor and usefulness. Read the guidelines and follow them, please."

**This periodical was #19 on the 2007 Top 50 Christian Publishers list.

$CHRISTIAN COMMUNICATOR, 9118 W. Elmwood Dr., #1G, Niles, IL 60714-5820. (847)296-3964. Fax (847)296-0754. E-mail: ljohnson@wordprocommunications.com. Website: www.ACWriters.com. American Christian Writers/Reg Forder, Box 110390, Nashville TN 37222. Toll-free (800)21-WRITE , fax (615)834-0450; ACWriters@aol.com (for samples, advertising or subscriptions). Lin Johnson, mng. ed. For Christian writers/speakers who want to improve their writing craft and speaking ability, stay informed about writing markets, and be encouraged in their ministries. Monthly (11X) mag.; 20 pgs.; circ. 3,000. Subscription $29.95. 70% unsolicited freelance. Complete ms/queries by e-mail only. Pays $5-10 on publication for 1st or reprint rts. Articles 650-1,000 wds. (22/yr.). Responds in 4-6 wks. Seasonal 6 mos. ahead. Accepts reprints (tell when/where appeared). Requires e-mail submission. Guidelines by e-mail; copy for 9x12 SAE/3 stamps to Nashville address. (Ads)

Poetry: Buys 22/yr. Free verse, haiku, light verse, traditional; to 20 lines. Poems on writing or speaking; $5. Send to Gretchen Sousa, gretloriat@earthlink.net.

Columns/Departments: Buys 80/yr. A Funny Thing Happened on the Way to Becoming a Communicator (humor), 75-300 wds.; Interviews (published authors or editors), 650-1,000 wds.; Speaker's Corner (techniques for speakers), 650-1,000 wds.

Tips: "I need editor profiles and articles for speaker's column."

CHRISTIANWRITERS.COM. Website: www.christianwriters.com. A free online writers' resource community to provide a supportive, family atmosphere where writers may easily access the tools and resources to create, market, and publish their work. Accepts articles, short fiction, poetry, and devotionals. Submit through Website. Guidelines on Website.

$CROSS & QUILL, 1624 Jefferson Davis Rd., Clinton SC 29325-6401. (864)697-6035. E-mail: CQarticles@cwfi-online.org, or cwfi@cwfi-online.org. Website: www.cwfi-online.org. Christian Writers Fellowship Intl. Sandy Brooks, ed./pub. For Christian writers, editors, agents, conference directors. Bimonthly newsletter; 16 pgs.; circ. 1,000+. Subscription $25; CWFI membership $45. 75% unsolicited freelance; 25% assigned. Complete ms; query for electronic submissions. Pays honorarium on publication for 1st or reprint rts. Articles 800-1,000 wds. (24/yr.); book reviews 100 wds. Responds in 2 mos. Seasonal 6 mos. ahead. Accepts reprints (tell when/where appeared). Regularly uses sidebars. Accepts e-mail submission to CQArticles@cwfi-online.org. Guidelines; copy $2/9x12 SAE/2 stamps. (Ads)

Poetry: Accepts 12/yr. Any type; to 12 lines. Submit max. 3 poems. Must pertain to writing/publishing.

Fillers: Accepts 12/yr. Anecdotes, cartoons, prayers; 25-100 wds. Pays in copies.

Columns/Departments: Accepts 36/yr. Writing Rainbows! (devotional), 500-600 wds.; Writers Helping Writers (how-to), 200-800 wds.; Editor's Roundtable (interview with editor), 200-800 wds.; Tots, Teens & In-Betweens (juvenile market), 200-800 wds.; BusinessWise (business side of writing), 200-800 wds.; Connecting Points (how-to on critique group), 200-800 wds.

Special Needs: Good "meaty" informational articles on children's writing; writing for teens; how-tos on organizing and operating writers' groups; program ideas for groups; and how to organize and run a writer's workshop, conference, or seminar.

Tips: "Most open to informational articles that explain how to improve writing skills, how to keep records, how to organize and run a writers' group. Keep in mind our audience is primarily writers and others associated with Christian publishing. Stick to informational, nuts and bolts type articles, and follow our guidelines."

$FELLOWSCRIPT, 20 Cross Rd., Dartmouth NS B2W 3G9, Canada. E-mail: query@inscribe.org. Website: www.inscribe.org. Inscribe Christian Writers' Fellowship. Joanna Malory, acq. ed. To provide encouragement, instruction, news, and helpful information to Christians who write. Quarterly newsletter; 28-44 pgs.; circ. 200. Subscription $40 (includes membership). 50% unsolicited freelance; 50% assigned. Query or complete ms; e-query OK. Accepts full mss by e-mail. Pays $5 or .025/wd. Cdn. on publication for 1st or reprint rts. Articles 700-1,200 wds. (40-50/yr.); book reviews (writing related), 150-300 wds. Responds in 2-4 wks. Seasonal 3-4 mos. ahead. Accepts simultaneous submissions & reprints (tell when/where appeared). Prefers requested ms by e-mail (copied into message). No kill fee. Uses some sidebars. Also accepts submissions from teens. Prefers NIV or NKJV. Guidelines (also by e-mail/Website); copy for $3.50 in Canadian stamps or IRCs. (Ads if writing related)

Fillers: Accepts 5-10/yr. Facts, prayers, tips; 300-500 wds. Pays $0-5.

Special Needs: Articles of practical help to writers, from beginners to advanced.

Contest: Fall contest in conjunction with Inscribe's Fall Conference every year in September (August deadline). Categories include fiction, poetry, children's stories, essays, and nonfiction. Details on Website, or write and ask to be put on mailing list.

Tips: "Most open to 700-1,200 words with strong take-away value for writers (at all levels, in most genres). Read our guidelines, follow them, and send us a good article."

$FICTION FIX NEWSLETTER: The Nuts and Bolts of Crafting Better Fiction. E-mail: administration@coffeehouseforwriters.com. Website: www.coffeehouseforwriters.com/news.html. Carol Lindsay, ed. For writers and aspiring writers of short stories and novels. Monthly newsletter; circ. 5,000. To subscribe, send blank e-mail to FictionFix-subscribe@topica.com. E-query only. Responds in 2-3 wks. Pays to $20 ($30-50 for assigned) within 10 days of publication for 1st electronic rts. How-to articles 300-1,500 wds. Prefers submission by e-mail (copied into message only/see guidelines for specifics). Guidelines on Website.

Columns/Departments: This Writer's Opinion (reviews of writing books), 300-500 wds.; The Writing Life (personal writing stories). No payment.

Tips: "Articles must be received by the 10th of the previous month. Articles received after the 10th will be considered for a later publication."

$FREELANCE WRITER'S REPORT, 45 Main St., PO Box A, North Stratford NH 03590-0167. (603)922-8383. E-mail: fwrcwm@writers-editors.com. Website: www.writers-editors.com. General/CNW Publishing Inc. Dana K. Cassell, ed. Covers marketing and running a freelance writing business. Monthly & online newsletter; 8 pgs. 25% freelance. Complete ms via e-mail (attached or copied into message). Pays .10/wd. on publication for one-time rts. Articles to 900 wds. (50/yr.). Responds within 1 wk. Seasonal 2 mos. ahead. Accepts simultaneous submissions & reprints (tell when/where appeared). Does not use sidebars. Guidelines on Website; copy for 6x9 SAE/2 stamps (for back copy); $4 for current copy.

Fillers: Prose fillers to 400 wds.

Contest: Open to all writers. Deadline March 15, 2008. Nonfiction, fiction, children's, poetry. Prizes; $100, $75, $50. Details on Website.

Tips: "No articles on the basics of freelancers; our readers are established freelancers. Looking for marketing and business building for freelance writers/editors/book authors."

$MERLYN'S PEN: Fiction, Essays, and Poems by America's Teens, PO Box 2550, Providence RI 02906-0550. Toll-free (800)247-2027. (401)751-3766. Fax (401)274-1541. E-mail: merlyn@merlynspen.org. Website: www.merlynspen.com. General. Jim Stahl, ed. Magazine; circ. 5,000. Subscription $29.95. Query; no e-query. Pays $20-200 on publication for all rts. Articles 500-5,000 wds.; fiction to 8,500 wds. Responds in 10-12 wks.

Poetry: Free verse, metric verse; $20-50.

Tips: Doing some revamping, so check Website to see if open to submissions.

($)MONEY THE WRITE WAY, PO Box 488, Dobbins CA 95935. (916)205-4763. E-mail: carmel@moneythewriteway.com. Website: www.moneythewriteway.com. Write Spirit Publishing. Carmel Mooney, pub. Educates, inspires, and supports Christian writers, travel writers, authors, and e-publishing enthusiasts in making money as a writer of integrity. Monthly e-zine; 8-15 pgs.; circ. 4,000. Subscription free. 80% unsolicited freelance; 10% assigned. Query; e-query OK. **PAYS IN COPIES,** free advertising for writer, and occasionally up to $10; for one-time rts. Articles 300-800 wds. (36/yr.); book reviews 300-500 wds. Responds in 2-4 wks. Seasonal 2 mos. ahead. Accepts simultaneous submissions & reprints (tell when/where appeared). Accepts mss by e-mail (attached file). Does not use sidebars. Prefers NIV. Guidelines; copy for #10 SAE or by e-mail. (Ads)

Fillers: Accepts 6-12/yr. Anecdotes, facts, ideas, quotes, tips; 50-100 wds. No payment (usually), or up to $5.

Columns/Departments: Accepts 36+/yr. Marketing for Writers—Marketing with Integrity, 300-800 wds.; monthly guest article (how-to or personal experience essay), 300-800 wds.; Boast Post (short pieces on personal writing accomplishments), 50-100 wds.

Special Needs: Christian writing: tips, resources, how-to, reviewing, travel writing, success stories, and marketing. Propose a column for us.

Contest: Occasionally sponsors writing contests.

Tips: "Most open to Boast Post (column), or how-to-write/marketing/breaking-in articles. Send a concise, focused query that is an example of writer's tone and expertise."

$NEW WRITER'S MAGAZINE, PO Box 5976, Sarasota FL 34277-5976. (941)953-7903. E-mail: newriters@aol.com. General/Sarasota Bay Publishing. George S. Haborak, ed. Bimonthly mag.; circ. 5,000. 95% freelance. Query or complete ms by mail. Pays $10-50 ($20-40 for fiction) on publication for 1st rts. Articles 700-1,000 wds. (50/yr.); fiction 700-800 wds. (2-6/yr.). Responds in 5 wks. Guidelines; copy $3.

Poetry: Buys 10-20/yr. Free verse, light verse; 8-20 lines. Pays $5 min. Submit max. 3 poems.

Fillers: Buys 25-45/yr. Writing-related cartoons; buys 20-30/yr.; pays $10 max. Anecdotes, facts, newsbreaks, short humor; 20-100 wds.; buys 5-15/yr. Pays $5 max.

Tips: "We like interview articles with successful writers."

NORTHWEST CHRISTIAN AUTHOR, Attn.: NCWA, PO Box 825, Enumclaw WA 98022. Toll-free (800)731-6292. (425)742-3168. E-mail: acquisitions@nwchristianwriters.org. Website: www.nwchristianwriters.org. Northwest Christian Writers Assn. Mike Owens, acq. ed. To encourage Christian authors to share the gospel through the written word and to promote excellence in writing. Bimonthly newsletter; 12 pgs.; circ. 200. Subscription $12; or $25 including membership. 40% unsolicited freelance; 60% assigned. Complete ms/cover letter; e-query OK. **PAYS 3 COPIES** for one-time or reprint rts. Not copyrighted. Articles 300-800 wds. (16/yr.); book reviews 100 wds. Responds in 2 wks. Accepts simultaneous submissions & reprints (tell when/where appeared). Prefers e-mail submission (attached file). Uses some sidebars. Also accepts submissions from teens. Guidelines on Website; no copy. (No ads)

Poetry: Accepts 3/yr. Free verse, light verse. Submit max. 3 poems.

Fillers: Anecdotes, tips; 50-250 wds.

Special Needs: How-tos on nonfiction and fiction writing. Focus on genre techniques.

Tips: "Most open to articles on writing techniques, particularly for specific genres. Stay within word count. E-queries should have 'NW Christian Author' in subject line. Include 1-2 sentence author bio with article."

$NOVEL WRITER MAGAZINE, 2060 Victoria St., Gorrie ON N0G 1X0, Canada. (519)335-6464. E-mail: novelwritermagazine@hotmail.com. Website: www.inspiredauthor.com, or www.novel-writer.com. Grace Publishing. Suzanne James, pub. How-to industry information; author interviews, how to write/get published, book reviews. Bimonthly mag.; 40-80 pgs. Subscription PDF $10 (print is individual copy only). Estab. 2006. 40% unsolicited freelance; 60% assigned. Query; no phone/e-query. Pays .02-.05/wd., and/or a subscription, on publication for one-time rts. Articles 1,000-3,000 wds.; reviews 300 wds. ($10). Responds in 4 wks. Seasonal 6 mos. ahead. Accepts reprints. Prefers accepted articles by e-mail (copied into message). No kill fee. Uses some sidebars. Also accepts submissions from children/teens. Guidelines/theme list on Website. (Ads) Incomplete topical listings.

Fillers: Buys several/yr. Facts, ideas, newsbreaks, short humor; 50-200 wds. Pays $1-5.

Tips: "One hundred percent of content must help fiction writers with writing, editing, conferences, etc."

ONCE UPON A TIME, 553 Winston Ct., St. Paul MN 55118. (651)457-6223. E-mail: audreyouat@comcast.net. Website: http://onceuponatimemag.com. Audrey B. Baird, ed./pub. Highly specialized magazine for children's writers and illustrators, offering help, instruction, encouragement in an over-the-fence-type friendly way. Quarterly mag.; 32 pgs.; circ. 1,000. Subscription $27. 50% unsolicited freelance. Complete ms/cover letter; no phone/fax/e-query. **PAYS IN COPIES** for one-time rts. Articles 100-900 wds. (80-100/yr.). Responds in 6 wks. Seasonal anytime. Accepts simultaneous submissions & reprints (tell when/where appeared—must be 1 yr. from last publication). Uses some sidebars. Guidelines (also on Website); copy $5. (Ads)

Poetry: Accepts 80-100/yr. Free verse, haiku, light verse, traditional; to 30 lines. Writing/illustrating related. Submit max. 6 poems. "About rhyming poetry: pay attention to rhythm—it's not enough to rhyme—rhyming poetry must have rhythm (and near rhyme is not enough). I'm willing to help and to edit and to suggest, but do your part first with revision until the piece is as good as you can get it."

Fillers: Accepts 20-30/yr. Anecdotes, cartoons, ideas, short humor, tips (all writing/illustrating related); to 100 wds.

Special Needs: How-to articles on writing and illustrating (by those qualified to write them) up to 800 wds.; short pieces on writing & illustrating, 100-400 wds.

Tips: "Send a good, tight article on the writing life—any aspect—that is either educational, informative, entertaining, humorous, or inspiring. We like a friendly, upbeat tone. Humor is always looked for. We get too many articles on rejection. I am open to them if you state what you learned from them or how you persevered in spite of them. Articles on good advice you've received that resulted in publication for you are always good. We like success stories and particularly look for how-to pieces. Perseverance is a strong theme for us. Read the writing books. Read the market guides. Attend conferences. Learn how to write before you attempt it."

OPINARI NEWSLETTER FOR BEGINNING AND ADVANCED CHRISTIAN WRITERS, 5113 W. Running Brook Rd., Columbia MD 21044. (443)745-1004. Fax (410)730-1353. E-mail: info@opinebooks.com. Website: www.opinari.com. Opine Publishing. Jeanne Purcell, ed. Information, ideas, and opportunities for new and advanced Christian writers. Quarterly newsletter/e-zine; 4 pgs. Subscription free (for subscribers only). 100% assigned freelance. Query; e-queries from advanced/published writers only. **NO PAYMENT.** Articles 300-450 wds. Responds in 3 wks. Accepts reprints (tell when/where appeared). Accepts submissions by e-mail (attached file). Guidelines/theme list by e-mail; free copy. (No ads)

Columns/Departments: My View (topics related to unique challenge of Christians who write for publication); 300-450 wds.

Special Needs: All articles/essays/ideas should relate to writing or the writer's life.

Tips: "Opinari is an approachable, friendly outreach to Christian writers. The editorial and philosophical priorities relate to (1) the writer's growth in, faith in, and relationship with Jesus Christ; and (2) the writer's work as stewardship devoted to Christ and developing professionally."

POETIC VOICES, PO Box 63, McDonaugh GA 30253. (770)507-3225. Fax (615)658-4078. E-mail: submissions@voicesofchrist.org. Website: www.voicesofchrist.org. Voices of Christ. Theresa H. Johnson, ed. To provide informational and educational content in the genre of poetry and to promote poets and poetry. Bimonthly e-zine/newsletter; circ. 5,000. Subscription free. 100% unsolicited freelance. Query/clips; e-query OK. Accepts full mss by e-mail. **NO PAYMENT** for one-time, reprint, electronic rts. Poetry; book reviews 250 wds. Responds in 8 wks. Seasonal 3 mos. ahead. Accepts simultaneous submissions & reprints (tell when/where appeared). Prefers e-mail submissions (copied into message or attached file). Also accepts submissions from children/teens. Prefers KJV. Guidelines by e-mail/Website; copy online. (Ads)

Poetry: Acceptances unlimited. Any type; 3-50 lines. Submit max. 3 poems. "Poetry is our main focus, specifically poetry that addresses social issues."

Tips: "Simply submit a query. We do, however, readily review and accept poetry that addresses current social issues of concern to the church and society that uphold Christian principles. In addition, we actively seek poetry that deals with end-time ministry."

$POETS & WRITERS MAGAZINE, 72 Spring St., New York NY 10012. E-mail: editor@pw.org. Website: www.pw.org. General. Submit to The Editors. Professional trade journal for poetry, fiction, and nonfiction writers. Subscription $19.95. Monthly mag.; circ. 70,000. Complete ms or query/clips by mail; e-query OK. Pays $150-500 on acceptance for 1st & nonexclusive rts. Articles 500-2,500 wds. (35/yr.). Responds in 6 wks. Seasonal 4 mos. ahead. Some kill fees 25%. Guidelines; copy $4.95.

Tips: "Most open to News & Trends, The Literary Life, and The Practical Writer (columns)."

$SHADES OF ROMANCE MAGAZINE, 7127 Minnesota Ave., St. Louis MO 63111. E-mail: sormag@yahoo.com. Website: www.sormag.com. Blog: www.sormag.blogspot.com. LaShaunda Hoffman, ed. A guide for readers and writers of multicultural romance and fiction. E-zine. E-query only. Pays $20 for articles, $25 for fiction within 30 days of publication (through PayPal) for electronic rts. Articles 500-800 wds. (6/yr.); short stories 500-1,500 wds. (6/yr.); devotions 200-500 wds. Responds in 2-4 wks. Seasonal 2 mos. ahead. Accepts simultaneous submissions & reprints (tell when/where appeared; pays $10). Accepts e-mail submissions (attached file). Does not use sidebars. Guidelines/themes by e-mail/Website; copy online. (Ads)

$SPIRIT-LED WRITER. E-mail: spiritwriter@att.net. Website: www.SpiritLedWriter.com. Lisa A. Crayton, pub./ed. Internet magazine for Christian beginning, intermediate, and advanced writers. Monthly e-zine. Query by e-mail (put "Query: [subject]" in subject line). Pays $10-20 on publication for one-time, reprint, and electronic rts. Articles to 1,200 wds. (70+/yr.); reviews to 500 wds. Responds in 8 wks. Accepts reprints. Submit accepted mss by e-mail (no attachments). Regularly uses sidebars. Also accepts submissions from teens. Guidelines by e-mail/Website; copy online. (Ads)

Columns/Departments: Buys several/yr. Musing Dept. (writing-related personal reflections), 700-900 wds.; God's Glory Dept. (writing success stories), 500-700 wds.; Business (articles on the business of writing), to 1,200 wds.; Children's Column (how-to on writing for youth), to 1,200 wds.; $10-20.

Special Needs: Writing-related devotionals; conference coverage (700-900 wds.); and book reviews of writing books, 250-500 wds. ($5-10, depending on whether they supply the book). Also articles on writing for youth or on advanced writing topics.

Tips: "Easiest to break in with a success story (God's glory), musing article, or devotional. We seek how-to and feature articles with a writing theme. We are not a general, Christian-living publication. We reject many manuscripts because they are general, not writing-related. Make it relevant to writing and writers."

TEACHERS & WRITERS, 520—8th Ave., Ste. 2020, New York NY 10018-4165. (212)691-6590. Fax (212)675-0171. E-mail: info@twc.org. Website: www.twc.org. Susan Karwaska, ed. (susan@twc.org). On teaching creative and imaginative writing for children. Quarterly & online mag.; circ. 3,000. Subscription $20. Query; phone/ fax/e-query OK. **PAYS IN COPIES.** Articles 3,000-6,000 wds. Guidelines by e-mail; copy $2.50.

$TICKLED BY THUNDER, 14076—86A Ave., Surrey BC V3W 0V9, Canada. (604)591-6095. E-mail: info@tickledbythunder.com. Website: www.tickledbythunder.com. Larry Lindner, ed. For writers wanting to better themselves. Quarterly chapbook (3-4X); 24 pgs.; circ. 1,000. Subscription $12 Cdn. (or $10 U.S.). 90% unsolicited freelance; 10% assigned. Complete ms/cover letter; e-query OK from subscribers only (use online form). Pays $2-5 (in Cdn. or U.S. stamps) on publication for one-time rts. Articles 1,500 wds. (5/yr.); fiction 2,000 wds. (20/yr.); book/music/video reviews 1,000 wds. Responds in 16 wks. Seasonal 6 mos. ahead. Accepts simultaneous submissions. Prefers requested ms on disk, no e-mail submission. Uses some sidebars. Also accepts submissions from children & teens. Guidelines (also by e-mail/ Website); copy $2.50/6x9 SAE. (Ads)

Poetry: Accepts 20-40/yr. Any type; to 40 lines. Submit max. 5-7 poems. "Try sending seasonal poetry well in advance."

Contest: For fiction (February 15 annual deadline) and poetry (February 15, May 15, August 15, and October 15 annual deadlines). Article contests for subscribers only (February 15, May 15, August 15, and October 15 deadlines). Send SASE for guidelines.

Tips: "Write a 300-word article describing how you feel about your successes/failures as a writer. Be specific, and focus—don't be at all general or vague; tell what works for you. Be original; say something classic in a new way. Use imagery. For fiction, surprise me. Write to put me on the edge of my seat—hold my attention—then wrap it up with something unexpected. Need book reviews of writing books."

$WIN-INFORMER, PO Box 11337, Bainbridge Island WA 98110. (206)842-9103. Fax (206)842-0536. E-mail: writersinfonetwork@juno.com. Website: www.christianwritersinfo.net. Writers Information Network. Elaine Wright Colvin, ed. Send books to be announced or reviewed to 5359 Ruby Pl. N.E., Bainbridge Island WA 98110. CBA industry news and trends to keep professional writers, editors, agents, and speakers in touch with the changing marketplace. Bimonthly mag.; 24-32 pgs.; circ. 1,000. Subscription $49.95 ($60 Canada/foreign in U.S. funds). 33% unsolicited; 20% assigned. Complete ms submitted in body of e-mail only. Pays $5-50 (or subscription) on acceptance for 1st rts. Articles 100-800 wds. (30/yr.); book reviews, 100-300 wds. Accepts e-mail submissions only. Responds in 1 mo. Uses some sidebars. Guidelines on Website; copy $10/9x12 SAE/4 stamps. (No ads, but likes to announce news of members' successes)

Poetry: Any type; writing related.

Fillers: Anecdotes, facts, ideas, newsbreaks, quizzes, quotes, prayers, short humor; 50-300 wds.; $10-20.

Columns/Departments: Columns are continuously changing to meet the needs of an evolving industry. Check a recent copy for current column needs.

Special Needs: "Hot news of our growing, changing market whenever and wherever you hear it—at a writers conference, in a magazine news announcement, from your editor or agent, at your writers group—pass it on. If you make it into a round-up article of what many industry insiders are saying, we'll even pay you. Our readers want to be kept on the cutting-edge of what is happening in the CBA industry."

Tips: "If it works for you, we want to hear about it. If you learn a hot tip, we'd love to share it. We are in a crowded marketplace and a tight book-publishing industry. We really do need each other! This industry is built on networking and relationships. We want tried and proven ideas—what's working for you and other professional writers and speakers. Give us articles on shopping your book proposal; keeping up with Web networking; balancing writing and blogging hours."

THE WRITE CONNECTION, 3706 N.E. Shady Lane Dr., Gladstone MO 64119. Phone/fax (816)459-8016. E-mail: HACWN@earthlink.net. Website: www.hacwn.org. Heart of America Christian Writers' Network. Jeanette Littleton, exec. ed.; Pat Mitchell, ed. Monthly newsletter; 4 pgs.; circ. 150. Subscription free with HACWN membership $25. 50% unsolicited freelance; 50% assigned. Complete ms/cover letter; phone/e-query OK. **NO PAYMENT** for 1st or reprint rts. Articles 400 wds. (15/yr.); book reviews 200 wds. Responds in 8 wks. Accepts simultaneous submissions; no reprints. Accepts requested mss by e-mail. Uses some sidebars. Also accepts submissions from teens. (Ads)

Poetry: Accepts 5/yr. Free verse, light verse, traditional; to 12 lines. Submit max. 3 poems.

Fillers: Accepts 25/yr. Anecdotes, facts, ideas, jokes, prayers, prose, quotes, short humor, tips—solely dealing with writing.

$THE WRITER, 21027 Crossroads Cir., Waukesha WI 53187. (262)796-8776. Fax (262)798-6468. E-mail: queries@writermag.com. Website: www.writermag.com. General. Elfrieda Abbe, ed.; Jeff Reich, mng. ed. How-to for writers; lists religious markets on Website. Monthly mag.; 68 pgs.; circ. 38,000. Subscription $32.95 (single issue $5.95). 80% unsolicited freelance. Query; no phone/fax query (prefers hard copy or e-query). Pays $75-500 for feature articles; book reviews ($50-varies); on acceptance for 1st rts. Features 600-2,900 wds. (60/yr.). Responds in 4-8 wks. Uses some sidebars. Guidelines on Website, copy $5.95. (Ads)

Fillers: Prose; writer-related cartoons $50. Send cartoons to jreich@writermag.com.

Columns/Departments: Buys 24+/yr. Freelance Success (shorter pieces on the business of writing); Off the Cuff (personal essays about writing; avoid writer's block stories). All 600-1,500 wds. Pays $100-300 for columns; $50-75 for reviews. Query 4 months ahead. See guidelines for full list of columns.

Special Needs: How-to on the craft of writing only.

Contests: Occasionally sponsors a contest.

Tips: "Get familiar first with our general mission, approach, tone, and the types of articles we do and don't do. Then, if you feel you have an article that is fresh and well suited to our mission, send us a query. Personal essays must provide takeaway advice and benefits for writers; we shun the 'navel-gazing' type of essay. Include plenty of how-to, advice, and tips on techniques. Be specific. Query for features six months ahead. All topics indicated must relate to writing."

$WRITER'S CHRONICLE: The Magazine for Serious Writers, The Association of Writers & Writing Programs, George Mason University, MSN 1E3, 4400 University Dr., Fairfax VA 22030-4444. (703)993-4301. Fax (703)993-4302. E-mail: chronicle@awpwriter.org. Website: www.awpwriter.org. D. W. Fenza, ed-in-chief. Bimonthly mag. Subscription $20. Pays $8/100 wds. on publication for 1st rts. No kill fee. Guidelines on Website.

Special Needs: Author interviews, essays, trends, and literary controversies. No poetry or fiction.

$WRITER'S DIGEST, 4700 E. Galbraith Rd., Cincinnati OH 45236. (513)531-2690. E-mail: wdsubmissions@fwpubs.com. Website: www.writersdigest.com. General/F & W Publications. Kara Gebhart Uhl, mng. ed. To inform, instruct, or inspire the freelancer and author. Monthly mag.; 76 pgs.; circ. 150,000. Subscription $27. 20% unsolicited; 60% assigned. Strongly prefers e-query (responds in 8 wks.). Pays .40-.50/wd. on acceptance for 1st & electronic (sometimes) rts. Articles 800-1,500 wds. (75/yr.). Responds to mail query in 2 mos. Seasonal 8 mos. ahead. Requires requested ms on disk or by e-mail (attached file or copied into message). Kill fee 25%. Regularly uses sidebars. Guidelines/editorial calendar on Website; copy $5.25 (attn: Lyn Menke). (Ads)

Contests: Sponsors annual contest for articles, short stories, poetry, and scripts. Also The National Self-Publishing Book Awards. Send SASE for rules.

Tips: "We're looking for fiction technique pieces by published authors."

$WRITERS' JOURNAL, PO Box 394, Perham MN 56573-0394. (218)346-7921. Fax (218)346-7924. E-mail: writersjournal@writersjournal.com. Website: www.writersjournal.com. Val-Tech Media/General. Leon Ogroske, ed. Advice, tools, and markets for writers, communicators, and poets. Bimonthly mag.; 68 pgs.; circ. 26,000. Subscription $19.97. 90% unsolicited freelance; 10% assigned. Complete ms/cover letter; phone/fax/e-query OK. Usually pays $30, plus subscription, on publication for one-time rts. Articles 1,000-2,500 wds. (30-40/yr.); fiction 2,000 wds. (contest entries only). Responds in 6-28 wks. Accepts simultaneous submissions; no reprints. Accepts requested ms by e-mail (copied into message). No kill fee. Uses some sidebars. Also accepts submissions from teens. Guidelines on Website; copy $5/SASE/$1.82 postage. (Ads)

Poetry: Esther M. Leiper, poetry ed. Buys 25/yr. All types; to 10 lines; $5/poem. Submit max. 4 poems.

Fillers: Buys 20/yr. Any type, 10-200 wds. Pays $1-10.

Contest: Runs several contests each year. Prizes up to $500. Categories are short story, horror/ghost, romance, travel writing, and fiction; 3 poetry; 2 photo. Send an SASE requesting guidelines.

Tips: "Be concise; no wordiness. Avoid personal essays. Write to the reader. We are looking for a well-written article on freelance income; articles on how to write better and how to sell what authors write. Also looking for articles on obscure income markets for writers. General story construction and grammar tips."

WRITERS MANUAL, Ste. 402, 7231—120th St., Delta BC V4C 6P5, Canada. E-mail: editor@writersmanual.com. Website: www.writersmanual.com (click on "Get Interviewed!"). Krista Barrett, ed-in-chief. Looking for author and/or freelance interviews. One-time rts.

$+WRITERS' NOTES, PO Box 11, Titusville NJ 08560. E-mail: editor@hopepubs.com. Website: www.writersnotes.com. Hopewell Publications LLC. Submit to The Editor. Features fiction, nonfiction, poetry, photos, graphic arts, and the writing craft. Semiannual mag.; circ. 1,500. Subscription $18.95. Open to freelance. Query; e-query OK. Pays $20-150 on publication for 1st rts. Articles 250-5,000 wds.; fiction 250-5,000 wds. Responds to queries in 3 wks.; submissions in 3 mos. Prefers hardcopy. Incomplete topical listings.

Special Needs: Novel excerpts.

WRITETOINSPIRE.COM. E-mail: editor@writetoinspire.com. Website: www.writetoinspire.com. Online publication. Provides good how-to information for Christian writers. **NO PAYMENT** for 1st or one-time rts. Articles 500-700 wds., written in an online style. Send submissions in body of e-mail (no attachments). Guidelines on Website.

WRITING CORNER. E-mail: deanna@biznessconcepts.com. Website: www.writingcorner.com. Deanna Lilly, ed. Online publication. Open to unsolicited freelance. Query or complete ms by e-mail (no attachments). **NO PAYMENT** for nonexclusive rts. Articles 600-900 wds.; fiction 600-900 wds. Responds in 2 wks. Accepts reprints. Guidelines on Website: www.writingcorner.com/admin/sub-guidelines.htm.

MARKET ANALYSIS

PERIODICALS IN ORDER BY CIRCULATION

ADULT/GENERAL

Guideposts 3,000,000
Columbia 1,600,000
Focus on the Family 1,500,000
In Touch 1,000,000
Stewardship 1,000,000
Angels on Earth 550,000
Marion Helpers 500,000
Spirituality for Today 495,000
Catholic Digest 400,000
Catholic Yearbook 400,000
Decision 400,000
Positive Thinking 400,000
Mature Living 318,000
St. Anthony Messenger 305,000
Charisma 250,000
Power for Living 250,000
Upscale Magazine 250,000
War Cry 250,000
Anglican Journal 215,000
Australian Catholics 200,000
Gospel Today 200,000
Liberty 200,000
Miraculous Medal 200,000
Today's Pentecostal Evangel 200,000
Family Room 180,000
Christianity Today 155,000
Cappers 150,000
Family Digest 150,000
Lutheran Journal 150,000
Standard 150,000
Company 120,000
Liguorian 120,000
Alabama Baptist 109,000
Lutheran Digest 105,000
Catholic Forester 100,000
CGA World 100,000
Discipleship Journal 100,000
Good News (KY) 100,000
On Mission 100,000
Men of Integrity 95,000
Today's Christian 75,000
Heartlight Internet 70,000+
Alive Now 70,000
Common Ground 70,000
Lookout 70,000
MESSAGE 70,000
ParentLife 70,000
United Church Observer 70,000
Christian Home & School 67,000
Celebrate Life 65,000
Marriage Partnership 60,000
Presbyterians Today 58,000
Creation 55,000
Mature Years 55,000
Live 54,500
Arlington Catholic 53,000
Discovery Years 52,600
Christian History 50,000
Community Spirit 50,000
Faith & Friends 50,000
Leaves 50,000
Wesleyan Life 50,000
Christian Standard 48,000
America 46,000
BGC World 46,000
Encompass 45,000
LarkNews.com 45,000
Messenger of St. Anthony 45,000
EFCA Today 44,000
Christian Motorsports 40,000
Parabola 40,000
Senior Living 40,000
U.S. Catholic 40,000
Cathedral Age 36,000
Highway News 35,000
Minnesota Christian 35,000
Lifeglow 34,000
Christian News NW 33,000
Faith & Family 32,000
Advance 30,000
Annals of St. Anne 30,000
Christian Computing 30,000
Christian Research 30,000
en confianza 30,000
Homeschooling Today 30,000
Kindred Spirit 30,000
Vibrant Life 30,000
World & I 30,000
Seek 29,000
CLEAR Living 28,000
Priority! 28,000
Focus on Your Child 25,000
LifeLine Journal 25,000
Pure Inspiration 25,000
Significant Living 25,000
Catholic Peace Voice 23,000
HonorBound 22,000
Friends Voice 21,000
African Voices 20,000
Believe! 20,000
Commonweal 20,000
Creation Illustrated 20,000
Eureka Street 20,000
Interim 20,000
Sports Spectrum 20,000
Trumpeter 20,000
Faith Today 18,000
Heartbeat 18,000
Montgomery's Journey 18,000
Canadian Mennonite 16,500
Covenant Companion 16,000
Marketplace 16,000
Over the Back Fence 15,000
Victory in Grace 15,000
Canada Lutheran 14,000
DisciplesWorld 14,000
Gems of Truth 14,000
St. Joseph's Messenger 14,000
Testimony 14,000
Bible Advocate 13,500
Light & Life 13,000
Books & Culture 12,000
Special Living 12,000
Spiritual Life 12,000
Evangel 11,000
Messenger/Sacred Heart 11,000
Christian Retailing 10,500
Messiah Magazine 10,000
Parents & Teens 10,000
Presbyterian Outlook 10,000
Regent Global Bus. Review 10,000
Spiritual Voice News 10,000
Vision 10,000
WHOLE Magazine 10,000
NRB Magazine 9,300
Montana Catholic 9,200
Fellowship 9,000
Haruah 9,000
Living Church 9,000
Sharing 9,000
Purpose 8,900
Aspiring Retail 8,000
Disciple's Journal 8,000
Friends Journal 8,000
Home Times 8,000
Arkansas Catholic 7,700
Science & Spirit 7,500
Wittenburg Door 7,500
Breakthrough Intercessor 7,000
Psychology for Living 7,000
White Wing Messenger 7,000
Creation Care 6,000
Gem 6,000
Impact 6,000
Image 5,200
AGAIN 5,000
Creative Nonfiction 5,000
Cross Currents 5,000
Leben 5,000
New Heart 5,000
Pentecostal Messenger 5,000
Prism 5,000
Purpose Magazine 5,000
Review for Religious 5,000
Social Justice Review 5,000
Way of St. Francis 5,000

Christian Civic League/ME 4,600
Cresset 4,500
Family Journal 4,500
Evangelical Advocate 4,000
Mensajero Ala Blanca 4,000
Quaker Life 4,000
Wireless Age 4,000
Catholic Insight 3,700
Culture Wars 3,500
Evangel 3,500
Sword and Trumpet 3,300
Evangel (OR) 3,000
Message/Open Bible 3,000
Perspectives 3,000
Prayer Closet 3,000
UrbanKingdom 3,000
Salvo Magazine 2,800
Mennonite Historian 2,600
Bread of Life 2,500
MovieGuide 2,500
Railroad Evangelist 2,500
Apocalypse Chronicles 2,000-3,000
Atlantic Catholic 2,000
Channels 2,000
Desert Call 2,000
Priscilla Papers 2,000
Mutuality 1,900
Jour./Church & State 1,700
Church Herald/Holiness 1,100
Brave Hearts 1,000
Connecting Point 1,000
Dovetail 1,000
DreamSeeker 1,000
Methodist History 800
Compass Direct 730
Ruminate 600
Storyteller 600
Christian Radio Weekly 500
Gold Country Families 450
Eternal Ink 440+
Anglican 300
Dreams & Visions 300
Silver Wings 300
Studio 300
Xavier Review 300
West Wind Review 250-500
Aujourd'hui Credo 250
Time of Singing 250
Your Backyard 250
Challenging Destiny 200
Ancient Paths 175
Pegasus Review 150
Angel Face 100
Haiku Hippodrome 100
Wildwood Reader 100
Reverent Submissions 85
Penwood Review 80-100

CHILDREN

American Girl 700,000
Focus/Clubhouse 101,100
Keys for Kids 100,000
High Adventure 87,000
Focus/Clubhouse Jr. 79,800
Pockets 67,000
Our Little Friend 45,000-50,000
Adventures 40,000
Celebrate 40,000
Primary Treasure 35,000
Discoveries 30,000
GUIDE 30,000
New Moon 30,000
Primary Street 20,000
Passport 18,000
Faces 15,000
SHINEbrightly 13,000
BREAD for God's Children 10,000
Nature Friend 10,000
Winner 9,000
Cadet Quest 8,000
Kids' Ark 8,000
Partners 6,519
Story Mates 6,250
Junior Companion 3,500
Primary Pal (KS) 2,900
Beginner's Friend 2,700
Skipping Stones 2,500

CHRISTIAN EDUCATION/LIBRARY

Christian School Education 70,000
Children's Ministry 60,000
Group 55,000
Catechist 52,000
Today's Catholic Teacher 45,000
RTJ 32,000
Resource 25,000
Momentum 23,000
Teach Kids! 12,000
Jour./Adventist Ed. 10,800
Teachers of Vision 10,000
Youth & CE Leadership 10,000
Christian Early Education 5,500
Christian Educator's Journal 4,200
Ideas Unlimited 4,200
Church & Synagogue Libraries 3,000
Kids' Ministry Ideas 2,500
Catholic Library World 1,000
Christian Librarian 800
Church Libraries 450
Jour./Christian Education 400
Jour./Ed. & Christian Belief 400
Jour./Research on C. E. 400
Jour./Christianity/Foreign Lang. 100

DAILY DEVOTIONALS

These Days 200,000
Secret Place 150,000
Our Journey 80,000
CLEAR Living 28,000
Daily Devotions for the Deaf 26,000
InDeed 26,000
Penned from the Heart 5,000

MISSIONS

One 100,000
Mission Frontiers 75,000
Catholic Missions/Canada 25,000
New World Outlook 24,000
Montgomery's Journey 18,000
PIME World 16,000
Leaders for Today 7,500
Evangelical Missions 7,000
Glad Tidings 5,000
PFI World Report 4,750
Women of the Harvest 4,000
Railroad Evangelist 2,500
Missiology 1,500
OpRev Equipper 1,500
Intl. Jour./Frontier 500
East-West Church & Ministry 430

MUSIC

CCM Magazine 70,000
Senior Musician 32,000
Creator 6,000
Tradition 3,500
Hymn 3,000
Christian Radio 500
Christian Music 300-1,200

NEWSPAPERS

Layman 450,000
Episcopal Life 280,000
Anglican Journal 200,000
Alpha News 195,000
Christian Examiner 180,000
Catholic New York 135,000
Nat. Catholic Reporter 120,000
Catholic Telegraph 100,000
Living 90,000
Pulpit Helps 75,000
Common Ground 70,000
Sword of the Lord 70,000
Our Sunday Visitor 68,000
Living Light News 65,000
Good News/S. Florida 64,000
Christian Citizen USA 60,000
Good News Journal 60,000
Arlington Catholic Herald 53,000
Chronicle/Kansas 50,000
Living 50,000
Together 50,000
Christian Ranchman 43,800
Good News, Etc. 42,000
Evangelical Times 40,000
Senior Living 40,000
Messianic Times 35,000
Minnesota Chr. Chronicle 35,000
Catholic Register 33,000
Christian Herald 31,000

Christian News NW 30,000
Citizen USA 30,000
Good News! 30,000
Interim 30,000
New Frontier 25,500
Christian Media 25,000
Life Gate 23,000
Indian Life 22,000
B.C. Catholic 20,000
Charlotte World 20,000
Holy City Chronicle 20,000
Heartbeat/CMA 18,000
Catholic Sentinel 16,000
Good News Today 16,000
Messenger 16,000
Christian Journal 15,000
Christian Voice 15,000
City Light News 12,000
Interchange 12,000
Christian Courier (WI) 10,000
Heartland Gatekeeper 10,000
Inland NW Christian 10,000
Network 10,000
Spiritual Voice News 10,000
Wisconsin Christian News 10,000
Star of Zion 9,200
Catholic New Times 8,500
Choice Newspaper 8,000
Disciple's Journal 8,000
Arkansas Catholic 7,700
New Freeman 7,500
Desert Voice 7,000
Living Stones News 7,000
Prairie Messenger 6,900
Home Times 6,000
SW KS Faith & Family 5,000
Christian Courier (Canada) 4,000
Christian Renewal 4,000
ChristianWeek 4,000
Island Catholic News 3,000
Atlantic Catholic 2,000
Christian Observer 2,000
Insight (for the blind) 2,000
B.C. Christian News 1,000
Hunted News 1,000
PrayerWorks 1,000
Anglican 300

PASTORS/LEADERS

Interpreter 225,000
Alpha News 195,000
Rick Warren's Ministry 177,000
Your Church 75,000
Church Life Inspiration 65,000
Leadership 55,000
Plugged In 50,000
Worship Leader 50,000
Rev. 45,000
Catholic Servant 41,000
Pray! 41,000
OUTreach 35,000
Technologies/Worship 35,000
Enrichment 33,000
Christian Century 30,000
Ministry Today 30,000
Pulpit Helps 25,000
Torch Legacy Leader 22,000
Lutheran Partners 20,000
Ministry & Liturgy 20,000
Youthworker 20,000
Ministry 19,000
Preaching Now 19,000
This Rock 15,870
Today's Parish 14,800
Net Results 12,000
Engage 10,000
Jour./Pastoral Care 10,000
Willow 10,000
Preaching 9,000
InSite 8,750
Sabbath School Leadership 8,100
Growth Points 8,000
Priest 6,500
Clergy Journal 6,000
Catechumenate 5,600
Let's Worship 5,500
Cross Currents 5,000
Review for Religious 5,000
Reformed Worship 4,600
Interpretation 4,500
African American Pulpit 4,000
Christian Management Report 3,500+
Lutheran Forum 3,200
Emmanuel 3,000
Single Adult Min. Jour. 3,000
Environment & Art 2,500
Word & World 2,500
Cornerstone Youth Resource 2,200
Church Worship 1,500
Parish Liturgy 1,200
Christian Ed. Jour. 750
Diocesan Dialogue 750
Ministry in Motion 700+
RevWriter Resource 500
Jour./Amer. Soc./Chur. Growth 400
Theological Digest 400
Sharing the Practice 250

TEEN/YOUNG ADULT

Brio 142,500
Essential Connection 120,000
Devo'Zine 100,000
Ignite Your Faith 100,000
Breakaway 96,000
Sharing the Victory 80,000
Bubblemag 50,000
Rock 50,000
Young Salvationist 48,000
Risen Magazine 45,000+
Steelroots 30,000
YouthWalk 30,000
Young & Alive 25,000
Insight 20,000
InTeen 20,000
Listen 20,000
Spirit 20,000
Credo 15,000
Student Leadership 8,500
TC Magazine 8,000
InsideOut 6,000
CLEAR Direction 5,300
Youth Compass 4,800
True Girl 3,500

WOMEN

Precious Times 350,000
Heart & Soul 300,000
More to Life 250,000-2,000,000
Today's Christian Woman 250,000
Journey 215,000
Lutheran Woman's Quarterly 200,000
Melody of the Heart 130,000
MOMSense 120,000
SpiritLed Woman 100,000
Share 95,000
Life Tools for Women 45,000
Dabbling Mum 40,000
At the Center 30,000
Godly Business Women 25,000
Horizons 25,000
Women's Ministry 25,000
History's Women 21,000
A Virtuous Woman 20,000+
First Lady 20,000
Inspired Living 20,000
Right to the Heart 15,000
Hope for Women 10,000
P31 Woman 10,000
Just Between Us 8,000
Together with God 7,500
CoLaborer 7,300
Esprit 5,000
Link & Visitor 4,000
Women Alive! 4,000
Tapestry (Canada) 3,200
ChurchWoman 3,000
Handmaiden 3,000
inSpirit 2,500
Hearts at Home 1,500
Making Waves 1,400
A Woman of Worth 100+

WRITERS

Writer's Digest 150,000
Poets & Writers 70,000
The Writer 38,000
Writers' Journal 26,000
Fiction Fix 5,000
Merlyn's Pen 5,000
New Writer's 5,000
Poetic Voices 5,000
Money the Write Way 4,000
Byline 3,000+

Christian Communicator 3,000
Teachers & Writers 3,000
Beginnings 1,500
Writers Notes 1,500
Cross & Quill 1,000+
Once Upon a Time 1,000
Tickled by Thunder 1,000
WIN-Informer 1,000
Advanced Christian Writer 500
Canadian Writer's Journal 385
FellowScript 200
NW Christian Author 200
Write Connection 150
Areopagus (UK) 100
The Write Touch 40

PERIODICAL TOPICS IN ORDER OF POPULARITY

NOTE: Following is a list of topics in order by popularity. To find the list of publishers interested in each of these topics, go to the Topical Listings for periodicals and find the topic you are interested in. The numbers indicate how many periodical editors said they were interested in seeing something of that type or on that topic. (*—new topic this year)

MISCELLANEOUS TALLIES

Canadian/Foreign Markets 77
Newspapers/Tabloids 99
Online Publications 146
Photographs 247
Take-home Papers 35
Young Writer Markets 116

TOPICS BY POPULARITY

1. Christian Living 266
2. Family Life 255
3. Interviews/Profiles 228
4. Inspirational 226
5. Current/Social Issues 219
6. Book Reviews 214
7. Personal Experience 211
8. Prayer 208
9. Poetry 198
10. Holiday/Seasonal 196
11. Faith 195
12. Spirituality 185
13. Relationships 182
14. Women's Issues 175
15. Devotionals/Meditations 172
16. Humor 172
17. Marriage 171
18. Evangelism/Witnessing 168
19. Christian Education 167
20. Parenting 164
21. Controversial Issues 162
22. True Stories 161
23. Discipleship 159
24. Church Outreach 150
25. Worship 148
26. Personal Growth 147
27. Leadership 139
28. Church Life 137
29. Missions 137
30. How-to 133
31. Health 132
32. Ethnic/Cultural Pieces 131
33. World Issues 131
34. Spiritual Life 130
35. Youth Issues 129
36. Encouragement 127
37. Essays 124
38. Historical 120
39. Theological 120
40. Fillers: Cartoons 118
41. Ethics 116
42. Death/Dying 112
43. Church Growth 111
44. News Features 111
45. Short Story: Adult/Religious 109
46. Men's Issues 108
47. Social Justice 108
48. Money Management 103
49. Bible Studies 102
50. Church History 102
51. Time Management 102
52. Opinion Pieces 100
53. Short Story: Contemporary 100
54. Stewardship 100
55. Singles Issues 98
56. Think Pieces 97
57. Divorce 96
58. Christian Business 95
59. Fillers: Anecdotes 95
60. Religious Freedom 95
61. Fillers: Short Humor 94
62. Celebrity Pieces 93
63. Church Traditions 90
64. Spiritual Warfare 90
65. Workplace Issues 86
66. Healing 85
67. Music Reviews 85
68. Short Story: Humorous 83
69. Spiritual Gifts 83
70. Salvation Testimonies 82
71. Book Excerpts 80
72. Environmental Issues 80
73. Fillers: Ideas 78
74. Homeschooling 75
75. Spiritual Renewal 75
76. Church Management 74
77. Fillers: Facts 73
78. Short Story: Biblical 73
79. Senior Adult Issues 72
80. Political 70
81. Doctrinal 69
82. Food/Recipes 69
83. Inner Life 68
84. Sports/Recreation 68
85. Video Reviews 68
86. Fillers: Prayers 67
87. Short Story: Adventure 67
88. Short Story: Historical 66
89. Writing How-to 66
90. Fillers: Quotes 64
91. How-to Activities (juv.) 64
92. Travel 64
93. Fillers: Word Puzzles 62
94. Crafts 61
95. Miracles 61
96. Religious Tolerance 61
97. Nature 60
98. Economics 59
99. Racism 58
100. Apologetics 57
101. Self-help 57
102. Short Story: Juvenile 57
103. Fillers: Prose 56
104. Short Story: Parables 55
105. Fillers: Quizzes 53
106. Creation Science 48
107. Fillers: Games 48
108. Short Story: Teen/Young Adult 47
109. Website Reviews 47
110. Short Story: Mystery/Suspense 46
111. Liturgical 45
112. Science 45
113. Fillers: Jokes 44
114. Fillers: Tips 44
115. Sociology 44
116. Peace Issues 43
117. Fillers: Newsbreaks 42
118. Short Story: Literary 42
119. Psychology 40
120. Photo Essays 39
121. Cults/Occult 38
122. Prophecy 38
123. Fillers: Party Ideas 37
124. Sermons 37
125. Short Story: Ethnic 37
126. Short Story: Allegory 36

127. Short Story: Fantasy 36
128. Exegesis 33
129. Nostalgia 32
130. Short Story: Science Fiction 32
131. Recovery 31
132. Short Story: Frontier 31
133. Homiletics 30
134. Movie Reviews 29
135. Fillers: Kid Quotes 28
136. Lifestyle Articles 26
137. Short Story: Romance 25
138. Short Story: Westerns 22
139. Short Story: Historical/ Romance 21
140. Short Story: Mystery/Romance 20
141. Short Story: Adult/General 19
142. Revival 18
143. Short Story: Skits 18
144. Short Story: Speculative 18
145. Short Story: Frontier/Romance 17
146. Short Story: Plays 17
147. Short Story: Sr. Adult Fiction 11
148. Fillers: Sermon Illustrations 6
149. Puppet Plays 5

SUMMARY OF INFORMATION ON CHRISTIAN PERIODICAL PUBLISHERS FOUND IN THE ALPHABETICAL LISTINGS

NOTE: Following is some general information based on averages of the information supplied by the periodical publishers in this guide. This information will be valuable in determining what numbers or percentages are typical in the various categories.

WANTS QUERY OR COMPLETE MANUSCRIPT

Of those periodicals that indicate a preference, 47 percent prefer or accept a complete manuscript, 37 percent want or will accept a query, 3 percent require a query, and 13 percent will accept either.

ACCEPTS PHONE QUERY

Every year fewer periodical publishers are accepting phone queries. Many seem now to prefer e-mail or even faxes to phone queries. It is suggested that you reserve phone queries for timely material that won't wait for the regular mailed query. If you phone in a query, be sure you have your idea well thought out and can present it succinctly and articulately.

ACCEPTS FAX QUERY

Most publishers have faxes, but many are asking for their fax number to be dropped from their listing—mostly because they prefer an e-mail query or are trying to avoid having complete manuscripts come by fax. Since a fax query will not have a SASE, it is suggested that you make fax queries only if you have your own fax machine or another means to accept their response.

ACCEPTS E-MAIL QUERY

At this point, almost every publisher has an e-mail address, but some are starting to ask that it not be listed to cut down on the growing number of messages they have to deal with. Some are now asking for e-mails/submissions using their online submission form.

SUBMISSIONS ON DISK

This question has almost become obsolete, as the majority of publishers that don't want a hard copy now want an e-mail submission. Individual listings will indicate which ones still want or accept a disk.

SUBMISSIONS BY E-MAIL

This area continues to show some significant changes in editors' perceptions of e-mail submissions. When asked if they would accept submissions by e-mail, almost a half said yes. Of those, 40 percent wanted the article copied into the message, 42 percent wanted them sent as an attached file, and the last 18 percent would accept them either way. Generally speaking, those who prefer the article copied into the message fear viruses, while those who prefer an attached copy don't like losing the coding when you copy it into the message.

PAYS ON ACCEPTANCE OR PUBLICATION

Of the publishers that indicated, 40 percent of the publishers pay on acceptance, while 60 percent pay on publication.

PERCENTAGE OF FREELANCE

Many of the publishers responded to the question about how much freelance material they use. Based on the figures we have, for the average publisher, 45 percent of the material purchased is unsolicited freelance and 55 percent is assigned.

CIRCULATION

In dividing the list of periodicals into three groups, according to size of circulation, the list comes out as follows: Publications with a circulation of 100,000 or more (up to 3,000,000) make up 15 percent of periodicals; publications with a circulation between 50,000 and 100,000, 10 percent; the remaining 75 percent have a circulation of 50,000 or less. If we break that last group into three more groups by circulation, we come out with circulations of 33,000-50,000 making up 10 percent; 18 percent with circulations of 17,000-32,000; and the remaining 72 percent with less than 17,000. That means that 52 percent of all the periodicals that reported their circulation are at a circulation of 17,000 or less. Overall, circulations seem to be dropping.

RESPONSE TIME

The average response time is just over eight weeks, one week longer than reported three years ago. Those who are writing and submitting regularly will have no problem confirming that most publishers are taking longer to respond to submissions.

REPRINTS

Nearly 50 percent of the periodicals included in the market guide accept reprints. Although until the last few years it was not necessary to tell a publisher where a piece had been published previously, that has changed. Most Christian publishers now want a tear sheet of the original publication and a cover letter telling when and where it appeared originally. Be sure to check the individual listings to see if a publisher wants to know when and where a piece has appeared previously. Most are also paying less for reprints than for original material.

PREFERRED BIBLE VERSION

The most preferred Bible version is the New International Version, the preference of more than half the publishers. Other preferred versions are the King James Version, the New Revised Standard Version, the New American Bible, New American Standard, Revised Standard Version, and New King James. The NIV seems a good choice for those who didn't indicate a preference, although the more conservative groups seem to favor the KJV.

GREETING CARD/GIFT/SPECIALTY MARKETS

This listing contains both Christian/religious card publishers and general publishers who have religious lines or produce some religious or inspirational cards. Keep in mind that the general companies may produce other lines of cards that are not consistent with your beliefs, and that for a general company, inspirational cards usually do not include religious imagery. These are all paying markets.

(+) Indicates new listing

NOTE: See the end of this listing for specialty product lists.

CARD PUBLISHERS

AFRICAN AMERICAN EXPRESSIONS, 10266 Rockingham Dr., Sacramento CA 95827-2515. Toll-free (800)684-1555. (916)424-5000. Fax (916)424-5053. E-mail: gperkins@black-gifts.com, or info@black-gifts.com. Website: www.black-gifts.com. Greg Perkins, pres. Christian card publishers and specialty products. Open to freelance; buys 5-10 ideas/yr. Prefers outright submissions. Pays $35 on acceptance. No royalty. Responds in 2 wks. Uses rhymed, unrhymed, traditional, and light verse. Produces invitations and conventional, humorous, informal, inspirational, juvenile, novelty, and religious cards. Needs anniversary, birthday, Christmas, friendship, get well, graduation, keep in touch, love, miss you, Mother's Day, new baby, relatives (all occasions), sympathy, valentines, wedding, and pastor appreciation. Holiday/seasonal 9 mos. ahead. Open to ideas for new card lines, calendars/journals, novelty/gift items, magnets, and stationery. No guidelines; free catalog.

ALEGRIA COLLECTION, PO Box 835008, Miami FL 33283-5008. (305)253-4646. Fax (305) 253-4604. E-mail: ventas@alegriacollection.com. Website: www.alegriacollection.com. Spanish greeting cards.

AMERICAN GREETINGS, One American Rd., Cleveland OH 44144-2398. (216)252-7300. Fax (216)252-6778. Website: www.americangreetings.com. Kathleen McKay, ed. No unsolicited material.

ARTFUL GREETINGS, PO Box 52428, Durham NC 27717. Toll-free (800)638-2733. (919)484-0100. Fax (919)484-3099. E-mail: myw@artfulgreetings.com. Website: www.artfulgreetings.com. Black art greeting cards and gifts.

BLESS HIS NAME GREETINGS, PO Box 414, Scott AR 72142. (501)612-0694. E-mail: Marie@blesshisnamegreetings.com, or publisher@blesshisnamegreetings.com. Website: www.blesshisnamegreetings.com. L. Marie Trotter, pub. A Christian/religious card publisher not currently accepting submissions.

BLUE MOUNTAIN ARTS INC., PO Box 4549, Boulder CO 80306. Toll-free (800)525-0642. (303)449-0536. Fax (303)447-0939. E-mail: editorial@sps.com. Website: www.sps.com. Submit to Editorial Department. General card publisher that does a few inspirational cards. Open to freelance; buys 50-100 ideas/yr. Prefers outright submissions. Pays $300 for all rts. for use on a greeting card, or $50 for one-time use in a book, on publication. No royalties. Responds in 12-16 wks. Uses unrhymed or traditional poetry; short or long, but no one-liners. Produces inspirational and sensitivity. Needs anniversary, birthday, Christmas, congratulations, Easter, Father's Day, friendship, get well, graduation, keep in touch, love, miss you, Mother's Day, new baby, please write, relatives, sympathy, thank you, valentines, wedding, reaching for dreams. Holiday/seasonal 3 mos. ahead. Open to ideas for new card lines. Send any number of ideas (1 per pg.). Open to ideas for gift books. Guidelines; no catalog.

Contest: Sponsors a poetry card contest online. Details on Website.

Tips: "We are interested in reviewing poetry and writings for greeting cards, and expanding our field of freelance poetry writers."

+C4YOURSELF GREETING CARDS, 1406 Sycamore St., Cincinnati OH 45202. (513)608-1878. E-mail: info@c4yourself.biz. Website: www.c4yourself.biz. Angela Morrow, creator. Christmas cards & cards for all occasions. Also does desk calendars. E-mail with card ideas.

CHRISTIAN INSPIRATIONS, Quadriga Art Inc., 30 E. 33rd St., New York NY 10016. (212)685-0751. Fax (212)889-6868. E-mail through Website: www.quadrigaart.com. Suzanne Kruck, VP. Christian card publisher. No unsolicited submissions; request permission in writing to send submissions. Pays on acceptance; no royalty. Responds in 4-6 wks. All types of verse, 4-6 lines. All kinds of cards and greetings, except Halloween and St. Patrick's. Seasonal 12 mos. ahead. Not open to new card lines or specialty products. No guidelines; catalog.

CREATIVE CHRISTIAN GIFTS, PO Box 915441, Longwood FL 32791-5441. Toll-free (866) 325-1857. (407)924-9186. E-mail: sales@creativechristiangifts.com. Website: www.creativechristiangifts.com. Renee Purner. Greeting cards & note cards.

CURRENT INC., PO Box 2559, Colorado Springs CO 80901. (719)594-4100. Fax (719)534-6259. Mar Porter, freelance coordinator. No freelance.

DAYSPRING CARDS INC., Box 1010, 21154 Hwy 16 East, Siloam Springs AR 72761. Fax (479)524-9477. E-mail: info@dayspring.com (type "write" in message or subject line). Website: www.dayspring.com. Christian/religious card publisher. Please read guidelines before submitting. Prefers outright submission. Pays $60/idea on acceptance for all rts. No royalty. Responds in 4-8 wks. Uses unrhymed, traditional, light verse, conversational, contemporary; various lengths. Looking for inspirational cards for all occasions, including anniversary, birthday, relative birthday, congratulations, encouragement, friendship, get well, new baby, sympathy, thank you, wedding. Also needs seasonal cards for friends and family members for Christmas, Valentine Day, Easter, Mother's Day, Father's Day, Thanksgiving, graduation, and Clergy Appreciation Day. Include Scripture verse with each submission. Send 10 ideas or less. Guidelines by phone or e-mail; no catalog.

Tips: Prefers submissions on 8 x 11 inch sheets, not 3x5 cards (one idea per sheet).

DESIGN DESIGN INC., 19 La Grave S.E., Grand Rapids MI 49503. (616)771-2448. Fax (616)774-2440. Website: www.designdesign.us. Rebecca Cooper, ed. A general card publisher that does a few inspirational and religious cards. Open to freelance submissions. Prefers outright submissions (but not of artwork). Rights purchased depend on product. Uses rhymed, unrhymed, traditional, and light verse. Produces anniversary, birthday, Christmas, congratulations, Easter, Father's Day, friendship, get well, graduation, Halloween, love, miss you, Mother's Day, new baby, relative (all occasions), St. Patrick's Day, sympathy, Thanksgiving, thank you, valentines, and wedding. Open to new card lines. Open to ideas for gift/novelty items, greeting books, magnets, and stationery. Guidelines for SASE; no catalog.

DESIGNER GREETINGS, PO Box 140729, Staten Island NY 10314. Toll-free (800)654-6960. (718)981-7700. Fax (866)981-0151. E-mail: info@designergreetings.com, or through Website: www.designergreetings.com. Fern Gimbelman, art dir. 50% freelance. Holiday/seasonal 6 mos. ahead. Responds in 2 mos. Pays on acceptance for greeting card rts. Guidelines on Website. Uses rhymed or unrhymed verse. Produces announcements, conventional, humorous, informal, inspirational, invitations, juvenile, sensitivity, soft line, studio. Up to 50% freelance.

+DICKSON'S LIFE PUBLISHING, 709 B Ave. East, Seymour IN 47274. (812)522-1308. Fax (812)522-1319. E-mail: rick@lawson-falle.com. Website: www.dicksonsgifts.com. Rick Tocquigny, pres. Christian/religious card publisher. Open to freelance; buys 25-50 ideas/yr. Prefers outright submissions. Pays $50 on acceptance for nonexclusive rts. Royalties 2-3%. Responds in 4 wks. Uses rhymed, unrhymed, traditional, light verse; under 75 wds. Produces all types of cards. Needs anniversary, birthday, Christmas, congratulations, Easter, Father's Day, friendship, get well, graduation, keep in touch, love, miss you, Mother's Day, new baby, please write, relative (all occasions), St. Patrick's Day, sympathy, Thanksgiving, thank you, valentines, wedding, adult baptism, mission trip blessings, confirmation, and first communion. Holiday/seasonal 18 mos. ahead. Open to ideas for new card lines; submit max. 3 ideas. Open to ideas for activity/coloring books, bookmarks, calendars/journals, gift/novelty items, magnets, mugs, plaques, stationery, t-shirts/apparel, and toys. No guidelines/catalog.

GIBSON GREETINGS, PO Box 371804, Cincinnati OH 45222-1804. E-mail: wcallah@gibsongreetings.com. Website: www.gibsongreetings.com. No freelance.

HEAVENLY DESIGNS, 118 Burnell Pl. S.E., Leesburg VA 20175. Toll-free (866)707-0113. Phone/fax (703)737-0113. E-mails: cindyjames@birthverse.com, or bjames@birthverse.com. Website: www.birthverse.com. Bob & Cindy James, owners. Inspirational greeting cards.

HERMITAGE ART CO. INC., 5151 N. Ravenswood Ave., Chicago IL 60640. Toll-free (800)621-7992. (773)561-3773. Fax (773)561-4422. E-mail: Office@hermitageart.com. Website: www.hermitageart.com. Color bulletins, bookmarks, specialty items.

INSPIRATIONART & SCRIPTURE INC., PO Box 5550, Cedar Rapids IA 52406-5550. Toll-free (800)728-5550. (319)365-4350. Fax (319)861-2103. E-mail: Customerservice@inspirationart.com. Website: www.inspirationart.com. Publishes Christian posters. Charles Edwards, creative dir. Open to freelance. Buys 20-30 ideas/yr. Prefers e-mail contact. Pays $150-250, 30 days after publication, for right to publish as a poster; or royalties 5% of net. Responds in 4 wks. Seasonal 6 mos. ahead. Open to new ideas for posters, bookmarks, or puzzles. Submit up to 3 ideas. Artist's guidelines on Website; catalog on Website or for $3.

LAURA LEIDEN CALLIGRAPHY INC., PO Box 141, Watkinsville GA 30677. (706)769-6989. Fax (706)769-0628. E-mail: llc@lauraleidencalligraphy.com. Website: www.lauraleidencalligraphy.com. Submit to: Freelance Submissions. General card publisher with one or more inspirational (not religious) lines, and producer of specialty products. Open to freelance. Buys 10-20 ideas/yr. Outright submission. Buys all rts. on acceptance. No royalties. Prefers rhymed verse; sentimental/nostalgic; 2-16 lines. Produces conventional, inspirational. Needs Anniversary, birthday, Christmas, Father's Day, friendship, get well, graduation, Mother's Day, new baby, mother, father, son, daughter, baby, animal lover, sympathy, wedding. Prefers 4-10 ideas/submission. Holiday/seasonal 8 mos. ahead. Not open to ideas for new card lines or specialty items. Also produces plaques. Send submissions to e-mail above; no catalog.

LAWSON FALLE PUBLISHING, 320 Pinebush Rd., Box 940, Cambridge ON N1R 5X9, Canada. Toll-free (800)265-8673. (821)623-7200, or (519)622-4310. Toll-free fax (800)565-2755. Fax (812)623-7201, or (519)620-8628. E-mail: lsandman@nalu.net. Website: www.dicksongifts.com. Dicksons Inc. Submit to Chief Editor. General card publisher with an inspirational line. Open to freelance; buys 20 ideas/yr. Prefer outright submission or e-mail contact. Buys rights to publish in CBA. Pays variable amounts. Royalties 3-5% of wholesale on publication. Responds in 3 wks. Prefers rhymed, unrhymed, traditional, and light verse, under 40 wds. Produces announcements, conventional, humorous, informal, inspirational, invitations, juvenile, novelty. Needs all types except Halloween, especially humorous birthday cards. Seasonal 18 mos. ahead. Not open to new card lines. Send 10 ideas. Open to ideas for calendars/journals, gift/novelty items, greeting books, and stationery. No guidelines or catalog.

Tips: "We need good but clean humor."

NORTHERN CARDS, Creative Department, 5694 Ambler Dr., Mississauga ON L4W 2K9, Canada. Toll-free (877)627-7444. (905)625-4944. Fax (905)625-5995. E-mail: artists@northerncards.com. Website: www.northerncards.com/docs/artists.shtml. Open to writers and artists. Greeting cards.

NOVO CARD PUBLISHERS INC., 3630 W. Pratt Ave., Lincolnwood IL 60712. Toll-free (800)624-2426. (847)763-0077. Fax (847)763-0020. E-mail: art@novocard.net. Website: www.novocard.net. Submit to Art Production. General card publisher that does a few inspirational and religious cards. Open to freelance; buys 10 ideas/yr. Prefers outright submissions. Pays $2/line on acceptance for all rts. No royalties. Responds in 5 wks. Uses traditional and light verse; 5-20 lines (nothing too brief). Produces baby announcements, conventional, humorous, inspirational, invitations, juvenile, religious, studio. Needs anniversary, birthday, Christmas, congratulations, Easter, Father's Day, friendship, get well, miss you, Mother's Day, new baby, relatives (all occasions), sympathy, Thanksgiving, thank you, valentines, wedding. Seasonal 6-8 mos. ahead. Open to ideas for new card lines. Submit enough ideas to show style. Guidelines/needs list; no catalog.

Tips: "We don't want anything too brief or too lengthy. We like verse that holds everyone's hearts, especially the male gender."

+OATMEAL STUDIOS, PO Box 138, Town Road 35, Rochester VT 05767. (802)767-3171.mail: Website: www.oatmealstudios.com. Dawn Abraham, editor. Needs: Mother's Day, Father's Day, Hanukkah, valentines, Easter, St. Patrick's Day, graduation, birthday, relative birthday, love, birthday making fun of getting older. Also does Post-it Notes for Computer Users or Teachers. Submit ideas on 3x5 index cards with your name and address on each one. Writer's guidelines and artist's guidelines on Website.

PLESH CREATIVE GROUP INC., 38 A Park St., Medfield MA 02052. (508)359-6400. Fax (508)359-6448. E-mail: PleshCreativeGroup@verizon.net. Website: www.PleshCreative.com. Submit to: Suzanne Comeau. General card publisher with a religious line. Open to freelance. Prefers outright submissions. Buys all rts. Pays $30-50 on acceptance. No royalties. Responds in several wks. Uses rhymed, unrhymed, traditional, and light verse; 8-10 lines or shorter. Produces conventional, humorous, inspirational, juvenile, religious.

PRINTESSDI, 742 Elmhurst Cir., Claremont CA 91711. (909)621-3790. Fax (206)339-3765. E-mail: cards@printessdi.com. Website: www.printessdi.com. Diane Cooley, design ed. A general card publisher with one or more inspirational lines. Open to freelance. Buys 5-10 ideas/yr. Prefers outright submissions (read guidelines first). Buys nonexclusive rts. Pays $5 ea. or merchandise, internet exposure for your work; on acceptance. No royalties. Responds in 3-4 wks. Open to new card lines. Prefers 4-12 ideas/submission, tied together by theme and/or style. Guidelines/needs list (also on Website); no catalog.

Tips: "Currently accepting 'how-to' articles (for Website) and artwork only. How to write a sympathy note, a thank-you note, an apology note, a love note, etc."

P. S. GREETINGS/FANTUS PAPER PRODUCTS, 5730 N. Tripp Ave., Chicago IL 60646-6723. Toll-free (800)621-8823. (773)267-6150. Fax (773)267-6055. E-mail: artdirector@psgreetings.com. Website: www.psgreetings.com. Submit to Design Director; Re: Freelance Writer. 80% freelance. Holiday/seasonal 6 mos. ahead. Responds in 1 mo. Pays flat fee on acceptance; no royalty. Rhymed or unrhymed verse. Produces conventional, humorous, inspirational, invitations, juvenile. Guidelines for #10 SASE (also on Website).

RED FARM STUDIO, 1135 Roosevelt Ave., Pawtucket RI 02861-0347. Toll-free (877)REDFARM. (401)728-9300. Fax (401)728-0350. E-mail: info@redfarm.com. Website: www.redfarmstudio.com. Thomas Scott, pres.; Steven Scott, VP; submit to Production Coordinator. General card publisher with a religious line. 100% freelance; buys 100 ideas/yr. Outright submission. Pays variable rates (about $4/line) within 1 mo. of acceptance for exclusive rts. No royalties. Responds in 2 mos. Use traditional and light verse; 1-4 lines. Produces announcements, invitations, religious. Needs anniversary, birthday, Christmas, friendship, get well, new baby, sympathy, wedding. Holiday 6 mos. ahead. Not open to ideas for new card lines. Submit any number of ideas. Guidelines/needs list for SASE.

BOB SIEMON DESIGNS INC., 3501 W. Segerstrom Ave., Santa Ana CA 92704-6497. (714)549-0678. Fax (714)979-2627. Website: www.bobsiemon.com. No freelance.

SOLE SOURCE GREETINGS, Attn: Art Submissions or Attn: Copy Submissions, 1 Idea Way, Caldwell ID 83605-6902. Toll-free (800)346-5860 or (800)285-1657. Toll-free fax (800)455-0642. E-mail through Website: www.solesourcegreetings.com. Send artwork via e-mail as a JPG or PDF file (see Website for size details). Check Website for samples of greetings. Open to: thinking of you, birthday, thank you, sympathy, new baby, congratulations, anniversary, wedding, etc. Also business-specific cards. Pays up to $500 for artwork; pays $25/message. Royalties 5% on retail sales; 2.5% on wholesale catalog sales.

WARNER PRESS INC., 1201 E. 5th St., PO Box 2499, Anderson IN 46018-9988. (765)644-7721. Fax (765)640-8005. E-mail: rfogle@warnerpress.org. Website: www.warnerpress.org. Karen Rhodes, product mktg. ed.; Robin Fogle, ed. asst. Producer of church resources (greeting cards, bulletins, coloring books, puzzle books). 30% freelance; buys 30-50 ideas/yr. Query for guidelines. Pays $30-35 on acceptance (for bulletins); material for bulletins cannot be sold elsewhere for bulletin use, but may be sold in any other medium. No royalties. Responds in 6-8 wks. Uses rhymed, unrhymed, traditional verse, and devotionals for bulletins; 16-24 lines. Accepts 10 ideas/submission. Guidelines for bulletins; no catalog.

Also Does: Also open to ideas for coloring books, church resource items.

+WORLD LIBRARY PUBLICATIONS, 3708 River Rd., Ste. 400, Franklin Park IL 60131. (847)233-2742. Fax (847)233-2762. E-mail: wrightj@jspaluch.com. Website: www.jspaluch.com. A division of J. S. Palach Co. John D. Wright, marketing dir. A music, liturgy, and art publisher with some greeting cards in their line. Open to freelance. Query. Pays on publication; pays some negotiable royalties. Traditional verse. Produces inspirational & religious cards; anniversary, birthday, Christmas, Easter, St. Patrick's Day, sympathy. Holiday/seasonal 10-12 mos. ahead. Not open to ideas for new card lines. Somewhat open to ideas for activity/coloring books, calendars/journals, puzzles, Sunday bulletins; all religious themed. Send any number of ideas. Guidelines; catalog for 9x12 SASE.

ADDITIONAL CARD PUBLISHERS

NOTE: Following is a list of card publishers who did not respond to our questionnaire. You may want to contact them on your own to see if they are open to freelance submissions.

APPALACHIAN BIBLE CO. INC., 506 Princeton Rd., Johnson City TN 37601.

BERG CHRISTIAN ENTERPRISES, 4525 S.E. 63rd Ave., Portland OR 97206. (503)777-4101.

BLACK FAMILY GREETING CARDS, 20 Cortlandt Ave., New Rochelle NY 10801. Bill Harte, pres.

BLACKSMITH CARDS & PRINTS, 37535 Festival Dr., Palm Desert CA 92211. Bob Smith, pres.

CD GREETING CARDS, PO Box 5084, Brentwood TN 37024-5084.

CRT CUSTOM PRODUCTS INC., 7532 Hickory Hills Ct., Whites Creek TN 37189.

DESIGNS FOR BETTER LIVING, 1716 N. Vista St., Los Angeles CA 90046.

KRISTIN ELLIOTT INC., 10 Industrial Way, Amesbury MA 01913-3223.

GOOD NEWS IN SIGHT, 2610 Mirror Lake Dr., Fayetteville NC 28303-5212.

GRACE PUBLICATIONS, PO Box 9432, Wyoming MI 49509-0432.

GREENLEAF INC., 951 S. Pine St., #250, Spartanburg SC 29302-3370. Greenleaf Foundation Inc.

HIGHER HORIZONS, PO Box 78399, Los Angeles CA 90016-0399.

LUCY & ME GALLERY, 13232 Riviera Pl. N.E., Seattle WA 98125-4645. Diane Roger, card ed.

ALFRED MAINZER INC., 3933—29th St, Long Island City NY 11101-3707. Toll-free (800)22-cards. (718)392-4200. Fax (718)392-2681.

MORE THAN A CARD, 5010 Baltimore Ave., Bethesda MD 20816.

OAKSPRINGS IMPRESSIONS, PO Box 572, Woodacre CA 94973-0572. (415)488-9194. Fax (415)488-0194.

FREDERICK SINGER & SONS INC., 215 Borden Ave., Long Island City NY 11101.

THESE THREE INC., 314 Washington Rd., #1001, South Hills PA 15216-1638. Jean P. Bridgers, card ed.

RANDALL WILCOX PUBLISHING, 826 Orange Ave., #544, Coronado CA 92118.

CAROL WILSON FINE ARTS, PO Box 17394, Portland OR 97217. Gary Spector, ed.

GAME MARKETS

NOTE: Some of the following markets for games, gift items, and videos have not indicated their interest in receiving freelance submissions. Contact these markets on your own for information on submission procedures before sending them anything. These are all paying markets.

+B EQUAL GAMES, The b EQUAL Co., 171 Birch St., #4, Redwood City CA 94062. Toll-free (800)233-0669. (650)298-9665. Fax (650)298-0054. Bible-based TV DVD games.

BIBLE GAMES CO., 14389 Cassell Rd., PO Box 237, Fredericktown OH 43019. Toll-free (800)824-2637. (740)694-8042. Fax (740)694-8072. E-mail: info@biblegamescompany .com. Website: www.biblegamescompany.com. JoAnn Vozar, operations mngr. Produces Bible games. 10% freelance. Buys 1-2 ideas/yr. Query. Pays on publication for all rts. (negotiable). Royalties 8%. Responds in 6-8 wks. Open to new ideas. One game per submission. Guidelines & catalog online.

Tips: "Send developed and tested game play, target market, and audience. Must be totally nonsectarian and fully biblical—no fictionalized scenarios." Board games, CD-ROMs, computer games, and video games.

CACTUS GAME DESIGN INC., 751 Tusquittee St., Hayesville NC 28904. (828)389-1536. Fax (828)389-1534. E-mail: rob@cactusgamedesign.com. Website: www.cactusgamedesign .com. Rob Anderson, pres. Produces card games, board games, and computer games. Open to freelance submissions. Buys 2-4 ideas/yr. Query by e-mail. Pays variable amounts on acceptance for game rts. Pays 5-15% royalty for complete games only. Responds in 4 wks. Open to new ideas for games. Guidelines (www.cactusgamedesign.com/inventors.php); catalog for .75 postage.

GOODE GAMES INTERNATIONAL, Original Family Fun Games, PO Box 1099, Nicholasville KY 40356. Toll-free (800)257-7767. (859)881-4513. E-mail: info@goodegames.com. Website: www.goodegames.com. Contact: Mike Goode.

TALICOR, 901 Lincoln Pkwy., Plainwell MI 49080. (269)685-2345. Fax (269)685-6789. E-mail: webmaster@Talicor.com. Website: www.Talicor.com. Lew Herndon, pres. Produces board games and puzzles. 100% freelance; buys 10 ideas/yr. Outright submissions. Pays variable rates on publication for all rts. Royalty 4-6%. Responds in 4 wks. Seasonal 6 mos. ahead. Open to new ideas for puzzles or toys. Submit 1-4 ideas. No guidelines; catalog for 9x12 SAE/$2.13 postage (mark "Media Mail").

WISDOM TREE, PO Box 8682, Tucson AZ 85738-8682. Fax (520)825-5702. E-mail: wisdom@ christianlink.com, or Thuff80691@aol.com. Website: www.wisdomtreegames.com. Brenda Huff, owner. Produces Bible-based computer games and does sales and marketing of Bible-based and family-friendly educational games. Responds in 1-6 wks. Seasonal 8 mos. ahead. Open to review of beta versions of computer games, computer software, or video games. Also networks with Christian Game Developers Group to put projects together. Catalog on request.

Special Needs: "Storybook/puzzle game engine."

GIFT/SPECIALTY ITEM MARKETS

+AGAPE WEAR, (410)676-0312. E-mail: Info@agapewear.org. Website: www.agapewear.org. Deborah Coleman, VP/Co-owner. Apparel.

ANCHOR WALLACE PUBLISHERS, 1000 Hwy 4 S., PO Box 7000, Sleepy Eye MN 56085-0007. Toll-free (800)533-3570. Toll-free fax (800)582-2352. E-mail: contactus@anchorwallace.com. Website: www.anchorwallace.com. Calendars and bulletins.

ARTBEATS, 129 Glover Ave., Norwalk CT 06850-1311. (203)847-2000. Fax (203)846-2105. E-mail: Richard@nygs.com, or mail@nygs.com. Website: www.NYGS.com. New York Graphic Society. Richard Fleischmann, pub. Produces prints and posters. Open to freelancers; purchases 100 ideas/yr. Outright submissions. Pays on publication. Royalties 10%. Responds in 3 wks. Does conventional, inspirational, juvenile, religious, and sensitivity prints and posters. Open to new ideas. Guidelines; no catalog.

ART 2 INSPIRE INC., 140 E. 52nd St., Ste. 2C, New York NY 10022. Toll-free (888)999-4188. (212)486-7700. Fax (212)486-7077. E-mail: info@art-2-inspire.com, or kingdavid18@aol.com. Website: www.Art-2-inspire.com. Catholic art posters.

BE ONE CHRISTIAN SPORTSWEAR, 3208 Merrywood Dr., Sacramento CA 95825. (916)483-7630. E-mail: beoneinchrist@aol.com. Website: www.BeOne.com. Christian clothing.

CARPENTREE INC., Carpentree Design, 2724 N. Sheridan, Tulsa OK 74115. Toll-free (800)736-2787. (918)582-3600. Fax (918)587-4329. E-mail from Website: www.carpentree.com. Submit to Design Dept. Produces framed art and verse. Buys several ideas/yr. Prefers outright submission. Rights purchased are negotiable. Pays on publication; negotiable royalty. Responds in 12-15 wks. Uses rhymed, unrhymed, and traditional verse for framed art; 4-16 lines. Open to ideas for new specialty items. Submit max 3-10 ideas. Open to ideas for framed art, tabletop items, and gift/novelty items. Guidelines; catalog $5/10x13 SAE.

CHRISTIAN ART GIFTS, 1025 N. Lombard Rd., PO Box 1443, Lombard IL 60148. Toll-free (800)521-7807. (630)599-0240. Fax (630)599-0245. Website: www.christianartgifts.com. Friendship cards, greeting books, bookmarks, mugs.

DESTINY IMAGE GIFTS, PO Box 310, Shippensburg PA 17257. Toll-free (800)722-6774. (717)532-3040. Fax (717)532-9291. E-mail: dlm@destinyimage.com. Website: www.destinyimage.com. Don Milam, ed. mngr. No unsolicited e-mail submissions; use online submission form. Gift products.

DEXSA: The Giving Company, PO Box 109, Hudson WI 54016. Toll-free (800)933-3972. (715)386-8701. Toll-free fax (888)559-1603. E-mail through Website: www.dexsa.com. John Larson, owner. Gifts.

+DOT GIBSON PUBLICATIONS, PO Box 117, Waycross GA 31502. Toll-free: (800)336-8095. (912)285-2848. Fax (912)285-0349. E-mail: info@dotgibson.com. Website: www.dotgibson.com. Dot Gibson, pub. (dot@dotgibson.com). Publishes inspirational gift books and children's books. Free catalog.

EAGLES WINGS, 2343 Clay St., Kissimmee FL 34741. (407)870-8800. Fax (407)932-0828. E-mail: info@eagleswings.com. Website: www.eagleswings.com. Apparel.

EXODUS WEAR, Exodus Enterprises, LLC, 9766—9th St., #401, Alta Loma CA 91737. Toll-free (888)3-EXODUS. Fax (909)899-7024. Website: www.exoduswear.com. Christian apparel.

GREENACRE WORKSHOP. Toll-free (800)851-7715. Fax (401)728-0350. E-mail: info@greenacreworkshop.com. Website: www.greenacreworkshop.com. Coloring/activity books; Paintables.

HERITAGE PUZZLE INC., PO Box 328, Pfafftown NC 27040-0328. Toll-free (888)348-3717. Toll-free fax (866)727-8209. E-mail: heritagepuzzle@triad.rr.com. Website: www.heritagepuzzle.com. Religious jigsaw puzzles.

JODY HOUGHTON DESIGNS INC., 30248 S.W. Thomas St., Unit 1002, Wilsonville OR 97070-8646. Toll-free (800)733-8253. E-mail: jody@jodyhoughton.com. Website: www.jodyhoughton.com.

KNOW HIM CHRISTIAN GEAR, 6200 S. Troy Cir., Ste. 140, Englewood CO 80111-6474. Toll-free (888)256-6944. (303)662-9512. Fax (303)662-9942. E-mail: Doug.Mckenna@knowhim.com. Website: www.KnowHim.com. Doug McKenna, pres. Christian apparel.

JAMES LAWRENCE COMPANY, 1501 Livingstone Rd., PO Box 188, Hudson WI 54016. Toll-free (800)546-3699. (715)386-3082. Fax (715)386-3699. E-mail: chuck@jameslawrencecompany.com. Website: www.jameslawrencecompany.com. Chuck Hetland, product development. Produces wall decor. Open to freelance. Buys variable number/yr. Prefers e-mail contact. Prefers exclusive rts. Pays $50-100/verse on acceptance. No royalties. Responds in 3-4 wks. Inspirational verse no shorter than 4 lines and no longer than 5 stanzas of 4 lines ea. Holiday 9-12+ mos. ahead. Open to new ideas for gift/novelty items, magnets, mugs, plaques. Send any number of ideas. No guidelines or catalog.

+LIGHTHOUSE CHRISTIAN PRODUCTS, 1050 Remington Rd., Schaumburg IL 60173. (847)519-1825. Fax (847)519-1844. E-mail: customerservice@lcpgifts.com. Website: www.lcpgifts.com. Christian gift products.

LIVING EPISTLES, 2232 S. Main St., #444, Ann Arbor MI 48103. Toll-free (800)294-8637. Fax (205)759-9889. E-mail: LivingEpistlesService@livingepistles.com. Website: www.livingepistles.com. Apparel.

LORENZ CORP., 501 E. Third St., Dayton OH 45401. Toll-free (800)444-1144, ext. 1. E-mail: info@lorenz.com. Website: www.lorenz.com. Gift products, stationery, book marks, buttons, postcards, posters, and more. Guidelines on Website.

MCBETH CORP, PO Box 400, Chambersburg PA 17201. Toll-free (800)876-5112. (717)263-5600. Fax (717)263-5909. E-mail: mcbethcorp@supernet.com. Website: www.wholesalecentral.com/mcbethcorp. Gifts, jewelry, calendars, Christmas items, activity books, greeting cards, and more.

MULTNOMAH GIFTS, a Division of Multnomah Books, 12265 Oracle Blvd., Ste. 200, Colorado Springs CO 80921. (719)590-4999. E-mail: info@waterbrookpress.com, or comments@multnomahbooks.com. Website: www.multnomahgifts.com. Produces 4-color gift books. Not open to freelance submissions. Guidelines; no catalog.

NOT OF THIS WORLD CLOTHING CO., 169 Radio Rd. #8, Corona CA 92879. (951)354-9528. Fax (951)354-9529. E-mail: info@notw.com. Website: www.notw.com. Shirts, wallets, belts, belt buckles.

POWERMARK: Comics Worth Reading, E. Hwy. CC, Ste. E104, Nixa MO 65714. Toll-free (877)769-2669. Fax (417)724-0119. E-mail: webmaster@powermarkcomics.com. Website: www.powermarkcomics.com. Contact: Steve Benintendi. Christian comic books.

PRINTS OF PEACE, PO Box 717, Camino CA 95709. (530)644-7044 or (530)621-4224. E-mail: design@printsofpeace.com. Website: www.printsofpeace.com.

RED LETTER 9, 2910 Kerry Forest Pkwy, D4, Tallahassee FL 32309. Toll-free (866)804-4833. Toll-free fax (866)804-4832. E-mail: info@redletter9.com. Website: www.redletter9.com. Apparel and gift items.

SOLID LIGHT CO., 7787 Graphics Way, Lewis Center OH 43035. Toll-free (800)726-9606. (740)548-1200. Fax (740)548-1223. Website: www.solidlightco.com. Apparel.

SONTEEZ CHRISTIAN T-SHIRTS, PO Box 44106, Phoenix AZ 85064. Toll-free (800)874-4485. E-mail: info@sonteez.com. Website: www.sonteez.com. T-shirts.

+VIDA ENTERTAINMENT, 201 East City Hall Ave., Norfolk VA 23451. Toll-free (877)YES-VIDA. (757)626-3102. E-mail: sales@vidaentertainment.com. Website: www.vidaentertainment.com. Books, DVDs, comics, & toys.

SOFTWARE DEVELOPERS

AMG SOFTWARE, 6815 Shallowford Rd. (37421), PO Box 22000, Chattanooga TN 37422. Toll-free (800)266-4977. (423)894-6060, ext. 275. Toll-free fax (800)265-6690 or (423)894-9511. E-mail: danp@amginternational.org. Website: www.amgpublishers.org. AMG International. Dan Penwell, dir. of prod. dev./acq. Bible software.

BAKER SOFTWARE, Box 6287, Grand Rapids MI 49516-6287. (616)676-9185. Fax (616)676-9573. Website: www.BakerBooks.com. Baker Publishing Group.

B & H SOFTWARE, 127 Ninth Ave. N., Nashville TN 37234. (615)251-3638. Website: www.broadmanholman.com.

BIBLESOFT, 22014—7th Ave. S., Seattle WA 98198-6235. (206)824-0547. Fax (206)824-1828. Website: www.biblesoft.com.

ELLIS ENTERPRISES INC., 5100 N. Brookline, #465, Oklahoma City OK 73112. (405)948-1766. Fax (405)917-2250. E-mail: mail@ellisenterprises.com. Website: www.ellisenterprises.com, or www.BibleLibrary.com. Contact: Dr. John Ellis. Produces the Micro Bible, Ultra Bible, Mega Bible, and Maxima Bible. Check out additional products on their Website.

LARIDIAN, 1733 Lake Terrace Rd. S.E., Cedar Rapids IA 52403. (319)378-4940. Fax (413)208-8477. E-mail: craigr@laridian.com, or support@laridian.com. Website: www.laridian.com. Craig Rairdin, pres. Send ideas by e-mail. Bible software for hand-held and palmtop computers.

LOGOS RESEARCH SYSTEMS, 1313 Commercial St., Bellingham WA 98225-4307. (360)527-1700. Fax (360)527-1707. E-mail: info@logos.com, or suggest@logos.com. Website: www.logos.com. Contact: Dan Pritchett (Dan@logos.com). Publishes the Logos Bible Software Series XScholar's Library, Pastor's Library, and Bible Study Library. Over 5,000 titles from more than 100 publishers now compatible with the system.

NAVPRESS SOFTWARE, 16002 Pool Canyon Rd., Austin TX 78734.

OLIVE TREE BIBLE SOFTWARE, PO Box 48271, Spokane WA 99228-1271. (509)465-0302. Fax (509)467-4976. E-mail: drew@olivetree.com. Website: www.OliveTree.com. Drew Hunter, pres. Bible software.

RIVER DEEP, 100 Pine St., Ste. 1900, San Francisco CA 94111. Toll-free (888)242-6747. (415)659-2000. Fax (415)659-2020. E-mail: info@riverdeep.net. Website: www.riverdeep.com. Software developer.

ZONDERVAN NEW MEDIA, 5300 Patterson St. S.E., Grand Rapids MI 49530. Toll-free (800)226-1122. (616)698-6900. Fax (616)698-3483. Website: www.zondervan.com. Contact: Britt Dennison. Software.

VIDEO/CD/DVD MARKETS

ALPHA OMEGA PUBLICATIONS, 804 N. 2nd Ave. E., Rock Rapids IA 51246. Toll-free (800)622-3070. Website: www.AOP.com. Videos & DVDs.

AMG PUBLISHERS/CD/CD-ROMS, 6815 Shallowford Rd. (37421), PO Box 22000, Chattanooga TN 37422. Toll-free (800)266-4977. (423)894-6060, ext. 275. Toll-free fax (800)265-6690 or (423)894-9511. E-mail: danp@amginternational.org. Website: www.amgpublishers.org. AMG International. Dan Penwell, dir. of prod. dev./acq. Bible CD-ROMs.

BIG IDEA INC., 230 Franklin Rd., #2A, Franklin TN 37064. Toll-free (800)295-0557. (615)224-2200. Website: www.bigidea.com. Query; no unsolicited ideas. Movies, videos, music, books, and games.

CANDLELIGHT MEDIA GROUP, 3323 State Hwy. 276, Emory TX 75440. Toll-free (800)747-2696. E-mail: info@candlelightmedia.com. Website: www.candlelightmedia.com. Videos, DVDs.

CLOUD TEN PICTURES, PO Box 1440, Niagara Falls NY 14302. (905)684-5561. Fax (905)684-7946. Website: www.cloudtenpictures.com. Film production and acquisition, video distribution, and marketing. Cloud Ten Pictures (maker of the Left Behind movies) is committed to making quality, Christian-themed films. For all inquiries, contact Producer and VP of Film: Andre van Heerden; andrev@cloudtenpictures.com.

CROWN VIDEO/CROWN COMEDY, 15397—117 Ave., Edmonton AB T5M 3X4, Canada. Toll-free (800)661-9467. (780)471-1417. Fax (780)474-0418. E-mail: info@crownvideo.com. Website: www.crownvideo.com. Precision Media Group. Distributor of Christian Films, stand-up comedy, and music.

DALLAS CHRISTIAN VIDEO, PO Box 450474, Garland TX 75045-0474. Toll-free (877)516-2900. Fax (972)644-5926. E-mail: DCV6681@aol.com. Website: www.dallaschristian video.com. Contact: Bob Hill. Videos.

RUSS DOUGHTEN FILMS INC., 5907 Meredith Dr., Des Moines IA 50322. Toll-free (800)247-3456. (515)278-4737. Fax (515)278-4738. E-mail: evangelism@rdfilms.com, or rdoughton@rdfilms.com. Website: www.rdfilms.com. Submit to Production Dept. Produces and distributes feature-length Christian movies. Open to ideas. Guidelines; free catalog.

GOSPEL COMMUNICATIONS, PO Box 455, Muskegon MI 49443-0455. Toll-free (800)467-7353. (231)774-3361. Fax (231)777-1847. E-mail: marilyn@gospelcommunications.org. Website: www.GospelFilmsDistribution.com. Contact: Marilyn Bush. Videos, DVDs, books, Bibles, and music.

TOMMY NELSON VIDEOS, PO Box 141000, Nashville TN 37214. E-mail: breeves@tommy nelson.com. Website: www.tommynelson.com. Contact: Bill Reeves, entertainment dir. Video producer.

PROPHECY PUBLICATIONS, PO Box 7000, Oklahoma City OK 73153. Toll-free (800)475-1111. Fax (405)636-1054. E-mail: Krissie@prophecyinthenews.com. Website: www .prophecyinthenews.com. Contact: J. R. Church. Religious education videos; fiction videos.

TYNDALE FAMILY VIDEO, 351 Executive Dr., Carol Stream IL 60188. (630)668-8300. Website: www.tyndale.com. Videos.

VISION VIDEO/GATEWAY FILMS, PO Box 540, Worcester PA 19490-0540. (610)584-3500. Fax (610)584-6643. E-mail: info@VisionVideo.com. Website: www.VisionVideo.com. Contact: Karen Rutt.

WACKY WORLD STUDIOS, 148 E. Douglas Rd., Oldsmar FL 34677-2939. (813)818-8277. Fax (813)818-8396. E-mail: info@wackyworld.tv. Website: www.wackyworld.tv. Full service custom art and design studio. Videos, DVDs.

WORLD WIDE PICTURES INC., PO Box 668029, Charlotte NC 28266-8029. Toll-free (800)745-4318. Fax: (704)401-3013. E-mail: info@wwp.org. Website: www.wwp.org. Billy Graham Assn. DVDs.

ZONDERVAN NEW MEDIA, 5300 Patterson St. S.E., Grand Rapids MI 49530. Toll-free (800)226-1122. (616)698-6900. Fax (616)698-3483. Website: www.zondervan.com. Contact: T. J. Rathbun. Videos.

SPECIALTY PRODUCTS TOPICAL LISTINGS

NOTE: Most of the following publishers are greeting card/specialty market publishers, but some will be found in the book publisher listings.

ACTIVITY/COLORING BOOKS

Cook, David C.
Dickson's Life Pub.
Greenacre Workshop
Knight George Pub.
McBeth Corp.
Rainbow Publishers
Warner Press
World Library Publications

AUDIOTAPES

AMG Publishers
AMG Software
Bible Games
Eldridge Plays
Fair Havens
McRuffy Press
MegaGrace Books
Tyndale House
W Publishing
Zondervan New Media

BOARD GAMES/ GAMES

Bethel Publishing
Bible Games
Big Idea
Cactus Game
Carson-Dellosa
Cook, David C.
Goode Games
Knight George Pub.
Master Books
Mission City Press
Morris, William
Review and Herald
Salt Works
Standard Publishing
Tyndale House
WinePress

BOOKMARKS

Christian Art Gifts
Christian Inspirations
Dickson's Life Pub.
Hermitage Art
InspirationArt
Lorenz
Warner Press

BULLETINS

Hermitage Art

CALENDARS/DAILY JOURNALS

Abingdon Press
African Amer. Expressions
American Tract
Anchor Wallace
Barbour
C4Yourself Greetings
Christian Inspirations
Dickson's Life Pub.
Group Publishing
Lawson Falle
McBeth Corp.
Neibauer Press
Tyndale House
Women of the Promise
World Library Publications

CD-ROMs

AMG Publishers
AMG Video/CD
Bible Games
Cactus Game
Cook, David C.
Fair Havens
Georgetown Univ. Press
Group Publishing
Our Sunday Visitor (bks.)

CHARTS

Rose Publishing

COMIC BOOKS

Cactus Game
Infuze
Kaleidoscope Press
Lighthouse Publishing
Nelson, Thomas
PowerMark
Vida Entertainment
ZonderKidz

COMPUTER GAMES

Bible Games
Big Idea
Cactus Game
Cook, David C.
Dean Press, Robbie
Grupo Nelson
Knight George Pub.
WinePress
Wisdom Tree
Wood Lake Books

COMPUTER SOFTWARE

AMG Publishers
AMG Software
B & H Software
Baker Software
BibleSoft
Ellis Enterprises
Laridian
Libros Liguori
Logos Research
NavPress Software
Olive Tree/Software
Regal
Resource Public.
River Deep
Wisdom Tree
Zondervan New Media

DVDs

Anglicans United
Big Idea
Candlelight Media
Crown Video
Gospel Communications
Vida Entertainment
Wacky World
WinePress
World Wide Pictures

GIFT BOOKS

Blue Mountain Arts
Christian Inspirations
Dot Gibson Public.
Multnomah Gifts
Review and Herald
Salt Works
Vida Entertainment

GIFT/NOVELTY ITEMS

Abingdon Press
African Amer. Expressions
Artful Greetings
Carpentree
Carson-Dellosa
Christian Art Gifts
Christian Inspirations
Cook, David C.
Design Design
Destiny Image
Dexsa
Dickson's Life Pub.
Hermitage Art
Houghton Designs, Jody

Lawrence Co., James
Lawson Falle
Lighthouse Christian
Lorenz
McBeth Corp.
Red Letter 9
Salt Works

GREETING BOOKS

Blue Mountain Arts
Christian Art Gifts
Christian Inspirations
Design Design
Houghton Designs, Jody
Lawson Falle

MAGNETS

African Amer. Expressions
Christian Inspirations
Design Design
Dickson's Life Pub.
Houghton Designs, Jody
Lawrence Co., James

MUGS

Christian Art Gifts
Christian Inspirations
Dickson's Life Pub.
Lawrence Co., James

MUSIC*

Gospel Communications

NOTECARDS

Creative Christian Gifts

PLAQUES

Christian Inspirations
Dickson's Life Pub.
Houghton Designs, Jody
Lawrence Co., James
Leiden, Laura

POSTCARDS

Abingdon Press
Houghton Designs, Jody
Lorenz
Warner Press

POSTERS

Art 2 Inspire
ArtBeats
InspirationArt
Life Cycle Books
Lorenz

PUZZLES

Bible Games
Christian Inspirations
Heritage Puzzle
InspirationArt
Rainbow Publishers
Talicor
World Library Publications

STATIONERY

African Amer. Expressions
Christian Inspirations
Design Design
Dickson's Life Pub.
Lawson Falle
Lorenz

SUNDAY BULLETINS

Anchor Wallace
Christian Inspirations
Warner Press
World Library Publications

T-SHIRTS/APPAREL

Active Disciple
Agape Wear
Be One Christian
Christian Inspirations
Dickson's Life Pub.
Eagles Wings
Exodus Wear
Know Him
Living Epistles
Not of This World
Red Letter 9
Solid Light
SonTeez

TOYS

Dickson's Life Pub.
Lighthouse Christian
Mission City Press
Standard Publishing
Talicor
Vida Entertainment

VIDEOS/VIDEO GAMES

Abingdon Press
Alpha Omega
AMG Video/CD
Anglicans United
Bible Games
Big Idea
Cactus Game
Candlelight Media
Cloud Ten
Cook, David C.
Crown Video
Dallas Christian Video
Destiny Image
Doughten Films, Russ
Editorial Unilit
Fair Havens
Focus on the Family
Focus on the Family (bks)
Gospel Communications
Group Publishing
Howard Books
Master Books
Nelson Videos, Tommy
Pauline Books
Prophecy Publications
Regal
Tyndale Family Video
Tyndale House
Victor Books
Vision Video
W Publishing
Wacky World
Wisdom Tree
Zondervan New Media

CHRISTIAN WRITERS' CONFERENCES AND WORKSHOPS

(*) Indicates information was not verified or updated by the conference director
(+) Indicates a new listing

Note: Visit the following Websites for information on these and other conferences: www.freelancewriting.com/conferences and www.screenwriter.com/insider/WritersCalendar.html. Link to the following conference sites at: www.stuartmarket.com.

ALABAMA

SOUTHERN CHRISTIAN WRITERS CONFERENCE. Tuscaloosa/First Baptist Church; June 2008. Contact: Joanne Sloan, SCWC, PO Box 1106, Northport AL 35473. (205)333-8603. Fax (205)339-4528. E-mail: SCWCworkshop@bellsouth.net. Attendance: 200+.

ARIZONA

AMERICAN CHRISTIAN WRITERS PHOENIX CONFERENCE. October 31-November 1, 2008; October 30-31, 2009. Contact: Reg A. Forder, Box 110390, Nashville TN 37222. Toll-free (800)21-WRITE. E-mail: ACWriters@aol.com. Website: www.ACWriters.com. Attendance: 40-80.

CATHOLIC SCREENWRITERS WORKSHOP. Tucson; February 25-28, 2008. Contact: Fr. Tom Santa, CssR, 7101 W. Picture Rocks Rd., Tucson AZ 85743-9645. Toll-free (866)737-5751. (520)744-3400. Fax (520)744-8021. E-mail: office@desertrenewal.org. Website: www.desertrenewal.org. Speaker: Virginia McCarthy.

ARKANSAS

ANNUAL ARKANSAS WRITERS CONFERENCE. Little Rock; June 6-7, 2008 (always 1st Friday & Saturday of June). Contact: Helen Austin, 7713 Harmon Dr., Little Rock AR 72227. (501)223-8633. E-mail: hmaustin@comcast.net. Website: www.geocities.com/penwomen. Attendance: 150-175. Sponsors 30 contests; one entry fee covers all contests.

CALIFORNIA

ACT ONE: WRITING PROGRAM. Hollywood; summer of 2008. Contact: Chris Riley, 2690 N. Beachwood Dr., Hollywood CA 90068. (323)464-0815. Fax (323)468-0315. E-mail: info@actoneprogram.com. Website: www.ActOneProgram.com. These are intensive training sessions for screenwriters, taught by professionals working in Hollywood. Offers track for television writers. No editors or agents in attendance. Limited to 30 students (by application).

AMERICAN CHRISTIAN WRITERS ANAHEIM CONFERENCE. October 24-25, 2008; October 23-24, 2009. Contact: Reg A. Forder, Box 110390, Nashville TN 37222. Toll-free (800)21-WRITE. E-mail: ACWriters@aol.com. Website: www.ACWriters.com. Attendance: 40-80.

ANTELOPE VALLEY CHRISTIAN WRITER'S CONFERENCE. Quartz Hill; May 2-3, 2008. Sponsored by the High Desert Christian Writer's Guild and Quartz Hill School of Theology. Theme: Streams in the Desert. Contact: Don Patterson, 6223 Almond Valley Way, Quartz Hill CA 93536. (661)722-0891. E-mail: donrpatterson@verizon.net. Website:www.avwriters.com.

BIOLA MEDIA CONFERENCE. La Mirada; April 2008. Contact: Craig Detweiler, Biola University, 13800 Biola Ave., La Mirada CA 90639. Toll-free (866)334-2266. Website: www.biola media.com.

CASTRO VALLEY CHRISTIAN WRITERS SEMINAR. Castro Valley; February 22-23, 2008. Contact: Pastor Jon Drury, 19300 Redwood Rd., Castro Valley CA 94546-3465. (510)886-6300. Fax (510)581-5022. E-mail: jond@redwoodchapel.org. Website: www.christianwriter.org. Doesn't usually have editors; no agents in attendance. Attendance: 200.

CHRISTIANS IN THEATRE ARTS (CITA) ANNUAL NETWORKING CONFERENCE. California; June 2008. Contact: Bryanne Barker, PO Box 26471, Greenville SC 29616. (864)679-1898. Fax (864)679-1899. E-mail: admin@cita.org. Website: www.cita.org. Usually offers an advanced track. Sponsors a play contest (rules on Website). Attendance: 350.

FICTION INTENSIVE, for fiction writers who want to go deeper. Tehachapi; June 2-8, 2008. Contact: Lauraine Snelling (instructor), PO Box 1530, Tehachapi CA 93581-1530. (661)823-0669. Fax (661)823-9427. E-mail: TLSnelling@yahoo.com. Website: www .LauraineSnelling.net. Attendance: limited to 10.

MOUNT HERMON CHRISTIAN WRITERS CONFERENCE. Mount Hermon (near Santa Cruz); March 14-18, 2008; April 3-7, 2009; also Mentoring Clinic November 2008 (see separate listing). Offers a Career Track for professional writers (details on Website). Also offers a teen track. Contact: David R. Talbott, Box 413, Mount Hermon CA 95041-0413. (831)355-4466. Fax (831)335-9413. E-mail: rachelw@mhcamps.org. Website: www.mount hermon.org/writers (no brochure; all details on Website). Speakers for 2008: Jerry B. Jenkins & Debbie Macomber. Many editors and agents in attendance. Offers partial scholarships. Attendance: 450.

MOUNT HERMON MENTORING CLINIC. Mount Hermon (near Santa Cruz); October (usually last week). Contact: David Talbott, PO Box 413, Mount Hermon CA 95041-0413. (831)335-4466. Fax (831)335-9413. E-mail: rachelw@mhcamps.org. Website: www.mount hermon.org/writersclinic. Offers a marketing track. No editors; maybe agents in attendance. Attendance: 100-150 in groups of 10 to an instructor/mentor.

ORANGE COUNTY CHRISTIAN WRITERS FELLOWSHIP WRITERS DAY. April 2008. Contact: John DeSimone, dir.; Peg Matthew Rose, ed., PO Box 982, Lake Forest CA 92630. (714)538-7070. Fax (949)458-1807. E-mail: editor@occwf.org. Website: www.occwf.org. See Website for list of faculty and conference location. Attendance: 120.

SAN DIEGO CHRISTIAN WRITERS GUILD FALL CONFERENCE. San Diego; September 2008. Contact: Jennie Gillespie, PO Box 270403, San Diego CA 92198. (760)294-3269. E-mail: info@sandiegocwg.org. Website: www.sandiegocwg.org. Editors and agents in attendance. Attendance: 180.

SANTA BARBARA CHRISTIAN WRITERS CONFERENCE. Westmont College; October 4, 2008 (always 1st Saturday of October). Contact: Opal Mae Dailey, PO Box 42429, Santa Barbara CA 93140. Phone/fax (805)682-0316 (call first for fax). E-mail: opalmaedailey@aol.com. Attendance: 50.

SCBWI WRITERS & ILLUSTRATORS CONFERENCE IN CHILDREN'S LITERATURE. New York City, early February 2008; Los Angeles, early August 2008. Society of Children's Book Writers & Illustrators. Contact: Lin Oliver, 8271 Beverly Blvd., Los Angeles CA 90048. (323) 782-1010. Fax (323)782-1892. E-mail: scbwi@scbwi.org. Website: www.scbwi.org. Includes a track for professionals. Editors and agents in attendance. Attendance: 900.

WRITERS SYMPOSIUM BY THE SEA. San Diego/Point Loma Nazarene University; February 6-8, 2008. Contact: Dean Nelson, Professor, Journalism Dept., PLNU, 3900 Lomaland Dr., San Diego CA 92106. (619)849-2592. Fax (619)849-2566. E-mail: deannelson@point loma.edu. Website: www.pointloma.edu/writers. Sometimes has editors in attendance. Speaker: Philip Yancey. Attendance: 500.

COLORADO

AD LIB CHRISTIAN ARTS RETREAT. St. Malo Retreat and Conference Center/Allenspark; September/October 2008. Contact: Judith Deem Dupree, PO Box 365, Pine Valley CA 91962-0365. Phone/fax (619)473-8683, or (303)823-9938. E-mail: adlib_pv@sbcglobal.net. Website: www.adlibchristianarts.org. Retreat and forum for literary, visual, and performing arts. Designed as a forum and format for renewal. Solitude, fellowship, issues and ideas, critiquing. Notable speakers. No "working" editors or agents. Attendance: 35-40.

+AMERICAN CHRISTIAN WRITERS DENVER CONFERENCE. September 13, 2008; September 12, 2009. Contact: Reg Forder, Box 110390, Nashville TN 37222. Toll-free (800)21-WRITE. E-mail: ACWriters@aol.com. Website: www.ACWriters.com. Attendance: 40-80.

COLORADO CHRISTIAN WRITERS CONFERENCE. Estes Park; May 14-17, 2008 at the YMCA of the Rockies. Director: Marlene Bagnull, LittD, 316 Blanchard Rd., Drexel Hill, PA 19026-3507. Phone/fax (610)626-6833. E-mail: mbagnull@aol.com. Website: www.writehis answer.com/Colorado. Conferees choose 6 hour-long workshops from 42 offered or a Fiction or Nonfiction Clinic (by application) plus one 6.5 hour continuing session from 7 offered. Nangie U 202 & 404 with Nancy Rue and Angie Hunt by application. One-on-one appointments, paid critiques, editors panels, and general sessions. Thursday evening concert by Marty Goetz. Teens Write Saturday afternoon, plus teens are welcome to attend the entire conference at 60% off. Contest (registered conferees only) awards four $100 discounts off May 13-16, 2009 conference. Faculty of 60 authors, editors, and agents. Attendance: 260.

GLEN EYRIE FICTION WRITER'S CONFERENCE. Colorado Springs; January 2008. Contact: Craig Dunham, 3820 N. 30th, Colorado Springs CO 80904. Toll-free (800)944-4536. (719) 272-7748. Fax (719)272-7448. Website: www.gleneyriegroup.org. Some editors/agents in attendance. Attendance: 100.

GMA MUSIC IN THE ROCKIES CONFERENCE. Estes Park; July 27-August 2, 2008. Contact: John W. Styll, dir., 1205 Division St., Nashville TN 37203. (615)242-0303. Fax (615)254-9755. Website: www.gospelmusic.org. Offers advanced track and teen track; critiques, talent, competition, and seminars. A & R and industry reps on site; teaching and judging. Attendance: 1,200.

JERRY B. JENKINS CHRISTIAN WRITERS GUILD WRITING FOR THE SOUL CONFERENCE. Colorado Springs; January 31-February 3, 2008; February 12-15, 2009. Sponsored by the Jerry B. Jenkins Christian Writers Guild. Held at the luxurious 5-star, 5-diamond Broadmoor Hotel. Host: Jerry B. Jenkins. Speakers for 2008 include: Lee Strobel, Robin Jones Gunn, Richard Lederer. More than 30 editor and agents in attendance. Payment plans available. Special meal rates offered for nonparticipating spouses or parents of teens. Offers multiple general sessions with national keynote speakers and in-depth workshops on 6 tracks; plus appointments with publisher's reps. Contact: Paul Finch, 5525 N. Union Blvd., Ste. 200, Colorado Springs CO 80918. Toll-free (866)495-5177. Fax (719)495-5181. E-mail: paul@christianwritersguild.com. Website: www.christianwritersguild.com. Attendance: 450.

CONNECTICUT

WESLEYAN WRITERS CONFERENCE. Wesleyan University/Middletown; June 15-20, 2008 (tentative, see Website). Contact: Anne Greene, Director, 294 High St., Rm. 207, Middletown CT 06459. (860)685-3604. Fax (860)685-2441. E-mail: agreene@wesleyan.edu. Website: www.wesleyan.edu/writers. Includes an advanced track. Editors and agents in attendance. Offers fellowship and scholarship awards. Attendance: 100.

DELAWARE

DELAWARE CHRISTIAN WRITERS CONFERENCE, Word of Life Christian Center, Newark; April 17-19, 2008. E-mail: Delawarewriter@yahoo.com. Website: www.DelawareChristianWritersConference.com. Director: John Riddle, 6 Basset Pl., Bear DE 19701. (302)834-4910. Editors, agents, advanced track, young writers program, writing contests, editorial appointments, and evaluations.

FLORIDA

AMERICAN CHRISTIAN WRITERS ORLANDO CONFERENCE. July 11-12, 2008; November 21, 2009. Contact: Reg A. Forder, Box 110390, Nashville TN 37222. Toll-free (800)21-WRITE. E-mail: ACWriters@aol.com. Website: www.ACWriters.com. Attendance: 40-80.

FLORIDA CHRISTIAN WRITERS CONFERENCE. Bradenton; February 28-March 2, 2008. Contact: Billie Wilson, 2344 Armour Ct., Titusville FL 32780. (321)269-5831. Fax (321)264-0037. E-mail: billiewilson@cfl.rr.com. Website: www.flwriters.org. Offers advanced track. Editors and agents in attendance. Offers partial scholarships. Offers awards in 11 categories: Poetry, Drama/Screenwriting, Children's book or short story, Curriculum; Short Story for teens or adults, Article, Devotional, Novel, Nonfiction book, Best Work for First-time Author, plus Writer of the Year. Attendance: 225.

INTERNATIONAL CHRISTIAN RETAIL SHOW. (Held in a different location each year.) July 13-17, 2008 in Orlando; July 12-16, 2009 in Denver CO. Contact: Scott Graham, Box 62000, Colorado Springs CO 80962-2000. Toll-free (800)252-1950. (719)265-9895. Fax (719)272-3510. E-mail: sgraham@cbaonline.org. Website: www.christianretailshow.com. Entrance badges available through book publishers or Christian bookstores. Attendance: 14,000.

WORD WEAVERS CHRISTIAN WRITERS GROUP ANNUAL RETREAT. Lake Yale; February 2008. Contact: Eva Marie Everson, 122 Fairway Ten Dr., Casselberry FL 32707-4823. Phone/fax (407)695-9366. E-mail: PenNhnd@aol.com. Speaker: Don Aycock.

GEORGIA

AMERICAN CHRISTIAN WRITERS ATLANTA CONFERENCE. May 2-3, 2008; May 1-2, 2009. Contact: Reg Forder, Box 110390, Nashville TN 37222. Toll-free (800)21-WRITE. E-mail: ACWriters@aol.com. Website: www.ACWriters.com. Attendance: 40-80.

CATCH THE WAVE WRITERS CONFERENCE. Woodstock; October 2008. Contact: Cindy Simmons, 6409 Bells Ferry Rd., Woodstock GA 30189-2324. (770)928-2795. Fax (770)924-6935. E-mail: Cynthiasimmons@christianauthorsguild.org. Website: www.christianauthorsguild.org. Sponsors a contest. Editors in attendance. Attendance: 30-40.

GEORGIA CHRISTIAN WRITERS' SPRING FESTIVAL. Atlanta area; May 3, 2008 (first Saturday in May each year). Contact: Lloyd Blackwell, 3049 Scott Rd. N.E., Marietta GA 30066. (770)421-1203. E-mail: lloydblackwell@worldnet.att.net.

SOUTHEASTERN WRITERS CONFERENCE. Epworth-by-the-Sea, St. Simons Island; June 15-19, 2008. Contact: Sheila Hudson, registrar, 161 Woodstone Dr., Athens GA. E-mail: info@southeasternwriters.com. Website: www.southeasternwriters.com. For brochure, e-mail: purple@southeasternwriters.com. Attendance: limited to 100. Awards cash prizes to attendees in every genre, and free manuscript critiques. Agent in residence. Register from Website or by mail.

ILLINOIS

KARITOS CHRISTIAN ARTS CONFERENCE. Bolingbrook; August 2008. Contact: Bob Hay, 24 N. Belmont Ave., #B, Arlington Heights IL 60004-6174. (847)749-1284. Website: www.karitos.com. Features workshops in all areas of the arts, including writing. Also general sessions and evening celebrations. Attendance: 300-400.

WRITE-TO-PUBLISH CONFERENCE. Wheaton (Chicago area); June 4-7, 2008. Contact: Lin Johnson, 9118 W. Elmwood Dr., #1G, Niles IL 60714-5820. (847)296-3964. Fax (847)296-0754. E-mail: lin@WriteToPublish.com. Website: www.WriteToPublish.com. Offers advanced track (prerequisite: 1 published book). Majority of faculty are editors; also has agents. Attendance: 250.

INDIANA

ADVANCE 2008 (CBA). (held in a different location each year). January 28-February 1, 2008. Contact: CBA, Box 62000, Colorado Springs CO 80962-2000. Toll-free (800)252-1950. (719)265-9895. Website: www.cbaonline.org. Entrance badges available through book publishers or Christian bookstores.

AMERICAN CHRISTIAN WRITERS FORT WAYNE CONFERENCE. Quality Inn; April 18-19, 2008; March 27-28, 2009. Contact: Reg A. Forder, Box 110390, Nashville TN 37222. Toll-free (800) 21-WRITE. E-mail: ACWriters@aol.com. Website: www.ACWriters.com. Attendance: 40-80.

AMERICAN CHRISTIAN WRITERS INDIANAPOLIS CONFERENCE. April 12, 2008; June 6, 2009. Contact: Reg A. Forder, Box 110390, Nashville TN 37222. Toll-free (800)21-WRITE. E-mail: ACWriters@aol.com. Website: www.ACWriters.com. Attendance: 40-80.

BETHEL COLLEGE CHRISTIAN WRITERS' WORKSHOP. Bethel College/Mishawaka; spring 2009. Contact: English Dept. Chair, 1001 W. McKinley Ave., Mishawaka IN 46544. (574)257-3427. Website: www.BethelCollege.edu/writersworkshop. Editors sometimes in attendance; no agents. Sometimes offers full or partial scholarships. Attendance: 130.

EARLHAM SCHOOL OF RELIGION: THE MINISTRY OF WRITING COLLOQUIUM. Richmond; October 24-25, 2008; late October 2009. Editors in attendance. Contact: '08 Writing Colloquium, Susan Yands, Earlham School of Religion, 228 College Ave., Richmond IN 47374-4095. Toll-free (800)432-1377. (765)983-1423. Fax (765)983-1688. E-mail: yanossu@earlham.edu. Website: www.esr.earlham.edu. 2008 speaker: Robert Wicks. Attendance: 200.

MIDWEST WRITERS WORKSHOP. Muncie/Ball State University Alumni Center; July 25-27, 2008 (always the last Thursday, Friday, and Saturday of July). Contact: Dept. of Journalism, Ball State University, Muncie IN 47306-0484. Director: Jama Kehoe Bigger. (765)282-1055. E-mail: midwestwriters@yahoo.com. Website: www.midwestwriters.org. Sponsors a contest. Editors and agents in attendance. Offers full scholarships. Attendance: 150.

IOWA

IOWA SUMMER WRITING FESTIVAL. University of Iowa/Iowa City; June/July 2008. This is a general writer's conference that comes highly recommended for good, solid instruction. Contact: Amy Margolis, Iowa Summer Writing Festival, C215 Seashore Hall, University of Iowa, Iowa City IA 52242-5000. (319)335-4160. Fax (319)335-4039. E-mail: iswfestival@uiowa.edu. Website: www.uiowa.edu/~iswfest. For two months, June and July, you can sign up for either one-week workshops or weekend workshops on a wide variety of topics. Write for a catalog of offerings (available in February).

+OKOBOJI CHRISTIAN WRITERS RETREAT. Okoboji; September 26-27, 2008. Contact: Denise Triggs, PO Box 281, Okoboji IA 51355. (712)332-7191. E-mail: Denise@waterfallsmin.com. Website: www.waterfallsretreats.com. Attendance: 40.

QUAD-CITIES CHRISTIAN WRITERS' CONFERENCE. Eldridge; April 11-12, 2008. Contact: Twila Belk, 4350 Tanglewood Rd., Bettendorf IA 52722. (563)332-1622. E-mail: iamstraightway@aol.com. Website: www.gottatellsomebody.com. Special track for pastors. Speakers: Dr. Dennis Hensley, Lin Johnson, Sally John, Frank Ball, Cynthia Ruchti, Myrna Strasser, and others. No editors or agents in attendance. Offers a limited number of scholarships. Attendance 100+.

KANSAS

CALLED TO WRITE. Girard; April 4-5, 2008. Contact: Deborah Vogts, 17300 Ness Rd., Erie KS 66733. (620)244-5619. E-mail: debvogts@terraworld.net. Website: www.christianwritersgirard.org. Blog: www.christianwritersfellowshipblogspot.com. Sponsors a contest for attendees only. Attendance: 50-60.

KENTUCKY

AMERICAN CHRISTIAN WRITERS LOUISVILLE CONFERENCE. May 31, 2008; May 30, 2009. Contact: Reg A. Forder, Box 110390, Nashville TN 37222. Toll-free (800)21-WRITE. E-mail: ACWriters@aol.com. Website: www.ACWriters.com. Attendance: 40-80.

KENTUCKY CHRISTIAN WRITERS' CONFERENCE. Elizabethtown; June 20-21, 2008. Contact: Judy Sliger, registrar, PMB 235, 803 N. Dixie Ave., Elizabethtown KY 42701. E-mail: registrar@kychristianwriters.com. Website: www.kychristianwriters.com. Keynote speaker: Karen Moore Artl. Editors in attendance. Workshops and appointments with editors. Attendance: 100.

MARYLAND

AMERICAN CHRISTIAN WRITERS BALTIMORE CONFERENCE. April 5, 2008; March 21, 2009. Contact: Reg Forder, Box 110390, Nashville TN 37222. Toll-free (800)21-WRITE. E-mail: ACWriters@aol.com. Website: www.ACWriters.com. Attendance: 40-80.

SANDY COVE CHRISTIAN WRITERS CONFERENCE & MENTORING RETREAT. Sandy Cove/North East; September 28-October 1, 2008. Offers Advanced and Teen Tracks. Contact: Jim Watkins, Writers' Conference Director, Sandy Cove Ministries, 60 Sandy Cove Rd., North East MD 21901. Toll-free (800)234-2683. E-mail: info@sandycove.org. Website: www.sandycove.org/docs/writers.php. Editors and agents in attendance. Attendance: 150.

MASSACHUSETTS

CAPE COD ANNUAL SUMMER WRITERS' CONFERENCE and **YOUNG WRITERS' WORKSHOP** (ages 12-16). Craigville Conference Center; August 17-22, 2008. Contact: Jacqueline M. Loring, exec. dir., PO Box 408, Osterville MA 02655-0408. (508)420-0200. Fax (508)420-0212. E-mail: writers@capecodwriterscenter.org. Website: www.capecodwriterscenter.org. Offers an advanced track. Editors and agents in attendance. Weeklong workshops are $125; personal conferences $50; and manuscript evaluations $125 (also open to writers not attending the conference). Deadline for submissions is July 15. Attendance: 200. Young Writers Workshop runs concurrent with conference.

MICHIGAN

ACW DETROIT CONFERENCE. Detroit; fall 2008. Contact: Pam Perry, pres., 33011 Tall Oaks, Farmington MI 48336. (248)426-2300. Fax (248)471-2422. E-mail: PamPerry@ministrymarketing.com. Website: www.ministrymarketing.com. Offers class/track for advanced writers. Attendance: 300. Editors/agents in attendance.

AMERICAN CHRISTIAN WRITERS GRAND RAPIDS CONFERENCE. June 20-21, 2008; June 26-27, 2009. Contact: Reg Forder, Box 110390, Nashville TN 37222. Toll-free (800)21-WRITE. E-mail: ACWriters@aol.com. Website: www.ACWriters.com. Attendance: 40-80.

+FAITHWRITERS CONFERENCE. Livonia (Detroit area); August 8-9, 2008. Contact: Scott Lindsay. E-mail: support@faithwriters.com. Website: www.faithwriters.com/conference.php. Attendance: 200.

MARANATHA CHRISTIAN WRITERS SEMINAR. Maranatha Bible & Missionary Conference/Muskegon; September 2008. Contact: Maranatha, 4759 Lake Harbor Rd., Muskegon MI 49441-5299. (231)798-2161. E-mail: info@maranatha-bmc.org. Website: www.WriteWithPurpose.org. Editors in attendance. Attendance: 50.

ORIGINAL & ADVANCED SPEAK UP WITH CONFIDENCE SEMINARS. Cornerstone University, Grand Rapids MI, June 2008; Western Seminary, Portland OR, March 2008 (see separate listing). For details & to register, go to: www.carolkent.org, click on "Speak Up Seminars." Contact: Carol Kent, 3141 Winged Foot Dr., Lakeland FL 33803-5437. Toll-free in U.S. (888)870-7719; outside U.S. (810)982-0898. Fax (810)987-4163. E-mail: Speakupinc@aol.com. Website: www.SpeakUpSpeakerServices.com. Speakers: Carol Kent, Jennie Afman Dimkoff, Bonnie Emmorey, Dr. Don & Anne Denmark, Ginger Shaw, and Kathe Wunnenberg. Speaking seminars. Offers advanced training and opportunities to be coached in small groups. Also offers a workshop on writing for speakers who write for publication. Offers seminars in other locations—see Website. Attendance: 100.

MINNESOTA

AMERICAN CHRISTIAN WRITERS MINNEAPOLIS CONFERENCE. August 8-9, 2008; August 14-15, 2009. Contact: Reg Forder, Box 110390, Nashville TN 37222. Toll-free (800)21-WRITE. Website: www.ACWriters.com. Attendance: 40-80.

MINNESOTA CHRISTIAN WRITERS SPRING & FALL SEMINARS. Minneapolis/St. Paul; spring seminar, March or April 2008; fall seminar, early November 2008. Contact: Delores Topliff, 6901 Ives Ln. N., Maple Gove MN 55369. (763)315-1014. E-mail: dtopliff@yahoo.com. Website: www.mnchristianwriters.org. No editors or agents in attendance. Attendance: 40.

THE WRITING ACADEMY SEMINAR. Mount Olivet Retreat Center outside Minneapolis; August 7-11, 2008. Sponsors year-round correspondence writing program and annual seminar in various locations. Contact: Mar Korman, 1128 Mule Lake Dr. N.E., Outing MN 56662. (218)792-5144. E-mail: jflz20@mcleodusa.net. Website: www.wams.org. Attendance: 30. Sponsors a contest open to nonattendees (rules are posted on Website).

WRITING SEMINARS/NORTH HENNEPIN COMMUNITY COLLEGE/WRITERS' CRUISE. Minneapolis; new classes every Monday and Thursday, year round. Instructor: Louise B. Wyly. Topics include Fiction I, II, III; children and teen writing; personal experiences; Beginning & Advanced; The Artist's Way; and memoirs. Now offers a Creative Writing Certificate. Attendance: 24 (2 classes each quarter). Contact: Louise Wyly, 6315—55th Ave. N., Apt. 219, Minneapolis MN 55428-3581. (763)533-6207. E-mail: Lsnowbunny@aol.com. Website: www.nhcc.edu (click on "Training and Development"); watch NHCC Bulletin for details, or call (612)424-0880 to inquire. Also sponsors a Writers' Alaskan Cruise; details available.

MISSOURI

AMERICAN CHRISTIAN WRITERS SPRINGFIELD CONFERENCE. August 16, 2008; August 22, 2009. Contact: Reg A. Forder, Box 110390, Nashville TN 37222. Toll-free (800)21-WRITE. E-mail: ACWriters@aol.com. Website: www.ACWriters.com. Attendance: 40-80.

HEART OF AMERICA CHRISTIAN WRITERS' NETWORK CONFERENCES. Kansas City, November 2008, Mentoring Retreat Spring 2008; check Website for dates of additional events. Contact: Mark and Jeanette Littleton, 3706 N.E. Shady Lane Dr., Gladstone MO 64119. Phone/fax (816)459-8016. E-mail: HACWN@earthlink.net. Website: www.HACWN.org. Offers classes for new and advanced writers. Has editors and agents in attendance. Contest details on brochure. Attendance: 150.

NEBRASKA

MY THOUGHTS EXACTLY WRITERS RETREAT. St. Benedict Retreat Center/Schuyler; October 2008. Contact: Cheryl Paden, PO Box 1073, Fremont NE 68026-1073. (402)727-6508. Geared toward the beginning writer. Attendance: 10.

NEVADA

AMERICAN CHRISTIAN WRITERS LAS VEGAS CONFERENCE. Las Vegas; October 25, 2008. Contact: Reg Forder, Box 110390, Nashville TN 37222. Toll-free (800)21-WRITE. E-mail: ACWriters@aol.com. Website: www.ACWriters.com. Attendance: 40-80.

NEW HAMPSHIRE

WRITERS WORKSHOPS BY MARY EMMA ALLEN. Taught as requested by writer's groups, conferences, schools, and libraries. Topics include: Workshops for Young Writers (for schools and home-parenting groups); Workshops for Teachers and Home-parenting Parents; Writing for Children Workshop; Travel Writing Workshop; Writing for Regional Markets; Poetry Writing Workshop; Writing Family History Workshop; Self-Publishing Workshop; Writer & the Internet Workshop; Writing for the Weekly Newspaper Workshop; Writing Columns for Newspaper, Magazine, and Online Publications; and Writing for Publication Workshop. Contact: Mary Emma Allen (instructor), 55 Binks Hill Rd., Plymouth NH 03264. (603)536-2641. Fax (603)536-4851. E-mail: me.allen@juno.com. Website: http://maryemmallen.blogspot.com.

NEW MEXICO

THE GLEN WORKSHOP. St. John's College/Santa Fe; July/August 2008. Includes fiction, poetry, nonfiction, memoir, on-site landscape painting, figure drawing, collage and mixed media, and several master classes. Contact: Gregory Wolfe, Image, 3307 Third Ave. W., Seattle WA 98119. (206)281-2988. Fax (206)281-2335. E-mail: glenworkshop@imagejournal.org. Website: www.imagejournal.org/glen. No editors/agents in attendance. Attendance: 200.

GLORIETA CHRISTIAN WRITERS' CONFERENCE. Glorieta (18 mile N. of Santa Fe); October 22-26, 2008; October 14-18, 2009. Editors and agents in attendance. Contact: Marita Littauer, 2201 San Pedro Dr. N.E., Bldg 1, Ste. 225, Albuquerque, NM 87110. Toll-free (800)433-6633. (505)899-4283. Fax (505)899-9282. E-mail: info@glorietaCWC.com. Website: www.glorietaCWC.com. Editors and agents in attendance. No scholarships. Attendance: 300-350.

SOUTHWEST WRITERS MINI WORKSHOPS. Albuquerque; various times during the year (check Website for dates). Contact: Wendy Bickel, 3721 Morris St. N.E., Ste. A, Albuquerque NM 87111-3611. (505)265-9485. E-mail: swwriters@juno.com. Website: www.southwest writers.com. General conference. Sponsors the Southwest Writers Contests annually and monthly (see Website). Agents and editors in attendance. Occasionally gives full scholarships. Attendance: 50.

NEW YORK

ANNUAL INTERNATIONAL CONFERENCE ON HUMOR, HOPE AND HEALING. Saratoga Springs; April 2008. General. Contact: The HUMOR Project Inc., 480 Broadway, Ste. 210, Saratoga Springs NY 12866. (518)587-8770. Toll-free fax (800)600-4242. E-mail: info@humorproject.com. Website: www.humorproject.com.

NORTH CAROLINA

AMERICAN CHRISTIAN WRITERS CHARLOTTE CONFERENCE. Marriott Executive Park; March 28-29, 2008. Contact: Reg Forder, Box 110390, Nashville TN 37222. Toll-free (800)21-WRITE. E-mail: ACWriters@aol.com. Website: www.ACWriters.com. Attendance: 40-80.

AMERICAN CHRISTIAN WRITERS GREENSBORO CONFERENCE. March 14, 2009. Contact: Reg A. Forder, Box 110390, Nashville TN 37222. Toll-free (800)21-WRITE. E-mail: AC Writers@aol.com. Website: www.ACWriters.com. Attendance: 40-80.

BLUE RIDGE MOUNTAIN CHRISTIAN WRITERS CONFERENCE. LifeWay Ridgecrest Conference Center; May 18-22, 2008. Contact: Ron Pratt, LifeWay Christian Resources, One Lifeway Plaza, Nashville TN 37234-0106. (615)251-2065. Fax (615)277-8232. E-mail: ron .pratt@lifeway.com, or Yvonne Lehman, PO Box 188, Black Mountain NC 28770. Website: www.lifeway.com/christianwriters. Editors and agents in attendance. Sponsors a contest & critiques. Attendance: 400+.

BONEFIRE! CRUISE 2008. April. Contact: Dr. Gail M. Hayes, PO Box 71017, Durham NC 27722-1017. (919)471-1783. E-mail: gmhayes@daughtersoftheking.org. Website; www .daughtersoftheking.org. Cruise open to all writers.

FAITH-BASED ARTS CONFERENCE. Durham; June 2008. Conference Director, PO Box 99374, Raleigh NC 27624-9374. E-mail: fbliterary@nc.rr.com. Website: www.fbfictionlovers.com. Editors & agents in attendance.

+SHE SPEAKS CONFERENCE. Charlotte; June 2008 (usually 3rd weekend). Contact: LeAnn Rice, Proverbs 31 Ministries, 616-G Matthews-Mint Hill Rd., Matthews NC 28105. (704)849-2270. Fax (704)849-7267. E-mail: office@Proverbs31.org. Website: www.SheSpeaksConference .com. Offers a track for advanced writers and teens. Sponsors an annual contest (theme varies). Speakers include: Lysa TerKeurst, Renee Swope, and acquisitions editors from major publishing houses. Editors & agents in attendance. Sometimes offers scholarships.

OHIO

AMERICAN CHRISTIAN WRITERS COLUMBUS CONFERENCE. June 6-7, 2008; June 12-13, 2009. Hosted by Columbus Christian Writers Assn./Pat Zell, (937)593-9207. Contact: Reg Forder, Box 110390, Nashville TN 37222. Toll-free (800)21-WRITE. E-mail: ACWriters@ aol.com. Website: www.ACWriters.com. Attendance: 40-80.

AMERICAN CHRISTIAN WRITERS DAYTON CONFERENCE. August 2, 2008; August 8, 2009. Contact: Reg A. Forder, Box 110390, Nashville TN 37222. Toll-free (800)21-WRITE. E-mail: ACWriters@aol.com. Website: www.ACWriters.com. Attendance: 40-80.

DAYTON CHRISTIAN WRITERS GUILD CONFERENCE. Dayton: July 11-12, 2008. Contact: Tina V. Toles, PO Box 251, Englewood OH 45322-2227. Phone/fax (937)836-6600. Cell: (937)371-6083. E-mail: daytonwriters@ureach.com. Website: www.dougtoles.com. Attendance 30-80.

NORTHWEST OHIO CHRISTIAN WRITERS SEMINAR. Toledo; September 2008. Contact: Linda Tippitt. E-mail: andamija@bex.net. No editors or agents in attendance. Attendance: 50.

PEN TO PAPER LITERARY SYMPOSIUM. Dayton; October 3-4, 2008. Contact: Valerie Coleman, Pen of the Writer, PMB 175—5523 Salem Ave., Dayton OH 45426. (937)307-0760. E-mail: info@penofthewriter.com. Website: www.penofthewriter.com. Editors and agents in attendance.

WRITE ON! WORKSHOPS. Dayton; March 29, 2008. Contact: Valerie Coleman, Pen of the Writer, PMB 175—5523 Salem Ave., Dayton OH 45426. (937)307-0760. E-mail: info@penofthewriter.com. Website: www.penofthewriter.com. Editors in attendance. Attendance: 25.

OKLAHOMA

AMERICAN CHRISTIAN WRITERS OKLAHOMA CITY CONFERENCE. La Quinta Hotel; February 22-23, 2008; February 27-28, 2009. Contact: Reg Forder, Box 110390, Nashville TN 37222. Toll-free (800)21-WRITE. E-mail: ACWriters@aol.com. Website: www.ACWriters.com. Attendance: 40-80.

OREGON

HEART TALK. A workshop for women beginning to speak or write for publication. Portland/Western Seminary; March 12-15, 2008 (speaking). Beverly Hislop, dir. of the Women's Center for Ministry. Contact: Women's Center for Ministry, Western Seminary, 5511 S.E. Hawthorne Blvd., Portland OR 97215-3367. (503)517-1931. Fax (503)517-1889. E-mail: wcm@westernseminary.edu. Website: www.westernseminary.edu/women. Attendance: 125. Editors and possibly agents in attendance. Offers partial scholarships based on need. Conference alternates between writing one year and speaking the next. The 2008 speaker's conference will keynote Carol Kent. Workshops and editors/publicists available for consultation. Check Website for details.

OREGON CHRISTIAN WRITERS COACHING CONFERENCE. Corban College, Salem; July 28-31, 2008. Website: www.OregonChristianWriters.org. Includes about 7 hours of training under a specific coach/topic. Offers advanced track. Editors and agents in attendance. Attendance: 250.

PENNSYLVANIA

GREATER PHILADELPHIA CHRISTIAN WRITERS' CONFERENCE. Philadelphia Biblical University, Langhorne; celebrating 25 years of ministry August 7-9, 2008. Founder and director: Marlene Bagnull, LittD, 316 Blanchard Rd., Drexel Hill, PA 19026-3507. Phone/fax (610)626-6833. E-mail: mbagnull@aol.com. Website: www.writehisanswer.com/Philadelphia. Conferees choose six hour-long workshops from 42 offered or a Fiction or Nonfiction Clinic (by application) plus one 6.5-hour continuing session from 7 offered. Nancy Rue and Angie Hunt (by application) offering Nangie U 202 and 404. One-on-one appointments, paid critiques, editors panels, and general sessions. Contest (registered conferees only) awards four $100 discounts off 2009 conference. Especially encourages African American writers. Faculty of 50-60 authors, editors, and agents. Attendance: 250.

+HIGHLIGHTS FOUNDATION FOUNDERS WORKSHOPS. Honesdale; dates unspecified. Contact: Kent Brown, Highlights Foundation, 814 Court St., Honesdale PA 18431. (570)253-1192. Fax (570)253-0179. E-mail: contact@highlightsfoundation.org. Website: www.HighlightsFoundation.org. Editors in attendance. Modest grants may be available. For children's writers. Targeted workshops that allow you to select a topic that fits your writing needs—from sports to nature, from magazine to books, from fiction to nonfiction, and from picture books to young adult novels. General.

HIGHLIGHTS FOUNDATION WRITERS WORKSHOP AT CHAUTAUQUA, July 12-19, 2008. Contact: Kent Brown, Highlights Foundation, 814 Court St., Honesdale PA 18431. (570)253-1192. Fax (570)253-0179. E-mail: contact@highlightsfoundation.org. Website: www.highlightsfoundation.org. For children's writers and illustrators. Week-long conference. Offers full and partial scholarships (applications received through January 2008). General.

MERCER COUNTY ANNUAL ONE-DAY WRITERS' WORKSHOP (sponsored by St. David's Writers' Conference); Stoneboro; April 19, 2008. Contact: Evelyn Minshull, 724 Airport Rd., Mercer PA 16137, (724)475-3239, eminshull@hotmail.com; or Gloria Clover, 26 Everbreeze Dr., Hadley PA 16130, (724)253-2635; gloworm@certainty.net. Websites: www.gloriaclover.com; www.stdavidswriters.com. Attendance: 140-180.

MONTROSE CHRISTIAN WRITERS CONFERENCE. Montrose; July 20-25, 2008. Contact: Patti Souder, c/o Montrose Bible Conference, 5 Locust St., Montrose PA 18801-1112. (570)278-1001. Fax (570)278-3061. E-mail: mbc@montrosebible.org/writers.htm. Website: www.montrosebible.org. Tracks for advanced writers and teens. Editors & agents in attendance. Attendance: 90. Provides a few partial scholarships.

REVWRITER WRITERS CONFERENCE. Bucks County; no decision yet made on holding this conference in 2008. Contact: RevWriter, Rev. Susan M. Lang, PO Box 81, Perkasie PA 18944. (215)453-5066. Fax (215)453-8128. E-mail: sue@revwriter.com. Website: www.revwriter.com.

ST. DAVIDS CHRISTIAN WRITERS' CONFERENCE. Grove City College, Grove City; June 2008. Offers writer's retreat and a special pastor's day. Contest in 10 categories for attendees only. Lora Zill, director. Contact: Audrey Stallsmith, registrar, 87 Pines Rd. E., Hadley PA 16130-1019. (724)253-2738. Fax (724)946-3689. E-mail: registrar@stdavidswriters.com. Website: www.stdavidswriters.com. Attendance: 70.

SUSQUEHANNA VALLEY WRITERS SATURDAY WORKSHOP. Lewisburg; April 2008. Contact: Marsha Hubler. (570)837-0002. Website: www.marshahubler.com.

WEST BRANCH CHRISTIAN WRITERS MINI-CONFERENCE. Montoursville; October 25, 2008 (tentative). Contact: Roberta Updegraff, 332 S. Pine Run Rd., Linden PA 17744. (570)584-2280. E-mail: bobbiup@suscom.net. Editors in attendance. Classes geared for beginners, but includes classes for more experienced. Also sponsors a contest (personal essay, poetry, nonfiction, devotional). Attendance: 90.

TENNESSEE

AMERICAN CHRISTIAN WRITERS MEMPHIS CONFERENCE. March 15, 2008; April 18, 2009. Contact: Reg A. Forder, Box 110390, Nashville TN 37222. Toll-free (800)21-WRITE. E-mail: ACWriters@aol.com. Website: www.ACWriters.com. Attendance: 40-80.

AMERICAN CHRISTIAN WRITERS MENTORING RETREAT. Nashville; May 9-10, 2008; May 15-16, 2009. Contact: Reg Forder, Box 110390, Nashville TN 37222. Toll-free (800)21-WRITE. E-mail: ACWriters@aol.com. Website: www.ACWriters.com. Attendance: 40-80.

COLLEGIATE JOURNALISM CONFERENCE. Nashville; October 2008 (usually 1st or 2nd weekend). Contact: Debbie Vann, (615)782-8664. E-mail: dvann@sbc.net. Website: www.bpnews.net/journalism. Attendance: 120-150.

TEXAS

ACFW NATIONAL CONFERENCE. Dallas; September 18-21,2008 (usually third week). Contact: ACFW Conference Committee, PO Box 101066, Palm Bay FL 32910-1066. (574)370-0988. E-mail: pr@acfw.com. Website: www.acfw.com. Offers advanced track. Contest. Speaker 2008: Angela Hunt. Editors & agents in attendance. Attendance: 400.

AMERICAN CHRISTIAN WRITERS DALLAS CONFERENCE. Dallas North; February 15-16, 2008; February 20-21, 2009. Contact: Reg Forder, Box 110390, Nashville TN 37222. Toll-free (800)21-WRITE. E-mail: ACWriters@aol.com. Website: www.ACWriters.com. Attendance: 40-80.

+AMERICAN CHRISTIAN WRITERS HOUSTON CONFERENCE. February 14, 2009. Contact: Reg Forder, Box 110390, Nashville TN 37222. Toll-free (800)21-WRITE. E-mail: AC Writers@aol.com. Website: www.ACWriters.com. Attendance: 40-80.

AUSTIN CHRISTIAN WRITERS' WORKSHOP. February 2008. Contact: Lin Harris, 129 Fox Hollow Cove, Cedar Creek TX 78612-4844. (512)601-2216. Fax (240)208-3201. E-mail: linharris@austin.rr.com. Attendance: 100.

EAST TEXAS CHRISTIAN WRITERS CONFERENCE. Marshall/East Texas Baptist University; June 6-7, 2008 (1st Friday & Saturday of June annually). Contact: Dr. Jerry Hopkins, East Texas Baptist University, 1209 N. Grove St., Marshall TX 75670. (903)923-2083. E-mail: Jhopkins@ETBU.edu. Website: www.ETBU.edu/news/CWC/default.htm.

+ECPA CHRISTIAN BOOK EXPO DALLAS 2009. Dallas; March 20-22, 2009. This event, a first for the Evangelical Christian Publishers Association, will bring together publishers, authors, and consumers. ECPA is inviting publishers, ministries, authors, and booksellers to exhibit in this open-to-the-public event. For more information, contact Mark Kuyper, (480)966-3998.

INSPIRATIONAL WRITERS ALIVE!/AMARILLO SEMINAR. March 29, 2008 (always first Saturday after Easter). Contact: Jerry McClenagan, 6808 Cloud Crest, Amarillo TX 79124. (806) 355-7117. E-mail: jerrydalemc@sbcglobal.net. Attendance: 50. Sponsors an annual contest.

NORTH TEXAS CHRISTIAN WRITERS' CONFERENCE. Keller; September 12-13, 2008 (second Friday & Saturday after Labor Day). Contact: Frank Ball, NTCW Conference, Cross Timbers Community Church Keller Campus, 1000 Randol Mill Ave., Roanoke TX 76262. (817) 915-1688. E-mail: frank.ball@ntchristianwriters.com. Website: www.ntchristianwriters .com. Speakers: Cecil Murphey & Judy Bodmer. No editors or agents in attendance. Offers partial scholarships. Sponsors a contest for conference registrants only. Attendance: 250.

TEXAS CHRISTIAN WRITERS CONFERENCE. Houston; August 2, 2008. Contact: Martha Rogers, 6038 Greenmont, Houston TX 77092-2332. (713)686-7209. E-mail: martha lrogers@sbcglobal.net. Website: www.martharogers.com. Editors & agents in attendance. Sponsors a contest: Inspirational Writers Alive! Open Competition; May 15 deadline. Attendance: 70. If you want to start another group in Texas, contact Martha Rogers.

YWAM HANDS-ON SCHOOL OF WRITING AND WRITERS TRAINING WORKSHOPS. Lindale; September-December 2008. Contact: Carol Scott, PO Box 1380, Lindale TX 75771-1380. (903)882-9663. Fax (903)882-1161. E-mail: writing@ywamwoodcrest.com. Website: www.ywamwoodcrest.com. List of workshops on Website or for SASE. Attendance: 10-20.

UTAH

+AMERICAN CHRISTIAN WRITERS SALT LAKE CITY CONFERENCE. September 20, 2008; September 19, 2009. Contact: Reg Forder, Box 110390, Nashville TN 37222. Toll-free (800)21-WRITE. E-mail: ACWriters@aol.com. Website: www.ACWriters.com. Attendance: 40-80.

WASHINGTON

AMERICAN CHRISTIAN WRITERS SPOKANE CONFERENCE. September 26-27, 2008; September 25-26, 2009. Contact: Reg Forder, Box 110390, Nashville TN 37222. Toll-free (800)21-WRITE. E-mail: ACWriters@aol.com. Website: www.ACWriters.com. Attendance: 40-80.

IMAGE FESTIVAL OF LITERATURE AND THE ARTS. Conference for 2008 unconfirmed. Contact: Julie Mullins, Program Director, Image, 3307 Third Ave. W., Seattle WA 98119. (206) 281-2988. Fax (206)281-2335. E-mail: Image@imagejournal.org. Website: www.image journal.org.

NORTHWEST CHRISTIAN WRITERS RENEWAL (formerly Seattle Pacific Writer's Renewal), Northshore Baptist Church, Bothell; May 2-3, 2008. Contact: Judy Bodmer, 11108 NE 141 Pl., Kirkland WA 98034. (425)488-2900. E-mail: conference@nwchristianwriters.org. Website: www.nwchristianwriters.org. Keynote speaker: Cecil Murphey. Editors and agents in attendance. Attendance: 125.

WRITER'S WEEKEND AT THE BEACH. Ocean Park; February 22-24, 2008. Contact: Birdie Etchison/Pat Rushford, PO Box 877, Ocean Park WA 98640-0877. (360)665-6576. E-mail: etchison@pacifier.com. Website: www.patriciarushford.com. (Registration form on Website.) Sponsors a limerick contest. Sometimes editors & agents in attendance. Offers scholarships for students. Attendance: 40-50.

WISCONSIN

GREEN LAKE CHRISTIAN WRITER'S CONFERENCE. Green Lake; early August 2008. Contact: Julie Miller or Pat Zimmer, Green Lake Conference Center, W2511 State Hwy. 23, Green Lake WI 54941-9300. Toll-free (800)558-8898. (920)294-7365. Fax (920)294-3848. E-mail for information: patzimmer@glcc.org. Website: www.glcc.org. Has editors & agents in attendance. Attendance: 50. Sponsors a contest. Also provides Christian Writer's Weeks when you can stay at the conference center for writing time; January, March, November (may vary).

+LIGHTHOUSE CHRISTIAN WRITERS FALL SEMINAR, Oconto; September 2008. Contact: Lois Wiederhoeft, 901 Aubin, PO Box 42, Peshtigo WI 54157. (715)582-1024. E-mail: 2loisann@myway.com. Website: www.mychristiansite.com/ministries/lhchristianwriters/fall.html.

WFCA ANNUAL SPRING CONFERENCE. Appleton; April 19, 2008. Contact: Andrea Boeshaar or Patti Wolf, Wisconsin Fellowship of Christian Authors, 803 Steeple Hill Rd., West Bend WI 53095. (414)355-5202. E-mail: andrea@andreaboeshaar.com. Website: www.wisconsin christianauthors.com. Register on Website. Special tracks for teens and advanced writers. No editors, some agents in attendance. Attendance: 50-75.

CANADA/FOREIGN

AMERICAN CHRISTIAN WRITERS CARIBBEAN CRUISE. November 29-December 7, 2008; November 28-December 5, 2009. Contact: Reg A. Forder, Box 110390, Nashville TN 37222. Toll-free (800)21-WRITE. E-mail: ACWriters@aol.com. Website: www.ACWriters.com. Attendance: 15-30.

+ASSOCIATION OF CHRISTIAN WRITERS (UK) MEMBERS CONFERENCE. Hoddesdon, Herts UK. Contact: Brian Vincent, dir., 31 Newlands Rd., Ruishton, Taunton, SOM., TA3 5J2, United Kingdom. Phone 01823-442 372. E-mail from Website: www.christianwriters.org.uk. Membership (900) open. Sponsors an occasional writers' weekend for members only. Next one in June 2009. Editors in attendance; no agents. No scholarships.

COMIX35 CHRISTIAN COMICS TRAINING SEMINAR. Various international locations & dates. Contact: Nathan Butler, PO Box 26747, Albuquerque NM 87125-7470. E-mail: comix35@comix35.org. Website: www.comix35.org. Speakers: Nate Butler & others. Often has editors in attendance; no agents. Attendance: 15-20. Sponsors a contest (details on Website).

+CRUISIN' FOR CHRIST. Caribbean cruise; August/September 2008. Contact: Kendra Norman-Bellamy (blessed_to_write@yahoo.com) E-mail: Cruisin_For_Christ@yahoo.com. Website: www.CruisinForChrist.homestead.com. Writing workshops onboard.

INSCRIBE CHRISTIAN WRITERS' FELLOWSHIP FALL CONFERENCE. Edmonton AB, Canada; September 2008. Contact: Eunice Matchett, 4304—45th St., Drayton Valley AB T7A 1G7, Canada. (780)542-7950. Fax (780)514-3702. E-mail: senappi@telusplanet.net. Website: www.inscribe.org (click on "Events"). Some editors in attendance, no agents. Runs two tracks: beginners and intermediate/advanced. Sponsors a fall contest open to nonmembers; details on Website. Attendance: 50.

LITTWORLD CONFERENCE. Sao Paulo, Brazil; November 2008 (held every two years on even years). Contact: John D. Maust, director, 351 S. Main Pl., Ste. 230, Carol Stream IL 60188-2455. (630)260-9063. Fax (630)260-9265. E-mail: MaiLittWorld@sbcglobal.net. Website: www.littworld.org. Editors in attendance. Attendance: 140.

WRITE! CANADA. Guelph, Ontario; June 2008. Contact: The Word Guild, PO Box 34, Port Perry ON L9L 1A2, Canada. (905)294-6482. Fax (905)471-6912. E-mail: events@thewordguild.com. Website: www.thewordguild.com. Hosted by The Word Guild, an association of Canadian writers and editors who are Christian. Editors and agents in attendance. Contests for attendees. Attendance: 240. Also sponsors one-day conferences in various Canadian cities.

WRITING SERVICES INSTITUTE (WSI)/MARSHA L. DRAKE, #109—4351 Rumble St., Burnaby BC V5J 2A2, Canada. Phone/fax (604)321-3555. Offers several correspondence and online courses: Write for Fun and Profit; Write for Success; Write Fiction from Plot to Print; Write with Power; Write for You; Magazine Article Writing; Write Yes!; Write Now; Young Author's Tutorial; Write Write—with Computers; and Write On! Write or e-mail for details and information on correspondence courses. Also writes company histories, biographies, résumés, and offers online tutorial. Charges negotiable fees for consultation, editing, and critique. See www.vsb-adult-ed.com for further information on courses and author biography.

CONFERENCES THAT CHANGE LOCATIONS

ACT ONE: SCREENWRITING WEEKENDS. See Website for dates and locations. Contact: Lauri Deason, conference coordinator, 2690 Beachwood Dr., Lower Fl., Hollywood CA 90068. (323)464-0815. Fax (323)468-0315. E-mail: info@ActOneProgram.com. Website: www.ActOneprogram.com. Open to anyone who is interested in learning more about the craft of screenwriting. Speakers vary: Sheryl Anderson, Thom Parham, Dean Batali, Chris & Kathy Riley. No editors or agents in attendance. Attendance: 75.

AMERICAN CHRISTIAN FICTION WRITERS CONFERENCE. Rotates cities; September (3rd weekend) 2008. Contact: Robin Miller, pres., PO Box 101066, Palm Bay FL 32910-1066. E-mail: pr@acfw.com. Website: www.ACFW.com. Offers an advanced track. Speaker 2008: Angela Hunt. Editors and agents in attendance. Sponsors 2 contests (details on Website). Offers 10 scholarships each year to ACFW members only.

AMERICAN CHRISTIAN WRITERS CONFERENCES. Various dates and locations (see individual states where held). Also sponsors an annual Caribbean cruise in November/December. Contact: Reg A. Forder, Box 110390, Nashville TN 37222. Toll-free (800)21-WRITE. E-mail: ACWriters@aol.com. Website: www.ACWriters.com. Attendance 30-40.

AUTHORIZEME. Various locations and dates. Contact: Sharon Norris Elliott, PO Box 1519, Inglewood CA 90308-1519. (310)508-9860. Fax (323)567-8557. E-mail: AuthorizeMe@

sbcglobal.net. Website: www.AuthorizeMe.net. AuthorizeMe is a 12-hour, hands-on seminar that teaches you how to get your book idea out of your head, down onto paper, and into a professional book proposal. Seminars offered nationwide. For a list of scheduled seminars, or to sponsor a seminar in your area, check Website.

CATHOLIC PRESS ASSOCIATION ANNUAL CONVENTION. Location unannounced; late May or early June 2008. Contact: Thomas Conway, exec. dir., 3555 Veterans Memorial Hwy., Unit O, Ronkonkoma NY 11779-7636. (631)471-4730. Fax (631)471-4804. E-mail: cathjour@catholicpress.com. Website: www.catholicpress.org. For media professionals. Annual book awards. Attendance: 400.

CHILDREN'S AUTHORS' BOOTCAMPS. Held in several locations each year; various dates. General. Contact: Bootcamp c/o Linda Arms White, PO Box 231, Allenspark CO 80510. Phone/fax (303)747-1014. E-mail: CABootcamp@msn.com. Website: www.WeMakeWriters.com. Upcoming dates and details on Website.

CHRISTIAN LEADERS AND SPEAKERS SEMINARS (The CLASSeminar). Sponsors several seminars across the country each year. Check Website for CLASSeminar dates and locations. For anyone who wants to improve their communication skills for either the spoken or written word, for professional or personal reasons. Speakers: Florence Littauer and Marita Littauer. Contact: Marita Littauer, 2201 San Pedro Dr. N.E., Bldg. 1, Ste. 225, Albuquerque, NM 87110-4133. (505) 899-4283. Fax (505) 899-9282. E-mail: info@classervices.com. Website: www.classervices.com. Attendance: 75-100.

EVANGELICAL PRESS ASSOCIATION CONVENTION, Portland OR (held in different location each year), May 7-9, 2008; Indianapolis IN, May 6-8, 2009. Contact: Doug Trouten, dir., PO Box 28129, Crystal MN 55428. (763)535-4793. Fax (763)535-4794. E-mail: director@epassoc.org. Website: www.epassoc.org. Attendance: 300-400. Annual convention for editors of evangelical periodicals; freelance communicators welcome.

+THE EXPERTIZING WORKSHOP. Held in Boston, New York, and San Francisco; every 3 mos. (October, January, April, July). Contact: Alyza Harris, Expertizing.com, PO Box 590239, Newton MA 02459. (617)630-0945. E-mail: Alyza@Expertizing.com, or alyza@PublishingGame.com. Website: www.Expertizing.com, or www.Expertizing.com/forum.htm. Learn how to get more media attention for your book and business. Speaker: Fern Reiss. Attendance: Limited to 6.

INTERNATIONAL CHRISTIAN RETAIL SHOW. Orlando FL (held in a different location each year); July 13-17, 2008. Contact: CBA, Box 62000, Colorado Springs CO 80962-2000. Toll-free (800)252-1950. (719)265-9895. Website: www.cbaonline.org. Entrance badges available through book publishers or Christian bookstores. Attendance: 14,000. Future dates: July 12-16, 2009, Denver CO, Colorado Convention Center.

JERRY B. JENKINS CHRISTIAN WRITERS GUILD. PO Box 88196, Black Forest CO 80908. Toll-free (866)495-5177. Fax (719)495-5181. E-mail: contactus@christianwritersguild.com. Website: www.christianwritersguild.com. Owned by Jerry B. Jenkins, author of the Left Behind series. Students enrolled in correspondence courses are personally mentored by seasoned professional writers or editors. The Guild also offers annual memberships, a critique service, associated benefits (advocacy, supplemental insurance, etc.), conferences, and contests. Call for a Free Starter Kit.

MENTORING CLINICS WITH CECIL MURPHEY. Various dates & locations. Contact: Cecil Murphey. (678)694-1111. E-mail: cec_haraka@msn.com. Participants must have a manuscript in process and a laptop computer with a USB port. Limited to 8 students.

THE PUBLISHING GAME WORKSHOP. Various cities throughout the year (check Website for dates and locations). Workshops held every 3 mos. (September, December, March, and June). Contact: Alyza Harris, Peanut Butter and Jelly Press, PO Box 590239, Newton MA 02459. Phone/fax (617)630-0945. E-mail: info@PublishingGame.com, or Alyza@publishinggame.com. Website:

www.PublishingGame.com (dates, locations, and registration forms on Website). Speaker: Fern Reiss. Editors and agents in attendance. Attendance: limited to 18.

SPAN's SMALL PUBLISHERS MARKETING CONFERENCE. Sponsored by the Small Publishers Assn. of North America. A marketing-specific, information-packed conference for authors, self-publishers, and independent presses. Contact: Scott Flora, 1618 W. Colorado Ave., Colorado Springs CO 80904-4029. (719)475-1726. Fax (719)471-2182. E-mail: scott@spannet.org. Website: www.SPANnet.org/conference.htm. Check Website to see if being held during 2008.

WINSUN COMMUNICATIONS WRITING SEMINARS/MARK LITTLETON. Various dates and locations. Available for your conference at your location. Contact: Mark Littleton, WINSUN Communications, 3706 N.E. Shady Lane Dr., Gladstone MO 64119. Phone/fax: (816)459-8016. E-mail: mlittleton@earthlink.net.

"WRITE HIS ANSWER" SEMINARS & RETREATS. Various locations around U.S.; dates throughout the year; a choice of focus on periodicals or books (includes self-publishing or mastering the craft). Contact: Marlene Bagnull, LittD, 316 Blanchard Rd., Drexel Hill PA 19026-3507. Phone/fax (610)626-6833. E-mail: mbagnull@aol.com. Website: www.writehisanswer.com/Writing_Seminars.htm. Attendance: 20-60. One- and two-day seminars by the author of *Write His Answer: A Bible Study for Christian Writers.*

AREA CHRISTIAN WRITERS' CLUBS, FELLOWSHIP GROUPS, AND CRITIQUE GROUPS

(+) A plus sign before a listing indicates a new listing.

ALABAMA

CHRISTIAN FREELANCERS. Tuscaloosa. Contact: Joanne Sloan, 4195 Waldort Dr., Northport AL 35473. (205)333-8603. E-mail: cjosloan@bellsouth.net. Membership (25) open.

OAKWOOD COLLEGE LITERARY GUILD/ACW CHAPTER. Huntsville. Contact: Dr. Cicely Daly, 3903 Nelson Dr. N.W., Huntsville AL 35810-3919. (256)852-8656. Fax (256)726-7042. E-mail: cdaly@oakwood.edu. Membership (12) open. Sponsors a seminar, usually first week of December at Oakwood College.

ARIZONA

EAST VALLEY CHRISTIAN WRITERS. Mesa. Contact: Brenda Jackson, 519 E. 8th Ave., Mesa AZ 85204. E-mail: BrendaAtTheRanch@yahoo.com. Membership (8) open.

+FOUNTAIN HILLS CHRISTIAN WRITERS GROUP. Contact: Jewell Johnson, 14223 N. Westminster Pl., Fountain Hills AZ 85268. (480)836-8968. E-mail: tykeJ@juno.com. Membership (16-25) open. ACW Chapter.

ARKANSAS

LITTLE ROCK/ACW CHAPTER. Little Rock. Contact: Carole Geckle, 5800 Ranch Rd., Little Rock AR 72223. (501)228-2477. E-mail: cgeckle@familylife.com. Membership (20) open.

SILOAM SPRINGS WRITERS. Contact: Rosemary M. Matthews, 2626 S. Mount Olive, Siloam Springs AR 72761-2658. (479)524-3506. E-mail: Rosie1st2000@yahoo.com. Membership (28) open. Periodically sponsors a contest open to nonmembers, and a seminar in September.

CALIFORNIA

BAY AREA WRITERS CRITIQUE GROUP. Fremont. Contact: Dianne Smith, 55 Montalban Dr., Fremont CA 94536-1679. (510)791-7804. E-mail: dmsfremont55@sbcglobal.net. Membership (6) open to experienced writers only.

CASTRO VALLEY CHRISTIAN WRITERS GROUP. Contact: Pastor Jon Drury, 19300 Redwood Rd., Castro Valley CA 94546-3465. (510)886-6300. E-mail: jdrury@redwoodchapel.org. Website: www.christianwriter.org. Membership (10) open. Sponsoring a Christian Writers Seminar, February 22-23, 2008; February 2009. Keynote speaker 2008: Karen O'Connor.

CHINO VALLEY CHRISTIAN WRITERS CRITIQUE GROUP. Chino. Contact: Nancy I. Sanders, 6361 Prescott Ct., Chino CA 91710-7105. (909)590-0226. E-mail: jeffandnancys@gmail.com. Website: www.nancyisanders.com. Membership (15) open. This group wrote a book called *Writing to Give God the Glory: A Potpourri of Devotions, Encouragement, & Tips for the Christian Who Writes.* Available at www.stuartmarket.com.

CHRISTIAN WRITERS' GROUP INTERNATIONAL. Santa Anna. Contact: Penelope Alexander, PO Box 1122, Huntington Beach CA 92647-1122. (714)979-3098. Membership (1) open.

+CHRISTIAN WRITERS GUILD OF SANTA BARBARA. Contact: Opal Mae Dailey, (805)682-0316/(805)252-9822. E-mail:opalmaedailey@aol.com, or cwfsb@sbcglobal.net. Meets monthly. Membership open.

+CHRISTIAN WRITERS NETWORK. Paradise (near Chico). Contact: Cornelia Dresser (530)872-5597/connied@copper.net; or Barbara Larsen (530)872-5119. Membership open.

DIABLO VALLEY CHRISTIAN WRITERS GROUP. Danville. Marcy Weydemuller, leader. Contact: Cynthia Herrmann, 65 S. "C" St., Tracy CA 95376. (209)607-5118. E-mail: cherrmn@pacbell.net. Membership (10-14) open.

HIGH DESERT CHRISTIAN WRITERS GUILD. Quartz Hill. Contact: Don Patterson, 6223 Almond Valley Way, Quartz Hill CA 93536. (661)722-5695. E-mail: don@theology.edu. Website: www.theology.edu/writers. Membership (30) open. Presents the Sable Quill-Pacesetter Award each year to the writer in the group who has shown the most progress or professional achievement. Cosponsors the Antelope Valley Christian Writers Conference, May 2-3, 2008.

+LODI WRITERS ASSOCIATION, (general membership, not just Christian). Contact: Dee Porter, PMB 265, 1030 S. Huttchins St. #4, Lodi CA 95240-5251. Phone/fax (209)334-0603. E-mail: crcomm@lodinet.com. Membership (70) open. Sponsors a one-day seminar.

NOVEL IDEA CHRISTIAN WRITERS SWARM. Norwalk/Cerritos. Contact: Derrell B. Thomas, 11239½ Ferina St., Norwalk CA 90650-5507. (562)292-9997. E-mail: derrell.writer@gmail.com. Membership (15) open.

ORANGE COUNTY CHRISTIAN WRITERS FELLOWSHIP. Various groups meeting throughout the county. Contact: Peggy Matthews Rose (editor@occwf.org) or write OCCWF, PO Box 982, Lake Forest CA 92630. Membership (200+) open. Annual membership includes a bimonthly newsletter, information on local critique groups, advance notice of writing opportunities through an e-mail list, and reduced fees for annual Spring Writer's Day (usually on a Saturday in April; see Website for details). Conference includes keynote speakers, workshops, and consultations. See Website for details: www.occwf.org.

PEGGY LESLIE'S CRITIQUE GROUP/SAN DIEGO CHRISTIAN WRITERS GUILD. El Cajon. Contact: Peggy Leslie, 329 Quail Run, El Cajon CA 92019. (619)447-6258. E-mail: gnpleslie@cox.net. Website: www.sandiegocwg.org. Membership (6) open.

SACRAMENTO CHRISTIAN WRITERS. Citrus Heights. Contact: Beth Miller Self, 2012 Rushing River Ct., Elverta CA 95626-9756. (916)992-8709. E-mail: cwbself@msn.com. Website: www.scwriters.org. Membership (25) open. Sponsors a contest. Sponsors a seminar every 5 years; the next one, in 2010, will be their 30th anniversary as a group.

SAN DIEGO COUNTY CHRISTIAN WRITERS' GUILD. Contact: Jennie & Robert Gillespie, PO Box 270403, San Diego CA 92198. (760)294-3269. E-mail: info@sandiegocwg.org. Website: www.sandiegocwg.org. Membership (100+) open. To join their Internet newsgroup, e-mail your name and address to: info@sandiegocwg.com. Sponsors 10 critique groups, fall seminar (September 2008), and spring awards banquet.

SANTA CLARA VALLEY CHRISTIAN WRITER'S GROUP. Cupertino. Contact: Richard M. Hinz, 550 S. 4th St., Apt. E, San Jose CA 95112, (408)297-3336, Rickhinz@yahoo.com. Or, Bob Schaetzle, (408)739-9516, heb_6@hotmail.com. Membership (14) open.

S.C.U.M. San Leandro. Contact: John B. Olson, 1261 Estrudillo Ave., San Leandro CA 94577. (510)357-4441. E-mail: johno@litany.com. Membership (12) open.

+SECRET GARDEN WRITERS GROUP, Castro Valley CA. Contact: Susy Flory or Gini Monroe. (510)828-5360. E-mail: irishbreakfast@comcast.net. Membership (8) open.

SONRISE CHRISTIAN WRITERS. East of Sacramento. Contact: Marlys Norris, PO Box 5144, Fair Oaks CA 95628. (916)961-0575. E-mail: marlysj@sbcglobal.net. Membership (10) open.

SOUTH VALLEY CHRISTIAN WRITERS/ACW CHAPTER. Group connects by e-mail only. Contact: Mary E. Kirk, 2151 Sunnyside Ave., #123, Clovis CA 93611-4023. (559)298-2715. E-mail: mkirk81@sbcglobal.net. Membership open.

TEMECULA CHRISTIAN WRITERS CRITIQUE GROUP. Contact: Rebecca Farnbach, 41403 Bitter Creek Ct., Temecula CA 92591-1545. (951)699-5148. Fax (951)699-4208. E-mail: sunbrook@hotmail.com. Membership (12) open. Part of San Diego Christian Writers Guild.

+WORDSMITHS (Professional Christian writers). Montclair. Contact: Nancy I. Sanders, 6361 Prescott Ct., Chino CA 91710-7105. E-mail: jeffandnancys@gmail.com. Membership (6) open (contact for membership information).

+THE WRITE BUNCH. Stockton. Contact: Shirley Cook, 3123 Sheridan Way, Stockton CA 95219. (209)477-8375. E-mail: shirleymcp@sbcglobal.net. Membership (7) open.

COLORADO

WORDS FOR THE JOURNEY CHRISTIAN WRITERS GUILD/ROCKY MOUNTAIN REGION. Parker. Contact: Sharen Watson, (303)346-9784. E-mail: sharen@wordsforthejourney.org. Website: www.wordsforthejourney.org. Membership (100+) open. See separate listing for Texas region.

DELAWARE

DELMARVA CHRISTIAN WRITERS' FELLOWSHIP. Georgetown. Contact: Candy Abbott, PO Box 777, Georgetown DE 19947-0777. (302)856-6649. Fax (302)856-7742. E-mail: candy.abbott@verizon.net. Website: www.delmarvawriters.com. Membership (36) open.

FLORIDA

ADVENTURES IN CHRISTIAN WRITING. Orlando. Contact: Joanna Adicks Wallace, 1107 E. Amelia St., Orlando FL 32803-5327. (407)841-2157. E-mail: joannaw@quixnet.net. Membership (20) open.

BRANDON CHRISTIAN WRITERS/ACW CHAPTER. Contact: Ruth C. Ellinger, 1405 S. Lithia Pinecrest Rd., Brandon FL 33511-6719. (813)685-7387. E-mail: Writer@Ruthellinger.com. Membership (10) open.

BROWARD ACW CHAPTER. Coral Springs. Contact: Lynne Cooper Sitton, 105 N.W. 104th Ter., Coral Springs FL 33071-7364. (954)341-2627. Chapter of ACW South Florida. E-mail: LynneCSitton@cs.com. Membership (10) open. Website: http://groups.yahoo.com/group/ACWSouthFlorida.

HOBE SOUND WRITERS GROUP/ACW CHAPTER; Hobe Sound. Contact: Faith Tofte, 9342 Bethel Way, Hobe Sound FL 33455. (772)545-4023. E-mail: faithtofte@bellsouth.net. Membership (5) open.

MIAMI-DADE ACW CHAPTER. Miami. Contact: Pat Fulton, Bird Road Community Church, 8476 Bird Rd., Miami FL 33155-3226. E-mail: patful01@msn.com. Chapter of ACW South Florida. Membership (20-25) open. Meetings alternate locations with Broward Chapter. Website: http://groups.yahoo.com/group/ACWSouthFlorida.

MID-FLORIDA CHRISTIAN WRITERS. Winter Garden. Contact: Joy Shelton, 1040 Glensprings Ave., Winter Garden FL 34787. (407)654-9076. Fax (407)654-9079. E-mail: JoySprinkles@aol.com. Membership (10) open.

SUNCOAST CHRISTIAN WRITERS. Clearwater. Contact: Elaine Creasman, 13014—106th Ave. N., Largo FL 33774-5602. Phone/fax (727)595-8963. E-mail: emcreasman@aol.com. Membership (10) open.

WORD WEAVERS. Longwood. Contact: Eva Marie Everson, 122 Fairway Ten Dr., Casselberry FL 32707-4823. (407)414-8188. E-mail: PenNhnd@aol.com. Membership (50+) open. Yearly contest for members. Planning a conference for February 2008 in Lake Yale.

GEORGIA

ATLANTA CHRISTIAN WRITERS/ACW CHAPTER. Contact: Susan Schreer Davis, 3750 Apple Way, Marietta GA 30066. (770)971-2381. E-mail: sschreer@bellsouth.net. Membership (15) open.

CENTRAL GEORGIA CHRISTIAN WRITERS. Meets online only. Contact: Judy Davis, 100 Wesleyan Dr., Warner Robins GA 31093. (478)922-5599. E-mail: JudyPDoris@cox.net. Website: http://cgcwriters.blogspot.com. Membership (20) open.

CHRISTIAN AUTHORS GUILD. Woodstock. Contact: Mike Anderson, PO Box 2673, Woodstock GA 30188. (770)928-2588. Fax (770)924-6935. E-mail: info@christianauthorsguild.org. Website: www.christianauthorsguild.org. Membership (66) open. Sponsors a contest and an annual fall conference in October.

EAST METRO ATLANTA CHRISTIAN WRITERS/ACW CHAPTER. Covington. Contact: Colleen Jackson, PO Box 2896, Covington GA 30015. (404)444-7514. E-mail: cjac401992@aol.com. Website: www.emacw.org. Membership (35) open. Sponsoring a seminar; date and location to be decided.

GEORGIA WRITERS ASSN./CHRISTIAN WRITERS POD. Woodstock/Marietta. Contact: Lloyd Blackwell, 3049 Scott Rd. N.E., Marietta GA 30066. (770)421-1203. E-mail: lloydblackwell@worldnet.att.net. Membership (63) open. Meets twice monthly. Sponsors a contest, an annual cooperative published book, and a seminar in September.

NORTHEAST GEORGIA WRITERS. Gainesville. Contact: Elouise Whitten, 660 Crestview Ter., Gainesville GA 30501-3110. (770)532-3007. E-mail: elouisewhitten@netzero.net. Membership (38) open. Sponsors contest open to members. Sponsors a conference in even years at Brenau University in Gainsville.

IDAHO

+ACW SANDPOINT. Contact: Anita Aurit, 403 Louis Ln., Sandpoint ID 83864. (208)610-0626. E-mail: AnitaAurit@gmail.com. Website: www.heroes.com/ACW.htm. Group blog: http://acwsandpoint.blogspot.com. Membership open.

INDIANA

OPEN DOOR CHRISTIAN WRITERS. Westport. Contact: Janet Teitsort, PO Box 129, Westport IN 47283-0129. Phone/fax (812)591-2210. E-mail: Janetteitsort@comcast.net. Membership (12) open.

IOWA

APPLES OF GOLD WRITERS OF IOWA. Marion. Contact: Kimn Swenson Gollnick, 550 Edinburgh Ave., Marion IA 52302-5614. (319)373-2302. E-mail: kimn.gollnick@gmail.com. Website: www.KIMN.net. Membership (10-12) open.

CEDAR RAPIDS CHRISTIAN WRITER'S GROUP. Contact: Susan Fletcher, 513 Knollwood Dr. S.E., Cedar Rapids IA 52403. (319)365-9844. E-mail: skmcfate@msn.com. Membership (4) open.

+CHRISTIAN WRITERS FELLOWSHIP OF OSKALOOSA. Contact: Judith Vander Wege, 808 Penn Blvd., Oskaloosa IA 52577. (641)673-5071. E-mail: judithvanderwege@mahaska.org. Membership open (new group). For critique, encouragement, and motivation.

KANSAS

CHRISTIAN WRITERS FELLOWSHIP. Girard. Contact: Deborah Vogts, 17300 Ness Rd., Erie KS 66733. (620)244-5619. E-mail: debvogts@gmail.com. Website: www.ChristianWriters Fellowship.blogspot.com. Membership (35) open. Sponsors a contest and a seminar April 4-5, 2008 (see separate listing).

+CREATIVE WRITERS FELLOWSHIP: North Newton, Hesston, Moundridge. Contact: Esther Groves, 405 West Bluestem, Apt. H4, North Newton KS 67117-8069. Membership (20) open.

KENTUCKY

JACKSON CHRISTIAN WRITERS CLUB. Vancleave. Contact: Donna Woodring, PO Box 10, Vancleve KY 41385-0010. (606)693-5000, ext. 174. E-mail: donnaw@kmbc.edu. Membership (5) open. Meets occasionally.

LOUISVILLE CHRISTIAN WRITERS/ACW CHAPTER. Contact: Lana Jackson, pres., 8516 Missionary Ct., Louisville KY 40291-4436. (502)968-3602. E-mail: LanaHJackson@insight bb.com. Website: www.LCWriters.com. Membership (22) open.

LOUISIANA

SOUTHERN CHRISTIAN WRITERS GUILD. Mandeville. Contact: Grace Booth or Marlaine Peachey, 806 Harmony Ln., Mandeville LA 70471. (985)626-4282. Fax (985)624-3108. E-mail: mpeachey@cityofmandeville.com. Website under construction. Membership (15) open (rebuilding group after hurricane). Presents quarterly workshops. Dues $25/yr.

MAINE

MAINE FELLOWSHIP OF CHRISTIAN WRITERS. China. Contact: Beth Rogers, 720 Essex St., Bangor ME 04401. (207)942-1616. E-mail: BethR58@aol.com. Membership (15) open.

MARYLAND

ANNAPOLIS FELLOWSHIP OF CHRISTIAN WRITERS. Annapolis. Contact: Jeri Sweany, 3107 Ervin Ct., Annapolis MD 21403-4620. (410)267-0924. Membership (10-15) open.

BALTIMORE AREA CHRISTIAN WRITERS/ACW CHAPTER. Owings Mills. Contact: Theresa Wilson, PO Box 47182, Windsor Mill MD 21244-3571. (443)804-3435. E-mail: acwriters group@aol.com. Website: www.writersinthemarketplace.org. Membership (27) open. Local host for ACW conference, April 5, 2008.

+MCC WRITERS' GROUP. Joppa. Contact: Virginia Colclasure or Dawn Sexton, c/o Mountain Christian Church, 1824 Mountain Rd., Joppa MD 21085. (410)877-1824. E-mail: Vcolclasure @clearviewcatv.net. Spring & fall writing seminars. Sponsors breakaway critique groups. Membership open.

THIRD SATURDAY CHRISTIAN WRITERS GROUP. Howard County. Contact: Claire K. DeBakey. (443)413-6790. E-mail: c.debakey@att.net. Membership (12+) open.

WISE PEN CHRISTIAN WRITERS GUILD. Baltimore. Contact: Anne Perry, 5714 Denwood Ave., Baltimore MD 21206. (442)919-4777. Nonfiction group. Membership (6) open. Sponsors a seminar in May in Baltimore.

MASSACHUSETTS

CENTRAL MASSACHUSETTS CHRISTIAN WRITERS FELLOWSHIP. Sturbridge. Contact: Barbara Shaffer, 168 Warren Rd., Brimfield MA 01010-9615. (413)245-9620. Membership (10) open.

MICHIGAN

AMERICAN CHRISTIAN WRITERS DETROIT. Contact: Pamela Perry, 33011 Tall Oaks St., Farmington MI 48336-4551. (248)426-2300. Fax (248)471-2422. E-mail: PamPerry@ministrymarketingsolutions.com. Website: www.ministrymarketingsolutions.com. Membership (175) open. Sponsors a fall seminar in Detroit.

THE CALLED AND READY WRITERS. Detroit. Contact: Wanda Burnside, 20700 Civic Center Dr., Ste. 170, Southfield MI 48076. (248)663-2363. Fax (313)861-7578. E-mail: mwwginc@aol.com. Website: www.thecalledandreadywriters.org. Sponsoring a spring conference, May or June 2008. Fall retreat, workshops, seminars, and special book signing events. Poetry critique available. Membership (70) open (over 25 published book authors).

CAPSTONE COMPOSERS. Bancroft. Contact: Rebecca L. Durling, 6986 Cole Rd., Bancroft MI 48414. (989)634-9237. Fax (989)634-5984. E-mail: durfar@michonline.net. Membership (10) open.

EAT, MEET AND CRITIQUE/ACW CHAPTER. Grandville. Contact: Flavia Crowner, 211 S. Maple St., Fennville MI 49408. E-mail: flacro@datawise.net. Membership (10) open.

MINNESOTA

MINNESOTA CHRISTIAN WRITERS GUILD. Edina (Minneapolis area). Contact: Sharon M. Knudson, pres., 724 N. Oak Dr., Vadnais Heights MN 55127-7959. (651)695-0609. Fax: same/call first. E-mail: sharonknudson@hotmail.com. Website: www.mnchristianwriters.org. Membership (140) open. Sponsors a spring contest for members only and annual spring (March) and fall (October) seminars in Minneapolis/St. Paul. Monthly meetings (Sept.-May); monthly newsletter. Sponsors critique circles throughout Minnesota.

MISSISSIPPI

BYHALIA CHRISTIAN WRITERS/ACW CHAPTER. Byhalia. Contact: Marylane Wade Koch, 2573 W. Church St., Byhalia MS 38611-9576. (662)838-2451. E-mail: mwkoch@att.net. Membership (24) open.

MISSOURI

CHRISTIAN WRITERS WORKSHOP OF ST. LOUIS/ACW CHAPTER. Brentwood area. Contact: Ruth Houser, 3148 Arnold-Tenbrook Rd., Arnold MO 63010-4732. (636)464-1187. E-mail: HouserRA@juno.com. Membership (15-20) open.

HEART OF AMERICA CHRISTIAN WRITERS' NETWORK. Kansas City. Contact: Mark and Jeanette Littleton, 3706 N.E. Shady Lane Dr., Gladstone MO 64119. Phone/fax (816)459-8016. E-mail: HACWN@earthlink.net. Website: www.HACWN.org. Membership (180) open. Sponsors monthly meetings, weekly critique groups, professional writer's fellowships, a contest (open to nonmembers), a newsletter, marketing e-mails, and two conferences: a major one in November and a mentoring conference in April.

OZARKS CHAPTER OF AMERICAN CHRISTIAN WRITERS. Springfield. Meets monthly. Contact: Jeanetta Chrystie, pres., OCACW, 5042 E. Cherry Hills Blvd., Springfield MO 65809. (417)832-8409. E-mail: DrChrystie@mchsi.com. Susan Willingham, newsletter ed.; OzarksACW@yahoo.com. Guidelines on Website: www.ClearGlassView.org/OzarksACW. New group; membership open.

MONTANA

WRITERS IN THE BIG SKY. Helena. Contact: Lenore Puhek, 1215 Hudson St., Helena MT 59601-1848. (406)443-2552. E-mail: lpuhek@mt.net. Membership (9) open.

NEBRASKA

CENTRAL NEBRASKA FELLOWSHIP OF CHRISTIAN WRITERS, ARTISTS, AND MUSICIANS (C-WAM). Kearney. Contact: Carolyn Scheidies, 415 E. 15th, Kearney NE 68847-6959. (308)234-3849. E-mail: crscheidies@hotmail.com (put C-WAM in subject line). Membership (15) open.

MY THOUGHTS EXACTLY WRITERS GROUP. Fremont. Contact: Cheryl A. Paden, PO Box 1073, Fremont NE 68025. (402)727-6508. Membership (6-8) open. Periodically sponsors a writers' retreat; October 2008.

WORDSOWERS CHRISTIAN WRITER'S GROUP/ACW CHAPTER. Omaha. Contact: Kelly Haack, 16268 Orchard Cir., Omaha NE 68135-1336. (402)593-7936. E-mail: haackkj@cox.net. Membership (20) open.

NEW JERSEY

NORTH JERSEY CHRISTIAN WRITER'S GROUP. Ringwood. Contact: Louise Bergmann DuMont, PO Box 36, Ringwood NJ 07456. (973)962-9267. E-mail: LouiseDumont@gmail.com. Website: www.louisedumont.com. Writers blog: www.njcwg.blogspot.com. Membership (32) open. E-mail for information. Usually sponsors a spring conference.

NEW MEXICO

SOUTHWEST WRITERS. Albuquerque. Contact: Larry Greely, pres., 3721 Morris St. N.E., Ste. A, Albuquerque NM 87111-3611. (505)265-9485. E-mail: swwriters@juno.com. Website: www.southwestwriters.com. Membership (700) open. Sponsors an annual and a monthly contest (open to nonmembers), a series of mini-conferences in Albuquerque (see Website for dates) and afternoon workshops in the months without mini-conferences. Semiannual e-lert notices are open to nonmembers. General.

NEW YORK

BROOKLYN WRITER'S CLUB. Contact: Ann Dellarocco, PO Box 184, Bath Beach Sta., Brooklyn NY 11214-0184. (718)680-4084. Membership (10-20) open.

NEW YORK CHRISTIAN WRITERS GROUP. Manhattan. Contact: Marilyn Driscoll, 350—1st Ave., New York, NY 10010 (Manhattan). (212)529-6087. E-mail: madrisc@rcn.com. Membership (8) open.

THE SCRIBBLERS/ACW CHAPTER. Riverhead. Contact: Bill Batcher, pres., c/o First Congregational Church, 103 First St., Riverhead NY 11901. E-mail: bbatcher@optonline.net. Membership (12) open. Meets monthly and sponsors biannual writing retreats.

SOUTHERN TIER CHRISTIAN WRITERS' FELLOWSHIP. Johnson City. Contact: Jean Jenkins, 3 Snow Ave., Binghamton NY 13905-3810. (607)797-5852. E-mail: jdjenkins2@verizon.net. Membership (10) open.

NORTH CAROLINA

COVENANT WRITERS. Cherryville. Contact: Robert Redding, 3392 Hwy. 274, Cherryville NC 28021-9634. (704)445-4962. E-mail: minwriter@yahoo.com. Membership (10) open.

SIX SERIOUS SCRIBES. Cary. Contact: Katherine W. Parrish, 103 Chimney Rise Dr., Cary NC 27511-7214. (919)467-1924. E-mail: servantsong@aol.com. Critique group. Membership (6) not currently open, but encourages others to start similar groups in the area.

OHIO

COLUMBUS CHRISTIAN WRITERS ASSN. Contact: Barbara Taylor Sanders, (614)306-3637. E-mail: BTSanders@columbus.rr.com. Membership (25) open.

CREATIVE FORCE AT NORTHGATE/ACW CHAPTER. Sunbury. Contact: Lark Lamontagne, 450 Township Rd. 208, Marengo OH 43334-5301. (740)625-6032. Fax (740)625-6572. E-mail: llamontagne@att.net. Membership (10) open.

DAYTON CHRISTIAN SCRIBES. Kettering. Contact: Cynthia Hinkle, 28 Stanton Dr., Springboro OH 45066. (937)886-9037. E-mail: cynthia.hinkle@sbcglobal.net. Membership (35) open.

DAYTON CHRISTIAN WRITERS' GUILD. Englewood. Contact: Tina Toles, PO Box 251, Englewood OH 45322. (937)836-6600. E-mail: daytonwriters@ureach.com. Membership (50) open.

+FAITH WRITERS. Milford. Contact: Sharon Siepel or Shaunna Howat, 5910 Price Rd., Milford OH 45150. (513)831-3770, ext. 112. E-mail: ssiepel@faithchurch.net. Membership (30) open. Also sponsors Faith Writers II, for serious writers.

+FRIENDS WRITERS GROUP/ACW CHAPTER. Canton. Contact: Diana Collins, 5455 Market Avenue N., Canton OH 44714. (330)492-8212. E-mail: FriendsWritersGroup@neo.rr.com. Membership open.

LEBANON AREA WRITERS. Contact: Mary Busha, 1370 Deerfield Road, #B, Lebanon, OH 45036. (513) 228-1205. Email: joyofwriting45@yahoo.com. Membership (12) open.

+MIDDLETOWN AREA CHRISTIAN WRITERS, Franklin. Contact: Donna J. Shepherd. (513)423-1627. E-mail: donnashepherd@cinci.rr.com. Website: www.middletownwriters.blogspot.com. Membership (15) open.

NORTHWEST OHIO CHRISTIAN WRITERS. Bowling Green. Contact: Charles Miller, 721 Colima, Toledo OH 43609. (419)382-0450. E-mail: panoochisoul@bex.net. Membership (65) open. Sponsors a Saturday seminar in September.

OKLAHOMA

FELLOWSHIP OF CHRISTIAN WRITERS (FCW), PO Box 700635, Tulsa, OK 74170-0635. Website: http://fellowshipofchristianwriters.org. Founded as Tulsa Christian Writers, FCW has helped to encourage, equip, launch, and inspire hundreds of writers for over 26 years. Membership (80-100) open; includes local and at-large group membership. Local group meets monthly in Tulsa. FCW membership benefits include a monthly 8-10 page newsletter, eligibility to members-only contests, book and tape discounts, free access to online critique groups, and a link on FCW Website to your Website. FCW also conducts a Free List Serve with over 750 members at Yahoo Groups—http://groups.yahoo.com/group/FCW—or send an email to FCW-subscribe@yahoogroups.com. Local membership $35/yr. At-large membership $25/yr. Contact: Lavon Lewis at the PO Box or via e-mail: Lavon@fellowshipofchristianwriters.org.

WORDWRIGHTS, OKLAHOMA CITY CHRISTIAN WRITERS. Contact: Milton Smith, 6457 Sterling Dr., Oklahoma City OK 73132-6804. (405)721-5026. E-mail: HisWordMatters@yahoo.com. Website: www.shadetreecreations.com. Membership (20) open. Occasional contests for members only. Cosponsors an annual writers' conference with American Christian Writers, February 22-23, 2008, in Oklahoma City; send an SASE for information.

OREGON

+GOD'S WORDSMITHS—ADVANCED. King City. Contact: Crystal Ortmann, 11625 S.W. King George Dr., King City OR 97224-2624. (503)804-8673. Fax (503)372-0529. E-mail: cjortmann@earthlink.net. Membership (3) open. Serious, published writers only; prefer those who have published books.

OREGON CHRISTIAN WRITERS. Contact: Duane Young, PO Box 20147, Keizer OR 97307-0147. E-mail from Website: www.oregonchristianwriters.org. Meets for 3, all-day Saturday conferences annually: February 16, 2008, in Salem; May 17, 2008, in Eugene; and October 18, 2008, in Portland. Newsletter published one month before each one-day conference. Annual 4-day Coaching Conference July 28-31, 2008, at Corban College in Salem. Occasionally sponsors a contest. Membership (450) open.

PORTLAND CHRISTIAN WRITERS GROUP. Contact: Stan Baldwin, (503)659-2974. Serious group; must write regularly. Waiting list available.

ROYAL PEN-DANTS. Salem/Portland area. Primarily for those writing for children. Contact: Carole Farmen. (503)362-2148. E-mail: cfarmen@msn.com. Membership (6) open only to committed, producing writers.

SALEM I CHRISTIAN WRITERS GROUP. Contact: Sam Hall, 6840 Macleay Rd. S.E., Salem OR 97301. (503)363-7586. E-mail: samhallarch@msn.com. Membership (9) not currently open.

WORDSMITHS. Gresham. Contact: Susan Thogerson Maas, 27526 S.E. Carl St., Gresham OR 97080-8215. (503)663-7834. E-mail: susan.maas@verizon.net. Membership (8-10) open. Christian and general writers.

WRITER'S DOZEN CRITIQUE GROUP. Springfield. Contact: Denise Nash, PO Box 1053, Leaburg OR 97489. (541)896-3816. E-mail: dcarlson@efn.org. Membership (12) not currently open.

PENNSYLVANIA

ARTISTS' JUNCTION WRITER'S GATHERING. Lancaster. Contact: Deb or Jan, PO Box 282, Lancaster PA 17608. (717)295-2533. E-mail: aji@artistsjunction.org. Website: www.artistsjunction.org. Membership open.

THE FIRST WORD. Sewickley. Contact: Shirley S. Stevens, 712 Ridge Ave., Pittsburgh PA 15202-2223. (412)761-2618. E-mail: poetcat@comcast.net. Membership (15) open. Affiliated with the St. Davids Christian Writers' Conference.

GREATER PHILADELPHIA CHRISTIAN WRITERS' FELLOWSHIP. Newton Square. Contact: Marlene Bagnull, 316 Blanchard Rd., Drexel Hill, PA 19026. Phone/fax (610)626-6833. E-mail: Mbagnull@aol.com. Website: www.writehisanswer.com. Membership (25) open. Meets one Thursday morning a month, October-June. Sponsors annual writers' conference (August 7-9, 2008) and contest (open to registered conferees only).

INDIANA CHRISTIAN WRITERS FELLOWSHIP. Indiana PA. Contact: Jan Woodard, 270 Sunset Dr., Indiana PA 15701. (724)465-5886. E-mail: prayercafe@hotmail.com. Membership (8) open. Quarterly meetings with retreats and breakfasts.

INDIAN VALLEY CHRISTIAN WRITERS FELLOWSHIP/ACW CHAPTER. Telford (Bucks County). Contact: Cheryl Wallace, 952 Route 113, Sellersville PA 18960-2962. (215)453-0415. E-mail: wallacewriter@earthlink.net. Membership (20+) open.

INSPIRATIONAL WRITERS' FELLOWSHIP. Brookville. Contact: Jan R. Sady, 2026 Langville Rd., Mayport PA 16240-5610. (814)856-2560. E-mail: janfran@windstream.net. Membership (15) open. Sponsors a conference in October.

JOHNSTOWN CHRISTIAN WRITERS' GUILD. Contact: Betty Rosian, 108 Deerfield Ln., Johnstown PA 15905-5703. (814)255-4351. E-mail: wordsforall@atlanticbb.net. Membership (12-15) open.

WEST BRANCH CHRISTIAN WRITERS. Williamsport. Contact: Cindy Emmet Smith, 131 Center St., Milton PA 17847-1717. (570)742-0789. E-mail: cswriter@yahoo.com. Membership (15) open. Sponsors an annual one-day mini-conference each fall, usually in October in Montoursville PA.

SOUTH CAROLINA

COLUMBIA CHRISTIAN WRITERS. Contact: Kim Andrysczyk, 201 Sutton Way, Irmo SC 29063. (803)781-3510. E-mail: kimbocraig@juno.com. Meets monthly. Membership (6) open.

GREENVILLE CHRISTIAN WRITERS GROUP. Contact: Nancy Parker, 3 Ben St., Greenville SC 29601. (864)232-1705. E-mail: Nancy@jjparker.com. Membership (20) open.

WRITING 4 HIM. Spartanburg. Contact: Linda Gilden, PO Box 2928, Spartanburg SC 29304. E-mail: Linda@lindagilden.com. Membership (20) open.

TENNESSEE

+SOUTHERN TENNESSEE CHRISTIAN WRITERS GROUP. Winchester area. Contact: Linda Winn, 138 Bluff Dr., Winchester TN 37398. (931)962-8801. E-mail: lhwinn@comcast.net. Membership open.

WEST TENNESSEE WORD WEAVERS/ACW CHAPTER. Henderson. Contact: Margaret Payne, 420 Melodie Cir., Henderson TN 38340. Membership (16) open. Sponsors a contest open to nonmembers.

TEXAS

AUSTIN CHRISTIAN WRITERS' GUILD. Contact: Lin Harris, 129 Fox Hollow Cv., Cedar Creek TX 78612-4844. (512)601-2216. Fax (240)208-3201. E-mail: linharris@austin.rr.com. Website: http://home.austin.rr.com/linharris/acwg.html. Membership (100) open. Meetings, critique groups, workshops, and conferences announced on Website.

CHRISTIAN WRITERS GROUP OF GREATER SAN ANTONIO. Universal City/San Antonio area. Contact: Brenda Blanchard, First Baptist Church, 1401 Pat Booker Rd., Universal City TX 78148-3928. (210)658-6394. E-mail: ZBGP1@aol.com. Has 4-6 speakers/yr. & one 1/2 day seminar. Membership (30) open.

DALLAS CHRISTIAN WRITERS GUILD. Plano. Contact: Jan Winebrenner, 2709 Winding Hollow, Plano TX 75093. E-mail: janwrite@earthlink.net. Website: www.dallaschristianwriters.com. Membership (30) open.

DENTON CHRISTIAN WRITERS GUILD. Denton. Contact: Sonjia Bradshaw, 3821 Willowick Dr., Denton TX 76210. E-mail: sonjia.bradshaw@dentonchristianwriters.com. Website: www.dentonchristianwriters.com. Membership (4) open.

INSPIRATIONAL WRITERS ALIVE! Groups meet in Houston, Pasadena, Jacksonville, Amarillo, Humble, and Port Neches. Contact: Martha Rogers, 6038 Greenmont, Houston TX 77092-2332. (713)686-7209. E-mail: marthalrogers@sbcglogal.net. Membership (130 statewide) open. Sponsors summer seminar, August 2008, monthly newsletter, and annual contest (January 1-May 15) open to nonmembers.

INSPIRATIONAL WRITERS ALIVE!/AMARILLO CHAPTER. Contact: Helen Luecke, 2921 S. Dallas, Amarillo TX 79103. (806)376-9671. Sponsors a seminar, March 29, 2008.

INSPIRATIONAL WRITERS ALIVE!/EAST TEXAS CHAPTER. Jacksonville. Contact: Maxine Holder, director & founding member, 4785 FM 1248 S., Rusk TX 75785-5254. (903)795-3986. E-mail: mholder@aol.com. Membership (15) open. Sponsors a contest through First Baptist chapter/Houston. Sponsors a biannual conference in Tyler TX; May 2008. Speaker: Jory Sherman.

NORTH TEXAS CHRISTIAN WRITERS/ACW CHAPTERS. Meetings held in Argyle, Arlington, Denton, Fort Worth, Keller, Lewisville. Contact: Frank Ball, PO Box 820802, Fort Worth TX 76182-0802. (817)915-1688. E-mail: frank.ball@ntchristianwriters.com. Website: www.ntchristianwriters.com. Membership (100+) open. Sponsors an annual seminar the second Friday and Saturday after Labor Day; September 12-23, 2008.

ROCKWALL CHRISTIAN WRITERS' GROUP. Lake Pointe Church/Rockwall. Contact: Leslie Wilson, 535 Cullins Rd., Rockwall TX 75032-6017. (972)772-3442. Cell: (214)505-5336. E-mail: les5points@aol.com. Website: http://rcwg.blogspot.com. Membership (20) open. Assists with the Greenville Christian Writers' Conference.

+WORDS FOR THE JOURNEY CHRISTIAN WRITERS GUILD/SOUTHEAST TEXAS REGION. The Woodlands. Contact: Linda Kozar. (281)362-1791. E-mail: lindakozar@mac.com. Website: www.wordsforthejourney.org. Membership (100+) open. See separate listing for Rocky Mountain CO Region.

UTAH

UTAH CHRISTIAN WRITERS FELLOWSHIP/ACW CHAPTER. Salt Lake City area. Contact: Julie Scott, PO Box 3, Bountiful UT 84011-0003. (801)294-5485. E-mail: julie.compelled2Tell@mac.com. Membership (20) open.

VERMONT

NEW ENGLAND CHRISTIAN WRITERS/ACW CHAPTER. Northwest VT. E-mail: vtwriters@freelist.org. Membership (10) open.

VIRGINIA

CAPITAL CHRISTIAN WRITERS. Fairfax. Leader: Betsy Dill, PO Box 873, Centreville VA 20122-0873. Phone/fax (703)803-9447. E-mail: ccwriters@gmail.com. Website: www.ccwriters.org. Meets the second Monday of odd numbered months. Contests for members only. Printed anthology for qualifying members in 2007. Membership (50-75) open.

NEW COVENANT WRITER'S GROUP. Newport News. Contact: Mary Tatem, 451 Summer Dr., Newport News VA 23606-2515. Phone/fax (757)930-1700. E-mail: rwtatem@juno.com. Membership (9) open.

PENINSULA CHRISTIAN WRITERS/ACW CHAPTER. Tabb (York County). Contact: Yvonne Ortega, PO Box 955, Yorktown VA 23692. E-mail: yvonne143@verizon.net. Membership (20) open.

RICHMOND CHRISTIANS WHO WRITE/ACW CHAPTER. Contact: Rev. Thomas C. Lacy, 12114 Walnut Hill Dr., Rockville VA 23146-1854. (804)749-4050. Fax (804)749-4939. E-mail: RichmondCWW@aol.com. Blog: http://rcww.blogspot.com. Membership (50) open.

TIDEWATER CHRISTIAN WRITERS FORUM/ACW CHAPTER. Norfolk. Contact: Peter D. Mallett, 1270 Pall Mall St., #A, Norfolk VA 23513. (757)889-9917. E-mail: F18Pete@aol.com. Website: http://groups.yahoo.com/group/TidewaterChristianWF. Membership (8) open. ACW Chapter 3055 (www.acwriters.com).

WASHINGTON

ADVENTIST WRITERS ASSOCIATION OF WESTERN WASHINGTON. Renton. Contact: Maylan Schurch, 18235—153rd Ave. S.E., Renton WA 98058. (206)625-9206. E-mail: maylans@aol.com. Membership open. Sponsors annual writers' conference in late June.

MEMOIR WRITERS. Federal Way. Contact: Bernice Large, 1013 S. 325th St., Federal Way WA 98003-5933. (253)946-2782. E-mail: belrge@comcast.net. Membership (15) open.

NORTHWEST CHRISTIAN WRITERS ASSN. Bothell WA. Contact: Athena Dean, PO Box 428, Enumclaw WA 98022-0428. Toll-free (800)731-6292. Fax (360)802-9992. E-mail: president@nwchristianwriters.org. Website: www.nwchristianwriters.org. Membership (135) open. Meets monthly. bimonthly newsletter. Taking over leadership of the Seattle Pacific Writers' Renewal, now called Northwest Christian Writers Renewal (see separate listing).

SPOKANE CHRISTIAN WRITERS. Contact: Ruth McHaney Danner, PO Box 18425, Spokane WA 99228-0425. (509)328-3359. E-mail: ruth@ruthdanner.com. Membership (10) open.

WALLA WALLA VALLEY CHRISTIAN SCRIBES. College Place. Contact: Helen Heavirland, PO Box 146, College Place WA 99324-0146. Phone/fax (541)938-3838. E-mail: hlh@bmi.net. Membership (8) open.

WENATCHEE CHRISTIAN WRITERS' FELLOWSHIP. Contact: Barbara A. Greig, 206 Woodring St., #5, Cashmere WA 98815-1081. (509)782-3129. E-mail: bgreig@juno.com. Membership (10) open.

WRITERS IN THE ROUGH/ACW CHAPTER. Arlington. Contact: Darlene Paterson, 18408 Hawksview Dr., Arlington WA 98223-4638. (360)474-0756. E-mail: dpat777@verizon.net. Membership (12) open.

WISCONSIN

LIGHTHOUSE CHRISTIAN WRITERS. Oconto. Contact: Lois Wiederhoeft, 901 Aubin, Lot 115, Peshtigo WI 54157. (715)582-1024. E-mail: 2loisann@myway.com. Or, Mary Jansen, PO Box 187, Mountain WI 54149; (715)276-1706. Website: www.mychristiansite.com/ministries/lhchristianwriters. Membership (12) open. Sponsors a fall seminar.

+THE LIVING WORD/ACW CHAPTER. Superior. Contact: Amy Trees, pres., 1421 E. 5th St., Superior WI 54880. E-mail: TheLivingWordSuperior@yahoogroups.com. Website: http://adtrees.bravehost.com/LivingWord.html. Membership (21) open.

WORD AND PEN CHRISTIAN WRITERS CLUB/ACW CHAPTER. Menasha. Contact: Chris Stratton, 107 E. McArthur St., Appleton WI 54911-2109. (920)739-0752. E-mail: wordandpen@mychristiansite.com. Website: www.mychristiansite.com/ministries/wordandpen. Membership (9) open.

WORDSMITHS (W.R.W.A.). Marinette/Menominee. Wisconsin Regional Writers Assn. (general group that includes Christians). Contact: Mildred Utke, 2709 Northland Cir. Dr., Marinette WI 54143-4277. (715)735-0127. Membership (4) open.

WRITER'S CRITIQUE GROUP. Fort Atkinson. Contact: James B. Robar, N2963 Buena Vista Rd., Fort Atkinson WI 53538. (920)568-1677. E-mail: jim@jamesbrobar.com. Membership (4) open.

CANADIAN/FOREIGN

ASSOCIATION OF CHRISTIAN WRITERS. Hoddesdon, Herts UK. Contact: Brian Vincent, dir., 31 Newlands Rd., Ruishton, Taunton, SOM., TA3 5J2, United Kingdom. Phone 01823-442 372. E-mail from Website: www.christianwriters.org.uk. Membership (900) open. Sponsors an occasional writers' weekend for members only. Next one in 2009.

FRASER VALLEY CHRISTIAN WRITERS GROUP. Abbotsford BC. Contact: Helmut Fandrich, 2461 Sunnyside Pl., Abbotsford BC V2T 4C4, Canada. Phone/fax (604)850-0666. E-mail: helmut7@coneharvesters.com. Membership (20) open.

INSCRIBE CHRISTIAN WRITERS' FELLOWSHIP. Edmonton (various locations across Canada). Contact: Eunice Matchett, 4304—45 St., Drayton Valley AB T7A 1G7, Canada. (780)542-7950. E-mail: scrappi@telusplanet.net. Website: www.inscribe.org. Membership (250) open. Sponsors a newsletter and 2 contests, details on Website (one open to non-members). Also sponsors annual conference in September.

NEW ZEALAND CHRISTIAN WRITERS GUILD. Contact: Janet Fleming, Box 115, Kaeo 0448, New Zealand. (MJflamingos@xtra.co.nz), or Janet Pointon (Pointon@ihug.co.nz). Website: www.nzcwg.bravehost.com. Membership (150) open. Workshops, biannual weekend retreat, local groups, home study courses, and bimonthly magazine.

SWAN VALLEY CHRISTIAN WRITERS GUILD, Swan River, MB. Contact: Addy Oberlin, Box 132, Swan River MB R0L 1Z0, Canada. Phone/fax (204)734-4269. E-mail: waltadio@mts .net. Membership (10) open. Sponsors a children's contest.

NATIONAL/INTERNATIONAL GROUPS (no state location)

AMERICAN CHRISTIAN FICTION WRITERS, Rachel Hauck, pres.; PO Box 101066, Palm Bay FL 32910. Phone/fax (321)984-4018. E-mail: pres@acfw.com. Website: www.ACFW.com. E-mail loop, online courses, critique groups, and newsletter for members. Send membership inquiries to address above. Membership (1,100) open. Sponsors a contest open to nonmembers. Sponsoring a seminar, September 2008.

AMERICAN CHRISTIAN WRITERS SEMINARS. Sponsors conferences in various locations around the country (see individual states for dates and places). Call or write to be placed on mailing list for any conference. Events are Friday and Saturday unless otherwise noted. Brochures usually mailed three months prior to event. Contact: Reg Forder, Box 110390, Nashville TN 37222. Toll-free (800)21-WRITE. Website: www.ACWriters.com.

CHRISTIAN WRITERS FELLOWSHIP INTL. (CWFI). Contact: Sandy Brooks, 1624 Jefferson Davis Rd., Clinton SC 29325-6401. (864)697-6035. E-mail: cwfi@cwfi-online.org. Website: www.cwfi-online.org. To contact Sandy Brooks personally: sandybrooks@cwfi-online.org. No meetings, but offers market consultations, critique service, writers books, and conference workshop tapes. Connects writers living in the same area, and helps start writers' groups. Membership (1,000+) open.

+CHRISTIAN WRITERS' GROUP INTL. (CWGI). Website: http://christianwritersgroup.org. An international organization of born-again Christians who write. Purpose: to assist Christians as they fulfill their calling to write by offering resources, information, education, support, networking, and interaction with Christian writers, editors, and publishers. Includes critique and prayer subgroups for members only. Periodically offers CWGI members scholarships to writing conferences. Editors and publishers are welcome. To join, send a blank e-mail to CWG-subscribe@yahoogroups.com, or sign up at http://groups.yahoo.com/group/CWGI. Executive director: Brandy Brow. Membership (700+) open.

FAITH, HOPE & LOVE is the inspirational chapter of Romance Writers of America. Dues for the chapter are $24/yr., but you must also be a member of RWA to join (dues $75/yr.). Chapter offers these services: online list service for members, a Web page, 20-pg. bimonthly newsletter, annual contest, monthly online guest chats with multipublished authors and industry professionals, connects critique partners by mail or e-mail, and latest romance-market information. To join, contact RWA National Office, 16000 Stuebner Airline Rd., Ste. 140, Spring TX 77379. (832)717-5200. Fax (832)717-5201. Website: www.rwanational.org. Or go to FHL Website: www.faithhopelove-rwa.org. Inspirational Readers Choice Contest by subgenre categories for published works; deadline April 1; cash prizes. Send SASE for guidelines. Membership (150+) open.

JERRY B. JENKINS CHRISTIAN WRITERS GUILD. Contact: Kerma Murray, 5525 N. Union Blvd., Ste. 200, Black Forest, CO 80918. Toll-free (866) 495-5177. E-mail: ContactUs@ChristianWritersGuild.com. Website: www.ChristianWritersGuild.com. This international organization of more than 1,500 members offers annual memberships, mentor-guided correspondence courses for adults (two-year Apprentice and advanced one-year Journeyman) and youth (Pages: ages 9-12, and Squires: 13 and up), writing contests, conferences, critique service, writers resource books, monthly newsletter, and more. Critique service accepts prose samples of 1-15 pages. Professional writing assessment covers proper language usage, pacing, presentation, purpose, and persuasiveness. Call for pricing structure. Members receive 10% off.

NATIONAL ASSN. OF WOMEN WRITERS. General. Contact: Sheri McConnell, 24165 IH-10 W., Ste. 217-637, San Antonio TX 78257. Toll-free phone/fax (866)821-5829. E-mail: naww@onebox.com. Website: www.naww.org. Over 40 chapters across the U.S. (see Website for list of locations, under "Chapters" link). Membership (3,000+) open. Sponsors regional events across the U.S. and national TeleSummits.

PEN-SOULS (prayer and support group, not a critique group). Conducted entirely by e-mail. Contact: Janet Ann Collins, 632 Pelton Way, Grass Valley CA 95945. (530)272-4905. E-mail: jan@janetanncollins.com. Membership (13) open.

THE WRITING ACADEMY. Contact: Inez Schneider, new member coordinator, 4010 Singleton Rd., Rockford IL 61114. (815)877-9675. Website: www.wams.org. Membership (75) open. Sponsors year-round correspondence writing program and annual seminar in August (held in various locations); currently in Minneapolis.

EDITORIAL SERVICES

The following listing is included because so many writers contact me looking for experienced/qualified editors who can critique or evaluate their manuscripts. These people from all over the country offer this kind of service. I cannot personally guarantee the work of all of those listed, so you may want to ask for references or samples of their work.

The following abbreviations indicate what kinds of work they are qualified to do:

B—brochures
BCE—book contract evaluation
CA—coauthoring
GE—general editing/ manuscript evaluation
GH—ghostwriting
LC—line editing or copyediting
NL—newsletters
SP—special projects

The following abbreviations indicate the types of material they evaluate:

A—articles
BP—book proposals
BS—Bible studies
D—devotionals
E—essays
F—fillers
GB—gift books
JN—juvenile novels
NB—nonfiction books
N—novels
PB—picture books
P—poetry
QL—query letter
S—scripts
SS—short stories
TM—technical material

(+) Indicates new listing

ARIZONA

CARLA'S MANUSCRIPT SERVICE/CARLA BRUCE, 10229 W. Andover Ave., Sun City AZ 85351-4509. Phone/fax (623)876-4648. E-mail: Carlaabruce@cox.net. Call/e-mail/write with deposit of $100. GE/LC/GH/typesetting/PDF files for publishers. Edits A/SS/P/F/N/NB/BP/QL/BS/GB/TM/E/D. Charges $25/hr. or gives a project estimate after evaluation. Does ghost-writing for pastors and teachers; professional typesetting. Twenty-three years ghostwriting/editing; 12 years typesetting.

CALIFORNIA

CHRISTIAN COMMUNICATOR MANUSCRIPT CRITIQUE SERVICE/SUSAN TITUS OSBORN, 3133 Puente St., Fullerton CA 92835-1952. (714)990-1532. Toll-free (877)428-7992. (714)990-1532. Fax (714)990-0310. E-mail: Susanosb@aol.com. Website: www.christian communicator.com. Call/e-mail/write. For book, send material with $125 deposit. Staff of 18 editors. GE/LC/GH/CA/SP/BCE. Edits A/SS/P/F/N/NB/BP/JN/PB/QL/BS/GB/TM/E/D/S. $75 for short pieces/picture books. Three-chapter book proposal $125. Additional editing $30/hr. Thirty years' experience.

CITY BOY EDITORIAL SERVICE/STEVEN HUTSON, 5022 Avenue N, Ste. 102-128, Palmdale CA 93551. (661)722-4896. Toll-free fax (866)501-4280. E-mail: steve@hutsonbooks.com. Website: www.hutsonbooks.com/editorial. Call/e-mail. GE/LC/CA/SP/WS. Edits A/SS/N/NB/JN/BS/GB/E/D. Published author; on faculty of Antelope Valley Christian Writers Conference. Proofreading $1/pg.; copyediting $1.95/hr.; 3-chapter critique $95 (up to 100 pgs.). Other projects at $30/hr., or upon discussion with client.

EDITORIAL & PRODUCTION SERVICES/DESTA GARRETT, dg-ink Book Design, PO Box 1182, Daly City CA 94017-1182. (650)994-2662. Fax (650)991-3050. E-mail: dg@dg-ink.net. Website: www.dg-ink.net, includes work samples. Write/call/e-mail. GE/LC/B/NL/SP. Complete editing and production for author, including for self-publishing using Adobe InDesign Creative Suite. Edits A/SS/NB/BS/TM/E/D/educational material. Has 20 years' experience doing all aspects of editing, production, and publishing of all types of material for nonprofit Christian foundation, up to large illustrated, indexed research books. Charges $50/hr.; $40/hr. for Christian authors with Christian material.

EDITORIAL SERVICES/KATHY IDE, 203 Panorama Ct., Brea CA 92821. (714)529-1212. Fax (714)529-5267. E-mail: Kathy@kathyide.com. Website: www.KathyIde.com. E-mail contact. GE/LC/GH/CA/B/NL/SP/WS, writing coach. Edits A/SS/F/N/NB/BP/QL/JN/BS/GB/D/S. Charges by the hour (mention this listing and get a $5/hr. discount). Freelance author, editor (full-time since 1998), and speaker. Has done proofreading and editing for Moody, Thomas Nelson, Barbour/Heartsong, and WinePress.

+GET PUBLISHED IN AMERICA.COM/B. K. NELSON, 1565 Paseo Vida, Palm Springs CA 92262. Toll-free (800)371-0076. (760)778-8800. Fax (760)778-0034. E-mail: bknelson4@cs.com. Website: www.bknelson.com. E-mail/write. LC/GH. Edits SS/N/NB/BP/QL/JN/PB/BS/GB/TM/S.

VICKI HESTERMAN, PhD/EDITING & WRITING SERVICES, PO Box 6788, San Diego CA 92166. E-mail: vickihesterman@earthlink.net (cc it to backup address: vhesterman@hotmail.com/indicate "Christian editor query" in subject line). E-mail or mail only; will follow-up with phone call. GE/LC/GH/CA/SP. Edits A/SS/F/N/NB/BP/QL/JN/PB/BS/GB/TM/E/D/photo books, memoirs. Cost depends on scope and condition of project. Send sample pages and explain your project for an estimate of cost. Edits/develops nonfiction material, including editorials; works with book and article writers and publishers as coauthor, line editor, or in editorial development. Book editor, book author, university writing professor, newspaper reporter, writing curriculum development, documentary photography.

DARLENE HOFFA, 512 Juniper St., Brea CA 92821. (714)990-5980. E-mail: jack.darlene.hoffa@roadrunner.com. E-mail contact. GE. Edits A/F/NB/BP/D. Nineteen years' experience; author of 11 books. Charges $20/hr. or $1.50/ms pg.

LIGHTHOUSE EDITING/DR. LON ACKELSON, 13326 Community Rd., #11, Poway CA 92064-4754. (858)748-9258. Fax (858)748-7431. E-mail: Isaiah68LA@sbcglobal.net. Website: www.lighthouseedit.com. E-mail/write. GE/LC/GH/CA/B/NL/BCE. Edits A/SS/N/NB/BP/QL/BS/E/D. Charges $35 for article/short story critique; $60 for 3-chapter book proposal. Send SASE for full list of fees. Editor since 1981; senior editor 1984-2002.

KAREN O'CONNOR COMMUNICATIONS/KAREN O'CONNOR, 10 Pajaro Vista Ct., Watsonville CA 95076. E-mail: karen@karenoconnor.com. Website: www.karenoconnor.com. E-mail. GE/LC. Book proposal commentary/editing. Edits A/F/NB/BP/QL/D. One-hour free evaluation; $90/hr. or flat fee depending on project. Has 32 years of writing/editing; 20+ years teaching writing; 50 published books and hundreds of magazine articles.

SHIRL'S EDITING SERVICE/SHIRL THOMAS, 9379 Tanager Ave., Fountain Valley CA 92708-6557. (714)968-5726. E-mail: Shirlth@verizon.net. E-mail (preferred)/write, and send material with $100 deposit. GE/LC/GH/SP/rewriting/analysis. Edits A/SS/P/F/N/NB/BP/QL/GB/D/greeting cards/synopses. Consultation/evaluation, $100; evaluation/critique, $65/hr.; copyediting $65/hr.; content editing/rewriting $75/hr.

LAURAINE SNELLING/KMB COMMUNICATIONS INC., 19872 Highline Rd., Tehachapi CA 93561-7796. (661)823-0669. Fax (661)823-9427. E-mail: TLsnelling@yahoo.com. Website: www.LauraineSnelling.net. E-mail contact. GE. Edits SS/N/JN. Charges $50/hr. with $100 deposit, or by the project after discussion with client. Award-winning author of 60 books (YA and adult fiction, 2 nonfiction); teacher at writing conferences.

THE STRONG WORD COMMUNICATION SERVICES/ANITA PALMER, 5800 Lake Murray Blvd., Unit 14, La Mesa CA 91942. (619)208-7202. Fax (619) 697-1823. E-mail: anita@thestrongword.com. Website: www.thestrongword.com. E-mail contact. GE/LC/GH/B/NL/SP. Edits A/SS/N/NB/BP/QL/JN/PB/BS/GB/E/D/memoirs. Published author. Former newspaper and magazine editor with 25 years' experience; experienced in media relations and marketing. Have freelanced for most of the major Christian publishing houses and some general houses. Quick, trustworthy, and reliable. Competitive rates; happy to negotiate: per project, per hour, or per page.

THE WORD WORKS/SONJA L. STRUTHERS, 40960 California Oaks Rd., Ste. 272, Murrieta CA 92562-4615. Phone/fax (951)696-5631. E-mail: info@mywriter.net. Website: www.mywriter.net. Call/e-mail. GE/LC/GH/B/NL/SP/WS. Edits: A/SS/NB/BP/QL/TM/E. Graduate of Irvine College Writing Program; award-winning editor & publisher for Inland Empire Mensa. Offers quote upon review of project only.

COLORADO

ALPHA TRANSCRIPTION/CHERYL A. COLCHIN, 1832 S. Lee St., Unit G, Lakewood CO 80232-6255. (303)978-0880. E-mail: alphatranscription@juno.com. Call/e-mail/write. Typing for authors, preferably from cassette tapes, but will consider legible longhand material. Rate determined after discussion with client. Has worked with Dr. Larry Crabb, David Wilkerson, literary agent and authors since 1988.

EDIT RESOURCE/ERIC & ELISA STANFORD, 7645 N. Union Blvd., PMB 235, Colorado Springs CO 80920. (719)599-7808. E-mail: info@editresource.com. Websites: www.editresource.com, www.inspirationalghostwriting.com, www.bookproposals.net. E-mail contact. GE/LC/GH/CA/NL/SP/copywriting/proposal development. Edits A/F/N/NB/BP/QL/BS/GB/E/D/book doctoring. Rates determined after discussion with client. Combined 35 years of professional editing experience.

OMEGA EDITING/MICHAEL P. COLCHIN, 1832 S. Lee St., Ste. G, Lakewood CO 80232-6255. (303)978-0880. E-mail: omegaediting@juno.com. Write/call/e-mail. GE/LC/GH/CA/B/NL/SP. Edits A/SS/NB/BP/QL/BS/TM/D. Charges $45 & up, or by the project after discussion with client. Works in partnership with authors and publishers as ghostwriter, coauthor, editor, or in editorial development. Published book and article author; 13 years' experience as freelance editor.

THE PERFECT PAPER/PATRICIA UNGER, 16695 Von Neuman Dr., Monument CO 80132. Phone/fax (719)481-4688. E-mail: dpunger@comcast.net. Website: www.theperfectpaper.com. Call/e-mail/send with $25 deposit. GE/LC/GH/B/NL/SP/BCE/PP/transcription. Edits A/SS/P/F/N/NB/BP/QL/JN/E/D/S. Charges $2.50-3.50/page for smaller projects (up to 30 pgs.); $60/hr. for projects over 30 pgs. Twenty years' experience proofreading and copyediting.

SCRIBBLE COMMUNICATIONS/BRAD LEWIS, Colorado Springs CO. (719)260-8651. E-mail: brad.lewis@scribblecommunications.com. Website: www.scribblecommunications.com. Call/e-mail. GE/GH/CA. Edits A/NB/BS/D/Website content. Edited 80+ nonfiction books; senior editor of the *New Men's Devotional Bible* (Zondervan); content editor for *New Living Translation Study Bible* (Tyndale). Charges by project, mutually agreed upon with publisher, and stated in editor's/author's agreement.

A WAY WITH WORDS/RENEE GRAY-WILBURN, Colorado Springs CO. (719)265-6626. E-mail: waywords@earthlink.net. Call/e-mail. LC/GH/CA/B/NL/SP. Edits A/SS/F/N/NB/JN/PB/BS/GB/TM/E/D. Line editing/copyediting: $20-25/hr. & up. Project prices negotiable. Has had a writing company for over 10 years. Provides editorial services for independent authors, Christian publishers, ministries, and small businesses (proofed nearly 100 books). Open to coauthoring opportunities.

THE WELL-WRITTEN WORD/NICKIE DUMKE, 1877 Polk Ave., Louisville CO 80027-1117. Phone/fax (303)666-8253. E-mail: dumke@earthlink.net. Website: www.food-allergy.org. Call/e-mail. GE/LC/GH/CA/NL/SP/health and medical editing and writing. Edits A/SS/F/N/NB/JN/PB/BS/GB/TM/E/D/cookbooks. Fifteen years' experience in writing, editing, and publishing; author of 5 books and several booklets. Charges $35/hr.; flat rate for project after evaluating material.

FLORIDA

EDITORIAL SERVICES/SHARON LEE ROBERTS, 240 San Marco Dr., Venice FL 34285. (941)484-0773. Fax (941)488-0847. E-mail: prose-and-poetry@peoplepc.com Call/e-mail/fax/write. GE/LC. Edits A/SS/P/F/PB/D. Charges $25/hr. for critique/evaluation/line editing/copyediting ($25 minimum) or $2.50/pg., or negotiable fee for project. Published author of 3 children's storybooks and hundreds of articles, short stories, and poems for children and adults. Former editorial assistant for *Living Streams*, a Christian writer's magazine.

EDITORIAL SERVICES/DIANE E. ROBERTSON, PO Box 364, Venice FL 34284-0364. (941)484-4936. E-mail: PSWRITER1@netzero.net. Write/e-mail. GE/LC/GH. Edits A/SS/F/N/NB/BP/QL/PB/BS/E/S. Writer, novelist, magazine associate editor, former magazine editor, experienced copywriter and copyeditor. Competitive and reasonable rates; e-mail a brief description of project to get an estimate or copy of rate sheet. Charges $40/hr. for 10 pages or less; otherwise charges $750 for 40 hours work.

EDITORIAL SERVICES/LESLIE SANTAMARIA, Winter Springs FL. E-mail: santamaria@mpinet.net. E-mail first. GE/LC. Edits A/SS/N/NB/BP/QL/JN/BS/TM/E/D. Critiques: $65 for short pieces/picture books; $100 for 3-chapter book proposals. Editing services: $25/hr. Published author and book reviewer with extensive book and magazine editing experience and a BA in English.

LIGHTPOST COMMUNICATIONS/SEAN FOWLDS, 305 Pinecrest Rd., Mount Dora FL 32757-5929. (352)383-2485. E-mail: sfowlds@earthlink.net. E-mail contact. GE/LC/B/NL/SP/copy for Websites. Edits A/SS/P/F/NB/BP/QL/PB/BS/GB/TM/E/D/S. Offers speaking, writing, and editing services. Negotiated sliding scale starting at $35/hr. Former editor of a national publication.

GEORGIA

BONNIE C. HARVEY, PhD, 5579B Chamblee Dunwoody Rd., Ste. 357, Atlanta GA 30038. (404)299-6149. Fax (404)297-6651. E-mail: BoncaH@aol.com. Website: www.bookimprove.com. Call/e-mail/write to discuss terms & payment. GE/LC/GH/CA/SP/theology. Edits A/SS/P/N/NB/QL/JN/BS/GB/E/D/S/theological and academic articles. Does critiquing, editing, book consulting, book proposals, and rewriting. Charges $20/hr. for reading/critiquing; $20/hr. for proofreading; $25/hr. for editing, $45-75/hr. for rewriting. Has PhD in English; 14 years teaching college-level English; teaches English and writing classes at Kennesaw University; over 27 years' experience as editor; has ghostwritten books and authored 22 books. Does agenting, see separate listing.

EDITORIAL SERVICES/GLORIA SPENCER, 6433 Rockland Rd., Lithonia GA 30038. (678)526-0101. E-mail: gfespencer@aol.com. E-mail contact. GE/LC/GH. Edits A/SS/N/NB/BP/BS/D. Over 15 years' experience editing fiction/nonfiction books, articles, and book proposals. Charges $15/hr. or by the project after initial free consultation.

ON-TIME EDITORIAL SERVICES/LEIGH DELOZIER, 1009 Crown River Pkwy., McDonough GA 30252. (770)914-3812. Fax (866)321-9914. E-mail: leighdelozier@bellsouth.net.

Website: www.leighdelozier.net or www.soulrestministries.net. Call/e-mail/write. GE/LC/B/NL/SP/WS. Edits A/SS/QL/GB/E/D/brochures & other marketing materials. Fees by the hour, page, or project, depending on the work. Proofreading $25/hr.; editing/rewriting $35-75/hr. BS in Journalism; 17 years' experience in publishing and public relations; published writer.

POSITIVE DIFFERENCE COMMUNICATIONS/ROSS WEST, 100 Martha Dr., Rome GA 30165-4138. (706)232-9325. Fax (706)235-2716. E-mail: rwest@positivedifference.com. Website: www.positivedifference.com. Call/write/e-mail. GE/LC/GH. Edits A/NB/BS. Charges by the page or provides a project cost estimate. Published professional; author of two books and several articles; more than 20 years' editing experience.

ILLINOIS

AFFORDABLE NOVEL CRITIQUE SERVICE/SALLY BRADLEY, 1249 Winslowe Dr., #301, Palatine IL 60074-8519. (847)666-8560. E-mail: sallysbradley@comcast.net, or sally@sallybradley.com. Website: www.sallybradley.com. E-mail or write. GE/detailed critique of first 25 pages of novels only. BA in English, former editor for Christian publisher, contest judge, member of Christian PEN (Proofreaders and Editors Network). Charges for up to 100 pages listed on Website; over 100 pages, contact via e-mail for quote.

ALICE 'N INK/ALICE PEPPLER, 6007 N. Sheridan Rd., Apt. 6, Chicago IL 60660-3061. (773)878-5943. E-mail: apeppler@aol.com. Website: www.apeppler.com. Call/e-mail/write. GE/LC/B/NL. Edits A/SS/P/F/N/NB/BP/QL/JN/PB/BS/GB/E/D ($25/hr.). Three-chapter book proposal, including market analysis $103; additional editing $30/hr. Publishing experience of 25 years. Published author of Christian books, articles, poetry, monographs. Quality work; quick turnaround.

AMY BADOWSKI'S EDITING SERVICE, 649 Frances Ave., Loves Park IL 61111. E-mail: Amy.Badowski@gmail.com. GE/LC. Edits A/SS/N/NB/BP/JN/E/D. BA English Studies, magna cum laude. Pursuing MA. Teaching. Charges $40-100 for articles; $250-750 for books.

THE WRITER'S EDGE, PO Box 1266, Wheaton IL 60189. E-mail: info@writersedgeservice.com. Website: www.WritersEdgeService.com. No phone calls. A manuscript screening service for 90 cooperating Christian publishers. Charges $95 to evaluate a book proposal and if publishable, they will send a synopsis of it to 90 publishers who might be interested. If not publishable they will tell how to improve it. If interested, send an SASE for guidelines and a Book Information Form; request a form via e-mail or copy from Website. The Writer's Edge now handles previously published books, including self-published books or those that are out of print and available for reprint. Requires a different form, but cost is the same. Reviews novels, nonfiction books, juvenile novels, Bible studies, devotionals, biography, and theology, but no poetry. See Website for details.

INDIANA

DENEHEN INC./DR. DENNIS E. HENSLEY, 6824 Kanata Ct., Fort Wayne IN 46815-6388. (260)485-9891. E-mail: dnhensley@hotmail.com. E-mail/write. GE/LC/GH. Edits A/SS/P/F/N/NB/QL/JN/BS/E/D/comedy/academic articles/editorials/Op-Ed pieces/columns/speeches/interviews. Rate sheet for SASE. Author of 50 books; PhD in English; University English professor; columnist for *Writer's Journal* and *Advanced Christian Writer.*

EDITORIAL SERVICES/BARBARA BUIS, 4978 S. County Rd. 75 West, Greencastle IN 46135. (765)247-9974. E-mail: truk4jsuschrst@yahoo.com. Call/Write. LC/Transcription from tapes. Edits A/SS/N/BS/D. Charges $1.50/pg.

+EDITORIAL SERVICES/JAMES HENDRIX, 107 W. Sherwood Ter., Fort Wayne IN 46807-2846. (260)458-9236. E-mail: JHendrix1@verizon.net. E-mail contact. GE/LC/CA/B/NL/SP/writing coach. Edits A/SS/F/N/NB/BP/QL/JN/PB/BS/GB/TM/E/D/S. Professional freelance writer for 10 years. E-mail for rates.

EDITORIAL SERVICES/APRIL STIER, 7768 N. 100 E., Ossian IN 46777-9360. (260)402-1883. E-mail: april_lynn@mac.com. E-mail/write. GE/LC/CA. Edits A/SS/F/N/NB/BP/QL/BS/GB/E/D. Charges $20/hr. for proofreading/copyediting; $27/hr. for line editing, and $250 and up for manuscript evaluation. Send SASE or e-mail for rate sheet. BA in English, AA in writing, BA in Biblical Studies; published writer.

EDITORIAL SERVICES/NANCY SWANSON, 2900 N. Apperson Way, Trailer 54, Kokomo IN 46901-1402. E-mail: sannanvan@yahoo.com. Write/e-mail. GE/LC/GH/CA/B/NL/SP. Edits A/SS/P/F/N/NB/JN/BS/E/D/S. Rates currently under revision; projects priced as mutually agreed. Former English teacher; editing course; 30+ years' experience editing.

XARIS COM/JAMES WATKINS, 318 N. Lenfesty Ave., Marion IN 46952. (765)618-7913. E-mail: jim@jameswatkins.com. Website: www.jameswatkins.com. E-mail contact. GE. Edits A/NB/BP/BS/D. Award-winning author of 12 books & 2,000 articles & editor; 20+ years' experience. Charge $50 for 2,000 words of critique, editing, market suggestions; $5/pg. for content editing; $15/pg. for rewriting; $50/hr. for Website evaluation/consulting.

IOWA

EDITORIAL SERVICES/KATHY GODFREY, 1409 Division St. #3, Burlington IA 52601-4243. (319)753-0145. E-mail: grantsandedits@yahoo.com. Write/call/e-mail. GE/LC/B/NL/SP/writing coach/grant writing. Edits A/SS/P/F/N/NB/BP/QL/JN/PB/BS/GB/TM/E/D/S. Writer for local newspaper; copyedited several Christian books. Charges $25, plus $2/pg.

KENTUCKY

EDITORIAL SERVICES/MARILYN A. ANDERSON, 127 Sycamore Dr., Louisville KY 40223-2956. (502)244-0751. Fax (502)452-9260. E-mail: shelle12@aol.com. Call/e-mail. GE/LC. Edits A/F/NB/BS/TM/E/D. Charges $15-20/hr. for proofreading; $25/hr. for extensive editing; or negotiable by the job or project. Holds an MA and BA in English; former high school English teacher; freelance consultant since 1993. References available. Contributing member of The Christian PEN.

BETTY L. WHITWORTH, 11740 S. Hwy 259, Leitchfield KY 42754. (270)257-2461. E-mail: Blwhit@bbtel.com. Call/e-mail. GE. Edits A/SS/N/NB/JN/D. Typing fees based on project (reasonable). Editing for novels and nonfiction books: $50 deposit with first 100 pgs., fee based on amount of work. Send entire manuscript for everything else. Retired English teacher, newspaper columnist for 18 yrs., published over 1,000 stories/articles; author of 4 books; have worked with over 60 writers.

MARYLAND

+EDITORIAL SERVICES/RHONDA OWEN-SMITH, 2916 Old Court Rd., Pikesville MD 21208. (410)602-8970. Fax (410)602-1056. E-mail: mapress@aol.com. E-mail/write. Does marketing, PR, media, publicity, direct response. Twenty-five years of relevant experience; published author; master's degree. Résumé & references available. Charges $25/hr. with 4 hr. minimum. All work based on contractual terms.

MASSACHUSETTS

WORD PRO/BARBARA WINSLOW ROBIDOUX, 127 Gelinas Dr., Chicopee MA 01020-4813. (413)592-4386. Fax (413)594-8375. E-mail: Ebwordpro@aol.com. Call/e-mail. GE/LC/writing coach. Edits A/SS/F/NB/BP/QL/TM/E/D. Fee quoted upon request. BA in English; 18 years as freelancer; book reviewer; on staff of TCC Manuscript critique service.

MICHIGAN

CALLED AND READY WRITERS CONSULTATION SERVICE/MARY EDWARDS/WANDA J. BURNSIDE, PO Box 211018, Detroit MI 48221. (313)491-3504. Fax (313)861-7578. E-mail: wtvision@hotmail.com. Website: www.thecalledandreadywriters.org. E-mail/$50 deposit. GE/LC/GH/CA/B/NL/SP/WS/BCE/PP/writing coach. Edits A/SS/P/F/N/NB/BP/QL/JN/PB/BS/GB/E/D/S/gospel tracts. Forty years' experience in editing. Has member and non-member rates. Charges by the page or type of project.

+EDITORIAL SERVICES/TIFFANY COLTER, 14665 Fike Rd., Riga MI 49276. (517)486-5418. E-mail: greatcommission2@aol.com. Website: www.writingcareercoach.com. E-mail contact. GE/writing coach. Edits A/SS/N/NB/BP/QL. Offers a 12-wk. online course on writer business development with coaching/feedback, $35 (audit for $50). BA, published in national and local periodicals, contest judge, business owner. Charges $20 for 15 pgs.; for longer mss will give a quote. Free e-lessons on Website.

+EDITORIAL SERVICES/MICHELLE LEWIS, 1227 Oakdale Ave., Niles MI 49120. (269)591-0672. Fax (269)357-0003. E-mail: editorialdragon@gmail.com. E-mail contact. GE/LC/CA/B/NL/SP/PP/scholarly work/dissertations. Edits A/SS/P/F/N/NB/BP/QL/JN/PB/BS/GB/TM/E/D/S/academic writing. Bachelor of Arts in English with a writing concentration. Editor for local Christian newspaper, published articles, writing tutor at Bethel College Writing Center. Charges $10-15/hr., depending on type and length of project. Usually requires a deposit before starting work; remainder on completion.

WALLIS EDITORIAL SERVICES/DIANA WALLIS, 547 Cherry St. S.E., #6C, Grand Rapids MI 49503-4755. (616)459-8836. E-mail: WallisEdit@sirus.com. Call/e-mail. GE/LC/SP/WS/proofreading. Edits A/N/NB/JN/BS/TM/D/advertising and promotional copy, Website content, educational materials for students and parents/teachers, catalog copy. Rates per project rather than per hour. Calvin College graduate, 15 years freelancing for publishers, corporations, and ad agencies; details on request.

THE WRITE SPOT/ARLENE KNICKERBOCKER, Where Quality and Economy Unite, PO Box 424, Davision MI 48423-9318. (810)793-0316. E-mail: writer@thewritespot.org. Website: www.thewritespot.org. E-mail contact. GE/LC/GH/CA/B/NL/SP/classes and speaking/writing coach. Edits: A/SS/P/F/NB/BP/QL/BS/E/D. Over 10 years of published credits; references available. Prices on Website.

MINNESOTA

NORTH COUNTRY TRANSCRIPTION (Psalm 96:12 NASB): Writing, Editing and Secretarial Services/CONNIE PETTERSEN. (218)927-6176. E-mail: pett289@mlecmn.net. Call/write. Manuscript typing; edits for punctuation/spelling/grammar, etc. Has published short fiction, over 250 nonfiction articles as newspaper feature/news writer; 30 years' secretarial/transcription experience. Types novels/nonfiction mss, résumés, etc. Software: Microsoft Office/Corel. Transcription by digital voice files. Fees: base @ .15 a 65-character line or $15/hr, plus postage. Free estimates. Confidentiality guaranteed. References.

MISSOURI

BLUE MOUNTAIN EDITORIAL SERVICE/BARBARA WARREN, Rte. 3 Box 3200, Exeter MO 65647. (417)835-3235. E-mail: barbarawarren@mo-net.com. Website: www.barbarawarren bluemountainedit.com. E-mail contact. GE/content editor/writing coach. Edits A/SS/N/BP/QL/JN/GB/E/D. Charges $20/hr. Twenty years' experience.

EDITORIAL SERVICES/J. TAYLOR LUDWIG, 6040 Sutherland Ave., St. Louis MO 63109-2246. (314)457-0026. E-mail: tludwig4@sbcglobal.net. E-mail contact. GE/LC. Edits A/SS/P/F/N/NB/BP/QL/JN/PB/BS/GB/TM/E/D/S. Charges $1.50/12 pt., double-spaced page, plus postage. Has M.A. in Media Communications; editor for Christian book publisher; book author.

THERE'S AN ANGEL IN YOUR INKWELL/CAROL NEWMAN, PO Box 480835, Kansas City MO 64148-0835. (913)681-1168. Fax (913)681-1173. E-mail: carol@angelinyourinkwell .com. Website: www.angelinyourinkwell.com. E-mail contact. GE/GH. Edits A/SS/P/F/NB/BP/QL/E/D. Variable rates according to project; average $40/hr.; 1/2 hr. free consultation. Twenty years national inspirational writer, teacher, and writing coach.

NEW HAMPSHIRE

AMGD ENTERPRISES/SALLY WILKINS, PO Box 273, Amherst NH 03031-0273. (603)673-9331. E-mail: SEDWilkins@aol.com. E-mail contact. GE/LC/B/NL. Edits A/F/NB/BP/QL. Published nonfiction adult and juvenile books and articles; edited 2 successful book proposals; experienced critiquer. Rate sheet for SASE.

NEW MEXICO

+EDITORIAL SERVICES/JEANNE SHANNON, 1217 Espejo St. N.E., Albuquerque NM 87112-5215. (505)296-0691. Fax (505)296-6124. E-mail: jspoetry@aol.com. Website: www.thewildflowerpress.com. E-mail contact. GE/LC. Edits A/SS/P/F/N/NB/BP/QL/JN/BS/TM/E. Published author; several years' experience as a technical writer/editor; MA in English; currently a small press publisher. Charges $1.25/pg. for copyediting/line editing; $25/hr. for more comprehensive editing.

NEW YORK

EDITORIAL SERVICES/STERLING DIMMICK, 311 Chemung St., Apt. 5, Waverly NY 14892-1463. (607)565-4247. E-mail: sterlingdimmick@hotmail.com. Call. GE/LC/GH/CA/SP. Edits A/SS/P/F/N/NB/BP/QL/JN/PB/BS/GB/TM/E/D/S. Has an AAS in Journalism; BA in Communication Studies. Charges $20/hr. or by the project.

EDITORIAL SERVICES/LAURIE GRAZIANO, 658 E. 34th St., Brooklyn NY 11203-6102. E-mail: grazianolau@yahoo.com. E-mail/write. Research/interviews/instructional. Will write A/P/F/D/greeting card copy. Experienced writer, contributing editor, staff writer, regular columnist. Charges by the project $15-75, or by the project.

NORTH CAROLINA

ANNA W. FISHEL, 3416 Hunting Creek Dr., Pfafftown NC 27040. (336)924-5880. E-mail: awfishel@triad.rr.com. Call/write/e-mail. GE/CA/SP. Edits A/SS/P/N/NB/JN/E/D. Charges by the hour. Estimates offered. Two decades of professional editing experience; editor with major Christian publishing house for over 10 years; published author of 6 children's books.

PREP PUBLISHING/PATTY SLEEM, 1110 1/2 Hay St., Fayetteville NC 28305. (910)483-6611. Fax (910)483-2439. E-mail: preppub@aol.com. Website: www.prep-pub.com. Write. GE/LC/SP. Edits N/NB. Project price based on written query and initial free telephone consultation. BA in English, MBA from Harvard, author of more than 25 books.

OHIO

JOY OF WRITING/MARY BUSHA, 1370-B Deerfield Road, Lebanon, OH 45036. (513) 228-1205. Email: joyofwriting45@yahoo.com. Write/call/e-mail. GE/LC/GH/CA/writing coach. Edits A/SS/N/NB/BP/QL/JN/PB/BS/GB/D. Offers workshops/seminars. Over 30 years of editorial and writing experience. Rates upon request.

OKLAHOMA

EPISTLEWORKS CREATIONS/JOANN RENO WRAY, 8409 S. Elder Ave., Broken Arrow OK 74011-8286. (918)451-4017. Cell: (918)695-4528. E-mail: epistle1@epistleworks.com. Website: http://epistleworks.com. Call/write/e-mail (prefers). GE/LC/GH/CA/B/NL/SP/research. Edits A/SS/P/F/N/NB/BP/D. Charges start at $25/hr. Accepts checks, money orders, or payment by PayPal. See site for details on services. Most editing requires min. $30 deposit. Binding estimates given. Graphic designs for logos, Website design, promotional materials, and more. Offers e-mail classes on writing. Available as speaker/teacher. Experienced artist, writer, and editor since 1974.

TWEEN WATERS EDITORIAL SERVICES/TERRI KALFAS, PO Box 1233, Broken Arrow OK 74013-1233. (918)346-7960. Fax (918)455-0794. E-mail: tlkalfas@cox.net. E-mail contact. GE/LC/GH/CA/B/SP/BCE. Edits A/N/NB/BP/QL/BS/TM/D/project management/book doctoring. Multiple editorial and freelance writing services. Twenty years' experience as reporter, writer, editor, editorial development director, and director of publishing. Equally skilled in copywriting for catalogs, direct marketing, and fund-raising. Former tech school writing instructor. Award-winning fiction writer. Available as conference speaker and workshop teacher. Charges $3 per pg./$25/hr./negotiable on special projects.

VERSATILE PEN/CHRISTY PHILLIPPE, 8816 S. 73rd East Ave., Tulsa OK 74133-4865. (918) 749-0098. E-mail: christy6871@aol.com. E-mail contact. GE/LC/B/NL/SP/research/indexing. Edits A/SS/N/NB/BS/GB/E/D. Thirteen years' experience in Christian publishing; former editor; ghostwritten books on bestseller list; former college English instructor. Charges vary.

WINGS UNLIMITED/CRISTINE BOLLEY, 712 N. Sweetgum Ave., Broken Arrow OK 74012-2156. (918)250-9239. Fax (918)250-9597. E-mail: WingsUnlimited@aol.com. Website: www.wingsunlimited.com. E-mail. GE/GH/CA/SP. Edits NB/D. Charges by the page; negotiated in advance. Former editorial acquisition editor with 25 yrs.' experience in book development of best-selling titles and author/coauthor/ghostwriter of 30+ titles. Also available to teach workshops at writer's conferences.

THE WRITE WORD/IRENE MARTIN, PO Box 300332, Midwest City OK 73140. E-mail: write1word@aol.com. Write/e-mail (detailing project). GE/critiques. Edits SS/F. (No nonfiction or autobiographies unless you want advice on presenting them as fiction.) Charges $3/pg., min. $15 for 5 pgs. Editing and writing workshops on a project-by-project basis. Has MEd and MA in English Creative Writing; published novelist; instructor/editor for Writer's Digest School; former university writing instructor.

OREGON

BALDWIN WRITERS SERVICES/STANLEY C. BALDWIN, 12900 S.E. Nixon, Portland OR 97222. (503)659-2974. E-mail: scbaldwin@juno.com. Evaluation of your organizational publication; Writers Workshops; manuscript critiquing by mail, contract evaluation. Send an SASE for rate sheet.

EDITING GALLERY LLC/CAROL L. CRAIG, 2622 Willona Dr., Eugene OR 97408. (541)342-7300. E-mail: carollcraig@comcast.net. Website: www.editinggallery.com. E-mail contact. GE/LC/writing coach. Edits N/BP/QL/JN/memoirs/synopses. English major. Charges $75/hr.

I'LL READ IT! EDITORIAL SERVICES/DONNA FLEISHER, PO Box 871, Lincoln City OR 97367. (541)994-2630. E-mail: donna@illreadit.com. Website: www.illreadit.com. Call/e-mail/write. GE/LC/writing coach. Edits SS/N/JN. Charges $300 flat fee for critique on entire manuscript, and $200 for a complete line edit. Prefers to work on hard copy; uses cassette tapes for the critique. Beginning novelists with a complete manuscript should check out her teaching series on writing Christian fiction available for a small fee on her Website. After listening to the series and making the first round of edits, then talk to her about the full critique.

PICKY, PICKY INK/SUE MIHOLER, 1075 Willow Lake Road N., Salem OR 97303-5790. (503)393-3356. E-mail: miholer@wvi.com. E-mail contact. LC. Edits A/NB/BS/D. Charges $30 an hour or negotiable by job. Freelance editor for several book publishers since 1998. "Write it right."

SALLY STUART, 1647 S.W. Pheasant Dr., Aloha OR 97006. (503)642-9844. Fax (503)848-3658. E-mail: stuartcwmg@aol.com. Website: www.stuartmarket.com. Call/write/e-mail. GE/BCE/agent contracts. Edits A/SS/N/NB/BP/GB/JN/E. No poetry or picture books. Charges $40/hr. for critique; $45/hr. for consultations. Contact for availability (not available April-June). For books, send a copy of your book proposal: cover letter, chapter-by-chapter synopsis for nonfiction (5-page overall synopsis for fiction), and the first three chapters, double spaced. Comprehensive publishing contract evaluation $80-150. Author of 35 books and 40+ years' experience as a writer, teacher, marketing expert.

+TERRYFLO WRITERS' HELPS/FLORENCE C. BLAKE, 4865 Hwy. 234, #176, White City OR 97503. E-mail: terryfloblake@yahoo.com. E-mail contact. LC/B/NL/SP. Edits A/SS/F/E/D/tracts. Freelance writers since 1999 with over 200 sales, community college writing teacher, senior contributing editor for general publication. Charges $2/double-spaced page.

PENNSYLVANIA

ANGAH CREATIVE SERVICES/DANIELLE CAMPBELL-ANGAH, 961 Taylor Dr., Folcroft PA 19032. (610)457-8300. E-mail: dcangah@angahcreative.com. Website: www.angahcreative.com. Ten years' writing experience; 5 years' editing experience.

IMPACT COMMUNICATIONS/DEBRA PETROSKY, 604 Chestnut St., 1st Fl., Irwin PA 15642. (724)863-5906. E-mail: editing4u@aol.com. Call/e-mail. GE/LC/B/back-cover text. Edits N/NB/TM. Has edited over 80 books. Charges $20/hr.; per page rates available.

MICHELLE T. HUEY EDITORIAL SERVICES, 121 Homestead Ln., Glen Campbell PA 15742-8404. (814)845-7683. Fax (call first). E-mail: writeon4writers@yahoo.com. Website: www.writeon4writers.com. E-mail contact. GE/LC/GH/B/NL/SP/WS. Edits A/SS/N/NB/QL/BS/GB/E/D/S. English/composition/journalism teacher for 20 yrs.; newspaper reporter, feature writer, editor, columnist for 10 yrs.; writing mentor for The Christian Writers Guild and The Writing Academy. Charges $30/hr. (estimates given); follows rates suggested at www.writersmarket.com/content/howmuch3.asp.

STRONG TOWER PUBLISHING/HEIDI NIGRO, PO Box 973, Milesburg PA 16853-0973. E-mail: strongtowerpubs@aol.com. Website: www.strongtowerpublishing.com. E-mail contact. GE/LC/NL/WS/PP/rewriting/developmental editing/writing coach. Edits A/SS/P/F/N/NB/BS/GB/TM/E/D. Specializes in general theological and eschatological mss. Twenty years' experience in editing in book and magazine publishing. Manuscript evaluation, $59-109; proofing, $2 per 250-word-page; copyediting, $4/250-word-page; developmental editing and book development $40 per hour or by project. Other projects negotiable. Provides free 5-page sample edit. Theological manuscripts must be consistent with basic statement of faith.

WORDS FOR ALL REASONS/ELIZABETH ROSIAN, 108 Deerfield Ln., Johnstown PA 15905-5703. (814)255-4351. E-mail: wordsforallreasons@yahoo.com. Website: www.101steps.zoomshare.com. Call/e-mail/write/total payment. GE/LC/GH/CA. Edits A/SS/F/N/NB/BP/QL/BS/E/D. Over 35 years' experience writing, teaching, and editing; over 1,000 articles in print, plus 7 books and many books edited for publication. Fast turnaround time. Charges $20/hr. Rate sheet on Website.

WRITE HIS ANSWER MINISTRIES/MARLENE BAGNULL, LittD, 316 Blanchard Rd., Drexel Hill PA 19026-3507. Phone/fax: (610)626-6833. E-mail: mbagnull@aol.com. Website: www.writehisanswer.com. Call/write. GE/LC/typesetting. Edits A/SS/N/NB/BP/JN/BS/D. Charges $35/hr.; estimates given. Call or write for information on At-Home Writing Workshops, a correspondence study program. Author of 5 books; compiler/editor of 3 books; over 1,000 sales to Christian periodicals.

TENNESSEE

CHRISTIAN WRITERS INSTITUTE MANUSCRIPT CRITIQUE SERVICE, PO Box 110390, Nashville TN 37222. Toll-free (800)21-WRITE. E-mail: ACWriters@aol.com. Website: www.ACWriters.com. Call/write. GE/LC/GH/CA/SP/BCE. Edits A/SS/P/F/N/NB/BP/JN/PB/BS/TM/E/D/S. Send SASE for rate sheet and submission slip.

EDITORIAL SERVICES/KIM PETERSON, 1114 Buxton Dr., Knoxville TN 37922. Write. GE/LC/GH/CA/B/SP/PP/mentoring/writing coach. Edits A/P/F/N/NB/BP/QL/JN/PB/GB/TM/E/D. Freelance writer; former college-level writing instructor; freelance editor; conference speaker. Charges $25/hr.

EDIT PLUS/CHARLES STROHMER, PO Box 4325, Sevierville TN 37876. (865)453-7120. Fax (865)428-0029. E-mail: wiselife@esper.com. Call/e-mail. GE/LC/CA/NL/SP. Edits A/NB/BP/QL/BS/TM/E/D. Twenty years' experience as author and editor for major Christian publishers. Call/e-mail to discuss project and rates. Rates vary according to the type of work, e.g., ms evaluation, line editing, rewriting, or book proposal.

TEXAS

+ASSURANCE EDITING SERVICES/MAUREEN B. MCCLAIN, PO Box 1051, Sanger TX 76266-1051. (940)458-3814. E-mail: Assuranceedit@juno.com. Call/e-mail/write. LC. Edits A/SS/P/F/N/NB/BP/QL/JN/BS/GB/E/D. Published book and devotional writer; freelancer for 10 years. E-mail for prices.

EDITORIAL SERVICES/DAYLE SHOCKLEY, 25510 Foxbriar, Spring TX 77373. (281)350-2902. E-mail: dayle@dayleshockley.com. Website: www.dayleshockly.com. Write/e-mail. GE/GH/NL/SP/PP. Edits A/SS/NB/BP/GB/E/D. Freelancer since 1987; special contributor to the *Dallas Morning News* since 1999; author of 3 books and dozens of articles. Contact for rates.

+FACETS BUSINESS COMMUNICATIONS/GEM SMITH, PO Box 79216, Houston TX 77279. (713)780-4676. E-mail: gem@facetscom.com. Website: www.facetscom.com. Call/e-mail. GE/LC/B/NL/SP/WS/content development. Edits A/SS/N/NB/BP/BS/TM/E/D/S. Published freelance writer/editor/speaker for 30 years. Has worked with technical/scientific material and authors with English as a second language. Works by the hour with deposit, after discussing project with client. Average is $35-50/hr.

PWC EDITING/PAUL W. CONANT, 527 Bayshore Pl., Dallas TX 75217-7755. (972)913-9123. Fax (972)557-7558. E-mail: editor@pwc-editing.com. Website: www.pwc-editing.com. Contact by e-mail. LC/NL/SP/PowerPoint/MS Word/Excel. Edits N/NB/BS/TM/D/S/dissertations/textbooks/Web pages. Writer, editor; proofreader for book publishers and magazines. Dissertations, $18/hr.; short works, $25/hr.; negotiable terms for long works.

+RENAISSANCE LITERARY SERVICES/JO REAVES, PO Box 248, Trenton TX 75490-7270. Phone/fax (903)989-2815. E-mail: editor@renaissanceliteraryservices.com. Website: www.renaissanceliteraryservices.com. E-mail contact. GE/LC/B/NL/SP/WS/PowerPoint/interior layout & design/audio transcription. Edits A/SS/P/F/N/NB/BP/QL/JN/PB/BS/GB/TM/E/D/S. Undergraduate and graduate work in languages and linguistics; managing editor of 3 newspapers; university professor (communications); 23 years' experience as professional editor; published author of 3 books. Charges $3-4/pg., depending on level of editing; additional rates on Website.

THE WRITE WAY EDITORIAL SERVICES/JANET K. CREWS/B. KAY COULTER, 806 Hopi Trl., Temple TX 76504-5008. (254)778-6490 or (254)939-1770. E-mails: janetcrews@sbcglobal.net or kaycoulter@sbcglobal.net. Website: www.writewayeditorial.com. Call/e-mail. GE/LC/GH/CA/B/NL/SP/scan to Word document/voice to Word document/graphics. Edits A/SS/N/NB/BP/QL/JN/BS/GB/D. Published author of 3 books; contributor to 2 books; 4 years with this editorial service; certified copyeditor. Free estimate; 20% of estimate as a deposit; $30/hr. Contact for additional details.

UTAH

RIVERWRITERS.COM/KATHLEEN WRIGHT. Sandy UT. Phone/fax (801)572-5227. E-mail: kathleen@riverwriters.com. Website: www.riverwriters.com. E-mail contact. GE/fiction coaching. Edits N/QL/fiction synopsis. Also a writing coach. Charges by the hour; e-mail for current rate. BA in journalism, 20+ years' editing/writing experience. Clients include beginning writers through multipublished award winners.

VIRGINIA

EDITOR FOR YOU/MELANIE RIGNEY, 4201 Wilson Blvd., #110328, Arlington VA 22203-1859. (703)863-3940. E-mail: editor@editorforyou.com. Website: www.editorforyou.com or www.melanierigney.com. Contact by e-mail. GE/LC/conference speaking. Edits N/NB/BP/QL/E. Charges .0125/wd. for copyediting; $65/hr. for content editing & coaching (provides a binding ceiling on number of hours); fees vary for ms evaluation. Editor of *Writer's Digest* magazine for 5 years; book editor/manager of Writer's Digest Books for 3 years; 29 years of editing experience.

EDITORIAL SERVICES/SKYLAR HAMILTON BURRIS, PO Box 7505, Fairfax Station VA 22039. (571)331-1481. E-mail: SSburris@msn.com. Website: www.editorskylar.com. E-mail contact. LC/NL/WS. Edits A/SS/F/N/NB/BP/JN/BS/GB/E/D. Charges authors $2/double-spaced pg. for editing. Charges businesses $35/hr. (for newsletter editing, writing, design). Specializes in working with self-publishing and POD authors. BA and MA in English. Eight years as a magazine editor; 10+ years' newsletter editing and design. Free sample edit of 2 pages.

SCRIVEN COMMUNICATIONS/KATHIE NEE SCRIVEN, 1902 Stevens Rd., #1406, Woodbridge VA 22191-2748. Phone/fax (703)492-6442. Cell (703)408-1184. Contact by phone. GE/LC/SP/WS. Edits A/SS/P/F/N/NB/BP/QL/JN/PB/BS/E/D/S. Charges $25-30/hr (rates vary depending on amount of rewriting needed, type of project, and turnaround time). Free half-hour consultation and estimate given. Discount for ministries. Brochure available for SASE. Has a BS in mass communication/journalism; 20 years' experience in print media; has edited over 40 books plus over 50 smaller projects; worked as an editor for several publications, plus several years' marketing experience. Specializes in spiritual growth books for adults.

SOLUTIONS UNLIMITED/SHARLENE PRITCHETT WADE, PO Box 1, Fisherville VA 22939. (540)241-1599. E-mail: solutions@rockbridge.net. Call/e-mail. GE/LC/GH/CA/B/NL/SP. Edits A/P/F/NB/GB/E/D. Competitive pricing by page or project. Creator of several works, newsletter designer, author, editor, encourager.

WASHINGTON

BRISTOL EDITING SERVICES/SANDRA E. HAVEN, PO Box 1000, Carlsborg WA 98324-1000. (360)582-9478. E-mail: services@bristolservicesintl.com. Website: www.bristolservices intl.com. E-mail contact. GE/SP. Edits A/SS/N/NB/BP/QL/JN/E. Critique (comprehensive edit) is .01/wd. Edits complete manuscripts as well as offering a "Write as We Go" service for writers working on book-length manuscripts. Fees and services fully explained on Website, or send SASE for services and rate sheet. Editor of Writers' Intl. Forum, 1990-1999 (award-winning publication); contributing editor to *1995 Novel & Short Story Writer's Market;* profiled as a leading editor for young writers in latest *Market Guide for Young Writers;* 16 years' experience in general editing.

BY BRENDA: WRITER & DESIGNER/BRENDA WILBEE, 7463 Leeside Dr., Blaine WA 98230. (360)746-0308. E-mail: BeeWilbee@gmail.com. Website: www.BrendaWilbee.com. E-mail contact. LC/GH/B/NL/SP/WS/PP/graphic design. Edits A/SS/F/N/NB/D. Has M.A. in Professional Writing; A.A. in Graphic Design; author of 9 CBA books and over 100 articles; long-time contributor to *Daily Guideposts.*

DOCUMENT DRIVEN/JANICE HUSSEIN, 16420 S.E. McGillivray, #103-103, Vancouver WA 98683. (503)789-6245. E-mail: Janiceh@gorge.net. Website: www.documentdriven.com. Call/e-mail. GE/LC. Edits N/QL/synopsis; submission critiques. MS in Writing/Publishing; MBA. Fee scale on Website; charges by project.

KALEIDOSCOPE PRESS/PENNY LENT, 2507—94th Ave. E., Edgewood WA 98371-2203. (253)848-1116. E-mail: K.press@earthlink.net. Call/e-mail/write; send negotiated deposit. GE/LC/GH/CA/B/NL/SP/BCE. Edits A/SS/P/F/N/NB/BP/QL/JN/PB/BS/GB/TM/E/D/S. Also market analysis, newsletters, brochures (graphic design & layout). All editing contracted by negotiated agreement. Discount given on larger projects. Thirty-eight years as published author on radio, in magazines, newspapers, and 11 books. Ghost writer and editor for 6 book publishers.

LOGOS WORD DESIGNS INC./LINDA L. NATHAN, PO Box 735, Maple Falls WA 98266-0735. (360)599-3429. Fax (360)392-0216. E-mail: linda@logosword.com. Website: www.logos word.com. Call/e-mail. GE/LC/GH/CA/B/NL/SP/résumés, consultations, writing assistance, manuscript submission services. Edits A/SS/F/N/NB/BP/QL/JN/PB/BS/TM/E/D/S/academic, legal, apologetics, conservative political. Over 30 years' experience in wide variety of areas, including publicity, postdoctoral; BA Psychology; some MA work. See Website or e-mail/call for rates.

MARION DUCKWORTH, 15917 N.E. 41st St., Vancouver WA 98682-7473. (360)896-8599. E-mail: mjduck@comcast.net. Call/e-mail/write. GE/SP. Edits A/SS/F/N/NB/BP/QL/BS; also does consultations. Charges $25/hr. for critique or consultation. Negotiates on longer projects. Author (for over 25 years) of 17 books and 300 articles; writing teacher for over 25 years; extensive experience in general editing and manuscript evaluation.

WORD SOURCE INC./MONICA COGLAS, PO Box 12575, Mill Creek WA 98082-0575. (425)481-4847. E-mail: wordsourceinc@verizon.net. E-mail/write/$20 deposit. GE/LC/B. Edits A/SS/N/NB/BP/QL/JN/PB/BS/GB/E/D. National award-winning author, business editor, newsletter editor, critique service, contest judge, and legal secretary. Charges $25/hr. or $5/pg. (4-page min.). Payment agreement must be signed in advance.

WISCONSIN

BRIAR PEN EDITORIAL SERVICES/SALLIE BACHAR, N1261 Briarwood Ln., Merrill WI 54452. (715)536-2450. E-mail: sallie.2@netzero.com. Call/e-mail/write. GE/LC. Edits A/SS/F/NB/E/D. Charges $25/hr. Associate editor of a national Christian magazine, published author, columnist, and journalist with over 10 years' experience.

MARGARET HOUK: EDITING SERVICES, West 2355 Valleywood Ln., Appleton WI 54915-8712. (920)687-0559. Fax (920)687-0259. E-mail: marghouk@juno.com. Call/write. GE/LC. Edits A/F/NB/BP/QL/E/D (all for teens or adults). Charges *Writer's Market* suggested rates. Author of 5 books and 700 articles; has taught writing and manuscript marketing for many years.

CANADIAN/FOREIGN

AOTEAROA EDITORIAL SERVICES/VENNESSA NG, PO Box 228, Oamaru 9444, New Zealand. Phone 0064273033738. (A U.S. based number is available to clients). E-mail: editor@aotearoaeditorial.com. Website: www.aotearoaeditorial.com. E-mail contact. GE/LC. Edits SS/N/BP. Page rates vary depending on project: start from .50/critique, $1/basic proofread, and $2.50/Copyedit. (Rates are in U.S. dollars and can be paid by PayPal.) Six years' critiquing experience.

BERYL HENNE, 711—60 Bridge St. W., Belleville ON K8P 1J3, Canada. (613)961-1791. E-mail: b.henne@sympatico.ca. Write or e-mail. GE/LC/B/NL/SP. Edits A/SS/NB/BS/TM/E/D. Charges $25/hr., will negotiate on larger projects. Has 5 years book and magazine editing, plus 18 years freelancing. Has worked with many self-publishing authors.

DORSCH EDITORIAL/AUDREY DORSCH, 1275 Markham Rd., #305, Toronto ON M1H 3A2, Canada. (416)439-4320. Fax (416)439-5089. E-mail: audrey@dorschedit.ca. Website: www.dorschedit.ca. Audrey Dorsch, ed. Editorial services: substantive editing, copyediting, indexing, proofreading, layout.

WENDY SARGEANT, PO Box 656, Capalaba QLD 4157, Australia. Phone 0427 870 330. Fax 07 32072263 (call first, Eastern Standard Time). E-mail: WendySargeant@bigpond.com. Website: www.editorsqld.com/freelance/Wendy_Sargeant.htm. Copy writing, editing, proofreading, research, feature writing. Special interests: technical material, business humor, children's books, educational books (primary, secondary, tertiary, and above), fiction, history, legal. Manuscript assessor and instructional designer with The Writing School. Award-winning author published in major newspapers and magazines. Editing educational manuals. Project officer and instructional designer for Global Education Project, United Nationals Assoc. Information specialist for Australian National University. See Wendy's writing under scribeofspirit.com.

CHRISTIAN LITERARY AGENTS

The references in these listings to "published authors" refer to those who have had one or more books published by royalty publishers, or who have been published regularly in periodicals. If a listing indicates that the agent is "recognized in the industry," it means they have worked with the Christian publishers long enough to be recognized (by the editors) as credible agents.

Note: Visit www.agentresearch.com to find more information on agents, or contact Professor Jim Fisher, Criminal Justice Dept., Edinboro University of Pennsylvania, Edinboro PA 16444, (814)732-2409, e-mail: Jfisher@edinboro.edu. Another site, www.sfwa.org/beware/agents.html, is sponsored by the Science Fiction and Fantasy Writers of America. At the site for the Association of Authors' Representatives, www.aar-online.org, you will find a list of agents who don't charge fees, except for office expenses. You may also send for their list of approved agents (send $7 with a #10 SAE/1 stamp) to: PO Box 237201, Ansonia Station, New York NY 10003. I also suggest that you check out any potential agents at their local Better Business Bureau or local attorney general's office. For additional agent sites: http://fictionaddiction.net/agents.html; www.anotherealm.com/prededitors.

As the information is available, listings will indicate which agents belong to the Association of Authors' Representatives Inc. (address above). Those members have subscribed to a set code of ethics. However, lack of such a designation does not indicate the agent is unethical; most Christian agents are not members. If they do happen to be members, it should give an extra measure of confidence. For a full list of member agents, go to: www.publishersweekly.com/aar.

(+) Indicates new listing

AARON AAMES AGENCY, 7834 Alabama Ave., Canoga Park CA 91304-4905. Fax (818)346-4313. Agent: Aaron Aames. Estab. 2006 (bought out previous agents). Not yet recognized in industry. No clients yet. Open to unpublished authors and new clients. Handles religious/inspirational fiction and nonfiction for all ages, screen plays, TV/movie scripts, crossover & general.

Contact: Letter. Accepts simultaneous submissions. Responds in 3-4 wks.

Commission: 15%.

Fees: None.

Tips: "Be patient, polite, and don't quit. SASE required."

AGENT RESEARCH & EVALUATION INC., 425 N. 20th St., Philadelphia PA 19130. (215)563-1867. Fax (215)563-6797. E-mail: info@agentresearch.info. Website: www.agentresearch.info. This is not an agency but a service that tracks the public record of literary agents and helps authors use the data to obtain effective literary representation. Charges fees for this service. Offers a free "agent verification" service at the site. (Answers the question of whether or not the agent has created a public record of sales.) Also offers a newsletter, *Talking Agents E-zine,* free if you send your e-mail address. See Jerry Jenkins's comments on this service on their Website, in the "Story So Far" section.

ALIVE COMMUNICATIONS, 7680 Goddard St., Ste. 200, Colorado Springs CO 80920. (719)260-7080. Fax (719)260-8223. E-mail: submissions@alivecom.com. Website: www.alivecom.com. Agents: Rick Christian, president; Lee Hough, Beth Jusino, Bruce Nuffer. Well known in the industry. Estab. 1989. Represents 100+ clients. New clients on referral only. Handles adult and teen novels and nonfiction, gift books, children's books, crossover and general market books. Deals in both Christian (70%) and general market (30%). Member Author's Guild & AAR.

Contact: E-mail to: submissions@alivecom.com. Responds in 6 wks. to referrals; may not respond to unsolicited submissions.

Commission: 15%

Fees: Only extraordinary costs with client's pre-approval; no review/reading fee.

Tips: If you have a referral, send material by mail and be sure to mark envelope "Requested Material." Unable to return unsolicited materials.

AMBASSADOR AGENCY, PO Box 50358, Nashville TN 37205. (615)370-4700. Fax (615)661-4344. E-mail: Wes@AmbassadorAgency.com. Website: www.AmbassadorAgency.com. Agent: Wes Yoder. Estab. 1973. Recognized in the industry. Represents 20 clients. Open to unpublished authors and new clients. Handles adult nonfiction, crossover books. Also has a Speakers Bureau.

Contact: E-mail.

THE ANDERSON LITERARY AGENCY INC., 435 Convent Ave., Ste. 5, New York NY 10031. (212)234-0692, or (212)234-0693. E-mail: gilesa@rcn.com. Agent: Giles Anderson. Open to unpublished authors and new clients. General agent. Handles adult religious nonfiction.

AUTHORCOACHING.COM: An Agent/Coaching Service for Inspirational Authors, PO Box 428, Newburg PA 17240. (717)423-6621. Fax (717)423-6944. E-mail: keith@authorcoaching.com. Website: www.AuthorCoaching.com. Coach: Keith Carroll. Estab. 2000. Deals with all inspirational material.

Contact: By letter, fax, phone, e-mail.

Fees: Visit Website for detailed description of fees.

+BENREY LITERARY, PO Box 12721, New Bern NC 28561. (252)638-5787. E-mail: janet@benreyliterary.com. Website: www.BenreyLiterary.com. Agent: Janet Benrey. Estab. 2006. Recognized in the industry. Represents 15 clients. Prefers referrals from current clients, or to meet writers at writer's conferences. Handles adult religious/inspirational novels (romance, contemporary women's, mystery, true crime); nonfiction (Christian living); general (thriller or cozy).

Contact: Requires e-queries.

Commission: 15%; foreign 20%.

MEREDITH BERNSTEIN LITERARY AGENCY, 2095 Broadway, Ste. 505, New York NY 10023. (212)799-1007. Fax (212)799-1145. Agents: Meredith Bernstein. Estab. 1981. Represents 85 clients. Open to unpublished authors and new clients. Handles nonfiction & fiction on spirituality. Member AAR.

Contact: Query with SASE. Considers simultaneous queries.

Commission: 15%; foreign 20%.

Fees: Charges $75/yr. disbursement fee.

Tips: "We obtain most of our new clients through conferences and referrals from others."

BIG SCORE PRODUCTIONS INC., PO Box 4575, Lancaster PA 17604. (717)293-0247. Fax (717) 293-1945. E-mail: bigscore@bigscoreproductions.com. Website: www.bigscoreproductions.com. Agents: David A. Robie, Sharon Hanby Robie. Recognized in industry. Estab. 1995. Represents 40-50 clients. Open to unpublished and new clients. Handles all types of fiction and nonfiction, gift books, general, crossover books, self-help, health, history, business, teen/children, and general nonfiction.

Contact: Query by e-mail only (query or proposal with outline and table of contents). No longer accepts queries or proposals by mail.

Commission: 15%, foreign and film 20-25%.

Fees: Photocopying, overnight, etc. No reading fees.

Tips: "Very open to taking on new clients. BigScore deals extensively with the general market, as well as the Christian market. Submit a well-prepared proposal that will take minimal fine tuning for presentation to publishers. Fiction: Your work must be extremely well written. Nonfiction: You must be highly marketable and media savvy. The more established in speaking or your profession, the better."

+BLUMER LITERARY AGENCY, 350 Seventh Ave., Ste. 2003, New York NY 10001-5013. (212)947-3040. Agent: Olivia B. Blumer. Member AAR. Estab. 2002. Represents 34 clients. Open to unpublished authors and new clients. Handles adult religious/inspirational nonfiction. General agent.

Contact: Query by mail only. Responds in 2-6 weeks.

Commission: 15%; foreign 20%.

Fees: Office expenses only.

BOOKS & SUCH/JANET KOBOBEL GRANT, 52 Mission Circle, Ste. 122, PMB 170, Santa Rosa CA 95409-5370. (707)538-4184. E-mail: representation@booksandsuch.biz. Website: www.booksandsuch.biz. Agents: Janet Kobobel Grant, Wendy Lawton, Etta Wilson. Well recognized in industry. Estab. 1997. Represents 100 clients. Open to new or unpublished authors (with recommendation only). Handles fiction and nonfiction for all ages, picture books, gift books, crossover, and general books.

Contact: E-mail query (no attachments); no phone query. Accepts simultaneous submissions. Responds in 6-8 wks.

Commission: 15%.

Fees: No fees.

Tips: "Especially looking for women's nonfiction. Also fiction that depicts everyday life and everyday faith struggles. Always interested in a strong nonfiction manuscript."

CURTIS BROWN LTD., 10 Astor Pl., New York NY 10003-6935. (212)473-5400. West Coast office: 1750 Montgomery St., San Francisco CA 94111. (415)954-8566. Agent: Perry Knowlton, chairman; Ellen C. Geiger. Member AAR. General agent; handles adult religious/inspirational novels & nonfiction.

Contact: Query with SASE; no fax/e-query. Submit outline or sample chapters. Responds in 3 wks. to query; 5 wks. to ms.

Fees: Charges for photocopying & some postage.

BROWNE & MILLER LITERARY ASSOCIATES, 410 S. Michigan Ave., Ste. 460, Chicago IL 60605. (312)922-3063. Fax (312)922-1905. E-mail: mail@browneandmiller.com. Website: www.browneandmiller.com. Agent: Danielle Egan-Miller. Estab. 1971. Recognized in the industry. Represents 75+ clients, mostly general, but also select Christian fiction writers. Open to new clients and talented unpublished authors, but most interested in experienced novelists looking for highly professional, full-service representation including rights management. Handles teen and adult fiction, adult nonfiction, and gift books for the general market; adult Christian fiction only. Member AAR, RWA, MWA, and The Author's Guild.

Contact: E-query to mail@browneandmiller.com, or mailed query letter/SASE.

Commission: 15%, foreign 20%.

PEMA BROWNE LTD., 11 Tena Pl., Valley Cottage NY 10989-2215. (845)268-0029. E-mail: ppbltd@optonline.net. Website: www.pemabrowneltd.com. Agent: Pema Browne. Recognized in industry. Estab. 1966. Represents 20 clients (2 religious). Open to unpublished authors; very few new clients at this time. Handles novels and nonfiction for all ages; picture books/novelty books, gift books, crossover books. Only accepts mss not previously sent to publishers; no simultaneous submissions. Responds in 6-8 wks.

Contact: Letter query with credentials; no phone, fax or e-query. Must include SASE. No simultaneous submissions. No attachments.

Commission: 20% U.S. & foreign; illustrators 30%.

Fees: None.

Tips: "Check at the library in reference section, in *Books in Print,* for books similar to yours. Have good literary skills, neat presentation. Know what has been published and research the genre that interests you."

SHEREE BYKOFSKY ASSOCIATES INC., 577 Second Ave., PMB 109, New York NY 10016. E-mail: Submitbee@aol.com. Website: www.shereebee.com. Agent: Sheree Bykofsky. Estab. 1984. Agent is a former editor and an author. Represents a limited number of clients. Open to unpublished authors and new clients. Handles adult religious/inspirational fiction and nonfiction. Member AAR.

Contact: Query with SASE; e-query OK; no phone calls, or unsolicited mss. Accepts simultaneous submissions, if notified. Responds to queries in 1 wk; mss in 1 mo.

Commission: 15%; foreign 20%.

Fees: No fees.

Tips: "I get new clients through the recommendations of others. No poetry, children's material, or screenplays."

CAMBRIDGE LITERARY ASSOCIATES, 135 Beach Rd., Unit C3, Salisbury MA 01952-2255. (978)499-0374. Fax (978)499-9774. Website: www.cambridgeliterary.com. Agent: Michael R. Valentino. Represents 20 clients. Accepting submissions only from well-published authors. Open to adult and teen fiction and nonfiction, screenplays, TV/movie scripts, and general books, crossover books. Member AAR.

Contact: Query letter by mail.

Commission: 15%; 20% foreign.

Fees: None.

Tips: "Christian fiction has become increasingly popular, especially works dealing with contemporary issues. Touch the readers where they live."

CASTIGLIA LITERARY AGENCY, 1155 Camino del Mar, Ste. 510, Del Mar CA 92014. (858)755-8761. Fax (858)755-7063. E-mail: JacLAgency@aol.com. Agents: Julie Castiglia and Sally Van Haitsma. Estab. 1993. Recognized in the industry. Represents 50 clients. Open to unpublished authors (with credentials) and selected new clients by referrals from editors, clients or published professionals. Handles adult religious/inspirational nonfiction, Christian fiction, and general crossover books. Member AAR.

Contact: Letter only/SASE. No phone/fax/e-query.

Commission: 15%; 25% foreign.

Fees: For excessive postage and copying, FedEx or messenger service.

Tips: "I do not look at unsolicited manuscripts."

+DONNA COFFEN, LITERARY AGENT/PUBLICIST, PO Box 822, Huntsville TX 77342. (936)291-2220. E-mail: donnacoffen@sbcglobal.net. Website: www.literaryagentpublicist.com. Agent: Donna Coffen. Estab. 2006. Represents 3 clients. Open to unpublished authors and new clients (in Texas only). Handles novels & nonfiction for all ages, picture books, poetry books, articles, short stories, poetry.

Contact: By letter, phone, or e-mail. Accepts simultaneous submissions. Responds in 4 wks.

Commission: 15%; foreign 20%.

Fees: Charges a $35 reading fee.

CS INTERNATIONAL, 43 W. 39th St., New York NY 10018. (212)921-1610. E-mail: csliterary@aol.com. Agent: Cynthia Neeseman. Handles adult fiction and nonfiction; screenplays; and seeks foreign sales for translations of books published in the U.S.

Contact: Query.

+THE BLYTHE DANIEL AGENCY INC., 4044 Cherry Plum Dr., Colorado Springs CO 80920. (719)213-3427. E-mail: blythe@theblythedanielagency.com. Website: www.theblythedanielagency.com. Agent: Blythe Daniel. Recognized in the industry. Estab. 2005. Represents 10 clients. Open to unpublished authors with a platform and new clients. Handles adult religious/inspirational novels, nonfiction for all ages, and crossover books.

Contact: By e-mail. Accepts simultaneous submissions. Responds in 4 weeks.

Commission: 15%; foreign 20%.

Fees: Only agreed-upon expenses.

Tips: "Preferences are authors who have a solid proposal on the topic of their book, including research on their audience, comparison to competitor's books, why they want to write on the topic, and what the author uniquely brings to the topic."

+DANIEL LITERARY GROUP, 1701 Kingsbury Dr., Ste. 100, Nashville TN 37215. E-mail: greg@danielliterarygroup.com. Website: www.danielliterarygroup.com. Agent: Greg Daniel. Estab. 2007. Open to unpublished authors and new clients.

DEFIORE & CO., 72 Spring St., Ste. 304, New York NY 10012. (212)925-7744. Fax (212)925-9803. E-mail: submissions@defioreandco.com. Website: www.defioreandco.com. Agents: Brian Defiore, Laurie Abkemeier, and Kate Garrick. Estab. 1999. Represents 35 clients. Open to new and unpublished authors. General agent; handles religious/inspirational nonfiction. Member of AAR.

Contact: Query with SASE, or e-query (no attachments).

Commission: 15%; foreign 20%.

Fees: Charges office expenses after book has sold.

JOELLE DELBOURGO ASSOCIATES, 516 Bloomfield Ave., Ste. 5, Montclair NJ 07042. (973) 783-6800. Fax (973)783-6802. E-mail: joelle@delbourgo.com. Website: www.delbourgo.com. Agent: Joelle Delbourgo. Open to unpublished authors and new clients. Handles adult religious nonfiction, adult and teen novels, short stories, crossover books, general books.

Contact: Query with SASE; no e-query. Accepts simultaneous submissions. Responds in 3 wks.

Commission: 15%; foreign 20%.

Fees: Writers are responsible for reasonable expenses.

DYSTEL & GODERICH LITERARY MANAGEMENT INC., 1 Union Square W., Ste. 904, New York NY 10003. (212)627-9100. Fax (212)627-9313. E-mail: Miriam@dystel.com. Website: www.dystel.com. Agents: Jane Dystel, Miriam Goderich, Stacey Glick, Michael Bourret, Jim McCarthy, and Lauren Abramo. Estab. 1994. Recognized in the industry. Represents 5-10 religious book clients. Open to unpublished authors and new clients. Handles fiction and nonfiction for adults, gift books, general books, crossover books. Member AAR.

Contact: Query letter with bio. Brief e-query; no simultaneous queries. Responds to queries in 3-5 wks.; submissions in 2 mos.

Commission: 15%; foreign 19%.

Fees: Photocopying is author's responsibility.

Tips: "Send a professional, well-written query to a specific agent."

EAMES LITERARY SERVICES, 4117 Hillsboro Rd., Ste. 251, Nashville TN 37215. Website: www.eamesliterary.com. Agents: John Eames (John@eamesliterary.com) and Ahna Phillips (Ahna@eamesliterary.com). Open to unpublished authors and new clients. Handles adult religious/inspirational novels & nonfiction.

EPIC LITERARY AGENCY. 7107 S. Yale Ave., #327, Tulsa OK 74136. (918)267-3248. Fax (918)267-3244. E-mail: KevinD@EpicLiterary.com, or info@EpicLiterary.com. Website: www.EpicLiterary.com. Agent: Kevin D. Decker. Estab. 1996. Represents up to 12 clients. Not currently open to unpublished authors; possibly open to new clients. Handles children's novels & nonfiction, picture books, screenplays, TV/movie scripts, gift books, crossover books.

Commission: 15%; foreign 20%.

Fees: Charges only for special travel or out-of-ordinary expenses.

Tips: "Please query first; we do not accept unsolicited manuscripts."

FARRIS LITERARY AGENCY INC., PO Box 570069, Dallas TX 75357-0069. (972)203-8804. Fax (972)226-1799. E-mail: farris1@airmail.net, or agent@farrisliterary.com. Website: www.farrisliterary.com. Agents: Mike Farris and Susan Morgan Farris. Open to unpublished authors and new clients. Handles Christian adult and teen fiction, spiritual or inspirational nonfiction, screenplays, general books, crossover books.

Contact: Mail or e-mail query (no attachments).

Commission: 15%; foreign 20%.

Fees: Expense for copies and postage only.

Tips: "Please keep your query to one page and allow 2 weeks for a response to queries and 4-6 weeks for response to submissions."

SARA A. FORTENBERRY LITERARY AGENCY, 1001 Halcyon Ave., Nashville TN 37204. (615)385-9074. Recognized in the industry. Estab. 1995. Represents 30 clients. Open to unpublished authors or new clients only by referral. Handles adult nonfiction and novels, picture books, gift books, and general books, crossover books.

Contact: Unpublished authors query by mail; published authors by phone or mail. Query letters should be accompanied by referral, book proposal, and SASE.

Commission: 15%; foreign 10%, plus subagent commission.

Fees: Standard expenses directly related to specific projects (copies, messenger, overnight shipping, and postage).

Tips: "For my purposes, a published author is one who has had a book published by a commercial (royalty) publisher."

SAMUEL FRENCH INC., 45 W. 25th St., New York NY 10010-2751. (212)206-8990. Fax (212) 206-1429. E-mail: info@samuelfrench.com. Website: www.samuelfrench.com, www.bakersplays.com. Agent: Roxane Heinz-Bradshaw. Estab. 1830. Handles rights to some religious/inspirational stage plays. Owns a subsidiary company that also publishes religious plays.

Contact: Query or send complete manuscript.

Commission: Varies.

Fees: None.

FULL CIRCLE LITERARY, LLC., 7676 Hazard Center Dr., Ste. 500, San Diego CA 92108. (858)824-9269. E-mail: kidsquery@fullcircleliterary.com. Website: www.fullcircleliterary.com. Estab. 2004. Agents: Lilly Ghahremani & Stefanie Von Borstel. Open to unpublished authors and new clients. General agent with one religious client. Handles teen/YA novels and picture books.

Contact: Query by mail or e-mail. Accepts simultaneous submissions. Responds in 4-6 weeks.

Commission: 15%.

Fees: No fees.

Tips: "Very limited Christian list—accepting teen/YA and children's picture books submissions only."

THE GARAMOND AGENCY, 12 Horton St., Newburyport MA 01950. (978)462-5060. E-mail: lisa.adams@garamondagency.com, or query@garmondagency.com. Website: www.garamondagency.com. Agent: Lisa Adams. Open to unpublished authors and new clients. General agent. Handles adult religious nonfiction.

Contact: Query with SASE; no e-query.

GENESIS CREATIVE GROUP, 28126 Peacock Ridge, Ste. 104, Rancho Palos Verdes CA 90275. Fax (310)541-9532. E-mail: KenRUnger@aol.com. Agent: Ken Unger. Estab. 1998; developing recognition in industry. Represents 10 clients. Open to new clients. Handles completed screenplays only; no books.

Contact: Send one-page query with personal information, project description, and target market, by mail or e-mail only. No phone calls; no unsolicited manuscripts.

Commission: 15%; may vary by type of project.
Fees: Office fees for long distance calls and postage only.
Tips: "We formed this company to represent material to film and television community. We want material that presents values based on Judeo-Christian tradition."

GOLDEN LITERARY AGENCY, 210 S. Holman Way, Golden CO 80401. (303)947-3524. Fax (303)384-9055. E-mail: goldenliterary@msn.com. Website: www.goldenliterary.com. Agent: Mary Ann Jeffreys. Estab. 2004. Recognized in the industry. Represents 6 clients with religious books. Open to unpublished authors and new clients. Handles adult Christian fiction & nonfiction; teen/young adult novels; Bible studies; or how-to-minister books. No children's books, poetry, or drama.
Contact: Proposal by mail or e-mail (preferred).
Commission: 15%; foreign 20%.
Fees: Office expenses only.
Tips: "Looking for authors who are passionate about their writing."

SANFORD J. GREENBURGER ASSOCIATES INC., 55 Fifth Ave., New York NY 10003. (212)206-5600. Fax (212)463-8718. Website: www.greenburger.com. Agents: Heide Lange, Faith Hamlin, Dan Mandel, Matthew Bialer, Jeremy Katz, Tricia Davey. Estab. 1945. Represents 500 clients. Open to unpublished authors and new clients. General agent; handles adult religious/inspirational nonfiction. Member of AAR.
Contact: Query/proposal/3 sample chapters to Heide Lange by mail with SASE, or by fax; no e-query. Accepts simultaneous queries. Responds in 6-8 wks. to query; 2 mos. to ms.
Commission: 15%; foreign 20%.
Fees: Charges for photocopying and foreign submissions.

GROSVENOR LITERARY AGENCY, 5510 Grosvenor Ln., Bethesda MD 20814. Phone/fax (301)564-6231. E-mail: deb@gliterary.com. Website: www.gliterary.com. Agent: Deborah Grosvenor. Estab. 1995. Represents 30 clients. Open to few unpublished authors and new clients. General agent; handles adult religious/inspirational nonfiction.
Contact: Letter. Responds in 1-2 mos.
Commission: 15%; foreign 20%.
Fees: None.

JOY HARRIS LITERARY AGENCY, 156 Fifth Ave., Ste. 617, New York NY 10010. (212)924-6269. Fax (212)924-6609. Agent: Joy Harris. Represents 100 clients. Handles religious/inspirational fiction. Member of AAR.
Contact: Proposal/outline or sample chapters. Responds in 2 mos.
Commission: 15%; foreign 20%.
Fees: Charges some office expenses.

HARTLINE LITERARY AGENCY, 123 Queenston Dr., Pittsburgh PA 15235. (412)829-2483. Fax (412)829-2432. E-mail: joyce@hartlineliterary.com. Website: www.hartlineliterary.com. Agents: Joyce A. Hart, adult novels (romance, mystery/suspense, women's fiction) and nonfiction; Tamela Hancock Murray, children's and young adult fiction, adult fiction (romance, mystery/suspense, women's) and nonfiction, tamela@hartlineliterary.com; Terry Burns, YA, children's, adult fiction & nonfiction, terry@hartliterary.com. Recognized in industry. Estab. 1992. Represents 150 clients. Open to published authors (or selected unpublished). Handles novels and nonfiction for all ages, gift books, general books, crossover books. No poetry.
Contact: E-mail preferred. Accepts simultaneous submissions. Responds in 12 wks.
Commission: 15%; foreign 20%.
Fees: Office expenses (very few); no reading fee.
Tips: "Be sure to include your biography and publishing history with your proposal. Please ask for our literary guidelines if you have questions about preparing proposals.

Working together we can make sure your manuscript gets the exposure and attention it deserves."

+THE HARVEY LITERARY AGENCY, LLC., 5579-B Chamblee Dunwoody Rd., Ste. 357, Dunwoody GA 30338. (404)299-6149. Fax (404)297-6651. E-mail: BoncaH@aol.com. Website: www.bookimprove.com. Agent: Dr. Bonnie C. Harvey. Represents 25+ clients. Recognized in the industry. Open to unpublished authors and new clients. Handles adult novels & nonfiction, juvenile & children's books.

Contact: By e-mail, letter, or phone.

Commission: 15%; foreign negotiable.

Fees: Office expenses.

JEFF HERMAN AGENCY, PO Box 1522, Stockbridge MA 01262. (413)298-0077. Fax (413)298-8188. E-mail: Jeff@jeffherman.com. Website: www.jeffherman.com. Agents: Jeff Herman and Deborah Herman. Estab. 1987. Recognized in the industry. Represents 20+ clients with religious books. Open to unpublished authors and new clients. Handles adult nonfiction (recovery/healing, spirituality), gift books, general books, crossover.

Contact: Query by mail/SASE; or by e-mail or fax. Accepts simultaneous submissions & e-queries.

Commission: 15%; foreign 10%.

Fees: No reading or management fees; just copying and shipping.

Tips: "I love a good book from the heart. Have faith that you will accomplish what has been appointed to you."

HIDDEN VALUE GROUP, 1240 E. Ontario Ave., Ste. 102-148, Corona CA 92881. Phone/fax (951)549-8891. E-mail: bookquery@hiddenvaluegroup.com. Website: www.HiddenValueGroup.com. Agents: Jeff Jernigan & Nancy Jernigan. Estab. 2001. Recognized in the industry. Represents 17+ clients with religious books. Open to previously published authors only. Handles adult novels and nonfiction, gift books, and crossover books. No poetry, articles, or short stories.

Contact: Prefers letter; e-mail OK. Accepts simultaneous submissions. Responds in 3-4 wks.

Commission: 15%; foreign 15%.

Fees: None.

Tips: "Women's nonfiction is of great interest. Make sure the proposal includes author bio, 2 sample chapters, and manuscript summary."

HORNFISCHER LITERARY MANAGEMENT, PO Box 50544, Austin TX 78763. E-mail: queries@hornfischerlit.com, or jim@hornfischerlit.com. Website: www.hornfischerlit.com. Agent: James D. Hornfischer. Estab. 2001. Represents 45 clients. Open to unpublished authors and new clients (with referrals from clients). Considers simultaneous submissions. Responds in 1 mo. General agent; handles adult religious/inspirational nonfiction.

Contact: E-query only for fiction; query or proposal for nonfiction (proposal package, outline, and 2 sample chapters). Considers simultaneous queries. Responds to queries in 6-8 wks.

Commission: 15%; foreign 25%.

ANDREA HURST LITERARY MANAGEMENT, 5050 Laguna Blvd., Ste. 112-330, Elk Grove CA 95758. (916)429-7725. E-mail: judy@andreahurst.com. Website: www.andreahurst.com. Agent: Judy Mikalonis. Fiction authors must be previously published. Handles adult nonfiction (Christian and mainstream), YA fiction, adult fiction (no romance, historical, science fiction, or supernatural thrillers).

WILLIAM K. JENSEN LITERARY AGENCY, 119 Bampton Ct., Eugene OR 97404. Phone/fax (541)688-1612. E-mail: Bill@wkjagency.com. Website: www.wkjagency.com. Agent: William K. Jensen. Estab. 2005. Recognized in the industry. Represents 30 clients. Open to unpublished authors and new clients. Handles adult fiction (no science fiction or fantasy), nonfiction for all ages, picture books, gift books, crossover books.

Contact: E-mail only. Accepts simultaneous submissions. Responds in 12 wks.

Commission: 15%.

Fees: No fees.

Tips: "I have contracted 38 books in the first 19 months of business."

NATASHA KERN LITERARY AGENCY INC., PO Box 1069, White Salmon WA 98672. (509)493-3803. Fax (509)493-3826. E-mail: natashakern@natashakern.com. Website: www.natashakern.com. Agent: Natasha Kern. Recognized in the industry. Estab. 1987. Represents 40 clients, 14 religious. Open to unpublished authors and new clients. Handles adult religious/inspirational fiction, crossover books, general books.

Contact: Accepts queries by letter; 3 pg. synopsis & 3 sample pgs.; no SASE required. Responds in 2-4 wks. to queries; 8 wks. to mss.

Commission: 15%; 20% foreign (includes foreign-agent commission).

Fees: No reading fee.

Tips: "We represent a wide range of inspirational fiction and nonfiction; adult only." See submission guidelines on Website.

LINDA KONNER LITERARY AGENCY, 10 W. 15th St., Ste. 1918, New York NY 10011. (212) 691-3419. E-mail: ldkonner@cs.com. Agent: Linda Konner. Open to unpublished authors and new clients. General agent. Handles adult religious/spirituality nonfiction.

Contact: Query with SASE. Accepts simultaneous submissions and e-queries. Responds in 1-2 wks. No unsolicited mss.

Commission: 15%; foreign 25%.

Tips: "Writers must be experts in their fields."

THE STEVE LAUBE AGENCY, 5025 N. Central Ave., #635, Phoenix AZ 85012-1502. (602)336-8910. E-mail: info@stevelaube.com. Website: www.stevelaube.com. Agent: Steve Laube. Estab. 2004. Well recognized in the industry. Represents 60+ clients. Open to new and unpublished authors. Handles adult Christian fiction and nonfiction, history, theology, how-to, health, Christian living. No YA, children's books, or poetry. Accepts simultaneous submissions. Responds in 6-8 wks.

Contact: Letter with proposal and sample chapters by mail is preferred; use guidelines on Website. No e-queries.

Commission: 15%; foreign 20%.

Fees: No fees.

Tips: "Looking for fresh and innovative ideas. Make sure your proposal contains an excellent presentation."

+LEATHER BOUND WORDS, 1493 Campton Ct., St. Louis MO 63368. (314)346-3548. E-mail: tgrady@leatherboundwords.com. Website: www.leatherboundwords.com. Agent: Thomas Grady. Estab. 2006. Not recognized in the industry. Represents 0 religious books. Open to unpublished authors and new clients. Considers simultaneous submissions. Responds in 5-10 days on queries/proposals, 3 mos. on mss. Represents adult novels & nonfiction; crossover books.

Contact: E-query. Accepts simultaneous submissions. Responds in 4-6 wks.

Commission: 15%; foreign 20%.

Fees: Office fees only, on permission.

THE LESCHER AGENCY INC., 47 E. 19th St., New York NY 10003. (212)529-1790. Fax (212)529-2716. E-mail: susanlescher@aol.com. Agent: Susan Lescher. Handles spiritual fiction & nonfiction.

Contact: Query by mail or e-mail.

LEVINE GREENBERG LITERARY AGENCY INC., 307—7th Ave., Ste. 2407, New York NY 10001. (212)337-0934. Fax (212)337-0948. Website: www.levinegreenberg.com. Agent: James Levine. West Coast Office: 112 Auburn St., San Refael CA 94901. (415)785-1582. Fax (415)785-1583. Agent: Arielle Eckstut. Estab. 1989. Represents 250 clients. Open to unpublished authors and new clients. General agent; handles adult religious/inspirational nonfiction. Member AAR.

Contact: See guidelines/submission form on Website; prefers e-query.

Commission: 15%; foreign 20%.

Fees: Office expenses.

Tips: "Our specialties include spirituality and religion."

LITERARY AND CREATIVE ARTISTS INC., 3543 Albemarle St. N.W., Washington DC 20008. (202)362-4688. Fax (202)362-8875. E-mail: muriel@lcadc.com, or lca9643@lcadc.com. Website: www.lcadc.com. Agent: Muriel Nellis. AAR member. Open to unpublished authors and new clients. General agent. Handles adult religious nonfiction. Submission guidelines on Website. Responds in 3 wks.

THE LITERARY GROUP INTL., The Stanford Bldg., 51 E. 25th St., Ste., 401, New York NY 10010. (212)274-1616. Fax (212)274-9876. E-mail: Fweimann@theliterarygroup.com, or js@theliterarygroup.com. Website: www.theliterarygroup.com. Agents: Frank Weimann, Ian Kleinert. Recognized in the industry. Estab. 1986. Represents 300 clients (120 for religious books). Open to new and unpublished authors. Handles adult fiction and nonfiction, history, general, crossover, gift books, how-to, health, spiritual guidance.

Contact: Letter.

Commission: 15%; foreign 20%.

Fees: No fees.

Tips: "Looking for fresh, original spiritual fiction and nonfiction. We offer a written contract which may be canceled after 30 days."

LITERARY MANAGEMENT GROUP INC., PO Box 40965, Nashville TN 37204. (615)812-4445. E-mail: brucebarbour@literarymanagementgroup.com. Website: www.literarymanagement group.com. Agents: Bruce R. Barbour & Margaret Langstaff. Estab. 1995. Well recognized in the industry. Represents 100+ clients. Open to published authors who have a platform and a compelling story or idea. Handles nonfiction only. Other services offered: book packaging and consulting.

Contact: E-mail preferred. Will review proposals, no unsolicited mss.

Commission: 15%; foreign 20%.

Fees: No fees or expenses on agented books.

Tips: "Follow guidelines, proposal outline, and submissions format on Website. Use Microsoft Word. Study the market and know where your book will fit in."

THE LITERATI, 138 Old Liberty Pike, Franklin TN 37064. (615)943-6851. E-mail: info@the literati.net. Website: www.theliterati.net. Agents: Angela DePriest (fiction); Dan DePriest (nonfiction). Estab. 2005. Recognized in the industry. Represents 13 clients. Open to unpublished authors and new clients. Handles adult/teen/children's novels & nonfiction, crossover books, general books.

Contact: E-mail preferred. Accepts simultaneous submissions. Responds in 1-3 weeks.

Commission: 15%; foreign 15-20% (20% if sub-agent involved).

Fees: Charges only for photocopying or legal fees. No fees to exceed $50 without prior consent.

Tips: "For initial submission, please send a one-page synopsis only of your book. We will contact you when we want to see more. This ultimately saves us time, and we'll be able to contact you faster."

STERLING LORD LITERISTIC INC., 65 Bleecker St., New York NY 10012. (213)780-6050. Fax (212)780-6095. E-mail: claudia@sll.com, or info@sll.com. Website: www.sll.com. Agent: Claudia Cross. Recognized in the industry. Represents 10 clients with religious books. Open to unpublished clients with referrals and to new clients. Handles adult and teen Christian fiction, spiritual adult nonfiction, gift books, crossover books, general books.

Contact: Letter, fax or (e-query with referral only). Accepts simultaneous submissions, if informed. Responds in 4-6 wks.

Commission: 15%; foreign 20%.

Fees: "We charge for photocopy costs for mss or costs above and beyond the usual cost of doing business."

LUKEMAN LITERARY MANAGEMENT INC., 157 Bedford Ave., Brooklyn NY 11211-2037. Website: www.lukeman.com. Agent: Noah Lukeman. Estab. 1996. Recognized in the industry. Represents 10 clients. Rarely open to unpublished authors or new clients (most are already publishing). Handles adult religious/inspirational novels and nonfiction.

Contact: Not accepting submissions at this time. Check Website for availability.

Commission: 15%; foreign 20%.

Fees: None.

+MACGREGOR LITERARY, 2373 N.W. 185th Ave., Ste. 165, Hillsboro OR 97124. E-mail: chip@macgregorliterary.com. Website: www.MacGregorLiterary.com. Agent: Chip MacGregor. Estab. 2006. Recognized in the industry. Represents 30 clients. Open to unpublished authors, if writing is great, and new clients. Handles adult religious/inspirational novels, nonfiction, & crossover books.

Contact: E-mail query to: submissions@macgregorliterary.com. Accepts simultaneous submissions. Responds in 4 wks.

Commission: 15%; foreign 20%.

Fees: No fees or expenses except in special situations.

Tips: "My authors are paid directly by the publisher. I use an at-will agreement (not a term agreement). I've represented numerous award winners and CBA bestsellers. Committed to representing books that make a difference."

MANUS & ASSOCIATES LITERARY AGENCY, 425 Sherman Ave., Ste. 200, Palo Alto CA 94306. (650)470-5151. Fax (650)470-5159. E-mail: manuslit@manuslit.com. Website: www.manuslit.com. Agents: Jillian Manus, Penny Nelson, Dena Fischer, and Jandy Nelson. Members AAR. Estab. 1994. Represents 10 clients. Not yet recognized in the industry. Open to unpublished authors and new clients. Handles adult religious/inspirational novels & nonfiction.

Contact: Query by mail/fax/e-query (no attachments). For fiction, send first 30 pages, bio, and SASE. For nonfiction, send proposal/sample chapters. Responds in 8 weeks.

Commission: 15%.

MARCH MEDIA INC. See Books and Such.

MCHUGH LITERARY AGENCY, 1033 Lyon Rd., Moscow ID 83843-9167. (208)882-0107. E-mail: elisabet@moscow.com. Agent: Elisabet McHugh. Estab. 1995. Represents 49 clients. Recognized in the industry. Open to unpublished authors and new clients. General agent; handles adult and teen religious/inspirational nonfiction, crossover books, general books.

Contact: E-mail first.

Commission: 15%; foreign 20%.

Fees: None, but clients provide copies of manuscripts.

Comments: "Be professional!"

WILLIAM MORRIS LITERARY AGENCY, 1325 Avenue of the Americas, New York NY 10019. (212)586-5100. E-mail: vs@wma.com. Website: www.wma.com. Agent: Valerie Summers.

Recognized in the industry. Estab. 1898. Hundreds of clients with religious books. Not open to unpublished authors or new clients. Handles all types of material. Member AAR.

Contact: Send query/synopsis, publication history by mail/SASE. No fax/e-query. No unsolicited mss.

Commission: 15%; foreign 20%.

Fees: None.

+NAPPALAND LITERARY AGENCY, 367 Hawthorne Dr., Loveland CO 80538. (970)635-0641. Fax (970)635-9869. E-mail: literary@nappaland.com, nappaland@aol.com. Website: www.nappaland.com. Nappaland Communications Inc. Agent: Mike Nappa. Estab. 1995. Handles literary nonfiction, cultural concerns, Christian living, women's issues, suspense fiction, and women's fiction.

+THE NASHVILLE AGENCY, PO Box 110909, Nashville TN 37222. Toll-free (866)333-8663. (615)263-4143. E-mail: submissions@thenashvilleagency.com. Website: www.thenashville agency.com. Agent: Jonathan Clements. Handles adult inspirational novels & nonfiction.

Contact: E-mail query. Responds in 6 wks.

+B. K. NELSON INC., 1565 Paseo Vida, Palm Springs CA 92264. (760)778-8800. Fax (760)778-0034. E-mail: bknelson4@cs.com. Website: www.BKNelson.com. Agent: John Benson. Estab. 1988. Represents 6 clients with religious books. Open to unpublished authors and new clients. Handles novels & nonfiction for all ages, screenplays, TV/movie scripts, gift books.

Contact: By fax or e-mail. "Inquire with name, credentials, log line, genre, address, phone, fax, and e-mail."

Commission: 20%; foreign 10%.

Fees: No fees.

Tips: "If nonfiction, submit query and subsequently a proposal professionally done. If fiction, query and subsequently submit an outline and 3 chapters, not to exceed 50 pages."

+NUNN COMMUNICATIONS INC., 1612 Ginger Dr., Carrollton TX 75007. (972)394-NUNN. E-mail: info@nunncommunications.com. Website: www.nunncommunications.com. Agent: Leslie Nunn Reed. Estab. 1995. Represents 20 clients. Recognized in the industry. Not open to unpublished authors. Handles adult nonfiction, gift books, crossover books, and general books.

Contact: By e-mail. Responds in 4-6 wks.

Commission: 15%.

Fees: Charges office expenses if over $100.

+ALLEN O'SHEA LITERARY AGENCY, LLC., 615 Westover Rd., Stamford CT 06902. (203)359-9965. Fax (203)357-9909. E-mail: MA615@aol.com. Website: www.publishersmarket place.com/members/AllenOShea. Agents: Marilyn Allen and Coleen O'Shea. Estab. 2003. Represents 4 clients with religious books. Recognized in the industry. Open to unpublished authors (with credentials & platform) and new clients. No simultaneous submissions. Responds in 4 wks. Handles teen novels and adult nonfiction.

Contact: Query by mail or e-mail.

Commission: 15%; foreign 15-25%.

Fees: For photography and overseas mailing.

Tips: "We specifically like nonfiction."

KATHI J. PATON LITERARY AGENCY, PO Box 2240, New York NY 10101-2240. (908)647-2117. E-mail: KJPLitBiz@optonline.net. Agent: Kathi Paton. Estab. 1987. Handles adult religious/inspirational nonfiction.

Contact: Prefers e-mail query.

Commission: 15%; foreign 20%.

Fees: For photocopying.

PATRICK-MEDBERRY ASSOCIATES, 27023 McBean Pkwy, #103, Valencia CA 91355. Phone/fax (818)980-5820. E-mail: patrickmedberry@sbcglobal.net. Agents: Peggy Patrick & C. J. Medberry. Estab. 2005. Newly established management company specializing in Christian writers, directors, and producers, as well as religious and inspirational novels, screenplays, TV/movie scripts, crossover books, general books, and screenplays. Open to unpublished authors and new clients.

Contact: Query by letter, fax, or e-mail; no calls.

Commission: 10%.

Fees: None.

PELHAM LITERARY AGENCY, 2451 Royal St. James Dr., El Cajon CA 92019-4408. (619)447-4468. E-mail: jmeals@pelhamliterary.com. Website: www.pelhamliterary.com. Agent: Jim Meals. Recognized in the industry. Estab. 1993. Open to unpublished authors and new clients. Handles adult and teen novels and nonfiction, crossover books.

Contact: Brief query letter preferred; e-query OK. Provides a list of published clients and titles. Accepts simultaneous submissions. Responds in 6 wks.

Commission: 15%; foreign 20%.

Fees: Charges for postage and copying only. Also offers an optional extensive critique for $200. Information on Website.

Tips: "We are actively seeking writers for the Christian fiction market, although also open to Christian nonfiction. We specialize in genre fiction and enjoy working with new writers."

ALICKA PISTEK LITERARY AGENCY, 302A W. 12th St., #124, New York NY 10014. E-mail: info@apliterary.com. Website: www.alickapistek.com. Agent: Alicka Pistek. Open to unpublished authors and new clients. General agent. Handles adult religious nonfiction.

Contact: E-query only. Responds in 8-10 wks.

QUICKSILVER BOOKS ONLINE, 508 Central Park Ave., #5101, Scarsdale NY 10583. Phone/fax (914)722-4664. E-mail: QBOnline@artsnet.net. Website: www.quicksilverbooks.com. Agent: Bob Silverstein. Estab. 1987. Represents 50 clients. Open to unpublished authors and new clients. General agent; handles adult religious/inspirational nonfiction.

Contact: Query by e-mail. Considers simultaneous submissions. Responds in 2-5 wks.

Commission: 15%; foreign 20%.

Fees: No fees.

RED WRITING HOOD INK, 2019 Attala Rd. 1990, Kosciusko MS 39090. (662)674-0636. Fax (662)796-3095. E-mail: info@redwritinghoodink.net. Website: www.redwritinghood ink.net. Agent: Sheri Ables. Estab. 1997. Recognized in the industry. Represents 4 clients with religious books. No unpublished authors; open to new clients. Handles novels and nonfiction for teen/young adults and adults; gift books; crossover books; some general titles.

Contact: No simultaneous submissions; responds in 3-4 wks.

Commission: 15%; 20% foreign.

RICIA MAINHARDT AGENCY, 612 Argyle Rd., #L5, Brooklyn NY 11230. (718)434-1893. Fax (718)434-2157. E-mail: ricia@ricia.com. Website: www.ricia.com. Handles adult and young adult fiction, nonfiction, picture books, and early readers. Submission guidelines on Website.

Contact: For fiction send a 3-5 page synopsis with first 20-30 pages (ending at a chapter break); for nonfiction, a chapter-by-chapters synopsis and 2 chapters; for children's send complete ms. Call for e-mail submissions instructions.

Fees: No reading fees.

RLR ASSOCIATES, LTD., Literary Dept., 7 W. 51st St., New York NY 10019. (212)541-8641. Fax (212)541-6052. Also has a California office. E-mail: sgould@rlrassociates.net. Website: www.rlrliterary.net. Scott Gould, literary assoc. Estab. 1972. Represents 50+ clients. Open to unpublished authors and new clients. General agency; handles adult religious/inspirational nonfiction.

Contact: Query with SASE. Considers simultaneous submissions. Responds in 5 wks.

Commission: 15%; foreign 20%.

ROSENBAUM & ASSOCIATES LITERARY AGENCY, 310 Shadow Creek Dr., Brentwood TN 37027. (615)834-8564. Fax (615)834-8560. E-mail: bucky@rosenbaumagency.com. Website: www.rosenbaumagency.com. Agent: Bucky Rosenbaum. Estab. 2006. Well recognized in the industry. Represents 30-40 clients. Open to a limited number of new clients and unpublished authors by referral only. Handles mostly adult nonfiction, and some general books, crossover books.

Contact: Unpublished query by mail/SASE; published authors by phone or e-mail. Accepts simultaneous submissions.

Commission: 15%; foreign 20%.

Fees: Only extraordinary costs with client's permission; no reading fees.

Tips: "Request a product proposal template by e-mail."

RITA ROSENKRANZ LITERARY AGENCY, 440 West End Ave., Ste. 15D, New York NY 10024-5358. (212)873-6333. Agent: Rita Rosenkranz. Estab. 1990. Represents 30 clients. Open to unpublished authors and new clients. General agent; handles adult religious/inspirational nonfiction. Member AAR.

Contact: Proposal package (outline and sample chapter); no fax/e-query. Accepts simultaneous submissions. Responds in 2 wks. to query.

Commission: 15%; foreign 20%.

Tips: "A strong cover letter is very important. Be sure to identify competition to your book, and be sure it's a valid project."

GAIL ROSS LITERARY AGENCY, 1666 Connecticut Ave. N.W., #500, Washington DC 20009. (202)328-3282. Fax (202)328-9162. E-mail: jennifer@gailross.com. Website: www.gailross.com. Contact: Jennifer Manguera. Estab. 1988. Represents 200 clients. Open to unpublished authors and new clients (mostly through referrals). General agent; handles adult religious/inspirational nonfiction, history, health, and business books.

Contact: Query with outline, sample pages, résumé/SASE; no e-query. Accepts simultaneous queries.

Commission: 15%; foreign 25%.

Fees: Office expenses.

DAMARIS ROWLAND AGENCY, 5 Peter Cooper Rd., #13H, New York NY 10010. (212)475-8942. Cell (917)538-3916. Fax (212)358-9411. Agent: Damaris Rowland. Estab. 1994. Represents 40 clients. Open to unpublished authors and new clients. No New Age material. Very selective.

Contact: Query letter.

Commission: 15%; foreign 20%.

Fees: Some office expenses.

PETER RUBIE LITERARY AGENCY, LTD., 240 W. 35th St., Ste. 500, New York NY 10001. (212)279-1776. Fax (212)279-0927. E-mail: peterrubie@prlit.com. Website: www.prlit.com. Agent: Peter Rubie. Open to unpublished authors and new clients. General agent. Handles adult religion/spirituality nonfiction.

Contact: Query/SASE; accepts e-query. Responds in 2-3 mos.

Commission: 15%; foreign 20%.

SCHIAVONE LITERARY AGENCY INC., 236 Trails End, West Palm Beach FL 33413-2135. Phone/fax (561)966-9294. E-mail: profschia@aol.com. Website: www.publishersmarketplace.com/members/profschia. Agent: James Schiavone, EdD. Recognized in the industry. Estab. 1997. Represents 6 clients. Open to unpublished and new clients. Handles adult, teen, and children's fiction and nonfiction; celebrity biography; general books; crossover books.

Contact: Query letter/SASE; one-page e-mail query (no attachments).

Commission: 15%, foreign 20%.

Fees: No reading fees; authors pay postage only.

Tips: Works primarily with published authors; will consider first-time authors with excellent material. Actively seeking books on spirituality, major religions, and alternative health. Very selective on first novels.

SUSAN SCHULMAN LITERARY AGENCY, 454 W. 44th St., New York NY 10036. (212)713-1633. Fax (212)581-8830. E-mail: schulman@aol.com. Website: www.schulmanagency.com.owner. Agent: Susan Schulman; Rights & Permissions: Eleanora Tevis; Submissions Editor: Linda Migalti Kiss. Estab. 1980. Building recognition in the Christian marketplace; well-established in general publishing. Represents 12 clients with religious books. Open to unpublished authors and new clients. Handles books for, by, and about women and women's issues and interests, including spiritual studies, historically based fiction and nonfiction, contemporary women's fiction, parenting, relationships, social trends, inspirational collections, especially if on one topic, as well as children's books, including early readers, picture books, young adult fiction and limited nonfiction. Member AAR.

Contact: Prefers mail contact; e-query OK. Responds only if interested. Accepts simultaneous submissions. Responds in 2-3 wks.

Commission: 15%; foreign 20% (shared 50/50 with foreign co-agent).

Fees: Only agreed-upon office expenses. No fees.

Tips: "We are interested in sophisticated religious and spiritual material, especially nonfiction or historically based fiction or nonfiction, as well as personal memoirs, all appropriate for a well-educated audience."

SCOVIL, CHICHAK, GALEN LITERARY AGENCY, 276 Fifth Ave., Ste. 708, New York NY 10001. (212)679-8686. Fax (212)679-6710. E-mail: annaghosh@scglit.com, or info@scglit.com. Website: www.scglit.com. Agent: Anna Ghosh. Open to unpublished authors and new clients. General agent. Handles adult religious/spirituality nonfiction. Submission guidelines on Website.

SCRIBBLERS HOUSE, LLC, PO Box 1007, Cooper Station, New York NY 10276-1007. E-mail: query@scribblershouse.net, or from Website: www.scribblershouse.net. Agents: Stedman Mays & Garrett Gambino. Estab. 2003. Not recognized in the industry. Some clients with spiritual books. Open to unpublished and new clients, but very selective. Handles adult nonfiction.

Contact: Prefers e-query; go to Website for instruction. Accepts simultaneous submissions. Responds in 8-12 wks.

Fees: Office expenses; no reading or other fees.

Tips: "See Website for most up-to-date information."

SE LITERARY PROPERTIES, PO Box 67385, St. Pete Beach FL 33706. E-mail: stephen@excellentnovels.com. Website: www.seliterary.homestead.com. Agent: Stephen Everett.

Contact: Mail or e-mail (no attachments).

Commission: 15%.

Fees: Office expenses only.

SERENDIPITY LITERARY AGENCY, LLC, 305 Gates Ave., Brooklyn NY 11216. (718)230-7689. Fax (718)230-7829. E-mail: rbrooks@serendipitylit.com. Website: www.serendipitylit.com. Agent: Regina Brooks. Member AAR. Estab. 2000. Represents 50 clients; 3 with religious books. Recognized in the industry. Open to unpublished authors and new clients. General agent; handles fiction & nonfiction for all ages, picture books, gift books, crossover books, general books. No science fiction.

Contact: By e-mail or letter; no faxes. Accepts simultaneous submissions. Responds in 8-12 wks.

Commission: 15%; foreign 20%.

Fees: None.

THE SEYMOUR AGENCY, 475 Miner Street Rd., Canton NY 13617. (315)386-1831. E-mail: marysue@slic.com. Website: www.theseymouragency.com. Agent: Mary Sue Seymour. Estab. 1992. Member of AAR. Ellen Feig (efeig@hotmail.com) handles film rts. Recognized in the industry. Represents 25 religious clients. Open to unpublished authors and new clients (prefers published authors). Handles romance novels, Christian chick lit, Christian historical romance, and nonfiction for all ages, general books, crossover books.

Contact: Query letter or e-mail with first 50 pages of ms; no fax query. For nonfiction, send proposal with chapter one. Simultaneous query OK. Responds in 1 mo. for queries and 2-3 mos. for mss.

Commission: 15% for unpublished authors; 12.5% for published authors; foreign 20%.

Fees: None.

Tips: "E-mail loglines for scripts to Ellen Feig, an attorney, who will also review contracts."

THE SHEPARD AGENCY, 73 Kingswood Dr., Bethel CT 06801. (203)790-4230. Fax (203)798-2924. E-mail: shepardagcy@mindspring.com. Website: http://home.mindspring.com/~shepardagcy. Agent: Jean Shepard. Recognized in the industry. Estab. 1987. Represents 11 clients. Open to unpublished authors; no new clients at this time. Handles fiction and nonfiction for all ages; no picture books; especially business, reference, professional, self-help, cooking, and crafts. Books only.

Contact: By e-mail.

Commission: 15%; foreign variable.

Fees: None except long-distance calls and copying.

KEN SHERMAN & ASSOCIATES, 9507 Santa Monica Blvd., Beverly Hills CA 90210. (310)273-3840. Fax (310)271-2875. E-mail: ken@kenshermanassociates.com. Agent: Ken Sherman. Estab. 1989. Represents 50 clients. Open to unpublished authors and new clients. Handles adult religious/inspirational novels, nonfiction, screenplays and TV/movie scripts.

Contact: By referral only. Responds in 1 mo.

Commission: 15%; foreign 20%; dramatic rts. 15%.

Fees: Charges office expenses and other negotiable expenses.

WENDY SHERMAN ASSOCIATES, 450 Seventh Ave., Ste. 2307, New York NY 10123. (212)279-9027. Fax (212)279-8863. E-mail: tracy@wsherman.com. Website: www.wsherman.com. Agents: Wendy Sherman, Michelle Brower, Emmanuelle Alspaugh. Open to unpublished authors and new clients. General agents. Handle adult religious nonfiction.

Contact: Query by mail/SASE or send proposal/1 chapter. No phone/fax query. Guidelines on Website.

Commission: 15%; foreign 20%.

JACQUELINE SIMENAUER LITERARY AGENCY, PO Box A.G., Mantoloking NJ 08738-0390. (732)262-0783. Open to unpublished authors. Handles spiritual fiction & nonfiction.

Contact: For fiction, query with first 3 chapters, synopsis, bio, and SASE. For nonfiction, send query with SASE. Simultaneous & e-query OK.

Commission: 15%; foreign 20%.

MICHAEL SNELL LITERARY AGENCY, PO Box 1206, Truro MA 02666-1206. (508)349-3718. Agent: Michael Snell. Estab. 1978. Represents 200 clients. Open to unpublished authors and new clients. General agent: handles adult religious/inspirational nonfiction.

Contact: Query with SASE. No simultaneous submissions. Responds in 1-2 wks.

Commission: 15%; foreign 15%.

SPENCERHILL ASSOCIATES, LTD./KAREN SOLEM, 24 Park Row, PO Box 374, Chatham NY 12037. (518)392-9293. Fax (518)392-9554. E-mail: ksolem@klsbooks.com. Agent: Karen Solem. Recognized in the industry. Estab. 2001. Represents 15 clients. Not currently open to unpublished authors or new clients. Handles adult novels and nonfiction, general books, crossover books.

Contact: A brief e-mail query is OK. If sending a proposal with chapters, send by mail.

Commission: 15%; foreign 20%.

Fees: Photocopying and Express Mail charges only.

STEELE-PERKINS LITERARY AGENCY, 26 Island Ln., Canandaigua NY 14424. (585)396-9290. Fax (585)396-3579. E-mail: pattiesp@aol.com. Agent: Pattie Steele-Perkins. Member AAR. Handles inspirational romance novels.

Contact: Proposal/3 chapters. Considers simultaneous submissions. Responds in 6 weeks. E-mail instead of calling.

Commission: 15%.

LESLIE H. STOBBE, 300 Doubleday Rd., Tryon NC 28782. (828)859-5964. Fax (978)945-0517. E-mail: lstobbe@alltel.net. Well recognized in the industry. Estab. 1993. Represents 75 clients. Open to unpublished authors and new clients. Handles adult fiction and nonfiction.

Contact: By e-mail or letter.

Commission: 15%

Fees: None.

Tips: "I will not accept clients whose theological positions in their book differ significantly from mine."

STONE MANNERS AGENCY, 6500 Wilshire Blvd., Ste. 550, Los Angeles CA 90048. (323)655-1313. Fax (323)655-7676. Agent: Michael Sheehy. Handles religious/inspirational TV/film screenplays as well as general screenplays.

Contact: Queries only.

SUITE A MANAGEMENT TALENT & LITERARY AGENCY, 120 El Camino Dr., Ste. 202, Beverly Hills CA 90212. (310)278-0801. Fax (310)278-0807. E-mail: suite-A@juno.com. Agent: Lloyd D. Robinson. Recognized in the industry. Estab. 2001. Several clients. Open to new and unpublished clients (if published in other media). Specializes in screenplays and novels for adaptation to TV movies.

Commission: 10%

Comments: Representation limited to adaptation of novels and true-life stories for film and television development. Work must have been published for consideration.

MARK SWEENEY & ASSOCIATES, 28540 Altessa Way, Ste. 201, Bonita Springs FL 34135. (239)594-1957. Fax (239)594-1935. E-mail: sweeney2@comcast.net. Agent: Mark Sweeney. Recognized in the industry. Estab. 2003. Open to unpublished authors and new clients on a restricted basis. Handles adult religious/inspirational novels & nonfiction for all ages, crossover books, general books.

Contact: E-mail.

Commission: 15%; foreign 20%.

Fees: None.

TALCOTT NOTCH LITERARY SERVICES, 276 Forest Rd., Milford CT 06460. (203)877-1146. Fax (203)876-9517. E-mail: editorial@talcottnotch.net. Website: www.talcottnotch.net. Agent: Gina Panettieri. Not yet recognized in the industry; building a Christian presence. Estab. 2003. Represents 25 clients (2 with religious books). Open to unpublished authors and new clients. Accepts simultaneous submissions; responds in 6 wks. Handles nonfiction & fiction, crossover & general market books for all ages.

Contact: By e-mail or letter.

Commission: 15%; foreign 20%.

Fees: None.

Tips: "While Christian and religious books are not our main focus, we are open to unique and thought-provoking works from all writers. We specifically seek nonfiction in areas of parenting, health, women's issues, arts & crafts, self-help, and current events. We are open to academic/scholarly work as well as commercial projects."

3 SEAS LITERARY AGENCY, PO Box 8571, Madison WI 53708. (608)221-4306. E-mail: threeseaslit@aol.com. Website: www.threeseaslit.com. Agent: Michelle Grajkowski. Estab. 2000. Represents 40 clients. Open to unpublished authors and new clients. General agent; handles adult religious/inspirational novels & nonfiction.

Contact: Query with proposal/first 3 chapters. Considers simultaneous submissions. Responds in 2-3 mos.

Commission: 15%; foreign 20%.

TOAD HALL INC., RR 2 Box 2090, Laceyville PA 18623. (570)869-2942. Fax (570)869-1031. E-mail: toadhallco@aol.com. Website: www.laceyville.com/toad-hall. Agent: Sharon Jarvis. Not yet known in the industry. Estab. 1983. Represents 1 religious client. Not open to unpublished authors or new clients. Handles adult religious/inspirational nonfiction; fiction only from published authors.

Contact: Letter or e-mail. Do not send any text unless requested.

Commission: 15%; foreign 10%.

Fees: Office expenses (photocopying, bank fees, special postage). $50 fee to read the first 50 pages plus synopsis/table of contents and provide a detailed written analysis.

Tips: "All queries should include (1) the category, (2) the word count, (3) brief summary, (4) bio, (5) SASE." Has their own small press, plus a partnership with an independent e-book company for authors considering self-publishing or a co-op arrangement.

TRIDENT MEDIA GROUP, LLC., 41 Madison Ave., 36th Fl., New York NY 10010. (212)262-4810. Fax (212)262-4849. E-mail: pfedorko@tridentmediagroup.com. Website: www.tridentmediagroup.com. Agent: Paul Fedorko. Open to unpublished authors and new clients. General agent. Handles adult religious nonfiction.

Contact: No unsolicited mss. Query/SASE first; send outline and sample chapters on request. Responds to queries in 3 wks.; mss in 6 wks.

VAN DIEST LITERARY AGENCY, PO Box 1482, Sisters OR 97759. (541)549-0477. Fax (541)549-1213. E-mail: DVanDiest@outlawnet.com. Website: www.ChristianLiteraryAgency.com. Agents: David & Sarah Van Diest. Estab. 2004. Represents 20 clients. Open to unpublished authors and new clients. Recognized in the industry. Handles teen & adult novels, nonfiction for all ages, crossover books.

Contact: By e-mail. Responds in 4 wks.

Commission: 15%; 25% for first-time authors.

WATERSIDE PRODUCTIONS INC., 2376 Oxford Ave., Cardiff-by-the-Sea CA 92007. (760)632-9190. Fax (760)632-9295. E-mail: webrown@waterside.com. Website: www.waterside.com. Agent: William E. Brown. Christian agent in a highly regarded general agency. Interested in handling Christian books, or books which otherwise challenge and engage readers from a Judeo-Christian perspective. Prefers nonfiction, but will look at fiction (the bar is very high). In addition to spiritually oriented books, devotions, theology, chick lit and mom lit, list includes business books: leadership, marketing, sales, business development.

Contact: Query via online form (see Website). Considers simultaneous submissions.

Commission: 15%; foreign 25%.

WESTPHAL LITERARY AGENCY, PO Box 148, Shelby IN 46377. (219)552-9027. E-mail: PennieWest@aol.com. Agents: Richard & Pennie Westphal. Estab. 2004. Recognized in the industry. Represents 10 clients with religious books. Open to unpublished authors and new clients. Handles adult & teen novels & nonfiction, short stories, stage plays, and general books.

Contact: Query with SASE or by e-mail.

Commission: 15%; foreign 15%.

Fees: Charges $125 annually for office expenses.

Tips: "Best to query first and follow our submission guidelines. In general books, we want nothing overtly sexual."

+WHALIN LITERARY AGENCY, 23623 N. Scottsdale Rd., Ste. D-3 #481, Scottsdale AZ 85255. (480)575-8622. E-mail: query@whalinagency.com. Website: www.whalinagency.com. Agent: W. Terry Whalin. Estab. 2007. Open to unpublished authors and new clients. Handles adult religious/inspirational novels & nonfiction.

Contact: No e-mail query unless requested.

Commission: 15%; foreign 20%.

Tips: Submission guidelines on Website.

WINSUN LITERARY AGENCY, 3706 N.E. Shady Ln. Dr., Gladstone MO 64119. Phone/fax (816)459-8016. E-mail: mlittleton@earthlink.net. Agents: Mark Littleton, pres.; Elizabeth Hey, assoc. agent. Recognized in the industry. Represents 30 clients. Somewhat open to unpublished authors and open to new clients. Handles fiction and nonfiction for all ages, picture books, gift books. Mainly for CBA, but some for ABA.

Contact: E-mail is best.

Commission: 15%; foreign 20%.

Fees: Postage and copying for new clients only.

Tips: "Send only your absolutely best work, i.e., work that has been rewritten to perfection, put through critique groups, and so on."

WOLGEMUTH & ASSOCIATES INC., 8600 Crestgate Cir., Orlando FL 32819. (407)909-9445. Fax (407)909-9446. E-mail: rwolgemuth@cfl.rr.com. Agent: Robert D. Wolgemuth; Andrew D. Wolgemuth (awolgemuth@cfl.rr.com); Erik S. Wolgemuth (ewolgemuth@cfl.rr.com). Well recognized in the industry. Estab. 1992. Represents 45 clients. No new clients or unpublished authors. Handles mostly adult nonfiction; most other types of books handled only for current clients.

Contact: By letter.

Commission: 15%.

Fees: None.

Tips: "We work with authors who are either best-selling authors or potentially best-selling authors. Consequently, we want to represent clients with broad-market appeal."

WOMACK PUBLISHING AGENCY, PO Box 2163, Merced CA 95344. (209)658-2226. E-mail: WomackAgency@aol.com. Agent: David A. Womack. Estab. 1998. Recognized in the industry. Represents 25 clients. Open to unpublished authors and new clients. Handles Christian or Catholic fiction & nonfiction for adults, some general books.

Contact: Prefers e-mail. No simultaneous submissions. Responds in 2 wks.

Commission: 15%; foreign 20%.

Fees: No up-front fees.

WORDSERVE LITERARY GROUP, 10152 S. Knoll Cir., Highlands Ranch CO 80130. (303)471-6675. Website: www.wordserveliterary.com. Agent: Greg Johnson. Estab. 2003. Represents 20+ clients. Recognized in the industry. Open to one or two unpublished authors and new clients/yr. Handles novels & nonfiction for all ages, gift books, crossover books, general books.

Contact: Query letter with SASE to start. Responds in 4 wks.

Commission: 15%; foreign 10-15%.

Fees: None.

Tips: "Nonfiction: First impressions count. Make sure your proposal answers all the questions on competition, outline, audience, felt need, etc. Fiction: Make sure your novel is completed before you submit a proposal (synopsis, plus 5 chapters)."

THE WRITER'S EDGE. See listing under Editorial Services—Illinois.

WRITERS HOUSE, 21 W. 26th St., New York NY 10010. (212)685-2400. Fax (212)685-1781. E-mail: azuckerman@writerhouse.com. Website: www.writershouse.com. Agent: Albert Zuckerman. Estab. 1974. Represents 440 clients. General agency; handles adult religious/inspirational fiction. Member of AAR.

Contact: One-page query by mail/SASE. No e-mail/fax queries. Responds in 1 mo. to query.

Commission: 15%; foreign 20%.

Fees: No fees.

Tips: "See Website for details. Write a compelling query so we'll ask to see your manuscript."

YATES & YATES, LLP, 1100 W. Town and Country Rd., Ste. 1300, Orange CA 92868-4654. (714)480-4000. Fax (714)480-4001. E-mail: email@yates-yates.com. Website: www.yates-yates.com. Estab. 1989. Recognized in the industry. Represents 50+ clients. Not currently open to unpublished authors or new clients. Handles adult novels, nonfiction for adults and teens, TV/Movie scripts, general books, crossover books.

Contact: E-mail.

Commission: Negotiable

Fees: Negotiable.

+ZACHARY SHUSTER HARMSWORTH LITERARY AND ENTERTAINMENT AGENCY, 1776 Broadway, Ste. 1405 (212)765-6900. Fax (212)765-6490; and 535 Boylston St., Ste. 1103, Boston MA 02116. (617)262-2400. Fax (617)262-2468. E-mail: mchappell@zshliterary.com. Website: www.zshliterary.com. Agent: Mary Beth Chappell (Boston office). Recognized in the industry. Represents 10 religious clients. Open to unpublished authors and new clients. Handles adult & teen religious/inspirational novels & adult nonfiction, crossover books, secular books.

Contact: E-mail query letter. Accepts simultaneous submissions. Responds in 2 wks. or queries, 8 wks. on full mss. Commission: 15%; foreign & film 20%.

Fees: Office expenses only.

Tips: "We are looking for inspirational fiction, Christian nonfiction, especially that which focuses on the emerging/emergent church or that which would appeal to readers in their 20s and 30s, and teen/YA series."

ADDITIONAL AGENTS

NOTE: The following agents did not return a questionnaire, but most have been identified as secular agents who handle religious/inspirational manuscripts. Be sure to send queries first if you wish to submit to them. Always check out an agent thoroughly before committing to work with him or her. Ask for references and a list of books represented, check with the Better Business Bureau, and ask your writing friends.

AVATAR LITERARY AGENCY, 3389 Sheridan St., Ste. 308, Hollywood FL 33021. Agent: Karen Weiss.

DAVID BLACK LITERARY AGENCY, 156 Fifth Ave., Ste. 608, New York NY 10010. Agent: David Black. Handles religious nonfiction.

Contact: Query by mail. No e-query. Not currently accepting unsolicited queries.

DUNOW, CARLSON & LERNER, 27 W. 20th St., Ste. 1003, New York NY 10011. Agent: Betsy Lerner. Open to unpublished authors and new clients. General agent. Handles adult religious nonfiction.

+K J LITERARY SERVICES, LLC, 1540 Margaret Ave., Grand Rapids MI 49507. (616)551-9797. E-mail: kim@kjliteraryservices.com. Website: www.kjliteraryservices.com. Agent: Kim Zeilstra.

DENISE MARCIL LITERARY AGENCY, 156—5th Ave, Ste. 625, New York NY 10011. Agent: Denise Marcil. General agent. Handles religious nonfiction. Member of AAR.

THE AMY RENNERT AGENCY, 98 Main St., #302, Tiburon CA 94920. E-mail: arennert@pacbell.net. Agent: Amy Rennert. Open to unpublished authors and new clients. General agent. Handles adult religious nonfiction.

Contact: Query with SASE; no e-query.

SOBEL WEBER ASSOCIATES, 146 E. 19th St., New York NY 10003. Agent: Nat Sobel. Open to unpublished authors and new clients. General agent. Handles adult religious nonfiction.

STEPHANIE VON HIRSCHBERG LITERARY AGENCY, 1385 Baptist Church Rd., Yorktown Heights NY 10598. (914)243-9250.

WILSON MEDIA, PO Box 613, Hastings-on-Hudson NY 10706. E-mail: wilsonmedia@verizon.net. Agent: Robert Wilson. Open to unpublished authors and new clients. General agent. Handles adult religious nonfiction.

CONTESTS

Below is a listing of all the contests mentioned throughout this guide, plus additional contests that will be of interest. Some are sponsored by book publishers or magazines, some by conferences or writers' groups. The contests are arranged by genre or type of material they are looking for, such as poetry, fiction, nonfiction, etc. Send an SASE to each one you are interested in to obtain a copy of their complete contest rules and guidelines, or check their Website. A listing here does not guarantee the legitimacy of a contest. For guidelines on evaluating contests and to determine if a contest is legitimate, go to: www.sfwa.org/beware/contests.html. Also note that many contests had not set deadlines and final details for the next year's contests when this guide was written, so always get a copy of their current guidelines before entering.

See end of this section for a list of Websites for major literary awards.

(+) indicates a new listing.

CHILDREN/YOUNG ADULT CONTESTS, WRITING FOR

DELACORTE DELL YEARLING CONTEST FOR FIRST MIDDLE-GRADE NOVEL, Random House Inc., 1745 Broadway, 9th Fl., New York NY 10019. Website: www.randomhouse.com/kids/writingcontests/index.html#middlegrade. Contemporary and historical fiction manuscripts, 96-160 pgs., for ages 9-12. Submit between April 1 and June 30. Prizes: $1,500, book contract, and $7,500 advance.

+DELACORTE DELL YEARLING CONTEST FOR FIRST YOUNG ADULT NOVEL, Random House Inc., 1745 Broadway, 9th Fl., New York NY 10019. Website: www.randomhouse.com/kids/writingcontests/index.html#youngadult. Contemporary and historical fiction manuscripts, 100-224 pgs., for ages 12-18. Submit between October 1 and December 31. Prizes: $1,500, book contract, and $7,500 advance.

HIGHLIGHTS FOR CHILDREN FICTION CONTEST, 803 Church St., Honesdale PA 18431. (570)253-1080. Website: www.highlights.com. Offers 3 prizes of $1,000 each for stories up to 800 words for children; for beginning readers to 500 words. See Website for guidelines and current topic. No crime, violence, or derogatory humor. No entry fee or form required. Entries must be postmarked between January 1 and February 28.

CORETTA SCOTT KING BOOK AWARD, Coretta Scott King Task Force, American Library Assn., 50 E. Huron St., Chicago IL 60611. Toll-free (800)545-2433. E-mail: feedback@ala.org. Website: www.ala.org. Annual award for children's books by African American authors and/or illustrators published the previous year. Books must fit one of these categories: preschool to grade 4; grades 5-8; grades 9-12. Deadline: December 1 each year. Guidelines on Website. Prizes: a plaque, a set of encyclopedias, and $1,000 cash. Recipients are authors and illustrators of African descent whose distinguished books promote an understanding and appreciation of the "American Dream."

+LEE & LOW BOOKS NEW VOICES AWARD, 95 Madison Ave., New York NY 10016. E-mail: info@leeandlow.com. Website: www.leeandlow.com. Annual award for a children's fiction or nonfiction picture book story by a writer of color; to 1,500 wds. Deadline: between May 1 and October 31. Prizes: $1,000 plus publication; & $500 for Honor Award Winner. Guidelines on Website.

+MILKWEED PRIZE FOR CHILDREN'S LITERATURE, Milkweed Editions, 1011 Washington Ave. S., Ste. 300, Minneapolis MN 55415. (612)332-3192. E-mail: editor@milkweed.org. Website: www.milkweed.org. Annual prize for unpublished novel intended for readers 8-13; 90-200 pgs. Prize: $5,000 advance against royalties and publication. Guidelines on Website.

POCKETS WRITING CONTEST, PO Box 340004, Nashville TN 37203-0004. (615)340-7333. Fax (615)340-7267. E-mail: pockets@upperroom.org. Website: www.pockets.org. United Methodist. Lynn W. Gilliam, ed. Devotional magazine for children (6-11 yrs.). Fiction-writing contest; submit between 3/1 and 8/15 every yr. Prize: $1,000 and publication in *Pockets*. Length: 1,000-1,600 wds. Must be unpublished and not historical fiction. Previous winners not eligible. Send to Pockets Fiction Contest at above address, designating "Fiction Contest" on outside of envelope. Send SASE for return and response.

SKIPPING STONES YOUTH HONOR AWARDS, PO Box 3939, Eugene OR 97403. (541)342-4956. E-mail: editor@skippingstones.org. Website: www.skippingstones.org. Interfaith/multicultural. Arun N. Toké, exec. ed.; Nina Forsberg, asst. ed. A multicultural awareness and nature appreciation magazine for young people 7-17, worldwide. Annual Book Awards for published books and authors. Deadline: February 1. Annual Youth Honor Awards for students 7-17. Deadline June 25. Send SASE for guidelines.

FICTION CONTESTS

AMERICAN CHRISTIAN FICTION WRITERS CONTEST, President; PO Box 101066, Palm Bay FL 32910-1066. Phone/fax (321)984-4018. Website: www.ACFW.com. E-mail loop, online courses, critique groups, and newsletter for members. Sponsors a contest open to non-members. See Website for current contest.

+BAAL HAMON SHORT STORY CONTEST, 28 Akinniranye St., PO Box 2338, Akure, Ondo State, Nigeria. Phone: +234 (0)34 216 339. E-mail: info@baalhamon.com. Website: www.baalhamon.com. Short Story Contest. Guidelines by e-mail (info@baalhamon.com).

BOSTON REVIEW SHORT STORY CONTEST, Boston Review, 35 Medford St., Ste. 302, Somerville MA 02143. Website: www.bostonreview.net. Prize: $1,000 (plus publication) for an unpublished short story to 4,000 words. Entry fee: $20. Deadline: October 1. Details on Website.

BULWER-LYTTON FICTION CONTEST. For the worst opening line to a novel. Deadline: April 15. Website: www.bulwer-lytton.com. Rules on Website.

CANADIAN WRITER'S JOURNAL SHORT FICTION CONTEST, White Mountain Publications, Box 1178, New Liskeard ON P0J 1P0, Canada. (705)647-5424. Canada-wide toll-free (800)258-5451. Website: www.cwj.ca. Sponsors semiannual short fiction contests. Deadline: March 31 and September 30. Length: to 1,200 wds. Entry fee: $5. Prizes: $100, $50, $25. All fiction needs for CWJ are filled by this contest. E-mail: cwc-calendar@cwj.ca.

+ALEXANDER PATTERSON CAPON PRIZE FOR FICTION, New Letters, UMKC, University House, 5101 Rockhill Rd., Kansas City MO 64110. (816)235-1168. E-mail: new letters@umkc.edu. Website: www.newletters.org. Deadline: May 18. Entry fee: $15. Prize: $1,500.

CHARACTERS ANNUAL SHORT STORY CONTEST, PO Box 708, Newport NH 03773-0708. (603)863-5896. E-mail: hotdog@nhvt.net. Website: www.cdavisnh.com. Annual Short Story Contest. Deadline: August 30. Prizes: Six prizes in 2 categories: adult authors and children authors (to age 16). All genres to 1,500 words. Entry fee: $3 per story. Prize: $50. Details in Website.

THE CHRISTY AWARDS, 1571 Glastonbury Rd., Ann Arbor MI 48103. Phone/fax (734)663-7931. E-mail: CA2000DK@aol.com. Website: www.christyawards.com. Awards in 9 fiction genres for excellence in Christian fiction. Nominations made by publishers, not authors. For submission guidelines and other information, see Website. Awards are presented at an Annual Christy Awards Banquet held Friday prior to the annual ICRS convention in July.

THE FLANNERY O'CONNOR AWARD FOR SHORT FICTION, University of Georgia Press, 330 Research Dr., Athens GA 30602. Website: www.ugapress.uga.edu. For collections of short fiction, 200-275 pgs. Prize: $1,000, plus publication under royalty book contract. Entry fee: $20. Deadline: between April 1 and May 31 (postmark). Guidelines on Website.

+JOHN GARDNER MEMORIAL PRIZE FOR FICTION, *Harpur Palate,* English Dept., Binghamton University, Box 6000, Binghamton NY 13920. Website: http://harpurpalate.binghampton.edu/johngardner.html. Unpublished short story of 8,000 words or less. Deadline: between January 1 and March 31. Entry fee: $15. Prize: $500, plus publication in the summer issue of *Harpur Palate.* Details on Website.

GLIMMER TRAIN PRESS FICTION CONTESTS. Sponsors 3 fiction contests during the year: Fiction Open, Very Short Fiction Award, and Short-Story Award for New Writers. General. Lengths and deadlines vary. Entry fee: $15. Prizes: $1,200 and publication, $500 and $300. Open to all writers, all themes. Submit original, unpublished stories. Glimmer Train Press, 1211 N.W. Glisan St., #207, Portland OR 97209. (503)221-0836. Website: www.glimmertrain.com.

C. S. LEWIS CONTESTS. Check Website for current contests: www.cslewisclassics.com.

THE MARY MCCARTHY PRIZE IN SHORT FICTION, PO Box 4456, Louisville KY 40204. (502)458-4028. E-mail: sarabandeb@aol.com. Website: www.sarabandebooks.org. Prize: $2,000 and publication of a collection of short stories, novellas, or a short novel (150-250 pgs.), plus a standard royalty contract. Deadline: between January 1 and February 15. Entry fee: $25.

NATIONAL WRITERS ASSOCIATION NOVEL WRITING CONTEST, The National Writers Assn., 3140 S. Peoria #295, Aurora CO 80014. (303)841-0246. Website: www.nationalwriters.com. Deadline: April 1. Entry fee: $35. Prizes $500, $250, $150. Details and entry form on Website.

NATIONAL WRITERS ASSOCIATION SHORT STORY CONTEST, The National Writers Assn., 10940 S. Parker Rd., #508, Parker CO 80134. (303)841-0246. Website: www.nationalwriters.com. Deadline: July 1. Entry fee: $15. Prizes $50, $100, $200. Guidelines on Website.

NELLIGAN PRIZE FOR SHORT FICTION, Colorado Review, Dept. of English, Colorado State University, Fort Collins CO 80523. Website: www.coloradoreview.colostate.edu/NPSF/sub.html. Best unpublished short story. First prize: $1,000, plus publication in *Colorado Review.* Entry fee: $10. Deadline: March 15 (varies).

+OPERATION FIRST NOVEL. Sponsored by the Jerry B. Jenkins Christian Writers Guild, 5525 N. Union Blvd., Ste. 200, Colorado Springs CO 80918. For unpublished novelists who are students or annual members of the Christian Writers Guild. Prize: publication by Tyndale House Publishers, plus $20,000 advance against royalties. Length: 75,000-100,000 wds. Deadline: October 2008 (check Website for exact date). No entry fee. For contest rules, go to www.ChristianWritersGuild.com/contest.

+KATHERINE ANNE PORTER PRIZE FOR FICTION, Literary Contest/Fiction, University of Tulsa, 600 S. College Ave., Tulsa OK 74104. (618)631-3080. E-mail: nimrod@utulsa.edu. Website: www.utulsa.edu/nimrod/awards.html. Quality prose and fiction by emerging writers of contemporary literature, unpublished. Deadline: between January 1 and April 30. Entry fee: $20. Prizes: $2,000 and publication; $1,000 and publication.

+RED HEN PRESS SHORT FICTION AWARD, Attn: Short Fiction Award, Red Hen Press, PO Box 3537, Granada Hills CA 91394. Website: www.redhen.org. Open to all writers and themes, and open to previously published work; up to 25 pgs. Deadline: June 30. Entry fee: $15. Prize: $1,000, plus publication in the *Los Angeles Review.* Guidelines on Website.

+SERENA MCDONALD KENNEDY AWARD, Snake Nation Press, 110 W. Force St., Valdosta GA 31601. (229)244-0752. Website: www.snakenationpress.org. Novellas to 50,000 words, or short story collection to 200 pgs. (published or unpublished). Deadline: April 30. Entry fee: $20. Prize: $1,000 and publication. Guidelines on Website.

TAMARAK AWARD, 600 U.S. Trust Bldg., 730 S. 2nd Ave., Minneapolis MN 55402. Website: www.minnesotamonthly.com. Short fiction to 4,000 wds. Prize: $10,000. Winning story to be published in the fall issue of *Minnesota Monthly.* For residents of Minnesota, North Dakota, South Dakota, Iowa, Wisconsin, and Michigan only. Spring deadline. Details on Website.

+PETER TAYLOR PRIZE FOR THE NOVEL, Knoxville Writers' Guild, PO Box 2565, Knoxville TN 37901-2565. Website: www.knoxvillewritersguild.org/guide.htm. For unpublished novels, 40,000 words or more. Deadline: between February 1 and April 30. Entry fee: $25. Prizes: $1,000 and publication. Guidelines on Website.

TOBIAS WOLFF AWARD IN FICTION, Mail Stop 9053, Western Washington University, Bellingham WA 98225. (360)650-4863. E-mail: bhreview@cc.wwu.edu. Website: www.wwu.edu/~bhreview. Short story or novel excerpt to 8,000 wds. Deadline: postmarked between December 1 and March 15. Entry fee: $15 for first story/chapter; $10 each additional. Prize: $1,000, plus publication. Details on Website.

WORD SMITTEN'S TENTEN FICTION COMPETITION, Word Smitten LLP, PO Box 5067, St. Petersburg FL 33737. E-mail: award@wordsmitten.com. Website: www.wordsmitten.com. Annual contest for a short story of exactly 1,010 words. Deadline: July 1. Entry fee: $18. Prize: $1,010, plus publication.

WRITER'S JOURNAL ANNUAL FICTION CONTEST, Val-Tech Media, PO Box 394, Perham MN 56573. E-mail: writersjournal@writersjournal.com. Website: www.writersjournal.com. Deadline: January 30. Entry fee: $15. Maximum 5,000 wds. Prizes: $500, $200, $100, plus publication. Sponsors several contests; see Website.

+THE WRITERS WEEKLY.COM 24-HOUR SHORT STORY CONTEST. A quarterly contest sponsored by Booklocker.com Inc., PO Box 2399, Bangor ME 04402-2399. (207)262-9696. Fax (207)262-5544. E-mail: angela@booklocker.com. Website: www.booklocker.com.

NONFICTION CONTESTS

AMY WRITING AWARDS. A call to present spiritual truth reinforced with biblical references in general, nonreligious publications. First prize is $10,000 with a total of $34,000 given annually. To be eligible, submitted articles must be published in a general, nonreligious publication and must be reinforced with at least one passage of Scripture. Deadline is January 31 of following year. For details and a copy of last year's winning entries, contact: The Amy Foundation, PO Box 16091, Lansing MI 48901-6091. (517)323-6233. E-mail: amyfoundtn@aol.com. Website: www.amyfound.org.

ANNUAL FAMILY HISTORY WRITING CONTEST, Attn: Writing Contest, 417 Irving Dr., Burbank CA 91504-2408. E-mail: scgs@scgsgenealogy.com. Website: www.scgsgenealogy.com. Southern California Genealogy Society. Two categories, 1,000-2,000 wds., or under 1,000 wds. Published or unpublished family or local history articles, character sketches, or memoirs. Prizes: $50-250. Deadline: November 1-December 31. No e-mail entries. Details on Website.

ANNUAL SIMON SCANLON WRITING AWARDS, The Way, 1112—26th St., Sacramento CA 95816-5610. E-mail: ofmcaway@att.net. Website: www.sbfranciscans.org. Sponsored by The Way of St. Francis. Articles: 1,500-2,000 wds. Prizes: $250-1,000. Deadline: October 4. Details on Website.

+AWP CREATIVE NONFICTION PRIZE, Assoc. of Writers and Writing programs, Carty House, Mail Stop 1E3, George Mason University, Fairfax VA 22030. (703)993-4301. E-mail: awp@awpwriter.org. Website: www.awpwriter.org. For authors of book-length manuscripts; submit only 150-300 pgs. Deadline: between January 1 and February 28. Entry fee: $20. Prize: $2,000. Send SASE for guidelines.

+THE BECHTEL PRIZE, Teachers and Writers Magazine Contest, 520 Eighth Ave., Ste. 2020, New York NY 10018. (212)691-6590. E-mail: info@twc.org. Website: www.twc.org/bechtel_prize.htm. Contemporary writing articles to 5,000 words. Deadline: May or June (varies). Entry fee: none. Prize: $3,500, plus publication.

ERMA BOMBECK WRITING COMPETITION. Website: www.wcpl.lib.oh.us/adults/erma.html. Entry fee: none. Prizes: $100 prize in each category and free registration in writer's conference. Personal essay (humor or human interest), 450 wds. Deadline: January (varies). Use online entry form.

THE BROSE PRIZE, The Brose Foundation, Lake Forest College, 555 N. Sheridan, Lake Forest IL 60045. (847)735-5175. Fax (847)735-6192. E-mail: rmiller@lfc.edu. Offered only every 10 years for unpublished work; next contest 2010. Deadline: September 1, 2010. Prizes: $4,000-$15,000. Entries become the property of the college. Open to a book or treatise on the relationship between any discipline or topic and the Christian religion. Send SASE for guidelines.

+DOROTHY CHURCHILL CAPON PRIZE FOR ESSAY, New Letters, UMKC, University House, 5101 Rockhill Rd., Kansas City MO 64110. (816)235-1168. E-mail: newletters@umkc.edu. Website: www.newletters.org. Deadline: May 18. Entry fee: $15. Prize: $1,500.

THE DABBLING MUM.COM CONTESTS, 508 W. Main St., Beresford SD 57004. (605)763-2549. E-mail: dm@thedabblingmum.com. Website: www.thedabblingmum.com. Alyice Edrich, ed. Balance your life while you glean from successful entrepreneurs, parents, and Christians—just like you. Every 2-3 months they have an essay contest (http://thedabblingmum.com/contests/index.htm).

ANNIE DILLARD AWARD IN CREATIVE NONFICTION. Essays on any subject to 8,000 wds. Deadline: between December 1 and March 15. Entry fee: $15 for first; $10 each additional. First prize: $1,000. Unpublished works only, to 8,000 wds. Manuscripts to: Bellingham Review, Mail Stop 9053, Western Washington University, Bellingham WA 98225. (360)650-4863. E-mail: bhreview@cc.wwu.edu. Website: www.wwu.edu/~bhreview. Details on Website.

+EVENT CREATIVE NONFICTION CONTEST, *The Douglas College Review,* PO Box 2503, New Westminster BC V3L 5B2, Canada. (604)527-5293. E-mail: event@douglas.bc.ca. Website: http://event.douglas.bc.ca. Previously unpublished creative nonfiction to 5,000 wds. Deadline: mid-April. Entry fee; $29.95. Prizes: Three $500 prizes and publication in *Event.*

+GRAYWOLD PRESS NONFICTION PRIZE, 2402 University Ave., Ste. 203, St. Paul MN 55114. (651)641-0036. Website: www.graywolfpress.org/Company_Info/Submission_Guidelines/Graywolf_Press_Nonfiction_Prize_Submission_Guidelines. For the best literary nonfiction book by a writer not yet established in the genre. Deadline: between September 1 and 30. Entry fee: none. Prize: $12,000.

GUIDEPOSTS CONTEST, 16 E. 34th St., New York NY 10016. (212)251-8100. Website: www.guideposts.org. Interfaith. Writers Workshop Contest held on even years with a late June deadline. True, first-person stories (yours or someone else's), 1,500 wds. Needs one spiritual message, with scenes, drama, and characters. Winners attend a week-long seminar (all expenses paid) on how to write for *Guideposts*.

+JEBAIRE YOUTH ESSAY CONTEST, Attn: Contest, PO Box 843, Snellville GA 30078. (770)823-9017. E-mail: info@jebairepublishing.com. Website: www.jebairepublishing.com. Shannon Clark, contest coordinator (SClark@jebairepublishing.com). Sponsors an annual contest for youth, ages 9-16. Essays 700-1,200 words on specific topics. Deadline: between April 1 and June 15. Guidelines available on Website or by e-mail. Submissions must be mailed to above address. Twenty winners will have their work published in a nonfiction anthology and receive a copy of the book.

CORETTA SCOTT KING AWARDS, American Library Assn., 50 E. Huron St., Chicago IL 60611. Toll-free (800)545-2433, ext. 4294. E-mail: olos@ala.org. Website: www.ala.org. Offered annually to an African American author and illustrator to promote understanding and appreciation of culture and the contributions of all people. Prize: $1,000, plus a set of encyclopedias. Guidelines on Website.

+RICHARD J. MARGOLIS AWARD of Blue Mountain Center, c/o Margolis & Assocs., 533 Boyston St., Boston MA 02116. (617)267-9700. Website: www.margolis.com/award. Given annually to a promising young journalist or essayist whose work combines warmth, humor, wisdom, and concern with social justice. Deadline: July 1. Prize: $5,000. Guidelines on Website.

NATIONAL WRITERS ASSOCIATION NONFICTION CONTEST, 10940 S. Parker Rd., #508, Parker CO 80134. (303)841-0246. Fax (303)841-2607. Website: www.nationalwriters.com. Annual nonfiction contest. Deadline: December 31. Entry fee: $18. Prizes: $50, $100, $200. Send SASE for guidelines.

OPERATION FIRST BOOK (nonfiction). Sponsored by the Jerry B. Jenkins Christian Writers Guild, 5525 N. Union Blvd., Ste. 200, Colorado Springs CO 80918. For unpublished authors who are students or annual members of the Christian Writers Guild. Winner receives publication by Tyndale House Publishers, plus $10,000 advance against royalties. Length: 75,000-100,000 wds. Deadline: September 2008 (check Website for exact date). Entry fee: none. For contest rules, go to www.ChristianWritersGuild.com/contest.

+LAMAR YORK PRIZE FOR NONFICTION, *The Chatahoochi Review,* George Perimeter College, 2101 Womack Rd., Dunwoody GA 30338. Website: www.gpc.edu/~gpccr. Essays up to 5,000 wds. Deadline: between October 1 and January 31. Entry fee: $10. Prize: $1,000 and publication in *The Chatahoochi Review.* Guidelines on Website.

PLAY/SCRIPTWRITING/SCREENWRITING CONTESTS

+ANNUAL FAITH AND VALUES SCREENWRITING COMPETITION. (204)292-4095. E-mail: info@ambassadorcommunication.biz. Website: www.ambassadorcommunications.biz/faithandvalues.html. Honors the best in faith-based TV series pilots and feature-length screenplays. Claire Hutchinson, contest coordinator. Monetary prizes. Winning scripts considered for representation by a WGA agent and read by Fox Faith and 10 other faith-based production companies. Deadline: February 1 (may vary).

+ANNUAL SCRIPTAPALOOZA SCREENPLAY COMPETITION. (323)654-5809. E-mail: info@scriptapalooza.com. Website: www.scriptapalooza.com. Deadline: April 13. Prize: $10,000. Details on Website.

+AUSTIN FILM FESTIVAL SCREENWRITERS COMPETITION, 1604 Nueces St., Austin TX 78701. (512)478-4795. E-mail: info@austinfilmfestival.com. Website: www.austinfilmfestival.com. Offers two first prizes for unpublished screenplays in the Adult/Family and Comedy categories. Deadline: May 15 (postmark). Entry fee: $40. Prizes: $5,000, plus travel expenses and admission to the festival.

+BAKER'S PLAYS HIGH SCHOOL PLAYWRITING COMPETITION, 45 W. 25th St., New York NY 10010. Plays may be about any subject and any length as long as the play can be reasonably produced by high school students on a high school stage. Deadline: January 30 (may vary). Guidelines on Website: www.bakersplays.com.

CITA PLAY DEVELOPMENT COMPETITION, PO Box 26471, Greenville SC 29616. E-mail: admin@cita.org. Website: www.CITA.org. (click on "Playwriting"). To encourage Christian playwrights, the writing of new plays and musicals that are informed by a biblical world-view in influencing our culture and furthering the Kingdom of God. Info on upcoming competitions will be listed on Website as available.

CITA THEATRICAL SKETCH WRITING CONTEST, Lin Sexton, 501 Coronado Way, Modesto CA 95350. E-mail: information@cita.org. Website: www.CITA.org. Details will be listed on Website when competitions are available.

KAIROS PRIZE FOR SPIRITUALLY UPLIFTING SCREENPLAYS. John Templeton Foundation. E-mail: contact@kairosprize.com. Website: www.kairosprize.com. Biannual. For first-time screenwriters with a religious message. Prizes: $25,000, $15,000, $10,000. Guidelines on Website.

+MOONDANCE INTERNATIONAL FILM FESTIVAL COMPETITION, 970—9th St., Boulder CO 80302. E-mail: info@moondancefilmfestival.com. Website: www.moondancefilmfestival .com. Open to films, screenplays, and features. Deadline: April 1. Entry fee: $25-75. Prize: winning entries screened at festival. Details by e-mail.

+NATIONAL CHILDREN'S THEATRE FESTIVAL, Actor's Playhouse at the Miracle Theatre, 280 Miracle Mile, Coral Gables FL 33134. (305)444-9293, ext. 615. E-mail: maulding@actors playhouse.org. Website: www.actorsplayhouse.org. Annual playwriting prize offering $500 and full production of winning musical, and author's transportation and lodging at the festival. Deadline: June 1. Entry fee: $10 (entry form on Website). Earl Maulding, festival dir.

NICHOLL FELLOWSHIPS IN SCREENWRITING, 1313 N. Vine St, Hollywood CA 90028-8107. (310)247-3010. E-mail: nicholl@oscars.org. Website: www.oscars.org/nicholl/index.html. International contest held annually, open to any writer who has not optioned or sold a treatment, teleplay, or screenplay for more than $5,000. Up to five $30,000 fellowships offered each year to promising authors. Guidelines/required application form on Website.

+MILDRED & ALBERT PANOWSKI PLAYWRITING AWARD, Award Coordinator, Forest Roberts Theatre, Northern Michigan University, Marquette MI 49855-5364. Website: www.nmu.edu/theatre. Unpublished, unproduced, full-length plays. Deadline: November 15. Prizes: $2,000, a summer workshop, a fully mounted production, and transportation to Marquette. Send SASE for guidelines and application.

+SLAMDANCE SCREENPLAY COMPETITION, Slamdance Inc., 5634 Melrose Ave., Los Angeles CA 90038. E-mail: mail@slamdance.com. Website: www.slamdance.com/screencomp. John Stoddard, dir. Annual contest. Deadline: May 18 (may vary). Entry fee: $40. First prize: $7,000. Details on Website. Accepts screenplays in every genre, both feature and short length.

THE WRITERS NETWORK ANNUAL SCREENPLAY & FICTION COMPETITION, Fade In Magazine, 287 S. Robertson Blvd., #467, Beverly Hills CA 90211. (310)275-0287. E-mail: writers net@aol.com. Website: www.fadeinonline.com. Deadline: May 31. Must submit online. Over $10,000 in cash prizes. Guidelines on Website.

POETRY CONTESTS

ANHINGA PRIZE FOR POETRY, PO Box 10595, Tallahassee FL 32302. (850)521-9920. Fax: (850)442-6363. E-mail: info@anhinga.org. Website: www.anhinga.org. A $2,000 prize for original poetry book in English. Winning manuscript published by Anhinga Press. For poets trying to publish a first or second book of poetry. Submissions: 48-80 pages. Number pages and include $25 reading fee. Deadline: between February 15 and May 1 each year. Details on Website.

ANNUAL CAVE CANEM POETRY PRIZE. Supports the work of African American poets with excellent manuscripts who have not found a publisher for their first book. Deadline: May 15. Prize: $500, publication by a national press, and 50 copies of the book. Details on Website: www.cavecanempoets.org. Mailing address: 2008 Cave Canem Poetry Prize, Cave Canem Foundation Inc., 584 Broadway, Ste. 508, New York NY 10012. E-mail: ccpoets@verizon.net.

MURIEL CRAFT BAILEY MEMORIAL POETRY AWARD, CWG Poetry Contest 2008, 4956 St. John Dr., Syracuse NY 13215. E-mail: poetry@comstockreview.org. Awarded annually. Deadline: July 1. Prizes: $100 to $1,000. Finalists published in the *Comstock Review.*

Unpublished poems to 40 lines. Entry fee: $4 for each poem (no limit on number of submissions). Details on Website: www.comstockreview.org.

BLUE MOUNTAIN ARTS/SPS STUDIOS POETRY CARD CONTEST, PO Box 1007, Boulder CO 80306. (303)449-0536. E-mail: poetrycontest@sps.com. Website: www.sps.com. Biannual contest (even years). Deadline: June 1. Rhymed or unrhymed original poetry (unrhymed preferred). Poems also considered for greeting cards or anthologies. Prizes: $300, $150, $50.

BOSTON REVIEW ANNUAL POETRY CONTEST. Deadline: June 1. First prize: $1,500, plus publication. Submit up to 5 unpublished poems. Entry fee: $20 (includes a subscription to *Boston Review*). Submit manuscripts in duplicate with cover note. Send manuscript and fee to: Poetry Contest, Boston Review, 35 Medford St., Ste. 302, Somerville MA 02143. Website: www.bostonreview.net

VIRGINIA BRENDEMUEHL PRIZE FOR POETRY, Rock & Sling: A Journal of Literature, Art and Faith, PO Box 30865, Spokane WA 99223. Fax (509)276-2971. E-mail: editors@rockandsling.org. Website: www.rockandsling.org. Kris Christensen, Susan Cowger, Laurie Klein, eds. A literary journal created to give forum to the spiritual journey, while exploring the Christian point of view. Prize: $1,000, plus publication. Deadline: July 31. Entry fee: $10/3 poems. Send SASE for guidelines. Prize: $1,000, plus publication. Deadline: July 30 (postmark). Send SASE and $10, payable to *Rock & Sling*, for 1-3 poems.

CHRISTIAN NEWS TODAY FREE POETRY CONTEST. E-mail: publisher@christiannewstoday.com. Website: www.christiannewstoday.com/poems.html. Any length or type; need to be poems of faith. Deadline: may vary. Prize: a surprise gift bag, plus having their poem featured on the main page of Website for 30 days. E-mail submissions.

DIAMOND EYES POETRY CONTEST, PO Box 7276, Woodland Park CO 80863-0203. Toll-free (888)769-9931. E-mail: Submit@depublishing.com. Website: www.depublishing.com. Jessica Adriel, sr. ed. Sponsors a poetry contest and publishes poetry books only from winners of that contest. Poetry is published in a gift book with inspirational photos. Accepts poetry on a number of topics (see list on Website). Submit anytime. Entry fee: $7.

DREAM HORSE PRESS NATIONAL POETRY CHAPBOOK PRIZE, PO Box 2080, Aptos CA 95001-2080. E-mail: dreamhorsepress@yahoo.com. Send 16-24 pages of poetry (paginated). Entry fee: $15. Deadline: May 31 (may vary). Prize: $500 and 25 copies of chapbook. See Website for details: www.dreamhorsepress.com. Electronic submissions OK, with electronic fee payment.

+DREAM HORSE PRESS ORPHIC PRIZE FOR POETRY (book prize), PO Box 2080, Aptos CA 95001-2080. E-mail: dreamhorsepress@yahoo.com. Send 48-80 pages of poetry (paginated). Entry fee: $25. Deadline: December 1 (may vary). Prize: $1,000 and 15 copies of chapbook. See Website for details: www.dreamhorsepress.com. Electronic submissions OK, with electronic fee payment.

49TH PARALLEL POETRY AWARD, Mail Stop 9053, Western Washington University, Bellingham WA 98225. (360)650-4863. E-mail: bhreview@cc.wwu.edu. Website: www.wwu.edu/~bhreview. Contact: Brenda Miller. Poems in any style or on any subject. Deadline: between December 1 and March 15. Entry fee: $15 for first entry; $10 for each additional entry. First prize: $1,000 and publication. Detail on Website.

GRIFFIN POETRY PRIZE. Contact: Ruth Smith, mngr., The Griffin Trust for Excellence in Poetry, 6610 Edwards Blvd., Mississauga ON L5T 2V6, Canada. (905)565-5993. E-mail: info@griffinpoetryprize.com. Website: www.griffinpoetryprize.com. Prizes: two $50,000 awards (one to a Canadian and one to a poet from anywhere in the world) for a collection of poetry published in English during the preceding year. All submissions must come from publishers. Deadline: December 31. Details on Website.

KATHRYN HANDLEY PROSE-POEM PRIZE, Soul Making Literary Competition, National League of American Pen Women, Nob Hill, San Francisco Branch, 1544 Sweetwood Dr., Colma CA 94015-2029. E-mail: pennobhill@aol.com. Website: www.soulmakingcontest.us. One-page poems only (single- or double-spaced). Up to 3 poems/entry. Deadline: November 30. Entry fee: $5. Prizes $25, $50, $100.

SARA HENDERSON HAY PRIZE, The Pittsburgh Quarterly, 6336 Crombie St., Pittsburgh PA 15217. Enter up to 3 poems, no more than 100 lines each. Prize: $600. Entry fee: $10. Details: www.city-net.com/~tpq.

TOM HOWARD/JOHN H. REID POETRY CONTEST, 351 Pleasant St., PMB 222, Northampton MA 01060. Website: www.winningwriters.com/tompoetry.htm. Deadline: between December 15 and September 30. Poetry in any style or genre. Published poetry accepted. Entry fee: $6 for every 25 lines. Prizes: $1,000, $400, $200, plus additional cash prizes. Details on Website.

BARBARA MANDIGO KELLY PEACE POETRY AWARDS, Nuclear Age Peace Foundation, PMB 121, 1187 Coast Village Rd., Ste. 1, Santa Barbara CA 93108-2794. (805)965-3443. E-mail: communications@napf.org. Website: www.wagingpeace.org. Annual series of awards to encourage poets to explore and illuminate positive visions of peace and the human spirit. Deadline: July 1. Prizes: $1,000 for Adult; $200 for Youth 13-18 years; and $200 for Youth ages 12 and under. Adult entry fee: $15 for up to 3 poems (no youth fee).

THOMAS MERTON POETRY OF THE SACRED CONTEST. Poetry that expresses, directly or indirectly, a sense of the holy or that, by mode of expression, evokes the sacred. The tone may be religious, prophetic, or contemplative. Deadline: December 31. First prize: $500; three Honorable Mentions, $100 each. Submit 1 poem. Entry fee: none. Submit to: The Thomas Merton Prize, The Thomas Merton Foundation, 2117 Payne St., Louisville KY 40206-2011, or e-mail to: hgraffy@mertonfoundation.org. Details: call (502)899-1991 or visit Website: www.mertonfoundation.org.

KATHRYN A. MORTON PRIZE IN POETRY, Sarabande Books, PO Box 4456, Louisville KY 40204. (502)458-4028. E-mail: info@sarabandebooks.org. Website: www.sarabande books.org. Prize: $2,000, plus publication of a book of poetry. Submit: minimum of 48 pages of poetry. Entry fee: $25. Deadline: January 1 through February 15.

NATIONAL WRITERS ASSOCIATION POETRY CONTEST, The National Writers Assn., 3140 S. Peoria, #295, Aurora CO 80014. Website: www.nationalwriters.com. Annual poetry contest. Entry fee: $10. Prizes: $25, $50, $100. Details and entry form on Website.

+NEW LETTERS PRIZE FOR POETRY, New Letters, UMKC, University House, 5101 Rockhill Rd., Kansas City MO 64110. (816)235-1168. E-mail: newletters@umkc.edu. Website: www.newletters.org. Deadline: May 18. Entry fee: $15. Prize: $1,500.

THE OPEN WINDOW ANNUAL POETRY ANTHOLOGY CONTEST, Hidden Brook Press, 109 Bayshore Rd., RR#4, Brighton ON K0K 1H0, Canada. (613)475-2368. E-mail: writers@ hiddenbrookpress.com. Website: www.hiddenbrookpress.com/an-ow.htm. Deadline: November 30 (may vary). Enter 3 poems maximum; to 60 lines. Prizes: 10 cash prizes from $10 to $100. Entry fee: $15. Details on Website.

POETRY SOCIETY OF VIRGINIA POETRY CONTESTS, PO Box 35685, Richmond VA 23235. Website: www.poetrysocietyofvirginia.org. Sponsors a number of poetry contests. Categories for adults and students. Prizes: $10-100. Entry fee per poem for nonmembers: $3. List of contests on Website.

SEEDS POETRY CHAPBOOK CONTEST, Hidden Brook Press, 109 Bayshore Rd., RR#4, Brighton ON K0K 1H0, Canada. (613)475-2368. E-mail: writers@hiddenbrookpress.com. Website: www.hiddenbrookpress.com. All types of poetry; published or unpublished. Deadline: October 1. Entry fee: $15 for 3 poems. Prizes: ten from $10 to $100.

SILVER WINGS CONTEST, PO Box 2340, Clovis CA 93613-2340. (559)347-0194. E-mail: cloviswings@aol.com. Jackson Wilcox, ed. Annual poetry contest on a theme. Deadline: December 31. Send SASE for details. Winners published in March issue. $325 in prizes. Entry fee: $3 entry fee.

SLIPSTREAM ANNUAL POETRY CHAPBOOK COMPETITION, Box 2071, Niagara Falls NY 14301. Website: www.slipstreampress.org/contest.html. Prize: $1,000, plus 50 copies of chapbook. Deadline: December 1. Send up to 40 pages of poetry. Reading fee: $15.

HOLLIS SUMMERS POETRY PRIZE, Ohio University Press, 19 Circle Dr., The Ridges, Athens OH 45701. (740)593-1155. E-mail: oupress@ohio.edu. For unpublished collection of original poems, 60-95 pgs. Entry fee: $15. Deadline: October 31. Prize: $1,000, plus publication in book form. Details on Website: www.ohiou.edu/oupress/poetryprize.htm.

THE MAY SWENSON POETRY AWARD, Utah State University Press, 7800 Old Main Hill, Logan UT 84322-7800. (435)797-1362. Website: www.usu.edu/usupress. Collections of original poetry, 50-100 pgs. Deadline: September 30. Prize: $1,000, publication, and royalties. Reading fee: $25. Details on Website.

TIME OF SINGING POETRY CONTESTS, PO Box 149, Conneaut Lake PA 16316. E-mail: timesing@zoominternet.net. Website: www.timeofsinging.bizland.com. Lora Zill, ed. Sponsors 1-2 annual poetry contests on specific themes or forms. Entry fee: $2/poem. Cash prizes. Details on Website.

KATE TUFTS DISCOVERY AWARD, Claremont Graduate University, 160 E. 10th St., Harper East B7, Claremont CA 91711-6165. (909)621-8974. E-mail: tufts@cgu.edu. Presented annually for a first or very early work by a poet of genuine promise. Prize: $10,000. Work submitted must be a book published between September 15, 2007, and September 15, 2008. Deadline: September 15. Details and entry form on Website: www.cgu.edu/tufts.

UTMOST NOVICE CHRISTIAN POETRY CONTEST, Utmost Christian Writers Foundation, 121 Morin Maze, Edmonton AB T6K 1V1, Canada. E-mail: nnharms@telusplanet.net. Website: www.utmostchristianwriters.com. Nathan Harms. Entry fee: $10/poem (10 poems max.). Prizes: $500, $300, $100; 15 honorable mentions $50 ea.; Best Rhyming Poem $250. Deadline: August 31 (may vary). Details on Website.

WAR POETRY CONTEST, 351 Pleasant St., PMB 222, Northhampton MA 01060. E-mail: warcontest@winningwriters.com. Website: www.winningwriters.com/annualcontest.htm. Sponsored by Winning Writers. Submit 1-3 unpublished poems on the theme of war, up to 500 lines total. Prizes: $1,500 first prize; $5,000 in total prizes. Deadline: between November 15 and May 31. Entry fee: $15.

YALE SERIES OF YOUNGER POETS COMPETITION, PO Box 209040, New Haven CT 06520. (203)432-0960. Fax (203)432-0948. E-mail: robert.flynn@yale.edu. Website: www.yale.edu/yup. Robert Flynn, ed./religion. Yale Series of Younger Poets competition. Open to poets under 40 who have not had a book of poetry published. Submit manuscripts of 48-64 pgs. Deadline: between October 1 and November 15. Entry fee: $15. Publishes one book each year. Details: on Website. Send complete manuscript.

MULTIPLE-GENRE CONTESTS

AMERICAN LITERARY REVIEW CONTESTS, PO Box 311307, University of North Texas, Denton TX 76203. E-mail: americanliteraryreview@yahoo.com. Website: www.engl.unt.edu/alr. Now sponsors three contests: short fiction, creative nonfiction, and poetry. Prize: $1,000 and publication in fall issue of the magazine. Entry fee: $15. Deadline: between June 1 and September 1. Details on Website.

+ANNUAL GREEN LAKE WRITERS CONTEST, Green Lake Conference Center, Attn: Program,

W2511 State Rd. 23, Green Lake WI 54941. Poetry, fiction, nonfiction, and general inspiration. Deadline: June 4. Prizes: $50, $25, and $15 in each category. You do not have to be present or attend conference to enter. Entry fee: $5 (for poetry) or $10 (other genres) for each entry.

BAKELESS LITERARY PUBLICATION PRIZES, Bread Loaf Writers Conference, Middlebury College, Middlebury VT 05753. E-mail: bakeless@middlebury.edu. Website: www.bakelessprize.org. Book series competition for new authors of literary works of poetry, fiction, and nonfiction. Entry fee: $10. Deadline: between September 15 and November 1. Details on Website.

BEST NEW CANADIAN CHRISTIAN AUTHOR CONTEST, The Word Guild, Box 34, Port Perry ON L9L 1A2, Canada. E-mail: admin@thewordguild.com. Website: www.thewordguild.com. Encourages first-time authors to write fiction and nonfiction books expressing Christian faith in a clear, original, and inspiring way. Deadline: November 30. Entry fees: $50 Cdn. (without a critique); $125 (with a critique). Prize: $1,000 advance and publication by Castle Quay Books Canada. Details on Website.

BYLINE CONTESTS, PO Box 111, Albion NY 14411-0111. (585)355-8172. Website: www.BylineMag.com. General market. Robbi Hess, ed. Sponsors many contests year round; details included in magazine, on Website, or send SASE for flier.

+CANTICLE WRITING CONTEST. Blog: http://heidihesssaxton.blogspot.com. Heidi Saxton, ed. Check blog for details on current contest. Winners published in *Canticle* magazine.

CHICKEN SOUP FOR THE SOUL CONTESTS. Website: www.chickensoup.com. See Website for list of current contests.

+CHRISTIAN SMALL PUBLISHER BOOK OF THE YEAR. Website: www.christianpublishers.net. Honors books produced by small publishers each year for outstanding contributions to Christian life. Categories: nonfiction, fiction, children's. Books need to have been published this year or last. Deadline: November 15. Eligible small publisher must have annual revenues of $350,000 or less. Details and nomination form on Website.

COLUMBIA FICTION/POETRY/NONFICTION CONTEST, 415 Dodge Hall, 2960 Broadway, New York NY 10027. Website: www.columbiajournal.org/contests.htm. Length: 20 double-spaced pages or up to 5 poems. Entry fee: $12. Prize: $500 in each category, plus publication. Deadline: January 15 (varies).

+CRAZY HORSE FICTION PRIZE & LYNDA HULL MEMORIAL POETRY PRIZE, Crazy Horse, Dept. of English, College of Charleston, 66 George St., Charleston SC 29424. E-mail: crazyhorse@cofc.edu. Website: http://crazyhorse.cofc.edu. Deadline: between September 1 and December 16. Reading fee: $15. Prizes: $2,000 in each category. Winners published in *Crazy Horse.* Guidelines on Website.

ECPA CHRISTIAN BOOK AWARD, 9633 S. 48th St., Ste. 140, Phoenix AZ 85044. (480)966-3998. E-mail: info@ecpa.org. Website: www.ECPA.org. Presented annually to the best books in Christian publishing. Awards recognize books in 6 different categories: Bibles, Fiction, Children & Youth, Inspiration & Gift, Bible Reference & Study, and Christian Life. Only ECPA members in good standing can nominate products. Deadline: January each year. Awards are presented annually at the International Christian Retail Show.

E.F.S. RELIGIOUS FICTION & NONFICTION WRITING COMPETITION, E.F.S. Enterprises Inc., 2844 Eighth Ave., Ste. 6E, New York NY 10039. (212)283-8899. E-mail: info@efs-enterprises.com. Website: www.efs-enterprises.com. Inspirational/religious fiction or nonfiction. Deadline: August 31. Entry fee: $25. Prizes: Publishing contract for grand prize winner; $50 for 1st place. Details & entry form on Website.

EVANGELICAL PRESS ASSOCIATION ANNUAL CONTEST, PO Box 28129, Crystal MN 55428. (763)535-4793. E-mail: director@epassoc.org. Website: www.epassoc.org. Sponsors annual contest for member publications.

+FAULKNER-WISDOM CREATIVE WRITING COMPETITION, Faulkner House, 624 Pirate's Alley, New Orleans LA 70116. (504)586-1609. E-mail: Faulkhouse@aol.com. Website: www.wordsandmusic.org. Unpublished novels, novellas, short stories, essays, and poetry. Deadline: between January 15 and May 1 (postmark). Entry fees: $10-35. Prizes: $750-7,500. Guidelines on Website.

FREEFALL SHORT FICTION & POETRY CONTEST. The Alexandra Writers' Centre Society, 922 9th Ave. S.E., Calgary AB T2G 0S4, Canada. Website: www.alexandrawriters.org/ctest.html. Deadline: October 1. Fiction to 3,000 wds.; 5 poems. Prizes: $200 & $100 Cdn. in both categories. Entry fee: $20.

+FREELANCE WRITER'S REPORT CONTEST, 45 Main St., PO Box A, North Stratford NH 03590-0167. (603)922-8383. E-mail: fwrcwm@writers-editors.com. Website: www.writers-editors.com. Dana K. Cassell, ed. Open to all writers. Deadline: March 15. Nonfiction, fiction, children's, poetry. Prizes: $100, $75, $50. Details on Website.

INSIGHT WRITING CONTEST, 55 W. Oak Ridge Dr., Hagerstown MD 21740-7301. (301)393-4038. Fax (301)393-4055. E-mail: insight@rhpa.org. Website: www.insightmagazine.org. Review and Herald/Seventh-day Adventist. Dwain N. Esmond, ed. A magazine of positive Christian living for Seventh-day Adventist high schoolers. Sponsors short story and poetry contests; includes a category for students 22 or under. Prizes: $50-$250. Deadline: June 1. Submit by e-mail. Details on Website.

INTERNATIONAL LIBRARY OF PHOTOGRAPHY FREE PHOTO CONTEST, 3600 Crondall Ln., Ste. 101, Owings Mills MD 21117. Website: www.picture.com/contest/enter.asp. Ongoing contest. Prize: $100,000 in prizes to amateur photographers. Submit photos electronically on Website. Details on Website.

LABELLE LETTRE CONTESTS, 2122 S. Silver Lake Rd., Castle Rock WA 98611. E-mail: admin@labellelettre.com. Website: www.labellelettre.com. Sponsors 4 contests/yr.; various genres and themes. Deadlines: February 1, May 1, August 1, November 1. Entry fee: $8. Prizes: $150, $75, $50; plus critique. Details and themes on Website.

MINISTRY & LITURGY VISUAL ARTS AWARDS, 160 E. Virginia St., #290, San Jose CA 95112. (408)286-8505. Fax (408)287-8748. E-mail: mleditor@rpinet.com. Website: www.rpinet.com/ml, or www.rpinet.com/vaaentry.pdf. Resource Publications Inc. Nick Wagner, ed. dir. To help liturgists and ministers make the imaginative connection between liturgy and life. Visual Arts Awards. Prize: $100. Entry fee: $30. Different deadline for each category (see Website).

MISSISSIPPI REVIEW PRIZE, The Center for Writers, University of Southern Mississippi, PO Box 5144, Hattiesburg MS 39406. (601)266-4321. E-mail: rief@mississippireview.com. Website: www.mississippireview.com/contest.html. Fiction & Poetry. Prize: $1,000 in each category. Deadline: April 1 to October 1. Entry fee: $15.

MOM'S CHOICE AWARDS. The Just For Mom Foundation. Website: www.momschoiceawards.org. Various award categories. Details on Website.

NEW MILLENNIUM AWARDS. Website: www.newmillenniumwritings.com/awards.html. Prizes: $1,000 award for each category. Best Poem, Best Fiction, Best Nonfiction, Best Short-Short Fiction (fiction and nonfiction 6,000 wds.; short-short fiction to 1,000 wds.; 3 poems to 5 pgs. total). Entry fee: $17 each. Deadline: June 17 (may vary). Guidelines on Website. Enter online or off.

+RUMINATE POETRY AND FICTION CONTEST, 140 N. Roosevelt Ave., Fort Collins CO 80521. (970)449-2726. E-mail: editor@ruminatemagazine.com. Website: www.ruminatemagazine.com. Brianna Van Dyke, ed. An intimate and hip publication of faith literature and art. Annual poetry & fiction contest. Entry fee: $15. Deadline: June 1. Prizes: $300 1st prize; $150 to runner-up. Details on Website.

MONA SCHREIBER PRIZE FOR HUMOROUS FICTION AND NONFICTION, 15442 Vista Haven Pl., Sherman Oaks CA 91403. E-mail: brashcyber@pcmagic.net. Website: www.brash

cyber.com. Humorous fiction and nonfiction to 750 wds. Prizes: $500, $250, and $100. Entry fee: $5. Deadline: December 1.

SHARING THE PRACTICE AWARDS, 100 S. Chestnut St., Kent OH 44240-3402. (330)678-0187. E-mail: pjbinder2@juno.com.. Website: www.apclergy.org. Academy of Parish Clergy/Ecumenical/Interfaith. Growth toward excellence through sharing the practice of parish ministry. Book of the Year Award ($100+), Top Ten Books of the Year list, Parish Pastor of the Year award ($200+). Inquire by e-mail.

SOUL-MAKING LITERARY COMPETITION, Webhallow House, 1544 Sweetwood Dr., Colma CA 94015-2029. E-mail: PenNobHill@aol.com. Website: www.SoulMakingContest.us/page3.html. Lists various competitions: prose and poetry. Prizes: up to $100. Entry fee: $5. Guidelines on Website.

+SOUTHWEST WRITERS ANNUAL CONTEST, 3721 Morris NE, Ste. A, Albuquerque NM 87111-3611. (505)265-9485. E-mail: swriters@juno.com. Website: www.southwestwriters.org. Novels, short stories, short nonfiction, and others. Includes inspirational/spiritual novels. Deadline: May 1 (varies). Prizes: Cash prizes in each category of $150, $100, $75; plus a $1,000 Storyteller Award selected from the first-place winners. Guidelines on Website or by mail.

THE STORYTELLER CONTESTS, 2441 Washington Rd., Maynard AR 72444. (870)647-2137. Fax (870)647-2454. E-mail: storyteller1@hightowercom.com. Contest Website: www.storyteller1.UPCsites.org. Fossil Creek Publishing. Regina Cook Williams, ed./pub.; Ruthan Riney, review ed. Family audience. Offers 1 or 2 paying contests per year, along with People's Choice Awards, and Pushcart Prize nominations.

TICKLED BY THUNDER CONTESTS, 14076—86A Ave., Surrey BC V3W 0V9, Canada. (604)591-6095. E-mail: info@tickledbythunder.com. Website: www.tickledbythunder.com. Larry Lindner, ed. Sponsors 9 writing contests each year in various genres. Prizes: $5-150 Cdn. Details on Website or by mail.

THE WRITER CONTESTS, 21027 Crossroads Cir., Waukesha WI 53189. (262)796-8776. E-mail: editor@writermag.com. Website: www.writermag.com. General. How-to for writers. Occasionally sponsors a contest. Check Website.

WRITER'S DIGEST, 4700 E. Galbraith Rd., Cincinnati OH 45207. (513)531-2690, ext. 1483. Fax (513)531-1843. E-mail: wdsubmissions@fwpubs.com. Website: www.writersdigest.com. Sponsors annual contests for articles, short stories, poetry, children's fiction, self-published books, and scripts (categories vary). Deadlines: vary according to contest. Prizes: $25,000 or more for each contest. See Website for list of current contests and rules.

WRITERS' JOURNAL CONTESTS, PO Box 394, Perham MN 56573-0394. (218)346-7921. Fax (218)346-7924. E-mail: writersjournal@writersjournal.com. Website: www.writersjournal.com. Val-Tech Media. Leon Ogroske, ed. Runs several contests each year. Prizes: up to $300. Categories are short story, horror/ghost, romance, travel writing, and fiction; 3 poetry; 2 photo. Different starter lines and deadlines for each category (see Website). Details on Website, or send SASE.

WRITERS' UNION OF CANADA AWARDS & COMPETITIONS, 90 Richmond St. E., Ste. 200, Toronto ON M5C 1P1, Canada. (416)703-8982. Fax (416)504-9090. E-mail: info@writersunion.ca. Website: www.writersunion.ca/compete.htm. Various competitions. Prizes: $500-10,000. Details on Website.

YOUNG SALVATIONIST CONTEST, PO Box 269, Alexandria VA 22313-0269. (703)684-5500. Fax (703)684-5539. E-mail: ys@usn.salvationarmy.org. Website: http://publications.salvationarmyusa.org. The Salvation Army. Laura Ezzell, mng. ed. For teens & young adults in the Salvation Army. Sponsors a contest for fiction, nonfiction, poetry, original art, and photography. Send SASE for details.

RESOURCES FOR CONTESTS

ADDITIONAL CONTESTS. You will find some additional contests sponsored by local groups and conferences that are open to nonmembers. See individual listings in those sections.

BYLINE MAGAZINE CONTEST LISTINGS. Website: www.bylinemag.com.

CHECK FOR LITERARY SCAMS. For help in determining if a contest is legitimate or not, go to: www.windpub.com/literary.scams

FREELANCE WRITING: WEBSITE FOR TODAY'S WORKING WRITER. Website: www.freelancewriting.com/contests.html.

KIMN SWENSON GOLLNICK'S WEBSITE. Contest listings. Website: www.KIMN.net.

OZARK CREATIVE WRITERS CONTESTS. Contact: Clarissa Willis, 2603 W. Walnut, Johnson City TN 37604. (423)929-1049. E-mail: ozarkcreativewriters@earthlink.net. Website: www.ozarkcreativewriters.org/AwardsContest.htm. Sponsors 25-30 contests each year.

MAJOR LITERARY AWARDS

AUDIES: www.audiopub.org
CALDECOTT MEDAL: www.ala.org
EDGAR: www.mysterywriters.org
HEMINGWAY FOUNDATION/PEN AWARD: www.pen-ne.org
HUGO: http://worldcon.org/hugos.html
NATIONAL BOOK AWARD: www.nationalbook.org
NATIONAL BOOK CRITICS CIRCLE AWARD: www.bookcritics.org
NEBULA: http://dpsinfo.com/awardweb/nebulas
NEWBERY: www.ala.org
NOBEL PRIZE FOR LITERATURE: www.nobelprize.org/literature
PEN/FAULKNER AWARD: www.penfaulkner.org
PULITZER PRIZE: www.pulitzer.org
RITA: www.rwanational.com
WHITBREAD AWARD: www.whitbread-bookawards.co.uk

DENOMINATIONAL LISTING OF BOOK PUBLISHERS AND PERIODICALS

An attempt has been made to divide publishers into appropriate denominational groups. However, due to the extensive number of denominations included, and sometimes incomplete denominational information, some publishers inadvertently may have been included in the wrong list. Additions and corrections are welcome.

ANTIOCHIAN ORTHODOX

Book Publishers:
Conciliar Press
Periodicals:
AGAIN
The Handmaiden

ASSEMBLIES OF GOD

Book Publishers:
Gospel Publishing House
Periodicals:
Enrichment
High Adventure
HonorBound
Live
Testimony
Today's Pentecostal Evangel
WT Online

BAPTIST, FREE WILL

Book Publishers:
Randall House
Randall House Digital
Periodicals:
Heartbeat
Together with God

BAPTIST, SOUTHERN

Book Publishers:
B & H Publishing
Baylor Univ. Press
Founders Press
New Hope Publishers
Southern Baptist Press
Periodicals:
Founders Journal
Journey
Let's Worship
Mature Living
On Mission
ParentLife

BAPTIST (other)

Book Publishers:
Earthen Vessel (Reformed)
Judson Press (American)
Mercer Univ. Press
Periodicals:
African American Pulpit (American)
BGC World
Courage (Regular)
Friends Journal
Heartbeat (Free Will)
Link & Visitor
Living My Faith (Regular)
Primary Pal/IL (Regular)
Real Faith in Life (Regular)
Secret Place (American)
Sword of the Lord (Independent)

CATHOLIC

Book Publishers:
ACTA Publications
Alba House
American Catholic Press
Canticle Books
Catholic Book Publishing
Cistercian Publications
HarperOne (Cath. bks.)
Libros Liguori
Liguori Publications
Liturgical Press
Loyola Press
Oregon Catholic Press
Our Sunday Visitor
Pauline Books
Paulist Press
Pflaum Publishing
Regnery Publishing
St. Anthony Messenger
Tau-Publishing
Periodicals:
America
Angel Face
Annals of St. Anne
Arkansas Catholic
Arlington Catholic Herald
Atlantic Catholic
Australian Catholics
Bread of Life
Canticle
Catechist
Catechumenate
Catholic Digest
Catholic Forester
Catholic Insight
Catholic Library World
Catholic Missions in Canada
Catholic New York
Catholic Peace Voice
Catholic Register
Catholic Sentinel
Catholic Servant
Catholic Telegraph
Catholic Yearbook
CGA World
Columbia
Commonweal
Culture Wars
Desert Call
Diocesan Dialogue
Emmanuel
Environment & Art
Faith & Family
Family Digest
Interim
Island Catholic News
Leaves
Liguorian
Marian Helper
Messenger (KY)
Messenger/Sacred Heart
Messenger/St. Anthony
Miraculous Medal
Montana Catholic
National Catholic Reporter
New Freeman
One
Our Sunday Visitor
Parish Liturgy
Prairie Messenger
Priest
Promise
Review for Religious
RTJ
Seeds
Share
Social Justice Review
Spirit
Spiritual Life
St. Anthony Messenger
St. Joseph's Messenger
This Rock
Today's Catholic Teacher
Today's Parish
True Girl
U.S. Catholic
Venture
Visions
Way of St. Francis

CHRISTIAN CHURCH/ CHURCH OF CHRIST

Book Publishers:
Chalice Press (Disciples of Christ)
College Press (Church of Christ)
Star Bible
Periodicals:
DisciplesWorld (Disciples of Christ)

CHURCH OF GOD (Anderson, IN)

Book Publishers:
Reformation Publishers
Warner Press

CHURCH OF GOD (Cleveland, TN)

Book Publisher:
Pathway Press
Periodical:
Youth and CE Leadership

CHURCH OF GOD (holiness)

Periodicals:
Beginner's Friend
Church Herald and Holiness Banner
Gems of Truth
Junior Companion
Primary Pal (KS)
Youth Compass

CHURCH OF GOD (other)

Periodicals:
Bible Advocate (Seventh-day)
Gem
Now What? (Seventh-day)
White Wing Messenger (Church of God of Prophecy)

CHURCH OF THE NAZARENE

Book Publishers:
Beacon Hill Press
Lillenas (music)
Periodicals:
Adventures
Celebrate
Credo Magazine
Discoveries
Passport
Resource

EPISCOPAL/ANGLICAN

Book Publishers:
Forward Movement
Latimer Press
Morehouse Publishing
Periodicals:
Episcopal Life
Interchange
Living Church
Sewanee Theological Review

LUTHERAN

Book Publishers:
Augsburg Fortress
Augsburg/Worship & Music
Concordia
Concordia Academic
Congregational Life & Learning
Langmarc Publishing
Lutheran University Press
Lutheran Voices
Northwestern Publishing
Periodicals:
Canada Lutheran (ELCC)
Canadian Lutheran
Cresset
Esprit (ELCC)
Lutheran Digest
Lutheran Forum
Lutheran Journal
Lutheran Partners (ELCA)
Lutheran Woman's Quarterly (MO Synod)
Word & World (ELCA)

MENNONITE

Book Publisher:
Kindred Books
Periodicals:
Canadian Mennonite
Evangel (OR)
Mennonite Historian
Messenger, The
Partners
Purpose
Story Mates

METHODIST, FREE

Periodicals:
Evangel
Light and Life

METHODIST, UNITED

Book Publishers:
Abingdon Press
Dimensions for Living
United Methodist Publishing House
Periodicals:
Alive Now
Good News/KY
Interpreter
Mature Years
Methodist History
New World Outlook
Pockets
Upper Room

PENTECOSTAL, UNITED

Periodicals:
InsideOut
Vision (adult)

PRESBYTERIAN

Book Publishers:
P & R Publishing
Presbyterian Publishing
Periodicals:
Channels (PCC)
Glad Tidings
Horizons/women (USA)
Interpretation
Layman (USA)
Presbyterian Outlook (USA)
Presbyterians Today

QUAKER/FRIENDS

Book Publishers:
Barclay Press
Friends United Press
Periodicals:
Fruit of the Vine
Quaker Life

REFORMED CHURCHES

Periodicals:
Perspectives
Reformed Worship
Vision (MI)

SEVENTH-DAY ADVENTIST

Book Publishers:
Pacific Press
Review and Herald
Periodicals:
Connected
Cornerstone Youth Resources
Guide Magazine
Insight (MD)
Journal/Adventist Ed
Kids' Ministry Ideas
Liberty
Message
Our Little Friend
Primary Treasure
Sabbath School Leadership
Vibrant Life

WESLEYAN CHURCH

Book Publisher:
Wesleyan Publishing House
Periodicals:
Light from the Word
Vista
Wesleyan Life

MISCELLANEOUS DENOMINATIONS

Evangelical Covenant Church
Covenant Companion
inSpirit Magazine
Evangelical Free Church
EFCA Today
Foursquare Gospel Church
Advance
Grace Brethren Churches
BMH Books
Open Bible Standard Churches
MESSAGE of the Open Bible
Orthodox Church in America
Divine Ascent
Plymouth Brethren
Chapter Two (books)
United Church of Canada
Aujourd'hui Credo
Fellowship Magazine
Theological Digest & Outlook
United Church Observer
United Church of Christ
Pilgrim Press
United Church Press

LIST OF BOOK PUBLISHERS AND PERIODICALS BY CORPORATE GROUP

Following is a listing of book publishers, followed by a list of periodicals, that belong to the same group or family of publications.

BARBOUR PUBLISHING

Barbour Publishing
Heartsong Presents
Heartsong Presents Mysteries

CHRISTIANITY TODAY, INTL.

Books & Culture
Christian History & Biography
Christianity Today
Christianity Today Movies
Christian Music Today
Ignite Your Faith
Leadership
Marriage Partnership
Men of Integrity
PreachingToday.com
Today's Christian
Today's Christian Woman
Your Church

CHRISTIAN MEDIA

Apocalypse Chronicles
Christian Media
Sound Body

DAVID C. COOK

Honor Books
Lion Publishing (books)
Scripture Press
Victor Books
Acquire the Fire
Power for Living
Quiet Hour
The Rock

FOCUS ON THE FAMILY

Focus on the Family (books)
Boundless Webzine
Breakaway
Brio
Brio and Beyond
Clubhouse
Clubhouse Jr.
en confianza
Focus on the Family
Focus on Your Child
Teen Phases
Tween Ages

BILLY GRAHAM EVANG. ASSN.

Decision
Decision Online
Passageway.org

GROUP PUBLICATIONS INC.

Group Publishing
Children's Ministry
Group Magazine
Rev. Magazine

GUIDEPOSTS

GuidepostsBooks
Ideals Children's Books
Ideals Press
Angels on Earth
Guideposts
Ideals Magazine
Positive Thinking

HARPERCOLLINS

Avon Inspire
HarperOne
ZonderKidz
Zondervan

THE NAVIGATORS

NavPress
NavPress Th1nk
Pray! Books
Pray!

THOMAS NELSON PUBLISHERS

J. Countryman
Editorial Betania
Editorial Caribe
Editorial Catolica
Editorial Diez Puntos
Grupo Nelson
Leader Latino
Nelson, Fiction, Thomas
Tommy Nelson
W Publishing Group

RANDOM HOUSE

Multnomah Books
WaterBrook Press

THE SALVATION ARMY

Faith & Friends
Good News!
New Frontier
Priority!
War Cry
Young Salvationist

STANDARD PUBLISHING

Standard Publishing (books)
Christian Standard
Devotions
The Lookout
Seek

STRANG COMMUNICATIONS

Charisma
Charisma House (books)
CharismaKids (books)
Creation House (co-publishing)
FrontLine (books)
Publicaciones Casa (books)
Realms (books)
Siloam (books)
Christian Retailing
Ministry Today
SpiritLed Woman

THE UPPER ROOM

Upper Room Books
Alive Now
Devo'Zine
The Upper Room
Weavings

URBAN MINISTRIES

Direction
InTeen
J.A.M.: Jesus and Me
Juniorway
Precepts for Living
Preschool Playhouse
Primary Street
Young Adult Today

GLOSSARY OF TERMS

NOTE: This is not intended to be an exhaustive glossary of terms. It includes primarily those terms you will find within the context of this market guide.

Advance. Amount of money a publisher pays to an author up front, against future royalties. The amount varies greatly from publisher to publisher, and is often paid in two or three installments (on signing contract, on delivery of manuscript, and on publication).

All rights. An outright sale of your material. Author has no further control over it.

Anecdote. A short, poignant, real-life story, usually used to illustrate a single thought.

Assignment. When an editor asks a writer to write a specific piece for an agreed-upon price.

As-told-to story. A true story you write as a first-person account, but about someone else.

Audio books. Books available on CDs.

Avant-garde. Experimental; ahead of the times.

Backlist. A publisher's previously published books that are still in print a year after publication.

B & W. Abbreviation for a black and white photograph.

Bar code. Identification code and price on the back of a book read by a scanner at checkout counters.

Bible versions. AMP—Amplified Bible; ASV—American Standard Version; CEV—Contemporary English Version; ESV—English Standard Version; GNB—Good News Bible; HCSB—Holman Christian Standard Bible; ICB—International Children's Bible; KJV—King James Version; MSG—The Message; NAB—New American Bible; NAS—New American Standard; NEB—New English Bible; NIrV—New International Reader's Version; NIV—New International Version; NJB—New Jerusalem Bible; NKJV—New King James Version; NLT—New Living Translation; NRSV—New Revised Standard Version; RSV—Revised Standard Version; TLB—The Living Bible; TNIV—Today's New International Version.

Bimonthly. Every two months.

Bio sketch. Information on the author.

Biweekly. Every two weeks.

Bluelines. Printer's proofs used to catch errors before a book is printed.

Book proposal. Submission of a book idea to an editor; usually includes a cover letter, thesis statement, chapter-by-chapter synopsis, market survey, and 1-3 sample chapters.

Byline. Author's name printed just below the title of a story, article, etc.

Camera-ready copy. The text and artwork for a book that are ready for the press.

Chapbook. A small book or pamphlet containing poetry, religious readings, etc.

Circulation. The number of copies sold or distributed of each issue of a publication.

Clips. See "Published Clips."

Column. A regularly appearing feature, section, or department in a periodical using the same heading; written by the same person or a different freelancer each time.

Concept statement. A 50-150 word summary of your proposed book.

Contributor's copy. Copy of an issue of a periodical sent to the author whose work appears in it.

Copyright. Legal protection of an author's work.

Cover letter. A letter that accompanies some manuscript submissions. Usually needed only if you have to tell the editor something specific or to give your credentials for writing a piece of a technical nature. Also used to remind the editor that a manuscript was requested or expected.

Credits, list of. A listing of your previously published works.

Critique. An evaluation of a piece of writing.

Defamation. A written or spoken injury to the reputation of a living person or organization. If what is said is true, it cannot be defamatory.

Derivative work. A work derived from another work, such as a condensation or abridgement. Contact copyright owner for permission before doing the abridgement and be prepared to pay that owner a fee or royalty.

Devotional. A short piece that shares a personal spiritual discovery, inspires to worship, challenges to commitment or action, or encourages.

Editorial guidelines. See "Writer's guidelines."

Electronic submission. The submission of a proposal or article to an editor by electronic means, such as by e-mail or on disk.

Endorsements. Flattering comments about a book; usually carried on the back cover or in promotional material.

EPA/Evangelical Press Assn. A professional trade organization for periodical publishers and associate members.

E-proposals. Proposals sent via e-mail.

E-queries. Queries sent via e-mail.

Eschatology. The branch of theology that is concerned with the last things, such as death, judgment, heaven, and hell.

Essay. A short composition usually expressing the author's opinion on a specific subject.

Evangelical. A person who believes that one receives God's forgiveness for sins through Jesus Christ, and believes the Bible is an authoritative guide for daily living.

Exegesis. Interpretation of the Scripture.

Feature article. In-depth coverage of a subject, usually focusing on a person, an event, a process, an organization, a movement, a trend or issue; written to explain, encourage, help, analyze, challenge, motivate, warn, or entertain as well as to inform.

Filler. A short item used to "fill" out the page of a periodical. It could be a timeless news item, joke, anecdote, light verse or short humor, puzzle, game, etc.

First rights. Editor buys the right to publish your piece for the first time.

Foreign rights. Selling or giving permission to translate or reprint published material in a foreign country.

Foreword. Opening remarks in a book introducing the book and its author.

Freelance. As in 50% freelance: means that 50% of the material printed in the publication is supplied by freelance writers.

Freelancer or freelance writer. A writer who is not on salary but sells his material to a number of different publishers.

Free verse. Poetry that flows without any set pattern.

Galley proof. A typeset copy of a book manuscript used to detect and correct errors before the final print run.

Genre. Refers to type or classification, as in fiction or poetry. Such types as westerns, romances, mysteries, etc., are referred to as genre fiction.

Glossy. A black-and-white photo with a shiny, rather than matte, finish.

Go-ahead. When a publisher tells you to go ahead and write up or send your article idea.

Haiku. A Japanese lyric poem of a fixed 17-syllable form.

Hard copy. A typed manuscript, as opposed to one on disk or in an e-mail.

Holiday/seasonal. A story, article, filler, etc., that has to do with a specific holiday or season. This material must reach the publisher the stated number of months prior to the holiday/season.

Homiletics. The art of preaching.

Honorarium. If a publisher indicates they pay an honorarium, it means they pay a small flat fee, as opposed to a set amount per word.

Humor. The amusing or comical aspects of life that add warmth and color to an article or story.

Interdenominational. Distributed to a number of different denominations.

International Postal Reply Coupon. See "IRC."
Interview article. An article based on an interview with a person of interest to a specific readership.
IRC or IPRC. International Postal Reply Coupon: can be purchased at your local post office and should be enclosed with a manuscript sent to a foreign publisher.
ISBN number. International Standard Book Number; an identification code needed for every book.
Journal. A periodical presenting news in a particular area.
Kill fee. A fee paid for a completed article done on assignment that is subsequently not published. Amount is usually 25-50% of original payment.
Libel. To defame someone by an opinion or a misquote and put his or her reputation in jeopardy.
Light verse. Simple, lighthearted poetry.
Little/Literary. Small circulation publications whose focus is providing a forum for the literary writer, rather than on making money. Often do not pay, or pay in copies.
Mainstream fiction. Other than genre fiction, such as romance, mystery, or science fiction. Stories of people and their conflicts handled on a deeper level.
Mass market. Books intended for a wide, general market, rather than a specialized market. These books are produced in a smaller format, usually with smaller type, and are sold at a lower price. The expectation is that their sales will be higher.
Ms. Abbreviation for manuscript.
Mss. Abbreviation for more than one manuscript.
Multiple submissions. Submitting more than one piece at a time to the same publisher, usually reserved for poetry, greeting cards, or fillers, not articles. Also see "Simultaneous submissions."
NASR. Abbreviation for North American serial rights.
Newsbreak. A newsworthy event or item sent to a publisher who might be interested in publishing it because it would be of interest to his particular readership.
Nondenominational. Not associated with a particular denomination.
Not copyrighted. Publication of your piece in such a publication will put it into public domain and it is not then protected. Ask that the publisher carry your copyright notice on your piece when it is printed.
Novella. A short novel starting at 20,000 words—35,000 words maximum. Length varies from publisher to publisher.
On acceptance. Periodical or publisher pays a writer at the time manuscript is accepted for publication.
On assignment. Writing something at the specific request of an editor.
One-time rights. Selling the right to publish a story one time to any number of publications (usually refers to publishing for a nonoverlapping readership).
On publication. Publisher pays a writer when his/her manuscript is published.
On speculation/On spec. Writing something for an editor with the agreement that he will buy it only if he likes it.
Overrun. The extra copies of a book printed during the initial print run.
Over the transom. Unsolicited articles that arrive at a publisher's office.
Payment on acceptance. See "On acceptance."
Payment on publication. See "On publication."
Pen name/Pseudonym. Using a name other than your legal name on an article or book in order to protect your identity or the identity of people included, or when the author wishes to remain anonymous. Put the pen name in the byline under the title, and your real name in the upper, left-hand corner.
Permissions. Asking permission to use the text or art from a copyrighted source.

Personal experience story. A story based on a real-life experience.

Personality profile. A feature article that highlights a specific person's life or accomplishments.

Photocopied submission. Sending an editor a photocopy of your manuscript, rather than an original. Some editors prefer an original.

Piracy. To take the writings of others just as they were written and put your name on them as the author.

Plagiarism. To steal and use the ideas or writings of another as your own, rewriting them to make them sound like your own.

Press kit. A compilation of promotional materials on a particular book or author, usually organized in a folder, used to publicize a book.

Public domain. Work that has never been copyrighted, or on which the copyright has expired. Subtract 75 from the current year, and anything copyrighted prior to that is in public domain.

Published clips. Copies of actual articles you have had published, from newspapers or magazines.

Quarterly. Every three months.

Query letter. A letter sent to an editor telling about an article you propose to write and asking if he or she is interested in seeing it.

Reporting time. The number of weeks or months it takes an editor to get back to you about a query or manuscript you have sent in.

Reprint rights. Selling the right to reprint an article that has already been published elsewhere. You must have sold only first or one-time rights originally, and wait until it has been published the first time.

Review copies. Books given to book reviewers or buyers for chains.

Royalty. The percentage an author is paid by a publisher on the sale of each copy of a book.

SAE. Self-addressed envelope (without stamps).

SAN. Standard Account Number, used to identify libraries, book dealers, or schools.

SASE. Self-addressed, stamped envelope. Should always be sent with a manuscript or query letter.

SASP. Self-addressed, stamped postcard. May be sent with a manuscript submission to be returned by publisher indicating it arrived safely.

Satire. Ridicule that aims at reform.

Second serial rights. See "Reprint rights."

Semiannual. Issued twice a year.

Serial. Refers to publication in a periodical (such as first serial rights).

Sidebar. A short feature that accompanies an article and either elaborates on the human interest side of the story or gives additional information on the topic. It is often set apart by appearing within a box or border.

Simultaneous rights. Selling the rights to the same piece to several publishers simultaneously. Be sure everyone is aware that you are doing so.

Simultaneous submissions. Sending the same manuscript to more than one publisher at the same time. Usually done with nonoverlapping markets (such as denominational or newspapers) or when you are writing on a timely subject. Be sure to state in a cover letter that it is a simultaneous submission and why.

Slander. The verbal act of defamation.

Slanting. Writing an article so that it meets the needs of a particular market.

Slush pile. The stack of unsolicited manuscripts that have arrived at a publisher's office.

Speculation. See "On speculation."

Staff-written material. Material written by the members of a magazine staff.

Subsidiary rights. All those rights, other than book rights, included in a book contract such as paperback, book club, movie, etc.

Subsidy publisher. A book publisher who charges the author to publish his book, as opposed to a royalty publisher who pays the author.

Synopsis. A brief summary of work from one paragraph to several pages long.

Tabloid. A newspaper-format publication about half the size of a regular newspaper.

Take-home paper. A periodical sent home from Sunday school each week (usually) with Sunday school students, children through adults.

Think piece. A magazine article that has an intellectual, philosophical, or provocative approach to a subject.

Third world. Reference to underdeveloped countries of Asia and Africa.

Trade magazine. A magazine whose audience is in a particular trade or business.

Traditional verse. One or more verses with an established pattern that is repeated throughout the poem.

Transparencies. Positive color slides, not color prints.

Unsolicited manuscript. A manuscript an editor didn't specifically ask to see.

Vanity publisher. See "Subsidy publisher."

Vignette. A short, descriptive literary sketch or a brief scene or incident.

Vitae/Vita. An outline of one's personal history and experience.

Work-for-hire. Signing a contract with a publisher stating that a particular piece of writing you are doing for him is work-for-hire. In the agreement you give the publisher full ownership and control of the material.

Writers' guidelines. An information sheet provided by a publisher that gives specific guidelines for writing for the publication. Always send an SASE with your request for guidelines.

GENERAL INDEX

This index includes periodicals, books, and greeting cards/specialty markets, as well as some of the organizations/resources and specialty lists or areas you may need to find quickly. Conferences, groups, and editorial services are listed alphabetically by state in those sections (not in the index). Check the table of contents for the location of supplementary listings.

Note: Due to the many changes in the market, and to help you determine the current status of any publisher you might be looking for, all markets will be listed in this index. If they are not viable markets, their current status will be indicated here. The following codes will be used: (ABD) asked to be deleted, (BA) bad address or contact information, (ED) editorial decision, (NF) no freelance, (NR) no recent response, (OB) out of business, (UTC) unable to contact. These changes will be noted in this listing for five years before being dropped altogether.